THE

WRITER'S
HANDBOOK
2003

Barry Turner has worked on both sides of publishing, as an editor and marketing director and as an author. He started his career as a journalist with *The Observer* before moving on to television and radio. He has written over twenty books including *A Place in the Country*, which inspired a television series, and a best selling biography of the actor, Richard Burton.

His recent work includes a radio play, travel articles, serialising books for *The Times*, editing the magazine *Country* and writing a one-man show based on the life of the legendary theatre critic, James Agate. This is his sixteenth year as editor of *The Writer's Handbook* and his fifth as editor of *The Statesman's Yearbook*.

THE
WRITER'S
HANDBOOK
2003

EDITOR

BARRY TURNER

MACMILLAN

First published 1988
This edition published 2002 by
Macmillan
an imprint of Pan Macmillan Ltd
Pan Macmillan, 20 New Wharf Road,
London N1 9RR
Basingstoke and Oxford
Associated companies throughout the world
www.panmacmillan.com

ISBN 0 333 90811 2

9 8 7 6 5 4 3 2

A CIP catalogue record for this book is available from the British Library

Credits

Publisher *Morven Knowles*
Editor *Barry Turner*
Editorial Assistant *Jill Fenner*
Poetry Editor *Peter Finch*
Contributors *Carole Blake*
  David Hooper
  Kate Pool
  Bob G Ritchie
  James Roose-Evans
  Gareth Shannon
  Mick Sinclair
Tax and Finance Adviser *Ian Spring*

Typeset by Heronwood Press, Medstead, Hants
Printed and bound in Great Britain by Mackays of Chatham plc, Kent

Contents

The Broader View

Leading agent Carole Blake claims there is more to international book sales than the American market

Authors measure their success in different ways but many look to the American market as some sort of Holy Grail, believing that success there is the ultimate goal. I would not deny that becoming a bestseller in America can greatly benefit your career – and your bank balance – but it is much harder and rarer for non-American authors to achieve than is generally realised. The English-language markets around the world (the primary ones being the UK, US, Australia and Canada) vary enormously and American writers' work often achieves much greater success in Britain, Australia, and Europe than non-American writers can expect within America.

Why is this? I think it's partly tied in to the general spread of American popular culture. The English-speaking world is used to accepting American music, film, television: we are comfortable with American culture. A relatively large proportion of our population travels abroad too. The other way around doesn't work quite so well: a smaller percentage of Americans travel extensively outside their own borders, so they are less familiar with overseas societies. However, they are experts on all things American. If non-American authors choose to set their fiction in America, or people their novels with American characters, the slightest wrong note or nuance will jar. And it is true to say that American readers seem more interested in American stories, characters and authors.

What can you do to crack this conundrum? It's certainly not a good idea to set out to write a novel especially for the American market: all too often American publishers will turn it down, or if it does get published, the American public won't buy it in sufficient quantities. And the bigger danger is losing the markets where you are already succeeding: in Britain or Australia, or the European countries where publishers might already be buying your translation rights.

I believe that if a writer already has a publisher in their home market, they should continue to write the very best books they are capable of, continue to build on sales they already have, and continue to submit to American publishers in the belief that the biggest English-language market will eventually recognise their worth.

After all, there are dozens of other languages to aim for (we have sold Michael Ridpath's financial thrillers to thirty-two languages so far, and many of our other clients to a couple of dozen languages) and for the most part fiction doesn't date so novels can still be sold to fresh markets – America included – years after first publication. As your list of translation sales grows, it demonstrates the broad appeal of your work and so becomes another sales aid in persuading yet more publishers in other markets to assess your work.

Just to demonstrate the sheer perversity of publishing markets internationally, my author Julian Stockwin, who writes in that very British genre of historical maritime adventure (Britannia ruling the waves!), had his books snapped up at auction in America within a couple of weeks of making the first submission. It's quality of storytelling and use of language that count.

Many agencies take enormous pride in the wide spread of languages to which they sell their authors. While languages like Bulgarian, Croatian, Estonian, Icelandic and Turkish may be small with correspondingly modest advances, collectively they can add up to a reasonable income and, of course, they add to the worldwide recognition of the author's work. Languages such as German, Japanese, French and Italian can add considerably to an author's wealth, sales and prestige. It is not uncommon for British authors to earn more, and sell more, in say German, than they do in their own language: even though the German market is nothing like as strong as it used to be a few years ago, it is still achieving substantial sales for translated books. One of my novelists once received such a big cheque for earned royalties (over and above the initial advance) that she was able to buy a country cottage with that one sum.

I love to track the sales of my authors around the world: there are sometimes delicious surprises. Many years ago Maeve Haran's first novel, *Having It All*, was published. It had been an instant success in English, and had sold to more than twenty languages. I asked the Polish publisher why she thought it had done so well in Polish, when the setting was the world of television in London. I realised I was confusing location with theme, when the Polish editor told me that her market had responded to it because it dealt with career women juggling the demands of home and career: 'Polish women have always had to work,' she said, and therefore they recognised and empathised with the dilemmas dramatised in the storyline. All of Maeve's novels sell hundreds of thousands of copies in their German translations too.

And that demonstrates another firmly held belief of mine about fiction: that to make a book work internationally you don't need to use exotic locations. Unpublished novelists often send their work to me with a letter that states that they know the work will appeal internationally 'because it is set in Moscow, Berlin, New York and Rome'. I'm afraid that only tells me that there will be a lot of scenes in airports and that the writer perhaps doesn't understand that it is experiences and emotions that unite worldwide audiences, not simply the location for the action.

I do firmly believe that good writing can be international: quality storytelling appeals to audiences around the world who will buy English-language editions exported by the original publisher, and will also form eager audiences for translated editions. The fiercely competitive trade in rights that takes place at book fairs around the world demonstrates that. Writing as different as Barbara Erskine's romantic mysteries, Lawrence Norfolk's intellectually demanding literary novels (one of them with footnotes!), Anna Davis' edgy modern fiction, Ann Granger's genre mysteries, and John Harvey's thoughtful detective novels all sell to publishers in dozens of languages. Some are successful in America, some not yet. But their accumulated sales are very impressive indeed.

Publishers in the smaller-language markets need to be very clever indeed to compete not only with each other but also with the exported English-language books. The Dutch and Scandinavian markets in particular include a high proportion of readers who are happy to read in English, and for the more literary authors especially there will be readers in these countries who prefer to read the original English edition rather than a translation. This puts extra pressure on the translating publishers to ensure the quality of their translated texts, while trying to get the book out as quickly as the original English edition, at the lowest selling price, even though they have to add the time and expense of the translation into an edition that will have to compete in the bookshops of Amsterdam or Copenhagen with the lower-priced English-language edition.

Raising the profile of their translated edition means the publisher must be innovative in getting publicity for the book and the author and this often leads to an invitation for the author to visit at the time of publication. No wonder writers often feel enormous admiration, loyalty and affection for their foreign-language publishers. And receiving your own book with a range of different covers, translated into Lithuanian, Romanian or Slovak, is thrilling.

One other thought. Selling foreign-language rights is very difficult for the un-agented author. Publishers in the non-English markets are offered so much – from authors in their own language, from English writers around the world and of course from all the other languages – that the likelihood of them selecting a title from a source they are unfamiliar with is remote. But not necessarily impossible. I have heard of an English novelist whose first novel was published in Dutch, by a marvellously entrepreneurial publisher in Amsterdam who publishes him still, before it was bought by a British publisher.

America isn't the only market to aim for, and English certainly isn't the only language market that appreciates our writers. Broader horizons are out there.

Carole Blake is Joint Managing Director of Blake Friedmann Literary Agency.

UK Publishers

AA Publishing

The Automobile Association, Fanum House, Basingstoke, Hampshire RG21 4EA
☎01256 491573 Fax 01256 491974

Managing Director *Stephen Mesquita*
Editorial Director *Michael Buttler*

Publishes maps, atlases and guidebooks, motoring, travel and leisure. About 100 titles a year.

Abacus

See **Time Warner Books UK**

ABC-Clio

Old Clarendon Ironworks, 35a Great Clarendon Street, Oxford OX2 6AT
☎01865 311350 Fax 01865 311358
Email oxford@abc-clio.ltd.uk
Website www.abc-clio.com

Acquisitions Editors *Dr Robert G. Neville, Simon Mason*

Formerly Clio Press Ltd. *Publishes* academic and general reference works, social sciences and humanities. Markets, outside North America, the Web, CD-ROM publications and reference books of the American parent company.
Royalties paid twice-yearly.

Abington Publishing

See **Woodhead Publishing Ltd**

Absolute Classics

See **Oberon Books**

Absolute Press

Scarborough House, 29 James Street West, Bath BA1 2BT
☎01225 316013 Fax 01225 445836
Email sales@absolutepress.demon.co.uk
Website www.absolutepress.demon.co.uk

Managing/Editorial Director *Jon Croft*

FOUNDED 1979. *Publishes* food and wine-related subjects as well as travel guides. About 10 titles a year. SERIES *Outlines* Monographs on gay and lesbian creative artists; *Gay Times Travel Guides* Launched in 2001, co-published with *Gay Times*. No unsolicited mss. Synopses and ideas for books welcome.
Royalties paid twice-yearly.

Abson Books London

5 Sidney Square, London E1 2EY
☎020 7790 4737 Fax 020 7790 7346
Email absonbooks@aol.com

Chairman *M.J. Ellison*

FOUNDED 1971 in Bristol. *Publishes* language glossaries and curiosities. No unsolicited mss; synopses and ideas for books welcome.
Royalties paid twice-yearly.

Academic Press

See **Harcourt Publishers International**

Academy Group Ltd

John Wiley & Sons, 4th Floor, International House, 7 High Street, Ealing Broadway, London W5 5DB
☎020 8326 3800 Fax 020 8326 3801

Chairman *John Jarvis*
Commissioning Editor *Maggie Toy*
Approx. Annual Turnover £2 million

FOUNDED 1969. Became part of the **John Wiley & Sons, Inc.** group in 1997. *Publishes* architecture and design. Welcomes unsolicited mss, synopses and ideas.
Royalties paid annually.

Acair Ltd

Unit 7, 7 James Street, Stornoway, Isle of Lewis HS1 2QN
☎01851 703020 Fax 01851 703294
Email acair@sol.co.uk

Specialising in matters pertaining to the Gaidhealtachd, Acair publishes books in Gaelic and English on Scottish history, culture and the Gaelic language. 75% of their children's books are targeted at primary school usage and are published exclusively in Gaelic.
Royalties paid twice-yearly.

Actinic Press

See **Cressrelles Publishing Co. Ltd**

Acumen Publishing Limited

15A Lewins Yard, East Street, Chesham, Buckinghamshire HP5 1HQ
☎01494 794398 Fax 01494 784850
Email steven.gerrard@acumenpublishing.co.uk
Website www.acumenpublishing.co.uk

Managing Director *Steven Gerrard*

FOUNDED in 1998 as an independent publisher for the higher education market. *Publishes* academic books on philosophy, history and politics. 10 titles in 2001. No unsolicited mss. Synopses and ideas for books welcome; send written proposal as per Acumen guidelines.
Royalties paid annually.

Addison Wesley Longman
See **Pearson Education**

Adlard Coles Nautical
See **A.&C. Black (Publishers) Ltd**

African Books Collective
The Jam Factory, 27 Park End Street, Oxford OX1 1HU
☎01865 726686 Fax 01865 793298
Email abc@africanbookscollective.com
Website www.africanbookscollective.com

FOUNDED 1990. Collectively owned by its 17 founder publishers. Exclusive distribution in N. America, UK, Europe and Commonwealth countries outside Africa for 61 African participating publishers. Concentration is on scholarly/academic, literature and children's books. Mainly concerned with the promotion and dissemination of African-published material outside Africa. Supplies African-published books to African libraries and organisations and *publishes* resource books on African publishing. TITLES *African Writers' Handbook; African Publishers Networking Directory; Women in Publishing and the Book Trade in Africa; The Electronic African Bookworm: A Web Navigator.*

Age Concern Books
1268 London Road, London SW16 4ER
☎020 8765 7200 Fax 020 8765 7211
Email books@ace.org.uk
Website www.ageconcern.org.uk
Approx. Annual Turnover £400,000

Publishing arm of Age Concern England. *Publishes* related non-fiction only. No fiction. About 18 titles a year. Unsolicited mss, synopses and ideas welcome for new practical handbooks.

Airlife Publishing Ltd
101 Longden Road, Shrewsbury, Shropshire SY3 9EB
☎01743 235651 Fax 01743 232944
Email editor@airlifebooks.com
Website www.airlifebooks.com
Editorial Head *Peter Coles*

Approx. Annual Turnover £3 million

Specialist aviation titles for pilots, historians and enthusiasts. Also twentieth century naval and military history. About 70 titles a year. TITLES *Airlife's World Aircraft; John 'Cat's Eyes' Cunningham; U-boat Tankers; Pilot's Weather.* Unsolicited mss, synopses and ideas for books welcome.
Royalties paid annually; twice-yearly by arrangement.

Ian Allan Publishing Ltd
Riverdene Business Park, Molesey Road, Hersham, Surrey KT12 4RG
☎01932 266600 Fax 01932 266601
Email info@ianallanpub.co.uk
Website www.ianallanpub.co.uk
Chairman *David Allan*
Managing Director *Tony Saunders*

Specialist transport publisher – atlases, maps, railway, aviation, road transport, military, maritime, reference. About 80 titles a year. Send sample chapter and synopsis with s.a.e. Manages distribution and sales for third party publishers.
IMPRINTS **Dial House** Sporting titles; **Midland Publishing** (see entry); **OPC** Railway titles.

J.A. Allen & Co.
An imprint of Robert Hale Ltd, Clerkenwell House, 45–47 Clerkenwell Green, London EC1R 0HT
☎020 7251 2661 Fax 020 7490 4958
Email allen@halebooks.com
Publisher *Caroline Burt*
Approx. Annual Turnover £750,000

FOUNDED 1926 as part of J.A. Allen & Co. (The Horseman's Bookshop) Ltd. Bought by **Robert Hale Ltd** in 1999. *Publishes* equine and equestrian non-fiction. About 20 titles a year. Mostly commissioned but willing to consider unsolicited mss of technical/instructional material related to all aspects of horses and horsemanship.
Royalties paid twice-yearly.

Allen Lane
See **Penguin Group (UK)**

Allison & Busby
Suite 111, Bon Marche Centre, 241 Ferndale Road, London SW9 8BJ
☎020 7738 7888 Fax 020 7733 4244
Email all@allisonbusby.co.uk
Website www.allisonandbusby.co.uk
Publishing Director *David Shelley*

FOUNDED 1967. *Publishes* literary fiction, crime fiction, biography and writers' guides. About 40 titles a year. TITLES *Little Green Men* Christopher Buckley; *The Encyclopaedia of Cult Children's TV* Richard Lewis; *Homage* Julian Rathbone. Send synopses with two sample chapters, not full mss. No replies without s.a.e.

Authors' Rating With one of the youngest publishing directors in the business (David Shelley is in his mid-20s), the reborn A&B is concentrating on fiction with a youth bias. The *Internet Writer's Handbook* is no relation.

Alpha Press
See **Sussex Academic Press**

Amber Lane Press Ltd
Cheorl House, Church Street, Charlbury, Oxfordshire OX7 3PR
☎01608 810024 Fax 01608 810024
Email jamberlane@aol.com
Chairman *Brian Clark*
Managing Director/Editorial Head *Judith Scott*
FOUNDED 1979 to publish modern play texts. *Publishes* plays and books on the theatre. About 4 titles a year. TITLES *Strange Fruit* Tony Marchant; *A Madhouse in Goa* Martin Sherman; *Kiss of the Spider Woman* Manuel Puig (play texts); *Strindberg and Love* Eivor Martinus. 'Expressly *not* interested in poetry.' No unsolicited mss. Synopses and ideas welcome.
Royalties paid twice-yearly.

AMCD (Publishers) Ltd
PO Box 182, Altrincham, Cheshire WA15 9UA
Email web@amcd.co.uk
Website www.amcd.co.uk
Managing Director *John Adams*
FOUNDED 1988. *Publishes* financial directories, books on China, local history, business books and foreign language dictionaries. Took over the Jensen Business Books imprint in 1993 and is well placed in electronic reference after developing its own software. In conjunction with JHC (Technology) Ltd, AMCD offers publishers access to the electronic book market with their reference, dictionary and directory Pop-Up© software packages which can handle most languages. About 5 titles a year. Welcomes ideas (by e-mail only) for business books, children's books and books on European history, China or the Far East. No poetry, fiction or historical romance.
Royalties paid twice yearly.

Amsco
See **Omnibus Press**

Andersen Press Ltd
20 Vauxhall Bridge Road, London SW1V 2SA
☎020 7870 8703/8700 Fax 020 7233 6263
Email andersenpress@randomhouse.co.uk
Website www.andersenpress.co.uk
Managing Director/Publisher *Klaus Flugge*
Editorial Director *Janice Thomson*
Editor, Fiction *Audrey Adams*
FOUNDED 1976 by Klaus Flugge and named after Hans Christian Andersen. *Publishes* children's high-quality picture books and fiction. Seventy per cent of the books are sold as co-productions abroad. TITLES *Elmer* David McKee; *One Little Angel* Ruth Brown; *I Want My Potty* Tony Ross; *Badger's Parting Gifts* Susan Varley; *little.com* Ralph Steadman; *Cat in the Manger* Michael Foreman; *Preston Pig Books* Colin McNaughton; *Junk* Melvin Burgess. Unsolicited mss welcome for picture books; synopsis in the first instance for books for young readers up to age 12. No poetry or short stories.
Royalties paid twice-yearly.

Authors' Rating The secret of Andersen's success is publishing children's books that are loved by adults. That and a wicked sense of fun that has been known to upset the education establishment – and hooray for that.

Chris Andrews Publications
15 Curtis Yard, North Hinksey Lane, Oxford OX2 0NA
☎01865 723404 Fax 01865 725294
Email chris.andrews@virgin.net
Website www.cap-ox.co.uk
Managing Director *Chris Andrews*
Approx. Annual Turnover £350,000
FOUNDED 1982. *Publishes* coffee table scenic travel guides. Also calendars, diaries, cards and posters. 10 titles in 2001 (including calendars and diaries). TITLES *Romance of Oxford; Romance of the Cotswolds.* Unsolicited synopses and ideas for travel/guide books will be considered; phone in the first instance. Also owns the **Oxford Picture Library** (see under **Picture Libraries**).

The Angel's Share
See **Neil Wilson Publishing Ltd**

Anness Publishing Ltd
Hermes House, 88–89 Blackfriars Road, London SE1 8HA
☎020 7401 2077 Fax 020 7633 9499

Email info@anness.com
Website www.nbn.books.com

Chairman/Managing Director *Paul Anness*
Publisher/Partner *Joanna Lorenz*

FOUNDED 1989. *Publishes* highly illustrated co-edition titles: general non-fiction – cookery, crafts, interior design, gardening, photography, decorating, lifestyle and children's. About 400 titles a year. IMPRINTS **Lorenz Books**; **Aquamarine**; **Hermes House**; **Peony Press**; **Southwater**.

Anthem Press
See **Wimbledon Publishing Company**

Antique Collectors' Club
Sandy Lane, Old Martlesham, Woodbridge, Suffolk IP12 4SD
☎01394 389950 Fax 01394 389999
Email sales@antique-acc.com
Website www.antique-acc.com

Managing Director *Diana Steel*
Sales Director *Mark Eastment*

FOUNDED 1966. Has a five-figure membership spread over the UK and the world. The Club's magazine *Antique Collecting* is sold on a subscription basis (currently £25 p.a.) and is published 10 times a year. It is sent free to members who may also buy the Club's books at special pre-publication prices. *Publishes* specialist books on antiques and collecting, the decorative arts, architecture and gardening. The price guide series was introduced in 1968 with the first edition of *The Price Guide to Antique Furniture*. Subject areas include furniture, silver/jewellery, metalwork, glass, textiles, art reference, ceramics, horology. Recent TITLES *Tiaras* Geoffrey Munn; *Frederick Sandys* Betty Elzea; *20th Century Ceramic Designers* Andrew Casey; *Scottish Wild Flowers* Mary McMurtrie. Unsolicited synopses and ideas for books welcome; no mss.
Royalties paid quarterly as a rule, but can vary.

Anvil Press Poetry Ltd
Neptune House, 70 Royal Hill, London SE10 8RF
☎020 8469 3033 Fax 020 8469 3363
Email anvil@anvilpresspoetry.com
Website www.anvilpresspoetry.com

Editorial Director *Peter Jay*

FOUNDED 1968 to promote English-language and foreign poetry, both classic and contemporary, in translation. English list includes Peter Levi, Dick Davis, Dennis O'Driscoll and Carol Ann Duffy. Translated books include Bei Dao, Celan, Dante, Lalic, Baudelaire, Lorca and Neruda. Preliminary enquiry required for translations. Unsolicited book-length collections of poems are welcome from writers whose work has appeared in poetry magazines. Please enclose adequate return postage.

Authors' Rating With a little help from the Arts Council, Anvil has become one of the foremost publishers of living poets.

Apollos
See **Inter-Varsity Press**

Apple
See **Quarto Publishing** under **UK Packagers**

Appletree Press Ltd
The Old Potato Station, 14 Howard Street South, Belfast BT7 1AP
☎028 9024 3074 Fax 028 9024 6756
Email reception@appletree.ie
Website www.appletree.ie

Managing Director *John Murphy*
Publishing Manager *Paul Harron*

FOUNDED 1974. *Publishes* cookery and other small-format gift books, plus general non-fiction of Irish and Scottish interest. TITLES *Little Cookbook* series (about 40 titles); *Ireland: The Complete Guide*. No unsolicited mss; send initial letter or synopsis.
Royalties paid twice-yearly in the first year, annually thereafter. For the *Little Cookbook* series, a standard fee is paid.

Aquamarine
See **Anness Publishing Ltd**

Arc Publications
Nanholme Mill, Shaw Wood Road, Todmorden, Lancashire OL14 6DA
☎01706 812338 Fax 01706 818948
Email arc.publications@virgin.net
Website www.arcpublications.co.uk

Publishers *Rosemary Jones, Angela Jarman*
General Editor *Tony Ward*
Associate Editors *John Kinsella* (International), *Jo Shapcott* (UK), *Jean Boase-Beier* (Translations)

FOUNDED in 1969 to specialise in the publication of contemporary poetry from new and established writers both in the UK and abroad. AUTHORS Sarah Day and John Tranter (Australia), Donald Atkinson, Chris Emery and Michael Haslam (UK), Tadeusz Rosewicz

(Poland), Cevat Çapan (Turkey), Richard Howard, Michael Harper and Thomas Lux (USA), Mika Haugova (Slovakia), Arjen Duinker (Holland). 13 titles a year. Authors submitting material should ensure that it is compatible with the current list, include a history of published works and enclose an s.a.e. if they wish mss to be returned. Electronic submissions are not accepted. IMPRINT **Arc Music** specialises in profiles of contemporary composers (particularly where none have existed hitherto) and symposia which take a 'new approach' to well-visited territory. Commissioned work only.

Arcadia Books

15–16 Nassau Street, London W1W 7AB
☎020 7436 9898 Fax 020 7436 9898
Email info@arcadiabooks.co.uk
Website www.arcadiabooks.co.uk
Managing Director *Gary Pulsifer*

Small, independent publishing house, FOUNDED in 1996, specialising in translated fiction from around the world. *Publishes* literary fiction, gay fiction, biography, autobiography, gender studies, travel writing. About 20 titles in 2001. TITLE *The Deposition of Father McGreevy* Brian O'Doherty. Does not welcome unsolicited material.

Royalties paid twice-yearly.

Argentum

See **Aurum Press Ltd**

Aris & Phillips Ltd

Teddington House, Warminster, Wiltshire BA12 8PQ
☎01985 213409 Fax 01985 212910
Email Aris.Phillips@btinternet.com
Website www.arisandphillips.com
Managing/Editorial Director *Adrian Phillips*
Editor, Hispanic Classics *Lucinda Phillips*

FOUNDED 1972 to publish books on Egyptology. A family firm which has remained independent for 30 years. *Publishes* academic, classical, oriental and hispanic. About 20 titles a year. TITLES *Campo Libre* (series); *The Tomb and Beyond* Naguib Kanawati; *Fecundity Figures* John Baines; *Late Egyptian Grammar* Friedrich Junge. Also publishes books for the Griffith Institute, the British School of Archaeology in Iraq, and the Gibb Memorial Trust, Australian Centre for Egyptology. With such a highly specialised list, unsolicited mss and synopses are not particularly welcome, but synopses will be considered.

Royalties paid twice-yearly.

Arnold

See **Hodder Headline Ltd**

Arrow

See **Random House Group Ltd**

Artech House

46 Gillingham Street, London SW1V 1AH
☎020 7596 8750 Fax 020 7630 0166
Email jlancashire@artechhouse.co.uk
Website www.artechhouse.com
Managing Director (USA) *William M. Bazzy*
Senior Commissioning Editor *Dr Julie Lancashire*

FOUNDED 1969. European office of Artech House Inc., Boston. *Publishes* electronic engineering, especially telecommunications, computer communications, computing, optoelectronics, signal processing, digital audio and video, intelligent transportation systems and technology management (books, software and videos). 60–70 titles a year. Unsolicited mss and synopses in the specialised areas listed are considered.

Royalties paid twice-yearly.

Ashgate Publishing Ltd

Gower House, Croft Road, Aldershot, Hampshire GU11 3HR
☎01252 331551 Fax 01252 317446 (Ashgate)/344405 (Gower)/3685954 (Lund Humphries)
Email info@ashgatepub.co.uk
Website www.ashgate.com *and* www.gowerpub.com
Chairman *Nigel Farrow*

FOUNDED 1967. *Publishes* business and professional titles under the **Gower** imprint and humanities, social sciences, law and legal studies under the **Ashgate** imprint. In December 1999 acquired **Lund Humphries**, publisher of art books and exhibition catalogues.

DIVISIONS **Ashgate** *Sarah Markham* Social sciences; *John Smedley* History/Variorum collected studies; *Rachel Lynch* Music and history; *Erika Gaffney* Literary studies; *Sarah Lloyd* Philosophy and religion; *Pamela Edwardes* Art history; *John Hindley* Aviation studies. **Gower** *Jo Burges, Jonathan Norman* Business, management and training; *John Irwin* Law and legal studies. **Lund Humphries** *Lucy Myers*. Access the websites for information on submission of material.

Ashgrove Publishing

55 Richmond Avenue, London N1 0LX
☎020 7713 7540 Fax 020 7713 7541
Email gmo73@dial.pipex.com

Website www.ashgrovepublishing.com
Chairman/Managing Director *Brad Thompson*
Approx. Annual Turnover £75,000

Acquired by Hollydata Publishers in 1999, Ashgrove has been publishing for over twenty years. *Publishes* mind, body, spirit, health, cookery, sports. 7 titles in 2001. No unsolicited mss; approach with letter and outline in the first instance.
Royalties paid twice-yearly.

Ashmolean Museum Publications

Ashmolean Museum, Beaumont Street, Oxford OX1 2PH
☎01865 278009 Fax 01865 278018
Email publications@ashmus.ox.ac.uk
Website www.ashmol.ox.ac.uk
Publisher/Editorial Head *Ian Charlton*

The Ashmolean Museum, which is wholly owned by Oxford University, was FOUNDED in 1683. The first publication appeared in 1890 but publishing did not really start in earnest until the 1960s. *Publishes* European and Oriental fine and applied arts, European archaeology and ancient history, Egyptology and numismatics, for both adult and children's markets. About 8 titles a year. No fiction, American/African art, ethnography, modern art or post-medieval history. Most publications are based on and illustrated from the Museum's collections.

IMPRINTS **Ashmoleum Museum Publications**; **Griffith Institute** (Egyptology imprint). Recent TITLES *Embroideries and Samplers From Islamic Egypt; Jules Flandrin Paintings; Twentieth Century Sculpture; Uccello's Hunt in the Forest; Modern Chinese Art; French Drawings and Watercolours*. No unsolicited mss.
Royalties paid annually.

Associated University Presses (AUP)

See **Golden Cockerel Press Ltd**

Athlone

See **The Continuum International Publishing Group Limited**

Atlantic Europe Publishing Co. Ltd

Greys Court Farm, Greys Court, Nr Henley on Thames, Oxfordshire RG9 4PG
☎01491 628188 Fax 01491 628189
Email info@AtlanticEurope.com
Website www.AtlanticEurope.com *and* www.curriculumVisions.com

Directors *Dr B.J. Knapp, D.L.R. McCrae*

Closely associated, since 1990, with Earthscape Editions packaging operation. *Publishes* full-colour, highly illustrated children's non-fiction in hardback for international co-editions and text books. Not interested in any other material. Main focus is on National Curriculum titles, especially in the fields of mathematics, science, technology, social history and geography. About 25 titles a year. Unsolicited synopses and ideas for non-fiction curriculum-based books welcome by e-mail only – does not accept material sent by post.
Fees paid.

AUP (Associated University Presses)

See **Golden Cockerel Press Ltd**

Aurum Press Ltd

25 Bedford Avenue, London WC1B 3AT
☎020 7637 3225 Fax 020 7580 2469
Email editorial@aurumpress.co.uk
Managing Director *Bill McCreadie*
Editorial Director *Piers Burnett*
Approx. Annual Turnover £3 million

FOUNDED 1977. Formerly owned by Andrew Lloyd Webber's Really Useful Group, now owned jointly by Piers Burnett, Bill McCreadie and Sheila Murphy, all of whom worked together in the 1970s for André Deutsch. Committed to producing high-quality, illustrated/non-illustrated adult non-fiction in the areas of general human interest, art and craft, lifestyle, sport and travel. About 60 titles a year. IMPRINTS **Argentum** Practical photography books; **Jacqui Small** High-quality lifestyle books.
Royalties paid twice-yearly.

Authentic Lifestyle

See **Paternoster Publishing**

AuthorsOnline

15–17 Maidenhead Street, Hertford, Hertfordshire SG14 1DW
☎01992 586788 Fax 01992 586787
Email theeditor@authorsonline.co.uk
Website www.authorsonline.co.uk
Owner *AuthorsOnLine Ltd.*
Managing Director *Gary Lee*
Editor *Richard Fitt*
Approx. Annual Turnover £1 million

FOUNDED 1997. *Publishes* new and reverted rights work in both electronic format via their website and traditional hard-copy. All genre welcome. Also offers a service to help authors self-publish in both formats. Submit mss by post or e-mail. Further information available via the website.

Autumn Publishing Ltd
North Barn, Appledram Barns, Birdham Road, Near Chichester, West Sussex PO20 7EQ
☎01243 531660 Fax 01243 774433
Email autumn@autumnpublishing.co.uk
Website www.autumnpublishing.co.uk
Managing Director *Michael Herridge*
Editorial Director *Ingrid Goldsmid*
FOUNDED 1976. Publisher of children's puzzle, activity and sticker books. About 50 titles a year. Unsolicited synopses and ideas for books welcome if they come within relevant subject areas.
Payment varies according to contract; generally a flat fee.

Award Publications Limited
1st Floor, 27 Longford Street, London NW1 3DZ
☎020 7388 7800 Fax 020 7388 7887
Email info@awardpublications.co.uk

FOUNDED 1958. *Publishes* children's books, both fiction and reference. 40 titles in 2001. IMPRINT **Horus Editions**. No unsolicited mss, synopses or ideas.

Azure
See **Society for Promoting Christian Knowledge**

Baillière Tindall
See **Harcourt Publishers International**

Duncan Baird Publishers
Castle House, 75–76 Wells Street, London W1T 3QH
☎020 7323 2229 Fax 020 7580 5692
Email james@dbairdpub.co.uk
Managing Director *Duncan Baird*
Editorial Director *Bob Saxton*
Approx. Annual Turnover £5 million
FOUNDED in 1992 to publish and package co-editions overseas and went on to launch its own publishing operation in 1998. *Publishes* illustrated cultural reference, world religions, health, mind, body and spirit, lifestyle, graphic design. 30 titles in 2001. No unsolicited mss. Synopses and ideas welcome; approach in writing in the first instance with s.a.e. No fiction or UK-only subjects.
Royalties paid twice-yearly.

Bantam/Bantam Press
See **Transworld Publishers**

Barefoot Books Ltd
124 Walcot Street, Bath BA1 5BG
☎01225 322400 Fax 01225 322499
Email edit@barefootbooks.com
Website www.barefootbooks.com
Publisher *Tessa Strickland*
FOUNDED in 1993. *Publishes* high-quality children's picture books, particularly new and traditional stories from a wide range of cultures. 30 titles in 2001. TITLES *The Genius of Leonardo*; *The Gigantic Turnip*; *Tales From Old Ireland*. No unsolicited mss.
Royalties paid twice-yearly.

Authors' Rating Writers of children's books would do well to keep track of Barefoot which, from small beginnings, is building a quality list that must be the envy of bigger publishers.

Baring & Rogerson
See **Eland Publishing Ltd**

Barny Books
The Cottage, Hough on the Hill, Near Grantham, Lincolnshire NG32 2BB
☎01400 250246/01522 790009
Fax 01400 251737
Managing Director/Editorial Head *Molly Burkett*
Business Manager *Tom Cann*
Approx. Annual Turnover £10,000
FOUNDED with the aim of encouraging new writers and illustrators. *Publishes* mainly children's books but moving into adult fiction and non-fiction. TITLES *Iron Jim* Andy Howarth; *Once Upon a Wartime* (series); *Hell, Fire and Damnation* Mario Martinez; *Trusty the Traitor* Ben Bartlett. Too small a concern to have the staff/resources to deal with unsolicited mss. Writers with strong ideas should approach Molly Burkett by letter in the first instance. Also runs a readership and advisory service for new writers (£10 fee for short stories or illustrations; £25 fee for full-length stories).
Royalties Division of profits 50/50.

Authors' Rating A gutsy small publisher with a sense of fun which appeals to youngsters.

Barrington Stoke
10 Belford Terrace, Edinburgh EH4 3DQ
☎0131 315 4933 Fax 0131 315 4934
Email info@barringtonstoke.co.uk

Website www.barringtonstoke.co.uk
Chairman *Patience Thomson*
Managing Director *Lucy Juckes*
Editorial Head *Samantha Parkinson*
Approx. Annual Turnover £310,000
FOUNDED in 1998 to publish books for 'reluctant, disenchanted and under-confident' young readers. Produces a series of audio books and issues teachers' notes to accompany teenage fiction titles. 24 titles in 2001. DIVISIONS **Fiction for 8–13-year-olds**; **4u2read.OK**; **Teenage Fiction** TITLES *Living With Vampires; Tod in Biker City; Runaway Teacher.* No unsolicited material. Books commissioned via literary agents only.
Royalties paid twice-yearly.

B.T. Batsford Ltd

64 Brewery Road, London N7 9NT
☎020 7697 3000 Fax 020 7697 3001
Email info@batsford.com
Website www.batsford.com
Chairman *John Needleman*
Publisher *Roger Huggins*
Approx. Annual Turnover £2 million
FOUNDED in 1843 as a bookseller, and began publishing in 1874. Acquired by **Chrysalis** in 1999. A world leader in books on chess, arts and craft. *Publishes* non-fiction: archaeology, bridge and chess, cinema, crafts and hobbies, fashion and costume, graphic design and gardening. About 100 titles a year.
Royalties paid twice in first year, annually thereafter.

BBC Books

BBC Worldwide Ltd , 80 Wood Lane, London W12 0TT
☎020 8433 2000 Fax 020 8433 3707
Website www.bbcworldwide.com
Head of Books *Tracey Smith*
Approx. Annual Turnover £450 million
Publishes TV tie-in and some stand-alone titles, including books which, though linked with BBC television or radio, may not simply be the 'book of the series'. Also TV tie-in titles for children. 100 titles a year. TITLES *Gary Rhodes' New British Classics* and *At the Table*; *A History of Britain* Simon Schama; and autobiographies – Terry Wogan, Steve Redgrave, Esther Rantzen. Unsolicited mss (which come in at the rate of about 40 weekly) are rarely accepted. However, strong ideas well expressed will always be considered, and promising letters stand a chance of further scrutiny.
Royalties paid twice-yearly.

Authors' Rating What with The Tweenies and Delia Smith, BBC Worldwide can hardly go wrong – except perhaps with those who question why such a profitable organisation needs to hike up the annual licence fee. BBC Worldwide is now Britain's ninth biggest book publisher with a growth rate that rivals would die for. The biggest expansion is in children's books and talking books. The BBC archive is a treasure trove still waiting to be fully explored. But more new titles can be expected now that BBC has bought Cover to Cover, a leading producer of unabridged readings on tape. So far BBC has fought shy of full-length readings. This will now change. All writers, including those not yet broadcasting names, are likely to benefit.

Bedford Square Press

See **NCVO Publications**

Belair

See **Folens Limited**

Belitha Press

Chrysalis Children's Books, 64 Brewery Road, London N7 9NT
☎020 7967 3000 Fax 020 7967 3003
Email info@belithapress.co.uk
Website www.belithapress.co.uk
Publisher *Chester Fisher*
FOUNDED 1980. Part of the children's division of **Chrysalis Books**. *Publishes* children's non-fiction in all curriculum areas. About 125 titles a year. All titles are expected to sell in at least four co-editions. TITLES *Start Writing; Art for All; History Mysteries; Monster Machines.* No unsolicited mss. Synopses and ideas for books welcome from experienced children's writers.

Ben Gunn

See **SB Publications**

David Bennett Books

Chrysalis Children's Books, 64 Brewery Road, London N7 9NT
☎020 7967 3000 Fax 020 7967 3003
Email info@db-books.co.uk
Website www.db-books.co.uk
Managing Editor *Helen Mortimer*
FOUNDED 1989. Part of the children's division of **Chrysalis Books**. *Publishes* children's picture and novelty books, interactive and board books, baby gifts and non-fiction for babies and toddlers. No unsolicited mss.

Berg Publishers

150 Cowley Road, Oxford OX4 1JJ
☎01865 245104 Fax 01865 791165
Email enquiry@berg.demon.co.uk
Website www.bergpublishers.com

Editorial & Managing Director *Kathryn Earle*
Production Director *Sara Everett*

Publishes scholarly books in the fields of history, fashion, cultural studies, social sciences and humanities. About 52 titles a year plus two journals, *Fashion Theory* and *Textile: The Journal of Cloth and Culture*. TITLES *Bound to Please: A History of the Victorian Corset* Leigh Summers; *Fashion Under the Occupation* Dominique Veillon (English trans.); *British Subjects: An Anthropology of Britain* ed. Nigel Rapport; *The Changing Face of Football: Racism, Identity and Multiculture in the English Game* Les Back, Tim Crabbe, John Solomos. IMPRINT **Oswald Wolff Books**. No unsolicited mss. Synopses and ideas for books welcome.
Royalties paid annually.

Berghahn Books

3 Newtec Place, Magdalen Road, Oxford OX4 1RE
☎01865 250011 Fax 01865 250056
Email editorialUK@berghahnbooks.com
Website www.berghahnbooks.com

Chairman/Managing Director *Marion Berghahn*
Approx. Annual Turnover £700,000

FOUNDED 1994. Academic publisher of books and journals. 65 titles in 2001. TITLES *The History of the Armenian Genocide; Western Historical Thinking; Displacement, Forced Settlement and Conservation*. No unsolicited mss; will consider synopses and ideas for books. Approach by e-mail in the first instance. No fiction or trade books.
Royalties paid annually. Overseas associate Berghahn Books Inc., New York.

Berkswell Publishing Co. Ltd

PO Box 420, Warminster, Wiltshire BA12 9XB
☎01985 840189 Fax 01985 840243
Email John.Stidolph@btinternet.com

Managing Director *John Stidolph*

FOUNDED 1974. *Publishes* churches, heritage, country sports, biography, books about Wessex and *The Churchwarden's Yearbook*. No fiction.

About 4 titles a year. Unsolicited mss, synopses and ideas for books welcome.
Royalties paid according to contract.

Berlitz Publishing Co. Ltd

Suite 120, 24–25 Nutford Place, London W1H 5YN
☎020 7569 3160 Fax 020 7725 7013
Email publishing@berlitz.co.uk
Website www.berlitz.com

Managing Director *R. Kirkpatrick*

FOUNDED 1970. Acquired by the Langenscheidt Publishing Group in February 2002. *Publishes* travel and language-learning products only: travel guides, phrasebooks and language courses. SERIES *Pocket Guides; Berlitz Complete Guide to Cruising and Cruise Ships; Phrase Books; Pocket Dictionaries; Business Phrase Books; Self-teach: Rush Hour Commuter Cassettes; Think & Talk; Berlitz Kids*. No unsolicited mss.

BeWrite Books

See entry under **Electronic Publishing and Other Services**

BFI Publishing

British Film Institute, 21 Stephen Street, London W1T 1LN
☎020 7255 1444 Fax 020 7636 2516
Website www.bfi.org.uk

Head of Publishing *Andrew Lockett*
Approx. Annual Turnover £600,000

FOUNDED 1980. Part of the **British Film Institute**. *Publishes* academic, educational and general film/television-related books. About 30 titles a year. TITLES *Film Classics* (series); *Modern Classics* (series); *The Cinema Book*, revised edition, eds. Pam Cook and Mieke Bernink; *BFI Film & Television Handbook* (annual) Eddie Dyja. Unsolicited synopses preferred to complete mss.
Royalties paid annually.

BFP Books

Focus House, 497 Green Lanes, London N13 4BP
☎020 8882 3315 Fax 020 8886 5174

Chief Executive *John Tracy*
Commissioning Editor *Stewart Gibson*

FOUNDED 1982. The publishing arm of the Bureau of Freelance Photographers. *Publishes* illustrated books on photography, mainly aspects of freelancing and marketing pictures. No unsolicited mss but ideas welcome.

Big Fish

Chrysalis Children's Books, 64 Brewery
Road, London N7 9NT
☎020 7967 3000 Fax 020 7967 3003
Email info@bigfishonline.co.uk
Website www.bigfishonline.co.uk
Publisher *Chester Fisher*
Part of the children's division of **Chrysalis
Books**. *Publishes* children's non-fiction in all
curriculum areas. About 125 titles a year. All
titles are expected to sell in at least four co-
editions. No unsolicited mss. Synopses and
ideas for books welcome from experienced
children's writers.

Clive Bingley Books

See **Facet Publishing**

Birlinn Ltd

West Newington House, 10 Newington
Road, Edinburgh EH9 1QS
☎0131 668 4371 Fax 0131 668 4466
Email info@birlinn.co.uk
Website www.birlinn.co.uk
Managing Editor *Hugh Andrew*
FOUNDED 1992. Acquired **John Donald
Publishers** in 1999 (see entry). *Publishes* local
and military history, Gaelic, humour, Highland
history, adventure, Scottish reference, guide-
books and folklore. 70 titles in 2001. No unso-
licited mss; synopses and ideas welcome.
Royalties paid.

Black & White Publishing Ltd

99 Giles Street, Edinburgh EH6 6BZ
☎0131 625 4500 Fax 0131 625 4501
Email mail@blackandwhitepublishing.com
Website www.blackandwhitepublishing.com
Director *Campbell Brown*
FOUNDED 1990. *Publishes* general fiction and
non-fiction, including memoirs, sport, cookery, humour and guidebooks. Text only submissions via website or synopsis and sample
chapter by post with s.a.e. or return postage.
IMPRINT **Itchy Coo** Scots language resources
for use in schools.
Royalties paid twice-yearly.

A.&C. Black (Publishers) Ltd

Alderman House, 37 Soho Square, London
W1D 3QZ
☎020 7758 0200 Fax 020 7758 0222
Email enquiries@acblack.com
Website www.acblack.com
Chairman *Nigel Newton*

Managing Director *Jill Coleman*
Approx. Annual Turnover £10 million
Publishes children's and educational books,
including music, for 3–15-year-olds, arts and
crafts, ceramics, fishing, ornithology, nautical,
reference, sport, theatre and travel. About 125
titles a year. Acquisitions brought the Herbert
Press' art, design and general books, Adlard
Coles' sailing list and Christopher Helm's and
Pica Press's natural history and ornithology lists
into A.&C. Black's stable. Bought by
Bloomsbury Publishing in May 2000.
IMPRINTS **Adlard Coles Nautical**;
Christopher Helm; **The Herbert Press**;
Pica Press. TITLES *New Mermaid* drama series;
Who's Who; *Writers' & Artists' Yearbook*; *Know
the Game* sports series; *Blue Guides* travel series;
Rockets and *Graffix* children's series. Initial
enquiry appreciated before submission of mss.
Royalties Payment varies according to con-
tract.

Black Ace Books

PO Box 6557, Forfar DD8 2YS
☎01307 465096 Fax 01307 465494
Website www.blackacebooks.com
Managing Directors *Hunter Steele, Boo Wood*
FOUNDED 1991. *Publishes* new fiction, Scottish
and general; some non-fiction including bi-
ography, history, philosophy and psychology.
36 titles in print. IMPRINTS **Black Ace Books**,
Black Ace Paperbacks TITLES *Succeeding at
Sex and Scotland, Or the Case of Louis Morel*
Hunter Steele; *La Tendresse* Ken Strauss MD;
Count Dracula (The Authorized Version) Hagen
Slawkberg; *Caryddwen's Cauldron* Paul Hilton;
The Sinister Cabaret John Herdman. No chil-
dren's, poetry, cookery, DIY, religion. 'No
submissions at all, please, without first checking
our website for details of current requirements
and submission guidelines.'
Royalties paid twice-yearly.

Black Dagger Crime

See **Chivers Press Ltd**

Black Lace

See **Virgin Books Ltd**

Black Sheep Books

PO Box 538, Hemel Hempstead,
Hertfordshire HP2 5GT
☎01442 257600 Fax 01442 252848
Email blacksheepbooks@supanet.com
Website www.blacksheepbooks.co.uk
Crime/Thrillers *Jack Crane*

General *Mark Evans*
Children's *Lisa Goode*
Approx. Annual Turnover £110,000

FOUNDED 1996. 'Bridges the gap between conventional publishers and literary agents by producing and promoting introductory publications. Look out for the Big Black Bus, mobile book fair.' Produces books by new writers in small print runs with a view to placing them with a larger publisher. *Publishes* true crime, crime fiction, thrillers, general fiction and non-fiction, children's. 20 titles in 2003. 'New writers preferred. We are receptive to any exciting material in any genre.' Submissions should be by post with s.a.e. or via the website.
Royalties paid twice-yearly.

Black Spring Press Ltd

Burbage House, 83–85 Curtain Road, London EC2A 3BS
☎020 7613 3066 Fax 020 7613 0028
Email general@dexterhaven.demon.co.uk

Directors *Robert Hastings, Alexander Hastings*

FOUNDED 1986. *Publishes* fiction and non-fiction, literary criticism, biography. About 5 titles a year. TITLES *The Lost Weekend* Charles Jackson; *The Big Brass Ring* Orson Welles; *The Tenant* Roland Topor; *The Terrible News* collection of Russian short stories by Zamyatin, Babel, Kharms, *et al.* No unsolicited mss.
Royalties paid twice-yearly.

Black Swan

See **Transworld Publishers**

Blackie & Co. Publishers

107–111 Fleet Street, London EC4A 2AB
☎020 7936 9021 Fax 020 7936 9100
Email editors@blackiepublishers.com
Website www.blackiepublishers.com

Editorial Head *Bettina Croft*
Managing Editor *Alison Taylor Foddy*
Consultant Editors *Dr Susan Forsyth PhD, Gill Smith, Laura Nuttall*

FOUNDED 1999. *Publishes* fiction and non-fiction, biography, autobiography, heritage, educational, literature – romance including historical fiction and non-fiction, women's issues, the environment, crime, science fiction/fantasy, computers/the Internet, religious, some illustrated children's, popular and academic. About 70–90 titles a year. TITLES *As the Dawn Breaketh* Bernard Hyde-Tingley; *Bill Tidy's Sporting Legends*; *Heart of Shadows (Lord Byron and the Supernatural)* Derek Fox and Mike

Vardy; *Straws in the Wind* Polly Harris. Talking Tapes/CDs produced. Authors considered for e-books in 2003. No unsolicited mss.
Royalties paid annually.

Authors' Rating Liable to ask authors to contribute towards costs of publication.

Blackstaff Press Ltd

Blackstaff House, Wildflower Way, Apollo Road, Belfast BT12 6TA
☎028 9066 8074 Fax 028 9066 8207
Email info@blackstaffpress.com
Website www.blackstaffpress.com

Director/Editorial Head *Anne Tannahill*

FOUNDED 1971. *Publishes* mainly, but not exclusively, Irish interest books, fiction, poetry, history, politics, illustrated editions, natural history and humour. About 25 titles a year. Unsolicited mss considered, but preliminary submission of synopsis plus short sample of writing preferred. Return postage *must* be enclosed.
Royalties paid twice-yearly.

Authors' Rating This Belfast publisher is noted for a strong backlist, 'wonderfully well-presented catalogues and promotional material'.

Blackwell Publishing

Osney Mead, Oxford OX2 0EL
☎01865 206206 Fax 01865 721205
Website www.blackwellpublishing.com

Also at: 108 Cowley Road, Oxford OX4 1JF
☎01865 791100 Fax 01865 791347

Chief Executive *René Olivieri*
President *Robert Campbell*
Chairman *Nigel Blackwell*

The holding company for Blackwell Science, Blackwell Publishers and Danish academic publisher Blackwell Munksgaard.

Blackwell Science (at Osney Mead address) FOUNDED 1939. *Publishes* medical, professional and science. About 400 titles a year, plus 350 journals, available online.

Blackwell Publishers (at Cowley Road address) FOUNDED 1926. *Publishes* journals and textbooks in social sciences, business and humanities. About 300 titles a year and over 250 journals.

Authors' Rating Blackwell Science's main business is in scientific journals, mostly produced in partnership with learned societies, and medical publishing. Much of the growth is in mainland Europe where Blackwell Science has offshoots in Berlin, Paris and Vienna.

John Blake Publishing Ltd

3 Bramber Court, 2 Bramber Road, London
W14 9PB
☎020 7381 0666 Fax 020 7381 6868
Email words@blake.co.uk
Managing Director *John Blake*
Deputy Managing Director *Rosie Ries*
FOUNDED 1991 and expanding rapidly. Bought
the assets of Smith Gryphon Ltd in 1997 and
acquired Metro Publishing in 2001. *Publishes*
mass-market non-fiction. No fiction, children's, specialist or non-commercial. About
100 titles a year. No unsolicited mss; synopses
and ideas welcome. Please enclose s.a.e.
Royalties paid twice-yearly.

Authors' Rating Now there are two. John
Blake, partner and brother of David Blake, has
set up this new operation to commission front
list while the original Blake Publishing will
concentrate on back list. But the formula for
success – sensational titles linked to the famous
and infamous – stays the same. Think of Blake's
top seller for last year, *Brooklyn*, a spoof diary of
the Beckham's baby, and you get the idea.

Blandford Press

See **Octopus Publishing Group**

Bloodaxe Books Ltd

Highgreen, Tarset, Northumberland
NE48 1RP
☎01434 240500 Fax 01434 240505
Email editor@bloodaxebooks.demon.co.uk
Website www.bloodaxebooks.demon.com
Managing/Editorial Director *Neil Astley*

Publishes poetry, literature and criticism, and
related titles by British, Irish, European, Commonwealth and American writers. 95 per cent
of the list is poetry. About 30 titles a year.
TITLES include three major anthologies, *The
Bloodaxe Book of 20th Century Poetry* Edna
Longley (ed.); *The New Poetry* Hulse, Kennedy
and Morley (eds.); *Sixty Women Poets* Linda
France (ed.); *Selected Poems* Jenny Joseph; *Poems*
J.H. Prynne; *Poems 1960–2000* Fleur Adcock;
recent collections by Selima Hill, Helen
Dunmore and Peter Reading. Unsolicited
poetry mss welcome; send a sample of no more
than 10 poems with s.a.e., 'but if you don't read
contemporary poetry, don't bother'. No e-mail
attachments. Authors of other material should
write in the first instance.
Royalties paid annually.

Authors' Rating Assisted by regional Arts
Council funding, Bloodaxe is one of the liveliest and most innovative of poetry publishers
with a list that takes in some of the best of the
younger poets.

Bloomsbury Publishing Plc

38 Soho Square, London W1D 3HB
☎020 7494 2111 Fax 020 7434 0151
Website www.bloomsburymagazine.com
Chairman/Chief Executive *Nigel Newton*
Publishing Directors *Alexandra Pringle,*
  Liz Calder, Kathy Rooney, Arzu Tahsin,
  Sarah Odedina, Jonathan Glasspool
Approx. Annual Turnover £26 million

FOUNDED 1986 by Nigel Newton, David
Reynolds, Alan Wherry and Liz Calder. Over
the following years Bloomsbury titles were to
appear regularly on *The Sunday Times* bestseller
list and many of its authors have gone on to
win prestigious literary prizes. In 1991 Nadine
Gordimer won the **Nobel Prize for
Literature**; Michael Ondaatje's *The English
Patient* won the 1992 **Booker Prize**; in 1997
Anne Michaels' *Fugitive Pieces* won both the
Orange Prize for Fiction and the Guardian
Fiction Prize. J.K. Rowling's *Harry Potter and
the Philosopher's Stone, Harry Potter and the
Chamber of Secrets* and *Harry Potter and the
Prisoner of Azkaban* won the **Nestlé Smarties
Book Prize** in 1997, 1998 and 1999 respec-
tively. Margaret Atwood's *The Blind Assassin*
won the **Booker Prize** in 2000. Published *The
Encarta World English Dictionary* in 1999.
Acquired **A.&C. Black (Publishers) Ltd** in
May 2000.
  Publishes literary fiction and non-fiction,
including general reference; also audiobooks.
AUTHORS include J.K. Rowling, Margaret
Atwood, T.C. Boyle, Daniel Goleman, David
Guterson, John Irving, Jay McInerney, Will
Self, Hunter S. Thompson, Rupert Thomson,
Joanna Trollope. Unsolicited mss and synopses
welcome; no poetry.
  Royalties paid twice-yearly.

Authors' Rating All praise to Harry Potter
whose record breaking sales have sent
Bloomsbury adrenaline rocketing. J.K.
Rowling now accounts for some 40 per cent of
Bloomsbury's turnover. But let no one suggest
that the company is lapsing into self satisfaction. The hunt is on for other strong sellers as
investment in overseas marketing and electronic publishing takes off. The problem for
new writers, of course, is finding a way
through the crowd of other hopefuls besieging
the Soho offices. Have a go by all means but
don't expect a quick response.

BMJ Books

BMA House, Tavistock Square, London
WC1H 9JR
☎020 7387 4499   Fax 020 7383 6662
Email jhudson@bmjbooks.com
Website www.bmjbooks.com
Chairman *Stella Dutton*
Managing Director *John Hudson*
Approx. Annual Turnover £2 million
FOUNDED 1988. Part of the British Medical
Journal Publishing Group. Book publishing
developed initially from collections of BMJ
articles but majority of titles now commis-
sioned independently of the Journal. *Publishes*
books on clinical medicine aimed at medical
professionals. 41 titles in 2001. No unsolicited
mss; will consider e-mailed synopses and ideas
for books.
Royalties paid twice-yearly.

Boatswain Press

See **Kenneth Mason Publications Ltd**

Bobcat

See **Omnibus Press**

The Bodley Head

See **Random House Group Ltd**

The Book Guild Ltd

Temple House, 25 High Street, Lewes,
East Sussex BN7 2LU
☎01273 472534   Fax 01273 476472
Email info@bookguild.co.uk
Website www.bookguild.co.uk
Chairman *George M. Nissen, CBE*
Managing Director *Carol Biss*
FOUNDED 1982. *Publishes* fiction, human inter-
est, media, children's fiction, academic, natural
history, naval and military, biography, art. About
80 titles a year. Expanding mainstream list plus
developing the human interest/media genre.
DIVISIONS
Photography/Travel *Healey's World* Denis
Healey. **Autobiography** *Vodka on Ice; A Year
with the Russians in Antarctica* Charles
Swithinbank. **Human Interest** *Collision Course*
Admiral Sir Raymond Lygo; *Flying Made It
Happen* Charles Hughesdon. **Food and Drink**
A Treasury of Persian Cuisine Shirin Simmons.
Children's *Nell of the Seas* Mark Scott. **Fiction**
Tales of Love and War Julian Fane; *Nothing Purple
Nothing Black* Paul Crawford; *Swimming in Circles*

Fanny Frewen. Unsolicited mss, ideas and synopses welcome.
Royalties paid twice-yearly.

Authors' Rating Regularly advertises for
authors who may be asked to cover their own
production costs. But in promoting its services,
The Book Guild is more up-front with its clients
than the typical vanity publisher who promises
the earth and delivers next to nothing.

Book House

See **Salariya Book Company Ltd** under
UK Packagers

Border Lines Biographies

See **Seren**

Boulevard Books &
The Babel Guides

71 Lytton Road, Oxford OX4 3NY
☎01865 712931   Fax 01865 712931
Email raybabel@dircon.co.uk
Website www.babelguides.com
Managing Director *Ray Keenoy*
Specialises in contemporary world fiction by
young writers in English translation. Existing or
forthcoming series of fiction from Brazil, Italy,
Latin America, Low Countries, Greece, and
elsewhere. The Babel Guides series of popular
guides to fiction in translation started in 1995.
DIVISONS
Latin American *Ray Keenoy* TITLE *Hotel
Atlantico* J.G. Noll. **Italian** *Fiorenza Conte* TITLE
The Toy Catalogue Sandra Petrignani. **Brazil** *Dr
David Treece* TITLE *The Jaguar*. **Low Countries**
Prof. Theo Hermans. **Greece** *Marina Coriolano-
Likourezos*. **Babel Guides to Fiction in
Translation** Series Editor *Ray Keenoy* TITLES
*Babel Guide to Italian Fiction in Translation; Babel
Guide to the Fiction of Portugal, Brazil & Africa in
Translation; Babel Guide to French Fiction in English
Translation; Babel Guide to Jewish Fiction; Babel
Guide to Scandinavian Fiction*. Suggestions and
proposals for translations of contemporary fiction
welcome. Also seeking contributors to forth-
coming Babel Guides (all literatures).
Royalties paid annually.

Bounty

See **Octopus Publishing Group**

Bowker

Windsor Court, East Grinstead House,
East Grinstead, West Sussex RH19 1XA
☎01342 336149   Fax 01342 336192

Website www.bowker.co.uk

Group Publishing Director *Gerard Dummett*
Managing Director *Charles Halpin*
Publisher *Geraldine Turpie*

Part of the Cambridge Information Group (CIG), based in Maryland in the USA. *Publishes* library reference, library science, bibliography, biography, business and professional directories. TITLES *Books In Print; Ulrich's Periodicals Directory.* Unsolicited material will not be read. *Royalties* paid annually.

Boxtree
See **Macmillan Publishers Ltd**

Marion Boyars Publishers Ltd
24 Lacy Road, London SW15 1NL
☎020 8788 9522 Fax 020 8789 8122
Email marion.boyars@talk21.com
Website www.marionboyars.co.uk

Editor *Julia Silk*
Editor, Non-fiction *Ken Hollings*

FOUNDED 1975, formerly Calder and Boyars. *Publishes* biography and autobiography, fiction, literature and criticism, music, philosophy, psychology, sociology and anthropology, theatre and drama, film and cinema, women's studies. About 30 titles a year. AUTHORS include Georges Bataille, Ingmar Bergman, Heinrich Böll, Hortense Calisher, Jean Cocteau, Carlo Gébler, Julian Green, Ivan Illich, Pauline Kael, Ken Kesey, Toby Litt, Kenzaburo Oe, Hubert Selby, Igor Stravinsky, Frederic Tuten, Eudora Welty, Judith Williamson, Tom Wiseman, Hong Ying. Unsolicited mss not welcome for fiction or poetry; submissions from agents only. Unsolicited synopses and ideas welcome for non-fiction.
Royalties paid annually. *Overseas associates* Marion Boyars Publishers Inc., 237 East 39th Street, New York, NY 10016, USA.

Boydell & Brewer Ltd
PO Box 9, Woodbridge, Suffolk IP12 3DF
☎01394 411320

Publishes non-fiction only, principally medieval studies. All books commissioned. No unsolicited material.

Bradt Travel Guides
19 High Street, Chalfont St Peter, Buckinghamshire SL9 9QE
☎01753 893444 Fax 01753 892333
Email info@bradt-travelguides.com
Website www.bradt-travelguides.com

Managing Director *Hilary Bradt*
Editorial Head *Tricia Hayne*
Approx. Annual Turnover £450,000

FOUNDED in 1974 by Hilary Bradt. *Specialises* in travel guides to off-beat places. 13 titles in 2001. SERIES country guides and island guides (Azores, Falklands, St Helena); wildlife guides (Galapagos, Arctic, Antarctica); and the 'Eccentric' series (Britain, London, America). No unsolicited mss; synopses and ideas for travel guidebooks (not travelogues) welcome.
Royalties paid twice-yearly.

Brassey's/Conway/Putnam
64 Brewery Road, London N7 9NT
☎020 7697 3000 Fax 020 7697 3001
Website www.brasseys.com

Chairman *John Needleman*

Long-standing independent publishers acquired by **Chrysalis** in 1999. *Publishes* books and journals on defence, military history, international relations, military technology, naval and maritime history, ship modelling as well as aeronautical subjects and aviation manufacturers.
IMPRINTS **Brassey's** Military history and technology; **Conway Maritime Press** Naval history, maritime culture and ship modelling; **Putnam Aeronautical Books** Technical and reference.
Royalties paid annually.

Nicholas Brealey Publishing
3–5 Spafield Street, London EC1R 4QB
☎020 7239 0360 Fax 020 7239 0370
Email rights@nbrealey-books.com
Website www.nbrealey-books.com

Managing Director *Nicholas Brealey*

FOUNDED 1992. Innovative books for business that address the most critical and interesting issues of the new century – from business to consumer behaviour, from self-help to leadership, from global change to cross-cultural understanding. Recently acquired the US publisher Intercultural Press, a specialist publisher in the field of crossing cultures. 20 titles a year. TITLES *Shackleton's Way; Power Up Your Mind; The Rich and How They Got That Way; The Soul of the New Consumer; The Power Laws; The 80/20 Principle; Riding the Waves of Culture; The Dance of Change.* No fiction, poetry or leisure titles. No unsolicited mss; synopses and ideas welcome.
Royalties paid twice-yearly.

Authors' Rating Looks to be succeeding in breaking away from the usual computer-speak business manuals to publish information and literate texts. Lead titles have a distinct trans-Atlantic feel.

The Breedon Books Publishing Co. Ltd

Breedon House, 3 Parker Centre, Derby
DE21 4SZ
☎01332 384235 Fax 01332 364063
Email anton@breedonpublishing.co.uk
Editorial Director *A.C. Rippon*
Approx. Annual Turnover £1 million

FOUNDED 1983. *Publishes* local history, heritage, old photographs and sport. 50 titles in 2001. Unsolicited mss, synopses and ideas welcome if accompanied by s.a.e. No poetry or fiction.
Royalties paid annually.

Breese Books Ltd

164 Kensington Park Road, London W11 2ER
☎020 7727 9426 Fax 020 7229 3395
Email MBreese999@aol.com
Website www.sherlockholmes.co.uk *and* www.abracadabra.co.uk
Chairman/Managing Director *Martin Ranicar-Breese*

FOUNDED in 1975 to produce specialist conjuring books and then went on to become a leading publisher of Sherlock Holmes pastiches. TITLES *Breese's Guide to Modern First Editions* (produced on a regular basis for book collectors) and 36 Sherlock Holmes articles by eight authors. No unsolicited submissions; Breese Books works with a regular team of authors.

Brepols Publishers

1 Jane Street, Saltaire, Shipley, West Yorkshire
BD18 3HA
Email simon.forde@brepols.com
Editorial Director *Simon Forde*

UK office of the Belgian academic publisher. FOUNDED 1796. *Publishes* scholarly monographs and collections in any field of pre-modern humanities. 150 titles a year. IMPRINT **Harvey Miller Publishers** Editorial Director *Johan Van Der Beke* FOUNDED 1974. *Publishes* academic studies in medieval and Renaissance art history only. 10–12 titles a year. No unsolicited mss; synopses and ideas welcome. E-mail contact preferred.
Royalties paid twice-yearly.

Brimax

See **Octopus Publishing Group**

Bristol Classical Press

See **Gerald Duckworth & Co. Ltd**

British Academic Press

See **I.B. Tauris & Co. Ltd**

The British Academy

10 Carlton House Terrace, London
SW1Y 5AH
☎020 7969 5200 Fax 020 7969 5300
Email secretary@britac.ac.uk
Website www.britac.ac.uk
Publications Officer *James Rivington*
Publications Assistant *Vicky Baldwin*

FOUNDED 1902. The primary body for promoting scholarship in the humanities, the Academy publishes many series stemming from its own long-standing research projects, or series of lectures and conference proceedings. Main subjects include history, philosophy and archaeology. About 15 titles a year. SERIES *Auctores Britannici Medii Aevi; Early English Church Music; Fontes Historiae Africanae; Records of Social and Economic History.* Proposals for these series are welcome and are forwarded to the relevant project committees. The British Academy is a registered charity and does not publish for profit.
Royalties paid only when titles have covered their costs.

The British Library

96 Euston Road, London NW1 2DB
☎020 7412 7704 Fax 020 7412 7768
Email blpublications@bl.uk
Publishing Manager *David Way*
Approx. Annual Turnover £950,000

FOUNDED 1979 as the publishing arm of The British Library to publish works based on the historic collections and related subjects. *Publishes* bibliographical reference, manuscript studies, illustrated books based on the Library's collections, and book arts. TITLES *The British Library Guide to Calligraphy, Illumination and Heraldry; The British Library Writers' Lives Series; Encyclopedia of Ephemera; Medieval Herbals.* About 50 titles a year. Unsolicited mss, synopses and ideas welcome if related to the history of the book, book arts or bibliography. No fiction or general non-fiction.
Royalties paid annually.

The British Museum Press

46 Bloomsbury Street, London WC1B 3QQ
☎020 7323 1234 Fax 020 7436 7315
Website www.britishmuseum.co.uk
Managing Director *Andrew Thatcher*
Managing Editor *Teresa Francis*

The book publishing division of The British

Museum Company Ltd. FOUNDED 1973 as British Museum Publications Ltd; relaunched 1991 as British Museum Press. *Publishes* ancient history, archaeology, ethnography, art history, exhibition catalogues, guides, children's books, and all official publications of the British Museum. Around 50 titles a year. TITLES *Egypt; Indigo; Sutton Hoo: Burial Ground of Kings?; The Atlantic Celts: Ancient People or Modern Invention?; The Classical Cookbook; How to Read Egyptian Hieroglyphs.* Synopses and ideas for books welcome.
Royalties paid twice-yearly.

Brockhampton Press Ltd
See **Caxton Publishing Group**

Andrew Brodie Publications
PO Box 23, Wellington, Somerset
TA21 8YX
☎01823 665345 Fax 01823 665345
Email andrew@andrewbrodie.co.uk
Website www.andrewbrodie.co.uk
Chairman *Andrew Brodie*
Approx. Annual Turnover £500,000
FOUNDED 1992. *Publishes* children's books. 43 titles in 2001. TITLES *Spelling Today* series; *Handwriting Today; Numeracy Today; Homework Today; Spelling for Literacy.* Unsolicited mss, synopses and ideas for books welcome; send a letter in the first instance.
Royalties paid annually.

John Brown Publishing Ltd
The New Boathouse, 136–142 Bramley Road, London W10 6SR
☎020 7565 3000 Fax 020 7565 3050
Chairman *John Brown*
Managing Director *Dean Fitzpatrick*
FOUNDED 1987. Magazine publisher. TITLES include *theAAMagazine, Waitrose Food Illustrated* and *The Oldie.*

Brown, Son & Ferguson, Ltd
4–10 Darnley Street, Glasgow G41 2SD
☎0141 429 1234 Fax 0141 420 1694
Email info@skipper.co.uk
Website www.skipper.co.uk
Chairman/Joint Managing Director
T. Nigel Brown
FOUNDED 1850. *Specialises* in nautical textbooks, both technical and non-technical. Also Scottish one-act/three-act plays. Unsolicited mss, synopses and ideas for books welcome.
Royalties paid annually.

Bryntirion Press
Bryntirion, Bridgend, Mid-Glamorgan
CF31 4DX
☎01656 655886 Fax 01656 665919
Email office@evangelicalmvt-wales.org
Press Manager *Huw Kinsey*
Owned by the Evangelical Movement of Wales. *Publishes* Christian books in English and Welsh. TITLES *Christian Handbook; Walk Worthy; Reformation: Yesterday, Today and Tomorrow.* No unsolicited mss; synopses and ideas welcome.
Royalties paid annually.

Bucknell University Press
See **Golden Cockerel Press Ltd**

Burns & Oates
See **The Continuum International Publishing Group Limited**

Business Books
See **Random House Group Ltd**

Business Education Publishers Ltd
The Solar Building, Doxford International, Sunderland, Tyne & Wear SR3 3XW
☎0191 525 2400 Fax 0191 520 1815
Email info@bepl.com
Website www.bepl.com
Managing Director *Mrs A. Murphy*
Approx. Annual Turnover £400,000
FOUNDED 1981. *Publishes* business education, economics and law for BTEC and GNVQ reading. Currently expanding into further and higher education, computing, IT, business, travel and tourism, occasional papers for institutions and local government administration. Unsolicited mss and synopses welcome.
Royalties paid annually.

Buster Books
See **Michael O'Mara Books Ltd**

Butterworth-Heinemann International
See **Reed Educational & Professional Publishing**

Butterworths
See **Reed Elsevier plc**

Butterworths Tolley
Tolley House, 2 Addiscombe Road, Croydon, Surrey CR9 5AF
☎020 8686 9141 Fax 020 8686 3155
Email customer-services@butterworths.com

Website www.butterworths.com
Managing Director Paul Virik
Part of Reed Elsevier Legal Division. DIVISIONS
Tolley Publishing; Charles Knight Publishing; Payroll Alliance; Butterworths Tax Publications.

C&B (Collins & Brown)
64 Brewery Road, London N7 9NT
☎020 7697 3000 Fax 020 7697 3001
Website www.chrysalis.co.uk
Publishing Director Colin Ziegler
FOUNDED 1989. Acquired by **Chrysalis** in
April 2001. Publishes illustrated non-fiction.
About 250 titles a year. IMPRINT **Collins & Brown** Lifestyle and interiors, gardening,
health, mind, body and spirit, photography,
practical art and craft. No unsolicited mss; outlines with s.a.e. only.
Royalties paid twice-yearly.

Cadogan Guides
Network House, 1 Ariel Way, London
W12 7SL
☎020 8600 3550 Fax 020 8600 3599
Email cadoganguides@morrispub.co.uk
Editorial Director Vicki Ingle
FOUNDED 1982. Publishes three series of travel
guides: to countries and regions, cities and for
parents (Take the Kids). Most titles are commissioned. No unsolicited material.

Authors' Rating American ownership has not
saved the company from the post-September
11th downturn in the travel book market. But
UK sales are holding up, suggesting that proposed titles should have appeal for Brits abroad.

Calder Publications Ltd
51 The Cut, London SE1 8LF
☎020 7633 0599 Fax 020 7928 5930
Email info@calderpublications.com
Website www.calderpublications.com
Chairman/Managing Director/Editorial Head John Calder
Formerly John Calder (Publishers) Ltd. A publishing company which has grown around the
tastes and contacts of John Calder, the iconoclast
of the literary establishment. The list has a reputation for controversial and opinion-forming
publications; Samuel Beckett is perhaps the most
prestigious name. The list includes all of
Beckett's prose and poetry. Publishes autobiography, biography, drama, literary fiction, literary

criticism, music, opera, poetry, politics, sociology, ENO opera guides. SERIES Thought Bites
Short polemical texts on current political and
social issues. AUTHORS Antonin Artaud,
Marguerite Duras, Martin Esslin, Erich Fried,
P.J. Kavanagh, Robert Menasse, Robert Pinget,
Luigi Pirandello, Alain Robbe-Grillet, Nathalie
Sarraute, L.F. Celine, Eva Figes, Claude Simon,
Howard Barker (plays). No new material accepted.
Royalties paid annually.

Authors' Rating Known for his patronage of
eccentric talents, John Calder is one of the few
publishers to carry the flag for the English language '... which is in great danger of disappearing under the American vernacular'.

California University Press
See **University Presses of California,
Columbia & Princeton Ltd**

Cambridge University Press
The Edinburgh Building, Shaftesbury Road,
Cambridge CB2 2RU
☎01223 312393 Fax 01223 315052
Website www.cambridge.org
Chief Executive Stephen R.R. Bourne
The oldest printer and publisher in the world
with long-established branches in the USA and
Australia and more recently established
branches in Spain, Africa, South America and
East Asia. Winner of The Queen's Award for
Export Achievement in 1998. Over the last ten
years, Cambridge has opened many new offices
around the world. Its books are sold in more
than 200 countries. Publications include the
Cambridge Histories and Companions, encyclopedias and dictionaries; the **Canto** series;
popular science and scientific and medical reference; major ELT courses; coursebooks for the
National Curriculum; Cambridge Reading; and
Cambridge Low Price Editions for the developing world. Publishes academic/educational and
reference books for English-language markets
worldwide, at all levels from primary school to
postgraduate, together with a list of Spanish
titles. Also ELT, Bibles and over 140 academic
journals. Over 23,000 authors in 106 different
countries and about 1800 new titles a year.
PUBLISHING GROUPS
Bibles C.J. Wright **ELT** C.J.F. Hayes **Science
Publishing** A.E. Crowden **Humanities and
Social Sciences** R. Fisher **Professional
Publishing** R.W.A. Barling **Education** A.C.
Gilfillan **Journals** C. Guettler. Synopses and
ideas for educational, ELT and academic books

are welcome (and preferable to the submission of unsolicited mss). No fiction or poetry.
Royalties paid twice-yearly.

Authors' Rating There has been some worry of late that CUP is slipping behind its main rivals. The point at issue is the future of e-publishing on which CUP has taken a cautious line. But there is a case for letting others make the expensive mistakes. Meanwhile, CUP retains its traditional strength in the academic market with an increasing number of titles which reach out to the general reader.

Camden Press Ltd
43 Camden Passage, London N1 8EA
☎020 7226 4673
Chairman *Bob Borzello*
FOUNDED 1985. *Publishes* social issues; all books are launched in connection with major national conferences. DIVISION **Publishing for Change** *Bob Borzello* TITLE *Living with the Legacy of Abuse.* IMPRINT **Mindfield** TITLES *Hate Thy Neighbour: The Race Issue; Therapy on the Couch.* No unsolicited material. Approach by telephone in the first instance.
Royalties paid annually.

Camden Softcover Large Print
See **Chivers Press Ltd**

Campbell Books
See **Macmillan Publishers Ltd**

Candle Books
See **Angus Hudson Ltd** under **UK Packagers**

Canongate Books Ltd
14 High Street, Edinburgh EH1 1TE
☎0131 557 5111 Fax 0131 557 5211
Email info@canongate.co.uk
Website www.canongate.net
Publisher *Jamie Byng*
Managing Director *David Graham*
Approx. Annual Turnover £2.7 million
FOUNDED 1973. *Publishes* a wide range of literary fiction and non-fiction. Historically there is a strong Scottish slant to the list but its output is increasingly international and Canongate has a growing reputation for originating unusual projects (typified by the Pocket Canons Bible series). Key AUTHORS include Michel Faber, Robert Sabbag, Laura Hird, Charles Bukowski, Anthony Bourdain, John Fante, Richard Brautigan, Dorit Rabinyan, Martin Strong, Will Ferguson, Jennifer Clement, Knut Hamsun, Chester

Himes, Iceberg Slim, Yann Martel and Toni Davidson. Also works closely with **Grove/Atlantic** in New York, developing a reciprocal relationship whereby Canongate US is publishing 20 books a year in America and Atlantic UK is distributed alongside Canongate in the UK and Commonwealth.

IMPRINTS **Canongate Classics** Adult paperback series dedicated solely to important works of Scottish literature; **Canongate Crime** Paperback series featuring writers from all around the world, includes **Canongate Crime Classics** dedicated to reprinting lost classics of the genre; **Canongate International** Fiction in translation; **Mojo Books** An imprint in collaboration with Emap's *Mojo* magazine that combines informed, incisive music writing with Canongate's extensive list of existing music titles.
Royalties paid twice-yearly.

Authors' Rating Now under the wing of a US publisher, Canongate has the opportunity to broaden its activities without losing its independence. Grove/Atlantic, though bigger than its Scottish partner, has the same tradition of imaginative publishing. The match promises well for authors and readers.

Canterbury Press Norwich
See **Hymns Ancient & Modern Ltd**

Canto
See **Cambridge University Press**

Capall Bann Publishing
Freshfields, Chieveley, Berkshire RG20 8TF
☎01635 247050/248711
Fax 01635 247050/248711
Email capallbann1@virgin.biz.com
Website www.capallbann.co.uk
Chairman *Julia Day*
Editorial Head *Jon Day*
FOUNDED 1993 with three titles and now have over 200 in print. Family-owned and -run company which *publishes* British traditions, folklore, computing, boating, animals, alternative healing, environmental, Celtic lore, mind, body and spirit. About 40 titles a year. TITLES *Practical Spirituality; Celtic Lore; Handbook of Fairies; Talking to the Earth; Bruce Roberts' Boatbuilding.* Unsolicited proposals for books welcome. No e-mailed submissions – correspondence only, please. No fiction or poetry.
Royalties paid twice-yearly.

Jonathan Cape Ltd
See **Random House Group Ltd**

Capstone Publishing Ltd

8 Newtec Place, Magdalen Road, Oxford
OX4 1RE
☎01865 798623 Fax 01865 240941
Email info@wiley-capstone.co.uk
Website www.capstoneideas.com

Joint Managing Directors *Mark Allin,*
Richard Burton

FOUNDED 1997. Part of **John Wiley & Sons**.
Publishes business books. 45 titles in 2001.
Unsolicited synopses and ideas for books welcome; write or e-mail in the first instance with synopsis, c.v. and one or two sample chapters. *Royalties* paid twice-yearly.

Carcanet Press Ltd

4th Floor, Conavon Court, 12–16 Blackfriars
Street, Manchester M3 5BQ
☎0161 834 8730 Fax 0161 832 0084
Email pnr@carcanet.u-net.com
Website www.carcanet.co.uk

Chairman *Kate Gavron*
Managing Director/Editorial Director
Michael Schmidt

In the last thirty years Carcanet has grown from an undergraduate hobby into a substantial venture. Robert Gavron bought the company in 1983 and it has established strong European, Commonwealth and American links. Winner of the **Sunday Times Small Publisher of the Year** award in 2000, it took over the Oxford Poets list from **Oxford University Press** in 1999 which it now publishes as a distinct imprint. Primarily a poetry publisher but also *publishes* academic, literary biography, fiction in translation and translations. About 60 titles a year, including the *PN Review* (six issues yearly). AUTHORS Homero Aridjis, John Ashbery, Eavan Boland, Joseph Brodsky, Donald Davie, Natalia Ginzburg, Robert Graves, Elizabeth Jennings, Edwin Morgan, Les Murray, Frederic Raphael, Leonardo Sciascia, Iain Crichton Smith, Pedro Tamen, Charles Tomlinson. Poetry submissions (hard copy only): 6–10 poems with covering letter and return postage if the material is to be sent back. Prospective writers should familiarise themselves with the Carcanet list.
Royalties paid annually.

Authors' Rating Ever in the forefront of imaginative publishing, Carcanet has taken a step closer to the source of its literary creativity by setting up a postgraduate Writing School at Manchester Metropolitan University. (See entry under **Writers' Courses, Circles and Workshops**.)

Cardiff Academic Press

St Fagans Road, Fairwater, Cardiff CF5 3AE
☎029 2056 0333 Fax 029 2055 4909
Managing Director *R.G. Drake*
Academic publishers.

Carfax Publishing

See **Taylor & Francis Group plc**

Carlton Publishing Group

20 Mortimer Street, London W1T 3JW
☎020 7612 0400 Fax 020 7612 0401
Email enquiries@carltonbooks.co.uk
Website www.carlton.com

Managing Director *Jonathan Goodman*
Publishing Director *Piers Murray Hill*
Approx. Annual Turnover £17 million

FOUNDED 1992. Owned by Carlton Communications, Carlton's books are aimed at the mass market for subjects such as TV tie-ins, lifestyle, computer games, sport, health, New Age, puzzles, popular science and rock'n'roll. *Publishes* illustrated leisure and entertainment. Prime UK customers include the Book Club and WHSmith.

DIVISIONS **Carlton Books**; **André Deutsch** Autobiography, biography, history, military history, humour and the arts; **Granada Media**; **Manchester United Books**. No unsolicited mss; synopses and ideas welcome. No novels, science fiction, poetry or children's fiction.

Authors' Rating Linked to the largest programme producer in the ITV network, Carlton Books has built a reputation on co-editions for the international market and television tie-ins. Noted for speed of taking a book from first idea to publication.

Carroll & Brown Publishers Limited

20 Lonsdale Road, London NW6 6RD
☎020 7372 0900 Fax 020 7372 0460
Email mail@carrollandbrown.co.uk
Managing Director *Amy Carroll*
Approx. Annual Turnover £3.5 million

FOUNDED in 1989 as a packaging operation and commenced publishing in 2000. *Publishes* practical cookery, health, gardening, lifestyle, mind, body and spirit. TITLES *Are You Psychic?; Walking for Health; Weeds: Friend or Foe?; Beads of Faith.* Synopses and ideas for illustrated books welcome; approach in writing in the first instance. No fiction.
Payment Fees or royalties paid.

Frank Cass & Co Ltd

Crown House, 47 Chase Side, Southgate,
London N14 5BP
☎020 8920 2100   Fax 020 8447 8548
Email info@frankcass.com
Website www.frankcass.com
Chairman *Frank Cass*
Managing Director *Stewart Cass*
Managing Editor (Books) *Andrew Humphrys*
Managing Editor (Journals) *Anthony Bastock*

Publishes books and journals in the fields of politics, international relations, military and security studies, history, Middle East and sports studies, economics, development studies.

DIVISIONS **Woburn Press** Educational list: history of education, education policy and practice TITLES *Her Majesty's Inspectorate of Schools Since 1944* John E. Dunford; *Going Comprehensive in England and Wales* Alan C. Kercknoff. IMPRINTS **Vallentine Mitchell/ Jewish Chronicle Publications** (see entry). Unsolicited mss considered but synopsis with covering letter preferred.
Royalties paid annually.

Cassell Illustrated

See **Octopus Publishing Group**

Cassell Military/Cassell Reference

See **The Orion Publishing Group Limited**

Castle Publications

See **Nottingham University Press**

Kyle Cathie Ltd

122 Arlington Road, London NW1 7HP
☎020 7692 7215   Fax 020 7692 7260
Email general.enquiries@kyle-cathie.com

FOUNDED 1990 to publish and promote 'books we have personal enthusiasm for'. *Publishes* non-fiction: cookery, food and drink, health and beauty, mind, body & spirit, gardening, homes and interiors, reference and occasional books of classic poetry. TITLES *Little Black Dress Diet* Michael van Straten; *Entertain* Ed Bain; *Ballymaloe Cookery* Darina Allen; *Spells for the Witch In You* Marina Baker. About 25 titles a year. No unsolicited mss. 'Synopses and ideas are considered in the fields in which we publish.'
Royalties paid twice-yearly.

Catholic Truth Society (CTS)

40–46 Harleyford Road, London SE11 5AY
☎020 7640 0042   Fax 020 7640 0046
Email f.martin@cts-online.org.uk
Website www.cts-online.org.uk

Chairman *Rt. Rev. Peter Smith*
General Secretary *Fergal Martin*
Approx. Annual Turnover £750,000

FOUNDED originally in 1868 and re-founded in 1884. *Publishes* religious books – Roman Catholic; a variety of doctrinal, moral, biographical, devotional and liturgical publications, including a large body of Vatican documents and sources. Unsolicited mss, synopses and ideas welcome if appropriate to their list.
Royalties paid annually.

Causeway Press Ltd

PO Box 13, 129 New Court Way, Ormskirk,
Lancashire L39 5HP
☎01695 576048   Fax 01695 570714
Chairman/Managing Director
   M. Haralambos
Approx. Annual Turnover £2 million

FOUNDED in 1982. *Publishes* educational textbooks only. 10 titles in 2001. TITLES *Mathematics for AQA; Mathematics for Edexcel; Psychology in Focus; GCSE Business Studies; Media Studies.* Unsolicited mss, synopses and ideas welcome.
Royalties paid annually.

Cavendish Publishing Limited

The Glass House, Wharton Street, London
WC1X 9PX
☎020 7278 8000   Fax 020 7278 8080
Email info@cavendishpublishing.com
Website www.cavendishpublishing.com
Managing Director *Sonny Leong*

FOUNDED 1990. *Publishes* academic law books. 100 titles in 2001. No unsolicited mss; send synopsis accompanied by a letter in the first instance.
Royalties paid twice-yearly. *Overseas associate* Cavendish Publishing (Australia) Pty Ltd.

Caxton Publishing Group

20 Bloomsbury Street, London WC1B 3JH
☎020 7636 7171   Fax 020 7636 1922
Email office@caxtonpublishing.com
Website www.caxtonpublishing.com
Chairman *Stephen Hill*
Managing Director *John Maxwell*
Approx. Annual Turnover £4 million

FOUNDED 1999. *Specialises* in reprinting out-of-print works for the 'value' market worldwide and commissioning new general non-fiction publications in reference, cookery, gardening and children's. 200 titles a year.
DIVISIONS/IMPRINTS **Brockhampton Press Ltd** Children's fiction and non-fiction. **Caxton**

Editions Ltd General non-fiction, reference and military. **Knight Paperbacks Ltd** Fiction. No unsolicited mss; synopses and ideas welcome; send letter in the first instance.
Royalties paid twice-yearly.

CBA Publishing
Bowes Morrell House, 111 Walmgate, York YO1 9WA
☎01904 671417 Fax 01904 671384
Website www.britarch.ac.uk
Publications Officer *Jane Thorniley-Walker*
Approx. Annual Turnover £80,000

Publishing arm of the **Council for British Archaeology**. *Publishes* academic archaeology reports, practical handbooks, yearbook, *British Archaeology* (bi-monthly magazine), *Young Archaeologist* (Young Archaeologists' Club magazine), monographs, archaeology and education. TITLES *Our Changing Coast; A Survey of the Intertidal Archaeology of Langstone Harbour; Prehistoric Roman and Post-Roman Landscapes of the Great Ouse Valley.*
Royalties not paid.

CBD Research Ltd
Chancery House, 15 Wickham Road, Beckenham, Kent BR3 5JS
☎020 8650 7745 Fax 020 8650 0768
Email cbd@cbdresearch.com
Website www.cbdresearch.com
Chairman *G.P. Henderson*
Managing Director *S.P.A. Henderson*
Approx. Annual Turnover £500,000

FOUNDED 1961. *Publishes* directories and other reference guides to sources of information. About 6 titles a year. No fiction.
IMPRINT **Chancery House Press** Non-fiction of an esoteric/specialist nature for 'serious researchers and the dedicated hobbyist'. Unsolicited mss, synopses and ideas welcome.
Royalties paid quarterly.

Centaur Press
See **Open Gate Press**

Century
See **Random House Group Ltd**

Chadwyck-Healey Ltd.
ProQuest Information and Learning Ltd, The Quorum, Barnwell Road, Cambridge CB5 8SW
☎01223 215512 Fax 01223 215513
Website www.proquest.co.uk
General Manager *Steven Hall*

Part of US company, ProQuest Information and Learning Ltd, the new name for Bell & Howell. *Publishes* humanities and literary databases on the Web, CD-ROM and microform. Key TITLES include *KnowUK; Literature Online; The English Poetry Database; Periodical Contents Index; KnowEurope.* No unsolicited mss. Synopses and ideas welcome for reference works only.
Royalties paid annually.

Chambers Harrap Publishers Ltd
7 Hopetoun Crescent, Edinburgh EH7 4AY
☎0131 556 5929 Fax 0131 556 5313
Email admin@chambersharrap.com
Website www.chambersharrap.com
Managing Director *Maurice Shepherd*
Administrator *Stephanie Gloyer*

Publishes dictionaries and reference. The imprint was founded in the early 1800s to publish self-education books, but soon diversified into dictionaries and other reference works. The acquisition of Harrap Publishing Group's core business strengthened its position in the dictionary market, adding bilingual titles, covering almost all the major European languages, to its English-language dictionaries. About 25 titles a year. Send synopsis with accompanying letter rather than completed mss.

Chancery House Press
See **CBD Research Ltd**

Channel 4 Books
See **Macmillan Publishers Ltd**

Geoffrey Chapman
See **The Continuum International Publishing Group Limited**

Paul Chapman Publishing Ltd
See **Sage Publications**

Chapman Publishing
4 Broughton Place, Edinburgh EH1 3RX
☎0131 557 2207 Fax 0131 556 9565
Email editor@chapman-pub.co.uk
Website www.chapman-pub.co.uk
Managing Editor *Joy Hendry*

A venture devoted to publishing works by the best of the Scottish writers, both up-and-coming and established, published in *Chapman*, Scotland's leading literary magazine. Has expanded publishing activities considerably over the last three years and is now publishing a wider range of works though the broad policy stands. *Publishes* poetry, drama, short stories, books of contemporary importance in 20th-century Scotland. About 4 titles a year. TITLES *Ye Cannae Win* Janet Paisley; *Clan McHine* Ian McDonough; *Wild Women Series – Wild Women of a Certain Age* Magi Gibson. No unsolicited mss; synopses and ideas for books welcome. *Royalties* paid annually.

Chapmans Publishers
See **The Orion Publishing Group Ltd**

Charnwood
See **F.A. Thorpe (Publishing)**

Chartered Institute of Personnel and Development
CIPD House, Camp Road, London SW19 4UX
☎020 8263 3387 Fax 020 8263 3850
Email publish@cipd.co.uk
Website www.cipd.co.uk

Part of CIPD Enterprises Limited. *Publishes* people management and training titles. A list of 200 titles. TITLES *The Motivation Handbook; HR Forecasting and Planning; Essentials of Employment Law.* Unsolicited mss, synopses and ideas welcome.
Royalties paid annually.

Chatham Publishing
See **Gerald Duckworth & Co Ltd**

Chatto & Windus Ltd
See **Random House Group Ltd**

Cherrytree Books
See **Evans Brothers Ltd**

Chicken House Publishing
2 Palmer Street, Frome, Somerset BA11 1DS
☎01373 454488 Fax 01373 454499
Email doublecluck.com
Chairman/Managing Director *Barry Cunningham*

Children's publishing house FOUNDED in 2000. *Publishes* books 'that are aimed at real children' – fiction, original picture books, gift books and fun non-fiction. Aiming to publish about 25 titles a year. 'We are always on the lookout for new talent.' Unsolicited material welcome; send letter with synopsis and sample chapters.
Royalties paid twice-yearly.

Authors' Rating A new kid on the street, Chicken House, according to its founder, Barry Cunningham, is a 'small, creative company which has made strategic alliances around the world'. These alliances certainly give new authors a strong international profile – just the thing in an ever more competitive market.

Child's Play (International) Ltd
Ashworth Road, Bridgemead, Swindon, Wiltshire SN5 7YD
☎01793 616286 Fax 01793 512795
Email allday@childs-play.com
Website www.childs-play.com
Chief Executive *Neil Burden*

FOUNDED in 1972, Child's Play is an independent publisher specialising in learning through play, whole child development, life-skills and values. *Publishes* books, games and A-V materials. TITLES Books: *Big Hungry Bear; There Was an Old Lady; Puzzle Island; Children of the Sun; Ten Beads Tall; Pocket Pals; Sliders; Roly Poly Books; Book Buddies; Mrs Honey's Tree; Big Books and Storysacks*; Games: *Dizzy Bizzy; Safe Places; Arithmetic Lotto.* Unsolicited mss welcome. Send s.a.e. for return or response. Expect to wait two months for a reply.
Royalties Outright or royalty payments are subject to negotiation.

Chimera
See **Pegasus Elliot Mackenzie Publishers Ltd**

Chivers Press Ltd
Windsor Bridge Road, Bath BA2 3AX
☎01225 335336 Fax 01225 310771
Email sales@chivers.co.uk
Website www.chivers.co.uk
Managing Director *Julian R. Batson*
Approx. Annual Turnover £9 million

Publishes reprints for libraries mainly, in large-print editions, including biography and autobiography, children's, crime, fiction and spoken word cassettes. No unsolicited material.
IMPRINTS
Chivers Large Print; **Gunsmoke Westerns**; **Galaxy Children's Large Print**; **Camden Softcover Large Print**; **Paragon Softcover Large Print**; **Windsor Large Print**; **Black Dagger Crime**. **Chivers Audio Books** (see entry under **Audio Books**).
Royalties paid twice-yearly.

Christian Focus Publications
Geanies House, Fearn, Tain, Ross-shire IV20 1TW
☎01862 871011 Fax 01862 871699
Email info@christianfocus.com
Website www.christianfocus.com

Chairman *R.W.M. Mackenzie*
Managing Director *William Mackenzie*
Publishing Executive *Willie Mackenzie*
Children's Editor *Catherine Mackenzie*
Approx. Annual Turnover £1.2 million
FOUNDED 1979 to produce children's books for the co-edition market. Now a major producer of Christian books. *Publishes* adult and children's books, including some fiction for children but not adults. No poetry. About 80 titles a year. Unsolicited mss, synopses and ideas welcome from Christian writers. Publishes for all English-speaking markets, as well as the UK.
IMPRINTS **Christian Focus** General books; **Mentor** Study books; **Christian Heritage** Classic reprints.
Royalties paid annually.

Christian Heritage
See **Christian Focus Publications**

Chrome Dreams
See entry under **Audio Books**

Chrysalis Books Ltd
64 Brewery Road, London N7 9NT
☎020 7697 3000 Fax 020 7697 3001
Website www.chrysalisbooks.co.uk
Chairman *John Needleman*
The holding company for the book publishing division of the media group, Chrysalis Group Plc.
IMPRINTS **Brassey's** (see entry), incorporating **Conway Maritime Press** and **Putnam Aeronautical Books**; **B.T. Batsford** (see entry); **C&B (Collins & Brown)** (see entry); **Pavilion Books Ltd** (see entry); **Robson Books** (see entry); **Salamander Books Ltd** (see entry); **Greenwich Editions** Promotional books and gifts; **Ramboro Books** Remainder books; **Vega** Mind, body and spirit.
DIVISION **Chrysalis Children's Books** Head of Division *Steve Evans*; Publisher *Chester Fisher* IMPRINTS **Big Fish** (see entry); **Belitha Press** (see entry); **David Bennett Books** (see entry); **Pavilion Children's Books** (see entry); **Zigzag** (see entry).

Authors' Rating Growing rapidly by acquisitions, Chrysalis is noted for a mixed bag of illustrated books. US co-editions account for half the company's sales.

Churchill Livingstone
See **Harcourt Publishers International**

Cicerone Press
2 Police Square, Milnthorpe, Cumbria LA7 7PY
☎01539 562069 Fax 01539 563417
Email info@cicerone.co.uk
Website www.cicerone.co.uk
Managing/Editorial Director *Jonathan Williams*
FOUNDED 1969. Guidebook publisher for outdoor enthusiasts. About 20 titles a year. No fiction or poetry. TITLES *Walks and Climbs in the Pyrenees; Tour of Mont Blanc; Walking in Hampshire* and *Long Distance Walking* series of guides. No unsolicited mss; synopses and ideas considered.
Royalties paid twice-yearly.

Cico Books
1st Floor, 32 Great Sutton Street, London EC1V 0NB
☎020 7253 7960 Fax 020 7253 7967
Email mail@cicobooks.co.uk
Managing Director *Mark Collins*
Publisher *Cindy Richards*
FOUNDED in 1999 by Mark Collins and Cindy Richards (both formerly with **Collins & Brown**) 'to offer flexibility by being small, selling co-edition rights to overseas publishers'. *Publishes* lifestyle and interiors, mind, body and spirit. About 12 titles a year. No unsolicited mss, synopses or ideas.
Royalties paid twice-yearly.

Clarion
See **Elliot Right Way Books**

T.&T. Clark
59 George Street, Edinburgh EH2 2LQ
☎0131 225 4703 Fax 0131 220 4260
Email ggreen@tandtclark.co.uk
Website www.tandtclark.co.uk
Managing Director/Editorial Head *Geoffrey Green*
FOUNDED 1821. Part of the **Continuum International Publishing Group Ltd**. *Publishes* religion, theology and philosophy for academic and professional markets. About 35 titles a year, including journals. TITLES *Church Dogmatics* Karl Barth; *The Romans Debate* Karl Donfried; *In the Beginning* Joseph Ratzinger. Unsolicited mss, synopses and ideas for books welcome.
Royalties paid twice-yearly.

James Clarke & Co.

PO Box 60, Cambridge CB1 2NT
☎01223 350865 Fax 01223 366951
Email publishing@jamesclarke.co.uk
Website www.jamesclarke.co.uk

Managing Director *Adrian Brink*

Parent company of **The Lutterworth Press** (see entry). *Publishes* scholarly and academic works, mainly theological, directory and reference titles. TITLES *Libraries Directory* (book and CD-ROM versions); *Encyclopedia of the Middle Ages; Deep Economy: Caring for Ecology, Humanity and Religion; Literature and Sacrament: the Sacred and the Secular in John Donne.* Approach in writing with ideas in the first instance.

Peter Collin Publishing Ltd

32–34 Great Peter Street, London SW1P 2DB
☎020 7222 1155 Fax 020 7222 1551
Email info@pcp.co.uk
Website www.petercollin.com

Chairman *P.H. Collin*

FOUNDED 1985. *Publishes* dictionaries, including specialised dictionaries in English for students and specialised bilingual dictionaries for translators (French, German, Swedish, Spanish, Greek, Chinese, Hungarian). Also *publishes Aspect Guides*, including the French Entrée series, and specialist guides to London. About 20 titles a year. Synopses and ideas welcome. No unsolicited mss; copy must be supplied on disk.

Royalties paid twice-yearly.

Collins

See **HarperCollins Publishers Ltd**

Collins & Brown

See **C&B**

Colonsay Books

See **House of Lochar**

Colourpoint Books

Unit D5, Ards Business Centre, Jubilee Road, Newtownards, Co. Down BT23 4YH
☎028 9182 0505 Fax 028 9182 1900
Email info@colourpoint.co.uk
Website www.colourpoint.co.uk

Partners *Sheila M. Johnston, Norman Johnston*

FOUNDED 1993. *Publishes* school textbooks and transport (covering mainland Britain as well as Northern Ireland), plus books of Irish interest. No fiction. 17 titles in 2001. Approach in writing in the first instance; include return postage, please.

Royalties paid twice-yearly.

Columbia University Press

See **University Presses of California, Columbia & Princeton Ltd**

Compendium Publishing Ltd

1st Floor, 43 Frith Street, London W1V 5TE
☎020 7287 4570 Fax 020 7494 0583
Email compendiumpub@aol.com

Managing Director *Alan Greene*
Editorial Director *Simon Forty*

FOUNDED 1996. *Publishes* and packages for international publishing companies – general non-fiction: history, reference, hobbies, children's, transport and militaria. 40 titles in 2001. No unsolicited mss; synopses and ideas preferred.

Royalties paid twice-yearly.

Condor

See **Souvenir Press Ltd**

Conran Octopus

See **Octopus Publishing Group**

Constable & Robinson Ltd

3 The Lanchesters, 162 Fulham Palace Road, London W6 9ER
☎020 8741 3663 Fax 020 8748 7562
Email enquiries@constablerobinson.com
Website www.constablerobinson.com

Non-Executive Chairman *Benjamin Glazebrook*
Managing Director *Nick Robinson*
Directors *Jan Chamier, Nova Jayne Heath, Adrian Andrews*
Approx. Annual Turnover £5 million

Constable & Co FOUNDED in 1890 by Archibald Constable, a grandson of Walter Scott's publisher. Robinson Publishing Ltd FOUNDED in 1983 by Nick Robinson. In December 1999 Constable and Robinson combined their individual shareholdings into a single company.

IMPRINTS **Constable** (Hardbacks) Editorial Director *Carol O'Brien Publishes* biography and autobiography, crime fiction, general and military history, psychology, travel, climbing, landscape photography and outdoor pursuits guidebooks. **Robinson** (Paperbacks) Senior Commissioning Editor *Krystyna Green Publishes* crime, science fiction, *Daily Telegraph* health books, the Mammoth series, psychology, true crime, military history and *Smarties* children's books. Unsolicited sample chapters, synopses and ideas for books welcome. No mss; no e-mail submissions. Enclose return postage.

Authors' Rating The merging of two small but highly regarded independent publishers promises well for authors who enjoy close attention from their editors. The broad scope of the fiction and non-fiction lists suggests a flexible response to book proposals.

Consultants Bureau
See **Kluwer Academic/Plenum Publishers**

Consumers' Association
See **Which? Books/Consumers' Association**

The Continuum International Publishing Group Limited
The Tower Building, 11 York Road, London SE1 7NX
☎020 7922 0880 Fax 020 7922 0881
Website www.continuumbooks.com
Chairman & Managing Director *Philip Sturrock*
Approx. Annual Turnover £11million
FOUNDED in 1999 by a buy-out of the academic and religious publishing of **Cassell** and the acquisition of Continuum New York. *Publishes* academic, religious and general books. 300 titles in 2000. DIVISIONS **Academic** *Janet Joyce* Textbooks, reference books and monographs in the humanities, social sciences, business and computing studies, education and performing arts. IMPRINTS **Pinter**; **Leicester University Press**; **Mansell**; **Athlone**; **Sheffield Academic Press** TITLES *Directory of Publishing; Companion to 20th Century Theatre; Reflective Teaching in the Primary School.* **Religious** *Robin Baird-Smith* IMPRINTS **Geoffrey Chapman**; **Mowbray**; **T.&T. Clark** (see entry); **Burns & Oates**; **Sheed & Ward**; **The Handsel Press** TITLES *Pilgrims in Rome; Jerome Biblical Commentary.* **General Books** *Robin Baird-Smith Publishes* authors such as Christopher Booker, John Bayley and Anthony O'Hear. Unsolicited synopses and ideas within the subject areas listed above welcome; approach in writing in the first instance. *Overseas associate* The Continuum International Publishing Group Inc., New York.
Royalties paid twice-yearly.

Authors' Rating The rapidly expanding religious and academic list owes much to the skilful acquisition of small but interesting companies such as Sheed & Ward and Sheffield Academic Press. A trade publishing division was set up last year which should help with declared policy of selling religious books in general shops.

Conway Maritime Press
See **Brassey's**

Thomas Cook Publishing
PO Box 227, Peterborough PE3 8XX
☎01733 416477 Fax 01733 416688
Managing Director *Kevin Fitzgerald*
Approx. Annual Turnover £1.7 million
Part of the Thomas Cook Group Ltd, publishing commenced in 1873 with the first issue of Cook's Continental Timetable. *Publishes* guidebooks, maps and timetables. About 20 titles a year. No unsolicited mss; synopses and ideas welcome as long as they are travel-related.
Royalties paid annually.

Leo Cooper
See **Pen & Sword Books Ltd**

Corgi
See **Transworld Publishers**

Cornwall Books
See **Golden Cockerel Press Ltd**

Coronet
See **Hodder Headline Ltd**

Countryside Books
2 Highfield Avenue, Newbury, Berkshire RG14 5DS
☎01635 43816 Fax 01635 551004
Email info@countrysidebooks.co.uk
Website www.countrysidebooks.co.uk
Publisher *Nicholas Battle*
FOUNDED 1976. *Publishes* local interest paperbacks on regional subjects, generally by English county. Local history, genealogy, walking and photographic, aviation and military, some transport. Over 300 titles available. Unsolicited mss and synopses welcome but no fiction, poetry, natural history or personal memories.
Royalties paid twice-yearly.

Cressrelles Publishing Co. Ltd
10 Station Road Industrial Estate, Colwall, Malvern, Worcestershire WR13 6RN
☎01684 540154 Fax 01684 540154
Email simonsmith@cressrelles4drama.fsbusiness.co.uk
Managing Director *Leslie Smith*
Publishes a range of local interest books, drama and chiropody titles. IMPRINTS **Actinic Press** Specialises in chiropody; **J. Garnet Miller Ltd** Plays and theatre texts; **Kenyon-Deane** Plays and drama textbooks.

Croom Helm
See **Routledge**

Crossway
See **Inter-Varsity Press**

The Crowood Press Ltd
The Stable Block, Crowood Lane, Ramsbury,
Marlborough, Wiltshire SN8 2HR
☎01672 520320 Fax 01672 520280
Email enquiries@crowood.com
Website www.crowood.com
Chairman *John Dennis*
Managing Director *Ken Hathaway*

Publishes sport and leisure titles, including animal and land husbandry, climbing and walking, maritime, country sports, equestrian, fishing and shooting; also chess and bridge, crafts, dogs, gardening, natural history, aviation, military history and motoring. About 70 titles a year. Preliminary letter preferred in all cases.
Royalties paid annually.

James Currey Publishers
73 Botley Road, Oxford OX2 0BS
☎01865 244111 Fax 01865 246454
Email editorial@jamescurrey.co.uk
Website www.jamescurrey.co.uk
Chairman *James Currey*
Managing Director/Editorial Director
Douglas H. Johnson

FOUNDED 1985. A specialist publisher. *Publishes* academic paperback books on Africa, the Caribbean and Third World: history, anthropology, economics, sociology, politics and literary criticism. Approach in writing by post with synopsis if material is 'relevant to our needs'.
Royalties paid annually.

Curzon Press
See **Routledge**

Custom Publishing
See **The Orion Publishing Group Limited**

Cygnus Arts
See **Golden Cockerel Press Ltd**

Dalesman Publishing Co. Ltd
Stable Courtyard, Broughton Hall, Skipton,
North Yorkshire BD23 3AZ
☎01756 701381 Fax 01756 701326
Email editorial@dalesman.co.uk
Website www.dalesman.co.uk
Editor *Terry Fletcher*

Publishers of *Dalesman, Cumbria and Lake District* and *Peak District* magazines, and regional books covering Yorkshire, the Lake District and the Peak District. Subjects include crafts and hobbies, geography and geology, guidebooks, history and antiquarian, humour, travel and topography. Will consider mss on subjects listed above. About 20 titles a year.
Royalties paid annually.

Terence Dalton Ltd
Water Street, Lavenham, Sudbury, Suffolk
CO10 9RN
☎01787 249291 Fax 01787 248267
Website www.lavenhamgroup.co.uk
Director/Editorial Head *Elisabeth Whitehair*

FOUNDED 1967. Part of the Lavenham Group Plc, a family company. *Publishes* non-fiction and currently contract-publishes water and environment books for Chartered UK Institution. No unsolicited mss; send synopsis with two or three sample chapters. Ideas welcome.
Royalties paid annually.

The C.W. Daniel Co. Ltd
1 Church Path, Saffron Walden, Essex
CB10 1JP
☎01799 521909 Fax 01799 513462
Email cwdaniel@dial.pipex.com
Website www.cwdaniel.com
Managing Director *Ian Miller*
Approx. Annual Turnover £1 million

FOUNDED in 1902 by a man who knew and was a follower of Tolstoy, the company was taken over by its present directors in 1973. Output increased following the acquisition in 1980 of health and healing titles from the Health Science Press, the purchase of Neville Spearman Publishers' metaphysical list in 1985 and the list of L.N. Fowler in 1998. *Publishes* New Age: alternative healing and metaphysical. About 15 titles a year. No fiction, diet or cookery. Unsolicited synopses and ideas welcome; no unsolicited mss.
Royalties paid annually.

Darf Publishers Ltd
277 West End Lane, London NW6 1QS
☎020 7431 7009 Fax 020 7431 7655
Website www.darfpublishers.co.uk
Chairman/Managing Director
M.B. Fergiani
Editorial Head *A. Bentaleb*
Approx. Annual Turnover £500,000

FOUNDED 1982 to publish books and reprints on the Middle East, history, theology and

travel. *Publishes* geography, history, language, literature, oriental, politics, theology and travel. About 10 titles a year. TITLES *Moslems in Spain; Travels of Ibn Battuta; The Barbary Corsairs; Elementary Arabic; Travels in Syria and the Holy Land.*
Royalties paid annually. *Overseas associates* Dar Al-Fergiani, Cairo, Tripoli and Tunis.

Darton, Longman & Todd Ltd
1 Spencer Court, 140–142 Wandsworth High Street, London SW18 4JJ
☎020 8875 0155 Fax 020 8875 0133
Email mail@darton-longman-todd.co.uk
Editorial Director *Brendan Walsh*
Approx. Annual Turnover £1 million
FOUNDED in 1959. In July 1990 DLT became a common ownership company, owned and run by staff members. A leading ecumenical, predominantly Christian, publisher, with a strong emphasis on spirituality, theology and the ministry and mission of the Church. About 50 titles a year. TITLES *Jerusalem Bible; New Jerusalem Bible; God of Surprises; Landmarks.* Sample material for books on theological or spiritual subjects considered.
Royalties paid twice-yearly.

David & Charles Children's Books
See **Gullane Children's Books**

David & Charles Publishers
Brunel House, Forde Close, Newton Abbot, Devon TQ12 4PU
☎01626 323200 Fax 01626 323317
Email mail@davidandcharles.co.uk
Website www.davidandcharles.co.uk
Managing Director *Budge Wallis*
FOUNDED 1960 as a specialist company. *Publishes* illustrated non-fiction for international markets, specialising in needlecraft, crafts, art techniques, practical photography, interiors and equestrian. No fiction, poetry or memoirs. About 50 titles a year. TITLES *Stitcher's Bible; Dolls' House Details; Watercolour in a Weekend; Photos That Sell; Enlightened Equitation; The Complete Equine Veterinary Manual.* Unsolicited mss will be considered if return postage is included; synopses and ideas welcome for the subjects listed above.
Royalties paid twice-yearly.

Authors' Rating It is hard to keep track of David & Charles as it gets pushed from one owner to another. The latest, Providence Equity, says that it is business as usual but authors could be forgiven for feeling a tad confused.

Christopher Davies Publishers Ltd
PO Box 403, Swansea, West Glamorgan SA1 4YF
☎01792 648825 Fax 01792 648825
Managing Director/Editorial Head
Christopher T. Davies
Approx. Annual Turnover £50,000
FOUNDED 1949 to promote and expand Welsh-language publications. By the 1970s the company was publishing over 50 titles a year but a subsequent drop in Welsh sales led to the establishment of a small English list which has continued. *Publishes* biography, cookery, history, sport and literature of Welsh interest. About 3 titles a year. TITLES *An A–Z of Wales and the Welsh; Welsh Birthplaces; A Journey Through Gower; Who's Who in Welsh History.* No unsolicited mss. Synopses and ideas for books welcome.
Royalties paid twice-yearly.

Authors' Rating A favourite for Celtic readers and writers.

Giles de la Mare Publishers Ltd
PO Box 25351, London NW5 1ZT
☎020 7485 2533 Fax 020 7485 2534
Email gilesdelamare@dial.pipex.com
Chairman/Managing Director *Giles de la Mare*
Approx. Annual Turnover £45,000
FOUNDED 1995 and commenced publishing in April 1996. *Publishes* mainly non-fiction, especially art and architecture, biography, history, music. TITLES *Married to the Amadeus* Muriel Nissel; *Venice: An Anthology Guide* Milton Grundy; *History at War* Noble Frankland; *Duchess of Cork Street* Lillian Browse; *Erasmus Darwin* Desmond King-Hele; *Shakespeare and the Prince of Love* Anthony Arlidge; *Flint Architecture of East Anglia* Stephen Hart; *19th Century British Painting* Luke Herrmann; *Handsworth Revolution* David Winkley. Unsolicited mss, synopses and ideas welcome after initial telephone call.
Royalties paid twice-yearly.

Dean
See **Egmont Books**

Debrett's Peerage Ltd
Brunel House, 55a North Wharf Road, London W2 1XR
☎020 7915 9633 Fax 020 7753 4212
Email people@debretts.co.uk
Website www.debretts.co.uk
Chairman *Christopher Haines*
FOUNDED 1769. The company's main activity

(in conjunction with **Macmillan**) is the quin-quennial *Debrett's Peerage and Baronetage* (published in 2000) and annual *Debrett's People of Today* (also available on CD-ROM and online). Debrett's general books are published under licence through **Headline**.

Royalties paid quarterly.

Dedalus Ltd
Langford Lodge, St Judith's Lane, Sawtry, Cambridgeshire PE28 5XE
☎01487 832382 Fax 01487 832382
Email DedalusLimited@compuserve.com
Website www.dedalusbooks.com
Chairman *Juri Gabriel*
Managing Director *Eric Lane*
Approx. Annual Turnover £200,000

FOUNDED 1983. *Publishes* contemporary European fiction and classics and original literary fiction. 14 titles in 2001. TITLES *The Dedalus Book of Absinthe; The Arabian Nightmare* Robert Irwin; *Memoirs of a Byzantine Eunuch; Faster Than Light* John Lucas; *Music in a Foreign Language* Andrew Crumey (winner of the **Saltire Best First Book Award** in 1994). Welcomes submissions for original fiction and books suitable for its list but 'most people sending work in have no idea what kind of books Dedalus publishes and merely waste their efforts'. Author guidelines on website. Particularly interested in intellectually clever and unusual fiction. A letter about the author should always accompany any submission. No replies without s.a.e.

DIVISIONS/IMPRINTS **Original Fiction in Paperback**; **Contemporary European Fiction 1992–2002**; **Dedalus European Classics**; **Empire of the Senses**; **Literary Concept Books**.
Royalties paid annually.

Authors' Rating A small, quality publisher which actually recognises that good books can come from foreign language writers.

University of Delaware
See **Golden Cockerel Press Ltd**

JM Dent
See **The Orion Publishing Group Ltd**

André Deutsch Ltd
See **Carlton Publishing Group**

Dial House
See **Ian Allan Publishing Ltd**

Digital Octopus
See **Octopus Publishing Group**

Dinas
See **Y Lolfa Cyf**

Diva Books
See **Millivres Prowler Group**

John Donald Publishers Ltd
West Newington House, 10 Newington Road, Edinburgh EH9 1QS
☎0131 668 4371 Fax 0131 668 4466
Website www.birlinn.co.uk
Managing Director *Hugh Andrew*

Bought by **Birlinn Ltd** in 1999. *Publishes* academic and scholarly, archaeology, architecture, textbooks, guidebooks, local, military and social history. About 20 titles a year. New books are published as an imprint of Birlinn Ltd.
Royalties paid annually.

Donhead Publishing Ltd
Lower Coombe, Donhead St Mary, Shaftesbury, Dorset SP7 9LY
☎01747 828422 Fax 01747 828522
Email jillpearce@donhead.com
Website www.donhead.com
Contact *Jill Pearce*

FOUNDED 1990 to specialise in publishing how-to books for building practitioners; particularly interested in architectural conservation material. *Publishes* building, architecture and heritage only. 6 titles a year. TITLES *Preserving Post-War Heritage; Stone Cleaning; Architecture 1900; Encyclopaedia of Architectural Terms; Gauged Brickwork; Cleaning Historic Buildings; Brickwork; Practical Stone Masonry; Conservation of Timber Buildings; Surveying Historic Buildings; English Heritage Directory of Building Limes; Heritage, Sands and Aggregates; Creative Re-use of Buildings; Journal of Architectural Conservation* (3 issues yearly). Unsolicited mss, synopses and ideas welcome.

Dorling Kindersley Ltd
Part of the Penguin Group, 80 Strand, London WC2R 0RL
☎020 7010 3000 Fax 020 7010 6060
Website www.dk.com
Chief Executive *Anthony Forbes Watson*
Managing Director *Andrew Welham*
Publisher *Christopher Davis*

FOUNDED 1974. Packager and publisher of illustrated non-fiction: cookery, crafts, gardening, health, travel guides, atlases, natural history and children's information and fiction. Launched a US imprint in 1991 and an Australian imprint in 1997. Acquired Henderson Publishing in 1995 and was purchased by Pearson plc for £311 million in 2000.

DIVISIONS Adult: **Travel/Reference** Publisher *Douglas Amrine*; **General/Lifestyle** Publisher *John Roberts*. Children's: **Reference** Publisher *Miriam Farby*; **PreSchool/Primary** Publisher *Sophie Mitchell*. IMPRINTS **Ladybird**; **Ladybird Audio**; **Funfax**; **Eyewitness Guides**; **Eyewitness Travel Guides**. TITLES *BMA Complete Family Health Encyclopedia*; *RHS A–Z Encyclopedia of Garden Plants*; *Children's Illustrated Encyclopedia*; *The Way Things Work*. Unsolicited synopses/ideas for books welcome.

Authors' Rating Having closed the Family Learning and CD-ROM divisions, the focus is on 'soft learning' products for the trade and education markets. Most titles are team efforts with writers and illustrators working closely with an in-house editor.

Doubleday
See **Transworld Publishers**

Ashley Drake Publishing Ltd
PO Box 733, Cardiff CF14 2YX
☎029 2056 0343 Fax 029 2056 1631
Email post@ashleydrake.com
Website www.ashleydrake.com

Managing Director *Ashley Drake*
Approx. Annual Turnover £100,000

FOUNDED 1995. *Publishes* academic, trade and Welsh-language books. 20 titles in 2003. No unsolicited mss; synopses and ideas for the Welsh Academic Press and St David's Press imprints welcome. No scientific or computing books.

IMPRINTS
Welsh Academic Press English language academic, scholarly humanities and social sciences. **St David's Press** Sport, music, cookery and general trade. **Morgan Publishing** General trade. **Y Ddraig Fach** Welsh-language titles for children. **Gwasg Addysgol Cymru** Welsh-language educational titles.
Royalties paid annually.

Drake Educational Associates
St Fagans Road, Fairwater, Cardiff CF5 3AE
☎029 2056 0333 Fax 029 2055 4909
Managing Director *R.G. Drake*
Educational publishers.

Dreamstar Books
Lasyard House, Underhill Street, Bridgnorth, Shropshire WV16 4BB
☎01746 761298 Fax 01746 767440
Email editor@corvedalegroup.co.uk
Website www.corvedalegroup.co.uk

Owner *Corvedale Publishing Ltd*
Editor *Mark Horton-Oliver*

FOUNDED 2000. *Publishes* illustrated children's fiction with series potential and cassette narration possibilities. Works closely with a number of charities and donates part of the proceeds from book sales to them. Unsolicited material welcome; approach by post or e-mail.
Royalties paid twice-yearly.

Dref Wen
28 Church Road, Whitchurch, Cardiff CF14 2EA
☎029 2061 7860
Email info.drefwen@btinternet.com

Chairman *R. Boore*
Managing Director *G. Boore*

FOUNDED 1970. *Publishes* Welsh language and bilingual children's books, Welsh and English educational books for Welsh learners.
Royalties paid annually.

Duck Editions/Duckbacks
See **Gerald Duckworth & Co. Ltd**

Gerald Duckworth & Co. Ltd
61 Frith Street, London W1D 3JL
☎020 7434 4242 Fax 020 7434 4420
Email info@duckworth-publishers.co.uk
Website www.ducknet.co.uk

COO *Gillian Hawkins*
Approx. Annual Turnover £2 million

FOUNDED 1898 by Gerald Duckworth. Original publishers of Virginia Woolf. Other early authors include Hilaire Belloc, John Galsworthy, D.H. Lawrence and George Orwell. Duckworth is a general trade publisher with eminent authors such as Beryl Bainbridge, D.J. Taylor and John Bayley in addition to a strong academic division.
IMPRINTS/DIVISIONS **Bristol Classical Press** Classical texts and modern languages; **Chatham Publishing** Maritime history; **Duck Editions** Contemporary literary fiction and non-fiction; **Duckworth Academic**; **Duckworth General**; **Duckbacks**. No unsolicited mss; synopses and sample chapters only. Enclose s.a.e. or return postage for response/return.
Royalties paid twice-yearly at first, annually thereafter.

Duncan Petersen Publishing Limited

31 Ceylon Road, London W14 0PY
☎020 7371 2356 Fax 020 7371 2507
Email dp@appleonline.net

Director *Andrew Duncan*

FOUNDED 1986. Publisher and packager of childcare, business, antiques, birds, nature, atlases, walking and travel books. IMPRINT **Duncan Petersen** SERIES *Charming Small Hotel Guides; Independent Traveller's Guides; Backroads Driving Guides; On Foot* (city walking guides). Unsolicited synopses and ideas for books welcome.
Fees paid.

Martin Dunitz Ltd

The Livery House, 7–9 Pratt Street, London NW1 0AE
☎020 7482 2202 Fax 020 7267 0159
Website www.dunitz.co.uk

Managing Director *Martin Dunitz*
Production Director *Rosemary Allen*
Journals Publisher *Máire Collins*

Acquired by the **Taylor & Francis Group plc** in 1999. *Publishes* specialist medical and dentistry atlases, texts, pocketbooks, slide atlases and CD-ROMs aimed at an international market. Particular areas of focus are psychiatry, neurology, cardiology, orthopaedics, dermatology, oncology and bone metabolism. The company won the Queen's Award for Export Achievement in 1991. 90–100 titles a year. Unsolicited synopses and ideas welcome but no mss. TITLES *International Journal of Cardiovascular Interventions, International Journal of Psychiatry in Clinical Practice, Journal of Cosmetic and Laser Therapy; Amyotrophic Lateral Sclerosis and Other Motor Neuron Disorders; The Cerebellum.*
Royalties paid twice-yearly.

Eagle/Little Eagle
See **Inter Publishing Ltd**

Earthlight
See **Simon & Schuster UK Limited**

Earthscan Publications
See **Kogan Page Ltd**

Ebury Press
See **Random House Group Ltd**

Economist Books
See **Profile Books**

Eden
See **Transworld Publishers**

Edinburgh University Press

22 George Square, Edinburgh EH8 9LF
☎0131 650 4218 Fax 0131 662 0053
Website www.eup.ed.ac.uk

Chairman *Timothy Rix*
Managing Director *Timothy Wright*
Editorial Director *Jackie Jones*
Editor, Polygon *Alison Bowden*

Publishes academic and scholarly books (and journals): gender studies, geography, history – ancient, classical, medieval and modern, Islamic studies, linguistics, literary criticism, media and cultural studies; philosophy, politics, Scottish studies, theology and religious studies. About 100 titles a year.
IMPRINTS **Polygon** Fiction and poetry, general trade books, Scottish literary, cultural and oral history; **Polygon@Edinburgh** Scottish politics and culture. No unsolicited mss for EUP titles; mss welcome for Polygon (not poetry) and Polygon@Edinburgh but must be accompanied by s.a.e. for reply/return; letter/synopsis preferred in the first instance.
Royalties paid annually.

Egmont Books

239 Kensington High Street, London W8 6SA
☎020 7761 3500 Fax 020 7761 3510
Email <firstname>.<lastname>ecb.egmont.com
Also at: Unit 7, Millbank House, Riverside Park, Bollin Walk, Wilmslow, Cheshire SK9 1BJ
☎01625 543800

Managing Director *Susannah McFarlane*
Fiction *Cally Poplak*
Picture Books *Rebecca Elgar*
Learning, Baby and Toddler *Nina Filipek*
(at Wilmslow address)
Approx. Annual Turnover £19.6 million

Part of the Egmont Group (Copenhagen), Egmont Books comprises the original imprints of Heinemann Young Books and Methuen Children's Books (both over 100 years old), and Hamlyn Children's Books. *Publishes* children's picture books, fiction and non-fiction; licensed characters for children. About 350 titles a year.
IMPRINTS **Mammoth** TITLES *The Ghost of Thomas Kempe; The Little Prince; Tintin.* **Heinemann; Methuen** TITLES *Thomas the Tank Engine; Winnie-the-Pooh;* **Dean.** No unsolicited mss. Synopses and sample chapters welcome; approach in writing with s.a.e. marked for the attention of 'The Reader'. 'We regret that we

are unable to return unsolicited material without s.a.e.'

Royalties paid twice-yearly.

Authors' Rating Reorganisation, including the merger of Egmont World with Egmont Children's Books, has given more freedom to commissioning editors to back their judgement. Improved sales suggest that devolution pays. Egmont has refined its list to focus more on really strong sellers. The emphasis now is on fiction and picture books. A sturdy back list helps to keep the show on the fast track.

Eland Publishing Ltd

Third Floor, 61 Exmouth Market, Clerkenwell, London EC1R 4QL
☎020 7833 0762 Fax 020 7833 4434
Email info@travelbooks.co.uk *or* info@sicklemoon.co.uk
Website www.travelbooks.co.uk *or* www.sicklemoon.co.uk

Directors *Rose Baring, John Hatt, Barnaby Rogerson*
Approx. Annual Turnover £100–200,000

Reprint publisher established by travel writer and editor John Hatt in 1982. Classic travel literature of the world. 6 titles in 2001. IMPRINTS **Sickle Moon Books** *Barnaby Rogerson* Reprints of travel literature and history of the Islamic world. **Baring & Rogerson Books** *Barnaby Rogerson* Poetry of travel. TITLES *Sultan in Oman* Jan Morris; *First Poems* Edward Barker. Ideas for books welcome; send letter or e-mail.
Royalties paid annually.

Element

See **HarperCollins Publishers Ltd**

11:9

See **Neil Wilson Publishing Ltd**

Edward Elgar Publishing Ltd

Glensanda House, Montpellier Parade, Cheltenham, Gloucestershire GL50 1UA
☎01242 226934 Fax 01242 262111
Email info@e-elgar.co.uk
Website www.e-elgar.co.uk

Chairman *Alex Ryan*
Managing Director *Edward Elgar*

FOUNDED 1986. International publisher in economics, the environment, public policy and social sciences. 213 titles in 2001. TITLES *Who's Who in Economics* (3rd ed.); *Handbook of Environmental and Resource Economics*; *Who's Who in the Management Sciences*. No unsolicited mss; synopses and ideas in the subject areas

listed above welcome. Approach by letter or e-mail; no telephone inquiries.
Royalties paid annually.

Elliot Right Way Books

Kingswood Buildings, Lower Kingswood, Tadworth, Surrey KT20 6TD
☎01737 832202 Fax 01737 830311
Email info@right-way.co.uk
Website www.right-way.co.uk

Managing Directors *A. Clive Elliot, Malcolm G. Elliot*

FOUNDED 1946 by Andrew G. Elliot. *Publishes* paperback how-to and educative titles on an unlimited variety of home reference, indoor and outdoor leisure pursuits, careers and business. Subjects include cookery, family financial and legal matters, public speaking, weddings, jokes, parenting, etiquette, English skills, driving, fishing, horse riding, drawing, music, puzzles, crosswords and quizzes, job seeking, running your own company. IMPRINTS **Right Way** Instructional paperbacks in B format for the most popular subjects; **Right Way Plus** Larger C format for more specialised subjects; **Clarion** B format for promotional/ultra low-price range. Unsolicited mss, synopses and ideas for books welcome.
Royalties paid annually.

Aidan Ellis Publishing

Whinfield, Herbert Road, Salcombe, South Devon TQ8 8HN
☎01548 842755 Fax 01548 844356
Email aidan@aepub.demon.co.uk
Website www.demon.co.uk/aepub

Partners/Editorial Heads *Aidan Ellis, Lucinda Ellis*

FOUNDED in 1971. *Specialises* in general trade books and non-fiction. TITLES *Eternity Regained* Marguerite Yourcenar; *Reunited! Loved Ones Traced by the Red Cross* Michael Johnstone; *The Royal Gardens in Windsor Great Park* Charles Lyte; *Trees For Your Garden* Roy Lancaster; *Pesca* Ian B. Hart; *Guide du Fromage* Pierre Androuët; *Kenwood* John Carswell; *Presumed Dead* Eunice Chapman; *The Bird Table Book* Tony Soper. Ideas and synopses welcome (return postage, please).
Royalties paid twice-yearly.

Elm Publications/Training

Seaton House, Kings Ripton, Huntingdon, Cambridgeshire PE28 2NJ
☎01487 773254
Email sritchie@elm-training.co.uk

Website www.elm-training.co.uk
Managing Director *Sheila Ritchie*
FOUNDED 1977. *Publishes* textbooks, teaching aids, educational resources and educational software in the fields of business and management for adult learners. Books and teaching/training resources are generally commissioned to meet specific business, management and other syllabuses. 'We are actively seeking good training materials for business/management, especially tested and proven.' About 30 titles a year. Ideas are welcome; first approach by post or e-mail with outline, or by a brief telephone call.
Royalties paid annually.

Elsevier Science Ltd
The Boulevard, Langford Lane, Kidlington, Oxford OX5 1GB
☎01865 843000 Fax 01865 843010
Website www.elsevier.com
Chief Operating Officer *Gavin Howe*
Parent company **Reed Elsevier**, Amsterdam. Now incorporates Pergamon Press and **Harcourt Publishers International**. *Publishes* academic and professional reference books, scientific, technical and medical books, journals, CD-ROMs and magazines.
DIVISION **Elsevier and Pergamon** *Barbara Barrett, Chris Lloyd, Paul Evans.* Unsolicited mss, synopses and ideas for books welcome.
Royalties paid annually.

Emissary Publishing
PO Box 33, Bicester, Oxfordshire OX26 4ZZ
☎01869 323447 Fax 01869 324096
Editorial Director *Val Miller*
FOUNDED 1992. *Publishes* mainly humorous paperback books including the complete set of Peter Pook novels; no poetry or children's. Runs a biennial Humorous Novel Competition in memory of the late Peter Pook and publishes the winning novel (s.a.e. for details). No unsolicited mss or synopses.
Royalties paid twice-yearly.

Empiricus Books
See **Janus Publishing Company Ltd**

English Heritage (Publications)
23 Savile Row, London W1S 2ET
☎020 7973 3703 Fax 020 7973 3680
Website www.english-heritage.org.uk
Head of Publications and Design
Val Horsler

FOUNDED 1984 to publish English Heritage guidebooks and a range of academic material related directly to the work of the organisation. No unsolicited material.

Enitharmon Press
26B Caversham Road, London NW5 2DU
☎020 7482 5967 Fax 020 7284 1787
Email books@enitharmon.co.uk
Website www.enitharmon.co.uk
Director *Stephen Stuart-Smith*
FOUNDED 1967. An independent company with an enterprising editorial policy, Enitharmon has established itself as one of Britain's leading poetry presses. Patron of 'the new and the neglected', Enitharmon prides itself on the success of its collaborations between writers and artists. *Publishes* poetry, literary criticism, fiction, art and photography. TITLES *London in Poetry and Prose* Anna Adams; *Christmas Poems* U.A. Fanthorpe; *Adamah* Jeremy Hooker; *The Disappeared and Other Poems* Harold Pinter; *Defining the Times* Kathleen Raine. No unsolicited mss.
Royalties paid according to contract.

Epworth Press
c/o Methodist Publishing House, 4 John Wesley Road, Werrington, Peterborough, Cambridgeshire PE4 6ZP
☎01733 332202 Fax 01733 331201
Chairman *Dr John A. Newton, CBE*
Editor *Gerald M. Burt*
Publishes Christian books only: philosophy, theology, biblical studies, pastoralia and social concern. No fiction, poetry or children's. A series based on the text of the *Revised Common Lectionary*, entitled *Companion to the RCL*, was launched in 1998 and the two new series *Exploring Methodism* and *Thinking Things Through* continue. About 10 titles a year. TITLES *Reasonable Enthusiast* Henry D. Rack; *The Quiet, Wise Spirit – Edwin Smith and Africa* John Young; *John Wesley: The Evangelist Revival and the Rise of Methodism* John Munsey Turner. Unsolicited mss considered but write to enquire in the first instance. Authors wishing to have their mss returned must send sufficient postage.
Royalties paid annually.

Euromonitor
60–61 Britton Street, London EC1M 5UX
☎020 7251 8024 Fax 020 7608 3149
Website www.euromonitor.com
Chairman *R.N. Senior*
Managing Director *T.J. Fenwick*

Approx. Annual Turnover £14 million

FOUNDED 1972. International business information publisher specialising in library and professional reference books, market reports, electronic databases, journals and CD-ROMs. *Publishes* business reference, market analysis and information directories only. About 200 titles a year.

DIVISIONS **Market Analysis** *T. Kitchen*, *S. Holmes*; **Reference Books & Directories** *S. Hunter.* TITLES *Credit & Charge Cards: The International Market; Europe in the Year 2000; European Marketing Handbook; European Directory of Trade and Business Associations; World Retail Directory and Sourcebook.*
Payment is generally by flat fee.

Europa Publications Ltd
See **Taylor & Francis Group plc**

Evans Brothers Ltd
2A Portman Mansions, Chiltern Street, London W1U 6NR
☎020 7487 0920 Fax 020 7487 0921
Email sales@evansbrothers.co.uk
Website www.evansbooks.co.uk
Managing Director *Stephen Pawley*
International Publishing Director *Brian Jones*
UK Publisher *Su Swallow*
Approx. Annual Turnover £3.5 million
FOUNDED 1908 by Robert and Edward Evans. Originally published educational journals, books for primary schools and teacher education. After rapid expansion into popular fiction and drama, both were sacrificed to a major programme of educational books for schools in East and West Africa. A UK programme was launched in 1986 followed by the acquisition of Hamish Hamilton's non-fiction list for children in 1990. Acquired interests in Cherrytree Books and Zero to Ten in 1999. *Publishes* UK children's and educational books, and educational books for Africa, the Caribbean and Latin America. About 90 titles a year.
IMPRINTS **Cherrytree Books** Publisher *Angela Sheehan*; **Zero to Ten** (327 High Street, Slough, Berkshire SL1 1TX) Publisher *Anna McQuinn.* Unsolicited mss, synopses and ideas for books welcome.
Royalties paid annually. *Overseas associates* in Kenya, Cameroon, Sierra Leone; Evans Bros (Nigeria Publishers) Ltd.

Everyman
See **The Orion Publishing Group Ltd**

Everyman Publishers Plc
Gloucester Mansions, 140a Shaftesbury Avenue, London WC2H 8HD
☎020 7539 7600 Fax 020 7379 4060
Email books@everyman.uk.com
Website www.everyman.uk.com
Managing Director *David Campbell*
Approx. Annual Turnover £3.5 million
FOUNDED 1990 with acquisition of Everyman's Library (established 1906) bought from J.M. Dent. *Publishes* hardback classics of world literature, pocket poetry anthologies, children's books and travel guides. AUTHORS include Bulgakov, Bellow, Borges, Forster, Grass, Mann, Nabokov, Orwell, Rushdie, Updike and Waugh. No unsolicited mss.
Royalties paid annually.

University of Exeter Press
Reed Hall, Streatham Drive, Exeter, Devon EX4 4QR
☎01392 263066 Fax 01392 263064
Email uep@exeter.ac.uk
Website www.ex.ac.uk/uep/
Publisher *Simon Baker*
FOUNDED 1956. *Publishes* academic books: archaeology, classical studies, history, maritime studies, English literature (especially medieval), linguistics, European studies, modern languages and literature, film history, performance studies, Arabic studies and books on Exeter and the South West. About 30 titles a year. Proposals welcomed in the above subject areas.
Royalties paid annually.

Exley Publications Ltd
16 Chalk Hill, Watford, Hertfordshire WD19 4BG
☎01923 248328 Fax 01923 800440
Email editorial@exleypublications.co.uk
Website www.helenexleygiftbooks.com
Editorial Director *Helen Exley*
FOUNDED 1976. Independent family company. *Publishes* giftbooks, quotation anthologies and humour. About 35 titles a year. Only series ideas needed – no individual titles. No rhyming poetry, please.

Expert Books
See **Transworld Publishers**

Faber & Faber Ltd
3 Queen Square, London WC1N 3AU
☎020 7465 0045 Fax 020 7465 0034
Website www.faber.co.uk

Chief Executive *Stephen Page*
Approx. Annual Turnover £13 million

Geoffrey Faber founded the company in the 1920s, with T.S. Eliot as an early recruit to the board. The original list was based on contemporary poetry and plays (the distinguished backlist includes Eliot, Auden and MacNeice). *Publishes* poetry and drama, children's, fiction, film, music, politics, biography, wine.

DIVISIONS

Fiction Editor-in-Chief *Jon Riley* AUTHORS P.D. James, Peter Carey, Giles Foden, Michael Frayn, Kazuo Ishiguro, Barbara Kingsolver, Milan Kundera, Hanif Kureishi, John Lanchester, John McGahern, Rohinton Mistry, Lorrie Moore, Andrew O'Hagan, Jane Smiley; **Children's** *Suzy Jenvey* AUTHORS Philip Ardagh, Terry Deary, Russell Stannard; **Film** *Walter Donohue* and **Plays** *Peggy Paterson* AUTHORS Samuel Beckett, Alan Bennett, David Hare, Brian Friel, Patrick Marber, Harold Pinter, Tom Stoppard, Woody Allen, John Boorman, Joel and Ethan Coen, John Hodge, Martin Scorsese, Quentin Tarantino; **Music** *Belinda Matthews* AUTHORS Humphrey Burton, John Drummond, Alexander Goehr, Nicholas Kenyon, Harvey Sachs, Elizabeth Wilson; **Poetry** *Paul Keegan* AUTHORS Simon Armitage, Douglas Dunn, Seamus Heaney, Ted Hughes, Tom Paulin; **Non-fiction** *Julian Loose* AUTHORS John Carey, Simon Garfield, Adam Phillips, Jan Morris, Jenny Uglow.

Royalties paid twice-yearly.

Authors' Rating Faber is particularly strong on poetry and the performance arts. A pointer to the future is the poetry database set up as a joint venture with Chadwyck-Healey.

Facet Publishing

7 Ridgmount Street, London WC1E 7AE
☎020 7255 0590/0505 (text phone)
Fax 020 7255 0591
Email info@facetpublishing.co.uk
Website www.facetpublishing.co.uk

Managing Director *Janet Liebster*

Publishing arm of **CILIP: The Chartered Institute of Library and Information Professionals** (formerly the Library Association). *Publishes* library and information science, monographs, reference, IT training materials and bibliography aimed at library and information professionals. 25–30 titles a year.

IMPRINTS

Library Association Publishing; **Clive Bingley Books**; **Facet Publishing**. Over 200 titles in print, including *Walford's Guide to Reference Material* and *AACR2*. Unsolicited mss, synopses and ideas welcome provided material falls firmly within the company's specialist subject areas.

Royalties paid annually.

Fairleigh Dickinson University Press
See **Golden Cockerel Press**

Falmer Press
See **Taylor & Francis Group plc**

Fernhurst Books

Duke's Path, High Street, Arundel, West Sussex BN18 9AJ
☎01903 882277   Fax 01903 882715
Email sales@fernhurstbooks.co.uk
Website www.fernhurstbooks.co.uk

Chairman/Managing Director *Tim Davison*

FOUNDED 1979. For people who love watersports. *Publishes* practical, highly-illustrated handbooks on sailing and watersports. TITLES *Heavy Weather Crossing; First Aid Afloat; Simple Yacht Design; Staying Put! The Art of Anchoring; Helming to Win; The History of Surfing; Mirror Racing.* No unsolicited mss; synopses and ideas welcome.

Royalties paid twice-yearly.

David Fickling Books
See **Random House Group Ltd**

Findhorn Press Ltd

The Park, Findhorn, Moray IV36 3TE
☎01309 690582   Fax 01309 690036
Email books@findhorn.org
Website www.findhornpress.com

Directors *Karin Bogliolo, Thierry Bogliolo*
Approx. Annual Turnover £320,000

FOUNDED 1971. *Publishes* mind, body, spirit, New Age and healing. 13 titles in 2001. Unsolicited synopses and ideas welcome if they come within their subject areas. No children's books, fiction or poetry.

Royalties paid twice-yearly.

Firefly Publishing
See **Helter Skelter Publishing**

First & Best in Education Ltd

Unit K, Earlstrees Court, Earlstrees Road, Corby, Northamptonshire NN17 4HH
☎01536 399004   Fax 01536 399012
Email firstandbest9@themail.co.uk

Website www.firstandbest.co.uk
Publisher *Tony Attwood*
Editor *Anne Cockburn*
Publishers of over 1000 educational books of all types for all ages of children and for parents and teachers. All books are published as being suitable for photocopying and/or as electronic books. 'Looking for new authors of educational books all the time. No fiction, please.' TITLES *Raising Grades Through Study Skills; Parents Survival Guide Series; Business Sponsorship of Secondary Schools; Revision, Study and ·Exam Techniques Guide.* IMPRINTS **Multisensory Maths; School Improvement Reports.** In the first instance check the website or send s.a.e. for details of requirements and current projects to *Anne Cockburn,* Editorial Dept. at the address above.
Royalties paid twice-yearly.

Fitzgerald Publishing
89 Ermine Road, Ladywell, London SE13 5JJ
☎020 8690 0597
Email fitzgeraldbooks@yahoo.co.uk
Managing Editor *Tim Fitzgerald*
General Editor *Andrew Smith*
FOUNDED 1974. *Specialises* in scientific studies of insects and spiders. 1–2 titles a year. TITLES *The Tarantula; Keeping Spiders and Insects in Captivity; Tarantulas of the USA; Scorpions of Medical Importance* (books) and *Earth Tigers – Tarantulas of Borneo; Desert Tarantulas* (TV/video documentaries). Unsolicited mss, synopses and ideas for books welcome. Also considers video scripts for video documentaries.

Fitzjames Press
See **Motor Racing Publications**

Fitzroy Dearborn Publishers
310 Regent Street, London W1B 3AX
☎020 7636 6627 Fax 020 7636 6982
Email post@fitzroydearborn.co.uk
Website www.fitzroydearborn.com
Managing Director *Daniel Kirkpatrick*
Publisher *Roda Morrison*
Commissioning Editors *Mark Hawkins-Dady, Gillian Lindsey, Lesley Henderson*
Publishes reference books: the arts, history, literature, business, science and the social sciences. About 50 titles a year. TITLES *International Dictionary of Library Histories; Encyclopedia of Gardens; Censorship: A World Encyclopedia; Encyclopedia of the Enlightenment; Encyclopedia of Life Writing; Encyclopedia of American Poetry; Reader's Guide to Military History; The British Film*

Catalogue. Unsolicited mss, synopses and ideas welcome for reference books.
Royalties paid twice-yearly. *US associate* Fitzroy Dearborn Publishers, 919 North Michigan Ave., Suite 760, Chicago, IL 60611.

Fitzwarren Publishing
2 Orchard Drive, Aston Clinton, Aylesbury, Buckinghamshire HP22 5HR
☎01296 632627 Fax 01296 630028
Contact *Julie Stretton*
Publishes two or three books a year, mainly layman's handbooks on legal matters. All books published so far have followed a rigid 128-page format. Written approaches and synopses from prospective authors welcome. Authors, although not necessarily legally qualified, are expected to know their subject as well as a lawyer would.
Royalties paid twice-yearly.

Five Star
See **Serpent's Tail**

Flame
See **Hodder Headline Ltd**

Flamingo
See **HarperCollins Publishers Ltd**

Flicks Books
29 Bradford Road, Trowbridge, Wiltshire BA14 9AN
☎01225 767728
Email flicks.books@dial.pipex.com
Publishing Director *Matthew Stevens*
FOUNDED 1986. Devoted solely to publishing books on the cinema and related media. TITLES *Queen of the 'B's: Ida Lupino Behind the Camera* ed. Annette Kuhn; *By Angels Driven: The Films of Derek Jarman* ed. Chris Lippard. Unsolicited mss, synopses and ideas within the subject area are welcome.
Royalties paid annually or twice yearly.

Floris Books
15 Harrison Gardens, Edinburgh EH11 1SH
☎0131 337 2372 Fax 0131 347 9919
Email floris@floris.demon.co.uk
Managing Director *Christian Maclean*
Editors *Christopher Moore, Gale Winskill*
Approx. Annual Turnover £350,000
FOUNDED 1977. *Publishes* books related to the Steiner movement, including The Christian Community, as well as arts & crafts, children's (including fiction with a Scottish theme),

history, religious, science, social questions and Celtic studies. No unsolicited mss. Synopses and ideas for books welcome.
Royalties paid annually.

Fodor's
See **Random House Group Ltd**

Folens Limited
Apex Business Centre, Boscombe Road, Dunstable, Bedfordshire LU5 4RL
☎0870 609 1238 Fax 01582 475524
Email folens@folens.com
Website www.folens.com
Chairman *Dirk Folens*
Managing Director *Malcolm Watson*
FOUNDED 1987. Leading educational publisher. About 150 titles a year. IMPRINTS **Folens**; **Belair**. Unsolicited mss, synopses and ideas for educational books welcome.
Royalties paid annually.

Mary Ford Publications Ltd
See **Michael O'Mara Books Ltd**

Foulsham Publishers
The Publishing House, Bennetts Close, Slough, Berkshire SL1 5AP
☎01753 526769 Fax 01753 535003
Chairman *R.S. Belasco*
Managing Director *B.A.R. Belasco*
Approx. Annual Turnover £2.2 million
FOUNDED 1819 and now one of the few remaining independent family companies to survive takeover. *Publishes* non-fiction on most subjects including lifestyle, travel guides, family reference, cookery, diet, health, DIY, business, self improvement, self development, astrology, dreams, MBS. No fiction. IMPRINT **Quantum** Mind, body and spirit titles. TITLES *Classic 1000 Cocktails; A Brit's Guide to Orlando and Walt Disney World 2002.* Unsolicited mss, synopses and ideas welcome. Around 60 titles a year.
Royalties paid twice-yearly.

Foundery Press
See **Methodist Publishing House**

Fountain Press
Newpro UK Ltd., Old Sawmills Road, Faringdon, Oxfordshire SN7 7DS
☎01367 242411 Fax 01367 241124
Email sales@newprouk.co.uk
Publisher *H.M. Ricketts*

Approx. Annual Turnover £800,000
FOUNDED 1923 when it was part of the Rowntree Trust Social Service. Owned by the British Electric Traction Group until 1982 when it was bought out by H.M. Ricketts. Acquired by Newpro UK Ltd in July 2000. *Publishes* mainly photography and natural history. About 25 titles a year. TITLES *Photography Yearbook*; *Antique and Collectable Cameras*; *Camera Manual* (series). Unsolicited mss and synopses welcome.
Royalties paid twice-yearly.

Authors' Rating Highly regarded for production values, Fountain has the reputation for involving authors in every stage of the publishing process.

Fourth Estate Ltd
77–85 Fulham Palace Road, London W6 8JB
☎020 8741 4414 Fax 020 8307 4466
Email general@4thestate.co.uk
Website www.4thestate.co.uk
Managing Director *Christopher Potter*
Publishing Director *Courtney Hodell*
Approx. Annual Turnover £17 million
FOUNDED 1984. Acquired by **HarperCollins** in July 2000, Fourth Estate has a strong reputation for literary fiction and up-to-the-minute non-fiction. *Publishes* fiction, popular science, current affairs, biography, humour, self-help, travel, reference. About 100 titles a year.
DIVISIONS
Literary Fiction/Non-fiction; **General Fiction/Non-Fiction** TITLES *The Fowler Family Business* Jonathan Meades; *John Henry Days* Colson Whitehead; *The Corrections* Jonathan Franzen; *A Year of Wonders* Geraldine Brookes; *Spike Island* Philip Hoare; *The Healing Land* Rupert Isaacson; *England; The Making of the Myth* Maureen Duffy; *Annie's Box. Charles Darwin, his Daugher and Human Evolution* Randal Keynes; *1066 and the Hidden History of the Bayeaux Tapestry* Andrew Bridgeford. No unsolicited mss; synopses welcome.
Royalties paid twice-yearly.

Authors' Rating Having achieved a reputation for innovative, exciting publishing – Dava Sobel's *Longitude*, turned down by other publishers, started a whole genre of narrative histories on quirky subjects – Fourth Estate was bought by HarperCollins who installed Fourth Estate's creator, Victoria Barnsley as chief executive of the whole shooting match. Last year, Fourth Estate set up in New York as the first stage in taking on the American market.

Free Association Books Ltd
57 Warren Street, London W1T 5NR
☎020 7388 3182   Fax 020 7388 3187
Email fab@fa-b.com
Website www.fa-b.com
Managing Director/Publisher *T.E. Brown*

Publishes psychoanalysis and psychotherapy, psychology, cultural studies, sexuality and gender, women's studies, applied social sciences. TITLES *Reaching the Young Autistic Child* S. Janert; *Judo With Words* B. Berchan; *A Compendium of Lacanian Terms* Marks, Murphy and Glowinski; *Psychoanalytic Psychotherapy Trainings – A Guide* R.M. Jones. Always send a letter in the first instance accompanied by a book outline.

Royalties paid twice-yearly. *Overseas associates* ISBS, USA; Astam, Australia.

W.H. Freeman
Palgrave, Houndsmill, Basingstoke, Hampshire RG21 6XS
☎01256 329242   Fax 01256 330688
President *Elizabeth Widdicombe* (New York)
Sales & Marketing Director *Margaret Hewinson*

Following integration into the BFW (Bedford, Freeman, Worth) College Group, USA, Freeman now *publishes* academic educational and textbooks in biochemistry, biology and zoology, chemistry, geography and geology, mathematics and statistics, medical, natural history, neuroscience, palaeontology, physics. Freeman's editorial office is in New York (Basingstoke is a sales and marketing office only) but unsolicited mss can go through Basingstoke. Those which are obviously unsuitable will be sifted out; the rest will be forwarded to New York.

Royalties paid annually.

Samuel French Ltd
52 Fitzroy Street, London W1T 5JR
☎020 7387 9373   Fax 020 7387 2161
Email theatre@samuelfrench-london.co.uk
Website www.samuelfrench-london.co.uk
Chairman *Charles R. Van Nostrand*
Managing Director *Vivien Goodwin*

FOUNDED 1830 with the object of acquiring acting rights and publishing plays. *Publishes* plays only. About 50 titles a year. Unsolicited mss considered only after initial submission of synopsis and specimen scene. Such material should be addressed to the Performing Rights Department.

Royalties paid twice-yearly for books; performing royalties paid monthly, subject to a minimum amount.

Authors' Rating Thrives on the amateur dramatic societies who are forever in need of play texts. Editorial advisers give serious attention to new material but a high proportion of the list is staged before it goes into print. New writers are advised to try one-act plays, much in demand by the amateur dramatic societies but rarely turned out by established playwrights.

David Fulton (Publishers) Ltd
The Chiswick Centre, 414 Chiswick High Road, London W4 5TF
☎020 8996 3333   Fax 020 8742 8390
Email mail@fultonpublishers.co.uk
Website www.fultonpublishers.co.uk
Managing Director *David Hill*
Senior Commissioning Editors *Nina Stibbe, Helen Fairlie, Jude Bowen*
Approx. Annual Turnover £2.4 million

FOUNDED 1987. *Publishes* non-fiction: books for teachers and teacher training at B.Ed and PGCE levels for early years, primary, secondary and virtually all aspects of special education; geography for undergraduates. Currently developing a range of curriculum materials (in book form, packs, on CD-ROM and/or disk) for use by teachers in the classroom. In 1995, David Fulton set up a Fulton Fellowship in Special Education (see entry under **Bursaries, Fellowships and Grants**). About 100 titles a year. No unsolicited mss; synopses and ideas for books welcome.

Royalties paid twice-yearly.

Funfax
See **Dorling Kindersley Ltd**

Gaia Books Ltd
66 Charlotte Street, London W1T 4QE
☎020 7323 4010   Fax 020 7323 0435
Email info@gaiabooks.com
Website www.gaiabooks.co.uk
Also at: 20 High Street, Stroud, Gloucestershire GL5 1AZ
☎01453 752985 Fax 01453 752987
Managing Director *Joss Pearson*

FOUNDED 1983. *Publishes* ecology, health, natural living, gardening, interiors, and mind, body & spirit, mainly in practical self-help illustrated reference form for Britain and the international market. About 12 titles a year. TITLES *Healing Drinks; The Feng Shui Kitchen; The Healing Energies of Earth; The Edible Container Garden; Pilates; The Fertility Plan.* Most projects are conceived in-house but outlines and mss with s.a.e. considered. 'From submission of an idea to project go ahead may take up to a year. Authors become involved with the Gaia team in the editorial, design and promotion work needed to create and market a book.'

Gairm Publications
29 Waterloo Street, Glasgow G2 6BZ
☎0141 221 1971 Fax 0141 221 1971
Chairman *Prof. Derick S. Thomson*

FOUNDED 1952 to publish the quarterly Gaelic periodical *Gairm* and soon moved into publishing other Gaelic material. Acquired an old Glasgow Gaelic publishing firm, Alexander MacLaren & Son, in 1970. *Publishes* a wide range of Gaelic and Gaelic-related books: dictionaries, grammars, handbooks, children's, fiction, poetry, biography, music and song. TITLES *The Companion to Gaelic Scotland; Derick Thomson's collection of poems, Meall Garbh/The Rugged Mountain.* Catalogue available.

Galaxy Children's Large Print
See **Chivers Press Ltd**

J. Garnet Miller Ltd
See **Cressrelles Publishing Co. Ltd**

Garnet Publishing Ltd
8 Southern Court, South Street, Reading, Berkshire RG1 4QS
☎0118 959 7847 Fax 0118 959 7356
Email enquiries@garnet-ithaca.demon.co.uk
Website www.garnet-ithaca.co.uk
Editorial Manager *Emma G. Hawker*

FOUNDED 1992 and purchased Ithaca Press in the same year. *Publishes* art, architecture, photography, archive photography, cookery, travel classics, travel, comparative religion, Islamic culture and history, foreign fiction in translation. Core subjects are Middle Eastern but list is rapidly expanding to be more general. About 30 titles a year.

IMPRINTS

Garnet Publishing TITLES *The Story of Islamic Architecture; Traditional Greek Cooking; Jerusalem: Caught in Time* series. **Ithaca Press** Specialises in post-graduate academic works on the Middle East, political science and international relations. About 20 titles a year. TITLES *The Making of the Modern Gulf States; The Palestinian Exodus; French Imperialism in Syria; Philby of Arabia.* Unsolicited mss not welcome – write with outline and ideas first plus current c.v.

Royalties paid twice-yearly. *Sister companies*: All Prints, Beirut; Garnet France, Paris.

Gay Men's Press
See **GMP**

Geddes & Grosset
David Dale House, New Lanark ML11 9DJ
☎01555 665000 Fax 01555 665694
Publishers *Ron Grosset, R. Michael Miller*
Approx. Annual Turnover £3 million

FOUNDED 1989. Publisher of children's and reference books. Unsolicited mss, synopses and ideas welcome. No adult fiction.

Geological Society Publishing House
Unit 7, Brassmill Enterprise Centre, Brassmill Lane, Bath BA1 3JN
☎01225 445046 Fax 01225 442836
Email dawn.angel@geolsoc.org.uk *or* angharad.hills@geolsoc.org.uk
Website www.bookshop.geolsoc.org.uk
Commissioning Editor *Angharad Hills*

Publishing arm of the Geological Society which was founded in 1807. *Publishes* undergraduate and postgraduate texts in the earth sciences. 25 titles a year. Unsolicited mss, synopses and ideas welcome.

Stanley Gibbons Publications
5 Parkside, Christchurch Road, Ringwood, Hampshire BH24 3SH
☎01425 472363 Fax 01425 470247
Website www.stanleygibbons.co.uk
Chairman *P. Fraser*
Editorial Head *D. Aggersberg*

Long-established force in the philatelic world with over a hundred years in the business. *Publishes* philatelic reference catalogues and handbooks. Approx. 15 titles a year. Reference works relating to other areas of collecting may be considered. TITLES *Stanley Gibbons British Commonwealth Stamp Catalogue; Stamps of the World.* Foreign catalogues include Japan and Korea, Portugal and Spain, Germany, Middle East, Balkans, China. Monthly publication: *Gibbons Stamp Monthly* (see entry under **Magazines**). Unsolicited mss, synopses and ideas welcome. *Royalties* by negotiation.

Robert Gibson & Sons Glasgow Limited
57 Fitzroy Lane, Glasgow G3 3JD
☎0141 248 5674 Fax 0141 221 8219
Email Robert.GibsonSons@btinternet.com
Chairman/Managing Director
R.G.C. Gibson

FOUNDED 1850 and went public in 1886. *Publishes* educational books only. About 40 titles a year. Unsolicited mss preferred to synopses/ideas.
Royalties paid annually.

Ginn
See **Reed Educational & Professional Publishing**

GMP (Gay Men's Press)
PO Box 3220, Brighton, East Sussex BN2 5AU
☎01273 672823   Fax 01273 672159
Website www.prowler.co.uk
Commissioning Editor *Peter Burton*
Part of the **Millivres Prowler Group**. *Publishes* books gay fiction only, from literary to popular. TITLES *Brutal* and *Wasted* both by Aiden Shaw; *Orange Bitter, Orange Sweet* Anthony Macdonald. Send synopsis with sample chapters rather than complete mss. Unsolicited material not returned unless accompanied by s.a.e.
Royalties negotiable.

Golden Cockerel Press Ltd
16 Barter Street, London WC1A 2AH
☎020 7405 7979   Fax 020 7404 3598
Email aup.uk@btinternet.com
Directors *Tamar Lindesay, Andrew Lindesay*
FOUNDED 1980 to distribute titles for US-based Associated University Presses Inc., New Jersey. *Publishes* academic titles mostly: art, film, history, literary criticism, music, philosophy, sociology and special interest. About 120 titles a year.
IMPRINTS **AUP: Bucknell University Press**; **University of Delaware**; **Fairleigh Dickinson University Press**; **Lehigh University Press**; **Susquehanna University Press**. Also: **Cygnus Arts** Non-academic books on the arts; **Cornwall Books** Trade hardbacks.

Authors' Rating Very much attuned to American interests with trans-Atlantic spelling and punctuation predominating. Some writers may find the process wearisome but those who persevere win through to a wider market.

Gollancz
See **The Orion Publishing Group Limited**

Gomer Press
Wind Street, Llandysul, Ceredigion SA44 4QL
☎01559 362371   Fax 01559 363758
Email gwasg@gomer.co.uk
Website www.gomer.co.uk
Chairman/Managing Director *J.H. Lewis*

FOUNDED 1892. *Publishes* adult fiction and non-fiction, children's fiction and educational material in English and Welsh. About 100 titles a year (65 Welsh; 35 English). IMPRINTS **Gomer Press** *Bethan Mair, Gordon Jones, Francesca Rhyddesch*. **Pont Books** *Mairwen Prys Jones*. No unsolicited mss, synopses or ideas.
Royalties paid twice-yearly.

The Good Web Guide Ltd
21 Broadwall, London SE1 9PL
☎020 7261 9382   Fax 020 7401 6544
Email marketing@thegoodwebguide.com
Website www.thegoodwebguide.com
Chairman *David Teale*
Managing Director *Sarah Mahaffy*
Publishing Director *Elaine Collins*
FOUNDED 1999. *Publishes* guides to the best sites on the Internet, both as books and online. The guides are available at retail outlets or online; subscription available giving full access to the website where reviews ae constantly updated and added to. 12 titles in 2001. No unsolicited mss; send synopsis/idea by post or e-mail. No fiction or children's books.
Royalties paid twice-yearly.

Gordon & Breach
See **Taylor & Francis Group plc**

Gower
See **Ashgate Publishing Ltd**

GPC Books
See **University of Wales Press**

Graham & Trotman
See **Kluwer Law International**

Graham & Whiteside Ltd
See **Gale Group** under **US Publishers**

Graham-Cameron Publishing & Illustration
The Studio, 23 Holt Road, Sheringham, Norfolk NR26 8NB
☎01263 821333   Fax 01263 821334
Editorial Director *Mike Graham-Cameron*
Art Director *Helen Graham-Cameron*
FOUNDED 1984 as a packaging operation. *Publishes* illustrated factual books for children, adults, institutions and business; also biography, education and social history. TITLES *Up From the Country; In All Directions; The Holywell Story; Let's Look at Dairying*. *No* unsolicited mss.
Royalties paid annually.

Granada Media
See **Carlton Publishing Group**

Granta Books
2–3 Hanover Yard, Noel Road, London
N1 8BE
☎020 7704 9776   Fax 020 7354 3469
Website www.granta.com
Associate Publisher *Gail Lynch*
FOUNDED 1979. *Publishes* literary fiction and
general non-fiction. About 25 titles a year. No
unsolicited mss; synopses and sample chapters
welcome.
Royalties paid twice-yearly.

W. Green (Scotland)
See **Sweet & Maxwell Group**

Green Books
Foxhole, Dartington, Totnes, Devon
TQ9 6EB
☎01803 863260   Fax 01803 863843
Email edit@greenbooksco.uk
Website www.greenbooks.co.uk
Chairman *Satish Kumar*
Publisher *John Elford*
Approx. Annual Turnover £250,000
FOUNDED in 1987 with the support of a num-
ber of Green organisations. Closely associated
with *Resurgence* magazine. *Publishes* high-quality
books on a wide range of Green issues, inclu-
ding economics, politics and the practical appli-
cation of Green thinking. No fiction or books
for children. TITLES *Forest Gardening* Robert A.
de J. Hart; *Eco-Renovation* Edward Harland; *The
Growth Illusion* Richard Douthwaite; *The Green
Lanes of England* Valerie Belsey; *The Organic
Directory* ed. Clive Litchfield. No unsolicited
mss. Synopses and ideas welcome.
Royalties paid twice-yearly.

Green Print
See **The Merlin Press Ltd**

Greenhill Books/ Lionel Leventhal Ltd
Park House, 1 Russell Gardens, London
NW11 9NN
☎020 8458 6314   Fax 020 8905 5245
Email LionelLeventhal@compuserve.com
Website www.greenhillbooks.com
Managing Director *Lionel Leventhal*
FOUNDED 1984 by Lionel Leventhal (ex-Arms
& Armour Press). *Publishes* aviation, military
and naval books, and its Napoleonic Library

series. Synopses and ideas for books welcome.
No unsolicited mss.
Royalties paid twice-yearly.

Greenwich Editions
See **Chrysalis Books Ltd**

Gresham Books Ltd
46 Victoria Road, Summertown, Oxford
OX2 7QD
☎01865 513582   Fax 01865 512718
Email greshambks@btinternet.com
Website www.gresham-books.co.uk
Managing Director *Paul A. Lewis*
Approx. Annual Turnover £300,000
A small specialist publishing house. *Publishes*
hymn and service books for schools and
churches, school histories, also craftbound
choir and orchestral folders and Records of
Achievement. TITLES include music and
melody editions of *Hymns for Church and School*;
The School Hymnal; Praise and Thanksgiving. No
unsolicited material but ideas welcome.

Griffith Institute
See **Ashmolean Museum Publications Ltd**

Grisewood & Dempsey
See **Kingfisher Publications plc**

Grub Street
The Basement, 10 Chivalry Road, London
SW11 1HT
☎020 7924 3966/7738 1008
Fax 020 7738 1009
Email post@grubstreet.co.uk
Website www.grubstreet.co.uk
Managing Director *John Davies*
FOUNDED 1982. *Publishes* cookery, food and
wine, health, military and aviation history
books. About 20 titles a year. Unsolicited mss
and synopses welcome in the above categories.
Royalties paid twice-yearly.

Guild of Master Craftsman Publications Ltd
166 High Street, Lewes, East Sussex
BN7 1XU
☎01273 477374   Fax 01273 478606
Chairman *A.E. Phillips*
Approx. Annual Turnover £2 million
FOUNDED 1974. Part of G.M.C. Services Ltd.
Publishes woodworking, craft, photography and
gardening books, magazines and videos; also
books on dolls' houses and miniatures. 40 titles

in 2000. Unsolicited mss, synopses and ideas for books welcome. No fiction.
Royalties paid twice-yearly.

Guinness World Records Ltd
338 Euston Road, London NW1 3BD
☎020 7891 4567 Fax 020 7891 4501
Email info@guinnessrecords.com
Website www.guinnessworldrecords.com
Vice-President, Head of Brand *Ian Castello-Cortes*
Approx. Annual Turnover £20 million

FOUNDED in 1954 to publish *The Guinness Book of Records*, published in 35 languages and the highest-selling copyright book in the world. The company's television shows have gained a global audience of more than 100 million and are broadcast in over 30 countries. In addition to *Guinness World Records* the company publishes the annual industry-standard volume *British Hit Singles*. In 2001 Guinness World Records became part of the Gullane Entertainment Group. Contact from prospective researchers, editors and designers welcome.

Gullane Children's Books
Winchester House, 259–269 Old Marylebone Road, London NW1 5XJ
☎020 7616 7200 Fax 020 7616 7201
Editorial Director *Alison Ritchie*

FOUNDED 1994. Formerly David & Charles Children's Books; acquired by multimedia group, Gullane Entertainment in 2001. *Publishes* board books, novelty books, picture books and gift collections for children of 0–12 years. Unsolicited mss will not be returned.
Royalties paid twice-yearly.

Gunsmoke Westerns
See **Chivers Press Ltd**

Gwasg Addysgol Cymru
See **Ashley Drake Publishing Ltd**

Gwasg Carreg Gwalch
12 Iard yr Orsaf, Llanrwst, Conwy LL26 0EH
☎01492 642031 Fax 01492 641502
Email books@carreg-gwalch.co.uk
Website www.carreg-gwalch.co.uk
Managing Editor *Myrddin ap Dafydd*
FOUNDED in 1990. *Publishes* Welsh language; English books of Welsh interest – history, folklore, guides and walks. 90 titles in 2001. Unsolicited mss, synopses and ideas welcome.
Royalties paid.

Gwasg Prifysgol Cymru
See **University of Wales Press**

Hachette-Livre
French publishing conglomerate which embraces **Orion Publishing Group**, **Octopus Publishing Group** and **Watts Publishing Group**. For more information, see entry under **European Publishers**.

Authors' Rating Almost unnoticed, at least by British pundits, French publisher Hachette has joined the league of UK conglomerates. With Orion, Octopus and Watts, the share of the illustrated market claimed by Hachette is over 25 per cent.

Peter Halban Publishers
22 Golden Square, London W1F 9JW
☎020 7437 9300 Fax 020 7437 9512
Email books@halbanpublishers.com
Website www.halbanpublishers.com
Directors *Peter Halban, Martine Halban*
FOUNDED 1986. Independent publisher. *Publishes* biography, autobiography and memoirs, history, philosophy, theology, politics, literature and criticism, Judaica and world affairs. 6–8 titles a year. No unsolicited material. Approach by letter in first instance.
Royalties paid twice-yearly for first two years, thereafter annually in December.

Robert Hale Ltd
Clerkenwell House, 45–47 Clerkenwell Green, London EC1R 0HT
☎020 7251 2661 Fax 020 7490 4958
Email enquire@halebooks.com
Chairman/Managing Director *John Hale*
FOUNDED 1936. Family-owned company. *Publishes* adult fiction (but not interested in category crime, romance or science fiction) and non-fiction. No specialist material (education, law, medical or scientific). Acquired **NAG Press Ltd** in 1993 with its list of horological, gemmological, jewellery and metalwork titles, and **J.A. Allen & Co.** in 1999 with its extensive list of horse and dog books (see entry). Over 250 titles a year. TITLES Non-fiction: *New Age Encyclopaedia* Belinda Whitworth; *Andrea Bocelli* Antonia Felix; *F.M. Halford and the Dry Fly Revolution* Tony Hayter; *Field Archery* Michael Hamlett-Wood; *Roger Moore: His Films and Career* Gareth Owen and Oliver Bayan. Fiction: *Methuselah's Children* Robert A. Heinlein; *The Silent Voyage* James Pattinson; *The Curious Conspiracy* Michael

Gilbert. Unsolicited mss, synopses and ideas for books welcome.

Royalties paid twice-yearly.

Authors' Rating Smiled upon in a Society of Authors survey on author relations, Robert Hale has carved out a profitable niche for popular non-fiction.

Halsgrove

Halsgrove House, Tiverton Business Park, Lower Moor Way, Tiverton, Devon EX16 6SS
☎01884 243242 Fax 01884 243325
Email sales@halsgrove.com
Website www.halsgrove.com

Joint Managing Directors *Simon Butler, Steven Pugsley*

FOUNDED in 1990 from defunct Maxwell-owned publishing group. Grown into the region's largest publishing and distribution group, specialising in books, video and audio tapes. *Publishes* local history, cookery, biography and art, mainly in hardback. 130 titles in 2001. Also established a series of local interest magazines in southern England. No fiction or poetry. Unsolicited mss, synopses and ideas for books of regional interest welcome.

Royalties paid annually.

Hambledon and London

102 Gloucester Avenue, London NW1 8HX
☎020 7586 0817 Fax 020 7586 9970
Email office@hambledon.co.uk

Editorial Director *Martin Sheppard*
Commissioning Director *Tony Morris*

FOUNDED 1980 as The Hambledon Press. Winner of the **Sunday Times Award for Small Publishers** in 2001. *Publishes* history and biography. TITLES *Churchill: A Study in Greatness* Geoffrey Best; *The Ambassadors' Secret* John North; *Old Masters: Great Artists in Old Age* Thomas Dormandy; *Family Names and Family History* David Hey. No unsolicited mss; send preliminary letter. Synopses and ideas welcome.

Royalties paid twice-yearly. *Overseas distributor* New York University Press (USA and Canada).

Hamish Hamilton

See **Penguin Group (UK)**

Hamlyn Children's Books

See **Egmont Books**

Hamlyn Octopus

See **Octopus Publishing Group**

The Handsel Press

See **The Continuum International Publishing Group Limited**

Harcourt Publishers International

32 Jamestown Road, London NW1 7BY
☎020 7424 4200 Fax 020 7482 2293
Website www.harcourt-international.com

Managing Director, Health Sciences
Dominic Vaughan

Owned by **Elsevier Science**. *Publishes* scientific, technical and medical books, journals, educational & occupational test. No unsolicited mss.

IMPRINTS **Academic Press**; **Baillière Tindall**; **Churchill Livingstone**; **Mosby**; **W.B. Saunders**.

Authors' Rating After Wiley, the second fastest growing publisher by turnover of professional and education books.

Harlequin Mills & Boon Ltd

Eton House, 18–24 Paradise Road, Richmond, Surrey TW9 1SR
☎020 8288 2800 Fax 020 8288 2899
Website www.eharlequin.com *or*
www.millsandboon.co.uk

Managing Director *Andrew Low*
Editorial Director *Karin Stoecker*
Approx. Annual Turnover £22 million

FOUNDED 1908. Owned by the Canadian-based Torstar Group. *Publishes* romantic fiction and historical romance. Over 600 titles a year.

IMPRINTS
Mills & Boon Modern Romance *Tessa Shapcott*; **Mills & Boon Tender Romance** *Samantha Bell* (50–55,000 words) Contemporary romances with international settings, focusing on hero and heroine. **Mills & Boon Medical Romance** *Sheila Hodgson* (50–55,000 words) Modern medical practice provides a unique background to love stories. **Mills & Boon Historical Romance** *Linda Fildew* (75–80,000 words) Historical romances. **MIRA** *Linda Fildew* (minimum 100,000 words) Individual women's fiction. **Red Dress Ink™** *Samantha Bell* (90–110,000 words) Contemporary women's fiction. **Mills & Boon Sensual Romance**, **Mills & Boon Blaze** and **Silhouette Super Romance** titles are acquired through the Canadian office. **Silhouette Desire**, **Special Edition**, **Sensation** and **Intrigue** imprints are handled by US-based **Silhouette Books** (see entry under **US Publishers**). Please send query letter

in the first instance. Tip sheets and guidelines for the Mills & Boon series available from the website or Harlequin Mills & Boon Editorial Dept. (please send s.a.e.).

Royalties paid twice-yearly.

Authors' Rating A note of cynicism is entering the Mills & Boon list with more chick-lit titles revealing that love and sex do not always go together. But the staple M&B romance is still going strong providing a good income for writers who can adapt to the clearly defined M&B formula. Just think, M&B has a network of 12,000 authors worldwide and every title scores six figure sales.

Harley Books

Martins, Great Horkesley, Colchester, Essex CO6 4AH
☎01206 271216 Fax 01206 271182
Email harley@keme.co.uk
Website www.harleybooks.com
Managing Director *Basil Harley*

FOUNDED 1983. Natural history publishers specialising in entomological and botanical books. Mostly definitive, high-quality illustrated reference works. TITLES *The Moths and Butterflies of Great Britain and Ireland; Dragonflies of Europe; The Aurelian Legacy: British Butterflies and their Collectors; The Liverwort Flora of the British Isles.*

Royalties paid twice-yearly in the first year, annually thereafter.

HarperCollins Publishers Ltd

77–85 Fulham Palace Road, London W6 8JB
☎020 8741 7070 Fax 020 8307 4440
Website www.fireandwater.com
Also at: Westerhill Road, Bishopbriggs, Glasgow G64 2QT
☎0141 772 3200 Fax 0141 306 3119
CEO/Publisher *Victoria Barnsley*
Approx. Annual Turnover £160 million

HarperCollins is the second largest book publisher in the UK, with a wider range of books than any other publisher; from cutting-edge contemporary fiction to block-busting thrillers, from fantasy literature and children's stories to enduring classics. The wholly-owned division of News Corporation also *publishes* a selection of non-fiction including history, celebrity memoirs, biographies, popular science, mind, body and spirit, dictionaries, maps and reference books. HarperCollins is also the third largest education publisher in the UK. Authors include many award-winning and international bestsellers such as Paulo Coelho, Bernard Cornwell, Josephine Cox, Michael Crichton, Barbara Erskine, Jonathan Franzen, Cathy Kelly, Judith Kerr, Dean Koontz, Doris Lessing, Frank McCourt, Tony Parsons, Sidney Sheldon, Carol Shields, Nigel Slater and Barbara Taylor Bradford. About 1500 titles a year.

GENERAL BOOKS DIVISION **Managing Director** *Amanda Ridout* **Harper-Collins (Trade)** Publishing Directors *Nick Sayers* (Fiction); *Lynne Drew* (Fiction); *Michael Fishwick* (Non-fiction); *Arabella Pike* (Non-fiction); *Susan Watt* (Fiction/Non-fiction). IMPRINTS **Collins Crime** Publishing Director *Julia Wisdom;* **Collins Willow** Publishing Director *Michael Doggart* Sports titles; **Flamingo** Publishing Director *Philip Gwyn Jones* Literary fiction/non-fiction; **HarperCollins Entertainment** Publishing Director *Val Hudson* Media-related books from film companions to autobiographies and TV tie-ins; **Voyager** Publishing Director *Jane Johnson* Science fiction/fantasy; **Special Projects & Estates** Publishing Director *David Brawn* Authors include Agatha Christie, J.R.R. Tolkien, C.S. Lewis.

Thorsons/Element Managing Director *Belinda Budge* Mind, body and spirit titles covering health, natural therapies, relationships and personal development.

Collins Children's (Children's Division) Managing Director *Katie Fulford;* Publishing Directors *Gail Penston* (Picture Books & Properties); *Gillie Russell* (Fiction) Quality picture books and book and tape sets for under-7s; fiction for age 6 up to young adult.

Fourth Estate (see entry).

PerfectBound Editorial Director *Leo Hollis* Global e-books available on four e-book platforms via 20 retail websites worldwide.

HarperCollins Audio (see entry under **Audio Books**).

COLLINS Managing Director *Thomas Webster* IMPRINTS **Collins; Collins Gem; Collins New Naturalist Library; Times Books; Jane's** (Reference Division) Publishing Director *Myles Archibald* Encyclopedias, guides and handbooks, phrase books and manuals on popular reference, art instruction, illustrated, cookery and wine, crafts, DIY, gardening, military, natural history, pet care, Scottish, pastimes. **Collins/Times Maps and Atlases** (Cartographic Division) Publishing Directors *Juliet Lawler* (International titles); *Mike Cottingham* (UK titles) Maps, atlases, street plans and leisure guides; **Collins/COBUILD** (Dictionaries Division) Publishing Director

Lorna Sinclair Knight Bilingual and English dictionaries, English dictionaries for foreign learners.

Collins Education (Education Division) Managing Director *Elizabeth Campbell* Books, CD-ROMs and online material for UK schools and colleges; **Letterland** Home learning titles from pre-school to Further Education.

Authors' Rating Named publisher of the year and winning book of the year at the latest British Book Awards, HarperCollins is the second largest publisher in the UK with just over 10 per cent of the market. With Victoria Barnsley's appointment as chief executive, there will be more emphasis on the HarperCollins strong points – biography, fiction, and mind, body and spirit.

Harrap
See **Chambers Harrap Publishers Ltd**

Harvard University Press
Fitzroy House, 11 Chenies Street, London WC1E 7EY
☎020 7306 0603 Fax 020 7306 0604
Email info@HUP-MITpress.co.uk
Website www.hup.harvard.edu
Director *William Sisler*
General Manager *Ann Sexsmith*

European office of **Harvard University Press**, USA. *Publishes* academic and scholarly works in history, politics, philosophy, economics, literary criticism, psychology, sociology, anthropology, women's studies, biological sciences, classics, history of science, art, music, film, reference. All mss go to the American office: 79 Garden Street, Cambridge, MA 02138 (see entry under **US Publishers**).

The Harvill Press Ltd
20 Vauxhall Bridge Road, London SW1V 2SA
☎020 7840 8400 Fax 020 7233 6058
Website www.harvill.com
Publisher *Christopher MacLehose*
Editorial Director *Margaret Stead*

FOUNDED in 1946. Purchased by the **Random House Group** in March 2002. *Publishes* literature in translation (especially Russian, Italian and French), English literature, quality thrillers, illustrated books and Africana, plus an occasional literature anthology. 90–100 titles in 2000. AUTHORS Mikhail Bulgakov, Raymond Carver, Richard Ford, Jean-Christophe Grange, Peter Høeg, Robert Hughes, Giuseppe T. di Lampedusa, Henning Mankell, Peter Matthiessen, Haruki Murakami, Boris Pasternak, José Saramago, W.G. Sebald, Aleksandr Solzhenitsyn. Synopses and ideas welcome. No educational or technical books. *Royalties* paid twice-yearly.

Authors' Rating Now part of Random House, there are question marks over Harvill's future as a publisher of exciting new work and, most particularly, of translations from other European languages. Harvill's discovery of Henning Mankell, the Swedish crime writer, is one of the best things to have happened in recent fiction. May Random House do him proud.

Haynes Publishing
Sparkford, Near Yeovil, Somerset BA22 7JJ
☎01963 440635 Fax 01963 440825
Email info@haynes-manuals.co.uk
Website www.haynes.co.uk
Chairman *John H. Haynes, OBE*
Approx. Annual Turnover £33 million

FOUNDED in 1960 by John H. Haynes. Family-run business. The mainstay of its programme has been the *Owners' Workshop Manual*, first published in the mid 1960s and still running off the presses today. Indeed the company maintains a strong bias towards motoring and transport titles. Acquired Sutton Publishing Ltd in March 2000. *Publishes* DIY service and repair manuals for cars, motorbikes and leisure plus other related topics under the Haynes imprint and a broad range of general non-fiction under the Sutton imprint.

AUTOMOTIVE DIVISION
IMPRINT **Haynes** Editorial Director *Matthew Minter* Service and repair manuals; Editorial Director *Mark Hughes* Motoring, motor sport, cars, motorcycles, home, DIY and leisure titles. Unsolicited submissions welcome if they come within the subject areas covered. GENERAL PUBLISHING DIVISION
IMPRINT **Sutton Publishing Ltd** (see entry).
Royalties paid twice-yearly. *Overseas subsidiaries* Haynes Manuals Inc., California, USA, Editions Haynes S.A., France, Haynes Publishing Nordiska AB, Sweden.

Authors' Rating After some costly acquisitions, Haynes is back on form with Sutton Publishing leading the way into general publishing.

Hazleton Publishing
3 Richmond Hill, Richmond, Surrey TW10 6RE
☎020 8948 5151 Fax 020 8948 4111
Email info@hazletonpublishing.com

Website www.hazletonpublishing.com
Publisher/Managing Director *R.F. Poulter*
Publisher of the leading Grand Prix annual
Autocourse, now in its 51st edition. *Publishes* high-
quality motor sport titles including annuals.
TITLES *Motocourse; Rallycourse.* About 13 titles a
year. No unsolicited mss; synopses and ideas
welcome. Interested in all motor sport titles.
Royalties Payment varies.

Headline
See **Hodder Headline Ltd**

Heartline Books Limited
PO Box 22598, London W8 7GB
☎020 7376 3930 Fax 020 7376 0999
Email enquiries@heartlinebooks.co.uk
Website www.heartlinebooks.com
Founder/Publisher *Mary-Jo Wormell*
Managing Director *Robert Williams*
Senior Editor *Sue Curran*
FOUNDED on St Valentine's Day 2001 to *pub-
lish* romantic fiction only. 'We are interested in
contemporary romantic fiction only (no histor-
ical, sagas, etc.).' No unsolicited mss; submit
synopsis and three sample chapters initially,
addressed to the senior editor, *Sue Curran.*
Royalties paid twice-yearly.

William Heinemann
See **Random House Group Ltd**

Heinemann Educational
See **Reed Educational & Professional
Publishing**

Heinemann Young Books
See **Egmont Books**

Helicon Publishing Ltd
RM plc, New Mill House, 183 Milton Park,
Abingdon, Oxfordshire OX14 4SE
☎01235 826000 Fax 01235 823222
Email admin@helicon.co.uk
Website www.helicon.co.uk
General Manager *Michael Holyoke*
Approx. Annual Turnover £1 million
FOUNDED 1992 from the management buy-out
of former Random Century's reference division.
Led by David Attwooll, the buy-out included
the Hutchinson encyclopedia titles and databases,
along with other reference titles. Helicon's assets
including all intellectual property were purchased from WHSmith by RM plc in February
2002, the UK market leader in provision of software and services to the education sector. The

Helicon print list is published under licence by
Hodder Educational. Now operating as a division of RM Learning, Helicon Publishing is
maintaining its lead in electronic publishing,
especially in the area of online licensing, where it
has relationships with several key UK and US
blue-chip consumer and educational service
providers and is developing online reference
titles designed for the education sector. CD-
ROM TITLES include *The Penguin Hutchinson
Reference Suite; The Hutchinson Encyclopedia of
Music; The Hutchinson Educational Encyclopedia
2001; The Hutchinson Science Reference Suite; The
Hutchinson History Reference Suite.*

Christopher Helm Publishers Ltd
See **A.&C. Black (Publishers) Ltd**

Helm Information Ltd
The Banks, Mountfield, Nr Robertsbridge,
East Sussex TN32 5JY
☎01580 880561 Fax 01580 880541
Email amandahelm@helm-information.co.uk
Website www.helm-information.co.uk
Directors *Amanda Helm, Christopher Helm*
FOUNDED 1990. *Publishes* academic books for
students and university libraries. SERIES *The
Critical Assessments of Writers in English* (collected
criticism); *Literary Sources & Documents* (primary
source material on various themes/events/cul-
tural/aesthetic movements ranging from the
American Civil War to the Gothic Revival);
Sources & Documents in Art History (literary
sources of various art movements); *The Dickens
Companion.* Will consider ideas and proposals
provided they are relevant to the series above.
Royalties paid annually.

Helter Skelter Publishing
4 Denmark Street, London WC2H 8LL
☎020 7836 1151 Fax 020 7240 9880
Email helter@skelter.demon.co.uk
Website www.skelter.demon.co.uk
Contact *Sean Body*
FOUNDED 1995. *Publishes* music and film books
only. 10 titles a year. IMPRINTS **Helter Skelter
Publishing; Firefly Publishing.** Unsolicited
mss, synopses and ideas welcome.

Henderson Publishing
See **Dorling Kindersley Ltd**

Ian Henry Publications Ltd
20 Park Drive, Romford, Essex RM1 4LH
☎01708 749119 Fax 01708 736213
Managing Director *Ian Wilkes*

FOUNDED 1976. *Publishes* local history, transport history and Sherlockian pastiches. 8–10 titles a year. TITLES *Lestrade and the Ripper; Witch-Hunt; Essex Spas.* No unsolicited mss. Synopses and ideas for books welcome. *Royalties* paid twice-yearly.

The Herbert Press
See **A.&C. Black (Publishers) Ltd**

Hermes House
See **Anness Publishing Ltd**

Hermes Penton Science
See **Kogan Page Ltd**

Nick Hern Books
The Glasshouse, 49a Goldhawk Road, London W12 8QP
☎020 8749 4953 Fax 020 8735 0250
Email info@nickhernbooks.demon.co.uk
Website www.nickhernbooks.co.uk
Chairman/Managing Director *Nick Hern*
FOUNDED 1988. Fully independent since 1992. *Publishes* books on theatre and film: from how-to and biography to plays and screenplays. About 30 titles a year. No unsolicited playscripts. Synopses, ideas and proposals for other theatre material welcome. Not interested in material unrelated to the theatre or cinema.

University of Hertfordshire Press
Learning and Information Services, Hatfield Campus Learning Resources Centre, College Lane, Hatfield, Hertfordshire AL10 9AB
☎01707 284681 Fax 01707 284666
Email W.A.Forster@herts.ac.uk
Website www.herts.ac.uk/UHPress
Contact *Bill Forster*
FOUNDED 1992. *Publishes* academic books on gypsies, literature, regional/local history, parapsychology. 8 titles in 2001. IMPRINTS **Interface Collection**; **Hertfordshire Publications**; **University of Hertfordshire Press.** TITLES *English Gypsies and State Policies*; *Gypsies under the Swastika*; *Guidelines for Testing Psychic Claimants*.

Hesperus Press Limited
4 Rickett Street, London SW6 1RU
☎020 7610 3331 Fax 020 7610 3337
Website www.hesperuspress.com
Managing Director/Publisher *Alessandro Gallenzi*
FOUNDED 2001. *Publishes* classic fiction in paperback. AUTHORS include Joseph Conrad, Edgar Allan Poe, Alexander Pope, Mark Twain, Anton Chekhov. 30 titles in 2002. Welcomes synopses and ideas for books. Approach in writing. No non-fiction.
Royalties paid annually.

Hippo
See **Scholastic Ltd**

Historic Military Press
See **SB Publications**

HMSO
See **The Stationery Office Ltd**

Hobsons Publishing
Challenger House, 42 Adler Street, London E1 1EE
☎020 7958 5000 Fax 020 7958 5001
Website www.hobsons.com
Chairman *Martin Morgan*
Group Managing Director *Christopher Letcher*
FOUNDED 1973. A division of Harmsworth Publishing Ltd, part of the Daily Mail & General Trust. *Publishes* course and career guides, under exclusive licence and royalty agreements for CRAC (Careers Research and Advisory Bureau); computer software; directories and specialist titles for employers, government departments and professional associations. TITLES *Graduate Employment and Training; Degree Course Guides; The Which Degree Series; Which University* (CD-ROM); *The POST-GRAD Series: The Directory of Graduate Studies; The Directory of Further Education.*

Hodder & Stoughton
See **Hodder Headline Ltd**

Hodder Headline Ltd
338 Euston Road, London NW1 3BH
☎020 7873 6000 Fax 020 7873 6024
Group Chief Executive *Tim Hely Hutchinson*
Approx. Annual Turnover £125 million
Formed in June 1993 through the merger of Headline Book Publishing and Hodder & Stoughton. Headline was formed in 1986 and had grown dramatically, whereas Hodder & Stoughton was 125 years old with a diverse range of publishing. About 2000 titles a year. The company was acquired by WHSmith plc in 1999.
DIVISIONS
Headline Book Publishing Managing Director *Martin Neild.* **Non-fiction** Publishing Director *Heather Holden-Brown*; **Fiction** Publishing Director *Jane Morpeth. Publishes*

commercial and literary fiction (hardback and paperback) and popular non-fiction including autobiography, biography, food and wine, gardening, history, popular science, sport and TV tie-ins. IMPRINTS **Headline**; **Review**. AUTHORS Kate Adie, Catherine Alliott, Lyn Andrews, Colin Bateman, Martina Cole, Janet Evanovich, Sophie Grigson, Wendy Holden, Ken Hom, Matthew Jukes, Faye and Jonathan Kellerman, Hugh O'Farrell, Sheila O'Flanagan, James Patterson.

Hodder & Stoughton General Managing Director *Jamie Hodder-Williams*, Deputy Managing Director *Sue Fletcher*. **Non-fiction** *Roland Philipps*; **Sceptre** *Carole Welch*; **Fiction** *Carolyn Mays*; **Audio** (See entry under **Audio Books**). *Publishes* commercial and literary fiction; biography, autobiography, history, self-help, humour, travel and other general interest non-fiction; audio. IMPRINTS **Hodder & Stoughton**; **Lir**; **Coronet**; **Flame**; **New English Library**; **Sceptre**; **Mobius**. AUTHORS Dickie Bird, Melvyn Bragg, John le Carré, Justin Cartwright, Alex Ferguson, Charles Frazier, Elizabeth George, Amy Jenkins, Thomas Keneally, Stephen King, Ed McBain, Malcolm Gluck, Rosamunde Pilcher, Mary Stewart.

Hodder Children's Books Managing Director *Mary Tapissier*. IMPRINTS **Hodder Children's Books**; **Signature**; **Wayland**. AUTHORS David Almond, Enid Blyton, John Cunliffe, Lucy Daniels, Mick Inkpen, Joan Lingard, Hilary McKay, David Melling, Jenny Oldfield, Christopher Pike.

Hodder & Stoughton Religious Managing Director *Charles Nettleton*, Publishing Director *Judith Longman*, Bibles & Hodder Christian Books *David Moloney*. *Publishes* NIV Bibles, Christian books, autobiography, TV-tie-ins, gift books, self-help. IMPRINTS **Hodder & Stoughton**; **Hodder Christian Books**.

Hodder/Arnold Managing Director *Philip Walters*, Deputy Managing Director *Tim Gregson-Williams*. *Publishes* in the following areas: **Schoolbooks** *Lis Tribe*; **Consumer Education** *Katie Roden*; **Further Education/Higher Education Textbooks** *Tim Gregson-Williams*; **Health Sciences** *Georgina Bentliff*; **Journals/Reference Books** *Mary Attree*. IMPRINTS **Hodder & Stoughton Educational**; **Teach Yourself**; **Hodder & Stoughton**; **Arnold**.

Authors' Rating With ever tougher competition for bookshop shelf space, the WHSmith takeover of Hodder Headline three years ago has brought dividends for the publisher. Sales in WHSmith outlets are up by over 20 per cent. But sales through other bookstores are also on the increase, proving that Hodder Headline has lost none of its skill in judging the market. A new mind, body and spirit imprint, Hodder Mobius, signals expansion in a highly competitive but potentially profitable market.

Hodder/Arnold
See **Hodder Headline Ltd**

Honeyglen Publishing Ltd
56 Durrels House, Warwick Gardens, London W14 8QB
☎020 7602 2876   Fax 020 7602 2876
Directors *N.S. Poderegin, J. Poderegin*
FOUNDED 1983. A small publishing house whose output is 'extremely limited'. *Publishes* history, philosophy of history, biography and selective fiction. No children's or science fiction. TITLES *The Soul of India; A Child of the Century* Amaury de Riencourt; *With Duncan Grant in South Turkey* Paul Roche; *Vladimir, The Russian Viking* Vladimir Volkoff; *The Dawning* Milka Bajic-Poderegin; *Quicksand* Louise Hide. Unsolicited mss welcome.

Honno Welsh Women's Press
c/o U.T.C., King Street, Aberystwyth, Ceredigion SY23 2LT
☎01970 623150   Fax 01970 623150
Email editor@honno.co.uk
Website www.honno.co.uk
Editor *Gwenllian Dafydd*
FOUNDED in 1986 by a group of women who wanted to create more opportunities for women in publishing. A co-operative operation which *publishes* fiction (adult and teenage) and children's books, all with a Welsh connection. Also publishes poetry, short story and autobiographical anthologies. About 6 titles a year. Welcomes mss and ideas for books from women only. All material must have a Welsh connection and be sent as hard copy, not by e-mail.
Royalties paid annually.

Horus Editions
See **Award Publications Limited**

House of Lochar
Isle of Colonsay, Argyll PA61 7YR
☎01951 200232   Fax 01951 200232
Email Lochar@colonsay.org.uk
Website www.colonsay.org.uk/lochar.html
Chairman *Kevin Byrne*
Managing Director *Georgina Hobhouse*
Approx. Annual Turnover £95,000
FOUNDED 1995 on a tiny island, taking advan-

tage of new technology and mains electricity and taking over some 20 titles from Thomas and Lochar. About 10 titles a year. *Publishes* mostly Scottish – history, topography, transport and fiction. IMPRINTS **House of Lochar** TITLES *The Crofter and the Laird; The Clyde in Pictures; Alexander III.* AUTHORS (fiction) Neill Gunn, Naomi Mitchison, Marion Campbell. **Colonsay Books** TITLES *Summer in the Hebrides.* **West Highland Series** Mini walking guides. No poetry or books unrelated to Scotland or Celtic theme. Unsolicited mss, synopses and ideas welcome if relevant to subjects covered.

Royalties paid annually.

House of Stratus
Thirsk Industrial Park, Thirsk, North Yorkshire YO7 3BX
☎01845 527700 Fax 01845 527711
Email info@houseofstratus.com
Website www.houseofstratus.com
CEO *David Lane*

FOUNDED 1999. *Publishes* fiction and non-fiction. Backlist of over 1500 titles including C.P. Snow, Brian Aldiss, Nevil Shute and G.K. Chesterton. About 30 titles annually. Submissions should incorporate a synopsis, sample chapter and author c.v.
Royalties paid twice-yearly. Overseas offices in New York.

How To Books Ltd
3 Newtec Place, Magdalen Road, Oxford OX4 1RE
☎01865 793806 Fax 01865 248780
Email info@howtobooks.co.uk
Website www.howtobooks.co.uk
Publisher/Managing Director *Giles Lewis*

An independent publishing house, FOUNDED in 1991. *Publishes* non-fiction reference books. How To titles are practical, accessible books that encourage their readers to improve their lives and develop their skills. How To authors must have first-hand experience of the subject about which they are writing and are given guidance in the development of their books. Subjects covered include business & management, computers & the Net, home & family, career choices & career development, living & working abroad, personal finance, small business & self employment, study & student guides, creative writing.

Human Horizons
See **Souvenir Press Ltd**

Human Science Press
See **Kluwer Academic/Plenum Publishers**

Hunt & Thorpe
See **John Hunt Publishing Ltd**

John Hunt Publishing Ltd
46a West Street, New Alresford, Hampshire SO24 9AU
☎01962 736880 Fax 01962 736881
Email maria@johnhunt-publishing.com
Website www.johnhunt-publishing.com *and* www.o-books.net
Approx. Annual Turnover £1.5 million

Publishes children's and world religions only – about 25 a year. IMPRINTS **Hunt & Thorpe**; **John Hunt Publishing; Arthur James; O Books.** Unsolicited material welcome.

C. Hurst & Co.
38 King Street, London WC2E 8JZ
☎020 7240 2666 Fax 020 7240 2667
Email hurst@atlas.co.uk
Website www.hurstpub.co.uk
Chairman/Managing Director *Christopher Hurst*
Editorial Heads *Christopher Hurst, Michael Dwyer*

FOUNDED 1967. An independent company, cultivating a concern for literacy, detail and the visual aspects of the product. *Publishes* contemporary history, politics and social science. About 20 titles a year. TITLES *The Impact of War on Children* Graça Machel; *Diary of An African Journey* H. Rider Haggard; *Iceland's 1100 Years; The Mask of Anarchy: The Liberian Civil War; Inside Al Qaeda: Global Network of Terror; The Chinese Essay.* No unsolicited mss. Synopses and ideas welcome.
Royalties paid annually.

Hutchinson
See **Random House Group Ltd**

Hymns Ancient & Modern Ltd
St Mary's Works, St Mary's Plain, Norwich, Norfolk NR3 3BH
☎01603 612914 Fax 01603 624483
Email hymns@scm-canterburypress.co.uk
Chairman *Patrick Coldstream, CBE*
Chief Executive *G.A. Knights*
Publisher, Canterbury Press Norwich *Christine Smith*
Publisher, RMEP *Mary Mears*
Publisher, SCM Press *Alex Wright*
Approx. Annual Turnover £4.4 million

Publishes hymn books for churches, schools and other institutions. All types of liturgical and general religious books and material for religious and social education. Owns SCM-Canterbury Press Ltd controlling the IMPRINTS **SCM Press** (see entry). **Canterbury Press Norwich** Liturgical and general religious books TITLES *The Meaning of Miracles; This is My Faith; Runcie: On Reflection.* **Religious and Moral Education Press (RMEP)** Religious, social and moral books for primary and secondary schools, assembly material and books for teachers and administrators. **G.J. Palmer & Sons Ltd** TITLES *Church Times* (see entry under **Magazines**); *The Sign* and *Home Words* – two monthly nationwide parish magazine inserts. Ideas welcome; no unsolicited mss.
Royalties paid annually.

Icon Books Ltd
Grange Road, Duxford, Cambridge CB2 4QF
☎01763 208008 Fax 01763 208080
Email info@iconbooks.co.uk
Website www.iconbooks.co.uk
Managing Director *Peter Pugh*
Editorial Director *Richard Appignanesi*
Publishing Director *Jeremy Cox*
FOUNDED 1992. SERIES **Introducing** Graphic introductions to key figures and ideas in the history of science, philosophy, psychology, religion and the arts TITLE *Introducing Quantum Theory.* **Postmodern Encounters** Provocative mini-essays exploring a key theme in the work of a major thinker in psychology, philosophy and science TITLE *Nietzsche and Postmodernism.* **Ideas in Psychoanalysis** Mini-essays on key terms in psychoanalysis TITLE *Superego.* **Revolutions in Science** New narrative non-fiction exploring specific discoveries in the history of science TITLE *Dawkins vs. Gould.* IMPRINT **Wizard Books** Children's fiction and non-fiction.
Royalties paid twice yearly. *Overseas associate* Totem Books, USA, distributed by National Book Network.

I.M.P. Fiction Ltd
PO Box 14691, London SE1 2ZA
☎020 7357 8007 Fax 020 7357 8608
Email info@impbooks.com
Website www.impbooks.com
Managing Director *Kaye Roach*
FOUNDED 1998. *Publishes* 'innovative new cutting-edge' fiction. No crime or science fiction. 4 titles in 2001. Approach in writing, enclosing biography, synopsis, first three chapters and

s.a.e. Material will not be returned if postage and packing not provided.
Royalties paid twice-yearly.

The In Pinn
See **Neil Wilson Publishing Ltd**

Independent Music Press
PO Box 14691, London SE1 2ZA
☎020 7357 8007 Fax 020 7357 8608
Email info@impbooks.com
Website www.impbooks.com
Managing Director *Martin Roach*
FOUNDED 1992. *Publishes* music biography and youth culture. No jazz or classical. TITLES include biographies of Travis, Stereophonics, Oasis, Prodigy and Ian Hunter's *Diary of a Rock 'n' Roll Star.* 4 titles in 2001. Approach by letter or e-mail, enclosing biography, synopsis, first three chapters and s.a.e. if return of work required. Material will not be returned if postage and packing not provided.
Royalties paid twice-yearly.

Independent Voices
See **Souvenir Press Ltd**

Informa
Mortimer House, 37–41 Mortimer Street, London W1T 3JH
☎020 7453 2370 Fax 020 7453 2387
Website www.informa.com
Publisher *Fotini Liontou*
Part of LLP Professional Publishing, a trading division of Informa Publishing Group Ltd. *Publishes* a range of medical/tax business to business newsletters, special reports and books aimed at senior management and professional practices. 4 newsletter titles a year. Unsolicited synopses and ideas welcome. Initial approach in writing.

Inter Publishing Ltd
6–7 Leapale Road, Guildford, Surrey GU1 4JX
☎01483 306309 Fax 01483 579196
Email eaglepublishing1@aol.com
Managing Director *David Wavre*
Approx. Annual Turnover £500,000
FOUNDED 1990. *Publishes* religious plus some gift and art books. About 24 titles a year. IMPRINTS **Eagle; Little Eagle** Christian books for young children. Unsolicited mss, synopses and ideas for books welcome.
Royalties paid twice-yearly.

Inter-Varsity Press

38 De Montfort Street, Leicester LE1 7GP
☎0116 255 1754   Fax 0116 254 2044
Email ivp@uccf.org.uk
Website www.ivpbooks.com

Chairman *Ralph Evershed*
Chief Executive *Brian Wilson*

FOUNDED mid-'30s as the publishing arm of Universities and Colleges Christian Fellowship, it has expanded to wider Christian markets worldwide. *Publishes* Christian belief and lifestyle, reference and bible commentaries. About 50 titles a year. No secular material or anything which fails to empathise with orthodox Protestant Christianity.
IMPRINTS **IVP**; **Apollos**; **Crossway** TITLES *The Bible Speaks Today; The Care of Creation* Berry; *Matters of Life and Death* Wyatt. No unsolicited mss; synopses and ideas welcome. *Royalties* paid twice-yearly.

International Thomson Publishing

See **Thomson Learning**

Internet Handbooks

Unit 5 Dolphin Building, Queen Anne's Battery, Plymouth, Devon PL4 0LP
☎01752 262626   Fax 01752 262641
Email editor@internet-handbooks.co.uk
Website www.internet-handbooks.co.uk

Owner *Internet Handbooks Ltd*

Publishes practical step-by-step guides to help the reader get the most out of the Internet. TITLES *The Internet for Writers; Where to Find It On the Internet; Marketing Your Business on the Internet; Personal Finance on the Internet.* The Internet Handbooks website offers substantial and free online help on a broad range of topics for all Internet users.
Royalties paid annually.

Intrigue

See **Harlequin Mills & Boon Ltd**

Isis Publishing

7 Centremead, Osney Mead, Oxford OX2 0ES
☎01865 250333   Fax 01865 790358

Part of the Ulverscroft Group Ltd. *Publishes* large-print books – fiction and non-fiction – and unabridged audio books. Together with **Soundings** (see entry under **Audio Books**) produces around 4000 titles on audio tape and CD. AUTHORS Catherine Cookson, Stephen King, Terry Pratchett, Willy Russell. No unsolicited mss: Isis undertakes no original publishing.
Royalties paid twice-yearly.

Itchy Coo

See **Black and White Publishing Ltd**

Ithaca Press

See **Garnet Publishing Ltd**

IVP

See **Inter-Varsity Press**

Jacqui Small

See **Aurum Press Ltd**

Arthur James

See **John Hunt Publishing Ltd**

Jane's Information Group

163 Brighton Road, Coulsdon, Surrey CR5 2YH
☎020 8700 3700   Fax 020 8763 1006
Website www.janes.com

Managing Director *Alfred Rolington*

FOUNDED 1898 by Fred T. Jane with the publication of *All The World's Fighting Ships*. Now part of the Woodbridge Company Limited. In recent years management has been focusing on growth opportunities in its core business and in enhancing the performance of initiatives like Jane's information available online and on CD-ROM. *Publishes* magazines and yearbooks on defence, aerospace, security and transport topics, with details of equipment and systems; plus directories and strategic studies. Also *Jane's Defence Weekly* (see entry under **Magazines**).

DIVISIONS
Magazines *Karen Heffer Sean Howe* TITLES *Jane's Defence Weekly; Jane's International Defense Review; Jane's Airport Review; Jane's Defence Upgrades; Jane's Navy International; Jane's Islamic Affairs Analyst; Jane's Missiles and Rockets.* **Publishing for Defence, Aerospace, Transport** *Alan Condron* TITLES *Defence, Aerospace Yearbooks.* **Transport** *Alan Condron* TITLES *Transportation Yearbooks.* **Security** *John Boatman* TITLES *Jane's Intelligence Review; Foreign Report; Jane's Sentinel* (regional security assessment); *Police Review.* CD-ROM and electronic development and publication. Unsolicited mss, synopses and ideas for reference/yearbooks welcome.
Royalties paid twice-yearly. *Overseas associates* Jane's Information Group Inc., USA.

Janus Publishing Company Ltd

76 Great Titchfield Street, London W1P 7AF
☎020 7580 7664   Fax 020 7636 5756
Email publisher@januspublishing.co.uk

Managing Director *Sandy Leung*

Publishes fiction, human interest, memoirs, philosophy, mind, body and spirit, religion and theology, social questions, popular science, history, spiritualism and the paranormal, poetry and young adults. About 400 titles in print. IMPRINTS **Janus Books** Subsidy publishing; **Empiricus Books** Non-subsidy publishing. TITLES *The Anarchists in the Spanish Civil War; Nature of the Self; Healing Connections; Politics and Human Nature; Tales of French Corsairs and Revolutions; Child of the Thirties; Napoleon 1813.* Unsolicited mss welcome.

Royalties paid twice-yearly. Agents in the USA, Europe and Asia.

Authors' Rating Authors may be asked to cover their own productions costs but Janus seems to be moving into conventional publishing with its Empiricus imprint.

Jarrold Publishing
Whitefriars, Norwich, Norfolk NR3 1TR
☎01603 763300 Fax 01603 662748
Email publishing@jarrold.com
Website www.jarrold-publishing.co.uk
Managing Director *Caroline Jarrold*

Part of Jarrold & Sons Ltd, the printing and publishing company FOUNDED in 1770. *Publishes* UK tourism, travel, leisure, history and calendars. Material tends to be of a high pictorial content. About 30 titles a year. IMPRINTS **Pitkin**; **Unichrome**. Unsolicited mss, synopses and ideas welcome but before submitting anything, approach in writing to the editorial department.

Jensen Business Books
See **AMCD (Publishers) Ltd**

Jewish Chronicle Publications
See **Vallentine Mitchell**

Michael Joseph
See **Penguin Group (UK)**

Kahn & Averill
9 Harrington Road, London SW7 3ES
☎020 8743 3278 Fax 020 8743 3278
Email kahn@averill23.freeserve.co.uk
Managing Director *Mr M. Kahn*

FOUNDED 1967 to publish children's titles but now specialises in music titles. A small independent publishing house. *Publishes* music and general non-fiction. No unsolicited mss; synopses and ideas for books considered.
Royalties paid twice-yearly.

Karnak House
300 Westbourne Park Road, London
W11 1EH
☎020 7243 3620 Fax 020 7243 3620
Email karnakhouse@aol.com
Managing Director *Amon Saba Saakana*

FOUNDED 1979. *Specialises* in African and Caribbean studies. *Publishes* anthropology, education, Egyptology, history, language and linguistics, literary criticism, music, parapsychology, prehistory. No poetry, humour or sport. About 12 titles a year. No unsolicited mss; send introduction or synopsis with one sample chapter. Synopses and ideas welcome.

Royalties paid twice-yearly. *Overseas subsidiaries* The Intef Institute, and Karnak House, Illinois, USA.

Kenilworth Press Ltd
Addington, Buckingham, Buckinghamshire
MK18 2JR
☎01296 715101 Fax 01296 715148
Email editorial@kenilworthpress.co.uk
Website www.kenilworthpress.co.uk
Chairman/Managing Director *David Blunt*
Approx. Annual Turnover £500,000

FOUNDED in 1989 with the acquisition of Threshhold Books. The UK's principal instructional equestrian publisher, producing the official books of the British Horse Society, the famous *Threshold Picture Guides*, and a range of authoritative titles sold around the world. About 10 titles a year.

IMPRINT **Kenilworth Press** TITLES *British Horse Society Manuals; Dressage with Kyra; A Modern Horse Herbal; For the Good of the Rider; No Foot, No Horse; Threshold Picture Guides 1–46.* Unsolicited mss, synopses and ideas welcome but only for titles concerned with the care or riding of horses or ponies.
Royalties paid twice-yearly.

Kenyon-Deane
See **Cressrelles Publishing Co. Ltd**

Laurence King Publishing Ltd
71 Great Russell Street, London WC1B 3BP
☎020 7430 8850 Fax 020 7430 8880
Email enquiries@laurenceking.co.uk
Website www.laurenceking.co.uk

Chairman *Robin Hyman*
Managing Director *Laurence King*
Approx. Annual Turnover £5 million

FOUNDED in 1976 as a book packager under the name Calman & King Ltd, the Laurence King publishing division commenced operations in

1991. College and trade divisions were united in 2001 under Laurence King Publishing Ltd. *Publishes* illustrated books on art, architecture, graphic design, interior design, the decorative arts, film and religion. 40 titles in 2001. DIVISIONS **Professional & Trade** *Philip Cooper* TITLES *3D>2D: The Designers Republic*; *Experimental Houses*. **College & Fine Art** *Lee Ripley-Greenfield* TITLES *A World History of Art*; *A History of Western Architecture*. Unsolicited material welcome; send synopsis by post.
Royalties paid twice-yearly.

Kingfisher Publications Plc

New Penderel House, 283–288 High Holborn, London WC1V 7HZ
☎020 7903 9999 Fax 020 7242 4979
Email sales@kingfisherpub.com
Managing Director *John Richards*

Formerly Larousse plc until 1997 when the company name changed to Kingfisher Publications Plc. FOUNDED 1994 when owners, Groupe de la Cité (also publishers of the Larousse dictionaries in France), merged their UK operations of Grisewood & Dempsey and **Chambers Harrap Publishers Ltd** (see entry).

DIVISION **Kingfisher** *Gill Denton* Non-fiction Publishing Director FOUNDED in 1973 by Grisewood & Dempsey Ltd. *Publishes* children's fiction and non-fiction in hardback and paperback: story books, rhymes and picture books, fiction and poetry anthologies, young non-fiction, activity books, general series and reference. No unsolicited mss accepted.
Royalties paid twice-yearly where applicable.

Jessica Kingsley Publishers Ltd

116 Pentonville Road, London N1 9JB
☎020 7833 2307 Fax 020 7837 2917
Email post@jkp.com
Website www.jkp.com
Managing Director *Jessica Kingsley*
Senior Editor *Amy Lankester-Owen*

FOUNDED 1987. Independent publisher of books for professionals and academics on social and behavioural sciences, including special needs, arts therapies, child psychology, psychotherapy (including forensic psychotherapy), practical theology and social work. Over 100 titles a year. 'We are actively publishing and commissioning in autism and Asperger Syndrome. We welcome suggestions for books and proposals from prospective authors. Proposals should consist of an outline of the book, a contents list, assessment of the market, and author's c.v. and should be

addressed to Jessica Kingsley. Complete manuscript should not be sent.'
Royalties paid twice-yearly.

Kluwer Academic/Plenum Publishers

241 Borough High Street, London SE1 1GB
☎020 7940 7490 Fax 020 7940 7495
Email mail@plenum.co.uk
Website www.wkap.nl
Managing Director *Dr Ken Derham*
Editor *Joanna Lawrence*

FOUNDED 1966. A division of **Kluwer Academic/Plenum Publishing**, New York. The London office is the editorial base for the company's UK and European operations. *Publishes* postgraduate, professional and research-level scientific, technical and medical textbooks, monographs, conference proceedings and reference books. About 200 titles (worldwide) a year. IMPRINTS **Consultants Bureau**; **Kluwer Academic/Plenum Publishers**; **Plenum Press**; **Human Science Press**. Proposals for new publications will be considered, and should be sent to the editor.
Royalties paid annually.

Kluwer Law International

3rd Floor, 241 Borough High Street, London SE1 1GB
☎020 7940 8480 Fax 020 7940 8485
Publisher *Sian O'Neill*

FOUNDED 1995. Parent company: Wolters Kluwer Group. Kluwer Law International consists of three components: the law list of Graham & Trotman, Kluwer Law and Taxation and Martinus Nyhoff. *Publishes* international law. 200 titles a year. Unsolicited synopses and ideas for books on law at an international level welcome.
Royalties paid annually.

Charles Knight Publishing
See **Butterworths Tolley**

Knight Paperbacks Ltd
See **Caxton Publishing Group**

Kogan Page Ltd

120 Pentonville Road, London N1 9JN
☎020 7278 0433 Fax 020 7837 3768/6348
Email kpinfo@kogan-page.co.uk
Website www.kogan-page.co.uk *or* www.earthscan.co.uk
Managing Director *Philip Kogan*
Approx. Annual Turnover £8 million

FOUNDED 1967 by Philip Kogan to publish *The Industrial Training Yearbook*. In 1992 acquired Earthscan Publications. *Publishes* business and management reference books and monographs, education and careers, marketing, personal finance, personnel, small business, training and industrial relations, transport, plus journals. Further expansion is planned, particularly in the finance and high-tech, EC publications areas, yearbooks and directories, and international business reference. Has initiated a number of electronic publishing projects and provision of EP content. About 280 titles a year.

DIVISIONS
Kogan Page *Pauline Goodwin, Philip Mudd, Peter Chadwick*. **Earthscan Publications** *Jonathan Sinclair Wilson* Has close associations with the International Institute for Environment and Development and with the Worldwide Fund for Nature. *Publishes* Third World issues and their global implications, and general environmental titles, both popular and academic. About 50 titles a year. Unsolicited mss, synopses and ideas for books welcome. **Hermes Penton Science** *Publishes* hi-tech engineering science monographs collaboratively with Hermes Science, Paris.
Royalties paid twice-yearly.

Authors' Rating The doyen of business books is out of love with the bookshops – or so it seems as Philip Kogan takes his company deeper into the uncharted waters of electronic publishing. As for the hard print, more of Kogan Page's books will be sold direct. The way the market is at present, it should do wonders for royalty statements.

Ladybird
See **Dorling Kindersley Ltd**

Landmark Publishing Ltd
Ashbourne Hall, Cokayne Avenue, Ashbourne, Derbyshire DE6 1EJ
☎01335 347349 Fax 01335 347303
Email landmark@clara.net
Website www.landmarkpublishing.co.uk

Chairman *Mr R. Cork*
Managing Director *Mr C.L.M. Porter*
Approx. Annual Turnover £350,000

FOUNDED in 1996 following the demise of Moorland Publishing. *Publishes* itinerary-based travel guides, and industrial and local history. 26 titles in 2001. No unsolicited mss; telephone in the first instance.
Royalties twice-yearly.

Larousse Plc
See **Kingfisher Publications Plc**

Lawrence & Wishart Ltd
99A Wallis Road, London E9 5LN
☎020 8533 2506 Fax 020 8533 7369
Email lw@l-w-bks.demon.co.uk
Website www.l-w-bks.co.uk

Managing Director/Editor *Sally Davison*

FOUNDED 1936. An independent publisher with a substantial backlist. *Publishes* current affairs, cultural politics, economics, history, politics and education. 15–20 titles a year. TITLES *A New Modernity; Liberty or Death; The Struggle for Democracy in Britain 1780–1830; Rosa Luxemburg: An Intimate Portrait*.
Royalties paid annually, unless by arrangement.

The Learning Institute
Honeycombe House, Bagley, Wedmore, Somerset BS28 4TD
☎01934 713563 Fax 01934 713492
Email courses@inst.org
Website www.inst.org

Managing Director *Kit Sadgrove*

FOUNDED 1994 to publish home-study courses in vocational subjects such as garden design, writing and computing. *Publishes* subjects that show the reader how to work from home, gain a new skill or enter a new career. Interests include self-improvement, interior design, hobbies, parenting, health, careers, music and investment. TITLES *Become a Freelance Photographer; Master the Art of Painting*. Author's guidelines sent on receipt of s.a.e. No unsolicited mss; send synopses and ideas only.
Royalties paid quarterly.

Lehigh University Press
See **Golden Cockerel Press Ltd**

Leicester University Press
See **The Continuum International Publishing Group Limited**

Lennard Associates Ltd
Windmill Cottage, Mackerye End, Harpenden, Hertfordshire AL5 5DR
☎01582 715866 Fax 01582 715121
Email mailbox@lenqap.demon.co.uk

Chairman/Managing Director *Adrian Stephenson*

FOUNDED 1979. Publisher of sporting yearbooks; sponsored and commissioned projects only.

YEARBOOKS *The Cricketers' Who's Who; RFU Club Directory; Wooden Spoon Rugby World.* No unsolicited mss.
IMPRINTS **Lennard Publishing**; **Queen Anne Press**. Acquired the latter and most of its assets in 1992.
Payment Both fees and royalties by arrangement.

Letterland
See **HarperCollins Publishers Ltd**

Charles Letts
See **New Holland Publishers (UK) Ltd**

Lionel Leventhal Ltd
See **Greenhill Books**

Dewi Lewis Publishing
8 Broomfield Road, Heaton Moor, Stockport SK4 4ND
☎0161 442 9450 Fax 0161 442 9450
Email mail@dewilewispublishing.com
Website www.dewilewispublishing.com
Contacts *Dewi Lewis, Caroline Warhurst*
Approx. Annual Turnover £260,000
FOUNDED 1994. *Publishes* fiction, photography and visual arts. 18 titles in 2001. TITLES *Industry of Souls* Martin Booth (**Booker Prize** shortlist, 1998); *Wolfy and the Strudelbakers* Zvi Jagendorf (**Booker Prize** longlist, 2001); *Common Sense* Martin Parr; *New York 1954–5* William Klein. Submissions: see website for details.
Royalties paid twice-yearly.

Lexis-Nexis
See **Reed Elsevier plc**

John Libbey & Co. Ltd
PO Box 276, Eastleigh SO50 5YS
☎023 8065 0208 Fax 023 8065 0259
Email johnlibbey@aol.com
Website www.johnlibbey.com
Chairman/Managing Director *John Libbey*
FOUNDED 1979. *Publishes* medical books and cinema/animation books and journals. *Specialises* in epilepsy, neurology, nuclear medicine, nutrition and obesity. Synopses and ideas welcome. *Overseas subsidiary* John Libbey Eurotext Ltd, France.

Librapharm Ltd
Gemini House, 162 Craven Road, Newbury, Berkshire RG14 5NR
☎01635 522651 Fax 01635 36294
Website www.librapharm.com

Chairman *Mr M.W. Frost*
Managing Director *Dr P.L. Clarke*
Approx. Annual Turnover £500,000
FOUNDED 1995 as a partial buyout from Kluwer Academic Publishers (UK) academic list. *Publishes* medical and scientific books and periodicals. IMPRINT **Petroc Press**. TITLES *The Inner Consultation*; *Emergencies in General Practice*; *Thinking About Patients*. Journals: *Primary Care Psychiatry*; *Current Medical Research and Opinion*; *Paediatric and Perinatal Drug Therapy*. Unsolicited mss, synopses and ideas for medical books welcome.
Royalties paid twice-yearly.

Library Association Publishing
See **Facet Publishing**

Frances Lincoln Ltd
4 Torriano Mews, Torriano Avenue, London, NW5 2RZ
☎020 7284 4009 Fax 020 7267 5249
Email <firstname and initial of surname>
   @frances-lincoln.com
Website www.franceslincoln.com
Managing Director *John Nicoll*
FOUNDED 1977. *Publishes* highly illustrated non-fiction: gardening, art and interiors, health, crafts, children's picture and information books; and stationery. About 50 titles a year.
DIVISIONS
Adult Non-fiction *Jo Christian* TITLES *Chatsworth* Duchess of Devonshire; *The Gravel Garden* Beth Chatto; **Children's General Fiction and Non-fiction** *Janetta Otter-Barry* TITLES *The Wanderings of Odysseus* Rosemary Sutcliffe, illus. Alan Lee; **Stationery** *Anne Fraser* TITLES *RHS Diary and Address Book*; *National Gallery Diary and Address Book.* Synopses and ideas for books considered.
Royalties paid twice-yearly.

Linden Press
See **Open Gate Press**

Linford Romance/Linford Mystery/Linford Western
See **F.A. Thorpe (Publishing)**

Lion Publishing
Mayfield House, 256 Banbury Road, Oxford OX2 7DH
☎01865 302750 Fax 01865 302757
Email enquiry@lion-publishing.co.uk
Website www.lion-publishing.co.uk
Managing Director *Paul Clifford*

Approx. Annual Turnover £6.77 million
FOUNDED 1971. A Christian book publisher, strong on illustrated books for a popular international readership, with rights sold in over 100 languages worldwide. *Publishes* a diverse list with Christian viewpoint the common denominator. All ages, from board books for children to multi-contributor adult reference, educational, paperbacks and colour co-editions and gift books.

DIVISIONS **Adult** *Laura Derico*; **Children's and Giftlines** *Caroline Knight*. Unsolicited mss accepted provided they have a positive Christian viewpoint intended for a wide general and international readership.

Royalties paid twice-yearly.

Lir
See **Hodder Headline Ltd**

Little Tiger Press
An imprint of Magi Publications,
1 The Coda Centre, 189 Munster Road,
London SW6 6AW
☎020 7385 6333 Fax 020 7385 7333
Email info@littletiger.co.uk

Publisher *Monty Bhatia*
Editors *Ramona Reihill, Jude Evans*
Approx. Annual Turnover £4.5 million

Publishes children's picture and novelty books for ages 0–7. No texts over 1200 words. About 24 titles a year. Unsolicited mss, synopses and new ideas welcome, but please telephone first.

Royalties paid annually.

Little, Brown & Co. (UK)
See **Time Warner Books UK**

Liverpool University Press
4 Cambridge Street, Liverpool L69 7ZU
☎0151 794 2233 Fax 0151 794 2235
Website www.liverpool-unipress.co.uk

Managing Director/Editorial Head *Robin Bloxsidge*

LUP's primary activity is the publication of academic and scholarly books and journals but it also has a limited number of trade titles. Although its principal focus is on the arts and social sciences, in which it is active in a wide variety of disciplines, the LUP list includes some **STM** titles. 30–40 titles a year. TITLES *Liverpool 8; A Runner Among Falling Leaves: The Yew-Tree at the Head of the Strand; Design Culture in Liverpool 1880–1914; Public Sculpture of Glasgow; Public Art Collections in North-West England; The Long Road to Peace in Modern Ireland; Coastal Dune Management; A New History of the Isle of Man; Gladsongs and Gatherings: Poetry in its Social Context in Liverpool since the 1960s; Thomas Gray's Journal of His Visit to the Lake District in October 1769.*

Royalties paid annually.

Livewire Books for Teenagers
See **The Women's Press**

Lonely Planet Publications Ltd
10A Spring Place, London NW5 3BH
☎020 7428 4800 Fax 020 7428 4828
Email go@lonelyplanet.co.uk
Website www.lonelyplanet.com

Owner *Lonely Planet (Australia)*
Editorial Head *Katharine Leck*
Approx. Annual Turnover £30 million

FOUNDED in 1973 by Tony and Maureen Wheeler to document a journey from London across Asia to Australia. Since then, Lonely Planet has grown into a global operation with headquarters in Melbourne and offices in Paris, California and London. *Publishes* travel guidebooks, phrasebooks, travel literature, pictorial books, city maps, regional atlases, diving and snorkelling, walking, cycling, wildlife, health, restaurant, pre-departure guidebooks. Also operates a commercial travel slide library called **Lonely Planet Images** (lpi@lonelyplanet. com.au). No unsolicited mss; synopses and ideas welcome.

Royalties negotiable.

Authors' Rating The American tendency, post-September 11th, to worry about all things foreign has taken a knock at the travel book market. There are signs of recovery but authors with 'the greatest holiday adventure ever' sort of title may have to be patient.

Lorenz Books
See **Anness Publishing Ltd**

Peter Lowe (Eurobook Ltd)
PO Box 52, Wallingford, Oxfordshire
OX10 0XU
☎01865 858333 Fax 01865 858263
Email eurobook@compuserve.com

Managing Director *Peter Lowe*

FOUNDED 1968. *Publishes* popular science and illustrated adult non-fiction. No unsolicited mss; synopses and ideas (with s.a.e.) welcome. No adult fiction.

Lund Humphries
See **Ashgate Publishing Ltd**

The Lutterworth Press

PO Box 60, Cambridge CB1 2NT
☎01223 350865 Fax 01223 366951
Email publishing@lutterworth.com
Website www.lutterworth.com

Managing Director *Adrian Brink*

The Lutterworth Press dates back to the 18th century when it was founded by the Religious Tract Society. In the 19th century it was best known for its children's books and magazines, both religious and secular, including *The Boys' Own Paper*. Since 1984 it has been an imprint of **James Clarke & Co** (see entry). *Publishes* religious books for adults and children, adult non-fiction, children's fiction and non-fiction. TITLES *A History of Celibacy; The Divine Drama: the Old Testament as Literature; Socrates Café; Deviating Voices: Women and Orthodox Religious Traditions; Joanna Southcott: the Woman Clothed with the Sun.* Approach in writing with ideas in the first instance.

Royalties paid annually.

Macdonald & Co.

See **Time Warner Books UK**

McGraw-Hill Education

McGraw-Hill House, Shoppenhangers Road, Maidenhead, Berkshire SL6 2QL
☎01628 502500 Fax 01628 770224
Website www.mcgraw-hill.co.uk

Owned by US parent company, FOUNDED in 1888. Began publishing in Maidenhead in 1965, having had an office in the UK since 1899. *Publishes* business, economics, computing and engineering for the academic, student and professional markets. Around 50 titles a year. See website for author's guide and how to submit new book proposals.

Royalties paid twice-yearly.

Macmillan Publishers Ltd

The Macmillan Building, 4 Crinan Street, London N1 9XW
☎020 7833 4000 Fax 020 7843 4640
Website www.macmillan.com

Chief Executive *Richard Charkin*
Approx. Annual Turnover £304 million (Book Publishing Group)

FOUNDED 1843. Macmillan is one of the largest publishing houses in Britain, publishing approximately 1400 titles a year. In 1995, Verlagsgruppe Georg von Holtzbrinck, a major German publisher, acquired a majority stake in the Macmillan Group. In 1996, Macmillan bought Boxtree, the successful media tie-in publisher and, in 1997, purchased the Heinemann English language teaching list from Reed Elsevier. Unsolicited proposals, synopses and mss are welcome in all divisions of the company (with the exception of Macmillan Children's Books). Authors who wish to send material to Macmillan General Books should note that there is a central submissions procedure in operation. Send a synopsis and the first 3–4 chapters with a covering letter and return postage to the Submissions Editor, Pan Macmillan, 20 New Wharf Road, London N1 9RR.

DIVISIONS
Palgrave Brunel Road, Houndmills, Basingstoke, Hampshire RG21 6XS ☎01256 329242 Fax 01256 3479476 Managing Director *Dominic Knight*; Managing Director, Editorial *Ian Jacobs*; Publishing Director, Grove *Sara Lloyd*; **Academic** *Josie Dixon*; **College: Humanities & Social Sciences Division** *Frances Arnold*; **Business Textbooks** *Anna Faherty*; **Professional Business & Management Division** *Stephen Rutt*; **Journals** *David Bull. Publishes* textbooks, monographs and journals in academic and professional subjects. Publications in both hard copy and electronic format.

Macmillan Education Macmillan Oxford, 4 Between Towns Road, Oxford OX4 3PP ☎01865 405700 Fax 01865 405701 Email info@macmillan.com Website www.macmillan education.com Executive Chairman *Christopher Paterson*; Managing Director *Chris Harrison*; Publishing Directors *Sue Bale* (ELT), *Alison Hubert* (Education), *Ian Johnstone* (Internet). *Publishes* a wide range of ELT titles and educational materials for the international education market from Oxford and through 30 subsidiaries worldwide.

Pan Macmillan 20 New Wharf Road, London N1 9RR ☎020 7014 6000 Fax 020 7014 6001 Managing Director *David North*; Publishes under **Macmillan, Pan, Picador, Sidgwick & Jackson, Boxtree, Channel 4 Books, Macmillan Children's Books, Campbell Books**.

IMPRINTS
Macmillan (FOUNDED 1843) Publisher *Jeremy Trevathan*, Editorial Directors (fiction) *Imogen Taylor, Peter Lavery. Publishes* commercial and literary fiction including genre fiction, crime, thrillers, romantic, sci-fi, fantasy and horror. Publishing Director (Fiction) *Maria Rejt*; Editorial Director (non-fiction) *Georgina Morley. Publishes* autobiography, biography,

business and industry, economics, gift books, history, natural history, travel, philosophy, politics and world affairs, psychology, gardening and cookery, popular science. Editorial Director (reference) *Morven Knowles. Publishes* trade reference titles.

Pan (FOUNDED 1947) Publisher *Clare Harington. Publishes* fiction: novels, detective fiction, sci-fi, fantasy and horror. Serious non-fiction: history, biography, science. General non-fiction: sports and games, film and theatre, travel, gardening and cookery. Publishing Director (Fiction) *Maria Rejt.*

Picador (FOUNDED 1972) Publishing Director *Maria Rejt,* Senior Editorial Director *Ursula Doyle. Publishes* literary international fiction and non-fiction.

Sidgwick & Jackson (FOUNDED 1908) Publisher *Gordon Scott Wise. Publishes* popular non-fiction in hardback and trade paperback with strong personality or marketable identity, from celebrity and showbusiness to ancient mystery, music and true-life adventure to inspirational and branded books. Also military history list.

Macmillan Audio Books (See entry under **Audio Books**)

Boxtree Publisher *Gordon Scott Wise. Publishes* media tie-in titles, including TV, film, music and Internet, plus entertainment licences, pop culture, humour and event-related books. TITLES *Dilbert; Destiny's Child; Pizza Express; The Motley Fool; Who Wants to be a Millionaire?; James Bond; Purple Ronnie; Viz; Wallace & Gromit.* **Channel 4 Books** Publisher *Ms Charlie Carman. Publishes* TV tie-in titles – books that stand on their own merits and not just the 'book of the series'. About 50 titles a year. TITLES *Friends; Water Colour Challenge; Time Team; Dawson's Creek; Frasier; South Park.*

Macmillan Children's Books (New Wharf Road address) Managing Director *Kate Wilson*; **Fiction, Non-Fiction, Poetry** *Sarah Davies*; **Picture Books, Gift Books,** **Campbell Books** *Mandy Suhr.* IMPRINTS **Macmillan, Pan, Campbell Books, Young Picador.** *Publishes* novels, board books, picture books, non-fiction (illustrated and non-illustrated), poetry and novelty books in paperback and hardback. No unsolicited material.

Royalties paid annually or twice-yearly depending on contract.

Authors' Rating In any assessment of Macmillan it is hard to overemphasise the importance of the *Grove Dictionary of Music* which has turned out to be one of the single biggest ventures in recent publishing. But there is much else going for this wide-ranging publisher, as proved by the lineup of prize winners on the trade side which continues to actively seek new talent. Education and audio books are doing well and if media tie-ins are having a harder time, this probably says more about the failure of television to come up with fresh ideas. A recent union between Pan Macmillan and sister company Gill & Macmillan has given birth to Tivoli, a popular fiction imprint·aimed at the Irish market.

Mainstream Publishing Co. (Edinburgh) Ltd

7 Albany Street, Edinburgh EH1 3UG
☎0131 557 2959 Fax 0131 556 8720
Email editorial@mainstreampublishing.com
Website www.mainstreampublishing.com

Directors *Bill Campbell, Peter MacKenzie*
Approx. Annual Turnover £2.75 million

Publishes art, autobiography/biography, current affairs, health, sport, history, illustrated and fine editions, photography, politics and world affairs, popular paperbacks. Over 80 titles a year. TITLES *Bin Laden: Behind the Mask of the Terrorist* Adam Robinson; *Jihad!: The Secret War in Afghanistan* Tom Carew; *Terror on the Pitch: Osama bin Laden's Plot Against the 1998 World Cup* Adam Robinson. Ideas for books considered, but they should be preceded by a letter, synopsis and s.a.e. or return postage.

Royalties paid twice-yearly.

Authors' Rating Renowned for controversial political books that other publishers shy away from, Mainstream is also strong on sports titles. Though based in Edinburgh and in the forefront of the literary rejuvenation of the city, Mainstream makes its impact beyond the Scottish border. Keen on finding authors who 'can develop with us'.

Mammoth
See **Egmont Books**

Management Books 2000 Ltd

Forge House, Limes Road, Kemble, Cirencester, Gloucestershire GL7 6AD
☎01285 771441 Fax 01285 771055
Email m.b.2000@virgin.net
Website www.mb2000.com

Publisher *James Alexander*
Approx. Annual Turnover £500,000

FOUNDED 1993 to develop a range of books for executives and managers working in the modern world of business. 'Essentially, the books are working books for working managers, practical and effective.' *Publishes* business, management, self-development and allied topics as well as sponsored titles. About 30 titles a year. Unsolicited mss, synopses and ideas for books welcome.

Manchester United Books
See **Carlton Publishing Group**

Manchester University Press
Oxford Road, Manchester M13 9NR
☎0161 275 2310 Fax 0161 274 3346
Email mup@man.ac.uk
Website www.manchesteruniversitypress.co.uk
Publisher/Chief Executive *David Rodgers*
Head of Editorial and Humanities *Matthew Frost*
Approx. Annual Turnover £2 million
FOUNDED 1904. MUP is Britain's third largest university press, with a list marketed and sold worldwide. Remit consists of occasional trade publications but mainly A-level and undergraduate textbooks and research monographs. *Publishes* in the areas of: literature, cultural studies, TV, film, theatre and media, history and history of art, design, politics and law. About 130 titles a year.
DIVISIONS **Humanities** *Matthew Frost*; **History/Art History** *Alison Whittle*; **Politics and Law** *Tony Mason*. Unsolicited mss welcome.
Royalties paid annually.

George Mann Books
PO Box 22, Maidstone, Kent ME14 1AH
☎01622 759591 Fax 01622 209193
Chairman/Managing Director *George Mann*
FOUNDED 1972. *Publishes* original non-fiction and selected reprints. Not considering new fiction for publication. 'Will only consider and respond to authors who, in the present publishing climate, are prepared to support *some of the costs* of publication. Unsolicited material not accompanied by return postage will neither be read nor returned.'
Royalties paid annually.

Mansell
See **The Continuum International Publishing Group Limited**

Manson Publishing Ltd
73 Corringham Road, London NW11 7DL
☎020 8905 5150 Fax 020 8201 9233
Email manson@man-pub.demon.co.uk

Website www.manson-publishing.co.uk
Chairman/Managing Director *Michael Manson*
FOUNDED 1992. *Publishes* scientific, technical, medical and veterinary. 10 titles in 2001. No unsolicited mss; synopses and ideas will be considered.
Royalties paid twice-yearly.

Marston House
Marston House, Marston Magna, Yeovil, Somerset BA22 8DH
☎01935 851331 Fax 01935 851372
Managing Director/Editorial Head *Anthony Birks-Hay*
FOUNDED 1989. Publishing imprint of book packager Alphabet & Image Ltd. *Publishes* fine art, architecture, ceramics. 4 titles a year.
Royalties paid twice-yearly, or flat fee in lieu of royalties.

Kenneth Mason Publications Ltd
The Book Barn, Westbourne, Emsworth, Hampshire PO10 8RS
☎01243 377977 Fax 01243 379136
Chairman *Kenneth Mason*
Managing Director *Piers Mason*
Approx. Annual Turnover £500,000
FOUNDED 1958. *Publishes* diet, health, fitness, nutrition and nautical. No fiction. About 15 titles a year. IMPRINTS **Boatswain Press**; **Research Disclosure**. Initial approach by letter with synopsis only.
Royalties paid twice-yearly in first year, annually thereafter.

Kevin Mayhew Publishers
Buxhall, Stowmarket, Suffolk IP14 3BW
☎01449 737978 Fax 01449 737834
Email info@kevinmayhewltd.com
Website www.kevinmayhewltd.com
Chairman *Kevin Mayhew*
Managing Director *Gordon Carter*
Commissioning Editors *Kevin Mayhew, Jonathan Bugden*
Approx. Annual Turnover £4 million
FOUNDED in 1976. One of the leading sacred music and Christian book publishers in the UK. *Publishes* religious titles – liturgy, sacramental, devotional, also children's books and school resources. Unsolicited synopses and mss welcome; telephone prior to sending material, please.
IMPRINT **Palm Tree Press** *Kevin Mayhew*

Bible stories, colouring/activity and puzzle books for children.
Royalties paid annually.

Melrose Press Ltd
St Thomas Place, Ely, Cambridgeshire CB7 4GG
☎01353 646600 Fax 01353 646601
Email tradesales@melrosepress.co.uk
Website www.melrosepress.co.uk
Chairman *Richard A. Kay*
Managing Director *Nicholas S. Law*
Approx. Annual Turnover £2 million
FOUNDED 1960. Took on its present name in 1969. *Publishes* biographical who's who reference only (not including *Who's Who*, which is published by **A.&C. Black**).

Mentor
See **Christian Focus Publications**

Mercat Press
10 Coates Crescent, Edinburgh EH3 7AL
Email enquiries@mercatpress.com
Website www.mercatpress.com
Directors *Seán Costello, Tom Johnstone*
Established as a stand-alone company in 2002 in a management buy-out following the collapse of parent firm James Thin. The Press was FOUNDED in 1971 as an adjunct to the former Scottish bookselling chain. It began by publishing reprints of classic Scottish literature but now produces a wide range of new non-fiction titles. In 1992 the company acquired the bulk of the stock of Aberdeen University Press and the backlist expanded greatly as a result. In 1999 it took over some 60 titles from the Stationery Office's Scottish heritage list. New titles are added regularly. *Publishes* Scottish classics reprints and non-fiction of Scottish interest. This includes walking guides and historical and literary books. TITLES *West Highland Way, Official Guide* Bob Aitken and Roger Smith; *25 Walks* series; *McLevy: The Edinburgh Detective* James McLevy; *Scottish Birds* Robin Hull; *Gaelic Dictionary* Malcolm MacLennan. Unsolicited synopses of non-fiction Scottish interest books, preferably with sample chapters, are welcome. No new fiction or poetry.
Royalties paid annually.

The Merlin Press Ltd
PO Box 30705, London WC2E 8QD
☎020 7836 3020 Fax 020 7497 0309
Email info@merlinpress.co.uk

Website www.merlinpress.co.uk
Managing Director *Anthony W. Zurbrugg*
FOUNDED 1956. *Publishes* economics, history, philosophy, left-wing politics. No fiction. IMPRINTS **Merlin Press**; **Green Print**. TITLES *Socialist Register* (annual); *The Essential E.P. Thompson*; *Men and Power*. About 10 titles a year.
Royalties paid twice-yearly.

Merrell Publishers Ltd
42 Southwark Street, London SE1 1UN
☎020 7403 2047 Fax 020 7407 1333
Email mail@merrellpublishers.com
Managing Director *Hugh Merrell*
Approx. Annual Turnover £1.6 million
FOUNDED 1993. *Publishes* art, architecture, design and photography. 25 titles in 2001. Unsolicited synopses and ideas for books welcome. Send c.v. and synopsis giving details of the book's target markets and funding of illustrations.
Royalties paid annually.

Methodist Publishing House
4 John Wesley Road, Werrington, Peterborough, Cambridgeshire PE4 6ZP
☎01733 325002 Fax 01733 384180
Website www.mph.org.uk
Chair *Dudley Coates*
Chief Executive *Brian Thornton*
Approx. Annual Turnover £2 million
FOUNDED 1800. Owned by the Methodist Church. *Publishes* a wide range of books, magazines and resources which are sold to Christians in the UK and overseas. 21 titles in 2001. New bi-monthly magazine *Flame* with a target readership of 35,000. IMPRINTS **Epworth Press** (see entry); **Foundery Press** *Brian Thornton*. Unsolicited mss, synopses and ideas welcome; send sample chapter and contents with covering letter.
Royalties paid twice-yearly.

Methuen Children's Books
See **Egmont Books**

Methuen Publishing Ltd
215 Vauxhall Bridge Road, London SW1V 1EJ
☎020 7798 1600 Fax 020 7233 9827
Email <name>@methuen.co.uk
Website www.methuen.co.uk
Managing Director *Peter Tummons*
Publishing Director *Max Eilenberg*

FOUNDED 1889. Methuen was owned by Reed International until it was bought by Random House in 1997. Purchased by a management buy-out team in 1998. *Publishes* fiction and non-fiction; travel, sport, drama, film, performing arts, humour. 60 titles in 2001. DIVISIONS **General**; **Drama**; **Film**; **Theatre**. No unsolicited mss; synopses and ideas welcome. Prefers to be approached via agents or a letter of inquiry. No first novels, cookery books, personal memoirs.
Royalties paid twice-yearly.

Metro Publishing
See **John Blake Publishing Ltd**

Michelin Travel Publications
Hannay House, 39 Clarendon Road, Watford, Hertfordshire WD17 1JA
☎01923 205240 Fax 01923 205241
Website www.Via.Michelin.co.uk

FOUNDED 1900 as a travel publisher. *Publishes* travel guides, maps and atlases, children's I-Spy books. Travel-related synopses and ideas welcome; no mss.

Midland Publishing – An imprint of Ian Allan Publishing Ltd
4 Watling Drive, Hinckley LE10 3EY
☎01455 255490 Fax 01455 255495
Email midlandbooks@compuserve.com
Publisher *N.P. Lewis*

Publishes aviation, military and railways. No wartime memoirs. No unsolicited mss; synopses and ideas welcome.
Royalties paid quarterly.

Milet Publishing Limited
6 North End Parade, London W14 0SJ
☎020 7603 5477 Fax 020 7610 5475
Email info@milet.com
Website www.milet.com
Managing Directors *Sedat Turhan, Patricia Billings*

FOUNDED 1995. *Publishes* children's books in dual language and in English; world literature for adults and language books. Over 30 titles in 2001. DIVISIONS **Children's, English**; **Children's, Dual Language** *Patricia Billings* TITLES *Picture the World; The Lucky Grain of Corn*. **World Literature**; **Language Books** *Sedat Turhan* TITLE *Milet Bilingual Visual Dictionary*. Welcomes synopses and ideas for books. Send proposal, outline or synopsis with sample text and/or artwork, either by post or

e-mail. 'We like bold, original stories and artwork, both universal and/or multicultural.'
Royalties paid twice-yearly.

Harvey Miller Publishers
See **Brepols Publishers**

Miller's
See **Octopus Publishing Group**

Millivres Prowler Group
Worldwide House, 116/134 Bayham Street, London NW1 0BA
☎020 7482 2576 Fax 020 7284 0329
Publisher (Books) *Helen Sandler*

Following a merger, the Millivres Prowler Group is now the biggest gay media company in Europe. Publishes about 30 book titles a year as well as *Gay Times* and *Diva* magazines. IMPRINTS **Diva Books** Commissioning Editor *Helen Sandler* Literary and genre fiction and non-fiction with a lesbian slant; also erotic fiction TITLES *Diva Book of Short Stories*; Cameron McGill mysteries by Jenny Roberts. Send first three chapters and synopsis with covering letter. **Zipper Books** Commissioning Editor *Kathleen Bryson* Explicit gay men's erotic fiction TITLES *The Low Road; The Bad Boy's Book of Bedtime Stories*. Contact commissioning editor for guidelines. **GMP** (see entry).

Mills & Boon
See **Harlequin Mills & Boon Ltd**

Mindfield
See **Camden Press Ltd**

Minerva Press Ltd
6th Floor, St Georges House, 6 St Georges Way, Leicester LE1 1SH
☎0116 255 3222
Fax 0116 258 7200 (submissions)
Email submissions@minerva-press.co.uk
Website www.minerva-press.co.uk
Director *Michael Shore*

FOUNDED in 1992, but the imprint can be traced back to 1792. *Publishes* fiction and non-fiction; memoirs/biography, poetry, religion, philosophy, history and children's. 375 titles in 2001. TITLES *Tricks* Chris Dunn; *In Quest of the Lost Legions* Major Tony Clunn, MBE; *Jack the Ripper Through the Mists of Time* Peter Hodgson. Specialises in new authors. Unsolicited mss, synopses and ideas for books welcome.
Royalties paid twice-yearly. Offices in London and New Delhi.

Authors' Rating Liable to ask authors to contribute towards costs of publication.

MIRA
See **Harlequin Mills & Boon Ltd**

Mitchell Beazley
See **Octopus Publishing Group**

Mobius
See **Hodder Headline Ltd**

Mojo Books
See **Canongate Books Ltd**

Monarch Books
Concorde House, Grenville Place, London
NW7 3SA
☎020 8959 3668 Fax 020 8959 3678
Email monarch@angushudson.com
Editorial Director *Tony Collins*
An imprint of **Angus Hudson Ltd** (see entry under **UK Packagers**). *Publishes* an independent list of Christian books across a wide range of concerns. About 30 titles a year. IMPRINT **Monarch** Upmarket paperback list with Christian basis and strong social concern agenda including psychology, future studies, politics, mission, theology, leadership and spirituality. Unsolicited mss, synopses and ideas welcome. 'Regretfully, no poetry or fiction.'

Morgan Publishing
See **Ashley Drake Publishing Ltd**

Mosby
See **Harcourt Publishers International**

Motor Racing Publications
PO Box 1318, Croydon, Surrey CR0 5YP
☎020 8654 2711 Fax 020 8407 0339
Email mrp.books@virgin.net
Website www.oberon.co.uk/mrp
Chairman/Editorial Head *John Blunsden*
FOUNDED soon after the end of World War II to concentrate on motor-racing titles. Fairly dormant in the mid '60s but was reactivated in 1968 by a new shareholding structure. John Blunsden later acquired a majority share and major expansion followed in the '70s. About 6–12 titles a year. *Publishes* motor-sport history, classic and performance car collection and restoration, race track and off-road driving and related subjects. IMPRINTS **Fitzjames Press**; **Motor Racing Publications** No unsolicited mss. Send synopses and ideas in specified subject areas in the first instance.
Royalties paid twice-yearly.

Mowbray
See **The Continuum International Publishing Group Limited**

Multi-Sensory Learning Ltd
Highgate House, Groom's Lane, Creaton, Northampton NN6 8NN
☎01604 505000 Fax 01604 505001
Email info@msl-online.net
Website www.msl-online.net
Senior Editor *Philippa Attwood*
Publishes materials and books related to dyslexia; the multi-sensory learning course for dyslexic pupils needing literacy skills development, plus numerous other items on assessment, reading, maths, music, etc. for dyslexics. Keen to locate authors able to write materials for dyslexic people and for teachers of dyslexics.

Murdoch Books UK Ltd
Ferry House, 51–57 Lacy Road, London
SW15 1PR
☎020 8355 1480 Fax 020 8355 1499
CEO *Robert Oerton*
Publisher *Catie Ziller*
Approx. Annual Turnover £6 million
Owned by Australian media group Murdoch Magazines Pty Ltd. *Publishes* full-colour non-fiction: homes and interiors, gardening, cookery, craft, cake decorating and DIY. About 46 titles a year. Synopses and ideas for books welcome; no unsolicited mss.
Royalties paid twice-yearly.

John Murray (Publishers) Ltd
50 Albemarle Street, London W1S 4BD
☎020 7493 4361 Fax 020 7499 1792
Website www.johnmurray.co.uk
Chairman *John R. Murray*
Managing Director *Nicholas Perren*
FOUNDED 1768. Acquired by **Hodder Headline** in May 2002. *Publishes* general trade books, educational (secondary school and college textbooks) and Success Studybooks.
DIVISIONS **General Books** *Grant McIntyre*; **Educational Books** *Nicholas Perren*. Unsolicited material discouraged.
Royalties paid twice yearly.

Authors' Rating And so farewell to the august publisher of Byron, Austen and Darwin. Finding the competition from the conglomerates all too much, John Murray has sold out to Hodder Headline and its parent company, WHSmith. The education list was the chief attraction for the buyer. The hope now must be that the new management will continue the John Murray tradition of publishing quality books for the upper reaches of the market.

NAG Press Ltd
See **Robert Hale Ltd**

National Trust Publications
36 Queen Anne's Gate, London SW1H 9AS
☎020 7222 9251 Fax 020 7222 5097
Website www.nationaltrust.org.uk/bookshop
Chairman *Charles Nunneley*
Director-General *Fiona Reynolds*
Publisher *Margaret Willes*

Publishing arm of The National Trust, FOUNDED in 1895 by Robert Hunter, Octavia Hill and Hardwicke Rawnsley to protect and conserve places of historic interest and beauty. *Publishes* gardening, cookery, handbooks, social history, architecture, general interest and children's books. TITLES *Literary Trails; The Art of Dress; Flora Domestica; Living In Style; Vegetarian Recipes.* No unsolicited material.
Royalties paid twice-yearly.

Nautical Data Ltd
The Book Barn, Westbourne, Emsworth, Hampshire PO10 8RS
☎01243 389352 Fax 01243 379136
Email info@nauticaldata.com
Website www.nauticaldata.com
Managing Director *Piers Mason*
Approx. Annual Turnover £750,000

FOUNDED 1999. *Publishes* nautical almanacs, pilots and nautical reference. 23 titles in 2001. No unsolicited mss; synopses and ideas welcome. No fiction or non-nautical themes.
Royalties paid twice-yearly.

NCVO Publications
Regent's Wharf, 8 All Saints Street, London N1 9RL
☎020 7713 6161 Fax 020 7713 6300
Website www.ncvo-voc.org.uk
Head of Communications *Maria Kane*
Approx. Annual Turnover £140,000

FOUNDED 1928. Publishing imprint of the National Council for Voluntary Organisations, embracing former Bedford Square Press titles and NCVO's many other publications. The list reflects NCVO's role as the representative body

for the voluntary sector. *Publishes* directories, management and trustee development, finance and fundraising titles of primary interest to the voluntary sector. TITLES *The Voluntary Agencies Directory; The Good Trustee Guide; The Good Campaigns Guide; The Good Financial Management Guide; The Good Employment Guide.* No unsolicited mss as all projects are commissioned in-house.

Thomas Nelson & Sons Ltd
See **Nelson Thornes Limited**

Nelson Thornes Limited
Delta Place, 27 Bath Road, Cheltenham, Gloucestershire GL53 7Th
☎01242 267100 Fax 01242 221914
Email cservices@nelsonthornes.com
Website www.nelsonthornes.com
Managing Director *Oliver Gadsby*

FOUNDED in 2000 following the merger of Stanley Thornes (Publishers) Ltd and Thomas Nelson & Sons Ltd. Part of the Wolters Kluwer Group of companies. Educational publisher of printed and electronic product, from pre-school to Higher Education. Unsolicited mss, synopses and ideas for books welcome if appropriate to specialised lists.
Royalties paid annually.

Authors' Rating The merger of Nelson with Stanley Thornes has created the second largest education publisher in the UK (Pearson is the first). The most successful divisions such as health and science are helped by the dominant position in the market held by the parent company, Wolters Kluwer.

New Beacon Books Ltd
76 Stroud Green Road, London N4 3EN
☎020 7272 4889 Fax 020 7281 4662
Chairman *John La Rose*
Managing Director *Sarah White*
Approx. Annual Turnover £120,000

FOUNDED 1966. *Publishes* fiction, history, politics, poetry and language, all concerning black people. No unsolicited material.
Royalties paid annually.

New English Library
See **Hodder Headline Ltd**

New Holland Publishers (UK) Ltd
Garfield House, 86–88 Edgware Road, London W2 2EA
☎020 7724 7773 Fax 020 7258 1293 (editorial)
Email postmaster@nhpub.co.uk

Website www.newhollandpublishers.com
Managing Director *John Beaufoy*
Publishing Director *Yvonne McFarlane*
Approx. Annual Turnover £6 million

FOUNDED 1956. Relaunched in 1987 as a publisher of illustrated books for the international market. In 1993, NH acquired Charles Letts Publishing Division list and four years later the then parent company (New Holland Struik Group, South Africa) acquired Southern Book Publishers, while their sister company (New Holland Australia) acquired the natural history and lifestyle divisions of Reed Australia. With its HQ in London, New Holland Publishers (UK) Ltd has now become the International Publishing Division of Johnnic Communications, one of Africa's leading publishing groups. NHP also has offices in Australia and New Zealand. *Publishes* non-fiction, practical and inspirational books in categories including cookery and food, crafts, DIY, fishing, gardening, interior design, mind, body and spirit, natural history, indoor and outdoor sports, travel, travel guides and general books. No unsolicited mss; synopses and ideas welcome.

Nexus
See **Virgin Books Ltd**

Nexus Special Interests
Nexus House, Azalea Drive, Swanley, Kent BR8 8HY
☎01322 660070 Fax 01322 667633
Website www.nexusonline.com
Contact *Steve Carter*

Publishes aviation, engineering, leisure and hobbies, modelling, electronics, health, craft, wine and beer making, woodwork. Send synopses rather than completed mss.
Royalties paid twice-yearly.

NFER-Nelson Publishing Co. Ltd
Darville House, 2 Oxford Road East, Windsor, Berkshire SL4 1DF
☎01753 858961 Fax 01753 856830
Website www.nfer-nelson.co.uk
Director of Education *Anne Eastgate*

FOUNDED 1981. Part of Granada Learning Ltd. *Publishes* educational and psychological tests and training materials. Main interest is in educational, clinical and occupational assessment and training material. Unsolicited mss welcome.
Royalties vary according to each contract.

Nia
See **The X Press**

Nightingale Books
See **Pegasus Elliot Mackenzie Publishers Ltd**

James Nisbet & Co. Ltd
Pirton Court, Prior's Hill, Pirton, Hitchin, Hertfordshire SG5 3QA
☎01462 713444 Fax 01462 713444
Chairman *E.M. Mackenzie-Wood*

FOUNDED 1810 as a religious publisher and expanded into more general areas from around 1850 onwards. The first educational list appeared in 1926 but the company now concentrates on business studies with the education largely discontinued. About 5 titles a year. No fiction, leisure or religion. No unsolicited mss; synopses and ideas welcome.
Royalties paid twice-yearly.

NMS Publishing Limited
Royal Museum, Chambers Street, Edinburgh EH1 1JF
☎0131 247 4026 Fax 0131 247 4012
Email ltaylor@nms.ac.uk
Website www.nms.ac.uk
Chairman *Anna Ritchie*
Director *Lesley A. Taylor*
Approx. Annual Turnover £250,000

FOUNDED 1987 to *publish* non-fiction related to the National Museums of Scotland collections: academic and general; children's; archaeology, history, decorative arts worldwide, history of science, technology, natural history and geology, poetry. 10 titles in 2001. TITLES *Scots' Lives* series; *Scotland's Past in Action; Churches to Visit in Scotland; Caring for the Scottish Home; The Making of the Museum of Scotland*; and Clarissa Dickson Wright's *Hieland Foodie*. No unsolicited mss; only interested in synopses and ideas for books which are genuinely related to NMS collections and to Scotland in general.
Royalties paid twice-yearly.

No Exit Press
See **Oldcastle Books Ltd**

Nonesuch Press
See **Reinhardt Books Ltd**

Northcote House Publishers Ltd
Horndon House, Horndon, Tavistock, Devon PL19 9NQ
☎01822 810066 Fax 01822 810034
Email northcote.house@virgin.net
Website www.northcotehouse.com

Managing Director *Brian Hulme*
FOUNDED 1985. *Publishes* a series of literary critical studies, in association with the British Council, *Writers and their Work*; education management, literary criticism, educational dance and drama. A new series of study aids for A-level students and undergraduates in English literature is in preparation. 20 titles in 2001. 'Well-thought-out proposals, including contents and sample chapter(s), with strong marketing arguments welcome.'
Royalties paid annually.

Nottingham University Press
Manor Farm, Main Street, Thrumpton, Nottingham NG11 0AX
☎0115 983 1011 Fax 0115 983 1003
Email editor@nup.com
Website www.nup.com
Managing Editor *Dr D.J.A. Cole*
Approx. Annual Turnover £250,000
Initially concentrated on agricultural and food sciences titles but has now branched into new areas including engineering, lifesciences, medicine and law. TITLES *Global 2050; Lung Function Tests; Diet, Lipoproteins and Coronary Heart Disease; Nutrition of Sows and Boars; Writing and Presenting Scientific Papers.* **Castle Publications** TITLES *The Cricket Coach's Guide to Man Management; The Games Guide.*
Royalties paid twice-yearly.

O Books
See **John Hunt Publishing Ltd**

Oak
See **Omnibus Press**

Oberon Books
521 Caledonian Road, London N7 9RH
☎020 7607 3637 Fax 020 7607 3629
Email oberon.books@btinternet.com
Website www.oberonbooks.com
Publishing Director *James Hogan*
Managing Director *Charles D. Glanville*
A rapidly expanding company, Oberon *publishes* play texts (usually in conjunction with a production) and theatre books. *Specialises* in contemporary plays and translations of European classics. About 70 titles a year. IMPRINTS **Oberon Books; Absolute Classics**. Publishes over 250 writers and translators including Neil Bartlett, John Barton, Steven Berkoff, Ranjit Bolt, John Bowen, Howard Brenton, Ken Campbell, Andy de la Tour, Dario Fo, Trevor Griffiths, Sir Peter Hall, Christopher Hampton, Giles Havergal, Rolf Hochhuth, Bernard Kops, Ash Kotak, Henry Livings, Frederick Lonsdale, Robert David MacDonald, Adrian Mitchell, John Mortimer, Stephen Mulrine, Meredith Oakes, John Osborne, Philip Osment, Michael Pennington, David Pownall, Dennis Quilley, David Rudkin, Colin Teevan, Reza de Wet, John Whiting, Tennessee Williams, Charles Wood.

Octagon Press Ltd
PO Box 227, London N6 4EW
☎020 8348 9392 Fax 020 8341 5971
Website www.octagonpress.com
Managing Director *George R. Schrager*
Approx. Annual Turnover £100,000
FOUNDED 1972. *Publishes* philosophy, psychology, travel, Eastern religion, translations of Eastern classics and research monographs in series. 4–5 titles a year. Unsolicited material not welcome. Enquiries in writing only.
Royalties paid annually.

Octopus Publishing Group
2–4 Heron Quays, London E14 4JP
☎020 7531 8400 Fax 020 7531 8650
Website www.octopus-publishing.co.uk
Chief Executive *Derek Freeman*
Approx. Annual Turnover £45 million (Group)
Formed following a management buyout of Reed Consumer Books from Reed Elsevier plc in 1998. Bought by French publishers Hachette-Livre in 2001 and acquired Cassell Illustrated and the lists of Ward Lock and Blandford Press.

Conran Octopus
Fax 020 7531 8627
Email info-co@conran-octopus.co.uk
Website www.conran-octopus.co.uk
Editor *Lorraine Dickey* Quality illustrated lifestyle books, particularly interiors, design, cookery, gardening and crafts TITLES *The Essential House Book* Terence Conran; *Fork to Fork* Monty Don; *Passion for Seafood* Gordon Ramsey; *New Retail* Rasshied Din.

Hamlyn Octopus
Email info-ho@hamlyn.co.uk
Website www.hamlyn.co.uk
Managing Director *Alison Goff* Popular non-fiction, particularly cookery, gardening, craft, sport, health, film and music TITLES *Larousse Gastronomique; Hamlyn All Colour Cookbook;*

Hamlyn Book of Gardening; Hamlyn Book of DIY & Decorating.

Mitchell Beazley/Miller's
Fax 020 7537 0773
Email info-mb@mitchell-beazley.co.uk
Website www.mitchell-beazley.co.uk

Publisher/Managing Director *Jane Aspden* Quality illustrated reference books, particularly food and wine, gardening, interior design and architecture, antiques, general reference TITLES *Hugh Johnson's Pocket Wine Book; The New Joy of Sex; Miller's Antiques and Collectibles Price Guides.*

Philip's
Fax 020 7531 8460
Email george.philip@philips-maps.co.uk
Website www.philips-maps.co.uk

Managing Director *John Gaisford* World atlases, globes, astronomy, road atlases, encyclopaedias, thematic reference TITLES *Philip's Atlas of the World; Philip's Modern School Atlas; Philip's Guide to the Stars and Planets; Ordnance Survey Street Atlas; Philip's Navigator Road Atlas; Philip's Millennium Encyclopaedia; Philip's Atlas of World History.*

Brimax
Fax 020 7531 8607
Email brimax@brimax.octopus.co.uk
Managing Director *Des Higgins* Mass-market board and picture books for children, age groups 1–10.

Bounty
Fax 020 7531 8607
Email bountybooksinfo-bp@bountybooks.co.uk
Managing Director *Alison Goff* Bargain and promotional books. New, repackaged and reissued titles.

Cassell Illustrated
Fax 020 731 8624

Publishing Director *Polly Powell* Serious non-fiction covering a wide range of topics from history and cookery to fitness and art.

Digital Octopus
Fax 020 7537 0479

Managing Director *Ciaran Fenton* Digitally-formatted titles.

Octopus TV
Fax 020 7531 8469

Contact *Nicholas Price* Television programmes from Octopus publications.

Royalties paid twice-yearly/annually, according to contract in all divisions.

Oldcastle Books Ltd

18 Coleswood Road, Harpenden,
Hertfordshire AL5 1EQ
☎01582 761264   Fax 01582 761264
Email info@noexit.co.uk
Website www.noexit.co.uk *or*
  www.pocketessentials.com

Managing Director *Ion S. Mills*

FOUNDED 1985. *Publishes* crime/noir fiction, gambling non-fiction and 96pp mini-reference titles on film, ideas, history, music, etc. *No unsolicited mss.* Send synopses and ideas. IMPRINTS **No Exit Press** TITLES *Fierce Invalids Home from Hot Climates* Tom Robbins; *Mr Blue* Edward Bunker; **Oldcastle Books** TITLES *The Hand I Played* David Spanier; *Football Betting to Win* Jacques Black; **Pocketessentials** TITLES *Alfred Hitchcock; Vampire Films; Conspiracy Theories.*
Royalties paid twice-yearly.

Oldie Publications

65 Newman Street, London W1T 3EG
☎020 7436 8801   Fax 020 7436 8804
Website www.theoldie.co.uk

Chairman *Richard Ingrams*

FOUNDED in 1992. Book publishing arm of *The Oldie* magazine. *Publishes* compilations from the magazine, including cartoon books. TITLES *I Once Met; Dictionary For Our Time; The Fourth Oldie Annual; Jennifer's Diary: By One Fat Lady* Jennifer Paterson. No unsolicited mss; synopses and ideas (with return postage) welcome.

Michael O'Mara Books Ltd

9 Lion Yard, Tremadoc Road, London
SW4 7NQ
☎020 7720 8643   Fax 020 7627 8953
Email <firstname.lastname>
  @michaelomarabooks.com
Website www.mombooks.com

Chairman *Michael O'Mara*
Managing Director *Lesley O'Mara*
Approx. Annual Turnover £5 million

FOUNDED 1985. Independent publisher. *Publishes* general non-fiction, royalty, history, humour, children's novelties, anthologies and reference. TITLES *Diana: Her True Story* Andrew Morton; *Eye of the Storm* Peter Ratcliffe; the 'Little Book' series, including *WAN2TLK?.* IMPRINTS **Mary Ford Publications Ltd** Cake decorating; **Buster Books** Children's. Unsolicited mss, synopses and ideas for books welcome.
Royalties paid twice-yearly.

Authors' Rating Master of the art of creating bestsellers (think of *Diana: Her True Story* and

Posh & Becks), Michael O'Mara is looking to expand his humour list. But it is the oddball subjects that appeal to him. The text messaging bible, *WAN2TLK?*, which some others thought a crazy idea, has sold more than a million copies.

Omnibus Press

Music Sales Ltd, 8–9 Frith Street, London W1V 5TZ
☎020 7434 0066 Fax 020 7734 2246
Email chris.charlesworth@musicsales.co.uk
Website www.omnibuspress.com
Editorial Head *Chris Charlesworth*
FOUNDED 1971. Independent publisher of music books, rock and pop biographies, song sheets, educational tutors, cassettes, videos and software. IMPRINTS **Amsco; Bobcat; Oak; Omnibus; Wise Publications**. Unsolicited mss, synopses and ideas for books welcome.
Royalties paid twice-yearly.

Oneworld Publications

185 Banbury Road, Oxford OX2 7AR
☎01865 310597 Fax 01865 310598
Email info@oneworld-publications.com
Website www.oneworld-publications.com
Editorial Director *Juliet Mabey*
FOUNDED 1986. *Publishes* adult non-fiction across a range of subjects from world religions and social issues to psychology and philosophy. About 30 titles a year. SERIES include one on world religions (with authors such as Geoffrey Parrinder, Keith Ward, Klaus Klostermaier and John Hicks), concise encyclopedias on world religions and a series of short histories of countries. **One World Philosophers** series was launched in 2001. Lead TITLES for 2001: *God: A Guide For the Perplexed* Keith Ward; *The Koran: A Short Introduction* Farid Esack. No unsolicited mss; synopses and ideas welcome, but should be accompanied by s.a.e. for return of material and/or notification of receipt. No autobiographies, fiction, poetry or children's.
Royalties paid annually.

Onlywomen Press Ltd

40 St Lawrence Terrace, London W10 5ST
☎020 8354 0796 Fax 020 8960 2817
Email onlywomenpress@cs.com
Website www.onlywomenpress.com
Editorial Director *Lilian Mohin*
FOUNDED 1974. *Publishes* lesbian literature: fiction, poetry, literary criticism and political theory. Unsolicited mss and proposals welcome. Submissions must be accompanied by s.a.e. and explanatory letter.

OPC

See **Ian Allan Publishing Ltd**

Open Gate Press (incorporating Centaur Press 1954)

51 Achilles Road, London NW6 1DZ
☎020 7431 4391 Fax 020 7431 5129
Email books@opengatepress.co.uk
Managing Directors *Jeannie Cohen, Elisabeth Petersdorff*
FOUNDED in 1989 to provide a forum for psychoanalytic social and cultural studies. *Publishes* psychoanalysis, philosophy, social sciences, politics, literature, religion, animal rights, environment. SERIES *Psychoanalysis and Society*. Also publishes a journal of psychoanalytic social studies, *New Analysis*. IMPRINTS **Open Gate Press; Centaur Press; Linden Press**. Since the acquisition of Centaur Press, Open Gate Press is continuing its work, in particular the *Kinship Library* – a series on the philosophy, politics and application of humane education. No unsolicited mss.
Royalties paid twice-yearly.

Open University Press

Celtic Court, 22 Ballmoor, Buckingham, Buckinghamshire MK18 1XW
☎01280 823388 Fax 01280 823233
Email enquiries@openup.co.uk
Website www.openup.co.uk
Managing Director *John Skelton*
Approx. Annual Turnover £3 million
FOUNDED 1977 as an imprint independent of the Open University's course materials. *Publishes* academic and professional books in the fields of education, management, sociology, health studies, politics, psychology, women's studies. No economics or anthropology. Not interested in anything outside the social sciences. About 100 titles a year. No unsolicited mss; enquiries/proposals only.
Royalties paid annually.

Orbit

See **Time Warner Books UK**

Orchard Books

See **The Watts Publishing Group Ltd**

The Orion Publishing Group Limited

Orion House, 5 Upper St Martin's Lane, London WC2H 9EA
☎020 7240 3444 Fax 020 7240 4822
Chairman *Jean-Louis Lisimachio*

Chief Executive *Anthony Cheetham*
Group Managing Director *Peter Roche*
Approx. Annual Turnover £60 million

FOUNDED 1992 by Anthony Cheetham, Rosemary Cheetham and Peter Roche. Incorporates Weidenfeld & Nicolson, JM Dent, Chapmans Publishers and Cassell.

DIVISIONS

Orion Managing Director *Malcolm Edwards* IMPRINTS **Orion Fiction** Publishing Director *Jane Wood* Hardcover fiction; **Orion Media** Publishing Director *Trevor Dolby* Hardcover non-fiction; **Orion Children's** Managing Director *Judith Elliott* Children's fiction/non-fiction; **Gollancz** Editorial Directors *Simon Spanton, Jo Fletcher* Science fiction and fantasy.

 Weidenfeld & Nicolson Managing Director *Adrian Bourne* IMPRINTS **Weidenfeld Illustrated** Editor-in-Chief *Michael Dover* Illustrated non-fiction; **Weidenfeld General** Publishing Director *Richard Milner* General non-fiction and literary fiction; **Phoenix Press** Managing Director *Bing Taylor* History; **Cassell Reference** Publishing Director *Richard Milbank* General reference; **Cassell Military** Publishing Director *Ian Drury* Military non-fiction; **Custom Publishing** Managing Director *Mark Smith*.

 Paperback Division Managing Director *Susan Lamb* IMPRINTS **Orion; Phoenix; Everyman**.

Authors' Rating Nudging Transworld as the top publisher of paperback fast sellers, Orion wants to be up there with the lead players. Prospective bestseller writers take note. But niche publishing such as history (chiefly under the Weidenfeld imprint) is also likely to grow.

Osprey Publishing Ltd

Elms Court, Chapel Way, Botley, Oxford OX2 9LP
☎01865 727022 Fax 01865 727017/727019
Email info@ospreypublishing.com
Website www.ospreypublishing.com

Managing Director *William Shepherd*
Editor, Military/Military History *Jane Penrose*
Editor, Aviation *Tony Holmes*

Publishes illustrated history, military history and aviation from around the world; also bimonthly *Osprey Military Journal (OMJ)*. FOUNDED 1969, Osprey became independent from **Reed Elsevier** in February 1998. 130 titles in 2001.

 MILITARY SERIES *Order of Battle; Men-at-*

Arms; Elite; Campaign; New Vanguard; Warrior. HISTORY SERIES *Essential Histories.* AVIATION SERIES *Aircraft of the Aces; Combat Aircraft; Aviation Pioneers; Aviation Elites.* No unsolicited mss; synopses and ideas welcome.
 Royalties paid twice-yearly.

Peter Owen Ltd

73 Kenway Road, London SW5 0RE
☎020 7373 5628/7370 6093
Fax 020 7373 6760
Email admin@peterowen.com
Website www.peterowen.com

Chairman *Peter Owen*
Editorial Director *Antonia Owen*

FOUNDED 1951. *Publishes* biography, general non-fiction, English-language literary fiction and translations, history, literary criticism, the arts. 'No genre or children's fiction; the company only rarely takes on first novels.' AUTHORS Jane Bowles, Paul Bowles, Shusaku Endo, Anna Kavan, Jean Giono, Anaïs Nin, Jeremy Reed, Peter Vansittart. 35–40 titles a year. Unsolicited synopses welcome for non-fiction material; no highly illustrated books. Mss should be preceded by a descriptive letter and synopsis with s.a.e.
 Royalties paid twice-yearly. *Overseas associates* worldwide.

Authors' Rating Peter Owen has been described as 'a publisher of the old and idiosyncratic school'. He has seven Nobel prizewinners on his list to prove it.

Oxford University Press

Great Clarendon Street, Oxford OX2 6DP
☎01865 556767 Fax 01865 556646
Email enquiry@oup.co.uk
Website www.oup.co.uk

Chief Executive *Henry Reece*
Approx. Annual Turnover £375 million

A department of Oxford University, OUP started as the university's printing business and developed into a major publishing operation in the 19th century. *Publishes* academic works in all formats (print and online): dictionaries, lexical and non-lexical reference, scholarly journals, student texts, schoolbooks, ELT materials, music, bibles, paperbacks, and children's books. Around 6000 titles a year.

DIVISIONS

Academic *I.S. Asquith* Academic and higher education titles in major disciplines, dictionaries, non-lexical reference, journals and trade books. OUP welcomes first-class academic material in the form of proposals or accepted theses.

Education *K. Harris* National Curriculum courses and support materials as well as children's literature.
ELT *P.R. Mothersole* ELT courses and dictionaries for all levels.
Royalties paid twice-yearly. *Overseas branches/subsidiaries* Sister company in USA with branches or subsidiaries in Argentina, Australia, Brazil, Canada, China, East Africa, India, Japan, Malaysia, Mexico, Pakistan, Southern Africa, Spain and Turkey. Offices in Chile, France, Germany, Greece, Italy, New Zealand, Singapore, Taiwan, Thailand and Uruguay.

Authors' Rating After three outstanding years for turnover and profits, OUP is set to increase investment in new publishing. But much turns on market reaction to the *New Dictionary of National Biography*, one of the biggest projects of its kind in contemporary publishing. Following the acquisition of Blackstone Press, OUP now rivals Butterworths and Sweet & Maxwell as a leading law book publisher.

Palgrave
See **Macmillan Publishers Ltd**

Palm Tree Press
See **Kevin Mayhew Publishers**

G.J. Palmer & Sons Ltd
See **Hymns Ancient & Modern Ltd**

Pan
See **Macmillan Publishers Ltd**

Paragon Press Publishing/ Vista House Ltd
Paragon Press Publishing: Suite 676, 37 Store Street, London WC1W 7QF
☎020 7644 4816
Email editorial@paragonpress-publishing.com
Website www.paragonpress-publishing.com
Vista House Ltd: 27 Greenhead Road, Huddersfield, West Yorkshire HD1 4EN
☎01484 427200
Managing Editor/Paragon Press *Reggie Sharp*
Publishing Director/Vista House
H.L. Byram, Med, BA(Hons)
FOUNDED 1998. IMPRINTS **Paragon Fiction**; **Paragon Non-fiction**; **Paragon Children**; and **Paragon Summaries**, an educational series for secondary and tertiary education. Paragon Professional Services offers professional advice on all aspects of publishing and

writing. Initial enquiries by e-mail or telephone. Submission guidelines on the website. IMPRINTS **Vista House** Fiction and non-fiction; biography and memoirs. No children's. **Vista Originals** 'For first-time authors'.

Authors' Rating Liable to ask authors to contribute towards costs of publication.

Paragon Softcover Large Print
See **Chivers Press Ltd**

Paternoster Publishing
PO Box 300, Kingstown Broadway, Carlisle, Cumbria CA3 0QS
☎01228 554320 Fax 01228 593388
Website www.paternoster-publishing.com
Publishing Director *Mark Finnie*
Approx. Annual Turnover £2 million
A division of STL Ltd. IMPRINTS:

Paternoster Authentic Theology Editorial Controller *Jill Morris* FOUNDED 1936. *Publishes* academic, religion and learned/church/life-related journals. Over 80 titles a year. TITLES *Complete Short Works of J.I. Packer, All's Well* R.T. Kendall. **Authentic Lifestyle** Editorial Controller *Nancy Lush* FOUNDED 1966. *Publishes* Christian books on evangelism, discipleship and mission. About 30 titles a year. TITLES *Operation World* Patrick Johnstone; publishing for Spring Harvest, Evangelical Alliance, Keswick Convention, Icthus, Operation Christmas Child. Unsolicited mss, synopses and ideas for books welcome.
Royalties paid twice-yearly.

Pavilion Books Ltd
64 Brewery Road, London N7 9Nt
☎020 7697 3000 Fax 020 7697 3001
Email <firstinitialsurname>@chrysalisbooks.co.uk
Website www.pavilionbooks.co.uk
Publishing Director *Vivien James*
Acquired by **Chrysalis** in 2001. *Publishes* Illustrated books in biography, cookery, gardening, humour, art, interiors, music, sport and travel. Unsolicited mss not welcome. Ideas and synopses for non-fiction titles considered.
Royalties paid twice-yearly.

Pavilion Children's Books
Chrysalis Children's Books, 64 Brewery Road, London N7 9NT
☎020 7697 3000 Fax 020 7697 3003
Email pavilionchildrens@chrysalisbooks.co.uk
Website www.chrysalisbooks.co.uk

Managing Editor *Liz Flanagan*

Part of the children's division of **Chrysalis Books**. Fiction and non-fiction children's books with visual flair for ages 5–14 including picture and gift books. No unsolicited mss.

Pearson Education

Edinburgh Gate, Harlow, Essex CM20 2JE
☎01279 623623 Fax 01279 431059
Website www.pearsoned-ema.com

Contracts & Copyrights Department Manager *Brenda Gvozdanovic*

FOUNDED in 1998 following the merger of Addison Wesley Longman, Prentice Hall Europe, Financial Times Management and **Simon & Schuster**'s educational list. The biggest educational publisher in the world. *Publishes* for a range of curriculum subjects, including English language teaching for students at primary and secondary school level, college and university, as well as for professionals. All unsolicited mss should be addressed to the Manager, Contracts and Copyrights Department.

Royalties paid twice-yearly. *Overseas associates* worldwide.

Authors' Rating Authors should not worry overmuch about the downturn in press advertising and the fallout from the bursting of the dot.com bubble, both of which have hit hard at Pearson's wider media interests. The fact is, the book publishing divisions continue to do well. Penguin has its own *Writer's Handbook* rating but in education and business information, there are exciting prospects for doing more online. Pearson is now one of the world's largest education publishing companies.

Pegasus Elliot Mackenzie Publishers Ltd

Sheraton House, Castle Park, Cambridge CB3 0AX
☎01223 370012 Fax 01223 370040
Email editors@pegasuspublishers.com
Website www.pegasuspublishers.com

Senior Editor *D.W. Stern*
Editor *R. Sabir*

Publishes fiction and non-fiction, general interest, biography, autobiography, children's, history, humour, science fiction, poetry, travel, war, memoirs, crime and erotica, also Internet and E books. IMPRINTS **Vanguard Press**; **Nightingale Books**; **Chimera** TITLES *Virgins are in Short Supply* Kevin Laffan; *And Hitler Stopped Play* George Cooper; *The Green Berets*

in Korea Fred Hayhurst. Unsolicited mss, synopses and ideas considered if accompanied by return postage.

Royalties paid twice-yearly.

Authors' Rating Liable to ask authors to contribute to production costs.

Pen & Sword Books Ltd

47 Church Street, Barnsley, South Yorkshire S70 2AS
☎01226 734734 Fax 01226 734438
Email charles@pen-and-sword.co.uk
Website www.pen-and-sword.co.uk

Chairman *Sir Nicholas Hewitt*
Managing Director *Charles Hewitt*
Imprint Manager *Henry Wilson*

One of the leading military history publishers in the UK. *Publishes* non-fiction only, specialising in naval and aviation history, WW1, WW2, Napoleonic, autobiography and biography. Also publishes *Battleground* series for battlefield tourists. About 100 titles a year. IMPRINTS **Leo Cooper**; **Wharncliffe Publishing** (see entry). Unsolicited synopses and ideas welcome; no unsolicited mss.

Royalties paid twice-yearly.

Penguin Group (UK)

A Pearson Company, 80 Strand, London WC2R 0RL
☎020 7010 3000 Fax 020 7010 6060
Website www.penguin.co.uk

Group Chairman & Chief Exective *John Makinson*
CEO: Penguin UK, Dorling Kindersley Ltd *Anthony Forbes Watson*
Managing Director: Penguin *Helen Fraser*
Approx. Annual Turnover £121 million

Owned by Pearson plc. The world's best known book brand and for more than 60 years a leading publisher whose adult and children's lists include fiction, non-fiction, poetry, drama, classics, reference and special interest areas. Reprints and new work.

DIVISIONS
Penguin General Books Managing Director *Tom Weldon* Adult fiction and non-fiction is published in hardback under Michael Joseph, Viking and Hamish Hamilton imprints. Paperbacks come under the Penguin imprint. IMPRINTS **Viking/Penguin** Publisher *Juliet Annan* Publishing Director *Tony Lacey*; **Hamish Hamilton** Publishing Director *Simon Prosser*; **Michael Joseph/Penguin** Publishing

Director *Louise Moore*. Does not accept unsolicited mss.

Penguin Press Publishing Directors *Stuart Proffitt, Simon Winder, Stefan McGrath* Academic adult non-fiction, reference, specialist and classics. IMPRINTS **Allen Lane**; **Penguin Reference** Publishing Director *Nigel Wilcockson* No unsolicited mss.

Dorling Kindersley Ltd (see entry).

Frederick Warne Managing Director *Sally Floyer* Classic children's publishing and merchandising including *Beatrix Potter*™; *Flower Fairies*; *Orlando*. **Ventura** Publisher *Sally Floyer* Producer and packager of *Spot* titles by Eric Hill.

Ladybird (see **Dorling Kindersley Ltd**).

Puffin Managing Director *Francesca Dow* (poetry and picture books) Publishers *Rebecca McNally* (fiction), *Clare Hulton* (media and popular non-fiction). Leading children's paperback list, publishing in virtually all fields including fiction, non-fiction, poetry, picture books, media-related titles. No unsolicited mss; synopses and ideas welcome.

Penguin Audiobooks (see entry under **Audio Books**).

ePenguin Commissioning Editor *Jeremy Ettinghausen* e-books list launched in 2001.

Royalties paid twice-yearly. *Overseas associates* worldwide.

Authors' Rating An impressive range of best-sellers has done wonders for the Penguin profile which a few years ago was looking a bit sad. The challenge now is to make commercial sense of Dorling Kindersley, the illustrated books publisher bought by Penguin in 2000. DK is undoubtedly in better shape but its travel books have taken a dip and break-even is still some way off. Penguin has been praised by writers for raising royalty rates for heavily discounted sales of books in UK shops. Previously, when books were discounted at 50 per cent or more, Penguin, in line with other publishers, cut payments to authors to four-fifths of the full royalty. As from 2002, royalties will be reduced only when the discount reaches 52.5 per cent. The threshold for mass market paperbacks has been raised from 52.5 per cent to 55 per cent.

Peony Press
See **Anness Publishing Ltd**

PerfectBound
See **HarperCollins Publishers Ltd**

Pergamon Press
See **Elsevier Science Ltd**

Persephone Books
59 Lamb's Conduit Street, London
WC1N 3NB
☎020 7242 9292 Fax 020 7242 9272
Email sales@persephonebooks.co.uk
Website www.persephonebooks.co.uk
Managing Director *Nicola Beauman*

FOUNDED 1999. *Publishes* reprint fiction and non-fiction, mostly 'by women, for women and about women'. 8 titles a year. 2001 TITLES included *Family Roundabout* Richmal Crompton; *Little Boys Lost* Marghanita Laski; *The Making of a Marchioness* Frances Hodgson Burnett; *Kitchen Essays* Agnes Jekyll. No unsolicited material.

Royalties paid twice-yearly

Perseus Press/Public Affairs Ltd
PO Box 317, Oxford OX2 9RU
☎01865 860960 Fax 01865 862763
Email info@theperseuspress.com
Website www.theperseuspress.com *and*
www.publicaffairsbooks.com
President/CEO *Jack McKeown (US)*

UK subsidiary of the Perseus Books Group (see under **US Publishers**). *Publishes* general books. IMPRINTS **Perseus Press** *Don Fehr*; **Public Affairs Ltd** *Peter Osnos*. No unsolicited mss. Synopses and ideas welcome by e-mail or post.

Petroc Press
See **Librapharm Ltd**

Phaidon Press Limited
Regent's Wharf, All Saints Street, London
N1 9PA
☎020 7843 1000 Fax 020 7843 1010
Email <name>@phaidon.com
Website www.phaidon.com
Chairman/Publisher *Richard Schlagman*
Managing Director *Andrew Price*
Deputy Publisher *Amanda Renshaw*
Approx. Annual Turnover £18 million

Publishes quality books on the visual arts, including fine art, art history, architecture, design, photography, decorative arts, music and performing arts. Also producing videos. About 100 titles a year. DIVISIONS/SERIES (with Editorial Heads) **Architecture and Design** *Karen Stein*; **Art and Ideas Series** *Pat Barylski*; **Contemporary Art** *Gilda Williams*; **Art and Photography** *Amanda Renshaw*; **55 Series** *Kendall Clarke*; **Academic** *Bernard Dod*. Unsolicited mss welcome but 'only a small amount of unsolicited material gets published'.

Royalties paid twice-yearly.

Authors' Rating Ah, those seductive art books. The quality of illustrations is superb and since language is a minor barrier to sales, Phaidon is doing well on the Continent with subsidiaries in France and Germany.

Philip's
See **Octopus Publishing Group**

Phillimore & Co. Ltd
Shopwyke Manor Barn, Chichester, West Sussex PO20 6BG
☎01243 787636 Fax 01243 787639
Email bookshop@phillimore.co.uk
Website www.phillimore.co.uk
Chairman *Philip Harris*
Managing Director *Noel Osborne*
Approx. Annual Turnover £1.3 million
FOUNDED in 1897 by W.P.W. Phillimore, Victorian campaigner for local archive conservation in Chancery Lane, London. Became the country's leading publisher of historical source material and local histories. Somewhat dormant in the 1960s, it was revived by Philip Harris in 1968. *Publishes* British local and family history, including histories of institutions, buildings, villages, towns and counties, plus guides to research and writing in these fields. About 70 titles a year. No unsolicited mss; synopses/ideas welcome for local or family histories.' IMPRINT **Phillimore** *Noel Osborne* TITLES *Domesday Book; A History of Essex; Carlisle; The Haberdashers' Company; Channel Island Churches; Bolton Past; Warwickshire Country Houses.* *Royalties* paid annually.

Phoenix Press
See **The Orion Publishing Group Ltd**

Piatkus Books
5 Windmill Street, London W1T 2JA
☎020 7631 0710 Fax 020 7436 7137
Email info@piatkus.co.uk
Website www.piatkus.co.uk
Managing Director *Judy Piatkus*
Approx. Annual Turnover £5.7 million
FOUNDED 1979 by Judy Piatkus. The company is customer-led and is committed to publishing fiction, both commercial and literary, and non-fiction. *Specialises* in publishing books and authors 'who we feel enthusiastic and committed to as we like to build for long-term success as well as short-term!' *Publishes* fiction, biography and autobiography, health, mind, body and spirit, popular psychology, self-help, history, science, business and management, cook-

ery 'and other books that tempt us'. In 1996 launched a list of mass-market non-fiction and fiction titles. About 175 titles a year (70 of which are fiction).
DIVISIONS
Non-fiction *Gill Bailey* TITLES *Optimum Nutrition Bible* Patrick Holford; *Water Detox* Jane Scrivner; *One Last Time* John Edwards; *10 Day MBA* Steven Silbiger; *Bono* Laura Jackson. **Fiction** *Judy Piatkus* TITLES *Ex-Appeal* Zoë Barnes; *Big Trouble* Dave Barry; *The Villa* Nora Roberts; *Three Women* Marge Piercy; *Twisted Minds* Hilary Norman. Piatkus is expanding its range of books and welcomes synopses and first three chapters.
Royalties paid twice-yearly.

Authors' Rating 'Independent general publishing is alive and well and flourishing at Piatkus Books,' says Judy Piatkus, founder of the company. Authors praise an editorial team wedded to quality.

Pica Press
See **A.&C. Black (Publishers) Ltd**

Picador/Young Picador
See **Macmillan Publishers Ltd**

Piccadilly Press
5 Castle Road, London NW1 8PR
☎020 7267 4492 Fax 020 7267 4493
Email books@piccadillypress.co.uk
Website www.piccadillypress.co.uk
Publisher/Managing Director *Brenda Gardner*
Approx. Annual Turnover £1.1 million
FOUNDED 1983. Independent publisher of children's and parental books. 30 titles in 2001. Welcomes approaches from authors 'but we would like them to know the sort of books we do. It is frustrating to get inappropriate material. They should check in their local libraries, bookshops or look at our website. We will send a catalogue (please enclose s.a.e.).' No adult or cartoon-type material.
Royalties paid twice-yearly.

Pictorial Presentations
See **Souvenir Press Ltd**

Pimlico
See **Random House Group Ltd**

Pinter
See **The Continuum International Publishing Group Limited**

Pitkin
See **Jarrold Publishing**

Plenum Publishers/Plenum Press
See **Kluwer Academic/Plenum Publishers**

Pluto Press Ltd
345 Archway Road, London N6 5AA
☎020 8348 2724 Fax 020 8348 9133
Email pluto@plutobks.demon.co.uk
Website www.plutobooks.com
Managing Director *Roger Van Zwanenberg*
Publishing Director *Anne Beech*
FOUNDED 1970. Has developed a reputation for innovatory publishing in the field of non-fiction. *Publishes* academic and scholarly books across a range of subjects including cultural studies, politics and world affairs. About 60 titles a year. Key titles for 2001 included two studies of the Taliban and events in Afghanistan. Prospective authors are encouraged to consult the website for guidelines on submitting proposals.

Pocketessentials
See **Oldcastle Books Ltd**

Point
See **Scholastic Ltd**

The Policy Press
University of Bristol, 34 Tyndall's Park Road, Bristol BS8 1PY
☎0117 954 6800 Fax 0117 973 7308
Managing Director *Alison Shaw*
The Policy Press is a specialist publisher of policy studies. Material published, in the form of books, reports, practice guides and journals, is taken from research findings and provides critical discussion of policy initiatives and their impact, and also recommendations for policy change. 45–50 titles per year. No unsolicited mss; brief synopses and ideas welcome.

Politico's Publishing
8 Artillery Row, London SW1P 1RZ
☎020 7931 0090 Fax 020 7828 8111
Email publishing@politicos.co.uk
Website www.politicos.co.uk/publishing
Chairman *John Simmons*
Managing Director *Iain Dale*
Publishing Director *Sean Magee*
Approx. Annual Turnover £250,000
FOUNDED 1998. Sister company to Politico's Bookstore in Westminster. *Publishes* political

books. 27 titles in 2001. TITLES *In My Own Time* Jeremy Thorpe; *Cherie Blair* Linda McDougall; *Brief Encounters* Gyles Brandreth. Unsolicited mss, synopses and ideas welcome; telephone in the first instance.
Royalties paid annually.

Polity Press
65 Bridge Street, Cambridge CB2 1UR
☎01223 324315 Fax 01223 461385
Website www.polity.co.uk
FOUNDED 1984. All books are published in association with **Blackwell Publishers**. *Publishes* archaeology and anthropology, criminology, economics, feminism, general interest, history, human geography, literature, media and cultural studies, medicine and society, philosophy, politics, psychology, religion and theology, social and political theory, sociology. Unsolicited synopses and ideas for books welcome.
Royalties paid annually.

Polygon/Polygon@Edinburgh
See **Edinburgh University Press**

Pont Books
See **Gomer Press**

Pop Universal
See **Souvenir Press Ltd**

Portland Press Ltd
59 Portland Place, London W1B 1QW
☎020 7580 5530 Fax 020 7323 1136
Email editorial@portlandpress.com
Website www.portlandpress.com
Chairman *Professor A.J. Turner*
Managing Director *Rhonda Oliver*
Managing Editor *Pauline Starley*
Approx. Annual Turnover £2.5 million
FOUNDED 1990 to expand the publishing activities of the Biochemical Society (1911). *Publishes* biochemisty and medicine for graduate, post-graduate and research students. Expanding the list to include schools and general readership. 5 titles in 2001. TITLES *Neuronal Signal Transduction and Alzheimer's Disease; Virtual University?; Educational Environments for the Future.* Unsolicited mss, synopses and ideas welcome. No fiction.
Royalties paid twice-yearly.

Prentice Hall
See **Pearson Education**

Prestel Publishing Limited
4 Bloomsbury Place, London WC1A 2QA
☎020 7323 5004 Fax 020 7636 8004
Email sales@prestel-uk.co.uk
Website www.prestel.com
Chairman *Jürgen Tesch*
FOUNDED 1924. *Publishes* art, architecture, photography, children's and general illustrated books. No fiction. Unsolicited mss, synopses and ideas welcome. Approach by post or e-mail.

Princeton University Press
See **University Presses of California, Columbia & Princeton Ltd**

Prion Books Ltd
Imperial Works, Perren Street, London NW5 3ED
☎020 7482 4248 Fax 020 7482 4203
Managing Director *Barry Winkleman*
Editorial Director *Karen Ball*
Formerly a packaging operation, began publishing under the Prion imprint in 1987. *Publishes* non-fiction: humour, popular culture, historical and literary reprints, beauty, food and drink, sex, psychology and health. About 40 titles a year. Unsolicited mss, synopses and ideas welcome only with s.a.e. and *not* by e-mail.
Royalties paid twice-yearly.

Profile Books
58A Hatton Gardens, London EC1N 8LX
☎020 7404 3001 Fax 020 7404 3003
Email info@profilebooks.co.uk
Website www.profilebooks.co.uk
Managing Director *Andrew Franklin*
Approx. Annual Turnover £2 million
FOUNDED 1996. *Publishes* serious nonfiction including current affairs, history, politics, psychology, cultural criticism, business and management. Winner of the **Sunday Times Small Publisher of the Year Award** 1999/2000. AUTHORS include Alan Bennett, J.M. Coetzee, Francis Fukuyama and Peter Nichols.
IMPRINTS **Profile Books** *Andrew Franklin*; **Economist Books** *Stephen Brough*. No unsolicited mss.
Royalties paid twice-yearly.

Authors' Rating Profile has achieved impressive growth while maintaining author-friendly relations.

Psychology Press
See **Taylor & Francis Group plc**

Public Affairs Ltd
See **Perseus Press**

Public Record Office Publications
Public Record Office, Kew, Surrey TW9 4DU
☎020 8392 5271 Fax 020 8392 5266
Email jane.crompton@pro.gov.uk
Website www.pro.gov.uk
Publishing Manager *Jane Crompton*
Publishes books, guides and document packs relating to the thousand years of historical records held in the National Archives. Specialist areas: family history and military history. TITLES *Immigrants and Expats* Roger Kershaw; *Garbo: The Spy Who Saved D-Day*; *Oscar Wilde: Trial and Punishment*; *The Records of the Foreign Office 1782–1968* Michael Roper. Also publishes *Ancestors*, a bi-monthly subscription magazine of family history.

Publishing House
Trinity Place, Barnstaple, Devon EX32 9HJ
☎01271 328892 Fax 01271 328768
Email publishinghouse@vernoncoleman.com
Website www.vernoncoleman.com
Managing Director *Vernon Coleman*
Editorial Head *Sue Ward*
Approx. Annual Turnover £750,000
FOUNDED 1989. Self-publisher of fiction, health, humour, animals, politics. Over 60 books published. TITLES *Bodypower; Bilbury Chronicles; Second Innings; It's Never Too Late; How to Publish Your Own Book* all by Vernon Coleman. No submissions.

Puffin
See **Penguin Group (UK)**

Pushkin Press Ltd
123 Biddulph Mansions, Elgin Avenue, London W9 1HU
☎020 7266 9136 Fax 020 7266 9136
Email petra@pushkinpress.com
Website www.pushkinpress.com
Chairman *Melissa Ulfane*
Editorial Head *Diana Di Carcaci*
Contact *Petra Howard-Wuerz*
Approx. Annual Turnover £250,000
Publishes novels and essays in translation drawn from the best of classic and contemporary European literature.
Royalties paid twice-yearly.

Putnam Aeronautical Books
See **Brassey's**

Quadrille Publishing Ltd
Alhambra House, 27–31 Charing Cross Road, London WC2H 0LS
☎020 7839 7117 Fax 020 7839 7118
Chairman *Sue Thomson*
Managing Director *Alison Cathie*
Editorial Director *Jane O'Shea*

FOUNDED in 1994 by four ex-directors of Conran Octopus, with a view to producing a small list of top-quality illustrated books. *Publishes* non-fiction, including cookery, gardening, interior design and decoration, craft, health. 26 titles in 2002. TITLES *Think Pink* Tricia Guild; *RHS Colour Your Garden* Jill Billington; *The Diet Bible* Judith Wills. Synopses and ideas for books welcome. No fiction or children's books.
Royalties paid twice-yearly.

Quantum
See **Foulsham Publishers**

Quartet Books
27 Goodge Street, London W1T 2LD
☎020 7636 3992 Fax 020 7637 1866
Chairman *Naim Attallah*
Managing Director *Jeremy Beale*
Publishing Director *Stella Kane*
Approx. Annual Turnover £1 million

FOUNDED 1972. Independent publisher. *Publishes* contemporary literary fiction including translations, popular culture, biography, music, history, politics and some photographic books. Unsolicited sample chapters with return postage welcome; no poetry, romance or science fiction. Submissions by disk or e-mail are not accepted.
Royalties paid twice-yearly.

Queen Anne Press
See **Lennard Associates Ltd**

Quiller Press (An imprint of Quiller Publishing Ltd)
Wykey House, Wykey, Shrewsbury, Shropshire SY4 1JA
☎01939 261616 Fax 01939 261606
Email info@quillerbooks.com
Managing Director *Andrew Johnston*

Specialises in sponsored books and publications sold through non-book trade channels as well as bookshops. *Publishes* architecture, biography, business and industry, collecting, cookery, DIY, gardening, guidebooks, humour, reference, sports, travel, wine and spirits. About 10

titles a year. TITLES *Camper and Nicholson* Ian Dear; *Great British Food* Heather Hay Ffrench; *The Dunlop Slazenger Story* Brian Simpson. Most ideas originate in-house; unsolicited mss only if the author sees some potential for sponsorship or guaranteed sales.
Royalties paid twice-yearly.

Radcliffe Medical Press Ltd
18 Marcham Road, Abingdon, Oxfordshire OX14 1AA
☎01235 528820 Fax 01235 528830
Email contact.us@radcliffemed.com
Website www.radcliffe-oxford.com
Managing Director *Andrew Bax*
Editorial Director *Gillian Nineham*
Approx. Annual Turnover £1.5 million

FOUNDED 1987. Medical publishers which began by specialising in books for general practice and health service management. *Publishes* clinical, management, health policy books, training materials and CD-ROMs. 80 titles in 2000. Unsolicited mss, synopses and ideas welcome. No non-medical or medical books aimed at lay audience.
Royalties paid twice-yearly.

Radcliffe Press
See **I.B. Tauris & Co. Ltd**

Ramboro Books
See **Chrysalis Books Ltd**

The Ramsay Head Press
9 Glenisla Gardens, Edinburgh EH9 2HR
☎0131 662 1915 Fax 0131 662 1915
Email conrad.wilson@genie.co.uk
Managing Director *Conrad Wilson*

FOUNDED 1968 by Norman Wilson, OBE. A small independent family publisher. *Publishes* biography, cookery, Scottish fiction and non-fiction, plus the biannual literary magazine *InScotland*. About 3–4 titles a year. TITLES *When It Works It Feels Like Play* Tessa Ransford; *Interesting Times, Poetry by David Simpson*. Synopses and ideas for books of Scottish interest welcome.
Royalties paid twice-yearly.

The Random House Group Ltd
Random House, 20 Vauxhall Bridge Road, London SW1V 2SA
☎020 7840 8400 Fax 020 7233 6058
Email enquiries@randomhouse.co.uk
Website www.randomhouse.co.uk
Chief Executive/Chairman *Gail Rebuck*

Deputy Chairman *Simon Master*
Managing Director *Ian Hudson*

Random's increasing focus on trade publishing, both here and in the US, has been well rewarded, with sales continuing to grow over the last year. Random House Group Ltd is the parent company of three separate publishing divisions and of **Transworld** (see entry). The three divisions are: General Books, the Group's largest publishing division; Children's Books, and Ebury Press. General Books is divided into two operating groups, allowing hardcover editors to see their books through to publication in paperback. The literary imprints Jonathan Cape, Secker & Warburg, Yellow Jersey Press and Chatto & Windus work side by side with paperback imprints Vintage and Pimlico to form one group; trade imprints Century, William Heinemann and Hutchinson go hand-in-hand with Arrow to form the other group. Acquired The Harvill Press in March 2002.

IMPRINTS

Jonathan Cape Ltd ☎020 7840 8576 Fax 020 7233 6117 Publishing Director *Dan Franklin* Biography and memoirs, current affairs, fiction, history, photography, poetry, politics and travel. IMPRINT **Yellow Jersey**.

Secker & Warburg ☎020 7840 8649 Fax 020 7233 6117 Editorial Director *Geoff Mulligan* Principally literary fiction with some non-fiction.

Chatto & Windus Ltd ☎020 7840 8522 Fax 020 7233 6117 Publishing Director *Alison Samuel* Art, belles-lettres, biography and memoirs, current affairs, essays, fiction, history, poetry, politics, philosophy, translations and travel.

Century (including **Business Books**) ☎020 7840 8555 Fax 020 7233 6127 Publisher *Kate Parkin*, Publishing Director Non-fiction *Mark Booth* General fiction and non-fiction, plus business management, advertising, communication, marketing, selling, investment and financial titles.

The Harvill Press (see entry).

William Heinemann ☎020 7840 8400 Fax 020 7233 6127 Publishing Director Non-fiction *Ravi Mirchandani* Publishing Director Fiction *Kirsty Fowkes* General non-fiction and fiction, especially history, biography, science, crime, thrillers and women's fiction.

Hutchinson ☎020 7840 8564 Fax 020 7233 7870 Publishing Director *Sue Freestone* General fiction and non-fiction including notably belles-lettres, current affairs, politics, travel and history.

Arrow ☎020 7840 8516 Fax 020 7233 6127 Publishing Director *Andy McKillop* Mass-market paperback fiction and non-fiction.

Pimlico ☎020 7840 8630 Fax 020 7233 6117 Publishing Director *Will Sulkin* Large-format quality paperbacks in the fields of history, biography, popular culture and literature.

Vintage ☎020 7840 8531 Fax 020 7233 6127 Publisher *Caroline Michel* Quality paperback fiction and non-fiction. Vintage was founded in 1990 and has been described as one of the 'greatest literary success stories in recent British publishing'.

Random House Children's Books (at Transworld Publishers, 61–63 Uxbridge Road, London W5 5SA ☎020 8231 6800 Fax 020 8231 6767) Managing Director *Philippa Dickinson* IMPRINTS **Hutchinson** Publishing Director *Caroline Roberts*; **Jonathan Cape** Publishing Director *Tom Maschler*; **The Bodley Head**; **Hutchinson**; **Doubleday** Fiction Publisher *Penny Walker*; **David Fickling Books** Publishing Director *David Fickling*, Fiction Publisher *Annie Eaton*; **Corgi**; **Red Fox**.

Ebury Press ☎020 7840 8400 Fax 020 7840 8406 Publisher *Fiona MacIntyre* IMPRINTS **Ebury Press**; **Vermilion**; **Fodor's**. Art, antiques, biography, Buddhism, cookery, gardening, health and beauty, homes and interiors, personal development, spirituality, travel and guides, sport, TV tie-ins. About 150 titles a year. Unsolicited mss, synopses and ideas for books welcome.

Royalties paid twice-yearly for the most part.

Authors' Rating Random House is tops, at least in terms of UK book sales. The publisher claims just over 14 per cent of the market – well ahead of HarperCollins and Penguin. In less than a decade, this high-powered publisher has quadrupled turnover and made profits healthy enough to invest in an impressive range of new writers. Synopses and manuscripts may be passed on to freelance readers, but there is reasonable assurance that they are at least read.

Ransom Publishing Ltd

Ransom House, Unit 1, Brook Street, Watlington, Oxfordshire OX49 5PP
☎01491 613711 Fax 01491 613733
Email ransom@ransompublishing.co.uk
Website www.ransom.co.uk

Managing Director *Jenny Ertle*

FOUNDED 1995 by ex-McGraw-Hill publisher. Partnerships formed with, among others, Channel 4 and the ICL. *Publishes* educational and consumer multimedia, study packs and children's books. Over 40 CD-ROMs, most with educational support packs. TITLES include *The Early Learning* series; *The Little Monsters* series; *Whale of a Tale* series including maths, science, language and geography; *Tom Paint; The Castle Under Siege; The History of the Universe; The History of Life; Rivers* plus natural history CD-ROMs.

Reader's Digest Association Ltd

11 Westferry Circus, Canary Wharf, London E14 4HE
☎020 7715 8000 Fax 020 7715 8181
Email gbeditorial@readersdigest.co.uk
Website www.readersdigest.co.uk
Managing Director *Andrew Lynam-Smith*
Editorial Head *Cortina Butler*

Editorial office in the USA (see entry under **US Publishers**). *Publishes* gardening, natural history, cookery, history, DIY, travel and word books. About 20 titles a year.

Reaktion Books

79 Farringdon Road, London EC1M 3JU
☎020 7404 9930 Fax 020 7404 9931
Email info@reaktionbooks.co.uk
Website www.reaktionbooks.co.uk
Managing Director *Michael R. Leaman*

FOUNDED in Edinburgh in 1985, moved to London in 1987. *Publishes* art history, architecture, Asian studies, cultural studies, design, film, geography, history, photography and travel writing. About 30 titles a year. TITLES *Zoo: A History of Zoological Gardens in the West* Eric Baratay and Elisabeth Hardouin-Fugier; *Activism!: Direct Action, Hacktivism and the Future of Society* Tim Jordan; *Autopia: Cars and Culture* eds. Joe Kerr and Peter Wollen. No unsolicited mss; synopses and ideas welcome.
Royalties paid twice-yearly.

Reardon Publishing

56 Upper Norwood Street, Leckhampton, Cheltenham, Gloucestershire GL53 0DU
☎01242 231800
Website www.reardon.co.uk
Managing Editor *Nicholas Reardon*

FOUNDED in the mid 1970s. Family-run publishing house specialising in local interest and tourism in the Cotswold area. Member of the **Outdoor Writers Guild**. *Publishes* walking and driving guides, and family history for societies. 10 titles a year. TITLES *The Cotswold Way* (video); *The Cotswold Way Map; Cotswold Walkabout; Cotswold Driveabout; The Donnington Way; The Haunted Cotswolds*. Unsolicited mss, synopses and ideas welcome with return postage only. Also

distributes for other publishers such as Ordnance Survey.
Royalties paid twice-yearly.

Red Dress Ink™

See **Harlequin Mills & Boon Ltd**

Red Fox

See **Random House Group Ltd**

William Reed Directories

Broadfield Park, Crawley, West Sussex RH11 9RT
☎01293 613400 Fax 01293 610322
Email directories@william-reed.co.uk
Website www.william-reed.co.uk

Editorial Manager *Sulann Staniford*

William Reed Directories, a division of William Reed Publishing, was ESTABLISHED in 1990. Its portfolio includes 13 titles covering the food, drink, non-food, catering, retail and export industries. The titles are produced as directories, market research reports, exhibition catalogues and electronic publishing.

Reed Educational & Professional Publishing

Halley Court, Jordan Hill, Oxford OX2 8EJ
☎01865 311366 Fax 01865 314641
Website www.repp.co.uk

Chief Executive *John Philbin*

A member of the **Reed Elsevier plc** group, REPP incorporates Heinemann Educational, Ginn and Butterworth-Heinemann in the UK; Greenwood Heinemann and Rigby in the USA; Rigby Heinemann in Australia.

Heinemann Educational Fax 01865 314140 Managing Director *Bob Osborne*, Primary *Paul Shuter*, Secondary *Kay Symons*. Textbooks/literature/other educational resources for primary and secondary school and further education. Mss, synopses and ideas welcome.

Ginn & Co Fax 01865 314189 Managing Director *Paul Shuter*, Editorial Director *Jill Duffy*. Textbook/other educational resources for primary and secondary schools.

Butterworth-Heinemann International Linacre House, Jordan Hill, Oxford OX2 8EJ ☎01865 310366 Fax 01865 314541 Managing Director *Philip Shaw*, Engineering & Technology *Neil Warnock-Smith*, Business *Kathryn Grant*. Books and electronic products across business, technical and open-learning fields for students and professionals.
Royalties paid twice-yearly/annually, according to contract in all divisions.

Reed Elsevier plc

25 Victoria Street, London SW1H 0EX
☎020 7222 8420   Fax 020 7227 5799
Website www.reedelsevier.com
Also at: 125 Park Avenue, 23rd Floor, New
York, NY 10017, USA
☎001 212 309 5498 Fax 001 212 309 5480
Sara Burgerhartstraat 25, 1055 KV
Amsterdam, The Netherlands
☎00 31 20 485 2434

Chief Executive Officer (UK) *Crispin Davis*

Reed Elsevier plc is a world-leading publisher
and information provider, operating in four
core segments: science and medical, legal, education, business.

DIVISIONS **Reed Educational & Professional Publishing** (see entry); **Elsevier
Science** (see entry); **Butterworths** Halsbury
House, 35 Chancery Lane, London WC2A 1EL
☎020 7400 2500 Fax 020 7400 2842 *Publishes*
legal and accountancy textbooks, journals, law
reports, CD-ROMs and online services; **Lexis-
Nexis**; **Harcourt School Publishers** (see
entry under **US Publishers**); **Reed Business**
Quadrant House, The Quadrant, Sutton, Surrey
SM2 5AS ☎020 8652 3500.

Authors' Rating Radical restructuring has
given Reed Elsevier a new zest for commercial
life with legal, business and scientific publishing
all doing better than might have been expected
in a tight market. Reed Elsevier is investing
heavily in its online business. Education has
benefited from the acquisition of US publisher
Harcourt.

Regency House Publishing Limited

3 Mill Lane, Broxbourne, Hertfordshire
EN10 7AZ
☎01992 479988   Fax 01992 479966
Email regencyhouse@btinternet.com

Chairman *Brian Trodd*
Managing Director *Nicolette Trodd*
Approx. Annual Turnover £1 million

FOUNDED 1991. Publisher and packager of
mass-market non-fiction. No fiction. No
unsolicited material.
Royalties paid twice-yearly.

Reinhardt Books Ltd

Flat 2, 43 Onslow Square, London SW7 3LR
☎020 7589 3751

Chairman/Managing Director *Max
Reinhardt*
Director *Joan Reinhardt*

FOUNDED in 1887 as H.F.L. (Publishers), it was
acquired by Max Reinhardt in 1947, changing
its name to the present one in 1987. First publication under the new name was Graham
Greene's *The Captain and the Enemy*. Also publishes under the **Nonesuch Press** imprint.
AUTHORS include Mitsumasa Anno, Alistair
Cooke and Maurice Sendak. New books are
no longer considered.
Royalties paid according to contract.

Religious & Moral Educational Press (RMEP)
See **Hymns Ancient & Modern Ltd**

Research Disclosure
See **Kenneth Mason Publications Ltd**

Review
See **Hodder Headline Ltd**

Richmond House Publishing Company Ltd

Douglas House, 3 Richmond Buildings,
London W10 3HE
☎020 7437 9556   Fax 020 7287 3463
Email sales@rhpco.co.uk
Website www.rhpco.co.uk

Managing Directors *Gloria Gordon,
Spencer Block*

Publishes directories for the theatre and entertainment industries. TITLES *British Theatre
Directory 2002*; *Artistes and Agents 2002*; *London
Seating Plan Guide*. Synopses and ideas welcome.

Right Way/Right Way Plus
See **Elliot Right Way Books**

Robinson Publishing Ltd
See **Constable & Robinson Ltd**

Robson Books

64 Brewery Road, London N7 9NT
☎020 7697 3000   Fax 020 7697 3007
Email robson@chrysalisbooks.co.uk
Website www.chrysalisbooks.co.uk

Publisher *Jeremy Robson*
Senior Editor *Joanne Brooks*

FOUNDED 1973. Part of **Chrysalis**. *Publishes*
general non-fiction, including biography, cookery, gardening, guidebooks, health and beauty,
humour, travel, sports and games. About 70 titles
a year. Unsolicited synopses and ideas for books
welcome (s.a.e. essential for reply).
Royalties paid twice-yearly.

RotoVision

Sheridan House, 112/116A Western Road,
Hove, East Sussex BN3 1DD
☎01273 727268 Fax 01273 727269
Website www.rotovision.com

Managing Director *Ken Fund*
Publisher *Aidan Walker*

FOUNDED 1996. Rapidly-expanding visual arts publishers with a strong emphasis on education and inspiration. *Publishes* graphic design, photography, web design, advertising, film, architecture, practical art, lighting design, interiors, product design, packaging design. 38 titles in 2001. TITLES *Animation: 2D and Beyond* Jane Pilling; *Stage Design* Tony Davis; *No-Copy Advertising* Lazar Dzamic; *Colour for Websites* Molly Holzschlag. No unsolicited mss; written synopses and ideas welcome; no phone calls, please. No academic or fiction.
Flat fee paid.

Round Hall

See **Sweet & Maxwell Group**

Roundhouse Publishing Group

Millstone, Limers Lane, Northam, North Devon EX39 2RG
☎01237 474474 Fax 01237 474774
Email roundhouse.group@ukgateway.net

Editorial Head *Alan Goodworth*

ESTABLISHED 1991. *Publishes* cinema and media-related titles. TITLES *Cinema of Oliver Stone; Cinema of Stanley Kubrick; Cinema of Martin Scorsese; Italian Cinema.* Represents and distributes a broad range of non-fiction publishing houses throughout the UK and Europe. No unsolicited mss.
Royalties paid twice-yearly.

Routledge

11 New Fetter Lane, London EC4P 4EE
☎020 7583 9855 Fax 020 7842 2298
Website www.routledge.com

Managing Director *Roger Horton*
Publishing Directors *Claire L'Enfant, Alan Jarvis, Mary MacInnes*
Approx. Annual Turnover £35.5 million (Group)

Routledge was formed in 1987 through an amalgamation of Routledge & Kegan Paul, Methuen & Co., Tavistock Publications, and Croom Helm. Subsequent acquisitions include the Unwin Hyman academic list from **HarperCollins** (1991), *Who's Who* and historical atlases from **Dent/Orion** (1994), archaeology and ancient history titles from **Batsford** (1996), and the E & FN Spon imprint from ITP Science (1997). In 1998, Routledge became a subsidiary of **Taylor & Francis Group plc** (see entry). In 2001 Curzon Press combined with the imprint to form **Routledge Curzon** for Asian studies.

Publishes academic and professional books and journals in the social sciences, humanities, health sciences and the built environment for the international market. Subjects: addiction, anthropology, archaeology, architecture, Asian studies, biblical studies, the built environment, business and management, civil engineering, classics, heritage, construction, counselling, criminology, development and environment, dictionaries, economics, education, environmental engineering, geography, health, history, Japanese studies, journals, language, leisure studies and leisure management, linguistics, literary criticism, media and culture, Middle East, nursing, philosophy, politics, political economy, psychiatry, psychology, reference, social administration, social studies and sociology, therapy, theatre and performance studies, women's studies. No poetry, fiction, travel or astrology. About 900 titles a year. Send synopses with sample chapter and c.v. rather than complete mss.

Royalties paid annually and twice-yearly, according to contract.

Ryland Peters and Small Limited

Kirkman House, 12–14 Whitfield Street,
London W1T 2RP
☎020 7436 9090 Fax 020 7436 9790
Email info@rps.co.uk
Website www.rylandpeters.com

Managing Director *David Peters*
Publishing Director *Alison Starling*

FOUNDED 1996. *Publishes* highly illustrated lifestyle books aimed at an international market, covering gardening, cookery, interior design. No fiction. No unsolicited mss; synopses and ideas welcome.
Royalties paid twice-yearly.

Sage Publications

6 Bonhill Street, London EC2A 4PU
☎020 7374 0645 Fax 020 7374 8741
Website www.sagepub.co.uk

Managing Director *Stephen Barr*
Editorial Director *Ziyad Marar*

FOUNDED 1971. *Publishes* academic books and journals in humanities and the social sciences. Bought academic and professional books publisher Paul Chapman Publishing Ltd in 1998.
Royalties paid twice-yearly.

Saint Andrew Press

Church of Scotland, 121 George Street,
Edinburgh EH2 4YN
☎0131 225 5722 Fax 0131 220 3113
Email cofs.standrew@dial.pipex.com
Website www.standrewpress.com *or*
www.williambarclay.org
Head of Publishing *Ann Crawford*
Approx. Annual Turnover £225,000

FOUNDED in 1954. Owned by the Church of
Scotland. *Publishes* religious, Scottish environmental and children's books aimed at the
Christian retail market in the UK and internationally. About 20 titles a year. Lead titles in
2001 included six *New Daily Study Bible* volumes
by William Barclay (revised and updated, the
series has sold over 10 million copies worldwide); *Walking in Darkness and Light* Kathy
Galloway; *The Dream and the Grace* James Aitken.
'Saint Andrew Press is expanding and is actively
seeking high-quality writing that is thought-provoking and, above all, helps readers to wrestle
with the complexities of life today.' No unsolicited mss but proposals very welcome in synopsis form. Please approach in writing.
Royalties paid annually.

St David's Press

See **Ashley Drake Publishing Ltd**

St Pauls Publishing

187 Battersea Bridge Road, London
SW11 3AS
☎020 7978 4300 Fax 020 7978 4370
Email editions@stpauls.org.uk
Publisher *Andrew Pudussery*

Publishing division of the Society of St Paul.
Began publishing in 1914 but activities were
fairly limited until around 1948. *Publishes* religious material mainly: theology, scripture,
catechetics, prayer books, children's material
and biography. Unsolicited mss, synopses and
ideas welcome. About 30 titles a year.

Salamander Books Ltd

64 Brewery Road, London N7 9NT
☎020 7697 3000 Fax 020 7697 3010
Email salamander@chrysalisbooks.co.uk
Website www.salamanderbooks.com
Publisher *Colin Goer*
Editorial Director *Charlotte Davies*

FOUNDED 1973. Part of **Chrysalis**. *Publishes*
colour illustrated books on collecting, cookery,
interiors, gardening, music, crafts, military, aviation, pet care, sport and transport. About 60 titles

a year. No unsolicited mss but synopses and ideas
for the above subjects welcome.
Royalties Outright fee paid instead of royalties.

Sangam Books Ltd

57 London Fruit Exchange, Brushfield Street,
London E1 6EP
☎020 7377 6399 Fax 020 7375 1230
Email sangambks@aol.com
Executive Director *Anthony de Souza*

Traditionally an educational publisher of school
and college level textbooks. Also *publishes* art,
India, medicine, science, technology, social sciences, religion, plus some fiction in paperback.

Saqi Books

26 Westbourne Grove, London W2 5RH
☎020 7221 9347 Fax 020 7229 7492
Email saqibooks@dial.pipex.com
Website www.saqibooks.com
Chairman/Managing Director *André Gaspard*

FOUNDED 1981, initially as a specialist publisher
of books on the Middle East and Arab world but
now includes Central Asia, South Asia and
European fiction. *Publishes* fiction and non-
fiction – academic and illustrated. 20 titles in
2001. Welcomes unsolicited material; approach
by post or e-mail.
Royalties paid annually.

W.B. Saunders

See **Harcourt Publishers International**

Savitri Books Ltd

See entry under **UK Packagers**

SB Publications

19 Grove Road, Seaford, East Sussex
BN25 1TP
☎01323 893498 Fax 01323 893860
Email sales@sbpublications.swinternet.co.uk
Website www.sbpublications.swinternet.co.uk
Owner *Mrs Lindsay Woods*

FOUNDED 1987. *Specialises* in local history,
including themes illustrated by old picture postcards and photographs; also travel, guides (town,
walking), maritime history and railways. 25 titles
a year. IMPRINTS **Historic Military Press**; **Ben
Gunn** TITLES *Lewes Then and Now*; *Curiosities of
East Sussex*; *A Dorset Quiz Book*; *On Foot on the
East Sussex Downs*. Also provides marketing and
distribution services for local authors.
Royalties paid annually.

Sceptre

See **Hodder Headline Ltd**

Scholastic Ltd

Villiers House, Clarendon Avenue,
Leamington Spa, Warwickshire CV32 5PR
☎01926 887799   Fax 01926 883331
Website www.scholastic.co.uk

Chairman M.R. Robinson
Managing Director David Kewley
Approx. Annual Turnover £42 million

FOUNDED 1964. Owned by US parent company. *Publishes* children's fiction and non-fiction and education for primary schools.

DIVISIONS
Scholastic Children's Books Richard Scrivener Commonwealth House, 1–19 New Oxford Street, London WC1A 1NU ☎020 7421 9000 Fax 020 7421 9001 IMPRINTS **Scholastic Press** (hardbacks); **Hippo** (paperbacks); **Point** (paperbacks) TITLES *Horrible Histories; Goosebumps; Point Horror; His Dark Materials* trilogy by Philip Pullman.

Educational Publishing Anne Peel (Villiers House address) Professional books and classroom materials for primary teachers, plus magazines such as *Child Education, Junior Education, Junior Focus, Infant Projects, Nursery Education; Literacy Time, Numeracy Time.*

Red House Book Clubs Mike Crossley, Victoria Birkett Cotswold Business Park, Witney, Oxford OX8 5YT ☎01993 893456 Fax 01993 776813 The Book Club group sells to families at home through The Red House Book Club, through Scholastic School Book Clubs (five different clubs catering for children from 4–15), and through the Red House International Schools Club.

School Book Fairs Mike Robinson The Book Fair Division sells directly to children, parents and teachers in schools through 27,000 week-long book events held in schools throughout the UK.
Royalties paid twice-yearly.

Authors' Rating Another beneficiary of the Harry Potter phenomenon (via its children's book clubs), Scholastic also leads the intellectual sector of children's publishing with Philip Pullman who, by any literary standards, takes some beating. Fiction for 8 to 12-year-olds is seen as a growth sector. Noted for its author-friendly skills, Scholastic has strengthened its marketing base with the purchase of Grolier, the leading US pre-school book club.

SCM Press

9–17 St Albans Place, London N1 0NX
☎020 7359 8033   Fax 020 7359 0049
Email admin@scm-canterburypress.co.uk

Website www.scm-canterburypress.co.uk
Publishing Director Alex Wright
Approx. Annual Turnover £500,000

Publishes culturally-engaged theology, philosophy of religion, and religious ethics from an interdisciplinary and inter-faith perspective. About 35 titles a year. No unsolicited mss or proposals considered.
Royalties paid annually.

Authors' Rating Leading publisher of religious ideas with well-deserved reputation for fresh thinking. At SCM, 'questioning theology is the norm'.

Scottish Cultural Press/ Scottish Children's Press

Unit 13d, Newbattle Abbey Business Annexe, Newbattle Road, Dalkeith EH22 3LJ
☎0131 660 6366   Fax 0131 660 6414
Email info@scottishbooks.com

Directors Avril Gray, Brian Pugh

FOUNDED 1992. *Publishes* Scottish interest titles, including cultural literature, poetry, archaeology, local history. DIVISION **S.C.P. Children's Ltd** (trading as **Scottish Children's Press**) Children's fiction and non-fiction. Unsolicited mss, synopses and ideas welcome provided return postage is included, but telephone before sending material, please.
Royalties paid.

Scribner

See **Simon & Schuster UK Limited**

Seafarer Books

102 Redwald Road, Rendlesham,
Woodbridge, Suffolk IP12 2TE
☎01394 420789   Fax 01394 461314
Email info@seafarerbooks.com
Website www.seafarerbooks.com

Sole Proprietor Patricia M. Eve

FOUNDED 1968. *Publishes* sailing titles, with an emphasis on the traditional. AUTHORS Jack London, Erskine Childers, Adrian Seligman, Frank Mulville, Bjorn Larsson. No unsolicited mss; preliminary letter essential before making any type of submission.
Royalties paid twice-yearly.

Search Press Ltd

Wellwood, North Farm Road, Tunbridge
Wells, Kent TN2 3DR
☎01892 510850   Fax 01892 515903
Email searchpress@searchpress.com
Website www.searchpress.com

Managing Director *Martin de la Bédoyère*
Commissioning Editor *Rosalind Dace*
FOUNDED 1970. *Publishes* full-colour art, craft, needlecrafts – papermaking and papercrafts, painting on silk, art techniques and embroidery. No unsolicited mss; synopsis with sample chapter welcome.
Royalties paid annually.

Secker & Warburg
See **Random House Group Ltd**

Seren
First Floor, 38–40 Nolton Street, Bridgend CF31 3BN
☎01656 663018 Fax 01656 649226
Email seren@seren.force9.co.uk
Website www.seren-books.com
Chairman *Cary Archard*
Managing Director *Mick Felton*
Approx. Annual Turnover £150,000
FOUNDED 1981 as a specialist poetry publisher but has now moved into general literary publishing with an emphasis on Wales. *Publishes* poetry, fiction, literary criticism, drama, biography, art, history and translations of fiction. About 25 titles a year.
DIVISIONS
Poetry *Amy Wack* AUTHORS Owen Sheers, Tony Curtis, Sheenagh Pugh, Duncan Bush, Deryn Rees-Jones. **Drama** *Amy Wack* AUTHORS Edward Thomas, Charles Way, Lucinda Coxon. **Fiction, Art, Literary Criticism, History, Translations** *Mick Felton* AUTHORS Christopher Meredith, Leslie Norris, Richard John Evans.
IMPRINT **Border Lines Biographies** TITLES *Bruce Chatwin; Dennis Potter; Mary Webb; Wilfred Owen; Raymond Williams*, etc. Unsolicited mss, synopses and ideas for books welcome.
Royalties paid twice yearly.

Serpent's Tail
4 Blackstock Mews, London N4 2BT
☎020 7354 1949 Fax 020 7704 6467
Email info@serpentstail.com
Website www.serpentstail.com
Contact *Ben Cooper*
Approx. Annual Turnover £650,000
FOUNDED 1986. Winner of the **Sunday Times Small Publisher of the Year Award** (1989) and the Ralph Lewis Award for new fiction (1992). Serpent's Tail has introduced to British audiences a number of major internationally known writers. Noted for its strong emphasis on design and an eye for the unusual.

Publishes contemporary fiction, contemporary gay fiction and non-fiction, including works in translation, crime, popular culture and biography. No poetry, romance or fantasy. About 40 titles a year.
IMPRINTS
Serpent's Tail TITLES *Fearless Jones* Walter Mosley; *Whatever* Michel Houellebecq; *This is Serbia Calling* Matthew Collin; *Pornocopia* Laurence O'Toole. **Five Star** TITLES *Acid Casuals* Nicholas Blincoe; *Always Outnumbered, Always Outgunned* Walter Mosley; *Beneath the Blonde* Stella Duffy. Send preliminary letter outlining proposal with a sample chapter and s.a.e. No unsolicited mss. Prospective authors unfamiliar with Serpent's Tail are advised to study the list before submitting anything.
Royalties paid annually.

Authors' Rating A publisher noted for originality which means doing what the conglomerates are unwilling or unable to do. An exciting fiction list much praised by its own and other publishers' authors.

Severn House Publishers
9–15 High Street, Sutton, Surrey SM1 1DF
☎020 8770 3930 Fax 020 8770 3850
Email info@severnhouse.com
Website www.severnhouse.com
Chairman *Edwin Buckhalter*
Editorial *Amanda Stewart*
FOUNDED 1974. A leader in library fiction publishing. *Publishes* hardback fiction: romance science fiction, horror, fantasy, crime. About 140 titles a year. No unsolicited material. Synopses/proposals preferred through *bona fide* literary agents only.
Royalties paid twice-yearly. *Overseas associate* Severn House Publishers Inc., New York.

Sheed & Ward
See **The Continuum International Publishing Group Limited**

Sheffield Academic Press
See **The Continuum International Publishing Group Limited**

Sheldon Press
See **Society for Promoting Christian Knowledge**

Shepheard-Walwyn (Publishers) Ltd
Suite 604, The Chandlery, 50 Westminster Bridge Road, London SE1 7QY
☎020 7721 7666 Fax 020 7721 7667

Email books@shepheard-walwyn.co.uk
Website www.shepheard-walwyn.co.uk
Managing Director *Anthony Werner*
Approx. Annual Turnover £150,000
FOUNDED 1972. 'We regard books as food for
the mind and want to offer a wholesome diet
of original ideas and fresh approaches to old
subjects.' *Publishes* general non-fiction in three
main areas: Scottish interest; gift books in calligraphy and/or illustrated; history, political
economy, philosophy. About 5 titles a year.
Synopses and ideas for books welcome.
Royalties paid twice-yearly.

The Shetland Times Ltd
Prince Alfred Street, Lerwick, Shetland
ZE1 0EP
☎01595 693622 Fax 01595 694637
Email publishing@shetland-times.co.uk
Website www.shetland-books.co.uk
Managing Director *Robert Wishart*
Publications Manager *Charlotte Black*
FOUNDED 1872 as publishers of the local news-
paper. Book publishing followed thereafter
plus publication of monthly magazine, *Shetland
Life*. *Publishes* anything with Shetland connec-
tions – local and natural history, music, crafts,
maritime. Prefers material with a Shetland
theme/connection.
Royalties paid annually.

Shire Publications Ltd
Cromwell House, Church Street, Princes
Risborough, Buckinghamshire HP27 9AA
☎01844 344301 Fax 01844 347080
Email shire@shirebooks.co.uk
Website www.shirebooks.co.uk
General Manager *Sue Ross*
FOUNDED 1962. *Publishes* original non-fiction
paperbacks. About 25 titles a year. No unso-
licited material; send introductory letter with
detailed outline of idea.
Royalties paid annually.

Authors' Rating You don't have to live in the
country to write books for Shire but it helps.
With titles like *Church Fonts, Haunted Inns* and
Discovering Preserved Railways there is a distinct
rural feel to the list. Another way of putting it, to
quote owner John Rotheroe, Shire specialises in
'small books on all manner of obscure subjects'.

Short Books
15 Highbury Terrace, London N5 1UP
☎020 7226 1607 Fax 020 7226 4169
Website www.theshortbookco.com

Contacts *Rebecca Nicolson, Aurea Carpenter*
FOUNDED in May 2001 by two former journalists, Rebecca Nicolson and Aurea Carpenter,
Short Books aims to bridge the gap between
publishing and journalism producing informative, entertaining non-fiction at a conquerable
length (20,000 to 40,000 words). 15 titles in
2002. Lists include biographies – novella-length
portraits of the co-stars of history; journalism –
essays, investigations and reportage by authors
including Paul Theroux, Francis Wheen and
John Sutherland; children's books – lively
biographies of intriguing figures from the past.
No fiction.

Sickle Moon Books
See **Eland Publishing Ltd**

Sidgwick & Jackson
See **Macmillan Publishers Ltd**

Sigma Press
1 South Oak Lane, Wilmslow, Cheshire
SK9 6AR
☎01625 531035 Fax 01625 536800
Email info@sigma.press
Website www.sigmapress.co.uk
Chairman/Managing Director *Graham Beech*
FOUNDED in 1980 as a publisher of technical
books, Sigma Press now publishes mainly in
the leisure area. *Publishes* outdoor, local her-
itage, myths and legends, sports, dance and
exercise. Approx. 40 titles in 2000. No unso-
licited mss; synopses and ideas welcome. No
poetry or novels required.
    DIVISION **Sigma Leisure** TITLES *The Coniston
Tigers* (biography); *Walking the Wainwrights*; *Salsa
& Merengue Step-by-Step*; *How to Run a Marathon*;
The Bluebird Years.
Royalties paid twice-yearly.

Signature
See **Hodder Headline Ltd**

Silhouette
See **Harlequin Mills & Boon Ltd**

Simon & Schuster UK Limited
Africa House, 64–78 Kingsway, London
WC2B 6AH
☎020 7316 1900 Fax 020 7316 0331
CEO/Managing Director *Ian Chapman*
Publishers *Suzanne Baboneau* (Fiction), *Helen
    Gummer* (Non-fiction)
Editorial Directors, Scribner *Ben Ball,
    Tim Binding*

FOUNDED 1986. Offshoot of the leading American publisher. *Publishes* general fiction, including science fiction under its **Earthlight** imprint (Editor *John Jarrold*) and non-fiction in hardback and paperback. Literary fiction and non-fiction is published in trade paperback under the **Scribner** imprint. No academic or technical material.

Royalties paid twice-yearly.

Authors' Rating Judged by BookTrack to be the second fastest growing publisher in the UK, Simon & Schuster has success across the board with first time authors making the best-seller lists.

Skoob Russell Square

10 Brunswick Centre, off Bernard Street,
London WC1N 1AE
☎020 7278 8760   Fax 020 7278 3137
Email books@skoob.com
Website www.skoob.com

Editorial *M. Lovell*

Publishes literary guides, cultural studies, eso-terica/occult, poetry, new writing from the Orient. No unsolicited mss, synopses or ideas. TITLES *Skoob Directory of Secondhand Bookshops*; *Perspectives on Post-Colonial Literature* D.C.R.A. Goonetilleke; *The Space of City Trees* Arthur Yap.

Smith Gryphon Ltd
See **John Blake Publishing Ltd**

Colin Smythe Ltd

PO Box 6, Gerrards Cross, Buckinghamshire
SL9 8XA
☎01753 886000   Fax 01753 886469
Email sales@colinsmythe.co.uk
Website www.colinsmythe.co.uk
Managing Director *Colin Smythe*
Approx. Annual Turnover £2.2 million

FOUNDED 1966. *Publishes* Anglo-Irish litera-ture, drama; criticism and history. About 15 titles a year. No unsolicited mss. Also acts as lit-erary agent for a small list of authors including Terry Pratchett.

Royalties paid annually/twice-yearly.

Society for Promoting Christian Knowledge (SPCK)

Holy Trinity Church, Marylebone Road,
London NW1 4DU
☎020 7643 0382   Fax 020 7643 0391
Website www.spck.org.uk

Director of Publishing *Simon Kingston*

FOUNDED 1698, SPCK is the third oldest pub-lisher in the country. IMPRINTS **SPCK** Editorial Director *Joanna Moriaty* Theology, academic, liturgy, prayer, spirituality, biblical studies, educational resources, mission, pastoral care, gospel and culture, worldwide. **Sheldon Press** Editor *Liz Marsh* Popular medicine, health, self-help, psychology. **Triangle** Senior Editor *Alison Barr* Popular Christian paper-backs. **Azure** Senior Editor *Alison Barr* General spirituality.

Royalties paid annually.

Authors' Rating Religion with a strong social edge.

Southwater
See **Anness Publishing Ltd**

Souvenir Press Ltd

43 Great Russell Street, London WC1B 3PA
☎020 7580 9307/8 & 7637 5711/2/3
Fax 020 7580 5064

Chairman/Managing Director *Ernest Hecht*

Independent publishing house. FOUNDED 1951. *Publishes* academic and scholarly, animal care and breeding, antiques and collecting, archaeology, autobiography and biography, business and industry, children's, cookery, crafts and hobbies, crime, educational, fiction, gardening, health and beauty, history and anti-quarian, humour, illustrated and fine editions, magic and the occult, medical, military, music, natural history, philosophy, poetry, psycholo-gy, religious, sociology, sports, theatre and women's studies. About 55 titles a year. Souvenir's Human Horizons series for the dis-abled and their carers is one of the most pre-eminent in its field and recently celebrated 27 years of publishing for the disabled.

IMPRINTS/SERIES
Condor; **Human Horizons**; **Independent Voices**; **Pictorial Presentations**; **Pop Universal**; **The Story-Tellers**. TITLES *A Chocolate a Day Keeps the Doctor Away* John Ashton and Suzy Ashton; *Address Unknown* Kressman Taylor; *Venice Revealed* Paolo Barbaro; *A Language Older Than Words* Derrick Jensen; *Sizzling Chops & Devilish Spins – Ping-Pong and the Art of Staying Alive* Jerome Charyn; *Opium* Barbara Hodgson. Unsolicited mss con-sidered but initial letter of enquiry and outline always required in the first instance.

Royalties paid twice-yearly.

Authors' Rating In his fifty years of running Souvenir, Ernest Hecht has proved time and again that he has an eye for the bestseller – this is, after all, the man who launched Arthur Hailey – but his success owes as much to his love of the outrageous and a quirky sense of fun. Who else would have published a history of bottoms (*The Rear View*) or *Fairy Spells, Seeing and Communicating with the Fairies*?

SPCK
See **Society for Promoting Christian Knowledge**

Spellmount Ltd
The Old Rectory, Staplehurst, Kent TN12 0AZ
☎01580 893730 Fax 01580 893731
Email enquiries@spellmount.com
Website www.spellmount.com
Managing Director *Jamie Wilson*
Approx. Annual Turnover £400,000
FOUNDED 1983. *Publishes* history and military history. About 30 titles a year. Synopses/ideas for books in these specialist fields welcome, enclosing return postage.
Royalties paid biannually for two years, then annually.

Spiro Press
Robert Hyde House, 48 Bryanston Square, London W1H 2EA
☎020 7479 2000 Fax 020 7479 2222
Website www.spiropress.com
Head of Publishing *Carl Upsall*
Commissioning Editor *Susannah Lear*
Approx. Annual Turnover (Publishing Division) £1.6 million
Spiro Press, formerly The Industrial Society Publishing, is part of the Capita Group and has been publishing books for over 20 years. *Specialises* in business, management, self-development, training, staff development, human resources – books, manuals and special reports. TITLES *Inspirational Leadership – Henry V and the Muse of Fire*; *No Scruples?*; *The Book of Balanced Living*. SERIES *Fast Track*. Unsolicited mss, synopses and ideas welcome. No fiction or illustrated non-fiction.
Royalties paid twice-yearly.

E & FN Spon
See **Routledge**

Springer-Verlag London Limited
Sweetapple House, Catteshall Road, Godalming, Surrey GU7 3DJ
☎01483 418800 Fax 01483 415144
Email postmaster@svl.co.uk

Website www.springer.co.uk
Managing Director *John Watson*
Editorial Director *Beverley Ford*
Approx. Annual Turnover £5 million
The UK subsidiary of BertelsmannSpringer of Germany. *Publishes* science, technical and medical books and journals. About 150 titles a year, plus journals. Specialises in computing, engineering, medicine, mathematics, statistics, astronomy. All UK published books are sold through Springer's German and US companies as well as in the UK. Not interested in social sciences, fiction or school books but academic and professional science and amateur astronomy mss or synopses welcome.
Royalties paid annually.

Stainer & Bell Ltd
PO Box 110, 23 Gruneisen Road, London N3 1DZ
☎020 8343 3303 Fax 020 8343 3024
Email post@stainer.co.uk
Website www.stainer.co.uk
Managing Directors *Carol Y. Wakefield, Keith M. Wakefield*
Publishing Director *Nicholas Williams*
Approx. Annual Turnover £810,000
FOUNDED 1907 to publish sheet music. *Publishes* music and religious subjects related to hymnody. Unsolicited synopses/ideas for books welcome. Send letter enclosing brief précis.
Royalties paid annually.

Harold Starke Publishers Ltd
Pixey Green, Stradbroke, Near Eye, Suffolk IP21 5NG
☎01379 388334 Fax 01379 388335
Website red@eclat.force9.co.uk
Directors *Harold K. Starke, Naomi Galinski*
Publishes adult non-fiction, medical and reference. No unsolicited mss.
Royalties paid annually.

The Stationery Office Ltd
St Crispins, Duke Street, Norwich, Norfolk NR3 1PD
☎01603 622211 Fax 01603 694313 (Editorial)
Website www.thestationeryoffice.com
Chief Executive *Iain Burns*
Approx. Annual Turnover £250 million
Formerly HMSO, which was FOUNDED 1786. Became part of the private sector in October 1996. 11,000 new titles each year with 50,000

titles in print. Publisher of material sponsored by Parliament, government departments and other official bodies. Also commercial publishing in the following broad categories: business and professional, environment, transport, education and law.

STM
See **Liverpool University Press**

The Story-Tellers
See **Souvenir Press Ltd**

Straightline Publishing Ltd
29 Main Street, Bothwell, Glasgow G71 8RD
☎01698 853000   Fax 01698 854208
Director *Frank Docherty*
Editors *B. Taylor, P. Bellew*
FOUNDED 1989. *Publishes* magazines and directories – trade and technical – books of local interest. TITLES *Cabletalk; Information Builder.* No unsolicited material.
Royalties paid annually.

Summersdale Publishers Ltd
46 West Street, Chichester, West Sussex PO19 1RP
☎01243 771107   Fax 01243 786300
Email submissions@summersdale.com
Website www.summersdale.com
Directors *Stewart Ferris, Alastair Williams*
Editor *Elizabeth Kershaw*
Approx. Annual Turnover £1 million
FOUNDED 1990. *Publishes* travel literature and guides, fiction, biography, martial arts, self-help, cookery, humour and gift books. 50–60 titles a year. TITLES *La Bella Vita* Vida Adamoli; *The Lonely Sea and the Sky* Sir Francis Chichester; *Empire of the Soul* Paul William Roberts. No unsolicited mss; synopses and ideas welcome.
Royalties paid.

Susquehanna University Press
See **Golden Cockerel Press**

Sussex Academic Press
PO Box 2950, Brighton, East Sussex BN2 5SP
☎01273 699533   Fax 01273 621262
Email edit@sussex-academic.co.uk
Website www.sussex-academic.co.uk
Managing Director *Anthony Grahame*
Approx. Annual Turnover £185,000
FOUNDED 1994. Academic publisher. 25 titles in 2001. DIVISION/IMPRINT **Sussex Academic** TITLES *The Palestinian Refugees; The Creation of*

Political News; Human Rights and Religion. **Alpha Press** TITLES *Who Cares for Planet Earth?; Glimpses of the Divine.* No unsolicited material; send letter of inquiry in the first instance.
Royalties paid annually.

Sutton Publishing Ltd
Phoenix Mill, Thrupp, Stroud, Gloucestershire GL5 2BU
☎01453 731114   Fax 01453 731117
Managing Director *Keith Fullman*
Publishing Director *Peter Clifford*
FOUNDED 1978. Acquired by **Haynes Publishing** in March 2000. *Publishes* academic, archaeology, biography, countryside, history, military, regional interest, local history, pocket classics (lesser known novels by classic authors), transport. About 240 titles a year. Send synopses rather than complete mss.
Royalties paid twice-yearly.

Swan Hill Press (An imprint of Quiller Publishing Ltd)
Wykey House, Wykey, Shrewsbury, Shropshire SY4 1JA
☎01939 261616   Fax 01939 261606
Email info@quillerbooks.com
Managing Director *Andrew Johnston*
Specialises in practical books on all country and field sports activities. *Publishes* books on fishing, shooting, gundog training, falconry, equestrian, deer, cookery. About 15 titles a year. Unsolicited mss must include s.a.e.
Royalties paid twice-yearly.

Sweet & Maxwell Group
100 Avenue Road, London NW3 3PF
☎020 7393 7000   Fax 020 7393 7010
Email customerservices@sweetandmaxwell.co.uk
Website www.sweetandmaxwell.co.uk
Managing Director *Wendy Beecham*
FOUNDED 1799. Part of the Thomson Corporation. *Publishes* materials in all media; looseleaf works, journals, law reports, CD-ROMs and online. Over 1100 products, including 180 looseleafs, 40 periodicals, more than 40 digital products and online information services, and 200 new titles each year. Not interested in non-legal material. The legal and professional list is varied and contains academic titles as well as treatises and reference works in the legal and related professional fields.
IMPRINTS **Sweet & Maxwell; W. Green (Scotland); Round Hall.** Ideas welcome.

Writers with legal/professional projects in mind are advised to contact the Legal & Regulatory Business unit at the earliest possible stage in order to lay the groundwork for best design, production and marketing of a project. *Royalties* and fees paid according to contract.

Tango Books
See **Sadie Fields Productions Ltd** under **UK Packagers**

Taschen UK Ltd
13 Old Burlington Street, London W1X 3AJ
☎020 7437 4350 Fax 020 7437 4360
Website www.taschen.com

UK office of the German photographic, art and architecture publisher. Editorial office in Cologne (see entry under **European Publishers**).

I.B. Tauris & Co. Ltd
6 Salem Road, London W2 4BU
☎020 7243 1225 Fax 020 7243 1226
Website www.ibtauris.com
Chairman/Publisher *Iradj Bagherzade*
Managing Director *Jonathan McDonnell*
FOUNDED 1984. Independent publisher. *Publishes* general non-fiction and academic in the fields of international relations, current affairs, history, politics, cultural, media and film studies, Middle East studies. Joint projects with Cambridge University Centre for Middle Eastern Studies, Institute for Latin American Studies and Institute of Ismaili Studies. *Distributes* The New Press (New York) outside North America. *Represents* **Curzon Press** in the UK. IMPRINTS **Tauris Parke Books** Illustrated books on architecture, travel, design and culture. **Tauris Parke Paperbacks** Trade titles, including art and art history. **British Academic Press** Academic monographs. **Radcliffe Press** Colonial history and biography. Unsolicited synopses and book proposals welcome.
Royalties paid twice-yearly.

Tavistock Publications
See **Routledge**

Taylor & Francis Group plc
11 New Fetter Lane, London EC4P 4EE
☎020 7583 9855 Fax 020 7842 2298
Website www.tandf.co.uk
Chairman *Robert Kiernan*
Chief Executive *David Smith*
Approx. Annual Turnover £115 million

FOUNDED 1798 with the launch of *Philosophical Magazine* which has been in publication ever since (now a solid state physics journal). The Group is now a public company but with strong academic connections among the major shareholders. **Falmer Press** joined the group in 1979 and it doubled its size in the late 1980s with the acquisition of Crane Russak in 1986 and Hemisphere Publishing Co in 1988 (now called Taylor & Francis Asia Pacific). In 1995, acquired Lawrence Erlbaum Associates Ltd, renamed **Psychology Press**, and Brunner/Mazel in 1997, adding to the growing list of psychology publications. In 1996, **UCL Press Ltd** was purchased, adding further to its portfolio of publications in science and humanities. In 1997, Garland Publishing Inc., New York, and in 1998 Routledge Publishing Holdings Ltd, including Carfax Publishing and E & FN Spon were acquired. The most recent additions to the Taylor & Francis Group are **Europa Publications Ltd**, the reference book publisher covering international affairs, politics and economics, and **Martin Dunitz Ltd** (see entry) in 1999. Acquired the international journals division of Scandinavian University Press in 2000, adding over 60 academic journals, followed in 2001 by **Gordon & Breach** and **Curzon Press** (see **Routledge**). *Publishes* scientific, technical, education titles at university, research and professional levels. About 1700 titles a year. Unsolicited mss, synopses and ideas welcome.
Royalties paid yearly. *Overseas offices* Taylor & Francis Inc., Philadelphia, PA and New York; Taylor & Francis Asia Pacific, Singapore; Taylor & Francis AS, Norway and Sweden.

Authors' Rating One of those companies that barely registers with authors until they look at some of the famous imprints that are gathered under the corporate umbrella. Very much into higher education and reference, further expansion is predicted, particularly in the US. Plans are well ahead for making all the titles available in e-book format.

Teach Yourself
See **Hodder Headline Ltd**

Telegraph Books
1 Canada Square, Canary Wharf, London E14 5DT
☎020 7538 6826 Fax 020 7538 6064
Website www.telegraphbooksdirect.co.uk
Owner *Telegraph Group Ltd*
Publisher *Susannah Charlton*
Approx. Annual Turnover £3 million

Concentrates on Telegraph branded books in association/collaboration with other publishers. Also runs Telegraph Books Direct, a direct mail, phone-line bookselling service and off-the-page sales for other publishers' books. *Publishes* general non-fiction: journalism, business and law, personal finance, education, gardening, guides, sport, puzzles and games. About 50 titles a year. Only interested in books if a Telegraph link exists. No unsolicited material.
Royalties paid twice-yearly.

Texere Publishing Ltd

71-77 Leadenhall Street, London EC3A 3DE
☎020 7204 3644 Fax 020 7208 6701
Email david_wilson@etexere.com
Website www.etexere.co.uk
Owner *Texere LLC, New York*
Chairman *Myles Thompson*
Publisher *David Wilson*

FOUNDED 2000 when it purchased the **Orion** business list. Small publishing house that focuses on finance, business, economics, investment and current affairs, at both professional and trade level, particularly topics with a global appeal and including technology/science crossover into business and finance. No fiction. 22 titles in 2002. Unsolicited material welcome; telephone or e-mail *David Wilson* in the first instance.
Royalties paid twice-yearly.

Thames and Hudson Ltd

181A High Holborn, London WC1V 7QX
☎020 7845 5000 Fax 020 7845 5050
Email mail@thameshudson.co.uk
Website www.thamesandhudson.com
Managing Director *Thomas Neurath*
Editorial Head *Jamie Camplin*
Approx. Annual Turnover £23 million

Publishes art, archaeology, architecture and design, biography, fashion, garden and landscape design, graphics, history, illustrated and fine editions, mythology, music, photography, popular culture, style, travel and topography. 200 titles a year. SERIES *World of Art; New Horizons; Celtic Design; Hip Hotels; Most Beautiful Villages; Earth From the Air.* TITLES *David Hockney: Secret Knowledge; Sensation; The Shock of the New; David Bailey: Chasing Rainbows; Colour and Culture; The Book of Kells; The Dalai Lama's Secret Temple; The Eco-Design Handbook; Fashion Illustration Now; Ancient Egypt: The Great Discoveries; The Seventy Great Mysteries of the Ancient World.* Send preliminary letter and outline before mss.
Royalties paid twice-yearly.

Authors' Rating Fifty years in the business, Thames and Hudson has a fine record of publishing quality illustrated books on art and design. The World of Art series, a huge range of modestly priced, scholarly books, is probably the best of its kind anywhere in the world. Financial success rests on producing the sort of books that easily carry over to other languages.

Thomson Learning

High Holborn House, 50-51 Bedford Row, London WC1R 4LR
☎020 7067 2500 Fax 020 7067 2600
Website www.thomsonlearning.co.uk
CEO (Worldwide) *Bob Christie*
CEO (Thomson Learning EMA)
Charles Iossi
Publishing Director (Thomson Learning EMA) *Emma Mitchell*

FOUNDED 1993. Formerly International Thomson Publishing, part of the Thomson Corporation and as such has offices worldwide with the UK office being reported to by Copenhagen (for Europe), Turkey (Middle East) and South Africa. *Publishes* education. TITLES *Management and Cost Accounting* Drury; *Strategy – Process, Content, Contact* DeWitt and Meyer. Unsolicited material aimed at students is welcome but telephone in the first instance to check out the idea.
Royalties vary according to contract.

Stanley Thornes (Publishers) Ltd
See **Nelson Thornes Limited**

F.A. Thorpe (Publishing)

The Green, Bradgate Road, Anstey, Leicester LE7 7FU
☎0116 236 4325 Fax 0116 234 0205
Chairman *David Thorpe*
Group Chief Executive *Robert Thirbly*
Approx. Annual Turnover £6 million

FOUNDED in 1964 to supply large print books to libraries. Part of the Ulverscroft Group Ltd. *Publishes* fiction and non-fiction large print books. No educational, gardening or books that would not be suitable for large print. 444 titles in 2001. DIVISIONS **Charnwood**; **Ulverscroft**. IMPRINTS **Linford Romance**; **Linford Mystery**; **Linford Western**. No unsolicited material.

Thorsons
See **HarperCollins Publishers Ltd**

Time Warner Books UK

Brettenham House, Lancaster Place, London
WC2E 7EN
☎020 7911 8000 Fax 020 7911 8100
Email uk@TimeWarnerBooks.com
Website www.TimeWarnerBooks.co.uk
Chief Executive *David Young*
Publisher *Ursula Mackenzie*
Approx. Annual Turnover £36.8 million
FOUNDED 1988 as Little, Brown & Co. (UK).
Part of Time-Warner Inc. Began by importing
its US parent company's titles and in 1990
launched its own illustrated non-fiction list. Two
years later the company took over former
Macdonald & Co. *Publishes* hardback and paperback fiction, literary fiction, crime, science
fiction and fantasy; and general non-fiction,
including illustrated: architecture and design, fine
art, photography, biography and autobiography,
cinema, gardening, history, humour, travel, crafts
and hobbies, reference, cookery, wines and
spirits, DIY, guidebooks, natural history and
nautical.

IMPRINTS
Little, Brown *Ursula Mackenzie, Alan Samson,
Barbara Boote, Hilary Hale Tara Lawrence*
Hardback fiction and general non-fiction.
Abacus *Richard Beswick* Literary fiction and
non-fiction paperbacks; **Orbit** *Tim Holman*
Science fiction and fantasy; **Time Warner**
Alan Samson, Barbara Boote, Hilary Hale Mass-
market fiction and non-fiction paperbacks; **X
Libris** *Sarah Shrubb* Women's erotica;
Illustrated *Julia Charles* Hardbacks; **Virago**
(see entry). Approach in writing in the first
instance. No unsolicited mss.
Royalties paid twice-yearly.

Authors' Rating A quality publisher that
manages to cover an impressive range of new
writing. Much praised by authors for friendly
efficiency.

Times Books

See **HarperCollins Publishers Ltd**

Titan Books

144 Southwark Street, London SE1 0UP
☎020 7620 0200 Fax 020 7620 0032
Email editorial@titanmail.com
Managing Director *Nick Landau*
Editorial Director *Katy Wild*
FOUNDED 1981. Now a leader in the publication
of graphic novels and film and television tie-ins.
Publishes comic books/graphic novels, film and
television titles. About 100 titles a year.

IMPRINT **Titan Books** TITLES *Batman; Buffy
the Vampire Slayer, Farscape: The Illustrated Season
2 Companion; The Simpsons; Star Wars; Starring
Sherlock Holmes; Superman; Transformers; 200 AD.*
No unsolicited fiction or children's books. Ideas
for film and TV titles considered; send synop-
sis/outline with sample chapter. No e-mail submissions. Author guidelines available.
Royalties paid twice-yearly.

Tolley Publishing

See **Butterworths Tolley**

Transworld Publishers, A division of Random House Group Ltd

61–63 Uxbridge Road, London W5 5SA
☎020 8579 2652 Fax 020 8579 5479
Email info@transworld-publishers.co.uk
Website www.booksattransworld.co.uk
Chairman *Mark Barty-King*
Joint Managing Directors *Larry Finlay,
Patrick Janson-Smith*
Approx. Annual Turnover £72 million
FOUNDED 1950. A subsidiary of **Random
House, Inc.**, New York, which in turn is a
wholly-owned subsidiary of **Bertelsmann
AG**, Germany. *Publishes* general fiction and
non-fiction, gardening, sports and leisure.

DIVISIONS
Adult Trade *Patrick Janson-Smith* IMPRINTS
Bantam *Francesca Liversidge*; **Bantam Press**
Sally Gaminara; **Corgi**; **Black Swan** *Bill Scott-
Kerr*, **Doubleday** *Marianne Velmans*; **Eden**
Katrina Whone; **Expert Books** *Gareth Pottle.*
AUTHORS Kate Atkinson, Charlotte Bingham,
Bill Bryson, Lee Child, Catherine Cookson, Jilly
Cooper, Ben Elton, Nicholas Evans, Frederick
Forsyth, Robert Goddard, Germaine Greer,
Joanne Harris, Stephen Hawking, D.G.
Hessayon, Anne McCaffrey, Andy McNab,
Terry Pratchett, Willy Russell, Gerald Seymour,
Danielle Steel, Joanna Trollope, Mary Wesley.
Royalties paid twice-yearly. *Overseas associates*
Random House Australia Pty Ltd; Random
House New Zealand; Random House (Pty)
Ltd (South Africa).

Authors' Rating The leading publisher of
paperback fastsellers, Transworld is an object
lesson in making quality pay.

Travel Publishing Ltd

7A Apollo House, Calleva Park, Aldermaston,
Berkshire RG7 8TN
☎0118 981 7777 Fax 0118 982 0077
Email travel_publishing@msn.com
Website www.travelpublishing.co.uk

Directors *Peter Robinson, Chris Day*
FOUNDED in 1997 by two former directors of **Reed Elsevier plc**. *Publishes* travel, accommodation, food and drink guides to Britain and Ireland. 20 titles in 2001. SERIES **Hidden Places**; **Hidden Inns**; **Golfers Guides**; **Country Living Rural Guides** (in conjunction with *Country Living* magazine; **Off the Motorway** TITLES *Hidden Places of Sussex*; *Hidden Inns of Wales*; *Golfers Guide to Ireland*; *Country Living Rural Guide to England – East Anglia*. Welcomes unsolicited material; send letter in the first instance.
Royalties paid twice-yearly.

Treehouse Children's Books Ltd
2nd Floor, The Old Brewhouse, Lower Charlton Trading Estate, Shepton Mallet, Somerset BA4 5QE
☎01749 330529 Fax 01749 330544
Email richard.powell4@virgin.net
Co-Directors *Richard Powell, David Bailey*
Approx. Annual Turnover £1 million
FOUNDED 1992. *Publishes* children's pre-school books. 24 titles in 2001. No mss. Illustrations, synopses and ideas for books welcome; write in the first instance.
Fees paid; no royalties.

Trentham Books Ltd
Westview House, 734 London Road, Stoke-on-Trent, Staffordshire ST4 5NP
☎01782 745567/844699 Fax 01782 745553
Website www.trentham-books.co.uk
Directors *Dr Gillian Klein, Barbara Wiggins*
Approx. Annual Turnover £1 million
Publishes education (nursery, school to higher), social sciences, intercultural studies, gender studies and law for professional readers *not* for children and parents. Also academic and professional journals. No fiction, biography or poetry. Over 30 titles a year. Unsolicited mss, synopses and ideas welcome if relevant to their interests. Material only returned if adequate s.a.e. sent.
Royalties paid annually.

Triangle
See **Society for Promoting Christian Knowledge**

Trident Press Ltd
Empire House, 175 Piccadilly, London W1J 9TB
☎020 7491 8770 Fax 020 7491 8664
Email admin@tridentpress.com
Website www.tridentpress.com

Managing Director *Peter Vine*
Approx. Annual Turnover £550,000
FOUNDED 1997. *Publishes* TV tie-ins, natural history, travel, geography, underwater/marine life, history, archaeology, culture and fiction. DIVISIONS **Fiction/General Publishing** *Paula Vine;* **Natural History** *Peter Vine*. TITLES *Red Sea Sharks; The Elysium Testament; BBC Wildlife Specials; UAE in Focus.* No unsolicited mss; synopses and ideas welcome, particularly TV tie-ins. Approach in writing or *brief* communications by e-mail, fax or telephone.
Royalties paid annually.

Trotman & Co. Ltd
2 The Green, Richmond, Surrey TW9 1PL
☎020 8486 1150 Fax 020 8486 1161
Website www.trotmanpublishing.co.uk
Chairman *Andrew Fiennes Trotman*
Editorial Director *Amanda Williams*
Approx. Annual Turnover £3 million
Publishes general careers books, higher education guides, teaching support material, employment and training resources. About 50 titles a year. TITLES *Degree Course Offers; The Student Book; UCAS/Trotman Complete Guides; Students' Money Matters.* Unsolicited material welcome. Also active in the educational resources market, producing recruitment brochures.
Royalties paid twice-yearly.

20/20
See **The X Press**

UCL Press Ltd
See **Taylor & Francis Group**

Ulverscroft
See **F.A. Thorpe (Publishing)**

Unichrome
See **Jarrold Publishing**

University Presses of California, Columbia & Princeton Ltd
1 Oldlands Way, Bognor Regis, West Sussex PO22 9SA
☎01243 842165 Fax 01243 842167
Email lois@upccp.demon.co.uk
Publishes academic titles only. US-based editorial offices. Over 200 titles a year. Enquiries only.

Usborne Publishing Ltd
83–85 Saffron Hill, London EC1N 8RT
☎020 7430 2800 Fax 020 7430 1562
Email mail@usborne.co.uk

Website www.usborne.com
Managing Director Peter Usborne
Publishing Director Jenny Tyler
Approx. Annual Turnover £14 million
FOUNDED 1973. Publishes non-fiction, fiction, computer books, puzzle books and music for children and young adults. Some titles for parents. Up to 120 titles a year. Non-fiction books are written in-house to a specific format and therefore unsolicited mss are not normally welcome. Ideas which may be developed in-house are sometimes considered. Fiction for children may be considered. Keen to hear from new illustrators and designers.
Royalties paid twice-yearly.

Authors' Rating Ever inventive, Usborne has had great success with Internet-linked children's reference books and shrunk editions (four inches square) of established titles.

Vallentine Mitchell/Jewish Chronicle Publications

Crown House, 47 Chase Side, Southgate, London N14 5BP
☎020 8920 2100 Fax 020 8447 8548
Email info@vmbooks.com
Website www.vmbooks.com
Chairman Frank Cass
Publishes books of Jewish interest: Jewish history, philosophy and heritage, Holocaust studies. An imprint of **Frank Cass & Co Ltd**.

Vanguard Press

See **Pegasus Elliot Mackenzie Publishers Ltd**

Vega

See **Chrysalis Books Ltd**

Ventura

See **Penguin Group (UK)**

Vermilion

See **Random House Group Ltd**

Verso

6 Meard Street, London W1F 0EG
☎020 7437 3546 Fax 020 7734 0059
Website www.versobooks.com
Chairman George Galfalvi
Managing Director Gavin Everall
Approx. Annual Turnover £2 million
Formerly New Left Books which grew out of the *New Left Review*. Publishes politics, history, sociology, economics, philosophy, cultural

studies, feminism. TITLES *The Prophet Armed: Trotsky 1879–1921* Isaac Deutscher; *The Trial of Henry Kissinger* Christopher Hitchens; *Through the Looking Glass: A Dissenter Inside New Labour* Liz Davies; *The Assassination of Lumumba* Ludo de Witte; *The Clash of Fundamentalism* Tariq Ali; *Close Up: Iranian Cinema, Past, Present and Future* Hamid Dabashi; *Innocent in the House* Andy McSmith; *The Red Velvet Seat: Women's Writings on the Cinema: The First Fifty Years* eds. Lant and Periz. No unsolicited mss; synopses and ideas for books welcome.
Royalties paid annually. *Overseas office* in New York.

Authors' Rating Dubbed by the *Bookseller* as 'one of the most successful small independent publishers'.

Viking

See **Penguin Group (UK)**

Vintage

See **Random House Group Ltd**

Virago Press

Time Warner Books, Brettenham House, Lancaster Place, London WC2E 7EN
☎020 7911 8000 Fax 020 7911 8100
Website www.virago.co.uk
Publisher Lennie Goodings
Senior Editor Antonia Hodgson
Editor, Virago Modern Classics Jill Foulston
Approx. Annual Turnover £2.5 million
FOUNDED in 1973 by Carmen Callil, Virago *publishes* fiction and non-fiction books of quality by women. Approximately 50 new books a year in the areas of autobiography, biography, fiction, history, politics, psychology and women's issues. IMPRINTS **Virago Modern Classics** 20th-century reprints; **Virago Vs** AUTHORS Margaret Atwood, Maya Angelou, Gail Anderson-Dargatz, Nina Bawden, Jennifer Belle, Sarah Dunant, Marilyn French, Gaby Hauptman, Michele Roberts, Natasha Walter, Sarah Waters. Send synopsis and sample chapter and return postage with all unsolicited material.
Royalties paid twice-yearly.

Virgin Books Ltd

Thames Wharf Studios, Rainville Road, London W6 9HT
☎020 7386 3300 Fax 020 7386 3360
Website www.virgin-books.com
Chairman Mark Fisher
Managing Director KT Forster
Approx. Annual Turnover £10 million

The Virgin Group's book publishing company. *Publishes* non-fiction, reference and large-format illustrated books on entertainment and popular culture, particularly music and books about film, showbiz, sport, biography, autobiography and humour. Launched a series of travel guides in 1999. No poetry, short stories, individual novels, children's books.

DIVISIONS
Non-fiction IMPRINT **Virgin** Publishing Director *Christina Hippisley*; Music Scout *Stuart Slater*; **Sport** Editorial Director *Jonathan Taylor*; **Illustrated Books** Editor *Mark Chapman*; **Travel** Editorial Director *Carolyn Thorne*.
  Fiction IMPRINTS **Virgin**; **Black Lace** Senior Editor *Kerri Sharp* Erotic fiction 'written by women for women'; **Nexus** Editor *Paul Copperwaite* Erotic fiction.
  Royalties paid twice-yearly.

Vista House Ltd
See **Paragon Press Publishing/Vista House Ltd**

The Vital Spark
See **Neil Wilson Publishing Ltd**

Voyager
See **HarperCollins Publishers Ltd**

University of Wales Press
10 Columbus Walk, Brigantine Place, Cardiff CF10 4BY
☎029 2049 6899   Fax 029 2049 6108
Email press@press.wales.ac.uk
Website www.wales.ac.uk/press

Director *Susan Jenkins*
Deputy Director *Richard Houdmont*
Approx. Annual Turnover £500,000

FOUNDED 1922. *Publishes* academic and scholarly books in English and Welsh in four core areas: history, Welsh and Celtic Studies, European Studies, religion and philosophy. 60 titles in 2000. IMPRINTS **GPC Books**; **Gwasg Prifysgol Cymru**; **University of Wales Press** TITLES *Distant Fields – Eighteenth Century Fictions of Wales* Moira Dearnley; *Gendering the Crusades* ed. Susan B. Edgington and Sarah Lamont; *Ernest Gallner and Modernity* Michael Lessnoff. Unsolicited mss considered.
  Royalties paid annually.

Walker Books Ltd
87 Vauxhall Walk, London SE11 5HJ
☎020 7793 0909   Fax 020 7587 1123
Editorial Director *Vanessa Clarke*

Editors *Deirdre McDermott* (Picture books), *Caroline Royds* (Fiction and gift books), *Denise Johnstone-Burt* (Picture books, board and novelty)
Approx. Annual Turnover £31.7 million

FOUNDED 1979. *Publishes* illustrated children's books, children's fiction and non-fiction. About 300 titles a year. TITLES *Maisy Lucy Cousins*; *Where's Wally?* Martin Handford; *Five Minutes' Peace* Jill Murphy; *Can't You Sleep, Little Bear?* Martin Waddell & Barbara Firth; *Guess How Much I Love You* Sam McBratney and Anita Jeram; *Point Blanc* Anthony Horowitz. Unsolicited mss welcome.
  Royalties paid twice-yearly.

Authors' Rating One of the most exciting children's lists. Editors are on the lookout for original ideas.

Wallflower Press
5 Pond Street, Hampstead, London NW3 2PN
☎020 7431 6622   Fax 020 7431 6621
Email info@wallflowerpress.co.uk
Website www.wallflowerpress.co.uk

Editorial Director *Yoram Allon*
Chief Editor *Del Cullen*
Approx. Annual Turnover £100,000

FOUNDED 1999. *Publishes* academic and popular film studies and related media and cultural studies. 12 titles in 2001. Unsolicited mss, synopses and proposals welcome. No fiction or academic material not related to the moving image.
  Royalties paid annually.

Ward Lock
See **Octopus Publishing Group**

Ward Lock Educational Co. Ltd
BIC Ling Kee House, 1 Christopher Road, East Grinstead, West Sussex RH19 3BT
☎01342 318980   Fax 01342 410980
Email wle@lingkee.com
Website www.wardlockeducational.com

Owner *Ling Kee (UK) Ltd*

FOUNDED 1952. *Publishes* educational books (primary, middle, secondary, teaching manuals) for all subjects, specialising in maths, science, geography, reading and English and currently focusing on Key Stages 1 and 2.

Frederick Warne
See **Penguin Group (UK)**

Franklin Watts
See **The Watts Publishing Group Ltd**

The Watts Publishing Group Ltd

96 Leonard Street, London EC2A 4XD
☎020 7739 2929 Fax 020 7739 6487
Email <gm>@wattspub.co.uk

Managing Director *Marlene Johnson*

Part of Groupe Lagardere. *Publishes* children's non-fiction, reference, information, gift, fiction, picture and novelty. About 300 titles a year.

IMPRINTS **Franklin Watts** *Philippa Stewart* Non-fiction and information; **Orchard Books** *Ann-Janine Murtagh* Fiction, picture and novelty books. Unsolicited mss, synopses and ideas for books welcome.

Royalties paid twice-yearly. *Overseas associates* in Australia and New Zealand.

Wayland

See **Hodder Headline Ltd**

Weidenfeld & Nicolson

See **The Orion Publishing Group Ltd**

Welsh Academic Press

See **Ashley Drake Publishing Ltd**

Westworld International Ltd

Unit 3, 25 Putney Hill, London SW15 6BE
☎020 8788 2455
Email editor@westworldinternational.com
Website www.westworldinternational.com

Chairman/Editorial Head, Fiction *Paul Smith*
Managing Director/Editorial Head, Biography *Stephen Smith*
Approx. Annual Turnover £200,000

FOUNDED 1996. *Publishes* mass-market biography and fiction in paperback. 2 titles in 2001. Welcomes unsolicited material; contact by e-mail with short synopsis. 'We are only interested in fiction or true life stories.'

Royalties paid twice-yearly. *Overseas associate* Westworld Germany Inc.

Wharncliffe Publishing

47 Church Street, Barnsley, South Yorkshire S70 2AS
☎01226 734222 Fax 01226 734438
Email charles@pen-and-sword.co.uk
Website www.local-books.com

Chairman *Sir Nicholas Hewitt*
Managing Director *Charles Hewitt*
Imprint Manager *Barbara Bramall*

An imprint of **Pen & Sword Books Ltd**. Wharncliffe is the book and magazine publishing arm of an old-established, independently

owned newspaper publishing and printing house. *Publishes* local history throughout the UK, focusing on nostalgia and old photographs. SERIES *Aspects*. No unsolicited mss; synopses and ideas welcome.

Royalties paid twice-yearly.

Which? Books/ Consumers' Association

2 Marylebone Road, London NW1 4DF
☎020 7830 6000 Fax 020 7830 7660
Website www.which.net

Director *Sheila McKechnie*
Head of Publishing *Robert Gray*

FOUNDED 1957. Publishing arm of the Consumers' Association, a registered charity. *Publishes* non-fiction: information, reference and how-to books on travel, gardening, health, personal finance, consumer law, food, careers, DIY. Titles must offer direct value or utility to the UK consumer. 25–30 titles a year.

IMPRINT **Which? Books** TITLES *The Good Food Guide*; *The Good Skiing and Snowboarding Guide*; *The Which? Hotel Guide*; *The Which? Wine Guide*; *Wills and Probate*; *Be Your Own Financial Adviser*. No unsolicited mss; send synopses and ideas only.

Royalties, if applicable, paid twice-yearly.

J. Whitaker & Sons Ltd

Woolmead House West, Bear Lane, Farnham, Surrey GU9 7LG
☎01252 742500 Fax 01252 742501
Website www.whitaker.co.uk

Managing Director *Jonathan Nowell*

FOUNDED in 1858 by bookseller Joseph Whitaker and remained independent until acquired by BPI, American subsidiary of the Dutch group VNU, in 1999. Published *Whitaker's Almanac* from 1868 until the title was sold to the Stationery Office in 1997. Provides a range of services for the book trade including the **ISBN Agency**, BookBank, SourceData, Teleordering and Book Track. Also new Web services: LibWeb (for libraries); PubWeb (for publishers) and WhitakerWeb (for booksellers). *Publishes* bibliographic reference products. TITLES *Whitaker's Books in Print*; *Information Age*; *Directory of Publishers* (*The Red Book*); and the journal of the book trade, *The Bookseller*.

Whittet Books Ltd

Hill Farm, Stonham Road, Cotton, Stowmarket, Suffolk IP14 4RQ
☎01449 781877 Fax 01449 781898
Email annabel@whittet.dircon.co.uk

Managing Director *Annabel Whittet*

Publishes natural history, pets, poultry, horses, domestic livestock, rural interest. Unsolicited mss, synopses and ideas for books welcome. *Royalties* paid twice-yearly.

Whurr Publishers Ltd
19B Compton Terrace, London N1 2UN
☎020 7359 5979 Fax 020 7226 5290
Email info@whurr.co.uk
Website www.whurr.co.uk
Chairman/Managing Director *Colin Whurr*
Approx. Annual Turnover £1 million

FOUNDED in 1987. *Publishes* speech and language therapy, nursing, psychology, psychotherapy, audiology, special education including dyslexia, ADHD, autism and Downs syndrome. No fiction and general trade books. 50 titles in 2001. Unsolicited mss, synopses and ideas welcome within their specialist fields only. 'Whurr Publishers believes authors can be best served by a small, specialised company combining old-fashioned service with the latest publishing technology.'
Royalties paid twice-yearly.

Wild Goose Publications
Iona Community, 4th Floor, The Savoy Centre, 140 Sauchiehall Street, Glasgow G2 3DH
☎0141 332 6292 Fax 0141 332 1090
Email admin@ionabooks.com
Website www.iona.books.com
Editorial Head *Sandra Kramer*
Approx. Annual Turnover £200,000

The publishing house of the Iona Community, established in the Celtic Christian tradition of St Columba, *publishes* books, tapes and CDs on holistic spirituality, social justice, political and peace issues, healing, innovative approaches to worship, song and material for meditation and reflection.

Wiley Europe Ltd
Baffins Lane, Chichester, West Sussex PO19 1UD
☎01243 779777 Fax 01243 775878
Website www.wiley.co.uk
Managing Director *Dr John Jarvis*
Publishing Directors *Mike Davis, Stephen Smith*
Approx. Annual Turnover £57 million

FOUNDED 1807. US parent company. *Publishes* professional, reference trade and text books, scientific, technical and biomedical.

DIVISIONS
Architecture *Maggie Toy*; **Business** *Sarah Stevens*; **Business/Management** *Diane Taylor*; **Chemistry, Earth Sciences** *Sally Wilkinson*; **Computing** *Karen Mosman, Gaynor Redvers-Mutton*; **Finance** *Sally Smith, Samantha Whittaker*; **Management/Accounting** *Steve Hardman*; **Management/Marketing** *Claire Plimmer*; **Psychology** *Vivien Ward*; **Major Reference Works** *David Hughes*; **Medicine & Life Sciences** *Deborah Dixon*; **Technology & Engineering** *Ann-Marie Halligan*. Unsolicited mss welcome, as are synopses and ideas for books.
Royalties paid annually.

Authors' Rating When it comes to scientific, technical and medical books, Wiley is racing ahead. Academic authors are attracted by the American connection. Online publishing is set to increase.

Neil Wilson Publishing Ltd
Suite 303a, The Pentagon Centre, 36 Washington Street, Glasgow G3 8AZ
☎0141 221 1117 Fax 0141 221 5363
Email info@nwp.sol.co.uk
Website www.nwp.co.uk *or* www.11-9.co.uk
Chairman *Gordon Campbell*
Managing Director/Editorial Director *Neil Wilson*
11:9 Editorial Administrator *Liz Small*
Approx. Annual Turnover £300,000

FOUNDED 1992. *Publishes* Scottish interest and history, biography, humour and hillwalking, whisky; also cookery and Irish interest. About 10 titles a year. NWP manages the **11:9** fiction imprint for new Scottish writing, launched in 2000, which is financed under the New Directions Lottery fund, distributed by the Scottish Arts Council. In addition, three non-fiction IMPRINTS were launched in 2000: **The In Pinn** Outdoor pursuits; **The Angel's Share** Whisky, drink and food-related subjects; **The Vital Spark** Humour. Unsolicited mss, synopses and ideas welcome. No politics, academic or technical.
Royalties paid twice-yearly.

Philip Wilson Publishers Ltd
7 Deane House, 27 Greenwood Place, London NW5 1LB
☎020 7284 3088 Fax 020 7284 3099
Email pwilson@philip-wilson.co.uk
Website www.philip-wilson.co.uk
Chairman *Philip Wilson*
FOUNDED 1976. *Publishes* art, art history,

antiques and collectables. About 15 titles a year.

Wimbledon Publishing Company
75–76 Blackfriars Road, London SE1 8HD
☎020 7401 4200   Fax 020 7401 4201
Email editor@wpcpress.com
Website www.wpcpress.com
Managing Director *Kamaljit Sood*
General Manager *Noel McPherson*
FOUNDED in 1992 as a publisher of school texts, going on to launch a humanities list in 1998 that focuses on history, politics, economics, international affairs, literature and culture. 30 titles in 2001.
IMPRINTS **WPC Education** *K. Sood*; **Anthem Press** *Tom Penn, Caroline Broughton*. Welcomes mss; synopses and ideas for books.
Royalties paid annually. *Partner organisation* Stylus Publishing LLC, Sterling, VA, US.

Windhorse Publications
11 Park Road, Moseley, Birmingham B13 8AB
☎0121 449 9191   Fax 0121 449 9191
Email windhorse@compuserve.com
Chairman/Editorial Head *Jnanasiddhi*
Approx. Annual Turnover £250,000
FOUNDED 1977. *Publishes* meditation and Buddhism and biographies of Buddhists. Associated with the FWBO, a world-wide Buddhist movement. 10 titles in 2001 TITLES *Tales of Freedom; What is Sangha?; Meditating.* Unsolicited mss, synopses and ideas welcome; approach by letter or e-mail in the first instance.
Royalties paid quarterly.

Windsor Large Print
See **Chivers Press Ltd**

Wise Publications
See **Omnibus Press**

WIT Press
Ashurst Lodge, Ashurst, Southampton, Hampshire SO40 7AA
☎023 8029 3223   Fax 023 8029 2853
Email marketing@witpress.com
Website www.witpress.com
Owner *Computational Mechanics International Ltd, Southampton*
Chairman *Professor C.A. Brebbia*
Managing Director/Editorial Head *Lance Sucharov*
FOUNDED in 1980 as Computational Mechanics Publications to publish engineering analysis titles. Changed to WIT Press to reflect the increased range of publications. *Publishes* scientific and technical, mainly at postgraduate level and above, including architecture, environmental engineering, bioengineering. 50 titles in 2001. TITLES *The Sustainable Street; Medical Applications of Computer Modelling – The Respiratory System; Environmental Urban Noise.* Unsolicited mss, synopses and ideas welcome; approach by post or e-mail. No non-scientific or technical material or lower level (school- and college-level texts).
Royalties paid annually. *Overseas subsidiary* Computational Mechanics, Inc., Billerica, USA.

Wizard Books
See **Icon Books Ltd**

Woburn Press
See **Frank Cass & Co Ltd**

Oswald Wolff Books
See **Berg Publishers**

The Women's Press
34 Great Sutton Street, London EC1V 0LQ
☎020 7251 3007   Fax 020 7608 1938
Website www.the-womens-press.com
Managing Director *Emma Drew*
Approx. Annual Turnover £1 million
Part of the Namara Group. First title published in 1978. *Publishes* women only: quality fiction and non-fiction. Fiction usually has a female protagonist and a woman-centred theme. International writers and subject matter encouraged. Non-fiction: books for and about women generally; gender politics, race politics, disability, feminist theory, health and psychology, literary criticism. About 50 titles a year.
IMPRINTS
Women's Press Classics; **Livewire Books for Teenagers** Fiction and non-fiction series for young adults. Synopses and ideas for books welcome. No mss without previous letter, synopsis and sample material.
Royalties paid twice-yearly.

Authors' Rating Aims to move up the ranks of fiction publishers with at least one lead title each season.

Woodhead Publishing Ltd
Abington Hall, Abington, Cambridge CB1 6AH
☎01223 891358   Fax 01223 893694
Email wp@woodhead-publishing.com
Website www.woodhead-publishing.com
Chairman *Alan Jessup*

Managing Director *Martin Woodhead*
Approx. Annual Turnover £1.3 million

FOUNDED 1989. *Publishes* engineering, materials technology, textile technology, finance and investment, food technology, environmental science. TITLES *Welding International* (journal); *Reinforced Plastics Durability*; *Meat Science 6e*; *Base Metals Handbook*; *Foreign Exchange Options*. About 50 titles a year.
DIVISIONS **Woodhead Publishing** *Martin Woodhead*; **Abington Publishing** (in association with the Welding Institute) *Francis Dodds*. Unsolicited material welcome.
Royalties paid annually.

Wordsmill & Tate Publishers

88 Kingsway, Holborn, London
WC2B 6AA
☎020 7841 2715 Fax 020 7841 1001
Email <name>@wordsmill.com
Website www.wordsmill.com

Commissioning Editor *Matthew Tate*
Editorial Coordinator *Jane Barrington*

Independent publisher *specialising* in hardback and paperback general fiction and non-fiction, biography, autobiography, memoirs, children's and history. No poetry, erotica or cookery. About 35–40 titles a year. Unsolicited material welcome with return postage. First time authors should send synopsis and sample chapters only.
Royalties paid twice-yearly.

Wordsworth Editions Ltd

Cumberland House, Crib Street, Ware,
Hertfordshire SG12 9ET
☎01920 465167 Fax 01920 462267
Email enquiries@wordsworth-editions.com *or*
  Editorial: dennishart@wordsworth-editions.com
Website www.wordsworth-editions.co.uk

Directors *M.C.W. Trayler, E.G. Trayler*
Approx. Annual Turnover £4 million

FOUNDED 1987. *Publishes* classics of English and world literature, reference books, poetry, children's classics, military history. Recently launched a new series of myth, legend and folklore books. About 75 titles a year. No unsolicited mss.

WPC Education

See **Wimbledon Publishing Company**

X Libris

See **Time Warner Books UK**

The X Press

PO Box 25694, London N17 6FP
☎020 8801 2100 Fax 020 8885 1322
Email vibes@xpress.co.uk

Editorial Director *Dotun Adebayo*
Marketing Director *Steve Pope*

LAUNCHED in 1992 with the cult bestseller *Yardie*, The X Press is the leading publisher of Black-interest fiction in the UK. Also *publishes* general fiction and children's fiction. 28 titles in 2001. IMPRINTS **The X Press** TITLES *Yardie*; *Baby Father*. **Nia** TITLE *In Search of Satisfaction*. **20/20** TITLE *Curvy Lovebox*. Send mss rather than synopses or ideas (enclose s.a.e.). No poetry.
Royalties paid annually.

Authors' Rating A small company that has done an inestimable service by introducing Black writers to the publishing mainstream. Popular fiction is the mainstay but the list also covers reprints of classic Black fiction.

Y Ddraig Fach

See **Ashley Drake Publishing Ltd**

Y Lolfa Cyf

Talybont, Ceredigion SY24 5AP
☎01970 832304 Fax 01970 832782
Email ylolfa@ylolfa.com
Website www.ylolfa.com/

Managing Director *Garmon Gruffudd*
General Editor *Lefi Gruffudd*
Approx. Annual Turnover £800,000

FOUNDED 1967. Small company which publishes mainly in Welsh; has its own four-colour printing and binding facilities. *Publishes* Welsh language publications; Celtic language tutors; English language books for the Welsh and Celtic tourist trade; nationalism and music. About 30 titles a year. Expanding slowly. TITLES *My Kingdom of Books* Richard Booth; *The Welsh Learner's Dictionary* Heini Gruffudd; *The Fight for Welsh Freedom* Gwynfor Evans. IMPRINT **Dinas** Part-author-subsidised imprint for non-mainstream books of Welsh interest in English and Welsh. Write first with synopses or ideas.
Royalties paid twice-yearly.

Yale University Press (London)

23 Pond Street, London NW3 2PN
☎020 7431 4422 Fax 020 7431 3755

Managing Director/Editorial Director
John Nicoll

FOUNDED 1961. Owned by US parent company. *Publishes* academic and humanities. About 200 titles (worldwide) a year. Unsolicited mss and synopses welcome if within specialised subject areas.

Royalties paid annually.

Authors' Rating A publisher with a marvellous talent for turning out scholarly books which also appeal to the general reader. Academic writers who want to reach a wider audience should take note.

Roy Yates Books

Smallfields Cottage, Cox Green, Rudgwick, Horsham, West Sussex RH12 3DE
☎01403 822299 Fax 01403 823012

Chairman/Managing Director *Roy Yates*
Approx. Annual Turnover £120,000

FOUNDED 1990. *Publishes* children's books only. No unsolicited material as books are adaptations of existing popular classics suitable for translation into dual-language format.

Royalties paid quarterly.

Yellow Jersey

See **Random House Group Ltd**

Zambezi Publishing Ltd

PO Box 221, Plymouth, Devon PL2 2YJ
☎01752 367300 Fax 01752 350453
Email info@zampub.com
Website www.zampub.com

Chair *Sasha Fenton*
Managing Director *Jan Budkowski*

FOUNDED 1999. *Publishes* non-fiction: mind, body and spirit, New Age, self-help. 5 titles in 2001. IMPRINT **Zambezi Publishing** *Sasha Fenton* TITLES *Chinese Divinations*; *Fortune Telling by Tarot Cards*. No unsolicied mss or ideas for books; send synopsis and sample chapter by mail. Brief e-mail communication acceptable but *no* attachments, please.

Royalties paid twice-yearly.

Zastrugi Books

PO Box 2963, Brighton, East Sussex BN1 6AW
☎01273 566369 Fax 01273 566369/562720

Chairman *Ken Singleton*

FOUNDED 1997. *Publishes* English-language teaching books only. No unsolicited mss; synopses and ideas for books welcome.

Royalties paid twice-yearly.

Zed Books Ltd

7 Cynthia Street, London N1 9JF
☎020 7837 4014 Fax 020 7833 3960
Email hosie@zedbooks.demon.co.uk
Website www.zedbooks.demon.co.uk

Approx. Annual Turnover £1 million

FOUNDED 1976. *Publishes* international and Third World affairs, development studies, women's studies, environmental studies, cultural studies and specific area studies. No fiction, children's or poetry. About 50 titles a year.

DIVISIONS **Development & Environment** *Robert Molteno*; **Women's Studies, Cultural Studies**. TITLES *The Development Dictionary* ed. Wolfgang Sachs; *Staying Alive* Vandana Shiva; *The Autobiography of Nawal* Nawal El Saadawi. No unsolicited mss; synopses and ideas welcome though.

Royalties paid annually.

Zero to Ten

See **Evans Brothers Ltd**

Zigzag

Chrysalis Children's Books, 64 Brewery Road, London N7 9NT
☎020 7697 3000 Fax 020 7697 3003
Email zigzag@chrysalisbooks.co.uk
Website www.chrysalisbooks.co.uk

Editorial Head *Honor Head*

Part of the children's division of **Chrysalis Books**. Interactive non-fiction for ages 5–14 on popular subjects. Most books contain CD-ROMs and Internet links. No unsolicited mss.

Zipper Books

See **Millivres-Prowler Group**

The Closed Book

Barry Turner argues that book buyers and readers are not necessarily the same thing

It is one of the great mysteries of publishing, one that is scarcely acknowledged, let alone investigated. How many books, once bought, are never read? That the number is substantial, no one would dispute. The titles on any coffee or bedside table will include at least one volume with a fading marker stuck between the opening pages. Value judgement plays a part, of course. A classic of modern fiction for one reader can transpose into pretentious nonsense when viewed by another pair of eyes. But while it may be true that variety is the spice of culture, it does not account for the mass of books that achieve respectable sales without ever having much prospect of being read.

Many of them are part of that prodigious and ever-growing output for the gift market. Some 40 per cent of booksellers' business is done in the two months leading up to Christmas. This is the time of year (along with birthdays and other anniversaries) when friends and family try to make up for not buying a really useful present by nipping into Waterstone's for the latest TV spin-off. 'You'll love it, my dear; you won't be able to put it down.' Well, you don't and you can. Having taken off the jolly wrapper and noted the sticky circle where the discount price has been peeled away, it only remains to find a space on the shelves where the volume can repose, unloved and unread.

Publishing thrives on the gift market. The secret is to produce what people think other people will want. Right or wrong, it is no concern of the publisher as long as he makes a sale. Outside the bestseller list (rejected by those who don't want to be thought predictable), the ideal gift book is a hefty tome (substance is equated with generosity) on a subject that is at once intellectually flattering but not too demanding, racy but not offensive, dramatic but never threatening – in fact, thoroughly anodyne, the sort of book that Aunt Edna might read if she didn't spend so much time watching *EastEnders*. The doorstop biography fits the bill, one that has a sales appeal enhanced by association with a name familiar to all. Shakespeare, say, or Lord Byron. It is a fair guess that most biographies are bought as presents; it is an equally fair guess that few of the recipients have ever read beyond the introduction. Aside from the stray marker, the pristine pages and the uncrumpled jacket are the giveaway, though not quite so obvious as the uncut pages of nineteenth-century anthologies of speeches and sermons which pop up in secondhand bookshops still looking for willing readers.

The nearest modern equivalents to the literary dinosaurs are produced by the university presses. Nobody but nobody reads the great mass of academic books, not even the academics, unless they themselves happen to be writing books, in which case relevant titles will be skimmed for suitable quotes. This is called research. The sole justification for the standard academic's book – ill written, poorly edited and dry as dust – is to prove to the university powers, particularly those who make appointments, that the author is doing some serious work in between vacations. But if no one is reading the stuff where is the business that makes it all worthwhile? The answer is on the library shelves. Since the publisher does not have to shift many copies of an expensive title to turn in a modest profit, library sales at home and abroad keep the academic show on the road. Recently released figures from Cambridge University Press reveal an in-print backlist of 13,500 titles, of which 8,000 sell fewer than 100 copies a year. Yet the total annual income generated is around £40 million. Even so, this is one bonanza that can't last. The new technology gave a short-term boost to the market by making it easier and cheaper to print books but now, in the age of the Internet, there are ways of disseminating knowledge that do not depend on producing hard-print heavyweights. The academic market is in meltdown.

Not so the third prolific source of unread books. Self-improvement starts with the classics we like to keep against the day (it never arrives) when we have the time and patience to catch up on a misspent education. One day my Proust will come but not yet, not yet. One of the most successful publishers to be set up in the last decade is Wordsworth, which trades entirely in cheap reprints of books known more by author and title than by content. Wordsworth deserves credit for opening up a market previously dominated by Penguin's over-priced classics but don't let us kid ourselves that more sales can be equated with more readers. Comfort buying is the name of this highly profitable game.

In the fantasy world of self-improvement, the biggest cash prizes go to publishers and authors who promise everything and deliver next to nothing. If the skills of the average middle manager are anything to go by, the popularity of myriad books guaranteeing instant success in business has achieved little except to raise hopes beyond realistic expectations. Cookery books sell, appropriately, like hot cakes without denting the consumption of junk food. There is always bookshop room for another foreign-language kit, yet the linguistic abilities of the British tourist remain pathetically modest.

And what of all those science bestsellers that attempt to explain the meaning of life? Stephen Hawking's *A Brief History of Time* was a fixture on the upper reaches of the bestseller list for over a year. Are we any the wiser? Need I ask? But in the ranks of the great unread, Hawking et al are far outclassed by the defenders of spiritual values. The best bestseller of all time is the Bible. Call it a symbol of Christian culture, the literary equivalent of a security blanket, a source of aphorisms. What it is not is a book for reading.

That many, possibly most, books do go to furnish a room but do little else is plain. Does it matter? Only to the extent that the number of books published is often taken as a measure of national literacy. A more unreliable benchmark would be hard to imagine.

Irish Publishers

International Reply Coupons (IRCs)

For return postage, IRCs are required (*not* UK postage stamps). These are available from post offices: letters, 60 pence; mss according to weight.

An Gúm

Cúirt Fhreidric, Sr. Fhreidric Thuaidh, Baile Átha Cliath 1
☎00 353 1 889 2800 Fax 00 353 1 873 1140
Email gum@educ.irlgov.ie
Senior Editor *Seosamh Ó Murchú*
Editor *Antain Mag Shamhráin*

FOUNDED 1926. Formerly the Irish language publications branch of the Department of Education and Science. Has now become part of the North/South Language Body established under the Good Friday Agreement to provide general reading, textbooks and dictionaries in the Irish language. *Publishes* educational, children's, music, lexicography and general. Little fiction or poetry. About 50 titles a year. Unsolicited mss, synopses and ideas for books welcome. Also welcomes reading copies of first and second level school textbooks with a view to translating them into the Irish language.
Royalties paid annually.

Anvil Books

45 Palmerston Road, Dublin 6
☎00 353 1 497 3628 Fax 00 353 1 496 8263
Managing Director *Rena Dardis*

FOUNDED 1964 with emphasis on Irish history and biography. Expansion of the list followed to include more general interest Irish material and, in 1982, The Children's Press was established. *Publishes* Irish history, biography (particularly 1916–22), folklore and children's fiction (for ages 9–14). No adult fiction, poetry, fantasy, short stories or illustrated books for children under 9. About 7 titles a year. 'Because of promotional requirements, only books by Irish-based authors considered and only books of Irish interest.' Send synopsis only with IRCs (no UK stamps); unsolicited mss not returned.
Royalties paid annually.

Ashfield Press

See **Blackhall Publishing**

Attic Press Ltd

c/o Cork University Press, Crawford Business Park, Crosses Green, Cork
☎00 353 21 432 1725 Fax 00 353 21 431 5329
Email S.Wilbourne@ucc.ie
Website www.iol.ie/~atticirl/
Publisher *Sara Wilbourne*

FOUNDED 1988. Began life in 1984 as a forum for information on the Irish feminist movement. *Publishes* non-fiction (history, women's studies, politics, biography). About 5 titles a year. Does not accept unsolicited proposals in adult fiction.
Royalties paid twice-yearly.

Blackhall Publishing

27 Carysfort Avenue, Blackrock, Co. Dublin
☎00 353 1 278 5090 Fax 00 353 1 278 4446
Email blackhall@eircom.net
Website www.blackhallpublishing.com
Managing Director *Gerard O'Connor*
Commissioning Editor *Ruth Garvey*

Publishes business, management and law books. Main subject areas include accounting, finance, management, marketing and law books aimed at both students and professionals in the industry. TITLES *Effective Top Team Management Teams*; *Winning Lifetime Customers*; *The Business Coaching Revolution*; *Clearly Computing* series; *The Management Compass*; *Untangling Organizational Gridlock*. IMPRINTS **Ashfield Press** Irish-interest books, both fiction and non-fiction. TITLES *Music for Middlebrows*; *The Brothers Behan*. **Inns Quay** TITLE *Irish Business Law*. Unsolicited mss and synopses welcome.
Royalties paid annually.

Blackwater Press

c/o Folens Publishers, Hibernian Industrial Estate, Greenhills Road, Tallaght, Dublin 24
☎00 353 1 413 7200 Fax 00 353 1 413 7280
Email john.o'connor@folens.ie
Chief Executive *Dirk Folens*
Managing Director *John O'Connor*

Part of Folens Publishers. *Publishes* political,

sports, fiction (*Margaret Burns*) and children's (*Deidre Whelan*). 84 titles in 2000.

Bradshaw Books

Tigh Filí, Thompson House, MacCurtain Street, Cork
☎00 353 21 450 9274 Fax 00 353 21 455 1617
Email admin@cwpc.ie
Website www.tighfili.com
Managing Director *Maire Bradshaw*
Literature Office *Liz Willows*
FOUNDED 1985. *Publishes* poetry, short stories, women's issues, spiritual, children's books. 6 titles in 2001. Organisers of the annual Lit. Review Ireland poetry competition. SERIES *Cork Literary Review; Eurochild; Millennium Poets; Lit Review Ireland; Eurochild; 21st Century Poets*. Submit letter, synopsis, sample chapters and s.a.e.
Royalties not generally paid.

Brandon/Mount Eagle

Dingle, Co. Kerry
☎00 353 66 915 1463
Fax 00 353 66 915 1234
Website www.brandonbooks.com
Publisher *Steve MacDonogh*
Approx. Annual Turnover €445,000
FOUNDED in 1997. *Publishes* strong Irish fiction and some non-fiction. About 15 titles a year. Not seeking unsolicited mss.

Edmund Burke Publisher

Cloonagashel, 27 Priory Drive, Blackrock, Co. Dublin
☎00 353 1 288 2159 Fax 00 353 1 283 4080
Email deburca@indigo.ie
Website www.deburcararebooks.com
Chairman *Eamonn De Búrca*
Approx. Annual Turnover E320,000
Small family-run business publishing historical and topographical and fine limited-edition books relating to Ireland. TITLES *History of the County of Mayo* Knox; *King Charles II Irish Army List* Dalton; *History of Dun Laoghaire Harbour* De Courcy Ireland; *Great Book of Irish Genealogies* 5 Vols.; *Irish Flower Garden Replanted* Nelson and Walsh; *The Three Candles, a Bibliographical Catalogue* de Búrca. Unsolicited mss welcome. No synopses or ideas.
Royalties paid annually.

Butterworth Ireland Limited

26 Upper Ormond Quay, Dublin 7
☎00 353 1 872 8514 (Law)/8524 (Tax)
Fax 00 353 1 873 1378
Website www.butterworths.ie

Chairman *P. Virik (UK)*
Legal Editor – Managing *Louise Leavy*
List Development Editor – Tax *David Hession*
Legal Editor *Ciarán Toland*
Subsidiary of Lexis Nexis Butterworth Tolley, London, (**Reed Elsevier** is the holding company). Leading publisher of Irish law and tax titles. *Publishes* solely law and tax books and electronic products. Unsolicited mss, synopses and ideas welcome for titles within the broadest parameters of tax and law.
Royalties paid twice-yearly.

The Children's Press

See **Anvil Books**

The Chronicle of Ireland

Park House, Foxrock, Dublin 18
☎00 353 1 235 2657 Fax 00 353 1 285 0157
Email natcollom@aol.com
Managing Editor *Harry Walsh*
Publishes the Chronicle of Ireland series, a two-volume annual review of the coverage by the main national media of the political, commercial and social developments in Ireland, North and South. IMPRINT **"G" Gulliver Book**.

Cló Iar-Chonnachta

Indreabhán, Connemara, Galway
☎00 353 91 593307 Fax 00 353 91 593362
Email cic@iol.ie
Website www.cic.ie
Chairman/Director *Micheál Ó Conghaile*
Editor *Róisin Ní Mhianáin*
Approx. Annual Turnover €320,000
FOUNDED 1985. *Publishes* fiction, poetry, plays, teenage fiction and children's, mostly in Irish, including translations. Also publishes cassettes of writers reading from their own works. 15 titles in 2001. TITLES *Sna Fir* Micheál ó Conghaile; *Breandán Ó hEithir, Iomramh Aonair* Liam Mac Con Iomaire; *The Village Sings* Gabriel Fitzmaurice; *Out in the Open* Cathal ó Searcaigh.
Royalties paid annually.

The Columba Press

55A Spruce Avenue, Stillorgan Industrial Park, Blackrock, Co. Dublin
☎00 353 1 294 2556 Fax 00 353 1 294 2564
Email sean@columba.ie (editorial) *or*
    info@columba.ie (general)
Website www.columba.ie
Chairman *Neil Kluepfel*
Managing Director *Seán O'Boyle*
Approx. Annual Turnover €1.02 million

FOUNDED 1985. Small company committed to growth. *Publishes* religious and counselling titles. 30 titles in 2001. (Backlist of 225 titles.) TITLES *The Glenstal Book of Prayer* by the monks of Glenstal; *St Thérèse in Ireland* Audrey Healy and Eugene McCaffrey. Unsolicited ideas and synopses rather than full mss preferred.
Royalties paid twice-yearly.

Cork University Press
Crawford Business Park, Crosses Green, Cork, Co. Cork
☎00 353 21 490 2980 Fax 00 353 21 431 5329
Email corkunip@ucc.ie
Website www.corkuniversitypress.com
Publisher *Sara Wilbourne*
Editor *Lucy Freeman*
FOUNDED 1925. Relaunched in 1992, the Press *publishes* academic and some trade titles. 26 titles in 2001. TITLES *Irish Migrants in Britain, 1815–1914: Documentary History; The Tourists's Gaze: Travellers to Ireland, 1800–2000; Yeats, the Irish Literary Revival and the Politics of Print.* Two journals, *Irish Review* (biannual), an interdisciplinary cultural review, and *The Irish Journal of Feminist Studies* (biannual), are now part of the list. Unsolicited synopses and ideas welcome for textbooks, academic monographs, belles lettres, illustrated histories and journals.
Royalties paid twice-yearly.

CJ Fallon Limited
Lucan Road, Palmerstown, Dublin 20
☎00 353 1 616 6400 Fax 00 353 1 616 6499
Email editorial@cjfallon.ie
Website www.cjfallon.ie
Owner *Adare Printing Group*
Managing Director *Henry McNicholas*
Editorial Head *Niall White*
FOUNDED 1927. Educational publishers for first and second level schools in Ireland. Unsolicited mss, synopses and ideas welcome; approach in writing in the first instance. No non-educational material considered.
Royalties paid annually.

Flyleaf Press
4 Spencer Villas, Glenageary, Co. Dublin
☎00 353 1 283 1693 Fax 00 353 1 283 1693
Email Flyleaf@indigo.ie
Website www.flyleaf.ie
Managing Director *Dr James Ryan*
FOUNDED 1981. Concentrates on family history and Irish history as a background to family history. No fiction. TITLES *Irish Records; Longford*

and its People; Tracing Your Kerry Ancestors; Tracing Your Dublin Ancestors. Unsolicited mss, synopses and ideas for books welcome.
Royalties paid twice-yearly.

Four Courts Press Ltd
Fumbally Lane, Dublin 8
☎00 353 1 453 4668 Fax 00 353 1 453 4672
Email info@four-courts-press.ie
Website www.four-courts-press.ie
Chairman/Managing Director *Michael Adams*
Director *Martin Healy*
FOUNDED 1972. *Publishes* mainly scholarly books in the humanities. About 60 titles a year. Synopses and ideas for books welcome.
Royalties paid annually.

Gateway
See **Gill & Macmillan**

Gill & Macmillan
10 Hume Avenue, Park West, Dublin 12
☎00 353 1 500 9500 Fax 00 353 1 500 9599
Website www.gillmacmillan.ie
Managing Director *M.H. Gill*
Approx. Annual Turnover €9.5 million
FOUNDED 1968 when M.H. Gill & Son Ltd and Macmillan Ltd formed a jointly owned publishing company. *Publishes* biography/autobiography, history, current affairs, literary criticism (all mainly of Irish interest), guidebooks, cookery, popular fiction. Also educational textbooks for secondary and tertiary levels. About 100 titles a year. Contacts: *Hubert Mahony* (educational); *Fergal Tobin* (general); *Ailbhe O'Reilly* (tertiary textbooks). IMPRINTS **Newleaf** *Eveleen Coyle* Popular health, psychology, mind, body and spirit; **Gateway** Spirituality, cosmic issues, environment, alternative science. **Tivoli** *Alison Walsh* Popular fiction. Unsolicited synopses and ideas welcome.
Royalties paid subject to contract.

Goldcrest
See **Poolbeg Press Ltd**

Inns Quay
See **Blackhall Publishing**

Institute of Public Administration
57–61 Lansdowne Road, Dublin 4
☎00 353 1 269 7011 Fax 00 353 1 269 8644
Email Sales@ipa.ie
Website www.ipa.ie
Chairman *Paddy Donnelly*

Director-General *Patrick A. Hall*
Publisher *Tony McNamara*
Approx. Annual Turnover €900,000

FOUNDED 1957 by a group of public servants, the Institute of Public Administration is the Irish public sector management development agency. The publishing arm of the organisation is one of its major activities. *Publishes* academic and professional books and periodicals: history, law, politics, economics and Irish public administration for students and practitioners. 10 titles in 2001. TITLES *Administration Yearbook & Diary*; *Media and the Marketplace*; *The Ogham Stone*; *Investing in People*; *From Cottage to Crèche*. No unsolicited mss; synopses and ideas welcome. No fiction or children's publishing.
Royalties paid annually.

Irish Academic Press Ltd
44 Northumberland Road, Ballsbridge, Dublin 4
☎00 353 1 668 8244 Fax 00 353 1 660 1610
Email info@iap.ie
Website www.iap.ie

Chairman *Frank Cass* (London)
Managing Editor *Mike Milotte*

FOUNDED 1974. *Publishes* academic monographs and humanities. 17 titles in 2001. Unsolicited mss, synopses and ideas welcome.
Royalties paid annually.

Irish Management Institute
Sandyford Road, Dublin 16
☎00 353 1 207 8400 Fax 00 353 1 295 5150
Email bill.carroll@imi.ie
Website www.imi.ie

Chief Executive *Barry Kenny*
Approx. Annual Turnover €15 million

FOUNDED 1952. The Institute, owned by its members, both corporate and individual, works to improve the practice of management. Offers managers a wide range of management development services. *Publishes* a newsletter, *Management Focus* on a quarterly basis, distributed to members. Other publications include periodic economic reports and management research and texts. Mss, synopses and ideas relevant to Irish management practice welcome.
Royalties paid annually.

The Lilliput Press
62–63 Sitric Road, Arbour Hill, Dublin 7
☎00 353 1 671 1647 Fax 00 353 1 671 1233
Email info@lilliputpress.ie
Website www.lilliputpress.ie

Chairman *Kathy Gilfillan*

Managing Director *Antony Farrell*
Approx. Annual Turnover €255,000

FOUNDED 1984. *Publishes* non-fiction: literature, history, autobiography and biography, ecology, essays; criticism; fiction and poetry. About 20 titles a year. TITLES *Grattan: A Life*; *The Outer Edge of Ulster*, *Gander at the Gate* (autobiography); *Nature in Ireland*; *Hugh Lane 1875–1915* (biography); *Malinski* (fiction); *Images of Dublin* (photography). Unsolicited mss, synopses and ideas welcome. No children's or sport titles.
Royalties paid annually.

Marino Books
See **Mercier Press Ltd**

Mercier Press Ltd
5 French Church Street, Cork
☎00 353 21 427 5040 Fax 00 353 21 427 4969
Email books@mercier.ie
Website www.mercier.ie
Also at: 16 Hume Street, Dublin 2
☎00 353 1 661 5299 Fax 00 353 1 661 8583
Email books@marino.ie

Chairman *George Eaton*
Managing Director *John F. Spillane*

FOUNDED 1944. One of Ireland's largest publishers with a list of approx 250 Irish interest titles. IMPRINTS **Mercier Press** *Mary Feehan* Children's, politics, history, mind, body and spirit. **Marino Books** *Jo O'Donoghue* Fiction, current affairs, women's interest. TITLES *The Course of Irish History*; all of John B. Keane's works; *Beyond Prozac*; *The Celtic Tiger: The Inside Story of Ireland's Boom Economy*. Unsolicited mss, synopses and ideas welcome.
Royalties paid annually.

Merlin Publishing
16 Upper Pembroke Street, Dublin 2
☎00 353 1 676 4373 Fax 00 353 1 676 4368
Website www.merlin-publishing.com *or* drumshee.com

Managing Director *Selga Medenieks*
Commissioning Editor *Aoife Barrett*

FOUNDED 2000. Member of **Clé**. *Publishes* art, biography, children's fiction, general non-fiction, history, photography, literature, literary studies and gift books. About 50 titles a year (mainly Irish interest). IMPRINT **Wolfhound Press** FOUNDED 1974. Fiction, children's and some non-fiction. TITLES *Famine*; *Eyewitness Bloody Sunday*; *Father Browne's Titanic Album*. Unsolicited mss (with synopses and s.a.e.) welcome but by post only. See Merlin website for submission guidelines and proposal form.

Mount Eagle
See **Brandon/Mount Eagle**

Newleaf
See **Gill & Macmillan**

The O'Brien Press Ltd
20 Victoria Road, Rathgar, Dublin 6
☎00 353 1 492 3333 Fax 00 353 1 492 2777
Email books@obrien.ie
Website www.obrien.ie
Managing Director/Publisher *Michael O'Brien*
Editorial Director *Íde Ní Laoghaire*
FOUNDED 1974. *Publishes* business, true crime, biography, music, travel, sport, Celtic subjects, food and drink, history, humour, politics, reference. Children's publishing – mainly fiction for every age from tiny tots to teenage. Illustrated fiction SERIES *Pandas* (5 years+); *Flyers* (6 years+); *Red Flag* (8 years+). Novels (10 years+) – contemporary, historical, fantasy. Some non-fiction – mainly historical, and art and craft, resource books for teachers. No poetry, adult fiction or academic. Unsolicited mss (sample chapters only), synopses and ideas for books welcome. Submissions will not be returned.
Royalties paid annually.

Oak Tree Press
19 Rutland Street, Cork
☎00 353 21 431 3855 Fax 00 353 21 431 3496
Email info@oaktreepress.com
Website www.oaktreepress.com
Managing Director *Brian O'Kane*
FOUNDED 1992. Specialist publisher of business and professional books with a focus on small business start-up and development. Unsolicited mss and synopses welcome; send to the managing director, at the address above.
Royalties paid annually.

On Stream Publications Ltd
Currabaha, Cloghroe, Co. Cork
☎00 353 21 438 5798 Fax 00 353 21 438 5798
Email info@onstream.ie
Website www.onstream.ie
Chairman/Managing Director *Roz Crowley*
Approx. Annual Turnover €255,000
FOUNDED 1992. Formerly Forum Publications. *Publishes* academic, fiction, cookery, wine, general health and fitness, local history, railways, photography and practical guides. About

6 titles a year. TITLES *Keeping Resources Human – A Practical Guide to Retaining Staff; The Book of Scarves: 100 Ideas; Dealing With Chronic Pain;* A Pinch of This – Tastes of Home-Cooking. Synopses and ideas welcome. No children's books.
Royalties paid annually.

Poolbeg Press Ltd
123 Grange Hill, Baldoyle, Dublin 13
☎00 353 1 832 1477 Fax 00 353 1 832 1430
Email poolbeg@poolbeg.com
Website www.poolbeg.com
Publisher *Paula Campbell*
FOUNDED 1976 to publish the Irish short story and has since diversified to include all areas of fiction (literary and popular), children's fiction and non-fiction, and adult non-fiction: history, biography and topics of public interest. About 70 titles a year. AUTHORS first published by Poolbeg include Marian Hayes, Sheila O'Flanagan, Cathy Kelly and Patricia Scanlan. Unsolicited mss, synopses and ideas welcome (mss preferred). No drama.
IMPRINTS**Poolbeg** (paperback and hardback); **Poolbeg For Children; Goldcrest; Wren.**
Royalties paid twice-yearly.

Real Ireland Design Ltd
27 Beechwood Close, Boghall Road, Bray, Co. Wicklow
☎00 353 1 286 0799 Fax 00 353 1 282 9962
Managing Director *Desmond Leonard*
Producers of calendars, diaries, posters, greetings cards and books, servicing the Irish tourist industry. *Publishes* photography and tourism. About 2 titles a year. No fiction. Unsolicited mss, synopses and ideas welcome.
Royalties paid twice-yearly.

Royal Dublin Society
Science Section, Ballsbridge, Dublin 4
☎00 353 1 668 0866 Fax 00 353 1 660 4014
Email Annette Macdonald@rds.ie
Website www.rds.ie
President *Michael Jacobs*
FOUNDED 1731 for the promotion of agriculture, science and the arts, and throughout its history has published books and journals towards this end. *Publishes* conference proceedings, biology and the history of Irish science. TITLES *Agricultural Development for the 21st Century; The Right Trees in the Right Places; Agriculture & the Environment; Water of Life; Science, Technology & Realism; Science Centres for*

Ireland; *Blueprint for a National Irish Science Centre*; *Science Education in Crisis*; occasional papers in *Irish Science & Technology* series.
Royalties not generally paid.

Royal Irish Academy

19 Dawson Street, Dublin 2
☎00 353 1 676 2570   Fax 00 353 1 676 2346
Executive Secretary *Patrick Buckley*
Editor of Publications *Rachel McNicholls*

FOUNDED in 1785, the Academy has been publishing since 1787. Core publications are journals but more books published in last 14 years. *Publishes* academic, Irish interest and Irish language. About 7 titles a year. Welcomes mss, synopses and ideas of an academic standard.
Royalties paid annually, where applicable.

Salmon Publishing Ltd

See entry under **Poetry Presses**

Simon & Schuster/Town House

See **Town House and Country House**

Sitric Books

62–63 Sitric Road, Arbour Hill, Dublin 7
☎00 353 1 671 1682   Fax 00 353 1 671 1233
Chair *Vivienne Guinness*
Managing Director *Antony Farrell*

FOUNDED 2000. *Publishes* current affairs, biography and fiction. About 5 titles a year. TITLES *Diary of a Teddy Boy*; *The Beat*; *Promises to Keep: A woman's medical nightmare and her husband's search for the truth*; *She Moves Through the Boom*. Unsolicited mss, synopses and ideas welcome. No children's or sports titles.
Royalties paid annually.

Tír Eolas

Newtownlynch, Doorus, Kinvara, Co. Galway
☎00 353 91 637452   Fax 00 353 91 637452
Email info@tireolas.com
Website www.tireolas.com
Publisher/Managing Director *Anne Korff*
Approx. Annual Turnover €65,000

FOUNDED 1987. *Publishes* books and guides on ecology, archaeology, folklore and culture. TITLES *The Book of the Burren*; *The Shannon Floodlands*; *Not a Word of a Lie*; *The Book of Aran*; *Women of Ireland, A Biographic Dictionary*; *Kinvara, A Seaport Town on Galway Bay*; *A Burren Journal*; *The Shores of Connemara*. Unsolicited mss, synopses and ideas for books welcome. No specialist scientific and technical, fiction, plays, school textbooks or philosophy.
Royalties paid annually.

Tivoli

See **Gill & Macmillan**

Town House and Country House

Trinity House, Charleston Road, Ranelagh, Dublin 6
☎00 353 1 497 2399   Fax 00 353 1 497 0927
Email books@townhouse.ie
Managing Director *Treasa Coady*

FOUNDED 1980. *Publishes* commercial fiction, art and archaeology, biography and environment. About 20 titles a year. TITLES *Love Like Hate Adore* Deirdre Purcell; *Mary, Mary* Julie Parsons; *Now is the Time* Sr. Stanislaus Kennedy; *Wild Wicklow* Richard Nairn and Miriam Crowley. IMPRINT **Simon & Schuster/TownHouse** FOUNDED 2001. *Publishes* Fiction and nonfiction. Unsolicited mss, synopses and ideas welcome. No children's books.
Royalties paid twice-yearly.

Veritas Publications

7–8 Lower Abbey Street, Dublin 1
☎00 353 1 878 8177   Fax 00 353 1 878 6507
Email publications@veritas.ie
Website www.veritas.ie
Director *Maura Hyland*
Managing Editor *Toner Quinn*

FOUNDED 1969 to supply religious textbooks to schools and later introduced a wide-ranging general list. Part of the Catholic Communications Institute. *Publishes* books on religious, ethical, moral, societal and social issues. 30 titles a year. Unsolicited mss, synopses and ideas for books welcome.
Royalties paid annually.

Wolfhound Press

See **Merlin Publishing**

Wren

See **Poolbeg Press Ltd**

Irish Literary Agents

The Book Bureau Literary Agency

7 Duncairn Avenue, Bray, Co Wicklow
☎00 353 1 276 4996
Fax 00 353 1 276 4834
Contact *Geraldine Nichol*

Handles mainstream and adult literary fiction. 'Strong editorial support before submission to publishers.' Send preliminary letter, synopsis and first 5 chapters; return postage/IRCs essential. *Commission* Home 10%; Overseas 20%. Works with foreign associates.

The Lisa Richards Agency

46 Upper Baggot Street, Dublin 4
☎00 353 1 660 3534
Fax 00 353 1 660 3545
Email fogrady@eircom.net
Contact *Faith O'Grady*

FOUNDED 1998. *Handles* fiction and general non-fiction (biography, memoirs, popular history, science), children's books, and film, TV and theatre scripts. Approach with proposal and sample chapter for non-fiction, and 3–4 chapters and short synopsis for fiction. No reading fee. CLIENTS Terry Eagleton, Martin Malone, Pauline McLynn, Damian Owens, Homan Potterton. *Commission* Home 10%; UK 15%; US & Translation 20%; Film & TV 15%. *Overseas associate* **The Marsh Agency** for translation rights.

Russell Literary Agency

PO Box 5, Bantry, Co. Cork
☎00 353 87 233 1970
Email russellbooks@eircom.net
Contacts *Andrew Russell, Jane Russell*

FOUNDED 2002. *Handles* commercial and literary fiction and non-fiction. No plays, poetry, fantasy/science fiction. Unsolicited mss welcome. Send covering letter with c.v., synopsis and 3 sample chapters in the first instance. No reading fee. *Commission* Home 10%; USA & Translation 20%.

Jonathan Williams Literary Agency

Ferrybank House, 6 Park Road, Dun Laoghaire, Co. Dublin
☎00 353 1 280 3482 Fax 00 353 1 280 3482
Contact *Jonathan Williams*

FOUNDED 1980. *Handles* general trade books: fiction, auto/biography, travel, politics, history, music, literature and criticism, gardening, cookery, sport and leisure, humour, reference, social questions, photography. Some poetry, business and children's, but less of a speciality. No plays, science fiction, mind, body and spirit, computer books, theology, multimedia, motoring, aviation. No reading fee unless 'the author wants a very fast opinion'. Initial approach by phone or letter. *Commission* Home 10%; US 20%; Translation 15%. *Overseas associates* Piergiorgio Nicolazzini Literary Agency, Italy; Lora Fountain Agency, France; Jan Michael, The Netherlands; Nadia Lawrence, Germany.

Taking Off: A Writer's Diary

Bob G. Ritchie looks back on a year of progress

January

Ease myself gently into creative mode by blowing the dust off a story I wrote last year inspired by photographs of Americans watching Bobby Kennedy's funeral train go by in 1968. At 10,000 words it feels too long, but maybe it'll make a good radio play. Not quite sure why I like it, but the naive hopes dashed at the end of the 60s still strike an emotional resonance with me. Let's hope it's not an omen of the year to come.

February

Finish rewriting pilot episode of my comedy drama series about a couple who make over people's otherwise sad, pathetic, colourless lives. It's a shameless exploitation of some of the most popular programmes on TV – *Ground Force*, *Changing Rooms*, *Looking Good* and *Don't Try This At Home* – so cannot possibly fail.

March

Send the Bobby play and *Makeover* to Jessica Dromgoole at the BBC New Writing Initiative, then start work on a TV sitcom set in an intensive care unit. It has just the right level of utterly tasteless black humour that should appeal to Channel 4 viewers. According to a piece in the *IoS*, no one's developing sitcoms any more, so not sure why I'm trying my hand at allegedly the most difficult kind of writing. I can hardly kid myself being shortlisted in last year's BBC Talent is only one step from becoming the next Richard Curtis. But at least writing comedy is fun. Well, more fun than writing about a family watching a funeral train go by, anyway.

April

A small envelope arrives in the post. Good news? Indeed it is. A magazine wants to publish one of my stories. Feel immediately as if I could leap tall buildings. Especially since the editor is also hanging on to the other story I sent 'for possible publication in a future issue'.

May

Makeover is rejected by the BBC ('too whimsical'), so I visit brother in Cornwall for a few days' R&R. Return home to a phone message from a lively voiced American woman called Carol. I gather she works for a publisher. 'We really enjoyed reading the start of the novel you sent us and we'd sure like to see the rest. Give me a call as soon as you can.'

Carol. What a lovely name.

The problem is I haven't touched The Novel since I sent her the first chapter six months ago. I call her to confess the rest isn't in a fit state to be read. 'I'm on the third draft,' I lie. Actually on the ninth. 'Doesn't matter,' she says. 'Send it when you can.'

So I'm now committed to spending the next few weeks licking it into shape. Not exactly looking forward to it. Recall what it was like when I was working full-time on it last year: became so engrossed, hardly saw the light of day; social life stopped dead, almost forgot how to speak.

The Bobby play comes back. The BBC reader thinks it's 'rather like *The Wonder Years* – it too often relies on a sense of wistfulness for its effect'. I can't help agreeing, though I've never seen *The Wonder Years*. *Intensive Care* is also now back from the six independent TV production companies who expressed an interest. Pete Atkin, script editor at Hat Trick, says there are 'a lot of enjoyable aspects to it', but it doesn't 'go on and do anything'. Victoria Grew at Alomo comes to the same conclusion – 'it reads more like a long sketch than an episode of a long-running series' – but then adds 'I do really like your writing' and asks me to write to her and tell her about myself. I consider this request for about half a second, then send a long letter by return.

Meanwhile, having decided to enter this year's BBC Talent competition with a speculative script for *Casualty*, I am almost done with moving Charlie Fairhead and Co. around Holby A&E. Only a couple of days to the deadline, which is cutting it fine, even by my standards, but we are, after all, dealing with matters of life and death. Injured child, serious skull fracture, paracetamol overdose, self-inflicted burn, road rage, bankruptcy, divorce, reconciliation – I bet you don't get all that in *The Wonder Years*.

June

Back to The Novel. I can't decide how much of my hero's childhood to include, nor even what kind of childhood he should have. I've already regressed him to eleven years old, but he was a bit of a psychopath even then, so maybe his ex-hippie mother was the problem, something to do with the man with whom she had a passionate but violent relationship when she was only sixteen. And where did she come from? London? Too 1960s. The North? Too 1950s. East Anglia? Too Graham Swift. Wales? Too poetic. Ireland? Far too poetic. Must go further afield. America? Yes. Which, because my hero ends up in America, makes his journey a circle. Very satisfying. And very popular in Hollywood movies.

Well, you have to think of these things.

July

Two more TV companies want to see the pilot script of *Makeover*. I spend another week on rewrites before sending it off. It hardly resembles my initial concept now, but I suppose that's what rewriting is about; one can't be sentimental. Even so, I shed a tear in the early hours for the demise of two characters I've become quite attached to. They were conceived, were born, grew, lived their brief lives, died – and no one knew about them except me.

The Novel progresses slowly. I give the hero a disturbing dream and drop the word 'mutilation' in, almost as an aside. Very pleasing. A deliberately vague but sinister hint of things to come. Realise writing a novel is like laying clues in a treasure hunt. Can't just tell people to go from A to B – too dull. Have to proceed by hints, suggestions, casual remarks. On the other hand very difficult to achieve a sense of mystery when I know what happens in the end.

Or do I?

August

Another rejection of *Makeover*, this time from Parallax, Ken Loach's production company. As usual, I try to dwell on the encouraging phrases: 'makeover culture is rich material for a series', 'great funny dialogue', 'clearly differentiated and accessible characters'. Unfortunately it also 'starts and develops too slowly', 'stretches credibility a bit too far', and has 'distracting elements'. In argumentative mood I read the script again, but am eventually forced to agree. But two companies still have it, so I decide not to do any more rewriting. Instead, in what can only be explained as a fit of madness, I decide to turn it into a radio play. Oh, dear.

Paul Abbott, writer of *Clocking Off*, suggests in an interview on the BBC website that most aspiring writers spend too much time working away at their single masterpiece, instead of trying out lots of different ideas. I suddenly panic I might be guilty of the same thing and do a quick count of the projects I've tackled in the last two years. Six short stories, five novels (all right, no more than a few pages of notes for three of them), two TV dramas, two TV sitcoms, one TV comedy drama series and five radio plays. At the end I'm none the wiser. Is that enough?

With rapidly diminishing enthusiasm I resume The Novel when – oh joy – a little bird tells me the publisher has gone bust. Phone Carol to check: dead line. Note also that the new edition of *Writer's Handbook* no longer contains an entry. Feel huge weight lift from my shoulders. Celebrate by running into the street and punching the air. Attend dinner party and find myself giggling like an idiot throughout. Conclude with relief that I'm not meant to be a novelist.

As if in confirmation, the next day a large envelope arrives from the BBC. *Casualty* script no. 885C (that's mine) has made it onto the Talent shortlist. All right, it's only one of a hundred, but as Jenny explains in her letter (Jenny – what a lovely name, so much nicer than Carol), that means it has already been approved by two readers. The catch is if I make it to the final fifteen I must submit an original idea for a new series. The three winners will be selected on the basis of their script and their series idea.

Help! What series idea?

September

I reach the final fifteen (well, of course I do, as in all the best stories) and am rewarded with a day-long workshop at Pebble Mill, an advance against future commissions and a request – well, more of a demand – that I neither talk to the press nor accept any commission from 'the other lot' without consulting the BBC first. I mention this to my daughter. 'Wow,' she says. 'Heavy.'

At the workshop we all sit in a circle like a meeting of Alcoholics Anonymous, along with Mal Young (Head of Drama Series) and various producers, script editors and writers from *Casualty* and *Doctors*. One by one they tell us what they are looking for: complete originality within a rigid set of guidelines. In other words, the moon on a stick. When Mal asks everyone to name their favourite TV series, over half – somewhat disloyally, I think – choose US programmes. Mal himself confesses he would never miss an episode of *The Sopranos*. Perhaps being in charge of BBC drama series is like running the Mafia.

After a weekend of nailbiting, I'm told I'm not one of the three winners. Actually less disappointed than I expected to be. Way past the age when my photograph would look good in the *Radio Times*.

October

An invitation from the BBC. Would I like to attend a session at London's Soho Theatre with a few heads of radio drama and comedy? Mightily chuffed, feel as if my name has been added to some list. Actually the theatre is jammed with 2–300 other hopefuls, so the list obviously isn't short. The session is chaired by a familiar face from my day at Pebble Mill, Kate Rowland, Creative Director, New Writing. She's flanked by the Commissioning Editor for Radio 4 and the Heads of Drama and Entertainment. Each gives a little spiel about where they fit in the BBC hierarchy, which is all very interesting but not why we're here. What we want to know is why our efforts keep getting rejected.

One poor soul actually asks, point-blank. 'Well,' improvises Kate, desperately trying to remember his script from among the 10,000 they receive each year, 'it probably wasn't good enough.' 'But,' protests possibly the next Harold Pinter, 'you gave it second prize in the Alfred Bradley playwriting competition.' Embarrassed looks all round. 'Come and see me afterwards,' says Kate. 'This one obviously slipped through the net.'

Ah, I can hear everyone thinking, that's obviously what happened to mine too.

Call from Jenny. My *Casualty* script has been passed to *EastEnders* with a strong recommendation. 'And,' she adds, 'expect a letter from *Doctors* soon.' I visit my local to have a celebratory drink or two. A friend is unimpressed. 'Writing for *EastEnders*? That's going to be a bit depressing, isn't it?'

As promised, an envelope arrives with BBC logo on it. I tear open with trembling fingers. Scan quickly for word 'sorry', but fail to find it. Instead see 'enjoyed' and 'invite' and 'submit'. Decide now safe to read properly. *Doctors* want me to submit ideas. Yesss!!!

November

To Bristol to see the BBC Talent Showcase: the three winning scripts performed live by the actual living breathing casts of *Doctors* and *Casualty*. I try not to look too stupidly star-struck. Congratulate Linda, Syed and Paul. Am I bitter? Not at all. Another failed finalist and I decide our scripts weren't chosen because they use too much outside broadcast. Well, stands to reason.

December

Lunch with editor of this *Handbook*. Very convivial. Bring him up to date on my writing career – or lack of it – and he says he'd like me to do a follow-up to my article for next year's edition. Briefly I worry that I might be in danger of becoming the most famous failed writer in the country. Then he adds that if I get any actual commissions before the deadline I can do a piece on how to get into TV. Feel this might be a bit premature, but by the end of the second bottle of wine I'm ready to write entire 'how to' book.

Leave restaurant slightly worse for wear but in buoyant mood. Pop into Waterstone's and surreptitiously rearrange shelf so that *The Writer's Handbook* is more prominent. Even turn one round so my name is visible.

I know, I know. Pathetic. But, as the year has proved, writing is a competition. And I want to win.

Audio Books

Assembled Stories
PO Box 5212, Grantham, Lincolnshire
NG33 5SR
☎01476 571333 Fax 01476 571333
Email assembledstories@hotmail.com
Website www.assembledstories.com
Managing Director *Peter Joyce*

FOUNDED 1992. *Publishes* classic fiction on cassette and CD with all books read by Peter Joyce. 6 titles in 2001. TITLES *Idle Thoughts of an Idle Fellow* Jerome K. Jerome; *The Monkey's Paw* W.W. Jacobs. Ideas for cassettes welcome.

AudioBooksForFree.Com Plc
25 Green Lane, Amersham, Buckinghamshire
HP6 6AS
☎01494 431119 Fax 01494 583417
Email ToUs@AudioBooksForFree.Com
Website www.AudioBooksForFree.Com
Managing Director *Ruslan G. Fedorovsky*

FOUNDED 2000. *Publishes* fiction: thrillers, crime, science fiction only. 60 titles in 2001. AUTHORS Michael Hartland, James Herlihy, Robert Jordan, Jon Schiller, Patrick Walsh, Edgar Rice Burroughs.

Barrington Stoke
See entry under **UK Publishers**

BBC Spoken Word
Windsor Bridge Road, Bath BA2 3AX
☎01225 335336 Fax 01225 310771
Owner *BBC Worldwide Ltd*
Managing Director *Jan Paterson*

BBC Spoken Word consists of the following IMPRINTS:

BBC Cover to Cover (email@coverto cover.co.uk) Editorial Director *Helen Nicoll* Unabridged readings of classic and contemporary children's titles. Unsolicited work not accepted.

BBC Radio Collection (radio.collection @bbc.co.uk) ESTABLISHED 1988. BBC Radio Collection releases material associated with BBC Radio and Television. Almost all releases sourced from BBC Radio and Television. Unsolicited work not accepted. TITLES *BBC Radio Shakespeare*; *Alan Bennett*; *This Sceptred Isle*; *Hancock*; *Steptoe*; *Round The Horne*; *Agatha Christie*; *Sherlock Holmes*. **BBC Word for Word** Unabridged contemporary adult titles. **Chivers** (see entry).

Canongate Audio
See **Canongate Books** under **UK Publishers**

Cavalcade Story Cassettes
See **Chivers Audio Books**

Chivers Audio Books
Windsor Bridge Road, Bath BA2 3AX
☎01225 335336 Fax 01225 310771
Website www.chivers.co.uk
Managing Director *Julian Batson*

Acquired by BBC Worldwide, Chivers *publishes* a wide range of titles on both cassette and CD, primarily for the library and direct mail markets. Fiction, autobiogrpahy, non-fiction, children's and crime. IMPRINTS **Chivers Audio Books**, **Chivers Children's Audio Books**, **Cavalcade Story Cassettes**.

Chrome Dreams
12 Seaforth Avenue, New Malden, Surrey
KT3 6JP
☎020 8715 9781 Fax 020 8241 1426
Email ob@chromedreams.co.uk
Website www.chromedreams.co.uk
Managing Director *Rob Johnstone*

A small record and music management company FOUNDED 1998 to produce audio-biographies of current rock and pop artists and legendary performers on CD and, more recently, books on the same subjects. 64 titles in 2000. Ideas for biographies welcome.

Corgi Audio
Transworld Publishers, A division of the Random House Group Ltd, 61–63 Uxbridge Road, London W5 5SA
☎020 8579 2652 Fax 020 8231 6666
Joint Managing Directors *Larry Finlay, Patrick Janson-Smith*

Publishes fiction, autobiography, children's and humour. TITLES *Discworld Series* Terry Pratchett; *Down Under* Bill Bryson and other travel writing; *A Kentish Lad* Frank Muir; *The Horse Whisperer* Nicholas Evans.

Cover To Cover
See **BBC Spoken Word**

CSA Telltapes Ltd
6a Archway Mews, 241a Putney Bridge Road, London SW15 2PE
☎020 8960 8466   Fax 020 8968 0804
Email michelle@csatelltapes.demon.co.uk
Website www.csatelltapes.demon.co.uk
Managing Director *Clive Stanhope*
FOUNDED 1989. *Publishes* fiction, children's, short stories, poetry, travel, biographies. Over 100 titles to-date. Tends to favour quality/classic/nostalgic/timeless literature for the 30+ age group. TITLES *Carry on Jeeves* P.G. Wodehouse; *Alfie* Bill Naughton; *Just William – Home for the Holidays* Richmal Crompton; *Hideous Kinky* Esther Freud; *Room at the Top* John Braine; *Midwich Cuckoos* John Wyndham; *I Capture the Castle* Dodie Smith; *Classic Stories of the Old and New Testaments*.

CYP Children's Audio
The Fairway, Bush Fair, Harlow, Essex CM18 6LY
☎01279 444707   Fax 01279 445570
Email enquiries@cypmusic.co.uk
Website www.kidsmusic.co.uk
Managing Director *Mike Kitson*
FOUNDED 1978. *Publishes* children's material for those under 10 years of age; educational, entertainment, licensed characters (*Mr Men*; *Little Miss*; *Sesame Street*, *Mopatop's Shop*; *Animal Stories*). Ideas for cassettes welcome. TV music and soundtrack production service available.

Faber.Penguin Audiobooks
80 Strand, London WC2R 0RL
☎020 7010 3000   Fax 020 7010 6060
Email audio@penguin.co.uk
Website www.penguin.co.uk
3 Queen Square, London WC1N 3AU
☎020 7465 0045 Fax 020 7465 0108
Head of Audio Publishing *Anna Archer* (at Strand address)

A joint venture between **Penguin Books** and **Faber & Faber**. *Publishes* 5–10 titles per year, drawing on the strength of Faber's authors. AUTHORS include Ted Hughes, Philip Larkin, Garrison Keillor, Sylvia Plath, T.S. Eliot, Wendy Cope, William Golding, Seamus Heaney, Philip Ardagh.

57 Productions
See **Organisations of Interest to Poets**

Halsgrove
See entry under **UK Publishers**

HarperCollins AudioBooks
77–85 Fulham Palace Road, London W6 8JB
☎020 8741 7070   Fax 020 8307 4517 (adult)/ 8307 4291 (children's)

The HarperCollins audio list was launched in the late 1980s.

ADULT
Managing Director *Amanda Root*, Publisher *Rosalie George Publishes* a wide range including popular and classic fiction, non-fiction, Shakespeare and poetry. 60 titles in 2001. TITLES *Man and Boy* Tony Parsons; *The Blind Assassin* Margaret Atwood; *Atonement* Ian McEwan; *Iris: A Memoir* John Bayley; *The Last Precinct* Patricia Cornwell; *English Passengers* Matthew Kneale; Agatha Christie series.

CHILDREN'S DIVISION
Audiobooks Manager *Stella Paskins* Publishing Director *Gail Penston* (picture books), Senior Editor *Gillie Russell* (fiction) *Publishes* picture books/cassettes and story books/cassettes as well as single and double tapes for children aged 2–13 years. Fiction, songs, early learning, poetry etc. 40 titles in 2001. AUTHORS C.S. Lewis, Enid Blyton, Robin Jarvis, Colin and Jacqui Hawkins, Ian Whybrow, Lynne Reid Banks, Robert Westall, Jean Ure, Nick Butterworth, Judith Kerr.

Hodder Headline Audio Books
338 Euston Road, London NW1 3BH
☎020 7873 6000   Fax 020 7873 6024
Website www.hodder.co.uk
Publisher *Rupert Lancaster*
LAUNCHED 1994. *Publishes* fiction and non-fiction. Approx 30 titles in 2001. AUTHORS Louis de Bernières, Dickie Bird, John LeCarré, Alex Ferguson, Stephen King, Ellis Peters, Rosamunde Pilcher, Terry Waite, Mary Wesley.

Isis Audio Books
See **Isis Publishing** under **UK Publishers**

Ladybird Audiobooks
See **Dorling Kindersley Ltd** under **UK Publishers**

Laughing Stock Productions
81 Charlotte Street, London W1T 4PP
☎020 7637 7943   Fax 020 7436 1646

Managing Director *Colin Collino*
FOUNDED 1991. Issues a wide range of comedy cassettes from family humour to alternative comedy. 12–16 titles per year. TITLES *Red Dwarf; Shirley Valentine* (read by Willy Russell); *Rory Bremner; Peter Cook Anthology; Sean Hughes; John Bird and John Fortune; Eddie Izzard.*

Macmillan Audio Books

20 New Wharf Road, London N1 9RR
☎020 7014 6040 Fax 020 7014 6141
Email a.muirden@macmillan.co.uk
Website www.panmacmillan.co.uk
Owner *Macmillan Publishers Ltd*
Manager *Alison Muirden*
FOUNDED 1995. *Publishes* adult fiction, non-fiction and autobiography, focusing mainly on lead book titles and releasing audio simultaneously with hard or paperback publication. About 75 titles a year. AUTHORS Wilbur Smith, Ken Follett, Colin Dexter, Clare Francis, Minette Walters, Michael Ondaatje, Helen Fielding, James Herbert, Lynda La Plante, V.S. Naipaul, Agatha Christie, Sue Grafton, Peter Robinson, Matthew Reilly.

Mr Punch Productions

113 Brackenbury Road, London W6 0BQ
☎020 8741 0297
Email editor@mrpunch.com
Managing Director *Stewart Richards*
FOUNDED 1995. Independent producer of audio books – drama and non-fiction. Over 70 titles with SERIES including *Classic Journals; Hollywood Playhouse,* Oscar-winning films specially adapted for the radio and performed by many of the original stars; *Variety Bandbox,* archive variety radio; *Classic Radio Drama; Great British Trials,* dramatised versions of original trial transcripts. TITLES *Wisdens; The Letters & Journals of Lord Nelson; Wonderful Life; Rebecca; Scott of the Antarctic; Tales From the Old Testament.* 'Always interested in non-fiction ideas that are suitable for performing in the first person (single- or multi-voice production).'

Naxos AudioBooks

18 High Street, Welwyn, Hertfordshire AL6 9EQ
☎01438 717808 Fax 01438 717809
Email Naxos_Audiobooks@compuserve.com
Website www.naxosaudiobooks.com
Owner *HNH International, Hong Kong/Nicolas Soames*
Managing Director *Nicolas Soames*

FOUNDED 1994. Part of Naxos, the classical budget CD company. Publisher of the Year in the 2001 **Spoken Word Awards**. *Publishes* classic and modern fiction, non-fiction, children's and junior classics, drama and poetry. TITLES *Ulysses* Joyce; *King Lear* Shakespeare; *History of the Musical* Fawkes; *Just So Stories* Kipling.

Orion Audio Books (Division of the Orion Publishing Group Ltd)

Orion House, 5 Upper St Martin's Lane, London WC2H 9EA
☎020 7240 3444 Fax 020 7379 6518
Email prw@orionbooks.co.uk
Website www.orionbooks.co.uk
Publisher *Trevor Dolby*
Orion Audio has released over 150 titles since it was FOUNDED in 1998. *Publishes* fiction, non-fiction, humour, children's, poetry, science, crime and thrillers. 60 titles in 2001. AUTHORS Penny Vincenzi, Maeve Binchy, Ian Rankin, Robert Crais, Michael Connelly, Francesca Simon (*Horrid Henry* series), the Dave Pelzer trilogy, Vikram Seth, Kevin Crossley-Holland. Ideas for cassettes welcome.

Penguin Audiobooks

80 Strand, London WC2R 0RL
☎020 7010 3067 Fax 020 7010 6695
Email audio@penguin.co.uk
Website www.penguin.co.uk
Head of Audio Publishing *Anna Archer*
Launched in November 1993 and has rapidly expanded since then to reflect the diversity of Penguin Books' list. *Publishes* mostly fiction, both classical and contemporary, non-fiction, autobiography and an increasing range of children's titles under the **Puffin Audiobooks** imprint. Approx. 70 titles a year. Contemporary AUTHORS include: Dick Francis, Barbara Vine, Anne Fine, Gillian Cross, John Mortimer, Roald Dahl, Tom Clancy, Sue Townsend, Philip Ridley, Nick Hornby.

Puffin Audiobooks

See **Penguin Audiobooks**

Random House Audiobooks

20 Vauxhall Bridge Road, London SW1V 2SA
☎020 7840 8400 Fax 020 7233 6127
Owner *The Random House Group Ltd.*
Managing Director *Mark McCallum*
Manager *Georgie Marnham*

The audiobooks division of Random House started early in 1991. Acquired the Reed Audio list in 1997. *Publishes* fiction, non-fiction and self help. 23 titles in 2000. AUTHORS include John Grisham, Stephen Fry, Stephen Hawking, Sebastian Faulks, Peter Ackroyd and Ruth Rendell.

Rickshaw Productions

64 Fields Court, Warwick CV34 5HP
☎0780 3553214 Fax 01926 402490
Email rickprod@aol.com
Website www.rickshaw-audiobooks.com

Executive Producer *Ms L.J. Fairgrieve*

FOUNDED 1998. *Publishes* adult fiction and non-fiction. Looking for unpublished writers of any genre, particularly short stories (not interested in children's stories or poetry). TITLES *Chinese Classic Stories* (read by Martin Jarvis); *Chinese Women's Stories* (Miriam Margolyes); *The Carved Pipe/The Tall Woman and Her Short Husband* (Elizabeth Lindsay); *The Halfway-House Hotel* by Richard James (Peter Mimmack); *The Tailor of Salisbury* (Martin Jarvis). Ideas for new stories welcome.

Simon & Schuster Audio

Africa House, 64–78 Kingsway, London WC2B 6AH
☎020 7316 1900 Fax 020 7316 0332
Email rumana.haider@simonandschuster.co.uk
Website www.simonsays.co.uk

Audio Manager *Rumana Haider*

Simon & Schuster Audio began by distributing their American parent company's audio products. Moved on to repackaging products specifically for the UK market and in 1994 became more firmly established in this market with a huge rise in turnover. *Publishes* adult fiction, self help, business, Star Trek and Alien Voices titles. TITLES *Animal Instincts* Alan Titchmarsh; *The Time Machine* H.G. Wells; *Popcorn* Ben Elton; *The 7 Habits of Highly Effective People* Stephen R. Covey; *Deja Dead* Kathy Reichs; *Lethal Seduction* Jackie Collins; *Ramses* Christian Jacq; *Rhinoceros* Colin Forbes; *Last Man Standing* David Baldacci.

Smith/Doorstop Cassettes

The Poetry Business, The Studio, Byram Arcade, Huddersfield, West Yorkshire HD1 1ND
☎01484 434840 Fax 01484 426566
Email edit@poetrybusiness.co.uk
Website www.poetrybusiness.co.uk

Co-directors *Peter Sansom, Janet Fisher*

Publishes poetry, read and introduced by the writer. AUTHORS Carol Ann Duffy, Simon Armitage, Les Murray, Ian McMillan, Sujata Bhatt.

Soundings

Isis House, Kings Drive, Whitley Bay, Tyne & Wear NE26 2JT
☎0191 253 4155 Fax 0191 251 0662
Website www.isis-publishing.co.uk

FOUNDED in 1982. Part of the Ulverscroft Group Ltd. *Publishes* fiction and non-fiction; crime, romance. About 190 titles a year. AUTHORS include Angus McVicar, Barbara Cartland, Catherine Cookson, Olivia Manning, Derek Tangye, Lyn Andrews, Susan Sallis, Mary Jane Staples, Alexander Fullerton, Patrick O'Brian, Pamela Oldfield.

The Poetry Wars
Are Not Over Yet

Peter Finch

It would be great in 2003 to report an end to the poetry wars. Or indeed the end of any kind of war. But those disagreements on poetic style and metrical direction which began so long ago are still very much around. As ever, the battle is between the insiders and the outsiders, the left vs. the right, with both sides convinced that they are the ones who own the true poetic grail. The insiders are the ones who write what new readers often imagine real poetry to be. They are clear, crisp, and immediately comprehensible. They represent that Georgian line of narrative in verse that runs from Hardy through Betjeman and Larkin to Tony Harrison, Andrew Motion, Wendy Cope, Carol Ann Duffy, Sean O'Brien and the other bestsellers of the present day. The outsiders are the experimenters, the chancers, those of the innovative texts. They are the ones who embraced the difficult modernism of Eliot and Pound and then took poetry off to those rarefied places where, apparently, the public never bother to go. They made it new. Wallace Stevens was central. John Ashbery is his heir. Over here Edwin Morgan, Roy Fisher, Tom Leonard, Allen Fisher and others continue the process. Poetry should be different. It should generate sparks when you engage with it. Comprehension comes later. 'Poetry can communicate before it is understood,' said T.S. Eliot. Although there are exceptions, both sides generally occupy completely different slices of space-time. They have their positions and they stick to them. And they fight.

This, of course, is what makes being a poet alive in Britain so exciting. No hearts and flowers, thank God. Few slow rhymes in a somnambulant room. Instead Sean O'Brien, Forward Prize winner, bestseller and self-appointed guardian of the mainstream muse, blasts what he sees as a fraudulent, pretentious, tin-eared, and parasitic brigade for trying to foist a fog-laden art onto a public who don't want it. By way of response the measured and clear voice of Michael Schmidt, Carcanet Press founder and editor of the influential *PN Review*, points out that the English and the Irish continue to engage with modernism despite our Georgian and Romantic legacy. Why should O'Brien declare it out of bounds? Under the skin we are all the same colour. Poetry is a broad church.

I'm recounting this intemperate exchange as a way of marking the fact that poetry is as open a road as anyone could possibly want. In the twenty-first century we can create any sort of poetry, from formal sonnet to remixed samples, and still find an audience. Neil Astley, editor of Bloodaxe Books, first engaged with verse because he felt you could do what you liked with it. Poetry – a place of artistic freedom. Creativity's killer application. Install yours now.

Over the past twelve months poetry has continued to make inroads into public consciousness by being incorporated into advertisements (check the make-your-own cut-up verse cards handed out for free by Coffee Mania), films, TV programmes and newspapers. The image of the poet as a sort of fey figure of fun is long gone. The woman with the hand drill bashes verse in her lunchbreak, the guy with the pint and the soccer boots does his on the bus. Poetry is a people's art. It has come down from the lofts of academe. We can all get access, we can all join in.

What's helped? A few years of well-chosen intervention by organisations such as the Poetry Society, which have championed large projects that put verse into public places. Here poets and poetry have found themselves incorporated into the workplace at law firms, broadcasters, department stores, prisons, zoos, railways, North Sea oil platforms and more. Excited by the Poetry Society's success, funding bodies across the country have started their own projects. Poets have truly entered the community. Some might argue that they never really left. With a small Arts Council financial injection, Siân Williams' well-organised contemporary poetry tours have regularly been reaching places that poetry rarely gets to. Verse, too, has been appearing regularly among the advertisements on the London Tube. The brilliant *Poetry On The Underground* founded by Judith Chernaik has done more for the popularisation of poetry in ten years than half a century of inappropriate verse forced into the school curriculum. Similar schemes, putting poetry onto overground trains and buses, have appeared across the UK. What's interesting here is that the vehicles for popularisation are not books. Poetry today appears to be working best outside the claustrophobic confines of the slim volume. The single verse on a public wall, poems in the *Independent* and the *Daily Express*, Michael Lee's *Poems In The Waiting Room* project, which puts verse freesheets into medical practices across the country, the snippet read as a time-filler on radio: these routes into the national consciousness have become far more travelled than the pamphlets of yore.

The other great populariser has been William Sieghart's annual National Poetry Day, now over a decade old, along with his Forward Poetry prizes, a focus which, in the words of the Arts Council, 'presents poetry as something modern and relevant to all people's lives'. This slice of personal enthusiasm coupled with public acceptance has spawned a great raft of media interest in verse where none previously existed. Poetry – or at least the variety that wins prizes – has become sexy. Both the BBC and Classic FM, along with a host of others, have capitalised on the running series of the Nation's Favourites. Best-loved poems have been voted upon, listed, recanted, anthologised, performed, and sold again by the shedload. Sieghart has done more for the popularisation of poetry than two hundred years of the laureate. Not that the new man, Andrew Motion, is holding back. In his time-limited post he has already made poetry a serious part of regular life. He takes it to schools, he anthologises it, he keeps it in the news. His collaborations with the Proms and his involvement with the Queen's Golden Jubilee Poetry Competition among British schools, the world's largest ever, have ensured massive exposure for verse. He may not be everyone's favourite poet himself but he does his job well.

So poetry is blossoming. Do you join in? If you imagine that what's eating you is a God-sent unique talent and all you have to do is simply put pen to paper in order to bang the stanzas out then, probably, best not. Among poetry's thousands there are too many already who think that verse is simple stuff. Poetry may *pack*, but to do that it needs work. It is undeniable that some poems will emerge fully formed, virtually whole as they are. But those are very much the exceptions. Most work trickles out slowly – an idea, an image, a flash of a notion of how the thing might go. Then comes the hard stuff. The plan, the writes and rewrites, the cuts and changes, the hash and re-hash. If your poetry isn't going through this kind of process then the chances are that it won't amount to much. Poetry shouldn't be easy material which comes out of its creators like toothpaste. It should emerge with ponder, with doubt, and with difficulty all around. Is what you have on the sheet before you a poem? Does it amount to anything new, anything startling, anything splendid, a different, entrancing, engaging way of looking at the world? Ask yourselves these questions. Scratch the thing out, redo it. Throw away more than you keep. Learn to kill your babies. Keep only that which really rocks. Do that. Then read on.

What should you read?

The way in is first to discover what poetry actually is. To do this means putting some time in at the bookshop and at the library. Be as open and catholic as you can in your selection. Ensure you check out the whole scene – the past, the present, mainstream English literature along with work in translation, the obvious poets you find you like as well as those you find difficult. Appreciation will not come without effort. Stay the course.

Ask at your booksellers for their recommendations. Check Waterstone's or Blackwell's, which both stock poetry titles. The online booksellers Amazon and BOL both produce browsable lists. Most shops these days carry a basic stock, but if you need more then get hold of the Poetry Library's current list of shops with a specific interest in poetry. Enquire at your local library. Start with a recent anthology of contemporary verse. You'll be spoilt for choice here, the new millennium has rushed a whole crop of century-definers into print. To get a broad view of what's going on, you should read not only Edna Longley's *Bloodaxe Book of Twentieth Century Poetry*, Simon Armitage and Robert Crawford's Penguin *British and Irish Poetry Since the War*, Sean O'Brien's *The Firebox* (Picador), Michael Schmidt's *The Harvill Book of Twentieth-Century Poetry in English* (Harvill). Hulse, Kennedy and Morley's Bloodaxe *The New Poetry*, William Sieghart's *Poems Of The Decade* (Forward) and Iain Sinclair's *Conductors of Chaos* (Picador) but also Richard Caddel and Peter Quartermain's *Other: British and Irish Poetry since 1970* (Wesleyan), Keith Tuma's *Anthology of Twentieth-Century British & Irish* Poetry (OUP), Sarah-Jane

Lovett's *Oral* (Sceptre), Lemn Sissay's *The Fire People – A Collection of Contemporary Black British Poets* (Payback Press), Jeni Couzyn's *The Bloodaxe Book of Contemporary Women Poets*, Tony Frazer's *A State Of Independence* (Stride), *Poems For The Millennium Volume Two: From Postwar to Millennium* edited by Jerome Rothenberg and Pierre Joris (California) and *Postmodern American Poetry*, a really splendid selection edited by Paul Hoover (Norton). This last title might be harder to find but will be worth the effort. Fill in with a standard overview of poetry in English since Chaucer. Ted Hughes and Seamus Heaney's two Faber anthologies, *The Rattle Bag* and *The School Bag*, are good scatter guns. For a more balanced historical view try Christopher Rick's *The Oxford Book of English Verse*, Andrew Motion's *Here To Eternity* (Faber), Paul Keegan's *New Penguin Book of English Verse*, Helen Gardner's *New Oxford Book of English Verse* and the great *Norton Anthology of Poetry* or long-term standby *Palgrave's Golden Treasury* (OUP).

Progress to the literary magazine. Write off to a number of the magazine addresses that follow this article and ask the price of sample copies. Enquire about subscriptions. Expect to pay something, but it shouldn't break the bank. Check the websites listed further on in this article. It is important that poets read not only to familiarise themselves with what is currently fashionable and to increase their own facility for self-criticism, but also to help support the activity in which they wish to participate. Buy – this is vital for little mags, it is the only way in which they are going to survive.

OK, I'm well read. What next?

Are you personally convinced that your work is ready? If you are uncertain, then most likely that will be the view of everyone else. Check your text for glips and blips. Rework it. Root out any clichés or archaic poetry expressions such as O, doeth, bewilld'd and the like. Drop any of what Peter Sansom calls 'spirit of the age' poetry words. Do without shards, lozenges, lambent patina, and stippled seagulls. If you work with rhyme attempt to avoid the obvious. Check that any meter you may be using actually works. Try not to clank. If by this time your writing still sounds OK, then go ahead.

The Internet and World Wide Web

The Internet is not a diversion. For the poet, or for that rare beast, the non-contributing poetry consumer, it's now moved into high focus. No longer a simple extension of conventional print, it is now an actual substitute which you ignore at your peril. Growth over the past few years has been nothing short of enormous – from nothing to everything in five years. Not bad for a medium originally built as a military device. With the advent of inexpensive access and complimentary Web space an increasing number of poetry enthusiasts and publishers have set up sites. Some have abandoned conventional print to operate solely online; others have launched without ever having known ink and paper. Cyberspace – the place where it all happens – is a mirror of the conventional world. The electronic replicates the real. Here are online books, magazines, historical and contemporary archives, reference works, creative tools, discussion forums, and news round-ups. Many dedicate themselves entirely to poetry.

Journals

Online magazines range from those which carry extracts taken from their print-based cousins to completely innovative, interactive compilations which mix sound and action with the text. The Net is no static place. It provides movement, video, sound, and user-defined typeface along with actual text. Some mags (e-zines, online journals) offer playable recordings of their poets performing, others give space for readers to add criticism. An increasing number are opening chat rooms and forums where readers can exchange views. The difference between online and print-based journals becomes more apparent when you discover that what you get when you call them up is not simply an enhanced version of the current issue but access to the entire back catalogue, often with extras thrown in. All searchable, storable, and, for the time being anyway, free.

Geography dissolves online. America is no further away and no more costly to access than Britain. One of the great mags, John Tranter's *Jacket*, is based in Australia. It's just as easy to read as George Simmers' UK *Snakeskin*, Ethan Paquan's *Slope* or Rick Lupert's Los Angeles *Poetry Super Highway*. In fact, half the time, the user has no idea precisely where the site being accessed is physically based. Place ceases to matter, language takes over. Online journals can range from the terrible to the terrific. For my money the aforementioned *Jacket*, Susan Kelly-De Witt's *Perihelion*, the graphically superb UK *Boomerang*, where Neil Rollinson has managed to attract contributions from many highly reputable poets, Rupert Loydell's *Stride*, and Jennifer Ley's *Riding the Meridian* are some of the world's best. Not all is in English, either. For an experience of the Welsh strict meters have a look at *Cartref Cynghanedd ar y We* (The Home of Cynghanedd on the Web); no translations are offered, you get this as it comes.

How do you contribute? As with all poetry ventures, read first. Will you fit in? If you think so then send your poems by e-mail, included in the body of the text or as an attached plain text file, no s.a.e. needed. More than likely you'll get an instant answer. No more waiting around for six weeks before your poems return, rejected and dog-eared. Online can be lightning fast.

A variant of the journal is the resource site or portal – websites which offer not only new verse, chat rooms and reviews but information (listings of competitions, other journals, events, etc.) and the opportunity to buy new books. *The Opening Line* runs a writers' forum, lists groups and events and offers flash fiction and poetry. Rick Lupert's American *Poetry Superhighway* is a worldwide poetry data source. Ted Slade's *Poetry Kit* offers a large amount of UK-orientated poetry information, competition lists, resources and a whole raft of self-help articles. Carole Baldock at *Poettext* (one of a series of genre-specific book portals run by Ginna Clark's Ebtext) is heading the same way. One of the best lies within BBC Online's Arts pages. Here you can find a large resource of information, poetry, lists, a chat room, Real Audio files of classic and contemporary poets, and a host of DIY versemakers. Well worth a visit.

Cyberspace is huge. Some of the sites which list online journals, such as *Peter Howard's Poetry Contacts*, seem to go on for days. Starting your own mag is easy – frictionless, Bill Gates calls it – and size presents little difficulty. On the Web it is easy to put up more, so in terms of quality of content that often means less. Not only are the UK's computer-literate newbies up there but America, Canada, Japan, South America and Australia's too.

Competitions

Naturally there is an online variant to the more the traditional send £5 and your best work contests. Many of these canvass entries from the unconnected and offer Net publication as the prize. For some poets this will no doubt be sufficient reward. Others accept online entries and choose their winners by asking readers to vote – again online. The selling point for these competitions is judged to be the enormous audience supposedly sitting around out there in front of their screens. The potential is certainly large – three hundred million users already connected and with more joining every day. Yet how many actually bother to access poetry remains debatable.

Books

If you tire of contributing to the websites of others, then why not start your own? A whole collection of verse online will present relatively little difficulty. Most ISPs offer free Web space to users or, if you can put up with the adverts, you can claim a home for nothing at somewhere like Geocities. Building your own home page is certainly not beyond anyone capable of using a word processor. If you'd like to see the kind of thing that's possible have a look at the site of poet Matthew Francis, or for something more graphically challenging, Neil Rollinson's dark creation. You might also care to look at my own, *The Peter Finch Archive*. If you are reticent get a fan to set up a site devoted to your works. This has happened to David Gascoyne, to J.H. Prynne, Maya Angelou, Ivor Cutler, Benjamin Zephaniah and others. Most of us, however, seem to like the idea of self build. If you have a recording of yourself doing your stuff then get one jump ahead. Put the recording up there on the site too.

Hypertext

Naturally the Web has developed its own verse forms. Most of these straddle the boundaries between verse, sound, and image, much in the way that concrete poetry did half a century ago. Many critics dismiss the new work as simply moving graphic art but protagonists see the world very differently. In the launch for its *Artszone*, the BBC website chose rather than conventional works to feature four excellent hypertext poets (including Peter Howard and Robert Kendall). But hypertext poetry is better experienced than reported. *Webartery* will give you links to some of the leading practitioners.

Groups

To reduce the poet's traditional feeling of isolation the Net presents a number of opportunities. Worldwide poets, once they've got over the stunning breadth of Net facilities, are usually hard to shut up. E-mail provides one of their vehicles. Here bands of poets circulate their work, their criticisms, and their views of world literature. Join a group (no cost, just ask) and you'll find a daily delivery of e-mails in your inbox. Some groups are moderated, which means that contributions are filtered by a controlling individual, although most are free-for-alls. Discussion can range from the moronic to the stimulating. *The British and Irish Poets Group* established by Ric Caddel and *Poetryetc*, an outgrowth of the list begun by John Kinsella, are two worth trying.

A variant on e-mail discussion groups are Usenet Newsgroups. Newsgroups are read through their own dedicated software or standard e-mail programs (provided by your ISP as part of your subscription) and are open to contributions from anyone anywhere. Articles are not directly delivered, you need to pick them up, but the principle is the same. If you want to contribute then type it up and it's done. The largest poetry newsgroups, *rec.arts.poems* and *alt.arts.poetry.comments*, offer pretty varied fare. By their worldwide nature they tend to be American dominated and standards of contribution are not always that high. But they are places where you can get an instant reaction to your latest poem. There are also masterclasses out there with established poets offering online advice. The BBC, trAce, Chadwyck-Healey and the Poetry Society are some of the organisations which have offered virtual residencies with well-known bards.

Tools and resources

The Net offers a multitude of these. There are online spell-checkers (in many languages), thesauri, an anagram creator, Shakespeare and Bible concordances, a rhyming dictionary. The archives of universities (particularly in America) offer the great poetry of the past in comprehensive quantity. Download facsimile editions of *The Germ* (the first ever poetry magazine from 1850) or hear Seamus Heaney recite. Read the complete works of Blake, find out what powered the Beat generation, discover how Hardy worked, check the roots of modern verse. You can find not only the texts themselves but entire critical apparatuses, historical contexts, biographies, bibliographies, portraits, shoe sizes, and names of lovers for most of the greats. You can access information on poetry readings or check at the British Council for data on literature festivals. For a glimpse at the broader picture check UNESCO's huge World Poetry Directory. Students revel in posting their dissertations. Archives want their knowledge made available to everyone. Interested in a particular style? Haiku? Visual poetry? Traditional forms? They've all got their sites.

E-commerce

Shopping on the Net is now the preferred method for buying specialist material. Both the big Internet bookshops – BOL and Amazon – offer the hunter searchable lists for that difficult to obtain poetry title. Buying online is generally safe and swift, although, as with all mail order, only as good as the van that brings the package to your door. The UK *Poetry Book Society*, which acts as a poetry book club (see **Organisations of Interest to Poets**), and a number of the specialist publishers are also taking advantage of Internet sales.

How to find them

Use the search engine. The big ones – Yahoo, Google, HotBot, Excite, AltaVista – can return enormous lists in response to keying in the word *poetry*. I got 149,529 results out of AltaVista. Much easier is to log on to one of a number of poetry resource sites which run clickable lists of relevant pages. The UK Poetry Society, The Poetry Library and the *Poetry Review*'s 'web watcher', Peter Howard's home page, are worth consulting. Ted Slade's *Poetry Kit* posts a large number of contacts. And for a good worldwide look try *Pif Magazine*'s Pilot-Search literary Web search engine.

Where next?

New ideas arrive all the time. trAce, the major online writing project set up at Nottingham-Trent University with support from the Arts Council, is signposting many of the ways Net writing can go. It offers online poetry writing courses, resident poets, and access to Flash animation for the hypertext innovators among us. Peter Howard's site runs a number of online poetry generators. The user keys in basic vocab and the Java script does the rest. On the other hand you may prefer to use your own creative engines. Log on now.

Some Web and Internet addresses for poets

Annedd y Cynganeddwyr	www.cynghanedd.com
BBC	www.bbc.co.uk/arts/poetry/index.shtml
Boomerang (magazine)	www.boomeranguk.com
British Poets e-mail list	jiscmail.ac.uk/lists/british-poets.html
Chadwyck-Healey	lion.chadwyck.co.uk

Electronic Poetry Centre	wings.buffalo.edu/epc
Matthew Francis	www.7greenhill.freeserve.co.uk
Jacket (magazine)	www.jacket.zip.com.au
John Kinsella	www.geocities.com/SoHo/Square/1664/ kinsella.html
The Opening Line (workshops)	www.openingline.co.uk
Perihelion (magazine)	webdelsol.com/Perihelion
Peter Finch Archive	www.peterfinch.co.uk
Peter Howard's Poetry Page	www.hphoward.demon.co.uk/poetry
Pif Magazine	www.pifmagazine.com
Poetry Book Society	www.poetrybooks.co.uk
Poetry Kit	www.poetrykit.org
Poetryetc e-mail list	www.jiscmail.ac.uk/lists/poetryetc.html
The Poetry Library	www.poetrylibrary.org.uk
The Poetry Society (UK)	www.poetrysoc.com
Poetry Superhighway	poetrysuperhighway.com
Poettext	www.poettext.com
Riding the Meridian (magazine)	www.heelstone.com/meridian
Slope (magazine)	www.slope.org
Snakeskin (magazine)	homepages.nildram.co.uk/~simmers
Stride (magazine)	www.stridemagazine.co.uk
trAce	trace.ntu.ac.uk
Webartery	www.webartery.com
World Poetry Directory	www.unesco.org/poetry

WAP & SMS

WAP is the slow to load, cut-down version of the Internet used by cellphones. SMS are the ubiquitous text messages which are now the preferred method of communication among the young. Both have been exploited by verse. At www.wapdrive.com/boomerang you can browse new short poetry and at www.wapdrive/qj96 you can read a range of haiku. *Onesixty*, launched by Centrifugalforces at the Cheltenham Festival, is the world's first text-message magazine. Visit www.CentriFugalForces.co.uk/onesixty/ to find out more.

Commercial publishers

Despite the obvious possibilities of making something from poetry via traditional methods in the hard-copy commercial marketplace, the number of those conglomerate publishers involved is actually quite small. Where once there were a multitude of mainstream poetry imprints there are now only three or four. With obvious exceptions poetry is increasingly seen as the quality line which enhances a publisher's list. It is rarely there to make profit alone. Despite a decade or more of poetry booms the stuff is still basically a commercial risk. Slim volumes are slow sellers. Their editors are almost always part-time or have other jobs within the company and are never allowed to publish what they would really like.

The obvious exception to this approach is long-term market leader and envy of the whole business, **Faber & Faber**. Here editor Paul Keegan presides over a list which continues to be as important to the firm as when T.S. Eliot inaugurated it more than seventy years ago. The best poetry does transcend the limits of the traditional market, Faber believes. This is the imprint most poets would like to join. The greats of the twentieth century are here – Pound, Eliot, Plath, Hughes, Larkin. Seamus Heaney made half a million in sales when he won the Nobel Prize. Wendy Cope regularly sells into five figures. The imprint is built on distinctively designed class and the roster of contemporary poets includes some of the best we have – Simon Armitage, Derek Walcott, Don Paterson, Andrew Motion, Jo Shapcott, Hugo Williams, Paul Muldoon, Douglas Dunn. The press publishes up to sixty poetry titles each year and runs a competition in conjunction with the booksellers Ottakars. If you fancy your chances then send a brief covering letter and a sample of your writing (ten to twenty poems), not forgetting s.a.e., if you think this is where you'll fit in. The Faber website is at www.faber.co.uk.

Oxford University Press has transferred its contemporary list to Michael Schmidt at Carcanet. OUP are now a great historical repository with some highly desirable titles. But new verse needs to be sent somewhere else.

A commercial editor with excellent taste is **Cape**'s Robin Robertson. His list is by no means all things to all people. Peter Redgrove, John Hartley Williams, Anne Carson, John Burnside, Sharon Olds and Michael Longley are typical. Roberston, himself a fine poet, produces four to five titles annually – all books, no anthologies, and with a few sourced from the other side of the Atlantic. Worth trying? Yes, but potential contributors should never waste anyone's time by not looking at the list first. Poetry at fellow Random House press, **Chatto & Windus**, is in the hands of Rebecca Carter. Output is slightly lower than that at Cape and has recently included Fred D'Aguiar, Ruth Padel, and John Fuller. But unless supported by a strong recommendation from an established fellow practitioner Carter does not want to see unsolicited manuscripts. Do check their Ruth Padel handbook, *52 Ways of looking At a Poem*, her *Independent on Sunday* articles anthologised.

Both Chatto and Cape preview examples from their lists in the poem for the day section of the Random House website at www.randomhouse.co.uk.

The Harvill Press runs one of the smaller commercial poetry lists, publishing one or two new titles annually (although years can pass when output is nothing at all). Central are the works of Paul Durcan and the late Raymond Carver. They also publish Michael Schmidt's fine anthology *The Harvill Book of Twentieth Century Poetry in English*. Editor Ian Finbar will look at new manuscripts but chances are slim. New writers would be better off starting elsewhere.

Among the other commercial houses activity appears to be limited to nominal titles, anthologies or backlist obligations. **BBC Books** churns out the Nation's

Favourites, bestsellers at Smith's. **Cassell** anthologises the poems from the London Underground (which sell so well you'd think they'd be encouraged to try something else). **Hamish Hamilton** does John Updike. **Methuen** publishes Wole Soyinka and John Hegley. **John Murray** recycles Betjeman and prints anthologies of old chestnuts and travel verse. **Everyman** runs pocket poets and anthologies of comic verse and poetry of the sea. **Boxtree** presents Purple Ronnie. Some specialist interests are dealt with at **Lion** (Christian verse) and **Windhorse** (Buddhist) – but it isn't a lot.

The smaller operators

Not all commercial publishing is vast and conglomerate. A few independents still exist and on their lists poetry occasionally occurs. Francis Bickmore at **Canongate Books** publishes Anna Akhmatova, Jim Dodge, Antonia Fraser's *Scottish Love Poems* anthology and Alan Spence's Scottish haiku. Northern Ireland general publisher **Blackstaff Press** brings out one or two poetry titles annually, including Patrick Crotty's groundbreaking *Modern Irish Poetry*. Welsh family firm **Gwasg Gomer** produces neat editions of Gillian Clarke, Janet Dube, John Barnie, Nigel Jenkins and others. Their *Borders*, a bilingual collection from Grahame Davies and Elin ap Hywel, introduces Welsh verse to a wider audience. Check their site at www.gomer.co.uk. **Polygon** (which is an imprint of **Edinburgh University Press**) continues to mix Gaelic with English as part of its 'poetry for the new generation' policy. Alison Bowden is the editor. The press has at least half a dozen poets on the list including Donny O'Rourke, Roddy Gorman, Liz Lochhead, and W.N. Herbert. They also publish *Pocket Books*, a series which mixes poetry with photography. Check their *The Dream State: The New Scottish Poets*. Unsolicited poetry, they say, is not welcome. Others in the field include **Gill & Macmillan** and **Y Lolfa**.

Universities

With the collapse of **OUP**'s contemporary interest, activity among UK presses is sparse. Reprints and literary studies at **Cambridge**, the same at **Manchester**. At the **University of Wales Press**, which publishes a splendid series of collected works from Welsh poets, you need to be dead. American university presses such as Nebraska, **Princeton, Louisiana, Wisconsin, Chicago, Harvard, Michigan**, North Carolina, **Washington, Alabama** and **California**, along with **W.W. Norton**, do an increasing amount of verse but exclusively by Americans. No chances there.

Women

There were days when **Virago** was out front here but no longer. When the imprint became part of Little, Brown (now **Time Warner Books UK**) it became considerably less partisan. The press more or less only publishes poetry from novelists already elsewhere on their lists – Margaret Atwood, Michèle Roberts, Maya Angelou – along with genre anthologies. There are no plans for expansion. At **The Women's Press**, Virago's traditional competitor, the situation is much the same: original good intentions gone, to be replaced by reissuing Elizabeth Barrett Browning and keeping Alice Walker in print. The **Onlywomen Press**, however, has kept its interest. Lilian Mohin tries to publish two poetry titles annually. Judith Barrington, Kate Foley, Jackie Kay, U.A. Fanthorpe, and Sunjoto Namjoshi are typical. Check its anthology *Not For the Academy: Lesbian Poets*. Generally, however, women poets are better served by the poetry specialists. More of them anon.

The mass-market paperback

The popular end is where many poets imagine the best starting place to be. Paperback houses were founded to publish inexpensive reprints of hard-covered originals and, despite years of innovation and market posturing, to a large extent still fulfil this role. Being neither cheap nor (in sales terms) that popular, poetry does not really fit in. Among the carousels at airports you do not see it. Check the empires of **Arrow**, **Bantam**, **Corgi**, **Headline**, and **Mills & Boon**. If you discount the inspirational, you won't find a book of verse between them. **Vintage**, to its credit, publishes Fred D'Aguir's novels in verse and reprints of Iain Sinclair. Elsewhere nothing, although there are two exceptions.

At **Penguin**, where things are always different, poetry has a significant role. With its unfailing commercial ear the company has correctly assessed the market for contemporary and traditional verse and systematically and successfully filled it. Reprinting important volumes pioneered by less commercial poetry presses, originating historic and thematic anthologies, reviving classic authors and producing a multitude of translations en route, Penguin continues to provide an almost unrivalled introduction to the world of verse. But appearances aside, this is most certainly no place for the beginner. 'We publish almost no new or unknown poets. In fact we publish very little new poetry beyond a small circle of established poets. We concentrate on selecteds and general anthologies,' publishing director Tony Lacey told me. The company focuses on sure sellers such as James Fenton, Geoffrey Hill, Tony Harrison and Roger McGough. The main thrust remains the repackaging of selecteds from proven bards such as Derek Mahon, Carol Ann Duffy, and U.A. Fanthorpe, a good range of modern poets in translation and larger sets from the likes of William Empson, Allen Ginsberg, and John Ashbery. The company's poetry overview anthologies, the Simon Armitage and Robert Crawford edited *British and Irish Poetry Since the War*, Peter Forbes' *Scanning The Century*, and Paul Keegan's *New Penguin Book of English Poetry* are musts. Penguin also publishes a number of useful books about poetry including Ian Hamilton's *Against Oblivion*, short biographies of twentieth-century poets, and James Fenton's *An Introduction to English Poetry*, a book for readers and writers of English poetry on metre, genre, diction, etc. Despite these obvious winners Lacey sees the whole market for verse as small, despite the hype. Penguin online is at www.penguin.com

Penguin's nearest rival, **Picador**, the literary paperbacker of **Pan Macmillan**, is now exhibiting considerable vigour and is now widely regarded as one of the country's leading poetry publishers. Under the commanding eye of successful and non-metropolitan poet Don Paterson it has moved into high gear, putting out a stream of successful collections from new poets such as Paul Farley and Colette Bryce along with established names such as Glyn Maxwell, Peter Porter, Carol Ann Duffy, Kate Clanchy, Michael Donaghy and Forward Prize winner Sean O'Brien. With its reliable content, Picador is turning itself into a UK reference point. Paterson will bring out at least six new titles annually as well as an anthology. Recent examples include Sean O'Brien's critically acclaimed *The Firebox* and Carol Ann Duffy's anthology of love poems, *Hand in Hand*. Worth trying here? 'Certainly: ten poems better than a full-length ms, but establish some track record in the reputable journals first,' advises Paterson.

The specialists

Despite a blatant lack of success in the commercial marketplace, poetry is readily available. But where? With the specialist independents. These are the small army of semi-commercial operations scattered across the country. They are run by genuine poetry enthusiasts whose prime concern starts not with money but with the furtherance of their art. Often begun as classic small presses that soon outgrew the restraints of back-bedroom offices and under-the-stairs warehousing, they are now a real force on the poetry scene. You can find them in Waterstone's, you can see them in Blackwell's and at Ottakars. Most receive grant aid, without which their publishing programmes would be sunk. They are models of what poetry publishing should be – active, involving, alert, and exciting. They promote their lists through readings, tours, websites, and broadcasts, and they involve their authors in the production and sales of their books. Never before have new poets been faced with so many publishing opportunities. And if there is any criticism then this is it. Too many books jamming the market. Just how does the reader see through the flood? By reputation, I guess. Two have emerged well ahead of the pack – **Carcanet** and **Bloodaxe.** Along with Faber these two now dominate British poetry publishing.

Taking them alphabetically, the first of these is Neil Astley's acclaimed **Bloodaxe Books**. Publishing thirty titles annually, the press, although slowing in the face of booktrade upheavals, still brings out more poetry books than any other British imprint. Picking up poets dropped by the commercial operators as well as discovering new ones, this is certainly one of poetry's best proving grounds. Based in Northumberland and begun in Newcastle in the late 1970s, the press is unhindered by a past catalogue of classical wonders or an overly regional concern. It relentlessly pursues the new. Astley presents the complete service from thematic anthologies, world greats, and selecteds to slim volumes by total newcomers. The press has its own range of excellent handbooks to the scene, including *Getting Into Poetry* and *Writing Poems*, along with an increasing range of critical volumes. Best poetry sellers are its anthologies: Linda France's *Sixty Women Poets*, Neil Astley's own *Staying Alive: real poems for unreal times*, and its decade-framing anthology *The New Poetry*. With commendable concern to staying ahead, Bloodaxe has produced Edna Longley's great *Bloodaxe Book of Twentieth Century Poetry* and Herbert and Hollis' *Strong Words*, an important collection of manifestos and poetics. Bloodaxe relishes the chance to publish work from outside the standard English mainstream – Ireland, Scotland and Wales are all represented, as are our more traditional UK outsiders such as J.H. Prynne. It also gives prominence to major American, European and Commonwealth poets. There is a multimedia thrust – a series of poets on cassette and a revamped Bloodaxe website (www.bloodaxebooks.com). Typical poets include Helen Dunmore, Philip Gross, Selima Hill, Jem Poster, Denise Levertov and Imtiaz Dharker. Bloodaxe will not go rusty with age. Newcomers are advised to send a sample rather than a full collection. 'If you don't read contemporary poetry we are unlikely to be interested in your work,' comments Astley. A simple way to taste the imprint's range is to try its two house anthologies, *Poetry With An Edge* and *New Blood*.

The second, **Carcanet Press**, has been the consistent recipient of critical accolades. Publishing four Nobel Prize-winning authors and four Pulitzers helps. Although it is no longer exclusively a publisher of verse (Carcanet publishes limited amounts of fiction, criticism, and lives and letters), the press still gives poetry pre-eminence. In 1999 it took over the list of contemporary poets published by OUP. Carcanet currently has over 500 titles in print, reps in forty-two countries and a programme that brings out forty to sixty poetry titles annually. Managing Director Michael Schmidt agrees with Auden's observation that most people who read verse read it for some reason other than the poetry. He fights the tide with his own mainstream journal, *PN Review*. Carcanet has a policy of serious quality. 'I am strongly aware of the anti-modernist slant in a lot of poetry publishing, and publish to balance this,' he comments. 'Most submissions we receive come from people ignorant of the list to which they are submitting. Nothing is more disheartening than to receive a telephone call asking whether Carcanet publishes poetry.' The press has a four-part editorial programme: to publish new writing, to dust down substantial but neglected figures of this and earlier centuries, to encourage the translation of poetry and to publish poets' prose and work relating to modern poetry. Typical of their list are Ian Macmillan, John Ashbery, Gillian Clarke, Eavan Boland, Edwin Morgan, Les Murray, Sophie Hannah, Linda Chase and the bestseller, Elizabeth Jennings. Carcanet has an air of purpose about it. 'We avoid the Technicolor and pyrotechnic media razzmatazz,' says Schmidt. Have a look at its website www.carcanet.co.uk, which is complete with an online bookselling facility. New poets are welcome to submit but check both your own past performance as well Carcanet's style before you go ahead. Send six to ten pages of work and expect to wait six weeks for a reply. Carcanet's *New Poetries* and *Oxford Poets 2001* anthologies give an idea where the taste of the press is going next.

Production standards among other specialists can be equally as good as Carcanet and Bloodaxe although annual output is substantially less.

Anvil Press Poetry, founded by Peter Jay in 1968, is now England's longest-standing independent poetry publisher. More than thirty years on, Anvil still publishes its earliest poets – Gavin Bantock, Anthony Howell and Harry Guest – although Jay is careful to avoid cliques. The best of new English-language poets are constantly sought, and a sampler of these can be found in the *Anvil New Poets 3* anthology. In addition, Anvil has won a deserved reputation for publishing the best of poetry in translation from around the world – Tagore, Seferis, Bei Dao, Lorca, Hikmet. Anvil's bestselling poet is Carol Ann Duffy. Producing around a dozen titles a year, Anvil gives particular attention to typographical detail, jacket design, and quality of binding, making each publication exceptionally attractive. Potential contributors are strongly advised to read through Anvil's books first and, if still keen, expect to wait for up to three months after sending in. For those who wish to familiarise themselves with the flavour of the Anvil list, Jay's acclaimed anthology *The Spaces of Hope* gives a perfect starting point. Its informative website is at www.anvilpresspoetry.com

Enitharmon Press represents quality, cares about presentation, and operates 'at the unfashionable end' of the poetry publishing spectrum. Its books, often concerned with the process of bringing together word and image, are produced to the highest of standards. Enitharmon has little interest in fashion. The press is, as Anne Stevenson put it, 'dedicated to a poetry of the human spirit in an age of rampant commercialism'. Owner Stephen Stuart-Smith continues a policy of publishing between eight and twelve volumes annually by new, established and unjustly neglected poets. Typical of the list are Jane Duran, Myra Schneider, Vernon Scannell, Kevin Crossley-Holland and Anthony Thwaite. The press has seen a surge in interest in the anthology, bringing out volumes covering women's views of their parents, the *Exeter Riddles*, Sean Street's *Radio Anthology* and Anna Adam's *London in Poetry and Prose*. 'It seems unlikely that many new names will be added to the list, as the bookshop chains are so resistant to poetry that only well-known poets get their books stocked', which is a pity. We need more from publishers like Stuart-Smith. Visit www.enitharmon.co.uk for more information.

Seren Books is a Welsh-based literary house publishing novels, art books, short fiction, biographies and critical texts. Started by Cary Archard as an off-shoot of the magazine *Poetry Wales*, the imprint still maintains a solid interest in verse, publishing at least six new single-author volumes annually. In receipt of Arts Council of Wales sponsorship, the bias towards work from Wales and the border regions is both admirable and inevitable. Poetry editor Amy Wack reads *everything* submitted but admits that she has only ever accepted one unsolicited manuscript in her entire tenure. Poets should read more, she says. Editions are quality productions with plenty of attention paid to design inside and out. Typical recent poets include Pascale Petit, bestseller Owen Sheers, Samantha Rhydderch and Tony Curtis. The major bestseller is Dannie Abse's *Twentieth Century Anglo-Welsh Poetry*. A good press sampler is the anthology *Oxygen – New Poets from Wales*. It has also published its own guide to the scene, *The Poetry Business*.

Tony Ward's **Arc Publications**, based in Lancashire, brings out around fourteen poetry titles annually. 'We publish work that we believe [is] important, innovative, and of outstanding quality,' Ward told me. The imprint has Jean Boase-Beier, David Morley and John Kinsella on the board and maintains a backlist of approaching a hundred titles. Ivor Cutler, John Kinsella and Miklós Radnóti are top sellers. Unafraid to take risks, Arc's policy is to publish the best in contemporary poetry, in a reader-friendly medium, without in any way compromising the standards of quality for which the press has always been known and recognised. The Arc website is at www.arcpublications.co.uk Prospective poets should not expect a quick response (allow up to four months – no submissions by e-mail), and should most certainly familiarise themselves with the Arc list before sending. 'We do not wish to put writers off or dampen enthusiasm, but we have never yet accepted an unpublished author,' is the official line. You have been warned.

Ward has an excellent reputation as a printer to the poetry press community and does a splendid job also for David Tipton's **Redbeck Press**. Tipton, who came up the pamphlet route used by many a small press, has now driven Redbeck into the top echelon. He publishes everything from Nick Toczek's performance pieces to Gavin Bantock's floating world. His star title of recent times has been Debjani Chatterjee's 200-page *Redbeck Anthology of British South Asian Poetry*. Other Redbeck poets include John Freeman, Jim Burns, Barry Tebb, Kim Taplin, Martin Hayes, Tulio Mora, Jenny Swann and Alan Dent. Non-centralist to the core.

Rupert Loydell's **Stride** has gathered a good reputation for catholic taste and running risks. After thirty-three issues in hard copy his eponymous magazine has now moved to the Web (www.stridemagazine.co.uk). Based in the south-west, output is eight books annually. The backlist runs to more than 200 titles ranging from the totally unknown to the famous. Stride almost perfectly fills the gap between the avant garde and the user-friendly. No one else is operating here. 'Our books are as likely to discuss free jazz, techno music or drug culture as marvel at the effect of sunlight on water, question ideas or beliefs or explore the intricacies of languages and the visual arts; as likely to use collage and cut-up as reinvent the sonnet; more likely to challenge and excite than send you to sleep', is the official line. The arrival of an American editor, Ethan Paquin, emphasises Stride's international interests. The press runs individual collections, criticism, interviews, along with a range of excellent, alternative anthologies. Stride responds to submissions swiftly, invariably within three weeks and often within three days. Successes include Martin Stannard, David Grubb and Alan Halsey. The crisis in book sales has, however, caused Stride to look at new methods of production including publishing on demand. Visit its website at www.stridebooks.com for up-to-date information. Its anthology, *Ladder to the Next Floor*, offers a sampler of how the press got where it is.

Peterloo Poets, based in Cornwall, represents poetry without frills, without fuss, and most definitely without the avant-garde. Run by Harry Chambers, the press aims to publish quality work by new and neglected poets, some of them late starters (although if you have been flogging your stuff around the circuit for years and got nowhere then Chambers is unlikely to be your saviour); to co-publish with reputable presses abroad; and to establish a Peterloo list of succeeding volumes by a core of poets of proven worth. Heaney described Chambers as one of the 'great hearers and hearteners of the work being done in British and Irish poetry'. Peterloo, which represents a stable centre for many people's idea of what poetry is, runs an active backlist of nearly 200 titles. Bestsellers include U.A. Fanthorpe, whose *Collected Poems* are published in 2003, Elma Mitchell and Dana Gioia. Poets central to the list are William Scammell, David Sutton and John Whitworth. Recent additions include Owen Gallagher, Julian Stannard and Ann Alexander. Peterloo, now in its twenty-sixth year, runs its own poetry competition, first prize £2,000, which also has five £100 prizes in a 15–19 Age Group Section, and insists that prospective contributors to the press have had at least six poems in reputable magazines. Send a full ms accompanied by a stamped envelope large enough to carry your ms back to you. Chambers currently takes a couple of months to reply and is full to 2003.

Michael Hulse, a former editor at Stand, runs the recently established **Leviathan** with high production standards. His assembled editorial team includes John Kinsella and Anne Michaels. He publishes five or so titles annually of British and American work alongside classics and poetry from around the world, in English or translation. Poets published in Leviathan's first two years include Kit Wright, Jackie Wills, Roger Finch, Peter Goldsworthy, Giles Goodland and Stephanos Papadopoulous. In difficult times this is a brave venture

There are other presses with less prodigious outputs but whose editions are still up there with the best of them. In Northumberland, Margaret and Peter Lewis's **Flambard Press** has maintained its stature. Begun in 1991 it now publishes around six or so titles annually in the Bloodaxe style. With aid from Northern Arts the press is interested in new and neglected poets especially from the North and the Borders. Gerard Benson, Wanda Barford, Gladys Mary Coles, Joolz and Amanda White are typical poets. Check www.flambardpress.co.uk Gladys Mary Coles has developed her **Headland Publications** into a regular Peterloo clone and is now producing some fine books. Her interest centres on north-west England and north Wales. Bestsellers include Myra Schneider's *Making Worlds: The Headland Anthology of Women's Poetry*, Edmund Cusick, Brian Wake, Alison Chisholm and others. Ken Edwards' **Reality Street Editions** specialises in 'linguistically innovative writing by women and men on both sides of the Atlantic'. Publishing a small number of single-author volumes, translations and ground-breaking anthologies, the press takes the new poetry seriously. Typical authors include Barbara Guest, Cris Cheek, Lisa Robertson and Denise Riley. The press has also published book/CD packages and runs an excellent Internet site (freespace.virgin.net/reality.street). Currently, however, the press is not accepting new manuscripts. Nicholas Johnson's **Etruscan Books** carries the flame for UK avant-garde poetry and performance with a terrific series of readers, chapbooks and multi-contributor volumes along with a first-class anthology of contemporary material, *Foil*. If anyone is pushing the edge out then Johnson is, and he's doing it with style. Output is backed up by extensive poetry tours and festival appearances. He has recently been active with a Brian Catling extravaganza in the south-west, Gloucester, and Bristol. His published poets include Bob Cobbing, Tom Leonard, Helen Macdonald, Wendy Mulford, Sean Rafferty, Maggie O'Sullivan, Bill Griffiths and Tom Pickard.

Paul Beasley's poetry agency (see **Organisations of Interest to Poets**), **57 Productions**, represents performance poetry heartland and, realising that most of his material works better on audio, has concentrated on editions on cassette and CD. Recent successes have included a double Adrian Mitchell as well as performances by Jackie Kay, Gillian Clarke and Benjamin Zephaniah. Check its multi-artist *Poetry in Performance* CDs for a good taster.

In Huddersfield, Janet Fisher and Peter Sansom run **Smith/Doorstop**, the poetry imprint of their enterprising **Poetry Business** (see **Organisations of Interest to Poets**). The press, which has expanded steadily over the years, now produces six to eight excellent-looking full-length collections annually. Dorothy Nimmo, Martin Stannard, Dennis Casling, Susan Utting and Michael Laskey are typical authors. Smith/Doorstop also runs an annual poetry pamphlet competition (with publication as one of the prizes) as well as producing poetry on cassette. Its *Contemporary Poems*, edited by Peter Sansom and Lesley Jeffries, offers a good critical introduction to the scene. The Web address is www.poetrybusiness.co.uk

Jessie Lendennie runs **Salmon Publishing** from the Cliffs of Moher, Co. Clare with connections at Spruce Island, Alaska where they are planning a North American poetry centre and writers' retreat. The press publishes some of the best designed titles in the West. An Irish connection is pretty useful when trying here, although Salmon does look at material from further afield. Typical poets include Adrienne Rich, Rita Ann Higgins, Marvin Bell, Linda McCarriston, James Simmons and Mary O'Malley. Its anthology of contemporary Irish women poets, *The White Page/An Bhileog Bhan*, is a terrific achievement. Recent titles include a *Selected and New Poems* from fantasy/science fiction writer Ray Bradbury (his first to be published outside the US), a collection of never before published poems by Caitlin Thomas, and *In the Chair: Interviews with Poets from the North of Ireland* by John Brown. (Salmon has an excellent website at www.salmonpoetry.com) And if the poetry is not flowing you can book in to a Salmon Creative Writing Workshop for £100 for the weekend.

Peepal Tree is the largest independent publisher of Caribbean, South Asian and black British poetry. Founded in 1986, it now produces around ten poetry titles annually. Typical poets include Kwame Dawes, Marcia Douglas, Cyril Dabydeen and Anthony Kellman. Editors Jeremy Poynting and Hannah Banister read over 1,000 submissions annually and are not known for their speedy responses. Send five or six examples of your work along with a biographical note and wait. You can get a Peepal Tree catalogue and news updates by e-mail: hannah@peepal.demon.co.uk

Elsewhere Lewis Davies's **Parthian Books** under poetry editor Richard Gwyn puts out fine editions of Ifor Thomas, Patrick Jones and Lloyd Robson along with a new anthology of young Welsh contemporaries.

As technology continues to make life easier for publishers it becomes harder to draw the line between the poetry specialists and the classic small presses. Maybe by now such a division does not exist at all.

The traditional outlets

Poetry has a place in our national press but traditionally a small one. The *Independent, Daily Express* and the *Guardian* feature verse from time to time, as do some of the serious Sunday heavies. The *Times Literary Supplement* and the *London Review of Books* give over space on a regular basis but they do have their favourites. Among other journals the situation is fluid. Poetry gets in when someone on the staff shows an interest. Check your targets along the shelves at WH Smith's. Local newspapers and freesheets occasionally devote pages to contributions from readers, mostly dire doggerel and largely unpaid, although it *is* publication. If your paper doesn't do this try sending in. Much of this might sound quite reassuring for the poet but the truth is that were poetry to cease to exist overnight, then these publications would continue to operate without a flicker. Who, other than the poets, would notice?

The regional anthologies

Running in parallel with the high-ground literary approach of much of the poetry world are empires largely unknown to the taste-makers and ignored by the critics. The biggest, Ian and Tracy Walton's **Forward Press** in Peterborough, now turns over £2 million annually, has almost 5,000 titles in print, and reckons to account for the highest proportion of all *new* verse published in the UK. Depressed with 'twenty years of not being able to enjoy poetry' because it was inevitably obscure, the couple have moved from back kitchen to three-storey office block in the service of 600,000 active British verse scribblers. 'A high proportion of the thousands of letters we receive tell us that many people find poetry over-complex and difficult to understand' runs one of their brochures. For more than a decade since it was founded, **Forward Press** has enthusiastically promoted an 'accessible, sincere poetry which everyone can relate to'. The higher realms are not for them. Publishing under a number of imprints including **Poetry Now**, **Anchor Books**, **Young Writers**, and

Triumph House, the operation receives thousands of contributions annually. Poets are sourced in the main through editorial copy in regional newspapers. The contributors flow in their hundreds. 'It is a bit like amateur dramatics,' Ian told me, 'anyone can take part.'

Forward's outstanding success is built on its approachability. The Waltons and their team of young editors include as many as 160 poems in each anthology. Submissions under thirty lines are preferred. Costs are kept down by using in-house printing equipment – a Ryobi digital press – coupled to serviceable bindings. If you want to see your work in print, and for most contributors this is the whole raison d'être for writing, then you have to buy a copy. For many poets this will be their first appearance in book form and chances are they will purchase more than a single copy. This is not a traditional vanity operation. No one is actually being ripped off, nor are the publishers raking in exorbitant profits. Page for page their titles are not much more expensive than those of Cape or Faber and are cheaper than the output of some little presses. However, distribution is patchy – not that many Forward titles make the shelves of our national chains, although efforts have been made. As for many of the small presses, interested parties are encouraged to buy direct. Forward's critics claim that quality is being neglected in exchange for quantity. Dumb down your criteria for inclusion, cram the poems in, sell more copies. Undoubtedly the genuine literary achievement of appearing in one of Forward's books is questionable. But in mitigation it must be said that for some writers this will be their much-needed beginning (check Angela Macnab and Sally Spedding), and for others the only success they are ever going to get.

Forward's much criticised royalty payment scheme has been replaced with the Forward Press Top 100 Awards, which offers in excess of £10,000 to the best of the poets published annually in its many anthologies.

In addition to their schools and regional collections, Forward runs three magazines, *Poetry Now*, *Scribbler!* and *Wordsmith* (for young writers), a print and design service for self-publishers, and **Spotlight** – a joint publishing venture which showcases a dozen new poets a time. Its **Writers' Bookshop** imprint publishes a most useful series of reference books including subject and genre guides, directories and handbooks. Forward offers the complete poetry life. If *A Treasured Moment, Perception of Life, Inspire to Rhyme, In High Spirits, Message from Within* and *From A Distance* sound like your scene send for the group's information pack (Remus House, Coltsfoot Drive, Peterborough, PE2 9JX), ring on 01733 898105, fax on 01733 313524, check the website, www.forwardpress.co.uk or e-mail your request (liz@forwardpress.co.uk). You'll find no dubious accommodation address dealing here, but on the other hand few literary giants either.

Envious of Forward's success at catching the hearts and minds of most of the UK's poetry hobbyists, a good number of rival empire-builders have risen in their wake. Regional poetry anthologies, Best of Britain collections, compendiums of English, Scottish, Irish and Welsh verse abound. Contributions are sourced through notices on library walls, local freesheets, local radio, and direct

mail. These operations vary from the glossy to a number of pathetically produced, and one hopes short-lived, incarnations based in the non-metropolitan
sticks. No actual rip-off occurs and contributors get in whether they purchase or
not. But if you want to see your work then you must buy and the books can
cost upwards of £30. Before agreeing to contribute, check the press's output.
Do not submit blindly, research its backlist. It is what Faber would demand of
you. The rule applies to the whole poetry scene.

The small press and the little magazine

Small publishing ventures have been with us for quite a long time. And today it's
easier than ever to get a small mag into the marketplace or to bring out a book.
Technologically literate poets are everywhere. Publishing has been stripped of its
mystery. Access to decent printers and the computers that drive them are com-
monplace. Page make-up and word-processing software make it so easy to do.
Disposable income has gone up. Poets in growing numbers are able and willing
to establish competent one-person publishing operations, turning out neat, pro-
fessional-looking titles on a considerable scale.

These are the small presses and little magazines. They sell to non-traditional
markets, rarely finding space on bookshop shelves, where they are regarded as
unshiftable nuisances. Professional distribution remains the age-old problem and
is probably now utterly unsolvable, using conventional routes. However, the
answer is around the corner. As publication shifts into cyberspace the difficulties
of hard-copy distribution will fall away. Increasing numbers of small mags now
have versions of themselves on the Web. Publication there is so much easier
than by traditional routes. There are a number of journals which now only exist
in Internet form (see the section on the Internet, earlier in this article). Yet for
now, but not for much longer, small mags still go hand-to-hand among friends,
at slams, readings, concerts, creative-writing classes, literary functions, and via
subscriptions, and are liberally exchanged among all those concerned. The network is large. The question remains: is anyone out there not directly concerned
with the business of poetry actually reading it? But that is another story.

Statistically, the small presses and the little magazines are the largest publishers
of new poetry, in both range and circulation. They operate in a bewildering blur
of shapes and sizes everywhere from Brighton to Birmingham and Aberystwyth
to Aberdeen. For up-to-the moment data have a look at Daniel Trent's excellent, browsable small magazine information website at *Little Magazines*
– www.little-magazines.co.uk – which exhibits flair and information in equal
measure.

This country's best poetry magazines all began as classic littles. Between them *PN
Review*, *Ambit*, *Orbis* (now relaunched under the editorship of Carole Baldock), *Poetry
Review*, *Rialto*, *Acumen*, *Terrible Work*, *The North*, *Smiths Knoll*, *Arete*, *Envoi* and *Stand* do
not come up to even half the circulation of journals like *Shooting Times* or *Practical
Fishkeeping* – which says a lot about the way society values its poetry. Nonetheless,

taken as a group, they will get to almost everyone who matters. They represent poetry as a whole. Read these and you will get some idea of where the cutting edge is.

In the second division in terms of kudos lie the regional or genre specialists such as *HU* (Irish poetry), *Raw Edge* (new writing from the west Midlands), *The New Welsh Review, Poetry Wales, Poetry Ireland, Krax* (humorous verse), *Poetry Scotland, Writing Women, Poetry Church, Christian Poetry Review, Snapshots Haiku Magazine* and *Time Haiku*. All these magazines are well produced, sometimes with the help of grants, and all represent a specific point of view. In Wales there is *Barddas* for poets using the strict meters and in Scotland *Lallans* for poets working in Lowland Scots.

The vast majority of small magazines, however, owe no allegiance and range from quality round-ups like *Billy Liar, Tears in the Fence*, Martin Holroyd's chatty *Poetry Monthly*, ex-*Rialto* editor John Wakeman's splendid *SHOp, Obsessed With Pipework*, general literary magazines such as *The Reader* and annuals, such as the excellent *Tabla*, to irregulars like *The Yellow Crane* (interesting new poems), *Moodswing* (a pocket broadsheet), *Breathe* (helps keep poetry alive), *The Unruly Sun* (no dogma), *As Well As* (poetry that's a bit askew), *The Interpreter's House* (the best prose and verse that the editor can get), the anarchic *Cannon Fodder* and *Skald* (general poetry). Some, like *The Penniless Press*, are for the poor of pocket and the rich of mind, *Fire* goes for length and the otherwise unpublishable. If you can't find a magazine that suits you and your style then you can't be writing poetry. On the other hand if you're really sure you are and still can't get in anywhere, then start your own.

Among the small presses there is a similar range. Roland John's **Hippopotamus Press** publishes Peter Dale, Edward Lowbury and other safe hands; **Equipage**, **Writers Forum**, **Prest Roots Press** and **Shearsman Books** keep the modernist tradition right there at the front; **Rockingham Press**, with its four or five titles annually, stays safe, solid, and conventional; **Feather Books** publishes Christian verse; Brian Wake's **Driftwood**, revived after a thirty-year break, puts out Jim Mangnall, Peggy Poole, Richard Hill and others plus a CD by Henry Graham; **Dangaroo** has Third World and ethnic concerns. **The Collective** works the Welsh marches; magazines *Acumen, The Rialto* and *Poetry Monthly* are also pamphleteers; **Semicolon** and **Flarestack Publishing** do sterling work. **Y Lolfa** publishes unofficial bards. For the new writer these kinds of presses are the obvious place to try first. Indeed it is where many have. Who put out T.S. Eliot's first? A small publisher. Dannie Abse, Peter Redgrove, James Fenton and Dylan Thomas? The same. R.S. Thomas, Ezra Pound, and Edgar Allan Poe didn't even go that far – they published themselves.

Poetry for children

The thing to remember here is that children rarely buy poetry for themselves, nor are there poetry magazines aimed at them. On the other hand there are a great number of children's poets out there – Duffy, McGough, Henri and Patten would be much lesser authors if they'd ignored the under-eighteens. The schools system regularly pays poets to read to their classes and teach their children. Macmillan, Faber, Penguin, Walker and a few other publishers run specialist children's poetry lists. The market switches between the traditional and the hilarious – *Warning: Never Play Snap With a Shark* chosen by John Foster is a typical title. If you have appropriate work, send in a few samples marked for the attention of the children's poetry editor. But do not imagine this market to be easy nor a place where you can unload your adult failures. Kids do not suffer fools gladly. For more information check with the Poetry Society which publishes a number of poetry in schools checklists along with a handbook.

Cash

Despite a small number of very high value awards (£75,000 plus) made by various government agencies to the select few, a lot of writers new to the business are surprised to learn that their poetry will not make them much money. For most, being a poet is not really much of an occupation. You get better wages delivering papers. There will be the odd £20 from the better-heeled magazine, perhaps even as much as £60 or so from those periodicals lucky enough to be in receipt of a grant, but generally it will be free copies of the issues concerned, thank you letters, and little more. Those with collections to be published by a subsidised, specialist publisher can expect a couple of hundred as an advance on royalties. Those using the small presses can look forward to a handful of complimentary copies. On the Internet published poets usually get nothing at all (although there are some exceptions, check *Pif* for example). The truth is that poetry itself is undervalued. You can earn money writing about it, reviewing it, lecturing on it, teaching it, or, certainly, by giving public performances (£150 standard here, £1,000 plus if you are Roger McGough, much more if you are Seamus Heaney). In fact, most things in the poetry business will earn better money than the verse itself. This isn't capitalism, this is art.

Readings

Since the great Beat Generation, Albert Hall reading of 1964, there has been an ever-expanding phenomenon of poets on platforms, reading or reciting their stuff to an audience that can be anywhere between raptly attentive and fast asleep. Jaci Stephen, writing in the *Daily Mirror*, reckoned readings to be like jazz. 'Both involve a small group of people making a lot of noise, and then, just when you think it's all over, it carries on.' But I believe there can be a magic in the spoken poem. Not everything, certainly. But when it's good it can be sublime. Yet for some writers the whole thing has devolved so far as to become a branch of the entertainment industry or, in the case of poetry slams (see **Competitions**, below), an opportunity to show off enormously in front of friends. Whichever way you view it, it is certainly an integral part of the business and one in which the beginner is going to need to engage sooner or later. Begin by attending and see how others manage. Watch out for local events advertised at your local library, ring your local arts board or check www.liveliterature.net, the Arts Council of England's listings service (in Wales look at www.academi. org). Poets with heavy reputations can often turn out to be lousy performers, while many an amateur can really crack it out. Don't expect to catch every image as you listen. Readings are not places for total comprehension but rather for glancing blows. Treat it as fun and it will be. If you are trying things yourself for the first time, make sure you bring your books along to sell, stand upright, drop the shoulders, gaze at a spot at the back of the hall, and blow.

Music

Poetry has made many inroads into the music business. There was a time when this meant Spike Milligan standing up and spouting in front of a jazz band or a middle-of-the-road brass playing behind John Betjeman, but no longer. There are quite a number of poets now working with musicians, starting bands, or mixing in pre-recorded backing tracks. The advent of rap and hip-hop and the ready use of the speech sample as a component part of dance beats has turned the public ear. Dub poets – such as Linton Kwesi Johnson – have long used reggae as a backdrop for their words and the likes of Americans Sonja Sohn, Saul Williams and Dana Bryant have been softening up the cool crowd with their funk-backed hooks. This is certainly a non-traditional approach well away from poetry's conventional involvement with literature and with books. Check the clubs (and the events mounted by *Apples & Snakes* in London) to hear more and expect what you find to be nothing like what you expected. Poetry keeps moving. Thank the Lord for that.

Competitions and awards

Poetry competitions have been the vogue for decades now, with the most unlikely organisations sponsoring them. The notion here is that anonymity ensures fairness. Entries are made under pseudonyms so that if your name does happen to be Andrew Motion, then this won't help you much. Results seem to bear this out too. The big competitions run biennially by the **Arvon Foundation** with the help of commercial sponsors, the **Academi**'s *Cardiff International* and the **Poetry Society**'s *National* attract an enormous entry and usually throw up quite a number of complete unknowns among the winners. And why do people bother? Cash prizes can be large – thousands – but it costs at least a few pounds a poem to enter, and often much more than that. If it's cash you want, then Lottery scratchcards are a better bet. And there has been a trend for winners to come from places like Cape Girardeau, Missouri and Tibooburra, Australia. The odds are getting longer. Who won the last Arvon? I don't remember. But if you do fancy a try then it's a pretty innocent activity. You tie up a poem for a few months and you spend a little money. Winners' tips include reading the work of the judges to see how they do it, submitting non-controversial middle-of-the-road smiling things, and doing this just before the closing date so you won't have to wait too long. Try two or three of your best. Huge wodges are costly and will only convince the judges of your insecurity. Have a look at *The Ring Of Words* (Sutton Publishing), an excellent historical anthology of Arvon winners and runners-up. For contests to enter watch the small mags, write to your regional arts board, check out *The New Writer*, *Poetry London*, *Writer's News*, or the listings in *Orbis* magazine, look on the notice board at your local library, or write for the regularly updated list from **The Poetry Library** in London (see **Organisations of Interest to Poets**).

Combining both competition and reading is the **Poetry Slam**. Here all-comers are given the opportunity to strut their stuff for around three closely timed minutes before a usually not all that literary crowd. Points are awarded much in the style as that for ice skating. You get them for a combination of performance and audience reaction. Scatology and streetwise crowd-pleasing are more likely to get you through the rounds than closely honed work. The events, which involve much shouting, can be a lot of fun.

Poetry Awards are slightly different. These are usually made for published books, and convention generally requires your publisher to make the nomination rather than you. These glittering prizes are increasing both in value and impact. Both the annual **T.S. Eliot** and **Forward Prizes** are now worth £10,000 a time, with the poetry section of the **Whitbread Book Award** not far behind. To win one of these your book needs to be pretty hot.

Radio and TV

Centring on National Poetry day each year, the BBC continues to poll the nation for the favourite poems. Classic Poems, Love Poems, Twentieth Century Poems, Comic Poems, and Poetry of Journeys have all been listed. Recently the Nation's Favourite Children's Poem was the centre of a BBC-run competition for young people as well as a Ping Pong Poetry project which had more than 1,000 participants from fifty-one schools around the country. *Journeys* had the BBC commission ten new contemporary works. However, the broadcaster's enthusiasm has slid away from television. Coverage for poetry on screen has always been scant. It is so hard to make verse visually appealing. Some producers have tried, notably Peter Symes with Tony Harrison and Ian Macmillan at BBC2. Film-maker Brian Hill has produced a number of collaborations with Simon Armitage for Channel Four. Digital TV, however, with its almost insatiable appetite for material, is potentially a much better market. BBC Digital have already tried televised poetry slams.

Poetry can also occasionally be found ladled between the music on MTV but inevitably by the media-promoted bards. Most poetry on air actually sticks with radio. Sue Roberts is the editor of a poetry strand from Manchester. She is keen to offer drama with poetry and had several successes including *Room of Leaves* by Amanda Dalton. Viv Beeby at Bristol makes drama out of classic poetry as well as commissioning new work and making on-location broadcasts such as Ian Macmillan in *Maine Voices*. Also at Bristol, Sara Davies looks after Radio 4's regular long-running Sunday 4.30 strand with *Poetry Please* (a listeners' request show which uses only published material) and other programmes including the well-received *Adventures in Poetry*. There have also been a number of Bristol-produced late-night poetry-in-performance programmes featuring Roger McGough, Matt Harvey and Rory Motion.

Fiona Mclean produces poetry for Radio 3 including a series of Poetry Proms featuring the work of a range of writers including Jo Shapcott. Radio 1 puts poetry into some of its evening slots, showcasing poets who have high streetcred. BBC World has Michael Rosen presenting listeners' favourites on its *Poems by Post* programmes. Independent radio is trying verse as fillers.

Poetry on radio is a large but difficult market. The BBC is pretty definite about having no remit to use 'unpublished or amateur verse'. Programme ideas should always be directed to a programme-making department at the BBC rather than to Radio 4 or Radio 3. If you are determined to put your verse on air then local and regional radio offer better possibilities. Try sending in self-produced readings on cassette (if you are any good at it) or topical poetry that regional magazine programmes could readily use. Don't expect to be paid much.

Starting up

Probably the best place will be locally. Find out through the library or the nearest arts board which writers' groups gather in your area and attend. There you will meet others of a like mind, encounter whatever locally produced magazines there might be, and get a little direct feedback on your work. 'How am I doing?' is a big question for the emerging poet and although criticism is not all that hard to come by, do not expect it from all sources. Magazine editors, for example, will rarely have the time to offer advice. It is also reasonable to be suspicious of that offered by friends and relations – they will no doubt be only trying to please. Writers' groups present the best chance for poets to engage in honest mutual criticism. But if you'd prefer a more detached, written analysis of your efforts and are willing to pay a small sum, then you could apply to *Prescription*, the service operated nationally by the Poetry Society (22 Betterton Street, London WC2H 9BU), to the service run by The Arts Council of Wales (see **Arts Councils and Regional Arts Boards**) or to those run on an area basis by your local arts board. There are also a number of non-subsidised critical services which you will find advertised in writers' magazines.

Read: if it's all a mystery to you, try Tony Curtis' *How to Study Modern Poetry* (Macmillan); Matthew Sweeney and John Hartley Williams' *Teach Yourself Writing Poetry*, John Whitworth's *Writing Poetry* (A&C Black) or my own *The Poetry Business* (Seren). How real poets actually work can be discovered by reading C.B. McCully's the *Poet's Voice and Craft* (Carcanet) or *How Poets Work* (Seren). After all this, if you still think it's appropriate, try sending in.

How to do it

Increase your chances of acceptance by following simple, standard procedure:

- Type or print on a single side of the paper, A4 size, single-spacing with double between stanzas, exactly as you'd wish your poem to appear when printed.
- Give the poem a title, clip multi-page works together, include your name and address at the foot of the final sheet. Avoid files, plastic covers, stiffeners and fancy clips of any sort.
- Keep a copy, make a record of what you send where and when, leave a space to note reaction.
- Send in small batches – six is a good number – with a brief covering letter saying who you are. Leave justification, apology and explanation for your writers' group.
- Include a self-addressed, stamped envelope of sufficient size for reply and/or return of your work.
- Be prepared to wait some weeks for a response. Don't pester. Be patient. Most magazines will reply in the end.
- Never send the same poem to two places at the same time (and this includes e-zine vs. hard copy. The jury is still out on whether or not the inclusion of a poem on your own personal website actually counts as publication). If you've entered the poem for a competition then make sure you never simultaneously send it elsewhere.
- If you are thinking of sending your submission electronically *check* first. Most journals and publishers in the *Writer's Handbook* survey have said that they refuse to accept materials sent this way.
- Send your best. Work that fails to fully satisfy even the author is unlikely to impress anyone else.

Where?

Try the list that follows. This is by no means the whole UK small-press scene, but only those where potential contributors might stand a chance. Even here do not expect unrelenting positive responses: magazines get overstocked, editors change, addresses shift, policy alters, operators run out of steam. Be prepared to hunt around and for a lot of your work to come back. You can help improve things by buying copies. Send in an s.a.e. asking how much. The total market is vast and if you want to go further than the *Writer's Handbook* listings then you could consult the following: the *Small Press Guide* (which only covers journals – Writers' Bookshop, Remus House, Coltsfoot Drive, Woodston, Peterborough PE2 9JX), *Light's List of Literary Magazines*, which contains both UK and US addresses (John Light, Photon Press, The Lighthouse, 37 The Meadows, Berwick upon Tweed, Northumberland TD15 1NY), the Internet directory at *Little Magazines* (see **The Small Press and Little Magazine**, above) or Len Fulton's *Directory of Poetry Publishers* (Dustbooks) – the main American directory.

Scams and cons

With poetry overpopulated by participants it is not surprising that the con artist should make an appearance. There are plenty of people out there taking money off beginner writers and offering very little in return. The traditional vanity anthology, once the staple of the trickster, is now in retreat following a number of successful campaigns. Nonetheless variations and embellishments on the approach resurface steadily. These include offers to put your poetry to music set-ting you off on the road to stardom, readings of your verse by actors with deep voices to help you break into the local radio market (there isn't one), and further requests for cash to have entries on you appear in leather-bound directories of world poets. Everyone appears, including your uncle. There are bogus compe-titions where entry fees bear no relation to final prize money (or such prize money turns out never to be forthcoming) and the advertised 'publication of winners in anthology form' often means shelling out more for what will turn out to be a badly printed abomination crammed full of weak work. Poets should look very carefully at anything which offers framed certificates, scrolls or engraved wall hangings. They should also be wary of suggestions that they have come high in the State of Florida's Laureateship Contest (or some such like) and have been awarded a calligraphed testimonial. Presentation usually occurs at a three-day festival held in one of state's most expensive hotels. To get your bit of paper you need to stay for all three days and it is you who has to settle the bill. If you try your luck at a no-entry-fee, advertised in the Sunday papers inter-national competition don't be too surprised to find you've made it through round one – that happens to everyone. The scam begins with round two when they start to ask you for money.

How do you spot the tricksters? They change their names and addresses at will. They bill themselves as Foundations, Societies, Libraries, National Associations, Guilds. They sound so plausible. If you have the slightest suspicion then check with the Poetry Society (see **Organisations of Interest to Poets**). Some of the scams operated in the poetry-competition field have a warning website devoted to exposing them. Check windpub.org/literary.scams/ilp.htm for a full view. In the poetry world genuine advertisements for contributions are rare. And if anyone asks you for money then forget it. It is not the way things should be done.

The next step

Once you have placed a few poems you may like to consider publishing a booklet. There are as many small presses around as there are magazines. Start with the upmarket professionals by all means – Jonathan Cape, Faber & Faber – but be prepared for compromise. The specialists and the small presses are swifter and more open to new work.

If all else fails you could do it yourself. Blake did, so did Walt Whitman. Modern technology puts the process within the reach of us all and if you can put up a shelf, there is a fair chance you will be able to produce a book to go on it. Read my *How to Publish Yourself* (Allison & Busby). Remember that publishing the book may be as hard as writing it but marketing and selling it is quite something else. Check Alison Baverstock's *Marketing Your Book: An Author's Guide* (A&C Black) if you really want to get ahead.

The listings

None of the lists of addresses that follow is exhaustive. Publishers come and go with amazing frequency. There will always be the brand-new press on the lookout for talent and the projected magazine desperate for contributions. For up-to-the minute information check with some of the **Organisations of Interest to Poets** (see page 169). Poetry has a huge market. It pays to keep your ear to the ground. The magazines and presses listed here have all been active during the past eighteen months and most (although be warned, *not all*) have indicated a willingness to look at new work. Those with a positive uninterest in receiving unsolicited work have been excluded. In all cases check before sending. Ask to see a catalogue or a sample copy. Good luck.

Poetry Presses

Anvil Press Poetry Ltd
Neptune House, 70 Royal Hill, London
SE10 8RF
☎020 8469 3033 Fax 020 8469 3363
Email anvil@anvilpresspoetry.com
Website www.anvilpresspoetry.com

Contact *Peter Jay*

Contemporary British poetry and poetry in translation. See entry under **UK Publishers**.

Arc Publications
Nanholme Mill, Shaw Wood Road,
Todmorden, Lancs OL14 6DA
☎01706 812338 Fax 01706 818948
Email arc.publications@virgin.net
Website www.arcpublications.co.uk

Contact *Tony Ward*

Contemporary poetry from new and established writers both in the UK and abroad. See entry under **UK Publishers**.

Au Quai
8 Richmond Road, Staines, Middlesex
TW18 2AB
Email vennel@hotmail.com
Website www.indigogroup.co.uk/llpp/
 vennel.html

Contact *Richard Price*

Modern Scottish poetry; poetry in translation; poetry that takes its bearings from modernism. See also **Vennel Press** and **Southfields** presses.

Aural Images
5 Hamilton Street, Astley Bridge, Bolton,
Lancs BL1 6RJ

Contacts *Susan & Alan White*

Poetry, youth arts workshops.

BB Books
Spring Bank, Longsight Road, Copster Green,
Blackburn, Lancs BB1 9EU

Contact *Dave Cunliffe*

Post-Beat poetics and counterculture theoretic. Iconoclastic rants and anarchic psycho-cultural tracts. See also **Global Tapestry Journal**.

Best Medicine Press
49 Saunton Avenue, Hayes, Middlesex
Website www.geocities.com/captaindisaster

Contact *David Seaman*

Bloodaxe Books Ltd
Highgreen, Tarset, Northumberland
NE48 1RP
☎01434 240500 Fax 01434 240505
Email editor@bloodaxebooks.com
Website www.bloodaxebooks.com

Contact *Neil Astley*

Britain's leading publisher of new poetry. No submissions by e-mail attachments. See entry under **UK Publishers**.

Carcanet Press
4th Floor, Conavon Court, 12–16 Blackfriars
Street, Manchester M3 5BQ
☎0161 834 8730 Fax 0161 832 0084
Email pnr@carcanet.u-net.com
Website www.carcanet.co.uk

Contact *Michael Schmidt*

Major poetry publisher. See entry under **UK Publishers**.

Chapman Publishing
4 Broughton Place, Edinburgh EH1 3RX
☎0131 557 2207 Fax 0131 556 9565
Email editor@chapman-pub.co.uk
Website www.chapman-pub.co.uk

Contact *Joy Hendry*

Scottish writing. See entry under **UK Publishers**.

Cherrycroft Press
Popes Lane, Cookham Dean, Berks SL6 9NY

The Collective Press
Penlanlas Farm, Llantilio Pertholey, Y-fenni,
Gwent NP7 7HN
☎01873 856350 Fax 01873 859559
Email john.jones6@which.net
Website www.welshwriters.com

Contact *John Jones*

Non-profit promoter and publisher of contemporary poetry.

Community of Poets and Artists Press

Thyme Cottage, Bogshole Lane, Whitstable, Kent CT5 3AT
☎01227 281806
Email bennetta.artco@virgin.net
Website www.artistspress.co.uk
Contact *Philip Bennetta*

Dedicated to making artists books, hand-sewn poetry pamphlets, with online gallery and magazine.

Corbie Press

57 Murray Street, Montrose, Angus DD10 8JZ
Contact *Neil Mathers*

Scottish & European literature, art, philosophy, some poetry. See also **Epoch Magazine**.

Dagger Press

70 Dagger Lane, West Bromwich, West Midlands B71 4BS
☎0121 553 2029
Contact *Brian Morse*

Poetry pamphlets.

Day Dream Press

39 Exmouth Street, Swindon, Wilts SN1 3PU
☎01793 523927
Contact *Kevin Bailey*

See also **HQ, Haiku Quarterly**.

Diamond Twig

5 Bentinck Road, Newcastle upon Tyne NE4 6UT
☎0191 273 5326
Email diamond.twig@virgin.net
Website www.diamondtwig.co.uk
Contact *Ellen Phethean*

New writing by women in the north of England.

Dionysia Press

20a Mongomery Street, Edinburgh EH7 5JS
☎0131 478 0680 Fax 0131 478 2572
Contact *Denise Smith*

Collections of poetry, words, translations. See also **Understanding** magazine.

Disseminate

23 Caestory Avenue, Raglan, Usk, Monmouthshire NP15 2EH

Driftwood Publications

5 Timms Lane, Freshfield, Merseyside L37 7DW
☎0151 525 2285 Fax 0151 524 0216
Email brian@sefonarts.fsnet.co.uk
Contact *Brian Wake*

New work by new and established poets more suited to the page than the stage.

Enitharmon Press

26B Caversham Road, London NW5 2DU
☎020 7482 5967 Fax 020 7284 1787
Email books@enitharmon.co.uk
Website www.enitharmon.co.uk
Contact *Stephen Stuart-Smith*

Poetry and criticism. See entry under **UK Publishers**.

Erran Publishing

43 Willow Road, Carlton, Notts NG4 3BH
Email erranpublishing@hotmail.com
Website www.poetichours.homestead.com
Contact *Nick Clark*

Non-profit supprter of third world charities. See also **Poetic Hours** magazine.

Essence Press

8 Craiglea Drive, Edinburgh EH10 5PA
Email jaj@essencepress.co.uk
Website www.essencepress.co.uk
Contact *Julie Johnstone*

A distinctive space for writing inspired by nature and exploring our place within the natural world. See also **Island** press.

Etruscan Books

28 Fowler's Court, Fore Street, Buckfast, Devon TQ11 0AA
☎01364 643128 Fax 01364 643054
Contact *Nicholas Johnson*

Modernist, sound, visual poetry, Gaelic, lyric poetry, US/UK poets.

Everyman Press

53 West Vale, Neston, Cheshire CH64 9SE
Contact *Elizabeth Boyd*

See also **Eclipse** magazine.

Feather Books

PO Box 438, Shrewsbury, Shropshire SY3 0WN
☎01743 872177 Fax 01743 872177
Email john@waddysweb.freeuk.com

Website www.waddysweb.freeuk.com
Contact *Rev. J. Waddington-Feather*
Quarterly magazine of Christian poetry and prayers. See also **The Poetry Church** magazine and entry under **Small Presses**.

Firebird Press
104 Argyle Gardens, Upminster, Essex RM14 3EU
Website www.homestead.com/firebirdpress
Contact *Pamela Constantine*
Furthering a renaissance of the perennial values which make life meaningful and worthwhile. See also **Rebirth, Romantic Renaissance** and **The Solar Flame** magazines.

Flambard
Stable Cottage, East Fourstones, Hexham, Northumberland NE47 5DX
☎01434 674360 Fax 01434 674178
Email admin@signature-books.co.uk
Website www.flambardpress.co.uk
Contact *Peter Elfed Lewis*
Concentrates on poetry but also publishes fiction, expecially literary and crime

Flarestack Publishing
Redditch Library, 15 Market Place, Redditch B98 8AR
☎01527 63291 Fax 01527 68571
Email flare.stack@virgin.net
Contact *Charles Johnson*
Considers first collections for A5 stapled pamphlet publication. See also **Obsessed With Pipework** magazine.

Forward Press
Remus House, Coltsfoot Drive, Woodston, Peterborough PE2 9JX
☎01733 898105 Fax 01733 313524
Email aja@forwardpress.co.uk
Website www.forwardpress.co.uk
Contact *Ian Walton*
General poetry and short fiction anthologies. See also **Triumph House** press and **Poetry Now** magazine.

Four Quarters Press
7 The Towers, Stevenage, Hertfordshire SG1 1HE
Contact *Eric Ratcliffe*

Gallery Pamphlets
Ardingly College, Haywards Heath, West Sussex RH17 6SQ
Email floherus@aol.com
Contact *Mark Floyer*
Quality crafted poetry. See also **Konfluence** magazine.

Gallery Poets
37 Micklehill Drive, Shirley, Solihull, West Midlands B90 2PU

Headland Publications
Ty Coch, Galltegfa, Ruthin, Denbighshire LL15 2AR
☎0151 625 9128 Fax 0151 625 9128
Contact *Gladys Mary Coles*
Fine editions of poetry; anthologies.

Hippopotamus Press
22 Whitewell Road, Frome, Somerset BA11 4EL
☎01373 466653 Fax 01373 466653
Contact *Roland John*
First collections of verse from those with a track record in the magazines. See also **Outposts** magazine.

Honno Welsh Women's Press
Editorial Office, UTC, King Street, Aberystwyth, Ceredigion SY23 2LT
☎01970 623150 Fax 01970 623150
Email editor@honno.co.uk
Website www.honno.co.uk
Contact *Gwenllian Dafydd*
The Welsh women's press – novels, childrens fiction, short stories, poetry and autobiographical anthologies. See entry under **UK Publishers**.

Hub Editions
Longholm, East Bank, Wingland, Sutton Bridge, Spalding, Lincs PE12 9YS
Contact *Colin Blundell*
Poetry, experimental writing, challenges to status quo, high-class hand-made perfect bound products.

JazzClaw
36 Wolfe Road, Norwich, Norfolk NR1 4HT
☎01603 499784
Email david.searle@care4free.net
Website www.searlepublishing.co.uk
Contact *David Searle*

Avant-garde poetry and prose, surrealism, erotica, dark themes, experimental. See also **Searle Publishing**.

The King's England Press
21 Commercial Road, Goldthorpe,
Rotherham, S. Yorks S63 9BL
☎01226 270258
Email enquiries@kingsengland.demon.co.uk
Website www.kingsengland.demon.co.uk
Contact *Steve Rudd*
Children's books including poetry.

KT Publications
16 Fane Close, Stamford, Lincs PE12 9YS
Contact *Kevin Troop*

Modern poetry and short stories. Charges a reading fee of £14 per manuscript.

Leviathan
Bears Hay Farm, Brookhay Lane, Fradley
WS13 8RG
☎01543 411161 Fax 01543 410679
Email claire.brodmann@btinternet.com
Contact *Michael Hulse*
See also **Leviathan Quarterly** magazine.

Mariscat Press
3 Mariscat Road, Glasgow G41 4ND
☎0141 423 7291
Email dmariscatpress@hotmail.com
Contact *Hamish Whyte*
Currently publishing poetry pamphlets only.

Masque Publishing
PO Box 4194, Worthing, West Sussex
BN11 2GT
Contact *Lisa Stewart*
Prints small collections of poetry. See also **Decanto** magazine.

Mole Valley Press
Pippbrook, Dorking, Surrey RH4 1JS

The Moving Finger
PO Box 4867, Birmingham B3 3HD
Contact *Dave Reeves*
See also **Raw Edge** magazine.

New Hope International
20 Werneth Avenue, Gee Cross, Hyde,
Cheshire SK14 5NL
Email newhope@iname.com
Website www.nhi.clara.net/online.htm

Contact *Gerald England*
Poetry booklet publisher. Contact before submitting material.

Oasis Books
12 Stevenage Road, Fulham, London SW6 6ES
☎020 7736 5059
Contact *Ian Robinson*
Pamphlets of poetry and prose. See also **Oasis** magazine.

Object Permanence
Flat 3/2, 16 Ancroft Street, Glasgow G20 7HU
Website www.objectpermanence.co.uk
Contact *Peter Manson*

The One Time Press
Model Farm, Linstead Magna, Halesworth,
Suffolk IP19 0DT
☎01986 785422
Email pw@onetimepress.com
Website www.onetimepress.com
Contact *Peter Wells*
Poetry of the 1940s in illustrated limited editions.

Original Plus
Flat 3, 18 Oxford Grove, Ilfracombe, Devon
EX34 9HQ
☎01823 461725
Email smithsssj@aol.com
Website members.aol.com/smithsssj/index.html
Contact *Sam Smith*
Requires something extra – another language or markedly original. See also **The Journal** magazine.

Othername Press
14 Rosebank, Rawtenstall, Rossendale
BB4 7RD
Poetry and surrealism.

Oversteps Books
Oversteps, Froude Road, Salcombe, S. Devon
TQ8 8LH
☎01548 843713 Fax 01548 843713
Email oversteps@globalnet.co.uk
Contact *Anne Born*
Small poetry press publishing a couple of books a year.

Paradise Press
80 College Road, Isleworth, Middlesex
TW7 5DS
☎020 8568 3777

Email prdsprss@netscapeonline.co.uk
See entry under **Small Presses**.

Parthian Books
53 Column Road, Cathays, Cardiff
CF10 3EF
☎029 2034 1314 Fax 029 2034 1314
Email parthianbooks@yahoo.co.uk
Website www.parthianbooks.co.uk
Contact *Richard Davies*
New Welsh writing.

Partners In Poetry
289 Elmwood Avenue, Feltham, Middlesex
TW13 7QB
☎0777 919676
Email partners_writing_group@hotmail.com
Website www.homestead.com/
    partners_writing_group
Contact *Ian Deal*
Competitions and poetry pamphlets. See also **A
Bard Hair Day**, **Imagenation**, **Poet Tree**,
Seventh Sense and **The Word Life Journal**
magazines.

Peepal Tree Press Ltd
17 King's Avenue, Leeds, W. Yorks
LS6 1QS
☎0113 245 1703 Fax 0113 246 8368
Email hannah@peepal.demon.co.uk
Contact *Jeremy Poynting*
Best in Caribbean and south Asian writing
from around the world. See entry under **Small
Presses**.

Pen&Inc
School of English & American Studies,
University of East Anglia, Norwich, Norfolk
NR4 7TJ
☎01603 592783
Email info@penandinc.co.uk
Website www.penandinc.co.uk
Contact *Julia Bell*
A small press supported by the Regional Arts
Lottery programme. See also **Pretext** maga-
zine and **Reactions** press.

Peterloo Poets
The Old Chapel, Sand Lane, Calstock,
Cornwall PL18 9QX
☎01822 833473 Fax 01822 833989
Email poets@peterloo.fsnet.co.uk
Contact *Harry Chambers*
Contemporary English poetry.

Picture Poems
114 Broadway, Herne Bay, Kent CT6 8HA
☎01227 360525
Email picturepoems@hbaykent.freeserve.co.uk
Contact *Barbara Dordi*
Publisher of original artwork with poetry/
prose. See also **Equinox** magazine.

Pigasus Press
13 Hazely Combe, Arreton, Isle Of Wight
PO30 3AJ
☎01983 865668
Email pigasus.press@virgin.net
Website freespace.virgin.net/pigasus.press/
    index.htm
Contact *Tony Lee*
Science fiction poetry in irregular themed
anthologies.

Pipers' Ash Ltd
Pipers Ash, Church Road, Christian Malford,
Chippenham, Wilts SN15 4BW
☎01249 720563 Fax 0870 056 8916
Email pipersash@supamasu.com
Website www.supamasu.com
Contact *Mr A. Tyson*
See entry under **Small Presses**.

Planet
PO Box 44, Aberystwyth SY23 3ZZ
☎01970 611255 Fax 01970 611197
Email planet.enquiries@planetmagazine.org.uk
Website www.planetmagazine.org.uk
Contact *John Barnie*
Fiction, poetry, current affairs, arts and en-
vironment. See also **Planet** magazine and entry
under **Small Presses**.

Poems in the Waiting Room
PO Box 488, Richmond TW9 4SW
Email leelda@globalnet.co.uk
Contact *Michael Lee*
Pamphlets for medical waiting rooms.

The Poetry Business
The Studio, Byram Arcade, Huddersfield,
W. Yorks HD1 1ND
☎01484 434840 Fax 01484 426566
Email edit@poetrybusiness.co.uk
Website www.poetrybusiness.co.uk
Contacts *Peter Sansom, Janet Fisher*

Poetry Monthly Press
39 Cavendish Road, Long Eaton, Nottingham
NG10 4HY

☎0115 946 1267
Email martinholroyd@compuserve.com
Website ourworld.compuserve.com/
  homepage/martinholroyd
Contact *Martin Holroyd*
See also **Poetry Monthly** magazine.

Poets Anonymous
70 Aveling Close, Purley, Surrey
CR8 4DW
Email poets@poetsanon.org.uk
Website www.poetsanon.org.uk/index.htm
Contact *Peter L. Evans*

Anthologies & collections of predominately
south London poets. See also **Poetic Licence**
magazine.

QQ Press
York House, 15 Argyle Terrace, Rothesay,
Isle of Bute PA20 0BD
Contact *Alan Carter*

Collections of poetry plus poetry anthologies.
See also **Quantum Leap** magazine.

Ragged Raven Press
1 Lodge Farm, Snitterfield, Stratford upon
Avon, Warwickshire CV37 0LR
☎01789 730358   Fax 01789 730320
Email raggedravenpress@aol.com
Website www.raggedraven.co.uk
Contacts *Bob Mee, Janet Murch*
Poetry. See also **Iota** magazine.

Raunchland Publications
18 Canon Lynch Court, Dunfermline, Fife
KY12 8AU
Email raunchland@hotmail.com
Website www.raunchland.co.uk
Contact *John Mingay*

Limited edition poetry/graphics booklets and
online publications.

Reactions
School of English & American Studies,
University of East Anglia, Norwich, Norfolk
NR4 7TJ
☎01603 592783
Email info@penandinc.co.uk
Website www.penandinc.co.uk
Contact *Julia Bell*

Annual poetry anthology – welcomes new poets.
See also **Pretext** magazine and **Pen&Inc** Press.

Red Candle Press
9 Milner Road, Wisbech, Cambs PE13 2LR
Email rep@poetry7.fsnet.co.uk
Website www.members.tripod.com/
  redcandlepress
Contact *M.L. McCarthy*

Traditionalist poetry press. See also
Candelabrum Poetry Magazine.

Rive Gauche Publishing
69 Lower Redland Road, Bristol BS6 6SP
☎0117 974 5106
Contact *P.V.T. West*

Poetry by women writing and performing in
Bristol.

Route Publishing
School Lane, Glasshoughton, Castleford,
W. Yorks WF10 4QH
☎01977 603028   Fax 01977 512819
Email info@route-online.com
Website www.route-online.com
Contact *Ian Daley*

Short fiction and poetry. See entry under
Small Presses.

Salmon Poetry
Knockeve, Cliffs of Moher, Co. Clare,
Republic of Ireland
☎00 35 658 1941
Email info@salmonpoetry.com
Website www.salmonpoetry.com
Contact *Jessie Lendennie*

Contemporary Irish and international poetry.

Searle Publishing
36 Wolfe Road, Norwich, Norfolk NR1 4HT
☎01603 499784
Email david.searle@care4free.net
Website searlepublishing.co.uk
Contact *David Searle*

Run by writers for writers – unsolicited mss
welcome. See also **JazzClaw** press.

Semicolon Press
99 Lime Avenue, Leamington Spa,
Warwickshire CV32 7DG
Email don@semicolon.demon.co.uk
Poetry pamphlets.

Seren
First Floor, 38–40 Nolton Street, Bridgend
CF31 3BN
☎01656 663018   Fax 01656 649226
Email seren@seren.force9.co.uk

Website www.seren-books.com

Contact *Mick Felton*

Poetry, fiction, lit crit, biography, essays. See entry under **UK Publishers** and **Poetry Wales** magazine.

SMH Books
Pear Tree Cottage, Watersfield, Pulborough, W. Sussex RH20 1NG
☎01798 831260 Fax 01798 831906
Email smhbooks@email.com

Contact *Sandra M.H. Saer*

Real-life books, including poetry and memoirs.

Smith/Doorstop Books
The Studio, Byram Arcade, Westgate, Huddersfield, W. Yorks HD1 1ND
☎01484 434840 Fax 01484 426566
Email edit@poetrybusiness.co.uk
Website www.poetrybusiness.co.uk

Contact *Peter Sansom*

Contemporary books, pamphlets and audio cassettes (see entry under **Audio Books**).

Southfields
8 Richmond Road, Staines, Middlesex TW18 2AB
Email vennel@hotmail.com
Website www.indigogroup.co.uk/llpp/vennel.html

Contact *Richard Price*

Modern Scottish poetry; poetry in translation; poetry that takes its bearings from modernism. See also **Vennel** and **Au Quai** presses.

Spouting Forth Inc
Thrimblemill Library, Thrimblemill Road, Smethwick, Sandwell, W. Midlands B67 5RJ
☎0121 429 2039

Contact *Dave Reeves*

Performance poetry.

Stride Publications
11 Sylvan Road, Exeter, Devon EX4 6EW
Email editor@stridebooks.co.uk
Website www.stridebooks.co.uk

Contact *Rupert Loydell*

Innovative poetry, experimental fiction, essays and interviews. See entry under **Small Presses**.

Summer Palace Press
Cladnagerach, Kilbeg, Kilcar, Co Donegal, Republic of Ireland
☎00 353 733 8448 Fax 00 353 733 8448

Contacts *Kate & Joan Newman*

First collections of poetry, 64 pages, beautiful books.

Survivors' Poetry Scotland
4 C4 Templeton Centre, Templeton Street, Glasgow G40 1DA
☎0141 556 4554 Fax 0141 400 8442
Email sps@spscot.co.uk
Website www.spscot.co.uk

For survivors of the mental health system. See entry under **Organisations of Interest to Poets**.

Tabla
Dept of English, University of Bristol, 3–5 Woodland Road, Bristol BS8 1TB
Fax 0117 928 8860
Email stephen.james@bristol.ac.uk
Website www.bristol.ac.uk/tabla

Contact *Dr Stephen James*

Publisher of the annual *Tabla Book of New Verse*.

Talking Pen
12 Derby Crescent, Moorside, Consett, Co. Durham DH8 8DZ
☎01207 505724
Website www.newwritingnorth.com

Contact *Steve Unwin*

Short poems, short prose, light/dark psychologically charged. See also **Moodswing** magazine.

Thumbscrew Press
PO Box 657, Oxford OX2 6PH
Email tim.kendall@bristol.ac.uk
Website www.bristol.ac.uk/thumbscrew

Contact *Tim Kendall*

Pamphlets by new and established poets. See also **Thumbscrew** magazine.

Totem
60 Swinley House, Redhill Street, London NW1 4BB
☎020 7387 7216
Email ishmael@ciaroscuro.com

Contact *Fiifi Annobil*

Publishers of contemporary literature and art.

Triumph House
Remus House, Coltsfoot Drive, Woodston, Peterborough PE2 9JX
☎01733 898102 Fax 01733 313524

Email triumphhouse@forwardpress.co.uk
Website www.forwardpress.co.uk
Contact *Sarah Andrew*

A Christian poetry imprint publishing many anthologies annually.

United Press Ltd
44a St James Street, Burnley, Lancs
BB11 1NQ
☎01282 459533   Fax 01282 412679
Email mail@upltd.co.uk
Website www.upltd.co.uk
Contact *Peter Quinn*

Publishes poetry & prose including national poetry anthology.

Vennel Press
8 Richmond Road, Staines, Middlesex
TW18 2AB
Email vennel@hotmail.com
Website www.indigogroup.co.uk/llpp/
   vennel.html
Contact *Richard Price*

Modern Scottish poetry; poetry in translation; poetry that takes its bearings from modernism. See also **Au Quai** and **Southfields** presses.

Wanda Publications
Word And Action, 75 High Street, Wimborne, Dorset BH21 1HS
☎01202 889669
Email wanda@wordandaction.com
Contact *Jane Peters*

Poetry, stories, local history and world of instant theatre. See also **South** magazine.

Waywiser Press
9 Woodstock Road, London N4 3ET
Email waywiserpress@aol.com
Website www.waywiser-press.com

West House Books
40 Crescent Road, Nether Edge, Sheffield
S7 1HN
Email alan@nethedge.demon.co.uk
Contact *Alan Halsey*

Wild Honey Press
16a Ballyman Road, Bray, Co Wicklow
Republic of Ireland
Email poetry@wildhoneypress.com
Website www.wildhoneypress.com
Contact *Randolph Healey*

Innovative poetry.

The Windows Project
First Floor, Liver House, 96 Bold Street, Liverpool L1 4HY
☎0151 709 3688
Contact *David Ward*

See also **Smoke** magazine.

Writers Forum
89a Petherton Road, London N5 2QT
☎020 7226 2657
Contact *Bob Cobbing*

Innovative language and visual poetries. See also **And** magazine.

Writers' Own Publications
121 Highbury Grove, Clapham, Bedford
MK41 6DU
☎01234 365982
Contact *Mrs E.M. Pickering*

Booklets of 22–36 poems by a single author.

Zum Zum Books
Goshem, Bunlight, Drumnadrochit, Inverness-shire IV63 6XH
☎01456 450402
Contact *Neil Oram*

Wild, brilliant, deep, sensuous, philosophical poetry.

Poetry Magazines

Acumen
6 The Mount, Higher Furzeham, Brixham, Devon TQ5 8QY
☎01803 851098 Fax 01803 851098
Contact *Patricia Oxley*

Good poetry, intelligent articles and wide-ranging reviews. See also **The Long Poem Group Newsletter**.

Aireings
Dean Head Farm, Scotland Lane, Leeds, W. Yorks LS18 5HU
Contact *Jean Barker*

40-page poetry magazine published since 1980. Leans towards women's work.

Ambit
17 Priory Gardens, London N5 5QY
Website www.ambit.co.uk
Contact *Martin Bax*

Poetry, fiction, graphics, arts, reviews.

And
89a Petherton Road, London N5 2QT
☎020 7226 2657
Contacts *Bob Cobbing & Adrian Clarke*

Visual and linguistically innovative poetries. See also **Writers Forum** press.

Areopagus
101 Maytree Close, Winchester SO22 4JF
Fax 0870 1346384
Email jareo@bigfoot.com
Website www.churchnet.org.uk/areopagus/index.html
Contact *Julian Barritt*

A Christian based arena for creative writers.

Arete
8 New College Lane, Oxford OX1 3BN
☎01865 289193 Fax 01895 289194
Email craig.raine@new.ox.ac.uk
Website www.aretemagazine.com
Contact *Craig Raine*

Fiction, poetry, reportage, reviews.

As Well As
69 Orchard Croft, Harlow, Essex CM20 3BG
Contact *John Steer*

The literary magazine of the West Essex Literary Society.

Awen
38 Pierrot Steps, 71 Kursaal Way, Southend on Sea, Essex SS1 2UY
Email monomythal@zoom.co.uk
Contact *David John Tyrer*

Poetry and vignette-length fiction of any style/ genre. See also **Garbaj** and **Monomyth** magazines.

Banipal
PO Box 22300, London W13 8ZQ
☎020 8568 9747 Fax 020 8568 8509
Email banipal@compuserve.com
Contact *Margaret Obank*

Modern Arab literature in translation.

A Bard Hair Day
289 Elmwood Avenue, Feltham, Middlesex TW13 7QB
☎0777 919 3676
Email partners_writing_group@hotmail.com
Website www.homestead.com/partners_writing_group
Contact *Ian Deal*

General poetry and short story magazine. See also **Partners in Poetry** press, **Imagenation**, **Poet Tree**, **Seventh Sense** magazines and **The Word Life Journal**.

Barddas
Pen Rhiw, 71 Fford Pentrepoeth, Treforys, Swansea SA6 6AE
☎01792 792829
Contact *Alan Llwyd*

Barddoniaeth Gymreig – Welsh language poetry – especially in the strict meters.

Billy Liar
7/8 Trinity Chare, Quayside, Newcastle upon Tyne NE1 3DF
☎0191 296 6787 Fax 0191 296 6787
Email liar.republic@virgin.net

Contact *Paul Summers*

State of the nation through fiction, journalism, poetry, visual art and reviews.

The Black Rose
56 Marlescroft Way, Loughton, Essex
IG10 3NA
Fax 020 8508 1757
Email blackrose@coolvamp.btinternet.co.uk
Website www.expage.com/blackrosepoetry
Contact *Bonita Hall*

Quarterly poetry magazine, all styles considered; new poets welcome.

Braquemard
48 Clifton Street, Hull HU2 9AP
☎Email braquemard@hotmail.com
Website www.braquemard.fsnet.co.uk
Contact *David Allenby*

40 pages of excellent poetry, prose and artwork.

Breathe Poetry Magazine
2 Grimshoe Road, Downham Market,
Norfolk PE38 9RA
Contact *Sharon Sweet*

Should satisfy all of your reading and writing needs.

Brittle Star
83 Barretts Grove, London N16 8AP
Email brittlestar@poetic.co.uk
Website come.to/brittlestar

The Brobdignagian Times
96 Albert Road, Cork, Republic of Ireland
Contact *Giovanni Malito*

Poetry, very short fiction, cover art.

Buzz Words
Calvers Farm, Thelveton, Diss, Norfolk
IP21 4NG
Email zoeking@calversfarm.fsnet.co.uk
Website www.buzzwordsmagazine.co.uk
Contact *Zoe King*

Small magazine with an international flavour – new and established writers of fiction and poetry.

Cadenza
PO Box 1768, Rugby CV21 4ZA
☎01788 334302 Fax 01788 334702
Email jo.good@ntlworld.com
Website www.qwfmagazine.co.uk
Contact *Jo Good*

Poetry and prose – mainstream but stretches the emotional/linguistic envelope.

Candelabrum Poetry Magazine
9 Milner Road, Wisbech, Cambs PE13 2LR
Email rep@poetry7.fsnet.co.uk
Website www.members.tripod.com/
   redcandlepress
Contact *Leonard McCarthy*

Traditionalist poetry mag for people who like poetry rhythmic and shapely. See also **Red Candle Press**.

Cannon Fodder
11 Cholmley Villas, Portsmouth Road,
Thames Ditton, Surrey KT7 0XU
Email gillnet@cholmley11.freeserve.co.uk
Contact *Rivka – G*

The Cauldron
PO Box 241, Oakengates, Shropshire TF2 9XZ
☎01952 277872
Email editor@writersbrew.fsnet.co.uk
Website www.writersbrew.fsnet.co.uk
Contact *Amanda Gillies*

Magazine for new writers and rhyming poets with news, competitons, reviews.

Chapman
4 Broughton Place, Edinburgh, Scotland
EH1 3RX
☎0131 557 2207 Fax 0131 556 9565
Email editor@chapman-pub.co.uk
Website www.chapman-pub.co.uk
Contact *Joy M. Hendry*

The best in Scottish and international writing, well-established writers and the up-and-coming. See entries under **UK Publishers** and **Magazines**.

The Coffee House
Charnwood Arts, Loughborough Library,
31 Granby Street, Loughborough, Leics
LE11 3DU
☎01509 822558 Fax 01509 822559
Email charnwood-arts@ndirect.co.uk
Website www.charnwood-arts.org.uk
Contact *Deborah Tyler-Bennett*

A meeting place for the arts, poetry, prose and visual artwork.

Connections
13 Wave Crest, Whitstable, Kent CT5 1EH
Contact *Narissa Knights*

Poetry, short stories, articles, news and reviews

from new and established writers. Small payment.

Cork Literary Review
Bradshaw Books, Tigh Fili, Thompson House, Maccurtain Street, Cork, Republic of Ireland
☎00 353 21 450 9274   Fax 00 353 21 455 1617
Contact *Sheila O'Hagan*

Cornish Poetry Journal
Lower Wesley Terrace, Pensilva, Liskeard, Cornwall PL14 5PD

CPR International
Grendon House, 8 Laxay, Lochs, Isle Of Lewis HS2 9PJ
☎01851 830418   Fax 01851 830412
Email grendon.house@virginnet.co.uk
Website www.virginnet.co.uk/grendon.house
Contact *Frances T. Lewis*

Formerly *Christian Poetry Review*. Poetry and reviews – the shorter poem preferred.

Current Accounts
16–18 Mill Lane, Horwich, Bolton, Lancs BL6 6AT
Email rodriesco@cs.com

Poetry, short fiction, articles – magazine of the Bank Street Writers' Group.

Cyphers
3 Selskar Terrace, Ranelagh, Dublin 6, Republic of Ireland
Fax 00 353 1 497 8866
Contact *Eilean Ní Chuilleanain*

Irish literary magazine: poetry, prose, reviews.

Dandelion Arts Magazine
24 Frosty Hollow, East Hunsbury, Northants NN4 0SY
Contact *Jacqueline Gonzalez-Marina*
International arts magazine.

The Dark Horse
3b Blantyre Mill Road, Bothwell, South Lanarkshire G71 8DD
Email gjctdh@freename.co.uk
Contact *Gerry Cambridge*
Poetry.

The David Jones Journal
The David Jones Society, 48 Sylvan Way, Sketty, Swansea SA2 9JB
☎01792 206144   Fax 01792 205305

Email anne.price-owen@sihe.ac.uk
Contact *Anne Price-Owen*

Articles, poetry, information, reviews and inspired works.

Decanto
PO Box 4194, Worthing, West Sussex BN11 2GT
Contact *Lisa Stewart*

Non-conformist poetry magazine – any style considered, not just contemporary. See also **Masque Publishing** press.

The Devil
247 Gray's Inn Road, London WC1X 8JR
☎020 8994 7767
Email steve@thedevilmag.co.uk
Website www.thedevilmag.co.uk
Contact *Stephen Plaice*

Prose, poetry, fiction, reviews, major interviews.

Dial 174
21 Mill Road, Watlington, King's Lynn, Norfolk PE33 0HH
☎01553 811949
Contact *Joseph Hemmings*

Poetry, short storie, articles, travelogues, artwork, etc.

Dream Catcher
9 Berkeley Square, Lincoln LN6 8BN
☎01522 882238
Website www.openingline.co.uk/magazines/
 dreamcatcher
Contact *Paul Sutherland*

Poetry, prose, b&w photographs, from national & international contributors .

Earthlove
PO Box 11219, Paisley PA1 2WH
Poetry magazine for the environment.

Eastern Rainbow
17 Farrow Road, Whaplode Drove, Spalding, Lincs PE12 0TS
☎01406 330242
Email p-rance@yahoo.co.uk
Contact *Paul Rance*

Focuses on 20th century culture via poetry, prose and art. See also **Peace and Freedom** magazine.

Eclipse
53 West Vale, Neston, Cheshire CH64 9SE
Contact *Elizabeth Boyd*
Bi-monthly poetry mag – all types and styles welcome. See also **Everyman Press**.

The Engine
3 Ardgreenan Drive, Belfast BT4 3FQ
☎028 9065 9866   Fax 028 9032 2767
Email clitophon@yahoo.com
Contact *Paul Murphy*
Poetry mag with an interest in the experimental and avant garde.

Envoi
44 Rudyard Road, Biddulph Moor, Stoke-on Trent ST8 7JN
☎01782 517892
Contact *Roger Elkin*
Poetry, sequences, features, reviews, competitions.

Epoch Magazine
57 Murray Street, Montrose, Angus DD10 8JZ
Contact *Neil Mathers*
Scottish and European literature, art, philosophy, some poetry. See also **Corbie Press**.

Equinox
114 Broadway, Herne Bay, Kent CT6 8HA
☎01227 360525
Email picturepoems@hbaykent.freeserve.co.uk
Contact *Barbara Dordi*
Twice-yearly journal of contemporary poetry illustrated with original artwork in colour. See also **Picture Poems** press.

Eratica
Waterloo Press (Hove), 51 Waterloo Road, Hove, E. Sussex BN3 1AN
Contact *Simon Jenner*

Fan the Flames
c/o Brikhouse C S, The Barns, Sheepcote Lane, Silver End, Witham, Essex CM8 3PJ
Email editor@fantheflames.co.uk
Website www.fantheflames.co.uk
Contact *Emma Reed*
Poetry and prose quarterly, distributed throughout the UK and abroad.

Federation Magazine
Burslem School of Art, Queen Street, Stoke-on-Trent ST6 3EJ

☎01792 822327   Fax 01792 822327
Email thefwwcp@tiscali.co.uk
Website www.thefwwcp.d4f.net
Contact *Tim Diggles*
Articles and reviews on all aspects of interest to writers and publishers.

Feminist Review
c/o Women's Studies, University of North London, 166–220 Holloway Road, London N7 8DB
Short fiction and poetry.

Fire
Field Cottage, Old Whitehill, Tackley, Kidlington, Oxon OX5 3AB
☎01869 331300
Website www.poetical.org
Contact *Jeremy Hilton*
Poetry: alternative, unfashionable, experimental, spiritual, demotic; occasional experimental prose.

The Firing Squad
25 Griffiths Road, West Bromwich B71 2EH
☎07950 591455
Contact *Geoff Stevens*
Protest poetry broadsheet. See also **Purple Patch** magazine.

First Time
The Snoring Cat, 16 Marianne Park, Dudley Road, Hastings, E. Sussex TN35 5PU
Contact *Josephine Austin*
Biannual magazine designed to encourage first-time poets.

Flaming Arrows
County Sligo V E C, Riverside, Sligo, Republic of Ireland
☎00 353 71 45844
Email leoregan@eirecom.net
Contact *Leo Regan*
Stories, poetry, contemplative, metaphysical, spiritual themes grounded in senses.

The Frogmore Papers
42 Morehall Avenue, Folkestone, Kent CT19 4EF
Contact *Jeremy Page*

Garbaj
38 Pierrot Steps, 71 Kursaal Way, Southend on Sea, Essex SS1 2UY

Email monomythal@zoom.co.uk
Contact *D.S. Davidson*

Humourous/non-pc poetry, vignette-length fiction, fake news, etc. See also **Awen** and **Monomyth** magazines.

Gentle Reader Poetry
8 Heol Pen Y Bryn, Penyrheol, Penyrheol, Caerphilly CF83 2JX
☎029 2088 6369
Email lynne54@btinternet.com
Contact *Lynne E. Jones*

Quarterly fiction and poetry. Welcomes new poets.

Glass Beads
PO Box 36103, London SW1 4GQ
Email ruvi@well.com
Contact *Ruvi Simmons*

The Glass Head
72 Doncaster Road, Mexborough, S. Yorkshire
Contact *Ian Parks*

Limited-edition poetry pamphlets.

Global Tapestry Journal
Spring Bank, Longsight Road, Copster Green, Blackburn, Lancs BB1 9EU
☎01254 249128
Contact *Dave Cunliffe*

Global Bohemia, post-Beat and counterculture orientation. See also **BB Books** press.

Green Queen
BM Box 5700, London WC1N 3XX
Contact *Elsa Wallace*

Occasional magazine, Green issues, lesbian & gay fiction, articles, poetry.

How Do I Love Thee?
1 Blue Ball Corner, Water Lane, Winchester, Hants SO23 0ER
Email adrian.abishop@virgin.net
Website freespace.virgin.net/poetry.life/
Contact *Adrian Bishop*

The magazine for love poetry. See also **Poetry Life** magazine.

HQ Poetry Magazine (Haiku Quarterly)
39 Exmouth Street, Swindon, Wilts SN1 3PU
☎01793 523927
Contact *Kevin Bailey*

General poetry mag with slight bias towards imagistic/haikuesque work. See also **Day Dream Press**.

HU – The Honest Ulsterman
49 Main Street, Greyabbey, Co Down BT22 2NF
Contact *Tom Clyde*

Ireland's premier journal for new poems, prose, articles.

Imagenation
289 Elmwood Avenue, Feltham, Middx TW13 7QB
☎0777 919 3676
Email partners_writing_group@hotmail.com
Website www.homestead.com/
    partners_writing_group
Contact *Ian Deal*

The power of the imagination. See also **Partners in Poetry** press, **A Bard Hair Day**, **Poet Tree**, **Seventh Sense** magazines and **The Word Life Journal**.

Inclement
White Rose House, 8 Newmarket Road, Fordham, Ely, Cambs CB7 5LL
Contact *Michelle Foster*

All forms and styles of poetry.

The Interpreter's House
10 Farrell Road, Wootton, Beds MK43 9DU
Contact *Merryn Williams*

Poems and stories up to 2500 words; new and established writers.

Intimacy
15 Waterlow Road, Maidstone, Kent ME14 2TR
☎01622 670419
Contact *Adam McKeown*

Communication experienced as nakedness (Laure).

Iota
1 Lodge Farm, Snitterfield, Stratford upon Avon, Warwickshire CV37 0LR
☎01789 730358   Fax 01789 730320
Email raggedravenpress@aol.com
Website www.raggedravenpress.co.uk
Contacts *Bob Mee & Janet Murch*

Poetry, reviews; long and short poems welcome. No epics. See also **Ragged Raven Press**

Irish Pages
Linen Hall Library, 17 Donegall Square North, Belfast BT1 5GB
Contact *Chris Agee*
Irish and international poetry and prose.

Island
8 Craiglea Drive, Edinburgh EH10 7PA
Email jaj@essencepress.co.uk
Website www.essencepress.co.uk/island
Contact *Julie Johnstone*
A distinctive space for writing inspired by nature and exploring our place within the natural world. See also **Essence Press**.

JazzClaw
36 Wolfe Road, Norwich, Norfolk NR1 4HT
☎01603 499784
Email david.searle@care4free.net
Website www.searlepublishing.co.uk
Contact *David Searle*
Avant garde poetry and prose, surrealism, erotica, dark themes, experimental. See also **Searle Publishing**.

The Journal
Flat 3, 18 Oxford Grove, Ilfracombe, Devon EX34 9HQ
☎01272 862708
Email smithsssj@aol.com
Contact *Sam Smith*
Poems in translation alongside poetry written in English. See also **Original Plus** press.

Kickin' & Screamin'
5 Canberra Close, Greenmeadow, Cwmbran NP44 3ET
Poetry.

Konfluence
Ardingly College, Haywards Heath, W. Sussex RH17 6SQ
☎Email floherus@aol.com
Contact *Mark Floyer*
Good quality crafted poetry – West Country bias but no regional/generic exclusivity. See also **Gallery Pamphlets** press.

Krax
63 Dixon Lane, Wortley, Leeds, W. Yorks LS12 4RR
Contact *Andy Robson*
Light-hearted, contemporary poetry, short fiction and graphics.

Lallans
Scots Language Society, A K Bell Library, York Place, Perth PH2 8AP
☎01738 440199
Contact *John Law*
The literary magazine for writing in Scots.

Leviathan Quarterly
Bear Hays Farm, Brookhay Lane, Fradley WS13 8RG
☎01543 411161
Email claire.brodmann@btinternet.com
Contacts *Michael Hulse*
Publishes fiction, essays, poetry, art and criticism. See also **Leviathan** press.

Lilith the Liverbird
75 Melbury Road, Huyton, Liverpool L14 8UR
Email 10001b7800@blueyonder.co.uk
Website www.geocities.com/lillithpink
Contact *Lynn Owen*
Women writers living life on Merseyside.

Linear B Publishing
PO Box 17162, Edinburgh EH11 2WT

Links
Bude Haven, 18 Frankfield Rise, Tunbridge Wells, Kent TN2 5LF
Email linksmag@supanete.com
Contact *Bill Headdon*
Poetry magazine committed to quality writing and reviews.

London Magazine
30 Thurloe Place, London SW7 2HQ
Contact *Sebastian Barker*
Art, literature, memoirs and reviews.

The Long Poem Group Newsletter
6 The Mount, Higher Furzeham, Brixham, S. Devon TQ5 8QY
☎01803 851098 Fax 01803 851098
Email pwoxley@aol.com
Website www.bath.ac.uk/~exxdgdc
Contact *William Oxley*
Eight pages devoted to debating the long poem in our time. See also **Acumen** magazine.

M(onkey) K(ettle)
PO Box 4616, Kiln Farm, Milton Keynes MK14 2ZJ
Website www.monkeykettle.co.uk
Poems, prose, photos, articles.

Magma
43 Keslake Road, London NW6 6DH
Email magmapoems@aol.com
Website www.champignon.net/magma
Contact *David Boll*
New poetry plus poetry reviews and interviews.

Merseyside Arts Magazine
PO Box 21, Liverpool L19 3RX
☎0151 427 8297 Fax 0151 291 6280
Email ms.art.mag@cablenet.co.uk
Contact *Bernard F. Spencer*
Local current news, events and information on all arts-relating subjects.

Modern Poetry in Translation
MPT, School of Humanities, King's College London, Strand, London WC2R 2LS
☎020 7848 2360 Fax 020 7848 2145
Website www.kcl.ac.uk/mpt
Contact *Norma Rinsler*
Poems from everywhere, translated into English.

Monomyth
38 Pierrot Steps, 71 Kursaal Way, Southend on Sea, Essex SS1 2UY
Email monomythal@zoom.co.uk
Contact *David John Tyrer*
Poetry, prose and articles; all genres, styles and lengths considered. New writers welcome. See also **Awen** and **Garbaj** magazines.

Moodswing
12 Derby Crescent, Moorside, Consett, Co. Durham DH8 8DZ
☎01207 505724
Website www.newwritingnorth.com
Contact *Steve Urwin*
Short poems, short prose, light/dark psychologically charged. See also **Talking Pen** press.

Mslexia
PO Box 656, Newcastle upon Tyne NE99 2XD
☎0191 261 6656 Fax 0191 261 6636
Email postbag@mslexia.demon.co.uk
Website www.mslexia.co.uk
For women who write. See entry under **Magazines**

Multi – Storey
PO Box 62, Levenshulme, Manchester M19 1TH
Email stuff@multistorey.co.uk
Website www.multistorey.co.uk

Contact *Finella Davenport*
Biannual literary magazine.

Nerve
PO Box 3848, Glasgow G46 6AS
☎0141 272 3333
Contact *Dave Maderson*
Poetry, short stories, screenplays, articles and reviews.

Never Bury Poetry
Bracken Clock, Troutbeck Close, Hawkshaw, Bury, Lancs BL8 4LJ
☎01204 884080
Email nbpoetry@zen.co.uk
Website www.nbpoetry.care4free.net
Contact *Jean Tarry*
Quarterly founded 1989. International reputation. Each issue has a different theme.

New Departures/Poetry Olympics
PO Box 9819, London W11 2GC
☎020 7229 7850 Fax 020 7229 7850
Contact *Mike Horovitz*
Journal of the Poetry Olympics.

New Welsh Review
Chapter Arts Centre, Market Road, Canton, Cardiff CF5 1QE
☎029 2066 5529 Fax 029 2066 5529
Email nwr@welshnet.co.uk
Contact *Victor Golightly*
Wales's leading literary quarterly in English: short stories, poems, feature articles. See entry under **Magazines**.

Nomad
Survivors Press, 4 C4 Templeton Centre, 62 Templeton Street, Glasgow G40 1DA
☎0141 556 4554 Fax 0141 400 8442
Email sps@spscot.co.uk
Website www.spscot.co.uk
Contact *Gerry Loose*
Poetry and creative writing by survivors of the mental health system, of abuse or addiction.

Norfolk Poets and Writers
9 Walnut Close, Taverham, Norwich, Norfolk NR8 6YN ☎0798 917 4076
Email wwbuk@yahoo.co.uk
Website www.wendywebb.co.uk
Contact *Wendy Webb*
Heart in Norfolk. For writers and poets everywhere.

The North
The Studio, Byram Arcade, Huddersfield, W. Yorks HD1 1ND
☎01484 434840 Fax 01484 426566
Email edit@poetrybusiness.co.uk
Website www.poetrybusiness.co.uk
Contacts *Peter Sansom & Janet Fisher*
Contemporary poetry and articles, extensive reviews.

Northwords Magazine
PO Box 5725, Dingwall IV15 9WJ
Email editor@northwords.co.uk
Website www.northwords.co.uk
Contact *Robert Davidson*
Scottish literary magazine with a world view.

Oasis
12 Stevenage Road, Fulham, London SW6 6ES
☎020 7736 5059
Contact *Ian Robinson*
Poetry, short fiction, essays, reviews, etc. See also **Oasis Books** press.

Obsessed With Pipework
Redditch Library, 15 Market Place, Redditch B98 8AR
☎01527 63291 Fax 01527 68571
Email flare.stack@virgin.net
Contact *Charles Johnson*
Open quarterly; 'poetry to surprise and delight with a high-wire aspect'. See also **Flarestack Publishing** press.

Orbis
17 Greenhow Avenue, West Kirby, Wirral CH48 5EL
☎0151 625 1446
Email carolebaldock@hotmail.com
Contact *Carole Baldock*
An independent international quarterly of poetry and prose with many reader-friendly features.

Other Poetry
29 Western Hill, Durham DH1 4RL
Website www.otherpoetry.com
Contact *Michael Standen*
Thrice-yearly, 60–70 poems per issue. Selection process involves all four editors. Token payment.

Outposts
22 Whitewell Road, Frome, Somerset BA11 4EL
☎01373 466653 Fax 01373 466653

Contact *Roland John*
Longest surviving independent poetry magazine in the UK. See also **Hippopotamus Press**.

Page 84's Pseudo-Chaotic Magazines
P E F Productions, 196 High Road, London N22 8HH
Email page84direct@yahoo.co.uk
Website www.84spythere.freehosting.net
Poetry, anti-poetry, aphorism, comment and artwork mag showing work of Page 84 and guest artists.

Panda
46 First Avenue, Clase, Swansea SA6 7LL
☎01792 414837 Fax 01792 414837
Email esmond.j@ntlworld
Website www.geocities.com/slap_dash/
    Quarterly_poetry.html
Contact *Esmond Jones*
Poetry and prose.

The Paper
29 Vickers Road, Firth Park, Sheffield S5 6UY
Contact *DG Kennedy*
Poetry and prose.

Peace and Freedom
17 Farrow Road, Whaplode Drove, Spalding, Lincs PE12 0TS
☎01406 330242
Email p-rance@yahoo.co.uk
Contact *Paul Rance*
Poetry/prose/art mag – humanitarian, environmental, animal welfare. See also **Eastern Rainbow** magazine.

Peer Poetry International
26 (wh) Arlington House, Bath BA1 1QN
☎01225 445298
Email peerpoetryintl@tiny.com.uk
Contact *Paul Amphlett*
80-page (35 poets) eclectic rhymed/free verse poetry biannual.

The Penniless Press
100 Waterloo Road, Ashton, Preston, Lancs PR2 1EP
☎01772 736421
Contact *Alan Dent*
Quarterly for the poor pocket and the rich mind. Poetry, fiction, essays, reviews.

Pennine Ink Magazine
The Gallery, Mid-Pennine Arts, Yorke Street, Burnley, Lancs BB11 1HD
☎01282 703657
Contact *Laura Sheridan*

Good poetry reflecting traditional and modern trends.

Pennine Platform
1 HS Dept. University of Bradford, Bradford, W. Yorks BD7 1DP
Contact *Dr Ed Reiss*

The pick of poetry from the Pennines and beyond.

Planet
P O Box 44, Aberystwyth SY23 3ZZ
☎01970 611255 Fax 01970 611197
Email planet.enquiries@planetmagazine.org.uk
Website www.planetmagazine.org.uk
Contact *John Barnie*

The Welsh Internationalist – current affairs, arts, environment. See also **Planet** press.

PN Review
4th Floor, Conavon Court, 12–16 Blackfriars Street, Manchester M3 5BQ
☎0161 834 8730 Fax 0161 832 0084
Email pnr@carcanet.u-net.com
Website www.carcanet.co.uk
Contact *Michael Schmidt*

See **Carcanet Press** under **UK Publishers**.

Poet Tree
289 Elmwood Avenue, Feltham, Middlesex TW13 7QB
☎0181 751 8652
Website homestead.com/
  partners_writing_group
Contact *Ian Deal*

General poetry and short story magazine. **Partners in Poetry** press, **Imagenation**, **A Bard Hair Day**, **Seventh Sense** magazines and **The Word Life Journal**.

Poetic Hours
43 Willow Road, Carlton, Notts NG4 3BH
Email erranpublishing@hotmail.com
Website www.poetichours.homestead.com
Contact *Nick Clark*

Non-profit supporter of Third World charities. See also **Erran Publishing**.

Poetic Licence
70 Aveling Close, Purley, Surrey CR8 4DW
Email poets@poesanon.org.uk
Website www.poetsanon.org.uk
Contact *Peter L. Evans*

Original unpublished poems and drawings. See also **Poets Anonymous** press.

The Poetry Church
Feather Books, PO Box 438, Shrewsbury, Shropshire SY3 0WN
☎01743 872177 Fax 01743 872177
Email john@waddysweb.freeuk.com
Website www.waddysweb.com
Contact *Rev. J. Waddington-Feather*

Quarterly magazine of Christian poetry and prayers. See **Feather Books** under **Small Presses**.

Poetry Cornwall
1 Station Hill, Redruth, Cornwall TR15 2PP
Email les.merton@tesco.net
Contact *Les Merton*

Promoting today's Cornish poets and writers.

Poetry Ireland News
Bermingham Tower, Upper Yard, Dublin Castle, Dublin 2 Republic of Ireland
☎00 353 1 671 4632 Fax 00 353 1 671 4634
Email poetry@iol.ie
Website www.poetryireland.ie
Contact *Joseph Woods*

Bi-monthly newsletter. See also **Poetry Ireland Review** magazine.

Poetry Ireland Review/ Eigse Eireann
Bermingham Tower, Upper Yard, Dublin 2, Republic of Ireland
☎00 353 1 671 4632 Fax 00 353 1 671 4634
Email poetry@iol.ie
Website www.poetryireland.ie
Contact *Joseph Woods*

Quarterly journal of poetry and reviews. See also **Poetry Ireland News** magazine.

Poetry Life
1 Blue Bell Corner, Water Lane, Winchester, Hampshire SO23 0ER
Email adrian.abishop@virgin.net
Website freespace.virgin.net/poetry.life/
Contact *Adrian Bishop*

Publishing the best of modern poetry. See also **How Do I Love Thee?** magazine.

Poetry London
1a Jewel Road, London E17 4QU
Email editors@plondon.demon.co.uk
Website www.poetrylondon.co.uk
Contact *Pascale Petit*

Poetry, listings, reviews, features and information. (Formerly *Poetry London Newsletter*.)

Poetry Monthly
39 Cavendish Road, Long Eaton, Nottingham
NG10 4HY
☎0115 946 1267
Email martinholroyd@compuserve.com
Contact *Martin Holroyd*

Wellcrafted, dynamic, fresh and individual poems. See also **Poetry Monthly Press**.

Poetry Nottingham International
PO Box 6740, Nottingham NG5 1QG
Contact *Julie Lumsden*

Poetry, articles, letters, features, reviews: 48–56 pages quarterly.

Poetry Now
Remus House, Coltsfoot Drive, Woodston,
Peterborough PE2 9JX
☎01733 898101   Fax 01733 313524
Email poetrynow@forwardpress.co.uk
Website www.forwardpress.co.uk
Contact *Natalie Nightingale*

Incorporating *Rhyme Arrival* magazine – communicating across the barriers.

The Poetry of Surrender
Sub Verse, PO Box 71, Northolt UB5 4YY
☎020 8864 9851
Email elle.finn@btinternet.com
Website www.btinternet.com/~elle.finn/
    SubVerse.htm
Contact *Elle Finn*

Heartfelt poetic musings on the value of surrender, submission and submissive people.

Poetry Review
Poetry Society, 22 Betterton Street, London
WC2H 9BX
☎020 7420 9883   Fax 020 7240 4818
Email poetryreview@poetrysoc.com
Website www.poetrysoc.com
Contacts *Robert Potts & David Herd*

A quarterly forum on the state of poetry.

Poetry Scotland
3 Spittal Street, Edinburgh EH3 9DY
☎0131 229 7252

Contact *Sally Evans*
All-poetry broadsheet with Scottish emphasis.

Poetry Wales
1st & 2nd Floors, 38–40 Nolton Street,
Bridgend CF31 3BN
☎01656 663018   Fax 01656 649226
Email poetrywales@seren.force9.co.uk
Website www.seren-books.com
Contact *Robert Minhinnick*

Poetry, criticism, essays, from Wales and further afield. See also **Seren** under **UK Publishers**.

Poets Cornered
28 Victoria Street, Brighton, E. Sussex
BN1 3FQ
Contact *Gemma Boyd*

PQR – Poetry Quarterly Review
Coleridge Cottage, Nether Stowey, Somerset
TA5 1NQ
☎01278 732662
Email pqrrev@aol.com
Contacts *Derrick Woolf & Till Brading*

In-depth reviews of mainstream/small-press poetry – no unrequested poetry, please.

Premonitions
13 Hazely Combe, Arreton, Isle of Wight
PO30 3AJ
☎01983 865668
Email pigasus.press@virgin.net
Contact *Tony Lee*

Magazine of sf-horror stories and horror stories, plus genre poetry and art. See also **Pigasus Press**.

Presence
12 Grovehall Avenue, Leeds, W. Yorks
LS11 7EX
Email martin.lucas@talk21.com
Website members.netscapeonline.co.uk/
    haikupresence
Contact *Martin Lucas*

Haiku, senryu, tanka, renku and related poetry in English.

Pretext
School of English & American Studies,
University of East Anglia, Norwich, Norfolk
NR4 7TJ
☎01603 592689
Email info@penandinc.co.uk
Website www.penandinc.co.uk

Contact *Julia Bell*

New fiction and poetry – essays on the world of writing. See also **Reactions** and **Pen&Inc** presses.

Prop

3 Treen Road, Astley, Manchester M29 7HD
☎01942 893923
Email steven.blythe@talk21.com

Contact *Steven Blythe*

Poetry, short fiction plus related essays, reviews and interviews.

Pulsar

34 Lineacre Close, Grange Park, Swindon,
Wilts SN5 6DA
☎01793 875941
Email david.pike@virgin.net
Website www.btinternet.com/~pulsarpoetry

Contact *David Pike*

Hard hitting/inspirational poetry – quarterly.

Purple Patch

25 Griffiths Road, West Bromwich
B71 2EH
☎07950 591455

Contact *Geoff Stevens*

Poetry mag founded 1976 – includes reviews and gossip column. See also **The Firing Squad** magazine.

Quantum Leap

York House, 15 Argyle Terrace, Rothesay,
Isle of Bute PA20 0BD

Contact *Alan Carter*

User-friendly magazine – encourages new writers – all types of poetry. See also **QQ Press**.

Rain Dog

PO Box 68, Manchester M19 2XD
Email rd-poetry@yahoo.com
Website www.page27.co.uk/jan/ps

Contact *Jan Whalen*

Biannual. Original contemporary poetry, sequences, reviews. Poetry by women particularly welcome. Formerly *Soup Dragon*.

Raw Edge

PO Box 4867, Birmingham B3 3HD

Contact *Dave Reeves*

New writing, free from outlets in the West Midlands Arts area. Writers with a regional connection only. See also **The Moving Finger** press.

The Reader

The English Dept., University of Liverpool,
Liverpool L69 7ZR
Email readers@thereader.co.uk
Website www.thereader.co.uk

Contact *Jane Davis*

A magazine about writing worth reading. See entry under **Magazines**.

Rebirth

104 Argyle Gardens, Upminster, Essex
RM14 3EU
Website www.homestead.com/firebirdpress

Contact *Pamela Constantine*

International journal of the new renaissance movement. See also **Firebird Press**, **Romantic Renaissance** and **The Solar Flame** magazines.

Red Poets' Society

PO Box 661, Wrexham LL11 1QU

Contact *Mike Jenkins*

Annual periodical.

The Rialto

PO Box 309, Aylsham, Norwich, Norfolk
NR11 6LN
Website www.therialto.co.uk

Contact *Michael Mackmin*

Excellent poetry in a clear environment.

Rising

80 Cazenove Road, Stoke Newington,
London N16 6AA
Email timmywells@hotmail.com

Contact *Tim Wells*

The readers' wives of poetry mags.

Romantic Renaissance

104 Argyle Gardens, Upminster, Essex
RM14 3EU
Website www.homestead.com/firebirdpress

Contact *Pamela Constantine*

Journal of the new renaissance movement. See also **Firebird Press**, **Rebirth** and **The Solar Flame** magazines.

Roundyhouse

63 Bwlch Road, Fairwater, Cardiff
CF3 3BX
☎029 2065 3211
Email h.williams13@ntl.world.com

Contact *Herbert Williams*

Poems and articles on poetry.

Route Magazine
School Lane, Glass Houghton, Castleford,
W. Yorks WF10 4QH
☎01977 603028 Fax 01977 512819
Email info@route-online.com
Website www.route-online.com
Contact *Ian Daley*
Short fiction and articles by the most exciting
contemporary writers. See entry for **Route
Publishing** under **Small Presses**.

The Rue Bella
2fl, 15 Warrender Park Terrace, Edinburgh
EH19 1EG
Website www.ruebella.co.uk
Contact *Nigel Bird*
Poetry – new writers.

Scriptor
2 Chambers Cottages, Underlyn Lane,
Marden, Tonbridge, Kent TN12 9BD
Poetry, short stories, essays from the South East.

Seam
PO Box 3684, Danbury, Chelmsford, Essex
CM3 4GP
Contact *Maggie Freeman*
New poetry by established and new poets.

Seventh Sense
289 Elmwood Avenue, Feltham, Middlesex
TW13 7QB
☎0777 919 3676
Email partners_writing_group@hotmail.com
Website www.homestead.com/
    partners_writing_group
Contact *Ian Deal*
Dedicated to the ongoing spiritual quest. See
also **Partners in Poetry** press, **Imagenation**,
A Bard Hair Day, **Poet Tree** magazines and
The Word Life Journal.

Shearsman
58 Velwell Road, Exeter, Devon EX4 4LD
☎01392 434511 Fax 01392 434511
Email shearsman@appleonline.net
Website www.shearsman.co.uk
Contact *Tony Frazer*
Mainly poetry, some prose, some reviews.
Poetry in the modernist tradition.

The SHOp: A Magazine Of Poetry
Skeagh, Schull, Co Cork Republic of Ireland
Email wakeman@iol.ie

Contact *John Wakeman*
International but with emphasis on Irish poetry.

Skald
2 Greenfield Terrace, Hill Street, Menai
Bridge, Ynys Mon LL59 5AY
☎01248 716343 Email skald@globalnet.com
Website www.centralslate.cmnia.co.uk/Skald
Contact *Zoe Skoulding*
Poetry and artwork, English and Welsh.

Smiths Knoll
49 Church Road, Little Glemham,
Woodbridge, Suffolk IP13 0BJ
Email royblackman@ukonline.co.uk
Contacts *Roy Blackman & Michael Laskey*
Surprising, honest, well-crafted poems. No
e-mail submissions.

Smoke
The Windows Project, 1st Floor, Liver
House, 96 Bold Street, Liverpool L1 4HY
☎0151 709 3688
Contact *Dave Ward*
Poetry, graphics, short prose – 24pp – bian-
nual. See also **The Windows Project** press.

Snapshots
PO Box 35, Sefton Park, Liverpool L17 3EG
Contact *John Barlow*
Haiku.

The Solar Flame
104 Argyle Gardens, Upminster, Essex
RM14 3EU
Website www.homestead.com/firebirdpress
Contact *Pamela Constantine*
Journal of the emerging spiritual and cultural
renaissance. See also **Firebird Press**, **Rebirth**
and **Romantic Renaissance** magazines.

South
Wanda Publications, 75 High Street,
Wimborne, Dorset BH21 1HS
☎01202 889669 Fax 01202 881061
Email wanda@wanda.demon.co.uk
Contact *Jane Peters*
Poetry for the Southern Counties. See also
Wanda Publications press.

Spiked
7 Swansea Road, Norwich, Norfolk NR2 3HU
Email editors@spiked-magazine.co.uk
Website www.appleonline.net/theaa/spiked.htm
Ideas, literature and the arts for Norfolk.

Stand
School of English, University of Leeds, Leeds, W. Yorks LS2 9JT
☎ 0113 233 4794   Fax 0113 233 4791
Email stand@english.novel.leeds.ac.uk
Website saturn.vcu.edu/~dlatane/stand.html
Contact *John Glover*

Quarterly magazine of poetry, fiction, reviews and cultural criticism.

Staple
Padley Rise, Nether Padley, Grindleford
Hope Valley, Derbys S32 2HE
☎01433 631949   Email e.barrett@shu.ac.uk
Contact *Ann Atkinson*

Poetry, short fiction, articles. Three issues a year. Established 1982.

Still
1 Lambolle Place, Belsize Park, London NW3 4PD
Email still@into.demon.co.uk
Website www.into.demon.co.uk
Contact *Ai Li*

A literary journal with a zen approach to haiku and short verse.

The Stinging Fly
PO Box 6016, Dublin 8, Republic of Ireland
Email stingingfly@hotmail.com
Website www.stingingfly.org
Contact *Eabhan N. Shuileabhain*

Dublin's literary magazine. New Irish and international writing. Poetry, short fiction, author interviews and book reviews.

Tangled Hair
Snapshot Press, PO Box 132, Crosby, Liverpool L23 8XS
Contact *John Barlow*

Tanka.

Tears In The Fence
38 Hod View, Stourpaine, Nr Blandford Forum, Dorset DT11 8TN
☎01258 456803   Fax 01258 454026
Email esp@euphony.net
Website www.wanderingdog.co.uk
Contact *David Caddy*

A magazine looking for the unusual, perceptive, risk-taking, lived and visionary literature.

Temenos Academy Review
PO Box 203, Ashford, Kent TN25 5ZT
☎01233 813663
Email stephen.overy@ashfordtelecom.net
Contact *Grevel Lindop*

10th Muse
33 Hartington Road, Southampton, Hants SO14 0EW
Contact *Andrew Jordan*

Poetry, prose and graphics, ideally combining lyricism and the pastoral with experimental techniques.

Terrible Work
21 Overton Gardens, Mannamead, Plymouth, Devon PL3 5BX
Contact *Tim Alen*

New innovative and non-mainstream poetry plus reviews and art.

The Third Half
16 Fane Close, Stamford, Lincs PE9 1HG
☎01780 754193
Contact *Kevin Troop*

Publishes two poets per issue. Charges a reading fee of £14 per submission.

Thumbscrew
PO Box 657, Oxford OX2 6PH
Email tim.kendall@bristol.ac.uk
Website www.bristol.ac.uk/thumbscrew
Contact *Tim Kendall*

International journal of poetry and poetry criticism. See also **Thumbscrew Press**.

Time Haiku
Kings Head Hill, London E4 7JG
Contact *Dr Erica Facey*

Haiku magazine aimed at experts and beginners.

Tremblestone
Corporation Building, 10f How Street, The Barbican, Plymouth, Devon PL4 0DB
Contact *Kenny Knight*

New and established writers and reviews of poetry magazines.

Twa Dugs
111 Main Street, West Kilbride, Ayrshire KA23 9AR
Email ralph@rgarratt.freeserve.co.uk
Website www.write2write.com
Contact *Ralph Garratt*

Poems.

Under Surveillance
Flat 1, College Road, Brighton, East Sussex
BN2 1JA
Contact *Eddie Harriman*
Unpublished poetry, short prose, artwork of
any genre welcome.

Understanding
20a Mongomery Street, Edinburgh EH7 5JS
☎0131 478 0680 Fax 0131 478 2572
Contact *Denise Smith*
Poems, short stories, parts of plays, reviews,
articles. See also **Dionysia Press**.

The Unruly Sun
The Rising Arts Centre, 30 Silver Street,
Reading, Berks RG1 2ST
Email sawers@btinternet.com
Contact *Jennifer Hoskins*
Irregular poetry magazine.

Upstart!
19 Cawarden, Stantonbury, Milton Keynes
MK14 6AH
☎01908 317535
Contact *Carol Barac*
Literary magazine – published every two years.

Urthona
3 Coral Park, Henley Road, Cambridge
CB1 3EA
☎01223 472417 Fax 01223 566568
Email urthona.mag@virgin.net
Website www.urthona.com
Contact *Shantigarbha*
Art & Buddhism. Builds bridges between
Buddhism and Western culture.

Wasafiri
Dept of English, University of London, Mile
End Road, London E1 4NS
☎020 7882 3120 Fax 020 7882 3120
Email wasafiri@qmw.ac.uk
Website www.english.qmw.ac.uk/wasafiri
Contact *Susheila Nasta*
Literary journal of African, Asian, Caribbean
and black British writing. See entry under
Magazines.

The Word Life Journal
289 Elmwood Avenue, Feltham, Middlesex
TW13 7QB
☎0777 919 3676
Website www.homestead.com/
  partners_writing_group
Contact *Ian Deal*
Poetry magazine dedicated to the ongoing
romantic renaissance. See also **Partners in
Poetry** press, **Imagenation**, **Poet Tree**,
Seventh Sense and, **A Bard Hair Day** maga-
zines.

The Yellow Crane
20 Princes Court, The Walk, Roath, Cardiff
CF2 3AU
Contact *Jonathan Brookes*
Interesting new poems from South Wales and
beyond.

Organisations of Interest to Poets

A survey of some of the societies, groups and other bodies which may be of interest to practising poets. Organisations not listed should send details to the Editor for inclusion in future editions.

Academi – The Welsh National Literature Promotion Agency

3rd Floor, Mount Stuart House, Mount Stuart Square, Cardiff Bay, Cardiff CF10 5FQ
☎029 2047 2266 Fax 029 2049 2930
Email post@academi.org
Website www.academi.org

North West Wales Office: Ty Newydd, Llanystumdwy, Criceith, Gwynedd LL52 0LW

North East Wales Office: Yr Hen Carchar, 46 Clwyd Street, Ruthin, Denbighshire LL15 1HP

West Wales Office: Dylan Thomas Centre, Somerset Place, Swansea SA1 1RR

Chief Executive *Peter Finch*

The writers' organisation of Wales with special responsibility for literary activity, writers' residencies, writers on tour, festivals, writers' groups, readings, tours, exchanges and other development work. **Yr Academi Gymreig/The Welsh Academy** operates the Arts Council of Wales franchise for Wales-wide literature development. It has offices in Cardiff and fieldworkers based in North West, North East and West Wales. *Publishes* the Lottery-funded *Encyclopedia of Wales*, the Welsh-medium literary magazine *Taliesin*, the *Academi English-Welsh Dictionary*, co-publisher of *The New Welsh Review* along with a number of other projects. The Academi sponsors a range of annual contests including the John Tripp Award For Spoken Poetry and the prestigious **Cardiff International Poetry Competition**. Publishes *A470* a bi-monthly literary information magazine.

Apples & Snakes

Battersea Arts Centre, Lavender Hill, London SW11 5TN
☎020 7924 3410 Fax 020 7924 3763
Email info@applesandsnakes.org
Website www.applesandsnakes.org

Director *Geraldine Collinge*

Set up in 1982 as a platform for poetry which would be popular, relevant, cross-cultural and accessible to the widest possible range of people. A&S stretches the boundaries of Poetry in Education and performance. Presents fortnightly shows at the Battersea Arts Centre and occasional shows around London and the UK. Operates a successful poetry in education scheme.

Arts Councils and Regional Arts Boards

See section on **Arts Councils and Regional Arts Boards**, pages 572-75.

The Arvon Foundation

See entry under **Writers' Courses, Circles and Workshops**

Association of Small Press Poets

7 Pincott Place, London SE4 2ER
☎020 7277 8831 Fax 08707 403511
Email info@smallpresspoets.co.uk
Website www.smallpresspoets.co.uk

Coordinator *Ruth Booth*

Association of poets wishing to increase the sales of their work. *Publishes The Big Poetry Catalogue* as a sales tool, *Appraisal* newsletter and offers various competitions, appraisal services and discounts on Robooth Publications, the ASPP coordinator's own press. Membership charges, on a sliding scale, start at £18.

The British Haiku Society

Lenacre Ford, Woolhope, Hereford HR1 4RF
☎01432 860328
Website www.britishhaikusociety.org

General Secretary *David Walker*

FORMED in 1990. Promotes the appreciation and writing within the British Isles of haiku, senyru, tanka, haibun and renga by way of tutorials, workshops, exchange of poems, critical comment and information. The Society runs a haiku library and administers the annual James W. Hackett Award, the prestigious **Sasakawa** prize and the Nobuyuki Yuasa Sasakawa English Haibun Contest. *Publishes*

The Haiku Kit teaching pack and the quarterly journal, *Blithe Spirit*.

The Eight Hand Gang
5 Cross Farm, Station Road, Padgate,
Warrington WA2 0QG
Secretary *John F. Haines*

An association of SF poets. *Publishes Handshake*, a single-sheet newsletter of SF poetry and information available free in exchange for an s.a.e.

57 Productions
57 Effingham Road, Lee Green, London
SE12 8NT
☎020 8463 0866 Fax 020 8463 0866
Email paul57prods@yahoo.co.uk
Website www.57productions.com
Contact *Paul Beasley*

Specialises in the promotion of poetry and its production through an agency service, a programme of events and a series of audio publications. Services are available to event promoters, festivals, education institutions and the media. Poets represented include Jean 'Binta' Breeze, Adrian Mitchell, John Cooper Clarke and Lemn Sissay. 57 Productions' series of audio cassettes, CDs and Poetry in Performance compilations offer access to some of the most exciting poets working in Britain today.

The Football Poets
4 The Retreat, Butterow, Stroud,
Gloucestershire
☎01453 7573766
Email dave@footballpoets.org
Website www.footballpoets.org

The Stroud Football Poets exist to promote writing about football worldwide. Formed by Dennis Gould and Stuart Butler in 1995 the organisation runs football poetry readings and performances of plays. Their website is a fast and entertaining mix of literature and soccer. Performance bookings and membership enquiries should be directed to Crispin Thomas (crispin@ctmuk.freeserve.co.uk).

The Northern Poetry Library
Central Library, The Willows, Morpeth,
Northumberland NE61 1TA
☎01670 534524/534514 Fax 01670 534513
Email amenities@northumberland.gov.uk

Membership available to everyone in Cleveland, Cumbria, Durham, Northumberland and Tyne and Wear. Associate membership available for all

outside the region. Over 17,000 books and magazines for loan including virtually all poetry published in the UK since 1968. Postal lending available too.

The Poet's House/Teach na hÉigse
Clonbarra, Falcarragh, Co. Donegal, Republic of Ireland
☎00 353 74 65470 Fax 00 353 74 65471
Email phouse@iol.ie
Director *Janice Fitzpatrick Simmons*

Set in the heart of Donegal Gaeltacht, the centre offers a year-long residential MA aong with three ten-day summer courses (to apply send three poems). During each session there are three resident and six visiting poets. Recent poets have included Peter Sirr, Paul Durcan, Michael Longley, Menna Elfyn, Frank Ormsby and Medbh McGuckian.

The Poetry Book Society
Book House, 45 East Hill, London SW18 2QZ
☎020 8870 8403 Fax 020 8877 1615
Website www.poetrybooks.co.uk
Director *Clare Brown*

For readers, writers, students and teachers of poetry. FOUNDED in 1953 by T.S. Eliot and funded by the Arts Council, the PBS is a unique membership organisation and book club providing up-to-date and comprehensive information about poetry from publishers in the UK and Ireland. Members receive the quarterly *PBS Bulletin* packed with articles by poets, poems, news, listings and access to discounts of at least 25% off featured titles. These range from modern classics to contemporary works. The transactional website has over 1000 titles available at discount to members. There are three membership packages – two of which include a number of new books specially selected by the Society's panel of experts along with, at both primary and secondary levels, a special package for teachers. Subscriptions start at £10. The PBS also runs the annual **T.S. Eliot Prize** for the best collection of new poetry.

The Poetry Business
The Studio, Byram Arcade, Westgate,
Huddersfield, West Yorkshire HD1 1ND
☎01484 434840 Fax 01484 426566
Email edit@poetrybusiness.co.uk
Website www.poetrybusiness.co.uk
Directors *Peter Sansom, Janet Fisher*

FOUNDED in 1986, the Business *publishes The North* magazine and books, pamphlets and cassettes under the **Smith/Doorstop** imprint. It runs an annual competition and organises monthly writing Saturdays. Send an s.a.e. for full details.

Poetry Can

Unit 11, Kuumba Project, 20–22 Hepburn Road, Bristol BS2 8UD
☎0117 942 6976 Fax 0117 944 1478
Email hester@poetrycan.demon.co.uk
Website www.poetrycan.demon.co.uk
Director *Hester Cockcroft*

FOUNDED in 1995, Poetry Can is a poetry development agency working across the Bristol and Bath area. It organises events and projects, supports the creative and professional development of poets and *publishes* a bi-monthly bulletin of poetry news and activity.

Poetry Ireland/Eigse Eireann

Bermingham Tower, Upper Yard, Dublin Castle, Dublin, Republic of Ireland
☎00 353 1 671 4632 Fax 00 353 1 671 4634
Email poetry@iol.ie
Website www.poetryireland.ie
Writers in Schools scheme
☎ 00 353 1 674 9860
Director *Joseph Woods*

The national organisation for poetry in Ireland, with its four core activities being readings, publications, education and an information and resource service. Organises readings by Irish and international poets countrywide. Through its website, telephone, post and public enquiries, Poetry Ireland operates as a clearing house for everything pertaining to poetry in Ireland. Operates the Writers in Schools scheme.

Publishes Poetry Ireland News, a bi-monthly newsletter containing information on events, competitions and opportunities. *Poetry Ireland Review* is published quarterly and is the journal of record for poetry in Ireland; current editor: *Maurice Harmon*. The organisation also produces occasional publications, most recently, *Watching the River Flow, a Century in Irish Poetry*. As a member of the International Translation Network, it has produced 12 dual-language titles by foreign poets.

The Poetry Library

Royal Festival Hall, Level 5, London
SE1 8XX
☎020 7921 0943/0664 Fax 020 7921 0939
Email info@poetrylibrary.org.uk
Website www.poetrylibrary.org.uk

Librarian *Mary Enright*

FOUNDED by the Arts Council in 1953. A collection of 45,000 titles of modern poetry since 1912, from Georgian to Rap, representing all English-speaking countries and including translations into English by contemporary poets. Two copies of each title are held, one for loan and one for reference. A wide range of poetry magazines and ephemera from all over the world are kept along with casettes, records and videos for consultation, with many available for loan. There is a children's poetry section with teacher's resource collection.

An information service compiles lists of poetry magazines, competitions, publishers, groups and workshops which are available from the Library on receipt of a large s.a.e. or direct from the website. It also has a noticeboard for lost quotations through which it tries to identify lines or fragments of poetry which have been sent in by other readers.

General enquiry service available. Membership is free but proof of identity and address are essential to join. Open 11.00 am to 8.00 pm, Tuesday to Sunday. The Library's website is one of the best poetry resources on the Net.

Beside the Library is *The Voice Box*, a performance space especially for literature. For details of current programme ring 020 7921 0971.

Poetry London

1a Jewel Road, London E17 4QU
Email editors@plondon.demon.co.uk
Website www.poetrylondon.co.uk
Contacts *Dermot Dayanch* (listings), *Pascale Petit* (poetry editor), *Scott Verner* (reviews)

Published three times a year, *Poetry London* includes poetry by new and established writers, reviews of recent collections and anthologies, features on issues relating to poetry, and an encyclopædic listings section of virtually everything to do with poetry in the capital and the South East. The magazine also carries a limited coverage of events elsewhere.

The Poetry School

1a Jewel Road, London E17 4QU
☎020 8223 0401/8985 0090
Fax 020 8223 0401
Email poetryschl@aol.com
Website www.poetryschool.com
Coordinator *Mimi Khalvati*

Funded by London Arts, the School offers a core programme of tuition in reading and writing poetry through a series of workshops, courses, masterclasses and seminars. Tutors include Graham Fawcett, Alison Fell, Selima Hill, Patience Agbabi, Roddy Lumsden and others. The School also provides a forum for practitioners to share experiences, develop skills and extend appreciation of the traditional and innovative aspects of their art. Runs an extended special events programme including a double series of masterclasses and 20th century poetry lectures with international poets such as Marilyn Hacker and Galway Kinnell.

The Poetry Society

22 Betterton Street, London WC2H 9BU
☎020 7240 9880/Membership Dept: 020 7384 3261 Fax 020 7240 4818
Email info@poetrysoc.com
Website www.poetrysoc.com

Chair *Richard Price*
Director *Christina Patterson*

FOUNDED in 1909 which ought to make it venerable, the Society exists to help poets and poetry thrive in Britain. In the past decade it has undergone a renaissance, reaching out from its Covent Garden base to promote the national health of poetry in a range of imaginative ways. Membership costs £32 for individuals. *Poetry News* membership is £15. Current activities include:

- Quarterly, redesigned magazine of new verse, views and criticism, *Poetry Review*.
- Quarterly newsletter, *Poetry News*.
- Promotions, events and cooperation with Britain's many literature festivals, poetry venues and poetry publishers.
- Competitions and awards, including the annual **National Poetry Competition** with a £5000 first prize.
- A manuscript diagnosis service, *The Poetry Prescription*, which gives detailed reports on submissions. Reduced rates for members.
- Seminars, fact sheets, training courses, ideas packs.
- Provides information and advice, publishes books, posters and resources for schools and libraries. Education membership costs £45/£25 and includes *The Young Poetry Pack*, *The Poetry Book For Primary Schools* and *Jumpstart Poetry for the Secondary School*, colourful poetry posters for Keystages 1, 2, 3 and 4. Many of Britain's most popular poets – including Michael Rosen, Roger McGough and Jackie Kay – contribute, offering advice and inspiration. (The Society's education website is at www.poetryclass.net)
- The Poetry Café serving snacks and drink to members, friends and guests, part of The Poetry Place, a venue for many poetry activities – readings, poetry clinic, workshops and poetry launches. This space is available for bookings.

Recent projects include *Poetry Places*, a national programme of residencies, placements and projects.

Point

Ithaca, Apdo. 119, E–03590 Altea Spain
☎00 34 96 584 2350 Fax 00 34 96 688 2767
Email elpoeta@point-editions.com
Website www.point-editions.com
Also at: Schapenstraat 157, B–1750 Lennik, Belgium

Director *Germain Droogenbroodt*

FOUNDED as POetry INTernational in 1984, Point is based in Spain and Belgium. A multilingual publisher of contemporary verse from *established* poets, the organisation has brought out more than 60 titles in at least eight languages, including English. Editions run the original work alongside a verse translation into Dutch made in cooperation with the poet. The organisation's website features the world's best-known and unknown poets in English, Spanish and Dutch. Point also co-organises an annual international poetry festival.

Regional Arts Boards

See **Arts Councils and Regional Arts Boards**

Scottish Poetry Library

5 Crichton's Close, Canongate, Edinburgh EH8 8DT
☎0131 557 2876
Email inquiries@spl.org.uk
Website www.spl.org.uk

Director *Robyn Marsack*

A comprehensive reference and lending collection of work by Scottish poets in Gaelic, Scots and English, plus the work of British and international poets. Stock includes books, tapes, videos, news cuttings and magazines. Borrowing is free to all. Services include a postal lending scheme, for which there is a small fee, a mobile library that can visit schools and other centres by arrangement, exhibitions, bibliographies, publications, information and promotion in the field of poetry. Also available is an online catalogue and computer index to poetry and poetry periodicals. The membership scheme costs £20 annually. Members receive a newsletter and other benefits and support the library.

Second Light

9 Greendale Close, London SE22 8TG
Email dilys_wood@lineone.net
Director Dilys Wood

A network of over 250 women poets, established and lesser known, aged from late thirties upwards. Aims to develop and promote women's poetry especially among those who wish to realise their latent ability. *Publishes* a news letter, runs an annual poetry competition, holds residential workshops, readings and cooperates with established poetry publishers to produce anthologies of women's work.

Slam! Productions

20 Coxwell Street, Cirencester,
Gloucestershire GL7 2BH
☎01285 640470
Email slam@scarum.freeserve.co.uk
Website www.author.co.uk/slam

Directors Marcus Moore, Sara-Jane Arbury

UK poetry slam specialists who organise events at venues throughout the year, run slam workshops for both schools and adults, offer selected performers special events, provide a total UK slam information service (send for their leaflets) and produce *Spiel*, a regular e-mail poetry slam newsletter. Membership is free. Contact by e-mail preferred.

Survivors' Poetry

Diorama Arts Centre, 34 Osnaburgh Street,
London NW1 3ND
☎020 7916 5317 Fax 020 7916 0830
Email survivors@survivorspoetry.org.uk

A unique national literature organisation promoting poetry by survivors of mental distress through workshops, readings and performances to audiences all over the UK. It was FOUNDED in 1991 by four poets with first-hand experience of the mental health system. Survivors' community outreach work provides training and performance workshops and publishing

projects. A survivor may be defined as a person with a current or past experience of psychiatric hospitals; a recipient of ECT, tranquillisers or other medication; a user of counselling and therapy services; a survivor of sexual abuse or child abuse; anyone who has empathy with the experience of survivors.

Survivors' Poetry Scotland

4 C4 Templeton Centre, 62 Templeton Street, Glasgow G40 1DA
☎0141 556 4554 Fax 0141 400 8442
Email sps@spscot.co.uk
Website www.spscot.co.uk

Project Manager Aimara Reques
Administrator Wallace MacBain
Managing Editor Gerry Loose

Promotes poetry by suvivors of mental distress through a poetry magazine, Nomad, which appears three times a year; writing workshops (four a week in Glasgow); and monthly performance evenings. SPS has set up groups in Dumfries, Edinburgh, Dundee and Aberdeen.

Tŷ Newydd

Llanystumdwy, Cricieth, Gwynedd LL52 0LW
☎01766 522811 Fax 01766 523095
Email tynewydd@dial.pipex.com
Website www.tynewydd.org

Director Sally Baker

Run by the Taliesin Trust, an independent, Arvon-style residential writers centre established in the one-time home of Lloyd George in North Wales. The programme (in both Welsh and English) has a regular poetry content. (See also **Writers' Courses, Circles and Workshops**.) Fees start at £100 for weekends and £320 for week-long courses. Among the many tutors to-date have been: Gillian Clarke, U.A. Fanthorpe, Roger McGough, Carol Ann Duffy, Liz Lochhead, Peter Finch and Paul Henry. Send for the centre's descriptive leaflets and programme of courses.

Small Presses

Aard Press
c/o Aardverx, 31 Mountearl Gardens, London SW16 2NL
Managing Editors D. *Jarvis, Dawn Redwood*
FOUNDED 1971. *Publishes* artists' bookworks, experimental/visual poetry, 'zines, eonist literature, topographics, ephemera and international mail-art documentation. Very small editions. No unsolicited material or proposals.
Royalties not paid. No sale-or-return deals.

Abbey Press
Abbey Grammar School, Courtenay Hill, Newry, Co. Down BT34 2ED
☎028 3026 3142 Fax 028 3026 2514
Also at: 12 The Pines, Jordanstown, Newtonabbey, Co. Antrim BT37 0SE
☎028 9086 0230
Editor *Adrian Rice*
Administrator *Mel McMahon*
FOUNDED in 1997, Abbey Press is a fast growing literary publisher with a strong poetry list. Also *publishes* biography, memoirs, fiction, history, politics, Irish language and academic. Lists currently full.

AK Press/AKA Books
PO Box 12766, Edinburgh EH8 9YE
☎0131 555 5165 Fax 0131 555 5215
Email ak@akedin.demon.co.uk
Website www.akuk.com
Managing Editor *Alexis McKay*
AK Press grew out of the activities of AK Distribution which distributes a wide range of radical (anarchist, feminist, etc.) literature (books, pamphlets, periodicals, magazines), both fiction and non-fiction. *Publishes* anarchist politics and history, situationism and occasional fiction in both book and pamphlet form. About 12 titles a year. Proposals and synopses welcome if they fall within AK's specific areas of interest.
Royalties paid.

Akros Publications
33 Lady Nairn Avenue, Kirkcaldy, Fife KY1 2AW
☎01592 651522

Publisher *Duncan Glen*
FOUNDED 1965. *Publishes* poetry collections, pamphlets and anthologies; literary essays and studies; travel books with a literary slant; local histories and memoirs. About 10 titles a year. Also publishes 220 magazines. Ideas for books welcome; no unsolicited mss. No fiction.
Royalties paid twice-yearly.

The Alembic Press
Hyde Farm House, Marcham, Abingdon, Oxon OX13 6NX
☎01865 391391 Fax 01865 391322
Email AlembicPrs@aol.com
Website members.aol.com/alembicprs/
Owner *Claire Bolton*
FOUNDED 1976. Publisher of hand-produced books by traditional letterpress methods. Short print-runs. *Publishes* bibliography, book arts and printing, miniatures and occasional poetry. Book design and production service to like-minded authors wishing to publish in this manner. No unsolicited mss.

Allardyce, Barnett, Publishers
14 Mount Street, Lewes, East Sussex BN7 1HL
☎01273 479393 Fax 01273 479393
Website www.abar.net
Publisher *Fiona Allardyce*
Managing Editor *Anthony Barnett*
FOUNDED 1981. *Publishes* art, literature and music. About 3 titles a year. IMPRINT **Allardyce Book**. Unsolicited mss and synopses cannot be considered.

Alphard Press
See **ignotus press**

Anglo-Saxon Books
Frithgarth, Thetford Forest Park, Hockwold cum Wilton, Norfolk IP26 4NQ
☎01842 828430 Fax 01842 828332
Email tony@asbooks.co.uk
Website www.asbooks.co.uk
Managing Editor *Tony Linsell*
FOUNDED 1990 to promote a greater awareness of and interest in early English history and culture. Originally concentrated on Old English

texts but now also publishes less academic, more popular titles. *Publishes* English history, culture, language and society. About 5–10 titles a year. Unsolicited synopses welcome but return postage necessary.

Royalties paid at standard rate.

Athelney

1 Providence Street, King's Lynn, Norfolk PE30 5ET Fax 01842 828332

Managing Editor *John Cooper*

FOUNDED 2000. *Publishes* nationalism in general; English nationalism in particular. Unsolicited outlines/contents page/first chapter welcome. Please enclose return postage.

Royalties – standard rate.

AVERT

AIDS Education and Research Trust, 4 Brighton Road, Horsham, West Sussex RH13 5BA
☎01403 210202 Fax 01403 211001
Email info@avert.org
Website www.avert.org

Managing Editor *Annabel Kanabus*

Publishing arm of the AIDS Education and Research Trust, a national registered charity established 1986. *Publishes* books and leaflets about HIV infection and AIDS. About 3 titles a year. Unsolicited mss, synopses and ideas welcome.

Royalties paid accordingly.

M.&M. Baldwin

24 High Street, Cleobury Mortimer, Kidderminster DY14 8BY
☎01299 270110 Fax 01299 270110
Email mb@mbaldwin.free-online.co.uk

Managing Editor *Dr Mark Baldwin*

FOUNDED 1978. *Publishes* local interest/history, WW2 codebreaking and inland waterways books. Up to 5 titles a year. Unsolicited mss, synopses and ideas for books welcome (not general fiction).

Royalties paid.

Bardon Enterprises

6 Winter Road, Southsea, Hampshire PO4 9BT
☎07752 873831 Fax 023 9287 4900
Email info@bardon-enterprises.co.uk
Website www.bardon-enterprises.co.uk

Managing Director *W.B. Henshaw*

FOUNDED 1996. *Publishes* music, art, biography, poetry, academic books and sheet music. Total publications: 22 books; 54 pieces of music. Unsolicited mss, synopses and ideas welcome. Short run editions. 'Cost free publishing.'

Bards Original Publishing

Studio 1, 9 The Mount, Burtons' St Leonards, East Sussex TN38 0HR
☎01424 201029 Fax 01424 201029
Email bardsoriginal@hotmail.com

Managing Editor *Tony Gill*

FOUNDED 1999. *Publishes* books on cricket, including fiction. *Specialises* in cricket club histories from club level to national teams. Welcomes unsolicited mss, synopses and ideas for books. Initial approach by telephone.

Royalties paid.

BB Books

See entry under **Poetry Presses**

The Better Book Company

Warblington Lodge, The Gardens, Warblington, Near Havant, Hampshire PO9 2XH
☎023 9248 1160 Fax 023 9249 2819
Email editors@better-book.com

Managing Editor *James Jude Garvey*

FOUNDED 1996. *Publishes* fiction, histories, memoirs, poetry, religious, scientific, company histories. 80 titles in 2002. Offers a complete editorial, design, printing and marketing service to self-publishing authors in all genre. A free booklet, *A Complete Guide to Self-Publishing* is available on request.

Royalties

Between the Lines

9 Woodstock Road, London N4 3ET
☎020 8374 5526 Fax 020 8374 5736
Email btluk@aol.com
Website www.interviews-with-poets.com

Editorial Board *Peter Dale, Philip Hoy, J.D. McClatchy*

FOUNDED 1998. *Publishes* extended interviews with leading contemporary poets. To-date, nine volumes published (featuring W.D. Snodgrass, Michael Hamburger, Anthony Thwaite, Anthony Hecht, Donald Hall, Thom Gunn, Richard Wilbur, Seamus Heaney and Donald Justice). Others scheduled for publication include Ian Hamilton, Charles Simic, John Ashbery, Paul Muldoon, Hans Magnus Enzensberger, Peter Porter and Peter Dale). Each volume includes a career sketch, a comprehensive bibliography, a representative selection from the poets' critics and reviewers, an uncollected poem and photograph. New series for 2002/3 will feature three poets per volume.

The Bewildered Publishing Company Ltd

Argoed Hall, Tregaron, Ceredigion SY25 6JR
☎01974 298070 Fax 01974 298708
Email argoed.hall@btinternet.com

Publisher *John Wilson*

FOUNDED in 1999 'to provide a direct route to the book market for authors with an unconventional approach to writing and publishing'. *Publishes* humorous paperbacks. No unsolicited material; initial inquiry by telephone, e-mail or letter.
Royalties not paid.

Big Engine Co. Ltd

PO Box 185, Abingdon, Oxfordshire OX14 1GR
☎01235 204011 Fax 01235 204012
Email info@bigengine.co.uk
Website www.bigengine.co.uk

Managing Editor *Ben Jeapes*

FOUNDED 2000 'to give new writers exposure and to re-issue deserving out of print titles'. *Publishes* science fiction and fantasy. 5 titles in 2001. No unsolicited mss. Synopses and ideas welcome by letter or e-mail.
Royalties paid twice-yearly.

Black Cat Books

See **Neil Miller Publications**

BlackAmber Books Ltd

PO Box 10812, London SW7 4ZG
☎020 7373 3178 Fax 020 7373 3178
Email information@blackamber.com
Website www.blackamber.com

Publisher *Rosemarie Hudson*

FOUNDED 1998. Home of 'the best writing emanating from the vibrant, mostly young, immigrant-descended population'. A collection point for British and European Black and Asian literature. 'Gives an outlet for the creative voice of European racial minorities, demonstrating their strengths and place in a multi-cultural world.'

The Book Castle

12 Church Street, Dunstable, Bedfordshire LU5 4RU
☎01582 605670 Fax 01582 662431
Email bc@book-castle.co.uk
Website www.book-castle.co.uk

Managing Editor *Paul Bowes*

FOUNDED 1986. *Publishes* non-fiction of local interest (Bedfordshire, Hertfordshire, Buckinghamshire, Oxfordshire, Northamptonshire, the Chilterns). 10 titles a year. About 70 titles in print. Unsolicited mss, synopses and ideas for books welcome.
Royalties paid.

Book-in-Hand Ltd

20 Shepherds Hill, London N6 5AH
☎020 8341 7650 Fax 020 8341 7650
Email ak@book-in-hand.demon.co.uk

Contact *Ann Kritzinger*

Print production service for self-publishers. Includes design and editing advice to give customers a greater chance of selling in the open market.

Bookmarque Publishing

26 Cotswold Close, Minster Lovell, Oxfordshire OX29 0SX
☎01993 775179
Email bookmarque@btinternet.com

Managing Editor *John Rose*

FOUNDED 1987. Publishing business with aim of filling gaps in motoring history of which it is said 'there are many'. *Publishes* motoring history, motor sport and 'general' titles. About 8 titles a year. All design and typesetting of books done in-house. Unsolicited mss and synopses welcome on transport titles. S.a.e. required for reply or return of material or for advice on publishing your work.
Royalties paid.

Brantwood Books

PO Box 144, Orpington, Kent BR6 6LZ
☎01689 833117 Fax 01689 833117
Email philip45other@yahoo.co.uk

Publisher *Philip Turner*

FOUNDED 1997. *Publishes* highly illustrated, limited edition print runs of specialist cinema titles, ranging from Russian cinema architecture to 36-page illustrated guides to British, North American and worldwide cinema circuit histories. DIVISIONS **Brantwood Books** and **Outline Publications** UK/US cinema circuit and film studio histories; **Brantwood Biographical** Biographies of movie moguls, producers and directors; **Brantwood Miniature Life** Series of outline biographies of popular movie stars; **Brantwood Technical** Screen, film and camera/projection topics. Consideration given to ideas which can be adapted to a 32-page format; initial approach in writing, please.

Brilliant Publications

1 Church View, Sparrow Hall Farm, Edlesborough, Dunstable, Bedfordshire LU6 2ES
☎01525 229720 Fax 01525 229725
Email sales@brilliantpublications.co.uk
Website www.brilliantpublications.co.uk

Publisher *Priscilla Hannaford*

FOUNDED 1993. *Publishes* resource books for teachers, parents and others working with 0–13-year-olds. About 10–15 titles a year. SERIES *How to Dazzle at ...* (9–13-year-olds with special needs); *How to be Brilliant at ...* (7–11-year-olds); *How to Sparkle at ...* (5–7-year-olds); *Activities* (3–5-year-olds). Submit synopsis and sample pages in the first instance. 'We do not publish stories for children.' Potential authors are strongly advised to look at the format of existing books before submitting synopses.
Royalties paid twice-yearly.

Charlewood Press

7 Weavers Place, Chandlers Ford, Eastleigh, Hampshire SO53 1TU
☎023 8026 1192
Email gponting@clara.net
Website www.home.clara.net/gponting/index-page11.html

Managing Editors *Gerald Ponting, Anthony Light*

FOUNDED 1987. Publishes local history books on the Fordingbridge area, researched and written by the two partners, and leaflets on local walks.

Chrysalis Press

7 Lower Ladyes Hills, Kenilworth, Warwickshire CV8 2GN
☎01926 855223 Fax 01926 748202
Email brian.buckley1@ntlworld.com

Managing Editor *Brian Boyd*

FOUNDED 1994. *Publishes* fiction, literary criticism and biography. No unsolicited mss.
Royalties paid.

CK Publishing

151 Brookfield Road, Cheadle, Cheshire SK8 1EY
☎0161 491 6074
Email editor@ckpublishing.co.uk
Website www.ckpublishing.co.uk

Managing Editor *Calum Kerr*

Publishes novels; also *Writer's Muse*, a bi-monthly creative writing magazine featuring short stories, poetry, reviews, articles, biography, etc. Unsolicited mss welcome; no synopses or ideas. S.a.e. essential.
Royalties paid for book collections. No payment for *Writer's Muse* magazine – free copies.

Clinamen Press Ltd

Enterprise House, Whitworth Street West, Manchester M1 5WG
☎0161 237 3355 Fax 0161 237 3727
Email bstebbing@clinamen.net
Website www.clinamen.net

FOUNDED 1998. *Publishes* philosophy, literary criticism, cultural studies, photography, travel literature, fiction and art theory. No unsolicited mss; two sample chapters with covering letter welcome. See also **the-phone-book.com** under **Electronic Publishing & Other Services**.

CNP Publications

See **Lyfrow Trelyspen**

Codex Books

PO Box 148, Hove, East Sussex BN3 3DQ
☎01273 728000 Fax 01273 205502
Email codex@codex-books.co.uk
Website www.codex-books.co.uk

Managing Editor *Hayley Ann*

Publishes contemporary fiction and non-fiction. Music-related titles feature strongly along with cyber punk, pulp, experimental fiction, gay fiction and journalism. AUTHORS include Steve Aylett, Billy Childish, Stewart Home, Mark Manning (aka Zodiac Mindwarp), Martin Millar and Jeff Noon. Refer to website for submission guidelines.
Royalties paid.

Columbia Publishing Wales Limited

Glen More, 6 Cwrt y Camden, Brecon, Powys LD3 7RR
☎01874 625270 Fax 01874 625270
Email dafydd@columbiapublishing.co.uk
Website www.columbiapublishing.co.uk

Managing Editor *Dafydd Gittins*

FOUNDED 2000. *Publishes* fiction and non-fiction – books, film and music (mainly pop and rock). Subjects suitable for film or television. 2 titles in 2000. No unsolicited mss. Synopses and ideas welcome; approach by letter or e-mail in the first instance.
Royalties paid.

Copperfield Books

Hillbrook House, Lyncombe Vale Road, Bath
BA2 4LS
☎01225 442835   Fax 01225 319755
Email sales@www.darcybook.com
Website www.darcybook.com
Managing Director *John Brushfield*

Publishes paperback fiction and general non-fiction. No unsolicited mss; 'we only commission books to our own specification'.

The Cosmic Elk

68 Elsham Crescent, Lincoln LN6 3YS
☎01522 820922
Email cosmicelk@zoom.co.uk *or*
   cosmicelk@hotmail.com *or*
   heather.hobden@ntlworld.com
Contact *Heather Hobden*

FOUNDED 1988 to publish easily updated books on science, history and the history of science. Now also markets and distributes books, and writes and publishes associated products (such as the John Harrison tea towel). 'New work always welcome on science or history topics. Please e-mail first to discuss.'

Crescent Moon Publishing and Joe's Press

PO Box 393, Maidstone, Kent ME14 5XU
☎01622 729593
Email jrobinson@crescentmoon.org.uk
Website www.crescentmoon.org.uk
Managing Editor *Jeremy Robinson*

FOUNDED 1988 to publish critical studies of figures such as D.H. Lawrence, Thomas Hardy, André Gide, Walt Disney, Rilke, Leonardo da Vinci, Mark Rothko, C.P. Cavafy and Hélène Cixous. *Publishes* literature, criticism, media, art, feminism, painting, poetry, travel, guidebooks, cinema and some fiction. Literary magazine, *Passion*, launched February 1994. Quarterly. *Pagan America*, twice-yearly anthology of American poetry. About 15–20 titles per year. Do not send whole mss. Unsolicited synopses and ideas welcome but approach in writing first and send an s.a.e.
Royalties negotiable.

Critical Vision

See **Headpress**

Crossbridge Books

345 Old Birmingham Road, Bromsgrove
B60 1NX
☎0121 447 7897   Fax 0121 445 1063
Email crossbridgebooks@btinternet.com
Website www.crossbridgebooks.com
Managing Director *Eileen Mohr*

FOUNDED 1995. *Publishes* Christian books for adults and children. 1–2 titles a year including Trevor Dearing's latest books. No unsolicited mss; telephone in the first instance. No New Age or books not biblically Christian. IMPRINT **Mohr Books**.
Royalties paid twice-yearly.

Crown House Publishing

Crown Buildings, Bancyfelin, Carmarthen
SA33 5ND
☎01267 211345   Fax 01267 211882
Website www.crownhouse.co.uk
Editorial Director *David Bowman*
Publishing Director *Bridget Shine*

FOUNDED 1998. *Publishes* titles in the areas of psychology, education, Neuro-Linguistic Programming (NLP), personal growth, stress management, business, health and hypnosis. The aim of our list is to both demystify the latest psychological advances, particularly in the fields of NLP and hypnosis, and provide professional therapists, consultants and trainers with books detailing the latest cutting-edge developments in their field. Approx. 20 titles a year.
Royalties paid twice-yearly.

Culva House Publications

10 The Carrs, Sleights, Whitby, North Yorkshire YO21 1RR
☎01947 810819
Website www.culvahouse.co.uk
Managing Editor *Alan Whitworth*

FOUNDED in 1986 as a part-time self-publishing venture and grew into a full-time business in 2000. *Publishes* architecture and local history; biography. 6 titles in 2001. Unsolicited material welcome; approach by letter.
Royalties paid.

Day Books

Orchard Piece, Crawborough, Charlbury, Oxfordshire OX7 3TX
☎01608 811196   Fax 01608 811196
Email diaries@day-books.com
Website www.day-books.com
Managing Editor *James Sanderson*

FOUNDED in 1997 to *publish* a series of great diaries from around the world, one of the most recent being *Inside Stalin's Russia*. Unsolicited mss, synopses and ideas welcome. Include return postage if return of material is required.

Dionysia Press
See entry under **Poetry Presses**

The Dragonby Press
15 High Street, Dragonby, Scunthorpe, North Lincolnshire DN15 0BE
☎01724 840645
Email rah.williams@virgin.net
Website freespace.virgin.net/rah.williams/
Managing Editor *Richard Williams*

FOUNDED 1987 to publish affordable bibliography for reader, collector and dealer. About 3 titles a year. Unsolicited mss, synopses and ideas welcome for bibliographical projects only.
Royalties paid.

Dramatic Lines
PO Box 201, Twickenham TW2 5RQ
☎020 8296 9502 Fax 020 8296 9503
Email mail@dramaticlinespublishers.co.uk
Website www.dramaticlinespublishers.co.uk
Managing Editor *John Nicholas*

FOUNDED to promote drama for young people. Publications with a wide variety of theatrical applications including classroom use and school assemblies, drama examinations, auditions, festivals, theatre group performance and musicals. Unsolicited drama-related mss, proposals and synopses welcome; enclose s.a.e.
Royalties paid.

Education Now Publishing Cooperative Ltd
113 Arundel Drive, Bramcote Hills, Nottingham NG9 3FQ
☎0115 925 7261 Fax 0115 925 7261
Website www.gn.apc.org/edheretics
Managing Editors *Dr Roland Meighan, Philip Toogood*

A non-profit research and writing group set up in reaction to 'the totalitarian tendencies of the 1988 Education Act'. Its aim is to widen the terms of the debate about education and its choices. *Publishes* reports on positive educational initiatives such as flexi-schooling, mini-schooling, small schooling, home-based education and democratic schooling. 4–5 titles a year. No unsolicited mss or ideas. Enquiries only.
Royalties generally not paid.

Educational Heretics Press
113 Arundel Drive, Bramcote Hills, Nottingham NG9 3FQ
☎0115 925 7261 Fax 0115 925 7261
Website www.gn.apc.org/edheretics
Directors *Janet & Roland Meighan*

Non-profit venture which aims to question the dogmas of schooling in particular and education in general, and establish the logistics of the next learning system. No unsolicited material. Enquiries only.
Royalties not paid but under review.

EKO Publishing
Nant Yr Hafod Cottage, Llandegla, Wrexham, Denbighshire LL11 3BG
☎01978 790442
Email indesigneko@cs.com
Managing Editor *Brian W. Burnett*

FOUNDED 1996 to publish modern, lively books and magazines in and about Esperanto. Unsolicited mss, synopses and ideas welcome.
Royalties paid.

Enable Enterprises
PO Box 1974, Coventry CV3 1YG
☎0800 358 8484 Fax 0870 133 2447
Email writers@enableenterprises.net
Website www.enableenterprises.net
Contact *Simon Stevens*

Enable Enterprises provides a wide range of accessibilty and disability services including publications on relevant issues. It welcomes unsolicited material related to accessibility and disability issues.

Fand Music Press
The Barony, 16 Sandringham Road, Petersfield, Hampshire GU32 2AA
☎01730 267341 Fax 01730 267341
Email Paul@fandmusic.com
Website www.fandmusic.com
Managing Editor *Peter Thompson*

FOUNDED in 1989 as a sheet music publisher, Fand Music Press has expanded its range to include CD recordings and books on music. Recently started publishing poetry and short stories. 10 titles a year. No unsolicited mss. Write with ideas in the first instance.

Feather Books
PO Box 438, Shrewsbury, Shropshire SY3 0WN
☎01743 872177 Fax 01743 872177
Email john@waddysweb.freeuk.com
Website www.waddysweb.freeuk.com
Managing Director *Rev. John Waddington-Feather*
Directors *David Grundy, Tony Reavill*

FOUNDED 1980 to publish writers' group

work. All material has a strong Christian ethos. *Publishes* poetry (mainly, but not exclusively, religious); Christian mystery novels (the Revd. D.I. Blake Hartley series); Christian children's novels; seasonal poetry collections and *The Poetry Church* quarterly magazine. 20 titles a year. Produces poetry, drama and music CD/cassettes. No unsolicited mss, synopses or ideas. All correspondence to include s.a.e., please.

Fern House
19 High Street, Haddenham, Ely, Cambridgeshire CB6 3XA
☎01353 740222 Fax 01353 741987
Email info@fernhouse.com
Website www.fernhouse.com
Managing Editor *Rodney Dale*
FOUNDED 1995. *Publishes* non-fiction with a bias towards biography, reference and technology. 4 titles in 2000. Unsolicited synopses and ideas welcome but please avoid sending large e-mail attachments.
Royalties paid.

Five Leaves Publications
PO Box 81, Nottingham NG5 4ER
☎0115 969 3597
Email fiveleaf01@surfaid.org
Website www.fiveleaves.co.uk
Contact *Ross Bradshaw*
FOUNDED 1995 (taking over the publishing programme of Mushroom Bookshop), producing 6–8 titles a year. *Publishes* fiction, poetry, politics and Jewish interest. Publisher of several books by Michael Rosen. Titles normally commissioned.
Royalties and fees paid.

Forth Naturalist & Historian
University of Stirling, Stirling FK9 4LA
☎01259 215091 Fax 01786 464994
Email lindsay.corbett@stir.ac.uk
Website www.stir.ac.uk/departments/natural sciences/
Also at: 30 Dunmar Drive, Alloa, Clackmannanshire FK10 2EH
Honorary Secretary *Lindsay Corbett*
FOUNDED 1975 by the collaboration of Stirling University members and the Central Regional Council to promote interests and publications on central Scotland. Aims to provide a 'valuable local studies educational resource for mid-Scotland schools, libraries and people'. Runs an annual symposium: Man and the Landscape

('Conserving Biodiversity and Heritage' in 2000). *Publishes* naturalist, historical and environmental studies and maps, including 1890s maps 25″ to the mile – 24 of central Scotland areas/places with historical notes. Over 20 selected papers from the annual *The Forth Naturalist & Historian* (Vol. 24 in 2001) are published in pamphlet form. Welcomes papers, mss and ideas relevant to central Scotland.
Royalties not paid.

Foxbury Press
1 Step Terrace, Winchester, Hampshire SO22 5BW
☎01962 864037 Fax 01962 860524
Managing Editor *Robert Cross*
FOUNDED in 1982 as part of St Paul's Bibliographies which was subsequently sold. *Publishes* bibliography and history. 2 titles in 2001. Welcomes synopses and ideas for books in the subject areas listed above; approach by mail.
Royalties paid twice-yearly.

Frontier Publishing
Windetts, Kirstead, Norfolk NR15 1EG
☎01508 558174
Email frontier.pub@macunlimited.net
Website www.frontierpublishing.co.uk
Managing Editor *John Black*
FOUNDED 1983. *Publishes* travel, photography, sculptural history and literature. 2–3 titles a year. No unsolicited mss; synopses and ideas welcome.
Royalties paid.

Galactic Central Publications
Imladris, 25A Copgrove Road, Leeds, West Yorkshire LS8 2SP
Email philsp@compuserve.com
Website www.philsp.com
Managing Editor *Phil Stephensen-Payne*
FOUNDED 1982 in the US. *Publishes* science fiction bibliographies. About 4 titles a year. All new publications originate in the UK. Unsolicited mss, synopses and ideas welcome.

Glosa Education Organisation
PO Box 18, Richmond, Surrey TW9 2GE
Website www.glosa.org
Managing Editor *Wendy Ashby*
FOUNDED 1981. *Publishes* textbooks, dictionaries and translations for the teaching, speaking and promotion of Glosa (an international, auxiliary language); also a newsletter, *Plu Glosa*

Nota, and journal, *PGN*. Unsolicited mss and ideas for Glosa books welcome.

Grant Books

The Coach House, New Road, Cutnall Green, Droitwich, Worcestershire WR9 0PQ
☎01299 851588 Fax 01299 851446
Email golf@grantbooks.co.uk
Website www.grantbooks.co.uk
Managing Editor *H.R.J. Grant*

FOUNDED 1978. *Publishes* golf-related titles only: course architecture, history, biography, etc., but no instructional material. New titles and old, plus limited editions. About 6 titles a year. Unsolicited mss, synopses and ideas welcome.
Royalties paid.

Great Northern Publishing

PO Box 202, Scarborough, North Yorkshire YO11 3GE
☎01723 581329 Fax 01723 581329
Email books@greatnorthernpublishing.co.uk
Website www.greatnorthernpublishing.co.uk
Senior Editor *Diane Crowther*

Independent, family-owned company FOUNDED in 1999, originally as a journal/newsletter and general publisher. Offers full book and journal publishing and production services to individuals, businesses, charities, museums and other small publishers. *Publishes* non-fiction (particularly military), fiction in most genres but no romance, religious, political or feminist books. Also publishers of *The Great War* and *Jade* magazines. Mail order and Internet-based bookshop stocking selected titles alongside its own. No unsolicited mss; send letter in the first instance.
Royalties paid twice-yearly.

Grevatt & Grevatt

9 Rectory Drive, Newcastle upon Tyne NE3 1XT
Email skillingley@hotmail.com
Website grevatt-grevatt.freeservers.com/index.htm
Chairman/Editorial Head *Dr S.Y. Killingley*

FOUNDED 1981. Alternative publisher of works not normally commercially viable. Three books have appeared with financial backing from professional bodies. *Publishes* academic titles and conference reports, particularly language, linguistics and religious studies. Some poetry also. No unsolicited mss. Synopses and ideas should be accompanied by s.a.e. Offers typesetting, editing and other services; s.a.e. with enquiries.
Royalties paid annually (after first 500 copies).

GSSE

11 Malford Grove, Gilwern, Abergavenny, Monmouthshire NP7 0RN
☎01873 830872
Email GSSE@zoo.co.uk
Owner/Manager *David P. Bosworth*

Publishes newsletters (main publication, *OLS News*) and booklets describing classroom practice (at all levels of education and training). Ideas welcome – particularly from practising teachers, lecturers and trainers describing how they use technology in their teaching.
Royalties paid by arrangement.

Happy House

3b Castledown Avenue, Hastings, East Sussex TN34 3RJ
☎01424 434778
Email HappyHouse@flexiweb.themail.co.uk

FOUNDED 1992 as a self-publishing venture for a Dave Arnold/Martin Honeysett collaboration of poetry and cartoons.

Haunted Library

Flat 1, 36 Hamilton Street, Hoole, Chester, Cheshire CH2 3JQ
☎01244 313685 Fax 01244 313685
Email pardos@globalnet.co.uk
Website www.users.globalnet.co.uk/~pardos/GS.html
Managing Editor *Rosemary Pardoe*

FOUNDED 1979. *Publishes* the *Ghosts and Scholars M.R. James Newsletter* two or three times a year, featuring articles, news and reviews (no fiction).
Royalties not paid.

Headpress

40 Rossall Avenue, Radcliffe, Manchester M26 1JD
☎0161 796 1935 Fax 0161 796 1935
Email david.headpress@zen.co.uk
Website www.headpress.com
Managing Editor *David Kerekes*

FOUNDED 1991. *Publishes Headpress* journal, devoted to the strange and esoteric, and books on film, music, popular and underground culture, comic art and marginalia. No fiction or poetry. IMPRINT **Critical Vision**. Unsolicited material welcome; send letter in the first instance.
Royalties and flat fees paid.

Heart of Albion Press

2 Cross Hill Close, Wymeswold, Loughborough, Leicestershire LE12 6UJ
☎01509 880725 Fax 01509 881715

Email albion@indigogroup.co.uk
Website www.indigogroup.co.uk/albion/
Managing Editor *R.N. Trubshaw*
FOUNDED 1990 to publish local history.
Publishes folklore and mythology. Synopses
relating to these subjects welcome.
Royalties negotiable.

Hilmarton Manor Press
Calne, Wiltshire SN11 8SB
☎01249 760208 Fax 01249 760379
Email mailorder@hilmartonpress.co.uk
Chairman/Managing Director *Charles Baile
de Laperriere*
Publisher of fine art dictionaries and reference
only.
Royalties paid.

ignotus press
BCM-Writer, London WC1N 3XX
☎01530 831916 Fax 01530 831916
Email ignotuspress@hotmail.com
Publisher *Suzanne Ruthven*
'We are looking for positive, forward-looking
material (fiction and nonfiction) on all aspects of
western ritual magic, mysteries, spiritual development, traditional and hereditary witchcraft and
other paths which demonstrate the writer's grasp
of both traditional and contemporary esoteric
practice. No New Age idealism, fantasy, pseudo-
spirituality or neo-Hammer House of Horror
fiction.' Send s.a.e. for authors' guidelines before
submitting material for consideration.
IMPRINTS **Moonraker Books** (fiction) and
Alphard Press (self-help and development).
Royalties paid.

Infinity Junction
PO Box 64, Neston DO CH64 0WB
Email infin-info@infinityjunction.com
Website www.infinityjunction.com
Managing Editor *Neil Gee*
Established originally as an internet outlet for
self-published books, Infinity Junction became
a publisher in 2001, releasing 2 titles, including
an anthology of short stories. 'Authors are
strongly advised to read the information on the
website before contacting us. We cannot
undertake to read unsolicited mss.'

Inner Sanctum Publications
75 Greenleaf Gardens, Polegate, East Sussex
BN26 6PQ
☎01323 484058
Email books@ethericrealms.com

Website www.ethericrealms.com
Managing Editor *Mary Hession*
FOUNDED in 1999 to *publish* spiritual books.
Unsolicited mss, synopses and ideas welcome;
approach in writing in the first instance.
Royalties not paid.

Intellect Books
The Mill, Parnall Road, Fishponds, Bristol
BS16 3JG
☎0117 958 9910 Fax 0117 958 9911
Email info@intellectbooks.com
Website www.intellectbooks.com
Chairman *Masoud Yazdani*
Managing Director *Robin Beecroft*
A multidisciplinary publisher for both individual
and institutional readers. Tracks newest developments in digital creative media – art, film, television, theatre design, etc. – and examines
distinct theories in education, language, gender
study and international culture through scholarly
articles. Also publishes in AI, computer science
and human-computer interaction in books,
journals and website.
Royalties paid.

Iolo
38 Chaucer Road, Bedford MK40 2AJ
☎01234 301718/07909 934866
Fax 01234 301718
Email newplays@dedwyddjones.screaming.net
Managing Director *Dedwydd Jones*
Publishes Welsh theatre-related material and cam-
paigns for a Welsh National Theatre. Ideas on
Welsh themes welcome; approach in writing.

Ivy Books
351 Woodstock Road, Oxford OX2 7NX
Manager *A. Hardy*
Small press concentrating on academic works.

Ivy Publications
72 Hyperion House, Somers Road, London
SW2 1HZ
☎020 8671 6872 Fax 020 8671 3391
Proprietor *Ian Bruton-Simmonds*
FOUNDED 1989. *Publishes* educational, science,
fiction, philosophy, children's, travel, literary
criticism, history, film scripts. No unsolicited
mss; send two pages, one from the beginning
and one from the body of the book, together
with synopsis (one paragraph) and s.a.e. No
cookery, gardening or science fiction.
Royalties paid annually.

Judith Handbooks
See **Studymates Limited**

Kittiwake
3 Glantwymyn Village Workshops,
Nr Machynlleth, Montgomeryshire SY20 8LY
☎01650 511314 Fax 01650 511602/
eFax: 0870 132 7404
Email david@perrocarto.co.uk
Website perrocarto.co.uk
Managing Editor *David Perrott*
FOUNDED 1986. *Publishes* guidebooks only,
with an emphasis on careful design/produc-
tion. Unsolicited mss, synopses and ideas for
guidebooks welcome. Specialist research, writing, cartographic and electronic publishing services available.
Royalties paid.

The Lindsey Press
Unitarian Headquarters, 1–6 Essex Street,
Strand, London WC2R 3HY
☎020 7240 2384 Fax 020 7240 3089
Email ga@unitarian.org.uk
Convenor *Kate Taylor*
ESTABLISHED at the end of the 18th century as a
vehicle for disseminating liberal religion.
Adopted the name of The Lindsey Press at the
beginning of the 20th century (after Theophilus
Lindsey, the great Unitarian Theologian).
Publishes books reflecting liberal religious
thought or Unitarian denominational history.
Also worship material – hymn books, collections
of prayers, etc. No unsolicited mss; synopses and
ideas welcome.
Royalties not paid.

Logaston Press
Logaston, Woonton, Almeley, Herefordshire
HR3 6QH
☎01544 327344
Managing Editors *Andy Johnson,
Ron Shoesmith*
FOUNDED 1985. *Publishes* guides, archaeology,
social history, rural issues and local history for
Wales, the Welsh Border and West Midlands.
10–15 titles a year. Unsolicited mss, synopses
and ideas welcome. Return postage appreciated.
Royalties paid.

Luath Press Ltd
543/2 Castlehill, The Royal Mile, Edinburgh
EH1 2ND
☎0131 225 4326 Fax 0131 225 4324
Email gavin.macdougall@luath.co.uk
Website www.luath.co.uk
Managing Editor *G.H. MacDougall*
FOUNDED 1981. *Publishes* mainly books with a
Scottish connection. Current list includes guide
books, walking and outdoor, history, folklore,
politics and global issues, cartoons, fiction,
poetry, biography, food and drink, environment,
music and dance, sport and *On the Trail* SERIES.
About 20–30 titles a year. Unsolicited mss, syn-
opses and ideas welcome; 'committed to publish-
ing well-written books worth reading'.
Royalties paid.

Lyfrow Trelyspen
The Roseland Institute, Gorran, St Austell,
Cornwall
☎01726 843501 Fax 01726 843501
Email trelispen@care4free.net
Managing Editor *Dr James Whetter*
FOUNDED 1975. *Publishes* works on Cornish
history, biography, essays, etc. 1–2 titles a year.
Also **CNP Publications** which *publishes* the
quarterly journal *The Cornish Banner/An Baner
Kernewek*. Unsolicited mss, synopses and ideas
welcome.
Royalties not paid.

Marine Day Publishers
64 Cotterill Road, Surbiton, Surrey KT6 7UN
☎020 8399 7625
Managing Editor *Anthony G. Durrant*
FOUNDED 1990. Part of The Marine Press Ltd.
Publishes local history.
Royalties not paid.

Maypole Editions
22 Mayfair Avenue, Ilford, Essex IG1 3DQ
☎020 8252 3937
Contact *Barry Taylor*
Publisher of plays and poetry in the main. 2–3
titles a year. Unsolicited mss welcome provided
return postage is included. Poetry always welcome for collected anthologies and should be
approximately 30 lines of tight verse, broadly
covering social concerns, ethnic minority issues,
feminist incident, romance generally, travel and
lyric rhyming verse. No politics except evenly
comparative. The biannual collected anthology is
designed as a small press platform for first-time
poets who might not otherwise get into print,
and a permanent showcase for those already published who want to break into the mainstream.
Catalogue £1, plus A5 s.a.e. 'Please be patient
when sending work because of the huge volume
of submissions.' Exempt Charity Status.

Meadow Books
35 Stonefield Way, Burgess Hill, West Sussex
WH15 8DW
☎01444 239044
Website www.historyofnursing.homestead.com
Managing Director C. O'Neill
FOUNDED 1990. Published *A Picture of Health*
and *More Pictures of Health*.

Mercia Cinema Society
19 Pinder's Grove, Wakefield, West Yorkshire
WF1 4AH
☎01924 372748
Email mervyn.gould@virgin.net
Managing Editor *Paul Smith*
FOUNDED 1980 to foster research into the history of picture houses. *Publishes* books and booklets on the subject, including cinema circuits and chains. Books are often tied in with specific geographical areas. Unsolicited mss, synopses and ideas.
Royalties not paid.

Meridian Books
40 Hadzor Road, Oldbury, West Midlands
B68 9LA
☎0121 429 4397
Managing Editor *Peter Groves*
FOUNDED 1985 as a small home-based enterprise following the acquisition of titles from Tetradon Publications Ltd. *Publishes* walking and regional guides. 4–5 titles a year. Unsolicited mss, synopses and ideas welcome if relevant. Send s.a.e. if mss to be returned.
Royalties paid.

Mermaid Turbulence
Annaghmaconway, Cloone, Leitrim, Republic of Ireland
☎00 353 78 36134 Fax 00 353 78 36134
Managing Director *Mari-Aymone Djeribi*
FOUNDED in 1993 with the first issue of *element* – an international literary journal. *Publishes* essays, fiction, poetry, cookery, children's and artists' books. 7 titles in 2002. Unsolicited mss, synopses and ideas welcome. No pulp fiction. Approach in writing, enclosing s.a.e.
Royalties paid annually.

Merton Priory Press Ltd
67 Merthyr Road, Whitchurch, Cardiff
CF14 1DD
☎029 2052 1956 Fax 029 2062 3599
Email merton@dircon.co.uk
Website www.merton.dircon.co.uk

Managing Director *Philip Riden*
FOUNDED 1993. *Publishes* academic and mid-market history, especially local, industrial and transport history; also memoirs and autobiographies. About 6 titles a year. Full catalogue available.
Royalties paid twice-yearly.

Neil Miller Publications
Mount Cottage, Grange Road, Saint Michael's, Tenterden, Kent TN30 6EE
Managing Editor *Neil Miller*
FOUNDED 1994. *Publishes* anthologies of short tales with a twist, comedy, suspense, mystery, fantasy, science fiction, horror and the bizarre under the **Black Cat Books** imprint. Also *publishes* paperbacks: classics, rare tales, tales of the unexpected. New authors always welcome. Evaluation and critique service available for large mss. 'We seek short story writers, in any genre. We read all tales that are sent in. No unsolicited/unrequested mss, please. In the first instance, send £7.75 (or £9.95 for two publications) and large 45-pence s.a.e. for author's package, which includes free book listing hundreds of possible publication outlets for new authors, or our latest novel; please state preference. We have published 190 new authors since 1994. We will help and advise on anything well written and researched. Now accepting novels and short poems.'

Millers Dale Publications
7 Weavers Place, Chandlers Ford, Eastleigh, Hampshire SO53 1TU
☎023 8026 1192
Email gponting@clara.net
Website www.home.clara.net/gponting/
  index-page10.html
Managing Editor *Gerald Ponting*
FOUNDED 1990. *Publishes* books on local history related to central Hampshire. Also books related to slide presentations by Gerald Ponting. Ideas for local history books on Hampshire considered.

Minority Rights Group
379 Brixton Road, London SW9 7DE
☎020 7978 9498 Fax 020 7738 6265
Email minority.rights@mrgmail.org
Website www.minorityrights.org
Deputy Head of Communications *Angela Warren*
FOUNDED in the late 1960s, MRG works to raise awareness of minority issues worldwide. *Publishes* books, reports and educational material on minority rights. 8–10 titles a year.

Mohr Books
See **Crossbridge Books**

Moonraker Books
See **ignotus press**

Morton Publishing
PO Box 23, Gosport, Hampshire PO12 2XD
Managing Editor *Nik Morton*
FOUNDED 1994. *Publishes* fiction – genre
novellas (eg crime, science fiction, fantasy,
horror, western), max. 20,000 words; short
story anthologies – max. 4000 words per story.
Unsolicited synopses and ideas for books welcome; enclose s.a.e. Also offers literary agent
service of guidance and advice (fees on application)
Royalties paid annually.

Mr Educator Handbooks
See **Studymates Limited**

Need2Know
Remus House, Coltsfoot Drive, Woodston,
Peterborough PE2 9JX
☎01733 898103 Fax 01733 313524
Website www.forwardpress.co.uk
Managing Editor *Ann Johnson-Allen*
FOUNDED 1995 'to fill a gap in the market for
self-help books'. Need2Know is an imprint of
Forward Press (see entry under **Poetry
Presses**). *Publishes* contemporary health and
lifestyle issues. No unsolicited mss. Call in the
first instance.
Payment Advance plus 15% royalties.

Nimbus Press
18 Guilford Road, Leicester LE2 2RB
☎0116 270 6318 Fax 0116 270 6318
Email clifford.sharp@nimbuspress.co.uk
Website www.nimbuspress.co.uk
Managing Editor *Clifford Sharp*
Assistant Editor *Justin Moulder*
FOUNDED in 1991. *Publishes* mind, body and
spirit books from an open and inclusive
Christian perspective, Christian drama and
humour. About 4 titles a year.
Royalties paid.

Northern Lights
Cumbria County Council, Community
Regeneration, Arroyo Block, The Castle,
Carlisle, Cumbria CA3 8UR
☎01228 607306 Fax 01228 67299
Email susan.tranter@cumbriacc.gov.uk

Managing Editor *Susan Tranter*
FOUNDED in 2000 to publish 'the best new
poetry and short fiction from Cumbria'.
Publishes 4 pamphlets a year. Welcomes mss,
synopses and ideas from previously unpublished writers in Cumbria. Send letter in the
first instance.
Royalties not paid.

Norvik Press Ltd
School of Language, Linguistics & Translation
Studies, University of East Anglia, Norwich,
Norfolk NR4 7TJ
☎01603 593356 Fax 01603 250599
Email norvik.press@uea.ac.uk
Website www.uea.ac.uk/llt/norvik_press
Managing Editors *Janet Garton,*
Michael Robinson
Small academic press. *Publishes* the journal
Scandinavica and books related to Scandinavian
literature. About 4 titles a year. Interested in
synopses and ideas for books within its *Literary
History and Criticism* series. No unsolicited mss.
Royalties paid.

The Nostalgia Collection
Silver Link Publishing Ltd, The Trundle,
Ringstead Road, Great Addington, Kettering,
Northamptonshire NN14 4BW
☎01536 330588 Fax 01536 330588
Email sales@nostalgiacollection.com
Website www.nostalgiacollection.com
Managing Editor *Peter Townsend*
FOUNDED 1985 in Lancashire, changed hands
in 1990 and now based in Northamptonshire.
Small independent company specialising in
nostalgia titles including illustrated books on
towns and cities, villages and rural life, rivers
and inland waterways, industrial heritage, rail-
ways, trams, ships and other transport subjects.
Publishes post-war nostalgia on all aspects of
social history under the **Past and Present
Publishing** imprint.
Fees paid.

Nyala Publishing
4 Christian Fields, London SW16 3JZ
☎020 8764 6292
Fax 020 8764 6292/0115 981 9418
Email nyala.publish@geo-group.co.uk
Website www.geo-group.co.uk
Editorial Head *J.F.J. Douglas*
FOUNDED 1996. Publishing arm of Geo
Group. *Publishes* biography, travel and general
non-fiction. No unsolicited mss; synopses and

ideas considered. Also offers a wide range of printing and publishing services. 'Quality low-cost printing a speciality.'
Royalties paid twice-yearly.

Orpheus Publishing House
4 Dunsborough Park, Ripley Green, Ripley, Guildford, Surrey GU23 6AL
☎01483 225777 Fax 01483 225776
Email orpheuspubl.ho@btinternet.com
Managing Editor *J.S. Gordon*

FOUNDED 1996. *Publishes* 'well-researched and properly argued' books in the fields of occult science, esotericism and comparative philosophy/religion. 'Keen to encourage good (but sensible) new authors.' In the first instance, send maximum 3-page synopsis with s.a.e.
Royalties by agreement.

Outline Publications
See **Brantwood Books**

Palladour Books
Hirwaun House, Aberporth, Nr Cardigan, Ceredigion SA43 2EU
☎01239 811658 Fax 01239 811658
Email palladour@powellj33.freeserve.co.uk
Managing Editors *Jeremy Powell, Anne Powell*

FOUNDED 1986. Started with a twice-yearly issue of catalogues on the literature and poetry of World War I. Occasional catalogues on World War II poetry have also been issued. No unsolicited mss.
Royalties not paid.

Panacea Press Limited
86 North Gate, Prince Albert Road, London NW8 7EJ
☎020 7722 8464 Fax 020 7586 8187
Email ebrecher@panaceapress.net
Managing Editor *Erwin Brecher*

FOUNDED as a self-publisher but now open for non-fiction from other authors. Material of academic value considered provided it commands a wide general market. No unsolicited mss; synopses and ideas welcome. Approach by fax or letter. No telephone calls.
Royalties paid annually.

Paradise Press
80 College Road, Isleworth, Middlesex TW7 5DS
☎020 8568 3777
Email prdsprss@netscapeonline.co.uk
FOUNDED 1995. Considers only high quality

lesbian and gay fiction workshopped through **Gay Authors Workshop**.

Parapress Ltd
5 Bentham Hill House, Stockland Green Road, Tunbridge Wells, Kent TN3 0TJ
☎01892 512118 Fax 01892 512118
Email e.imlay.parapress@virgin.net
Website www.parapress.co.uk
Managing Editor *Elizabeth Imlay*
Production and Promotion *James Ewing*

FOUNDED 1993. *Publishes* animals, autobiography, biography, history, literary criticism, military and naval, music, self-help, sports. Some self-publishing. About 6 titles a year.

Parthian
53 Colum Road, Cardiff CF10 3EF
☎029 2034 1314 Fax 029 2034 1314
Email parthianbooks@yahoo.co.uk
Website www.parthianbooks.co.uk
Chairman *Gillian Griffiths*
Publisher *Richard Davies*

FOUNDED 1993. *Publishes* contemporary Welsh fiction, drama and poetry in English, also translations of Welsh language fiction. New writing magazine, *Human Conditions*, published annually. No unsolicited mss; synopses with sample chapters and ideas welcome.
Royalties paid annually.

Partnership Publishing Ltd
2 Market Street, Wellington, Telford, Shropshire TF1 1LP
☎01952 415334 Fax 01952 245077
Email info@publish.uk.ws
Managing Director *Steve Rooney*

Publisher of *Bus and Coach Professional*; *Professional Recovery*; *MOT Professional*; *Oakengates & District News*; *Wellington News*; *Dawley, Madeley, Broseley News*; *Vehicle Salvage Professional*. Offers full magazine publication services, including design and production, editorial and advertising sales service.

Past and Present Publishing
See **The Nostalgia Collection**

Paupers' Press
27 Melbourne Road, West Bridgford, Nottingham NG2 5DJ
☎0115 981 5063 Fax 0115 981 5063
Email stan2727uk@aol.com
Website members.aol.com/stan2727uk/pauper.htm

Managing Editor *Colin Stanley*

FOUNDED 1983. *Publishes* extended essays in booklet form (about 15,000 words) on literary criticism and philosophy. 'Sometimes we stray from these criteria and produce full-length books, but only to accommodate an exceptional ms.' About 6 titles a year. Limited hardback editions of bestselling titles. No unsolicited mss but synopses and ideas for books welcome. *Royalties* paid.

Peepal Tree Press Ltd

17 King's Avenue, Leeds, West Yorkshire LS6 1QS
☎0113 245 1703 Fax 0113 245 9616
Email info@peepaltreepress.com
Website www.peepaltreepress.com
Managing Editor *Jeremy Poynting*

FOUNDED 1985. *Publishes* fiction, poetry, drama and academic studies. *Specialises* in Caribbean, Black British and south Asian writing. About 18 titles a year. In-house printing and finishing facilities. AUTHORS include **Forward Poetry Prize**-winner Kwame Dawes. 'Please send an A5 s.a.e. with a 38p stamp for a copy of our submission guidelines.' Write or phone for a free catalogue.
Royalties paid.

The Penniless Press

100 Waterloo Road, Ashton, Preston, Lancashire PR2 1EP
Editor *Alan Dent*

Publishes quarterly magazine with literary, philosophical, artistic and political content, including reviews of poetry, fiction, non-fiction and drama. Prose of up to 3000 words welcome. No mss returned without s.a.e.
Payment Free copy of magazine.

Pipers' Ash Ltd

'Pipers' Ash', Church Road, Christian Malford, Chippenham, Wiltshire SN15 4BW
☎01249 720563 Fax 0870 0568916
Email pipersash@supamasu.com
Website www.supamasu.com
Managing Editor *Mr A. Tyson*

FOUNDED 1976. The company's publishing activities include individual collections of contemporary short stories, science fiction short stories, poetry, plays, short novels, local histories, children's fiction, philosophy, biographies, translations and general non-fiction. 18 titles a year. Synopses and ideas welcome; 'new authors with potential will be actively encouraged'. Offices in New Zealand and Australia.
Royalties paid annually.

Planet

PO Box 44, Aberystwyth, Ceredigion SY23 3ZZ
☎01970 611255 Fax 01970 611197
Email planet.enquiries@planetmagazine.org.uk
Website www.planetmagazine.org.uk
Managing Editor *John Barnie*

FOUNDED 1975 and relaunched in 1985 as publisher of the arts and current affairs magazine *Planet: The Welsh Internationalist* and branched out into book publishing in 1995. All books so far have been commissioned. Unsolicited synopses and ideas welcome.
Royalties paid.

Playwrights Publishing Co.

70 Nottingham Road, Burton Joyce, Nottinghamshire NG14 5AL
☎0115 931 3356
Email playwrightspublishingco@yahoo.com
Website geocities.com/
  playwrightspublishingco
Managing Editors *Liz Breeze, Tony Breeze*

FOUNDED 1990. *Publishes* one-act and full-length plays. Unsolicited scripts welcome. No synopses or ideas. Reading fees: £15 one act; £30 full length.
Royalties paid.

Pomegranate Press

Dolphin House, 51 St Nicholas Lane, Lewes, Sussex BN7 2JZ
☎01273 470100 Fax 01273 470100
Email sussexbooks@compuserve.com
Website ourworld.compuserve.com/
  homepages/sussexbooks
Managing Editor *David Arscott*

FOUNDED in 1992 by writer/broadcaster David Arscott, who also administers the **Sussex Book Club**. *Specialises* in books about Sussex. IMPRINT **Pomegranate Practicals** How-to books.
Royalties paid twice-yearly.

David Porteous Editions

PO Box 5, Chudleigh, Newton Abbot, Devon TQ13 0YZ
☎01626 853310 Fax 01626 853663
Email editorial@davidporteous.com
Website www.davidporteous.com
Publisher *David Porteous*

FOUNDED 1992 to produce high quality colour

illustrated books on hobbies and leisure for the UK and international markets. *Publishes* crafts, hobbies, art techniques and needlecrafts. No poetry or fiction. 3–4 titles a year. Unsolicited mss, synopses and ideas welcome if return postage included.

Royalties paid twice-yearly.

Power Publications
1 Clayford Avenue, Ferndown, Dorset BH22 9PQ
☎01202 875223 Fax 01202 875223
Email sales@powerpublications.co.uk

Contact *Mike Power*

FOUNDED 1989. *Publishes* local interest, pub walk guides and mountain bike guides. 2–3 titles a year. Unsolicited mss/synopses/ideas welcome.

Royalties paid.

Praxis Books
Crossways Cottage, Walterstone, Herefordshire HR2 0DX
☎01873 890695
Email author@rebeccatope.fsnet.co.uk
Website www.rebeccatope.com

Proprietor *Rebecca Smith*

FOUNDED 1992. *Publishes* reissues of the works of Sabine Baring-Gould, memoirs, diaries and general interest. 19 titles to date. Unsolicited mss accepted with s.a.e. No fiction, children's or humour. Editing service available. Flexible funding negotiable. 'I am most likely to accept work with a clearly identifiable market.'

Primrose Hill Press Ltd
58 Carey Street, London WC2A 2JB
☎020 7405 7484 Fax 020 7405 7459
Email info@primrosehillpress.co.uk
Website www.primrosehillpress.co.uk

Managing Director *Brian H.W. Hill*

FOUNDED in 1997, having taken over the stock and projects in progress of Silent Books Ltd. *Publishes* general art titles, wood engraving, poetry and books for the gift market, 'all high quality productions'. No fiction. About 12 titles a year. Unsolicited mss, synopses and ideas welcome.

QueenSpark Books
49 Grand Parade, Brighton, East Sussex BN2 2QA
☎01273 571710 Fax 01273 571710
Email info@queensparkbooks.org.uk
Website www.queensparkbooks.org.uk

A community writing and publishing group run mainly by volunteers who work together to write and produce books. Since the early 1970s they have published 70 titles, mainly featuring the lives of local people. No fiction or poetry. Writing workshops and groups held on a regular basis. New members welcome.

Radikal Phase Publishing House Ltd
Willow Court, Cordy Lane, Underwood, Nottinghamshire NG16 5FD
☎01773 764288 Fax 01773 764282
Email sales@radikalbooks.com
Website www.radikalbooks.com

Joint Managing Directors *Philip Gardiner, Kevin Marks*

FOUNDED 2001. *Publishes* radical revelation and technical electrical books. 4 titles in 2001. IMPRINTS **William Ernest** *Kevin Marks*; **Radikal Phase** *Philip Gardiner*. Welcomes unsolicited material; approach in writing in the first instance.

Royalties paid twice-yearly.

The Riverside Press
PO Box 388A, Surbiton, Surrey KT7 0ZT
☎020 8339 0945 Fax 020 8339 0945
Email ed@good-writing-matters.com
Website www.good-writing-matters.com

Managing Editor *Michael Russell*

FOUNDED 1998 to publish short-run titles from new writers. Mainly fiction but also special interest non-fiction. Editorial support service provided. No unsolicited mss. Send synopses/ ideas and three chapters only with covering letter.

The Robinswood Press
30 South Avenue, Stourbridge, West Midlands DY8 3XY
☎01384 397475 Fax 01384 440443
Email robinswoodpress@hotmail.com
Website www.robinswoodpress.com

Managing Editor *Christopher J. Marshall*

FOUNDED 1985. *Publishes* education, particularly teacher resources, SEN, including the Spotlight and Lifeboat Read and Spell ranges. Also collaborative publishing, e.g. with Camphill Foundation and Birmingham Royal Ballet. About 12–15 titles a year. Unsolicited mss, synopses and ideas welcome.

Royalties paid.

Romer Publications
PO Box 10120, NL–1001 EC Amsterdam, The Netherlands
☎00 31 20 676 9442 Fax 00 31 20 676 9442

Email harrymelkman@hotmail.com
Managing Editor *Hubert de Brouwer*
FOUNDED 1986. *Publishes* critical reflection on origins and legitimacy of established institutions; law and history. Unsolicited mss, synopses and ideas within the areas covered welcome.
Royalties paid.

Route
School Lane, Glasshoughton, Castleford, West Yorkshire WF10 4QH
☎01977 603028 Fax 01977 512819
Email books@route-online.com
Website www.route-online.com
Books Coordinator *Ian Daley*
FOUNDED 1986. *Publishes* contemporary fiction (novels and short stories). No local history, children's, autobiography, poetry, reference or nostalgia. Unsolicited mss discouraged; authors should send for fact sheet first. Write or ring for free catalogue.
Royalties paid.

SAKS Publications
PO Box 33504, London, E9 7YE
Email hotspotwriters@compuserve.com
Publisher *Kadija George*
FOUNDED 1996. *Publishes* Sable literary magazine for writers of African/Caribbean/Asian descent.

Serif
47 Strahan Road, London E3 5DA
☎020 8981 3990 Fax 020 8981 3990
Managing Editor *Stephen Hayward*
FOUNDED 1993. *Publishes* cookery, Irish and African studies and modern history; no fiction. Ideas and synopses welcome; no unsolicited mss.
Royalties paid.

Sherlock Publications
6 Bramham Moor, Hill Head, Fareham, Hampshire PO14 3RU
☎01329 667325
Email sherlock.publications@btinternet.com
Managing Editor *Philip Weller*
FOUNDED to supply publishing support to a number of Sherlock Holmes societes. *Publishes* Sherlock Holmes and other Conan Doyle studies only. About 14 titles a year. No unsolicited mss; synopses and ideas welcome.
Royalties not paid.

Spacelink Books
115 Hollybush Lane, Hampton, Middlesex TW12 2QY
☎020 8979 3148
Website spacelink.50megs.com
Managing Director *Lionel Beer*
FOUNDED 1967. Named after a UFO magazine published in the 1960/70s. *Publishes* non-fiction titles connected with UFOs, Fortean phenomena and paranormal events. No unsolicited mss; send synopses and ideas. Publishers of *TEMS News* for the Travel and Earth Mysteries Society. Distributors of a wide range of related titles and magazines.
Royalties and fees paid according to contract.

Stenlake Publishing
54–58 Mill Square, Catrine, Ayrshire KA5 6RD
☎01290 552233 Fax 01290 551122
Email david@stenlake.co.uk
Website www.stenlake.co.uk
Publishes local history, railways, shipping, aviation and industrial. 48 titles in 2001. Unsolicited mss, synopses and ideas welcome if accompanied by s.a.e. Also, freelance writers with experience in the above fields are sought for specific commissions.
Royalties or fixed fee paid.

Stone Flower Limited
PO Box 1513, Ilford IG1 3QU
Managing Editor *L.G. Norman*
FOUNDED 1989. *Publishes* biography, law, humour and general fiction. Will consider mss, synopses and ideas only if sent with s.a.e. or IRC. Approach in writing in the first instance.

Stride
11 Sylvan Road, Exeter, Devon EX4 6EW
Email editor@stridebooks.co.uk
Website www.stridebooks.co.uk
Managing Editor *Rupert Loydell*
FOUNDED in 1982 as a magazine and booklet series. Since the mid-1980s, the press has published paperback editions of imaginative new writing. *Publishes* poetry, experimental fiction, criticism, reviews, interviews, arts (particularly experimental music). 14 titles in 2001. Unsolicited mss preferred to synopses. Ideas for future books welcome. Approach in writing only (with s.a.e.).
Royalties sometimes paid; free copies usually.

Studymates Limited

PO Box 2, Bishops Lydeard, Somerset
TA4 3YE
☎01823 432002 Fax 01823 430097
Email info@studymates.co.uk
Website www.studymates.co.uk *or*
www.mr.educator.com

Managing Editor *Graham Lawler, MA*

FOUNDED 1998 as part of International Briefings
Ltd and taken over by education expert Graham
Lawler in July 2000. Studymates are academic
titles for students at university or college. Three
new lists are planned – **Studymates
Professional**, for the professional person to
improve their knowledge in the workplace;
Judith Handbooks, problem-solving books for
women that deal with emotional and day-to-
day practical issues; and **Mr Educator
Handbooks** for under-16s. Books both for
children, e.g. *Literacy Poems*, and for adults about
educating children. Ideas first in writing; authors
are asked to follow the layout of the author kit
available on the website.

Tamarind Ltd

PO Box 52, Northwood, Middlesex
HA6 1UN
☎020 8866 8808 Fax 020 8866 5627
Email info@tamarindbooks.co.uk
Website www.tamarindbooks.co.uk

Managing Editor *Verna Wilkins*

FOUNDED 1987 to publish picture books which
give Black children a high, unselfconscious,
positive profile. Won Gold Award for Best
Product, Nursery & Creche Exhibition, 1994;
featured BBC TV Words and Pictures: *Time to
Get Up, Dave and the Tooth Fairy*; Book of the
Month, Junior Education: *Profile of Benjamin
Zephaniah* 1999. All titles sold into both trade
and educational markets. Age range: 2–12.

Tarquin Publications

Stradbroke, Diss, Norfolk IP21 5JP
☎01379 384218 Fax 01379 384289
Email enquiries@tarquin-books.demon.co.uk
Website www.tarquin-books.demon.co.uk

Managing Editor *Gerald Jenkins*

FOUNDED 1970 as a hobby which gradually
grew and now *publishes* mathematical, cut-out
models, teaching and pop-up books. Other
topics covered if they involve some kind of
paper cutting or pop-up scenes. 6 titles in
2002. No unsolicited mss; letter with 1–2 page
synopses welcome.
Royalties paid.

Tartarus Press

Coverley House, Carlton-in-Coverdale,
Leyburn, North Yorkshire DL8 4AY
☎01969 640399 Fax 01969 640399
Email tartarus@pavilion.co.uk
Website www.tartaruspress.com

Proprietor *Raymond Russell*
Editor *Rosalie Parker*

FOUNDED 1987. *Publishes* fiction, short stories,
reprinted classic supernatural fiction and reference books. About 12 titles a year. 'Please do not
send submissions. We cater to a small, collectable
market; we solicit the fiction we publish.'

T.C.L. Publications

14 Webbs Drive, Pembroke SA71 4FB
☎01646 685637

Managing Editor *Duncan Haws*

FOUNDED 1966 as Travel Creatours Limited
(TCL). *Publishes* nautical books only – the
Merchant Fleet series (40 vols.). 3 titles in 2000.
Unsolicited mss welcome, 'provided they are
in our standard format and subject matters'.
Royalties paid.

Tindal Street Press Ltd

217 The Custard Factory, Gibb Street,
Birmingham B9 4AA
☎0121 773 8157/8 Fax 0121 693 5525
Email ehargrave@btinternet.com
Website www.tindalstreet.org.uk

Managing Editor *Emma Hargrave*

FOUNDED in 1998 to publish contemporary
original fiction from the English regions.
Publishes original fiction only – novels and
short story anthologies. No local history, memoirs or poetry. 6 titles in 2002. Approach with
a letter, synopsis and three chapters and include
s.a.e. for return of ms.
Royalties paid.

Trafford Publishing

Suite 6E, 2333 Government Street, Victoria,
British Columbia Canada V8T 4P4
☎001 250 383 6864 Fax 001 250 383 6804
Email editorial@trafford.com
Website www.trafford.com

Managing Editor *Bruce Batchelor*

FOUNDED 1995. A self-publishing venture offering 'on-demand publishing . . . serving authors
from 28 countries'. Books are usually published
and publicised within 6 to 8 weeks. Package
price is US$990. All genres welcome. Preferred
approach by e-mail.
Royalties paid.

Tuckwell Press Ltd

The Mill House, Phantassie, East Linton,
East Lothian EH40 3DG
☎01620 860164 Fax 01620 860164
Email tuckwellpress@sol.co.uk
Website www.tuckwellpress.co.uk
Managing Director *John Tuckwell*

FOUNDED 1995. *Publishes* history, archaeology, literature, ethnology, biography, architecture, gardening history, genealogy, palaeography, with a bias towards Scottish and academic texts, also north of England. 170 titles in print. No unsolicited mss but synopses and ideas welcome if relevant to subjects covered.
Royalties paid annually.

Wakefield Historical Publications

19 Pinder's Grove, Wakefield, West Yorkshire
WF1 4AH
☎01924 372748
Email kate@airtime.co.uk
Managing Editor *Kate Taylor*

FOUNDED 1977 by the Wakefield Historical Society to publish well-researched, scholarly works of regional (namely West Riding) historical significance. 1–2 titles a year. Unsolicited mss, synopses and ideas for books welcome.
Royalties not paid.

The Waywiser Press

9 Woodstock Road, London N4 3ET
☎020 8374 5526 Fax 020 8374 5736
Email waywiser-press@aol.com
Website www.waywiser-press.com
Editor *Philip Hoy*

FOUNDED 2001. Primarily a publisher of poetry but plans to publish other genres 'from time to time'. No unsolicited mss but will consider synopses, short extracts, ideas; approach in writing only with s.a.e.
Royalties paid.

Whittles Publishing

Roseleigh House, Latheronwheel, Caithness
KW5 6DW
☎01593 741240 Fax 01593 741360
Email info@whittlespublishing.com
Website www.whittlespublishing.com
Managing Editor *Dr Keith Whittles*

Publisher in civil and structural engineering and geomatics disciplines plus nautical/marine and nature writing. Unsolicited mss, synopses and ideas welcome on appropriate themes.
Royalties paid annually.

William Ernest

See **Radikal Phase Publishing House Ltd**

Witan Books & Publishing Services

Cherry Tree House, 8 Nelson Crescent, Cotes
Heath, via Stafford ST21 6ST
☎01782 791673
Managing Editor *Jeff Kent*

FOUNDED in 1980 for self-publishing and commenced publishing other writers in 1991. *Publishes* general books, including biography, education, environment, geography, history, politics, popular music and sport. 2 titles in 2001. Witan Publishing Services, which began as an offshoot to help writers get their work into print, offers guidance, editing, proofreading, etc. Unsolicited mss, synopses and ideas welcome (include s.a.e.).
Royalties paid.

Worple Press

12 Havelock Road, Tonbridge, Kent
TN9 1JE
☎01732 367466 Fax 01732 352057
Email theworpleco.@aol.com
Managing Editors *Peter Carpenter, Amanda Knight*

FOUNDED 1997. Independent publisher specialising in poetry, art and alternative titles. 4 titles a year. No unsolicited mss. Write or phone for catalogue and flyers.
Royalties paid.

Writers' Bookshop

Remus House, Coltsfoot Drive, Woodston,
Peterborough PE2 9JX
☎01733 898103 Fax 01733 313524
Email aja@forwardpress.com
Website www.forwardpress.com
Managing Editor *Ann Johnson-Allen*

Writers' Bookshop is an imprint of Forward Press (see entry under **Poetry Presses**). *Publishes* writers' aids in the form of directories and how-to guides. Best-known annual title is the *Small Press Guide*. For further information and an author brief, call *Ann Johnson-Allen*.

Electronic Publishing and Other Services

ABCtales

PO Box 34203, London NW5 1FX
☎020 7209 2607 Fax 020 7209 2594
Email mail@abctales.com
Website www.abctales.com

Owner *Burgeon Creative Ideas Ltd*
Editor *Emily Dubberley*

FOUNDED by A. John Bird, MBE, co-founder of the *Big Issue* magazine, Tony Cook and Gordon Roddick. ABCtales is a free website and monthly print magazine dedicated to publishing and developing new writing. Content is predominantly short stories and poetry but includes interviews and lifestyle features, photo essays, reviews (games, websites, film, music) and competitions. **youngABCtales** is the sister site for children. Anyone can upload creative writing to the website; the best work is selected for paid publication in the print magazine.

Authors OnLine

See entry under **UK Publishers**

BeWrite Books

363 Badminton Road, Nibley, Bristol
BS37 5JF
☎00 334 9335 9531 (editorial base in France)
Fax 00 334 9341 3509
Email info@bewrite.net
Website www.bewrite.net

Managing Director *Cait Myers*
Editorial Director *Neil Marr*

A multi-genre publishing house FOUNDED in 1999 and especially geared toward the encouragement and publication in electronic and print formats of first-time authors. Unsolicited mss and synopses welcome (e-mail preferred). 'All offers promptly acknowledged, decisions made quickly and draft manuscript-to-publication time shorter than most other publishing houses.'

Royalties paid quarterly (no advance).

Books 4 Publishing

Lasyard House, Underhill Street, Bridgnorth, Shropshire WV16 4BB
☎01746 761298 Fax 01746 767440
Email editor@books4publishing.com

Website www.books4publishing.com
Owner *Corvedale Publishing Ltd*
Managing Director *Mark Horton-Oliver*

FOUNDED 2000. *Specialises* in helping new and unpublished authors gain recognition for their work by displaying synopses and up to 5000 words on the Books 4 Publishing website. Planning to move into e-publishing. Mss, synopses and ideas welcome; initial enquiries by e-mail or post.

Chameleon HH Publishing

The Quarry House, East End, Witney, Oxfordshire OX29 6QA
☎01993 880223 Fax 01993 880236
Email marion@chameleonhh.co.uk & david@chameleonhh.co.uk
Website www.chameleonhh.co.uk

Directors *David Hall, Marion Hazzledine*

FOUNDED 1997. CD-ROM and Web publishers on behalf of commercial publishers, institutes, associations and government bodies. Produces web-updateable CDs – CD duplication, plus all artwork undertaken. Welcomes unsolicited mss for electronic publishing from self-publishers. Consulting and advice on CD-ROM and Web publishing.

Claritybooks.com

Colt Farm, Bromley Green Road, Ashford, Kent TN26 2EQ
Email editor@claritybooks.com
Website www.claritybooks.com

Publishes in a copyright protected, encrypted electronic format. Specialises in selling to users of hand-held computers/PDAs and combined PDA/mobile phones. Will consider all fiction and non-fiction categories from literary to genre, whether full length, novella or short stories. Particularly interested in book-length collected short stories. Professional/business 'how-to' books, good health/beauty/relationship guides, computing instruction. Children's books (not illustrated), especially structured readers, young fiction including virtual reality/ alternative ending. Educational study guides, tie-ins with current exam syllabi. Humourous works. Observational/commentary on modern sexual politics, working life and times. Licence limited to e-book sales via Internet only. Author retains all other rights. No charges to authors. Free text to digital scanning service where authors unable to provide digital copy. All communication by e-mail (no attachments). State target market and brief description of work. Authors may be invited to submit sample work either electronically or on paper according to preference (send s.a.e.).

Context Limited
Grand Union House, 20 Kentish Town Road, London NW1 9NR
☎020 7267 8989 Fax 020 7267 1133
Email postmaster@context.co.uk
Website www.context.co.uk

FOUNDED 1986. Electronic publisher of UK and European legal and offical information on CD-ROM, online and the Internet. TITLE JUSTIS Cartoons CD-ROM, developed jointly with the **Centre for the Study of Cartoons and Caricature** at the University of Kent (see entry under **Library Services**), contains over 18,000 political cartoons published in British newspapers from 1912 to 1990. No unsolicited mailshots; enquiries only.

Deunant Books
PO Box 25, Denbigh LL16 5ZQ
☎01745 870259 Fax 01745 870259
Email mail@deunantbooks.com
Website www.deunantbooks.com
Managing Director Les Broad

FOUNDED 2001. Internet publisher of art, biography, children's, fiction, science fiction, politics, short story compendia, poetry, travel (in English and Welsh). 9 titles in 2001. Currently exploring the incorporation of sound and video into and alongside written works. Welcomes unsolicited material; contact by phone, post or e-mail. 'All will be replied to personally.' No technical manuals that need regular updates.
Royalties paid quarterly.

ePublish Scotland
236 Magdala Terrace, Galashiels, Selkirkshire TD1 2HT
☎01896 752109
Email info@epublish-scotland.com
Website www.epublish-scotland.com
Managing Director John Brewer

FOUNDED 1999. *Publishes* in electronic format with an emphasis on educational material. 'We wish to expand our range of products and

encourage other authors to consider distributing their work through us.' Welcomes synopses and ideas; approach by e-mail in the first instance.

Fledgling Press Limited
7 Lennox Street, Edinburgh EH4 1QB
☎0131 332 6867
Email info@fledglingpress.co.uk
Website www.fledglingpress.co.uk
Director Zander Wedderburn

FOUNDED 2000. Internet publisher, aiming to be 'a launching pad for new authors. Special interest in authentic writing about the human condition, including autobiography, diaries, poetry and fictionalised variations on these.' Monthly competition (www.canyourwrite.com) with prizes for short pieces. Also free books and reports in the areas of shiftwork and working time. Send mss and other details by e-mail from the website or by post. Currently £20 fee for mounting accepted work. Links into short-run book production.

The Good Web Guide Ltd
See entry under **UK Publishers**

The Barrie James Literary Agency (including **New Authors Showcase**)
Rivendell, Kingsgate, Torquay, Devon TQ2 8QA
☎01803 326617
Email james@newauthors.org.uk
Website www.newauthors.org.uk
Contact Barrie E. James

FOUNDED 1997. Internet site for new writers and poets to display their work to publishers. No unsolicited mss. First approach should be by sending s.a.e.

NoSpine.com
25c Fonthill Road, London N4 3HY
☎020 7281 8326 Fax 0870 052 6882
Email info@nospine.com
Website www.nospine.com
Managing Director Andrew Gardner

An electronic self-publishing venture 'designed by authors for authors'. NoSpine accepts electronic mss and arranges sales and distribution in return for a commission on each sale. Authors retain complete control over their work, full copyright, and set their own sale prices of which they retain 80%. 'We are not a vanity publisher, nor a subsidy publisher. No author ever pays us a penny: in effect we are a writers'

cooperative.' All new submissions are refereed by the founding authors to screen out unacceptable or illegal material.

Online Originals

Priory Cottage, Wordsworth Place, London NW5 4HG
☎020 7267 4244
Website www.onlineoriginals.com
Managing Director David Gettman
Commissioning Editor Dr Christopher Macann

Publishes book-length works on the Internet only. Acquires global electronic rights (including print-on-demand and digital reading) in literary fiction, intellectual non-fiction, drama, fiction for young readers (ages 8–16). No poetry, fantasy, how-to, self-help, picture books, cookery, hobbies, crafts or local interest. 20 titles in 2001. TITLES *The Seed of Joy* William Amos; *Eden Park* Craig Filleyh; *Quintet* Frederick Forsyth. Unsolicited mss, synopses and ideas for books welcome. *All* authors must have Internet access. Submissions or enquiries on paper or diskette will be discarded. Guidelines available from the website address above.
   Royalties paid annually (50% royalties on standard price of £6 or $9).

PerfectBound

See **HarperCollins Publishers Ltd** under **UK Publishers**

Puff Adder Books

35A Lower Park Road, Brightlingsea, Colchester, Essex CO7 0JX
☎01206 303607
Email books@puff-adder.com
Website www.puff-adder.com
Publisher Karen Scott

Managing Editor Diana Hayden
FOUNDED 2001. *Publishes* literary fiction, writers' guides, general non-fiction, poetry and children's fiction. 40 titles in 2001. Also operate resource websites for writers (see **Author-Network**; **New Writers Consultancy** and **Writers' Circles** under **Useful Websites at a Glance**). Welcomes unsolicited material; send query letter and synopsis by e-mail in the first instance.
   Royalties 45%.

Self Publishing

See entry under **Useful Websites at a Glance**.

StoryZone

Ryman's Cottages, Little Tew, Oxfordshire OX7 4JJ
☎0845 458 8408
Website www.storyzone.co.uk

Online children's library. The stories, both published and unpublished, are selected by subject, reading age, author or title. The first page of the stories can be previewed free of charge. Minimum charge: £5 for 5 stories.

the-phone-book.com

Enterprise House, Whitworth Street West, Manchester M1 5WG
☎0161 237 5355 Fax 0161 237 3727
Email editor@the-phone-book.com
Website www.the-phone-book.com

FOUNDED 2001. *Publishes* ultra-short fiction of less than 150 words online to website and WAP site.

Triple Hitter

See entry under **Useful Websites at a Glance**.

WritersServices

See entry under **Useful Websites at a Glance**

The Party of the First Part

Book contracts are thick with legalese. Gareth Shannon gives an expert's view on what to look for

The contract is in the post. It arrives. It's on the doormat. You can hardly wait to open the envelope. Then you see the mass of small print and the eyes glaze over. But this is the moment to be strong. The document may contain some of the most boring words ever strung together. But they represent hard cash or, for unwary readers, the needless throwing away of income.

Start with the advance. The mega-deals make headlines but are not typical. An established writer may celebrate £20,000 plus but a first-time novelist is lucky to get more than £1,000, while educational and academic writers may settle for a few hundred. A reasonable advance for all but the top names is a sum equivalent to 60 per cent of the estimated royalties payable on the first edition. The advance should be non-returnable, except when the author fails to deliver a manuscript by the due date, or if it is not in line with what was agreed with the publisher. Usually, it is split three ways, part on signature of contract, part on delivery of the manuscript and part on publication.

What proportion of the advance will be due on signature? Ideally one-third (or more if you can present a good case) with the remaining two-thirds due on delivery and publication respectively. If you have a contract for several books, check whether all of the advance money will be added together and sit against future royalties from all books, or whether each book will be separately accounted for against its portion of the advance. Make sure the contract is clear on this point.

A popular misconception is that if an advance is not recovered by royalties on sales, in other words if there is an unearned advance, the publisher is bound to lose money. But the correlation between royalties and profit is not precise. A typical royalty is 10 per cent of the sale price of the book; a publisher's margin may be 15 or 20 per cent after overheads and trade discount are taken into account. It is possible, therefore, for an unearned advance to be absorbed into costs with the publisher still coming out at a profit. It all depends on the size of the advance, the level of sales and the publisher's margin over fixed costs. There are too many variables to produce a general rule. Just do not be too quick to assume that the publisher loses out.

Another unsafe assumption is that advances are bound to be higher if negotiated by an agent. This may be so for best-selling authors who put their work up for auction but down the scale there may not be much room for manoeuvre. Where an agent really proves his worth is in knowing the pitfalls of a publishing contract and helping his client to avoid them.

Much is written about royalties and what you can expect. In addition to *The Writer's Handbook*, both the Society of Authors and the Writers' Guild have a helpful advisory service for members, which can be used to gauge the fairness of an offer. Royalties – like the advance – are usually the first items to be agreed, even before there is sight of a contract, so find out as much as you can before saying yes. The rest of the contract follows the agent–publisher boilerplate, if there is one, with exceptional items held open for negotiation. It is likely that you can improve a contract significantly with some research and a little negotiation. No serious publisher is going to withdraw an offer to publish if you do not agree by return. Indeed, everyone expects that there will have to be some movement between an opening offer and the terms of a final signed contract. What is needed is an understanding of what it is reasonable to ask and what makes a changed offer worth accepting.

The writer who handles his own affairs is not entirely alone. After years of vigorous campaigning, the writers' unions have negotiated Minimum Terms Agreements (MTA) with several leading publishers. A copy of the standard MTA, which can be obtained from either the Society of Authors or the Writers' Guild (free of charge to members who send a stamped, addressed envelope), is a useful benchmark against which to judge a publisher's offer, though the standard MTA is to some extent a counsel of perfection. When it comes to signing on the dotted line, you may feel you have had to give way on a few points, but if the general principles of the MTA are followed, the chances of securing a reasonable deal are much enhanced.

Before looking at some of the major subsidiary rights deals it's worth stating an obvious truism that 'no two books are perceived equally'. One book hits its target market without any great effort on the part of publisher or author while another is declared out of print and appears now and then in one of those 'What I wish I had published' columns in the trade press, but which no one seems eager to reissue despite singing its praises. Yet another title appeals to the US market and the right to publish it there is sold for a small fortune, while many others, despite everyone's best efforts, slip further down the list of available titles at each passing book fair. What follows is a few guiding principles to deals which may, in the right circumstances, be relevant to your book.

Serial rights

For the right book, serialisation in a national newspaper can be one of the most lucrative rights to be exercised. Serialisation of extracts prior to the book's publication (first serial rights) is more lucrative than any press follow-up (second serial rights). Obviously the book must strike some chord with the newspaper – either from a similarity in philosophy, or because its subject would be of more than passing interest to its readers. Most agents jealously guard these rights but when they are controlled by the publisher the following splits in revenue are typical: first serial rights may be divided as high as 90:10 in the author's favour, while second serial rights are usually 75:25. The days of the political memoir and its accompanying big-money newspaper serial deal may have passed but there is still a sale to targeted markets both in the UK and overseas. Fees can range from a few hundred pounds to a hundred thousand plus. Anything that throws new light on people or events in the news will command higher fees. But don't expect to get the money by the first post. The contract may well specify that any earnings on serialisation must be set against the advance.

US rights

This has always been seen as the most important market for many books, yet there is still no easy route to achieving success in the US. In an ideal world, the US publisher will pay an advance and royalty to the UK publisher which is then shared with the author. A successful author – if not represented by an agent – might receive 85 per cent of this income, while a less well-known writer might receive around 60 per cent. Often, though, this is not the whole story. One publishing firm might have a successful track record of selling rights in the US and offer no more than 75 per cent of these proceeds to its authors. On the other hand, a newly formed company with no obvious connections might happily offer 85 per cent though with no realistic chance that these rights will be sold. If pressed to grant these rights to a publisher, there is nothing to be lost by asking about its experience in the US market. But don't forget that 60 or 75 per cent of something is better than holding on to the rights and then not exploiting them.

There are other deals where printed copies are sold to a US publisher at a fixed price. Under this type of arrangement, a book priced at £18 in the UK might be sold for around £5 with consequently little return for the publisher or the author. These situations are very similar to the co-edition market for illustrated books. Why do it, then? It's not the first choice but it is a way to present books to the US market and to try to build up recognition of both publisher and author. The author can expect 7.5 to 10 per cent of the publisher's income from this type of deal, the sums varying according to whether bound or unbound copies are sold.

Translation rights

A large market in Spanish and German-speaking countries for rights to works in English is frequently overlooked by authors. Deals tend to be on an advance and royalty basis, though small companies in emerging markets may try for a flat fee. An author can expect 75 to 80 per cent of any proceeds. Some agents and publishers use local agents for translation deals which means more commission deducted from any sums due to the author. Working alone, translation can be a leap of faith for an author who has no knowledge of overseas publishers, but a little research on the company's website, or a query to a local online writers' discussion group, can pay dividends.

Electronic verbatim text rights

The current theory is that this will one day be a lucrative source of income, although events have not seen this borne out so far. Most publishers now expect to be granted some form of electronic text right when they acquire a book and it pays to do some research on how near they are to exploiting these rights. There is little point in either an author or publisher controlling rights which they are not capable of exploiting fully.

Only a few years ago, it looked as though content providers (authors and publishers) would be able to license their works to websites and make a small fortune from such sales. Today, this idea seems to have vanished as most of the Internet's sites do not require any payment and the received wisdom is that this so-called 'free distribution' model is here to stay. Not everyone agrees, though. Leading newspapers are beginning to charge users to access areas of their sites. If anything the recent downturn in fortunes of this new economy might persuade site owners that a combination of free and paid access is the only way to survive. Then there are the large portal sites such as Yahoo! or BTInternet which can only survive by offering users content on a wide variety of subjects. Many of these portal sites will not pay for content while some expect the publisher to pay to make the material available. The argument is that it is a form of marketing for the publisher and there should be money available in a marketing budget for this showcasing. In these cases, there is precious little return for authors unless it is from increased book sales, although there should be the chance of commissions from content teams attached to a site. These content teams are the editorial hub of a website and are responsible for writing and commissioning the content that appears on it. Many of these teams have newspaper or magazine backgrounds so will be used to newspaper or magazine fee scales and writers should price their work accordingly. This market may be static at present but as sites are redesigned and new ones form it is likely that it will take off again. Those writers who have bothered to keep up to date with such developments will be in a good position to be first in with their work.

Gareth Shannon is Senior Consultant at Roger Palmer Limited Media Contracts. Previously he was Rights Manager at IPC Media Ltd, the magazine publisher, which he joined after five years as Assistant General Secretary at the Society of Authors.

For further reading and research investigate the websites of some of the US talent unions, e.g. www.nwu.org or www.asja.org. The Society of Authors' quarterly journal The Author *often analyses current issues in authors' contracts, supplementing the material contained in its* Quick Guide *series of booklets. Though written from the point of view of a publisher's rights department, Lynette Owen's book* Selling Rights *(fourth edition, Routledge, 2001) contains a wealth of background information that helps to put offered terms into economic perspective.*

Useful Websites at a Glance

Many of these and other useful websites for writers can be found in *The Internet for Writers* by Nick Daws (ISBN 1-84025-308-8), one of a series of books published by Internet Handbooks and *The Incredibly Indispensable Web Directory* by Clive and Bettina Zietman, published by Kogan Page (ISBN 0-7494-3617-4).

AbeBooks
www.abebooks.co.uk
The merging of AbeBooks and JustBooks in February 2002 has resulted in a second-hand and antiquarian online bookshop with over 35 million titles offered by nearly 10,000 book-sellers worldwide.

Academi (Welsh Academy/Yr Academi Gymreig)
www.academi.org
News of events, publications and funding for Welsh-based literary events. (See entry under **Professional Associations and Societies**.)

Alibris
www.alibris.com
Used, foreign, rare and out-of-print books online.

Alliance of Literary Societies
www.sndc.demon.co.uk/als.htm
Details of societies and events. (See entry under **Professional Associations and Societies**.)

Amazon Bookshop
www.amazon.co.uk
A wide range of online shopping, including books, music, videos and electronics. Access to more than 1.5 million UK published titles.

Ancestry
www.ancestry.com
Family history information – databases, articles and other sources of genealogical data.

The Arts Council of England
www.artscouncil.org.uk
Includes information on funding applications, publications and the National Lottery. (See entry under **Arts Councils and Regional Arts Board**s.)

Arvon Foundation
www.arvonfoundation.org

Information on the three Arvon centres in the UK. (See entry under **Writers' Courses, Circles and Workshops**.)

Association for Scottish Literary Studies
www.asls.org.uk
The educational charity promoting the languages and literature of Scotland. (See entry under **Professional Associations and Societies**.)

Association of Authors' Agents (AAA)
www.agentsassoc.co.uk
UK agents' organisation including list of current members. (See entry under **Professional Associations and Societies**.)

Association of Authors' Representatives (AAR)
www.aar-online.org
US agents' organisation including list of current members. (See entry under **Professional Associations and Societies**.)

Authors' Licensing and Collecting Society (ALCS)
www.alcs.co.uk
Details of membership, news, publications, legal issues and rights, plus links to related sites. (See entry under **Professional Associations and Societies**.)

Author-Network
www.author-network.com
Writers' resource site, operated by **Puff Adder Books**.

Author-Publisher Network
www.author.co.uk
Services for writers, information network, newsletter and online magazine. (See entry under **Professional Associations and Societies**.)

BBC
www.bbc.co.uk
Access to all BBC departments and services.

bibliofind
www.bibliofind.com
Over 20 million second-hand and rare books, periodicals and ephemera for sale online.

BOL
www.bol.com
Internet shopping, including books and music; a database of over 1.5 million titles.

Book2Book
www.book2book.co.uk
Established by a group of publishers, booksellers, website developers and trade journalists to provide up-to-date news, features and useful information for the book trade.

Booktrust
www.booktrust.org.uk
Book information service, guide to prizes and awards, links to other book organisations, factsheets for writers. (See entry under **Professional Associations and Societies**.)

British Association of Picture Libraries and Agencies (BAPLA)
www.bapla.org.uk
Free telephone referrals available from the BAPLA database through this website. (See entry under **Professional Associations and Societies**.)

British Centre for Literary Translation
www.literarytranslation.com
A joint website with the British Council containing workshops by leading translators, contacts and networks, and listings of translation conferences, seminars and events. (See entry under **Professional Associations and Societies**.)

British Council
www.britishcouncil.org
Information on the Council's English Language services, education programmes, science and health links, and information exchange. (See entry under **Professional Associations and Societies**.)

British Film Institute (bfi)
www.bfi.org.uk
Information on the services offered by the Institute. (See entry under **Professional Associations and Societies**.)

British Library
www.bl.uk
Reader service enquiries, access to main catalogues, information on collections, links to the various Reading Rooms and exhibitions. (See related entries under **Library Services**.)

Children's Writing Resource Center
www.write4kids.com
US website for children's writers', whether published or beginners. Includes special reports, advice, chat links, news on the latest bestsellers and links to related sites.

CILIP
www.cilip.org.uk
The professional body for librarians and information professionals. (See entry under **Professional Associations and Societies**.)

Complete Works of William Shakespeare
the-tech.mit.edu/Shakespeare/works.html
Access to the text of the complete works with search facility, quotations and discussion pages.

Copyright Advice and Anti-Piracy Hotline   www.copyright-info.org
Copyright advice and information. (See entry under **Professional Associations and Societies**.)

Copyright Licensing Agency Ltd (CLA)   www.cla.co.uk
Copyright information, customer support and information on CLA services. (See entry under **Professional Associations and Societies**.)

Crime Writers' Association (CWA)
www.thecwa.co.uk
Website of the professional crime writers' association. (See entry under **Professional Associations and Societies**.)

Daily Mirror
www.mirror.co.uk
The *Daily Mirror* newspaper online.

Dictionary of Slang
dictionaryofslang.co.uk
A guide to slang 'from a British perspective'. Research information; search facility.

The Eclectic Writer
www.eclectics.com/writing/writing.html
US website offering a selection of articles on

advice for writers on topics such as 'Proper Manuscript Format', 'Electronic Publishing', 'How to Write a Synopsis' and 'Motivation'. Also a Character Chart for fiction writers and an online discussion board.

Electronic Telegraph
www.telegraph.co.uk
The Daily Telegraph online – one of the first UK national newspapers to establish itself on the web.

Encyclopædia Britannica
www.eb.com
A subscription access to the entire *Encyclopædia Britannica* database as well as Merriam-Webster's *Collegiate Dictionary* and the *Britannica Book of the Year*. (A 30-day free trial is available.) EB online gives links to more than 130,000 sites selected, rated and reviewed by Britannica editors.

The English Association
www.le.ac.uk/engassoc
News, publications, conference and membership information. (See entry under **Professional Associations and Societies**.)

Federation of Worker Writers and Community Publishers (FWWCP)
www.thefwwcp.d4f.net
Links to members of the FWWCP, the Federation magazine, information on membership. (See entry under **Professional Associations and Societies**.)

Film Angel
www.filmangel.co.uk
Established in March 2000 by Hammerwood Films to create a shop window for writers and would-be film angels. Writers submit a short synopsis which can be displayed for a predetermined period, for a fee; would-be angels are invited to finance a production of their choice.

Filmmaker Store
www.filmmakerstore.com
Scriptwriting resources, listings and advice.

Financial Times
www.ft.com
Financial Times online.

Great Books Online
www.bartleby.com
An ever-expanding list of great books published online for reference, free of charge.

The Guardian
www.guardian.co.uk
Website of *The Guardian* and *The Observer* newspapers online.

Guide to Grammar and Style
www.andromeda.rutgers.edu/~jlynch/Writing
A guide to grammar and style which is organised alphabetically, plus articles and links to other grammatical reference sites.

Hansard
www.parliament.the-stationery-office.co.uk/pa/cm/cmhansrd.htm
The official record of debates and written answers in the House of Commons. The transcript of each day's business appears at noon on the following weekday.

House of Commons Research Library
www.parliament.uk/commons/lib/research/rpintro.htm
Gives access to the text of research reports prepared for MPs on a wide range of current issues.

HTML Writers Guild
www.hwg.org
US organisation offering resources, support, representation and education for web authors. (See entry under **Professional Associations and Societies**.)

The Independent
www.independent.co.uk
The Independent newspaper online.

Ingenta
www.ingenta.com
Established in 1998, Ingenta is the largest online academic research service in the UK. Formed through a public/private partnership with the University of Bath, the site offers 'free searching of millions of academic and professional articles from thousands of journals online'.

Institute of Linguists
www.iol.org.uk
Discussion forum, news on regional societies, job opportunities, 'Find a Linguist' service, and *The Linguist* magazine. (See entry under **Professional Associations and Societies**.)

Institute of Translation and Interpreting (ITI)
www.iti.org.uk
Website of the professional association of trans-

lators and interpreters, with the ITI Directory, publications, training and membership information. (See entry under **Professional Associations and Societies**.)

International Movie Database
www.imdb.com
Essential resource for film buffs and researchers with search engine for cast lists, screenwriters, directors and producers; film and television news, awards, film preview information, video releases.

Internet Bookshop
www.bookshop.co.uk
Online bookshop with 1.4 million UK and US titles.

Internet Classics Archive
classics.mit.edu
Includes 441 works of classical literature by 59 different authors. Mostly Greek and Roman works with some Chinese and Persian. All are in English translation

Journalism UK
www.journalismuk.co.uk
A website for UK-based journalists who write for text-based publications. Includes links to newspapers, magazines, e-zines, news sources plus information on jobs, training and organisations.

The Library Association
See **CILIP**

Mr William Shakespeare and the Internet
daphne.palomar.edu/Shakespeare
Guide to scholarly Shakespeare resources on the Internet.

National Union of Journalists (NUJ)
www.gn.apc.org/media
Represents those journalists who work in all sectors of publishing, print and broadcasting. (See entry under **Professional Associations and Societies**.)

New Writers Consultancy
www.new-writers-consultancy.com
Advice for writers and critiques, offered by Diana Hayden and Karen Scott of **Puff Adder Books**.

New Writing North
www.newwritingnorth.com
Essentially for writers based in the north of

England but also a useful source of advice and guidelines.

Novel Advice Newsletter
www.noveladvice.com
A free US journal aimed at the fiction writer; full text of current and past issues online.

PEN
www.pen.org.uk
Website of the English Centre of International PEN. News of events, membership details. (See entry under **Professional Associations and Societies**.)

PlaysOnTheNet
www.playsonthenet.com
Information and help for new playwrights. Launched in association with **Oneword Radio** in January 2002, the site offers the chance to get involved, whether as a writer or someone who enjoys reading and listening to new plays. The site features new works that can be downloaded.

Poets and Writers Online
www.pw.org
A US site containing publishing advice, a directory of writers, online bookstore, literary links, news, articles on aspects of writing, grants and awards.

Producers Alliance for Cinema and Television (PACT)
www.pact.co.uk
Publications, jobs in the industry, production companies, membership details. (See entry under **Professional Associations and Societies**.)

Publishers Association
www.publishers.org.uk
Information about the Association and careers in publishing; also 'Getting Published' pages. (See entry under **Professional Associations and Societies**.)

Pure Fiction
www.purefiction.com
Described as 'the website for anybody who loves to read – or aspires to write – bestselling fiction'. Contains book reviews, writing advice, a writers' showcase and an online bookshop.

Relax With a Book
www.relaxwithabook.com
Reviews, author interviews and competitions online.

Royal Society of Literature
www.rslit.org
Information on lectures, discussions and readings; membership details and prizes. (See entry under **Professional Associations and Societies**.)

Science Fiction Foundation Collection
www.liv.ac.uk/~asawyer/sffchome.html
The research library of the Science Fiction Foundation, based at the University of Liverpool. Includes links to the Foundation, the John Wyndham archive, the Foundation's journal and other SF collections and associations. (See entry under **Library Services**.)

Scottish Arts Council
www.sac.org.uk
Information on funding and events; 'Image of the Month' and 'Poem of the Month'. (See entry under Arts Councils and Regional Arts Boards.)

Scottish Book Trust
www.scottishbooktrust.com
Information on the Trust's activities and a link to their Book Information Service. (See entry under **Professional Associations and Societies**.)

Scottish Library Association
www.slainte.org.uk
Links to various services and major Scottish websites and information on people, organisations, libraries, events and resources of Scottish interest. (See entry under **Professional Associations and Societies**.)

Scottish Publishers Association
www.scottishbooks.org
Links to websites of members of the Association, information on activities and publications. (See entry under **Professional Associations and Societies**.)

Screenwriters and Playwrights Home Page
www.teleport.com/~cdeemer/scrwriter.html
A website resource for scriptwriters, maintained by US screenwriter Charles Deemer. Links to a discussion forum and 'Screenwright', an electronic screenwriting course.

Screenwriters Online
screenwriter.com/insider/news.html
Described as the '*only* professional screenwriter's site run by major screenwriters who get their scripts and screenplays made into movies'. Contains screenplay analysis, expert articles and *The Insider Report*.

Self Publishing
www.SelfPublishing.co.uk
Established to allow writers to advertise their books on the Internet. Mostly of appeal to self-published authors but open to everyone by publishing a 'taster' of one chapter of a novel or equivalent for other books.

Society for Freelance Editors and Proofreaders (SFEP)
www.sfep.org.uk
Basic information about the Society. (See entry under **Professional Associations and Societies**.)

Society of Authors
www.societyofauthors.org
Includes FAQs for new writers, diary of events, membership details, links to publishers' and other societies' websites. (See entry under **Professional Associations and Societies**.)

Society of Indexers
www.socind.demon.co.uk
Indexing information for publishers and authors, 'Electronic Indexers Available' pages. Membership information. (See entry under **Professional Associations and Societies**.)

South Bank Centre, London
www.sbc.org.uk
Links to the Royal Festival Hall, the Hayward Gallery and Poetry Library; news of literature events.

The Sun
www.the-sun.co.uk
Website of *The Sun* newspaper.

The Times
www.thetimes.co.uk
Website of *The Times* newspaper.

trAce Online Writing Centre
www.trace.ntu.ac.uk
Based at Nottingham Trent University, trAce is an online centre for writers and readers worldwide to share and critique their work, discuss favourite books and talk. Also holds occasional (live) conferences and workshops. Links to a wide range of sites for writers.

Triple Hitter
www.triplehitter.net
New website dedicated to 'aiding aspiring writers in obtaining their big break' by showcasing their work free of charge. Includes various interviews, links and helpful hints.

UK Children's Books Directory
www.ukchildrensbooks.co.uk
A directory of the online world of children's books.

The Arts Council of Wales
www.ccc-acw.org.uk
Information on publications, council meetings, the arts in Wales. Links to other arts websites. (See entry under **Arts Councils and Regional Arts Boards**.)

The Web Writer
www.geocities.com/Athens/Parthenon/8390/TOC.htm
A site for writers who want to write for publication on the web. Information and advice includes getting online, choosing a computer, saving money on your PC, dealing with Windows, software information, researching online, how to build a website, writing for the web, website issues.

Webster Dictionary/Thesaurus
www.m-w.com/home.htm
Merriam-Webster Online. Includes a search facility for words in the *Webster Dictionary* or *Webster Thesaurus*; word games, 'Word of the Day' and Language Info Zone.

Welsh Academy – see **Academi**

Welsh Books Council (Cyngor Llyfrau Cymru)
www.cllc.org.uk *and* www.gwales.com
Information about books from Wales, editorial and design services, 'Wales Book Day'. (See entry under **Professional Associations and Societies**.)

The Word Pool
www.wordpool.co.uk
Children's book review site with information on writing for children and a thriving discussion group for children's writers.

Word Pool Design
www.wordpooldesign.co.uk
Web design for writers, illustrators and publishers. 'Friendly advice and help from people who understand the world of books.'

WordCounter
www.wordcounter.com
Highlights the most frequently used words in a given text. Use as a guide to see what words are overused.

Writers' Guild of Great Britain
www.writersguild.org.uk
A wide range of information including rates of pay, articles on topics such as copyright, news, writers' resources and industry regulations. (See entry under **Professional Associations and Societies**.)

Writers, Artists and their Copyright Holders (WATCH)
www.watch-file.com
Database of copyright holders in the UK and North America. (See entry under **Professional Associations and Societies**.)

Writers' Circles
www.writers-circles.com
Offers free pages to writers' circles. Listings and information. Operated by **Puff Adder Books**.

Writernet
www.writernet.org.uk
Formerly New Playwrights Trust. Information, advice and guidance for writers on all aspects of the live and recorded performance.

WritersNet
www.writers.net
A directory of writers, editors, publishers and literary agents.

WritersServices
www.WritersServices.com
Established in March 2000 by Chris Holifield, former deputy MD and publisher at Cassell. Offers factsheets, book reviews, advice, links and other resources for writers including editorial services, contract vetting and self-publishing. (Enquiries to: info@writersservices.com)

UK Packagers

Aladdin Books Ltd
28 Percy Street, London W1T 2BZ
☎020 7323 3319 Fax 020 7323 4829
Managing Director *Charles Nicholas*

FOUNDED in 1979 as a packaging company but with joint publishing ventures in the UK and USA. *Commissions* children's fully illustrated, non-fiction reference books. About 40 titles a year. IMPRINTS **Aladdin Books** *Bibby Whittaker* Children's reference; **Nicholas Enterprises** *Charles Nicholas* Adult non-fiction; **The Learning Factory** *Charles Nicholas* Early learning concepts 0–4 years. TITLES *Encyclopedia of Awesome Dinosaurs; The Atlas of Animals*. Will consider synopses and ideas for children's non-fiction with international sales potential only. No fiction.
Fees usually paid instead of royalties.

The Albion Press Ltd
Spring Hill, Idbury, Oxfordshire OX7 6RU
☎01993 831094 Fax 01993 831982
Chairman/Managing Director *Emma Bradford*

FOUNDED 1984. *Commissions* illustrated trade titles, particularly children's. About 4 titles a year. TITLES *From a Distance* Jane Ray and Julie Gold; *The Little Mermaid and other Fairy Stories* Isabelle Brent. Unsolicited synopses and ideas for books not welcome.
Royalties paid; fees paid for introductions and partial contributions.

Alphabet & Image Ltd
See **Marston House** under **UK Publishers**

Amber Books Ltd
Bradleys Close, 74–77 White Lion Street, London N1 9PF
☎020 7520 7600 Fax 020 7520 7606/7
Email enquiries@amberbooks.co.uk
Website www.amberbooks.co.uk
Managing Director *Stasz Gnych*
Publishing Manager *Judith Samuelson*

FOUNDED 1989. *Commissions* military, aviation, transport, sport, combat, survival and fitness, naval history, crime and general reference. 40–50 titles in 2001. No fiction, cookery, gardening or lifestyle. IMPRINT **Brown Books**. No unsolicited material.
Fees paid.

Archival Facsimiles Limited
The Old Bakery, 52 Crown Street, Banham, Norwich, Norfolk NR16 2HW
☎01953 887277 Fax 01953 888361
Email erskpres@aol.com
Website www.erskine-press.com
Chief Executive *Crispin de Boos*

FOUNDED 1986. Specialist private publishers for individuals and organisations. Produces scholarly reprints and limited editions for academic/business organisations in Europe and the USA, ranging from leather-bound folios of period print reproductions to small illustrated booklets. Under the **Erskine Press** imprint *publishes* books on Antarctic exploration, general interest autobiographies and medical related 'Patient's Guides' (*Hip & Knee Replacement; Chronic Fatigue Syndrome*). No unsolicited mss. Ideas welcome.
Royalties paid twice-yearly.

AS Publishing
73 Montpelier Rise, London NW11 9DU
☎020 8458 3552 Fax 020 8458 0618
Managing Director *Angela Sheehan*

FOUNDED 1987. *Commissions* children's illustrated non-fiction. No unsolicited synopses or ideas for books, but approaches welcome from experienced authors, editors and illustrators in this field.
Fees paid.

BCS Publishing Ltd
2nd Floor, Temple Court, 109 Oxford Road, Cowley, Oxford OX4 2ER
☎01865 770099 Fax 01865 770050
Email bcs-publishing@dial.pipex.com
Managing Director *Steve McCurdy*
Approx. Annual Turnover £200,000

Commissions general interest non-fiction for the international co-edition market.

Bender Richardson White
PO Box 266, Uxbridge, Middlesex UB9 5BD
☎01895 832444 Fax 01895 835213
Email brw@brw.co.uk
Partners *Lionel Bender, Kim Richardson,
Ben White*
FOUNDED 1990 to produce illustrated non-fiction for children, adults and family reference for publishers in the UK and abroad. 40 titles in 2001. Unsolicited material not welcome.
Fees paid.

Book Packaging and Marketing
3 Murswell Lane, Silverstone, Towcester,
Northamptonshire NN12 8UT
☎01327 858380 Fax 01327 858380
Email martin@marixevans.freeserve.co.uk
Contact *Martin F. Marix Evans*
FOUNDED 1989. Essentially a project management service, handling books demanding close designer/editor teamwork or complicated multi-contributor administration, for publishers, business 'or anyone who needs one'. Mainly illustrated adult non-fiction including military, travel, historical, home reference and coffee-table books. No fiction or poetry. 5–8 titles a year. Proposals considered but rarely come to fruition; most books are bespoke by publishers. Additional writers are sometimes required for projects in development. TITLES *The Fall of France 1940*; *Contemporary Photographers*, 3rd ed.; *The Vital Guide To Major Battles of World War II*; *The Battles of the Somme 1916–18*; *The Military Heritage of Britain and Ireland*; *Passchendale and the Battle of Ypres*; *American Voices of World War I*.
Payment Authors contract direct with client publishers; fees paid on first print usually and royalties on reprint but this depends on publisher.

Breslich & Foss Ltd
20 Wells Mews, London W1T 3HQ
☎020 7580 8774 Fax 020 7580 8784
Email sales@breslichfoss.com
Directors *Paula Breslich, K.B. Dunning*
Approx. Annual Turnover £1 million
Packagers of non-fiction titles only, including art, children's, crafts, gardening and health. Unsolicited mss welcome but synopses preferred. Include s.a.e. with all submissions.
Royalties paid twice-yearly.

Brown Books
See **Amber Books Ltd**

Brown Wells and Jacobs Ltd
Forresters Hall, 25–27 Westow Street, London
SE19 3RY
☎020 8771 5115 Fax 020 8771 9994
Email postmaster@popking.demon.co.uk
Website www.bwj.org
Managing Director *Graham Brown*
FOUNDED 1979. *Commissions* non-fiction, novelty, pre-school and first readers, natural history and science. About 40 titles a year. Unsolicited synopses and ideas for books welcome. *Fees* paid.

Cameron Books (Production) Ltd
PO Box 1, Moffat, Dumfriesshire DG10 9SU
☎01683 220808 Fax 01683 220012
Email info@cameronbooks.co.uk
Website www.cameronbooks.co.uk
Directors *Ian A. Cameron, Jill Hollis*
Approx. Annual Turnover £400,000
Commissions contemporary art, film, design, collectors' reference, natural history, social history, decorative arts, architecture, gardening and cookery. About 6 titles a year. Unsolicited synopses and ideas for books welcome.
Payment varies with each contract.

Chancerel International Publishers Ltd
120 Long Acre, London WC2E 9ST
☎020 7240 2811 Fax 020 7836 4186
Email chancerel@chancerel.com
Website www.chancerel.com
Managing Director *W.D.B. Prowse*
FOUNDED 1976. *Commissions* and *publishes* language-teaching materials in English, German, French, Spanish, Italian and Japanese. Language teachers/writers often required as authors/consultants, especially native speakers other than English. *Payment* generally by flat fee but royalties sometimes.

Compendium Publishing Ltd
See entry under **UK Publishers**

Roger Coote Publishing
Gissing's Farm, Fressingfield, Eye, Suffolk
IP21 5SH
☎01379 588044 Fax 01379 588055
Email rgc@ndirect.co.uk
Director *Roger Goddard-Coote*
FOUNDED 1993. Packager of children's and adult non-fiction for trade, school and library markets. About 40 titles a year. No fiction. Include s.a.e. for return.
Fees paid; no royalties.

Diagram Visual Information Ltd

195 Kentish Town Road, London
NW5 2JU
☎020 7482 3633 Fax 020 7482 4932
Email diagramvis@aol.com

Managing Director *Bruce Robertson*

FOUNDED 1967. Producer of library, school, academic and trade reference books. About 10 titles a year. Unsolicited synopses and ideas for books welcome.

Fees paid; no payment for sample material/ submissions for consideration.

Direct Image Publishing

Beckside, Lindale, Grange over Sands, Cumbria LA11 6NA
☎015395 33443 Fax 015395 35794
Email elaine@directimageprod.demon.co.uk
Website www.directimageprod.co.uk

Co-directors *Chris Ware, Elaine Ware*

A sub-division of Direct Image Productions Ltd. FOUNDED in 1992 to support video training programmes. Two key areas: outdoor education; complimentary therapies. Builds training programmes and publishes teachers' resource material, usually as part of a video and book package. No unsolicited mss; approach with letter and outline of idea in the first instance.

Payment One-off fee paid.

Duncan Petersen Publishing Limited

See entry under **UK Publishers**

Eddison Sadd Editions

St Chad's House, 148 King's Cross Road, London WC1X 9DH
☎020 7837 1968 Fax 020 7837 2025
Email reception@eddisonsadd.co.uk

Managing Director *Nick Eddison*
Editorial Director *Ian Jackson*
Approx. Annual Turnover £3 million

FOUNDED 1982. Produces a wide range of popular illustrated non-fiction – mind, body, spirit and complementary therapies are particular strengths – with books published in 25 countries. Ideas and synopses are welcome but titles must have international appeal.

Royalties paid twice yearly; flat fees paid when appropriate.

Erskine Press

See **Archival Facsimiles Limited**

Expert Publications Ltd

Sloe House, Halstead, Essex CO9 1PA
☎01787 474744 Fax 01787 474700
Email expert@lineone.net

Chairman *Dr. D.G. Hessayon*

FOUNDED 1993. Produces the *Expert* series of books by Dr. D.G. Hessayon. Currently 21 titles in the series, including *The NEW Flower Expert*; *The Evergreen Expert*; *The Vegetable & Herb Expert*; *The Flowering Shrub Expert*; *The Container Expert*. No unsolicited material.

Haldane Mason Ltd

59 Chepstow Road, London W2 5BP
☎020 7792 2123 Fax 020 7221 3965
Email haldane.mason@dial.pipex.com

FOUNDED 1994. *Commissions* adult and children's illustrated non-fiction and young children's fiction. Adult list consists mainly of mind, body and spirit plus alternative health books under the Neals' Yard Remedies banner; children's age range 0–11. 20 titles in 2001. Unsolicited synopses and ideas welcome; approach in writing in the first instance. No adult fiction.

Fees paid.

Angus Hudson Ltd

Concorde House, Grenville Place, Mill Hill, London NW7 3SA
☎020 8959 3668 Fax 020 8959 3678
Email coed@angushudson.com

Managing Director *Nicholas Jones*
Approx. Annual Turnover £3.5 million

FOUNDED 1977. Leading packager of religious co-editions. *Commissions* Christian books for all ages and co-editioning throughout the world. About 150 titles a year. Publishes under **Candle Books** and **Monarch Books** (see entry under **UK Publishers**) imprints. Prototype dummies complete with illustrations welcome for consideration. Synopses for text books welcome; no unsolicited mss, please.

Royalties paid.

The Ilex Press Limited

The Old Candlemakers, West Street, Lewes, East Sussex BN7 2NZ
☎01273 487440 Fax 01273 487441
Email [surname]@ilexpress.co.uk

Managing Director *Sophie Collins*

FOUNDED 1999. Sister company of **The Ivy Press Limited**. *Commissions* titles on digital art, design and photography as well as on all aspects of website design and graphics software.

No fiction. Unsolicited synopses and ideas welcome; send a brief idea outline (3 or 4 pages) and a letter.
Fees paid.

The Ivy Press Limited
The Old Candlemakers, West Street, Lewes, East Sussex BN7 2NZ
☎01273 487440 Fax 01273 487441
Email [surname]@ivypress.co.uk
Managing Director *Sophie Collins*
FOUNDED 1996. Sister company of **The Ilex Press Limited**. *Commissions* illustrated non-fiction books covering subjects such as art, health, self-help, mind, body and spirit, and general reference. No fiction. 60 titles in 2001. Unsolicited synopses and ideas welcome; send a brief idea outline (3 or 4 pages) and a letter.
Fees paid.

The Learning Factory
See **Aladdin Books Ltd**

Lexus Ltd
60 Brook Street, Glasgow G40 4AB
☎0141 556 0440 Fax 0141 556 2202
Email pt@lexus.win-uk.net
Managing/Editorial Director *P.M. Terrell*
FOUNDED 1980. Compiles bilingual reference, language and phrase books. About 5 titles a year. TITLES *Rough Guide Phrasebooks; Harrap Study Aids; Hugo's Phrase Books; Oxford Italian Pocket Dictionary; Langenscheidt Chinese, Japanese, Korean* and *Vietnamese Dictionaries; Impact Specialist Bilingual Glossaries; Oxford Student's Japanese Learner.* No unsolicited material. Books are mostly commissioned. Freelance contributors employed for a wide range of languages.
Payment generally flat fee.

Lionheart Books
10 Chelmsford Square, London NW10 3AR
☎020 8459 0453 Fax 020 8451 3681
Email Lionheart.Brw@btinternet.com
Senior Partner *Lionel Bender*
Partner *Madeleine Samuel*
A design/editorial packaging team. Titles are primarily commissioned from publishers. Highly illustrated non-fiction for children aged 8–14, mostly natural history, history and general science. About 20 titles a year.
Payment generally flat fee.

Market House Books Ltd
2 Market House, Market Square, Aylesbury, Buckinghamshire HP20 1TN
☎01296 484911 Fax 01296 437073
Website www.mhbref.com
Directors *Dr Alan Isaacs, Dr John Daintith, Peter Sapsed*
FOUNDED 1970. Formerly Laurence Urdang Associates. Compiles dictionaries, encyclopedias and reference. About 15 titles a year. TITLES *Oxford Concise Medical Dictionary; Oxford Dictionary for Science Writers and Editors; Oxford Dictionary of Accounting; Bloomsbury Thesaurus; Larousse Thematica* (6 volume encyclopedia); *Collins English Dictionary; The Macmillan Encyclopedia; Grolier Bibliographical Encyclopedia of Scientists* (10 vols); *Oxford Paperback Encyclopedia; Penguin Biographical Dictionary of Women; Penguin Dictionary of Plant Sciences; New Penguin Dictionary of the Theatre; The Macmillan Dictionary of Philosophy; The Macmillan Dictionary of Phrase and Fable.* Unsolicited material not welcome as most books are compiled in-house.
Fees paid.

Marshall Editions Ltd
See **Quarto Publishing**

Monkey Puzzle Media Ltd
Gissing's Farm, Fressingfield, Eye, Suffolk IP21 5SH
☎01379 588044 Fax 01379 588055
Email rgc@ndirect.co.uk
Chairman/Managing Director *Roger Goddard-Coote*
Editorial Director *Edwina Conner*
FOUNDED 1998. Packager of adult and children's non-fiction for trade, school, library and mass markets. About 80 titles a year. No fiction or textbooks. Synopses and ideas welcome. Include s.a.e. for return.
Fees paid; no royalties.

Mike Moran Productions Ltd
33 Warner Road, Ware, Hertfordshire SG12 9JL
☎01920 466003 Fax 01920 466003
Email Mike.Moran@moran19.fsnet.co.uk
Website www.mikemoranphotography.co.uk
Chairman/Managing Director *Mike Moran*
Packager and publisher. TITLES *MM Publisher Database; MM Printer Database* (available in UK, European and international editions).

Nicholas Enterprises
See **Aladdin Books Ltd**

Orpheus Books Limited
2 Church Green, Witney, Oxfordshire
OX28 4AW
☎01993 774949 Fax 01993 700330
Email info@orpheusbooks.com
Chairman *Nicholas Harris*
FOUNDED 1993. *Commissions* children's non-fiction. 8 titles in 2001. No unsolicited material.
Fees paid.

Pinwheel Limited
Station House, 8–13 Swiss Terrace, London
SW6 7LU
☎020 7586 5100 Fax 020 7483 1999
Email sales@pinwheel.co.uk
Website www.pinwheel.co.uk
Managing Director *Sarah Fabiny*
Approx. Annual Turnover £1.6 million
FOUNDED 1995. Bought by Andromeda Oxford Ltd in 1999. *Commissions* children's novelty books for the under-fives. No reference, non-fiction or age 10 and above. 30 titles in 2001. Welcomes synopses and ideas for books; approach by letter or e-mail.
Fees paid instead of royalties.

Playne Books Limited
Chapel House, Trefin, Haverfordwest,
Pembrokeshire SA62 5AU
☎01348 837073 Fax 01348 837063
Email playne.books@virgin.net
Editorial Director *Gill Davies*
Design & Production *David Playne*
FOUNDED 1987. *Commissions* early learning titles for young children – fun ideas with an educational slant and novelty books. Also highly illustrated and practical books on any subject. Synopses and ideas by prior arrangement only.
Royalties paid 'on payment from publishers'. Fees sometimes paid instead of royalties.

Mathew Price Ltd
The Old Glove Factory, Bristol Road,
Sherborne, Dorset DT9 4HP
☎01935 816010 Fax 01935 816310
Email mathewp@mathewprice.com
Chairman/Managing Director *Mathew Price*
Approx. Annual Turnover £500,000
Commissions full-colour novelty picture books

and fiction for young children plus children's non-fiction for all ages.
Fees sometimes paid instead of royalties.

Quarto Publishing
The Old Brewery, 6 Blundell Street, London
N7 9BH
☎020 7700 6700 Fax 020 7700 4191
Website www.quarto.com
Chairman *Laurence Orbach*
FOUNDED 1976. Britain's largest book packager. Acquired Marshall Editions in 2002. *Commissions* illustrated non-fiction, including painting, graphic design, how-to, lifestyle, visual arts, history, cookery, gardening, crafts. *Publishes* under the Apple imprint. Unsolicited synopses/ideas for books welcome.
Payment Flat fees paid.

Regency House Publishing Limited
See entry under **UK Publishers**

Sadie Fields Productions Ltd
4C/D West Point, 36–37 Warple Way,
London W3 0RG
☎020 8996 9970 Fax 020 8996 9977
Email sheri@tangobooks.co.uk
Directors *David Fielder, Sheri Safran*
FOUNDED 1981. Children's books with international co-edition potential: pop-ups, three-dimensional, novelty, picture and board books, 1500 words maximum. About 30 titles a year. Approach with preliminary letter and sample material in the first instance. *Publishes* in the UK under the **Tango Books** imprint.
Royalties based on a per-copy-sold rate and paid in stages.

Salariya Book Company Ltd
25 Marlborough Place, Brighton, East Sussex
BN1 1UB
☎01273 603306 Fax 01273 693857
Email salariya@salariya.com
Website www.salariya.com *and* www.book-house.co.uk
Managing Director *David Salariya*
FOUNDED 1989. Children's information books – fiction, history, art, music, science, architecture, education and picture books. *Publishes* under its IMPRINT **Book House** Publisher *David Salariya* Highly illustrated non-fiction in all subjects for children, from pre-school to teenage.
Payment by arrangement.

Savitri Books Ltd

115J Cleveland Street, London W1P 5PN
☎020 7436 9932 Fax 020 7580 6330
Managing Director *Mrinalini S. Srivastava*
Approx. Annual Turnover £200,000
FOUNDED 1983 and since 1998, Savitri Books
has also become a publisher in its own right
(textile crafts). Keen to work 'very closely with
authors/illustrators and try to establish long-
term relationships with them, doing more books
with the same team of people'. *Commissions*
illustrated non-fiction, crafts, New Age and
nature. About 7 titles a year. Unsolicited synopses and ideas for books 'very welcome'.

Sheldrake Press

188 Cavendish Road, London SW12 0DA
☎020 8675 1767 Fax 020 8675 7736
Email mail@sheldrakepress.demon.co.uk
Website www.sheldrakepress.demon.co.uk
Publisher *Simon Rigge*
Approx. Annual Turnover £250,000
Publishes illustrated non-fiction: history, travel,
style, cookery and stationery. TITLES *The
Victorian House Book; The Shorter Mrs Beeton;
The Power of Steam; The Railway Heritage of
Britain; Wild Britain; Wild France; Wild Spain;
Wild Italy; Wild Ireland; Amsterdam: Portrait of a
City* and Kate Greenaway stationery books.
Synopses and ideas for books welcome, but not
interested in fiction.
Fees or royalties paid.

Stonecastle Graphics Ltd/ Touchstone

Old Chapel Studio, Plain Road, Marden,
Tonbridge, Kent TN12 9LS
☎01622 832590 Fax 01622 832592
Email touchstone@touchstone.ndirect.co.uk
Website www.touchstonedesign.co.uk
Partner *Paul Turner*
Partner/Editorial Head *Sue Pressley*
Approx. Annual Turnover £300,000
FOUNDED 1976. Formed additional design/
packaging partnership, Touchstone, in 1983.
Commissions illustrated non-fiction general books
– motoring, health, sport, leisure, home interest
and popular culture. 20 titles in 2001. TITLES *The
Encyclopedia of Golf Techniques; How to Draw the
Human Figure; The Beginner's Guide to Drawing
Cartoons; Calligraphy Techniques; Spooky Fun;
Scary Faces; Kid's Cookery; Kid's Gardening.*
Unsolicited synopses and ideas for books wel-
come. *Fees* paid.

Templar Publishing

Pippbrook Mill, London Road, Dorking,
Surrey RH4 1JE
☎01306 876361 Fax 01306 889097
Email editorial@templarco.co.uk
Website www.templarco.co.uk
Managing Director/Editorial Head
Amanda Wood
Approx. Annual Turnover £10 million
FOUNDED 1981. A division of The Templar
Company plc. *Commissions* quality novelty and
gift books, picture books and children's illus-
trated non-fiction. 100 titles a year. Synopses and
ideas for books welcome. 'We are particularly
interested in picture book mss and ideas for new
novelty concepts.' *Royalties* by arrangement.

Toucan Books Ltd

Third Floor, 89 Charterhouse Street, London
EC1M 6PE
☎020 7250 3388 Fax 020 7250 3123
Managing Director *Robert Sackville-West*
Approx. Annual Turnover £1,200,000
FOUNDED 1985. *Specialises* in international co-
editions and fee-based editorial, design and
production services to film. *Commissions* illus-
trated non-fiction only. About 20 titles a year.
TITLES *The Eventful Century; The Earth, Its
Wonders, Its Secrets; Leith's Cookery Bible;
Charles II; The Complete Photography Course;
Journeys into the Past* series; *People and Places.*
Unsolicited synopses and ideas for books wel-
come. No fiction or non-illustrated titles.
Royalties paid twice-yearly; fees paid in addi-
tion to or instead of royalties.

Touchstone

See **Stonecastle Graphics Ltd**

David West Children's Books

7 Princeton Court, 55 Felsham Road, Putney,
London SW15 1AZ
☎020 8780 3836 Fax 020 8780 9313
Email dww@btinternet.com
Website www.davidwestchildrensbooks.com
FOUNDED 1992. *Commissions* children's illustrated reference books. No fiction or adult
books. 70 titles in 2002. Unsolicited ideas and
synopses welcome; approach in writing in the
first instance. *Fees* and royalties paid annually.

Wordwright Publishing

8 St Johns Road, Saxmundham, Suffolk
IP17 1BE
☎01728 604204 Fax 01728 604029
Email wordwright@clara.co.uk

Contact *Charles Perkins*

FOUNDED by ex-editorial people 'so good writing always has a chance with us'. *Commissions* illustrated non-fiction: social history and comment, military history, women's issues, sport. *Specialises* in military and social history, natural history, science, art, cookery, and gardening. About 6–8 titles a year. Unsolicited synopses/ideas (a paragraph or so) welcome for illustrated non-fiction.

Payment usually fees but royalties (twice-yearly) paid for sales above a specified number of copies.

Working Partners Ltd
1 Albion Place, London W6 0QT
☎020 8748 7477 Fax 020 8748 7450
Email enquiries@workingpartnersltd.co.uk
Contacts *Ben Baglio, Rod Ritchie, Chris Snowdon*

Specialises in children's mass-market series fiction books. Creators of *Animal Ark*; *Puppy Patrol*; *Dolphin Diaries*; *Heartland*; *Sheltie*; *Survive!* No unsolicited mss.

Payment Both fees and royalties by arrangement.

Zoë Books Ltd
15 Worthy Lane, Winchester, Hampshire
SO23 7AB
☎01962 851318
Email enquiries@zoebooks.co.uk
Website www.zoebooks.co.uk
Managing Director *Imogen Dawson*
Director *Bob Davidson*

FOUNDED 1990. *Specialises* in full-colour information and reference books for schools and libraries worldwide. *Publishes* about 30 titles a year. Does *not* publish picture books or fiction. No freelance work available. Unsolicited material not considered.

Fees paid.

Book Clubs

David Arscott's Sussex Book Club
Dolphin House, 51 St Nicholas Lane, Lewes, Sussex BN7 2JZ
☎01273 470100 Fax 01273 470100
Email sussexbooks@compuserve.com
Website www.ourworld.compuserve.com/
  homepages/sussexbooks
FOUNDED January 1998. *Specialises* in books about the county of Sussex. Represents all the major publishers of Sussex books and offers a wide range of titles. Free membership without obligation to buy.

Artists' Choice
PO Box 3, Huntingdon, Cambridgeshire PE28 0QX
☎01832 710201 Fax 01832 710488
Website www.artists-choice.co.uk
Specialises in books for the amateur artist at all levels of ability.

Baker Books
Manfield Park, Cranleigh, Surrey GU6 8NU
☎01483 267888 Fax 01483 267409
Email bakerbooks@dial.pipex.com
Website www.bakerbooks.co.uk
Book clubs for schools: Rainbow for ages 2–5 and Funfare, ages 5–11. Two issues per term operated in the UK and overseas.

BCA (Book Club Associates)
Greater London House, Hampstead Road, London NW1 7TZ
☎020 7760 6500 Fax 020 7760 6901
With two million members, BCA is Britain's largest book club organisation. Consists of 31 book clubs, catering for general and specific interests. These include: Ancient & Medieval History Book Club, The Arts Guild, The Book Club of Ireland, Books For Children, The Christian Book Club, Computer Books Direct, Discovery, The English Book Club, Escape (female fiction), Fantasy and Science Fiction, History Guild, Home Software World, Mango, Military and Aviation Book Society, Mind, Body & Spirit, Moments, Mystery and Thriller Club, Quality Paperbacks Direct, Railway Book Club, Taste, World Books.

Bibliophile Books
5 Thomas Road, London E14 7BN
☎020 7515 9222 Fax 020 7538 4115
Email orders@bibliophilebooks.com
Website www.bibliophilebooks.com
New books covering a wide range of subjects at discount prices. Write, phone or fax for free catalogue issued 10 times a year.

Cygnus Books
PO Box 15, Llandeilo, Carmarthenshire SA19 6YX
☎01550 777701 Fax 01550 777569
Email enquiries@cygnus-books.co.uk
Website www.cygnus-books.co.uk
'Books for your next step in spirituality and complementary health care.' See website for over 1000 hand-picked titles. Also publishes *The Cygnus Review* magazine which features 50–60 reviews on new mind, body and spirit titles each month.

The Folio Society
44 Eagle Street, London WC1R 4FS
☎020 7400 4222 Fax 020 7400 4242
Fine editions of classic fiction, history and memoirs; also some children's classics.

Letterbox Library
71–73 Allen Road, London N16 8RY
☎020 7503 4801 Fax 020 7503 4800
Website www.letterboxlibrary.com
Children's book cooperative. Hard and soft-cover, non-sexist and multi-cultural books for children from one to teenage.

Poetry Book Society
See entry under **Organisations of Interest to Poets**

Readers' Union Ltd
Brunel House, Forde Close, Newton Abbot, Devon TQ12 2DW
☎01626 323200 Fax 01626 323318
Eight book clubs, all dealing with specific

interests: Country Review, The Craft Club, Craftsman Society, Equestrian Society, The Gardeners Society, Needlecrafts with Cross Stitch, Focal Point, Puzzles Plus.

Red House Book Clubs
See **Scholastic Ltd** under **UK Publishers**

Writers' News Bookshelf
PO Box 168, Wellington Street, Leeds, West Yorkshire LS1 1RF
☎0113 238 8333 Fax 0113 238 8330
Email janet.evans@writersnews.co.uk

Specialises in books for writers.

UK Literary Agents and Scouts

★ = Members of the **Association of Authors' Agents**

Sheila Ableman Literary Agency
122 Arlington Road, London NW1 7HP
☎020 7485 3409 Fax 020 7485 3409
Email sheila@ableman.freeserve.co.uk
Contact *Sheila Ableman*
FOUNDED 1999. *Handles* non-fiction including
history, science, biography and autobiography.
Specialises in TV tie-ins and celebrity ghost
writing. No poetry, children's, cookery, gardening or sport. Unsolicited mss welcome.
Approach in writing with publishing history,
c.v., synopsis, three chapters and s.a.e. for
return. No reading fee. *Commission* Home
15%; US & Translation 20%.

The Agency (London) Ltd★
24 Pottery Lane, Holland Park, London
W11 4LZ
☎020 7727 1346 Fax 020 7727 9037
Email info@theagency.co.uk
Contacts *Stephen Durbridge, Leah Schmidt,*
Sebastian Born, Julia Kreitman, Bethan Evans,
Hilary Delamere, Katie Haines, Wendy
Gresser, Ligeia Marsh
FOUNDED 1995. *Handles* children's fiction, TV,
film, theatre, radio scripts. No adult fiction or
non-fiction. Send letter with s.a.e. No reading
fee. *Commission* Home 10%; US various.

Gillon Aitken Associates Ltd★
29 Fernshaw Road, London SW10 0TG
☎020 7351 7561 Fax 020 7376 3594
Email reception@aitkenassoc.demon.co.uk
Contacts *Gillon Aitken, Clare Alexander*
FOUNDED 1977. *Handles* fiction and non-fic-
tion. No plays or scripts unless by existing
clients. Send preliminary letter, with half-page
synopsis and first 30 pp of sample material, and
return postage, in the first instance. No reading
fee. CLIENTS include Pat Barker, John
Cornwell, Linda Davies, Sarah Dunant,
Sebastian Faulks, Niall Ferguson, Helen
Fielding, Germaine Greer, Susan Howatch,
Candia McWilliam, V.S. Naipaul, Jonathan
Raban, Piers Paul Read, Gillian Slovo, Colin
Thubron, A.N. Wilson. *Commission* Home
10%; US 15%; Translation 20%.

Michael Alcock Management★
96 Farringdon Road, London EC1R 3EA
☎020 7837 8137 Fax 020 7837 8787
Email Alcockmgt@aol.com
Contacts *Michael Alcock, Anna Power*
FOUNDED 1997. *Handles* general non-fiction
including current affairs, biography and memoirs, history, lifestyle, health and personal
development; literary and commercial mainstream fiction. No unsolicited mss; approach
by letter in the first instance giving details of
writing and other media experience, plus synopsis. For fiction send first three chapters as
well. S.a.e. essential for response. No reading
fee. CLIENTS include Tamsin Blanchard, James
Burke, Barbara Currie, Tom Dixon, Yehudi
Gordon, Mark Griffiths, Joanna Hall, Lisa
Hilton, Lynne Robinson, Barnaby Rogerson,
Barry Turner, Lowri Turner. *Commission*
Home 15%; US and Translation 20%.

Darley Anderson
Literary, TV & Film Agency★
Estelle House, 11 Eustace Road, London
SW6 1JB
☎020 7385 6652 Fax 020 7386 9689/5571
Email darley.anderson@virgin.net
Contacts *Darley Anderson* (thrillers), *Kerith*
Biggs (crime/foreign rights), *Elizabeth*
Wright (women's fiction/love stories/'tear-
jerkers'), *Carrie Neilson* (TV/film, children's
books), *Hayley Wood* (non-fiction)
Run by an ex-publisher with a knack for spot-
ting talent and a tough negotiator. *Handles* commercial fiction and non-fiction; children's
fiction; also selected scripts for film and TV. No
academic books or poetry. *Special interests*
Fiction: all types of thrillers and young male fiction. All types of American and Irish novels. All
types of women's fiction. Also crime/mystery
and humour. Non-fiction: celebrity autobiographies, biographies, sports books, 'true life'
women in jeopardy, relevatory history and science, popular psychology, self-improvement,
diet, health, beauty, fashion, animals, humour/
cartoons, gardening, cookery, inspirational and
religious. Send letter and outline with first three
chapters; return postage/s.a.e. essential. CLIENTS

Richard Asplin, Anne Baker, Catherine Barry, Paul Carson, Caroline Carver, Lee Child, Martina Cole, John Connolly, Joseph Corvo, Margaret Dickinson, Rose Doyle, Joan Jonker, Rani Manicka, Carole Matthews, Lesley Pearse, Lynda Page, Allan Pease, Adrian Plass, Carmen Ryan, Mary Ryan, Fred Secombe, Rebecca Shaw, Peter Sheridan, Kwong Kuen Shan, Linda Taylor, Elizabeth Waite, David Wishart. *Commission* Home 15%; US 20%; Translation 20–25%; TV/Film/Radio 20%. *Overseas associates* APA Talent and Literary Agency (LA/Hollywood); Liza Dawson Associates (New York); and leading foreign agents throughout the world.

Anubis Literary Agency

79 Charles Gardner Road, Leamington Spa, Warwickshire CV31 3BG
☎01926 832644 Fax 01926 311607

Contacts *Steve Calcutt, Maggie Heavey*

FOUNDED 1994. *Handles* mainstream adult fiction, especially science fiction, fantasy, horror, crime and women's. Also literary fiction. Scripts for film and TV. No children's books, poetry, short stories, journalism, academic or non-fiction. No unsolicited mss; send a covering letter and brief (one-page) synopsis (s.a.e. essential). No telephone calls. No reading fee. CLIENTS include Lesley Asquith, Georgie Hale, Tim Lebbon, Adam Roberts, Elon Salmon, Steve Savile, Zoe Sharp. *Commission* Home 15%; US & Translation 20%. Works with the **Marsh Agency** on translation rights.

Artellus Limited

30 Dorset House, Gloucester Place, London NW1 5AD
☎020 7935 6972 Fax 020 7487 5957

Chairman *Gabriele Pantucci*
Director *Leslie Gardner*

FOUNDED 1986. Full-length and short mss; scripts for films. Crime, science fiction, historical, contemporary and literary fiction; non-fiction: art history, current affairs, biography, general history, science. No reading fee. Will suggest revision. Works directly in the USA and with agencies in Europe, Japan and Russia. *Commission* Home 10%; Overseas 12½–20%.

Author Literary Agents

53 Talbot Road, Highgate, London N6 4QX
☎020 8341 0442/07989 318245 (mobile)
Fax 020 8341 0442
Email agile@authors.co.uk

Contact *John Havergal*

FOUNDED 1997. New writing for book publishers and screen producers; also markets strong new content and design ideas for calendar, gift, greeting, game, toy, stationery and other markets. Send half-to-one-page (max.) outline and writing/work sample for quick saleability rating together with s.a.e. *Commission* Writing: Home 15%; Overseas & Translation 25%; Non-writing, e.g. illustration, plastic & digital media: Publishing 25%; Non-publishing 33.34% (all rates plus VAT).

The Bell Lomax Agency

James House, 1 Babmaes Street, London SW1Y 6HF
☎020 7930 4447 Fax 020 7925 0118
Email agency@bell-lomax.co.uk

Executives *Eddie Bell, Pat Lomax, Paul Moreton, June Bell*

ESTABLISHED 2002. *Handles* quality fiction and non-fiction, biography, children's, business and sport. No unsolicited mss without preliminary letter. No scripts. No reading fee.

Blake Friedmann Literary Agency Ltd★

122 Arlington Road, London NW1 7HP
☎020 7284 0408 Fax 020 7284 0442
Email <firstname>@blakefriedmann.co.uk
Website www.blakefriedmann.co.uk

Contacts *Carole Blake* (books), *Julian Friedmann* (film/TV), *Conrad Williams* (original scripts/radio), *Isobel Dixon* (books)

FOUNDED 1977. *Handles* all kinds of fiction from genre to literary; a varied range of specialised and general non-fiction, plus scripts for TV, radio and film. No poetry, juvenile, science fiction or short stories (unless from existing clients). *Special interests* commercial women's fiction, literary fiction, upmarket non-fiction. Unsolicited mss welcome but initial letter with synopsis and first two chapters preferred. Letters should contain as much information as possible on previous writing experience, aims for the future, etc. No reading fee. CLIENTS include Ted Allbeury, Jane Asher, Joanna Briscoe, Elizabeth Chadwick, Teresa Crane, Barbara Erskine, Maeve Haran, John Harvey, Ken Hom, Paul Johnston, Glenn Meade, Lawrence Norfolk, Joseph O'Connor, Michael Ridpath, Tim Sebastian. *Commission* Books: Home 15%; US & Translation 20%. Radio/TV/Film: 15%. *Overseas associates* throughout Europe, Asia and the US.

David Bolt Associates

12 Heath Drive, Send, Surrey GU23 7EP
☎01483 721118 Fax 01483 721118

Contact *David Bolt*

FOUNDED 1983. *Handles* fiction and general non-fiction. No books for small children or verse (except in special circumstances). No scripts. *Special interests* fiction, African writers, biography, history, military, theology. Preliminary letter with s.a.e. essential. Reading fee for unpublished writers. Terms on application. CLIENTS include Chinua Achebe, David Bret, Joseph Rhymer, Colin Wilson. *Commission* Home 10%; US & Translation 19%.

BookBlast Ltd

PO Box 20184, London W10 5AU
☎020 8968 3089 Fax 020 8932 4087
Website www.bookblast.com

Contact *Address material to the Company*

HANDLES traditional and underground fiction and non-fiction. No unsolicited mss. No submissions on disk, by fax or e-mail. Preliminary letter, synopsis, biographical information and s.a.e. essential, also names of agents and publishers previously contacted. Film, TV and radio rights mainly sold in works by existing clients. *Commission* Home 12%; US & Translation 20%; TV & Radio 15%; Film 20%.

Alan Brodie Representation Ltd
(incorporating Michael Imison Playwrights Ltd)

211 Piccadilly, London W1J 9HF
☎020 7917 2871 Fax 020 7917 2872
Email info@alanbrodie.com
Website www.alanbrodie.com

Contacts *Alan Brodie, Sarah McNair*

FOUNDED 1989. *Handles* theatre, film and TV scripts. No books. Preliminary letter plus professional recommendation and c.v. essential. No reading fee but s.a.e. required. *Commission* Home 10%; Overseas 15%.

Rosemary Bromley Literary Agency

Avington, Near Winchester, Hampshire SO21 1DB
☎01962 779656 Fax 01962 779656
Email juvenilia@clam.co.uk

Contact *Rosemary Bromley*

FOUNDED 1981. *Handles* non-fiction. Also scripts for TV and radio. No poetry or short stories. *Special interests* natural history, leisure, biography and cookery. No unsolicited mss. No fax or e-mail enquiries. Send preliminary letter with full details. Enquiries unaccompanied by return postage will not be answered. CLIENTS include Elisabeth Beresford, Linda Birch, Teresa Collard, estate of Fanny Cradock, Glenn Hamilton, Cathy Hopkins, Keith West, John Wingate. *Commission* Home 10%; US 15%; Translation 20%.

Bronte Literary Agency

PO Box 45, Brighouse, Calderdale, West Yorkshire HD6 2YQ
☎01484 544663
Email goodreading@bronteliterary.co.uk
Website www.bronteliterary.co.uk

Contact *John Ellison*

FOUNDED 2001. *Handles* fiction, non-fiction, children's, poetry. No political books. Approach by e-mail or letter in the first instance. No reading fee. *Commission* Home 15%; USA 20%; Translation rate negotiable.

Felicity Bryan★

2A North Parade, Banbury Road, Oxford OX2 6LX
☎01865 513816 Fax 01865 310055

Agents *Felicity Bryan, Catherine Clarke*
Contact *Michele Topham*

FOUNDED 1988. *Handles* fiction of various types and non-fiction with emphasis on history, biography, science and current affairs. No scripts for TV, radio or theatre. No crafts, how-to, science fiction or light romance. No unsolicited mss. Best approach by letter. No reading fee. CLIENTS include Karen Armstrong, Simon Blackburn, Humphrey Carpenter, John Charmley, Liza Cody, Artemis Cooper, A.C. Grayling, Angela Huth, Diarmaid MacCulloch, Sue MacGregor, James Naughtie, John Julius Norwich, Gemma O'Connor, Iain Pears, Rosamunde Pilcher, Matt Ridley, Miriam Stoppard, Roy Strong, John Sulston. *Commission* Home 10%; US & Translation 20%. *Overseas associates* Andrew Nurnberg, Europe; several agencies in US.

Brie Burkeman★

14 Neville Court, Abbey Road, London NW8 9DD
☎0709 223 9113 Fax 0709 223 9111
Email brie.burkeman@mail.com

Contact *Brie Burkeman*

FOUNDED 2000. *Handles* commercial and literary full-length fiction and non-fiction. Film, TV, theatre scripts. No academic, text, poetry, short stories, musicals or short films. No reading fee but return postage essential. Unsolicited e-mail attachments will be deleted without opening. Also independent film and TV consultant to literary agents. *Commission* Home 15%; Overseas 20%.

Juliet Burton Literary Agency
2 Clifton Avenue, London W12 9DR
☎020 8762 0148 Fax 020 8743 8765
Contact *Juliet Burton*
FOUNDED 1999. *Handles* fiction and non-fiction. *Special interests* crime and women's fiction. No plays, film scripts, articles, poetry or academic material. No reading fee. Approach in writing in the first instance; send synopsis and two sample chapters with s.a.e. No unsolicited mss. *Commission* Home 10%; US & Translation 20%.

Campbell Thomson & McLaughlin Ltd★
1 King's Mews, London WC1N 2JA
☎020 7242 0958 Fax 020 7242 2408
Contacts *John McLaughlin, Charlotte Bruton*
FOUNDED 1931. *Handles* fiction and general non-fiction, excluding children's. No plays, film/TV scripts, articles, short stories or poetry. No unsolicited mss or synopses. Preliminary letter with s.a.e. essential. No reading fee. *Overseas associates* Fox Chase Agency, Pennsylvania; Raines & Raines, New York.

Capel & Land Ltd★
29 Wardour Street, London W1D 6PS
☎020 7734 2414 Fax 020 7734 8101
Email robert@capelland.co.uk
Contact *Georgina Capel*
FOUNDED 2000. *Handles* fiction and non-fiction. Also film, TV, theatre and radio scripts. No children's or illustrated books. Send sample chapters and synopsis with covering letter in the first instance. No reading fee. CLIENTS Kunal Basu, Julie Burchill, Andrew Greig, Henry Porter, Andrew Roberts, Louis Theroux, Lucy Wadham. *Commission* Home, US & Translation 15%.

Casarotto Ramsay and Associates Ltd
National House, 60–66 Wardour Street, London W1V 3HP
☎020 7287 4450 Fax 020 7287 9128
Email agents@casarotto.uk.com
Website www.casarotto.uk.com

Film/TV/Radio *Jenne Casarotto, Tracey Hyde, Charlotte Kelly, Jodi Shields, Chris Cope, Elinor Burns*
Stage *Tom Erhardt, Mel Kenyon*
(**Books** *Handled by* **Lutyens and Rubinstein**)
Took over the agency responsibilities of Margaret Ramsay Ltd in 1992, incorporating a strong client list, with names like Alan Ayckbourn, Caryl Churchill, Willy Russell and Muriel Spark. *Handles* scripts for TV, theatre, film and radio. No unsolicited material without preliminary letter. CLIENTS include J.G. Ballard, Edward Bond, Simon Callow, David Hare, Terry Jones, Neil Jordan, Willy Russell. *Commission* Home 10%; US & Translation 20%. *Overseas associates* worldwide.

Celia Catchpole
56 Gilpin Avenue, London SW14 8QY
☎020 8255 7200 Fax 020 8288 0653
Contact *Celia Catchpole*
FOUNDED 1996. *Handles* children's books – artists and writers. No TV, film, radio or theatre scripts. No poetry. No unsolicited mss. *Commission* Home 10% (writers) 15% (artists); US & Translation 20%. Works with associate agents abroad.

Chapman & Vincent★
The Mount, Sun Hill, Royston, Hertfordshire SG8 9AT
☎01763 245005 Fax 01763 243033
Email ChapmanVincent@camnews.net
Contacts *Jennifer Chapman, Gilly Vincent*
A small agency whose clients come mainly from personal recommendation. The agency aims to look after only a limited number of predominantly non-fiction writers and is not actively seeking clients but happy to consider really original work. Does not handle poetry, thrillers, adventure, children's books or genre fiction. Please do not telephone or submit by fax or e-mail. Write with two sample chapters and enclose s.a.e. CLIENTS include George Carter, Leslie Geddes-Brown, Sara George, Rowley Leigh, John Miller, Dorit Peleg. *Commission* Home 15%; US & Europe 20%.

Mic Cheetham Literary Agency
11–12 Dover Street, London W1S 4LJ
☎020 7495 2002 Fax 020 7495 5777
Website www.miccheetham.com
Contact *Mic Cheetham*
ESTABLISHED 1994. *Handles* general and literary

O = handles foreign writer

fiction, crime and science fiction, and some specific non-fiction. No film/TV scripts apart from existing clients. No children's, illustrated books or poetry. No unsolicited mss. Approach in writing with publishing history, first two chapters and return postage. No reading fee. CLIENTS include Iain Banks, Carol Birch, Anita Burgh, Laurie Graham, Toby Litt, Ken MacLeod, China Miéville, Antony Sher. *Commission* Home 10%; US & Translation 20%. Works with **The Marsh Agency** for all translation rights.

Judith Chilcote Agency★
8 Wentworth Mansions, Keats Grove, London NW3 2RL
☎020 7794 3717
Email judybks@aol.com
Contact *Judith Chilcote*

FOUNDED 1990. *Handles* commercial fiction, TV tie-ins, health and nutrition, sport, cinema, self-help, popular psychology, biography and autobiography, cookery and current affairs. No academic, science fiction, children's, short stories, film scripts or poetry. *No approaches by e-mail.* Send letter with c.v., synopsis, three chapters and s.a.e. for return. No reading fee. *Commission* Home 15%; Overseas 20–25%.

Teresa Chris Literary Agency
43 Musard Road, London W6 8NR
☎020 7386 0633
Contact *Teresa Chris*

FOUNDED 1989. *Handles* crime, general, women's, commercial and literary fiction, and non-fiction: history, biography, health, cookery, lifestyle, sport and fitness, gardening, etc. *Specialises* in crime fiction and commercial women's fiction. No scripts. Film and TV rights handled by co-agent. No poetry, short stories, fantasy, science fiction or horror. Unsolicited mss welcome. Send query letter with first two chapters plus two-page synopsis (*s.a.e. essential*) in first instance. No reading fee. CLIENTS include Stephen Booth, Susan Clark, Tamara McKinley, Marguerite Patten, Danuta Reah, Kate Tremayne. *Commission* Home 10%; US 15%; Translation 20%. *Overseas associates* Thompson & Chris Literary Agency, USA; representatives in most other countries.

Mary Clemmey Literary Agency★
6 Dunollie Road, London NW5 2XP
☎020 7267 1290 Fax 020 7267 1290
Contact *Mary Clemmey*

FOUNDED 1992. *Handles* fiction and non-

fiction – high-quality work with an international market. No science fiction, fantasy or children's books. TV, film, radio and theatre scripts from existing clients only. No unsolicited mss. Approach by letter only giving a description of the work in the first instance. S.a.e. essential. No reading fee. US & Canadian clients: The Bukowski Agency, **Frederick Hill Associates**, Lynn C. Franklin Associates Ltd, The Miller Agency, **Roslyn Targ Literary Agency Inc**, Weingel-Fidel Agency Inc. *Commission* Home 10%; US & Translation 20%. *Overseas Associate* Elaine Markson Literary Agency, New York.

Jonathan Clowes Ltd★
10 Iron Bridge House, Bridge Approach, London NW1 8BD
☎020 7722 7674 Fax 020 7722 7677
Contacts *Ann Evans, Isobel Creed, Lisa Whadcock*

FOUNDED 1960. Pronounced 'clewes'. Now one of the biggest fish in the pond, and not really for the untried unless they are true high-flyers. Fiction and non-fiction, plus scripts. No textbooks or children's. *Special interests* situation comedy, film and television rights. No unsolicited mss; authors come by recommendation or by successful follow-ups to preliminary letters. CLIENTS include David Bellamy, Len Deighton, Elizabeth Jane Howard, Doris Lessing, David Nobbs, Gillian White and the estate of Kingsley Amis. *Commission* Home & US 15%; Translation 19%. *Overseas associates* **Andrew Nurnberg Associates**; Sane Töregard Agency.

Elspeth Cochrane Personal Management
14/2 Second Floor, South Bank Commercial Centre, 140 Battersea Park Road, London SW11 4NB
☎020 7622 0314 Fax 020 7622 5815
Email elspethc@dircon.co.uk
Contact *Elspeth Cochrane*

FOUNDED 1960. *Handles* fiction, non-fiction, biographies, screenplays. Subjects have included Richard Burton, Marlon Brando, Sean Connery, Clint Eastwood, Lord Olivier. Also scripts for all media, with special interest in drama. No unsolicited mss. Preliminary letter, synopsis and s.a.e. is essential in the first instance. CLIENTS include Royce Ryton, Robert Tanitch. *Commission* 12½% ('but this can change; the percentage is negotiable, as is the sum paid to the writer').

Rosica Colin Ltd

1 Clareville Grove Mews, London
SW7 5AH
☎020 7370 1080 Fax 020 7244 6441

Contact *Joanna Marston*

FOUNDED 1949. Handles all full-length mss,
plus theatre, film, television and sound broadcasting but few new writers being accepted.
Preliminary letter with return postage essential;
writers should outline their writing credits and
whether their mss have previously been submitted elsewhere. May take 3–4 months to
consider full mss; synopsis preferred in the first
instance. No reading fee. *Commission* Home
10%; US 15%; Translation 20%.

Conville & Walsh Limited★

118–120 Wardour Street, London W1V 3LA
☎020 7287 3030 Fax 020 7287 4545
Email <firstname>@convilleandwalsh.com

Directors *Clare Conville, Patrick Walsh* (book
rights), *Sam North* (film/TV rights),
Peter Tallack (popular science)

ESTABLISHED in 2000 by Clare Conville (ex-
A.P. Watt) and Patrick Walsh (ex-**Christopher
Little Literary Agency**). Handles literary and
commercial fiction plus serious and narrative
non-fiction. Clare Conville also represents many
successful children's authors. Particularly inter-
ested in first novelists plus scientists, historians
and journalists. CLIENTS Jez Alborough, John
Burningham, Kate Cann, Helen Castor, Tom
Conran, Michael Cordy, Mike Dash, Professor
John Emsley, Steve Erikson, Katy Gardner,
Christopher Hart, Dermot Healy, James
Holland, Tom Holland, Sebastian Horsley,
David Huggins, Viven Kelly, Guy Kennaway,
P.J. Lynch, Hector Macdonald, Harland Miller,
Jacqui Murhall, D.B.C. Pierre, Rebecca Ray,
Patrick Redmond, Candace Robb, Saira Shah,
Tahir Shah, Nicky Singer, Simon Singh, Doron
Swade, Dr Richard Wiseman, Adam Wishart,
Isabel Wolff and the estate of Francis Bacon.
Commission Home 15%; US & Translation 20%.

Jane Conway-Gordon★

1 Old Compton Street, London W1D 5JA
☎020 7494 0148 Fax 020 7287 9264

Contact *Jane Conway-Gordon*

FOUNDED 1982. Works in association with
Andrew Mann Ltd. Handles fiction and gen-
eral non-fiction. No poetry or science fiction.
Unsolicited mss welcome; preliminary letter
and return postage essential. No reading fee.
Commission Home 15%; US & Translation

20%. *Overseas associates* **McIntosh & Otis,
Inc.**, New York; plus agencies throughout
Europe and Japan.

Rupert Crew Ltd★

1A King's Mews, London WC1N 2JA
☎020 7242 8586 Fax 020 7831 7914
Email rupertcrew@compuserve.com
(correspondence only)

Contacts *Doreen Montgomery, Caroline
Montgomery*

FOUNDED 1927. International representation,
handling volume and subsidiary rights in fiction
and non-fiction properties. No plays or poetry,
journalism or short stories. Preliminary letter
and return postage essential. No reading fee.
Commission Home 15%; Elsewhere 20%.

Curtis Brown Group Ltd★

Haymarket House, 28/29 Haymarket, London
SW1Y 4SP
☎020 7396 6600 Fax 020 7396 0110
Email cb@curtisbrown.co.uk

Also at: 37 Queensferry Street, Edinburgh
EH2 4QS
☎0131 225 1286/1288 Fax 0131 225 1290

Chairman *Paul Scherer*
Group Managing Director *Jonathan Lloyd*
Directors *Mark Collingbourne* (Finance),
Fiona Inglis (MD, Australia)
Books, London *Jonathan Lloyd, Anna Davis,
Jonny Geller, Hannah Griffiths, Ali Gunn,
Camilla Hornby, Anthea Morton-Saner,
Peter Robinson, Vivienne Schuster, Mike Shaw,
Elizabeth Stevens*
Books, Edinburgh *Giles Gordon*
Foreign Rights *Diana Mackay, Carol Jackson,
Kate Cooper*
Film/TV/Theatre *Nick Marston* (MD,
Media Division), *Ben Hall, Philip Patterson*
Presenters *Sue Freathy, Julian Beynon*

Long-established literary agency, whose first
sales were made in 1899. Merged with John
Farquharson, forming the Curtis Brown Group
Ltd in 1989. Also represents directors, designers
and presenters. Handles a wide range of subjects
including fiction, general non-fiction, children's
books and associated rights (including multimedia) as well as film, theatre, TV and radio
scripts. Outline for non-fiction and short synopsis for fiction with two or three sample chapters
and autobiographical note. No reading fee.
Return postage essential. *Commission* Home
10%; US & Translation 20%. *Overseas associates*
in Australia, Canada and the US.

☐ = Contemporary
Q = Quality

Judy Daish Associates Ltd

2 St Charles Place, London W10 6EG
☎020 8964 8811 Fax 020 8964 8966
Contacts *Judy Daish, Sara Stroud, Tracey Elliston*
FOUNDED 1978. Theatrical literary agent. *Handles* scripts for film, TV, theatre and radio. No books. Preliminary letter essential. No unsolicited mss.

Caroline Davidson Literary Agency

5 Queen Anne's Gardens, London W4 1TU
☎020 8995 5768 Fax 020 8994 2770
Contacts *Caroline Davidson, Rebecca Connell*
FOUNDED 1988. *Handles* fiction and non-fiction, including archaeology, architecture, art, astronomy, biography, design, fitness, gardening, health, history, medicine, natural history, reference, science. Many highly illustrated books. Finished, polished first novels positively welcomed. No occult, short stories, children's, plays or poetry. Writers should send an initial letter giving details of the project and/or book proposal, including the first 50 pages of their novel if a fiction writer, together with c.v. and return postage. Submissions without the latter are not considered or returned. CLIENTS Susan Aldridge, Peter Barham, Nigel Barlow, Anna Beer, Amy Brown, Stuart Clark, Andrew Dalby, Emma Donoghue, Robert Feather, Chris Greenhalgh, Tom Jaine, Huon Mallalieu. *Commission* US, Home, Commonwealth, Translation 12½%; occasionally more (20%) if sub-agents are involved.

Merric Davidson Literary Agency

12 Priors Heath, Goudhurst, Cranbrook, Kent TN17 2RE
☎01580 212041 Fax 01580 212041
Email authors@mdla.co.uk
Contacts *Merric Davidson, Wendy Suffield*
FOUNDED 1990. *Handles* fiction, general non-fiction and children's books. No scripts. No academic, short stories or articles. Particularly keen on contemporary fiction. No unsolicited mss. Send preliminary letter with synopsis and biographical details. S.a.e. essential for response. No reading fee. CLIENTS include Alys Clare, Francesca Clementis, Murray Davies, Harold Elletson, Alison Habens, Frankie Park, Mark Pepper, Simon Scarrow, Luke Sutherland. *Commission* Home 10%; US 15%; Translation 20%.

Mark Dawson Literary Agency

30 Valentine Road, London E9 7AD
☎020 8986 3252 Fax 020 8986 3346
Email markj.dawson@virgin.net

Contacts *Mark Dawson, Mette Olsen*
FOUNDED in 2001 by author and media lawyer Mark Dawson. *Handles* thrillers, crime, science fiction, literary fiction. No TV, film, theatre, radio scripts or poetry. Send preliminary letter, synopsis and first two chapters in the first instance. No reading fee. CLIENTS Sean Doolittle, Christopher Kenworthy, Ray Nayler. *Commission* Home 10%; US & Translation 15%.

Felix de Wolfe

Garden Offices, 51 Maida Vale, London W9 1SD
☎020 7289 5770 Fax 020 7289 5731
Contact *Felix de Wolfe*
FOUNDED 1938. *Handles* quality fiction only, and scripts. No non-fiction or children's. No unsolicited mss. No reading fee. CLIENTS include Jan Butlin, Robert Cogo-Fawcett, Carolina Giametta, Brian Glover, Sheila Goff, Aileen Gonsalves, John Kershaw, Bill MacIlwraith, Angus Mackay, Gerard McLarnon, Braham Murray, Julian Slade, Jeff Sowson, Malcolm Taylor, David Thompson, Paul Todd, Dolores Walshe. *Commission* Home 12½%; US 20%.

Dorian Literary Agency (DLA)★

Upper Thornehill, 27 Church Road, St Marychurch, Torquay, Devon TQ1 4QY
☎01803 312095 Fax 01803 312095
Contact *Dorothy Lumley*
FOUNDED 1986. *Handles* general fiction, specialising in popular fiction: women's (from romance, historicals to contemporary); crime (from historical to noir and thrillers); sience fiction, fantasy (but cautious about humorous/soft fantasy, i.e. unicorns), dark fantasy and horror. Adult and young adult but no children's under 10, poetry or drama. Introductory letter with outline and 1–3 chapters (with return postage/s.a.e.) only, please. No enquiries or submissions by fax or e-mail. No reading fee. CLIENTS include Gillian Bradshaw, Stephen Jones, Brian Lumley, Amy Myers, Rosemary Rowe. *Commission* Home 10%; US 15%; Translation 20–25%. Works with agents in most countries for translation.

Toby Eady Associates Ltd

9 Orme Court, London W2 4RL
☎020 7792 0092 Fax 020 7792 0879
Email toby@tobyeady.demon.co.uk *or* jessica@tobyeady.demon.co.uk
Website www.tobyeadyassociates.co.uk
Contacts *Toby Eady, Jessica Woollard*

Handles fiction, and non-fiction. Approach by personal recommendation. No film/TV scripts or poetry. *Special interests* China, Middle East, Africa, India. CLIENTS INCLUDE Jung Chang, Fadia Faqir, Liu Hong, Ma Jian, David Landau, Kenan Makiya, Nuha Al Radi, Lin Ping, Amir Taheri, Annie Wang, Xinran Xue, Bernard Cornwell, Mark Burnell, John Carey, Kuki Gallmann, Francesca Marciano, Shyama Perera, Fiammetta Rocco, Rachel Seiffert, Ann Wroe. *Commission* Home 10–15%; Elsewhere 20%. *Overseas associates* USA: Ed Breslin; France: La Nouvelle Agence; Germany: Mohrbooks; Holland: Jan Michael; Scandinavia, Italy, Spain: Rosie Buckman; China: Joanne Wang.

Eddison Pearson Ltd
6 Swains Lane, London N6 6QU
☎020 7700 7763 Fax 020 7700 7866
Email box1@eddisonpearson.com

Contact *Clare Pearson*

FOUNDED 1995. *Handles* children's books and scripts, literary fiction and non-fiction, poetry. Please enquire in writing, enclosing s.a.e. E-mail enquiries also welcome. No unsolicited mss; send a brief sample of work in the first instance. No reading fee. *Commission* Home 10%; US & Translation 15%.

Edwards Fuglewicz★
49 Great Ormond Street, London WC1N 3HZ
☎020 7405 6725 Fax 020 7405 6726

Contacts *Ros Edwards, Helenka Fuglewicz*

FOUNDED 1996. *Handles* fiction (literary and commercial; not science fiction, horror or fantasy); non-fiction: biography, history, popular culture. No scripts. Unsolicited mss welcome; approach in writing in the first instance with covering letter giving brief c.v., up to three chapters and a synopsis (enclose s.a.e. for return of mss); disks and e-mail submissions not acceptable. No reading fee. *Commission* Home 15%; US & Translation 20%.

Faith Evans Associates★
27 Park Avenue North, London N8 7RU
☎020 8340 9920 Fax 020 8340 9410

Contact *Faith Evans*

FOUNDED 1987. Small agency. *Handles* fiction and non-fiction. No scripts. New clients by personal recommendation only; no unsolicited mss or phone calls, please. CLIENTS include Melissa Benn, Shyam Bhatia, Madeleine Bourdouxhe, Eleanor Bron, Carolyn Cassady, Caroline Conran, Helen Falconer, Alicia

Foster, Midge Gillies, Ed Glinert, Jim Kelly, Helena Kennedy, Seumas Milne, Tom Paulin, Sheila Rowbotham, Lorna Sage, Rebecca Stott, Hwee Hwee Tan, Marion Urch, Harriet Walter, Elizabeth Wilson. *Commission* Home 15%; US & Translation 20%. *Overseas associates* worldwide.

Lisa Eveleigh Literary Agency★
3rd Floor, 11/12 Dover Street, London W1S 4LJ
☎020 7399 2803 Fax 020 7399 2801
Email Eveleigh@dial.pipex.com

Contact *Lisa Eveleigh*

FOUNDED 1996. *Handles* literary and commercial fiction and non-fiction and children's books. No plays, scripts or poetry, science fiction or horror. Send synopsis with covering letter and c.v. rather than full ms. No reading fee but return postage essential. Please restrict e-mail contact to preliminary letter only. CLIENTS include Christina Balit, Philip Casey, Paul Heiney, Lisa Kopper, Irma Kurtz, Jonathan Meres, Libby Purves, Lori Reid, Grace Wynne-Jones. *Commission* Home 15%; US & Translation 20%.

Famous Pictures & Features Agency
See entry under **Picture Libraries**

John Farquharson★
See **Curtis Brown Group Ltd**

Film Rights Ltd
See **Laurence Fitch Ltd**

Laurence Fitch Ltd
Southbank Commercial Centre, 140 Battersea Park Road, London SW11 4NB
☎020 7720 2000 Fax 020 7720 6000
Email information@laurencefitch.com
Website www.laurencefitch.com

Contact *Brendan Davis*

FOUNDED 1952, incorporating the London Play Company (1922) and in association with Film Rights Ltd (1932). *Handles* children's and horror books, scripts for theatre, film, TV and radio only. No unsolicited mss. Send synopsis with sample scene(s) in the first instance. No reading fee. CLIENTS include Carlo Ardito, Hindi Brooks, John Chapman & Ray Cooney, John Graham, Glyn Robbins, Gene Stone, the estate of Dodie Smith, Edward Taylor. *Commission* UK 10%; Overseas 15%. *Overseas associates* worldwide.

Jill Foster Ltd

9 Barb Mews, Brook Green, London W6 7PA
☎020 7602 1263 Fax 020 7602 9336
Email agents@jflagency.com

Contacts *Jill Foster, Alison Finch, Simone Bassi, Simon Williamson*

FOUNDED 1976. *Handles* scripts for TV, drama and comedy. No fiction, short stories or poetry. No unsolicited mss; approach by letter in the first instance. No approaches by e-mail. No reading fee. CLIENTS include Ian Brown, Nick Doughty, Jan Etherington and Gavin Petrie, Phil Ford, Rob Gittins, Jenny Lecoat, Peter Tilbury, Susan Wilkins. *Commission* Home 12½%; Books, US & Translation 15%.

Fox & Howard Literary Agency

4 Bramerton Street, London SW3 5JX
☎020 7352 8691 Fax 020 7352 8691

Contacts *Chelsey Fox, Charlotte Howard*

FOUNDED 1992. A small agency, specialising in non-fiction, that prides itself on 'working closely with its authors'. *Handles* biography, history and popular culture, reference, business, gardening, mind, body and spirit, self-help, health. No unsolicited mss; send letter, synopsis and sample chapter with s.a.e. for response. No reading fee. CLIENTS Sarah Bartlett, Simon Collin, Professor Bruce King, Tony Clayton Lea, Marion Shoard, Maryon Stewart, Jane Struthers. *Commission* Home 10–15%; US & Translation 20%.

French's

78 Loudoun Road, London NW8 0NA
☎020 7483 4269 Fax 020 7722 0754

Contact *Mark Taylor*

FOUNDED 1973. *Handles* fiction and non-fiction; and scripts for all media, especially novels and screenplays. No religious or medical books. No unsolicited mss. 'For unpublished authors we offer a reading service at £70 per ms, exclusive of postage.' Interested authors should write in the first instance. *Commission* Home 10%.

Futerman, Rose & Associates★

Heston Court Business Estate, 19 Camp Road, Wimbledon, London SW19 4UW
☎020 8947 0188 Fax 020 8286 4861
Email guy@futermanrose.co.uk
Website www.futermanrose.co.uk

Contacts *Guy Rose, Alexandra Groom, Christopher Oxford*

FOUNDED 1984. *Handles* scripts for film, TV and theatre. Commercial fiction and non-fiction with film potential; biography and show busi-

ness. No unsolicited mss. Send preliminary letter with a brief resumé, detailed synopsis and s.a.e. CLIENTS Alexandra Connor, Frank Dickens, Martin Dillon, Iain Duncan Smith, Royston Ellis, Charles Fourie, Russell Warren Howe, Sue Lenier, John McVicar, Angela Meredith, Valerie Grosvenor Myer, Yvonne Ridley, Gordon Thomas, Simon Woodham. *Commission* Literature: 12½–17½%; Drama/Screenplays: 15–20%. *Overseas associates* worldwide.

Jüri Gabriel

35 Camberwell Grove, London SE5 8JA
☎020 7703 6186 Fax 020 7703 6186

Contact *Jüri Gabriel*

Handles quality fiction of all types, non-fiction and (almost exclusively for existing clients) film, TV and radio rights/scripts. Jüri Gabriel worked in television, wrote books for 20 years and is chairman of **Dedalus** publishers. No short stories, articles, verse or books for children. Unsolicited mss ('two-page synopsis and three sample chapters in first instance, please') welcome if accompanied by return postage and letter giving sufficient information about author's writing experience, aims, etc. CLIENTS include Nigel Cawthorne, Diana Constance, Miriam Dunne, Pat Gray, Robert Irwin, John Lucas, David Madsen, Richard Mankiewicz, David Miller, Prof. Cedric Mims, John Outram, Dr Stefan Szymanski, Frances Treanor, Dr Terence White, Dr Robert Youngson. *Commission* Home 10%; US & Translation 20%.

Eric Glass Ltd

25 Ladbroke Crescent, London W11 1PS
☎020 7229 9500 Fax 020 7229 6220
Email eglassltd@aol.com

Contact *Janet Glass*

FOUNDED 1934. *Handles* fiction, non-fiction and scripts for publication or production in all media. No poetry, short stories or children's works. No unsolicited mss. No reading fee. CLIENTS include Marc Camoletti, Charles Dyer and the estates of Rodney Ackland, Jean Cocteau, Philip King, Robin Maugham, Beverley Nichols, Jack Popplewell, Jean-Paul Sartre, Arthur Schnitzler. *Commission* Home 10%; US & Translation 20%. *Overseas associates* in the US, Australia, France, Germany, Greece, Holland, Italy, Japan, Poland, Scandinavia, South Africa, Spain.

David Godwin Associates

55 Monmouth Street, London WC2H 9DG
☎020 7240 9992 Fax 020 7395 6110
Email assistant@davidgodwinassociates.co.uk

Contacts *David Godwin*

FOUNDED 1996. *Handles* literary and general fiction, non-fiction, biography. No scripts, science fiction or children's. No reading fee. Send covering letter with first three chapters and s.a.e. for response. *Commission* Home 10%; Overseas 20%.

Annette Green Authors' Agency

6 Montem Street, London N4 3BE
☎020 7281 0009 Fax 020 7686 5884
Email annettekgreen@aol.com
Contact *Address material to the Company*

FOUNDED 1998. *Handles* literary and general fiction and non-fiction, upmarket popular culture, biography and memoirs. No dramatic scripts, poetry, or children's. Preliminary letter and s.a.e. essential. No reading fee. CLIENTS include Nick Barlay, Bill Broady, Dr Jerry Brotton, Emma Gold, Justin Hill, Max Kinnings, Maria McCann, Ian Marchant, Professor Charles Pasternak, Owen Sheers, Elizabeth Woodcraft. *Commission* Home 15%; US & Translation 20%.

Christine Green Authors' Agent★

6 Whitehorse Mews, Westminster Bridge Road, London SE1 7QD
☎020 7401 8844 Fax 020 7401 8860
Contact *Christine Green*

FOUNDED 1984. *Handles* fiction (general and literary) and general non-fiction. No scripts, poetry or children's. No unsolicited mss; initial letter and synopsis preferred. No reading fee but return postage essential. *Commission* Home 10%; US & Translation 20%.

Louise Greenberg★

The End House, Church Crescent, London N3 1BG
☎020 8349 1179 Fax 020 8343 4559
Email louisegreenberg@msn.com
Contact *Louise Greenberg*

FOUNDED 1997. *Handles* literary fiction and non-fiction. No poetry, health or sport. No reading fee. S.a.e. essential. *Commission* Home 10%; US & Translation 20%. *Dramatic associate* **Micheline Steinberg Playwrights**.

Greene & Heaton Ltd★

37 Goldhawk Road, London W12 8QQ
☎020 8749 0315 Fax 020 8749 0318
Contacts *Carol Heaton, Judith Murray, Antony Topping*

A small agency with a varied list of clients. *Handles* fiction (no science fiction, fantasy or children's books) and general non-fiction. No original scripts for theatre, film or TV. No reply to unsolicited submissions without s.a.e. and/or return postage. CLIENTS include Mark Barrowcliffe, Geraldine Bedell, Bill Bryson, Jan Dalley, Marcus du Sautoy, Colin Forbes, Michael Frayn, P.D. James, Mary Morrissy, William Shawcross, Sarah Waters. *Commission* Home 10%; US & Translation 20%.

Gregory & Company, Authors' Agents★ (formerly **Gregory & Radice**)

3 Barb Mews, London W6 7PA
☎020 7610 4676 Fax 020 7610 4686
Email info@gregoryandcompany.co.uk
Website www.gregoryandcompany.co.uk
Contact *Jane Gregory*
Editorial *Broo Doherty*
Rights *Jane Barlow, Claire Morris*

FOUNDED 1987. *Handles* all kinds of fiction and general non-fiction. *Special interest* fiction – literary, commercial, crime, suspense and thrillers. 'We are particularly interested in books which will also sell to publishers abroad.' No original plays, film or TV scripts (only published books are sold to film and TV). No science fiction, fantasy, poetry, academic or children's books. No reading fee. Editorial advice given to own authors. No unsolicited mss; send a preliminary letter with c.v., synopsis, first three chapters and future writing plans (plus return postage). Short submissions by fax or e-mail. *Commission* Home 15%; US, Translation, Radio/TV/Film 20%. Is well represented throughout Europe, Asia and US.

David Grossman Literary Agency Ltd

118b Holland Park Avenue, London W11 4UA
☎020 7221 2770 Fax 020 7221 1445
Contact *Material should be addressed to the Submissions Dept.*

FOUNDED 1976. *Handles* full-length fiction and general non-fiction – good writing of all kinds and anything healthily controversial. No verse or technical books for students. No original screenplays or teleplays (only works existing in volume form are sold for performance rights). Generally works with published writers of fiction only but 'truly original, well-written novels from beginners' will be considered. Best approach by preliminary letter giving full description of the work and, in the case of fiction, with the first 50 pages. All material must be accompanied by return postage. No approaches or submissions by fax or e-mail. No unsolicited mss. No reading fee. *Commission* Rates vary for different markets. *Overseas associates* throughout Europe, Asia, Brazil and the US.

The Rod Hall Agency Limited
3 Charlotte Mews, London W1T 4DZ
☎020 7637 0706 Fax 020 7637 0807
Email office@rodhallagency.com
Website www.rodhallagency.com
Contacts *Rod Hall, Clare Barker, Charlotte Mann*

FOUNDED 1997. *Handles* drama for film, TV and theatre. Does not represent writers of episodes for TV series where the format is provided but represents originators of series. CLIENTS include Simon Beaufoy (*The Full Monty*), Jeremy Brock (*Mrs Brown*), Lee Hall (*Billy Elliot*), Liz Lochhead (*Perfect Days*), Martin McDonagh (*The Beauty Queen of Leenane*). Introductory letter required with brief description of the work to be considered together with c.v. No reading fee. *Commission* Home 10%; US 15%; Translation 20%.

Margaret Hanbury Literary Agency*
27 Walcot Square, London SE11 4UB
☎020 7735 7680 Fax 020 7793 0316
Email maggie@mhanbury.demon.co.uk
Contact *Margaret Hanbury*

Personally run agency representing quality fiction and non-fiction. No plays, scripts, poetry, children's books, fantasy, horror. No unsolicited approaches at present. *Commission* Home 15%; Overseas 20%.

Roger Hancock Ltd
4 Water Lane, London NW1 8NZ
☎020 7267 4418 Fax 020 7267 0705
Email info@rogerhancock.com
Contact *Material should be addressed to the Company*

FOUNDED 1960. *Special interests* comedy drama and light entertainment. Scripts only. No books. Unsolicited mss not welcome. Initial phone call required. No reading fee. *Commission* Home 10%; Overseas 15%.

Antony Harwood Limited
109 Riverbank House, 1 Putney Bridge Approach, London SW6 3JD
☎020 7384 9209 Fax 020 7384 9206
Email mail@antonyharwood.com
Contacts *Antony Harwood, James Macdonald Lockhart*

FOUNDED 2000. *Handles* fiction and non-fiction.

Send letter and synopsis with return postage in the first instance. No reading fee. CLIENTS Peter F. Hamilton, Alan Hollinghurst, A.L. Kennedy, Douglas Kennedy, Chris Manby, George Monbiot, Tim Parks. *Commission* Home 10%; US & Translation 20%.

A.M. Heath & Co. Ltd*
79 St Martin's Lane, London WC2N 4RE
☎020 7836 4271 Fax 020 7497 2561
Contacts *Bill Hamilton, Sara Fisher, Sarah Molloy, Victoria Hobbs*

FOUNDED 1919. *Handles* fiction, general non-fiction and children's. No dramatic scripts, poetry or short stories. Preliminary letter and synopsis essential. No reading fee. CLIENTS include Joan Aiken, Christopher Andrew, Bella Bathurst, Anita Brookner, Helen Cresswell, Patricia Duncker, Geoff Dyer, Katie Fforde, Lesley Glaister, Graham Hancock, Hilary Mantel, Hilary Norman, Susan Price, John Sutherland, Adam Thorpe, Barbara Trapido. *Commission* Home 10–15%; US & Translation 20%; Film & TV 15%. *Overseas associates* in the US, Europe, South America, Japan and the Far East.

Rupert Heath Literary Agency
The Beeches, Furzedown Lane, Amport, Hampshire SP11 8BW
☎01264 771899 Fax 01264 771142
Email rupheath@hotmail.com
Contact *Rupert Heath*

FOUNDED 2000. *Handles* literary and general fiction and non-fiction, including history, biography and autobiography, current affairs, popular science, the arts and some popular culture. No scripts, short stories, poetry or children's. Approach with e-mail or letter (synopsis, sample chapter and s.a.e.). No reading fee. *Commission* Home 15%; US & Translation 20%. *Overseas associates* worldwide.

David Higham Associates Ltd*
5–8 Lower John Street, Golden Square, London W1F 9HA
☎020 7434 5900 Fax 020 7437 1072
Email dha@davidhigham.co.uk
Scripts *Nicky Lund, Georgina Ruffhead, Gemma Hirst*
Books *Anthony Goff, Bruce Hunter, Jacqueline Korn, Caroline Walsh, Veronique Baxter*

FOUNDED 1935. *Handles* fiction, general non-fiction (biography, history, current affairs, etc.) and children's books. Also scripts. Preliminary letter with synopsis essential in first instance. No reading fee. CLIENTS include John le Carré, Stephen Fry, Jane Green, James Herbert, Jeremy Paxman, Jacqueline Wilson. *Commission* Home 10%; US & Translation 20%.

Vanessa Holt Ltd★

59 Crescent Road, Leigh-on-Sea, Essex SS9 2PF
☎01702 473787 Fax 01702 471890
Email vanessa@holtlimited.freeserve.co.uk
Contact *Vanessa Holt*

FOUNDED 1989. *Handles* general fiction, non-fiction and non-illustrated children's books. No scripts, poetry, academic or technical. *Specialises* in crime fiction, commercial and literary fiction, and particularly interested in books with potential for sales abroad and/or to TV. No unsolicited mss. Approach by letter in first instance; s.a.e. essential. No reading fee. *Commission* Home 15%; US & Translation 20%; Radio/TV/Film 15%. Represented in all foreign markets.

Kate Hordern Literary Agency

18 Mortimer Road, Clifton, Bristol BS8 4EY
☎0117 923 9368 Fax 0117 973 1941
Email katehordern@compuserve.com
Contact *Kate Hordern*

FOUNDED 1999. *Handles* quality literary and commercial fiction including women's, suspense and genre fiction; also general non-fiction. No children's books. Approach in writing in the first instance with details of project. New clients taken on very selectively. Synopsis required for fiction; proposal/chapter breakdown for non-fiction. Sample chapters on request only. S.a.e. essential. No reading fee. CLIENTS Richard Bassett, Jeff Dawson, James Gray, Will Randall. *Commission* Home 15%; US & Translation 20%. *Overseas associates* Carmen Balcells Agency, Spain; Synopsis Agency, Russia and various agencies in Asia.

Valerie Hoskins Associates

20 Charlotte Street, London W1T 2NA
☎020 7637 4490 Fax 020 7637 4493
Email vha@vhassociates.co.uk
Contacts *Valerie Hoskins, Rebecca Watson*

FOUNDED 1983. *Handles* scripts for film, TV and radio. *Special interests* feature films, animation and TV. No unsolicited scripts; preliminary letter of introduction essential. No reading fee. *Commission* Home 12½%; US 20% (maximum).

Tanja Howarth Literary Agency★

19 New Row, London WC2N 4LA
☎020 7240 5553 Fax 020 7379 0969
Email tanja.howarth@virgin.net
Contact *Tanja Howarth*

FOUNDED 1970. Interested in taking on both fiction and non-fiction from British writers. No children's books, plays or poetry, but all other subjects considered providing the treatment is intelligent. *No unsolicited mss.* Also an established agent for foreign literature, particularly from the German language. *Commission* Home 15%; Translation 20%.

ICM

Oxford House, 76 Oxford Street, London W1D 1BS
☎020 7636 6565 Fax 020 7323 0101
Contacts *Greg Hunt, Cathy King, Hugo Young, Michael McCoy, Sue Rodgers, Jessica Sykes*

FOUNDED 1973. *Handles* film, TV and theatre scripts. No books. No unsolicited mss. Preliminary letter essential. No reading fee. *Commission* 10%. *Overseas associates* ICM, New York/Los Angeles.

IMG Literary UK

The Pier House, Strand on the Green, Chiswick, London W4 3NN
☎020 8233 5000 Fax 020 8233 5001
IMG Literary US, 825 Seventh Avenue, Ninth Floor, New York, NY 10009
☎001 212 489 5400 Fax 001 212 246 1118
Chairman *Mark H. McCormack*
Agents *Sarah Wooldridge (UK), Mark Reiter, David McCormick, Carolyn Krupp, Lisa Queen, Susan Reed (US),*
Handles celebrity books, commercial fiction, non-fiction, sports-related and how-to business books. No theatre, children's, poetry or academic books. *Commission* Home & US 20%; Elsewhere 25%.

Michael Imison Playwrights Ltd
See **Alan Brodie Representation Ltd**

Intercontinental Literary Agency★

33 Bedford Street, London WC2E 9ED
☎020 7379 6611 Fax 020 7379 6790
Email ila@ila-agency.co.uk
Contacts *Nicki Kennedy, Sam Edenborough*

FOUNDED 1965. *Handles* translation rights only for, among others, the authors of **PFD**, London; **LAW Ltd**, London; Harold Matson Co. Inc., New York.

International Literary Representation & Management LLC

186 Bickenhall Mansions, Bickenhall Street, London W1U 6BX
☎020 7224 1748 Fax 020 7224 1802
Email info@yesitive.com
Website www.yesitive.com

Vice President for Europe *Peter Cox*

European office of US agency. Represents authors with major international potential. Submissions considered only if the guidelines given on the website have been followed. Do not send unsolicited mss by post. No radio or theatre scripts. No reading fee. CLIENTS Daniel Altieri, Brian Clegg, Brian Cruver, Professor Devra Lee Davis, Dr Patrick Dixon, Senator Orrin Hatch, Commodore Scott Jones, USN, Michael J. Nelson, Michelle Paver, Saxon Roach, Tom Stevenson, Mary Tabor. *Commission* by agreement.

International Scripts

1A Kidbrooke Park Road, Blackheath, London SE3 0LR
☎020 8319 8666 Fax 020 8319 0801

Contacts *Bob Tanner, Pat Hornsey, Jill Lawson*

FOUNDED 1979 by Bob Tanner. *Handles* most types of books (non-fiction and fiction) and scripts for most media. No poetry, articles or short stories. Preliminary letter plus s.a.e. required. CLIENTS include Jane Adams, Zita Adamson, Simon Clark, Cory Daniells, Paul Devereux, Dr James Fleming, James Gibbins, Ed Gorman, Julie Harris, Robert A. Heinlein, Anna Jacobs, Anne Jones, Richard Laymon, Nick Oldham, Mary Ryan, John and Anne Spencer, Janet Woods, **Barrons** (USA), Masquerade Books (USA). *Commission* Home 15%; US & Translation 20%. *Overseas associates* include Ralph Vicinanza, USA; Thomas Schlück, Germany; Eliane Benisti, France.

Barrie James Literary Agency/ New Authors Showcase

See entry under **Electronic Publishing and Other Services**

Janklow & Nesbit (UK) Ltd

29 Adam & Eve Mews, London W8 6UG
☎020 7376 2733 Fax 020 7376 2915
Email queries@janklow.co.uk

Contacts *Tif Loehnis, Carl Parsons*

FOUNDED 2000. *Handles* fiction and non-fiction; commercial and literary. No unsolicited mss. Send full outline (non-fiction), synopsis and three sample chapters (fiction) plus informative covering letter and return postage. (See also **Janklow & Nesbit Associates**, New York, under **US Agents**.)

John Johnson (Authors' Agent) Limited★

Clerkenwell House, 45/47 Clerkenwell Green, London EC1R 0HT
☎020 7251 0125 Fax 020 7251 2172
Email johnjohnson@btinternet.com

Contacts *Andrew Hewson, Margaret Hewson, Elizabeth Fairbairn*

FOUNDED 1956. *Handles* general fiction and non-fiction. No science fiction, technical or academic material. Scripts from existing clients only. No unsolicited mss; send a preliminary letter and s.a.e. in the first instance. No reading fee. *Commission* Home 10%; US 15–20%; Translation 20%.

Jane Judd Literary Agency★

18 Belitha Villas, London N1 1PD
☎020 7607 0273 Fax 020 7607 0623

Contact *Jane Judd*

FOUNDED 1986. *Handles* general fiction and non-fiction: women's fiction, crime, thrillers, literary fiction, humour, biography, investigative journalism, health, women's interests and travel. 'Looking for good contemporary women's fiction but not Mills & Boon-type.' No scripts, academic, gardening or DIY. Approach with letter, including synopsis, first chapter and return postage. Initial telephone call helpful in the case of non-fiction. CLIENTS include Patrick Anthony, the John Brunner estate, Andy Dougan, Jill Mansell, Jonathon Porritt, Rosie Rushton, Manda Scott. *Commission* Home 10%; US & Translation 20%.

Juvenilia

Avington, Near Winchester, Hampshire SO21 1DB
☎01962 779656 Fax 01962 779656
Email juvenilia@clara.co.uk

Contact *Rosemary Bromley*

FOUNDED 1973. *Handles* young/teen fiction and picture books; non-fiction and scripts for TV and radio. No poetry or short stories unless part of a collection or picture book material. No unsolicited mss. Send preliminary letter with full details of work and biographical outline in first instance. Preliminary letters unaccompanied by return postage will not be answered. Enquiries by phone, fax or e-mail will not be answered.

CLIENTS include Paul Aston, Elisabeth Beresford, Linda Birch, Denis Bond, Terry Deary, Ann Evans, Gaye Hicyilmaz, Tom Holt, Tony Maddox, Phil McMylor, Anna Perara, Elizabeth Pewsey, Fran and John Pickering, Saviour Pirotta, Eira Reeves, Kelvin Reynolds, James Riordan, Peter Riley, Susan Rollings, Malcolm Rose, Cathy Simpson, Keith West. *Commission* Home 10%; US 15%; Translation 20%.

Tamar Karet Literary Agency
56 Priory Road, Crouch End, London N8 7EX
☎020 8340 6460 Fax 020 8348 8638
Email tamar@btinternet.com
Contact *Tamar Karet*
FOUNDED in 2001 by publisher with particular experience of fiction, social affairs and illustrated books. *Specialises* in fiction, travel, leisure, health, cookery, biography, history, social affairs and politics. No academic, children's, poetry, science fiction, horror, militaria or scripts. No unsolicited mss; no submissions by e-mail. Send synopsis and sample with s.a.e. *Commission* Home 15%; US & Translation 20%.

Michelle Kass Associates*
36–38 Glasshouse Street, London W1B 5DL
☎020 7439 1624 Fax 020 7734 3394
Contacts *Michelle Kass, Resham Naqvi*
FOUNDED 1991. *Handles* literary fiction and film primarily. Approach with telephone call/explanatory letter in the first instance. No reading fee. *Commission* Home 10%; US & Translation 15–20%.

Frances Kelly*
111 Clifton Road, Kingston upon Thames, Surrey KT2 6PL
☎020 8549 7830 Fax 020 8547 0051
Contact *Frances Kelly*
FOUNDED 1978. *Handles* non-fiction, including illustrated: biography, history, art, self-help, food & wine, complementary medicine and therapies, finance and business books; and academic non-fiction in all disciplines. No scripts except for existing clients. No unsolicited mss. Approach by letter with brief description of work or synopsis, together with c.v. and return postage. *Commission* Home 10%; US & Translation 20%.

Paul Kiernan
PO Box 120, London SW3 4LU
☎020 7352 5562
Contact *Paul Kiernan*
FOUNDED 1990. *Handles* fiction and non-fiction, including autobiography and biography, plus specialist writers for subjects such as cookery or gardening. Also scripts for TV, film, radio and theatre (but TV and film scripts from book-writing clients only). No unsolicited mss. Preferred approach is by letter or personal introduction. Letters should include synopsis and brief biography. No reading fee. CLIENTS include K. Banta, Lord Chalfont, Ambassador Walter J.P. Curley, Sir Paul Fox. *Commission* Home 15%; US 20%.

Knight Features
20 Crescent Grove, London SW4 7AH
☎020 7622 1467 Fax 020 7622 1522
Email peter@knightfeatures.co.uk
Contacts *Peter Knight, Samantha Ferris, Gaby Martin, Ann King-Hall, Andrew Knight*
FOUNDED 1985. *Handles* motor sports, cartoon books, puzzles, business, history, factual and biographical material. No poetry, science fiction or cookery. No unsolicited mss. Send letter accompanied by c.v. and s.a.e. with synopsis of proposed work. CLIENTS include David Kerr Cameron, Frank Dickens, Christopher Hilton, Gray Jolliffe, Angus McGill, Chris Maslanka, Barbara Minto. *Commission* dependent upon authors and territories. *Overseas associates* United Media, US; Auspac Media, Australia.

Labour and Management Limited
Milton House, Milton Street, Waltham Abbey, Essex EN9 1EZ
☎01992 711511/614527 Fax 01992 711511/614527
Email TriciaSumner@email.msn.com
Contact *Tricia Sumner*
FOUNDED 1995. *Specialises* in literary fiction, theatre, TV, radio and film. *Special interests* in multi-cultural, gay, feminist and anti-establishment writing. No new authors taken on except by recommendation. No unsolicited mss. CLIENTS include Marion Baraitser, Kathleen Kiirik Bryson, John R. Gordon, Barry Grossman, Angela Lanyon, Chris Madogh, Roland Moore, Jeremy Rayner. *Commission* Home 12½%; Overseas 20%.

LAW Ltd (Lucas Alexander Whitley)*
14 Vernon Street, London W14 0RJ
☎020 7471 7900 Fax 020 7471 7910
Email <firstname>@lawagency.co.uk
Contacts *Mark Lucas, Julian Alexander, Araminta Whitley, Philippa Milnes-Smith (children's), Alice Saunders, Celia Hayley,*

Lucinda Cook, Peta Nightingale, Helen Mulligan

FOUNDED 1996. *Handles* full-length commercial and literary fiction, non-fiction and children's books. No plays, poetry, textbooks or fantasy. Film and TV scripts handled for established clients only. Unsolicited mss considered; send brief covering letter, short synopsis and two sample chapters. S.a.e. essential. No e-mailed submissions. *Commission* Home 15%; US & Translation 20%. *Overseas associates* worldwide.

Cat Ledger Literary Agency★
20–21 Newman Street, London W1T 1PG
☎020 7861 8226 Fax 020 7861 8001
Contact *Cat Ledger*

FOUNDED 1996. *Handles* non-fiction: popular culture – film, music, sport, travel, humour, biography, politics; investigative journalism; fiction (non-genre). No scripts. No children's, poetry, fantasy, science fiction, romance. No unsolicited mss; approach with preliminary letter, synopsis and s.a.e. No reading fee. *Commission* Home 10%; US & Translation 20%.

Barbara Levy Literary Agency★
64 Greenhill, Hampstead High Street, London NW3 5TZ
☎020 7435 9046 Fax 020 7431 2063
Contacts *Barbara Levy, John Selby*

FOUNDED 1986. *Handles* general fiction, non-fiction, and film and TV rights. No unsolicited mss. Send detailed preliminary letter in the first instance. No reading fee. *Commission* Home 10%; US 20%; Translation by arrangement, in conjunction with **The Marsh Agency**. *US associate* Arcadia Ltd, New York.

Limelight Management★
33 Newman Street, London W1T 1PY
☎020 7637 2529 Fax 020 7637 2538
Email limelight.management@virgin.net
Contacts *Fiona Lindsay, Linda Shanks*

FOUNDED 1991. *Handles* general non-fiction: cookery, gardening, antiques, interior design, wine, art and crafts and health. No TV, film, radio or theatre. *Specialises* in illustrated books. Unsolicited mss welcome; send preliminary letter (s.a.e. essential). No reading fee. *Commission* Home 15%; US & Translation 20%.

The Christopher Little Literary Agency★
10 Eel Brook Studios, 125 Moore Park Road, London SW6 4PS

☎020 7736 4455 Fax 020 7736 4490
Email <firstname>@christopherlittle.net
Contacts *Christopher Little, Kellee Nunley*

FOUNDED 1979. *Handles* commercial and literary full-length fiction and non-fiction. No poetry, plays, science fiction, fantasy, textbooks, illustrated children's or short stories. Film scripts for established clients only. No unsolicited submissions. *Commission* Home 15%; US, Canada, Translation, Audio, Motion Picture 20%.

London Independent Books
26 Chalcot Crescent, London NW1 8YD
☎020 7706 0486 Fax 020 7724 3122
Proprietor *Carolyn Whitaker*

FOUNDED 1971. A self-styled 'small and idiosyncratic' agency. *Handles* fiction and non-fiction reflecting the tastes of the proprietors. All subjects considered (except computer books and young children's), providing the treatment is strong and saleable. Scripts handled only if by existing clients. *Special interests* boats, travel, travelogues, commercial fiction. No unsolicited mss; letter, synopsis and first two chapters with return postage the best approach. No reading fee. *Commission* Home 15%; US & Translation 20%.

The Andrew Lownie Literary Agency★
17 Sutherland Street, London SW1V 4JU
☎020 7828 1274 Fax 020 7828 7608
Email lownie@globalnet.co.uk
Website www.andrewlownie.co.uk
Contact *Andrew Lownie*

FOUNDED 1988. *Specialises* in non-fiction, especially history, biography, current affairs, military history, UFOs, reference and packaging celebrities and journalists for the book market. No poetry, short stories or science fiction. Formerly a journalist, publisher and himself the author of 12 non-fiction books, Andrew Lownie's CLIENTS include Theo Aronson, Juliet Barker, Guy Bellamy, the Joyce Cary estate, Peter Evans, Jonathan Fryer, Laurence Gardner, Timothy Good, Gloria Hunniford, Leo McKinstry, Julian Maclaren-Ross estate, Patrick MacNee, Norma Major, Sir John Mills, Nick Pope, John Rae, Richard Rudgley, Desmond Seward, Alan Whicker, Lawrence James, editors of the *Oxford Classical Dictionary* and *Cambridge Guide to Literature in English*. Approach with letter, synopsis, sample chapter and s.a.e. Translation rights handled by **The Marsh Agency**. *Commission* Worldwide 15%.

Lucas Alexander Whitley

See **LAW Ltd**

Lutyens and Rubinstein★

231 Westbourne Park Road, London
W11 1EB
☎020 7792 4855 Fax 020 7792 4833
Partners *Sarah Lutyens, Felicity Rubinstein*
Submissions *Susannah Godman*

FOUNDED 1993. *Handles* adult fiction and non-fiction books. No TV, film, radio or theatre scripts. Unsolicited mss accepted; send introductory letter, c.v., two chapters and return postage for all material submitted. No reading fee. *Commission* Home 15%; US & Translation 20%.

Duncan McAra

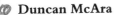

28 Beresford Gardens, Edinburgh EH5 3ES
☎0131 552 1558 Fax 0131 552 1558
Email duncanmcara@hotmail.com

Contact *Duncan McAra*

FOUNDED 1988. *Handles* fiction (literary fiction) and non-fiction, including art, architecture, archaeology, biography, military, travel and books of Scottish interest. Preliminary letter, synopsis and sample chapter (including return postage) essential. No reading fee. *Commission* Home 10%; Overseas 20%.

Bill McLean
Personal Management Ltd

23B Deodar Road, London SW15 2NP
☎020 8789 8191

Contact *Bill McLean*

FOUNDED 1972. *Handles* scripts for all media. No books. No unsolicited mss. Phone call or introductory letter essential. No reading fee. CLIENTS include Dwynwen Berry, Graham Carlisle, Jeff Dodds, Jane Galletly, Patrick Jones, Tony Jordan, Bill Lyons, Annie Marshall, John Maynard, Michael McStay, Les Miller, Ian Rowlands, Jeffrey Segal, Ronnie Smith, Barry Thomas, Frank Vickery, Mark Wheatley. *Commission* Home 10%.

Eunice McMullen
Children's Literary Agent Ltd

Low Ibbotsholme Cottage, Off Bridge Lane,
Troutbeck Bridge, Windermere, Cumbria
LA23 1HU
☎01539 448551 Fax 01539 442289
Email eunicemcmullen@totalise.co.uk

Contact *Eunice McMullen*

FOUNDED 1992. *Handles* all types of children's material in particular picture books. Has 'an excellent' list of picture book authors and illustrators. *No unsolicited scripts.* Telephone enquiries only. CLIENTS include Wayne Anderson, Reg Cartwright, Jason Cockcroft, Ross Collins, Siobhan Dodds, Richard Fowler, Charles Fuge, Susie Jenkin-Pearce, Angela McAllister, David Melling, Sue Porter, Susan Winter, David Wood. *Commission* Home 10%; US 15%; Translation 20%.

Andrew Mann Ltd★

1 Old Compton Street, London W1V 5PH
☎020 7734 4751 Fax 020 7287 9264
Email manscript@onetel.net.uk

Contacts *Anne Dewe, Tina Betts*

FOUNDED 1975. *Handles* fiction, general non-fiction and film, TV, theatre, radio scripts. No unsolicited mss. Preliminary letter, synopsis and s.a.e. essential. No reading fee. *Commission* Home 15%; US & Translation 20%. *Overseas associates* various.

Manuscript ReSearch

PO Box 33, Bicester, Oxfordshire OX26 4ZZ
☎01869 323447 Fax 01869 324096

Contact *Graham Jenkins*

FOUNDED 1988. Principally *handles* scripts suitable for film/TV outlets. Will only consider book submissions from established clients. Preferred first approach from new contacts is by letter with brief outline and s.a.e. *Commission* Home 10%; Overseas 20%.

Marjacq Scripts Ltd

34 Devonshire Place, London W1G 6JW
☎020 7935 9499 Fax 020 7935 9115
Email mark@marjacq.com
Website www.marjacq.com

Contact *Mark Hayward*

HANDLES general fiction and non-fiction, and screenplays. Special interest in crime, sagas and science fiction. No poetry, children's books or plays. Send synopsis and three chapters; will suggest revisions for promising mss. No reading fee. *Commission* Home 10%; Overseas 20%.

The Marsh Agency★

11/12 Dover Street, London W1S 4LJ
☎020 7399 2800 Fax 020 7399 2801
Email enquiries@marsh-agency.co.uk
Website www.marsh-agency.co.uk

Contact *Paul Marsh*

FOUNDED 1994. International rights specialists selling English and foreign language writing. No

TV, film, radio or theatre. No unsolicited mss. CLIENTS include several British and American agencies and publishers, and some individual authors. See also **Paterson Marsh Ltd**.

Martinez Literary Agency
60 Oakwood Avenue, Southgate, London N14 6QL
☎020 8886 5829

Contacts *Mary Martinez, Francoise Budd*

FOUNDED 1988. *Handles* high-quality fiction, children's books, arts and crafts, interior design, alternative health/complementary medicine, autobiography, biography, popular music, sport and memorabilia books. Not accepting any new writers. *Commission* Home 15%; US, Overseas & Translation 20%; Performance Rights 20%.

MBA Literary Agents Ltd★
62 Grafton Way, London W1T 5DW
☎020 7387 2076 Fax 020 7387 2042
Email <firstname>@mbalit.co.uk

Contacts *Diana Tyler, John Richard Parker, Meg Davis, Laura Longrigg, David Riding*

FOUNDED 1971. *Handles* fiction and non-fiction, TV, film, radio and theatre scripts. No unsolicited mss. Works in conjunction with agents in most countries. Also UK representative for **Writers House, Inc**, the Donald Maass Agency and the JABberwocky Agency. CLIENTS include Campbell Armstrong, A.L. Barker, estate of Harry Bowling, Jeffrey Caine, Glenn Chandler, Andrew Cowan, Patricia Finney, Maggie Furey, Sue Gee, Joanna Hines, B.S. Johnson estate, Robert Jones, Anne McCaffrey, Paul Magrs, Susan Oudot, Sir Roger Penrose, Anne Perry, Gervase Phinn, Christopher Russell, Jim Shields, Iain Sinclair, Steve Strange, Mark Wallington, Patrick Wilde, Paul Wilson, Valerie Windsor, The Chap Magazine. *Commission* Home 15%; Overseas 20%; Theatre/TV/Radio 10%; Film 10–20%.

Midland Exposure
4 Victoria Court, Oadby, Leicestershire LE2 4AF
☎0116 271 8332 Fax 0116 281 2188
Email partners@midlandexposure.co.uk
Website www.midlandexposure.co.uk

Partners *Cari Crook, Lesley Gleeson*

FOUNDED 1996. *Handles* short fiction for magazines only. *Specialises* in women's, teenage and children's magazine fiction. No books. 'Keen to encourage new writers.' Unsolicited mss welcome. Please ring for current reading fee. *Commission* Home 15–25%; US 20%.

Christy Moore Ltd
See **Sheil Land Associates Ltd**

William Morris Agency (UK) Ltd★
52/53 Poland Street, London W1F 7LX
☎020 7534 6800 Fax 020 7534 6900
Website www.wma.com

Managing Director *Stephanie Cabot*

London office FOUNDED 1965. Worldwide theatrical and literary agency with offices in New York, Beverly Hills and Nashville and associates in Sydney. *Handles* fiction, general non-fiction, TV and film scripts. No unsolicited film, TV or stage material *at all*. Mss for books with preliminary letter to Book Department. No reading fee. *Commission* TV 10%; UK Books 15%; US Books & Translation 20%.

Michael Motley Ltd
The Old Vicarage, Tredington, Tewkesbury, Gloucestershire GL20 7BP
☎01684 276390 Fax 01684 297355

Contact *Michael Motley*

FOUNDED 1973. *Handles* only full-length mss (i.e. 60,000+). No short stories or journalism. No science fiction, horror, poetry or original dramatic material. New clients by referral only. Unsolicited mss returned unread. No reading fee. *Commission* Home 10%; US 15%; Translation 20%. *Overseas associates* in all publishing centres.

Judith Murdoch Literary Agency★
19 Chalcot Square, London NW1 8YA
☎020 7722 4197

Contact *Judith Murdoch*

FOUNDED 1993. *Handles* full-length fiction only. No thrillers, science fiction/fantasy, children's, poetry or short stories. No unsolicited mss; approach in writing only enclosing first two chapters and brief synopsis. Return postage/s.a.e. essential. No reading fee. CLIENTS include Meg Hutchinson, Lisa Jewell, Pamela Jooste. Translation rights handled by **The Marsh Agency**. *Commission* Home 15%; US & Translation 20%.

The Narrow Road Company
182 Brighton Road, Coulsdon, Surrey CR5 2NF
☎020 8763 9895 Fax 020 8763 9329
Email narrowroad@freeuk.com

Contacts *Richard Ireson, Isabella Summers*

FOUNDED 1986. Part of the Narrow Road Group. Theatrical literary agency. *Handles* scripts for TV, theatre, film and radio. No novels or poetry. No unsolicited mss; approach by letter with c.v. and one-page synopsis. Interested in writers with some experience and original ideas. CLIENTS include Vanessa Brooks, David Halliwell, Alex Lowe, Brian Marshall.

William Neill-Hall Ltd
Old Oak Cottage, Ropewalk, Mount Hawke, Truro, Cornwall TR4 8DW
☎01209 891427 Fax 01209 891427
Email wneill-hall@msn.com
Contact *William Neill-Hall*

FOUNDED 1995. *Handles* general non-fiction, religion. No TV, film, theatre or radio scripts; no fiction or poetry. *Specialises* in religion, sport, history and current affairs. No unsolicited mss. Approach by phone or letter. Enclose return postage. No reading fee. CLIENTS include Mary Batchelor, George Carey, Richard Foster, Juliet Janvrin, Jennifer Rees Larcombe, Peter Owen-Jones, Eugene Peterson, David Pytches, Mary Pytches, Philip Yancey. *Commission* Home 10%; US 15%; Translation 20%.

The Maggie Noach Literary Agency★
22 Dorville Crescent, London W6 0HJ
☎020 8748 2926 Fax 020 8748 8057
Email m-noach@dircon.co.uk
Contact *Maggie Noach*

FOUNDED 1982. Pronounced 'no-ack'. *Handles* a wide range of well-written books including general non-fiction, especially biography, commercial fiction and non-illustrated children's books for ages 7–12. No scientific, academic or specialist non-fiction. No poetry, plays, short stories or books for the very young. Recommended for promising young writers but *very* few new clients taken on as it is considered vital to give individual attention to each author's work. Unsolicited mss not welcome. Approach by letter (*not by telephone or e-mail*), giving a brief description of the book and enclosing a few sample pages. Return postage essential. No reading fee. *Commission* Home 15%; US & Translation 20%.

Andrew Nurnberg Associates Ltd★
Clerkenwell House, 45–47 Clerkenwell Green, London EC1R 0HT
☎020 7417 8800 Fax 020 7417 8812
Email all@nurnberg.co.uk
Directors *Andrew Nurnberg, Sarah Nundy, D. Roger Seaton, Vicky Mark*
Associate Director *Anna Chodakowska*

FOUNDED in the mid-1970s. *Specialises* in foreign rights, representing leading authors and agents. Branches in Moscow, Bucharest, Budapest, Prague, Sofia, Warsaw and Riga. *Commission* Home 15%; US & Translation 20%.

Alexandra Nye
'Craigower', 6 Kinnoull Avenue, Dunblane, Perthshire FK15 9JG
☎01786 825114
Contact *Alexandra Nye*

FOUNDED 1991. *Handles* fiction and topical non-fiction. *Special interests* literary fiction and history. Unsolicited mss welcome (s.a.e. essential for return). Preliminary approach by letter, with synopsis, preferred. Reading fee for supply of detailed report. CLIENTS Dr Tom Gallagher, Harry Mehta, Robin Jenkins. *Commission* Home 10%; US 20%; Translation 15%.

David O'Leary Literary Agents
10 Lansdowne Court, Lansdowne Rise, London W11 2NR
☎020 7229 1623 Fax 020 7727 9624
Email d.o'leary@virgin.net
Contact *David O'Leary*

FOUNDED 1988. *Handles* fiction, both popular and literary, and non-fiction. Areas of interest include thrillers, history, popular science, Russia and Ireland (history and fiction). No poetry or science fiction. No unsolicited mss but happy to discuss a proposal. Ring or write in the first instance. No reading fee. CLIENTS include David Crackanthorpe, James Kennedy, Nick Kochan, Jim Lusby, Derek Malcolm, Ken Russell. *Commission* Home 10%; US 10%. *Overseas associates* Lennart Sane, Scandinavia/Spain/South America; Tuttle Mori, Japan.

Deborah Owen Ltd★
78 Narrow Street, Limehouse, London E14 8BP
☎020 7987 5119/5441 Fax 020 7538 4004
Contacts *Deborah Owen, Michael Shavit*

FOUNDED 1971. Small agency specialising in representing authors direct around the world. *Handles* international fiction and non-fiction (books which can be translated into a number of languages). No new authors. CLIENTS include Penelope Farmer, Amos Oz and Delia Smith. *Commission* Home 10%; US & Translation 15%.

Owen Robinson Literary Agents
20 Tolbury Mill, Bruton, Somerset BA10 0DY
☎01749 812008 Fax 01749 812008
Email jpr@owenrobinson.netlineuk.net
(enquiries only)

Contact *Justin Robinson*

FOUNDED 1998. *Handles* fiction and non-fiction. No plays, film scripts, poetry or short stories. No reading fee. No unsolicited mss. Approach in writing with s.a.e. in the first instance; send synopsis and three sample chapters subsequently. CLIENTS include Paul Garrison, Michael Holt, Sarah Lawson, Chrissie Loveday, Roger Nichols, Alistair Owen, Ann Taylor. *Commission* Home 10%; US & Translation 15–20%. Works with agents overseas.

Paterson Marsh Ltd★

11/12 Dover Street, London W1S 4LJ
☎020 7399 2800 Fax 020 7399 2801
Email steph@patersonmarsh.co.uk
Website www.patersonmarsh.co.uk
Contacts *Mark Paterson* (☎01206 825433; email mark@markpaterson.co.uk), *Paul Marsh, Stephanie Ebdon*

Formerly Mark Paterson & Associates, FOUNDED 1961. World rights representatives of authors and publishers handling many subjects, with specialisation in psychoanalysis and psychotherapy. CLIENTS range from Balint, Bion, Casement and Ferenczi, through to Freud and Winnicott; plus Hugh Brogan, Peter Moss and the estates of Sir Arthur Evans, Hugh Schonfield and Dorothy Richardson. No fiction, scripts, poetry, children's, articles, short stories or 'unsaleable mediocrity'. No unsolicited mss, but preliminary letter and synopsis with s.a.e. welcome. *Commission* 20% (including sub-agent's commission).

John Pawsey

60 High Street, Tarring, Worthing, West Sussex BN14 7NR
☎01903 205167 Fax 01903 205167
Contact *John Pawsey*

FOUNDED 1981. Experience in the publishing business has helped to attract some top names here, but the door remains open for bright, new ideas. *Handles* non-fiction: biography, politics, current affairs, popular culture, travel, sport, business and music; also fiction: crime, thrillers, suspense or 'genuine originals' but not science fiction, fantasy and horror. *Special interests* sport, current affairs and biography. No children's, drama scripts, poetry, short stories, journalism or academic. Preliminary letter with s.a.e. essential. No reading fee. CLIENTS include Jennie Bond, Dr David Lewis, David Rayvern Allen, Patricia Hall, Elwyn Hartley Edwards, Peter Hobday, Jon Silverman. *Commission* Home 10–15%; US & Translation

19–25%. *Overseas associates* in the US, Japan, South America and throughout Europe.

◗ Maggie Pearlstine Associates Ltd★

31 Ashley Gardens, Ambrosden Avenue, London SW1P 1QE
☎020 7828 4212 Fax 020 7834 5546
Email post@pearlstine.co.uk
Contact *Maggie Pearlstine*

FOUNDED 1989. Small, selective agency. *Handles* general non-fiction and fiction. *Special interest:* history, current affairs, biography and health. No children's, poetry, horror, science fiction, short stories or scripts. Seldom takes on new authors. Prospective clients should write an explanatory letter and enclose s.a.e. and the first chapter only. No submissions accepted by fax, e-mail or from abroad. No reading fee. CLIENTS Debbie Beckerman, John Biffen, Matthew Baylis, Kate Bingham, Menzies Campbell, Kim Fletcher, Fiona Harrold, Roy Hattersley, Rachel Holmes, Charles Kennedy, Mark Leonard, Eleanor Mills, Claire Macdonald, Dr Raj Persaud, Prof. Lesley Regan, Hugo Rifkind, Winifred Robinson, Jackie Rowley, Henrietta Spencer-Churchill, Alan Stewart, Prof. Robert Winston. Translation rights handled by **Gillon Aitken Associates Ltd**. *Commission* Home 12½% (fiction), 10% (non-fiction); US & Translation 20%; TV, Film & Journalism 20%.

Peters Fraser & Dunlop Group Ltd

See **PFD**

◗ PFD★

Drury House, 34–43 Russell Street, London WC2B 5HA
☎020 7344 1000
Fax 020 7836 9539/7836 9541
Email postmaster@pfd.co.uk
Website www.pfd.co.uk
Joint Chairmen *Anthony Jones, Tim Corrie*
Managing Director *Anthony Baring*
Books *Caroline Dawnay, Michael Sissons, Pat Kavanagh, Charles Walker, Rosemary Canter, Robert Kirby, Simon Trewin, James Gill*
Serial *Pat Kavanagh, Carol MacArthur*
Film/TV *Anthony Jones, Tim Corrie, Norman North, Charles Walker, Vanessa Jones, St. John Donald, Rosemary Scoular, Natasha Galloway, Jago Irwin, Louisa Thompson*
Actors *Maureen Vincent, Ginette Chalmers, Dallas Smith, Lindy King, Ruth Young, Lucy Brazier*
Theatre *Kenneth Ewing, St John Donald, Nicki Stoddart, Rosie Cobbe*

Children's *Rosemary Canter*
Multimedia *Rosemary Scoular*

FOUNDED 1988 as a result of the merger of A. D. Peters & Co. Ltd and Fraser & Dunlop, and was later joined by the June Hall Literary Agency. *Handles* all sorts of books including fiction and children's, plus scripts for film, theatre, radio and TV material. Prospective clients should write 'a full letter, with an account of what he/she has done and wants to do and enclose, when possible, a detailed outline and sample chapters'. Screenplays and TV scripts should be addressed to the 'Film & Script Dept.' Enclose s.a.e. No reading fee. The Children's Dept. does not accept unsolicited written material but welcomes work from illustrators seeking representation. CLIENTS include Julian Barnes, Alan Bennett, Alain de Botton, A.S. Byatt, estate of C.S. Forester, Nicci Gerrard, Robert Harris, Nick Hornby, Clive James, Russell Miller, estate of Nancy Mitford, John Mortimer, Andrew Motion, Douglas Reeman, Ruth Rendell, Anthony Sampson, Gerald Seymour, Tom Stoppard, Emma Thompson, Joanna Trollope, estate of Evelyn Waugh. *Commission* Home 10%; US & Translation 20%.

Pollinger Limited★

3rd Floor, Goldsmiths' House, 137–141 Regent Street, London W1B 4HZ
☎020 7025 7820 Fax 020 7025 7829
Email info@pollingerltd.com
Website www.pollingerltd.com

Chairman *Paul Woolf*
Managing Director *Lesley Pollinger*
Adult List *Lorella Belli*
Permissions/Foreign Rights *Heather Chalcroft*
Children's List *Linda Jennings*
Consultant *Gerald Pollinger*

FOUNDED 2002. A successor of Laurence Pollinger Limited (founded 1958) and Pearn, Pollinger & Higham. *Handles* all types of general trade adult and children's fiction and non-fiction books; intellectual property development, illustrators/photographers. CLIENTS include Roy Apps, Dougie Brimson, Michael Coleman, Adrienne Kennaway, Gary Latham, Nisha Minhas, Gary Paulsen, Nicholas Rhea and Sue Welford. Also the estates of H.E. Bates, Vera Chapman, Louis Bromfield, Erskine Caldwell, D.H. Lawrence, W.H. Robinson, Malcolm Saville, Clifford D. Simak and other notables. Unsolicited material considered *only* if preceded by letter or e-mail. *Commission* Home 15%;

Translation 20%. Overseas and media associates, including Oak Media.

Shelley Power Literary Agency Ltd★

13 rue du Pré Saint Gervais, 75019 Paris, France
☎00 33 1 42 38 36 49
Fax 00 33 1 40 40 70 08
Email shelley.power@wanadoo.fr

Contact *Shelley Power*

FOUNDED 1976. Shelley Power works between London and Paris. This is an English agency with London-based administration/accounts office and the editorial office in Paris. *Handles* general commercial fiction, quality fiction, business books, self-help, true crime, investigative exposés, film and entertainment. No scripts, short stories, children's or poetry. Preliminary letter with brief outline of project (plus return postage as from UK or France) essential. 'We do not consider submissions by e-mail.' No reading fee. *Commission* Home 10%; US & Translation 19%.

PVA Management Limited

Hallow Park, Worcester WR2 6PG
☎01905 640663 Fax 01905 641842
Email books@pva.co.uk

Managing Director *Paul Vaughan*

FOUNDED 1978. *Handles* non-fiction only. Please send synopsis and sample chapters together with return postage. *Commission* 15%.

Radala & Associates

17 Avenue Mansions, Finchley Road, London NW3 7AX
☎020 7794 4495 Fax 020 7431 7636
Email bt.press@lineone.net

Contacts *Richard Gollner, Néil Hornick, Anna Swan, Andy Marino*

FOUNDED 1970. *Handles* quality fiction, non-fiction, performing and popular arts, psychotherapy. Also provides or recommends editorial services and initiates in-house projects. Prospective clients should send a short letter plus synopsis (maximum 2pp), first two chapters, if a novel (double-spaced, numbered pages), and s.a.e. 'However, current industry pressures oblige us to consider only writers with solid publication/production track records.' For creative/editorial consultancy, apply to Robert Lambolle (☎020 8455 4564 or ziph@appleonline.net). *Commission* Home 10%; US 15–20%; Translation 20%. *Overseas associates* **Writers House, LLC.** (Al Zuckerman), New York; plus agents throughout Europe.

Real Creatives Worldwide
14 Dean Street, London W1D 3RX
☎020 7437 4188
Email realcreate@aol.com

Contacts *Mark Maco, Malcolm Rasala, Michael Schaeble, Darren Guthrie*

FOUNDED 1984. *Specialises* in drama, science, technology, factual and entertainment. Represents TV/film writers and directors, as well as designers, editors, producers and composers. 'Send letter or e-mail requesting a writer's submission agreement covering libel, defamation, plagiarism, etc.' Reading fee: £59.99. *Commission* Home & US 20%.

Rogers, Coleridge & White Ltd★
20 Powis Mews, London W11 1JN
☎020 7221 3717   Fax 020 7229 9084

Contacts *Deborah Rogers, Gill Coleridge, Patricia White, David Miller, Zoe Waldie, Peter Straus*
Foreign Rights *Ann Warnford-Davis, Laurence Laluyaux, Stephen Edwards*

FOUNDED 1967. *Handles* fiction, non-fiction and children's books. No poetry, plays or technical books. No unsolicited mss, please and no submissions by fax or e-mail. Rights representative in UK and translation for several New York agents. *Commission* Home 10%; US 15%; Translation 20%. *Overseas associate* ICM, New York.

Frederick Rosschild Security
PO Box 155, Great Yarmouth, Norfolk NR31 8GY

Contact *Frederick Rosschild*

FOUNDED 1994. *Handles* all types of fiction and non-fiction. Adult and children's books. Full-length novels, sagas and short stories. No plays or poetry. *Specialises* in debut writers. Initial contact should be by letter enclosing A5 envelope and £3 of loose stamps to cover p&p of information booklet. No telephone calls. (NB Office closed 30 November until 31 January.) *Commission* Home 12%; Foreign 24%. Translations from French and German into English (UK), and English (US) into English (UK) by negotiation.

Hilary Rubinstein Books
32 Ladbroke Grove, London W11 3BQ
☎020 7792 4282   Fax 020 7221 5291
Email hrubinstein@beeb.net

Contact *Hilary Rubinstein*

FOUNDED 1992. *Handles* fiction and non-fiction. No poetry or drama. Approach in writing in the first instance. No reading fee but return postage, please. CLIENTS include Lucy Irvine, Eric Lomax, Donna Williams. *Commission* Home 10%; US & Translation 20%. *Overseas associates* **Ellen Levine Literary Agency, Inc.**, New York; **Andrew Nurnberg Associates** (European rights).

Uli Rushby-Smith Literary Agency
72 Plimsoll Road, London N4 2EE
☎020 7354 2718   Fax 020 7354 2718

Contact *Uli Rushby-Smith*

FOUNDED 1993. *Handles* fiction and non-fiction, commercial and literary, both adult and children's. Film and TV rights handled in conjunction with a sub-agent. No plays or poetry. First approach with an outline, two or three sample chapters and explanatory letter (s.a.e. essential). No reading fee. *Commission* Home 15%; US & Translation 20%. Represents UK rights for **Curtis Brown**, New York (children's), 2.13.61 USA, Penguin (Canada), Penguin South Africa, the Alice Toledo Agency (NL) and Columbia University Press.

The Saddler Literary Agency
9 Curzon Road, London W5 1NE
☎020 8998 4868   Fax 020 8998 8851
Email john@saddler.fsnet.co.uk

Contact *John Saddler*

FOUNDED March 2001. John Saddler has been senior editor of **Black Swan**, an editorial director of **Fourth Estate**, publishing director of **Flamingo** and, until 2000, was publisher of Anchor Books, the literary imprint of **Transworld Publishers**. *Handles* fiction and non-fiction. Send preliminary letter with synopsis and return postage in the first instance. No reading fee. *Commission* Home 10%; US & Translation 20%.

Rosemary Sandberg Ltd
6 Bayley Street, London WC1B 3HB
☎020 7304 4110   Fax 020 7304 4109
Email rosemary@sandberg.demon.co.uk

Contact *Rosemary Sandberg*

FOUNDED 1991. In association with **Ed Victor Ltd**. *Handles* children's picture books and novels. *Specialises* in children's writers and illustrators. No unsolicited mss as client list is currently full. *Commission* 10%.

The Sayle Literary Agency★
Bickerton House, 25–27 Bickerton Road, London N19 5JT
☎020 7263 8681   Fax 020 7561 0529

Proprietor *Rachel Calder*

Handles fiction, crime and general. Non-fiction: current affairs, social issues, travel, biographies, historical. No plays, poetry, children's, textbooks, technical, legal or medical books. No unsolicited mss. Preliminary letter essential, including a brief biographical note and a synopsis plus two or three sample chapters. Return postage essential. No reading fee. CLIENTS Stephen Amidon, Pete Davies, Margaret Forster, Georgina Hammick, Phillip Knightley, Rory MacLean, Denise Mina, Malcolm Pryce, Kate Pullinger, Ronald Searle, Gitta Sereny, Stanley Stewart, William Styron, Mary Wesley. *Commission* Home 10%; US & Translation 20%. *Overseas associates* Elaine Markson Literary Agency; Darhansoff, Verrill and Feldman; Anne Edelstein Literary Agency, USA; translation rights handled by **The Marsh Agency**; film rights by **Sayle Screen Ltd**.

Sayle Screen Ltd

11 Jubilee Place, London SW3 3TD
☎020 7823 3883 Fax 020 7823 3363
Email info@saylescreen.com
Website www.saylescreen.com

Agents *Jane Villiers, Matthew Bates, Toby Moorcroft, Cathy Kehoe*

Specialises in writers and directors for film and television. Also deals with theatre and radio. Works in association with the **Sayle Literary Agency** representing film and TV rights in novels and non-fiction. CLIENTS include Shelagh Delaney, Marc Evans, Margaret Forster, Rob Green, Mark Haddon, Christopher Monger, Paul Morrison, Gitta Sereny, Sue Townsend, Mary Wesley. No unsolicited material without preliminary letter.

Seifert Dench Associates

24 D'Arblay Street, London W1F 8EH
☎020 7437 4551 Fax 020 7439 1355
Website www.seifert-dench.co.uk

Contacts *Linda Seifert, Elizabeth Dench, Michelle Arnold*

FOUNDED 1972. *Handles* scripts for TV and film. Unsolicited mss will be read, but a letter with sample of work and c.v. (plus s.a.e.) is preferred. CLIENTS include Peter Chelsom, Tony Grisoni, Stephen Volk. *Commission* Home 10–15%. *Overseas associates* include: William Morris/Sanford Gross and C.A.A., Los Angeles.

The Sharland Organisation Ltd

The Manor House, Manor Street, Raunds,
Northamptonshire NN9 6JW
☎01933 626600 Fax 01933 624860

Email tsoshar@aol.com

Contacts *Mike Sharland, Alice Sharland*

FOUNDED 1988. *Specialises* in national and international film and TV negotiations. Also negotiates multimedia, interactive TV deals and computer game contracts. *Handles* scripts for film, TV, radio and theatre; also non-fiction. Markets books for film and handles stage, radio, film and TV rights for authors. No scientific, technical or poetry. No unsolicited mss. Preliminary enquiry by letter or phone essential. *Commission* Home 15%; US & Translation 20%. *Overseas associates* various.

Vincent Shaw Associates Ltd

20 Jay Mews, Kensington Gore, London
SW7 2EP
☎020 7581 8215 Fax 020 7225 1079
Email vincentshaw@clara.net

Contact *Vincent Shaw*

FOUNDED 1954. *Handles* TV, radio, film and theatre scripts. No unsolicited material. *Commission* Home 10%; US & Translation by negotiation. *Overseas associate* Herman Chessid, New York.

Sheil Land Associates Ltd★ (incorporating **Richard Scott Simon Ltd 1971** and **Christy Moore Ltd 1912**)

43 Doughty Street, London WC1N 2LF
☎020 7405 9351 Fax 020 7831 2127
Email info@sheilland.co.uk

Agents, UK & US *Sonia Land, Luigi Bonomi, Sam Boyce, Vivien Green, Amanda Preston*

Film/Theatrical/TV *John Rush, Roland Baggot*

Foreign *Amelia Cummins, Helen Philpott*

FOUNDED 1962. *Handles* full-length general, commercial and literary fiction and non-fiction, including: social politics, business, history, military history, gardening, thrillers, crime, romance, fantasy, drama, biography, travel, cookery and humour, UK and foreign estates. Also theatre, film, radio and TV scripts. Welcomes approaches from new clients either to start or to develop their careers. Preliminary letter with s.a.e. essential. No reading fee. CLIENTS include Peter Ackroyd, John Blashford-Snell, Seve Ballesteros, Melvyn Bragg, Stephanie Calman, Catherine Cookson estate, Anna del Conte, Seamus Deane, Alan Drury, Erik Durschmied, Alan Garner, Bonnie Greer, Susan Hill, Richard Holmes, HRH The Prince of Wales, John Humphries, James Long, Richard Mabey, Colin McDowell,

Van Morrison, Patrick O'Brian estate, Esther Rantzen, Pam Rhodes, Jean Rhys estate, Richard and Judy, Martin Riley, Colin Shindler, Tom Sharpe, Brian Sykes, Jeffrey Tayler, Alan Titchmarsh, Rose Tremain, John Wilsher. *Commission* Home 15%; US & Translation 20%. *Overseas associates* **Georges Borchardt, Inc.** (Richard Scott Simon). UK representatives for **Farrar, Straus & Giroux, Inc**. US film and TV representation: CAA, APA, and others.

 Caroline Sheldon Literary Agency★
Thorley Manor Farm, Thorley, Yarmouth PO41 0SJ
☎01983 760205
Contact *Caroline Sheldon*

FOUNDED 1985. *Handles* adult fiction, in particular women's, both commercial and literary novels. Also full-length children's fiction. No TV/film scripts unless by book-writing clients. Send letter with all relevant details of ambitions and first four chapters of proposed book (enclose large s.a.e.). No reading fee. *Commission* Home 10%; US & Translation 20%.

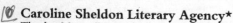 Dorie Simmonds Agency
67 Upper Berkeley Street, London W1H 7QX
☎020 7486 9228 Fax 020 7486 8228
Email dhsimmonds@aol.com
Contact *Dorie Simmonds*

Handles a wide range of subjects including general non-fiction and commercial fiction, children's books and associated rights. Specialities include contemporary personalities and historical biographies. Outline required for non-fiction; a short synopsis for fiction with 2–3 sample chapters, and a c.v. with writing experience/publishing history. No reading fee. Return postage essential. *Commission* Home & US 15%; Translation 20%.

Jeffrey Simmons
10 Lowndes Square, London SW1X 9HA
☎020 7235 8852 Fax 020 7235 9733
Contact *Jeffrey Simmons*

FOUNDED 1978. *Handles* biography and autobiography, cinema and theatre, fiction (both quality and commercial), history, law and crime, politics and world affairs, parapsychology and sport (but not exclusively). No science fiction/fantasy, children's books, cookery, crafts, hobbies or gardening. Film scripts handled only if by book-writing clients. *Special interests* personality books of all sorts and fiction from young writers (i.e. under 40) with a future. Writers become clients by personal introduction or by

letter, enclosing a synopsis if possible, a brief biography, a note of any previously published books, plus a list of any publishers and agents who have already seen the mss. *Commission* Home 10–15%; US & Foreign 15%.

Richard Scott Simon Ltd
See **Sheil Land Associates Ltd**

Sinclair-Stevenson
3 South Terrace, London SW7 2TB
☎020 7581 2550 Fax 020 7581 2550
Contact *Christopher Sinclair-Stevenson*

FOUNDED 1995. *Handles* biography, current affairs, travel, history, fiction, the arts. No scripts, children's, academic, science fiction/fantasy. Send synopsis with s.a.e. in the first instance. No reading fee. CLIENTS include Jennifer Johnston, J.D.F. Jones, Ross King, Christopher Lee, Andrew Sinclair and the estates of Alec Guinness, John Cowper Powys and John Galsworthy. *Commission* Home 10%; US 15%; Translation 20%. *Overseas associate* T.C. Wallace Ltd, New York. Translation rights handled by **David Higham Associates**.

Robert Smith Literary Agency Ltd★
12 Bridge Wharf, 156 Caledonian Road, London N1 9UU
☎020 7278 2444 Fax 020 7833 5680
Email robertsmith.literaryagency@virgin.net
Contact *Robert Smith*

FOUNDED 1997. *Handles* non-fiction; biography, health and nutrition, cookery, lifestyle, showbusiness and true crime. No scripts, fiction, poetry, academic or children's books. No unsolicited mss. Send a letter and synopsis in the first instance. No reading fee. CLIENTS Stewart Evans, Neil and Christine Hamilton, James Haspiel, Christine Keeler, Roberta Kray, Norman Parker, Mike Reid, Keith Skinner, Douglas Thompson, Christopher Warwick. *Commission* Home 15%; US & Translation 20%. *Overseas associates* Frédérique Poretta Literary Agency (France); Thomas Schlück Literary Agency (Germany).

Elaine Steel
110 Gloucester Avenue, London NW1 8HX
☎020 8348 0918 Fax 020 8341 9807
Email ecmsteel@aol.com
Contact *Elaine Steel*

FOUNDED 1986. *Handles* scripts, screenplays and books. No technical or academic. Initial phone call preferred. CLIENTS include Les Blair, Anna Campion, Michael Eaton, Brian Keenan, Troy

Kennedy Martin, Rob Ritchie, Albie Sachs, Ben Steiner. *Commission* Home 10%; US & Translation 20%.

Abner Stein*
10 Roland Gardens, London SW7 3PH
☎020 7373 0456 Fax 020 7370 6316
Contact *Abner Stein*

FOUNDED 1971. Mainly represents US agents and authors but *handles* some full-length fiction and general non-fiction. No scientific, technical, etc. No scripts. Send letter and outline in the first instance rather than unsolicited mss. *Commission* Home 10%; US & Translation 20%.

Micheline Steinberg Playwrights
409 Triumph House, 187–191 Regent Street, London W1R 7WF
☎020 7287 4383
Email steinplays@aol.com
Contacts *Micheline Steinberg, Ginny Sennett*

FOUNDED 1988. *Specialises* in plays for stage, TV, radio and film. Best approach by preliminary letter (with s.a.e.). Dramatic associate for **Pollinger Limited**. *Commission* Home 10%; Elsewhere 15%.

Shirley Stewart Literary Agency
3rd Floor, 21 Denmark Street, London WC2H 8NA
☎020 7836 4440 Fax 020 7836 3482
Director *Shirley Stewart*

FOUNDED 1993. *Handles* literary fiction and non-fiction. No scripts, children's, science fiction, fantasy or poetry. Will consider unsolicited material; send letter with two or three sample chapters in the first instance. S.a.e. essential. Submissions by fax or on disk not accepted. No reading fee. *Commission* Home 10%; US & Translation 20%. *Overseas associate* **Curtis Brown Ltd**, New York.

The Susijn Agency
3rd Floor, 64 Great Titchfield Street, London W1W 7QH
☎020 7580 6341 Fax 020 7580 8626
Email info@thesusijnagency.com
Website www.thesusijnagency.com
Contacts *Laura Susijn, Susy Behr*

FOUNDED April 1998. *Specialises* in selling rights worldwide in literary fiction and non-fiction. Preliminary letter, synopsis and first two chapters preferred. No reading fee. Also represents non-English language authors and publishers for UK, US and translation rights

worldwide. *Commission* Home 15%; US & Translation 15–20%.

The Tennyson Agency
10 Cleveland Avenue, Wimbledon Chase, London SW20 9EW
☎020 8543 5939 Fax 020 8543 5939
Email mail@literator.co.uk
Website www.literator.co.uk
Contact *Christopher Oxford*

New agency, FOUNDED in 2001, *specialising* in theatre, radio, television and film scripts. Other material considered on an ad hoc basis; humanities bias. No musicals, poetry, travel, military/historical, academic or sport. No unsolicited material; send introductory letter with résumé and proposal/outline of work. No reading fee. CLIENTS Vivienne Allen, Alastair Cording, Iain Grant, Philip Hurd-Wood, Walter Saunders, Diana Ward. *Commission* Home 12½%; US & Translation 15%.

J.M. Thurley Management
30 Cambridge Road, Teddington, Middlesex TW11 8DR
☎020 8977 3176 Fax 020 8943 2678
Email JMThurley@aol.com
Contact *Jon Thurley*

FOUNDED 1976. *Handles* full-length fiction, non-fiction, TV and films. Particularly interested in strong commercial and literary fiction. Will provide creative and editorial assistance to promising writers. No unsolicited mss; approach by letter in the first instance with synopsis and first three chapters plus return postage. No reading fee. *Commission* Home, US & Translation 15%.

Lavinia Trevor Agency*
The Glasshouse, 49A Goldhawk Road, London W12 8QP
☎020 8749 8481 Fax 020 8749 7377
Contact *Lavinia Trevor*

FOUNDED 1993. *Handles* general fiction (literary and commercial) and non-fiction, including popular science. No science fiction, poetry, academic, technical or children's books. No TV, film, radio, theatre scripts. Approach with a preliminary letter, a brief autobiography and first 50–100 typewritten pages. S.a.e. essential. No reading fee. *Commission* rate by agreement with author.

Jane Turnbull*
13 Wendell Road, London W12 9RS
☎020 8743 9580 Fax 020 8749 6079
Email jane.turnbull@btinternet.com

Contact *Jane Turnbull*

FOUNDED 1986. *Handles* fiction and non-fiction. No science fiction, sagas or romantic fiction. *Specialises* in biography, history, current affairs, health and diet. No unsolicited mss. Approach with letter in the first instance. No reading fee. Translation rights handled by **Gillon Aitken Associates Ltd**. *Commission* Home 10%; US & Foreign 20%.

Ed Victor Ltd★

6 Bayley Street, Bedford Square, London WC1B 3HE
☎020 7304 4100 Fax 020 7304 4111

Contacts *Ed Victor, Graham Greene, Maggie Phillips, Sophie Hicks, Lizzy Kremer*

FOUNDED 1976. *Handles* a broad range of material including children's books but leans towards the more commercial ends of the fiction and non-fiction spectrums. No poetry, scripts or academic. Takes on very few new writers. No unsolicited mss. After trying his hand at book publishing and literary magazines, Ed Victor, an ebullient American, found his true vocation. Strong opinions, very pushy and works hard for those whose intelligence he respects. Loves nothing more than a good title auction. CLIENTS include Eoin Colfer, Frederick Forsyth, A.A. Gill, Josephine Hart, Jack Higgins, Erica Jong, Nigella Lawson, Kathy Lette, Allan Mallinson, Anne Robinson and the estates of Douglas Adams, Raymond Chandler, Dame Iris Murdoch, Sir Stephen Spender and Irving Wallace. *Commission* Home & US 15%; Translation 20%.

Robin Wade Literary Agency

31 Ivory House, East Smithfield, London E1W 1AT
☎020 7488 4171 Fax 020 7488 4172
Email rw@rwla.com
Website www.rwla.com

Contact *Robin Wade*

FOUNDED 2001. *Handles* general fiction and non-fiction including children's books. No scripts, poetry, plays or short stories. Send detailed synopsis and two specimen chapters by e-mail with a brief biography. No reading fee. CLIENTS Louise Cooper, Lorna Read, James Rennie. *Commission* Home 10%; Overseas & Translation 20%. 'Fees negotiable if a contract has already been offered.'

Cecily Ware Literary Agents

19C John Spencer Square, London N1 2LZ
☎020 7359 3787 Fax 020 7226 9828

Email cware@dial.pipex.com

Contacts *Cecily Ware, Gilly Schuster, Warren Sherman*

FOUNDED 1972. Primarily a film and TV script agency representing work in all areas: drama, children's, series/serials, adaptations, comedies, etc. No unsolicited mss or phone calls. Approach in writing only. No reading fee. *Commission* Home 10%; US 10–20% by arrangement.

Warner Chappell Plays Ltd

See **Josef Weinberger Plays**

Watson, Little Ltd★

Capo Di Monte, Windmill Hill, London NW3 6RJ
☎020 7431 0770 Fax 020 7431 7225
Email sz@watsonlittle.com

Contacts *Sheila Watson, Mandy Little, Sugra Zaman*

Handles fiction and non-fiction. *Special interests* history, popular science, psychology, self-help and business books. No scripts. Not interested in authors who wish to be purely academic writers. Send preliminary ('intelligent') letter with synopsis. *Commission* Home 15%; US 24%; Translation 19%. *Overseas associates* worldwide. *Dramatic associate*: **The Sharland Organisation Ltd**.

A.P. Watt Ltd★

20 John Street, London WC1N 2DR
☎020 7405 6774 Fax 020 7831 2154
Email apw@apwatt.co.uk
Website www.apwatt.co.uk

Directors *Caradoc King, Linda Shaughnessy, Derek Johns, Joanna Frank, Georgia Garrett, Nick Harris*

FOUNDED 1875. The oldest-established literary agency in the world. *Handles* full-length type-scripts, including children's books, screenplays for film and TV. No poetry, academic or specialist works. No unsolicited mss accepted. CLIENTS Trezza Azzopardi, Quentin Blake, Marika Cobbold, Helen Dunmore, Nicholas Evans, Giles Foden, Esther Freud, Janice Galloway, Martin Gilbert, Nadine Gordimer, Linda Grant, Colin and Jacqui Hawkins, Reginald Hill, Michael Holroyd, Michael Ignatieff, Mick Jackson, Philip Kerr, Dick King-Smith, India Knight, John Lanchester, Alison Lurie, Jan Morris, Jill Murphy, Andrew O'Hagan, Susie Orbach, Tony Parsons, Caryl Phillips, Philip Pullman, Jancis Robinson, Jon Ronson, Elaine Showalter, Zadie Smith, Graham Swift, Colm Toibin, Fiona Walker and the estates of

Wodehouse, Graves and Maugham. *Commission* Home 10%; US & Translation 20%.

Josef Weinberger Plays

12–14 Mortimer Street, London W1T 3JJ
☎020 7580 2827 Fax 020 7436 9616
Email general.info@jwmail.co.uk
Website www.josef-weinberger.com

Contact *Michael Callahan*

Formerly Warner Chappell Plays, Josef Weinberger is now both agent and publisher of scripts for the theatre. No unsolicited mss; introductory letter essential. No reading fee. CLIENTS include Ray Cooney, John Godber, Peter Gordon, Debbie Isitt, Arthur Miller, Sam Shepard, John Steinbeck. *Overseas representatives* in the US, Canada, Australia, New Zealand, India, South Africa and Zimbabwe.

John Welch, Literary Consultant & Agent

Mill Cottage, Calf Lane, Chipping Camden, Gloucestershire GL55 6JQ
☎01386 840237 Fax 01386 840568
Email johnwelch@waitrose.com

Contact *John Welch*

FOUNDED 1992. *Handles* military history, aviation, history, biography and sport. No fiction, poetry, children's books or scripts for radio, TV, film or theatre. Already has a full hand of authors so no new authors being considered at present. CLIENTS include Alexander Baron, Michael Calvert, Timothy Jenkins, Sybil Marshall, Ewart Oakeshott, Norman Scarfe, Anthony Trew, Peter Trew, David Wragg. *Commission* Home 10%.

Dinah Wiener Ltd*

12 Cornwall Grove, Chiswick, London W4 2LB
☎020 8994 6011 Fax 020 8994 6044

Contact *Dinah Wiener*

FOUNDED 1985. *Handles* fiction and general non-fiction: auto/biography, popular science, cookery. No scripts, children's or poetry. Approach with preliminary letter in first instance, giving full but brief c.v. of past work and future plans. Mss submitted must include s.a.e. and be typed in double-spacing. CLIENTS include T.J. Armstrong, Valerie-Anne Baglietto, Malcolm Billings, Hugh Brune, Guy Burt, Victoria Corby, David Deutsch, Robin Gardiner, Jenny Hobbs, Mark Jeffery, Tania Kindersley, Michael Lockwood, Sarah Mason, Daniel Snowman, Peta Tayler, Rachel

Trethewey, Marcia Willett. *Commission* Home 15%; US & Translation 20%.

Janet Woodward Ltd

Parlington Hall, Aberford, West Yorkshire LS25 3EG
☎0113 281 3913 Fax 0113 281 3911
Email info@jwl.uk.com

Contacts *Janet Woodward, Pamela Dash*

International licensing agency specialising in starting new projects for the animation and gift industries. Worldwide representation. In-house studio. Current concepts include *Rambling Ted, Kit 'n' Kin, Child Hazel, Martin's Magic Mouse, Short 'n' Sweet, Colin New*. New creators should forward full-concept synopses with sample illustrations.

The Wylie Agency (UK) Ltd

17 Bedford Square, London WC2B 3JA
☎020 7908 5900 Fax 020 7908 5901
Email mail@wylieagency.co.uk

Handles fiction and non-fiction. No scripts or children's books. Approach in writing with three sample chapters, synopsis and s.a.e./return postage. No reading fee. *Commission* Home 10%; USA 15%; Translation 20%.

Zebra Agency

Broadland House, 1 Broadland, Shevington, Lancashire WN6 8DH
☎0794 958 4758
Email admin@zebraagency.co.uk
Website www.zebraagency.co.uk

Contacts *Dee Jones, Cara Wooi*

FOUNDED 1997. *Handles* non-fiction and general fiction including crime, suspense and drama, murder, mysteries, adventure, thrillers, horror and science fiction. Also scripts for TV, radio, film and theatre. No reading fee. Editorial advice given to new authors. No unsolicited mss; send preliminary letter giving publishing history and brief c.v., with synopsis and first three chapters of novel or 10 pp of script (plus return s.a.e.). No phone calls or submissions by fax or e-mail. *Commission* Home 10%; US & Translation 20%.

LITERARY SCOUTS

Literary scouts gather information from UK agents, publishers and editors on behalf of foreign clients. They only work with material that is already commissioned or being handled by an agent. They do not accept any unsolicited material.

Louise Allen-Jones
40 Lillieshall Road, Clapham Old Town,
London SW4 0LP
☎020 7720 2453 Fax 020 7498 1818
Email laj@bookscout.demon.co.uk
Contact *Louise Allen-Jones*

Scouts for Econ Ullstein List, Germany; The
English Agency, Japan; Bruna, The Netherlands;
Kinneret-Zmora, Israel; The Film Council, UK.

Badcock & Rozycki
Literary Scouts
1 Old Compton Street, London W1D 5JA
☎020 7734 7997 Fax 020 7734 6886

Contacts *June Badcock* (june@badcock-
rozycki.co.uk), *Barbara Rozycki*
(barbara@badcock-rozycki.co.uk),
Claire Holt (claire@badcock-rozycki.co.uk)

Scouts for Wilhelm Heyne Verlag, Marion von
Schröder Verlag and Diana Verlag, Germany;
Unieboek BV and Prometheus/Bert Bakker,
The Netherlands; RCS Libri Group, Italy;
Editions Jean-Claude Lattès, France; Ediciones
Salamandra, Spain; Ellinika Grammata, Greece;
Werner Söderström Osakeyhtiö, Finland;
Forum, Sweden; NW Damm & Son A/S,
Norway; Egmont Lademann A/S, Denmark;
Edda Media, Iceland.

Anne Louise Fisher
and Suzy Lucas
29 D'Arblay Street, London W1F 8EP
☎020 7494 4609 Fax 020 7494 4611
Email annelouise@alfisher.co.uk
Contacts *Anne Louise Fisher, Suzy Lucas*

Scouts for Doubleday Inc., Broadway Books and
Nan A. Talese, US; Librarie Plon-Perrin-Orban
and Pocket and Havas Poche, France; Karl
Blessing Verlag, Berlin Verlag and Siedler
Verlag, Germany; Arnoldo Mondadori Editore
and Oscar Mondadori, Italy; Albert Bonniers
Bokförlag, Sweden; Otava, Finland; Gyldendal
Norsk Forlag, Norway; De Boekerij and M
Publishers, The Netherlands; Plaza y Janés,
Grijalbo, Editorial Debate, Editorial Lumen and
Mondadori Iberica, Spain; Patakis Publications,
Greece.

Koukla Maclehose
Arundel House, 3 Westbourne Road, London
N7 8AR
☎020 7607 1336 Fax 020 7609 7775
Email koukla@atlas.co.uk
Contact *Koukla Maclehose*

Scouts for Tammi, Finland; Wählström &
Widstrand, Sweden; Pax, Norway; Rosinante,
Denmark; Meulenhoff, Holland and Arena,
The Netherlands; Hanser, Zsolnay, Sans Souci
and Nagel & Kimche, Germany; Gallimard,
and Denoël, France; Einaudi, Italy; Anagrama,
Spain; Asa, Portugal; Psichogios, Greece;
Keter, Israel.

Folly Marland
6 Elmcroft Street, London E5 0SQ
☎020 8986 0111 Fax 020 8986 0111
Email fmarland@pobox.com
Contact *Folly Marland*

Scouts for Scherz Verlag, Germany; Uitgeverij
Het Spectrum, The Netherlands; Sony
Magazines, Japan; Livani, Greece.

Britt Pfluger
8 Elder Avenue, Crouch End, London
N8 9TH
☎020 8348 1422 Fax 020 8348 1422
Contact *Britt Pfluger*

Scouts for Aufbau-Verlag, Germany.

Ros Ramsay
109a Queenstown Road, London SW8 3RH
☎020 7978 2162 Fax 020 7652 0212

Contacts *Ros Ramsay* (ros@rosramsay.com),
Kate Walwyn (kate@rosramsay.com)

Scouts for Kiepenheuer & Witsch, Germany;
Sperling & Kupfer, Italy; Ambo Anthos, The
Netherlands; Norstedts, Sweden; Kadokawa,
Japan; Hed Arzi, Israel; Slate Films, London.

Heather Schiller
1 Waldegrave Road, Brighton, East Sussex
BN1 6RG
☎01273 505477 Fax 01273 505477
Email heatherschiller@tinyonline.co.uk
Contact *Heather Schiller*

Scouts for BZZTÔH, The Netherlands;
Cappelens, Norway; Piper, Germany; Grup
62, Spain.

Jane Southern
11 Russell Avenue, Bedford MK40 3TE
☎01234 400147 Fax 01234 400146
Email jane.southern@ntlworld.com
Contact *Jane Southern*

Scouts for Hoffmann und Campe Verlag and
Bertelsmann Club, Germany; The House of
Books, The Netherlands; Belfond, Presses de la
Cité and France Loisirs, France.

Van Lear Limited

PO Box 21816, Parson's Green, London
SW6 5ZU
☎020 7610 6165 Fax 020 7610 6045
Email evl@vanlear.co.uk

Contact *Liz Van Lear*

Scouts for Droemer Knaur Schneekluth,
Germany; Planeta Group, Spain and Latin
America; Richters, Sweden; Artist House,
Japan; Oceanida, Greece; Dom Quixote,
Portugal; il Saggiatore, Italy; Veen Bosch &
Keuning, The Netherlands.

Kathy Van Praag

53 St John Street, Oxford OX1 2LQ
☎01865 556753 Fax 01865 556753
Email kvanpraag@aol.com

Contact *Van Kathy Praag*

Scouts for Rowohlt Verlag, Germany;
Distribuidora Record, Brazil.

National Newspapers

Departmental e-mail addresses are too numerous to include in this listing. They can be obtained from the newspaper's main switchboard or the department in question

Business a.m.
40 Torphichen Street, Edinburgh EH3 8JB
☎0131 330 0000 Fax 0131 330 0005
Email info@businessam.co.uk
Website www.businessam.co.uk
Owner *Bonnier Group (Sweden)*
Editor *John Penman*
Circulation 11,276

Subscription tabloid, launched in September 2000, aimed at the Scottish business community. Published Monday to Friday, the paper covers commerce, industry, finance and politics 'through Scottish eyes'. Includes *Investor* and *Business p.m.* sections.
 Deputy Editors *Paul Stokes/Richard Neville*

The Business
292 Vauxhall Bridge Road, London
SW1V 1SS
☎020 7961 0000
Owner *Barclay Brothers*
Editor-in-Chief *Andrew Neil*
Circulation 89,421

LAUNCHED in February 1998. National newspaper dedicated to business, finance and politics. No unsolicited material. All ideas must be discussed with the department's editor in advance.
 Political Editor *Andrew Porter*
 City Editor *Robert Bailhache*

Daily Express
Ludgate House, 245 Blackfriars Road, London
SE1 9UX
☎020 7928 8000 Fax 020 7620 1654
Website www.express.co.uk
Owner *Northern & Shell Media/Richard Desmond*
Editor *Chris Williams*
Circulation 907,772

Under owner Richard Desmond, publisher of *OK!* magazine, the paper features a large amount of celebrity coverage. The general rule of thumb is to approach in writing with an idea; all departments are prepared to look at an outline without commitment. Ideas welcome but already receives many which are 'too numerous to count'.
 News Editor *David Leigh*
 Diary (Hickey Column) *Kathryn Spencer*
 Features Editor *Heather O'Connor*
 City Editor *Stephen Kahn*
 Political Editor *Patrick O'Flynn*
 Sports Editor *Bill Bradshaw*
 Planning Editor (News Desk) should be circulated with copies of official reports, press releases, etc., to ensure news desk cover at all times.

Saturday magazine **Editor** *Martin Smith*
 Payment negotiable.

Daily Mail
Northcliffe House, 2 Derry Street, Kensington, London W8 5TT
☎020 7938 6000 Fax 020 7937 4463
Owner *Associated Newspapers/Lord Rothermere*
Editor *Paul Dacre*
Circulation 2.45 million

In-house feature writers and regular columnists provide much of the material. Photo-stories and crusading features often appear; it's essential to hit the right note to be a successful *Mail* writer. Close scrutiny of the paper is strongly advised. Not a good bet for the unseasoned. Accepts news on savings, building societies, insurance, unit trusts, legal rights and tax.
 News Editor *Tony Gallagher*
 City Editor *Alex Brummer*
 'Money Mail' Editor *Tony Hazell*
 Political Editor *David Hughes*
 Education Correspondent *Sarah Harris*
 Diary Editor *Nigel Dempster*
 Features Editor *Eric Bailey*
 Literary Editor *Jane Mays*
 Sports Editor *Colin Gibson*
 Femail *Lisa Collins*

Weekend: Saturday supplement **Editor** *Heather McGlone*

Daily Mirror

1 Canada Square, Canary Wharf, London
E14 5AP
☎020 7293 3000 Fax 020 7293 3409
Website www.mirror.co.uk
Owner *Trinity Mirror plc*
Editor *Piers Morgan*
Circulation 2.11 million

No freelance opportunities for the inexperienced, but strong writers who understand what the tabloid market demands are always needed.
   News Editor *Conor Hanna*
   Features Editor *Peter Willis*
   Political Editor *James Hardy*
   Business Editor *Clinton Manning*
   Education Editor *Dorothy Lepkowska*
   Showbusiness Diary Editor *Kevin O'Sullivan*
   Sports Editor *Dean Morse*

M magazine: Saturday supplement 'for young women' **Editor-in-Chief** *Tina Weaver*

Daily Record

One Central Quay, Glasgow G3 8DA
☎0141 309 3000 Fax 0141 309 3340
Website www.record-mail.co.uk
Owner *Trinity Mirror plc*
Editor-in-Chief *Peter Cox*
Circulation 567,368

Mass-market Scottish tabloid. Freelance material is generally welcome.
   News Editor *Tom Hamilton*
   Features Editor *Jill Mair*
   Business Editor *Colin Calder*
   Political Editor *Paul Sinclair*
   Sports Editor *Alan Thomson*
   Magazine Editor *Angela Dewar*

Scotland Means Business Quarterly business magazine, launched March 2002. **Editor** *Magnus Gardham*

Daily Sport

19 Great Ancoats Street, Manchester
M60 4BT
☎0161 236 4466 Fax 0161 236 4535
Website www.dailysport.co.uk
Owner *Sport Newspapers Ltd*
Editor *David Beevers*
Circulation 235,000

Tabloid catering for young male readership. Unsolicited material welcome; send to News Editor.
   News Editor *Justin Dunn*
   Sports Editor *Marc Smith*

Daily Star

Ludgate House, 245 Blackfriars Road, London
SE1 9UX
☎020 7928 8000 Fax 020 7922 7960
Owner *Richard Desmond*
Editor *Peter Hill*
Circulation 667,899

In competition with *The Sun* for off-the-wall news and features. Freelance opportunities available.
   Deputy Editor *Hugh Whittow*
   Features Editor *Dawn Neesom*
   Sports Editor *Jim Mansell*

The Daily Telegraph

1 Canada Square, Canary Wharf, London
E14 5DT
☎020 7538 5000 Fax 020 7513 2506
Website www.telegraph.co.uk
Owner *Conrad Black*
Editor *Charles Moore*
Circulation 1.01 million

Unsolicited mss not generally welcome – 'all are carefully read and considered, but only about one in a thousand is accepted for publication'. As they receive about 20 weekly, this means about one a year. Contenders should approach the paper in writing, making clear their authority for writing on that subject. No fiction.
   Home Editor *Richard Spencer* Tip-offs or news reports from *bona fide* journalists. Must phone the news desk in first instance. Maximum 200 words. *Payment* minimum £40 (tip).
   Arts Editor *Sarah Crompton*
   City Editor *Neil Collins*
   Political Editor *George Jones*
   Diary Editor *Charlie Methvin* Always interested in diary pieces; contact *Peterborough* (Diary column).
   Education *John Clare*
   Environment *Charles Clover*
   Features Editor *Richard Preston* Most material supplied by commission from established contributors. New writers are tried out by arrangement with the features editor. Approach in writing. Maximum 1500 words.
   Literary Editor *Kate Summerscale*
   Sports Editor *David Welch* Occasional opportunities for specialised items.
   Style Editor *Rachel Forder*
   Wellbeing Editor *Vicky Rands*
   Payment by arrangement.

Daily Telegraph Weekend: Saturday colour supplement. **Editor** *Rachel Simhon*

Financial Times
1 Southwark Bridge, London SE1 9HL
☎020 7873 3000 Fax 020 7873 3076
Email <firstname>.<lastname>@ft.com
Website www.ft.com
Owner *Pearson*
Editor *Andrew Gowers*
Circulation 494,074

FOUNDED 1888. UK and international coverage of business, finance, politics, technology, management, marketing and the arts. All feature ideas must be discussed with the department's editor in advance. Not snowed under with unsolicited contributions – they get less than any other national newspaper. Approach by e-mail with ideas in the first instance.

News Editor *William Lewis*
Features Editor *John Gapper*
Arts Editor *Peter Aspden*
Financial Editor *Jane Fuller*
Literary Editor *Jan Dalley*
Diary Editor *Sundeep Tucker*
Education *Jim Kelly*
Environment *Vanessa Houlder*
Political Editor *To be appointed*
Small Businesses *Katharine Campbell*
Sports Editor *David Owen*

Weekend FT and *the business*. **Editor** *Julia Cuthbertson*

How to Spend It Monthly magazine. **Editor** *Gillian de Bono*

The Guardian
119 Farringdon Road, London EC1R 3ER
☎020 7278 2332 Fax 020 7837 2114
Website www.guardian.co.uk
Owner *The Scott Trust*
Editor *Alan Rusbridger*
Circulation 404,630

Of all the nationals *The Guardian* probably offers the greatest opportunities for freelance writers, if only because it has the greatest number of specialised pages which use freelance work. But mss must be directed at a specific slot.

News Editor *Harriet Sherwood* No opportunities except in those regions where there is presently no local contact for news stories.
Arts Editor *Dan Glaister*
Literary Editor *Claire Armitstead*
Executive Financial Editor *Paul Murphy*
City Editor *Julia Finch*
On Line *Vic Keegan* Science, computing and technology. A good part of Thursday's paper, almost all written by freelancers. Expertise essential – but not a trade page; written for 'the in-terested man in the street' and from the user's point of view. Computing/communications (Internet) articles should be addressed to *Jack Schofield*; science articles to *Tim Radford*. Mss on disk or by e-mail to: neil.mcintosh@guardian.co.uk.

Diary Editor *Matthew Norman*
Education Editor *Will Woodward* Expert pieces on modern education welcome.
Environment *John Vidal*
Features Editor *Ian Katz* Receives up to 50 unsolicited mss a day; these are passed on to relevant page editors.
Guardian Society *David Brindle* Focuses on social change – the forces affecting us, from environment to government policies. Top journalists and outside commentators.
Media Editor *Janine Gibson* Nine pages a week, plus 'New Media'. Outside contributions are considered. All aspects of modern media, advertising and PR. Background insight important. Best approach is by e-mail (janine.gibson@guardian.co.uk)
Political Editor *Mike White*
Sports Editor *Ben Clissitt*
Women's Page *Clare Margetson* Runs three days a week. Unsolicited ideas used if they show an appreciation of the page in question. Maximum 800–1000 words. Write, e-mail (clare.margetson@guardian.co.uk) or fax on 020 7239 9935.

The Guardian Weekend: glossy Saturday issue. **Editor** *Katharine Viner*. *The Guide Tim Lusher*

The Herald (Glasgow)
200 Renfield Street, Glasgow G2 3PR
☎0141 302 7000 Fax 0141 302 7070
Website www.theherald.co.uk
Owner *Scottish Media Group (SMG)*
Editor *Mark Douglas-Home*
Circulation 96,615

The oldest national newspaper in the English-speaking world, The Herald, which dropped its 'Glasgow' prefix in February 1992, was bought by Scottish Television in 1996. Lively, quality, national Scottish daily broadsheet. Approach with ideas in writing or by phone in first instance.

News Editor *Magnus Llewelin*
Arts Editor *Keith Bruce*
Business Editor *Robert Powell*
Diary *Tom Shields*
Education *Liz Buie*
Sports Editor *Donald Cowey*
Herald Magazine *Kathleen Morgan*

The Independent

Independent House, 191 Marsh Wall, London E14 9RS

☎020 7005 2000 Fax 020 7005 2999

Website www.independent.co.uk

Owner *Independent Newspapers*
Editor *Simon Kelner*
Circulation 226,584

FOUNDED 1986. Particularly strong on its arts/media coverage, with a high proportion of feature material. Theoretically, opportunities for freelancers are good. However, unsolicited mss are not welcome; most pieces originate in-house or from known and trusted outsiders. Ideas should be submitted in writing.

News Editor *Adam Leigh*
Features *Laurence Earle*
Arts Editor *Ian Irvine*
Business Editor *Jeremy Warner*
Education *Richard Garner*
Environment *Michael McCarthy*
Literary Editor *Boyd Tonkin*
Political Editor *Andrew Grice*
Sports Editor *Paul Newman*
Travel Editor *Simon Calder*

The Independent Magazine: Saturday supplement. **Editor** *Lisa Markwell*. *The Information* **Editor** *Jacqueline Hunter*

Independent on Sunday

Independent House, 191 Marsh Wall, London E14 9RS

☎020 7005 2000

Fax 020 7005 2999

Website www.independent.co.uk/sindy/sindy.html

Owner *Independent Newspapers*
Editor *Tristan Davies*
Circulation 232,433

FOUNDED 1986. Regular columnists contribute most material but feature opportunites exist. Approach with ideas in first instance.

News Editor *Peter Victor*
Focus Editor *Catherine Pepinster*
Arts Editor *Marcus Field*
Comment Editor *Anne McElvoy*
Business Editor *Jason Nissé*
Literary Editor *Suzi Feay*
Environment *Geoffrey Lean*
Political Editor *To be appointed*
Sports Editor *Neil Morton*
Travel Editor *Victoria Summerley*

Review supplement. **Editor** *Andrew Tuck*

International Herald Tribune

6 bis, rue des Graviers, 92521 Neuilly, Paris, France

☎0033 1 4143 9300 Fax 0033 1 4143 9338

Email iht@iht.com

Website www.iht.com

Executive Editor *David Ignatius*
Managing Editor *Robert J. McCartney*
Deputy Editors *Katherine Knorr, Charles Mitchelmore*
Circulation 225,000

Published in France, Monday to Saturday, and circulated in Europe, the Middle East, North Africa, the Far East and the USA. General news, business and financial, arts and leisure. Uses regular freelance contributors. Contributor policy can be found on the website at: www.iht.com/contributor.htm

The Mail on Sunday

Northcliffe House, 2 Derry Street, Kensington, London W8 5TS

☎020 7938 6000 Fax 020 7937 3829

Owner *Associated Newspapers/Lord Rothermere*
Editor *Peter Wright*
Circulation 2.42 million

Sunday paper with a high proportion of newsy features and articles. Experience and judgement required to break into its band of regular feature writers.

News Editor *Paul Field*
Financial Editor *Ben Laurance*
Diary Editor *Nigel Dempster*
Features Editor/Women's Page *Sian James*
Books *Marilyn Warnick*
Political Editor *Simon Walters*
Sports Editor *Malcolm Vallerius*
Night & Day Editor *Christena Appleyard*
Review Editor *Jim Gillespie*

You – The Mail on Sunday Magazine: colour supplement. Many feature articles, supplied entirely by freelance writers. **Editor** *Sue Peart*.
Features Editor *Catherine Fenton*

Morning Star

1st Floor, Cape House, 787 Commercial Road, London E14 7HG

☎020 7538 5181 Fax 020 7538 5125

Email morsta@geo2.poptel.org.uk

Owner *Peoples Press Printing Society*
Editor *John Haylett*
Circulation 9,000

Not to be confused with the *Daily Star*, the

Morning Star is the farthest left national daily. Those with a penchant for a Marxist reading of events and ideas can try their luck, though feature space is as competitive here as in the other nationals.

News Editor *Dan Coysh*
Features & Arts Editor *Kevin Russell*
Political Editor *Mike Ambrose*
Foreign Editor *Brian Denny*
Sports Editor *Alex Reid*

News of the World

1 Virginia Street, London E98 1NW
☎020 7782 1000 Fax 020 7583 9504
Website www.newsoftheworld.co.uk

Owner *News International plc/Rupert Murdoch*
Editor *Rebekah Wade*
Circulation 3.92 million

Highest circulation Sunday paper. Freelance contributions welcome. News and features editors welcome tips and ideas.

News Editor *Greg Miskin*
Features Editor *Gary Thompson*
Business/City Editor *Peter Prendergast*
Political Editor *Ian Kirby*
Sports Editor *Mike Dunn*

Sunday Magazine: colour supplement. **Editor** *Judy McGuire*. Showbiz interviews and strong human-interest features make up most of the content, but there are no strict rules about what is 'interesting'. Unsolicited mss and ideas welcome.

The Observer

119 Farringdon Road, London EC1R 3ER
☎020 7278 2332 Fax 020 7713 4250
Email editor@observer.co.uk
Website www.observer.co.uk

Owner *Guardian Newspapers Ltd*
Editor *Roger Alton*
Circulation 460,084

FOUNDED 1791. Acquired by Guardian Newspapers from Lonrho in May 1993. Occupies the middle ground of Sunday newspaper politics. Unsolicited material is not generally welcome, 'except from distinguished, established writers'. Receives far too many unsolicited offerings already. No news, fiction or special page opportunities. The newspaper runs annual competitions which change from year to year. Details are advertised in the newspaper.

Executive Editor, News *Andy Malone*
Arts Editor *Jane Ferguson*
Review Editor *Lisa O'Kelly*

Comment Editor *Mike Holland*
City Editor *Richard Wachman*
Business Editor *Frank Kane*
Personal Finance Editor *Maria Scott*
Science Editor *Robin McKie*
Education Correspondent *Tracy McVeigh*
Environment Editor *Anthony Browne*
Literary Editor *Robert McCrum*
Travel Editor *Jeannette Hyde*
Sports Editor *Brian Oliver*

The Observer Magazine: glossy arts and lifestyle supplement. **Editor** *Allan Jenkins*

The Observer Sport Monthly: glossy magazine supplement launched in 2000. **Editor** *Matthew Tench*

The Observer Food Monthly: launched summer 2001. **Editor** *To be appointed*

Scotland on Sunday

Barclay House, 108 Holyrood Road, Edinburgh EH8 8AS
☎0131 620 8620 Fax 0131 620 8491
Website www.scotlandonsunday.com

Owner *Scotsman Publications Ltd*
Editor *Margot Wilson*
Circulation 86,132

Scotland's top-selling quality broadsheet. Welcomes ideas rather than finished articles.

News Editor *Peter Laing*
Features Editor *Deborah Collcutt*

Scotland on Sunday Magazine: colour supplement. **Editor** *Deborah Collcutt* Features on personalities, etc.

The Scotsman

Barclay House, 108 Holyrood Road, Edinburgh EH8 8AS
☎0131 620 8620
Fax 0131 620 8616 (Editorial)
Website www.scotsman.com

Owner *Scotsman Publications Ltd*
Editor *Iain Martin*
Circulation 78,209

Scotland's national newspaper. Many unsolicited mss come in, and stand a good chance of being read, although a small army of regulars supply much of the feature material not written in-house. See website for contact details.

News Editor *David Lee*
Business Editor *Ian Watson*
Education *Seonag MacKinnon*
Features Editor *Charlotte Ross*
Book Reviews *David Robinson*

The Sun

1 Virginia Street, London E98 1SN
☎020 7782 4000 Fax 020 7782 4108
Email <firstname>.<lastname>@the-sun.co.uk
Website www.the-sun.co.uk
Owner *News International plc/Rupert Murdoch*
Editor *David Yelland*
Circulation 3.35 million

Highest circulation daily. Populist outlook; very keen on gossip, pop stars, TV soap, scandals and exposés of all kinds. No room for non-professional feature writers; 'investigative journalism' of a certain hue is always in demand, however.

> **Head of News** *Graham Dudman*
> **Head of Features** *John Perry*
> **Head of Sport** *Steve Waring*
> **Woman's Editor** *Sharon Hendry*
> **Fashion Editor** *Erica Davies*

Sunday Express

Ludgate House, 245 Blackfriars Road, London SE1 9UX
☎020 7928 8000 Fax 020 7620 1654
Website www.express.co.uk
Owner *Northern & Shell Media/Richard Desmond*
Editor *Martin Townsend*
Circulation 901,846

The general rule of thumb is to approach in writing with an idea; all departments are prepared to look at an outline without commitment. Ideas welcome but already receives many which are 'too numerous to count'.

> **Deputy Editor** *Phil McNeill*
> **News Editor** *Jim Murray*
> **Features Editor** *Giulia Rhodes*
> **Business Editor** *Richard Phillips*
> **Political Editor** *Julia Hartley-Brewer*
> **Sports Editor** *Mike Scott*

S: Sunday supplement on celebrities, homes, food and health. **Editor** *Louise Robinson.* No unsolicited mss. All contributions are commissioned. Ideas in writing only. *Enjoy*: Sunday showbiz and travel supplement.

> *Payment* negotiable.

Sunday Herald

200 Renfield Street, Glasgow G2 3PR
☎0141 302 7800 Fax 0141 302 7809
Email editor@sundayherald.com
Website www.sundayherald.com
Owner *Scottish Media Group (SMG)*
Editor *Andrew Jaspan*
Circulation 54,316

Also at: 10 George Street, Edinburgh EH2 2DU
☎0131 200 8100 Fax 0131 200 8088
LAUNCHED February 1999. Scottish seven-section broadsheet.

> **Deputy Editor** *Richard Walker*
> **News Editor** *David Milne*
> **Political Editor** *Douglas Fraser*
> **Sports Editor** *David Dick*
> **Entertainment Editor** *Andrew Burnet*
> **Magazine Editor** *Jane Wright*

Sunday Mail

One Central Quay, Glasgow G3 8DA
☎0141 309 3000 Fax 0141 309 3587
Website www.sundaymail.co.uk
Owner *Trinity Mirror plc*
Editor *Allan Rennie*
Circulation 665,101

Popular Scottish Sunday tabloid.

> **News Editor** *Jim Wilson*
> **Features Editor** *Susie Cormack*

Seven Days: weekly supplement. **Editor** *Liz Steele.*

Mailsport Monthly: monthly magazine. **Editor** *George Cheyne*

Sunday Mirror

1 Canada Square, Canary Wharf, London E14 5AP
☎020 7293 3000
Fax 020 7293 3939 (news desk)
Website www.sundaymirror.co.uk
Owner *Trinity Mirror*
Editor *Tina Weaver*
Circulation 1.76 million

In general terms contributions are welcome, though the paper patiently points out it has more time for those who have taken the trouble to study the market. Initial contact in writing preferred, except for live news situations. No fiction.

> **News Editor** *Euan Stretch* The news desk is very much in the market for tip-offs and inside information. Contributors would be expected to work with staff writers on news stories. Approach by telephone or fax in the first instance.
> **Finance** *Anna Day*
> **Features Editor** *Jane Johnson* 'Anyone who has obviously studied the market will be dealt with constructively and courteously.' Cherishes its record as a breeding ground for new talent.
> **Sports Editor** *Steve McKenlay*

M Celebs: colour supplement. **Editor** *Mel Brodie*

Sunday People

1 Canada Square, Canary Wharf, London
E14 5AP
☎020 7293 3000 Fax 020 7293 3517
Website www.people.co.uk

Owner *Trinity Mirror plc*
Editor *Neil Wallis*
Circulation 1.34 million

Slightly up-market version of *The News of the World*. Keen on exposés and big-name gossip. Interested in ideas for investigative articles. Phone in first instance.

News Editor *Ian Edmonson*
Features Editor *Dawn Alford*
Political Editor *Nigel Nelson*
Sports Editor *Lee Clayton*
Travel Editor *Richard Allen*

The People Magazine. **Editor** *Amanda Cable*
Approach by phone with ideas in first instance.

Sunday Post

2 Albert Square, Dundee DD1 9QJ
☎01382 223131 Fax 01382 201064
Email mail@sundaypost.com
Website www.sundaypost.com

Owner *D.C. Thomson & Co. Ltd*
Editor *David Pollington*
Circulation 612,000

Contributions should be addressed to the editor.

Sunday Post Magazine: monthly colour supplement. **Editor** *Maggie Dun*

Sunday Sport

19 Great Ancoats Street, Manchester M60 4BT
☎0161 236 4466 Fax 0161 236 4535
Website www.sundaysport.co.uk

Owner *David Sullivan*
Editor *Paul Carter*
Circulation 195,810

FOUNDED 1986. Sunday tabloid catering for a particular sector of the male 15–35 readership. As concerned with 'glamour' (for which, read: 'page 3') as with human interest, news, features and sport. Unsolicited mss are welcome; receives about 90 a week. Approach should be made by phone in the case of news and sports items, by letter for features. All material should be addressed to the news editor.

News Editor *Justin Dunn* Off-beat news, human interest, preferably with photographs.

Features Editor *Sarah Stephens* Regular items: glamour, showbiz and television, as well as general interest.

Sports Editor *Marc Smith* Hard-hitting sports stories on major soccer clubs and their

personalities, plus leading clubs/people in other sports. Strong quotations to back up the news angle essential.

Payment negotiable and on publication.

The Sunday Telegraph

1 Canada Square, Canary Wharf, London
E14 5DT
☎020 7538 5000 Fax 020 7538 6242
Website www.telegraph.co.uk

Owner *Conrad Black*
Editor *Dominic Lawson*
Circulation 779,141

Right-of-centre quality Sunday paper which, although traditionally formal, has pepped up its image to attract a younger readership. Unsolicited material from untried writers is rarely ever used. Contact with idea and details of track record.

News Editor *Richard Ellis*
Features Editor *Anna Murphy*
City Editor *Robert Peston*
Political Editor *Colin Brown*
Education Editor *Martin Bentham*
Arts Editor *Susannah Herbert*
Environment Editor *David Harrison*
Literary Editor *Miriam Gross*
Diary Editor *Adam Helliker*
Sports Editor *Jon Ryan*

Sunday Telegraph Magazine **Editor** *Lucy Tuck*

The Sunday Times

1 Pennington Street, London E98 1ST
☎020 7782 5000 Fax 020 7782 5658
Website www.sunday-times.co.uk

Owner *News International plc/Rupert Murdoch*
Editor *John Witherow*
Circulation 1.43 million

FOUNDED 1820. Tendency to be anti-establishment, with a strong crusading investigative tradition. Approach the relevant editor with an idea in writing. Close scrutiny of the style of each section of the paper is strongly advised before sending mss. No fiction. All fees by negotiation.

News Editor *Charles Hymas* Opportunities are very rare.

News Review Editor *Eleanor Mills* Submissions are always welcome, but the paper commissions its own, uses staff writers or works with literary agents, by and large. The features sections where most opportunities exist are *Style* and *The Culture*.

Culture Editor *Helen Hawkins*
Business Editor *Rory Godson*
City Editor *Kirstie Hamilton*

Education Editor *Geraldine Hackett*
Science/Environment *Jonathan Leake*
Literary Editor *Caroline Gascoigne*
Sports Editor *Alex Butler*
Style Editor *Robert Johnston*

Sunday Times Magazine: colour supplement.
Editor *Robin Morgan* No unsolicited material.
Write with ideas in first instance.

The Times
1 Pennington Street, London E98 1TT
☎020 7782 5000 Fax 020 7488 3242
Website www.thetimes.co.uk
Owner *News International plc/Rupert Murdoch*
Editor *Robert Thomson*
Circulation 717,281

Generally right (though features can range in
tone from diehard to libertarian). *The Times*

receives a great many unsolicited offerings.
Writers with feature ideas should approach by
letter in the first instance. No fiction.
Deputy Editor *Ben Preston*
News Editor *John Wellman*
Features Editor *Anne Barrowclough*
Associate Editor *Brian MacArthur*
City/Financial Editor *Patience Wheatcroft*
Diary Editor *Jack Malvern*
Arts Editor *Sarah Vine*
Education *To be appointed*
Literary Editor *Erica Wagner*
Political Editor *Phil Webster*
Sports Editor *David Chappell*

Weekend Times Editor *Jane Wheatley*

The Times Magazine: Saturday supplement.
Editor *Gill Morgan*
Times 2 Editor *Sandra Parsons*

Up, Up and Away

Mick Sinclair reveals the secrets of successful travel writing

Travel writing is the stuff dreams are made of: first-class flights, luxury suites, the world's finest restaurants, and a sybaritic life only interrupted by short trips home to check your byline in prestigious magazines and bank fat royalty cheques from your bestselling books. Unfortunately, all that really is a dream. The reality is much more likely to involve dingy hotels, long hours in draughty bus stations and many months facing a computer screen hoping to meet an impossible deadline while saving up for a weekend at Butlins.

The 1990s were boom times for travel and consequently for travel writing. Travel supplements of newspapers and magazines expanded, bookshops began filling miles of shelving with travel-related titles. Be it fly-fishing, snowboarding or sitting in the sun in destinations from Alaska to Zanzibar, there was something written somewhere explaining exactly how, where and when to do it. All this should be good news for writers. So how to start?

Newspapers and magazines

Travel editors of newspapers and magazines are besieged with speculative copy, most of which begins with the author's journey to the airport and is in the bin before they reach takeoff speed. Finding a personal and offbeat take on somewhere familiar and a lively start – 'When the stench of the sewer hit my nostrils I knew I'd arrived in . . . ' – will have more chance of enticing the editor to read beyond the first sentence than vaguely offering an article 'about Paris' or 'my Mediterranean cruise'.

Avoid speculative pieces that will be outdated within a year, which is how long it may take for the piece to be used. Ideally, ensure payment is made on acceptance and not on publication as, aside from routine delays, earthquakes, riots and outbreaks of plague can all render an otherwise exceptional article unusable. Fact-based features, such as those focusing on recommended hotels or restaurants, are usually specifically commissioned from established writers and require different skills, not least the ability to make dozens of near-identical properties sound highly individual. As space for features is dictated by advertising, a downturn means fewer pages and less chance of being published. Along with changing tourism trends, general news can affect a travel editor's preferences: widespread publicity on the risk of deep-vein thrombosis on long-haul flights, for example, prompted greater focus on short-haul destinations.

Guide books

Guide books may seem a logical extension of newspaper or magazine travel articles but the two have little in common. True, the author needs to provide lively and accurate words for both, but for books this must continue, ideally without contradiction or ambiguity, for perhaps 300 pages and incorporate practical information without breaking the flow. Publishers commonly commission guides as a series rather than as individual titles and will be impressed as much with a would-be author's awareness of the series, its overall tone and target readership, as by detailed knowledge of a destination. With marketing arranged well in advance and publication dates set in stone, the writer must be able to meet deadlines, which could mean producing 30,000 quality words in six weeks or 100,000 inside four months.

The guide author has to become intimately familiar not only with the obvious tourist destinations of a region, along with its history, culture and cuisine, but also with a broad swath of its life and society that might span contemporary politics, nightclub culture, environmental issues, football teams and even the most popular TV soaps. They need, too, a breadth of general knowledge that might shame the average encyclopaedia. Los Angeles, for example, might be Hollywood, freeways and sun-kissed beaches but it is also the huge Getty Center, which means producing informed accounts of Renaissance paintings and illustrated medieval manuscripts.

Modern guides generally conform to a very precise design, rarely allowing the author to wax lyrical as mood dictates. Each page requires an exact number of words and that the text on each page be self-contained, enabling the next page to start with a fresh heading. For aesthetic reasons, the publisher may also expect each page to neatly divide into a specific number of paragraphs, sometimes at the expense of grammatical correctness or even literal sense. Additionally, the same page might contain a sidebar of stand-alone text related to but separate from the main page text. A valued writer is one able to effortlessly describe the world's greatest museum in twenty-five words (preferably less) or expand coverage of a hole in the ground ('curious geological phenomenon') to make interesting reading while filling a gap caused by a design miscalculation.

All being well, guides appear in revised form about every two years. It is important for authors to ensure that it is they who will have the option of providing this updated material for a suitable fee (assuming a royalty is not paid; see Currency exchange, below). A good job on the first edition should mean the subsequent revision being a relatively simple matter of checking phone numbers, opening times and other straightforward practical information. Publishers' budgets, or the lack of them, mean that updates do not necessarily bring a return visit but may instead entail long sessions on the phone or, increasingly, the Internet. Revisions might be complicated by design changes, requiring existing text to be rewritten even if it has not dated, and by publishers' reluctance on cost grounds to change photos.

Leading UK guide publishers often sell as many, or more, books in the US than they do at home. Such co-editions can complicate matters, particularly when the US partner takes an active role in deciding content. Aside from confirming that the two nations really are divided by a common language, the American end will want more emphasis on top-of-the-range restaurants and accommodations, and no mention of anything unpleasant: quoting local murder rates, even to show they are falling, is definitely out.

Travelogues

Despite the success of Bill Bryson and Peter Mayle, publishers unfailingly inform authors contemplating similar undertakings – first-hand accounts of potentially life-changing journeys through landscapes populated by all manner of exotic characters – that such books do not sell. Unfortunately, they are right most of the time, although there are unknowns that do unexpectedly well, such as Chris Stewart with *Driving Over Lemons*. Without a track record, authors will need to have had the experience and written most of the book before touting the idea to a publisher, and should be particularly careful to find a suitable niche: a year of mine-clearing in Cambodia might have little appeal to a major publisher but may tickle the fancy of a small house specialising in developing-nation issues.

Writers hoping to break into travel authorship by recounting a thrill-a-minute tale of death-defying adventure will probably find swimming the Atlantic with a pack of sharks or crossing Antarctica on a toboggan to be much easier than convincing a publisher to commission an account of the exploit. Unless, of course, the author has the contacts to arrange a TV documentary (ideally a series) beforehand, in which case publishers will be beating a path to the author's door before the phrase 'spin-off' can even be uttered.

Rounding up the usual clichés

There was a time when travel writing was reliable and dependable, not for the informed commentary on the subject matter but for the number of clichés that could be strung together in describing a place where markets are 'colourful', where waterfalls always 'cascade' and where sunsets are unfailingly 'glorious'. Readers and publishers alike are nowadays alert to the above and use of 'paradise' or 'Mecca' to describe anything above average and 'contrasts' (perhaps the one thing every place on earth can claim) employed in almost any context. Writers should also watch out for lazily describing ethnic areas as 'vibrant', praising a restaurant's 'sinful' desserts, and recommending a place for its 'pulsating' nightlife. Admittedly some clichés are unavoidable because the cliché is true; some apparently, since copyeditors seem surprisingly keen to insert them, are desirable.

Having avoided clichés, certain recurring phrases and other travel-writing quirks can be mulled over. What exactly is 'authentic' cuisine? Why does anybody need to know exactly how many rooms a hotel has? Do architects actually 'build' buildings or do they really only 'design' them? Do buildings date from when they were started, finished or formally opened: should San Francisco's Grace Cathedral, for example, be dated as 1910 (cornerstone laid), 1928 (construction begins) or 1964 (consecration)?

Currency exchange

'How wonderful,' your friends will say, 'being paid to travel.' Sadly, a wallet filled with boarding passes does not impress a bank manager. Along with the common misconception that travel writers spend all their time travelling is the idea that they get paid for doing so. For newspaper and magazine articles, the payment will almost certainly be the organ's minimum rate per word regardless of how long the writer was away. Some guide book publishers pay a royalty, which is preferable in most instances though sales are, obviously, directly proportional to the popularity of the destination: even the definitive *Backpacking in Tristan da Cunha* will not make its author rich. The majority of guide publishers pay a fee per word akin to that of a moderately paying magazine and, regrettably, expect all rights to be assigned in return.

For a new title, fee-paying publishers usually add an amount to the basic fee to cover 'expenses' which is normally defined (if it is defined at all) as costs of flights and accommodation with very little extra for sustenance, despite the expectation of extensive restaurant recommendations, and certainly nothing for time spent away from home working perhaps seven days a week and twelve hours a day. Complain about this to the publisher and the words 'free' and 'holiday' will be heard. Royalty paying guide publishers commonly offer nothing more than an advance on the royalty.

Another widely held belief is that the travel writers' world is awash with freebies. There are exceptions, such as orchestrated affairs when selected hacks, likely to be chosen for their susceptibility to gin and tonic, are chaperoned throughout and expected to repay the hospitality with reams of uncritical praise. In most cases, however, free accommodation and free food are rarities. Local hotel and restaurant owners are unlikely to be falling over themselves to be mentioned in anything other than specialist publications or by local reviewers. Mainstream guide books typically include hundreds of hotels and dining places, leaving little incentive for a particular establishment to offer complimentary or even discounted rates to travel writers.

Researching a guide can indeed be a hungry business. My first involved eating nothing but crispbread for five days in Iceland and taking a tedious 'midnight sun' (remarkably similar to the 'midday sun') evening bus tour of a fjord solely because the trip included hot buns. Horrifying though it is to those who take close heed of restaurant recommendations, the under-nourished author has likely scanned the dining sections of local magazines and newspapers for clues and followed them up by peering into restaurant windows to assess the atmosphere and the clientele, quickly noting down a few items from the menu before heading to a local supermarket to build an evening meal from unhealthy snack food.

Travels in cyberspace

Thanks to computers and the Internet, travel research has become much easier and cheaper. Many local newspapers are online, restaurants, hotels and museums often have websites, and tourist information sites have listings, links and suggestions. Though far from infallible, these sources can lessen the terror of blank spaces and looming deadlines, as well as providing up-to-the minute news.

The rise in travel-related websites through the late 1990s appeared to expand opportunities for writers. In fact, most content was licensed from established publishers with the text originators seldom seeing any additional remuneration. The dot.com crash ended any fears that the Web would render traditional travel writing obsolete but did leave writers needing to become as familiar with the nooks and crannies of cyberspace as with those of the real world, locating the most useful Web pages to recommend to readers in much the same way as they might hunt down, say, a remote Greek taverna. This can bring unexpected benefits, such as making what might be an outdated destination account suddenly seem impressively contemporary.

Happy trails?

Despite the pitfalls, potholes and run-ins with publishing staff whose idea of a trip is the two-week package kind, travel writing exceptionally rewards its practitioners with more exotic experiences, meetings with memorable people and insights into the workings of the world in a year than most people encounter in a lifetime. The hours might be long and the pay might be poor, but the view from the travel writer's eyrie is always an exceptional one.

Mick Sinclair has written on travel and other subjects for newspapers and magazines here and abroad. He is also author of sixteen books, the latest of which is Cities of the Imagination: San Francisco, *published by Signal Books.*

Regional Newspapers

ENGLAND

Berkshire

Reading Evening Post
8 Tessa Road, Reading, Berkshire
RG1 8NS
☎0118 918 3000 Fax 0118 959 9363
Email editorial@reading-epost.co.uk
Owner *Guardian Media Group*
Editor *Andy Murrill*
Circulation 23,802

Unsolicited mss welcome; one or two received every day. Fiction rarely used. Interested in local news features, human interest, well-researched investigations. Special sections include holidays & travel (Monday); food page; children's page (Tuesday); style page (Wednesday); business (Wednesday & Friday); motoring and motorcycling; gardening; rock music (Friday).

Cambridgeshire

Cambridge Evening News
Winship Road, Milton, Cambridge
CB4 6PP
☎01223 434434 Fax 01223 434415
Owner *Cambridge Newspapers Ltd*
Editor *Colin Grant*
Circulation 40,776

News Editor *Helen King*
  Business Editor *Jenny Chapman*
  Sports Editor *Chris Gill*

Cheshire

**Chronicle Newspapers
(Chester & North Wales)**
Chronicle House, Commonhall Street,
Chester CH1 2AA
☎01244 340151 Fax 01244 340165
Email elangton@chron8.demon.co.uk
Website www.iccheshireonline.co.uk

Owner *Trinity Mirror Plc*
Editor-in-Chief *Eric Langton*

All unsolicited feature material will be considered.

Cleveland

Evening Gazette
Borough Road, Middlesbrough, Cleveland
TS1 3AZ
☎01642 234242 Fax 01642 249843
Owner *Trinity International Holdings plc*
Editor *Steve Dyson*
Circulation 61,000

Special pages: business, motoring, home, computing, recruitment.
  News Editor *Chris Styles*
  Features Editor/Women's Page *Kathryn Armstrong*
  Business *Helen Logan*
  Sports Editor *Allan Boughey*
  Councils *Sandy McKenzie*
  Education *Julie Martin*
  Consumer *Michelle Ruane*
  Health *Helen Sturdy*

Hartlepool Mail
New Clarence House, Wesley Square,
Hartlepool TS24 8BX
☎01429 274441 Fax 01429 869024
Email post@hartmail.demon.co.uk
Website www.hartlepoolmail.co.uk

Owner *Johnston Press Plc*
Editor *Harry Blackwood*
Circulation 23,614

  News Editor *Gavin Ledwith*
  Sports Editor *Roy Kelly*

Cumbria

News & Star
Newspaper House, Dalston Road, Carlisle,
Cumbria CA2 5UA
☎01228 612600 Fax 01228 612601
Owner *Cumbrian Newspaper Group Ltd*
Editor *Keith Sutton*
Circulation 25,375

Assistant Editor *Nick Turner*
  Deputy Editor *Steve Johnston*
  Sports Editor *Mike Gardner*
  Women's Page *Jane Loughran*

North West Evening Mail
Abbey Road, Barrow in Furness, Cumbria
LA14 5QS
☎01229 821835 Fax 01229 840164
Email news@nwemail.co.uk
Website www.nwemail.co.uk
Owner *Robin Burgess*
Editor *Bill Myers*
Circulation 20,815
All editorial material should be addressed to the editor.
   Sports Editor *Leo Clarke*

Derbyshire
Derby Evening Telegraph
Northcliffe House, Meadow Road, Derby
DE1 2DW
☎01332 291111 Fax 01332 253027
Owner *Northcliffe Newspapers Group Ltd*
Editor *Mike Norton*
Circulation 60,691
Weekly business supplement.
   News Editor *Michael Hill*
   (newsdesk@derbytelegraph.co.uk)
   Features Editor/Women's Page *Sarah Newton* (sarahnewton@derbytelegraph. co.uk)
   Sports Editor *Dave Parkinson* (sports@derbytelegraph.co.uk)
   Motoring Editor *Bob Maddox*

Devon
Evening Herald
17 Brest Road, Derriford Business Park,
Derriford, Plymouth, Devon PL6 5AA
☎01752 765500 Fax 01752 765527
Email news@westcountrypublications.co.uk
Website www.thisisplymouth.co.uk
Owner *Northcliffe Newspapers Group Ltd*
Editor *Alan Qualtrough*
Circulation 48,054
All editorial material to be addressed to the editor or the **News Editor** *John Casey*.

Express & Echo
Heron Road, Sowton, Exeter, Devon
EX2 7NF
☎01392 442211
Fax 01392 442294/442287 (editorial)
Email echonews@westcountrypublications. co.uk
Website www.thisisexeter.co.uk

Owner *Westcountry Publications Limited*
Editor *Steve Hall*
Circulation 30,978
Weekly supplements: *Business Week; Property Echo; Wheels; Weekend Echo.*
   Head of Content *Sue Kemp*
   Features Editor/Women's Page *Richard Best*
   Sports Editor *Simon Mills*

Herald Express
Harmsworth House, Barton Hill Road,
Torquay, Devon TQ2 8JN
☎01803 676000 Fax 01803 676299 (editorial)
Email editor@thisissouthdevon.co.uk
Website www.thisissouthdevon.co.uk
Owner *Northcliffe Newspapers Group Ltd*
Editor *B. Hanrahan*
Circulation 30,174
Drive scene, property guide, *What's On Now* – leisure guide, Monday sports, special pages, rail trail, Saturday surgery, nature and conservation column. Supplements: *Gardening* (weekly); *Visitors Guide* and *Antiques & Collectables* (fortnightly); *Devon Days Out* (every Saturday in summer and at Easter and May Bank Holidays). Unsolicited mss generally not welcome. All editorial material should be addressed to the editor in writing.

Sunday Independent
Burrington Way, Plymouth, Devon PL5 3LN
☎01752 206600 Fax 01752 206164
Owner *Newsquest*
Editor *Nikki Rowlands*
Circulation 38,958
Tabloid Sunday covering the whole of the West Country from Bristol to Weymouth and Land's End. News stories/tips, news features. All editorial should be addressed to the editor. *Payment* by arrangement.

Western Morning News
17 Brest Road, Derriford Business Park,
Derriford, Plymouth, Devon PL6 5AA
☎01752 765500 Fax 01752 765535
Website www.thisisplymouth.co.uk
Owner *Northcliffe Newspapers Group Ltd*
Editor *Barrie Williams*
Circulation 53,050
Unsolicited mss welcome, but must be of topical and local interest and addressed to the **News Editor** *Ian Mean*.
   Sports Editor *Rick Cowdery*

Dorset

Daily Echo

Richmond Hill, Bournemouth, Dorset
BH2 6HH
☎01202 554601 Fax 01202 292115
Owner *Newsquest Media Group Ltd (a Gannett company)*
Editor *Neal Butterworth*
Circulation 45,090

FOUNDED 1900. Has a strong features content and invites specialist articles, particularly on unusual and contemporary subjects but only with a local angle. Supplements: business, education, homes and gardens, motoring, what's on, *Weekender*. Regular features on weddings, property, books, local history, green issues, the Channel coast. All editorial material should be addressed to the **News Editor** *Andy Martin*.
Payment on publication.

Dorset Evening Echo

Fleet House, Hampshire Road, Granby
Industrial Estate, Weymouth, Dorset DT4 9XD
☎01305 830930 Fax 01305 830956
Owner *Newsquest Media Group Ltd (a Gannett company)*
Editor *David Murdock*
Circulation 20,430

Farming, by-gone days, films, arts, showbiz, brides, children's page, motoring, property, weekend leisure and entertainment including computers and gardening.
News Editor *Paul Thomas*
Sports Editor *Paul Baker*

County Durham

The Northern Echo

Priestgate, Darlington, Co. Durham DL1 1NF
☎01325 381313 Fax 01325 380539
Email echo@nne.co.uk
Website www.thisisthenortheast.co.uk
Owner *Newsquest (North East) Ltd (a Gannett company)*
Editor *Peter Barron*
Circulation 70,358

FOUNDED 1870. Freelance pieces welcome but telephone first to discuss submission.
News Editor *Nigel Burton* Interested in reports involving the North East or North Yorkshire. Preferably phoned in.
Features Editor *Nick Morrison* Background pieces to topical news stories relevant to the area. Must be arranged with the features editor before submission of any material.

Business Editor *Jonathan Jones*
Sports Editor *Nick Loughlin*
Payment and length by arrangement.

Essex

Evening Echo

Newspaper House, Chester Hall Lane, Basildon, Essex SS14 3BL
☎01268 522792 Fax 01268 469281
Owner *Newsquest Media Group (a Gannett company)*
Editor *Martin McNeill*
Circulation 42,000

Relies almost entirely on staff and regular outside contributors, but will very occasionally consider material sent on spec. Approach the editor in writing with ideas. Although the paper is Basildon-based, its largest circulation is in the Southend area.

Evening Gazette (Colchester)

Oriel House, 43–44 North Hill, Colchester, Essex CO1 1TZ
☎01206 506000 Fax 01206 508274
Email newsdesk@thisisessex.co.uk
Website www.thisisessex.co.uk
Owner *Newsquest (Essex)*
Editor *Irene Kettle*
Circulation 28,206

Monday – Friday daily newspaper servicing north and mid-Essex including Colchester, Harwich, Clacton, Braintree, Witham, Maldon and Chelmsford. Unsolicited mss not generally used. Relies heavily on regular contributors.
Features Editor *Iris Clapp*

Gloucestershire

The Citizen

St John's Lane, Gloucester GL1 2AY
☎01452 424442
Fax 01452 420664 (Editorial)
Owner *Northcliffe Newspapers Group Ltd*
Editor *Spencer Feeney*
Circulation 34,813

All editorial material to be addressed to the **News Editor** *Matt Holmes*.

Gloucestershire Echo

1 Clarence Parade, Cheltenham, Gloucestershire GL50 3NY
☎01242 271900 Fax 01242 271848
Owner *Northcliffe Newspapers Group Ltd*
Editor *Anita Syvret*

Circulation 25,426

All material, other than news, should be addressed to the editor.

News Editor Blaise Tapp

Hampshire

The News
The News Centre, Hilsea, Portsmouth, Hampshire PO2 9SX
☎023 9266 4488 Fax 023 9267 3363
Email newsdesk@thenews.co.uk
Website www.portsmouth.co.uk
Owner Portsmouth Printing & Publishing Ltd
Editor Mike Gilson
Circulation 73,161

Unsolicited mss not generally accepted. Approach by letter.
   News Editor Colin McNeill
   Features Editor John Millard General subjects of S.E. Hants interest. Maximum 600 words. No fiction.
   Sports Editor Colin Channon Sports background features. Maximum 600 words.

The Southern Daily Echo
Newspaper House, Test Lane, Redbridge, Southampton, Hampshire SO16 9JX
☎023 8042 4777 Fax 023 8042 4770
Owner Newscom Plc
Editor Ian Murray
Circulation 60,343

Unsolicited mss 'tolerated'. Approach the editor in writing with strong ideas; staff supply almost all the material.

Kent

Kent Messenger
6 & 7 Middle Row, Maidstone, Kent ME14 1TG
☎01622 695666 Fax 01622 757227
Email kentmessenger@thekmgroup.co.uk
Website www.kentonline.co.uk
Owner Kent Messenger Group
Circulation 48,425

Associate Director, Editorial Simon Irwin
Very little freelance work is commissioned.

MedwayToday
395 High Street, Chatham, Kent ME4 4PQ
☎01634 830600 Fax 01634 829484
Email medwaytoday@thekmgroup.co.uk
Owner Kent Messenger Group

Editor Bob Dimond
Circulation 21,567
Business Editor Trevor Sturgess
   Community Editor David Jones
   Sports Editor Mike Rees

Lancashire

Bolton Evening News
Newspaper House, Churchgate, Bolton, Lancashire BL1 1DE
☎01204 522345 Fax 01204 365068
Email ben_editorial@lancashire.newsquest. co.uk
Website www.thisislancashire.co.uk
Owner Newsquest Media Group Ltd (a Gannett company)
Editor Steve Hughes
Circulation 42,035

Business, children's page, travel, local services, motoring, fashion and cookery.
   News Editor John Horne
   Features Editor/Women's Page Angela Kelly

Evening Chronicle
PO Box 47, Union Street, Oldham, Lancashire OL1 1EQ
☎0161 633 2121 Fax 0161 652 2111
Email oec@compuserve.com
Owner Hirst Kidd & Rennie Ltd
Editor Jim Williams
Circulation 32,206

Motoring, food and wine, women's page, business page.
   News Editor Mike Attenborough
   Women's Page Janice Barker

The Gazette (Blackpool)
PO Box 20, Avroe House, Avroe Crescent, Blackpool, Lancashire FY4 2DP
☎01253 400888 Fax 01253 361870
Owner RIM
Circulation 35,598
Managing Director/
Editor-in-Chief Philip Welsh
Associate Editor Neil Hepburn

Unsolicited mss welcome in theory. Approach in writing with an idea. Supplements: The Result (sport, Monday); Eve (women, Tuesday); Wheels (motoring, Wednesday); Property (Thursday); Big Weekend (entertainment, Friday); LIFE! magazine (entertainment & leisure, Saturday).

Lancashire Evening Post

Olivers Place, Eastway, Fulwood, Preston,
Lancashire PR2 9ZA
☎01772 254841 Fax 01772 880173
Website www.prestononline.co.uk
Owner *Regional Independent Media*
Editor *Simon Reynolds*
Circulation 48,831

Unsolicited mss are not generally welcome;
many are received and not used. All ideas in
writing to the editor.

Lancashire Evening Telegraph

Newspaper House, High Street, Blackburn,
Lancashire BB1 1HT
☎01254 678678 Fax 01254 680429
Website www.thisislancashire.co.uk
Owner *Newsquest Media Group Ltd (a Gannett
company)*
Editor *Kevin Young*
Circulation 43,919

News stories and feature material with an East
Lancashire flavour (a local angle, or written by
local people) welcome. Approach in writing
with an idea in the first instance. No fiction.
   News Editor *Andrew Turner*
   Features Editor *John Anson*

Leicestershire

Leicester Mercury

St George Street, Leicester LE1 9FQ
☎0116 251 2512 Fax 0116 253 0645
Website www.thisisleicestershire.co.uk
Owner *Northcliffe Newspapers Group Ltd*
Editor *Nick Carter*
Circulation 104,926
   Head of News *Richard Bettsworth*
   Features Editor *Alex Dawon*

Lincolnshire

Grimsby Telegraph

80 Cleethorpe Road, Grimsby,
N.E. Lincolnshire DN31 3EH
☎01472 360360 Fax 01472 372257
Email newsdesk@grimsbytelegraph.co.uk
Owner *Northcliffe Newspapers Group Ltd*
Editor *To be appointed*
Circulation 45,000

Sister paper of the *Scunthorpe Evening Telegraph*.
Unsolicited mss generally welcome. Approach in
writing. No fiction. Weekly supplements:

Business Telegraph; *Homes and Gardens*; *Drive*
(motoring); *Sports Telegraph* (Saturday). All material to be addressed to the **News Editor**
D. Atkin. Particularly welcomes hard news
stories – approach in haste by telephone.
   Special Publications Editor *B. Farnsworth*

Lincolnshire Echo

Brayford Wharf East, Lincoln LN5 7AT
☎01522 820000 Fax 01522 804493
Email editor@lincolnshireecho.co.uk
Owner *Northcliffe Newspapers Group Ltd*
Editor *Michael Sassi*
Circulation 29,206

Best buys, holidays, motoring, dial-a-service,
restaurants, sport, leisure, home improvement,
record reviews, gardening corner, stars. All editorial material to be addressed to the editor.

Scunthorpe Evening Telegraph

4–5 Park Square, Scunthorpe, N. Lincolnshire
DN15 6JH
☎01724 273273 Fax 01724 273101
Owner *Northcliffe Newspapers Group Ltd*
Editor *Michelle Lalor*
Circulation 24,292

All correspondence should go to the **Assistant
Editor** *Jane Manning*.

Greater London

Evening Standard

Northcliffe House, 2 Derry Street, London
W8 5EE
☎020 7938 6000 Fax 020 7937 2648
Website www.thisislondon.com
Owner *Associated Newspapers/Lord Rothermere*
Editor *Veronica Wadley*
Circulation 418,958

Long-established evening paper, serving Londoners with both news and feature material.
Genuine opportunities for London-based
features. Produces a weekly colour supplement,
ES The Evening Standard Magazine, a weekly listings magazine *Hot Tickets* and regular weekly
supplements: *Just the Job* (Monday), *Homes &
Property* (Wednesday) and *ES Wheels* (Friday).
   Joint Deputy Editors *Andrew Bordiss, Ian
MacGregor*
   Associate Editor (Features) *Nicola Jeal*
   News Editor *Ian Walker*
   Features Editor *Bernice Davison*
   Sports Editor *Simon Greenberg*
   Editor, *ES* *Mimi Spencer*
   Editor, *Hot Tickets* *Mark Booker*

Greater Manchester

Manchester Evening News

164 Deansgate, Manchester M60 2RD
☎0161 832 7200 Fax 0161 834 3814
Website www.manchesteronline.co.uk

Owner *Manchester Evening News Ltd*
Editor *Paul Horrocks*
Circulation 173,446

One of the country's major regional dailies. Initial approach in writing preferred. No fiction. *Personal Finance* (Mon); *Health* (Tues); *Homes & Property* (Wed); *Small Business* (Thurs); *Lifestyle* (Fri/Sat); *Holidays* (Sat).

News Editor *Ian Wood*
Features Editor *Maggie Henfield* Regional news features, personality pieces and showbiz profiles considered. Maximum 1200 words.
Sports Editor *Peter Spencer*
Women's Page *Diane Cooke*
Payment based on house agreement rates.

Merseyside

Daily Post

PO Box 48, Old Hall Street, Liverpool
L69 3EB
☎0151 227 2000 Fax 0151 236 4682
Website www.icliverpool.co.uk

Owner *Trinity Mirror Plc*
Editor *Alastair Machray*
Circulation 72,776

Unsolicited mss welcome. Receives about six a day. Approach in writing with an idea. No fiction. Local, national/international news, current affairs, profiles – with pictures. Maximum 800–1000 words.

Features Editor *Jane Haase*
News Editor *Andrew Edwards*
Sports Editor *Richard Williamson*
Women's Page *Susan Lee*

Liverpool Echo

PO Box 48, Old Hall Street, Liverpool
L69 3EB
☎0151 227 2000 Fax 0151 236 4682
Email letters@liverpoolecho.co.uk

Owner *Liverpool Daily Post & Echo Ltd*
Editor *Mark Dickinson*
Circulation 157,999

One of the country's major regional dailies. Unsolicited mss welcome; initial approach with ideas in writing preferred.

News Editor *Andrew Edwards*
Features Editor *Jane Wolstenholme*

Sports Editor *Ken Rogers*
Women's Editor *Susan Lee*

Norfolk

Eastern Daily Press

Prospect House, Rouen Road, Norwich,
Norfolk NR1 1RE
☎01603 628311 Fax 01603 623872
Website www.EDP24.co.uk

Owner *ARCHANT} Regional*
Editor *Peter Franzen*
Circulation 72,233

Most pieces by commission only. Supplements: *Centro* (daily); education (Tuesday); motoring, business, property pages, agriculture, employment (all weekly); *Event* full-colour magazine (Friday); Saturday full colour magazine.

Deputy Editor *James Ruddy*
Assistant Editor (News) *Paul Durrant*
Features Editor *David Macaulay*
Sports Editor *David Thorpe*
Magazine Editor *Steve Snelling*

Evening News

Prospect House, Rouen Road, Norwich,
Norfolk NR1 1RE
☎01603 628311 Fax 01603 219060
Email david.bourn@ecng.co.uk
Website www.ecn.co.uk

Owner *Eastern Counties Newspapers Group Ltd*
Editor *David Bourn*
Circulation 36,458

Includes special pages on local property, motoring, children's page, pop, fashion, arts, entertainments and TV, gardening, local music scene, home and family.

Assistant Editor *Tim Williams*
  (tim.williams@ecng.co.uk)
Deputy Editor *Roy Strowger*
  (roy.strowger@ecng.co.uk)
Features Editor *Derek James*

Northamptonshire

Chronicle and Echo

Upper Mounts, Northampton NN1 3HR
☎01604 467000 Fax 01604 467190

Owner *Northamptonshire Newspapers*
Editor *Mark Edwards*
Circulation 27,778

Unsolicited mss are 'not necessarily unwelcome but opportunities to use them are rare'. Approach in writing with an idea. No fiction.

Supplements: *Sports Chronicle* (Monday); *Property Week* (Wednesday); *What's On Guide* (Thursday); *Weekend Motors* (Friday).
News Editor *Richard Edmondson*
Features Editor/Women's Page *Hilary Scott*
Sports Editor *Steve Pitts*

Evening Telegraph
Newspaper House, Ise Park, Rothwell Road, Kettering, Northamptonshire NN16 8GA
☎01536 506100 Fax 01536 506195
Email etnewsdesk@northantsnews.co.uk
Website www.northantsnews.com
Owner *Johnston Press Plc*
Managing Editor *David Penman*
Circulation 33,346

Northamptonshire Business Guide (weekly); *Entertainment Guide* and *Jobs* supplements (Thursday); and *Home & Garden* – monthly lifestyle supplement including gardening, films, eating out, etc.
News Editor *Nick Tite*
Sports Editor *Ian Davidson*

Nottinghamshire
Evening Post Nottingham
Castle Wharf House, Nottingham NG1 7EU
☎0115 948 2000 Fax 0115 964 4032
Owner *Northcliffe Newspapers Group Ltd*
Editor *Graham Glen*
Circulation 92,000

Unsolicited mss occasionally used. Good local interest only. Maximum 800 words. No fiction. Send ideas in writing.
News Editor *Claire Lumley*
Deputy Editor *Jon Grubb*
Sports Editor *Tim Walters*

Oxfordshire
Oxford Mail
Osney Mead, Oxford OX2 0EJ
☎01865 425262 Fax 01865 425554
Email news@nqo.com
Website www.thisisoxford.co.uk
Owner *Newsquest (Oxfordshire) Ltd*
Editor *Jim McClure*
Circulation 35,000

Unsolicited mss are considered but a great many unsuitable offerings are received. Approach in writing with an idea, rather than by phone. No fiction. All fees negotiable.

Shropshire
Shropshire Star
Ketley, Telford, Shropshire TF1 5HU
☎01952 242424 Fax 01952 254605
Owner *Shropshire Newspapers Ltd*
Editor *Sarah-Jane Smith*
Circulation 89,619

No unsolicited mss; approach the editor with ideas in writing in the first instance. No news or fiction.
Head of Supplements *Sharon Walters*
Limited opportunities; uses mostly in-house or syndicated material. Maximum 1200 words.
Sports Editor *Dave Bollinger*

Somerset
The Bath Chronicle
Windsor House, Windsor Bridge Road, Bath BA2 3AU
☎01225 322322 Fax 01225 322291
Owner *BUP Plc*
Editor *David Gledhill*
Circulation 17,501

Local news and features especially welcomed.
Deputy Editor *John McCready*
News Editor *Paul Wiltshire*
Features Editor *Liz Burcher*
Sports Editor *Tony Harrison*

Evening Post
Temple Way, Bristol BS99 7HD
☎0117 934 3000 Fax 0117 934 3575
Email mail@epost.co.uk
Website www.epost.co.uk
Owner *Bristol United Press plc*
Editor *Mike Lowe*
Circulation 70,284

News Editor *Kevan Blackadder*
Features Editor *Bill Davis*
Sports Editor *Chris Bartlett*

Western Daily Press
Temple Way, Bristol BS99 7HD
☎0117 934 3000 Fax 0117 934 3574
Email WDEditor *or* WDNews *or* WDFeats@bepp.co.uk
Website www.westpress.co.uk
Owner *Bristol Evening Post & Press Ltd*
Editor *Terry Manners*
Circulation 51,427

Sports Editor *Bill Beckett*
Women's Page *Lynda Cleasby*

Staffordshire

Burton Mail
65–68 High Street, Burton upon Trent,
Staffordshire DE14 1LE
☎01283 512345 Fax 01283 515351
Email editorial@burtonmail.co.uk
Owner *Burton Daily Mail Ltd*
Editor *Paul Hazeldine*
Circulation 18,456

Fashion, health, wildlife, environment, nostalgia,
financial/money (Monday); consumer (Tuesday); women's world, rock (Wednesday); property (Thursday); motoring, farming, what's on
(Friday); what's on, leisure (Saturday).
News/Features Editor *Andrew Parker*
Sports Editor *Rex Page*
Women's Page *Bill Pritchard*

The Sentinel/Sentinel Sunday
Sentinel House, Etruria, Stoke on Trent,
Staffordshire ST1 5SS
☎01782 602525 Fax 01782 280781
(Sentinel)/201167 (Sentinel Sunday)
Website www.thisisstaffordshire.co.uk
Owner *Staffordshire Sentinel Newspapers Ltd*
Editor-in-Chief *Sean Dooley*
Circulation 85,368 (Sentinel)

Weekly sports final supplement. All material
should be sent to the **Head of Content** *Martin
Tideswell.*

Suffolk

East Anglian Daily Times
Press House, 30 Lower Brook Street, Ipswich,
Suffolk IP4 1AN
☎01473 230023 Fax 01473 211391
Email EADT@ecng.co.uk
Website www.eadt.co.uk
Owner *Eastern Counties Newspapers Group Ltd*
Editor *Terry Hunt*
Circulation 44,157

FOUNDED 1874. Unsolicited mss generally not
welcome; three or four received a week and
almost none are used. Approach in writing in the
first instance. No fiction. Supplements: Young
Readers' section (Monday); Business (Tuesday);
Job Quest (Wednesday); Property (Thursday);
Motoring (Friday); Magazine (Saturday).
News Editor *Aynsley Davidson* Hard news
stories involving East Anglia (Suffolk, Essex
particularly) or individuals resident in the area
are always of interest.
Features *Julian Ford* Mostly in-house, but

will occasionally buy in when the subject is of
strong Suffolk/East Anglian interest. Photo
features preferred (extra payment). Special
advertisement features are regularly run. Some
opportunities here. Maximum 1000 words.
Sports Editor *Nick Garnham*
Women's Page *Victoria Hawkins*

Evening Star
30 Lower Brook Street, Ipswich, Suffolk
IP4 1AN
☎01473 230023 Fax 01473 225296
Owner *Eastern Counties Newspaper Group*
Editor *Nigel Pickover*
Circulation 30,391
News Editor *Colin Adwent*
Sports Editor *Mike Horne*

East Sussex

The Argus
Argus House, Crowhurst Road, Hollingbury,
Brighton, East Sussex BN1 8AR
☎01273 544544 Fax 01273 505703
Email simonb@argus-btn.co.uk
Website www.theargus.co.uk
Owner *Newsquest (Sussex) Ltd*
Editor-in-Chief *Simon Bradshaw*
Circulation 50,285
News Editor *Rebecca Stephens*
Sports Editor *Chris Giles*

Tyne & Wear

Evening Chronicle
Groat Market, Newcastle upon Tyne, Tyne
and Wear NE1 1ED
☎0191 232 7500 Fax 0191 232 2256
Email ec.news@ncjmedia.co.uk
Website www.evening-chronicle.co.uk
Owner *Trinity Mirror Plc*
Editor *Paul Robertson*
Circulation 107,346

Receives a lot of unsolicited material, much of
which is not used. Family issues, gardening,
pop, fashion, cooking, consumer, films and
entertainment guide, home improvements,
motoring, property, angling, sport and holidays. Approach in writing with ideas.
News Editor *Mick Smith*
Features Limited opportunities due to fulltime feature staff.
Sports Editor *Paul New*
Women's Interests *Kay Jordan*

Gazette

Chapter Row, South Shields, Tyne & Wear
NE33 1BL
☎0191 455 4661 Fax 0191 456 8270
Website www.southtynesidetoday.co.uk

Owner *Northeast Press Ltd*
Editor *Rob Lawson*
Circulation 23,332

News Editor *Gary Welford*
 Sports Editor *John Cornforth*
 Women's Page *Caroline Sword*

The Journal

Thomson House, Groat Market, Newcastle
upon Tyne, Tyne & Wear NE1 1ED
☎0191 232 7500
Fax 0191 232 2256/201 6044
Email jnl.newsdesk@ncjmedia.co.uk
Website www.the-journal.co.uk

Owner *Trinity Mirror Plc*
Editor *Gerard Henderson*
Circulation 51,936

Daily platforms include farming and business.
Monthly full-colour business supplement: *The
Journal Northern Business Magazine.*
 Deputy Editor *Anne Edwards*
 Sports Editor *Kevin Dinsdale*
 Arts & Entertainment Editor *David
 Whetstone*
 Environment Editor *Tony Henderson*
 Business Editor *Peter Jackson*

Sunday Sun

Newcastle Chronicle & Journal Ltd, Groat
Market, Newcastle upon Tyne, Tyne & Wear
NE1 1ED
☎0191 201 6330 Fax 0191 230 0238
Email peter.montellier@ncjmedia.co.uk

Owner *Trinity Mirror Plc*
Editor *Peter Montellier*
Circulation 95,672

All material should be addressed to the appropriate editor (phone to check), or to the editor.
 Sports Editor *Dylan Younger*

Sunderland Echo

Echo House, Pennywell, Sunderland, Tyne &
Wear SR4 9ER
☎0191 501 5800 Fax 0191 534 4861
Email andrew.smith@northeast-press.co.uk

Owner *Johnston Press Plc*
Group Editorial Director *Andrew Smith*
Circulation 57,703

All editorial material to be addressed to the **News**

Editor *Patrick Lavelle* (echo.news@northeast-
press.co.uk).

Warwickshire

Coventry Evening Telegraph

Corporation Street, Coventry CV1 1FP
☎024 7663 3633 Fax 024 7655 0869
Email news@coventry-telegraph.co.uk
Website www.IcCoventry.co.uk

Owner *Trinity Mirror Plc*
Editor *Alan Kirby*
Circulation 82,417

Unsolicited mss are read, but few are pub-
lished. Approach in writing with an idea. No
fiction. All unsolicited material should be
addressed to the editor. Maximum 600 words
for features.
 News Editor *John West*
 Features Editor *Steve Chilton*
 Sports Editor *Roger Draper*
 Women's Page *Steve Chilton*
 Payment negotiable.

Leamington Spa Courier

32 Hamilton Terrace, Leamington Spa,
Warwickshire CV32 4LY
☎01926 457755 Fax 01926 451690
Email editorial@leamingtoncourier.co.uk
Website www.leamingtononline.co.uk

Owner *Central Counties Newspapers*
Editor *Martin Lawson*
Circulation 13,410

One of the Leamington Spa Courier Series
which also includes the *Warwick Courier* and
Kenilworth Weekly News. Unsolicited feature
articles considered, particularly matter with a
local angle. Telephone with idea first.
 News Editor *Richard Parker*

West Midlands

Birmingham Evening Mail

28 Colmore Circus, Queensway, Birmingham
B4 6AX
☎0121 236 3366 Fax 0121 233 0271

Owner *Trinity Mirror Plc*
Editor *Roger Borrell*
Circulation 138,828

Freelance contributions are welcome, particularly topics of interest to the West Midlands
and Women's Page pieces offering original and
lively comment.
 News Editor *Carole Cole*
 Features Editor *Alison Handley*
 Women's Page *Diane Parkes*

Birmingham Post

28 Colmore Circus, Queensway, Birmingham
B4 6AX
☎0121 236 3366 Fax 0121 625 1105
Owner *Trinity Mirror Plc*
Publisher & Editor *Dan Mason*
Circulation 21,833

One of the country's leading regional newspapers. Freelance contributions are welcome. Topics of interest to the West Midlands and pieces offering lively, original comment are particularly welcome.

Head of News *Richard McComb*
Head of Features *Phil Brown*

Express & Star

Queen Street, Wolverhampton, West
Midlands WV1 1ES
☎01902 313131 Fax 01902 319721
Owner *Midlands News Association*
Editor *Adrian Faber*
Circulation 170,873

Deputy Editor *Richard Ewels*
Assistant Editors *Shirley Tart, Roy Williams*
Head of News *John Bray*
Features Editor *David Hotchkiss*
Business Editor *Jim Walsh*
Sports Editor *Steve Gordos*
Women's Editor *Anne-Laure Domenichini*

Sunday Mercury (Birmingham)

28 Colmore Circus, Queensway, Birmingham
B4 6AZ
☎0121 236 3366 Fax 0121 234 5877
Email sundaymercury@mrn.co.uk
Owner *Trinity Mirror Plc*
Editor *David Brookes*
Circulation 100,407

Head of Content *Tony Larner*
Assistant Editor (Sport) *Lee Gibson*

Wiltshire

Evening Advertiser

100 Victoria Road, Swindon, Wiltshire
SN1 3BE
☎01793 528144 Fax 01793 542434
Email editor@newswilts.co.uk
Website www.thisiswiltshire.co.uk
Owner *Newsquest (Wiltshire) Ltd*
Editor *Simon O'Neill*
Circulation 26,343

Copy and ideas invited. 'All material must be strongly related or relevant to the town of Swindon or the county of Wiltshire.' Little scope for freelance work. Fees vary depending on material.

Deputy Editor *Pauline Leighton*
News Editor *Mark Drew*
Sports Editor *Neville Smith*

Worcestershire

Evening News

Berrow's House, Hylton Road, Worcester
WR2 5JX
☎01905 748200 Fax 01905 748009
Owner *Newsquest (Midlands South) Ltd*
Editor *Stewart Gilbert*
Circulation 23,102

Local events (Tuesday); jobs/careers (Wednesday); property (Thursday); showbiz/what's on, motoring/Pulse pop page (Friday); holidays/what's on (Saturday).

Deputy Editor *Mark Higgitt*
News Editor *Tina Faulkner*
Features Editor/Women's Page *Dave Chapman*
Sports Editor *Paul Ricketts*

Yorkshire

The Doncaster Star

40 Duke Street, Doncaster, South Yorkshire
DN1 3EA
☎01302 344001 Fax 01302 768340
Email rob.hollingworth@rim.co.uk
Owner *Sheffield Newspapers Ltd*
Editor/News Editor *Rob Hollingworth*
Circulation 9,716

All editorial material to be addressed to the editor.

Sports Editor *Steve Hossack*

Evening Courier

PO Box 19, King Cross Street, Halifax,
West Yorkshire HX1 2SF
☎01422 260200 Fax 01422 260341
Website www.halifaxtoday.co.uk
Owner *Johnston Press Plc*
Editor *Edward Riley*
Circulation 29,000

News Editor *John Kenealy*
Features Editor *William Marshall*
Sports Editor *Ian Rushworth*
Women's Page *Diane Crabtree*

Evening Press

PO Box 29, 76–86 Walmgate, York YO1 9YN
☎01904 653051 Fax 01904 612853
Email newsdesk@ycp.co.uk
Website www.thisisyork.co.uk
Owner *Newsquest Media Group (a Gannett company)*
Editor *Elizabeth Page*
Circulation 42,074

Unsolicited mss not generally welcome, unless submitted by journalists of proven ability. *Business Press Pages* (Tuesday); *Property Press* (Thursday); *Friday Night Fever* – what's on (Friday); *8 Days* TV supplement (Saturday).
News Editor *Fran Clee*
Picture Editor *Martin Oates*
Sports Editor *Martin Jarred*
Payment negotiable.

Huddersfield Daily Examiner

Queen Street South, Huddersfield,
West Yorkshire HD1 2TD
☎01484 430000 Fax 01484 437789
Owner *Trinity Mirror Plc*
Editor *John Williams*
Circulation 35,218

Home improvement, home heating, weddings, dining out, motoring, fashion, services to trade and industry.
Deputy Editor *John Bird*
News Editor *Neil Atkinson*
Features Editor *Andrew Flynn*
Sports Editor *John Gledhill*
Women's Page *Hilarie Stelfox*

Hull Daily Mail

Blundell's Corner, Beverley Road, Hull, East Yorkshire HU3 1XS
☎01482 327111 Fax 01482 584353
Website www.thisishull.co.uk
Owner *Northcliffe Newspapers Group Ltd*
Editor *John Meehan*
Circulation 85,000
   Content Editor *Tracy Fletcher*
   Features Editors *Lucy Smith*, *Matt Stephenson*

Scarborough Evening News

17–23 Aberdeen Walk, Scarborough, North Yorkshire YO11 1BB
☎01723 363636 Fax 01723 383825
Email editorial@scarborougheveningnews.co.uk
Website www.scarboroughtoday.co.uk
Owner *Yorkshire Regional Newspapers Ltd*
Editor *Paul Napier*

Circulation 17,154

Special pages include property (Monday); motoring (Tuesday/Friday).
   Deputy Editor *Sue Wilkinson*
   News Editor *Neil Pickford*
   Sports Editor *Charles Place*
   All other material should be addressed to the editor.

The Star

York Street, Sheffield, South Yorkshire
S1 1PU
☎0114 276 7676 Fax 0114 272 5978
Owner *Sheffield Newspapers Ltd*
Editor *Peter Charlton*
Circulation 102,749

Unsolicited mss not welcome, unless topical and local.
   News Editor *Bob Westerdale* Contributions only accepted from freelance news reporters if they relate to the area.
   Features Editor *Richard Smith* Very rarely requires outside features, unless on specialised subject.
   Sports Editor *Martin Smith*
   Women's Page *Jo Davison*
   Payment negotiable.

Telegraph & Argus (Bradford)

Hall Ings, Bradford, West Yorkshire
BD1 1JR
☎01274 729511 Fax 01274 723634
Website www.thisisbradford.co.uk
Owner *Newsquest Media Group Ltd (a Gannett company)*
Editor *Perry Austin-Clarke*
Circulation 51,838

No unsolicited mss – approach in writing with samples of work. No fiction.
   Assistant Editor (News & Features) *Damian Bates* Local features and general interest. Showbiz pieces. 600–1000 words (maximum 1500).
   Sports Editor *Rob Stewart*

Yorkshire Evening Post

Wellington Street, Leeds, West Yorkshire
LS1 1RF
☎0113 243 2701 Fax 0113 238 8536
Email eped@ypn.co.uk
Owner *Regional Independent Media*
Editor *Neil Hodgkinson*
Circulation 100,596

Evening sister of the *Yorkshire Post*.
   News Editor *David Helliwell*

Features Editor *Anne Pickles*
Sports Editor *Phil Rostron*
Women's Page *Jayne Dawson*

Yorkshire Post

Wellington Street, Leeds, West Yorkshire
LS1 1RF
☎0113 243 2701 Fax 0113 238 8537
Email yp.editor@ypn.co.uk
Owner *Regional Independent Media*
Editor *Tony Watson*
Circulation 75,836

A serious-minded, quality regional daily with a generally conservative outlook. Three or four unsolicited mss arrive each day; all will be considered but initial approach in writing preferred. All submissions should be addressed to the editor. No fiction, poetry or family histories. **Head of Content** *John Furbisher*
Features Editor *Mick Hickling* Open to suggestions in all fields (though ordinarily commissioned from specialist writers).
Sports Editor *Bill Bridge*
Women's Page *Jill Armstrong*

NORTHERN IRELAND

Belfast News Letter

46–56 Boucher Crescent, Belfast BT12 6QY
☎028 9068 0000 Fax 028 9066 4412
Owner *Century Newspapers Ltd*
Editor *Geoff Martin*
Circulation 33,853

Weekly supplements: *Farming Life*; *Business News Letter*, *Female Times*; *The Guide*; *Sports Ulster*.
Deputy Editor *Mike Chapman*
News Editors *Ric Clark, Steven Moore*
Features Editor *Geoff Hill*
Sports Editor *Brian Millar*
Fashion & Lifestyle/Property Editor
Sandra Chapman
Business Editor *Adrienne McGill*
Agricultural Editor *David McCoy*

Belfast Telegraph

Royal Avenue, Belfast BT1 1EB
☎028 9026 4000 Fax 028 9055 4506/4540
Owner *Independent News & Media (UK)*
Editor *Edmund Curran*
Circulation 111,329

Weekly business, property and recruitment supplements.
Deputy Editor *Jim Flanagan*
News Editor *Paul Connolly*

Features Editor *John Caruth*
Sports Editor *John Laverty*
Business Editor *Nigel Tilson*

The Irish News

113/117 Donegall Street, Belfast BT1 2GE
☎028 9032 2226 Fax 028 9033 7505
Owner *Irish News Ltd*
Editor *Noel Doran*
Circulation 51,677

All material to appropriate editor (phone to check), or to the news desk.
Head of Content *Fiona McGarry*
Sports Editor *Thomas Hawkins*
Arts Editor/Women's Page *Joanna Braniff*

Sunday Life

124–144 Royal Avenue, Belfast BT1 1EB
☎028 9026 4301 Fax 028 9055 4507
Email betty.arnold@belfasttelegraph.co.uk
Website www.sundaylife.co.uk
Owner *Independent News & Media (UK)*
Circulation 96,612
Editor/General Manager *Martin Lindsay*
Deputy Editor *Martin Hill*
Sports Editor *Jim Gracey*

SCOTLAND

The Courier and Advertiser

80 Kingsway East, Dundee DD4 8SL
☎01382 223131 Fax 01382 454590
Email courier@dcthomson.co.uk
Website www.thecourier.co.uk
Owner *D.C. Thomson & Co. Ltd*
Editor *Adrian Arthur*
Circulation 90,263

Circulates in East Central Scotland. Features occasionally accepted on a wide range of subjects, particularly local/Scottish interest – including finance, insurance, agriculture, motoring, modern homes, lifestyle and fitness. Maximum length, 500 words.
News Editor *Arliss Rhind*
Features Editor/Women's Page *Shona Lorimer*
Sports Editor *Graeme Dey*

Daily Record (Glasgow)

See **National Newspapers**

Evening Express (Aberdeen)

PO Box 43, Lang Stracht, Mastrick, Aberdeen
AB15 6DF
☎01224 690222 Fax 01224 344106

Email d.martin@ajl.co.uk
Owner *Northcliffe Newspapers Group Ltd*
Editor *Donald Martin*
Circulation 68,191

Circulates in Aberdeen and the Grampian region. Local, national and international news and pictures, sport. Family platforms include *What's On*, *Counter* (consumer news), *Eating Out Guide*, *Family Days Out*. Unsolicited mss welcome 'if on a controlled basis'.

News Editor *Richard Prest* Freelance news contributors welcome.
Payment negotiable.

Evening News

Barclay House, 108 Holyrood Road, Edinburgh EH8 8AS
☎0131 620 8620 Fax 0131 620 8696
Website www.edinburghnews.com
Owner *Scotsman Publications Ltd*
Editor *Ian Stewart*
Circulation 90,000

FOUNDED 1873. Circulates in Edinburgh, Fife, Central and Lothian. Coverage includes: entertainment, gardening, motoring, shopping, fashion, health and lifestyle, showbusiness. Occasional platform pieces, features of topical and/ or local interest. Unsolicited feature material welcome. Approach the appropriate editor in writing.

Associate Editor (News) *David Lee*
Sports Editor *Martin Dempster*
Payment NUJ/house rates.

Evening Telegraph

80 Kingsway East, Dundee DD4 8SL
☎01382 223131 Fax 01382 454590
Owner *D.C. Thomson & Co. Ltd*
Editor *Alan Proctor*
Circulation 29,465

Circulates in Tayside, Dundee and Fife. All material should be addressed to the editor.

Evening Times

200 Renfield Street, Glasgow G2 3PR
☎0141 302 7000 Fax 0141 302 6677
Email TimesEditorial@scottishmedia.com
Owner *S.M.G.*
Editor *Charles McGhee*
Circulation 110,585

Circulates in Glasgow and the west of Scotland. Supplements: *Job Search; Home Front; Woman; Times Out* (leisure); *Times Out Weekend Extra*.
News Editor *Hugh Boag*
Features Editor *Ken McNab*

Sports Editor *David Stirling*
Women's Editor *Kim Miller*

Greenock Telegraph

2 Crawfurd Street, Greenock PA15 1LH
☎01475 726511 Fax 01475 783734
Owner *Clyde & Forth Press Ltd*
Editor *Stewart Peterson*
Circulation 19,872

Circulates in Greenock, Port Glasgow, Gourock, Kilmacolm, Langbank, Bridge of Weir, Inverkip, Wemyss Bay, Skelmorlie, Largs. Unsolicited mss considered 'if they relate to the newspaper's general interests'. No fiction. All material to be addressed to the editor.

The Herald/Sunday Herald (Glasgow)

See **National Newspapers**

Paisley Daily Express

14 New Street, Paisley PA1 1YA
☎0141 887 7911 Fax 0141 887 6254
Email pde@s-un.co.uk
Owner *Scottish & Universal Newspapers Ltd*
Editor *Norman Macdonald*
Circulation 9,067

Circulates in Paisley, Linwood, Renfrew, Johnstone, Elderslie, Neilston and Barrhead. Unsolicited mss welcome only if of genuine local (Paisley) interest. The paper does not commission work and will consider submitted material. Maximum 1000–1500 words. All submissions to the editor.

News Editor *Anne Dalrymple*
Sports Reporters *Michelle Evans*, *Matt Vallance*

The Press and Journal

PO Box 43, Lang Stracht, Mastrick, Aberdeen AB15 6DF
☎01224 690222 Fax 01224 663575
Owner *Northcliffe Newspapers Group Ltd*
Editor *Derek Tucker*
Circulation 104,548

A well-established daily that circulates in Aberdeen, Grampians, Highlands, Tayside, Orkney, Shetland and the Western Isles. Most material is commissioned but will consider ideas.

News Editor *Fiona McWhirr* Wide variety of hard or off-beat news and features relating especially, but not exclusively, to the north of Scotland.

Sports Editor *Jim Dolan*
Women's Page *Victoria Murchie*
Payment by arrangement.

Scotland on Sunday (Edinburgh)
See **National Newspapers**

The Scotsman (Edinburgh)
See **National Newspapers**

Sunday Mail (Glasgow)
See **National Newspapers**

Sunday Post (Dundee)
See **National Newspapers**

WALES

Evening Leader
Mold Business Park, Wrexham Road, Mold, Clwyd CH7 1XY
☎01352 707707 Fax 01352 752180
Owner *North Wales Newspapers*
Editor-in-Chief *Mark Rossiter*
Circulation 30,976

Circulates in Wrexham, Flintshire, Deeside and Chester. Special pages/features: motoring, travel, arts, women's, children's, photography, local housing, information and news for the disabled, music and entertainment.
> **News Editor** *Joanne Shone*
> **Features Editor** *Debra Greenhouse*
> **Sports Editor** *Nick Harrison*

South Wales Argus
Cardiff Road, Maesglas, Newport, Gwent NP20 3QN
☎01633 810000 Fax 01633 777202
Owner *Newsquest*
Editor *Gerry Keighley*
Circulation 30,000

Circulates in Newport, Gwent and surrounding areas.
> **News Editor** *Alison Gow*
> **Sports Editor** *Carson Wishart*

South Wales Echo
Thomson House, Havelock Street, Cardiff CF10 1XR
☎029 2022 3333 Fax 029 2058 3624
Website www.icwales.com
Owner *Trinity Mirror Plc*
Editor *Alastair Milburn*
Circulation 75,959

Circulates in South and Mid Glamorgan and Gwent.
> **Head of News & Design** *Nick Machin*

Head of Features & Development *Neil Cammies*
Head of Sport *Carl Difford*

South Wales Evening Post
Adelaide Street, Swansea, West Glamorgan SA1 1QT
☎01792 510000 Fax 01792 514697
Email postbox@swwp.co.uk
Website www.thisissouthwales.co.uk
Owner *Northcliffe Newspapers Group Ltd*
Editor *To be appointed*
Circulation 60,427

Circulates throughout south west Wales.
> **News Editor** *Jonathan Isaacs*
> **Features Editor** *Andy Pearson*
> **Sports Editor** *David Evans*

Wales on Sunday
Thomson House, Havelock Street, Cardiff CF10 1XR
☎029 2022 3333 Fax 029 2058 3725
Owner *Trinity Mirror plc*
Editor *Alan Edmunds*
Circulation 62,286

LAUNCHED 1989. Tabloid with sports supplement. Does not welcome unsolicited mss.
> **News Editor** *Ceri Gould*
> **Features/Women's Page** *Mike Smith*
> **Sports Editor** *Paul Abbandonato*

The Western Mail
Thomson House, Havelock Street, Cardiff CF10 1XR
☎029 2058 3583 Fax 029 2058 3652
Email nfowler@wme.co.uk
Website www.icwales.com
Owner *Trinity Mirror Plc*
Editor *Neil Fowler*
Circulation 64,172

Circulates in Cardiff, Merthyr Tydfil, Newport, Swansea and towns and villages throughout Wales. Mss welcome if of a topical nature, and preferably of Welsh interest. No short stories or travel. Approach in writing to the editor. 'Usual subjects already well covered, e.g. motoring, travel, books, gardening. We look for the unusual.' Maximum 1000 words. Opportunities also on women's page. Supplements: Saturday Magazine; Education; Welsh Homes; Country and Farming; Business; Sport; Motoring.
> **Assistant Editor** *Mark Tattersall*
> **Head of Content** *Lee Wenham*
> **Sports Editor** *Philip Blanche*

CHANNEL ISLANDS

Jersey Evening Post
PO Box 582, Jersey, Channel Islands
JE4 8XQ
☎01534 611611 Fax 01534 611622
Email editorial@jerseyeveningpost.com
Website www.thisisjersey.com
Owner *Jersey Evening Post Ltd*
Editor *Chris Bright*
Circulation 23,081

Special pages: gardening, motoring, property, boating, technology, young person's (16–25), women, food and drink, personal finance, rock reviews, health, business.
   News Editor *Sue Le Ruez*

Features Editor *Elaine Hanning*
Sports Editor *Ron Felton*

Guernsey Press & Star
Braye Road, Vale, Guernsey, Channel Islands
GY1 3BW
☎01481 240240 Fax 01481 240235
Email newsroom@guernsey-press.com
Website www.guernsey-press.com
Owner *Guiton Group*
Editor *Richard Digard*
Circulation 16,000

Special pages include children's and women's interest, gardening and fashion.
   News Editor *James Falla*
   Sports Editor *Rob Batiste*
   Women's Page *Suzanne Heneghan*

Freelance Rates – Newspapers

Freelance rates vary enormously. The following minimum rates, set by the **National Union of Journalists**, should be treated as guidelines. The NUJ has no power to enforce minimum rates on newspapers that do not recognise the Union. It is up to freelancers to negotiate the best deal they can.

National newspapers

(Including *The Herald, Sunday Herald, Daily Record, Sunday Mail, The Scotsman, Scotland on Sunday, Evening Standard*)

Features (including reviews, obituaries, etc) Broadsheet rates start at under £220 per 1000 words and as low as £100 in Scotland, but sums of over £500 are common. Tabloids often pay considerably more than broadsheets though items are usually shorter.

News News may be paid for per 1000 words or by the day. When payment is by the word, the minimum should be £230 per 1000 words or pro rata. (Applies to all areas of news reporting, including sport.)

Day Rates A low minimum of £125 for a six- or seven-hour shift. Accept day rates only if required to be in the office for the day.

Exclusives These can command very high fees, depending on how much the newspaper wants the story. A prominent position for the piece should command £550 or more. A guaranteed minimum of at least £280 should be negotiated in case it appears further down the page in a shorter form.

Colour Supplements Higher rates of payment should apply.

Crosswords 15 × 15 squares and under: at least £120; 15 × 15 squares and over: at least £150.

Regional & provincial newspapers (England & Wales)

According to the NUJ, freelance rates in many papers in this area (especially in provincials) have remained static over the last few years – 'a fact that makes individual negotiation all the more important, and which makes positive recommendations impossible'. The 'lineage' system (payment per line of text published – usually four words) is common in provincials, at around £2–3 per ten lines, and 20–30 pence per line thereafter, for both news and features. 'Payment on dailies and Sundays is still way below acceptable levels.'

Crosswords At least £70.

Magazines

ABCtales
See entry under **Electronic Publishing and Other Services**

Abraxas
57 Eastbourne Road, St Austell, Cornwall PL25 4SU
☎01726 64975 Fax 01726 64975
Email palnew7@hotmail.com
Website www.AbraxasMagazine.com
Owner *Paul Newman*
Editors *Paul Newman, Pamela Smith-Rawnsley*
FOUNDED 1991. QUARTERLY incorporating the *Colin Wilson Newsletter*. Unsolicited mss welcome after a study of the magazine – initial approach by phone or letter preferred.
Features Essays, translations and reviews. Welcomes provocative, lively articles on little-known literary figures and new slants on psychology, existentialism and ideas. Maximum length 2000 words. *Payment* nominal if at all.
Fiction One story per issue. Maximum 2000 words. Favours compact, obsessional stories.
Poetry Double-page spread – slight penchant for the surreal but open to most styles.
Payment free copy of magazine.

Acclaim
See **The New Writer**

Accountancy
40 Bernard Street, London WC1N 1LD
☎020 7833 3291 Fax 020 7833 2085
Owner *Institute of Chartered Accountants in England and Wales*
Editor *Brian Singleton-Green*
Circulation 60,611
FOUNDED 1889. MONTHLY. Written ideas welcome.
Features *Brian Singleton-Green* Accounting/tax/business-related articles of high technical content aimed at professional/managerial readers. Maximum 2000 words.
Payment by arrangement.

Accountancy Age
32–34 Broadwick Street, London W1A 2HG
☎020 7316 9236/Features: 020 7316 9611
Fax 020 7316 9250
Email accountancy_age@vnu.co.uk
Website www.accountancyage.com
Owner *VNU Business Publications*
Editor *Damian Wild*
News Editor *Gavin Hinks* (020 7316 9242)
Circulation 77,806
FOUNDED 1969. WEEKLY. Unsolicited mss welcome. Ideas may be suggested in writing provided they are clearly thought out.
Features *Liz Loxton* Topics right across the accountancy, business and financial world. Maximum 2000 words.
Payment negotiable.

Ace Tennis Magazine
9–11 North End Road, London W14 8ST
☎020 7605 8000 Fax 020 7602 2323
Email Dominic.Bliss@acemag.co.uk
Owner *Tennis GB*
Editor *Dominic Bliss*
Circulation 47,973
FOUNDED 1996. MONTHLY specialist tennis magazine. News (250 words max.) and features (2000 words max.). No unsolicited mss; send feature synopses by e-mail in the first instance. No tournament reports.
Payment £200 per 1000 words.

Active Life
16 Ennismore Avenue, London W4 1SF
Email hhodge@lexicon-uk.com
Website www.activelifemag.com
Owner *Maturetimes Ltd*
Editor *Helene Hodge*
FOUNDED 1990. MONTHLY magazine aimed at over 50s. General consumer interests including travel, finance, property and leisure. Opportunities for freelancers in all departments, including fiction. Approach in writing with synopsis of ideas. Authors' notes available on receipt of s.a.e.

Acumen
See under **Poetry Magazines**

Aeroplane
IPC Media Ltd., King's Reach Tower, Stamford Street, London SE1 9LS
☎020 7261 5849 Fax 020 7261 5269
Email aeroplane_monthly@ipcmedia.com

Website www.aeroplanemonthly.com
Owner *IPC Country & Leisure Media Ltd*
Editor *Michael Oakey*
Circulation 34,500

FOUNDED 1973. MONTHLY. Historic aviation and aircraft preservation from its beginnings to the 1960s. No post-1960 aircraft types; no poetry. Will consider news items and features written with authoritative knowledge of the subject, illustrated with good quality photographs.

News *Tony Harmsworth* Maximum 500 words. **Features** *Michael Oakey* Maximum 3000 words. *Payment* £60 per 1000 words; £10–40 per picture used. Approach by letter in the first instance.

African Affairs

Dept of Historical & Cultural Studies, Goldsmiths College, University of London, New Cross, London SE14 6NW
☎020 7919 7486   Fax 020 7919 7398
Email afraf@compuserve.com
Owner *Royal African Society*
Editors *David Killingray, Stephen Ellis*
Circulation 2250

FOUNDED 1901. QUARTERLY learned journal publishing articles on recent political, social and economic developments in sub-Saharan countries. Also included are historical studies that illuminate current events in the continent. Unsolicited mss welcome. Maximum 8000 words.

No payment.

Air International

PO Box 100, Stamford, Lincolnshire
PE9 1XQ
☎01780 755131   Fax 01780 757261
Email malcolm.english@keypublishing.com
Owner *Key Publishing Ltd*
Editor *Malcolm English*

FOUNDED 1971. MONTHLY. Civil and military aircraft magazine. Unsolicited mss welcome but initial approach by phone or in writing preferred.

Air Pictorial

HPC, Drury Lane, St Leonards on Sea, East Sussex TN38 9BJ
☎01424 720477   Fax 01424 443693
Email editor@airpictorial.com
Owner *Hastings Printing Company*
Editor *Barry C. Wheeler*
Circulation 21,000

FOUNDED 1939. MONTHLY review of aviation

for those interested in military, commercial and business aircraft and equipment – old and new. Will consider articles on military and civil aircraft, airports, air forces, current and historical subjects. No fiction. **Features** 'New writers always welcome and if the copy is not good enough it is returned with guidance attached.' Maximum 5000 words. **News** Items are always considered from new sources. Maximum 300 words. *Payment* negotiable.

AirForces Monthly

PO Box 100, Stamford, Lincolnshire
PE9 1XQ
☎01780 755131   Fax 01780 757261
Email edafm@keypublishing.com
Owner *Key Publishing Ltd*
Editor *Alan Warnes*
Circulation 25,787

FOUNDED 1988. MONTHLY. Modern military aircraft magazine. Unsolicited mss welcome but initial approach by phone or in writing preferred.

Amateur Gardening

Westover House, West Quay Road, Poole, Dorset BH15 1JG
☎01202 440840   Fax 01202 440860
Owner *IPC Media*
Editor *Tim Rumball*
Circulation 55,454

FOUNDED 1884. WEEKLY. New contributions are welcome especially if they are topical and informative. All articles/news items should be supported by colour pictures (which may or may not be supplied by the author).

Features Topical and practical gardening articles. Maximum 1000 words.

News Compiled and edited in-house generally but all stories welcomed.

Payment negotiable.

Amateur Photographer

IPC Media Ltd., King's Reach Tower, Stamford Street, London SE1 9LS
☎020 7261 5100/0870 444 5000 (switchboard)   Fax 020 7261 5404
Email amateurphotographer@ipcmedia.com
Website www.amateurphotographer.com
Owner *IPC Media*
Editor *Garry Coward-Williams*
Circulation 30,600

FOUNDED 1884. WEEKLY. For the competent amateur with a technical interest. Freelancers are used but writers should be aware that there is ordinarily no use for words without pictures.

Amateur Stage
Hampden House, 2 Weymouth Street,
London W1W 5BT
☎020 7636 4343 Fax 020 7636 2323
Email cvtheatre@aol.com
Owner *Platform Publications Ltd*
Editor *Charles Vance*

Some opportunity here for outside contributions. Topics of interest include amateur premières, technical developments within the amateur forum and items relating to landmarks or anniversaries in the history of amateur societies. Approach in writing only (include s.a.e. for return of mss).
No payment.

Ancestors
See **Public Record Office Publications** under **UK Publishers**

Angler's Mail
IPC Media Ltd., King's Reach Tower,
Stamford Street, London SE1 9LS
☎020 7261 5778 Fax 020 7261 6016
Email anglersmail@ipcmedia.com
Owner *IPC Media*
Editor *Roy Westwood*
News Editor *Thomas Petch*
Circulation 46,466

FOUNDED 1965. WEEKLY. Angling news and matches. Interested in pictures, stories and tip-offs. No features. Approach the news editor by telephone.
Payment £10–40 per 200 words; pictures, £20–40.

Animal Action
Wilberforce Way, Southwater, Horsham,
West Sussex RH13 9RS
☎0870 010 1181 Fax 0870 753 0048
Email publications@rspca.org.uk
Website www.rspca.org.uk
Owner *RSPCA*
Editor *Michaela Miller*
Circulation 80,000

BI-MONTHLY. RSPCA youth membership magazine. Articles (pet care, etc.) are written in-house. Good-quality animal photographs welcome.

Animalprints
Worthing Animal Aid, PO Box 4065,
Worthing, West Sussex BN11 3JL
☎01903 877144
Email WorthingAnimalAid@btinternet.com

Owner *Worthing Animal Aid*
Editor *Lilian Taylor*
Circulation 500

FOUNDED 1999. QUARTERLY magazine that aims to advance the animal movement. Welcomes contributions that are well researched, subtly thought provoking and have the potential for stimulating discussion. Approach in writing.
Payment Complimentary copies of relevant issue.

The Antique Dealer and Collectors' Guide
PO Box 805, Greenwich, London SE10 8TD
☎020 8691 4820 Fax 020 8691 2489
Email antiquedealercollectorsguide@ukbusiness.com
Website www.antiquecollectorsguide.co.uk
Owner *Statuscourt Ltd*
Publisher *Philip Bartlam*
Circulation 12,500

FOUNDED 1946. TEN ISSUES YEARLY. Covers all aspects of the antiques and fine art worlds. Unsolicited mss welcome.
Features Practical but readable articles on the history, design, authenticity, restoration and market aspects of antiques and fine art. Maximum 2000 words. *Payment* rates by arrangement.
News Items on events, sales, museums, exhibitions, antique fairs and markets. Maximum 300 words.

Antique Interiors International
Loudham Hall, Loudham, Suffolk IP13 0NN
☎01728 747505 Fax 01728 747868
Owner *Antique Publications*
Editor-in-Chief *Alistair Hicks*
Circulation 22,000

FOUNDED 1986. QUARTERLY. Amusing coverage of antiques, art and interiors. Unsolicited mss not welcome. Approach by phone or in writing in the first instance. Interested in freelance contributions on international art news items.

Antiques & Art Independent
PO Box 1945, Comely Bank, Edinburgh EH4 1AB
☎07000 268478 Fax 07000 268478
Email antiquesnews@hotmail.com
Website www.antiquesnews.co.uk
Owner *Gallery UK Ltd*
Publisher/Editor *Tony Keniston*
Circulation 21,000

FOUNDED 1997. BI-MONTHLY. Up-to-date information for the British antiques and art trade, circulated to dealers and collectors throughout the UK. News, photographs, gossip and controversial views on all aspects of the fine art and antiques world welcome. Articles on antiques and fine arts themselves are not featured. Approach in writing with ideas.

Apollo Magazine

1 Castle Lane, London SW1E 6DR
☎020 7233 6640 Fax 020 7630 7791
Email editorial@apollomag.com
Owner *Paul Z. Josefowitz*
Editor *David Ekserdjian*

FOUNDED 1925. MONTHLY. Specialist articles on art and antiques, exhibition and book reviews, exhibition diary, information on dealers and auction houses. Unsolicited mss welcome. Interested in specialist, usually new research in fine arts, architecture and antiques. Not interested in crafts or practical art, photography or art after 1945.

Aquarist & Pondkeeper

TRMG, Winchester Court, 1 Forum Place, Hatfield, Hertfordshire AL10 0RN
☎01707 273999 Fax 01707 269333
Email aandpeditor@btinternet.com
Owner *TRMG*
Editor *Derek Lambert*
Circulation 20,000

FOUNDED 1924. MONTHLY. Covers all aspects of aquarium and pondkeeping: conservation, herpetology (study of reptiles and amphibians), news, reviews and aquatic plant culture. Unsolicited mss welcome. Ideas should be submitted in writing first.

Features Good opportunities for writers on any of the above topics or related areas. 1500–3000 words, plus illustrations. **News** Very few opportunities.

Architects' Journal

151 Rosebery Avenue, London EC1R 4GB
☎020 7505 6700 Fax 020 7505 6701
Website www.ajplus.co.uk
Owner *Emap Construct*
Editor *Isabel Allen*
Circulation 16,441

WEEKLY trade magazine dealing with all aspects of the industry. No unsolicited mss. Approach in writing with ideas.

Architectural Design

John Wiley & Sons, 4th Floor, International House, Ealing Broadway Centre, London W5 5DB

☎020 8326 3800 Fax 020 8326 3801
Owner *John Wiley & Sons Ltd*
Executive Editor *Maggie Toy*
Editor *Helen Castle*
Senior Production Editor *Mariangela Palazzi-Williams*
Circulation 5,000

FOUNDED 1930. BI-MONTHLY. Sold as a book as well as a journal, *AD* charts theoretical and topical developments in architecture. Format consists of 128pp, the first part dedicated to a theme compiled by a specially commissioned guest editor; the back section (AD+) carries series and more current one-off articles. Unsolicited mss not welcome generally, though journalistic contributions will be considered for the back section.

The Architectural Review

151 Rosebery Avenue, London EC1R 4GB
☎020 7505 6725 Fax 020 7505 6701
Website www.arplus.com
Owner *Emap Construct*
Editor *Peter Davey*
Circulation 23,211

MONTHLY professional magazine dealing with architecture and all aspects of design. No unsolicited mss. Approach in writing with ideas.

Arena

Block A, 2nd Floor, Exmouth House, Pine Street, London EC1R 0JH
☎020 7689 9999 Fax 020 7689 0901
Owner *Emap élan East*
Editor *Anthony Noguera*
Circulation 38,182

Style and general interest magazine for men. Intelligent feature articles and profiles.

Features Fashion, lifestyle, film, television, politics, business, music, media, design, art, architecture and sport.

Art Monthly

4th Floor, 26 Charing Cross Road, London WC2H 0DB
☎020 7240 0389 Fax 020 7497 0726
Email info@artmonthly.co.uk
Website www.artmonthly.co.uk
Owner *Britannia Art Publications*
Editor *Patricia Bickers*
Circulation 6000

FOUNDED 1976. TEN ISSUES YEARLY. News and features of relevance to those interested in modern and contemporary visual art. Unsolicited mss welcome. Contributions should be addressed to the deputy editor, accompanied by s.a.e.

Features Always commissioned. Interviews and articles of up to 1500 words on art theory, individual artists, contemporary art history and issues affecting the arts (e.g. funding and arts education). Exhibition reviews of 750–1000 words; book reviews of 750–1000 words.

News Brief reports (250–300 words) on art issues.

Payment negotiable.

The Art Newspaper
70 South Lambeth Road, London SW8 1RL
☎020 7735 3331 Fax 020 7735 3332
Email feedback@theartnewspaper.com
Website www.theartnewspaper.com
Owner *Umberto Allemandi & Co. Publishing*
Editor *Anna Somers Cocks*
Circulation 22,000

FOUNDED 1990. MONTHLY. Tabloid format with hard news on the international art market, news, museums, exhibitions, archaeology, conservation, books and current debate topics. Length 250–2000 words. No unsolicited mss. Approach with ideas in writing. Commissions only.

Payment £120 per 1000 words.

The Artist
Caxton House, 63–65 High Street, Tenterden, Kent TN30 6BD
☎0158076 3673 Fax 0158076 5411
Website www.theartistmagazine.co.uk
Owner/Editor *Sally Bulgin*
Circulation 20,000

FOUNDED 1931. MONTHLY. Art journalists, artists, art tutors and writers with a good knowledge of art materials are invited to write to the editor with ideas for practical and informative features about art, materials, techniques and artists.

Artscene
Dean Clough Industrial Park, Halifax, West Yorkshire HX3 5AX
☎01422 322527 Fax 01422 322518
Email artscene@btconnect.com
Owner *Yorkshire and Humberside Arts*
Editor *Victor Allen*
Circulation 25,000

FOUNDED 1973. MONTHLY. Listings magazine for Yorkshire and Humberside. No unsolicited mss. Approach by phone with ideas.

Features Profiles of artists (all media) and associated venues/organisers of events of interest. Topical relevance vital. Maximum length 1500 words. *Payment* £100 per 1000 words.

News Artscene strives to bring journalistic values to arts coverage – all arts 'scoops' in the region are of interest. Maximum length 500 words. *Payment* £100 per 1000 words.

Asian Times
Unit 2, 65 Whitechapel Road, London E1 1DU
☎020 7650 2000 Fax 020 7650 2001
Website www.ethnicmedia.co.uk
Owner *Ethnic Media Group*
Editor *Gary Khangura*
Circulation 28,525

FOUNDED 1983. WEEKLY community paper for the Asian community in Britain. Interested in relevant general, local and international issues. Approach in writing with ideas for submission.

Athletics Weekly
83 Park Road, Peterborough, Cambridgeshire PE1 2TN
☎01733 898440 Fax 01733 898441
Email results@athletics-weekly.co.uk
Website www.athleticsweekly.com
Owner *Descartes Publishing*
Editor *Jason Henderson*
Circulation 20,000

FOUNDED 1945. WEEKLY. Covers track and field, road, fell, cross-country, race walking, athletic features and sports politics.

News *Steve Landells* Maximum 400 words.

Features *Tony Ward* Maximum 2000 words. Approach in writing.

Payment negotiable.

Attitude
Ludgate House, 245 Blackfriars Road, London SE1 9UX
☎020 7928 8000 Fax 020 7922 7600
Email attitude@express.co.uk
Owner *Northern & Shell plc*
Editor *Adam Mattera*
Circulation 60,000

FOUNDED 1994. MONTHLY. Style magazine aimed primarily, but not exclusively, at gay men. Celebrity, fashion and cultural coverage. Brief summaries of proposed features, together with details of previously published work, should be sent by post or fax only. 'It sounds obvious, but anyone wanting to contribute to the magazine should read it first.'

The Author
84 Drayton Gardens, London SW10 9SB
☎020 7373 6642
Owner *The Society of Authors*

Editor *Derek Parker*
Manager *Kate Pool*
Circulation 8,500

FOUNDED 1890. QUARTERLY journal of the **Society of Authors**. Most articles are commissioned.

Auto Express

30 Cleveland Street, London W1T 4JD
☎020 7907 6200 Fax 020 7907 6234
Email editorial@autoexpress.co.uk
Website www.autoexpress.co.uk
Owner *Dennis Publishing*
Editor *David Johns*
News & Features Editor *Richard Yarrow*
Circulation 95,000

FOUNDED 1989. WEEKLY consumer motoring title with news, drives, tests, investigations, etc. **Features** Welcomes ideas. No fully-written articles – features will be commissioned if appropriate and good enough. Maximum 2000 words. *Payment* £350 per 1000 words. **News** News stories and tip-offs welcome. Fillers, 150 words max.; leads, 300 words. Approach by e-mail.

Autocar

60 Waldegrave Road, Teddington, Middlesex TW11 8LG
☎020 8943 5630 Fax 020 8267 5759
Email autocar@haynet.com
Owner *Haymarket Magazines Ltd*
Editor *Rob Aherne*
Circulation 77,403

FOUNDED 1895. WEEKLY. All news stories, features, interviews, scoops, ideas, tip-offs and photographs welcome.
News *Phil McNamara*
Payment negotiable.

B Magazine

17–18 Berners Street, London W1T 3LN
☎020 7664 6470 Fax 020 7070 3401
Email letters@bmagazine.co.uk
Website www.atticfutura.co.uk
Owner *Attic Futura*
Editor *Gina Johnson*
Circulation 192,733

MONTHLY glossy magazine aimed at women in their mid-twenties. Will consider real-life stories, emotional issues and celebrity features. Ideas for features should be sent to *Kerry Smith*. No short stories or opinion pieces. Approach in writing or by e-mail.

Baby Magazine

Higbury wViP, 53–79 Highgate Road, London NW5 1TW
☎020 7331 1000 Fax 020 7331 1225
Email newbaby@wvip.co.uk
Website www.newbabymagazine.co.uk
Owner *Highbury wViP*
Editor *Jackie Guthrie*
Circulation 40,000

MONTHLY. For parents-to-be and parents of children up to two years old. No unsolicited mss.
Features Send synopsis of feature with covering letter in the first instance. Unsolicited material is not returned.

Baby's Best Buys

Higbury wViP, 53–79 Highgate Road, London NW5 1TW
☎020 7331 1000 Fax 020 7331 1241
Email dan.bromage@wvip.co.uk
Owner *Highbury wViP*
Editor *Dan Bromage*

QUARTERLY. Comprehensive product testing for parenting equipment and maternity wear.

Balance

Diabetes UK, 10 Parkway, London NW1 7AA
☎020 7424 1000 Fax 020 7424 1001
Email balance@diabetes.org.uk
Owner *Diabetes UK*
Editor *Martin Cullen*
Circulation 250,000

FOUNDED 1935. BI-MONTHLY. Unsolicited mss are not accepted. Writers may submit a brief proposal in writing. Only topics relevant to diabetes will be considered.
Features Medical, diet and lifestyle features written by people with diabetes or with an interest and expert knowledge in the field. General features are mostly based on experience or personal observation. Maximum 1500 words. *Payment* NUJ rates.
News Short pieces about activities relating to diabetes and the lifestyle of people with diabetes. Maximum 150 words.

The Banker

149 Tottenham Court Road, London W1P 9LL
☎020 7896 2507 Fax 020 7896 2586
Website www.thebanker.com
Owner *FT Business*
Editor *Stephen Timewell*
Circulation 24,000

FOUNDED 1926. MONTHLY. News and features on banking, finance and capital markets world-wide and technology.

BBC Gardeners' World Magazine

Woodlands, 80 Wood Lane, London
W12 0TT
☎020 8433 3959 Fax 020 8433 3986
Email gwletters@bbc.co.uk
Website www.gardenersworld.com
Owner *BBC Worldwide Publishing Ltd*
Editor *Adam Pasco*
Circulation 300,511

FOUNDED 1991. MONTHLY. Gardening advice, ideas and inspiration. No unsolicited mss. Approach by phone or in writing with ideas – interested in features about exceptional small gardens. Also interested in any exciting new gardens showing good design and planting ideas. 'The magazine aims to be the first to bring news of new trends and developments, and always welcomes ideas from contributors.'

BBC Good Food

Woodlands, 80 Wood Lane, London
W12 0TT
☎020 8433 2000 Fax 020 8433 3931
Website www.bbcworldwide.com
Owner *BBC Worldwide Publishing Ltd*
Editor *Orlando Murrin*
Circulation 322,614

FOUNDED 1989. MONTHLY food and drink magazine with television and radio links. No unsolicited mss.

BBC Good Homes Magazine

Woodlands, 80 Wood Lane, London
W12 0TT
☎020 8433 2391 Fax 020 8433 2691
Website www.bbcgoodhomes.com
Owner *BBC Worldwide Publishing Ltd*
Editor *Julie Savill*
Circulation 121,312

FOUNDED 1998. MONTHLY. Interiors, garden-ing, property, home shopping. No non-homes related features, fiction or puzzles. **Features** *Gill Smith* Readers' homes; property features from specialists. Approach by letter with cut-tings.

BBC History Magazine

Room A1050, Woodlands, 80 Wood Lane, London W12 0TT
☎020 8433 2433 Fax 020 8433 2931
Email bbchistory@galleon.co.uk
Website www.historymagazine.co.uk

Owner *BBC Worldwide Publishing Ltd*
Editor *Greg Neale*
Circulation 52,000

FOUNDED 2000. MONTHLY. General news and features on British and international history, with books and CD reviews, listings of history events, TV and radio history programmes and regular features for those interested in history and current affairs. Will consider submissions from academic or otherwise expert historians/ archaeologists as well as, occasionally, from his-torically literate journalists who include expert analysis and historiography with a well-told narrative. Ideas for regular features are wel-come. Also publishes cartoons, a monthly quiz and crossword. 'We cannot guarantee to acknowledge all unsolicited mss.' **Features** should be pegged to anniversaries or forth-coming books/TV programmes, current affairs topics, etc. 750–3000 words. **News** 400–500 words. Send short letter or e-mail with synop-sis, giving appropriate sources, pegs for publi-cation dates, etc. *Payment* negotiable.

BBC Homes & Antiques

Woodlands, 80 Wood Lane, London
W12 0TT
☎020 8433 3490 Fax 020 8433 3867
Website www.bbcworldwide.com/antiques
Owner *BBC Worldwide Publishing Ltd*
Editor *Judith Hall*
Circulation 165,388

FOUNDED 1993. MONTHLY traditional home interest magazine with a strong bias towards antiques and collectables. Opportunities for freelancers are limited; most features are com-missioned from regular stable of contributors. No fiction, health and beauty, fashion or gen-eral showbusiness. Approach with ideas by phone or in writing.
  Features *Caroline Wheater* At-home features: inspirational houses – people-led items. Pieces commissioned on recce shots and cuttings. Guidelines available on request. Celebrity features: 'at homes or favourite things' – send cuttings of relevant work published. Maximum 1500 words.
  Special Pages Regular feature – 'Memories'. Maximum 800 words.
  Payment negotiable.

BBC Music Magazine

Room A1004, Woodlands, 80 Wood Lane, London W12 0TT
☎020 8433 2000 Fax 020 8433 3292
Email music.magazine@bbc.co.uk

Website www.bbcmusicmagazine.com
Owner *BBC Worldwide Publishing Ltd*
Editor *Helen Wallace*
Circulation 121,046 (worldwide)

FOUNDED 1992. MONTHLY. All areas of classical music. Not interested in unsolicited material. Approach with ideas only, by fax.

BBC Top Gear Magazine

Woodlands, 80 Wood Lane, London
W12 0TT
☎020 8433 3716 Fax 020 8433 3754
Website www.topgear.com
Owner *BBC Worldwide Publishing Ltd*
Editor *Kevin Blick*
Circulation 150,000

FOUNDED 1993. MONTHLY companion magazine to the popular TV series. No unsolicited material as most features are commissioned.

BBC Wildlife Magazine

Broadcasting House, Whiteladies Road,
Bristol BS8 2LR
☎0117 973 8402 Fax 0117 946 7075
Email wildlife.magazine@bbc.co.uk
Owner *BBC Worldwide Publishing Ltd*
Editor *Rosamund Kidman Cox*
Circulation 50,811

FOUNDED 1963 (formerly *Wildlife*, née *Animals*). MONTHLY. Unsolicited mss generally not welcome.

Features Most features commissioned from writers with expert knowledge of wildlife or conservation subjects. Maximum 2500 words. *Payment* £200–450.

News Most news stories commissioned from known freelancers. Maximum 800 words. *Payment* £80–120

Bee World

IBRA, 18 North Road, Cardiff CF10 3DT
☎029 2037 2409 Fax 029 2066 5522
Email mail@ibra.org
Website www.ibra.org.uk
Owner *International Bee Research Association*
Editor *Dr P.A. Munn*
Circulation 1700

FOUNDED 1919. QUARTERLY. High-quality factual journal, including peer-reviewed articles, with international readership. Features on apicultural science and technology. Unsolicited mss welcome but authors should write to the editor for guidelines before submitting material.

Bella

H. Bauer Publishing, Academic House,
24–28 Oval Road, London NW1 7DT
☎020 7241 8000 Fax 020 7241 8056
Owner *H. Bauer Publishing*
Editor-in-Chief *Jackie Highe*
Circulation 468,937

FOUNDED 1987. WEEKLY. Women's magazine specialising in real-life, human interest stories.

Features *Sue Ricketts* Contributions welcome for some sections of the magazine: readers' letters, 'Blush with Bella' and 'Bella Rat'.

Fiction *Linda O'Byrne* Maximum 1000–1200 words. Send s.a.e. for guidelines.

Best

197 Marsh Wall, London E14 9SG
☎020 7519 5500 Fax 020 7519 5516
Email best@natmags.co.uk
Owner *National Magazine Company*
Editor *Louise Court*
Circulation 430,433

FOUNDED 1987. WEEKLY women's magazine. Multiple features, news, short stories on all topics of interest to women. Important for would-be contributors to study the magazine's style which differs from many other women's weeklies. Approach in writing with s.a.e.

Features Maximum 1500 words. No unsolicited mss.

Fiction Short story slot; unsolicited mss accepted. Maximum 1000 words. Send s.a.e. for guidelines.

Payment negotiable.

Best of British

Ian Beacham Publishing, Bank Chambers,
27a Market Place, Market Deeping,
Lincolnshire PE6 8EA
☎01778 342814
Email mail@british.fsbusiness.co.uk
Website www.bestofbritishmag.co.uk
Owner *Ian Beacham Publishing*
Editor *Peter Kelly*
Editor-in-Chief *Ian Beacham*

FOUNDED 1994. MONTHLY magazine celebrating all things British, both past and present. Emphasis on nostalgia – memories from the 1940s, 1950s and 1960s. Study of the magazine is advised in the first instance. All preliminary approaches should be made in writing.

Best Solutions

IBIS, 38 Broad Street, Earls Barton,
Northamptonshire NN6 0ND
☎01604 466500 Fax 01604 466480

Website www.bestsolutions.co.uk
Owner *Grahame White*
Editor *Graham Cole*

FOUNDED 1996. QUARTERLY 32pp business to business consultancy magazine. No unsolicited mss. Interested in business solution articles (1000 words). Approach in writing.

The Big Issue

1–5 Wandsworth Road, London
SW8 2LN
☎020 7526 3200 Fax 020 7526 3201
Email editorial@bigissue.com
Website www.bigissue.com
Editor-in-Chief *A. John Bird*
Editor *Matthew Collin*
Circulation 122,679

FOUNDED 1991. WEEKLY. An award-winning campaigning and street-wise general interest magazine sold in London, the Midlands, the North East and South of England. Separate regional editions sold in Manchester, Scotland, Wales and the South West.

Features Interviews, campaigns, comment, opinion and social issues reflecting a varied and informed audience. Balance includes social issues but mixed with arts and cultural features. Freelance writers used each week – commissioned from a variety of contributors. Best approach is to e-mail or post synopses to assistant editor, *Sam Hart* with examples of work in the first instance. Maximum 1500 words. *Payment* £160 for 1000 words.

News *Gibby Zobel* Hard-hitting exclusive stories with emphasis on social injustice aimed at national leaders.

Arts *Tina Jackson* Interested in interviews and analysis ideas. Reviews written in-house. Send synopses to arts editor.

Bird Life Magazine

RSPB, The Lodge, Sandy, Bedfordshire
SG19 2DL
☎01767 680551 Fax 01767 683262
Email derek.niemann@rspb.org.uk
Owner *Royal Society for the Protection of Birds*
Editor *Derek Niemann*
Circulation 90,000

FOUNDED 1965. BI-MONTHLY. Bird, wildlife and nature conservation for 8–12-year-olds (RSPB Wildlife Explorer members). No unsolicited mss. No 'captive/animal welfare' articles.

Features Unsolicited material rarely used.

News News releases welcome. Approach in writing in the first instance.

Birds

RSPB, The Lodge, Sandy, Bedfordshire
SG19 2DL
☎01767 680551 Fax 01767 683262
Email rob.hume@rspb.org.uk
Owner *Royal Society for the Protection of Birds*
Editor *R.A. Hume*
Circulation 585,000

QUARTERLY magazine which covers not only wild birds but also wildlife and related conservation topics. No interest in features on pet birds or 'rescued' sick/injured/orphaned ones. Content refers mostly to RSPB work so opportunities for freelance work on other subjects are limited but some freelance submissions are used in most issues. Phone to discuss.

Birdwatch

3D/F Leroy House, 436 Essex Road, London
N1 3QP
☎020 7704 9495 Fax 020 7704 2767
Website www.birdwatch.co.uk
Owner *Solo Publishing*
Editor *Dominic Mitchell*
Circulation 15,000

FOUNDED 1992. MONTHLY magazine featuring illustrated articles on all aspects of birds and birdwatching, especially in Britain. No unsolicited mss. Approach in writing with synopsis of 100 words maximum. Annual **Birdwatch Bird Book of the Year** award (see entry under **Prizes**).

Features *Dominic Mitchell* Unusual angles/personal accounts, if well-written. Articles of an educative or practical nature suited to the readership. Maximum 2000 words.

Fiction *Dominic Mitchell* Very little opportunity although occasional short story published. Maximum 1500 words.

News *David Mairs* Very rarely use external material.

Payment £40 per 1000 words.

Bizarre

9 Dallington Street, London EC1V 0BQ
☎020 7687 7000 Fax 020 7687 7096
Email bizarre@ifgmags.com
Website www.bizarremag.com
Editor *Joe Gardiner*
Circulation 105,220

FOUNDED 1997. MONTHLY magazine featuring amazing stories and images from around the world. No fiction, poetry, illustrations, short snippets.

Features *Joe Gardiner* Particularly interested in reportage. Maximum 2000 words. Approach in writing

Payment negotiable.

Black Beauty & Hair

2nd Floor, Culvert House, Culvert Road, Battersea, London SW11 5HD
☎020 7720 2108 Fax 020 7498 3023
Email info@blackbeauty.co.uk
Website www.blackbeautyandhair.com
Owner *Hawker Consumer Publications Ltd*
Editor *Irene Shelley*
Circulation 21,499

BI-MONTHLY with one annual special: *The Hairstyle Book* in October; and a *Bridal Supplement* in the April/May issue. Black hair and beauty magazine with emphasis on authoritative articles relating to hair, beauty, fashion, health and lifestyle. Unsolicited contributions welcome.

Features Beauty and fashion pieces welcome from writers with a sound knowledge of the Afro-Caribbean beauty scene plus bridal features. Minimum 1000 words.

Payment £100 per 1000 words.

Bliss Magazine

Endeavour House, 189 Shaftesbury Avenue, London WC2H 8JG
☎020 7208 3478 Fax 020 7208 3591
Email christina.reeves@ecm.emap.com
Owner *Emap élan*
Editor *Helen Johnston*
Circulation 255,653

FOUNDED 1995. MONTHLY teenage lifestyle magazine for girls. No unsolicited mss; 'call the deputy editor (*Rachel Jane*) with an idea and then send it in.'

News *Katie Masters* Worldwide teenage news. Maximum 200 words. *Payment* £50–100.

Features Real life teenage stories with subjects willing to be photographed. Reports on teenage issues. Maximum 2000 words. *Payment* £350.

The Book Collector

PO Box 12426, London W11 3GW
☎020 7792 3492 Fax 020 7792 3492
Email info@thebookcollector.co.uk
Website www.thebookcollector.co.uk
Owner *The Collector Ltd*
Editor *Nicolas J. Barker*

FOUNDED 1950. QUARTERLY magazine on

bibliography and the history of books, book-collecting, libraries and the book trade.

Book World Magazine

2 Caversham Street, London SW3 4AH
☎020 7351 4995 Fax 020 7351 4995
Owner *Christchurch Publishers Ltd*
Editor *James Hughes*
Circulation 5500

FOUNDED 1980. MONTHLY news and reviews for serious book collectors, librarians, antiquarian and other booksellers. No unsolicited mss. Interested in material relevant to literature, art and book collecting. Send letter in the first instance.

Bookdealer

Suite F22, Park Hall Estate, 40 Martell Road, West Dulwich, London SE21 8EN
☎020 8761 5570 Fax 020 8761 5570
Editor *Barry Shaw*

WEEKLY trade paper which acts almost exclusively as a platform for people wishing to buy or sell rare/out-of-print books. Twelve-page editorial only; occasional articles and book reviews by regular freelance writers.

Books

39 Store Street, London WC1F 7DS
☎020 7692 2900 Fax 020 7419 2111
Editor *Liz Thomson*
Circulation 80,000

Formerly *Books and Bookmen*. Free consumer magazine dealing chiefly with features about authors and reviews of books. Carries few commissioned pieces.

Payment negotiable.

The Bookseller

Endeavour House, 5th Floor, 189 Shaftesbury Avenue, London WC2H 8TJ
☎020 7420 6006 Fax 020 7420 6103
Website www.theBookseller.com
Owner *VNU Entertainment Media*
Editor *Nicholas Clee*

Trade journal of the publishing and book trade – the essential guide to what is being done to whom. Trade news and features, including special features, company news, publishing trends, bestseller data, etc. Unsolicited mss rarely used as most writing is either done in-house or commissioned from experts within the trade. Approach in writing first.

Features *Jenny Bell*
News *Joel Rickett*

Boxing Monthly

40 Morpeth Road, London E9 7LD
☎020 8986 4141 Fax 020 8986 4145
Email bm@boxing-monthly.demon.co.uk
Website www.boxing-monthly.co.uk

Owner *Topwave Ltd*
Editor *Glyn Leach*
Circulation 30,000

FOUNDED 1989. MONTHLY. International coverage of professional boxing; previews, reports and interviews. Unsolicited material welcome. Interested in small hall shows and grass-roots knowledge. No big fight reports. Approach in writing in the first instance.

Boyz

2nd Floor, Medius House, 63–69 New Oxford Street, London WC1A 1DG
☎020 7845 4300 Fax 020 7845 4309
Email hudson@boyz.co.uk

Editor *David Hudson*
Circulation 55,000

FOUNDED 1994. WEEKLY entertainment and features magazine aimed at a gay readership covering clubs, fashion, TV, films, music, theatre, celebrities and the UK gay scene in general. Unsolicited mss are looked at but not often used.

Brides

Vogue House, Hanover Square, London W1S 1JU
☎020 7499 9080 Fax 020 7460 6369

Owner *Condé Nast Publications Ltd*
Editor *Sandra Boler*
Circulation 64,620

BI-MONTHLY. Much of the magazine is produced in-house, but a good, relevant feature on cakes, jewellery, music, flowers, etc. is always welcome. Maximum 1000 words. Prospective contributors should telephone with an idea in the first instance.

British Birds

The Banks, Mountfield, Robertsbridge, East Sussex TN32 5JY
☎01580 882039 Fax 01580 882038
Email editor@britishbirds.co.uk

Editor *Dr R. Riddington*
Circulation 7,000

FOUNDED 1907. MONTHLY ornithological journal. Features main papers on topics such as behaviour, distribution, ecology, identification and taxonomy; annual *Reports on Rare Birds in Great Britain*; bird news from official national correspondents throughout Europe and sponsored competitions for Bird Photograph of the Year and Bird Illustrator of the Year. Unsolicited mss welcome from ornithologists only.

Features Well-researched, original material relating to Western Palearctic birds welcome.

News *Bob Scott/Adrian Pitches* Items ranging from conservation to humour. Maximum 200 words.

Payment for photographs, drawings, paintings and main papers.

British Chess Magazine

The Chess Shop, 44 Baker Street, London W1U 7RT
☎020 7486 8222 Fax 020 7486 3355
Email bcmchess@compuserve.com
Website www.bcmchess.co.uk

Director/Editor *John Saunders*

FOUNDED 1881. MONTHLY. Emphasis on tournaments, the history of chess and chess-related literature. Approach in writing with ideas. Unsolicited mss not welcome unless from qualified chess experts and players.

British Medical Journal

BMA House, Tavistock Square, London WC1H 9JR
☎020 7387 4499 Fax 020 7383 6418
Email editor@bmj.com
Website www.bmj.com

Owner *British Medical Association*
Editor *Professor Richard Smith*

One of the world's leading general medical journals.

British Philatelic Bulletin

Royal Mail, Gavrelle House, 2–14 Bunhill Row, London EC1Y 8HQ
☎020 7847 3321 Fax 020 7847 3359

Owner *Royal Mail*
Editor *John Holman*
Circulation 25,000

FOUNDED 1963. MONTHLY bulletin giving details of forthcoming British stamps, features on older stamps and postal history, and book reviews. Welcomes photographs of interesting, unusual or historic letter boxes.

Features Articles on all aspects of British philately. Maximum 1500 words.

News Reports on exhibitions and philatelic events. Maximum 500 words. Approach in writing in the first instance.

Payment £45 per 1000 words.

British Railway Modelling

The Maltings, West Street, Bourne,
Lincolnshire PE10 9PH
☎01778 391176 Fax 01778 425437
Email johne@warnersgroup.co.uk
Website www.brmodelling.com
Owner *Warners Group Publications Plc*
Managing Editor *David Brown*
Editor *John Emerson*
Circulation 18,347

FOUNDED 1993. MONTHLY. A general magazine
for the practising modeller. No unsolicited mss
but ideas are welcome. Interested in features on
quality models, from individual items to complete layouts. Approach in writing.

Features Articles on practical elements of
the hobby, e.g. locomotive construction, kit
conversions, etc. Layout features and articles on
individual items which represent high standards
of the railway modelling art. Maximum length
6000 words (single feature). *Payment* up to £60
per published page.

News News and reviews containing the
model railway trade, new products, etc.
Maximum length 1000 words. *Payment* up to
£60 per published page.

Broadcast

33-39 Bowling Green Lane, London
EC1R 0DA
☎020 7505 8045 Fax 020 7505 8050
Owner *Emap Communications*
Editor *Lucy Rouse*
Circulation 14,297

FOUNDED 1960. WEEKLY. Opportunities for
freelance contributions. Write to the relevant
editor in the first instance.

Features *Katy Elliott/David Wood* Any
broadcasting issue. Maximum 1500 words.

News *Colin Robertson* Broadcasting news.
Maximum 350 words.
Payment £200 per 1000 words.

Brownie

17–19 Buckingham Palace Road, London
SW1W 0PT
☎020 7834 6242 Fax 020 7828 5791
Email MarionT@guides.org.uk
Website www.guides.org.uk
Owner *The Guide Association*
Editor *Marion Thompson*
Circulation 16,500

FOUNDED 1962. MONTHLY. Aimed at Brownie
members aged 7–10.

Articles Crafts and simple make-it-yourself
items using inexpensive or scrap materials.

Fiction Brownie content an advantage. No
adventures involving unaccompanied children
in dangerous situations – day or night. Maximum 650 words.
Payment £50 per 1000 words pro rata.

Bukowski Journal

PO Box 11271, Wood Green, London
N22 8BF
Email bukzine@aol.com
Website www.bukzine.co.uk
Owner/Editor *Rikki Hollywood*
Circulation 1000

FOUNDED 1999 to promote the work of
American barfly and author, Charles Bukowski.
'A platform for lovers and haters of his work.'
Welcomes provocative, lively articles, essays,
illustrations on Bukowski or like-minded souls
such as Robert Crumb, Dan Fante, etc.
Approach by e-mail or letter. *Payment* Free copy
of journal.

The Burlington Magazine

14–16 Duke's Road, London WC1H 9SZ
☎020 7388 1228 Fax 020 7388 1230
Email editorial@burlington.org.uk
Website www.burlington.org.uk
Owner *The Burlington Magazine*
Publications Ltd
Editor *Caroline Elam*

FOUNDED 1903. MONTHLY. Unsolicited contributions welcome on the subject of art history
provided they are previously unpublished. All
preliminary approaches should be made in
writing.

Exhibition Reviews Usually commissioned,
but occasionally unsolicited reviews are published if appropriate. Maximum 1000 words.

Articles Maximum 4500 words. *Payment*
£100 (maximum).

Shorter Notices Maximum 2000 words.
Payment £50 (maximum).

Bus and Coach Professional

2 Crown Street, Wellington, Telford,
Shropshire TF1 1LP
☎01952 415334 Fax 01952 245077
Email editorial@busandcoach.com
Website www.busandcoach.com

Editorial Director *Steve Rooney*

MONTHLY magazine for executives and senior
managers in the bus and coach industry.
'Strong on news and features. Some opportunities for well-written freelance material if
relevant to our requirement. Phone or e-mail
before submission.'

Business Brief

PO Box 582, Five Oaks, St Saviour, Jersey
JE4 8XQ
☎01534 611600   Fax 01534 611610
Email mspeditorial@msppublishing.com
Owner *MSP Publishing*
Editor *Peter Body*
Circulation 6000

FOUNDED 1989. MONTHLY magazine covering business developments in the Channel Islands and how they affect the local market. Styles itself as the magazine for business people rather than just a magazine about business. Interested in business-orientated articles only – 800 words maximum. Approach the editor by telephone initially.
Payment negotiable.

Business Life

One Oxendon Street, London SW1Y 4EE
☎020 7925 2544   Fax 020 7976 1087
Owner *Cedar Communications*
Editor *Alex Finer*
Circulation 193,000

TEN ISSUES YEARLY including two double issues. 'Business with a lifestyle twist; lifestyle with a business twist.' Distributed on European airline routes. Unsolicited mss not welcome. Few opportunities for freelancers. Approach with ideas in writing only.

Business Traveller

Condor House, 5–14 St Paul's Churchyard, London EC4N 8BE
☎020 7778 0000   Fax 020 7778 0022
Website www.businesstraveller.com
Owner *Perry Publications*
Editor-in-Chief *Julia Brookes*
Circulation 42,000

MONTHLY. Consumer publication. Opportunities exist for freelance writers but unsolicited contributions tend to be about leisure travel rather than business travel. Would-be contributors are advised to study the magazine or the website first. Approach in writing with ideas.
Payment varies.

Camcorder User

Highbury wViP, 53–79 Highgate Road, London NW5 1TW
☎020 7331 1000   Fax 020 7331 1242
Email rob.hull@wvip.co.uk
Website www.camuser.co.uk
Owner *Highbury wViP*
Editor *Robert Hull*
Circulation 15,000

FOUNDED 1988. MONTHLY magazine dedicated to camcorders, with features on creative technique, shooting advice, new equipment, accessory round-ups and interesting applications on location. Unsolicited mss, illustrations and pictures welcome. *Payment* negotiable.

Campaign

22 Bute Gardens, London W6 7HN
☎020 8267 4683   Fax 020 8267 4914
Website www.campaignlive.com
Owner *Haymarket Publishing Ltd*
Editor *Caroline Marshall*
Circulation 17,700

FOUNDED 1968. WEEKLY. Lively magazine serving the advertising and related industries. Freelance contributors are best advised to write in the first instance.
Features Articles of 1500–2000 words.
News Relevant news stories of up to 320 words.
Payment negotiable.

Camping and Caravanning

Greenfields House, Westwood Way, Coventry, Warwickshire CV4 8JH
☎024 7669 4995   Fax 024 7669 4886
Owner *Camping and Caravanning Club*
Editor *Nick Harding*
Circulation 154,076

FOUNDED 1901. MONTHLY. Interested in journalists with camping and caravanning knowledge. Write with ideas for features in the first instance.
Features Outdoor pieces in general, plus items on specific regions of Britain. Maximum 1200 words. Illustrations to support text essential.

Canal and Riverboat

PO Box 618, Norwich, Norfolk NR7 0QT
☎01603 708930   Fax 01603 708934
Email bluefoxfilms@netscapeonline.co.uk
Website www.canalandriverboat.com
Owner *A.E. Morgan Publications Ltd*
Editor *Chris Cattrall*
Circulation 20,000

Covers all aspects of waterways, narrow boats and cruisers. Contributions welcome. Make initial approach in writing.
Features Waterways, narrow boats and motor cruisers, cruising reports, practical advice, etc. Unusual ideas and personal comments are particularly welcome. Maximum 2000 words. Articles should be supplied in PC Windows format disk. *Payment* around £50 per page.
News Items of up to 300 words welcome

on the Inland Waterways System, plus photographs if possible. *Payment* £15.

Car Mechanics

Kelsey Publishing Ltd, PO Box 13, Westerham, Kent TN16 3WT
☎01733 891431 Fax 01733 352749
Email carmechanics@kelsey.co.uk
Owner *Kelsey Publishing*
Editor *Peter Simpson*
Circulation 35,000

MONTHLY. Practical guide to maintenance and repair of post–1978 cars for DIY and the motor trade. Unsolicited mss, with good-quality colour prints or transparencies, 'at sender's risk'. Ideas preferred. Initial approach by letter or phone welcome and strongly recommended, 'but please read a recent copy first for style'.

Features Good, technical, entertaining and well-researched material welcome, especially anything presenting complex matters clearly and simply.

Payment by arrangement ('but generous for the right material').

Caravan Life

Warners Group Publications plc, The Maltings, West Street, Bourne, Lincolnshire PH10 9PH
☎01778 391165 Fax 01778 425437
Email mikelec@warnersgroup.co.uk
Editor *Michael Le Caplain*
Circulation 17,000

FOUNDED 1987. Magazine for experienced caravanners and enthusiasts providing practical and useful information and product evaluation. Opportunities for caravanning, relevant touring and travel material, also monthly reviews of the best tow cars, all with good-quality colour photographs.

Caravan Magazine

IPC Media Ltd., Focus House, Dingwall Avenue, Croydon, Surrey CR9 2TA
☎020 8774 0600 Fax 020 8774 0939
Email caravan@ipcmedia.com
Website www.caravan.com
Owner *IPC Media*
Editor *Rob McCabe*
Circulation 17,744

FOUNDED 1933. MONTHLY. Unsolicited mss welcome. Approach in writing with ideas. All correspondence should go direct to the editor.

Features Touring with strong caravan bias, technical/DIY features and how-to section. Maximum 1500 words.

Payment by arrangement.

Caribbean Times

Unit 2, 65 Whitechapel Road, London
E1 1DU
☎020 7650 2000 Fax 020 7650 2001
Website www.ethnicmedia.co.uk
Owner *Ethnic Media Group*
Editor *Ron Shillingford*
Circulation 25,190

FOUNDED 1981. WEEKLY community paper for the African and Caribbean communities in Britain. Interested in general, local and international issues relevant to these communities. Approach in writing with ideas for submission.

Carmarthenshire Life

Swan House Publishing, Swan House, Bridge Street, Newcastle Emlyn, Carmarthenshire SA38 9DX
☎01239 710632 Fax 01239 710632
Email davidfielding@themail.co.uk
Owner *Swan House Publishing*
Editor *David Fielding*

FOUNDED 1995. MONTHLY county magazine with articles on local history, issues, characters, off-beat stories with good colour or b&w photographs. No country diaries, short stories or poems. Most articles are commissioned from known freelancers but 'always prepared to consider ideas from new writers'. No mss. Send cuttings of previous work (published or not) and synopsis to the editor.

Cat World

Avalon Court, Star Road, Partridge Green, West Sussex RH13 8RY
☎01403 711511 Fax 01403 711521
Email editor@catworld.co.uk
Website www.catworld.co.uk
Owner *Ashdown Publishing Ltd*
Editor *Jo Rothery*
Circulation 20,000

FOUNDED 1981. MONTHLY. Unsolicited mss welcome but initial approach in writing preferred. No poems.

Features Lively, first-hand experience features on every aspect of the cat. Breeding features and veterinary articles by acknowledged experts only. Preferred length 750 or 1700 words. Accompanying pictures should be good quality and sharp.

News Short, concise, factual or humorous items concerning cats. Maximum 100 words.

Submissions on disk (MS Word) if possible, with accompanying hard copy and s.a.e. for return or by e-mail.

Catholic Gazette

The Chase Centre, 114 West Heath Road,
London NW3 7TX
☎020 8458 3316 Fax 020 8905 5780
Email catholic.gazette@cms.org.uk
Website www.cms.org.uk/gazette
Owner *Catholic Missionary Society*
Editor *Peter Wilson*
Circulation 1600

FOUNDED 1910. MONTHLY. Covers the work
of the Catholic Missionary Society – evangeli-
sation, scripture and prayer features. Interested
in items on what is going on in the Catholic
Church in England and Wales. Maximum
2000 words for features with *payment* of £15
for first page and £10 thereafter. 'Rear Light'
– personal comment page: maximum 400
words. *Payment* £15. Approach in writing.

The Catholic Herald

Lamb's Passage, Bunhill Row, London
EC1Y 8TQ
☎020 7588 3101 Fax 020 7256 9728
Email editorial@catholicherald.co.uk
Website www.catholicherald.co.uk
Editor *Dr William Oddie*
Deputy Editor *Luke Coppen*
Literary Editor *Damian Thompson*
Circulation 22,000

WEEKLY. Interested mainly in straight Catholic
issues but also in general humanitarian matters,
social policies, the Third World, the arts and
books.
Payment by arrangement.

CCC Magazine

IPC Focus Network, Focus House, Dingwall
Avenue, Croydon, Surrey CR9 2TA
☎020 8774 0946 Fax 020 8774 0935
Email ccc@ipcmedia.com
Owner *IPC Media*
Editor *Steve Kirk*
Circulation 25,000

FOUNDED 1963. MONTHLY. Unsolicited mss
welcome but prospective contributors are advised to make initial contact in writing.
Features Technical articles on current
motorsport and unusual sport-orientated road
cars. Length by arrangement.
Payment negotiable.

Chapman

4 Broughton Place, Edinburgh EH1 3RX
☎0131 557 2207 Fax 0131 556 9565
Email editor@chapman-pub.co.uk
Website www.chapman-pub.co.uk
Owner/Editor *Joy Hendry*
Circulation 2000

FOUNDED 1970. Scotland's quality literary magazine. Features poetry, short works of fiction,
criticism, reviews and articles on theatre, politics,
language and the arts. Unsolicited material welcome if accompanied by s.a.e. Approach in writing unless discussion is needed. Priority is given
to full-time writers.
Features Topics of literary interest, especially Scottish literature, theatre, culture or
politics. Maximum 5000 words.
Fiction Short stories, occasionally novel
extracts if self-contained. Maximum 6000
words. *Payment* by negotiation.
Special Pages Poetry, both UK and non-
UK in translation (mainly, but not necessarily,
European). *Payment* by negotiation.

Chat

IPC Media Ltd., King's Reach Tower,
Stamford Street, London SE1 9LS
☎020 7261 6565 Fax 020 7261 6534
Website www.ipc.media.co.uk/pubs/chat.htm
Owner *IPC Connect*
Editor *Paul Merrill*
Circulation 478,230

FOUNDED 1985. WEEKLY general interest
women's magazine. Unsolicited mss considered;
approach in writing with ideas. Not interested in
contributors 'who have never bothered to read
Chat and therefore don't know what type of
magazine it is'.
Features *Anna Kingsley* Human interest and
humour. Maximum 1000 words. *Payment* up
to £600 maximum.
Fiction *Olwen Rice* Maximum 800 words.

Cheshire Life

3 Tustin Court, Portway, Preston, Lancashire
PR2 2YQ
☎01772 722022 Fax 01772 736496
Website www.cheshirelife.co.uk
Owner *Life Magazines*
Editor *Patrick O'Neill*
Circulation 15,000

FOUNDED 1934. MONTHLY. Homes, gardens,
personalities, business, farming, conservation,
property, heritage, books, fashion, arts, science
– anything which has a Cheshire connection.

Child Education

Scholastic Ltd, Villiers House, Clarendon
Avenue, Leamington Spa, Warwickshire
CV32 5PR
☎01926 887799 Fax 01926 883331

Website www.scholastic.co.uk
Owner *Scholastic Ltd*
Editor *Jeremy Sugden*
Circulation 45,000

FOUNDED 1923. MONTHLY magazine aimed at teachers of children aged 4–7 years. Practical articles from teachers about education for this age group are welcome. Maximum 900 words. Approach in writing with synopsis.

Choice

Kings Chambers, 39–41 Priestgate, Peterborough, Cambridgeshire PE1 1FR
☎01733 555123 Fax 01733 427500
Email choice.bayardpresse@talk21.com
Owner *Bayard Presse (UK) Ltd*
Editor *Sue Dobson*
Circulation 100,000

MONTHLY full-colour, lively and informative magazine for people aged 50 plus which helps them get the most out of their lives, time and money after full-time work.
   Features Real-life stories, hobbies, interesting (older) people, British heritage and countryside, involving activities for active bodies and minds, health, relationships, book/entertainment reviews. Unsolicited mss read (s.a.e. for return of material); write with ideas and copies of cuttings if new contributor. No phone calls, please.
   Rights/Money All items affecting the magazine's readership are written by experts. Areas of interest include pensions, state benefits, health, finance, property, legal.
   Payment by arrangement.

Christian Herald

Christian Media Centre, 96 Dominion Road, Worthing, West Sussex BN14 8JP
☎01903 821082 Fax 01903 821081
Email news@christianherald.org.uk
Website www.christianherald.org.uk
Owner *Christian Media Centre Ltd*
Editor *Russ Bravo*
Circulation 15,000

WEEKLY. Evangelical, inter-denominational newspaper for committed Christians. News, bible-based comment and incisive features. No poetry. Contributors' guidelines available.
   Payment Christian Media rates.

Church Music Quarterly

Cleveland Lodge, Westhumble, Dorking, Surrey RH5 6BW
☎01306 872800 Fax 01306 887260
Email cmq@rscm.com
Website www.rscm.com
Owner *Royal School of Church Music*
Editor *Esther Jones*
Circulation 17,000

QUARTERLY. Contributions welcome. Telephone in the first instance.
   Features Articles on church music or related subjects considered. Maximum 2000 words.
   Payment £60 per page.

Church of England Newspaper

20–26 Brunswick Place, London N1 6DZ
☎020 7417 5800 Fax 020 7216 6410
Email cen@parlicom.com
Website www.churchnewspaper.com
Owner *Parliamentary Communications Ltd*
Editor *Colin Blakely*
Circulation 9,500

FOUNDED 1828. WEEKLY. Almost all material is commissioned but unsolicited mss are considered.
   Features *Jonathan Wynne-Jones* Preliminary enquiry essential. Maximum 1200 words.
   News *Claire Shelley* Items must be sent promptly and should have a church/Christian relevance. Maximum 200–400 words.
   Payment negotiable.

Church Times

33 Upper Street, London N1 0PN
☎020 7359 4570 Fax 020 7226 3073
Email news@churchtimes.co.uk *or*
features@churchtimes.co.uk
Website www.churchtimes.co.uk
Owner *Hymns Ancient & Modern*
Editor *Paul Handley*
Circulation 35,700

FOUNDED 1863. WEEKLY. Unsolicited mss considered.
   Features *Prudence Fay* Articles and pictures (any format) on religious topics. Maximum 2000 words. *Payment* £100 per 1000 words.
   News *Helen Saxbee* Occasional reports (commissions only) and up-to-date photographs.
   Payment by arrangement.

Classic Bike

EMAP Automotive, Media House, Lynchwood, Peterborough Business Park, Peterborough, Cambridgeshire PE2 6EA
☎01733 468465 Fax 01733 468466
Email classic.bike@emap.com
Owner *Emap Active Ltd*
Editor *Brian Crichton*
Circulation 50,000

FOUNDED 1978. MONTHLY. Mainly pre-1972

classic motorcycles with a heavy bias to British marques. Approach in writing.

News Genuine news with good illustrations, if possible, suitable for a global audience. Maximum 400 words.

Features British motorcycle industry inside stories, technical features 'that can be understood by all', German, Spanish and French machine features, people. Maximum 2000 words.

Special Pages How-to features, oddball machines, stunning pictures, features with a fresh slant.

Payment £100–125 per 1000 words, plus pictures.

Classic Boat

Focus House, Dingwall Avenue, Croydon, Surrey CR9 2TA
☎020 8744 0603 Fax 020 8744 0943
Email cb@ipcmedia.com
Website www.classicboat.co.uk

Owner *IPC Media*
Editor *Dan Houston*
Circulation 16,264

FOUNDED 1987. MONTHLY. Traditional boats and classic yachts, old and new; maritime history. Unsolicited mss, particularly if supported by good photos, are welcome. Sail and power boat pieces considered. Approach in writing with ideas. Interested in well-researched stories on all nautical matters. News reports welcome. Contributor's notes available (send s.a.e.).

Features Boatbuilding, boat history and design, events, yachts and working boats. Material must be well-informed and supported where possible by good-quality or historic photos. Maximum 3000 words. Classic is defined by excellence of design and construction – the boat need not be old and wooden! *Payment* £75–100 per published page.

News New boats, restorations, events, boatbuilders, etc. Maximum 500 words. *Payment* according to merit.

Classic Cars

Media House, Peterborough Business Park, Lynchwood, Peterborough PE2 6EA
☎01733 468219 Fax 01733 468888
Email classic.cars@emap.com

Owner *Emap Automotive Ltd*
Editor *Martyn Moore*
Circulation 53,135

FOUNDED 1973. THIRTEEN ISSUES YEARLY. International classic car magazine containing entertaining and informative articles about classic cars, events and associated personalities. Contributions welcome.

Classical Guitar

1 & 2 Vance Court, Trans Britannia Enterprise Park, Blaydon on Tyne NE21 5NH
☎0191 414 9000 Fax 0191 414 9001
Email classicalguitar@ashleymark.co.uk
Website www.classicalguitarmagazine.com

Owner *Ashley Mark Publishing Co.*
Editor *Colin Cooper*

FOUNDED 1982. MONTHLY.

Features *Colin Cooper* Usually written by staff writers. Maximum 1500 words. *Payment* by arrangement.

News *Thérèse Wassily Saba* Small paragraphs and festival concert reports welcome. *No payment.*

Reviews *Tim Panting* Concert reviews of up to 250 words are usually written by staff reviewers.

Classical Music

241 Shaftesbury Avenue, London WC2H 8TF
☎020 7333 1742 Fax 020 7333 1769
Email classical.music@rhinegold.co.uk
Website www.rhinegold.co.uk

Owner *Rhinegold Publishing Ltd*
Editor *Keith Clarke*

FOUNDED 1976. FORTNIGHTLY. A specialist magazine using precisely targeted news and feature articles aimed at the music business. Most material is commissioned but professionally written unsolicited mss are occasionally published. Freelance contributors may approach in writing with an idea but should familiarise themselves beforehand with the style and market of the magazine.

Payment negotiable.

Classics

Berwick House, 8–10 Knoll Rise, Orpington, Kent BR6 0PS
☎01689 887200 Fax 01689 838844
Email classics@splpublishing.co.uk

Owner *SPL Publishing Ltd*
Editor *Andrew Charman*

FOUNDED 1997. MONTHLY how-to magazine for classic car owners, featuring everything from repairing and restoring to buying, selling and enjoying all types of cars from the 1950s to 1980s. Includes vehicle comparison tests, price guide, practical advice and technical know-how from experts and owners, plus hundreds of readers' free ads.

Features Illustrated features on classic car maintenance, repair and restoration with strong technical content and emphasis on DIY.

News All classic car related news stories and topical photos.

Climber

Warners Group Publications plc, West Street, Bourne, Lincolnshire PE10 9PH
☎01778 391117

Owner *Warners Group Publications plc*
Editor *Bernard Newman*

FOUNDED 1962. MONTHLY. Unsolicited mss welcome (they receive about ten a day). Ideas welcome.

Features Freelance features (accompanied by photographs) are accepted on climbing and mountaineering in the UK and abroad, but the standard of writing must be extremely high. Maximum 2000 words. *Payment* negotiable.

News No freelance opportunities as all items are handled in-house.

Club International

2 Archer Street, London W1D 7AW
☎020 7292 8000 Fax 020 7734 5030
Email swiftly@pr-org.co.uk *or*
  claireb@pr-org.co.uk

Owner *Paul Raymond*
Editor *Robert Swift*
Circulation 180,000

FOUNDED 1972. MONTHLY. Features and short humorous items aimed at young male readership aged 18–30.

Features Maximum 1000 words.
Shorts 200–750 words.
Payment negotiable.

Coin News

Token Publishing Ltd, Orchard House, Duchy Road, Heathpark, Honiton, Devon EX14 1YD
☎01404 46972 Fax 01404 44788
Email info@tokenpublishing.com
Website www.tokenpublishing.com

Owners *J.W. Mussell, Carol Hartman*
Editor *J.W. Mussell*
Circulation 10,000

FOUNDED 1964. MONTHLY. Contributions welcome. Approach by phone in the first instance.

Features Opportunity exists for well-informed authors 'who know the subject and do their homework'. Maximum 2500 words.
Payment £20 per 1000 words.

Company

National Magazine House, 72 Broadwick Street, London W1F 9EP
☎020 7439 5000 Fax 020 7312 3797
Website www.company.co.uk

Owner *National Magazine Co. Ltd*
Editor *Sam Baker*
Circulation 261,117

MONTHLY. Glossy women's magazine appealing to the independent and intelligent young woman. A good market for freelancers: 'We look for great newsy features relevant to young British women'. Keen to encourage bright, new, young talent, but uncommissioned material is rarely accepted. Feature outlines are the only sensible approach in the first instance. Maximum 1500–2000 words. Features to *Lindsay Frankel*, Features Editor.

Payment £250 per 1000 words.

Compass Sport

Ballencrieff Cottage, Ballencrieff Toll, Bathgate, West Lothian EH48 4LD
☎01506 632728 Fax 01506 635444
Email pages@clara.net
Website www.compasssport.com

Owner *Pages Editorial & Publishing Services*
Editor *Suse Coon*

BI-MONTHLY orienteering magazine covering all disciplines of the sport including mountain marathons, mountain bike O, ski O and trail O. Includes profiles and articles on relevant topics, with subsections on fixtures, junior news and mountain marathons which are compiled by sub-editors. Letters, puzzles and competition. Phone or e-mail to discuss content and timing.

Payment by arrangement.

Computer Arts Special

30 Monmouth Street, Bath BA1 2BW
☎01225 442244 Fax 01225 732295
Website www.computerarts.co.uk

Owner *The Future Network*
Editor *Garrick Webster*

FOUNDED 1999. MONTHLY. The world of computer arts – 3D, web design, photoshop, digital video. No unsolicited mss. Interested in tutorials, profiles, tips, software and hardware reviews. Approach by post or e-mail.

Computer Weekly

Quadrant House, The Quadrant, Sutton, Surrey SM2 5AS
☎020 8652 3122 Fax 020 8652 8979

Email computer.weekly@rbi.co.uk
Website www.cw360.com
Owner *Reed Business Information*
Editor *Karl Schneider*
Circulation 143,000

FOUNDED 1966. Freelance contributions welcome.

Features *Martin Couzins* Always looking for good new writers with specialised industry knowledge. Maximum 1800 words.

News Some openings for regional or foreign news items. Maximum 300 words.

Payment negotiable.

Computing, The IT Newspaper

32–34 Broadwick Street, London W1A 2HG
☎020 7316 9000 Fax 020 7316 9160
Email computing@vnu.co.uk
Website www.computing.co.uk
Owner *VNU Business Publications Ltd*
Editor *Colin Barker*
Deputy Editor *Mike Gubbins*
Circulation 110,000

FOUNDED 1973. WEEKLY newspaper for IT professionals. Unsolicited technical articles welcome. Please enclose s.a.e. for return.

News *Bryan Glick*
Payment negotiable.

Condé Nast Traveller

Vogue House, Hanover Square, London W1S 1JU
☎020 7499 9080 Fax 020 7493 3758
Email cntraveller@condenast.co.uk
Website www.cntraveller.co.uk
Owner *Condé Nast Publications*
Editor *Sarah Miller*
Circulation 80,000

FOUNDED 1997. MONTHLY travel magazine. Proposals rather than completed mss preferred. Approach in writing in the first instance. No unsolicited photographs. 'The magazine has a no freebie policy and no writing can be accepted on the basis of a press or paid-for trip.'

Conservative Heartland

WRAP Communications Ltd, 302A Tower Bridge Business Complex, London SE16 4DG
☎020 7231 0707 Fax 020 7231 1232
Email info@wrapcom.com
Website www.wrapcom.com
Owner *Wrap Communications/The Conservative Party*
Editor *Henry Macrory*
Circulation 244,000

FOUNDED 1999. THREE ISSUES YEARLY. Conservative Party magazine. Lifestyle articles, political comment and information. No unsolicited material; approach by telephone or e-mail with idea in the first instance.

Features Ideas for stories about relevant political issues ('not necessarily the most obvious') with human interest angle. Maximum 1000 words. *Payment* £250 per 1000 words.

News Stories about Party initiatives in constituencies and regions. Maximum 300 words. *Payment* £75 per 300 words.

Contemporary Review

PO Box 1242, Oxford OX1 4FJ
☎01865 201529 Fax 01865 201529
Email editorial@contemporaryreview.co.uk
Website www.contemporaryreview.co.uk
Owner *Contemporary Review Co. Ltd*
Editor *Dr Richard Mullen*

FOUNDED 1866. MONTHLY. Covers international affairs and politics, literature and the arts, history and religion. No fiction. Maximum 3000 words.

Literary Editor *Dr James Munson* Monthly book section with reviews which are always commissioned.

Payment £5 per page.

CosmoGIRL!

National Magazine House, 72 Broadwick Street, London W1F 9EP
☎020 7439 5000 Fax 020 7439 5400
Email cosmogirl.mail@natmags.co.uk
Website www.cosmogirl.co.uk
Owner *National Magazine Co. Ltd*
Editor *Celia Duncan*
Circulation 170,629

FOUNDED 2001. MONTHLY glossy magazine for 'fun, fearless teens'. Fashion, beauty advice and boys. **Features** *Miranda Eason* Interested in ideas – send synopsis by mail – no finished articles.

Cosmopolitan

National Magazine House, 72 Broadwick Street, London W1F 9EP
☎020 7439 5000 Fax 020 7439 5016
Owner *National Magazine Co. Ltd*
Editor *Lorraine Candy*
Circulation 463,010

MONTHLY. Designed to appeal to the mid-twenties, modern-minded female. Popular mix of articles, with emphasis on relationships and careers, and hard news. No fiction. Will rarely use unsolicited mss but always on the look-out for 'new writers with original and relevant ideas and a strong voice'. Send short synopsis of idea. All would-be writers should be familiar with the magazine.

Payment about £250 per 1000 words.

Cotswold Life
Cumberland House, Oriel Road,
Cheltenham, Gloucestershire GL50 1BB
☎01242 255334 Fax 01242 254035
Email info@cotswoldlife.co.uk
Owner *Loyalty & Conquest Communications Ltd*
Publisher *Peter Waters*
Circulation 10,000

FOUNDED 1968. MONTHLY. News and features on life in the Cotswolds. Contributions welcome.

Features Interesting places and people, reminiscences of Cotswold life in years gone by, and historical features on any aspect of Cotswold life. Approach in writing in the first instance. Maximum 1500–2000 words.

Payment by negotiation.

Counselling at Work
Association for Counselling at Work, BACP,
1 Regent Place, Rugby, Warwickshire
CV21 2PJ
☎0870 443 5252
Email acw@bacp.co.uk
Owner *British Association for Counselling and Psychotherapy*
Editor *Ian Macwhinnie*
Circulation 1600

FOUNDED 1993. QUARTERLY official journal of the Association for Counselling at Work, a division of B.A.C. Looking for well-researched articles (500–2400 words) about *any* aspect of workplace counselling. Mss from those employed as counsellors or in welfare posts are particularly welcome. Photographs accepted. No fiction or poetry. Send A4 s.a.e. for writer's guidelines and sample copy of the journal.

No payment.

Country Homes and Interiors
IPC Media Ltd., King's Reach Tower,
Stamford Street, London SE1 9LS
☎020 7261 6451 Fax 020 7261 6895
Owner *IPC Media*
Editor *Deborah Barker*
Circulation 103,169

FOUNDED 1986. MONTHLY. The best approach for prospective contributors is with an idea in writing as unsolicited mss are not welcome.

Features *Jean Carr* Monthly personality interviews of interest to an intelligent, affluent

readership (women and men), aged 25–44. Maximum 1200 words.

Houses *Arabella St John Parker* Country-style homes with excellent design ideas. Length 1000 words.

Payment negotiable.

Country Life
IPC Media Ltd., King's Reach Tower,
Stamford Street, London SE1 9LS
☎020 7261 7058 Fax 020 7261 5139
Website www.countrylife.co.uk
Owner *IPC Media*
Editor *Clive Aslet*
Circulation 43,491

ESTABLISHED 1897. WEEKLY. *Country Life* features articles which relate to architecture, countryside, wildlife, rural events, sports, arts, exhibitions, current events, property and news articles of interest to town and country dwellers. Strong informed material rather than amateur enthusiasm. 'We regret we cannot be liable for the safe custody or return of any solicited or unsolicited materials.'

Payment variable, depending on word length and picture size.

Country Living
National Magazine House, 72 Broadwick Street, London W1F 9EP
☎020 7439 5000 Fax 020 7439 5093
Website www.countryliving.co.uk
Owner *National Magazine Co. Ltd*
Editor *Susy Smith*
Circulation 162,156

Magazine aimed at both country dwellers and town dwellers who love the countryside. Covers people, conservation, wildlife, houses (gardens and interiors) and rural businesses. No unsolicited mss.

Payment negotiable.

Country Smallholding
Community Media Ltd, Fair Oak Close,
Exeter Airport Business Park, Clysts Honiton,
Nr Exeter, Devon EX5 2UL
☎01392 447766 Fax 01392 446841
Email editorial@countrysmallholding.com
Website www.countrysmallholding.com
Owner *CML*
Editor *Sara Priddle*
Circulation 21,000

FOUNDED 1975. MONTHLY magazine for small farmers, smallholders, practical landowners and for anyone looking for a new home in the country. Articles welcome on organic growing, keeping poultry, livestock and other animals, crafts, cookery, herbs, building and energy. Articles should be detailed and practical, based on first-hand knowledge and experience.

Country Sports

The Old Town Hall 367 Kennington Road, London SE1 4PT
☎020 7582 5432 Fax 020 7793 8484

Owner *Countryside Alliance*
Editors *Nigel Henson, Henny Goddard*
Circulation 60,000

FOUNDED 1996. QUARTERLY magazine on country sports and conservation issues. No unsolicited mss.

Country Walking

Bretton Court, Bretton, Peterborough, Cambridgeshire PE3 8DZ
☎01733 264666 Fax 01733 465353

Owner *Emap Plc*
Editor *Nicola Dela-Croix*
Circulation 54,163

FOUNDED 1987. MONTHLY magazine containing walks, features related to walking and things you see, country crafts, history, nature, photography, etc., plus pull-out walks guide containing 25+ routes every month. Very few unsolicited mss accepted. An original approach to subjects welcomed. Interested in book reviews, news cuttings. No poor-quality pictures. Approach by letter or e-mail with ideas.
   Features *Emma Kendall* Send synopsis.
   Special Pages 'Down your way' section walks. Accurately and recently researched walk and fact file. Points of interest along the way and pictures to illustrate. Please contact for guidelines (unsolicited submissions not often accepted for this section).
   Payment not negotiable.

The Countryman

23 Sheep Street, Burford, Oxfordshire OX18 4LS
Owner *Countryman Publishing Ltd*
Editor *David Horan*
Circulation 27,683

FOUNDED 1927. MONTHLY. Unsolicited mss with s.a.e. welcome; about 120 received each week. Contributors are strongly advised to study the magazine's content in the first instance. Articles supplied with top quality illustrations (colour transparencies, archive b&w prints and line drawings) are far more likely to be used. Maximum article length 1500 words.

The Countryman's Weekly
(incorporating Gamekeeper and Sporting Dog)

Yelverton, Devon PL20 7PE
☎01822 855281 Fax 01822 855372
Email cmansweekly@aol.com

Publisher *Vic Gardner*
Editor *Kelly Gardner*

FOUNDED 1895. WEEKLY. Unsolicited material welcome.
   Features On any country sports topic. Maximum 1000 words.
   Payment rates available on request.

County

26C High Street, Watlington, Oxfordshire OX49 5PY
☎01491 614040 Fax 01491 614041

Owners *Mr and Mrs Watts*
Editor *Mrs Ashlyn Watts*
Circulation 50,000

FOUNDED 1986. QUARTERLY lifestyle magazine featuring homes, interiors, gardening, fashion and beauty, motoring, leisure and dining. Welcomes unsolicited mss. All initial approaches should be made in writing.

The Cricketer International

Ridge Farm, Lamberhurst, Kent TN3 8ER
☎01892 893000 Fax 01892 893010
Email editorial@cricketer.co.uk
Website www.cricketer.com

Owner *Ben G. Brocklehurst*
Editor *Peter Perchard*
Circulation 30,000

FOUNDED 1921. MONTHLY. Unsolicited mss considered. Ideas in writing only. No initial discussions by phone. All correspondence should be addressed to the editor.

Crimewave

5 Martins Lane, Witcham, Ely, Cambridgeshire CB6 2LB
☎01353 777931
Email ttapress@aol.com
Website www.ttapress.com

Owner *TTA Press*
Editor *Andy Cox*

FOUNDED 1998. QUARTERLY B5 colour magazine of crime fiction. 'The UK's only magazine specialising in crime short stories, publishing the very best from across the spectrum.' Every issue contains stories by authors who are household names in the crime fiction world but room is found for lesser known and unknown writers. *Taking Care of Frank* by Antony Mann (Crimewave 2) and *Prussian Snowdrops* (Crimewave 4) won the **CWA/Macallan Short Story Dagger** award in 1999 and 2001 respectively. Submissions welcome (not via e-mail) with appropriate return postage. Potential contributors are advised to study the magazine. Contracts exchanged upon acceptance. *Payment* on publication.

Cumbria and Lake District Magazine
Stable Courtyard, Broughton Hall, Skipton, North Yorkshire BD23 3AZ
☎01756 701381 Fax 01756 701326
Email editorial@dalesman.co.uk
Website www.dalesman.co.uk
Owner *Dalesman Publishing Co. Ltd*
Editor *Terry Fletcher*
Circulation 16,434

FOUNDED 1951. MONTHLY. County magazine of strong regional and countryside interest, focusing on the Lake District. Unsolicited mss welcome. Maximum 1500 words. Approach in writing or by phone with feature ideas.

Cutting Teeth
Arts & Cultural Department Office, 17B Castlemilk Arcade, Glasgow G45 9AA
☎0141 634 2603 Fax 0141 631 1484
Email cuttingteeth@fringemedia.co.uk
Website www.fringemedia.co.uk
Editor *John Ferry*

THREE ISSUES YEARLY. New Scottish writing by established and previously unpublished writers. Interested in unpublished poetry, short stories (maximum 3000 words) and reviews. Initial approach by e-mail.

Cycle Sport
IPC Media Ltd., Focus House, Dingwall Avenue, Croydon CR9 2TA
☎020 8774 0828 Fax 020 8686 0947
Owner *IPC Media*
Editor *To be appointed*
Circulation 20,667

FOUNDED 1993. MONTHLY magazine dedicated to professional cycle racing. Unsolicited ideas for features welcome.

Cycling Weekly
IPC Media Ltd, Focus House, Dingwall Avenue, Croydon, Surrey CR9 2TA
☎020 8774 0811 Fax 020 8774 0952
Owner *IPC Media*

Editor *Robert Garbutt*
Circulation 30,657

FOUNDED 1891. WEEKLY. All aspects of cycle sport covered. Unsolicited mss and ideas for features welcome. Approach in writing with ideas. Fiction rarely used.
Features Cycle racing, coaching, technical material and related areas. Maximum 2000 words. Most work commissioned but interested in seeing new work. *Payment* around £60–120 per 1000 words (quality permitting).
News Short news pieces, local news, etc. Maximum 300 words. *Payment* £15 per story.

The Dalesman
Stable Courtyard, Broughton Hall, Skipton, North Yorkshire BD23 3AZ
☎01756 701381 Fax 01756 701326
Email editorial@dalesman.co.uk
Owner *Dalesman Publishing Co. Ltd*
Editor *Terry Fletcher*
Circulation 50,680

FOUNDED 1939. Now the biggest-selling regional publication of its kind in the country. MONTHLY magazine with articles of specific Yorkshire interest. Unsolicited mss welcome; receives approximately ten per day. Initial approach in writing or by phone. Maximum 1500 words.
Payment negotiable.

Dance Theatre Journal
Laban Centre London, Laurie Grove, London SE14 6NH
☎020 8692 4070 Fax 020 8694 8749
Email dtj@laban.co.uk
Website www.dantheatrejournal.co.uk
Owner *Laban Centre London*
Editor *Ian Bramley*
Circulation 2000

FOUNDED 1982. QUARTERLY. Interested in features on every aspect of the contemporary dance scene, particularly issues such as the funding policy for dance, critical assessments of choreographers' work and the latest developments in the various schools of contemporary dance. Unsolicited mss welcome. Length 1000–3000 words.
Payment varies 'according to age and experience'.

Dance Today!
The Dancing Times Ltd, Clerkenwell House, 45–47 Clerkenwell Green, London EC1R 0EB
☎020 7250 3006 Fax 020 7253 6679
Email dancetoday!@dancing-times.co.uk

Website www.dancing-times.co.uk
Owner *The Dancing Times Ltd*
Editor *Bronya Seifert*
Circulation 4000

FOUNDED 1956 as *Ballroom Dancing Times*. Relaunched as *Dance Today!* in 2001. MONTHLY magazine for anyone interested in dance, particularly social dance. Unsolicited contributions welcome; send c.v. with sample work by post or e-mail.

The Dancing Times

Clerkenwell House, 45–47 Clerkenwell Green, London EC1R 0EB
☎020 7250 3006 Fax 020 7253 6679
Email DT@dancing-times.co.uk
Website www.dancing-times.co.uk
Owner *The Dancing Times Ltd*
Editor *Mary Clarke*

FOUNDED 1910. MONTHLY. Freelance suggestions welcome from specialist dance writers and photographers only. Approach in writing.

Darkness Rising

117 Birchanger Lane, Birchanger, Hertfordshire CM23 5QF
Email michael@micksims.force9.co.uk
Website www.maynard-sims.com
Editors *Mick Sims, Len Maynard*

THREE ISSUES YEARLY. Anthology of supernatural stories and novellas of any length. Ghost stories, horror, psychological, traditional and modern. New writers and rare fiction from the past. Prefers hard copy submissions or e-mail with Word file attachment. Enclose s.a.e. for any enquiries requiring a response. Full details and guidelines on the website. *Payment* Free copy of relevant issue.

Darts World

28 Arrol Road, Beckenham, Kent BR3 4PA
☎020 8650 6580 Fax 020 8654 4343
Website www.dartsworld.com
Owner *World Magazines Ltd*
Editor *A.J. Wood*
Circulation 24,500

Features Single articles or series on technique and instruction. Maximum 1200 words.
Fiction Short stories with darts theme. Maximum 1000 words.
News Tournament reports and general or personality news required. Maximum 800 words.
Payment negotiable.

Dateline Magazine

Pollet House, St Peter Port, Guernsey GY1 1WF
☎0870 766262 Fax 01481 735353
Email magazine@dateline.co.uk
Owner *One Saturday Plc*
Editor *Nicky Boult*
Circulation 7000

FOUNDED 1976. MONTHLY magazine for single people. Unsolicited mss welcome.
Features Anything of interest to, or directly concerning, single people. Maximum 2000 words.
News Items required at least six weeks ahead. Maximum 2500 words.
Payment from £45 per 1000 words; £10 per illustration/picture used.

Day by Day

Woolacombe House, 141 Woolacombe Road, Blackheath, London SE3 8QP
☎020 8856 6249
Owner *Loverseed Press*
Editor *Patrick Richards*
Circulation 25,000

FOUNDED 1963. MONTHLY. News commentary and digest of national and international affairs, with reviews of the arts (books, plays, art exhibitions, films, opera, musicals) and county cricket and Test reports among regular slots. Unsolicited mss welcome (s.a.e. essential). Approach in writing with ideas. Contributors are advised to study the magazine in the first instance. (Specimen copy 95p.) UK subscription: £12; Europe £17; RoW £19.
News *Ronald Mallone* Interested in themes connected with non-violence and social justice only. Maximum 600 words.
Features No scope for freelance contributions here.
Poems *Michael Gibson* Short poems in line with editorial principles considered. Maximum 20 lines.
Payment negotiable.

Dazed & Confused

112 Old Street, London EC1V 1BD
☎020 7336 0766 Fax 020 7336 0966
Email dazed@confused.co.uk
Website www.confused.co.uk
Owner *Waddell Ltd*
Editor *Rachel Newsome*
Circulation 80,000

FOUNDED 1992. MONTHLY. Cutting edge fashion, music, art interviews and features. No unsolicited material. Approach in writing with ideas in the first instance.

Decanter

First Floor, Broadway House, 2–6 Fulham Broadway, London SW6 5UE
☎020 7610 3929 Fax 020 7381 5282
Email editorial@decantermagazine.com
Website www.decanter.com
Editor *Amy Wislocki*
Circulation 35,000

FOUNDED 1975. Glossy wines magazine. Feature ideas welcome – by e-mail or fax. No fiction.

News/Features All items and articles should concern wines, food and related subjects.

Derbyshire Life and Countryside

Heritage House, Lodge Lane, Derby DE1 3HE
☎01332 347087 Fax 01332 290688
Owner *B.C. Wood*
Editor *Vivienne Irish*
Circulation 11,783

FOUNDED 1931. MONTHLY county magazine for Derbyshire. Unsolicited mss and photographs of Derbyshire welcome, but written approach with ideas preferred.

Descent

51 Timbers Square, Cardiff CF24 3SH
☎029 2048 6557 Fax 029 2048 6557
Email descent@wildplaces.co.uk
Owner *Wild Places Publishing*
Editor *Chris Howes*
Assistant Editor *Judith Calford*

FOUNDED 1969. BI-MONTHLY magazine for cavers and mine enthusiasts. Submissions welcome from freelance contributors who can write accurately and knowledgeably on any aspect of caves, mines or underground structures.

Features General interest articles of under 1000 words welcome, as well as short foreign news reports, especially if supported by photographs/illustrations. Suitable topics include exploration (particularly British, both historical and modern), expeditions, equipment, techniques and regional British news. Maximum 2000 words.

Payment on publication according to page area filled.

Desire

1 Fentiman Road, London SW8 1LD
☎020 7820 8844 Fax 020 7627 5808
Website www.desire.co.uk
Owner *Moondance Media Ltd*

Editor *Ian Jackson*

FOUNDED 1994. SIX ISSUES YEARLY. Britain's first erotic magazine for both women and men, celebrating sex and sensuality with a mix of articles, columns, features, reviews, interviews, fantasy and poetry (1000–2500 words).

For sample copy of magazine plus contributors' guidelines and rates, please enclose 4x first class stamps.

Director

116 Pall Mall, London SW1Y 5ED
☎020 7766 8950 Fax 020 7766 8840
Email director-ed@iod.com
Editor *Joanna Higgins*
Circulation 50,000

1991 Business Magazine of the Year. Published by Director Publications Ltd. for members of the Institute of Directors. Wide range of features from political and business profiles and management thinking to employment and financial issues. Also book reviews. Regular contributors used. Send letter with synopsis/published samples rather than unsolicited mss. Strictly no 'lifestyle' writing.

Payment negotiable.

Disability Now

6 Market Road, London N7 9PW
☎020 7619 7323 Fax 020 7619 7331
Email editor@disabilitynow.org.uk
Website www.disabilitynow.org.uk
Publisher *SCOPE*
Editor *Mary Wilkinson*
Circulation 25,399

FOUNDED 1984. Leading MONTHLY newspaper for disabled people in the UK – people with a wide range of physical disabilities, as well as their families, carers and relevant professionals. Freelance contributions welcome. No fiction. Approach in writing.

Features Covering new initiatives and services, personal experiences and general issues of interest to a wide national readership. Maximum 1000 words. Disabled contributors welcome.

News Maximum 300 words.

Special Pages Possible openings for cartoonists.

Payment by arrangement.

Disabled Motorist

DDMC, Cottingham Way, Thrapston, Northamptonshire NN14 4PL
☎01832 734724 Fax 01832 733816
Email ddmc@ukonline.co.uk
Website www.ukonline.co.uk/ddmc

Owner *Disabled Drivers' Motor Club*
Editor *Lesley Browne*
Circulation 18,000

MONTHLY publication of the Disabled Drivers' Motor Club, an organisation which aims to promote and protect the interests and welfare of disabled people and help and encourage them in gaining increased mobility. Various discounts available for members; membership costs £10 p.a. (single), £15 (joint). The magazine includes information for members plus members' letters. Approach in writing with ideas. Unsolicited mss welcome.

Diva, lesbian life and style

Worldwide House, 116–134 Bayham Street, London NW1 0BA
☎020 7482 2576 Fax 020 7284 0329
Email edit@divamag.co.uk
Website www.divamag.co.uk

Owner *Millivres-Prowler Group*
Editor *Gillian Rodgerson*

FOUNDED 1994. MONTHLY journal of lesbian news and culture. Welcomes news, features, short fiction and photographs. No poetry. Contact the news editor with news items and *Gillian Rodgerson* with features, fiction and photographs. Approach in writing in the first instance.

Dog World

Somerfield House, Wotton Road, Ashford, Kent TN23 6LW
☎01233 621877 Fax 01233 645669
Website www.dogworld.co.uk

Owner *Dog World Ltd*
Editor *Simon Parsons*
Circulation 26,000

FOUNDED 1902. WEEKLY newspaper for people who are seriously interested in pedigree dogs. Unsolicited mss occasionally considered but initial approach in writing preferred.

Features Well-researched historical items or items of unusual interest concerning dogs. Maximum 1000 words. Photographs of unusual 'doggy' situations occasionally of interest. *Payment* up to £50; photos £15.

News Freelance reports welcome on court cases and local government issues involving dogs.

Eastern Eye

Unit 2, 65 Whitechapel Road, London E1 1DU
☎020 7650 2000 Fax 020 7650 2001
Website www.ethnicmedia.co.uk

Owner *Ethnic Media Group*
Editor *Mujibul Islam*
Circulation 40,000

FOUNDED 1989. WEEKLY community paper for the Asian community in Britain. Interested in relevant general, local and international issues. Approach in writing with ideas for submission.

The Ecologist

Unit 18, Chelsea Wharf, 15 Lots Road, London SW10 0QJ
☎020 7351 3578 Fax 020 7351 3617
Email sally@theecologist.org
Website www.theecologist.org

Owner *Ecosystems Ltd*
Editor *Zac Goldsmith*
Managing Editor *Malcolm Tait*
Circulation 20,000

FOUNDED 1970. MONTHLY. Unsolicited mss welcome but best approach is a brief (one-side, A4) proposal to the editor, outlining experience and background and summarising suggested article. Writers should study the magazine for style before submission.

Features Radical approach to political, economic, social and environmental issues, with an emphasis on rethinking the basic assumptions that underpin modern society. Articles of between 500 and 3000 words.

Payment £160 per first 1000 words, £100 per 1000 thereafter.

The Economist

25 St James's Street, London SW1A 1HG
☎020 7830 7000 Fax 020 7839 2968
Website www.economist.com

Owner *Pearson/individual shareholders*
Editor *Bill Emmott*
Circulation 141,335 (UK sales)

FOUNDED 1843. WEEKLY. Worldwide circulation. Approaches should be made in writing to the editor. No unsolicited mss.

The Edge

65 Guinness Buildings, Hammersmith, London W6 8BD
☎020 7460 9444
Email davec@theedge.abelgratis.co.uk
Website www.theedgeabelgratis.co.uk

Editor *Dave Clark*

QUARTERLY. Reviews and features: film (indie arts), books, popular culture. Fiction: modern crime/horror/SF/erotica/slipstream.   Sample issue £3.50 post-free (cheques payable to 'The

Edge'). Writers' guidelines available for s.a.e. or by e-mail.

Payment up to £60 per 1000 words.

Edinburgh Review

22A Buccleuch Place, Edinburgh EH8 9LN
☎0131 651 1415
Email edinburgh.review@ed.ac.uk

Publisher *Centre for the History of Ideas in Scotland*
Circulation 750

FOUNDED 1969. THREE ISSUES YEARLY. Articles and fiction on Scottish and international literary, cultural and philosophical themes. Unsolicited contributions are welcome (1600 are received each year), but prospective contributors are strongly advised to study the magazine first. Allow up to six months for a reply.

Features Interest will be shown in accessible articles on philosophy and its relationship to literature or visual art.

Fiction Scottish and international. Maximum 6000 words.

Electrical Times

Highbury Business Communications, Ann Boleyn House, 9–13 Ewell Road, Cheam, Surrey SM3 8BZ
☎020 8722 6000 Fax 020 8722 6095

Owner *Highbury Business Communications*
Editor *Richard Simmonds*
Circulation 12,900

FOUNDED 1891. MONTHLY. Aimed at electrical contractors, designers and installers. Unsolicited mss welcome but initial approach preferred.

Elle

Endeavour House, 189 Shaftesbury Avenue, London WC2H 8JG
☎020 7437 9011 Fax 020 7208 3599

Owner *Emap élan Publications*
Editor *Sarah Bailey*
Deputy Editor *Margi Conklin*
Features Director *Lisa Grainger*
Circulation 210,861

FOUNDED 1985. MONTHLY fashion glossy. Prospective contributors should approach the relevant editor in writing in the first instance, including cuttings.

Features Maximum 2000 words.

First Word Short articles on current/cultural events, fashion and beauty. Maximum 500 words.

Payment about £250 per 1000 words.

Empire

7th Floor, Endeavour House, 189 Shaftesbury Avenue, London WC2H 8JG
☎020 7859 8450 Fax 020 7859 8613
Website www.empireonline.co.uk

Owner *Emap élan Network*
Editor *Emma Cochrane*
Circulation 160,305

FOUNDED 1989. Launched at the Cannes Film Festival. MONTHLY guide to the movies which aims to cover the world of films in a 'comprehensive, adult, intelligent and witty package'. Although most of *Empire* is devoted to films and the people behind them, it also looks at the developments and technology behind television and video plus music, multimedia and books. Wide selection of in-depth features and stories on all the main releases of the month, and reviews of over 100 films and videos. Contributions welcome but approach in writing first.

Features Behind-the-scenes features on films, humorous and factual features.

Payment by agreement.

The Engineer

50 Poland Street, London W1F 7AX
☎020 7970 4106 Fax 020 7970 4189
Website www.e4engineering.com

Owner *Centaur Communications*
Editor *Sean Brierley*
Circulation 38,000

FOUNDED 1856. WEEKLY news magazine for the UK manufacturing industry.

Features Most outside contributions are commissioned but good ideas are always welcome. Maximum 2000 words.

News Scope for specialist regional freelancers, and for tip-offs. Maximum 500 words.

Technology Technology news from specialists, and tip-offs. Maximum 500 words.

Payment by arrangement.

The English Garden

Romsey Publishing Ltd, Glen House, Stag Place, London SW1E 5AQ
☎020 7233 9191 Fax 020 7630 8084
Email editorial@theenglishgarden.co.uk

Owner *Romsey Publishing Ltd*
Editor *Julia Watson*
Circulation 95,917

FOUNDED 1996. MONTHLY. Features on beautiful gardens with practical ideas on design and planting. No unsolicited mss.

Features *Janine Wookey* Maximum 1000–1200 words. Approach in writing in the first instance; send synopsis of 150 words with strong design and planting ideas, or sets of photographs of interesting gardens. 'No stately home or estate gardens with teams of gardeners.'

English Nature Magazine

English Nature, Northminster House, Peterborough, Cambridgeshire PE1 1UA
☎01733 455191 Fax 01733 455436
Email gordon.leel@english-nature.org.uk
Website www.english-nature.org.uk
Owner *English Nature*
Editor *Gordon Leel*
Circulation 16,000

FOUNDED 1992. BI-MONTHLY magazine which explains the work of English Nature, the government adviser on wildlife and conservation policies. No unsolicited material.

The Erotic Review

EPS, 4th Floor, 1 Maddox Street, London W1S 2PZ
☎020 7437 8887 Fax 020 7437 3528
Email editrice@eroticreview.org
Website www.eroticreview.org
Owner *The Erotic Review Limited*
Editor *Rowan Pelling*
Circulation 30,000

FOUNDED 1997. MONTHLY erotic literary magazine containing articles, humour, fiction, poetry and art work. Unsolicited material welcome. No pornography. Approach in writing enclosing a brief sample of work and s.a.e.
Features Esoteric, humorous or real-life experiences. Maximum 2000 words. *Payment* £40–100. **Fiction** Erotic short stories. Maximum 2000 words. *Payment* £50–100.

ES (Evening Standard magazine)

See entry under **Regional Newspapers**

Esquire

National Magazine House, 72 Broadwick Street, London W1F 9EP
☎020 7439 5000 Fax 020 7439 5675
Owner *National Magazine Co. Ltd*
Editor *Peter Howarth*
Circulation 62,007

FOUNDED 1991. MONTHLY. Quality men's general interest magazine. No unsolicited mss or short stories.

Essentials

IPC Media Ltd., King's Reach Tower, Stamford Street, London SE1 9LS
☎020 7261 6970 Fax 020 7261 5262
Owner *IPC Media*
Editor *Karen Livermore*
Circulation 176,078

FOUNDED 1988. MONTHLY women's interest magazine. Unsolicited mss (not originals) welcome if accompanied by s.a.e. Initial approach in writing preferred. Prospective contributors should study the magazine thoroughly before submitting anything. No fiction. **Features** Maximum 2000 words (double-spaced on A4).
Payment negotiable, but minimum £100 per 1000 words.

Essex Life & Countryside

G13 Dugard House, Peartree Road, Stanway, Colchester, Essex CO3 5JX
☎01206 571348 Fax 01206 366982
Submissions to: PO Box 6657, Bishop's Stortford CM23 4WB
Owner *ECNG Lifestyle*
Editor *Carmen Konopka*
Circulation 10,000

FOUNDED 1952. MONTHLY. Unsolicited material of Essex interest welcome. **Features** must include photos. No general interest material. Maximum 1400 words. *Payment* £25 per page.

The Essex Magazine

See **The Journal Magazines**

Eve

BBC Worldwide, Room AG200, 80 Wood Lane, London W12 0TT
☎020 8433 3767 Fax 020 8433 3359
Email eve@bbc.co.uk
Website www.allabouteve.co.uk
Owner *BBC Worldwide Publishing Ltd*
Editor *Jane Bruton*
Features Editor *Victoria Woodhall*
Circulation 121,157

FOUNDED 2000. MONTHLY. Wide-ranging general interest – aimed at the intelligent 30+ woman. No unsolicited material. Send introductory letter, *recent* writings and outlines for ideas aimed at a specific section. It is essential that would-be contributors familiarise themselves with the magazine.

Eventing

See **Horse and Hound**

Evergreen

PO Box 52, Cheltenham, Gloucestershire GL50 1YQ
☎01242 537900 Fax 01242 537901

Editor R. *Faiers*
Circulation 75,000

FOUNDED 1985. QUARTERLY magazine featuring articles and poems about Britain. Unsolicited contributions welcome.

Features Britain's natural beauty, towns and villages, nostalgia, wildlife, traditions, odd customs, legends, folklore, crafts, etc. Length 250–2000 words.

Payment £15 per 1000 words; poems £4.

Executive Woman

2 Chantry Place, Harrow, Middlesex HA3 6NY
☎020 8420 1210 Fax 020 8420 1691
Email info@execwoman.com
Website www.execwoman.com

Owner *Saleworld*
Editor *Angela Giveon*
Circulation 85,000

FOUNDED 1987. BI-MONTHLY magazine for female executives in the corporate field and female entrepreneurs.

Features New and interesting business issues and 'Women to Watch'. Health and conferencing, profiles, technology, beauty, fashion, training and arts items. 600–1200 words.

Legal/Financial Opportunities for lawyers/accountants to write on issues in their field. Maximum 600 words.

Payment negotiable.

The Face

2nd Floor, Block A, Exmouth House, Pine Street, London EC1R 0JL
☎020 7689 9999 Fax 020 7689 0300

Owner *Emap élan*
Editor *Neil Stevenson*
Circulation 55,329

FOUNDED 1980. Magazine of the style generation, concerned with who's what and what's cool. Profiles, interviews and stories. No fiction. Acquaintance with the 'voice' of *The Face* is essential before sending mss on spec.

Features New contributors should write to the features editor with their ideas. Maximum 3000 words.

Diary No news stories.

Family Circle

IPC Media Ltd., King's Reach Tower, Stamford Street, London SE1 9LS
☎020 7261 5000 Fax 020 7261 5929
Email rebecca_holloway@ipcmedia.com

Owner *IPC Media*
Editor *Gillian Carter*
Circulation 180,134

FOUNDED 1964. MONTHLY. Little scope for freelancers as most material is produced in-house. Unsolicited material is rarely used, but it is considered. Prospective contributors are best advised to e-mail ideas to the relevant editor.

Features *Emma Burstall*
Style *Amanda Cooke*
Food and Wine *Heather Mairs*
Home *Lucy Searle*
Payment by arrangement.

Family Tree Magazine

61 Great Whyte, Ramsey, Huntingdon, Cambridgeshire PE26 1HJ
☎01487 814050 Fax 01487 711361
Email family-tree-magazine@mcmail.com
Website www.family-tree.co.uk

Owner *ABM Publishing Ltd*
Editor *Sue Fearn*
Circulation 45,000

FOUNDED 1984. MONTHLY. News and features on matters of genealogy. Not interested in own family histories. Approach in writing with ideas. All material should be addressed to *Sue Fearn*.

Features Any genealogically related subject. Maximum 2400 words. No puzzles or fictional articles.

Payment £40 per 1000 words (news and features).

Fancy Fowl

TP Publications, Barn Acre House, Saxtead Green, Suffolk IP13 9QJ
☎01728 685832 Fax 01728 685842
Email ff@prestige.typo.co.uk

Owner *TP Publications*
Editor *Liz Fairbrother*
Circulation 3000

FOUNDED 1979. MONTHLY. Devoted entirely to poultry, waterfowl, turkeys, geese, pea fowl, etc. – management, breeding, rearing and exhibition. Outside contributions of knowledgeable, technical poultry-related articles and news welcome. Maximum 1000 words. Approach by letter.
Payment negotiable.

Farmers Weekly

Quadrant House, Sutton, Surrey SM2 5AS
☎020 8652 4911 Fax 020 8652 4005
Email farmers.weekly@rbi.co.uk
Website www.fwi.co.uk

Owner *Reed Business Information*
Editor *Stephen Howe*
Circulation 89,000

WEEKLY. 1996 Business Magazine of the Year.

For practising farmers and those in the ancillary industries. Unsolicited mss considered.

Features A wide range of material relating to farmers' problems and interests: specific sections on arable and livestock farming, farm life, practical and general interest, machinery and business.

News General farming news.

Payment negotiable.

Farmers Guardian

PO Box 18, Olivers Place, Eastway, Fulwood, Preston, Lancashire PR2 9GU
☎01772 557225   Fax 01772 204939

Owner *CMP Information*
Editor *Michael Finch*
Circulation 55,000

WEEKLY publication containing news of direct concern to farmers and the agricultural supply trade.

Fast Car

Berwick House, 8–10 Knoll Rise, Orpington, Kent BR6 0PS
☎01689 887200   Fax 01689 838844
Email fastcar@splpublishing.co.uk

Owner *SPL Publishing Ltd*
Editor *Steve Chalmers*
Circulation 114,310

FOUNDED 1987. THIRTEEN ISSUES YEARLY. Lad's magazine about perfomance tuning and modifying cars. Covers all aspects including the latest street styles and music. Features cars and their owners, product tests and in-car entertainment. Also includes a free reader ads section.

Features Innovative ideas in line with the above and in the *Fast Car* writing style. Generally four pages in length. No Kit-car features, race reports or road test reports of standard cars. Copy should be as concise as possible. *Payment* negotiable.

News Any item in line with the above.

FHM

Mappin House, 4 Winsley Street, London W1W 8HF
☎020 7504 6000   Fax 020 7504 6300
Website www.fhm.co.uk

Owner *Emap Plc*
Editor *David Davies*
Circulation 570,719

FOUNDED in 1986 as a free fashion magazine, FHM evolved to become more male oriented but without much public acclaim until Emap bought the title in 1994. Since then it has become the best-selling men's magazine in the UK covering all areas of men's lifestyle. Published MONTHLY with 15 international editions worldwide.

The Field

IPC Media Ltd., King's Reach Tower, Stamford Street, London SE1 9LS
☎020 7261 5198   Fax 020 7261 5358
Email lucy_higginson@ipc.co.uk
Website www.thefield.co.uk

Owner *IPC Media*
Editor *Jonathan Young*
Circulation 33,718

FOUNDED 1853. MONTHLY magazine for those who are serious about the British countryside and its pleasures. Unsolicited mss (and transparencies) welcome but initial approach should be made in writing.

Features Exceptional work on any subject concerning the countryside. Most work tends to be commissioned.

Payment varies.

Film Review

Visual Imagination Ltd, 9 Blades Court, Deodar Road, London SW15 2NU
☎020 8875 1520   Fax 020 8875 1588
Website www.visimag.com

Owner *Visual Imagination Ltd*
Editor *Neil Corry*
Circulation 50,000

MONTHLY. Reviews, profiles, interviews and special reports on films. Unsolicited material considered.

Payment negotiable.

Fine Food Digest

PO Box 1525, Gillingham, Dorset SP8 4WA
☎01747 822290   Fax 01747 822289
Email bobfarrand@btinternet.com

Owner/Editor *Robert Farrand*
Circulation 4200

FOUNDED 1980. SIX ISSUES YEARLY. Serves the speciality food retail trade. Small budget for freelance material.

First Down

175 Tottenham Court Road, London W1T 7NU
☎020 7323 1988   Fax 020 7637 0862
Email firstdown@indmags.co.uk
Website www.first-down.co.uk

Owner *Independent Magazines (UK) Ltd*
Editor *Keith Webster*
Circulation 15,000

FOUNDED 1986. WEEKLY American football

tabloid paper. Features and news. Welcomes contributions; approach in writing.

Fishing News

Telephone House, 69–77 Paul Street, London EC2A 4LQ
☎020 7017 4531 Fax 020 7017 4536
Email tim.oliver@informa.com
Website www.fishingnews.co.uk

Owner *Informa Group Plc*
Editor *Tim Oliver*
Circulation 11,400

FOUNDED 1913. WEEKLY. All aspects of the commercial fishing industry in the UK and Ireland. No unsolicited mss; telephone inquiry in the first instance. Maximum 600 words for news and 1500 words for features. *Payment* £100 per 1000 words.

The Fix

5 Martins Lane, Witcham, Ely, Cambridgeshire CB6 2LB
☎01353 777931
Email ttapress@aol.com
Website www.ttapress.com

Owner *TTA Press*
Editor *Andy Cox*

FOUNDED 1994. BI-MONTHLY. Features detailed contributors' guidelines of international short story publications, plus varied articles, news, views, reviews and interviews.

Features Unsolicited articles welcome on any aspect of short story publishing: market information, writing, editing, illustrating, interviews and reviews. All genres. Submissions should include adequate return postage. 'Please study the magazine: this will greatly enhance your chances of acceptance.'

Flight International

Quadrant House, The Quadrant, Sutton, Surrey SM2 5AS
☎020 8652 3882 Fax 020 8652 3840
Email flight.international@rbi.co.uk
Website www.flightinternational.com

Owner *Reed Business Information*
Editor *Murdo Morrison*
Circulation 52,222

FOUNDED 1909. WEEKLY. International trade magazine for the aerospace industry, including civil, military and space. Unsolicited mss considered. Commissions preferred - phone with ideas and follow up with letter. E-mail submissions encouraged.

Features *Murdo Morrison* Technically informed articles and pieces on specific geographi-

cal areas with international appeal. Analytical, in-depth coverage required, preferably supported by interviews. Maximum 1800 words.

News *Emma Kelly* Opportunities exist for news pieces from particular geographical areas on specific technical developments. Maximum 350 words.

Payment NUJ rates.

Flora International

The Fishing Lodge Studio, 77 Bulbridge Road, Wilton, Salisbury, Wiltshire SP2 0LE
☎01722 743207 Fax 01722 743207

Publisher/Editor *Maureen Foster*
Circulation 16,000

FOUNDED 1974. BI-MONTHLY magazine for flower arrangers and florists. Unsolicited mss welcome. Approach in writing with ideas. Not interested in general gardening articles.

Features Fully illustrated, preferably with b&w photos or illustrations/colour transparencies. Flower arranging, flower gardens and flowers. Floristry items written with practical knowledge and well illustrated are particularly welcome. Maximum 1000 words.

Profiles/Reviews Personality profiles and book reviews.

Payment £50 per 1000 words plus additional payment for suitable photographs.

FlyPast

PO Box 100, Stamford, Lincolnshire PE9 1XQ
☎01780 755131 Fax 01780 757261
Email flypast@keypublishing.com

Owner *Key Publishing Ltd*
Editor *Ken Ellis*
Circulation 50,577

FOUNDED 1981. MONTHLY. Historic aviation and aviation heritage, mainly military, Second World War period up to c.1970. Unsolicited mss welcome.

Focus

See **British Science Fiction Association** under **Professional Associations**

Focus

Origin Publishing, 14th Floor, Tower House, Fairfax Street, Bristol BS1 3BN
☎0117 927 9009 Fax 0117 934 9008
Website www.originpublishing.co.uk

Owner *Origin Publishing*
Editor *Emma Bayley*
News Editor *Graham Southorn*
Circulation 50,000

FOUNDED 1996. MONTHLY. Popular science

and discovery. Welcomes *relevant* summaries of original ideas. Material should be sent by post.

For Women

Fantasy Publications, 4 Selsdon Way, London E14 9EL
☎020 7308 5090
Email ecoldwell@nasnet.co.uk
Editor *Liz Beresford*
Circulation 60,000

FOUNDED 1992. SIX-WEEKLY magazine of erotic and sex interest for women – health and sex, erotic fiction and erotic photography. No homes and gardens articles. Approach in writing in the first instance. Send e-mail or s.a.e. for submission guidelines.

Features Relationships and sex. Maximum 2500 words. *Payment* £100 per 1000 words.

Fiction *Elizabeth Coldwell* Erotic short stories. Maximum 3000 words. *Payment* £150 total.

Fortean Times: The Journal of Strange Phenomena

PO Box 2409, London NW5 4NP
☎020 8552 5466 Fax 020 7485 5002
Email sieveking@forteantimes.com
Website www.forteantimes.com
Owners/Editors *Bob Rickard/Paul Sieveking*
Circulation 30,000

FOUNDED 1973. MONTHLY. Accounts of strange phenomena and experiences, curiosities, mysteries, prodigies and portents. Unsolicited mss welcome. Approach in writing with ideas. No fiction, poetry, rehashes or politics.

Features Well-researched and referenced material on current or historical mysteries, or first-hand accounts of oddities. Maximum 3000 words, preferably with good relevant photos/illustrations.

News Concise copy with full source references essential.
Payment negotiable.

Foundation: The International Review of Science Fiction

c/o Middlesex University, White Hart Lane, London N17 8HR
Email farah@fjm3.demon.co.uk
Owner *Science Fiction Foundation (reg. Charity 1041052)*
Editor *Dr Farah Mendlesohn*

THRICE-YEARLY publication devoted to the critical study of science fiction.
Payment None.

France Magazine

Cumberland House, Oriel Road, Cheltenham, Gloucestershire GL50 1BB
☎01242 216050 Fax 01242 216074
Email editorial@francemag.com
Website www.francemag.com
Owner *Eastern Counties Newspaper Group*
Editor *Philip Faiers*
Circulation 61,000

FOUNDED 1989. BI-MONTHLY magazine containing all things of interest to Francophiles – in English. Approach in writing in the first instance.

Freelance Market News

Sevendale House, 7 Dale Street, Manchester M1 1JB
☎0161 228 2362, ext 210 Fax 0161 228 3533
Email fmn@writersbureau.com
Editor *Angela Cox*

MONTHLY. News and information on the freelance writers' market, both inland and overseas. Includes market information, competitions, seminars, courses, overseas openings, etc. Short articles (700 words maximum). Unsolicited contributions welcome. *Payment* £50 per 1000 words.

The Freelance

See **National Union of Journalists** under **Professional Associations and Societies**

FT Expat

4th Floor, 149 Tottenham Court Road, London W1P 9LL
☎020 7896 2000 Fax 020 7896 2229
Email ftexpat.threads@ft.com
Website www.FTExpat.com
Owner *Financial Times Business*
Managing Editor *Hugh Fasken*
Circulation 50,000

FOUNDED January 2001. MONTHLY magazine aimed at British and non-British expatriates and international investors. Unsolicited mss considered, if suitable to the interests of the readership.

Features Up to 1200 words on finance, property, employment opportunities and other topics likely to appeal to readership, such as living conditions in countries with substantial expatriate populations.
Payment negotiable.

Garden Answers (incorporating Practical Gardening)

Bretton Court, Bretton, Peterborough, Cambridgeshire PE2 8DZ
☎01733 264666 Fax 01733 282695

Owner *Emap Active Publications Ltd*
Editor *Gail Major*
Circulation 71,613

FOUNDED 1982. MONTHLY. 'It is unlikely that unsolicited manuscripts will be used, as articles are usually commissioned and must be in the magazine style.' Prospective contributors should approach the editor in writing. Interested in hearing from gardening writers on any subject, whether flowers, fruit, vegetables, houseplants or greenhouse gardening.

Garden News

Bretton Court, Bretton, Peterborough, Cambridgeshire PE3 8DZ
☎01733 264666 Fax 01733 282695

Owner *Emap Active Publications Ltd*
Editor *Sarah Page*
Circulation 75,000

FOUNDED 1958. Britain's biggest-selling, full-colour gardening WEEKLY. News and advice on growing flowers, fruit and vegetables, plus colourful features on all aspects of gardening especially for the committed gardener. News and features welcome, especially if accompanied by top-quality photos or illustrations. Contact the editor before submitting any material.

The Garden, Journal of the Royal Horticultural Society

Bretton Court, Bretton Centre, Peterborough, Cambridgeshire PE3 8DZ
☎01733 264666 Fax 01733 282655
Email thegarden@rhs.org.uk
Website www.rhs.org.uk

Owner *The Royal Horticultural Society*
Editor *Ian Hodgson*
Circulation 300,000

FOUNDED 1866. MONTHLY journal of the Royal Horticultural Society. Covers all aspects of the art, science and practice of horticulture and garden making. 'Articles must have depth and substance.' Approach by letter with a synopsis in the first instance. Maximum 2500 words.

Gardens Illustrated

BBC Worldwide, Woodlands, 80 Wood Lane, London W12 0TT
☎020 8433 1353 Fax 020 8433 2680
Website www.gardensillustrated.com

Owner *BBC Worldwide Publishing Ltd*
Editor *Rosie Atkins*
Circulation 32,120

FOUNDED 1993. TEN ISSUES YEARLY. 'Britain's most distinguished garden magazine' with a world-wide readership. The focus is on garden design, with a strong international flavour. Unsolicited mss are rarely used and it is best that prospective contributors approach the editor with ideas in writing, supported by photographs.

Gardens Monthly

SPL, Berwick House, 8–10 Knoll Rise, Orpington, Kent BR6 0PS
☎01689 887200 Fax 01689 876438
Email gardens@splpublishing.co.uk

Owner *SPL Publishing Ltd*
Editor *Helen Griffin*

LAUNCHED April 2000. Aimed at all gardeners, from beginners to more serious growers, of specialist plants who want inspiration and advice. Covers design, plants, garden style, practical techniques and equipment.

Gay Times

Worldwide House, 116–134 Bayham Street, London NW1 0BA
☎020 7482 2576 Fax 020 7284 0329
Website www.prowler.co.uk

Owner *Millivres-Prowler Group*
Editor *Vicky Powell*
Circulation 65,000

Covers all aspects of gay life, plus general interest likely to appeal to the gay community, art reviews and news. Regular freelance writers used. *Payment* negotiable.

Gibbons Stamp Monthly

Stanley Gibbons, 5 Parkside, Christchurch Road, Ringwood, Hampshire BH24 3SH
☎01425 472363 Fax 01425 470247
Email gibbonsstampmonthly@ stanleygibbons.com
Website www.stanleygibbons.com

Owner *Stanley Gibbons Ltd*
Editor *Hugh Jefferies*
Circulation 22,000

FOUNDED 1890. MONTHLY. News and features. Unsolicited mss welcome. Make initial approach in writing or by telephone to avoid disappointment.

Features *Hugh Jefferies* Unsolicited material of specialised nature and general stamp features welcome. Maximum 3000 words but longer pieces can be serialised. *Payment* £30–50 per 1000 words.

News *Michael Briggs* Any philatelic news item. Maximum 500 words. *No payment.*

Girl About Town

Independent House, 191 Marsh Wall, London
E14 9RS
☎020 7005 5550 Fax 020 7005 0222
Website www.londoncareers.net

Owner *Independent Magazines*
Editor-in-Chief *Bill Williamson*
News/Style Pages *Dee Pilgrim*
Circulation 85,000

FOUNDED 1972. Free WEEKLY magazine for
women aged 18 to 35. Unsolicited mss may be
considered. No fiction.

Features Standards are 'exacting'. Commissions only. Some chance of unknown writers
being commissioned. Maximum 1500 words.

Payment negotiable.

Glamour

Hanover House, Hanover Square, London
W1S 1JU
☎020 7499 9080 Fax 020 7491 2551

Owner *Condé Nast*
Editor *Jo Elvin*
Circulation 436,579

FOUNDED 2001. Handbag-size glossy women's
magazine – fashion, beauty and celebrities. No
unsolicited mss; send ideas for features in synopsis form to the Features Editor *Miranda Levy*.

Gliding and Motorgliding International

281 Queen Edith's Way, Cambridge
CB1 9NH
☎01223 247725 Fax 01223 413793
Email bryce.smith@virgin.net
Website www.glidingmagazine.com

Owner *Soaring Society of America*
Editor *Gillian Bryce-Smith*

FOUNDED November 1998 for international
gliding and motorgliding enthusiasts. Few
opportunities for freelance writers. Now on
the Internet as the first gliding magazine to be
electronic only. *No payment.*

Golf Monthly

IPC Media Ltd., King's Reach Tower,
Stamford Street, London SE1 9LS
☎020 7261 7237 Fax 020 7261 7240
Email jane_carter@ipcmedia.com

Owner *IPC Media*
Editor *Jane Carter*
Circulation 81,361

FOUNDED 1911. MONTHLY. Player profiles,
golf instruction, general golf features and
columns. Not interested in instruction material

from outside contributors. Unsolicited mss
welcome. Approach in writing with ideas.

Features Maximum 1500–2000 words.
Payment by arrangement.

Golf Weekly

Bushfield House, Orton Centre,
Peterborough, Cambridgeshire PE2 5UW
☎01733 288035 Fax 01733 288025
Email golf.weekly@emap.com

Owner *Emap Active Publications Ltd*
Editor *Peter Masters*
Circulation 20,000

FOUNDED 1890. WEEKLY. Unsolicited material
welcome from full-time journalists only. 'Always
looking for photographic and written news contributions.' For features, approach in writing in
first instance; for news, e-mail, fax or phone.

Features Maximum 1500 words.
News Maximum 300 words.
Payment negotiable.

Golf World

Bushfield House, Orton, Peterborough,
Cambridgeshire PE2 5UW
☎01733 237111 Fax 01733 288025
Website www.golferworld.co.uk

Owner *Emap Active Publications Ltd*
Editor *Neil Pope*
Circulation 57,581

FOUNDED 1962. MONTHLY. No unsolicited
mss. Approach in writing with ideas.

Good Holiday Magazine

3A High Street, Esher, Surrey KT10 9RP
☎01372 468140 Fax 01372 470765
Email info@goodholidayideas.com
Website www.goodholidayideas.com

Editor *John Hill*
Circulation 100,000

FOUNDED 1985. QUARTERLY aimed at better-off
holiday-makers rather than travellers. Worldwide destinations including Europe and domestic. No unsolicited material. Consult journalist
guidelines on the website in the first instance.

Payment negotiable.

Good Housekeeping

National Magazine House, 72 Broadwick
Street, London W1F 9EP
☎020 7439 5000 Fax 020 7439 5591
Website www.natmags.co.uk

Owner *National Magazine Co. Ltd*
Editor-in-Chief *Lindsay Nicholson*
Circulation 405,140

FOUNDED 1922. MONTHLY glossy. No unsolicited mss. Write with ideas in the first instance to the appropriate editor.

Features *Kerry Fowler* Most work is commissioned but original ideas are always welcome. No ideas are discussed on the telephone. Send short synopsis, plus relevant cuttings, showing previous examples of work published. No unsolicited mss.

Health *Julie Powell*. Submission guidelines as for features; no unsolicited mss.

Good Motoring

Station Road, Forest Row, East Sussex
RH18 5EN
☎01342 825676 Fax 01342 824847
Email gem@gemrecovery.org.uk
Website www.roadsafety.org.uk

Owner *Guild of Experienced Motorists*
Editor *Derek Hainge*
Circulation 52,000

FOUNDED 1932. QUARTERLY motoring, road safety and travel magazine. Occasional general features. 1500 words maximum. Prospective contributors should approach in writing only.

Good News

50 Loxwood Avenue, Worthing, West Sussex
BN14 7RA
☎01903 824174 Fax 01903 824174

Owner *Good News Fellowship*
Editor *Donald Banks*
Circulation 22,000

FOUNDED 2001. MONTHLY evangelistic newspaper which welcomes contributions. No fiction. Send for sample copy of writers' guidelines in the first instance. No poetry or children's stories.

News Items of up to 500 words (preferably with pictures) 'showing God at work, and human interest photo stories. "Churchy" items not wanted. Testimonies of how people have come to personal faith in Jesus Christ and the difference it has made are always welcome. They do not need to be dramatic!'

Women's Page Relevant items of interest welcome.
Payment negotiable.

Good Ski Guide

145–147 Ewell Road, Surbiton, Surrey
KT6 6AW
☎020 8786 2950 Fax 020 8786 2951
Email info@goodskiguide.com
Website www.goodskiguide.com

Owner *Profile Media Group plc*

Editor *Owen Jones*
Circulation 50,000

FOUNDED 1976. FIVE ISSUES YEARLY. Unsolicited mss welcome from writers with a knowledge of skiing and ski resorts. Prospective contributors are best advised to make initial contact in writing as ideas and work need to be seen before any discussion can take place. *Payment* negotiable.

The Goodlife Magazine

165A Finborough Road, London SW10 9AP
☎020 7373 7282 Fax 020 7373 3215
Email goodlifemedia@btconnect.com

Owner/Editor *Eileen Spence-Moncrieff*
Circulation 40,000

FOUNDED 1988. Features on fashion, interiors, restaurants, theatre, social scene, health and beauty. No unsolicited mss.

GQ

Vogue House, Hanover Square, London
W1R 0AD
☎020 7499 9080 Fax 020 7495 1679
Website www.gq-magazine.co.uk

Owner *Condé Nast Publications Ltd*
Editor *Dylan Jones*
Circulation 125,885

FOUNDED 1988. MONTHLY. Men's style magazine. No unsolicited material. Write or fax with an idea in the first instance.

Granta

2–3 Hanover Yard, Noel Road, London
N1 8BE
☎020 7704 9776 Fax 020 7704 0474
Email editorial@granta.com
Website www.granta.com

Editor *Ian Jack*
Deputy Editors *Liz Jobey, Sophie Harrison*

QUARTERLY magazine of new writing, including fiction, memoirs, reportage and photography, published in paperback book form. Highbrow, diverse, contemporary, with a thematic approach. Unsolicited mss (including fiction) considered. A lot of material is commissioned. Vital to read the magazine first to appreciate its very particular fusion of cultural and political interests. No reviews, news articles or poetry. Access the website for guidelines. *Payment* negotiable.

The Great Outdoors

See **TGO**

Guardian Weekend

See under **National Newspapers (The Guardian)**

Guiding magazine

17–19 Buckingham Palace Road, London
SW1W 0PT
☎020 7834 6242 Fax 020 7828 5791
Website www.guides.org.uk
Owner *The Guide Association*
Acting Editor *Victoria Wheater*
Circulation 28,000

FOUNDED 1914. MONTHLY. Unsolicited mss
welcome provided topics relate to the Movement and/or women's role in society. Ideas in
writing appreciated in first instance. No nostalgic, 'when I was a Guide', pieces, please.

Activity Ideas Interesting, contemporary
ideas and instructions for activities for girls aged
5 to 18+ to do during unit meetings – crafts,
games (indoor/outdoor), etc.

Features Topics that can be useful in the
Guide programme. 650–1200 words.

News Guide activities. Maximum 100–150
words.

Payment £70 per 1000 words.

Hair

IPC Media Ltd., King's Reach Tower,
Stamford Street, London SE1 9LS
☎020 7261 6975 Fax 020 7261 7382

Owner *IPC Media*
Editor *Kate Barlow*
Circulation 172,950

FOUNDED 1977. BI-MONTHLY hair and beauty
magazine. No unsolicited mss, but always
interested in good photographs. Approach with
ideas in writing.

Features Fashion pieces on hair trends and
styling advice. Maximum 1000 words.

Payment negotiable.

Hairflair

Hairflair Magazines Ltd, Freebournes House,
Freebournes Road, Witham, Essex CM8 3US
☎01376 534540 Fax 01376 534546

Owner *Hairflair Magazines Ltd*
Editor *Ruth Page*
Circulation 60,000

FOUNDED 1982. BI-MONTHLY. Original and
interesting hair and beauty-related features
written in a young, lively style to appeal to a
readership aged 16–35 years. Unsolicited mss
not welcome, although freelancers are used.

Features Hair and beauty. Maximum 2500
words.

Payment negotiable.

Harpers & Queen

National Magazine House, 72 Broadwick
Street, London W1F 9EP
☎020 7439 5000 Fax 020 7439 5506
Owner *National Magazine Co. Ltd*
Editor *Lucy Yeomans*
Circulation 86,039

MONTHLY. Up-market glossy combining the
stylish and the streetwise. Approach in writing
(not phone) with ideas.

Features *Harriet Green* Ideas only in the first
instance.

News Snippets welcome if very original.
Payment negotiable.

Health & Efficiency

Burlington Court, Carlisle Street, Goole,
East Yorkshire DN14 5EG
☎01405 769712/764206 Fax 01405 763815
Email newfreedom@btinternet.com
Website www.healthandefficiency.co.uk

Owner *New Freedom Publications Ltd*
Editor *Mark Nisbet*
Circulation 15,000

FOUNDED 1898. MONTHLY naturist magazine.
Features Will consider short features on social
nudism, longer features on nudist holidays and
nudist philosophy. 90% of every issue is by freelance contributors. 1000–1500 words. **News**
'We are always on the lookout for national and
international nudist news stories.' 250–500
words. No soft porn, 'sexy' stories or sleazy photographs. Approach by post, e-mail or telephone.

Health & Fitness Magazine

Highbury wViP, 53–79 Highgate Road,
London NW5 1TW
☎020 7331 1184 Fax 020 7331 1108
Website www.hfonline.co.uk

Owner *Highbury wViP*
Editor *Mary Comber*
Circulation 65,000

FOUNDED 1983. MONTHLY. Will consider
ideas; approach in writing in the first instance.

Health Education

The Health Education Unit, Research and
Graduate School of Education, University of
Southampton, Southampton SO17 1BJ
☎023 8059 3707
Email skw@soton.ac.uk
Website www.emeraldinsight.com

Owner *Emerald*
Editor *Dr Katherine Weare*
Circulation 2000

FOUNDED 1992. SIX ISSUES YEARLY. Health education journal with an emphasis on schools and young people. Professional readership.

Heat

Endeavour House, 189 Shaftesbury Avenue, London WC2H 8JG
☎020 7437 9011 Fax 020 7859 8670
Email heat@emap.com
Website www.heatmagazine.co.uk
Owner *Emap élan Network*
Editor *Mark Frith*
Circulation 355,304

FOUNDED January 1999. WEEKLY entertainment magazine dealing with TV, film and radio information, fashion and features, with an emphasis on celebrity interviews and news. Targets 18- to 40-year-old readership, male and female. Articles written both in-house and by trusted freelancers. No unsolicited mss.

Hello!

Wellington House, 69–71 Upper Ground, London SE1 9PQ
☎020 7667 8700 Fax 020 7667 8716
Website www.hellomagazine.com
Owner *Hola!* (Spain)
Editor-in-Chief *To be appointed*
Circulation 526,947

WEEKLY. Owned by a Madrid-based publishing family, *Hello!* has grown faster than any other British magazine since its launch here in 1988. The magazine is printed in Madrid, with editorial offices both there and in London. Major colour features plus regular news pages. Although much of the material is provided by regulars, good proposals do stand a chance. Approach with ideas in the first instance. No unsolicited mss.

Features Interested in celebrity-based features, with a newsy angle, and exclusive interviews from generally unapproachable personalities.
Payment by arrangement.

Here's Health

Greater London House, Hampstead Road, London NW1 7EJ
☎020 7874 0200 Fax 020 7347 1897
Email helen.lim@emap.com
Website www.thinknatural.com/hereshealth
Owner *Emap Esprit*
Editor *Colette Harris*
Circulation 37,502

FOUNDED 1956. MONTHLY. Full-colour magazine dealing with alternative medicine, nutrition, natural health, wholefoods, supplements, organics and the environment. Prospective contributors should bear in mind that this is a specialist magazine with a pronounced bias towards alternative/complementary medicine, using expert contributors on the whole. No completed articles. Contact Features Editor *Lisa Howells* with ideas in the first instance.
Payment negotiable.

Heritage Scotland

28 Charlotte Square, Edinburgh EH2 4ET
☎0131 243 9300 Fax 0131 243 9397
Email igardner@nts.org.uk
Owner *National Trust for Scotland*
Editor *Ian Gardner*
Circulation 138,878

FOUNDED 1983. THREE ISSUES YEARLY. Magazine containing heritage/conservation features. No unsolicited mss.

Hi-Fi News

Focus House, Dingwall Avenue, Croydon, Surrey CR9 2TA
☎020 8774 0846 Fax 020 8774 0940
Email hi-finews@ipcmedia.com
Owner *IPC Media*
Editor *Steve Harris*
Circulation 18,415

FOUNDED 1956. MONTHLY. Write in the first instance with suggestions based on knowledge of the magazine's style and subject. All articles must be written from an informed technical or enthusiast viewpoint.
Payment negotiable, according to technical content.

High Life

One Oxendon Street, London SW1Y 4EE
☎020 7925 2544 Fax 020 7321 2942
Email high.life@cedarcom.co.uk
Website www.cedarcom.co.uk
Owner *Cedar Communications*
Editor *Mark Jones*
Circulation 211,215

FOUNDED 1973. MONTHLY glossy. British Airways in-flight magazine. Almost all the content is commissioned. No unsolicited mss. Few opportunities for freelancers.

History Today

20 Old Compton Street, London W1D 4TW
☎020 7534 8000 Fax 020 7534 8008
Email p.furtado@historytoday.com
Website www.historytoday.com

Owner *History Today Trust for the Advancement of Education*
Editor *Peter Furtado*
Circulation 29,269

FOUNDED 1951. MONTHLY. General history and archaeology worldwide, history behind the headlines. Serious submissions only; no 'jokey' material. Approach by post or e-mail.

Home

SPL, Berwick House, 8–10 Knoll Rise, Orpington, Kent BR6 0PS
☎01689 887200 Fax 01689 896847
Email ksleeman@splpublishing.co.uk
Owner *Highbury House Communications*
Editor *Sarah Giles*

MONTHLY magazine with ideas, information and inspiration for the home. Features include style, design, home products, gardens and cookery. Synopses and ideas welcome; approach in writing. No health and lifestyle articles.

Home & Country

104 New Kings Road, London SW6 4LY
☎020 7731 5777 Fax 020 7736 4061
Owner *National Federation of Women's Institutes*
Editor *Susan Seager*
Circulation 55,000

FOUNDED 1919. MONTHLY. Official full-colour journal of the Federation of Women's Institutes, containing articles on a wide range of subjects of interest to women. Strong environmental country slant with crafts and cookery plus gardening appearing every month. Unsolicited mss, photos and illustrations welcome.
Payment by arrangement.

Home & Family

Mary Sumner House, 24 Tufton Street, London SW1P 3RB
☎020 7222 5533 Fax 020 7222 1591
Owner *MU Enterprises Ltd*
Editor *Jill Worth*
Circulation 60,000

FOUNDED 1976. QUARTERLY. Unsolicited mss considered. No fiction or poetry. Features on family life, social problems, marriage, Christian faith, etc. Maximum 1000 words.
Payment 'modest'.

Homes & Gardens

IPC Media Ltd., King's Reach Tower, Stamford Street, London SE1 9LS
☎020 7261 5000 Fax 020 7261 6247

Owner *IPC Media*
Editor *Isobel McKenzie-Price*
Circulation 148,106

FOUNDED 1919. MONTHLY. Almost all published articles are specially commissioned. No fiction or poetry. Best to approach in writing with an idea, enclosing snapshots if appropriate.

Horse and Hound

IPC Media Ltd., King's Reach Tower, Stamford Street, London SE1 9LS
☎020 7261 6315 Fax 020 7261 5429
Email jenny_sims@ipcmedia.com
Owner *IPC Media*
Editor *Lucy Higginson*
Circulation 67,100

FOUNDED 1884. WEEKLY. The oldest equestrian magazine on the market. Contains regular veterinary advice and instructional articles, as well as authoritative news and comment on fox hunting, international and national showjumping, horse trials, dressage, driving and endurance riding. Also weekly racing and point-to-points, breeding reports and articles. Regular books and art reviews, and humorous articles and cartoons are frequently published. Plenty of opportunities for freelancers. Unsolicited contributions welcome.
    Also publishes a sister monthly publication, *Eventing*, which covers the sport of horse trials comprehensively.
    Payment NUJ rates.

Horse and Rider

Haslemere House, Lower Street, Haslemere, Surrey GU27 2PE
☎01428 651551 Fax 01428 654108
Email djm@djmurphy.co.uk
Website www.horseandridermagazine.co.uk
Owner *D.J. Murphy (Publishers) Ltd*
Editor *Alison Bridge*
Assistant Editor *Danielle Pascoe*
Circulation 46,000

FOUNDED 1949. MONTHLY. Adult readership, largely horse-owning. News and instructional features, which make up the bulk of the magazine, are almost all commissioned. New contributors and unsolicited mss are occasionally used. Approach the editor in writing with ideas.

Hotline

John Brown Contract Publishing, The New Boathouse, 136–142 Bramley Road, London W10 6SR
☎020 7565 3000 Fax 020 7565 3060
Email info@johnbrown.co.uk

Website www.johnbrownpublishing.com
Editor *Siân Phillips*
Circulation 4 million (readership)
FOUNDED 1997. QUARTERLY on-board magazine for Virgin trains. Lifestyle and news-based features. No unsolicited material.

House & Garden

Vogue House, Hanover Square, London W1S 1JU
☎020 7499 9080 Fax 020 7629 2907
Website www.condenast.co.uk
Owner *Condé Nast Publications Ltd*
Editor *Susan Crewe*
Circulation 150,593

FOUNDED 1947. MONTHLY. Most feature material is produced in-house but occasional specialist features are commissioned from qualified freelancers, mainly for the interiors, wine and food sections and travel.

Features *Liz Elliot* Suggestions for features, preferably in the form of brief outlines of proposed subjects, will be considered.

House Beautiful

National Magazine House, 72 Broadwick Street, London W1F 9EP
☎020 7439 5000 Fax 020 7439 5625
Owner *National Magazine Co. Ltd*
Editor *Sarah Whelan*
Circulation 192,409

FOUNDED 1989. MONTHLY. Lively magazine offering sound, practical information and plenty of inspiration for those who want to make the most of where they live. Over 100 pages of easy-reading editorial. Regular features about decoration, DIY, food, gardening and home finance. Approach in writing with synopses or ideas in the first instance.

i-D Magazine

124 Tabernacle Street, London EC2A 4SA
☎020 7490 9710 Fax 020 7251 2225
Email editor@i-dmagazine.co.uk
Website www.i-dmagazine.com
Owner *Levelprint*
Editor *Avril Mair*
Circulation 66,000

FOUNDED 1980. MONTHLY lifestyle magazine for both sexes with a fashion bias. International. Very hip. Does not accept unsolicited contributions but welcomes new ideas from the fields of fashion, music, clubs, art, film, technology, books, sport, etc. No fiction or poetry. 'We are always looking for freelance non-fiction writers with new or unusual ideas.' A different theme each issue – past themes have included Green politics, taste, films, sex, love and loud dance music – means it is advisable to discuss feature ideas in the first instance.

Ideal Home

IPC Media Ltd., King's Reach Tower, Stamford Street, London SE1 9LS
☎020 7261 6505 Fax 020 7261 6697
Owner *IPC Media*
Assistant Editor *Ailsa Macdonald*
Circulation 244,870

FOUNDED 1920. MONTHLY glossy. Unsolicited feature articles are welcome if appropriate to the magazine. Prospective contributors wishing to submit ideas should do so in writing to the editor. No fiction.

Features Furnishing and decoration of houses, kitchens or bathrooms; interior design, soft furnishings, furniture and home improvements, lifestyle, travel, etc. Length to be discussed with editor.

Payment negotiable.

The Illustrated London News

20 Upper Ground, London SE1 9PF
☎020 7805 5562 Fax 020 7805 5911
Website www.ilng.co.uk
Owner *James Sherwood*
Editor *Alison Booth*
Circulation 47,547

FOUNDED 1842. BIANNUAL: Christmas and Summer issues, plus the occasional special issue to coincide with particular events. Although the *ILN* covers issues concerning the whole of the UK, its emphasis remains on the capital and its life. Travel, wine, restaurants, events, cultural and current affairs are all covered. There are few opportunities for freelancers but all unsolicited mss are read (receives about five a week). The best approach is with an idea in writing. Particularly interested in articles relating to events and developments in contemporary London, and about people working in the capital. All features are illustrated, so ideas with picture opportunities are particularly welcome.

Image Magazine

Upper Mounts, Northampton NN1 3HR
☎01604 467000 Fax 01604 467190
Email image@northantsnews.co.uk
Owner *Northamptonshire Newspapers Ltd*
Editor *Ruth Supple*

Circulation 12,000

FOUNDED 1905. MONTHLY general interest regional magazine. No unsolicited mss. Approach by phone or in writing with ideas. No fiction.

Features Local issues, personalities, businesses, etc., of Northamptonshire, Bedfordshire, Buckinghamshire interest. Maximum 500 words. *Payment* negotiable.

News No hard news as such, just monthly diary column.

Other Regulars on motoring, fashion, beauty, lifestyle, travel and horoscopes. Maximum 500 words.

In Britain

Glen House, Stag Place, London SW1E 5AQ
☎020 7233 9191 Fax 020 7630 8084
Email inbritain@romseypublishing.com

Editor *Andrea Spain*
Circulation 40,000

FOUNDED in the 1930s. BI-MONTHLY. Travel magazine of the British Tourist Authority. Not much opportunity for unsolicited work – approach (by e-mail) with ideas and samples. Words and picture packages preferred (good quality transparencies only).

In Style

IPC Media Ltd., Kings Reach Tower, Stamford Street, London SE1 9LS
☎020 7261 5000

Owner *IPC Media*
Editor *To be appointed*
Features/Fashion Features Director
Vanessa Friedman
Senior Editors *Polly Williams, Laura Campbell*
Fashion Director *Paula Reed*
Circulation 151,000

LAUNCHED March 2001. MONTHLY. UK edition of US fashion, beauty, celebrity and lifestyle magazine. Unsolicited material welcome; send by e-mail to individual editors.

Independent Magazine

See under **National Newspapers (The Independent)**

Inspirations For Your Home

SPL Publishing, Berwick House, 8–10 Knoll Rise, Orpington, Kent BR6 0PS
☎01689 887200 Fax 01689 896847

Owner *SPL Publishing Ltd*
Editor *Andrée Frieze*
Circulation 97,000

Homes and interiors with practical hands-on approach – decorating, design, house features, makeovers, creative living and gardens. Will consider unsolicited synopses on these subjects.

Insurance Age

Informa House, 30–32 Mortimer Street, London W1W 7RE
☎020 7017 4232 Fax 020 7436 8392
Website www.insuranceage.com

Owner *Informa*
Editor *Joanna Malvern*
Circulation 22,050

FOUNDED 1979. MONTHLY publication circulated to insurance brokers. Covers general insurance (*not* life and pensions). No unsolicited mss. Interested in exclusive stories linked to the insurance broker market, risk managers, loss adjusters and claims managers.

News *Joanna Malvern* Maximum 400 words.
Features *Michelle Worvell* Maximum 1200 words.
Payment negotiable.

International Rugby News

175 Tottenham Court Road, London W1T 7NU
☎020 7323 1944 Fax 020 7323 1943
Website www.rugbynews.net

Owner *Independent Magazines Ltd*
Editor *Graeme Gillespie*
Circulation 44,000

FOUNDED 1987. Contains news, views and features on the UK and the world rugby scene, with special emphasis on clubs, schools, fitness and coaching. Welcomes unsolicited material.

Interzone: Science Fiction & Fantasy

217 Preston Drove, Brighton, East Sussex BN1 6FL
☎01273 504710
Website www.sfsite.com/interzone

Owner/Editor *David Pringle*
Circulation 10,000

FOUNDED 1982. MONTHLY magazine of science fiction and fantasy. Unsolicited mss are welcome 'from writers who have a knowledge of the magazine and its contents'. S.a.e. essential for return.

Fiction 2000–6000 words. *Payment* £30 per 1000 words.

Features Book/film reviews, interviews with writers and occasional short articles. Length by arrangement. *Payment* negotiable.

Investors Chronicle
Maple House, 149 Tottenham Court Road,
London W1T 7LB
☎020 7896 2525 Fax 020 7896 2054
Email ceri.jones@ft.com
Website www.investorschronicle.co.uk

Owner *Pearson*
Deputy Editor *Rosie Carr*
Commissioning Editor *Richard Andersen*
Circulation 51,121

FOUNDED 1860. WEEKLY. Opportunities for freelance contributors in the survey section only. All approaches should be made in writing. Over forty surveys are published each year on a wide variety of subjects, generally with a financial, business or investment emphasis. Copies of survey list and synopses of individual surveys are obtainable from the surveys editor.
Payment negotiable.

J17
Endeavour House, 189 Shaftesbury Avenue,
London WC2H 8JG
☎020 7208 3408 Fax 020 7208 3590

Owner *Emap élan Publications*
Editor *Helen Bazauye*
Circulation 180,351

FOUNDED 1983. MONTHLY. News, articles and quizzes of interest to girls aged 13–17. Ideas are sought in all areas. Prospective contributors should send ideas to the deputy editor.
Beauty *Lara Williamson*
Features/News *Kate Hodges*
Payment by arrangement.

Jane's Defence Weekly
Sentinel House, 163 Brighton Road,
Coulsdon, Surrey CR5 2YH
☎020 8700 3700 Fax 020 8763 1007
Email jdw@janes.co.uk
Website www.janes.com

Owner *Jane's*
Editor *Clifford Beal*
Circulation 25,500

FOUNDED 1984. WEEKLY. No unsolicited mss. Approach in writing with ideas in the first instance.
Features Current defence topics (politics, strategy, equipment, industry) of worldwide interest. No history pieces. Maximum 2000 words.

Jazz Journal International
3 & 3A Forest Road, Loughton, Essex
IG10 1DR
☎020 8532 0456/0678 Fax 020 8532 0440

Owner *Jazz Journal Ltd*
Editor-in-Chief *Eddie Cook*
Circulation 8000+

FOUNDED 1948. MONTHLY. A specialised jazz magazine, for record collectors, principally using expert contributors whose work is known to the editor. Unsolicited mss not welcome, with the exception of news material (for which no payment is made). It is not a gig guide, nor a free reference source for students.

Jersey Now
PO Box 582, Five Oaks, St Saviour, Jersey,
Channel Islands JE4 8XQ
☎01534 611743 Fax 01534 611610
Email mspeditorial@msppublishing.com

Owner *MSP Publishing*
Managing Editor *Peter Body*
Circulation 25,000

FOUNDED 1987. QUARTERLY lifestyle magazine for Jersey covering homes, gardens, the arts, Jersey heritage, motoring, boating, fashion and technology. Upmarket glossy aimed at an informed and discerning readership. Interested in Jersey-orientated articles only – 1200 words maximum. Approach the deputy editor initially. *Payment* negotiable.

Jewish Chronicle
25 Furnival Street, London EC4A 1JT
☎020 7415 1500 Fax 020 7405 9040
Email jconline@jchron.co.uk

Owner *Kessler Foundation*
Editor *Edward J. Temko*
Circulation 50,000

WEEKLY. Unsolicited mss welcome if 'the specific interests of our readership are borne in mind by writers'. Approach in writing, except for urgent current news items. No fiction. Maximum 1500 words for all material.
Features *Gerald Jacobs*
Leisure/Lifestyle *Alan Montague*
Home News *Barry Toberman*
Foreign News *Jenni Frazer*
Supplements *Angela Kiverstein*
Payment negotiable.

Jewish Quarterly
PO Box 35042, London NW1 7XH
☎020 7284 1117 Fax 020 7284 1117

Publisher *Jewish Literary Trust Ltd*
Editor *Matthew Reisz*

FOUNDED 1953. QUARTERLY illustrated magazine featuring Jewish literature and fiction, politics, art, music, film, poetry, history, dance, community, autobiography, Hebrew, Yiddish, Israel and the Middle East, Judaism, interviews, Zionism, philosophy and holocaust studies. Features a major books and arts section. Unsolicited mss welcome but letter or phone call preferred in first instance.

Jewish Telegraph

Jewish Telegraph Group of Newspapers, 11 Park Hill, Bury Old Road, Prestwich, Manchester M25 0HH
☎0161 740 9321 Fax 0161 740 9325
Email editor@jewishtelegraph.com
Website www.jewishtelegraph.com

Editor *Paul Harris*
Circulation 16,000

FOUNDED 1950. WEEKLY publication with local, national and international news and features. (Separate editions published for Manchester, Leeds, Liverpool and Glasgow.) Unsolicited features on Jewish humour and history welcome.

The Journal Magazines (Norfolk, Suffolk, Cambridgeshire)/ The Essex Magazine

The Old County School, Northgate Street, Bury St Edmunds, Suffolk IP33 1HP
☎01284 701190 Fax 01284 701680
Email info@acornmagazines.co.uk

Owner *Acorn Magazines Ltd*
Editor *Pippa Bastin*
Circulation 12,000 each

FOUNDED 1990. MONTHLY magazines covering items of local interest – history, people, conservation, business, places, food and wine, fashion, homes and sport.

Features 750–1500 words maximum, plus pictures. Approach the deputy editor by phone with ideas in the first instance.

Just Seventeen

See J17

Kent Life

Datateam Publishing Ltd, London Road, Maidstone, Kent ME15 8LY
☎01622 687031 Fax 01622 757646

Publisher *Datateam Publishing Ltd*
Editor *Ian Trevett*
Circulation 10,000

FOUNDED 1962. MONTHLY. Strong Kent interest plus fashion, food, books, gardening, wildlife, motoring, property, sport, interiors with local links. Unsolicited mss welcome. Interested in anything with a genuine Kent connection. No fiction or non-Kentish subjects. Approach in writing with ideas. Maximum length 1500 words. *Payment* negotiable.

Kerrang!

Mappin House, 4 Winsley Street, London W1N 7AR
☎020 7436 1515 Fax 020 7312 8910
Website www.kerrang.com

Owner *Emap Performance*
Editor *Paul Rees*
Circulation 76,841

FOUNDED 1980. WEEKLY rock, punk and nu-metal magazine. 'Written by fans for fans.' Will consider ideas for features but not actively seeking new contributors unless expert in specialist fields such as Black metal and nu-metal.

The Lady

39–40 Bedford Street, London WC2E 9ER
☎020 7379 4717 Fax 020 7836 4620

Editor *Arline Usden*
Circulation 41,242

FOUNDED 1885. WEEKLY. Unsolicited mss are accepted provided they are not on the subject of politics or religion, or on topics covered by staff writers or special correspondents, i.e. fashion and beauty, health, cookery, household, gardening, finance and shopping.

Features Well-researched pieces on British and foreign travel, historical subjects or events; interviews and profiles and other general interest topics. Maximum 1200 words for illustrated two-page articles; 900 words for one-page features; 430 words for first-person 'Viewpoint' pieces. All material should be addressed to the editor with s.a.e. enclosed. Photographs supporting features may be supplied as colour transparencies or b&w prints. Telephone enquiries about features are not encouraged.

Lakeland Walker

Messrs Warners, Manor Lane, Bourne, Lincolnshire PE10 9PH
☎01778 391000

Contact *Michael Cowton*

FOUNDED 1996. EIGHT ISSUES YEARLY. News and features relating to the Lake District and walking in the area – wildlife, local history, places to visit, local transport. Maximum 1000–1500 words. Unsolicited material welcome.

Land Rover World

Focus House, Dingwall Avenue, Croydon, Surrey CR9 2TA
☎020 8686 2599 Fax 020 8774 0937

Owner *IPC Media*

Editor *Luke Evans*
Circulation 30,000

FOUNDED 1994. MONTHLY. Incorporates *Practical Land Rover World* and *Classic Land Rover World*. Unsolicited material welcome, especially if supported by high-quality illustrations.

Features All articles with a Land Rover theme of interest. Potential contributors are strongly advised to examine previous issues before starting work.

Payment negotiable.

LG

Upper Mounts, Northampton NN1 3HR
☎01604 467043 Fax 01604 467190

Owner *Northamptonshire Newspapers Ltd*
Editor *Ruth Supple*
Circulation 6000

Formerly *Looking Good*, FOUNDED 1984. Relaunched in 2002 as *LG*, a QUARTERLY magazine aimed at women aged 18–30. Fashion and beauty, lifestyle, true life stories. Contributions occasionally considered but majority of work is done in-house.

Life&Soul Magazine

PO Box 119, Chipping Norton OX7 6GR
☎01993 832578 Fax 01993 832578
Email editor@lifeandsoul.com
Website www.lifeandsoul.com

Publisher *Karma Publishing Ltd*
Editor *Roy Stemman*
Circulation 3000

QUARTERLY. The only magazine in the world dealing with all aspects of reincarnation – from people who claim to recall their past lives spontaneously to those who have been regressed. It also examines other evidence for immortality, including near-death experiences and spirit communication.

Lincolnshire Life

County Life Ltd, PO Box 81, Lincoln LN1 1HD
☎01522 527127 Fax 01522 560035
Email editorial@lincolnshirelife.co.uk
Website www.lincolnshirelife.co.uk

Publisher *A.L. Robinson*
Executive Editor *Judy Theobald*
Circulation 10,000

FOUNDED 1961. MONTHLY county magazine featuring geographically relevant articles on local culture, history, personalities, etc. Maximum 1000–1500 words. Contributions supported by three or four good-quality photographs are always welcome. Approach in writing.

Payment varies.

The Lincolnshire Poacher

County Life Ltd, PO Box 81, Lincoln LN1 1HD
☎01522 527127 Fax 01522 560035
Email editorial@lincolnshirelife.co.uk
Website www.lincolnshirelife.co.uk

Publisher *A.L. Robinson*
Executive Editor *Judy Theobald*
Circulation 5000

QUARTERLY county magazine featuring geographically relevant but nostalgic articles on history, culture and personalities of Lincolnshire. Maximum 1000–1500 words. Contributions supported by three or four good-quality photography/illustrations appreciated. Approach in writing.

Payment varies.

The List

14 High Street, Edinburgh EH1 1TE
☎0131 558 1191 Fax 0131 557 8500
Email editor@list.co.uk
Website www.list.co.uk

Owner *The List Ltd*
Publisher *Robin Hodge*
Editor *Mark Fisher*
Circulation 17,500

FOUNDED 1985. FORTNIGHTLY. Events guide covering Glasgow and Edinburgh. Interviews and profiles of people working in film, theatre, music and the arts. Maximum 1200 words. No unsolicited mss. Phone with ideas. News material tends to be handled in-house.

Payment £100.

Literary Review

44 Lexington Street, London W1F 0LW
☎020 7437 9392 Fax 020 7734 1844
Email litrev@dircon.co.uk
Website www.litreview.com

Editor *Nancy Sladek*
Circulation 15,000

FOUNDED 1979. MONTHLY. Publishes book reviews (commissioned), features and articles on literary subjects. Prospective contributors are best advised to contact the editor in writing. Unsolicited mss not welcome. Runs a monthly competition, the Literary Review Grand Poetry Competition, on a given theme. Open to subscribers only. Details published in the magazine.

Payment varies.

Living France

Picture House Publishing, 79 High Street, Olney, Buckinghamshire MK46 4EF
☎01234 713203 Fax 01234 711507
Email enquiries@livingfrance.com
Website www.livingfrance.com

Publisher *Trevor Yorke*
Editor *Lucy-Jane Cypher*

FOUNDED 1989. MONTHLY. A Francophile magazine catering for those with a passion for France, French culture and lifestyle. Covers all aspects of holidaying, living and working in France. Property section for those owning or wishing to buy a property in France. No un-solicited mss; approach in writing with an idea.

Loaded

IPC Media Ltd., King's Reach Tower, Stamford Street, London SE1 9LS
☎020 7261 5562 Fax 020 7261 5557
Email simon_guirao@ipc.co.uk

Owner *IPC Media*
Editor *Keith Kendrick*
Circulation 308,711

FOUNDED 1994. MONTHLY men's lifestyle magazine featuring music, sport, sex, humour, travel, fashion, hard news and popular culture. Will consider material which comes into these categories; approach in writing in the first instance. No fiction or poetry.

Logos

5 Beechwood Drive, Marlow, Buckinghamshire SL7 2DH
☎01628 477577 Fax 01628 477577
Email logos-marlow@dial.pipex.com

Owner *Whurr Publishers Ltd*
Editor *Gordon Graham*
Associate Editor *Betty Graham*

FOUNDED 1990. QUARTERLY. Aims to 'deal in depth with issues which unite, divide, excite and concern the world of books', with an inter-national perspective. Each issue contains 6–8 articles of between 3500–7000 words. 'Logos is a professional forum, not a scholarly journal.' Suggestions and ideas for contributions are wel-come, and should be addressed to the editor. 'Guidelines for Contributors' available. Contri-butors write from their experience as authors, publishers, booksellers, librarians, etc.

No payment.

London Hotel Magazine

165A Finborough Road, London SW10 9AP
☎020 7373 7282 Fax 020 7373 3215

Owner/Editor *Eileen Spence-Moncrieff*

FOUNDED 1995. Features on antiques, fashion, galleries, events and attractions, restaurants, social pages, theatre directories, business. Circulated to 115 major hotels.

London Review of Books

28 Little Russell Street, London WC1A 2HN
☎020 7209 1101 Fax 020 7209 1102
Email edit@lrb.co.uk
Website www.lrb.co.uk

Owner *LRB Ltd*
Editor *Mary-Kay Wilmers*
Circulation 38,660

FOUNDED 1979. FORTNIGHTLY. Reviews, essays and articles on political, literary, cultural and scientific subjects. Also poetry. Unsolicited contributions welcome (approximately 50 received each week). No pieces under 2000 words. Contact the editor in writing. Please include s.a.e.

Payment £150 per 1000 words; poems, £75.

Looking Good

See **LG**

Machine Knitting Monthly

PO Box 1479, Maidenhead, Berkshire SL6 8YX
☎01628 783080 Fax 01628 633250
Email rpa@surf3.net
Website www.machineknittingmonthly.co.uk

Owner *RPA Publishing Ltd*
Editor *Anne Smith*

FOUNDED 1986. MONTHLY. Unsolicited mss considered 'as long as they are applicable to this specialist publication. We have our own regu-lar contributors each month but we're always willing to look at new ideas from other wri-ters.' Approach in writing in the first instance.

Management Today

174 Hammersmith Road, London W6 7JP
☎020 7413 4956
Email management.today@haynet.com

Owner *Haymarket Business Publications Ltd*
Editor-in-Chief *Rufus Olins*
Circulation 93,394

General business topics and features. Ideas wel-come. Send brief synopsis to the editor.

marie claire

2 Hatfields, London SE1 9PG
☎020 7261 5240 Fax 020 7261 5277

Owner *European Magazines Ltd*
Editor *TBA*

Circulation 382,094

FOUNDED 1988. MONTHLY. An intelligent glossy magazine for women, with strong international features and fashion. No unsolicited mss. Approach with ideas in writing. No fiction.

Features *Charlotte Moore* Detailed proposals for feature ideas should be accompanied by samples of previous work.

Market Newsletter

Focus House, 497 Green Lanes, London N13 4BP
☎020 8882 3315 Fax 020 8886 5174
Email info@thebfp.com
Owner *Bureau of Freelance Photographers*
Editor *John Tracy*
Deputy Editor *Stewart Gibson*
Circulation 7000

FOUNDED 1965. MONTHLY. Circulated to members of the Bureau of Freelance Photographers (annual membership fee: £45 UK; £60 Overseas). News of current markets – magazines, books, cards, calendars, etc. – and the type of submissions (mainly photographs) they are currently looking for. Includes details of new magazine launches, publication revamps, etc. Also profiles of particular markets and photographers. Limited scope for non-members to contribute.

Marketing Week

12–26 Lexington Street, London W1R 4HQ
☎020 7970 4000 Fax 020 7970 6721
Email mw.editorial@chiron.co.uk
Website www.marketing-week.co.uk
Owner *Centaur Communications*
Editor *Stuart Smith*
Circulation 41,000

WEEKLY trade magazine of the marketing industry. Features on all aspects of the business, written in a newsy and up-to-the-minute style. Approach with ideas in the first instance.

Features *Daney Parker*
Payment negotiable.

Match

Bushfield House, Orton Centre,
Peterborough, Cambridgeshire PE2 5UW
☎01733 237111 Fax 01733 288150
Owner *Emap Active Ltd*
Editor *Simon Caney*

FOUNDED 1979. WEEKLY. The UK's biggest-selling football magazine aimed at 10–15-year-olds. Most material is generated in-house by a strong news and features team. Some freelance

material used if suitable. No submissions without prior consultation with editor, either by phone or in writing. Work experience placements often given to trainee journalists and students; the majority of staff are recruited through this route.

Features/News Good and original material is always considered. Maximum 500 words.
Payment negotiable.

Matrix

See **British Science Fiction Association** under **Professional Associations**

Maxim

30 Cleveland Street, London W1T 4JD
☎020 7907 6410 Fax 020 7907 6439
Email editorial@maxim-magazine.co.uk
Owner *Dennis Publishing*
Editor *Tom Loxley*
Circulation 276,640

ESTABLISHED 1995. MONTHLY glossy men's lifestyle magazine featuring sex, travel, health, motoring and fashion. No fiction or poetry. Approach in writing in the first instance, sending outlines of ideas only together with examples of published work.

Mayfair

2 Archer Street, Piccadilly Circus, London W1D 7AW
☎020 7292 8000 Fax 020 7734 5030
Email mayfair@pr-org.co.uk
Owner *Paul Raymond Publications*
Editor *Danny King*
Circulation 331,760

FOUNDED 1966. THIRTEEN ISSUES YEARLY. Unsolicited material accepted if pertinent to the magazine and if accompanied by suitable illustrative material. 'We will *only* publish work if we can illustrate it.' Interested in features and humour aimed at men aged 18–80; 800–1000 words. Punchy, bite-sized humour, top ten features, etc. 'Must make the editor laugh.' Also considers erotica.

Mayfair Times

102 Mount Street, London W1K 2TH
☎020 7629 3378 Fax 020 7629 9303
Email sjg@wetherell.co.uk
Owner *Mayfair Times Ltd*
Editor *Stephen Goringe*
Circulation 20,000

FOUNDED 1985. MONTHLY. Features on Mayfair of interest to both residential and commercial readers. Unsolicited mss welcome.

Medal News

Orchard House, Duchy Road, Heathpark,
Honiton, Devon EX14 1YD
☎01404 46972 Fax 01404 44788
Email info@tokenpublishing.com
Website www.tokenpublishing.com

Owners *J.W. Mussell, Carol Hartman*
Editor *J.W. Mussell*
Circulation 5000

FOUNDED 1989. MONTHLY. Unsolicited material welcome but initial approach by phone or in writing preferred.

Features 'Opportunities exist for well-informed authors who know the subject and do their homework.' Maximum 2500 words.
Payment £20 per 1000 words.

Media Week

Quantum House, 19 Scarbrook Road,
Croydon, Surrey CR9 1LX
☎020 8565 4323 Fax 020 8565 4394
Email weeked@qpp.co.uk
Website www.mediaweek.co.uk

Owner *Quantam Business Media*
Editor *Patrick Barrett*
Circulation 20,555

FOUNDED 1986. WEEKLY trade magazine. UK and international coverage on all aspects of commercial media. No unsolicited mss. Approach in writing with ideas.

Melody Maker

See **New Musical Express**

Men's Health

7–10 Chandos Street, London W1G 9AD
☎020 7291 6000 Fax 020 7291 6053
Website www.menshealth.co.uk

Owner *Rodale Press*
Editor *Simon Geller*
Circulation 215,517

FOUNDED 1994. MONTHLY men's healthy lifestyle magazine covering health, fitness, nutrition, stress and sex issues. No unsolicited mss; will consider ideas and synopses tailored to men's health. No fiction, celebrities, sportsmen or extreme sports. Approach in writing in the first instance.

MiniWorld Magazine

Focus House, Dingwall Avenue, Croydon,
Surrey CR9 2TA
☎020 8774 0600 Fax 020 8774 0937
Email miniworld@ipcmedia.co.uk
Website www.miniworld.co.uk

Owner *IPC Media*
Editor *Monty Watkins*
Circulation 37,000

FOUNDED 1991. MONTHLY car magazine devoted to the Mini. Unsolicited material welcome but prospective contributors are advised to contact the editor.

Features Maintenance, tuning, restoration, technical advice, classified, sport, readers' cars and social history of this cult car.
Payment negotiable.

Mizz

IPC Media Ltd., King's Reach Tower,
Stamford Street, London SE1 9LS
☎020 7261 6319 Fax 020 7261 6032

Owner *IPC Media*
Executive Editor *Lucie Tobin*
Deputy Editor *Leslie Sinoway*
Circulation 144,933

FOUNDED 1985. FORTNIGHTLY magazine for the 10–14-year-old girl.

Features 'We have a full features team and thus do not accept freelance features.'
Fiction Maximum 1000 words.

Mojo

Mappin House, 4 Winsley Street, London
W1W 8HF
☎020 7436 1515 Fax 020 7312 8296
Email mojo@ecm.emap.com

Owner *Emap-Metro*
Editor *Pat Gilbert*
Circulation 96,837

FOUNDED 1993. MONTHLY magazine containing features, reviews and news stories about rock music and its influences. Receives about five mss per day. No poetry, think-pieces on dead rock stars or similar fan worship.

Features Amateur writers discouraged except as providers of source material, contacts, etc. *Payment* negotiable.
News All verifiable, relevant stories considered.
Reviews Write to Reviews Editor with relevant specimen material.

Moneywise

RD Publications Ltd, 11 Westferry Circus,
Canary Wharf, London E14 4HE
☎020 7715 8465 Fax 020 7715 8725
Website www.moneywise.co.uk

Owner *Reader's Digest Association*
Editor *David Ellis*
Circulation 105,000

FOUNDED 1990. MONTHLY. No unsolicited

mss; initial approach in writing with c.v. preferred.

More!

Endeavour House, 189 Shaftesbury Avenue, London WC2H 8JG
☎020 7208 3165 Fax 020 7208 3595
Email more.letters@emap.com
Owner *Emap élan Publications*
Editor *Marian Jones*
Features Director *Ceri Roberts*
Editorial Enquiries *Fran Lee*
Circulation 290,059

FOUNDED 1988. FORTNIGHTLY women's magazine aimed at the working woman aged 16–24. Features on sex and relationships plus news. Most items are commissioned; approach features director with idea. Prospective contributors are strongly advised to study the magazine's style before submitting anything.

Mother and Baby

Greater London House, Hampstead Road, London NW1 7EJ
☎020 7874 0200
Owner *Emap Esprit*
Editor *Dani Zur*
Circulation 84,871

FOUNDED 1956. MONTHLY. Welcomes suggestions for feature ideas about pregnancy, newborn basics, practical babycare, baby development and childcare subjects. Approaches may be made by telephone or in writing to the **Features Editor** *Una Rice*.

Motor Boat & Yachting

IPC Country & Leisure Media Limited, King's Reach Tower, Stamford Street, London SE1 9LS
☎020 7261 5333 Fax 020 7261 5419
Email mby@ipcmedia.com
Website www.mby.com
Owner *AOL Time Warner*
Editor *Alan Harper*
Circulation 19,736

FOUNDED 1904. MONTHLY for those interested in motor boats and motor cruising.
Features *Alan Harper* Cruising features and practical features especially welcome. Illustrations/photographs (mostly colour) are just as important as text. Maximum 3000 words. *Payment* from £100 per 1000 words or by arrangement.
News *Tom Isitt* Factual pieces. Maximum 200 words. *Payment* up to £50 per item.

Motorcaravan Motorhome Monthly (MMM)

PO Box 44, Totnes, Devon TQ9 5XB
Website www.mmmonline.co.uk
Owner *Warners Group Publications Plc*
Editor *Mike Jago*
Circulation 30,500

FOUNDED 1966. MONTHLY. 'There's no money in motorcaravan journalism but for those wishing to cut their first teeth ...' Unsolicited mss welcome if relevant, but ideas in writing preferred in first instance.
Features Caravan site reports. Maximum 500 words.
Travel Motorcaravanning trips (home and overseas). Maximum 2000 words.
News Short news items for miscellaneous pages. Maximum 200 words.
Fiction Must be motorcaravan-related and include artwork/photos if possible. Maximum 2000 words.
Special pages DIY – modifications to motorcaravans. Maximum 1500 words.
Owner Reports Contributions welcome from motorcaravan owners. Contact the editor for requirements. Maximum 2000 words.
Payment varies.

Ms London

Independent House, 191 Marsh Wall, London E14 9RS
☎020 7005 5959 Fax 020 7005 5999
Website www.londoncareers.net
Owner *Independent Magazines*
Editor-in-Chief *Bill Williamson*
Circulation 85,000

FOUNDED 1968. WEEKLY. Aimed at working women in London, aged 18–35. No unsolicited mss.
Features Content is varied and topical, ranging from celebrity interviews to news issues, fashion, health, careers, relationships and home-buying. Approach in writing only with ideas in the first instance, enclosing sample of published writing. Material should be London-angled, sharp or humorous and fairly sophisticated in content. Maximum 1500 words. *Payment* about £130 per 1000 words on publication.
News Handled in-house but follow-up feature ideas welcome.

Mslexia (For Women Who Write)

PO Box 656, Newcastle upon Tyne NE99 2XD
☎0191 261 6656 Fax 0191 261 6636
Email postbag@mslexia.demon.co.uk

Website www.mslexia.co.uk

Owner *Mslexia Publications Limited*
Editor *Debbie Taylor*
Circulation 10,000

FOUNDED 1997. QUARTERLY. Articles, advice, reviews, interviews, events for women writers plus new poetry and prose. Will consider fiction, poetry, features and letters but contributors *must* send for guidelines first.

Music Week
Ludgate House, 245 Blackfriars Road, London SE1 9UR
☎020 8742 2828   Fax 020 7579 4011

Owner *CMP Information*
Editor-in-Chief *Ajax Scott*
Circulation 13,900

Britain's only WEEKLY music business magazine. No unsolicited mss. Approach in writing with ideas.

Features Analysis of specific music business events and trends.

News Music industry news only.

Musical Opinion
2 Princes Road, St Leonards on Sea, East Sussex TN37 6EL
☎01424 715167   Fax 01424 712214
Email musicalopinion2@aol.com
Website www.musicalopinion.com

Owner *Musical Opinion Ltd*
Editor *Denby Richards*
Circulation 5000

FOUNDED 1877. QUARTERLY with four free supplements in intervening months. Classical music content, with topical features on music, musicians, festivals, etc., and reviews (concerts, festivals, opera, ballet, jazz, CDs, DVDs, videos, books and printed music). International readership. No unsolicited mss; commissions only. Ideas always welcome though; approach by phone, fax or e-mail, giving telephone number. It should be noted that topical material has to be submitted six months prior to events. Not interested in review material, which is already handled by the magazine's own regular team of contributors.
Payment negotiable.

My Weekly
80 Kingsway East, Dundee DD4 8SL
☎01382 223131   Fax 01382 452491
Email myweekly@dcthomson.co.uk

Owner *D.C. Thomson & Co. Ltd*
Editor *Harrison Watson*

Circulation 305,407

A traditional women's WEEKLY. D.C. Thomson has long had a policy of encouragement and help to new writers of promise. Ideas welcome. Approach in writing.

Features Particularly interested in human interest pieces (1000–1500 words) which by their very nature appeal to all age groups.

Fiction Three stories a week, ranging in content from the emotional to the off-beat and unexpected. 1000–4000 words. Also serials.
Payment negotiable.

The National Trust Magazine
36 Queen Anne's Gate, London SW1H 9AS
☎020 7222 9251   Fax 020 7222 5097
Email enquiries@thenationaltrust.org.uk

Owner *The National Trust*
Editor *Gaynor Aaltonen*
Circulation 1.41 million

FOUNDED 1968. THREE ISSUES YEARLY. Conservation of historic houses, coast and countryside in England, Northern Ireland and Wales. No unsolicited mss. Approach in writing with ideas.

The Naturalist
c/o University of Bradford, Bradford, West Yorkshire BD7 1DP
☎01274 234212   Fax 01274 234231
Email m.r.d.seaward@bradford.ac.uk

Owner *Yorkshire Naturalists' Union*
Editor *Prof. M.R.D. Seaward*
Circulation 5000

FOUNDED 1875. QUARTERLY. Natural history, biological and environmental sciences for a professional and amateur readership. Unsolicited mss and b&w illustrations welcome. Particularly interested in material – scientific papers – relating to the north of England.
No payment.

Nature
The Macmillan Building, 4–6 Crinan Street, London N1 9XW
☎020 7833 4000   Fax 020 7843 4596
Email nature@nature.com
Website www.nature.com

Owner *Macmillan Magazines Ltd*
Editor *Philip Campbell*
Circulation 61,000

Covers all fields of science, with articles and news on science and science policy only. Little scope for freelance writers.

Needlecraft

30 Monmouth Street, Bath BA1 2BW
☎01225 442244 Fax 01225 732398
Email needlecraft@futurenet.co.uk
Owner *Future Publishing*
Editor *Debora Bradley*
Circulation 23,500

FOUNDED 1991. MONTHLY. Needlework projects with full instructions covering cross stitch, needlepoint, embroidery, patchwork and quilting. Will consider ideas or sketches for projects covering any of the magazine's topics. Initial approaches should be made in writing.

Features on the needlecraft theme. Discuss ideas before sending complete mss. Maximum 1000 words.

Technical pages on 'how to' stitch, use different threads, etc. Only suitable for experienced writers.

Payment negotiable.

New Beacon

105 Judd Street, London WC1H 9NE
☎020 7388 1266
Website www.rnib.org.uk
Owner *Royal National Institute for the Blind*
Editor *Ann Lee*
Circulation 6000

FOUNDED 1917. MONTHLY (except August). Published in print, braille and on tape and disk. Unsolicited mss welcome. Approach with ideas in writing. Personal experiences by writers who have a sight difficulties (partial sight or blindness), and authoritative items by professionals or volunteers working in the field of sight difficulties welcome. Maximum 1500 words.

Payment negotiable.

New Humanist

Bradlaugh House, 47 Theobald's Road, London WC1X 8SP
☎020 7430 1371 Fax 020 7430 1271
Email jim.herrick@rationalist.org.uk
Owner *Rationalist Press Association*
Editor *Jim Herrick*
Circulation 5000

FOUNDED 1885. QUARTERLY. Unsolicited mss welcome. No fiction.

Features Articles with a humanist perspective welcome in the following fields: religion (critical), humanism, human rights, philosophy, current events, literature, history and science. 2000 words. *Payment* nominal, but negotiable.

Book Reviews 750–1000 words, by arrangement with the editor.

New Impact

Anser House, Courtyard Offices, 3 High Street, Marlow, Buckinghamshire SL7 1AX
☎01628 475570 Fax 01628 475570
Email curious@anserhouse.co.uk
Website www.anserhouse.co.uk
Owner *D.E. Sihera*
Editor *Elaine Sihera*
Features Editor *Carole Hughes*
Circulation 10,000

FOUNDED 1993. BI-MONTHLY. Celebrates diversity, enterprise and achievement from a minority ethnic perspective. Unsolicited mss welcome. Interested in training, arts, features, personal achievement, small business features, profiles of personalities especially for a multicultural audience. Promotes the British Diversity Awards each November and the Windrush Awards each June, the Register of Diversity Managers among employers and managing the diversity maze for practitioners.

News Local training/business features – some opportunities. Maximum length 550 words. *Payment* negotiable.

Features Original, interesting pieces with a deliberate multicultural/diversity focus. Personal/professional successes and achievements welcome. Maximum length 1000 words. *Payment* negotiable.

Fiction Short stories, poems – especially from minority writers. Not interested in romantic/sexual narratives. Maximum length 1500 words. *Payment* negotiable.

Special Pages Interviews with personalities – especially Asian, African Caribbean. Maximum length 1200 words. *Payment* negotiable.

New Internationalist

55 Rectory Road, Oxford OX4 1BW
☎01865 728181 Fax 01865 793152
Email ni@newint.org
Website www.newint.org/
Owner *New Internationalist Trust*
Co-Editors *Vanessa Baird, David Ransom, Katharine Ainger*
Circulation 70,000

Radical and broadly leftist in approach, but unaligned. Concerned with world poverty and global issues of peace and politics, feminism and environmentalism, with emphasis on the Third World. Difficult to use unsolicited material as they work to a theme each month and features are commissioned by the editor on that basis. The way in is to send examples of published or unpublished work; writers of interest are taken up.

New Musical Express
IPC Media Ltd., King's Reach Tower,
Stamford Street, London SE1 9LS
☎020 7261 6472 Fax 020 7261 5185
Website www.nme.com
Owner *IPC Media*
Editor *Ben Knowles*
Circulation 70,456

Britain's best-selling musical WEEKLY. Now
incorporates *Melody Maker*. Freelancers used,
but always for reviews in the first instance.
Specialisation in areas of music (or film, which
is also covered) is a help.
   Reviews: Books/Film *Victoria Segal* **LPs**
John Robinson **Live** *Andy Capper*. Send in
examples of work, either published or specially
written samples.

New Nation
Unit 2, 65 Whitechapel Road, London
E1 1DU
☎020 7650 2000 Fax 020 7650 2001
Website www.ethnicmedia.co.uk
Owner *Ethnic Media Group*
Editor *Michael Eboda*
Circulation 30,000

FOUNDED 1996. WEEKLY community paper for
the Black community in Britain. Interested in
relevant general, local and international issues.
Approach in writing with ideas for submission.

New Scientist
1st Floor, 151 Wardour Street, London
W1F 8WE
☎020 7331 2701 Fax 020 7331 2772 (News)
Website www.newscientist.com
Owner *Reed Business Information Ltd*
Editor-in-Chief *Dr Alun Anderson*
Editor *Jeremy Webb*
Circulation 135,000

FOUNDED 1956. WEEKLY. No unsolicited mss.
Approach with ideas – one A4-page synopsis –
by fax.
   Features Commissions only, but good ideas
welcome. Maximum 3500 words.
   News *Daniel Clery* Mostly commissions, but
ideas for specialist news welcome. Maximum
1000 words.
   Reviews *Maggie McDonald* Reviews are
commissioned.
   Forum *Richard Fifield* Unsolicited material
welcome if of general/humorous interest and
related to science. Maximum 1000 words.
   Payment negotiable.

The New Shetlander
11 Mounthooly Street, Lerwick, Shetland
ZE1 0BJ
☎01595 693816 Fax 01595 696787
Email shetland@zetnet.co.uk
Owner *Shetland Council of Social Service*
Editors *Alex Cluness, John Hunter*
Circulation 1900

FOUNDED 1947. QUARTERLY literary magazine
containing short stories, essays, poetry, historical articles, literary criticism, political comment, arts and books. The magazine has two
editors and an editorial committee who all look
at submitted material. Interested in considering
short stories, poetry, historical articles with a
northern Scottish or Scandinavian flavour, literary pieces and articles on Shetland. As a
rough guide, items should be between 1000
and 2000 words although longer mss are considered. Initial approach in writing, please.
   Payment Complimentary copy.

New Statesman
Victoria Station House, 191 Victoria Street,
London SW1E 5NE
☎020 7828 1232 Fax 020 7828 1881
Website www.newstatesman.co.uk
Publisher *Spencer Neal*
Editor *Peter Wilby*
Deputy Editor *Cristina Odone*
Circulation 26,000

WEEKLY magazine, the result of a merger
(1988) of *New Statesman* and *New Society*.
Coverage of news, book reviews, arts, current
affairs, politics and social reportage. Unsolicited
contributions with s.a.e. will be considered.
No short stories.
   Books *Jason Cowley*
   Arts *Frances Stonor Saunders*

New Theatre Quarterly
Oldstairs, Kingsdown, Deal, Kent
CT14 8ES
☎01304 373448
Email simontrussler@lineone.net
Website www.uk.cambridge.org
Publisher *Cambridge University Press*
Editors *Clive Barker, Simon Trussler*

FOUNDED 1985 (originally launched in 1971 as
Theatre Quarterly). Articles, interviews, documentation and reference material covering all
aspects of live theatre. Recommend preliminary e-mail enquiry before sending contributions. No theatre reviews or anecdotal material.

New Welsh Review

Chapter Arts Centre, Market Road, Cardiff CF5 1QE
☎029 2066 5529 Fax 029 2066 5529
Email nwr@welshnet.co.uk

Owner *New Welsh Review Ltd*
Editor *Victor Golightly*
Circulation 900

FOUNDED 1988. QUARTERLY Welsh literary magazine in the English language. Welcomes material of literary and cultural interest to Welsh readers and those with an interest in Wales. Approach in writing in the first instance.

Features Maximum 3000 words. *Payment* £25 per 1000 words.

Fiction Maximum 5000 words. *Payment* £40–80 average.

News Maximum 400 words. *Payment* £10–30.

New Woman

Endeavour House, 189 Shaftesbury Avenue, London WC2H 8JG
☎020 7437 9011 Fax 020 7208 3585
Email lizzi.hosking@emap.com
Website www.newwomanonline.co.uk

Owner *Hachette/Emap élan Ltd*
Editor *Sara Cremer*
Circulation 305,088

MONTHLY women's interest magazine. Winner of the PPA 'Magazine of the Year' award in 1998 and the BSME 'Editor of the Year' in 2001. Aimed at women aged 25–35. An 'entertaining, informative and intelligent' read. Main topics of interest include men, sex, love, health, careers, beauty and fashion. Uses mainly established freelancers but unsolicited ideas submitted in synopsis form will be considered. Welcomes ideas from male writers for humorous 'men's opinion' pieces.

Features/News *Lauren Libbert* Articles must be original and look at subjects or issues from a new or unusual perspective.

The New Writer

PO Box 60, Cranbrook, Kent TN17 2ZR
☎01580 212626 Fax 01580 212041
Email editor@thenewwriter.com
Website www.thenewwriter.com

Publisher *Merric Davidson*
Editor *Suzanne Ruthven*
Poetry Editor *Abi Hughes-Edwards*

FOUNDED 1996. Published BI-MONTHLY following the merger between *Acclaim* and *Quartos* magazines. TNW continues to offer practical 'nuts and bolts' advice on poetry and prose but with the emphasis on *forward-looking* articles and features on all aspects of the written word that demonstrate the writer's grasp of contemporary writing and current editorial/publishing policies. Plenty of news, views, competitions, reviews and regional gossip in the Newsletter section; writers' guidelines available with s.a.e.

Features Unsolicited mss welcome. Interested in lively, original articles on writing in its broadest sense. Approach with ideas in writing in the first instance. No material is returned unless accompanied by s.a.e. *Payment* £20 per 1000 words.

Fiction Publishes short-listed entries from guest writers and subscriber-only submissions. *Payment* £10 per story.

Poetry Unsolicited poetry welcome. Both short and long unpublished poems, providing they are original and interesting. *Payment* £3 per poem.

New Writing Scotland

Association for Scottish Literary Studies, c/o Department of Scottish History, 9 University Gardens, University of Glasgow G12 8QH
☎0141 330 5309 Fax 0141 330 5309
Email d.jones@scothist.arts.gla.ac.uk
Website www.asls.org.uk

Contact *Duncan Jones*

ANNUAL anthology of contemporary poetry and prose in English, Gaelic and Scots, produced by the **Association for Scottish Literary Studies** (see entry under **Professional Associations and Societies**). Will consider poetry, drama, short fiction or other creative prose but not full-length plays or novels, though self-contained extracts are acceptable. Contributors should be Scottish by birth or upbringing, or resident in Scotland. Maximum length of 3500 words is suggested. Send no more than two short stories and six poems. Submissions should be accompanied by two s.a.e.s (one for receipt, the other for return of mss). Mss, which must be sent by 31 January, should be typed, double-spaced, on one side of the paper only with the sheets secured at top left-hand corner. Provide covering letter with full contact details but do not put name or address on individual work(s). Prose pieces should carry an approximate word count.

newBOOKS.mag

15 Scots Drive, Wokingham, Berkshire RG41 3XF
Email guypringle@waitrose.com

Owner/Editor *Guy Pringle*
Circulation 15,000

FOUNDED 2000. BI-MONTHLY magazine for readers and reading groups with extracts from the best new fiction and free copies to be claimed. No unsolicited contributions.

Newcastle Life
See **North East Times**

19
IPC Media Ltd., King's Reach Tower, Stamford Street, London SE1 9LS
☎020 7261 6410 Fax 020 7261 7634

Owner *IPC Media*
Editor *To be appointed*
Circulation 118,001

FOUNDED 1968. MONTHLY women's magazine aimed at 18–25-year-olds. Aims for a 50/50 balance between fashion/lifestyle aspects and newsier, meatier material, e.g. women in prison, boys, abortion, etc. 40% of the magazine's feature material is commissioned, ordinarily from established freelancers. 'But we're always keen to see bold, original, vigorous writing from people just starting out.'
Features Approach in writing with ideas.

North East Times
Tattler House, Beech Avenue, Fawdon, Newcastle upon Tyne NE3 2RN
☎0191 284 4495 Fax 0191 285 9606
Email northeasttimes@onyxnet.co.uk

Owner *Chris Robinson (Publishing) Ltd*
Editor *Chris Robinson*
Circulation 10,000

MONTHLY county magazine incorporating *Newcastle Life*. No unsolicited mss. Approach with ideas in writing. Not interested in any material that is not applicable to ABC1 readers.

The North
See **Poetry Magazines**

Now
IPC Media Ltd., King's Reach Tower, Stamford Street, London SE1 9LS
☎020 7261 6274

Owner *IPC Media*
Editor *Jane Ennis*
Circulation 552,744

FOUNDED 1996. WEEKLY magazine of celebrity gossip, news and topical features aimed at the working woman. Unlikely to use freelance contributions due to specialist content – e.g. exclusive showbiz interviews – but ideas will be considered. Approach in writing; no faxes.

Nursing Times
Greater London House, Hampstead Road, London NW1 7EJ
☎020 7874 0500 Fax 020 7874 0505

Owner *Emap Healthcare*
Editor *To be appointed*
Circulation 56,838

A large proportion of *Nursing Times'* feature content is from unsolicited contributions sent on spec. Pieces on all aspects of nursing and health care, both practical and theoretical, written in a lively and contemporary way, are welcome. Commissions also.
Payment varies/NUJ rates apply to commissioned material from union members only.

OK! Magazine
Ludgate House, 245 Blackfriars Road, London SE1 9UX
☎020 7928 8000 Fax 020 7579 4607

Owner *Northern & Shell Media/Richard Desmond*
Editor *Nic McCarthy*
Circulation 486,858

FOUNDED 1996. WEEKLY celebrity-based magazine. Welcomes interviews and pictures on well known personalities, and ideas for general features. Approach by phone or fax in the first instance.

The Oldie
65 Newman Street, London W1T 3EG
☎020 7436 8801 Fax 020 7436 8804
Email theoldie@theoldie.co.uk
Website www.theoldie.co.uk

Owner *Oldie Publications Ltd*
Editor *Richard Ingrams*
Circulation 30,000

FOUNDED 1992. MONTHLY general interest magazine with a strong humorous slant for the older person. Submissions welcome; enclose s.a.e. No poetry.

OLS (Open Learning Systems) News
11 Malford Grove, Gilwern, Abergavenny, Monmouthshire NP7 0RN
☎01873 830872
Email GSSE@zoo.co.uk

Owner/Editor *David P. Bosworth*
Circulation 300

FOUNDED 1980. QUARTERLY dealing with the application of open, flexible, distance learning and supported self-study at all educational/training levels. Interested in open-access learning and the application of educational technology to learning situations. Case studies particularly welcome. Not interested in theory of education alone, the emphasis is strictly on applied policies and trends.

Features Learning programmes (how they are organised); student/learner-eye views of educational and training programmes with an open-access approach. Sections on teleworking and lifelong learning. Approach the editor by e-mail or in writing.

No payment for 'news' items. Focus items will negotiate.

Opera
36 Black Lion Lane, London W6 9BE
☎020 8563 8893 Fax 020 8563 8635
Email editor@operamag.clara.co.uk
Website www.opera.co.uk

Owner *Opera Magazine Ltd*
Editor *John Allison*
Circulation 11,500

FOUNDED 1950. MONTHLY review of the current opera scene. Almost all articles are commissioned and unsolicited mss are not welcome. All approaches should be made in writing.

Opera Now
241 Shaftesbury Avenue, London
WC2H 8TF
☎020 7333 1740 Fax 020 7333 1769
Email opera.now@rhinegold.co.uk
Website www.rhinegold.co.uk

Publisher *Rhinegold Publishing Ltd*
Editor-in-Chief *Ashutosh Khandekar*
Deputy Editor *Antonia Couling*

FOUNDED 1989. BI-MONTHLY. News, features and reviews aimed at those involved as well as those interested in opera. No unsolicited mss. All work is commissioned. Approach with ideas in writing.

Orbis
See **Poetry Magazines**

Organic Gardening
Sandvoe, North Roe, Shetland ZE2 8RY
☎01806 533319 Fax 01806 533319
Email organic.gardening@virgin.net

Editor *Gaby Bartai Bevan*
Circulation 20,000

FOUNDED 1988. MONTHLY. Articles and features on all aspects of gardening based on organic methods. Unsolicited material welcome; 800–2000 words for features and 100–300 for news items. Poetry not published. Prefers 'hands-on'

accounts of projects, problems, challenges and how they are dealt with. Approach in writing.
Payment by arrangement.

OS (Office Secretary) Magazine
Brookmead House, Thorney Leys Business Park, Witney, Oxfordshire OX8 7GE
☎01993 894500 Fax 01993 778884

Owner *The Media Office*
Editor *Emma Smith*
Circulation 44,500

FOUNDED 1986. BI-MONTHLY. Features articles of interest to secretaries and personal assistants aged 25–60. No unsolicited mss.

Features Informative pieces on technology and practices, office and employment-related topics. Length 1000 words.
Payment by negotiation.

Palmtop Magazine
Palmtop Publications, PO Box 188, Bicester, Oxfordshire OX6 0GP
☎01869 249287 Fax 01869 246043
Email editor@palmtop.co.uk
Website www.palmtop.co.uk

Owners *Mr S. Clack, Miss R.A. Rolfe*
Editor *Mr S. Clack*
Circulation 12,000

FOUNDED 1994. BI-MONTHLY users' magazine for Psion hand-held computers. No unsolicited mss; approach by telephone or e-mail in the first instance.

PC Format
Future Publishing, 30 Monmouth Street, Bath BA1 2BW
☎01225 442244 Fax 01225 732295
Email pcfmail@futurenet.co.uk
Website www.futurenet.co.uk

Owner *Future Publishing*
Senior Editor *Dan Hutchinson*
Circulation 76,337

FOUNDED 1991. FOUR-WEEKLY magazine covering everything for the consumer PC – games, hardware, Internet creativity. Welcomes feature ideas in the first instance; approach by telephone, e-mail or in writing.

Pembrokeshire Life
3 Pisgah, Cresselly, Kilgetty, Pembrokeshire SA68 0TD
☎01646 651725

Owner *Swan House Publishing*
Editor *Keith Johnson*

FOUNDED 1989. MONTHLY county magazine

with articles on local history, issues, characters, off-beat stories with good colour or b&w photographs. No country diaries, short stories, poems. Most articles are commissioned from known freelancers but 'always prepared to consider ideas from new writers'. No mss. Send cuttings of previous work (published or not) and synopsis to the editor.

People Management
Personnel Publications Limited, 17 Britton Street, London EC1M 5TP
☎020 7880 6200 Fax 020 7336 7635
Email editorial@peoplemanagement.co.uk
Website www.peoplemanagement.co.uk
Editor *Steve Crabb*
Circulation 107,648
FORTNIGHTLY magazine on human resources, industrial relations, employment issues, etc. Welcomes submissions but apply for 'Guidelines for Contributors' in the first instance. **Features** *Jane Pickard* **News** *Rima Manocha* **Law at Work** *Jill Evans*.

The People's Friend
80 Kingsway East, Dundee DD4 8SL
☎01382 462276/223131 Fax 01382 452491
Email peoplesfriend@dcthomson.co.uk
Owner *D.C. Thomson & Co. Ltd*
Editor *Margaret McCoy*
Circulation 397,080
The *Friend* is basically a fiction magazine, with two serials and several short stories each week. FOUNDED in 1869, it has always prided itself on providing 'a good read for all the family'. All stories should be about ordinary, identifiable characters with the kind of problems the average reader can understand and sympathise with. 'We look for the romantic and emotional developments of characters, rather than an over-complicated or contrived plot. We regularly use period serials and, occasionally, mystery/adventure.' Guidelines on request with s.a.e.
Short Stories Can vary in length from 1000 words or less to as many as 4000.
Serials Long-run serials of 10–15 instalments or more preferred. Occasionally shorter.
Articles Short fillers welcome.
Payment on acceptance.

Period Living & Traditional Homes
Endeavour House, 189 Shaftesbury Avenue, London WC2H 8JG
☎020 7208 3507 Fax 020 7208 3597
Owner *Emap élan Ltd*

Editor *Garry Mason*
Deputy Editor *Andrew Lilwall-Smith*
Circulation 80,023
FOUNDED 1992. Formed from the merger of *Period Living* and *Traditional Homes*. Covers interior decoration in a period style, period house profiles, traditional crafts, renovation of period properties.
Payment varies according to length/type of article.

Personal Finance
Arnold House, 36–41 Holywell Lane, London EC2A 3SF
☎020 7827 5454 Fax 020 7827 0567
Owner *Charterhouse Communications plc*
Editor *Martin Fagan*
Circulation 50,000
ESTABLISHED 1994. MONTHLY finance magazine.
Features All issues relating to personal finance, particularly investment, insurance, banking, mortgages, savings, borrowing, health care and pensions. No corporate articles or personnel issues. Write to the editor with ideas in the first instance. No unsolicited mss. *Payment* £200 per 1000 words.
News All items written in-house.

The Philosopher
Centre for Lifelong Learning, Newcastle University, Newcastle upon Tyne NE1 7RU
Website www.philsoc.freeserve.co.uk
Owner *The Philosophical Society*
Editor *Martin Cohen*
FOUNDED 1913. BIANNUAL journal of the Philosophical Society of Great Britain with an international readership made up of members, libraries and specialist booksellers. Wide range of interests, but leaning towards articles that present philosophical investigation which is relevant to the individual and to society in our modern era. Accessible to the non-specialist. Will consider articles and book reviews. Notes for Contributors available; send s.a.e. or see website.
As well as short philosophical papers, will accept:
News about lectures, conventions, philosophy groups. Ethical issues in the news. Maximum 1000 words.
Reviews of philosophy books (maximum 600 words); discussion articles of individual philosophers and their published works (maximum 2000 words).

Miscellaneous items, including graphics, of philosophical interest and/or merit.
Payment free copies.

Piano
241 Shaftesbury Avenue, London WC2H 8TF
☎020 7333 1724 Fax 020 7333 1736
Email pianomagazine@mail.com
Website www.rhinegold.co.uk
Owner *Rhinegold Publishing*
Editor *Jeremy Siepmann*
Deputy Editor *Joanna Sallnow*
Circulation 11,000

FOUNDED 1993. BI-MONTHLY magazine containing features, profiles, technical information, news, reviews of interest to those with a serious amateur or professional concern with pianos or their playing. No unsolicited material. Approach with ideas in writing only.

Picture Postcard Monthly
15 Debdale Lane, Keyworth, Nottingham NG12 5HT
☎0115 937 4079 Fax 0115 937 6197
Email reflections@argonet.co.uk
Website www.postcardcollecting.co.uk
Owners *Brian & Mary Lund*
Editor *Brian Lund*
Circulation 4000

FOUNDED 1978. MONTHLY. News, views, clubs, diary of fairs, sales, auctions, and well-researched postcard-related articles. Might be interested in general articles supported by postcards. Unsolicited mss welcome. Approach by phone or in writing with ideas.

Pilot
The Clock House, 28 Old Town, Clapham, London SW4 0LB
☎020 7498 2506 Fax 020 7498 6920
Email pilotmagazine@compuserve.com
Website www.pilotweb.co.uk
Publisher *Market Link Publishing Ltd*
Editor *Philip Whiteman*
Circulation 25,048

FOUNDED 1968. MONTHLY magazine for private plane pilots. No staff writers; the entire magazine is written by freelancers – mostly regulars. Unsolicited mss welcome but ideas in writing preferred. Perusal of any issue of the magazine will reveal the type of material bought. 700 words of 'Advice to would-be contributors' sent on receipt of s.a.e. (mark envelope 'Advice').

Features *Philip Whiteman* Many articles are unsolicited personal experiences/travel accounts from pilots of private planes; good photo coverage is very important. Maximum 5000 words. *Payment* £100–700 (first rights). Photos £30–120 each.

News *Mike Jerram* Contributions need to be as short as possible. See *Pilot Notes* and *Old-Timers* in the magazine.

Pink Paper
2nd Floor, Medius House, 63–69 New Oxford Street, London WC1A 1DG
☎020 7845 4300 Fax 020 7845 4309
Email editorial@pinkpaper.co.uk
Editor *Tristan Reid-Smith*
Circulation 55,000

FOUNDED 1987. WEEKLY. Only national newspaper for lesbians and gay men covering politics, social issues, health, the arts and all areas of concern to lesbian/gay people. Unsolicited mss welcome. Initial approach by post with an idea preferred. Interested in profiles, reviews, in-depth features and short news pieces.
Payment by arrangement.

Planet: The Welsh Internationalist
See **Planet** under **Small Presses**

PN Review
See under **Poetry Magazines**

Poetry Ireland Review
See under **Poetry Magazines**

Poetry Review
See under **Poetry Magazines**

Poetry Scotland
See under **Poetry Magazines**

Poetry Wales
See under **Poetry Magazines**

Pony
D.J. Murphy (Publishers) Ltd, Haslemere House, Lower Street, Haslemere, Surrey GU27 2PE
☎01428 651551 Fax 01428 653888
Email pony@djmurphy.co.uk (text only)
Website www.ponymag.com
Owner *D.J. Murphy (Publishers) Ltd*
Editor *Janet Rising*
Assistant Editor *Zoe Cannon*
Circulation 32,114

FOUNDED 1948. Lively MONTHLY aimed at 10–16-year-olds. News, instruction on riding, stable management, veterinary care, interviews. Approach in writing with an idea.

Features welcome. Maximum 900 words.
News Written in-house. Photographs and illustrations (serious/cartoon) welcome.
Payment £65 per 1000 words.

Popular Crafts

Nexus House, Azalea Drive, Swanley, Kent BR8 8HU
☎01322 660070 Fax 01322 616319
Email debbie.moss@nexusmedia.com
Website www.popularcrafts.com
Owner *Highbury-Nexus*
Editor *Debbie Moss*
Circulation 32,000

FOUNDED 1980. MONTHLY. Covers crafts of all kinds. Freelance contributions welcome – copy needs to be lively and interesting. Approach in writing with an outline of idea and photographs.
Features Project-based under the following headings: Homecraft; Needlecraft; Popular Craft; Kidscraft; News and Columns. Any craft-related material including projects to make, with full instructions/patterns supplied in all cases; profiles of crafts people and news of craft group activities or successes by individual persons; articles on collecting crafts; personal experiences and anecdotes.
Payment on publication.

PR Week

174 Hammersmith Road, London W6 7JP
☎020 8267 4429 Fax 020 8267 4509
Website www.prweekuk.com
Owner *Haymarket Business Publications Ltd*
Editor *Kate Nicholas*
Circulation 18,200

FOUNDED 1984. WEEKLY. Contributions accepted from experienced journalists. Approach in writing with an idea.
News *Gidon Freeman*
Payment negotiable.

Practical Boat Owner

Westover House, West Quay Road, Poole, Dorset BH15 1JG
☎01202 440820 Fax 01202 440860
Website www.pbo.co.uk
Owner *IPC Media*
Editor *Rodger Witt*
Circulation 52,800

FOUNDED 1967. MONTHLY magazine of practical information for cruising boat owners. Receives about 1500 mss per year. Interested in hard facts about gear, equipment, pilotage and renovation, etc. from experienced yachtsmen.
Features Technical articles about main-tenance, restoration, modifications to cruising boats, power and sail up to 45ft, or reader reports on gear and equipment. European pilotage articles and cruising guides. Approach in writing with synopsis in the first instance.
Payment negotiable.

Practical Caravan

60 Waldegrave Road, Teddington, Middlesex TW11 8LG
☎020 8267 5629 Fax 020 8267 5725
Email practical.caravan@haynet.com
Website www.practicalcaravan.com
Owner *Haymarket Magazines Ltd*
Editor *Carl Rodgerson*
Circulation 47,037

FOUNDED 1967. MONTHLY. Contains caravan reviews, travel features, investigations, products, park reviews. Unsolicited mss welcome on travel relevant only to caravanning/touring vans. No motorcaravan or static van stories. Approach with ideas by phone or letter.
Features Must refer to caravanning, towing. Written in friendly, chatty manner. Features with pictures/transparencies welcome but not essential. Maximum length 2000 words.
Payment negotiable.

Practical Fishkeeping

Bretton Court, Bretton, Peterborough, Cambridgeshire PE3 8DZ
☎01733 264666 Fax 01733 465246
Email steve.windsor@ecm.emap.com
Owner *Emap Active Publications Ltd*
Editor *Karen Youngs*
Circulation 25,000

MONTHLY. Practical articles on all aspects of fishkeeping. Unsolicited mss welcome. Approach in writing with ideas. Quality photographs of fish always welcome. No fiction or verse.

Practical Gardening

See **Garden Answers**

Practical Parenting

IPC Media Ltd., King's Reach Tower, Stamford Street, London SE1 9LS
☎020 7261 5058 Fax 020 7261 6542
Owner *IPC Media*
Editor-in-Chief *Jayne Marsden*
Circulation 56,501

FOUNDED 1987. MONTHLY. Practical advice on pregnancy, birth, babycare and childcare, 0–3 years. Submit ideas in writing with synopsis or send mss on spec. Interested in feature articles of up to 3000 words in length, and in

readers' experiences/personal viewpoint pieces of between 750–1000 words. All material must be written for the magazine's specifically targeted audience and in-house style.
Payment negotiable.

Practical Photography
Bretton Court, Bretton, Peterborough, Cambridgeshire PE3 8DZ
☎01733 264666 Fax 01733 465246
Email practical.photography@emap.com
Owner *Emap Active Publications Ltd*
Editor *William Cheung*
Circulation 77,654

THIRTEEN ISSUES YEARLY All types of photography, particularly technique-orientated pictures. No unsolicited mss. Preliminary approach may be made by telephone. Always interested in new ideas.
Features Anything relevant to the world of photography, but not 'the sort of feature produced by staff writers'. Features on technology and humour are two areas worth exploring. Bear in mind that there is a three-month lead-in time. Maximum 2000 words.
News Only 'hot' news applicable to a monthly magazine. Maximum 400 words.
Payment varies.

Practical Wireless
Arrowsmith Court, Station Approach, Broadstone, Dorset BH18 8PW
☎01202 659910 Fax 01202 659950
Email <name>@pwpublishing.ltd.uk
Website www.pwpublishing.ltd.uk
Owner *P.W. Publishing*
Editor *Rob Mannion*
Circulation 20,000

FOUNDED 1932. MONTHLY. News and features relating to amateur radio, radio construction and radio communications. Unsolicited mss welcome. Author's guidelines available (send s.a.e.). Approach by phone with ideas in the first instance. Copy should be supported where possible by artwork, either illustrations, diagrams or photographs.
Payment £54–70 per page.

Practical Woodworking
Nexus Media, Nexus House, Azalea Drive, Swanley, Kent BR8 8HU
☎01322 660070 Fax 01332 616319
Email practical.woodworking@ nexusmedia.com
Owner *Nexus Media Ltd*
Editor *Mark Chisholm*

FOUNDED 1965. MONTHLY. Contains articles relating to woodworking – projects, techniques, new products, tips, letters, etc. Unsolicited mss welcome. No fiction. Approach with ideas in writing or by phone.
Features Projects, techniques, etc. *Payment* £60–75 per published page.

Prediction
Focus House, Dingwall Avenue, Croydon, Surrey CR9 2TA
☎020 8774 0600 Fax 020 8774 0939
Owner *IPC Media*
Editor *To be appointed*
Circulation 35,000

FOUNDED 1936. MONTHLY. Covering astrology and occult-related topics. Unsolicited material in these areas welcome (about 200–300 mss received every year). Writers' guidelines available on request.
Astrology Pieces should be practical and of general interest. Charts and astro data should accompany them, especially if profiles.
Features Articles on mysteries of the earth, alternative medicine, psychical/occult experiences and phenomena are considered.
News & Views Items of interest to readership welcome. Maximum 300 words.

Pregnancy Magazine
Highbury wViP, 53–79 Highgate Road, London NW5 1TW
☎020 7331 1000 Fax 020 7331 1241
Email dan.bromage@wvip.co.uk
Owner *Highbury wViP*
Editor *Dan Bromage*

BI-MONTHLY magazine for mothers-to-be, giving them the facts they need for successful pregnancy and birth.

Press Gazette
Quantum House, 19 Scarbrook Road, Croydon, Surrey CR9 1LX
☎020 8565 4200 Fax 020 8565 4395
Email pged@qpp.co.uk
Owner *Quantum*
Editor *Philippa Kennedy*
Deputy Editor *Jon Slattery*
Circulation 9500

WEEKLY magazine for all journalists – in regional and national newspapers, magazines, broadcasting, and online – containing news, features and analysis of all areas of journalism, print and broadcasting. Unsolicited mss welcome; interested in profiles of magazines, broadcasting companies and news agencies, personality profiles, technical and current affairs relating to the world of journalism. Approach with ideas by phone, e-mail, fax or in writing.

Pride

Hamilton House, 55 Battersea Bridge Road, London SW11 3AX
☎020 7228 3110 Fax 020 7228 3129

Owner Carl Cushnie Junior
Editor To be appointed
Circulation 36,000

FOUNDED 1991. MONTHLY lifestyle magazine for Black women with features, beauty, arts and fashion. No unsolicited material; approach in writing with ideas.

Features Issues pertaining to the Black community. 'Ideas and solicited mss are welcomed from new freelancers.' Maximum 2000 words. **Fiction** Publishes the occasional short story. Unsolicited mss welcome. Maximum 3000 words. **Beauty** Freelancers used for short features. Maximum 1000 words.

Prima

National Magazine House, 72 Broadwick Street, London W1F 9EP
☎020 7439 5000
Email prima@natmags.co.uk
Website www.natmags.co.uk

Owner National Magazine Company
Editor Maire Fahey
Circulation 380,181

FOUNDED 1986. MONTHLY women's magazine.

Features Coordinator Verity Watkins Mostly practical and written by specialists, or commissioned from known freelancers. Unsolicited mss not welcome.

Private Eye

6 Carlisle Street, London W1D 3BN
☎020 7437 4017 Fax 020 7437 0705
Email strobes@private-eye.co.uk

Owner Pressdram
Editor Ian Hislop
Circulation 188,081

FOUNDED 1961. FORTNIGHTLY satirical and investigative magazine. Prospective contributors are best advised to approach the editor in writing. News stories and feature ideas are always welcome, as are cartoons. All jokes written in-house.

Payment in all cases is 'not great', and length of piece varies as appropriate.

Prospect

4 Bedford Square, London WC1B 3RD
☎020 7255 1281 Fax 020 7255 1279
Email editorial@prospect-magazine.co.uk *or* publishing@prospect-magazine.co.uk
Website www.prospect-magazine.co.uk

Owner Prospect Publishing Limited
Editor David Goodhart
Circulation 18,165

FOUNDED 1995. MONTHLY. Essays, reviews and research on current/international affairs and cultural issues. No news features. Unsolicited contributions welcome, although more useful to approach in writing with ideas in the first instance.

Psychic News

The Coach House, Stansted Hall, Stansted, Essex CM24 8UD
☎01279 817050 Fax 01279 817051
Email pn@snu.org.uk
Website www.snu.org.uk

Owner Psychic Press 1995 Ltd
Editor Lyn Guest de Swarte
Circulation 40,000

FOUNDED 1932. *Psychic News* is the world's only WEEKLY spiritualist newspaper. It covers subjects such as psychic research, hauntings, ghosts, poltergeists, spiritual healing, survival after death, and paranormal gifts. Unsolicited material considered.

Publishing News

39 Store Street, London WC1E 7DS
☎020 7692 2900 Fax 020 7419 2111
Email mailbox@publishingnews.co.uk
Website www.publishingnews.co.uk

Editor Jane Ellis

WEEKLY newspaper of the book trade. Hardback and paperback reviews and extensive listings of new paperbacks and hardbacks. Interviews with leading personalities in the trade, authors, agents and features on specialist book areas.

Punch

Suite 5, 3 Hans Crescent, London SW1X 0LN
☎020 7225 6716 Fax 020 7225 6845
Email edit@punch.co.uk
Website www.punch.co.uk

Owner Liberty Publishing
Editor Richard Brass

FOUNDED in 1841 and RELAUNCHED in 1996. BI-WEEKLY investigative and gossip magazine. Ideas are welcome but telephone in the first instance. *Payment* negotiable.

Q

Mappin House, 4 Winsley Street, London
W1W 8HF
☎020 7436 1515 Fax 020 7312 8247
Website www.q4music.com

Owner *Emap Performance*
Editor *Danny Eccleston*
Circulation 200,636

FOUNDED 1986. THIRTEEN ISSUES YEARLY.
Glossy aimed at educated popular music enthusiasts of all ages. Few opportunities for freelance writers. Unsolicited mss are strongly discouraged. Prospective contributors should approach in writing only.

Q-News, The Muslim Magazine

Dexion House, 2–4 Empire Way, Wembley,
Middlesex HA9 0EF
☎020 7262 3287 Fax 020 8903 0820
Email info@q-news.com
Website www.q-news.com

Owner *Fuad Namdi*
Editor *Shagufta Yaqub*
Circulation 15,000

FOUNDED 1992. MONTHLY British Muslim community magazine covering news, features, current affairs. Regular health column, film/book/events reviews, Islamic religious/spiritual articles, art, culture, civilisation, history, etc. Interested in hearing from specialists on issues affecting the Muslim community, local/regional news and analysis.
    Features *Shagufta Yaqub* 'Writers wishing to focus on areas of interest to our readership will gain access and credibility among the relevant people.' 3000 words maximum. **News** *Fareena Alam* Analysis on news and current affairs – alternative rather than mainstream viewpoint preferred. 2000 words maximum. **Fiction** *Shagufta Yaqub* 'An area we would like to develop. The right person could use this opportunity as a launch pad into their career.' 2000 words maximum. Approach by e-mail.
    Payment None.

Quartos Magazine

See **The New Writer**

QWF Magazine

PO Box 1768, Rugby CV21 4ZA
☎01788 334302 Fax 01788 334702
Email jo@qwfmagazine.co.uk
Website www.qwfmagazine.co.uk

Editor *Jo Good*

BI-MONTHLY small press magazine. FOUNDED in 1994, as a showcase for the best in women's short story writing – original and thought-provoking. Only considers stories that are previously unpublished and of less than 4000 words; articles must be less than 1000 words and of interest to the writer. Include covering letter, s.a.e. and brief biography with mss. Also runs script appraisal service and regular short story competitions. For further information and detailed guidelines for contributors, contact the editor at the address above or access the website.

Racecar Engineering

Focus House, Dingwall Avenue, Croydon
CR9 2TA
☎020 8774 0946 Fax 020 8774 0935
Email racecar@ipcmedia.com

Owner *IPC Media*
Editor *Charles Armstrong-Wilson*
Circulation 15,000

FOUNDED 1990. MONTHLY. In-depth features on motorsport technology plus news and products. Interested in receiving news and features from freelancers. **Features** Informed insight into current motorsport technology. 3000 words maximum. **News** New cars, products or business news relevant to motorsport. No items on road cars or racing drivers. 500 words maximum. Call or e-mail to discuss proposal.

Racing Post (incorporating **The Sporting Life**)

1 Canada Square, Canary Wharf, London
E14 5AP
☎020 7293 3000 Fax 020 7293 3758
Email editor@racingpost.co.uk
Website www.racingpost.co.uk

Owner *Trinity Mirror Plc*
Editor *Chris Smith*

FOUNDED 1986. DAILY horse racing paper with some general sport. In 1998, following an agreement between the owners of *The Sporting Life* and the *Racing Post*, the two papers merged.

Radio Times

80 Wood Lane, London W12 0TT
☎020 8433 3400 Fax 020 8433 3160
Email radio.times@bbc.co.uk
Website www.radiotimes.com

Owner *BBC Worldwide Limited*
Acting Editor *Liz Vercoe*
Circulation 1.2 million

WEEKLY. UK's leading broadcast listings magazine. The majority of material is provided by freelance and retained writers, but the topical-

ity of the pieces means close consultation with editors is essential. Very unlikely to use unsolicited material. Detailed BBC, ITV, Channel 4, Channel 5 and satellite television and radio listings are accompanied by feature material relevant to the week's output.
Payment by arrangement.

Rail

Bretton Court, Bretton, Peterborough, Cambridgeshire PE3 8DZ
☎01733 264666 Fax 01733 282720

Owner *Emap Active Publications Ltd*
Managing Editor *Nigel Harris*
Circulation 33,000

FOUNDED 1981. FORTNIGHTLY magazine dedicated to modern railway. News and features, and topical newsworthy events. Unsolicited mss welcome. Approach by phone with ideas. Not interested in personal journey reminiscences. No fiction.
Features By arrangement with the editor. All modern railway British subjects considered. Maximum 2000 words. *Payment* varies/negotiable.
News Any news item welcome. Maximum 500 words. *Payment* varies (up to £100 per 1000 words).

Railway Gazette International

Quadrant House, Sutton, Surrey SM2 5AS
☎020 8652 8608 Fax 020 8652 3738
Website www.railwaygazette.com

Owner *Reed Business Information*
Editor *Murray Hughes*

FOUNDED 1835. MONTHLY magazine written for senior railway managers and engineers worldwide. 'No material for railway enthusiast publications.' Telephone to discuss ideas in the first instance.

The Railway Magazine

IPC Media Ltd., King's Reach Tower, Stamford Street, London SE1 9LS
☎020 7261 5533/5821 Fax 020 7261 5269
Email railway@ipcmedia.com
Website www.ipcmedia.com

Owner *IPC Media*
Editor *Nick Pigott*
Circulation 33,132

FOUNDED 1897. MONTHLY. Articles, photos and short news stories of a topical nature, covering modern railways, steam preservation and railway history, welcome. Maximum 2000 words, with sketch maps of routes, etc., where

appropriate. Unsolicited mss welcome. No poetry.
Payment negotiable.

The Rambler

2nd Floor, Camelford House, 87–90 Albert Embankment, London SE1 7TW
☎020 7339 8500 Fax 020 7339 8501
Email ramblers@london.ramblers.org.uk

Owner *Ramblers' Association*
Editor *Christopher Sparrow*
Circulation 130,000

QUARTERLY. Official magazine of the Ramblers' Association, available to members only. Unsolicited mss welcome. S.a.e. required for return.
Features Freelance features are invited on any aspect of walking in Britain. Length 450–650 words, preferably with good photographs. No general travel articles.

Reader's Digest

11 Westferry Circus, Canary Wharf, London E14 4HE
☎020 7715 8000 Fax 020 7715 8716
Website www.readersdigest.co.uk

Owner *Reader's Digest Association Ltd*
Editor-in-Chief *To be appointed*
Circulation 1.01 million

Although in theory, a good market for general interest features of around 2500 words very few are ever accepted. However, 'a tiny proportion' comes from freelance writers, all of which are specially commissioned. Toughening up its image with a move into investigative journalism. Opportunities exist for short humorous contributions to regular features – 'Life's Like That', 'Humour in Uniform'. Issues a helpful booklet called 'Writing for Reader's Digest', available by post at £4.50.
Payment up to £200.

The Reader

English Department, University of Liverpool, Liverpool L69 7ZR
Email readers@thereader.co.uk
Website www.thereader.co.uk

Editor *Jane Davis*
Circulation 1200

FOUNDED 1997. BIANNUAL. Poetry, short fiction, literary articles and essays, thought, reviews, recommendations. Contributions from internationally lauded and new voices. Welcomes articles/essays about reading, maximum 2000 words. *Payment* up to £50. Recommendations for good reading, maximum 1000 words.

Payment £30 approx. Short stories, maximum 2500 words. *Payment* £50 approx. No theoretical style literary discourses. Approach in writing.

Record Collector

43–45 St Mary's Road, Ealing, London W5 5RQ
☎020 8579 1082 Fax 020 8566 2024
Email editor@rcmag.demon.co.uk
Managing Editor *Peter Doggett*
Editor *Andy Davis*

FOUNDED 1979. MONTHLY. Detailed, well-researched articles welcome on any aspect of record collecting or any collectable artist in the field of popular music (1950s–1990s), with complete discographies where appropriate. Unsolicited mss welcome. Approach with ideas by phone.
Payment negotiable.

Red

Endeavour House, 189 Shaftesbury Avenue, London WC2H 8JG
☎020 7208 3358 Fax 020 7208 3218
Email ruth.adams@emap.com
Website www.redmagazine.co.uk
Owner *Emap élan Network Ltd*
Editor *Trish Halpin*
Circulation 173,774

FOUNDED 1998. MONTHLY magazine aimed at the 30-something woman. Will consider ideas sent in 'on spec' but tends to rely on regular contributors.

Report

ATL, 7 Northumberland Street, London WC2N 5DA
☎020 7930 6441 Fax 020 7782 1618
Owner *Association of Teachers and Lecturers*
Editor *Heather Pinnell*
Circulation 160,000

FOUNDED 1978. EIGHT ISSUES YEARLY during academic terms. Contributions welcome. All submissions should go directly to the editor. Articles should be no more than 800 words and must be of practical interest to the classroom teacher and F.E. lecturers.

Right Now!

PO Box 2085, London W1A 5SX
☎0845 601 3243 Fax 0845 601 3243
Email rightnow@compuserve.com
Website www.right-now.org
Owner *Right Now! Press Ltd*
Editor *Derek Turner*

Circulation 3000

FOUNDED 1993. QUARTERLY far right-wing conservative commentary. Welcomes well-documented disputations, news stories and features about British heritage ('the more politically incorrect, the better!'). No fiction or poems. Initial approach in writing.
No payment.

Rugby World

IPC Media Ltd., 23rd Floor, King's Reach Tower, Stamford Street, London SE1 9LS
☎020 7261 6830 Fax 020 7261 5419
Website www.rugbyworld.com
Owner *IPC Media*
Editor *Paul Morgan*
Circulation 38,500

FOUNDED 1960. MONTHLY. Features of special rugby interest only. Unsolicited contributions welcome but s.a.e. essential for return of material. Prior approach by phone or in writing preferred.

Runner's World

7–10 Chandos Street, London W1M 0AD
☎020 7291 6000 Fax 020 7291 6080
Email rwedit@rodale.co.uk
Website www.runnersworld.co.uk
Owner *Rodale Press*
Editor *Steven Seaton*
Circulation 53,164

FOUNDED 1979. MONTHLY magazine giving practical advice on all areas of distance running including products and training, travel features, news and cross-training advice. Personal running-related articles, famous people who run or off-beat travel articles are welcome. No elite athlete or training articles. Approach with ideas in writing in the first instance.

Running Fitness

2nd Floor, Arcade Chambers, Westgate Arcade, Peterborough, Cambridgeshire PE1 1PY
☎01733 347559 Fax 01733 352749
Owner *Kelsey Publishing*
Editor *Paul Larkins*
Circulation 26,000

FOUNDED 1985. MONTHLY. Instructional articles on running, fitness, and lifestyle, plus running-related activities and health.
Features Specialist knowledge an advantage. Opportunities are wide, but approach with ideas in first instance.
News Opportunities for people stories, especially if backed up by photographs.

Sable

See **SAKS Publications** under **Small Presses**

Safeway The Magazine

Redwood, 7 Saint Martin's Place, London WC2N 4HA
☎020 7747 0788 Fax 020 7747 0799
Editor *Julie Barton Breck*
Circulation 1.8 million

FOUNDED 1996. MONTHLY in-store magazine covering food and recipes, beauty, health, shopping, gardens, travel and features. Regular freelancers are employed and although outside material is rarely used ideas will be considered for beauty, health, travel and features. Approach in writing in the first instance.

Saga Magazine

Saga Publishing, Embrook, Sandgate, Kent CT20 3SE
☎01303 771523 Fax 01303 776699
Website www.saga.co.uk
Owner *Saga Publishing Ltd*
Editor *Emma Soames*
Circulation 1.17 million

FOUNDED 1984. MONTHLY magazine that sets out to celebrate the role of older people in society, reflecting their achievements, promoting their skills, protecting their interests, and campaigning on their behalf. A warm personal approach, addressing the readership in an up-beat and positive manner, required. It has a hard core of celebrated commentators/writers (e.g. Clement Freud, Keith Waterhouse) as regular contributors. Articles mostly commissioned or written in-house but exclusive celebrity interviews welcome if appropriate/relevant. Length 1000–1200 words (maximum 1600).

Sailing Today

4 Chapel Row, Bath BA1 1HN
☎01225 470074 Fax 01225 313325
Email feedback@sailingtoday.co.uk
Owner *Madforsport Ltd*
Editor *John Goode*

FOUNDED 1997. MONTHLY practical magazine for cruising sailors. *Sailing Today* covers owning and buying a boat, equipment and products for sailing and is about improving readers' skills, boat maintenance and product tests. Most articles are commissioned but will consider practical features and cruise stories with photos. Approach by telephone or in writing in the first instance.

Sailing with Spirit

4 South View, Nether Heyford, Northampton NN7 3NH
☎01327 342566
Email sws@onlinehealing.org
Website www.onlinehealing.org/sws/
Editor *Keith Beasley*
Circulation 2000

FOUNDED 1996. QUARTERLY holistic magazine for Northamptonshire. Contributors must have local connections and expertise or first-hand experience in matters spiritual, organic or 'green'.

Sainsbury's The Magazine

20 Upper Ground, London SE1 9PD
☎020 7633 0266 Fax 020 7401 9423
Owner *New Crane Publishing*
Editor *Sue Robinson*
Consultant Food Editor *Delia Smith*
Circulation 361,609

FOUNDED 1993. MONTHLY featuring a main core of food and cookery with features, health, beauty, fashion, home, gardening and news. No unsolicited mss. Approach in writing with ideas only in the first instance.

The Salisbury Review

33 Canonbury Park South, London N1 2JW
☎020 7226 7791 Fax 020 7354 0383
Email salisbury-review@easynet.co.uk
Website easyweb.easynet.co.uk/~salisbury-review
Editor *A.D. Harvey*
Managing Editor *Merrie Cave*
Consulting Editors *Roger Scruton, Sir Richard Body, Dennis O'Keeffe*
Circulation 1700

FOUNDED 1982. QUARTERLY magazine of conservative thought. Editorials and features from a right-wing viewpoint. Unsolicited material welcome.
   Features Maximum 4000 words.
   Reviews Maximum 1000 words.
   No payment.
   company:Scotland on Sunday Magazine
See under **National Newspapers (Scotland on Sunday)**

The Scots Magazine

D.C. Thomson & Co., 2 Albert Square, Dundee DD1 9QJ
☎01382 223131 Fax 01382 322214
Email mail@scotsmagazine.com
Website www.scotsmagazine.com

Owner *D.C. Thomson & Co. Ltd*
Editor *John Methven*
Circulation 55,000

FOUNDED 1739. MONTHLY. Covers a wide field of Scottish interests ranging from personalities to wildlife, climbing, reminiscence, history and folklore. Outside contributions welcome; 'staff delighted to discuss in advance by letter or e-mail'.

The Scottish Farmer

SMG Magazines, 200 Renfield Street, Glasgow G2 3PR
☎0141 302 7700 Fax 0141 302 7799
Email news.sf@smg.plc.uk

Owner *SMG Magazines*
Editor *Alasdair Fletcher*
Circulation 22,000

FOUNDED 1893. WEEKLY. Farmer's magazine covering most aspects of Scottish agriculture. Unsolicited mss welcome. Approach with ideas in writing.
   Features *Alasdair Fletcher* Technical articles on agriculture or farming units. 1000–2000 words.
   News *John Duckworth* Factual news about farming developments, political, personal and technological. Maximum 800 words.
   Weekend Family Pages Rural and craft topics.

Scottish Field

Special Publications, Royston House, Caroline Park, Edinburgh EH5 1QJ
☎0131 551 2942 Fax 0131 551 2938
Email editor@scottishfield.co.uk

Owner *Oban Times*
Editor *Archie Mackenzie*

FOUNDED 1903. MONTHLY. Scotland's quality lifestyle magazine. Unsolicited mss welcome but writers should study the magazine first.
   Features Articles of general interest on Scotland and Scots abroad with good photographs or, preferably, colour slides. Approx 1000 words.
   Payment negotiable.

Scottish Home & Country

42A Heriot Row, Edinburgh EH3 6ES
☎0131 225 1724 Fax 0131 225 8129
Email magazine@swri.demon.co.uk

Owner *Scottish Women's Rural Institutes*
Editor *Liz Ferguson*
Circulation 12,000

FOUNDED 1924. MONTHLY. Scottish or rural-related issues, health, travel and general interest. Unsolicited mss welcome. Commissions are rare and tend to go to established contributors only.

Scottish Rugby Magazine

First Press Publishing, 1 Central Quay, Glasgow G3 8DA
☎0141 309 1400 Fax 0141 248 1099
Email editor@scottishrugby.co.uk

Senior Editor *Alex Macleod*
Circulation 19,200

FOUNDED 1990. MONTHLY. Features, club profiles, etc. Approach in writing with ideas.

ScottishGolf

ScottishGolf, Gateway East, Technology Park, Dundee DD2 1SW
☎01382 429064 Fax 01382 429001

Owner *ScottishGolf*
Editor *Martin Vousden*
Circulation 40,000

FOUNDED mid-1980s. MONTHLY. Features and results, in particular the men's events. No unsolicited mss. Approach in writing with ideas.

Scouting Magazine

Gilwell House, Gilwell Park, Chingford, London E4 7QW
☎020 8433 7100 Fax 020 8433 7103

Owner *The Scout Association*
Editor *Anna Sorensen*
Circulation 20,000

MONTHLY magazine for adults connected to or interested in the Scout Movement. Interested in Scouting-related submissions only.
   Payment by negotiation.

Screen

Gilmorehill Centre for Theatre, Film and Television, University of Glasgow, Glasgow G12 8QQ
☎0141 330 5035 Fax 0141 330 3515
Email screen@arts.gla.ac.uk
Website www.screen.arts.gla.ac.uk

Publisher *Oxford University Press*
Editors *Annette Kuhn, John Caughie, Simon Frith, Karen Lury, Jackie Stacey, Sarah Street*
Editorial Assistant *Caroline Beven*
Circulation 1200

QUARTERLY refereed academic journal of film and television studies for a readership ranging from undergraduates to screen studies academics and media professionals. There are no specific qualifications for acceptance of articles.

Straightforward film reviews are not normally published. Check the magazine's style and market in the first instance.

Screen International

33–39 Bowling Green Lane, London EC1R 0DA
☎020 7505 8056 Fax 020 7505 8117
Website www.screendaily.com
Owner *Emap Communications*
Managing Editor *Leo Barraclough*

International trade paper of the film, video and television industries. Expert freelance writers are occasionally used in all areas. No unsolicited mss. Approach with ideas in writing.
Features *Louise Tutt*
Payment negotiable on NUJ basis.

Screentrade Magazine

Screentrade Media, PO Box 144, Orpington, Kent BR6 6LZ
☎01689 833117 Fax 01689 833117
Email philip45other@yahoo.co.uk
Owner *Screentrade Media*
Editor *Philip Turner*
Circulation 3000+

FOUNDED 2002. QUARTERLY journal for British and European film distributors and exhibitors. Interested in items on cinema projection in its various forms, cinema building history, nostalgia, showmanship, book reviews, managerial matters, wry observations on the industry. Also film and producer/director retrospectives. No film reviews or film star interviews. **Features** Most contributions are from within the industry. Items on the state of cinema exhibition, cinema architecture, interviews with key industry personnel sometimes required. 1500–3000 words. **News** Topical items (if substantiated) welcome. Events coverage (e.g. festivals) from an exhibitor's viewpoint preferred.
Payment negotiable.

Scriptwriter Magazine

2 Elliott Square, London NW3 3SU
☎020 7586 4853 Fax 020 7586 4853
Email julian@scriptwritermagazine.com
Website www.scriptwritermagazine.com
Owner *Scriptease Ltd*
Editor *Julian Friedmann*
Circulation 1500

LAUNCHED November 2001. Six issues per year. Magazine for professional scriptwriters covering all aspects of the craft and business of writing for the small and large screen.

Interested in serious, in-depth analysis; maximum 1500–3500 words. E-mail with synopsis sample material and c.v. *Payment* £20 per 1000 words.

Sea Breezes

Units 28–30, Spring Valley Industrial Estate, Braddan, Isle of Man IM2 2QS
☎01624 626018 Fax 01624 661655
Email seabreezes@manninmedia.co.im
Website www.manninmedia.co.im
Owner *Print Centres*
Editor *Captain A.C. Douglas*
Circulation 15,000

FOUNDED 1919. MONTHLY. Covers virtually everything relating to ships and seamen. Unsolicited mss welcome; they should be thoroughly researched and accompanied by relevant photographs. No fiction, poetry, or anything which 'smacks of the romance of the sea'.
Features Factual tales of ships, seamen and the sea, Royal or Merchant Navy, sail or power, nautical history, shipping company histories, epic voyages, etc. Length 1000–4000 words. 'The most readily acceptable work will be that which shows it is clearly the result of first-hand experience or the product of extensive and accurate research.'
Payment £14 per page (about 800 words).

She Kicks

The Design Works, William Street, Gateshead, Tyne and Wear NE10 0JP
☎0191 420 8383 Fax 0191 420 4950
Website www.shekicks.net
Editor *Jennifer O'Neill*
Circulation 30,000

FOUNDED 1996. BI-MONTHLY. The only magazine for women football players. Contributions welcome.
Features *Jennifer O'Neill* International reports, player and team profiles, diet, health and fitness, tactics, training advice, play improvement, fund-raising. 1500 words maximum.
News *Wilf Frith* Match reports, team news, transfers, injuries, results and fixtures. 600 words maximum.
Payment negotiable.

She Magazine

National Magazine House, 72 Broadwick Street, London W1F 9EP
☎020 7439 5000 Fax 020 7312 3981
Owner *National Magazine Co. Ltd*
Editor *Eve Cameron*

Circulation 176,183

Glossy MONTHLY for the thirty-something woman, addressing her needs as an individual, a partner and a parent. Talks to its readers in an intelligent, humorous and sympathetic way. Features should be about 1200 words long. Approach with ideas in writing. No unsolicited material.
Payment negotiable.

Ships Monthly

IPC Country & Leisure Media Ltd, 222 Branston Road, Burton-upon-Trent, Staffordshire DE14 3BT
☎01283 542721 Fax 01283 546436
Email shipsmonthly@ipcmedia.com
Owner *IPC Country & Leisure Media Ltd*
Editor *Iain Wakefield*
Circulation 22,000

FOUNDED 1966. MONTHLY A4 format magazine for ship enthusiasts. News, photographs and illustrated articles on all kinds of ships – mercantile and naval, sail and steam, past and present. No yachting. Most articles are commissioned; prospective contributors should telephone in the first instance.

Shoot Monthly Magazine

IPC Media Ltd., King's Reach Tower, Stamford Street, London SE1 9LS
☎020 7261 6287 Fax 020 7261 6019
Email shoot@ipcmedia.com
Owner *IPC Media*
Editor *Colin Mitchell*
Circulation 22,318

FOUNDED 1969. MONTHLY football magazine. No unsolicited mss. Present ideas for news, features or colour photo-features to the editor by letter or e-mail.
Features Hard-hitting, topical and off-beat.
News Items welcome, especially exclusive gossip and transfer speculation.
Payment negotiable.

Shooting Times & Country Magazine

IPC Media Ltd., King's Reach Tower, Stamford Street, London SE1 9LS
☎020 7261 6180 Fax 020 7261 7179
Owner *IPC Media*
Editor *Robert Gray*
Circulation 27,040

FOUNDED 1882. WEEKLY. Covers shooting, fishing and related countryside topics. Unsolicited mss considered. *Payment* negotiable.

Shout Magazine

D.C. Thomson & Co., Albert Square, Dundee, Tayside DD1 9QJ
☎01382 223131 Fax 01382 200880
Email shout@dcthomson.co.uk
Owner *D.C. Thomson Publishers*
Editor *Maria T. Welch*
Circulation 111,069

FOUNDED 1993. FORTNIGHTLY. Pop music, quizzes, emotional, beauty, fashion, soap features. Welcomes ideas for fiction, horoscope features and quizzes. Queries by telephone welcome.
Fiction *Maria Welch* Supernatural/spooky stories welcome. Maximum 1500 words. *Payment* £100.

Shout!

PO Box YR46, Leeds, West Yorkshire LS9 6XG
☎0113 248 5700 Fax 0113 295 6097
Email shoutmag@cwcom.net
Website www.shoutmag.demon.co.uk
Owner/Editor *Mark Michalowski*
Circulation 7000

FOUNDED 1995. MONTHLY lesbian/gay and bisexual news, views, arts and scene for Yorkshire; lgb health and politics. Interested in reviews of Yorkshire lgb events, happenings, news, analysis – 300 to maximum 1000 words. No fiction, fashion or items with no reasonable relevance to Yorkshire and the north.
Payment £40 per 1000 words.

Shropshire Magazine

77 Wyle Cop, Shrewsbury, Shropshire SY1 1UT
☎01743 362175
Owner *Shropshire Newspapers Ltd*
Editor *Sarah-Jane Smith*

FOUNDED 1950. MONTHLY. Unsolicited mss welcome but ideas in writing preferred.
Features Personalities, topical items, historical (e.g. family) of Shropshire; also general interest: homes, weddings, antiques, etc. Maximum 1000 words.
Payment negotiable 'but modest'.

Sight & Sound

British Film Institute, 21 Stephen Street, London W1T 1LN
☎020 7255 1444 Fax 020 7436 2327
Website www.bfi.org.uk/sightandsound
Owner *British Film Institute*
Editor *Nick James*

FOUNDED 1932. MONTHLY. Topical and critical articles on international cinema, with regular columns from the USA and Europe. Length 1000–5000 words. Relevant photographs appreciated. Also book, film and video release reviews. Unsolicited material welcome. Approach in writing with ideas.

Payment by arrangement.

The Sign

See **Hymns Ancient & Modern Ltd** under **UK Publishers**

Ski and Board

The White House, 57–63 Church Road, Wimbledon, London SW19 5SB
☎020 8410 2000 Fax 020 8410 2001
Email s&b@skiclub.co.uk
Website www.skiclub.co.uk

Owner *Ski Club of Great Britain*
Editor *Arnie Wilson*

FOUNDED 1903. FOUR ISSUES YEARLY. Features from established ski/snowboard writers only.

The Skier and Snowboarder Magazine

Mountain Marketing Ltd., PO Box 386, Sevenoaks, Kent TN13 1AQ
☎0845 310 8303 Fax 01732 779266
Email skierandsnowboarder@hotmail.com

Publisher *Mountain Marketing Ltd*
Editor *Frank Baldwin*
Circulation 20,000

Official magazine to the World Ski and Snowboard Association, UK. SEASONAL. From July to May. FIVE ISSUES YEARLY. Outside contributions welcome.

Features Various topics covered, including race reports, resort reports, fashion, equipment update, dry slope, school news, new products, health and safety. Crisp, tight, informative copy of 800 words or less preferred.

News All aspects of skiing news covered.
Payment negotiable.

Slimming

Greater London House, Hampstead Road, London NW1 7EJ
☎020 7347 1854 Fax 020 7347 1863
Email claire.selsby@emap.com

Owner *Emap Esprit*
Editor *Alison Hall*
Circulation 106,029

FOUNDED 1969. ELEVEN ISSUES YEARLY.

Leading magazine about slimming, diet and health. Opportunities for freelance contributions on general health (diet-related); psychology related to health and fitness; celebrity interviews. It is best to approach with an idea in writing.

Payment negotiable.

Smallholder

Hook House, Wimblington March, Cambridgeshire PE15 0QL
☎01354 741182 Fax 01354 741182
Email hook.house@virgin.net
Website www.smallholder.co.uk

Owner *Newsquest*
Editor *Liz Wright*
Circulation 20,000

FOUNDED 1982. MONTHLY. Outside contributions welcome. Send for sample magazine and editorial schedule before submitting anything. Follow up with samples of work to the editor so that style can be assessed for suitability. No poetry or humorous but unfocused personal tales.

Features New writers always welcome, but must have high level of technical expertise – 'not textbook stuff'. Illustrations and photos welcomed and paid for. Length 750–1500 words.

News All agricultural and rural news welcome. Length 200–500 words.
Payment negotiable ('but modest').

Smash Hits

Mappin House, Winsley Street, London W1W 8HF
☎020 7436 1515 Fax 020 7636 5792
Website www.smashhits.net

Owner *Emap Performance*
Editor *To be appointed*
Circulation 200,212

FOUNDED 1979. FORTNIGHTLY. Top of the mid-teen market. Unsolicited mss are not accepted, but prospective contributors may approach in writing with ideas.

Snooker Scene

Cavalier House, 202 Hagley Road, Edgbaston, Birmingham B16 9PQ
☎0121 454 2931 Fax 0121 452 1822

Owner *Everton's News Agency*
Editor *Clive Everton*
Circulation 16,000

FOUNDED 1971. MONTHLY. No unsolicited mss. Approach in writing with an idea.

Somerset Life Magazine
23 Market Street, Crewkerne, Somerset
TA18 7JU
☎01460 270000 Fax 01460 270022
Owner *Archant*
Managing Editor *Jenny Nicholls*
Circulation 9000

FOUNDED 1991. MONTHLY magazine with features on any subject of interest (historical, geographical, arts, crafts) to people living in Somerset. Length 600–1000 words, preferably with illustrations. Unsolicited mss welcome but initial approach in writing preferred.
Payment negotiable.

The Spectator
56 Doughty Street, London WC1N 2LL
☎020 7405 1706 Fax 020 7242 0603
Email editor@spectator.co.uk
Website www.spectator.co.uk
Owner *The Spectator (1828) Ltd*
Editor *Boris Johnson*
Deputy Editor *Stuart Reid*
Circulation 60,776

FOUNDED 1828. WEEKLY political and literary magazine. Prospective contributors should write in the first instance to the relevant editor. Unsolicited mss welcome, but no 'follow up' phone calls, please.
Books *Mark Amory*
Payment nominal.

The Sporting Life
See **Racing Post**

Springboard – Writing To Succeed
144 Alexandra Road, Great Wakering, Essex
SS3 0GW
☎01702 216247
Email slieberman@tinyonline.co.uk
Owner/Editor *Sandra Lieberman*
Circulation 100

FOUNDED 1990. QUARTERLY. *Springboard* is not a market for writers but a forum from which they can find encouragement and help. Provides articles, news, market information, competition/folio news directed at helping writers to achieve success.

Staffordshire Life
The Publishing Centre, Derby Street, Stafford
ST16 2DT
☎01785 257700 Fax 01785 253287
Email editor@staffordshirelife.co.uk
Owner *The Staffordshire Newsletter*
Editor *Philip Thurlow-Craig*

Circulation 20,000

FOUNDED 1982. ELEVEN ISSUES YEARLY. Full-colour county magazine devoted to Staffordshire, its surroundings and people. Contributions welcome. Approach in writing with ideas.
Features Maximum 1200 words.
Fashion Copy must be supported by photographs.
Payment NUJ rates.

The Stage (incorporating Television Today)
Stage House, 47 Bermondsey Street, London
SE1 3XT
☎020 7403 1818 Fax 020 7357 9287
Email editor@thestage.co.uk
Website www.thestage.co.uk
Owner *The Stage Newspaper Ltd*
Editor *Brian Attwood*
Circulation 41,500

FOUNDED 1880. WEEKLY. No unsolicited mss. Prospective contributors should write with ideas in the first instance.
Features Preference for middle-market, tabloid-style articles. 'Puff pieces', PR plugs and extended production notes will not be considered. Maximum 800 words. Profiles: 1200 words.
News News stories from outside London are always welcome. Maximum 300 words.
Payment £100 per 1000 words.

Stamp Magazine
Focus House, Dingwall Avenue, Croydon
CR9 2TA
☎020 8774 0772 Fax 020 8774 0939
Email steve_fairclough@ipcmedia.com
Owner *IPC Media*
Editor *Steve Fairclough*
Circulation 12,000

FOUNDED 1934. MONTHLY news and features on the world of stamp collecting from the past to the present day. Interested in articles by experts on particular countries or themes such as subject matter illustrated on stamps – dogs, politics, etc. Approach in writing.
News *David Stanford* News of latest stamp issues or industry news. Maximum 500 words.
Features *Steve Fairclough* Any features welcome on famous stamps, rarities, postmarks, postal history, exhibitions, postcards, personal collections, auctions. Must be illustrated with colour images ('we can arrange for photography of original stamps'). Maximum 2500 words, or 5000 for 2-part expert piece.
Payment negotiable.

Stand Magazine
See under **Poetry Magazines**

Staple
See under **Poetry Magazines**

The Strad
Orpheus Publications, SMG Plc, 3
Waterhouse Square, 138–142 Holborn,
London EC1N 2NY
☎020 7882 1040 Fax 020 7882 1020
Email thestrad@orpheuspublications.com
Website www.thestrad.com

Owner *SMG Plc*
Editor *Joanna Pieters*
Circulation 17,500

FOUNDED 1890. MONTHLY for classical string
musicians, makers and enthusiasts. Unsolicited
mss accepted occasionally 'though acknowl-
edgement/return not guaranteed'.

Features Profiles of string players, teachers,
luthiers and musical instruments, also relevant
research. Maximum 2000 words.
Reviews *Naomi Sadler, Kristen Thorner.*
Payment £130 per 1000 words.

Suffolk and Norfolk Life
Barn Acre House, Saxtead Green, Suffolk
IP13 9QJ
☎01728 685832 Fax 01728 685842

Owner *Today Magazines Ltd*
Editor *Kevin Davis*
Circulation 17,000

FOUNDED 1989. MONTHLY. General interest,
local stories, historical, personalities, wine, travel,
food. Unsolicited mss welcome. Approach by
phone or in writing with ideas. Not interested in
anything which does not relate specifically to
East Anglia.

Features *Kevin Davis* Maximum 1500
words, with photos.
News *Kevin Davis* Maximum 1000 words,
with photos.
Special Pages *William Locks* Study the magazine for guidelines. Maximum 1500 words.
Payment £30–40.

Sugar Magazine
17 Berners Street, London W1T 3LN
☎020 7664 6440 Fax 020 7703 3409

Owner *Attic Futura*
Editor *To be appointed*
Editorial Director *Lysanne Currie*
Circulation 385,165

FOUNDED 1994. MONTHLY. Everything that
might interest the teenage girl. No unsolicited
mss. Will consider ideas or contacts for real-life
features. No fiction. Approach in writing in
the first instance.

Sunday Post Magazine
See under **National Newspapers (Sunday
Post, Dundee)**

Sunday Times Magazine
See under **National Newspapers (The
Sunday Times)**

Superbike Magazine
Focus House, Dingwall Avenue, Croydon,
Surrey CR9 2TA
☎020 8774 0600 Fax 020 8774 0951
Website www.ipcmedia.com

Publisher *Keith Foster*
Editor *Kenny Pryde*
Circulation 70,483

FOUNDED 1977. MONTHLY. Dedicated to all
that is best and most exciting in the world of
high-performance motorcycling. Unsolicited
mss, synopses and ideas welcome.

Surrey County
Datateam Publishing Ltd, London Road,
Maidstone, Kent ME15 8LY
☎01622 687031 Fax 01622 757646

Owner *Datateam Publishing Ltd*
Editor *Ian Trevett*
Circulation 10,000

FOUNDED 1970. MONTHLY. Strong Surrey
interest plus fashion, food, books, gardening
wildlife, motoring, property, sport, interiors
with local links. Unsolicited mss welcome.
Interested in anything with a genuine Surrey
connection. No fiction or non-Surrey subjects.
Approach in writing with ideas. Maximum
length 1500 words. *Payment* negotiable.

Sussex Life
Baskerville Place, 28 Teville Road, Worthing,
West Sussex BN11 1UG
☎01903 218719 Fax 01903 820193
Email ian@sussexlife.co.uk
Website www.sussexlife.com

Owner *Sussex Life Ltd*
Editor *Trudi Linscer*
Circulation 70,000

FOUNDED 1965. MONTHLY. Sussex and general
interest magazine. Regular supplements on
education, fashion, homes and gardens.
Interested in investigative, journalistic pieces
relevant to the area and celebrity profiles.

Unsolicited mss, synopses and ideas in writing welcome. Minimum 500 words.
Payment £15 per 500 words and picture.

Swimming Magazine

Harold Fern House, Derby Square, Loughborough, Leicestershire LE11 5AL
☎01509 618766   Fax 01509 618768
Owner *Amateur Swimming Association*
Editor *P. Hassall*
Circulation 20,000

FOUNDED 1923. MONTHLY about competitive swimming and associated subjects. Unsolicited mss welcome.

Features Technical articles on swimming, water polo, diving or synchronised swimming. Length and payment negotiable.

The Tablet

1 King Street Cloisters, Clifton Walk, London W6 0QZ
☎020 8748 8484   Fax 020 8748 1550
Email thetablet@tablet.co.uk
Website www.thetablet.co.uk
Owner *The Tablet Publishing Co Ltd*
Editor *John Wilkins*
Circulation 21,695

FOUNDED 1840. WEEKLY. Quality international Roman Catholic magazine featuring articles – political, social, cultural, theological or spiritual – of interest to concerned Christian laity and clergy. Unsolicited material welcome (1500 words) if relevant to magazine's style and market. All approaches should be made in writing.
Payment from about £75.

Take a Break

Academic House, 24–28 Oval Road, London NW1 7DT
☎020 7241 8000   Fax 020 7241 8052
Email tab.features@bauer.co.uk
Owner *H. Bauer Publishing Ltd*
Editor *John Dale*
Circulation 1.15 million

FOUNDED 1990. WEEKLY. True-life feature magazine. Approach with ideas in writing.

News/Features Always on the look-out for good, true-life stories. Maximum 1200 words. *Payment* negotiable.

Fiction Sharp, succinct stories which are well told and often with a twist at the end. All categories, provided it is relevant to the magazine's style and market. Maximum 1000 words. *Payment* negotiable.

Tatler

Vogue House, Hanover Square, London W1S 1JU
☎020 7499 9080   Fax 020 7409 0451
Website www.tatler.co.uk
Owner *Condé Nast Publications Ltd*
Editor *Geordie Greig*
Circulation 82,026

Up-market glossy from the Condé Nast stable. New writers should send in copies of either published work or unpublished material; writers of promise will be taken up. The magazine works largely on a commission basis: they are unlikely to publish unsolicited features, but will ask writers to work to specific projects.

Features *Vassi Chamberlain*

TGO (The Great Outdoors)

SMG Magazines, 200 Renfield Street, Glasgow G2 3PR
☎0141 302 7700   Fax 0141 331 6948
Email smg.mags@smg.plc.uk
Owner *SMG Ltd*
Editor *Cameron McNeish*
Circulation 22,000

FOUNDED 1978. MONTHLY. Deals with walking, backpacking and wild country topics. Unsolicited mss are welcome.

Features Well-written and illustrated items on relevant topics. Maximum 2500 words. Colour photographs only, please.

News Short topical items (or photographs). Maximum 300 words.
Payment £200–300 for features; £10–20 for news.

that's life!

Academic House, 24–28 Oval Road, London NW1 7DT
☎020 7241 8000   Fax 020 7241 8008
Owner *H. Bauer Publishing Ltd*
Editor *Christabel Smith*
Circulation 584,221

FOUNDED 1995. WEEKLY. True-life stories, puzzles, health, homes, parenting, cookery and fun.

Features *Dawn Smith* Maximum 1600 words. *Payment* £650.

Fiction *Emma Fabian* 1200 words. *Payment* £200–300.

The Third Alternative

5 Martins Lane, Witcham, Ely, Cambridgeshire CB6 2LB
☎01353 777931
Email ttapress@aol.com

Website www.ttapress.com
Owner *TTA Press*
Editor *Andy Cox*
FOUNDED 1993. Quarterly A4 colour magazine of horror, fantasy, science fiction and cross-genre fiction, plus interviews, profiles, comment, cinema and artwork. Publishes talented newcomers alongside famous authors. Unsolicited mss welcome if accompanied by s.a.e. or e-mail address for overseas submissions (no length restriction, but no novels or serialisations). Queries and letters welcome via e-mail but submissions as hard copy only. Potential contributors are advised to study the magazine. Contracts are exchanged upon acceptance; payment is upon publication. Winner of several British Fantasy Awards. The magazine is supported by **Eastern Arts** and the **Arts Council of England**.

This England

PO Box 52, Cheltenham, Gloucestershire GL50 1YQ
☎01242 537900 Fax 01242 537901
Owner *This England Ltd*
Editor *Roy Faiers*
Circulation 200,000
FOUNDED 1968. QUARTERLY, with a strong overseas readership. Celebration of England and all things English: famous people, natural beauty, towns and villages, history, traditions, customs and legends, crafts, etc. Generally a rural basis, with the 'Forgetmenots' section publishing readers' recollections and nostalgia. Up to one hundred unsolicited pieces received each week. Unsolicited mss/ideas welcome. Length 250–2000 words.
Payment £25 per 1000 words.

Time

Brettenham House, Lancaster Place, London WC2E 7TL
☎020 7499 4080 Fax 020 7322 1259
Website www.timeeurope.com
Owner *Time Warner, Inc.*
Editors (Europe, Middle East, Africa) *Ann Morrison, Donald Morrison*
Circulation 5.46 million
FOUNDED 1923. WEEKLY current affairs and news magazine. There are few opportunities for freelancers on *Time* as almost all the magazine's content is written by staff members from various bureaux around the world. No unsolicited mss.

Time Out

Universal House, 251 Tottenham Court Road, London W1T 7AB
☎020 7813 3000 Fax 020 7813 6001
Website www.timeout.com
Publisher *Lesley Gill*
Editor *Laura Lee Davies*
Circulation 86,000
FOUNDED 1968. WEEKLY magazine of news and entertainment in London.
Features *Jessica Cargill Thompson* 'Usually written by staff writers or commissioned, but it's always worth submitting an idea by post if particularly apt to the magazine.' 1000 words.
Consumer Section *Rachael Philipps* Fashion, shopping, travel, design, property.
Payment negotiable.

The Times Educational Supplement

Admiral House, 66–68 East Smithfield, London E1W 1BX
☎020 7782 3000 Fax 020 7782 3200
Email editor@tes.co.uk *or* newsdesk@tes.co.uk *or* friday@tes.co.uk
Website www.tes.co.uk
Owner *News International*
Editor *Bob Doe*
Circulation 127,283
FOUNDED 1910. WEEKLY. New contributors are welcome and should fax or e-mail ideas on one sheet of A4 for news, features or reviews to the editor.
Opinion *Jeremy Sutcliffe* 'Platform': a weekly slot for a well-informed and cogently argued viewpoint. Maximum 1200 words. 'Another Voice': a shorter comment on an issue of the day by non-education professionals. Maximum 700 words.
School Management *Neil Levis/***Governors** *Karen Thornton* Weekly pages on practical issues for school governors and managers. Maximum 800 words.
Research Focus *David Budge*
Further Education *Ian Nash* Includes post-16 education and training in colleges, work and the wider community. Aimed at everyone from teachers/lecturers to leaders and opinion formers in lifelong learning. News, features, comment and opinion on all aspects of college life welcome. Length from 350 words (news) to 1000 maximum (features).
Friday A weekly magazine with *The TES* which focuses on whole school issues, good practice, teaching as a career and the work/life balance:

Features *Sarah Bayliss* Unsolicited features are rarely accepted but ideas are welcome accompanied by cuttings and/or c.v. Length from 1000–2000 words. Strong storylines are expected.

Books *Geraldine Brennan*

Arts *Heather Neill*

Resources *Yolanda Brooks*

Talkback *Jill Craven* Short, first person pieces, maximum 650 words, are welcome for consideration. Humour from teachers is encouraged, especially for the 'Thank God it's Friday' column.

You and Your Job *Jill Craven*

Online (Computers in Education) *Merlin John* A magazine devoted to information and communications technology appearing with *The TES* six times a year.

TES Teacher *Joyce Arnold* New weekly magazine for classroom teachers appearing with *The TES* focusing on what individual teachers do in the classroom to teach pupils and subjects. Specific subject section each week. Maximum 800 words.

Special Issues Occasional pull-out magazines on topics including school management (*Neil Levis*), first appointments (*Susan Young*), business links (*Ian Nash*), school visits – *Going Places* – (*Yolanda Brooks*).

Primary *Diane Hofkins* A monthly A4 glossy magazine published separately from *The TES*. Articles should aim to help teachers think about their work or provide ideas for teaching. Maximum 1000 words. It is advisable to send in a proposal before submitting a completed article.

The Times Educational Supplement Scotland

Scott House, 10 South St Andrew Street, Edinburgh EH2 2AZ
☎0131 557 1133 Fax 0131 558 1155
Email scoted@tes.co.uk
Website www.tes.co.uk/scotland

Owner *TSL Education Ltd*
Editor *Neil Munro*
Circulation 9000

FOUNDED 1965. WEEKLY. Unsolicited mss welcome.

Features Articles on education in Scotland. Maximum 1000 words.

News Items on education in Scotland. Maximum 600 words.

The Times Higher Education Supplement

Admiral House, 66–68 East Smithfield, London E1W 1BX

☎020 7782 3000 Fax 020 7782 3300
Email editor@thes.co.uk
Website www.thes.co.uk

Owner *News International*
Editor *John O'Leary*
Circulation 28,300

FOUNDED 1971. WEEKLY. Unsolicited mss are welcome but most articles and *all* book reviews are commissioned. 'In most cases it is better to write, but in the case of news stories it is all right to phone.'

Books *Andrew Robinson*

Features *Mandy Garner* Most articles are commissioned from academics in higher education.

News *Mary Cook* Freelance opportunities very occasionally.

Science *Steve Farrar*

Science Books *Andrew Robinson*

Foreign *David Jobbins*

Payment by negotiation.

The Times Literary Supplement

Admiral House, 66–68 East Smithfield, London E1W 1BX
☎020 7782 3000 Fax 020 7782 3100
Website www.the-tls.co.uk

Owner *TSL Education Ltd*
Editor *Peter Stothard*
Circulation 35,000

FOUNDED 1902. WEEKLY review of literature. Contributors should approach in writing and be familiar with the general level of writing in the *TLS*.

Literary Discoveries *Alan Jenkins*

Poems *Mick Imlah*

News News stories and general articles concerned with literature, publishing and new intellectual developments anywhere in the world. Length by arrangement.

Payment by arrangement.

Titbits

2 Caversham Street, London SW3 4AH
☎020 7351 4995 Fax 020 7351 4995

Owner *Sport Newspapers Ltd*
Editor *James Hughes*
Circulation 150,000

FOUNDED 1895. MONTHLY. Consumer magazine for men covering show business and general interests. Ideas in writing welcome. Maximum 3000 words. News, features, particularly photofeatures (colour), and fiction. Always send letter or telephone first.

Payment negotiable.

Today's Golfer
Bushfield House, Orton Centre,
Peterborough, Cambridgeshire PE2 5UW
☎01733 237111 Fax 01733 288014
Owner *Emap Active Ltd*
Editor *Paul Hamblin*
Deputy Editor *John McKenzie*
Circulation 94,570

FOUNDED 1988. MONTHLY. Golf instruction, features, player profiles and news. Most features written in-house but unsolicited mss will be considered. Approach in writing with ideas. Not interested in instruction material from outside contributors.

Features/News *Kevin Brown* Opinion, player profiles and general golf-related features.

Top of the Pops Magazine
Room A1136, Woodlands, 80 Wood Lane,
London W12 0TT
☎020 8433 3910 Fax 020 8433 2694
Website www.beeb.com/totp
Owner *BBC Worldwide Publishing Ltd*
Editor *Corinna Shaffer*
Circulation 245,423

FOUNDED 1995. MONTHLY teenage pop music magazine with a lighthearted and humorous approach. No unsolicited material apart from pop star interviews.

Total Film
99 Baker Street, London W1U 6FP
☎020 7317 2600 Fax 020 7317 0275
Email totalfilm@futurenet.co.uk
Owner *Future Publishing*
Editor *Matt Mueller*
Circulation 83,100

FOUNDED 1997. MONTHLY reviews-based movie magazine. Interested in ideas for features, not necessarily tied in to specific releases, and humour items. No reviews or interviews with celebrities/directors. Approach by post or e-mail.

Traditional Woodworking
The Well House, High Street, Burton on Trent, Staffordshire DE14 1JQ
☎01283 742950 Fax 01283 742957
Owner *Waterways World*
Editor *Alan Kidd*

FOUNDED 1988. MONTHLY. Features workshop projects, techniques, reviews of the latest woodworking tools and equipment, general articles on woodworking and furniture making. Supplements: *Powertools Quarterly* and *Powertools Guide*.

Features Technical features and furniture projects welcome. The latter must include drawings and cutting lists. A photograph of the piece is required before commissioning. Approach in writing in the first instance. *Payment* negotiable.

Trail
Bretton Court, Bretton, Peterborough, Cambridgeshire PE3 8DZ
☎01733 264666 Fax 01733 282654
Website www.trailmag.com
Owner *Emap Active Publishing Ltd*
Editor *Ed Kenyon*
Circulation 36,450

FOUNDED 1990. MONTHLY. Gear reports, where to walk and practical advice for the hillwalker and long distance walker. Inspirational reads on people and outdoor/walking issues. Health, fitness and injury prevention for high level walkers and outdoor lovers. Approach by phone or in writing in the first instance.

Features *Matthew Swaine* Very limited requirement for overseas articles, 'written to our style'. Ask for guidelines. Maximum 2000 words.

Limited requirement for guided walks articles. Specialist writers only. Ask for guidelines. 750–2000 words (depending on subject).

Payment £80 per 1000 words.

Traveller
45–49 Brompton Road, London SW3 1DE
☎020 7589 0500 Fax 020 7581 1357
Website www.traveller.org.uk
Owner *Wexas International*
Editor *Jonathan Lorie*
Deputy Editor *Amy Sohanpaul*
Circulation 35,359

FOUNDED 1970. QUARTERLY.
Features High quality, personal narratives of remarkable journeys. Articles should be offbeat, adventurous, authentic. No mainstream destinations. For guidelines, see website. Articles must be accompanied by professional quality, original slides. Freelance articles considered. Maximum 1600 words. Initial contact by fax.

Payment £150 per 1000 words.

Trout Fisherman
EMAP Active Ltd, Bushfield House, Orton Centre, Peterborough, Cambridgeshire PE2 5UW
☎01733 237111 Fax 01733 465820

Owner *Emap Active Ltd*
Editor *Mark Sutcliffe*
Circulation 42,000

FOUNDED 1977. MONTHLY instructive magazine on trout fishing. Most of the articles are commissioned, but unsolicited mss and quality colour transparencies welcome.
Features Maximum 2500 words.
Payment varies.

TVTimes
IPC Media Ltd., King's Reach Tower, Stamford Street, London SE1 9LS
☎020 7261 7000   Fax 020 7261 7777

Owner *IPC Media*
Editor *To be appointed*
Circulation 627,095

FOUNDED 1955. WEEKLY magazine of listings and features serving the viewers of independent television, BBC, satellite and radio. Freelance contributions by commission only. No unsolicited contributions.

Ulster Tatler
39 Boucher Road, Belfast BT12 6UT
☎028 9068 1371   Fax 028 9038 1915
Email ulstertat@aol.com
Website www.ulstertatler.com

Owner/Editor *Richard Sherry*
Circulation 15,000

FOUNDED 1965. MONTHLY. Articles of local interest and social functions appealing to Northern Ireland's ABC1 population. Welcomes unsolicited material; approach by phone or in writing in the first instance.
Features *Noreen Dorman* Maximum 1500 words.
Fiction *Richard Sherry* Maximum 3000 words.

The Universe
St James's Buildings, Oxford Street, Manchester M1 6FP
☎0161 236 8856   Fax 0161 236 8892
Website www.the-universe.net

Owner *Gabriel Communications Ltd*
Editor *Joe Kelly*
Circulation 60,000

Occasional use of new writers, but a substantial network of regular contributors already exists. Interested in a very wide range of material: all subjects which might bear on Christian life. Fiction not normally accepted.
Payment negotiable.

Vector
See **British Science Fiction Association** under **Professional Associations**

The Vegan
Donald Watson House, 7 Battle Road, St Leonards on Sea, East Sussex TN37 7AA
☎01424 427393   Fax 01424 717064
Email editor@vegansociety.com
Website www.vegansociety.com

Owner *Vegan Society*
Editor *Rick Savage*
Circulation 5000

FOUNDED 1944. QUARTERLY. Deals with the ecological, ethical and health aspects of veganism. Unsolicited mss welcome. Maximum 2000 words.
Payment negotiable.

Verbatim
The Language Quarterly
PO Box 156, Chearsley, Aylesbury, Buckinghamshire HP18 0DQ
☎01844 208474
Email verbatim.uk@tesco.net
Website www.verbatimmag.com

Owner *Word, Inc.*
Editor *Erin McKean*

FOUNDED in 1974 by Laurence Urdang. QUARTERLY journal devoted to what is amusing, interesting and engaging about the English language and languages in general. Will consider unsolicited material but write for writer's guidelines in the first instance. For a sample copy of the magazine, send 50p (stamp or IRC).
Payment ranges from £20–300, 'depending on length, wit and other merit'.

Vogue
Vogue House, Hanover Square, London W1S 1JU
☎020 7499 9080   Fax 020 7408 0559
Website www.vogue.co.uk

Owner *Condé Nast Publications Ltd*
Editor *Alexandra Shulman*
Circulation 195,167

Condé Nast Magazines tend to use known writers and commission what's needed, rather than using unsolicited mss. Contacts are useful.
Features *Bronwyn Cosgrave* Upmarket general interest rather than 'women's'. Good proportion of highbrow art and literary articles, as well as travel, gardens, food, home interest and reviews.

The Voice Newspaper

234–244 Stockwell Road, London SW9 9UG
☎020 7737 7377 Fax 020 7274 8994
Email mike.best@the-voice.co.uk
Website www.voice-online.co.uk
Owner *Val McCalla*
Editor-in-Chief *Mike Best*
Circulation 40,000

FOUNDED 1982. WEEKLY newspaper for the Afro Caribbean community. News, features, arts, reviews and special pull-out of jobs and sport. Open to ideas for features, news and arts items; approach in writing.
Payment negotiable.

The Voice of Shooting

BASC, Marford Mill, Rossett, Wrexham
LL12 0HL
☎01244 573000 Fax 01244 573001
Owner *The British Association for Shooting and Conservation (BASC)*
Editor *Jeffrey Olstead*
Circulation 120,000

FOUR ISSUES PER YEAR. Good articles and stories on shooting, conservation and related areas may be considered although most material is produced in-house. Maximum 1500 words.
Payment negotiable.

Voyager

Mediamark Publishing International,
11 Kingsway, London WC2B 6PH
☎020 7212 9000 Fax 020 7212 9001
Email info@mediamark.co.uk
Owner *Mediamark/bmi british midland*
Editor *Howard Rombough*
Circulation 54,191

TEN ISSUES PER YEAR. In-flight magazine of bmi british midland. Lifestyle features and profiles, plus British Midland information. No unsolicited mss. Approach in writing with ideas in the first instance. No destination travel articles.

The War Cry

101 Newington Causeway, London SE1 6BN
☎020 7367 4900 Fax 020 7367 4710
Email warcry@salvationarmy.org.uk
Website www.salvationarmy.org.uk/warcry
Owner *The Salvation Army*
Editor *Major Nigel Bovey*
Circulation 80,000

FOUNDED 1879. WEEKLY magazine containing Christian comments on current issues. Unsolicited mss welcome if appropriate to contents. No fiction or poetry. Approach by phone with ideas.
News relating to Christian Church or social issues. Maximum length 500 words. *Payment* £20 per article.
Features Magazine-style articles of interest to the 'man/woman-in-the-street'. Maximum length 500 words. *Payment* £20 per article.

Wasafiri

Dept of English & Drama, Queen Mary College, University of London, Mile End Road, London E1 4NS
☎020 7882 3120 Fax 020 7882 3120
Email wasafiri@qmw.ac.uk
Website www.english.qmw.ac.uk/wasafiri
Editor *Susheila Nasta*
Managing Editor *Richard Dyer*
Reviews Editor *Paola Marchionni*

TRI-ANNUAL literary journal of African, Asian, Black British and Caribbean culture. Short stories, poetry, reviews, interviews, criticism and cross cultural debate, film and literature. Illustrations in b&w. Send double-spaced mss, in duplicate, with s.a.e. *Payment* negotiable.

The Water Gardener

Winchester Court, 1 Forum Place, Hatfield, Hertfordshire AL10 0RN
☎01707 273999 Fax 01707 276555
Email watergardener@trmg.co.uk
Website www.trmg.co.uk
Owner *TRMG*
Publisher *Susie Muir*

FOUNDED 1994. MONTHLY. Everything relevant to water gardening. Will consider photonews items and features on aspects of the subject; write with idea in the first instance. Maximum 2000 words. *Payment* by negotiation.

Waterways World

The Well House, High Street, Burton on Trent, Staffordshire DE14 1JQ
☎01283 742950 Fax 01283 742957
Email wwedit@the-wellhouse.com
Owner *Waterways World Ltd*
Editor *Hugh Potter*
Circulation 22,408

FOUNDED 1972. MONTHLY magazine for inland waterway enthusiasts. Unsolicited mss welcome, provided the writer has a good knowledge of the subject. No fiction.
Features *Hugh Potter* Articles (preferably illustrated) are published on all aspects of inland waterways in Britain and abroad, including

recreational and commercial boating on rivers and canals.

News *Chris Daniels* Maximum 500 words.
Payment £42 per 1000 words.

Waymark
IPROW, PO Box 78, Skipton, North Yorkshire BD23 4UP
Email comms@iprow.co.uk
Website www.iprow.co.uk
Editor *Clare Denby*
Circulation 1000

FOUNDED 1986. THREE ISSUES YEARLY. Journal of the Institute of Public Rights of Way Officers. Available to non-members by subscription.

News Most produced in-house but some opportunities for original/off-beat items. Maximum 500 words.

Features Ideas welcome on any topic broadly relating to the British countryside and public access to it. Controversial, thought provoking pieces readily considered. Maximum 1750 words.

Special Pages Cartoons or brief humorous items on an access or countryside/environmental theme welcome. Send ideas in writing with s.a.e. initially.

Wedding and Home
IPC Media Ltd., King's Reach Tower, Stamford Street, London SE1 9LS
☎020 7261 7471 Fax 020 7261 7459
Email weddingandhome@ipcmedia.com
Owner *IPC Media*
Editor *To be appointed*
Circulation 51,813

FOUNDED 1985. BI-MONTHLY offering ideas and inspiration for women planning their wedding. Most features are written in-house or commissioned from known freelancers. Unsolicited mss are not welcome, but approaches may be made in writing.

Weekly News
D.C. Thomson & Co. Ltd., Albert Square, Dundee DD1 9QJ
☎01382 223131 Fax 01382 201390
Email d.burness@dcthomson.co.uk
Owner *D.C. Thomson & Co. Ltd*
Editor *David Burness*
Circulation 206,302

FOUNDED 1855. WEEKLY. Newsy, family-orientated magazine designed to appeal to the busy housewife. 'We receive a lot of unsolicited articles and there is great loss of life among them.'

Usually commissions, but writers of promise will be taken up. Series include showbiz, royals and television. No fiction.
Payment negotiable.

West Lothian Life
Ballencrieff Cottage, Ballencrieff Toll, Bathgate, West Lothian EH48 4LD
☎01506 632728 Fax 01506 635444
Email pages@clara.net
Website home.clara.net/pages
Owner *Pages Editorial & Publishing Services*
Editor *Susan Coon*

QUARTERLY county magazine for people who live, work or have an interest in West Lothian. Includes three or four major features (1500 words) on successful people, businesses or initiatives. A local walk takes up the centre spread. Regular articles by experts on collectables, property, interior design, cookery and local gardening, plus news items, letters and a competition. Freelance writers used only for main features. Phone first to discuss content and timing.
Payment by arrangement.

What Car?
60 Waldegrave Road, Teddington, Middlesex TW11 8LG
☎020 8267 5688 Fax 020 8267 5750
Email whatcar@haynet.com
Website www.whatcar.co.uk
Owner *Haymarket Motoring Publications Ltd*
Editor *Steve Fowler*
Circulation 153,164

MONTHLY. The car buyer's bible, *What Car?* concentrates on road test comparisons of new cars, news and buying advice on used cars, as well as a strong consumer section. Some scope for freelancers. Testing is only offered to the few, and general articles on aspects of driving are only accepted from writers known and trusted by the magazine. No unsolicited mss.
Payment negotiable.

What Hi-Fi? Sound & Vision
38–42 Hampton Road, Teddington, Middlesex TW11 0JE
☎020 8943 5000 Fax 020 8267 5019
Website www.whathifi.com
Owner *Haymarket Magazines Ltd*
Managing Director *Kevin Costello*
Editor *Andy Clough*
Circulation 75,000

FOUNDED 1976. MONTHLY. Features on hi-fi and home cinema. No unsolicited contributions. Prior consultation with the editor essential.

Features General or more specific on hi-fi and home cinema pertinent to the consumer electronics market.

Reviews Specific product reviews. All material is now generated by in-house staff. Freelance writing no longer accepted.

What Investment

Arnold House, 36–41 Holywell Lane, London EC2A 3SF
☎020 7827 5454 Fax 020 7827 0567

Owner *Charterhouse Communications*
Editor *Sally Wright*
Circulation 37,000

FOUNDED 1982. MONTHLY. Features articles on a variety of savings and investment matters. All approaches should be made in writing.

Features Length 1200–1500 words (maximum 2000).
Payment NUJ rates minimum.

What Mortgage

Arnold House, 36–41 Holywell Lane, London EC2A 3SF
☎020 7827 5454 Fax 020 7827 0567
Website www.whatmortgageonline.co.uk

Owner *Charterhouse Communications*
Editor *Hilary Osborne*
Circulation 25,000

FOUNDED 1982. MONTHLY magazine on property purchase and finance. No unsolicited material; prospective contributors may make initial contact with ideas either by telephone or in writing.

Features Up to 1500 words on related topics are considered. Particularly welcome are new angles, ideas or specialities relevant to mortgages.
Payment £175 per 1000 words.

What Satellite TV

Highbury wViP, 53–79 Highgate Road, London NW5 1TW
☎020 7331 1000 Fax 020 7331 1241
Email wvwhatsat@wvip.co.uk
Website www.wotsat.com

Owner *Highbury wViP*
Editor *Geoff Bains*
Circulation 65,000

FOUNDED 1986. MONTHLY including news, technical information, equipment tests, programme background, listings. Contributions welcome – phone first.

Features *Geoff Bains* Unusual installations and users. In-depth guides to popular/cult shows. Technical tutorials.

News *Alex Lane* Industry and programming. 250 words maximum.

What's New in Building

City Reach, 5 Greenwich View Place, Millharbour, London E14 9NN
☎020 7861 6303 Fax 020 7861 6241

Owner *CMP Information*
Editor *Mark Pennington*
Circulation 31,496

MONTHLY. Specialist magazine covering new products for building. Unsolicited mss not generally welcome. The only freelance work available is rewriting press release material. This is offered on a monthly basis of 25–50 items of about 150 words each.
Payment £5.25 per item.

What's On in London

180–182 Pentonville Road, London N1 9LB
☎020 7278 4393 Fax 020 7837 5838
Email whatson@globalnet.co.uk
Website www.whatsoninlondon.co.uk

Owner *S.D. Shaw*
Editor *Michael Darvell*
Circulation 40,000

FOUNDED 1935. WEEKLY entertainment-based guide and information magazine. Features, listings and reviews. Always interested in well-thought-out and well-presented mss. Articles should have London/Home Counties connection, except during the summer when they can be of much wider tourist/historic interest, relating to unusual traditions and events. Approach the editor by telephone in the first instance.

Features *Graham Hassell*
Art *Fisun Güner*
Cinema *Jason Caro*
Pop Music *John Coleman*
Classical Music *Michael Darvell*
Theatre *Oliver Jones*
Events *Mark Wilsher*
Payment by arrangement.

Wild Times

RSPB, The Lodge, Sandy, Bedfordshire SG19 2DL
☎01767 680551 Fax 01767 683262
Email derek.niemann@rspb.org.uk

Owner *Royal Society for the Protection of Birds*
Editor *Derek Niemann*

FOUNDED 1965. BI-MONTHLY. Bird, wildlife and nature conservation for under 8-year-olds (RSPB Wildlife Explorer members). No unsolicited mss. No 'captive/animal welfare' articles.
Features Unsolicited material rarely used.

News News releases welcome. Approach in writing in the first instance.

Wine Magazine

Quest Magazines Ltd., 6–14 Underwood Street, London N1 7JQ
☎020 7549 2572 Fax 020 7549 2550
Email wine@wilmington.co.uk
Website www.connectingdrinks.com
Owner *Wilmington Publishing*
Editor *Chris Losh*
Circulation 35,000

FOUNDED 1983. MONTHLY. No unsolicited mss.

News/Features Wine, spirits, cigars, food and food/wine-related travel stories. Prospective contributors should approach in writing.

Wingbeat

RSPB, The Lodge, Sandy, Bedfordshire SG19 2DL
☎01767 680551 Fax 01767 683262
Email derek.niemann@rspb.org.uk
Owner *Royal Society for the Protection of Birds*
Editor *Derek Niemann*

FOUNDED 1965. BI-MONTHLY. Bird, wildlife and nature conservation for 14–18-year-olds (RSPB Wildlife Explorer members). No unsolicited mss. No 'captive/animal welfare' articles.

Features Unsolicited material rarely used.

News News releases welcome. Approach in writing in the first instance.

Wisden Cricket Monthly

c/o The New Boathouse, 136–142 Bramley Road, London W10 6SR
☎020 7565 3000 Fax 020 7565 3090
Email wcm@wisden.com
Owner *Wisden Cricket Magazines Ltd*
Editor *Stephen Fay*
Circulation 20,000

FOUNDED 1979. MONTHLY. Very few uncommissioned articles are used, but would-be contributors are not discouraged. Approach in writing.

Payment varies.

Woman

IPC Media Ltd, King's Reach Tower, Stamford Street, London SE1 9LS
☎020 7261 5000 Fax 020 7261 5997
Owner *IPC Media*
Editor *Carole Russell*
Circulation 646,643

FOUNDED 1937. WEEKLY. Long-running, pop-ular women's magazine which boasts a readership of over 2.5 million. No unsolicited mss. Most work commissioned. Approach with ideas in writing.

Features *Judy Yorke* Maximum 1250 words.
Books *Carole Russell*

Woman and Home

IPC Media Ltd., King's Reach Tower, Stamford Street, London SE1 9LS
☎020 7261 5176 Fax 020 7261 7346
Owner *IPC Media*
Editor *Sue James*
Circulation 253,008

FOUNDED 1926. MONTHLY. No unsolicited mss. Prospective contributors are advised to write with ideas, including photocopies of other published work or details of magazines to which they have contributed. S.a.e. essential for return of material. Most freelance work is specially commissioned.

Woman's Own

IPC Media Ltd., King's Reach Tower, Stamford Street, London SE1 9LS
☎020 7261 5550 Fax 020 7261 5346
Owner *IPC Media*
Editor *Elsa McAlonan*
Circulation 518,495

FOUNDED 1932. WEEKLY. Prospective contributors should contact the features editor *in writing* in the first instance before making a submission. No unsolicited fiction.

Woman's Realm

Merged with *Woman's Weekly* in 2001.

Woman's Weekly

IPC Media Ltd., King's Reach Tower, Stamford Street, London SE1 9LS
☎020 7261 6131 Fax 020 7261 6322
Owner *IPC Media*
Editor *Gilly Sinclair*
Deputy Editor *Geoffrey Palmer*
Circulation 504,531

FOUNDED 1911. Mass-market women's WEEKLY.

Features Inspiring, positive human interest stories, especially first-hand experiences, of up to 1200 words. Freelancers used regularly but tend to be experienced magazine journalists. Synopses and ideas should be submitted in writing.

Fiction *Gaynor Davies* Short stories 1000–2500 words; serials 12,000–30,000 words.

Guidelines for serials: 'a strong emotional theme with a conflict not resolved until the end'; short stories should have warmth and originality.

Women's Health

Highbury wViP, 53–79 Highgate Road, London NW5 1TW
☎020 7331 1000 Fax 020 7331 1108
Email womenshealth@wvip.co.uk
Owner *Highbury House Communications*
Editor *Tracey Smith*
Circulation 100,000

FOUNDED 1998. MONTHLY lifestyle magazine with a health twist, taking an irreverant approach. Aimed at ABC1 women of 25–39. No unsolicited mss. Will consider ideas for items with interesting angles on fitness and beauty plus alternative health and food. Approach in writing or by e-mail in the first instance.

Woodworker

Nexus House, Azalea Drive, Swanley, Kent BR8 8HU
☎01322 660070 Fax 01322 616319
Website www.getwoodworking.com
Owner *Nexus Special Interests*
Editor *Mark Ramuz*
Circulation 45,000

FOUNDED 1901. MONTHLY. Contributions welcome; approach with ideas in writing.
Features Articles on woodworking with good photo support appreciated. Maximum 2000 words. *Payment* £100 per 1000 words.
News Stories and photos (b&w) welcome. Maximum 300 words. *Payment* £10–25 per story.

World Fishing

Nexus House, Azalea Drive, Swanley, Kent BR8 8HU
☎01322 660070 Fax 01322 616324
Email adrian.tatum@nexusmedia.com
Owner *Nexus Media Ltd*
Editor *Adrian Tatum*
Circulation 5769

FOUNDED 1952. MONTHLY. Unsolicited mss welcome; approach by phone or in writing with an idea.
News/Features of a technical or commercial nature relating to the commercial fishing and fish processing industries worldwide (the magazine is read in 116 different countries). Maximum 1500 words.
Payment by arrangement.

The World of Embroidery

PO Box 42B, East Molesley, Surrey KT8 9BB
☎020 8943 1229 Fax 020 8977 9882
Email administrator@embroiderersguild.com
Website www.embroiderersguild.com
Owner *Embroiderers' Guild*
Editor *Polly Leonard*
Circulation 12,000

FOUNDED 1933. BI-MONTHLY. Features articles on embroidery techniques, historical and foreign embroidery, and contemporary artists' work with illustrations. Also reviews. Unsolicited mss welcome. Maximum 1000 words.
Payment negotiable.

The World of Interiors

Vogue House, Hanover Square, London W1S 1JU
☎020 7499 9080 Fax 020 7493 4013
Email interiors@condenast.co.uk
Website www.worldofinteriors.co.uk
Owner *Condé Nast Publications Ltd*
Editor *Rupert Thomas*
Circulation 65,183

FOUNDED 1981. MONTHLY. Best approach by fax or letter with an idea, preferably with reference snaps or guidebooks.
Features *Rupert Thomas* Most feature material is commissioned. 'Subjects tend to be found by us, but we are delighted to receive suggestions of interiors, archives, little-known museums, collections, etc. unpublished elsewhere, and would love to find new writers.'

World Soccer

IPC Media Ltd., King's Reach Tower, Stamford Street, London SE1 9LS
☎020 7261 5737 Fax 020 7261 7474
Website www.worldsoccer.com
Owner *IPC Media*
Editor *Gavin Hamilton*
Circulation 52,547

FOUNDED 1960. MONTHLY. Unsolicited material welcome but initial approach by phone or in writing preferred. News and features on world soccer.

World Wide Writers

PO Box 3229, Bournemouth, Dorset BH1 1ZS
☎01202 589828 Fax 01202 587758
Email writintl@globalnet.co.uk
Website www.worldwidewriters.com
Owner *Writers International Ltd*
Editor *Frederick E. Smith*

FOUNDED 1996. QUARTERLY. Welcomes short stories which must be original and not previously published or broadcast. Length 2500–5000 words.

Writers' Forum

PO Box 3229, Bournemouth, Dorset
BH1 1ZS
☎01202 589828 Fax 01202 587758
Email writintl@globalnet.co.uk
Website www.worldwidewriters.com
Owner *Writers International Ltd*
Editor *John Jenkins*
Circulation 25,000

FOUNDED 1993. BI-MONTHLY magazine covering all aspects of the craft of writing. Well written articles welcome. Write to the editor in the first instance.

Writers' News/Writing Magazine

PO Box 168, Wellington Street, Leeds, West Yorkshire LS1 1RF
☎0113 238 8333 Fax 0113 238 8330
Owner *Yorkshire Post Newspapers*
Editor *Derek Hudson*
Circulation 21,500(WN)/45,000(WM)

FOUNDED 1989. MONTHLY/BI-MONTHLY magazines containing news and advice for writers. *Writers' News* is exclusive to mail-order members who also receive *Writing Magazine*, a full-colour glossy publication, which is available on newsstands. No poetry or general items on 'how to become a writer'. Receive 1000 mss each year. Approach in writing.

News Exclusive news stories of interest to writers. Maximum 350 words.

Features How-to articles of interest to professional writers. Maximum 1500 words.

Yachting Monthly

IPC Media Ltd., King's Reach Tower, Stamford Street, London SE1 9LS
☎020 7261 6040 Fax 020 7261 7555
Email paul-gelder@ipcmedia.com
Website www.yachtingmonthly.com
Owner *IPC Media*
Editor *Sarah Norbury*
Deputy Editor *Paul Gelder*
Circulation 37,083

FOUNDED 1906. MONTHLY magazine for yachting and cruising enthusiasts – not racing. Unsolicited mss welcome, but many are received and not used. Prospective contributors should make initial contact in writing.

Features A wide range of features concerned with maritime subjects and cruising under sail;

well-researched and innovative material always welcome, especially if accompanied by colour transparencies. Maximum 2250 words.

Payment £80–110 per 1000 words.

Yachting World

IPC Media Ltd., King's Reach Tower, Stamford Street, London SE1 9LS
☎020 7261 6800 Fax 020 7261 6818
Email yachting_world@ipcmedia.com
Website www.yachting-world.com
Owner *IPC Media*
Editor *Andrew Bray*
Circulation 35,807

FOUNDED 1894. MONTHLY with international coverage of yacht racing, cruising and yachting events. Will consider well researched and written sailing stories. Preliminary approaches should be by phone for news stories and in writing for features.

Payment by arrangement.

Yorkshire Women's Life Magazine

PO Box 113, Leeds, West Yorkshire LS8 2WX
☎0113 262 1409
Publisher/Editor *Dawn Maria France*

FOUNDED 2001. THREE ISSUES YEARLY. Features of interest to women along with regional, national, international news and lifestyle articles. Past issues have covered anorexia nervosa, dealing with a monster boss, new female contraceptive. 'It is important to study the style of the magazine before submitting material. Send A4 s.a.e. with 38p stamp for copy of submission guidelines. Unsolicited mss and new writers actively encouraged; approach in writing in the first instance with s.a.e.'

You & Your Wedding

Silver House, 31–35 Beak Street, London W1R 3LD
☎020 7440 3838 (Editorial) Fax 020 7287 8655
Owner *NatMags Specialist Media (AIM) Ltd*
Editor *Carole Hamilton*
Circulation 62,145

FOUNDED 1985. BI-MONTHLY. Anything relating to weddings, setting up home, and honeymoons. No unsolicited mss. Ideas may be submitted in writing only, especially travel features. No phone calls.

You – The Mail on Sunday Magazine

See under **National Newspapers (The Mail on Sunday)**

Young Writer

Glebe House, Weobley, Hereford HR4 8SD
☎01544 318901 Fax 01544 318901
Email editor@youngwriter.org
Website www.youngwriter.org

Editor *Kate Jones*

Describing itself as 'The Magazine for Children with Something to Say', *Young Writer* is issued three times a year, at the back-to-school times of September, January and April. A forum for young people's writing – fiction and non-fiction, prose and poetry – the magazine is an introduction to independent writing for young writers aged 5–18.

Payment from £20 to £100 for freelance commissioned articles (these can be from adult writers).

Your Cat Magazine

Roebuck House, 33 Broad Street, Stamford, Lincolnshire PE9 1RB
☎01780 766199 Fax 01780 766416
Email suebpgroup@talk21.com
Website www.yourcat.co.uk

Owner *Bourne Publishing Group*
Editor *Sue Parslow*

FOUNDED 1994. MONTHLY magazine giving practical information on the care of cats and kittens, pedigree and non-pedigree, plus a wide range of general interest items on cats. Will consider 'true life' cat stories (maximum 900 words) and quality fiction. Send synopsis in the first instance. 'No articles written as though by a cat.'

Your Dog Magazine

Roebuck House, 33 Broad Street, Stamford, Lincolnshire PE9 1RB
☎01780 766199 Fax 01780 766416
Email sarahbpgroup@talk21.com

Owner *BPG (Stamford) Ltd*
Editor *Sarah Wright*
Circulation 26,000

FOUNDED 1995. MONTHLY. Practical advice for pet dog owners. Will consider practical features and some personal experiences (no highly emotive pieces or fiction). Telephone in the first instance.

News Maximum 300–400 words.
Features Maximum 2500 words; limited opportunities.
Payment negotiable.

Your Horse

Bretton Court, Bretton, Peterborough, Cambridgeshire PE3 8DZ
☎01733 264666 Fax 01733 465200

Owner *Emap Active Ltd*
Editor *Amanda Stevenson*
Circulation 61,000

For people who live, breath and have fun around horses. Most writing produced in-house but well-targeted articles will always be considered.

Yours Magazine

Homenene House, Orton Centre, Peterborough, Cambridgeshire PE2 5UW
☎01733 237111 Fax 01733 288129

Owner *Emap Esprit*
Editor *Christine Moss*
Circulation 360,186

FOUNDED 1973. MONTHLY plus four seasonal specials. Aimed at a readership aged 55 and over.

Features Best approach by letter with outline in first instance. Maximum 1000 words.
News Short, newsy items of interest to readership welcome. Length 300–500 words.
Fiction One or two short stories used in each issue.
Payment negotiable.

Zest

National Magazine House, 72 Broadwick Street, London W1F 9EP
☎020 7439 5000 Fax 020 7312 3750
Email zest.mail@natmags.co.uk
Website www.zest.co.uk

Owner *National Magazine Company*
Editor *Alison Pylkkanen*
Features Editor *Rebecca Frank*

FOUNDED 1994. MONTHLY. Health, beauty, fitness, nutrition and general well-being. No unsolicited mss. Prefers ideas in synopsis form; approach in writing.

Freelance Rates – Magazines

Freelance rates vary enormously. The following minimum rates, set by the **National Union of Journalists**, should be treated as guidelines. The NUJ has no power to enforce minimum rates on journals that do not recognise the Union. It is up to freelancers to negotiate the best deal they can.

Examples of NUJ categories for magazines:

Group A (large circulation, well-known titles with over £8000 per page of advertising) *Cosmopolitan, Hello!, marie claire, New Scientist, Radio Times, Woman, Woman's Own.*

Group B (consumer magazines with between £5000 and £8000 per page of advertising) *The Face, Time Out, Moneywise.*

Group C (special interest/large-circulation trade magazines with between £2500 and £5000 per page of advertising) *Accountancy Age, Architect's Journal.*

Group D (less than £2000 per page of advertising or carry little or no advertising) *Nursing Times.*

The following figures are the minimum rates which should be paid by magazines in the above groups for first use only:

Features (per 1000 words)

Group A	£450
Group B	£325
Group C	£250
Group D	£180

Cartoons (b&w)

	Group A	Group B & C	Group D
Minimum fee	£110	£90	£70
Feature strip (up to 4 frames)	£135	£120	£110

For colour, charge at least double these rates.

Crosswords

	Group A	Group B & C	Group D
15 × 15 squares and under	£170	£95	£90
Over 15 × 15 squares	£220	£150	£100

News Agencies

Associated Press Limited
12 Norwich Street, London EC4A 1BP
☎020 7353 1515
Fax 020 7353 8118 (Newsdesk)

Material is either generated in-house or by regulars. Hires the occasional stringer. No unsolicited mss.

Dow Jones Newswires
10 Fleet Place, London EC4M 7QN
☎020 7842 9900 Fax 020 7842 9361

A real-time financial and business newswire operated by Dow Jones & Co., publishers of *The Wall Street Journal*. No unsolicited material.

National News Press and Photo Agency
4–5 Academy Buildings, Fanshaw Street, London N1 5LQ
☎020 7684 3000 Fax 020 7684 3030

All press releases are welcome. Most work is ordered or commissioned. Coverage includes courts, tribunals, conferences, general news, etc. – words and pictures – as well as PR.

Press Association Ltd
292 Vauxhall Bridge Road, London SW1V 1AE
☎020 7963 7000/7830 (Newsdesk)
Fax 020 7963 7192 (Newsdesk)
Email copy@pa.press.net
Website www.pa.press.net

No unsolicited material. Most items are produced in-house though occasional outsiders may be used. A phone call to discuss specific material may lead somewhere 'but this is rare'.

Reuters
85 Fleet Street, London EC4P 4AJ
☎020 7250 1122

No unsolicited mss.

Solo Syndication Ltd
17–18 Hayward's Place, Clerkenwell, London EC1R 0EQ
☎020 7566 0360 Fax 020 7566 0388

FOUNDED 1978. *Specialises* in worldwide newspaper syndication of photos, features and cartoons. Professional contributors only.

Space Press NA
Bridge House, Blackden Lane, Goostrey, Cheshire CW4 8PZ
☎01477 533403/534440 Fax 01477 535756
Email Scoop2001@aol.com

Editor *John Williams*
Pictures *Emma Williams*

FOUNDED 1972. Press and picture agency covering Cheshire and the North West, North Midlands, including Knutsford, Macclesfield, Congleton, Crewe and Nantwich, Wilmslow, Alderley Edge, serving national, regional and local press, TV and radio. A member of the National Association of Press Agencies (NAPA).

Teamwork Sports Agency
6 Sharman Walk, Apperknowle, Sheffield, South Yorkshire S18 4BJ
☎01246 414767/07970 284848 (mobile)
Fax 01246 414767
Email Nicksport1@aol.com

Contact *Nick Johnson*

Provides written/broadcast coverage of sport in the South Yorkshire area.

Television and Radio

BBC TV and Radio

Website www.bbc.co.uk

Director-General *Greg Dyke*

The structure of the BBC includes four programming divisions: Drama, Entertainment and Children's; Factual and Learning; News; and Sport. Music Production is part of the Radio Division but also produces classical music programmes for television. A New Media division develops the BBC's interactive television and online activities.

TELEVISION

BBC Television Centre, Wood Lane, London W12 7RJ
☎020 8743 8000

Director, Television *Jana Bennett*
Controller, BBC1 *Lorraine Heggessey*
Controller, BBC2 *Jane Root*
Controller, BBC Four *Roly Keating*
Controller, BBC Choice *Stuart Murphy*

BBC Four, launched in March 2002 is a digital channel devoted soley to the arts. Programmes include *Readers and Writers*, a weekly book programme. BBC Choice is a digital entertainment channel aimed at younger audiences with programmes such as *Liquid News* — headline stories from the world of showbusiness.

RADIO

Broadcasting House, Portland Place, London W1A 1AA
☎020 7580 4468

Director of Radio & Music *Jenny Abramsky*
Controller, Radio 1 *Andy Parfitt*
Controller, Radio 2 *James Moir*
Controller, Radio 3 *Roger Wright*
Controller, Radio 4 *Helen Boaden*
Controller, Radio 5 Live *Bob Shennan*

Radio 1 is popular music; Radio 2 broadcasts light entertainment; Radio 3 is mainly classical and contemporary music; Radio 4 is news and current affairs with consumer matters, wildlife, science, gardening, etc. It also produces the bulk of drama, comedy, serials and readings. Radio 5 Live is the 24-hour news and sport station.

Drama, Entertainment and Children's Division

Director *Alan Yentob*

BBC *writersroom* runs targeted schemes and workshops linked directly to production. It accepts and assesses unsolicited scripts for film, single TV dramas and radio drama. Also runs *northern exposure* which focuses on new writing in the north of England, channelled through theatres in Liverpool, Manchester, Bradford, Leeds and Newcastle. To be considered for one of the schemes run by writersroom, send a sample full length drama script to: BBC writersroom, Room 222, BBC Broadcasting House, Portland Place, London W1A 1AA. For guidelines on unsolicited scripts please log on to www.bbc.co.uk/writersroom or send a large s.a.e. to *Jessica Dromgoole*, **New Writing Coordinator**, BBC Drama, Entertainment and Children's Programmes at the Broadcasting House address above. (For online information and advice, see separate entry for **The Writers Room**.)

DRAMA

Controller, Drama Commissioning *Jane Tranter*
Head of Continuing Drama *Mal Young*
Head of Films *David Thompson*
Head of Development, Serials *Sarah Brown*
Head of Development, Serials *Serena Cullen*
Head of Development, Films *Tracey Scoffield*
Head of Radio Drama *Gordon House*
Executive Producer *Jeremy Mortimer*
Executive Producer *David Hunter*
Executive Producer (Manchester) *Sue Roberts*
**Executive Producer (Birmingham)/
Editor, The Archers** *Vanessa Whitburn*
Executive Producer (World Service Drama) *Marion Nancarrow*

ENTERTAINMENT

Acting Head of Light Entertainment, Television *Jonathan Glazier*
Head of Comedy Entertainment, Television *Jon Plowman*
Producer *Bill Dare*
Editor, Radio Entertainment *John Pidgeon*

Programmes produced range from *Shooting Stars* and *Jonathan Creek* on television to *Just a Minute*;

I'm Sorry I Haven't a Clue and *The News Quiz* on Radio 4. Virtually every comic talent in Britain got their first break writing one-liners for topical comedy weeklies. For information on those programmes requiring non-commissioned submissions, join the mailing list for *Writer's Newsletter* – contact: claire.bartlett@bbc.co.uk

CBBC (CHILDREN'S)

Controller, CBBC *J. Nigel Pickard*
Head of Programmes *Dorothy Prior*
Head of Acquisitions *Theresa Plummer-Andrews*
Executive Producer,
    CBBC Drama *Elaine Sperber*
Head of Entertainment *Chris Bellinger*
Head of CBBC News/Executive
    Producer, Exchange *Roy Milani*
Head of CBBC Factual *Jeremy Daldry*
Editor, Blue Peter *Steve Hocking*
Executive Producer,
    CBBC Pre-school *Clare Elstow*
Executive Producer,
    CBBC Education *Sue Nott*
Creative Director, Children's
    Programmes, Scotland *Claire Mundell*

Factual and Learning Division

Joint Directors *Michael Stevenson,*
    Glenwyn Benson

ADULT LEARNING AND CHILDREN'S EDUCATION
Head of Learning Strategy and
    Partnerships *Paul Gerhardt*
Head of Children's Education *Frank Flynn*
Radio Production *Graham Ellis*
Head of Interactive *Liz Cleaver*

SPECIALIST FACTUAL
(includes Arts, History and Science)
Acting Controller *Keith Scholey*
BBC Milton Keynes
Walton Hall, Milton Keynes, MK7 6BH
☎01908 655588 Fax 01908 655300

Television and radio production of schools and college programmes, language courses, education for adults, plus multimedia and audiovisual material in partnership with the Open University. The Learning Zone broadcasts education, training and information programmes on BBC2 from midnight during the week.

GENERAL FACTUAL
(includes Leisure and Documentaries)
Controller *Anne Morrison*

News Division

Website www.news.bbc.co.uk
BBC News is the world's largest news-gathering organisation, with 2000 journalists, 250 specialist correspondents and 57 bureaux around the world. There are four specialist units: world affairs; economics and business; politics; and social affairs. BBC News serves: BBC1, BBC2, BBC Choice, Radios 1, 2, 3, 4 and 5 Live, BBC News 24, BBC Parliament, BBC World, BBC World Service, News Online, Ceefax.

Director, News *Richard Sambrook*
Deputy Director, News *Mark Damazer*
Head of Current Affairs *Peter Horrocks*
Head of Newsgathering *Adrian Van Klaveran*
Head of Interactive *Richard Deverell*
Head of Political Programmes *Fran Unsworth*
Head of Radio News *Stephen Mitchell*
Head of TV News *Roger Mosey*
Deputy Head of TV News *Rachel Attwell*

TELEVISION
Editor, 1 o'clock News *Chris Rybczynski*
Editor, 6 o'clock News *Jay Hunt*
Editor, 10 o'clock News *Mark Popescu*
Editor, Newsnight *George Entwhistle*
Editor, Breakfast News *Richard Porter*
Editor, Breakfast With Frost *Barney Jones*
Editor, World Service News Programmes
    To be appointed

RADIO
Editor, Today *Rod Liddle*
Editor, The World at One/World This
    Weekend/PM/Broadcasting House
    Kevin Marsh
Managing Editor, Five Live News
    Programmes *Ceri Thomas*
Editor, The World Tonight *Jenni Russell*

Ceefax
Room 7013, BBC Television Centre,
Wood Lane, London W12 7RJ
☎020 8576 1801
Editor, Ceefax *Paul Brannan*

Subtitling
Room 1468, BBC White City, Wood Lane,
London W12 7RJ
☎020 8752 7054/0141 339 8844 ext. 2128
A rapidly expanding service available via Ceefax page 888. Units based in both London and Glasgow.

Sport Division

Director, Sport *Peter Salmon*
Executive Editor, Football *Niall Sloane*

Sports news and commentaries across television and Radios 1, 4 and 5 Live, with the majority of output on Radio 5 Live. Regular programmes include *Sportsnight; Sports News* and *Sport on Five* .

BBC Religion

New Broadcasting House, Oxford Road, Manchester M60 1SJ
☎0161 200 2020 Fax 0161 244 3183
Head of Religion and Ethics *Alan Bookbinder*

Regular programmes for television include *Heaven & Earth; Songs of Praise; Everyman; Heart of the Matter*. Radio output includes *Good Morning Sunday; Sunday Half Hour; Choral Evensong; The Brains Trust; The Daily Service*.

BBC Talent

Website www.bbc.co.uk/talent

The BBC's search for new talent covers a wide range of areas including TV and radio producers, presenters, filmmakers, sitcom and comedy writers. Access the website for further information.

BBC World Service

PO Box 76, Bush House, Strand, London WC2B 4PH
☎020 7240 3456 Fax 020 7557 1900
Website www.bbc.co.uk/worldservice

Director *Mark Byford*
Director, English Networks & News, BBCWS *Phil Harding*

The World Service broadcasts in English and 42 other languages. The English service is round-the-clock, with news and current affairs as the main component. With over 150 million listeners, excluding countries where research is not possible, it reaches a bigger audience than its five closest competitors combined. The World Service is increasingly available throughout the world on local FM stations, via satellite and online as well as through short-wave frequencies. Coverage includes world business, politics, people/events/opinions, development issues, the international scene, developments in science and technology, sport, religion, music, drama, the arts. BBC World Service broadcasting is financed by a grant-in-aid voted by Parliament amounting to £173.2 million for 2002/2003.

The Writers Room

BBC, Room A400, Centre House, 56 Wood Lane, London W12 7SB
Email writersroom@bbc.co.uk
Website www.bbc.co.uk/writersroom

Online advice for new writers wishing to break into writing comedy and drama for for television and radio. Regular initiatives to encour-age new writing can be found on the website along with advice from professional writers and producers in the form of master classes, Q&As and pratical suggestions. The site is updated weekly and includes news and information plus a forum for writers to share views and discuss current output. 'We try to make a prompt personal reply to all e-mails.'

BBC Regions

BBC Northern Ireland

Broadcasting House, Ormeau Avenue, Belfast BT2 8HQ
☎028 9033 8000
Website www.bbc.co.uk/northernireland

Controller *Anna Carragher*
Head of Broadcasting *Tim Cooke*
Head of News & Current Affairs *Andrew Colman*
Editor, News Gathering *Michael Cairns*
Editor, Television News *Angelina Fusco*
Editor, Radio News *Kathleen Carragher*
Head of Drama *Robert Cooper*
Head of Entertainment, Events & Sport *Mike Edgar*
Editor, Entertainment *Alex Johnston*
Editor, Sport *Edward Smith*
Editor, Music Programmes *Declan McGovern*
Head of Factual and Learning *Bruce Batten*
Editor, Learning *Kieran Hegarty*
Editor, Popular Factual *Clare McGinn*
Editor, Factual Learning *Deirdre Devlin*
Producer, Religion *Bert Tosh*
Editor, Political Programmes *Lena Ferguson*
Editor, Text Services *Eddie Fleming*
Managing Director, Foyle *Ana Leddy*
Head of Programme Operations *Stephen Beckett*

Regular television programmes include *Newsline 6.30; Hearts and Minds* and *Country Times*. Radio stations: BBC Radio Foyle and BBC Radio Ulster (see entries).

BBC Scotland

Broadcasting House, Queen Margaret Drive, Glasgow G12 8DG
☎0141 338 2000
Website www.bbc.co.uk/scotland

Controller *John McCormick*
Controller, Network Development, Nations and Regions *Colin Cameron*
Head of Drama, Television *Barbara McKissack*
Head of Drama, Radio *Patrick Rayner*

Head of Comedy and Entertainment
Mike Bolland
Head of Factual Programmes *Andrea Miller*
Executive Editor New Media *Julie Adair*
Head of Programmes, Scotland *Ken MacQuarrie*
Head of Radio *Maggie Cunningham*
Head of Gaelic *Donalda MacKinnon*
Head of News and Current Affairs
Blair Jenkins
Head of Sport *Neil Fraser*
Commissioning Editor, Television
Ewan Angus

Headquarters of BBC Scotland with centres in Aberdeen, Dundee, Edinburgh and Inverness. Regular programmes include *Reporting Scotland* and *Sportscene* on television and *Good Morning Scotland* and *Fred Macaulay* on radio.

Aberdeen
Broadcasting House, Beechgrove Terrace, Aberdeen AB9 2ZT
☎01224 625233
Head of North *Andrew Jones*

News, plus some features, including the regular *Beechgrove Garden*. Second TV centre, also with regular radio broadcasting.

Dundee
Nethergate Centre, 66 Nethergate, Dundee DD1 4ER
☎01382 202481

News base only; contributors' studio.

Edinburgh
The Tun, Holyrood Road, Edinburgh EH8 8JF
☎0131 557 5677
Senior Producer, Arts & Features
Jane Fowler

News, current affairs, arts and features.

Inverness
7 Culduthel Road, Inverness 1V2 4AD
☎01463 720720
Editor *Ishbel MacLennan*
News features for Radio Scotland.

Radio Nan Gaidheal
Rosebank, Church Street, Stornoway, Isle of Lewis PA87 2LS
☎01851 705000
Editor *Marion MacKinnon*
The Gaelic radio service serving most of Scotland.

BBC Wales
Broadcasting House, Llandaff, Cardiff CF5 2YQ
☎029 2032 2000 Fax 029 2055 2973
Website www.bbc.co.uk/wales

Controller *Menna Richards*
Head of Programmes (Welsh Language)
Keith Jones
Head of Programmes (English Language)
Clare Hudson
Head of News & Current Affairs *Aled Eurig*
Head of Drama *Matthew Robinson*
Series Editor, Pobol y Cwm *Terry Dyddgen-Jones*

Headquarters of BBC Wales, with regional centres in Bangor, Aberystwyth, Carmarthen, Wrexham and Swansea. BBC Wales television produces up to 12 hours of English language programmes a week, 12 hours in Welsh for transmission on **S4C** and an increasing number of hours on network services. Regular programmes include *Wales Today; Newyddion* (Welsh-language daily news); *Wales on Saturday* and *Pobol y Cwm* (Welsh-language soap) on television and *Good Morning Wales; Good Evening Wales; Post Cyntaf* and *Post Prynhawn* on radio.

Bangor
Broadcasting House, Meirion Road, Bangor, Gwynedd LL57 2BY
☎01248 370880 Fax 01248 351443
Head of Centre *Marian Wyn Jones*

BBC Asian Network
BBC Pebble Mill, Epic House, Charles Street, Leicester LE1 3SH
☎0116 251 6688 Fax 0116 253 2004
Email asian.network@bbc.co.uk
Website www.bbc.co.uk/asiannetwork

Managing Editor *Vijay Sharma*

Commenced broadcasting in November 1996. Broadcasts to a Midlands audience during the day and nationwide coverage in the evening. Programmes in English, Bengali, Gujerati, Hindi, Punjabi and Urdu.

BBC Birmingham
Pebble Mill Road, Birmingham B5 7QQ
☎0121 432 8888 Fax 0121 432 8847
Website www.bbc.co.uk/birmingham

Head of Regional and Local Programmes
Roy Roberts
Output Editor *Charles Watkin*

Home of the Pebble Mill Studio. Output for the network includes: TV – *Doctors; Countryfile; Top Gear; Dalziel and Pascoe; Gardener's World; Real Rooms.* Radio – *The Archers; Shake, Rattle and Roll; Farming Today; Jazz Notes; Late Night Currie; Ramblings With Clare Balding.*

BBC Birmingham serves opt-out stations in Nottingham and Norwich:

BBC East Midlands (Nottingham)
East Midlands Broadcasting Centre, London Road, Nottingham NG2 4UU
☎0115 955 0500 Fax 0115 902 1983
Website www.bbc.co.uk/nottingham
Head of Regional and Local Programmes
  Alison Ford
Acting Output Editor *Kevin Hill*

BBC East (Norwich)
St Catherine's Close, All Saint's Green, Norwich, Norfolk NR1 3ND
☎01603 619331 Fax 01603 284455
Website www.bbc.co.uk/norfolk
Head of Regional and Local Programmes
  David Holdsworth
Output Editor *Tim Bishop*

BBC Bristol
Broadcasting House, Whiteladies Road, Bristol BS8 2LR
☎0117 973 2211
Head of General Factual TV *Tom Archer*
Head of Natural History Unit *Keith Scholey*
BBC Bristol is the home of the BBC's Natural History Unit, producing programmes such as *Blue Planet; Life of Mammals; Wildlife on One; The Natural World* and *The Really Wild Show* for BBC1 and BBC2. It also produces natural history programmes for Radio 4 and Radio 5 Live. The Features department produces a wide range of television programmes, including *999; Antiques Roadshow; Bargain Hunt* and *Vets in Practice* in addition to radio programmes specialising in history, travel, literature and human interest features for Radio 4.

BBC London
35 Marylebone High Street, London W1U 4QA
☎020 7224 2424
Executive Editor *Jane Mote* (Responsible for BBC London Live and Newsroom South East)
Editor, Newsgathering *Sandy Smith*

BBC North/BBC North West/ BBC North East & Cumbria
The regional centres at Leeds, Manchester and Newcastle make their own programmes on a bi-media approach, each centre having its own head of regional and local programmes.

BBC North (Leeds)
Broadcasting Centre, Woodhouse Lane, Leeds, West Yorkshire LS2 9PX
☎0113 244 1188
Head of Regional and Local Programmes
  Colin Philpott
Editor, Newsgathering *Jake Fowler*
Editor, Look North *Kate Watkins*
Assistant News Editors, Look North
  Denise Wallace, Ned Thacker
Political Editor, North of Westminster
  Len Tingle
Senior Broadcast Journalist, North of Westminster *Rod Jones*
Weeklies Editor, Close Up North
  Ian Cundall
Producers, Close Up North *Richard Taylor, Paul Greenan*

BBC North West (Manchester)
New Broadcasting House, Oxford Road, Manchester M60 1SJ
☎0161 200 2020
Head of Regional and Local Programmes
  Martin Brooks
Editor, Newsgathering *Michelle Mayman*
Producer, Northwest Tonight *Jim Clark*
Producer, Close Up North *Deborah van Bishop*
Producer, Northwestminster *Liam Fogarty*

BBC North East & Cumbria (Newcastle upon Tyne)
Broadcasting Centre, Barrack Road, Newcastle Upon Tyne NE99 2NE
☎0191 232 1313
Head of Regional and Local Programmes
  Olwyn Hocking
Editor, Newsgathering *Andrew Hartley*
Producer, Look North *Iain Williams*
Producer, North of Westminster *Michael Wild*
Producer, Close Up North *Jacqui Hodgson*

BBC South East (Tunbridge Wells)
The Great Hall, Mount Pleasant, Tunbridge Wells, Kent TN1 1QQ
☎01892 670000

Head of Regional and Local Programmes
Laura Ellis (Responsible for BBC South East
[TV], BBC Radio Kent and BBC Southern
Counties Radio)
Editor, Newsgathering *Rod Beards*
Executive Producer, First Sight
Dippy Chaudhary

BBC West/BBC South/ BBC South West

The three regional television stations, BBC
West, BBC South and BBC South West produce the nightly news magazine programmes,
as well as regular 30-minute local current affairs
programmes and parliamentary programmes.
Each of the regions operates a comprehensive
local radio service as well as a range of correspondents specialising in subjects like health,
education, business, local government, home
affairs and the environment.

BBC West (Bristol)
Broadcasting House, Whiteladies Road,
Bristol BS8 2LR
☎0117 973 2211
Head of Regional and Local Programmes
Andrew Wilson (Responsible for BBC West
[TV], BBC Radio Bristol, BBC Somerset
Sound, BBC Radio Gloucestershire and
BBC Wiltshire Sound)
Output Editors *Jane Kinghorn, Stephanie
Marshall*
Series Producer, Close Up West *James
MacAlpine*

BBC South (Southampton)
Broadcasting House, Havelock Road,
Southampton, Hampshire SO14 7PU
☎023 8022 6201
Head of Regional and Local Programmes
Eve Turner (Responsible for BBC South
[TV], BBC Radio Berkshire, BBC Radio
Oxford and BBC Radio Solent)
Output Editor *Cathy Burnett*
Series Producer, Southern Eye *Jane French*

BBC South West (Plymouth)
Broadcasting House, Seymour Road,
Mannamead, Plymouth, Devon PL3 5BD
☎01752 229201
Head of Regional and Local Programmes
Leo Devine (Responsible for BBC South
West [TV], BBC Radio Devon, BBC
Radio Cornwall, BBC Radio Guernsey and
BBC Radio Jersey)

News Editor *Roger Clark*
Editor, Current Affairs *Simon Willis*

BBC Local Radio

BBC Local Radio
Room 2661, Broadcasting House, London
W1A 1AA
☎020 7580 4468
Website www.bbc.co/england

There are 39 local BBC radio stations in England
transmitting on FM and medium wave. These
present local news, information and entertainment to local audiences and reflect the life of the
communities they serve. Each has its own newsroom which supplies local bulletins and national
news service. Many have specialist producers. A
comprehensive list of programmes for each is
unavailable and would soon be out of date. For
general information on programming, contact
the relevant station direct.

BBC Radio Berkshire
PO Box 104.4, Reading, Berkshire RG94 8FH
☎08459 311444 Fax 08459 311555
Website www.bbc.co.uk/radioberkshire
Editor *Phil Ashworth*

Restored to its original name in 2000 having
been merged with BBC Radio Oxford in 1995
to create BBC Thames Valley.

BBC Radio Bristol
PO Box 194, Bristol BS99 7QT
☎0117 974 1111 Fax 0117 923 9323
Email radio.bristol@bbc.co.uk
Website www.bbc.co.uk/radiobristol
Managing Editor *Jenny Lacey*
Wide range of feature material used.

BBC Radio Cambridgeshire
PO Box 96, 104 Hills Road, Cambridge
CB2 1LD
☎01223 259696 Fax 01223 460832
Email cambs@bbc.co.uk
Website www.bbc.co.uk/radiocambridgeshire
Editor *David Martin*

Commenced broadcasting in May 1982. Short
stories are broadcast occasionally.

BBC Radio Cleveland
PO Box 95FM, Broadcasting House,
Newport Road, Middlesbrough, Cleveland
TS1 5DG
☎01642 225211 Fax 01642 211356

Email radio.cleveland@bbc.co.uk
Website www.bbc.co.uk/radiocleveland
Managing Editor *Andrew Glover*
Material used is mainly local to Teesside, Co. Durham and North Yorkshire, and is almost exclusively news and current affairs.

BBC Radio Cornwall
Phoenix Wharf, Truro, Cornwall TR1 1UA
☎01872 275421 Fax 01872 275045
Email radio.cornwall@bbc.co.uk
Website www.bbc.co.uk/radiocornwall
Editor *Pauline Causey*
On air from 1983 serving Cornwall and the Isles of Scilly. Broadcasts 117 hours of local programmes weekly including news, phone-ins and specialist music. Chris Blount's afternoon programme includes interviews with local authors and arts-related features on Cornish themes.

BBC Coventry and Warwickshire
Holt Court, 1 Greyfriars Road, Coventry CV1 2WR
☎024 7686 0086 Fax 024 7657 0100
Email coventry.warwickshire@bbc.co.uk
Website www.bbc.co.uk/
    coventrywarwickshire
Managing Editor *Keith Beech*
Commenced broadcasting in January 1990 as CWR. Shares programmes with sister station, BBC Radio WM. News, current affairs, public service information and community involvement, relevant to its broadcast area: Coventry and Warwickshire.

BBC Radio Cumbria
Annetwell Street, Carlisle, Cumbria CA3 8BB
☎01228 592444 Fax 01228 511195
Email radio.cumbria@bbc.co.uk
Website www.bbc.co.uk/radiocumbria
Editor *Nigel Dyson*
Occasional opportunities for plays and short stories are advertised on-air.

BBC Radio Cymru
Broadcasting House, Llandaff, Cardiff CF5 2YQ
☎029 2032 2000 Fax 029 2055 5960
Email radio.cymru@bbc.co.uk
Website www.bbc.co.uk/cymru
Editor *Aled Glynne Davies*
Editor, Radio Cymru News *Rhian Gibson*
Welsh-language programmes only, including *Post Cyntaf*, *Chwaraeon* and *Gang Bangor*.

BBC Radio Derby
PO Box 104.5, Derby DE1 3HL
☎01332 361111 Fax 01332 290794
Email radio.derby@bbc.co.uk
Website www.bbc.co.uk/radioderby
Editor *Simon Cornes*
News and information (the backbone of the station's output), local sports coverage, daily magazine and phone-ins, minority interest, Asian and African Caribbean weekly programmes.

BBC Radio Devon
PO Box 1034, Broadcasting House, Seymour Road, Mannamead, Plymouth, Devon PL3 5YQ
☎01752 260323 Fax 01752 234599
Email radio.devon@bbc.co.uk
Website www.bbc.co.uk/radiodevon
Also at: Walnut Gardens, St David's Hill, Exeter, Devon EX4 4DB
☎01392 215651
Managing Editor *John Lilley*
Head of Programmes *Ian Timms*
Head of News *Sarah Solftley*
On air since 1983. Programmes include *Douglas Mounce with Show Time* – Saturday, 5.00 pm to 6.00 pm.

BBC Essex
198 New London Road, Chelmsford, Essex CM2 9XB
☎01245 616000 Fax 01245 492983
Email essex@bbc.co.uk
Website www.bbc.co.uk/essex
Editor *Margaret Hyde*
Broadcasts local and regional programmes for 20 hours every day aimed at a mature audience. Programmes are a mix of news, interviews, expert contributors, phone-ins, sport and special interest such as gardening.

BBC Radio Foyle
8 Northland Road, Londonderry BT48 7GD
☎028 7137 8600 Fax 028 7137 8666
Website www.bbc.co.uk/northernireland
Managing Editor *Ana Leddy*
News Producers *Eimear O'Callaghan, Paul McFadden*
Arts/Book Reviews *Colum Arbuckle*
Features *Michael Bradley*
Radio Foyle broadcasts about seven hours of original material a day, seven days a week to the north west of Northern Ireland. Other programmes are transmitted simultaneously with Radio Ulster. The output ranges from news,

sport, and current affairs to live music recordings and arts reviews.

BBC Radio Gloucestershire

London Road, Gloucester GL1 1SW
☎01452 308585 Fax 01452 309491
Email radio.gloucestershire@bbc.co.uk
Website www.bbc.co.uk/radiogloucestershire
Managing Editor *Mark Hurrell*

News and information covering the large variety of interests and concerns in Gloucestershire. Leisure, sport and music, plus African Caribbean and Asian interests. Regular book reviews and interviews with local authors.

BBC GLR

See **BBC London Live**

BBC GMR

PO Box 951, Oxford Road, Manchester M60 1SD
☎0161 200 2000 Fax 0161 236 5804
Email gmr@bbc.co.uk
Website www.bbc.co.uk/gmr
Managing Editor *Steve Taylor*
News Editor *Mark Elliot*
Programmes Editor *Lawrence Mann*

On air from 1970, originally as Radio Manchester. Became BBC GMR in 1988. One of the largest of the BBC local radio stations, broadcasting news, current affairs, phone-ins, help, advice and sport.

BBC Radio Guernsey

Commerce House, Les Banques, St Peter Port, Guernsey, Channel Islands GY1 2HS
☎01481 728977 Fax 01481 713557
Email radio.guernsey@bbc.co.uk
Website www.bbc.co.uk/radioguernsey
Managing Editor *Robert Wallace*

Opened with its sister station, BBC Radio Jersey, in March 1982. Broadcasts 80 hours of local programming a week.

BBC Hereford & Worcester

Hylton Road, Worcester WR2 5WW
☎01905 748485 Fax 01905 748006
Email bbchw@bbc.co.uk
Website www.bbc.co.uk/herefordworcester
Also at: 43 Broad Street, Hereford HR4 9HH
☎01432 355252 Fax 01432 356446
Managing Editor *James Coghill*

Holds competitions on an occasional basis for short stories, plays or dramatised documentaries with a local flavour.

BBC Radio Humberside

9 Chapel Street, Hull, North Humberside HU1 3NU
☎01482 323232 Fax 01482 621403
Email radio.humberside@bbc.co.uk
Website www.bbc.co.uk/radiohumberside
Editor *Helen Thomas*

On air since 1971. Occasionally broadcasts short stories by local writers and holds competitions for local amateur authors and playwrights.

BBC Radio Jersey

18 Parade Road, St Helier, Jersey, Channel Islands JE2 3PL
☎01534 870000 Fax 01534 732569
Email matthew.price@bbc.co.uk
Website www.bbc.co.uk/radiojersey
Managing Editor *Denzil Dudley*
Senior Broadcast Journalist *Matthew Price*

Local news, current affairs and community items.

BBC Radio Kent

The Great Hall, Mount Pleasant Road, Tunbridge Wells, Kent TN1 1QQ
☎01892 670000 Fax 01892 549118
Email radio.kent@bbc.co.uk
Website www.bbc.co.uk/radiokent
Managing Editor *Steve Taschini*

Occasional commissions are made for local interest documentaries and other one-off programmes.

BBC Radio Lancashire

Darwen Street, Blackburn, Lancashire BB2 2EA
☎01254 262411 Fax 01254 680821
Email radio.lancashire@bbc.co.uk
Website www.bbc.co.uk/radiolancashire
Editor *John Clayton*

Journalism-based radio station, interested in interviews with local writers. Contact *Jacquie Williams* and *Brett Davison*, 1.15 pm to 4.00 pm Monday to Friday (jacquie.williams@bbc.co.uk *or* brett.davison@bbc.co.uk).

BBC Radio Leeds

Broadcasting House, Woodhouse Lane, Leeds, West Yorkshire LS2 9PN
☎0113 244 2131 Fax 0113 242 0652
Email radio.leeds@bbc.co.uk
Website www.bbc.co.uk/radioleeds
Managing Editor *Ashley Peatfield*

One of the country's biggest local radio stations,

BBC Radio Leeds was also one of the first, coming on air in the 1960s as something of an experimental venture. The station is 'all talk', with a comprehensive news, sport and information service as the backbone of its daily output. BBC Radio Leeds has been a regular finalist for the title of Sony Regional Station of the Year. Has also won two Gold Sonys for best presentation.

BBC Radio Leicester
Epic House, Charles Street, Leicester LE1 3SH
☎0116 251 6688 Fax 0116 251 1463
Email radio.leicester@bbc.co.uk
Website www.bbc.co.uk/radioleicester

Editor *Liam McCarthy*

The first local station in Britain. Occasional interviews with local authors.

BBC Radio Lincolnshire
PO Box 219, Newport, Lincoln LN1 3XY
☎01522 511411 Fax 01522 511726
Email radio.lincolnshire@bbc.co.uk
Website www.bbc.co.uk/radiolincolnshire

Managing Editor *Charlie Partridge*

Unsolicited material considered only if locally relevant. Maximum 1000 words: straight narrative preferred, ideally with a topical content.

BBC London Live 94.9FM
35 Marylebone High Street, London
W1M 4AA
☎020 7224 2424 Fax 020 7208 9661
Email londonlive@bbc.co.uk
Website www.bbc.co.uk/londonlive

Editor *David Robey*

Formerly Greater London Radio (GLR), launched in 1988, London Live broadcasts news, information, travel bulletins, sport and music to Greater London and the Home Counties. Dotun Adebayo's *Word for Word* explores and celebrates poetry, the spoken word and song lyrics every Sunday between 1.00 pm and 3.00 pm.

BBC Radio Manchester
See **BBC GMR**

BBC Radio Merseyside
55 Paradise Street, Liverpool L1 3BP
☎0151 708 5500 Fax 0151 794 0988
Email radio.merseyside@bbc.co.uk
Website www.bbc.co.uk/radiomerseyside

Editor *Mick Ord*

First Friday – a monthly poetry slot between 1.30 pm and 2.00 pm on the first Friday of every month in the Roger Phillips lunchtime programme. Merseyside writers can offer poetry by e-mailing roger.phillips@bbc.co.uk or send copies with name/address attached, to 'First Friday Poetry', c/o BBC Radio Merseyside at the address above. Only the poets used will be acknowledged and contacted.

BBC Radio Newcastle
Broadcasting Centre, Barrack Road,
Newcastle upon Tyne NE99 1RN
☎0191 232 4141
Email radio.newcastle@bbc.co.uk
Website www.bbc.co.uk/radionewcastle

Editor *Sarah Drummond*
Senior Producer (Programmes)
  Sarah Miller

Commenced broadcasting in January 1971. The BBC's eighth biggest local radio station in England, Radio Newcastle reaches an audience of 229,000.

BBC Radio Norfolk
Norfolk Tower, Surrey Street, Norwich,
Norfolk NR1 3PA
☎01603 617411 Fax 01603 633692
Email norfolk@bbc.co.uk
Website www.bbc.co.uk/radionorfolk

Editor *David Clayton*

Good local ideas and material welcome for features/documentaries, but must relate directly to Norfolk.

BBC Radio Northampton
Broadcasting House, Abington Street,
Northampton NN1 2BH
☎01604 239100 Fax 01604 230709
Email northampton@bbc.co.uk
Website www.bbc.co.uk/radionorthampton

Managing Editor *David Clargo*

Books of local interest are regularly featured. Authors and poets are interviewed on merit. Poems and short stories are reviewed occasionally, but not broadcast. Runs regular competitions for local writers.

BBC Radio Nottingham
London Road, Nottingham NG2 4UU
☎0115 955 0500 Fax 0115 902 1983
Email radio.nottingham@bbc.co.uk
Website www.bbc.co.uk/radionottingham

Editor *Kate Squire*

Rarely broadcasts scripted pieces of any kind but interviews with authors form a regular part of the station's output.

BBC Radio Oxford

PO Box 95.2, Oxford OX2 7YL
☎08459 311444 Fax 08459 311555
Email radio.oxford@bbc.co.uk
Website www.bbc.co.uk/radiooxford
Managing Editor *Phil Ashworth*

Restored to its original name in 2000 having been merged with BBC Radio Berkshire in 1995 to create BBC Thames Valley. The station frequently carries interviews with local authors and offers books as prizes.

BBC Radio Scotland (Dumfries)

Elmbank, Lover's Walk, Dumfries
DG1 1NZ
☎01387 268008 Fax 01387 252568
Email dumfries@bbc.co.uk
Senior Producer *Willie Johnston*

Previously Radio Solway. The station mainly outputs news bulletins (four daily) although the station has become more of a production centre with programmes being made for Radio Scotland as well as BBC Radio 2 and 5 Live. Freelancers of a high standard, familiar with Radio Scotland, should contact the producer.

BBC Radio Scotland (Orkney)

Castle Street, Kirkwall, Orkney KW15 1DF
☎01856 873939 Fax 01856 872908
Senior Producer *John Fergusson*

Regular programmes include *Around Orkney* (weekday news programme) and *Bruck* (magazine programme).

BBC Radio Scotland (Selkirk)

Municipal Buildings, High Street, Selkirk
TD7 4JX
☎01750 21884 Fax 01750 22400
Contact *Ninian Reid*

Formerly BBC Radio Tweed. Local news bulletins.

BBC Radio Sheffield

Shoreham Street, Sheffield S1 4RS
☎0114 273 1177 Fax 0114 267 5454
Email radio.sheffield@bbc.co.uk
Website www.bbc.co.uk/radiosheffield
Station Editor *Gary Keown*
Programmes Editor *Emma Gilliam*
News Editor *David Holmes*

Writer interviews, writing-related topics and readings on the Rony Robinson show between 11.10 am and 11.30 am.

BBC Radio Shetland

Pitt Lane, Lerwick, Shetland ZE1 0DW
☎01595 694747 Fax 01595 694307
Senior Producer *Richard Whitaker*

Regular programmes include *Good Evening Shetland*. An occasional books programme highlights the activities of local writers and writers' groups.

BBC Radio Shropshire

2–4 Boscobel Drive, Shrewsbury, Shropshire
SY1 3TT
☎01743 248484 Fax 01743 237018
Email radio.shropshire@bbc.co.uk
Website www.bbc.co.uk/shropshire
Editor *Tony Fish*

On air since 1985. Unsolicited literary material rarely used, and then only if locally relevant.

BBC Radio Solent

Broadcasting House, Havelock Road,
Southampton, Hampshire SO14 7PW
☎023 8063 1311 Fax 023 8033 9648
Email radio.solent@bbc.co.uk
Website www.bbc.co.uk/radiosolent
Managing Editor *Mia Costello*

Broadcasting since 1970.

BBC Somerset Sound

Bedes House, Park Street, Taunton,
Somerset
☎01823 252437 Fax 01823 332539
Website www.bbc.co.uk/radiobristol/somerset
Editor *Jenny Lacey*

Informal, speech-based programming, with strong news and current affairs output and regular local-interest features, including local writing. Poetry and short stories on the *Adam Thomas Programme*.

BBC Southern Counties Radio

Broadcasting Centre, Guildford, Surrey
GU2 5AP
☎01483 306306 Fax 01483 304952
Email southern.counties.radio@bbc.co.uk
Website www.bbc.co.uk/southerncounties
Also at: Broadcasting House, 40–42 Queens, Brighton, East Sussex BN1 3XB
Managing Editor *Mike Hapgood*

Regular programmes include three individual breakfast shows: *Breakfast Live in Brighton with JoAnne Good/in Surrey with Ed Douglas/in Sussex with John Radford*.

BBC Radio Stoke

Cheapside, Hanley, Stoke on Trent,
Staffordshire ST1 1JJ
☎01782 208080 Fax 01782 289115
Email radio.stoke@bbc.co.uk
Website www.bbc.co.uk/radiostoke

Managing Editor *Mark Hurrell*

On air since 1968, one of the first eight 'experimental' BBC stations. Emphasis on news, current affairs and local topics. Music represents one fifth of total output. Unsolicited material of local interest is welcome – send to *Barbara Adams*.

BBC Radio Suffolk

Broadcasting House, St Matthew's Street,
Ipswich, Suffolk IP1 3EP
☎01473 250000 Fax 01473 210887
Email suffolk@bbc.co.uk *or*
radiosuffolk@bbc.co.uk
Website www.bbc.co.uk/suffolk

Managing Editor *David Peel*

Strongly speech-based, dealing with news, current affairs, community issues, agriculture, commerce, the arts, travel, sport, leisure. Programmes sometimes carry interviews with writers.

BBC Thames Valley

See **BBC Radio Berkshire**and **BBC Radio Oxford**

BBC Three Counties Radio

1 Hastings Street, Luton, Bedfordshire
LU1 5XL
☎01582 637400 Fax 01582 401467
Email 3cr@bbc.co.uk
Website www.bbc.co.uk/3counties

Managing Editor *Mark Norman*

Encourages freelance contributions from the community across a wide range of radio output, including interview and feature material. Interested in local history topics (five minutes maximum).

BBC Radio Ulster

Broadcasting House, Ormeau Avenue, Belfast
BT2 8HQ
☎028 9033 8000

Programmes broadcast from 6.30 am to midnight weekdays and from 6.55 am to midnight at weekends. Radio Ulster has won seven Sony awards in recent years. Programmes include: *Good Morning Ulster*; *John Bennett*; *Gerry Anderson*; *Talk Back*; *Just Jones*; *Evening Extra*; *On Your Behalf*; *Your Place and Mine* and *Across the Line*.

BBC Radio Wales

Broadcasting House, Llandaff, Cardiff CF5 2YQ
☎029 2032 2000 Fax 029 2032 2674
Email radio.wales@bbc.co.uk
Website www.bbc.co.uk/wales/radio

Editor *Julie Barton*
Editor, Radio Wales News *Geoff Williams*

Broadcasts news on the hour and half hour throughout weekday daytime programmes; hourly bulletins in the evenings and at weekends. Programmes include *Good Morning Wales*; *Roy Noble*; *Nicola Heywood Thomas* and *Kevin Hughes*. Access line number: 08700 100110.

BBC Wiltshire Sound

Broadcasting House, Prospect Place, Swindon,
Wiltshire SN1 3RW
☎01793 513626 Fax 01793 513650
Email wiltshire.sound@bbc.co.uk
Website www.bbc.co.uk/wiltshiresound

Editor *Tony Wargon*

Regular programmes include: *Peter Heaton-Jones's Mid-Morning Show* (reviews and author interviews).

BBC Radio WM

PO Box 206, Birmingham B5 7SD
☎0121 432 2000 Fax 0121 472 3174
Email radio.wm@bbc.co.uk
Website www.bbc.co.uk/radiowm

Managing Editor *Keith Beech*

Commenced broadcasting in November 1970 as BBC Birmingham. Speech-based station broadcasting to the West Midlands, South Staffordshire, North Worcestershire and North Warwickshire.

BBC Radio York

20 Bootham Row, York YO30 7BR
☎01904 641351 Fax 01904 610937
Email radio.york@bbc.co.uk
Website www.bbc.co.uk/radioyork

Editor *Barrie Stephenson*

Stories only accepted in reponse to occasional short story competitions.

Independent Television

Anglia Television

Anglia House, Norwich, Norfolk NR1 3JG
☎01603 615151 Fax 01603 761245
Email angliatv@angliatv.co.uk
Website www.angliatv.com

Managing Director *Graham Creelman*
Controller of Programmes *Neil Thompson*
Controller of News *Guy Adams*

Anglia Television is a major producer of programmes for the ITV network, including *Trisha* (Trisha Goddard's chat show) and major documentaries. Network drama is produced by Anglia's parent company, Granada.

Border Television plc

Television Centre, Durranhill, Carlisle, Cumbria CA1 3NT
☎01228 525101 Fax 01228 541384
Website www.border-tv.com

Deputy Chairman *James Graham, OBE*
Controller of Programmes *Neil Robinson*

Border's programming concentrates on documentaries rather than drama. Most scripts are supplied in-house but occasionally there are commissions. Apart from notes, writers should not submit written work until their ideas have been fully discussed.

Carlton Television, London Region

101 St Martin's Lane, London WC2N 4AZ
☎020 7240 4000 Fax 020 7240 4171
Website www.carlton.com

Chief Executive, Carlton Channels *Clive Jones*
Director of Programmes, Carlton Productions *Steve Hewlett*

Carlton Television holds four of the 15 regional ITV licences: Carlton – the weekday broadcaster for the London region; Carlton Central Region – covering the east, west and south Midlands; and Carlton West Country Region, HTV Wales and HTV West – covering the south west of England. Network drama includes *Crossroads; The Vice; Bertie and Elizabeth* and *Blue Dove*. See also **Carlton Productions** under **Film, TV and Video Production Companies**.

Carlton Broadcasting, Carlton Central Region

Gas Street, Birmingham B1 2JP
☎0121 643 9898 Fax 0121 634 4240
Website www.carlton.com/central
Managing Director, Carlton Broadcasting *Ian Squires*

Regular regional programmes include *Central Weekend* and *Asian Eye*.

Carlton Broadcasting, Carlton West Country Region

Langage Science Park, Western Wood Way, Plymouth, Devon PL7 5BG
☎01752 333333 Fax 01752 333444
Website www.carlton.com/westcountry
Managing Director *Mark Haskell*
Director of Programmes *Jane McCloskey*
Controller of News *Phil Carrodus*
Head of Current Affairs *Graham Smith*

Came on air in January 1993. News, current affairs, documentary and religious programming.

HTV Wales

The TV Centre, Culverhouse Cross, Cardiff CF5 6XJ
☎029 2059 0590 Fax 029 2059 7183
Website www.htvwales.co.uk
Controller/Director of Programmes *Elis Owen*

HTV West

Television Centre, Bath Road, Bristol BS4 3HG
☎0117 972 2722 Fax 0117 972 2400
Website www.htvwest.co.uk
Managing Director *Jeremy Payne*
Controller, HTV West & Director of Regional Programmes *Sandra Jones*

Channel 4

124 Horseferry Road, London SW1P 2TX
☎020 7396 4444 Fax 020 7306 8356
Website www.channel4.com
Director of Programmes *Tim Gardam*
Head of Film *Paul Webster*
Head of Entertainment *Danielle Lux*

COMMISSIONING EDITORS
Independent Film and Video *Adam Barker*
Head of Drama and Animation *Tessa Ross*
Head of Comedy *Caroline Leddy*
Documentaries *Peter Dale*
News, Current Affairs & Business *David Lloyd*
Sport *David Kerr*
Multicultural Programmes *Yasmin Anwar*
Arts, History and Religion *Janice Hadlow*
Controller of Acquisition *June Dromgoole*

Channel 4 started broadcasting as a national channel in November 1982. It enjoys unique status as the world's only major public service broadcaster funded entirely by its own commercial activities. All programmes are commissioned from independent production companies and are broadcast across the whole of the UK except those parts of Wales covered by S4C. Its FilmFour channel, launched in November 1998, is a premium pay-TV channel featuring modern independent cinema. A second digital channel, E4 was launched in January 2001, broadcasting a range of programmes similar to Channel 4.

Channel 5
22 Long Acre, London WC2E 9LY
☎020 7550 5555 Fax 020 7550 5554
Website www.channel5.co.uk

CEO *Dawn Airey*
Director of Programmes *Kevin Lygo*
Controller of Children's and Religious Programmes *Nick Wilson*
Senior Programme Controller *Chris Shaw*
Controller of Drama Programmes *Corinne Hollingworth*

Channel 5 Broadcasting Ltd won the franchise for Britain's third commercial terrestrial television station in 1995 and came on air at the end of March 1997. Regular programmes include *Family Affairs* (Monday to Friday soap opera) and *Open House* (Gloria Hunniford's daytime magazine show), plus documentaries, drama, films, children's programmes, sport and entertainment.

Channel Television
Television Centre, La Pouquelaye, St Helier, Jersey, Channel Islands JE1 3ZD
☎01534 816816 Fax 01534 816817
Website www.channeltv.co.uk
Also at: Television House, Bulwer Avenue, St Sampsons, Guernsey, Channel Islands GY2 4LA
☎01481 241888 Fax 01481 241878

Managing Director *Michael Lucas*
Director of Programmes *Karen Rankine*
Director of Sales *Gordon De Ste Croix*
Director of Resources & Transmission *Kevin Banner*

Channel Television is the Independent Television broadcaster to the Channel Islands, serving 143,000 residents, most of whom live on the main islands, Jersey, Guernsey, Alderney and Sark. The station has a weekly reach of more than 94% with local programmes (in the region of six hours each week) at the heart of the ITV service to the islands.

GMTV
The London Television Centre, Upper Ground, London SE1 9TT
☎020 7827 7000 Fax 020 7827 7249
Email talk2us@gmtv.co.uk

Website www.gmtv.co.uk
Managing Director *Paul Corley*
Director of Programmes *Peter McHugh*
Managing Editor *John Scammell*

Winner of the national breakfast television franchise. Jointly owned by Scottish Media Group, Carlton Communications, Walt Disney Company and Granada Group. GMTV took over from TV-AM on 1 January 1993, with live programming from 6.00 am to 9.25 am. Regular news headlines, current affairs, topical features, showbiz and lifestyle, sports and business, quizzes and competitions, travel and weather reports. Launched its digital service, GMTV2, in January 1999, with daily broadcasts from 6.00 am to 9.25 am. News reports, travel, health and lifestyle features, some simulcast with GMTV1. Children's programming on Saturdays.

Grampian Television Limited
Queen's Cross, Aberdeen AB15 4XJ
☎01224 846846 Fax 01224 846800
Website www.grampiantv.co.uk
Managing Director *Derrick Thomson*
Head of News and Current Affairs *Henry Eagles*

Extensive regional news and reports including farming, fishing and sports, interviews and leisure features, various light entertainment, Gaelic and religious programmes, and live coverage of the Scottish political, economic and industrial scene. Serves the area stretching from Fife to Shetland. Regular programmes include *North Tonight*; *Grampian Midweek* and *The People Show*.

Granada Television
Quay Street, Manchester M60 9EA
☎0161 832 7211 Fax 0161 953 0283
Website www.granadamedia.com

Director of Programmes *John Whiston*
Director of Production *Claire Poyser*
Controller of Regional Programmes *Kieron Collins*
Controller of Drama *Carolyn Reynolds*
Controller of Current Affairs and Features *Jeff Anderson*
Controller of Documentaries, History and Science *Bill Jones*

Opportunities for freelance writers are not great but mss from professional writers will be considered. All mss should be addressed to the head of scripts. Regular programmes include *Coronation Street* and *Tonight*.

HTV Wales/ HTV West
See **Carlton Television**

ITN (Independent Television News Ltd)

200 Gray's Inn Road, London WC1X 8XZ
☎020 7833 3000 Fax 020 7430 4868
Email contact@itn.co.uk
Website www.itn.co.uk

Chief Executive *Stewart Purvis*
Editor-in-Chief *Richard Tait*
Editor, ITN News for ITV *Nigel Dacre*
Editor, Channel 4 News *Jim Gray*
Editor, Channel 5 News *Gary Rogers*

Provider of the main national and international news for ITV, Channel 4 and Channel 5 and radio news for IRN. Programmes on ITV: *Lunchtime News; Evening News; News at Ten,* plus regular news summaries, and three programmes a day at weekends. Programmes on Channel 4 include the in-depth news analysis programmes *Channel 4 News* and *The Big Breakfast News.* Programmes on Channel 5: *5 News Early; 5 News at Noon; 5 News* plus regular updates. ITN also has operating control of *Euronews,* Europe's only pan-European broadcaster. Since August 2000, ITN broadcasts in its own right on ITN News Channel, a 24-hour news service available for television, video, audio and text format.

LWT (London Weekend Television)

The London Television Centre, Upper Ground, London SE1 9LT
☎020 7620 1620
Website www.itv.com/lwt

Chairman *Charles Allen*
Managing Director *Lindsay Charlton*
Director of Production *Tamara Howe*
Controller of Entertainment & Comedy
  Bob Massie
Controller of Drama *Michele Buck*
Controller of Arts *Melvyn Bragg*
Controller of Factual Programmes *Will Smith*

Makers of current affairs, entertainment and drama series such as *Blind Date; Surprise Surprise; Where the Heart Is; Night & Day; London's Burning* also *The South Bank Show* and *Jonathan Dimbleby.* Provides a large proportion of ITV's drama and light entertainment, and also for BSkyB and Channel 4.

Meridian Broadcasting

Television Centre, Southampton, Hampshire SO14 0PZ
☎023 8022 2555 Fax 023 8033 5050
Email viewerliaison@meridiantv.com
Website www.meridiantv.com

Managing Director *Mary McAnally*
Controller of Regional Programmes *Mark Southgate*
Director of News *Andy Cooper*

Meridian's studios in Southampton provide a base for network and regional productions. Regular regional programmes include the award-winning news service, *Meridian Tonight; Countryways* and *Grass Roots.*

S4C

Parc Tŷ Glas, Llanishen, Cardiff CF14 5DU
☎029 2074 7444 Fax 029 2075 4444
Email s4c@s4c.co.uk
Website www.s4c.co.uk

Chief Executive *Huw Jones*
Director of Programmes *Huw Eirug*

The Welsh 4th Channel, established by the Broadcasting Act 1980, is responsible for a schedule of Welsh and English programmes on the Fourth Channel in Wales. Known as S4C, the analogue service is made up of about 34 hours per week of Welsh language programmes and more than 85 hours of English language output from Channel 4. S4C Digital broadcasts in Welsh exclusively for 80 hours per week. Ten hours a week of the Welsh programmes are provided by the BBC; the remainder are purchased from HTV and independent producers. Drama, comedy and documentary are all part of S4C's programming.

Scottish Television Ltd

200 Renfield Street, Glasgow G2 3PR
☎0141 300 3000 Fax 0141 300 3030
Website www.stv.co.uk

Managing Director, Scottish TV
  Sandy Ross
Head of Features & Entertainment
  Agnes Wilkie
Senior News Producer *Paul McKinney*
Head of Sport & General Factual Programmes *Denis Mooney*
Head of Drama *Eric Coulter*

Scottish Television produces 16.5 hours of television a week for the central Scotland region. This is made up of news, current affairs and sport, and a wide-ranging portfolio of other programmes ranging from entertainment, documentary and religion to regional drama such as *High Road* and *New Found Land.* Scottish Television also produces a wide range of programming such as drama for other broadcasters including the ITV Network. The company is always interested in new ideas and proposals.

Teletext Ltd
101 Farm Lane, Fulham, London SW6 1QJ
☎020 7386 5000 Fax 020 7386 5002
Website www.teletext.co.uk
Managing Director *Mike Stewart*
Editor-in-Chief *John Sage*

On 1 January 1993, Teletext Ltd took over the electronic publishing service for both ITV, Channel 4 and Channel 5. Transmits a wide range of news pages and features, including current affairs, sport, TV listings, weather, travel, holidays, finance, games, competitions, etc. Also broadcasts on digital terrestrial (Channel 9), digital cable TV and the Web and mobile services.

Tyne Tees Television
Television Centre, Newcastle upon Tyne
NE1 2AL
☎0191 261 0181 Fax 0191 261 2302
Email tyne.tees@granadamedia.com
Website www.granadamedia.com
Managing Director *Margaret Fay*
Controller of Programmes *Graeme Thompson*
Head of New Media, TTTV Productions
  Malcolm Wright
Editor, Current Affairs and Features
  Jane Bolesworth
Managing Editor, News *Graham Marples*
Head of Network Features *Mark Robinson*
Head of Regional Affairs *Norma Hope*
Head of Sport *Roger Tames*

Programming covers religion, politics, news and current affairs, regional documentaries, business, entertainment, sport and arts. Regular programmes include *North East Tonight with Mike Neville* and *Around the House* (politics). In 2001, Tyne Tees produced a series of six new regional dramas – *First Cut* – showcasing writers and directors new to television.

UTV (Ulster Television)
Havelock House, Ormeau Road, Belfast
BT7 1EB
☎028 9032 8122 Fax 028 9024 6695
Website www.utvinternet.com
Director of Programming *Alan Bremner*
Head of News & Current Affairs
  Rob Morrison

Regular programmes on news and current affairs, politics, sport, education, music, light entertainment, arts, health and local culture.

Yorkshire Television
The Television Centre, Leeds, West Yorkshire
LS3 1JS
☎0113 243 8283 Fax 0113 244 5107
Website www.granadamedia.com
London office: Global House, 96–108 Great Suffolk Street, London SE1 0BE
☎020 7578 4304 Fax 020 7578 4320
Chairman *Charles Allen*
Managing Director *David Croft*
Director of Programmes, Yorkshire Tyne Tees Productions *John Whiston*
Controller of Drama, Yorkshire Tyne Tees Productions *Keith Richardson*
Controller of Drama, YTV *Carolyn Reynolds*
Controller of Comedy Drama and Drama Features *David Reynolds*

Part of Granada Media Group. Drama series, situation comedies, film productions and long-running series like *Emmerdale* and *Heartbeat*. Always looking for strong writing in these areas, but prefers to find it through an agent. Documentary/current affairs material tends to be supplied by producers; opportunities in these areas are rare but adaptations of published work as a documentary subject are considered. In theory, opportunity exists within series, episode material. Best approach is through a good agent.

Cable and Satellite Television

Artsworld
80 Silverthorne Road, London SW8 2XA
☎020 7819 1160 Fax 020 7819 1161
Email tv@artsworld.com
Website www.artsworld.com
Chairman *Sir Jeremy Isaacs*
Channel Director *Richard Melman*

Satellite arts channel, launched in November 2000. Broadcasts from 7.00 pm to midnight (repeated from 2.00 pm to 7.00 pm the following day) via BSkyB. Programmes include the series, *Great Books*.

British Sky Broadcasting Ltd (BSkyB)
6 Centaurs Business Park, Grant Way, Isleworth, Middlesex TW7 5QD
☎020 7705 3000 Fax 020 7705 3030
Website www.sky.com
Chief Executive *Tony Ball*
Chief Operating Officer *Richard Freudenstein*
Managing Director, Sky Sports *Vic Wakeling*

Director of Broadcasting & Production
 Mark Sharman
Head of Sky News *Nick Pollard*

Launched in 1989, British Sky Broadcasting gives over 15 million viewers (in 5.9 million households) access to movies, news, entertainment and sports channels, and interactive services on Sky digital. Launched in October 1998, Sky digital has more than 200 channels and offers a range of innovative interactive services. 2001 saw the introduction of the next-generation integrated digital satellite set-top box/personal video recorder, Sky+.

WHOLLY-OWNED SKY CHANNELS:

Sky Premier
Blockbusting action, comedy and romance, featuring recent box office hits.

Sky MovieMax
Contemporary hit movies, embracing all genres, from Hollywood's major studios.

Sky Cinema
Classic and popular movies from 70 years of cinema, including seasons and retrospectives.

Sky News
Award winning 24-hours news service with hourly bulletins and expert comment.

Sky One
The most frequently watched non-terrestrial channel with the accent on entertainment for 16–34-year-olds.

Sky Sports 1/Sky Sports 2/Sky Sports 3/Skysports News/Sky Sports Extra
Over 30,000 hours of sport are broadcast every year across the five Sky Sports channels. Sky Sports 1, 2 and 3 are devoted to live events, support programmes and in-depth sports coverage seven days a week. Two further channels are available on Sky digital: Skysports News provides sports news and the latest results and information 24 hours a day; Sky Sports Extra carries additional sports programming including the award-winning live interactive coverage.

Sky Travel
Magazine shows, documentaries and teleshopping.

JOINT VENTURES:
National Geographic; Nickelodeon; Nick Jr; The History Channel; Paramount; Paramount Comedy Channel; QVC; MUTV; Music Choice Europe; Granada Breeze; Granada Men & Motors; Granada Plus; Sky News Australia; Artsworld; Adventure One; The Biography Channel; Attheraces.

CNBC
10 Fleet Place, London EC4M 7QS
☎020 7653 9300 Fax 020 7653 9480
Email feedback@cnbceurope.com
Website www.cnbceurope.com
President *Rick Cotton*

A service of NBC and Dow Jones. 24-hour business and financial news service. Programmes include *Business Centre Europe; European Market Watch; Today's Business Europe; Squawk Box.*

CNN International
Turner House, 16 Great Marlborough Street, London W1F 7HS
☎020 7693 1000 Fax 020 7693 1001
Website www.europe.cnn.com

Senior Vice President, CNN International Europe, Middle East, Africa *Tony Maddox*
Editor, CNN.com Europe *Nick Wrenn*

CNN, the leading global 24-hour news network, is available to one billion people worldwide via the 35 CNN branded TV, Internet, radio and mobile services produced by CNN News Group, an AOL Time Warner company. CNN has major production centres in Atlanta, New York, Los Angeles, London, Hong Kong and Mexico City. The London bureau, the largest outside the USA, is CNN's European headquarters and produces over 50 hours of programming per week. There are 7 live business and news programmes, including *BizNews; Business International; World News Europe* and *World Business Tonight.* Weekly programmes include *Inside Europe*, a look at the cultural heritage of Europe and *International Correspondents*, a discussion programme featuring journalists and media figures.

MTV Networks Europe
180 Oxford Street, London W1D 1DS
☎020 7284 7777 Fax 020 7284 7788
Website www.mtv.co.uk
President & Chief Executive *Brent Hansen*

ESTABLISHED 1987. Europe's 24-hour music and youth entertainment channel, available on cable, via satellite and digitally. Transmitted from London in English across Europe.

NBC Europe
Unit 1/1, Harbour Yard, Chelsea Harbour, London SW10 0XD
☎020 7352 9205 Fax 020 7352 9628

Chairman *Patrick Cox*
Director of Programming *Bernhard Bertram*

24-hour European broad-based news, information and entertainment service in English, with additional programmes in German and advertisements in English and German.

Travel (Landmark Travel Channel)
66 Newman Street, London W1P 3LA
☎020 7636 5401 Fax 020 7636 6424
Website www.travelchannel.co.uk

Launched in February 1994. Broadcasts programmes and information on the world of travel. Destinations reports, lifestyle programmes plus food and drink, sport and leisure pursuits. Transmits from 7.00 am to 1.00 am throughout Europe and Africa.

National Commercial Radio

Classic FM
7 Swallow Place, London W1B 2AG
☎020 7343 9000 Fax 020 7344 2700
Website www.classicfm.com

Chief Executive *Ralph Bernard*
**Managing Director/Programme
   Controller** *Roger Lewis*
Managing Editor *Darren Henley*

Classic FM, Britain's largest national commercial radio station, started broadcasting in September 1992. Plays accessible classical music 24 hours a day and broadcasts news, weather, travel, business information, political/celebrity/general interest talks, features and interviews. Classic has gone well beyond its expectations, attracting 6.7 million listeners a week. Winner of the 'Station of the Year' Sony Award in April 2000.

Digital One
20 Southampton Street, London WC2E 7QH
☎020 7288 4600
Email info@digitalone.co.uk
Website www.ukdigitalradio.com

The UK's only national commercial digital radio network. Backed by radio group GWR and cable supplier ntl, Digital One began broadcasting on 15 November 1999. Channels include **Classic FM**, **Virgin Radio** and **Oneword**.

ITN Radio News Channel (Digital)
200 Gray's Inn Road, London WC1X 8XZ
☎020 7833 3000
Website www.itn.co.uk

Chief Editor *Nicholas Wheeler*

Launched in August 2000, the ITN Digital

News Channel broadcasts rolling news, 18 hours a day.

Oneword
Landseer House, 19 Charing Cross Road, London WC2H 0ES
☎020 7976 3030 Fax 020 7930 9460
Website www.oneword.co.uk

Managing Director *Ben Budworth*
Head of Programmes *Paul Kent*

The first commercial radio station dedicated solely to the transmission of plays, books, comedy and reviews for those who are 'looking for a break from unrelenting music on the radio'. Broadcasts between 6.00 am and midnight daily on the Digital One network in the UK, on Sky Digital (Channel 887) in Europe and worldwide on the Internet. Programmes include *Between the Lines*, a twice-daily conversation by Paul Blezard with different authors.

Relaxwithabook Radio
Greek Court, 14A Old Compton Street, London W1D 4TJ
☎020 7 Fax 020 7734 4952
Website www.relaxwithabook.com

Launched on Sky Digital 905 in December 2001, Relaxwithabook Radio is a conversation channel featuring author interviews with a new themed programme every day. The interviews can also be accessed on the supporting website (address above) where the books are discussed and can be ordered online.

TalkSport
PO Box 1089, London SE1 8WQ
☎020 7959 7800
Website www.talksport.net

Programme Director *Mike Parry*

Commenced broadcasting in February 1995 as Talk Radio UK. Re-launched January 2000 as TalkSport, the UK's first sports radio station. Broadcasts 24 hours a day. News items can be e-mailed to *Mike Parry* via the website.

Virgin Radio
1 Golden Square, London W1F 9DJ
☎020 7434 1215 Fax 020 7494 1055
Website www.virginradio.co.uk

Chief Executive *John Pearson*
Programme Director *Paul Jackson*

'Ten great songs in a row every hour, all day.' Bought by Chris Evans' Ginger Media Group in December 1997 and acquired by the Scottish Media Group in March 2000.

Independent Local Radio

96.3 Radio Aire/Magic 828
51 Burley Road, Leeds, West Yorkshire
LS3 1LR
☎0113 283 5500 Fax 0113 283 5501
Website www.radioaire.co.uk
Programme Director *Mike Bawden*

Music-based programming. 96.3 Aire FM caters for the 15–34–year–old listener while Magic 828 aims at the 25–44 age group with easy favourites.

Beacon FM/Classic Gold WABC
267 Tettenhall Road, Wolverhampton,
West Midlands WV6 0DE
☎01902 461383 Fax 01902 461299
Website www.koko.com
Programme Director *Steve Martin*

Part of the GWR Group plc. No outlets for unsolicited literary material.

Big AM
See **Signal One**

Radio Borders
Tweedside Park, Tweedbank, Galashiels
TD1 3TD
☎01896 759444 Fax 0845 345 7080
Website www.radioborders.com
Programme Controller *Danny Gallagher*
Head of News *Angeline McConville*

Music-based station with local and national news.

Breeze
See **Essex FM**

BRMB-FM 96.4/ 1152 Capital Gold
Nine Brindley Place, 4 Oozells Square,
Birmingham B1 2DJ
☎0121 245 5000 Fax 0121 245 5245
Website www.brmb.co.uk
Programme Controller *Adam Bridge*
News Editor *Kevin Pashby*

Music-based stations; no outlets for writers. Part of Capital Radio Plc.

Broadland 102/Classic Gold Digital Amber
47–49 Colegate, Norwich, Norfolk NR3 1DB
☎01603 630621
Fax 01603 671175 (newsroom)
Website www.koko.com

Programme Controller *Dave Brown*
Part of GWR Group plc. Popular music programmes and local news only.

1152 Capital Gold
See **BRMB-FM 96.4**

Capital Radio
30 Leicester Square, London WC2H 7LA
☎020 7766 6000 Fax 020 7766 6100
Website www.capitalfm.com
Group Programme Director *Keith Pringle*

Commenced broadcasting in October 1973 as the country's second commercial radio station (the first being LBC, launched a week earlier). Europe's largest commercial radio station. Main outlet is entertainment news bulletins, Monday to Thursday at 7.30 pm, called *Entertainment Capital*, covering pop music, films, TV and London events. The vast majority of material is generated in-house.

Central FM Ltd
201–203 High Street, Falkirk FK1 1DU
☎01324 611164 Fax 01324 611168
Website www.centralfm.co.uk
Managing Director *Evelyn Queen*
Programme Controller *Tom Bell*

Broadcasts music, sport and local news to central Scotland, 24 hours a day.

Century FM
Century House, PO Box 100, Church Street,
Gateshead NE8 2YY
☎0191 477 6666 Fax 0191 477 5660
Programme Controller *Giles Squire*

Music, talk, news and interviews, 24 hours a day.

CFM
PO Box 964, Carlisle, Cumbria CA1 3NG
☎01228 818964 Fax 01228 819444
Email cfmradio.com
Website www.cfmradio.com
Programme Controller *David Bain*
Head of Commercial Production
   Peter White
News Editor *Bill Macdonald*

Music, news and information station.

Channel 103 FM
6 Tunnell Street, St Helier, Jersey, Channel Islands JE2 4LU
☎01534 888103 Fax 01534 887799
Website www.channel103.com

Station Manager *Richard Johnson*
Music programmes, 24 hours a day.

Chiltern FM/Classic Gold Digital
Chiltern Road, Dunstable, Bedfordshire
LU6 1HQ
☎01582 676200
Fax 01582 676241 (newsroom)
Website www.koko.com

Programme Controller, FM *Trevor James*
**Programme Controller, Classic Gold
Digital** *Don Douglas*

Part of the GWR Group plc. Music-based programmes, broadcasting 24 hours a day.

Classic Gold 666/954
Hawthorn House, Exeter Business Park,
Exeter, Devon EX1 3QS
☎01392 444444 Fax 01392 444433

Programme Controller *Colin Slade*
Part of CGDL. No outlets for writers.

Classic Gold Digital – Breeze 1521
See **102.7 Mercury FM**

Classic Gold Digital 1332
See **102.7 Hereward FM**

Classic Gold Digital 1359
See **Mercia FM**

Classic Gold Digital 1557
See **Northants 96**

Classic Gold Digital 774
See **Severn Sound FM**

Classic Gold Digital Amber
See **Broadland 102**

Classic Gold GEM AM
See **96 TRENT FM**

Classic Gold Marcher
Marcher Sound Ltd., The Studios, Mold
Road, Wrexham LL11 4AF
☎01978 752202 Fax 01978 722209
Website www.marchergold.co.uk

Programme Controller *Graham Ledger*

Occasional features and advisory programmes.
Hour-long Welsh language broadcasts are aired
weekdays at 6.00 pm.

Classic Gold WABC
See **Beacon FM**

Clyde 1/Clyde 2
Clydebank Business Park, Clydebank G81 2RX
☎0141 565 2200 Fax 0141 565 2265
Website www.clyde1.com *or*
www.clyde2.com

Managing Director *Paul Cooney*

Programmes usually originate in-house or by
commission. All documentary material is made
in-house. Good local news items always considered. There are three book programmes presented by Alex Dickson each week on Clyde 2 at
10.00 pm – 10.30 pm: *Authors* (Monday) features
author interviews while *Hardback Bookcase*
(Tuesday) and *Paperback Bookcase* (Wednesday)
review latest titles.

Cool FM
See **Downtown Radio**

Downtown Radio/Cool FM
Newtownards, Co. Down, Northern Ireland
BT23 4ES
☎028 9181 5555 Fax 028 9181 5252
Email programmes@downtown.co.uk
Website www.downtown.co.uk

Managing Director *David Sloan*

Downtown Radio first ran a highly successful
short story competition in 1988, attracting over
400 stories. The competition is now an annual
event and writers living within the station's
transmission area are asked to submit material
during the winter and early spring. The competition is promoted in association with Eason
Shops. For further information, write to *Derek
Ray* at the station.

Essex FM/Breeze
Radio House, Clifftown Road, Southend on
Sea, Essex SS1 1SX
☎01702 333711 Fax 01702 333686
Website www.koko.com

Programme Director *Jeff O'Brien*

Music-based stations. Part of the GWR Group
plc. No real opportunities for writers' work as
such, but will occasionally interview local
authors of published books. Contact *Tracey
Cooper*, Head of News.

Forth One/Forth 2
Forth House, Forth Street, Edinburgh EH1 3LF
☎0131 475 1224 (One)/1226 (2)
Fax 0131 475 1221
Email richard@forthone.com *or*
   scott@forth2.com
Website www.forthonline.co.uk

Head of Forth One *Richard Wilkinson*
Head of Forth 2 *Scott Wilson*
News Editor *Paul Robertson*

News stories welcome from freelancers.
Music-based programming.

FOX FM

Brush House, Pony Road, Cowley, Oxford
OX4 2XR
☎01865 871000 Fax 01865 871037 (news)
Website www.foxfm.co.uk

Managing Director *Lyn Long*
Head of News *Antony Masters*

Owned by Capital Radio Plc. Music programmes. No outlet for creative writing.

Galaxy 101

Millennium House, 26 Baldwin Street, Bristol
BS1 1SE
☎0117 901 0101 Fax 0117 901 4666
Email newsdesk@galaxy101.co.uk
Website www.galaxy101.co.uk

Programme Controller *Tristan Bolitho*

Dance music, 24 hours a day.

Galaxy 102.2

See **100.7 Heart FM**

Gemini FM

Hawthorn House, Exeter Business Park,
Exeter, Devon EX1 3QS
☎01392 444444 Fax 01392 444433
Website www.koko.com

Programme Controller *Kevin Kane*

Part of GWR Group plc. No outlets for writers.

GWR FM

PO Box 2000, 1 Passage Street, Bristol
BS99 7SN
☎0117 984 3200 Fax 0117 984 3202
Website www.koko.com

Programme Controller *Paul Andrew*

Very few opportunities for writers. Almost all
material originates in-house. Part of the GWR
Group plc.

Hallam FM/Magic AM

Radio House, 900 Herries Road, Sheffield
S6 1RH
☎0114 209 1000 Fax 0114 285 3159
Website www.hallamfm.co.uk

Programme Director *Anthony Gay*

Music, news and features, 24 hours a day.

100.7 Heart FM/Galaxy 102.2

1 The Square, 111 Broad Street, Birmingham
B15 1AS
☎0121 695 0000 Fax 0121 695 0055
Email mail@heartfm.co.uk *or*
    mail@galaxy1022.co.uk
Website www.heartfm.co.uk

Managing Director *Paul Fairburn*
Programme Director, Heart FM
    Alan Carruthers
Programme Director, Galaxy *Neil Greenslade*

Heart FM commenced broadcasting music,
regional news and information in September
1994. Galaxy broadcasts today's dance and soul,
news and information.

102.7 Hereward FM/
Classic Gold Digital 1332

PO Box 225, Queensgate Centre,
Peterborough, Cambridgeshire PE1 1XJ
☎01733 460460 Fax 01733 281444
Website www.koko.com

Programme Controller *Paul Green*

Part of GWR Group plc. Not usually any
openings offered to writers as all material is
compiled and presented by in-house staff.

FM 103 Horizon

Broadcast Centre, Crownhill, Milton Keynes,
Buckinghamshire MK8 0AB
☎01908 269111 Fax 01908 564893
Website www.koko.com

Programme Controller *Trevor Marshall*

Part of the GWR Group plc. Music and news.

Invicta FM/Capital Gold

PO Box 100, Whitstable, Kent CT5 3YR
☎01227 772004 Fax 01227 774450
Website www.invictafm.com

Programme Controller *Mike Osborne*

Music-based station, serving listeners in Kent.
Part of Capital Radio Plc.

Island FM

12 Westerbrook, St Sampsons, Guernsey,
Channel Islands GY2 4QQ
☎01481 242000 Fax 01481 249676
Website www.islandfm.guernsey.net

Managing Director *Kevin Stewart*

Music-based programming.

Isle of Wight Radio

Dodnor Park, Newport, Isle of Wight
PO30 5XE

☎01983 822557 Fax 01983 821690
Email mail@iwradio.co.uk
Website www.iwradio.co.uk

Managing Director *Andy Shier*
Programme Manager *Tom Stroud*

Part of the Local Radio Company, Isle of Wight Radio is the island's only radio station broadcasting local news, music and general entertainment.

ITN News Direct 97.3 FM
See **LBC 1152 AM**

Key 103/Magic 1152
Castle Quay, Castlefield, Manchester M15 4PR
☎0161 288 5000 Fax 0161 288 5001
Website www.key103.co.uk

Programme Director *Andrew Robson*

Music-based programming.

LBC 1152 AM/
ITN News Direct 97.3 FM
200 Gray's Inn Road, London WC1X 8XZ
☎020 7430 8460 (LBC)/020 7312 8499 (News Direct) Fax 020 7430 4834
Email editor@lbc.co.uk *(LBC editorial queries)*
Website www.lbc.co.uk *and* ww.newsdirect.co.uk

Editor *Stuart Thomas*

LBC 1152 AM: news, views and information for London; ITN News Direct 97.3 FM: 24-hour rolling news station.

105.4 FM Leicester Sound
Granville House, Granville Road, Leicester LE1 7RW
☎0116 256 1300 Fax 0116 256 1305
Website www.koko.com

Managing Director *Chris Hughes*

Part of GWR Group plc. Predominantly a music station. Very occasionally, unsolicited material of local interest – 'targeted at our particular audience' – may be broadcast.

Magic 1152 (Manchester)
See **Key 103**

Magic 1152AM
(Newcastle upon Tyne)
See **Metro Radio**

Magic 1161
See **Viking FM**

Magic 1548
See **Radio City Ltd**

Magic 828
See **96.3 Radio Aire**

Magic AM
See **Hallam FM**

Medway's Mercury FM
Berkeley House, 186 High Street, Rochester, Kent ME1 1EY
☎01634 841111 Fax 01634 841122
Website www.koko.com

Managing Director *John Hirst*
Programme Director *Steve Joy*

A wide range of music programming plus news, views and local interest. Part of the GWR Group plc.

Mercia FM/
Classic Gold Digital 1359
Mercia Sound Ltd., Hertford Place, Coventry CV1 3TT
☎024 7686 8200 Fax 024 7686 8203

Managing Director *Carlton Dale*
Programme Controller *Louis Clark*

Music-based station.

102.7 Mercury FM/
Classic Gold – Breeze 1521
9 The Stanley Centre, Kelvin Way, Manor Royal, Crawley, West Sussex RH10 9SE
☎01293 519161 Fax 01293 560927
Email <firstname>.<surname>@musicradio. com
Website www.koko.com

Programme Controller *Simon Osborne*

Mercury FM plays contemporary music targeting 15–34 years. Breeze 1521 AM plays hits from the 1960s to the '90s, targeting 35 years-plus. Both services carry local, national and international news.

Metro Radio/Magic 1152AM
Swalwell, Newcastle upon Tyne NE99 1BB
☎0191 420 0971 (Metro)/420 3040 (Magic)
Fax 520191 488 8611
Website www.metroradio.co.uk

Programme Director *Tony McKenzie*

Very few opportunities for writers, but phone-in programmes may interview relevant authors.

Minster FM

PO Box 123, Dunnington, York YO1 5ZX
☎01904 488888 Fax 01904 488811
Website www.minsterfm.co.uk

Joint Station Managers *Sarah Barry, John Harding*

Music, local news and sport.

Moray Firth Radio

PO Box 271, Scorguie Place, Inverness
IV3 8UJ
☎01463 224433 Fax 01463 243224
Email gary.robinson@mfr.co.uk

Managing Director/Programme Controller *Gary Robinson*
Programme Organiser *Ray Atkinson*
Book Reviews *May Marshall*

Book reviews every Sunday morning at 7.00 am – 8.00 am.

Northants 96/ Classic Gold Digital 1557

19–21 St Edmunds Road, Northampton
NN1 5DY
☎01604 795600 Fax 01604 795601
Email reception@northants96.musicradio.com
Website www.koko.com

Programme Controller *Richard Neale*

Music and news, 24 hours a day. Part of the GWR Group plc.

NorthSound Radio

45 King's Gate, Aberdeen AB15 4EL
☎01224 337000 Fax 01224 400003
Website www.northsound.co.uk

Managing Director *Adam Findlay*
Programme Controller *Gerry Burke*

Features and music programmes 24 hours a day including, mid-morning (9.00 am – midday), *Northsound 2* feature programme.

Ocean Radio/Power 103.2 FM/ Capital Gold

Radio House, Whittle Avenue, Segensworth West, Fareham, Hampshire PO15 5SH
☎01489 589911 Fax 01489 589453
Email info@oceanradio.co.uk
Website www.oceanradiofm.com *or* www.powerfm.com *or* www.capitalgold.com

Programme Controller *Mark Sadler*

Music-based programming only. Part of Capital Radio Plc.

Orchard FM

Haygrove House, Shoreditch, Taunton, Somerset TA3 7BT
☎01823 338448 Fax 01823 321611
Email orchardfmnews@koko.com
Website www.koko.com

Programme Director *Steve Bulley*
News Team *Darren Bevan, Nicola Maxey, Kate Wakefield.*

Music-based programming only. Part of the GWR Group plc.

Plymouth Sound Radio

Earl's Acre, Alma Road, Plymouth, Devon PL3 4HX
☎01752 227272 Fax 01752 275605
Website www.koko.com

Programme Controller *Gavin Marshall*

Music-based station. No outlets for writers. Part of the GWR Group plc.

Power 103.2 FM

See **Ocean Radio**

Premier Christian Radio

Glen House, Stag Place, London SW1E 5AG
☎020 7316 1300 Fax 020 7233 6706
Email premier@premier.org.uk
Website www.premier.org.uk

Managing Director *Peter Kerridge*

Broadcasts programmes that reflect the beliefs and values of the Christian faith, 24 hours a day.

Q103FM

PO Box 103, Vision Park, Chivers Way, Histon, Cambridge CB4 9WW
☎01223 235255 Fax 01223 235161
Website www.koko.com

Managing Director *Lynda Couch-Smith*

Part of GWR Group plc. Music and news.

96.3 QFM

65 Sussex Street, Kenning Park, Glasgow G41 1DK
☎0141 429 9430 Fax 0141 429 9431
Email news@q-fm.com

Station Director *Esther Morton*
Programme Controller *Colin Paterson*

Music-based programming plus local information and news. Part of the Wireless Group.

Radio City Ltd/Magic 1548

Radio City Tower, St John's Beacon, 1 Houghton Street, Liverpool L1 1RL
☎0151 472 6800 Fax 0151 472 6821

Website www.radiocity.co.uk
Managing Director *Sean Marley*
Programme Director *Richard Maddock*

Opportunities for writers are very few and far between as this is predominantly a music station.

Radio XL 1296 AM

KMS House, Bradford Street, Birmingham B12 0JD
☎0121 753 5353 Fax 0121 753 3111
Station Manager *To be appointed*

Asian broadcasting for the West Midlands, 24 hours a day. Broadcasts *Love Express* featuring love stories and poems. Writers should send material for the attention of *Ambrin*.

Red Dragon FM/Capital Gold

Atlantic Wharf, Cardiff CF10 4DJ
☎029 2066 2066 Fax 029 2066 2060
Website www.reddragonfm.co.uk
Programme Controller *David Rees*
News Editor *Andrew Jones*

Acquired by Capital Radio in 1998. Music-based programming only.

Red Rose Radio

PO Box 301, St Paul's Square, Preston, Lancashire PR1 1YE
☎01772 477700 Fax 01772 477701
Website www.rockfm.co.uk
Programme Director *Marc Brow*

Music-based station. No outlets for writers.

Sabras Radio

Radio House, 63 Melton Road, Leicester LE4 6PN
☎0116 261 0666 Fax 0116 266 7776
Email don@sabrasradio.com
Website www.sabrasradio.com
Programme Controller *Don Kotak*

Programmes for the Asian community, broadcasting 24 hours a day.

Severn Sound FM/ Classic Gold Digital 774

Bridge Studios, Eastgate Centre, Gloucester GL1 1SS
☎01452 313200 Fax 01452 313213
Website www.koko.com
Managing Director *Neil Cooper*

Part of the GWR Group plc. Music and news.

SGR FM 97.1

Alpha Business Park, Whitehouse Road, Ipswich, Suffolk IP1 5LT
☎01473 461000/241111 (newsdesk)
Fax 01473 742200
Website www.sgrfm.co.uk
Managing Director *Mike Stewart*
Programme Controller *Mark Pryke*

Music-based programming.

Signal One/Big AM

Stoke Road, Shelton, Stoke on Trent, Staffordshire ST4 2SR
☎01782 441300 Fax 01782 441351
Website www.signalone.co.uk
Programme Controller *Kevin Howard*

Music-based station. No outlets for writers. Part of the Wireless Group.

Southern FM

PO Box 2000, Brighton, East Sussex BN41 2SS
☎01273 430111 Fax 01273 430098
Website www.southernfm.com
Programme Controller *Tony Aldridge*
News Manager *Laurence King*

Music, news, entertainment and competitions. Part of Capital Radio Plc.

Spectrum Radio

204–206 Queenstown Road, Battersea, London SW8 3NR
☎020 7627 4433 Fax 020 7627 3409
Email enquiries@spectrumradio.net
Website www.spectrumradio.net
Managing Director *Toby Aldrych*

Programmes for a broad spectrum of ethnic groups in London.

Spire FM

City Hall Studios, Malthouse Lane, Salisbury, Wiltshire SP2 7QQ
☎01722 416644 Fax 01722 416688
Website www.spirefm.co.uk
Station Director *Ceri Herford*

Music, news current affairs, quizzes and sport. Won the Sony Award for the best local radio station in 1994 and 1996.

Star 107.5 FM

1st Floor, The West Suite, Cheltenham Film Studios, Arle Court, Hatherly Lane, Cheltenham, Gloucestershire GL51 6PN
☎01242 699555 Fax 01242 699666

Email mail@star1075.co.uk
Website www.star1075.co.uk
Programme Controller *Ian Timms*
Formerly 107.5 CAT FM. Music-based programmes, broadcasting 24 hours a day.

Sun FM 103.4
PO Box 1034, Sunderland, Tyne & Wear
SR5 2YL
☎0191 548 1034 Fax 0191 548 7171
Website www.sun-fm.com
Programme Controller *Simon Grundy*
Music-based programmes only.

Sunrise Radio (Yorkshire)
Sunrise House, 30 Chapel Street, Bradford,
West Yorkshire BD1 5DN
☎01274 735043 Fax 01274 728534
Website www.sunriseradio.fm
**Programme Controller, Chief Executive
& Chairman** *Usha Parmar*
Programmes for the Asian community in
Bradford.

Sunshine 855
South Shropshire Communications Ltd., Unit
11, Burway Trading Estate, Bromfield Road,
Ludlow, Shropshire SY8 1EN
☎01584 873795 Fax 01584 875900
Website www.sunshine855.co.uk
Operations Director *Mrs G. Murfin*
Music, news and information, broadcast 24
hours a day.

Swansea Sound 1170 MW
See **The Wave FM**

Tay FM/Tay AM
Radio Tay Ltd., PO Box 123, Dundee
DD1 9UF
☎01382 200800 Fax 01382 423252
Email tayfm@radiotay.co.uk *and*
tayam@radiotay.co.uk
Website www.tayfm.co.uk *and*
www.tayam.co.uk
Managing Director/Programme Director
Ally Ballingall
Wholly-owned subsidiary of Scottish Radio
Holdings. Carries a 20-minute book programme every Sunday evening, presented by
Mabel Adams. Short stories and book reviews
of local interest are welcome. Send to the programme director.

107.8FM Thames Radio
Brentham House, 45c High Street, Hampton
Wick, Kingston upon Thames, Surrey
KT1 4DG
☎020 8288 1300 Fax 020 8288 1312
Email info@thamesradio.com
Website www.thamesradio.com
Station Manager *Greg Martin*
Programme Controller *Johnny Haywood*
Music-based programmes of current hits and
classic pop.

96 Trent FM/
Classic Gold GEM AM
29–31 Castlegate, Nottingham NG1 7AP
☎0115 952 7000 Fax 0115 912 9302
Email admin@trentfm.musicradio.com
Website www.koko.com
Managing Director *Chris Hughes*
Part of the GWR Group plc.

2CR-FM/Classic Gold 828
5–7 Southcote Road, Bournemouth, Dorset
BH1 3LR
☎01202 259259 Fax 01202 255244
Email newsbournemouth@musicradio.com
Website www.koko.com
Programme Controller *Craig Morris*
Wholly-owned subsidiary of the GWR Group
plc. Serves Dorset and Hampshire. All reviews/
topicality/press releases to the Programme
Controller, 2CR-FM at the address above.

2-Ten FM/Classic Gold
PO Box 2020, Reading, Berkshire RG31 7FG
☎0118 945 4400 Fax 0118 928 8513
(admin)/8809 (news)
Website www.koko.com
Programme Controller *Tim Parker*
A subsidiary of the GWR Group plc. Music-
based programming.

Viking FM/Magic 1161
Commercial Road, Hull, North Humberside
HU1 2SG
☎01482 325141 Fax 0845 585969
Website www.vikingfm.co.uk
Managing Director *Sue Timson*
Programme Controller *Stuart Baldwin*
News Co-ordinator *Jamie York*
Music-based programming. Part of the EMAP
Group.

The Wave FM /Swansea Sound 1170 MW

Victoria Road, Gowerton, Swansea SA4 3AB
☎01792 511964 (FM)/511170 (MW)
Fax 01792 511965 (FM)/511171 (MW)
Email admin@thewave.co.uk *or*
   admin@swanseasound.co.uk
Website www.the wave.co.uk *or*
   swanseasound.co.uk

Station Director *Andy Griffiths*
Programme Manager *Steve Barnes*
News Editor *Emma Thomas*

Music-based programming on FM while Swansea Sound is interested in a wide variety of material, though news items must be of local relevance. An explanatory letter, in the first instance, is advisable.

Wessex FM

Radio House, Trinity Street, Dorchester, Dorset DT1 1DJ
☎01305 250333 Fax 01305 250052
Website www.wessexfm.co.uk

Programme Manager *Stewart Smith*

Music, local news, information and features.

West Sound AM/West FM

Radio House, 54 Holmston Road, Ayr
KA7 3BE
☎01292 283662
Fax 01292 283665/262607 (news)
Website www.west-sound.co.uk
   or www.westfm.co.uk

Programme Director *Alan Toomey*

Music-based broadcasting.

102.4 Wish FM

Orrell Road, Wigan WN5 8HJ
☎01942 761024 Fax 01942 777694

Programme Controller *Craig Beck*

Music-based programming plus news and sport. Part of the Wireless Group.

Wyvern FM

5–6 Barbourne Terrace, Worcester WR1 3JZ
☎01905 612212/746644 (newsroom)
Fax 01905 746637
Website www.koko.com

Managing Director *Neil Cooper*
Programme Controller *Simon Monk*

Part of the GWR Group plc. Music-based pro-gramming.

Freelance Rates – Broadcasting

Freelance rates vary enormously. The following minimum rates should be treated as guidelines. Most work can command higher fees from employers. It is up to freelancers to negotiate the best deal they can. A useful source of information for newcomers to broadcasting is the **National Union of Journalists** northern freelance network on www.northern-freelance.net

BBC Guidelines for Freelance Minimum Rates

BBC – Published Material
(negotiated by the **Publishers Association** and the **Society of Authors**)

Domestic Radio

Plays/prose (per minute)	£14.03
Prose for dramatisation (per minute)	£10.94
Poems (per half-minute)	£14.03
Prose translation (per minute)	£9.36

World Service Radio (English)

Plays/prose (per minute)	£7.03
Prose for dramatisation (per minute)	£5.48
Poems (per half-minute)	£7.03
Prose translation (per minute)	£4.69

Television

Prose (per minute)	£20.64
Poems (per half-minute)	£23.97

BBC Radio Drama
(negotiated by the **Society of Authors** and the **Writers' Guild**)
A beginner in radio drama should receive at least £45.16 per minute for an original drama script. For an established writer – one who has three or more plays to his credit – the minimum rate per minute is £68.74.

An attendance payment of £39.26 per production is paid to established writers. The rate per script for *The Archers* is £697.

Daily Serial minimum rates:
1) Where the storyline, characters, format, etc. are provided, the minimum fee is £555;
2) Where the overall format and structure are provided but the writer provides the storyline, some characters, etc. the minimum fee is £735. (All fees cover one origination and one repeat.)

BBC Interviews and Talks
Continue to be under negotiation

Features/documentaries
Currently under negotiation but previous rates stood at: up to 7 minutes, £178.50; £25.50 per minute thereafter.

Independent Radio

For details of the **NUJ**/CRCA (Commercial Radio Companies Association) agreement on recommended rates, contact the NUJ Broadcasting Office (see **Professional Associations and Societies**).

Research
TV organisations which hire freelancers to research programme items should pay on a day rate which reflects the value of the work and the importance of the programme concerned.

Presentation
In all broadcast media, presenters command higher fees than news journalists. There is considerable variation in what is paid for presenting programmes and videos, according to their audience and importance. Day rates with television companies are usually about £140–160 a day.

Television Drama

For a 60-minute teleplay, the BBC will pay an established writer £7410 and a beginner £4703. The corresponding figures for ITV are £9245 for the established writer and £6568 for a writer new to television but with a solid reputation in other literary areas. ITV also has a 'beginner' category with a payment of £6296 for a 60-minute teleplay.

Day rates for attendance at read-throughs and rehearsals is £67 for the BBC and £74.40 for ITV.

(*NB* ITV rates currently under negotiation)

Feature Films

The **Writers' Guild** and **PACT** agreement of 1992 (still being re-negotiated) allows for a minimum guaranteed payment to the writer of £31,200 on a feature film with a budget in excess of £2 million; £19,000 on a budget from £750,000 to £2 million; £14,000 on a budget below £750,000. However, many in the industry pay rates which take inflation into account and negotiate a royalty provision for uses instead of fixed percentage payments.

Film, TV and Video Production Companies

Aardman
Gas Ferry Road, Bristol BS1 6UN
☎0117 984 8485 Fax 0117 984 8486
Website www.aardman.com
Head of Script Development *Mike Cooper*
Development Executive (Shorts & Series)
Helen Brunsdon

FOUNDED 1972. Award-winning animation studio producing films, television series, videos, commercials and new media properties. OUTPUT includes: *Rex the Runt; Morph Files; Creature Comforts; Wallace and Gromit; Angry Kid; Chicken Run*. No unsolicited submissions.

Absolutely Productions Ltd
8th Floor, Alhambra House, 27–31 Charing Cross Road, London WC2H 0AU
☎020 7930 3113 Fax 020 7930 4114
Email info@absolutely-uk.com
Website www.absolutely-uk.com
Executive Producer *Miles Bullough*

TV and film production company specialising in comedy and entertainment. OUTPUT *Absolutely* series 1–4 (Ch4); *mr don and mr george* (Ch4); *Squawkietalkie* (comedy wildlife programme for Ch4); *The Preventers* (ITV); *Scotland v England* (Ch4); *Barry Welsh is Coming* (HTV); *The Jack Docherty Show* (Ch5); *The Morwenna Banks Show* (Ch5); *Stressed Eric* (BBC2); *Armstrong & Miller* (Paramount/Ch4); *The Creatives* (BBC2); *Trigger Happy* (Ch4); *The Announcement* (Dakota Entertainment).

Abstract Images
117 Willoughby House, Barbican, London EC2Y 8BL
☎020 7638 5123
Email productions@abstract-images.co.uk
Contact *Howard Ross*

Television documentary and drama programming. Also theatre productions. OUTPUT includes *Balm in Gilead* (drama); *Road* (drama); *Bent* (drama); *God: For & Against* (documentary); *This Is a Man* (drama/doc). Encourages new writers; send synopsis in the first instance.

Acacia Productions Ltd
80 Weston Park, London N8 9Tb
☎020 8341 9392 Fax 020 8341 4879
Email acacia@dial.pipex.com
Website www.acaciaproductions.co.uk
Contact *J. Edward Milner*

Producer of award-winning television and video documentaries; also news reports, corporates and programmes for educational charities. No unsolicited mss. OUTPUT includes documentary series entitled *Last Plant Standing; A Farm in Uganda; Montserrat: Under the Volcano; Spirit of Trees* (8 progs.); *Vietnam: After the Fire; Macroeconomics – the Decision-makers; Greening of Thailand; A Future for Forests.*

Acrobat Television
107 Wellington Road North, Stockport, Cheshire SK4 2LP
☎0161 477 9090 Fax 0161 477 9191
Email info@acrobat-tv.co.uk
Contacts *David Hill, Annie Broom*

Corporate video producer. OUTPUT includes instructional video for the British Association of Ski Instructors; corporate videos for Neilson Sailing, Hepworth Building Products, The Simon Group and First Choice Ski. No unsolicited mss.

Alomo Productions
1 Stephen Street, London W1T 1AL
☎020 7691 6531 Fax 020 7691 6081

Alomo is a **FremantleMedia** company. Major producer of television drama and comedy. OUTPUT *Starting Out; Dirty Work; Goodnight Sweetheart; Birds of a Feather; Love Hurts; The New Statesman; Grown Ups; Unfinished Business; Cry Wolf*. New writers encouraged.

Anglo-Caribbean Productions
1a Gambole Road, Tooting Broadway, London SW17 0QJ
☎07970 715080 Fax 020 8801 7592
Email jasonyoung72@yahoo.com
Website www.anglocaribbean.plus.com
Producer *Jason Young*

Feature films and television serials. OUTPUT *To See Ourselves; The North Londoners; The House of Hope; The Young Professionals; It's Coming Home; The Black Englishman; Ska Special.* Material must be of an inter-racial nature in order to develop the profile of Black English characters. All scripts via agents only.

Anglo/Fortunato Films Ltd
170 Popes Lane, London W5 4NJ
☎020 8932 7676   Fax 020 8932 7491
Contact *Luciano Celentino*

Film, television and video producer/director of action comedy and psych-thriller drama. No unsolicited mss.

Antelope (UK) Ltd
The Highgate Business Centre, 33 Greenwood Place, London NW5 1LD
☎020 7428 3920   Fax 020 7428 3921
Email antelope@antelope.co.uk
Website www.antelope.co.uk
Managing Director *Mick Csáky*
Head of Production *Justin Johnson*

Film, television and video productions for drama, documentary and corporate material. OUTPUT *Cyberspace* (ITV); *Brunch* (Ch5); *The Pier* (weekly arts and entertainment programme); *Placido Domingo* (ITV); *Baden Powell – The Boy Man; Howard Hughes – The Naked Emperor* (Ch4 'Secret Lives' series); *Hiroshima*. No unsolicited mss: 'not reading any new material at present'.

Apex Television Production & Facilities Ltd
Vision Centre, Eastern Way, Bury St Edmunds, Suffolk IP32 7AB
☎01284 724900   Fax 01284 700004
Website www.apextv.co.uk
Contact *Bernard Mulhern*

Video producer: corporate drama, documentary, commercials and production for a wide range of international companies. Many drama-based training programmes. No scripts. All work is commissioned against a particular project.

Arena Films Ltd
2 Pelham Road, London SW19 1SX
☎020 8543 3990   Fax 020 8540 3992
Producer *David Conroy*
Film and TV drama.

Argus Video Productions
52 Church Street, Briston, Melton Constable, Norfolk NR24 2LE

☎01263 861152
Contact *Siri Taylor*

Producer of corporate, documentary and educational videos. OUTPUT includes *View & Do* series on leisure and hobby interests; *The Chainsaw Safety* and *Relaxation* series; and *Moving Postcard Series on East Anglia*. No unsolicited mss.

Ariel Productions Ltd
11 Albion Gate, Hyde Park Place, London W2 2LF
☎020 7262 7726   Fax 020 7262 7726
Producer *Otto Plaschkes*

Feature film and television producer. OUTPUT includes *Georgy Girl; Hopscotch; In Celebration; Butley; Doggin' Around*. Encourages new writers through involvement with the **National Film and Television School** and Screen Laboratory. No unsolicited mss.

Arlington Productions Limited
Pinewood Studios, Iver Heath, Buckinghamshire SL0 0NH
☎01753 651700   Fax 01753 656050

Television producer. Specialises in popular international drama, with *occasional* forays into other areas. 'We have an enviable reputation for encouraging new writers but only accept unsolicited submissions via agents.'

The Ashford Entertainment Corporation Ltd
182 Brighton Road, Coulsdon, Surrey CR5 2NF
☎020 8645 0667   Fax 020 8763 2558
Email info@ashford-entertainment.co.uk
Website www.ashford-entertainment.co.uk
Managing Director *Frazer Ashford*
Head of Production *Georgina Huxstep*

FOUNDED in 1996 by award-winning film and TV producer Frazer Ashford whose credits include *Great Little Trains* (Mainline Television for Westcountry/Ch4, starring the late Willie Rushton); *Street Life* and *Make Yourself at Home* (both for WTV). Produces theatrical films and television – drama, lifestyle and documentaries. Happy to receive ideas for documentaries but submit a one-page synopsis only in the first instance, enclosing s.a.e. 'Be patient, allow up to four weeks for a reply. Be precise with the idea; specific details rather than vague thoughts. Attach a back-up sheet with credentials and supporting evidence, ie, can you ensure that your idea is feasible?'

Assembly Film and Television Ltd

Riverside Studios, Crisp Road, London
W6 9RL
☎020 8237 1075 Fax 020 8237 1071
Email judithmurrell@riversidestudios.co.uk

Contacts *William Burdett-Coutts, Judith Murrell*

Television documentary producer. OUTPUT includes the Prudential Awards for the Arts; the London Comedy Festival; Ch4's Black Season, *In Exile: Sitcom*; BAFTA award-winning *Black Books: Sitcom* and Jo Brand's *Hot Potatoes* for BBC1. Welcomes unsolicited mss. 'We are always interested in looking at new writers.'

Beckmann Productions Ltd

Meadow Court, West Street, Ramsey, Isle of Man IM8 1AE
☎01624 816585 Fax 01624 816589
Email beckmann@enterprise.net
Website www.beckmanngroup.co.uk

Contacts *Stuart Semark, Michael Souter*

Isle of Man-based company. Video and television documentary. OUTPUT *Practical Guide to Europe* (travel series); *Maestro* (12-part series on classical composers); *Ivory Orphans; Ages in History.*

Black Coral Productions Ltd

2nd Floor, 241 High Street, London E17 7BH
☎020 8520 2830 Fax 020 8520 2358
Email bcp@coralmedia.co.uk
Website www.m4media.net

Contacts *Lazell Daley, Marcia Miller*

Producer of drama and documentary film and television. Committed to the development of new writing with a particular interest in short and feature-length dramas. Offers a script consultancy service for which a fee is payable. Runs courses – see **Blaze the Trail** under **Writers' Courses, Circles and Workshops**.

Blackwatch Productions Limited

752–756 Argyle Street, Anderston, Glasgow
G3 8UJ
☎0141 222 2640/2641 Fax 0141 222 2646
Email info@blackwatchtv.com

Company Director *Nicola Black*
Director *Paul Gallagher*
Research & Development Officer
  Heidi Proven
Production Manager *Amanda Keown*

Film, television, video producer of drama and documentary programmes. OUTPUT incudes *Designer Vaginas; Bonebrakers; Luv Bytes*; and *Can We Can We Carry On, Girls?* for Ch4. Also co-ordinates *Mesh*, animation scheme. Does not welcome unsolicited mss.

Blue Heaven Productions Ltd

116 Great Portland Street, London W1W 6PJ
☎020 7436 5552 Fax 020 7436 0888

Contact *Christine Benson*

Film and television drama and occasional documentary. OUTPUT *The Ruth Rendell Mysteries; Crime Story: Dear Roy, Love Gillian; Ready When You Are/Screen Challenge* (three series for Meridian Regional); *The Man who Made Husbands Jealous* (Anglia Television Entertainment/Blue Heaven). Scripts considered but treatments or ideas preferred in the first instance. New writing encouraged.

Brighter Pictures

See **Endemol UK plc**

British Lion
Screen Entertainment Ltd

Pinewood Studios, Iver, Buckinghamshire
SL0 0NH
☎01753 651700 Fax 01753 656391

Chief Executive *Peter R. E. Snell*

Feature film production. OUTPUT has included *A Man for All Seasons; Treasure Island; A Prayer for the Dying; Lady Jane; The Crucifer of Blood; Death Train.*

Bronco Films Ltd

The Producers Centre, 61 Holland Street, Glasgow G2 4NJ
☎0141 287 6817 Fax 0141 287 6815
Email broncofilm@btinternet.com
Website www.broncofilms.co.uk

Contact *Peter Broughan*

Film, television and video drama. OUTPUT includes *Rob Roy* (feature film) and *Young Person's Guide to Becoming a Rock Star* (TV series). No unsolicited mss.

Buccaneer Films

5 Rainbow Court, Oxhey, Hertfordshire
WD19 4RP
☎01923 254000/07740 902095 (mobile)
Fax 01923 254000
Email michael@gosling.com

Contact *Michael Gosling*

Corporate video production and still photography specialists in education and sport. No unsolicited mss.

Caravel Film Techniques Ltd

The Great Barn Studios, Cippenham Lane,
Slough, Berkshire SL1 5AU
☎01494 446662 Fax 01753 571383
Email Ajjcaraveltv.aol.com
Website www.caravelstudios.com

Contact *Anita See*

Film, video and TV: documentary, commercials and corporate. OUTPUT Promos for commercial TV, documentaries for BBC & ITV, sales and training material for corporate blue chip companies. No unsolicited scripts. Prepared to review mostly serious new writing.

Carlton Productions

35–38 Portman Square, London W1H 6NU
☎020 7486 6688 Fax 020 7486 1132
Website www.carltontv.com

**Managing Director/Director of
Programmes** *Steve Hewlett*
Director of Drama & Co-production
Jonathan Powell

Makers of independently produced TV drama for ITV. OUTPUT *Crossroads; The Vice; Bertie and Elizabeth; The Hunt; Pollyanna; Dirty Tricks; Blue Dove; Plain Jane; Peak Practice; Cadfael.* 'We try to use new writers on established long-running series.' Scripts from experienced writers and agents only.

Carnival (Films & Theatre) Ltd

12 Raddington Road, Ladbroke Grove,
London W10 5TG
☎020 8968 0968 Fax 020 8968 0155
Email info@carnival-films.co.uk
Website www.carnival-films.co.uk

Contact *Brian Eastman*

Film, TV and theatre producer. OUTPUT Film: *The Mill on the Floss* (BBC); *Firelight* (Hollywood Pictures/Wind Dancer Productions); *Up on the Roof* (Rank/Granada); *Shadowlands* (Savoy/Spelling); *In Hitler's Shadow* (Home Box Office); *Under Suspicion* (Columbia/Rank/LWT). Television: *As If* (Ch4/Columbia); *Lucy Sullivan is Getting Married* (ITV); *The Tenth Kingdom* (Sky/NBC); *Agatha Christie's Poirot* (ITV/LWT/A&E); *Every Woman Knows a Secret* and *Oktober* (both for ITV Network Centre); *The Fragile Heart* (Ch4); *Crime Traveller* (BBC); *Bugs 1–4* (BBC); *Anna Lee* (LWT); *All Or Nothing At All* (LWT); *Head Over Heels* (Carlton); *Jeeves & Wooster I–IV* (Granada); *Traffik* (Ch4); *Forever Green 1–3* (LWT); *Porterhouse Blue* (Ch4); *Blott on the Landscape* (BBC). Theatre: *What a Performance; Juno & the Paycock; Murder is Easy;*

Misery; Ghost Train; Map of the Heart; Shadowlands; Up on the Roof.

Cartwn Cymru

Ben Jenkins Court, 19A High Street, Llandaf,
Cardiff CF5 2DY
☎029 2057 5999 Fax 029 2057 5919
Email production@cartwn-cymru.demon.co.uk

Contact *Naomi Jones*

Animation production company. OUTPUT *Toucan 'Tecs* (YTV/S4C); *Funnybones* and *Turandot: Operavox* (both for S4C/BBC); *Testament: The Bible in Animation* (BBC2/S4C); *The Miracle Maker* (S4C/BBC/British Screen/Icon Entertainment International); *Faeries* (HIT Entertainment plc for CITV); *Otherworld* (animated feature film for SAC Films, British Screen, Arts Council of Wales).

Celador

39 Long Acre, London WC2E 9LG
☎020 7240 8101 Fax 020 7845 6977
Email tvhits@celador.co.uk
Website www.celador.co.uk

Head of Entertainment *Colman Hutchinson*
Creative Head of Films *Steve Knight*

Producer of TV and radio comedy and light entertainment. OUTPUT *Who Wants to be a Millionaire; Winning Lines; Commercial Breakdown; Britain's Brainiest ...; All About Me.* 'We are interested in original non-derivative sitcom scripts and entertainment formats. Some broadcast experience would be helpful. As a relatively small company our script-reading capacity is limited.'

Celtic Films Ltd

21 Grafton Street, London W1S 4EV
☎020 7409 2080 Fax 020 7409 2383
Email celticfilms@aol.com

Contact *Stuart Sutherland*

Film and television drama producer. OUTPUT includes 14 feature-length *Sharpe* TV films for Carlton and *A Life for a Life – The True Story of Stefan Kiszko* TV film for ITV. Supports new writing and welcomes unsolicited mss.

Central Office of Information Film & Video

Hercules Road, London SE1 7DU
☎020 7261 8667 Fax 020 7261 8776

Head of Department *Jackie Huxley*

Film, video and TV: drama, documentary, commercials, corporate and public information films. OUTPUT includes government commercials and corporate information. No scripts. New writing commissioned as required.

Chameleon Television Ltd

Television House, 104 Kirkstall Road, Leeds, West Yorkshire LS3 1JS
☎0113 244 4486 Fax 0113 243 1267
Email allen@chameleontv.com

Contacts *Allen Jewhurst, Kevin Sim, Anna Hall, Simon Wells*

Film and television drama and documentary producer. OUTPUT includes *The Reckoning* (USA/Ch4); *Dunblane* (ITV); *Foul Play* (Ch5); *St Hildas* and *Rules of the Game* (both for Ch4); *Divorces From Hell, New Voices* and *Shipman* (all for ITV). Scripts not welcome unless via agents but new writing is encouraged.

Chatsworth Television Limited

97–99 Dean Street, London W1D 3TE
☎020 7734 4302 Fax 020 7437 3301
Email television@chatsworth-tv.co.uk
Website www.chatsworth-tv.co.uk

Managing Director *Malcolm Heyworth*

Drama, factual and entertainment television producer. Interested in contemporary and factually based series.

The Children's Film & Television Foundation Ltd

The John Maxwell Building, Elstree Film & TV Studios, Shenley Road, Borehamwood, Hertfordshire WD6 1JG
☎020 8953 0844 Fax 020 8207 0860
Email annahome@cftf.onyxnet.co.uk

Chief Executive *Anna Home*

Involved in the development and co-production of films for children and the family, both for the theatric market and for TV.

Cinécosse

Riversfield Studios, Ellon, Aberdeenshire AB41 9EY
☎01358 722150 Fax 01358 720053
Email admin@cinecosse.co.uk
Website www.cinecosse.co.uk

Contact *Graeme Mowat*

Television and video documentary and corporate productions. OUTPUT includes *Scotland's Larder* (Scottish/Grampian TV); safety and training videos for industry; tourism promotional and sales information. All scripts are commissioned; no unsolicited material.

Cinema Verity Productions Ltd

11 Addison Avenue, London W11 4QS
☎020 7460 2777 Fax 020 7371 3329

Contact *Verity Lambert*

Leading television drama producer whose credits include *She's Out* by Lynda la Plante; *Class Act* by Michael Aitkens; *May to December* (BBC series); *Running Late* by Simon Gray (Screen 1); *The Cazalets* adapt. of *The Cazalet Chronicle* by Elizabeth Jane Howard (BBC). No unsolicited mss.

Circus Films

See **Elstree (Production) Co. Ltd.**

Clarion TV

Mill House, Wandle Road, Croydon, Surrey CR0 4SD
☎020 8681 3891 Fax 020 9303 0160
Email clariontv@btopenworld.com
Website www.completelycreative.co.uk

Director of Programming Operations
Kieran Matthew
Director of Programme Developments
Andrew Linton
Managing Director *Richard Hannah*

Specialises in producing factual entertainment, reality TV, documentaries and corporate material. In development: The Property Channel, a satellite specialist-programming channel; *Combating Cowboys*, a secret camera series shot in collaboration with the UK's trading standards authorities. Will consider submissions (address to *Richard Hannah*) but unable to return material.

Cleveland Productions

5 Rainbow Court, Oxhey, Near Watford, Hertfordshire WD19 4RP
☎01923 254000/07740 902095 (mobile)
Fax 01923 254000
Email michael@gosling.com

Contact *Michael Gosling*

Communications in sound and vision A/V production and still photography specialists in education and sport. No unsolicited mss.

Collingwood & Convergence Productions Ltd

10–14 Crown Street, Acton, London W3 8SB
☎020 8993 3666 Fax 020 8993 9595
Email info@crownstreet.co.uk

Producers *Christopher O'Hare, Terence Clegg, Tony Collingwood*
Head of Development *Helen Stroud*

Film and TV. Convergence Productions produces live action, drama documentaries; Tony Collingwood Productions specialises in children's animation. OUTPUT **Convergence**: *Theo* (film drama series); *Plastic Fantastic* (UK cosmetic surgery techniques, Ch5) and *David Starkey's Henry VIII* (Ch4 historical documentary). **Collingwood**: *RARG* (award-winning animated film); *Captain Zed and the Zee Zone* (ITV); *Daisy-Head Mayzie* (Dr Seuss animated series for Turner Network and Hanna-Barbera); *Animal Stories* (animated poems, ITV network); *Eddy and the Bear* (CITV). Unsolicited mss not welcome 'as a general rule as we do not have the capacity to process the sheer weight of submissions this creates. We therefore tend to review material from individuals recommended to us through personal contact with agents or other industry professionals. We like to encourage new writing and have worked with new writers but our ability to do so is limited by our capacity for development. We can usually only consider taking on one project each year, as development/finance takes several years to put in place.'

Company of Wolves
19–23 Wells Street, London W1P 3FP
☎020 7344 8090 Fax 020 7344 8091
Email cofwolves@aol.com

Contact *Stephen Woolley*

Leading feature film producer. OUTPUT has included *End Of the Affair; Butcher Boy; Interview With the Vampire; Michael Collins; Crying Game; Mona Lisa; Company of Wolves.* Forthcoming productions: *The Actors* (comedy set in Dublin); *The Borgias*; and *Double Down* (thriller starring Nick Nolte). No unsolicited material.

Convergence Productions Ltd
See **Collingwood & Convergence Productions Ltd**

Cosgrove Hall Films
8 Albany Road, Chorlton–cum–Hardy, Manchester M21 0AW
☎0161 882 2500 Fax 0161 882 2555
Email animation@chf.co.uk

Contacts *Mark Hall, Iain Pelling*

Children's animation producer; film video and television. OUTPUT includes *Noddy* and *Rotten Ralph* (both for BBC); *Lavender Castle* by Gerry Anderson; *The Fox Busters; Animal Shelf; Rocky & the Dodos*; Alison Uttley's *Little Grey Rabbit* (all for children's ITV); Terry Pratchett's *Discworld* (Ch4). 'We try to select writers on a

project-by-project basis.' Hosted the **Writers' Guild** workshop in 1998.

Creative Channel Ltd
Channel TV, Television Centre, St Helier, Jersey, Channel Islands JE1 3ZD
☎01534 816873 Fax 01534 816889
Email creative@channeltv.co.uk
Website www.channeltv.co.uk

Senior Producer *David Evans*

Part of the Channel Television Group. Producer of TV commercials and corporate material: information, promotional, sales, training and events coverage. CD and DVD production; promotional videos for all types of businesses in the Channel Islands and throughout Europe. No unsolicited mss; new writing/scripts commissioned as required. Interested in hearing from local writers resident in the Channel Islands.

Creative Film Makers Ltd
Pottery Lane House, 34A Pottery Lane, London W11 4LZ
☎020 7229 5131 Fax 020 7229 4999

Contacts *Michael Seligman, Nicholas Seligman*

Corporate and sports documentaries, commercials and television programmes. OUTPUT *The World's Greatest Golfers*, plus various corporate and sports programmes for clients like Nestlé, Benson & Hedges, Wimpey, Bouygues. 'Always open to suggestions but have hardly ever received unsolicited material of any value.' Keen nevertheless to encourage new writers.

The Creative Partnership
13 Bateman Street, London W1D 3AF
☎020 7439 7762
Email sally@thecreativepartnership.co.uk
Website www.thecreativepartnership.co.uk

Contacts *Christopher Fowler, Jim Sturgeon*

'Europe's largest "one-stop shop" for advertising and marketing campaigns for the film and television industries.' Clients include most major and independent film companies. No scripts. 'We train new writers in-house, and find them from submitted c.v.s. All applicants must have previous commercial writing experience.'

Cricket Ltd
Medius House, 63–69 New Oxford Street, London WC1A 1EA
☎020 7845 0300 Fax 020 7845 0303
Email team@cricket-ltd.com
Website www.cricket-ltd.com

Head of Production (Film & Video)
Jonathan Freer

Film and video, live events and conferences, print and design. 'Communications solutions for business clients wishing to influence targeted external and internal audiences.'

Cromdale Films Ltd
12 St Paul's Road, London N1 2QN
☎020 7226 0178

Contact *Ian Lloyd*

Film, video and TV: drama and documentary. OUTPUT *The Face of Darkness* (feature film); *Drift to Dawn* (rock music drama); *The Overdue Treatment* (documentary); *Russia, The Last Red Summer* (documentary). Initial phone call advised before submission of scripts.

Crown Business Communications Ltd
United House, 9 Pembridge Road, London W11 3JY
☎020 7727 7272 Fax 020 7727 9940
Email clarkea@crownbc.com
Website www.crownbc.com

Contact *Alex Clarke*

Leading producer of moving image, live, design, on-/off-line communications for major corporate clients. 'Always interested in talented writers, especially with a sector journalism or Internet experience.'

Cutting Edge Productions Ltd
27 Erpingham Road, Putney, London SW15 1BE
☎020 8780 1476 Fax 020 8780 0102
Email norridge@globalnet.co.uk

Contact *Julian Norridge*

Corporate and documentary video and television. OUTPUT includes US series on evangelicalism, 'Dispatches' on US tobacco and government videos. No unsolicited mss; 'we commission all our writing to order but are open to ideas.'

Cwmni'r Castell Ltd
10 Garth Road, Colwyn Bay, Conwy LL29 8AF
☎01492 512349 Fax 01492 514235
Email castell@enterprise.net

Contact *Elwyn Vaughan Williams*

Television light entertainment and corporate video producer. Welcomes material from new comedy writers.

Dakota Films Ltd
4 Junction Mews, London W2 1PN
☎020 7706 9407 Fax 020 7402 6111
Email info@dakota-films.demon.co.uk

Managing Director *Jonathan Olsberg*

Film and television drama. Feature films include: *Me Without You; Janice Beard 45wpm; Let Him Have It; Othello.* Currently developing a slate of films, including John Sayles' *Fade to Black* and John Duigan's *Head in the Clouds*, and a number of projects by new writers. Interested in working with new talent but does not consider unsolicited material.

Dareks Production House
58 Wickham Road, Beckenham, Kent BR3 6RQ
☎020 8658 2012 Fax 020 8325 0629
Email david@dareks.fsnet.co.uk

Contact *David Crossman*

Independent producer of corporate and broadcast television. 'We are interested in *short* (10–15 minute) narrative scripts – initial synopsis by e-mail, please.'

Devlin Morris Productions Ltd
97b West Bow, Edinburgh EH1 2JP
☎0131 226 7728 Fax 0131 226 6668
Email contact@devlinmorris-prod.sol.co.uk

Contacts *Morris Paton, Vivien Devlin*

Independent media production house encompassing international arts and travel writing as well as a range of drama, radio, film and television projects.

Direct Image Productions Ltd
See **Direct Image Publishing** under **UK Packagers**

Diverse Production Limited
Gorleston Street, London W14 8XS
☎020 7603 4567 Fax 020 7603 2148
Website www.diverse.co.uk

Contacts *Roy Ackerman, Narinder Minhas*

Broadcast television production with experience in popular prime-time formats, strong documentaries (one-offs and series), investigative journalism, science, business and history films, travel series, arts and music, talk shows, schools and education. OUTPUT includes *Secret Lives; Omnibus; Cutting Edge; Equinox; Modern Times; Dispatches; Without Walls; Panorama; The Big Idea; Empires and Emperors* and the *Little Picture Show.*

DMS Films Ltd
369 Burnt Oak Broadway, Edgware,
Middlesex HA8 5XZ
☎020 8951 6060 Fax 020 8951 6050
Email danny@argonaut.com
Producer *Daniel San*

Film drama producer. OUTPUT includes
Understanding Jane; Hard Edge; Strangers. Welcomes unsolicited screenplays; send synopsis or
outline in first instance.

Double-Band Films
Crescent Arts Centre, 2–4 University Road,
Belfast BT7 1NH
☎028 9024 3331 Fax 028 9023 6980
Email info@doublebandfilms.com
Website www.doublebandfilms.com
Contacts *Michael Hewitt, Dermot Lavery*

Documentary and drama programmes for film
and television. Has specialised in documentary
production for the past twelve years. OUTPUT
George Best's Body, Escobar's Own Goal and
Maradona: Kicking the Habit (all for Ch4); *Still
Life* (short drama film). Currently working on a
documentary about English and Argentinian
football for Ch4.

Drake A–V Video Ltd
89 St Fagans Road, Fairwater, Cardiff
CF5 3AE
☎029 2056 0333 Fax 029 2055 4909
Website www.drakegroup.co.uk
Contact *Ian Lewis*

Corporate A–V film and video, mostly promotional, training or educational. Scripts in these
fields welcome. Other work includes interactive multimedia and CD-ROM production.

The Drama House Ltd
Coach Road Cottage, Little Saxham, Suffolk
IP29 5LE
☎01284 810521 Fax 01284 811425
Email jack@dramahouse.co.uk
Website www.dramahouse.co.uk
Contact *Jack Emery*

Film and television producer. OUTPUT *Inquisition*
(Ch5); *Little White Lies* (BBC1); *Breaking the
Code* (BBC1); *Witness Against Hitler* (BBC1);
Suffer the Little Children (BBC2). Send two-page
synopsis only. All synopses read and returned if
accompanied by s.a.e. Interested especially in
new writers.

Charles Dunstan Communications Ltd
42 Wolseley Gardens, London W4 3LS
☎020 8994 2328 Fax 020 8994 2328
Contact *Charles Dunstan*

Producer of film, video and TV for documentary and corporate material. OUTPUT *Renewable
Energy* for broadcast worldwide in *Inside Britain*
series; *The Far Reaches* travel series; *The Electric
Environment.* No unsolicited scripts.

Ealing Films Limited
Beaumont House, 8 Beaumont Road, Poole,
Dorset BH13 7JJ
☎01202 706379 Fax 01202 706944
Managing Director *Eben Foggitt*
Head of Development *Anita Simpkins*

Film and television drama producer.

Ecosse Films
12 Quayside Lodge, Watermeadow Lane,
London SW6 2UZ
☎020 7371 0290 Fax 020 7736 3436
Email info@ecossefilms.com
Website www.ecossefilms.com
Contact *Josie Atkins*

Producer of feature films and television drama
such as *Charlotte Gray; Mrs Brown* and *Monarch
of the Glen.* Submissions through agents only;
no unsolicited scripts.

Eden Productions Ltd
24 Belsize Lane, London NW3 5AB
☎020 7435 3242 Fax 020 7794 1519
Email jancis@cix.co.uk *or* nlander@cix.co.uk
Contacts *Nicholas Lander, Jancis Robinson*

Producer of *Jancis Robinson's Wine Course;
Vintners' Tales with Jancis Robinson; Taste with
Jancis Robinson* and wine training videos for
British Airways. No unsolicited mss.

Edinburgh Film Productions
Traquair House, Innerleithen, Peeblesshire
EH44 6PP
☎01896 831188
Contact *R. Crichton*

Film, TV drama and documentary. OUTPUT
*Sara; Moonacre; Torch; Silent Mouse; The Curious
Case of Santa Claus; The Stamp of Greatness.* No
unsolicited scripts at present.

Elstree (Production) Co. Ltd
Shepperton Studios, Studios Road,
Shepperton, Middlesex TW17 0QD
☎01932 592680/1 Fax 01932 592682

Website www.elsprod.com

Contact *Greg Smith*

Produces feature films, TV drama and theatre. OUTPUT *Othello* (BBC); *Great Expectations* (Disney Channel); *Porgy & Bess* (with Trevor Nunn); *Old Curiosity Shop* (Disney Channel/ RHI); *London Suite* (NBC/Hallmark); *Animal Farm* and *David Copperfield* (both for Hallmark/ TNT). Co-owner of Circus Films with Trevor Nunn for feature film projects.

Endemol UK plc

Shepherd's Building Central, Charecroft Way, Shepherd's Bush, London W14 0EE
☎0870 333 1700   Fax 0870 333 1800

Chief Executive *Tom Barnicoat*
Chairman *Peter Bazalgette*
Creative Director *Tim Hincks*
Managing Director, Endemol UK productions *Nikki Cheetham*
Chief Executive, Initial *Malcolm Gerrie*
Managing Director, Initial *Laurence Jones*

Endemol UK plc is the largest 'non-broadcaster' entertainment producer in Britain. Its production brands – Endemol UK Productions, Initial and Brighter Pictures – are behind some of the biggest international television hits to come out of the UK. The group produces over 2500 hours of programming for the UK and its commercial activity spans interactive media, programme and format sales, consumer marketing, and advertiser related programming. Endemol UK is wholly owned by the leading European television multinational, Endemol, which in turn is 100%-owned by Spanish telecoms and media giant, Telfonica.

Excalibur Productions

Slack Top Farm, Heptonstall, West Yorkshire HX7 7HA
☎01422 843871   Fax 01422 843871

Contact *Jay Jones*

Most recent productions are medical documentaries including an investigation into diabetes control sponsored by Bayer Diagnostics, collaborative literary and cultural projects such as *The Boys From Savoy* with David Glass, and corporates for South Yorkshire Supertram and Datacolor International. Interested in ideas, scripts and possible joint development for broadcast, sell-through and experimental arts.

Fairline Productions Ltd

15 Royal Terrace, Glasgow G3 7NY
☎0141 331 0077   Fax 0141 331 0066
Email fairprods@aol.com

Contact *Leigh McMahon*

Television and video producer of documentary and corporate programmes and commercials. OUTPUT includes *Hooked*, a 15-part angling series (Discovery Channel) plus training and instructional videos for Forbo-Nairn Ltd, Royal Bank of Scotland, and Health & Safety Executive. No unsolicited scripts.

Farnham Film Company Ltd

34 Burnt Hill Road, Lower Bourne, Farnham, Surrey GU10 3LZ
☎01252 710313   Fax 01252 725855
Website www.farnfilm.com

Contact *Ian Lewis*

Television and film: children's drama and documentaries. Unsolicited mss usually welcome but prefers a letter to be sent in the first instance. Check website for current requirements.

Farrant Partnership

429 Liverpool Road, London N7 8PR
☎020 7700 4647   Fax 020 7697 0224
Email mail@farrant-partnership.com

Contact *James Farrant*

Corporate video productions.

Festival Film and Television Ltd

Festival House, Tranquil Passage, Blackheath, London SE3 0BJ
☎020 8297 9999   Fax 020 8297 1155
Email raymarshall@festivalfilm.com

Contact *Ray Marshall*

Specialises in television drama. In the last ten years has produced 15 Catherine Cookson mini-series for ITV, the latest of which was *A Dinner of Herbs*. Looking primarily for commercial TV projects, feature films (no horror or violence) and children's/family drama. Prefers submissions through an agent. Unsolicited work must be professionally presented or it will be returned unread.

Film and General Productions Ltd

4 Bradbrook House, Studio Place, London SW1X 8EL
☎020 7235 4495   Fax 020 7245 9853

Contacts *Clive Parsons, Davina Belling*

Film and television drama. Feature films include *True Blue* and *Tea with Mussolini*. Also *Seesaw* (ITV drama), *The Greatest Store in the World* (family drama, BBC) and *The Queen's Nose* (children's series, BBC). Interested in considering new writing but subject to prior telephone conversation.

The Firedog Motion Picture Corporation Ltd

182 Brighton Road, Coulsdon, Surrey CR5 2NF
☎020 8660 8663 Fax 020 8763 2558
Email info@firedogfilms.co.uk
Website www.firedogfilms.co.uk
Managing Director *Frazer Ashford*
Head of Production *Georgina Huxstep*

Member of the **Ashford Entertainment Group**. 'Happy to see film/drama ideas.' In the first instance, authors should send a one-page synopsis, their writing c.v. and a brief history/submission history of the project to-date.

Firehouse Productions

42 Glasshouse Street, London W1B 5DW
☎020 7439 2220 Fax 020 7439 2210
Email postie@hellofirehouse.com
Website www.hellofirehouse.com
Contacts *Julie-anne Edwards, Gavin Knight*

Corporate films and websites, commercials and DRTV. OUTPUT includes work for De Beers; BT, Video Arts and various agencies.

First Creative Ltd

Belgrave Court, Caxton Road, Fulwood, Preston, Lancashire PR2 9PL
☎01772 651555 Fax 01772 651777
Email mail@firstcreative.com
Contact *M. Mulvihill*

Video productions for documentary, corporate and multimedia material. Unsolicited scripts welcome. Open to new writing.

The First Film Company Ltd

38 Great Windmill Street, London W1D 7LU
☎020 7439 1640 Fax 020 7437 2062
Producers *Roger Randall-Cutler, Rob Cheek*
FOUNDED 1984. Cinema screenplays. All submissions should be made through an agent.

Flashback Television Limited

11 Bowling Green Lane, London EC1R 0BG
☎020 7490 8996 Fax 020 7490 5610
Email mailbox@flashbacktv.co.uk
Website www.flashbacktv.com
Contact *Tim Ball*

Producer of documentaries and factual entertainment including *Nigella Bites* (Ch4) and *Battle Stations* (A&E). In 2001, Flashback opened a new regional operation – Flashback Bristol.

Flick Media

15 Golden Square, London W1F 9JG
☎020 7734 7979 Fax 020 7287 9495
Website www.flickmedia.co.uk
Contact *Esther Knight*

Producer of film drama, including *Conspiracy of Silence* (feature film). No unsolicited scripts.

Flicks Films Ltd

101 Wardour Street, London W1F 0UG
☎020 7734 4892 Fax 020 7287 2307
Website www.flicksfilms.com
Managing Director/Producer *Terry Ward*
Film and video: children's animated series and specials. OUTPUT *The Mr Men; Little Miss; Bananaman; The Pondles; Nellie the Elephant; See How They Work With Dig and Dug; Timbuctoo.* Scripts specific to their needs will be considered. 'Always willing to read relevant material.'

Focus Films Ltd

The Rotunda Studios, Rear of 116–118 Finchley Road, London NW3 5HT
☎020 7435 9004 Fax 020 7431 3562
Email focus@pupix.demon.co.uk
Contacts *David Pupkewitz, Malcolm Kohll*
   (Head of Development)

Film producer. OUTPUT *The Book of Eve* (Canadian drama); *Julia's Ghost* (German co-production); *The 51st State* (feature film); *Secret Society* (comedy drama feature film); *Crimetime* (feature thriller); *Diary of a Sane Man; Othello.* Projects in development include *Mutant; 90 Minutes; Barry.* No unsolicited scripts.

Mark Forstater Productions Ltd

27 Lonsdale Road, London NW6 6RA
☎020 7624 1123 Fax 020 7624 1124
Contact *Mark Forstater*

Active in the selection, development and production of material for film and TV. OUTPUT *Monty Python and the Holy Grail; The Odd Job; The Grass is Singing; Xtro; Forbidden; Separation; The Fantasist; Shalom Joan Collins; The Silent Touch; Grushko; The Wolves of Willoughby Chase; Between the Devil and the Deep Blue Sea; Doing Rude Things.* No unsolicited scripts.

FremantleMedia Ltd

1 Stephen Street, London W1T 1AL
☎020 7691 6000 Fax 020 7691 6100
Website www.freemantlemedia.com
Chief Executive *Tony Cohen*
Chief Executive, UK Production *Alan Boyd*
Head of Entertainment *Richard Holloway*

FremantleMedia, formerly known as Pearson Television, is the production arm of the RTL Group, Europe's largest TV and radio company. Acquired Thames Television in 1993 (producer of *The Bill*) and Grundy Worldwide (*Neighbours*) in 1995. Further acquisitions were Witzend Productions (*Lovejoy*) and **Alomo Productions** (see entry) in 1996 and **TalkBack Productions** (see entry) in 2000. FremantleMedia produces more than 180 programmes in over 33 countries.

Full Moon Productions

rue Fenelon, Salignac Eyvigues,
Dordogne 24590, France
☎00 33 553 29 94 06 Fax 00 33 553 29 94 06
Email fullmoonproductions@worldonline.fr
Website www.salignacfoundation.com

Contact *Barry C. Paton, BSc.*

Production and logistics management in France. 'We are keen to explore new and innovative drama production for broadcast and/or film. Our script advisors can assess projects. No unsolicited scripts initally, please.' Initial contact should be by letter or e-mail. Also runs training courses in video production and screenwriting.

Gabriela Productions Limited

51 Goldsmith Avenue, London W3 6HR
☎020 8993 3158 Fax 020 8993 8216
Email only4contact@yahoo.com

Contact *W. Starecki*

Film and television drama and documentary productions, including *Blooming Youth* and *Dog Eat Dog* for Ch4 and *Spider's Web* for Polish TV. Welcomes unsolicited mss.

Gaia Communications

Sanctuary House, 35 Harding Avenue,
Eastbourne, East Sussex BN22 8PL
☎01323 734809/727183 Fax 01323 734809
Email mail@gaiacommunications.co.uk
Website www.gaiacommunications.co.uk

Producer *Robert Armstrong*
Script Editor *Loni Webb*

ESTABLISHED 1987. Video and TV corporate and documentary. OUTPUT *Discovering* (south east regional tourist and local knowledge series); *Holistic* (therapies and general information).

Gala Productions Ltd

25 Stamford Brook Road, London W6 0XJ
☎020 8741 4200 Fax 020 8741 2323
Email david@galaproductions.co.uk
Producer *David Lindsay*

TV commercials, promos, film and TV documentaries.

Noel Gay Television

Shepperton Studios, Studios Road,
Shepperton, Middlesex TW17 0QD
☎01932 592569 Fax 01932 592172
Email charles.armitage@virgin.net

CEO *Charles Armitage*

OUTPUT: *The Fear* (BBC Choice); *Second Chance* (Ch4); *Hububb* – Series 1–5 (BBC); *I-Camcorder* (Ch4); *Frank Stubbs Promotes* (Carlton/ITV); *10%ers* – Series 2 (Carlton/ITV); *Call Up the Stars* (BBC1); *Smeg Outs* (BBC video); *Red Dwarf* – 8xseries; *Dave Allen* (ITV); *Windrush* (BBC2). Joint ventures and companies include a partnership with Odyssey, a leading Indian commercials, film and TV producer, and the Noel Gay Motion Picture Company, whose credits include *Virtual Sexuality*; *Trainspotting* (with Ch4 and Figment Films); *Killer Tongue*; *Dog Soldiers*; *Fast Sofa*; and *Pasty Faces*. Associate NGTV companies are Grant Naylor Productions, **Rose Bay Film Productions** (see entry) and Pepper Productions. NGTV is willing to accept unsolicited material from writers but 1–2-page treatments only. No scripts, please.

Ginger Television

See **SMG & Ginger TV Productions Ltd**

GMT Productions Ltd

The Old Courthouse, 26A Church Street,
Bishop's Stortford, Hertfordshire CM23 2LY
☎01279 501622 Fax 01279 501644
Email patrick.wallis@virgin.net

Contacts *Patrick Wallis, Barney Broom*

Film, television and video: drama, documentary, corporate and commercials. No unsolicited mss.

Goldcrest Films International Ltd

65–66 Dean Street, London W1D 4PL
☎020 7437 8696 Fax 020 7437 4448
Email mailbox@goldcrest-films.com

Chairman *John Quested*
Contact *Abigail Walsh*

FOUNDED in the late 1970s. Formerly part of the Brent Walker Leisure Group but independent since 1990 following management buyout led by John Quested. The company's core activities are film production, post-production facilities and worldwide distribution. Scripts via agents only.

The Good Film Company

2nd Floor, 14–15 D'Arblay Street, London
W1V 3FP
☎020 7734 1331 Fax 020 7734 2997
Email productions@goodfilms.co.uk
Website www.goodfilms.co.uk

Contact *Yanina Barry*

Commercials and pop videos. CLIENTS include Hugo Boss, Cadbury's, Wella, National Express Coaches, Camel Cigarettes, Tunisian Tourist Board. *No* unsolicited mss.

Granada Film

4th Floor, 48 Leicester Square, London
WC2H 7FB
☎020 7389 8555 Fax 020 7930 8499

Head of Film *Pippa Cross*

Films and TV films. OUTPUT *The Hole*; *Bloody Sunday*; *House of Mirth*; *Longitude*; *My Left Foot*; *Jack & Sarah*; *Girls Night*. No unsolicited scripts. Supportive of new writing but often hard to offer real help as Granada are developing mainstream commercial projects which usually requires some status in talent areas.

Granite Film & Television Productions Ltd

Vigilant House, 120 Wilton Road, London
SW1V 1JZ
☎020 7808 7230 Fax 020 7808 7231

Contact *Simon Welfare*

Producer of television documentary programmes such as *Nicholas & Alexandra*; *Victoria & Albert* and *Arthur C. Clarke's Mysterious Universe*. No unsolicited mss.

Green Umbrella Ltd

The Production House, 147a St Michaels Hill, Bristol BS2 8DB
☎0117 973 1729 Fax 0117 946 7432
Email postmaster@umbrella.co.uk
Website www.umbrella.co.uk

Television documentary maker and children's drama producer. OUTPUT includes episodes for *The Natural World*, *Wildlife on One* and original series such as *Living Europe* and *Triumph of Life*. Unsolicited treatments relating to natural history and science subjects are welcome.

Greenwich Films Ltd

Studio 2B1, The Old Seager Distillery, Brookmill Road, London SE8 4JT
☎020 8694 2211 Fax 020 8694 2971

Contact *Liza Brown, Development Dept.*

Film, television and video: drama. 'We welcome new writers, though as a small outfit we prefer to meet them through personal contacts as we do not have the resources to deal with too many enquiries. No unsolicited mss, just outlines, please.'

Hammer Film Productions Ltd

92 New Cavendish Street, London W1W 6XJ
☎020 7637 2322 Fax 020 7323 2307

Contact *Terry Ilott*

Television and feature films. Please do not send unsolicited scripts or treatments.

Hammerwood Film Productions

110 Trafalgar Road, Portslade, East Sussex
BN41 1GS
☎01273 277333 Fax 01273 705451
Email filmangels@freenetname.co.uk
Website www.filmangel.co.uk

Contacts *Ralph Harvey, Petra Ginman*

Film, video and TV drama. OUTPUT *Boadicea – Queen of Death* (film; co-production with Pan-European Film Productions and Mirabilis Films); *Boadicea – A Celtic Tragedy* (TV series). In pre-production: *Road to Nirvana* (Ealing-style comedy); *The Black Egg* (witchcraft in 17th century England); *The Ghosthunter*; *A Symphony of Spies* (true stories of WW2 espionage and resistance required). 'Authors are recommended to access www.filmangel.co.uk (see **Useful Websites at a Glance**).'

Hartswood Films Ltd

Twickenham Studios, The Barons, St Margarets, Middlesex TW1 2AW
☎020 8607 8736 Fax 020 8607 8744
Email films.tv@hartswoodfilms.co.uk

Contact *Elaine Cameron*

Film and TV production for drama, comedy and documentary. OUTPUT *Men Behaving Badly* (BBC); *Is It Legal?* (Ch4); *Wonderful You* (ITV); *Border Cafe* (BBC1); *Coupling* (BBC).

Hat Trick Productions Ltd

10 Livonia Street, London W1F 8AF
☎020 7434 2451 Fax 020 7287 9791
Website www.hattrick.com

Contact *Denise O'Donoghue*

Television programmes. OUTPUT includes *Clive Anderson All Talk*; *Small Potatoes*; *The Wilsons*; *The Peter Principle*; *Whatever You Want*; *Confessions*; *Drop the Dead Donkey*; *Father Ted*; *Game On*; *Have I Got News For You*; *If I Ruled the World*; *Room 101*; *Whose Line Is It Anyway?*; *Clive Anderson Talks Back*; *Dicing with Debt*. The company's drama output includes: *A Very Open Prison; Boyz Unlimited; Crossing the Floor; Eleven Men Against Eleven; Gobble; Lord of Misrule; Mr White Goes to Westminster; Underworld; Sex 'n' Death*. Films: *The Suicidal Dog; Sleeping Dictionary; Bloody Sunday*.

Head to Head Communication Ltd

The Hook, Plane Tree Crescent, Feltham, Middlesex TW13 7AQ
☎020 8893 7766 Fax 020 8893 2777
Email amanda@hthc.co.uk

Contact *Amanda Anderson*

Producer of business and corporate communication programmes and events.

Healthcare Productions Limited

Unit 1.04 Bridge House, Three Mills, Three Mill Lane, London E3 3DU
☎020 8980 9444 Fax 020 8980 1901
Email penny@healthcareproductions.co.uk
Website www.healthcareproductions.co.uk

Contact *Penny Webb*

Television and video: documentary and drama. Produces training and educational material, in text, video and CD-ROM, mostly health-related, social care issues, law and marriage.

Jim Henson Productions Ltd

30 Oval Road, Camden, London NW1 7DE
☎020 7428 4000 Fax 020 7428 4001
Website www.henson.com *and*
   www.muppets.com

Contacts *Angus Fletcher, Sophie Finston*

Feature films and TV: family entertainment and children's. OUTPUT *Gulliver's Travels; Buddy; Muppet Treasure Island; The Muppet Christmas Carol; Muppets From Space; The Dark Crystal; Labyrinth; The Witches* (films); *Dinosaurs* (ABC); *Muppet Tonight* (BBC/Sky); *The Muppet Show* (ITV); *The Storyteller* (Ch4/BBC); *Dr Seuss; The Secret Life of Toys* (BBC); *The Animal Show* (BBC); *Mopatop's Shop* (ITV); *Brats of the Lost Nebula* (WB); *Farscape* (Sci-Fi/USA/BBC); *Bear in the Big Blue House* (Disney Channel/Ch5); *Jim Henson's Construction Site* (ITV); *The Hoobs* (Ch4); *Jack and the Beanstalk: The Untold Story* (CBS); *Telling Stories with Tomie de Paola* and *Donna's Day* (both for Odyssey); *The Fearing Mind* (Fox). Scripts via agents only.

Heritage Theatre Ltd

8 Clanricarde Gardens, London W2 4NA
☎020 7243 2750 Fax 020 7792 8584
Email rm@heritagetheatre.com
Website www.heritagetheatre.com

Contact *Robert Marshall*

Video recordings of successful stage plays, sold to the public in VHS and DVD format. 'It is possible to negotiate agreements before the production is staged.'

John Holloway

53 Daybrook Road, Wimbledon, London SW19 3DJ
☎020 8542 7721 Fax 020 8542 7721
Email jhvp@btinternet.com

Contact *John Holloway*

Corporate video. CLIENTS include the Post Office, IBM, British Gas, Freemans, Eastern Electricity, Customs & Excise.

Holmes Associates

The Studio, 37 Redington Road, London NW3 7QY
☎020 7813 4333 Fax 020 7916 9172
Email holmesassociates@blueyonder.co.uk

Contact *Andrew Holmes*

Prolific originator, producer and packager of documentary, drama and music television and films. See also **Open Road Films**. OUTPUT has included *Prometheus* (Ch4 'Film on 4'); *The Shadow of Hiroshima* (Ch4 'Witness'); *The House of Bernarda Alba* (Ch4/WNET/Amaya); *Piece of Cake* (LWT); *The Cormorant* (BBC/Screen 2); *John Gielgud Looks Back; Rock Steady; Well Being; Signals; Ideal Home?* (all Ch4); *Timeline* (with MPT, TVE Spain & TRT Turkey); *Seven Canticles of St Francis* (BBC2). Not currently producing TV drama/documentaries.

Hourglass Pictures Ltd

117 Merton Road, Wimbledon, London SW19 1ED
☎020 8540 8786 Fax 020 8542 6598
Email pictures@hourglass.co.uk
Website www.hourglass.co.uk

Director *Martin Chilcott*

Film and video: documentary, drama and commercials. OUTPUT includes television science documentaries and educational programming. Also health and social issues for the World Health Organization and product information for pharmaceutical companies. Open to new writing.

Icon Films

4 West End, Somerset Street, Bristol BS2 8NE
☎0117 924 8535 Fax 0117 942 0386
Email info@iconfilms.co.uk
Website www.iconfilms.co.uk

Contact *Harry Marshall*

Film and TV documentaries. OUTPUT *Yeti, Hunt for the Wildman* (Ch4/TLC); *A Different Ball Game* (National Geographic); *Quest for the True Cross* (Ch4/Discovery). Specialises in documentaries. Open-minded to new film-makers. Proposals welcome.

Ideal Image Ltd
Cherrywood House, Crawley Down Road, Felbridge, Surrey RH19 2PP
☎01342 300566 Fax 01342 312566

Contact *Alan Frost*

Producer of documentary and drama for film, video, TV and corporate clients. OUTPUT *The Pipeline; Beating the Market.* No unsolicited scripts.

Imari Entertainment Ltd
PO Box 158, Beaconsfield, Buckinghamshire HP9 1AY
☎01494 677147 Fax 01494 677147
Email info@imari-entertainment.com

Contacts *Jonathan Fowke, David Farey*

TV and video producer, covering all areas of drama and documentary. Also partner company, Imari Multi-media.

Initial
See **Endemol UK plc**

Isis Productions
106 Hammersmith Grove, London W6 7HB
☎020 8748 3042 Fax 020 8748 3046
Email isis@isis-productions.com

Directors *Nick de Grunwald, Jamie Rugge-Price*
Production Coordinator *Catriona Lawless*

Formed in 1991, Isis Productions focuses on the production of music and documentary programmes, and co-produces children's programmes under its Rocking Horse banner. OUTPUT *England's Other Elizabeth – Elizabeth Taylor* (BBC 'Omnibus'); *UB40* (ITV 'South Bank Show'); *Fabulous* (BSkyB); *Ivy's Genes* (human genome project, Ch4); *Classic Albums* (international series on the making of the greatest records in rock history, including films on Grateful Dead, Stevie Wonder, Jimi Hendrix, The Band); *Energize!* (kids-in-sport magazine series, Westcountry TV); *Behind the Reporting Line* (behind-the-scenes look at foreign news gathering with Foreign Editor John Simpson, BBC2); *Dido and Aeneas* (film of Purcell's opera, BBC2/Thirteen WNET/ZDF-Arte/NVC Arts); *The Making of Sgt Pepper* (60-min film, Buena Vista International/LWT – winner of Grand Prix at MIDEM).

Isolde Films Ltd
28 Narrow Street, London E14 8DQ
☎020 7702 8700 Fax 020 7702 8701

Contacts *Tony Palmer, Michela Antonello*

Film and TV: drama and documentary. OUTPUT *Wagner; Menuhin; Maria Callas; Testimony; In From the Cold; Pushkin; England, My England* (by John Osborne); *Kipling.* Unsolicited material is read, but please send a written outline first.

JAM Pictures and
Jane Walmsley Productions
8 Hanover Street, London W1S 1YE
☎020 7290 2676 Fax 020 7290 2677
Email producers@jampix.com

Contacts *Jane Walmsley, Michael Braham*

JAM Pictures was FOUNDED in 1996 to produce drama for film, TV and stage. Projects include: *Son of Pocahontas* (TV film, ABC); *Breakthrough* (feature co-production with Viacom Productions, Inc.); *One More Kiss* (feature, directed by Vadim Jean); *Bad Blood* (UK theatre tour); *Chalet Girls* (ITV sitcom). Jane Walmsley Productions, formed in 1985 by TV producer, writer and broadcaster, Jane Walmsley, has completed award-winning documentaries and features such as *Hot House People* (Ch4). No unsolicited mss. 'Letters can be sent to us, asking if we wish to see mss; we are very interested in quality material.'

Keo Films.com
Studio 2B, 151–157 City Road, London EC1V 1JH
☎020 7490 3580 Fax 020 7490 8419
Email keo@keofilms.com
Website www.keofilms.com

Contact *Katherine Perry*

Television documentaries and factual entertainment. OUTPUT includes BBC's 'QED': *The Maggot Mogul* and *Sleeping it Off*; plus *A Cook on the Wild Side; TV Dinners; Beast of the Amazon; Big Snake* and *Jungle Trip* ('To the Ends Of the Earth' series); *River Cottage; Return to River Cottage; The Real Deal; Agia Napa Fantasy Island; Shadow People; River Cottage Forever; Brown Britain; Going To Extremes.* All for Ch4. No unsolicited mss.

Kingfisher Television
Productions Ltd
Carlton Studios, Lenton Lane, Nottingham NG7 2NA
☎0115 964 5262 Fax 0115 964 5263

Contact *Tony Francis*

Broadcast television production.

Kismet Film Company

25 Old Compton Street, London W1D 5JW
☎020 7734 0099 Fax 020 7734 1222
Email kismetfilms@dial.pipex.com

Producer *Michele Camarda*
Head of Development *Nicole Stott*
Development Assistant *Asha Radwan*

Feature films. OUTPUT includes *Photographing Fairies*; *This Year's Love*; *Wonderland* and *Born Romantic*. Kismet can no longer accept unsolicited material. Involved in workshops such as PAL Writer's Workshop, **Equinoxe Screenwriting Workshops** and North by Northwest.

Kudos Productions Limited

65 Great Portland Street, London W1W 7LW
☎020 7580 8686 Fax 020 7580 8787
Email reception@kudosproductions.co.uk

Head of Development *Claire Parker*
Head of Drama *Jane Featherstone*

Film and television; drama and documentaries such as *Among Giants* (feature); *The Magician's House* and *Spooks* (BBC1 series) and *Psychos* (Ch4 series); *Confidence Lab* (BBC2 series). No unsolicited mss.

Lagan Pictures Ltd

21 Tullaghbrow, Tullaghgarley, Ballymena,
Co Antrim BT42 2LY
☎028 2563 9479/077 9852 8797 Fax 028 2563 9479

Producer/Director *Stephen Butcher*

Film, video and TV: drama, documentary and corporate. OUTPUT *A Force Under Fire* (Ulster TV). In development: *Into the Bright Light of Day* (drama-doc); *The £10 Float* (feature film); *The Centre* (drama series). 'We are always interested in hearing from writers originating from or based in Northern Ireland or anyone with, preferably unstereotypical, projects relevant to Northern Ireland. We do not have the resources to deal with unsolicited mss, so please write with a brief treatment/synopsis in the first instance.'

Landseer Film and Television Productions Ltd

140 Royal College Street, London NW1 0TA
☎020 7485 7333 Fax 020 7485 7573
Email mail@landseerfilms.com
Website www.landseerfilms.com

Directors *Derek Bailey, Ken Howard*

Film and video production: documentary, drama, music and arts. OUTPUT *Should Accidentally Fall* (BBC/Arts Council); *Nobody's Fool* ('South Bank Show' on Danny Kaye for LWT); *Swinger* (BBC2/Arts Council); *Auld Lang Syne* and *Retying the Knot* – The Incredible String Band (both for BBC Scotland); *Benjamin Zander* ('The Works', BBC2); *Zeffirelli* ('South Bank Show', LWT); *Death of a Legend* – Frank Sinatra ('South Bank Show' special); *Petula Clark* and *Bing Crosby* (both 'South Bank Show'); *Routes of Rock* (Carlton); *See You in Court* (BBC); *Nureyev Unzipped*, *Gounod's Faust*, *The Judas Tree*, *Ballet Boyz*, *4Dance* and *Bourne to Dance* (all for Ch4).

Lilyville Screen Entertainment Ltd

7 Lilyville Road, London SW6 5DP
☎020 7371 5940 Fax 020 7736 9431
Email tonycash@msn.com

Contact *Tony Cash*

Drama and documentaries for TV. OUTPUT *Poetry in Motion* (series for Ch4); 'South Bank Show': *Ben Elton* and *Vanessa Redgrave*; *Musique Enquête* (drama-based French language series, Ch4); *Landscape and Memory* (arts documentary series for the BBC); Jonathan Miller's production of the *St Matthew Passion* for the BBC; major documentary on the BeeGees for the 'South Bank Show'. Scripts with an obvious application to TV may be considered. Interested in new writing for documentary programmes.

London Scientific Films Ltd

Mill Studio, Crane Mead, Ware, Hertfordshire
SG12 9PY
☎01920 444399
Email lsf@londonscientificfilms.co.uk

Contact *Mike Cockburn*

Film and video documentary and corporate programming. No unsolicited mss.

Lucida Productions

Lucida Studios, 14 Havelock Walk, London
SE23 3HG
☎020 8699 5070

Contact *Paul Joyce*

Television and cinema: arts, adventure, current affairs, documentary, drama and music. OUTPUT has included *Motion and Emotion: The Films of Wim Wenders*; *Dirk Bogarde* – By Myself; *Sam Peckinpah* – Man of Iron; *Kris Kristofferson* – Pilgrim; *Wild One: Marlon Brando*; *Stanley Kubrick: 'The Invisible Man'*; *2001: the Making of a Myth* (Ch4). Currently in development for documentary and drama projects.

LWT United Productions
London Television Centre, Upper Ground,
London SE1 9LT
☎020 7620 1620
Controller of Drama *Michele Buck*

Television drama. OUTPUT *London's Burning;
Night and Day; Hornblower; Walking on the Moon*
by Martin Sadofski (drama-doc); *Touching Evil;
Where the Heart Is.*

Malone Gill Productions Ltd
27 Campden Hill Road, London W8 7DX
☎020 7937 0557 Fax 020 7376 1727
Email malonegill@cs.com
Contact *Georgina Denison*

Mainly documentary but also some drama.
OUTPUT includes *The Face of Russia* (PBS);
Vermeer ('South Bank Show'); *Highlanders* (ITV);
Storm Chasers; Nature Perfected and *The Feast of
Christmas* (all for Ch4); *The Buried Mirror:
Reflections on Spain and the New World* by Carlos
Fuentes (BBC2/Discovery Channel). Approach
by letter with proposal in the first instance.

Mike Mansfield Television Ltd
41–42 Berners Street, London W1T 3NB
☎020 7580 2581 Fax 020 7580 2582
Email mikemantv@aol.com
Contact *Mr Hilary McLaren*

Television for BBC, ITV, Ch4 and Ch5.
OUTPUT *Viva Diva!* (Shirley Bassey music
special) and *Jean Michel Jarre Pyramids New Year.*

Bill Mason Films Ltd
Orchard House, Dell Quay, Chichester, West
Sussex PO20 7EE
☎01243 783558
Email bill.mason@argonet.co.uk
Contact *Bill Mason*

Film and video: documentaries only. OUTPUT
*Racing Mercedes; The History of Motor Racing;
The History of the Motor Car.* No need for out-
side writing; all material is written in-house.
The emphasis is on automotive history.

Maverick Television
The Custard Factory, Gibb Street,
Birmingham B9 4AA
☎0121 771 1812 Fax 0121 771 1550
Email maverick@mavericktv.co.uk
Website www.mavericktv.co.uk
Contact *Clare Welch*

FOUNDED 1994. High quality and innovative
DVC programming in both documentary and
drama. Expanding into light entertainment and
more popular drama. OUTPUT *Trade Secrets*
(BBC2); *Picture This: Accidental Hero* (BBC2);
*Motherless Daughters, Highland Bollywood: Black
Bag, Health Alert: My Teenage Menopause,
Embarrassing Illnesses, Vee-TV* and *Home From
Home* (all for Ch4); *Long Haul* (Scottish Screen/
STV); *Learning to Love the Grey* (BBC/OU).

Maya Vision International Ltd
43 New Oxford Street, London WC1A 1BH
☎020 7836 1113 Fax 020 7836 5169
Website www.mayavisionint.com
Contact *John Cranmer*

Film and TV: drama and documentary. OUTPUT
Saddam's Killing Fields (for 'Viewpoint', Central
TV); *3 Steps to Heaven* and *A Bit of Scarlet* (feature
films for BFI/Ch4); *A Place in the Sun* and *North
of Vortex* (drama for Ch4/Arts Council); *The
Real History Show* (Ch4); *In the Footsteps of
Alexander the Great* (BBC2 documentary); *Hitler's
Search for the Holy Grail* (Ch4 documentary);
Conquistadors (BBC2 documentary). No unso-
licited material; commissions only.

MBP TV
Saucelands Barn, Coolham, Horsham, West
Sussex RH13 8QG
☎01403 741620 Fax 01403 741647
Email info@mbptv.com
Website www.mbptv.com
Contact *Phil Jennings*

Maker of film and video specialising in programmes covering equestrianism and the
countryside. No unsolicited scripts, but always
looking for new writers who are fully
acquainted with the subject.

MedSci Healthcare
Communications
Stoke Grange, Fir Tree Avenue, Stoke Poges,
Buckinghamshire SL2 4NN
☎01753 516644 Fax 01753 516965
Email kerry@medsci.co.uk
Website www.medsci.co.uk

Contacts *Peter Fogarty, Kerry Williams,
Louise Simmonds*

Training programmes, interactive CD-based
training, websites and medical video programmes for the pharmaceutical industry.

Melendez Films
Suite 501, Triumph House, 189–191 Regent
Street, London W1B 4JY
☎020 7434 0220 Fax 020 7434 3131

Contacts *Steven Melendez, Graeme Spurway*

Independent producer working with TV stations. Animated films aimed mainly at a family audience, produced largely for the American market, and prime-time network broadcasting. Also develops and produces feature films (eight so far). OUTPUT has included *Peanuts* (TV specials); *The Lion, the Witch and the Wardrobe; Babar the Elephant* (TV specials); *Dick Deadeye or Duty Done*, a rock musical based on Gilbert & Sullivan operettas. Synopses only, please. Enclose s.a.e. for return.

Mendoza Productions

75 Wigmore Street, London W1H 9LH
☎020 7935 4674 Fax 020 7935 4417
Email debz@mendozafilms.com

Contacts *Wynn Wheldon, Debby Mendoza*

Commercials, title sequences (e.g. Alan Bleasdale's *G.B.H.*); party political broadcasts. Currently in pre-production on a feature-length comedy film. Unsolicited mss welcome but 'comedies only, please'. Material will not be returned without s.a.e. Involved with the **Screenwriters' Workshop**.

Mersey Television Company Ltd

Campus Manor, Childwall Abbey Road, Liverpool L16 0JP
☎0151 722 9122 Fax 0151 722 1969
Website www.merseytv.com

Chairman *Prof. Phil Redmond*

The best known of the independents in the north of England. Makers of television drama. OUTPUT *Brookside; Hollyoaks* (both for Ch4).

Mission Pictures

23 Golden Square, London W1F 9JP
☎020 7734 6303 Fax 020 7734 6202
Email info@missionpictures.net

Contacts *Katie Goodson, Ed Rubin*

Feature films, including *Welcome to Sarajevo; Thunderpants; Gridlock'd; The Debt Collector; Splendor; A Texas Funeral; Some Voices; Very Annie-Mary.* Likes to encourage young talent but cannot consider unsolicited mss.

Moonstone Films Ltd

5 Linkenholt Mansions, Stamford Brook Avenue, London W6 0YA
☎020 8846 8511 Fax 0870 4017171
Email moonstonefilms@fsmail.net

Contact *Tony Stark*

Television: current affairs, science and history documentaries. OUTPUT *Arafat's Authority*, a critical look at the Palestinian authority in the West Bank and Gaza for BBC 'Correspondent'. Unsolicited mss welcome.

MW Entertainments Ltd

48 Dean Street, London W1D 5BF
☎020 7734 7707 Fax 020 7734 7727
Email development@michaelwhite.co.uk

Contact *Michael White*

High-output company whose credits include *Widow's Peak; White Mischief; Nuns on the Run* (co-production with HandMade Films Ltd); *The Comic Strip Series.* Also theatre projects, including *Notre-Dame de Paris; Fame; Me and Mamie O'Rourke; She Loves Me; Crazy for You.* Contributions are passed by Michael White to a script reader for consideration.

Newgate Company

13 Dafford Street, Larkhall, Bath, Somerset BA1 6SW
☎01225 318335

Contact *Jo Anderson*

A commonwealth of established actors, directors and playwrights, Newgate originally concerned itself solely with theatre writing (at the Bush, Stratford, Roundhouse, etc.). However, in the course of development, several productions fed into a list of ongoing drama for BBC TV/Ch4. Looking to develop this co-production strand for film, television and radio projects with other 'Indies'.

Northlight Productions Ltd

The Media Village, Grampian Television, Queen's Cross, Aberdeen AB15 4XJ
☎01224 646460 Fax 01224 646450
Email tv@northlight.co.uk
Website www.northlight.co.uk

Contact *Robert Sproul-Cran*

Film, video and TV: drama, documentary and corporate work. OUTPUT ranges from high-end corporate fund-raising videos to *Thicker Than Water*, a drama series currently in development; *Equinox: Lethal Seas* (documentary on whirlpools for Ch4/Discovery); two schools' series for Ch4 including *Chez Mimi*, 5-part drama sitcom in French. Scripts welcome. Has links with EAVE (European Audio-Visual Entrepreneurs) and Media.

Octopus TV

See **Octopus Publishing Group** under **UK Publishers**

Omnivision

Pinewood Studios, Iver Heath,
Buckinghamshire SL0 0NH
☎01753 656329 Fax 01753 631146
Email info@omnivision.co.uk
Website www.omnivision.co.uk

Contacts *Christopher Morris, Steve Rowsell*

TV and video producers of documentary, corporate, news and sport programming. Also equipment and facilities hire. Interested in ideas; approach by letter or e-mail.

ON Communication

5 East St Helen Street, Abingdon, Oxford
OX14 5EG
☎01235 537400 Fax 01235 530581
Email ON@oncomms-tv.co.uk
Website www.oncomms-tv.co.uk

Contact *Mrs Sharon Frost*

An independent production company FOUNDED in 1985 to produce high-quality factual programming, including science, current affairs, authored documentaries for television, as well as for corporate and heritage markets.

Open Media

The Mews Studio, 8 Addison Bridge Place,
London W14 8XP
Email contact@openmedia.co.uk

Contact *Araminta Phillips*

Broadcast television: OUTPUT *After Dark; The Secret Cabaret; James Randi Psychic Investigator; Opinions; Is This Your Life?; Don't Quote Me; Brave New World; The Talking Show; Natural Causes; Equinox; Dispatches.*

Open Road Films

The Studio, 37 Redington Road, London
NW3 7QY
☎020 7813 4333 Fax 020 7916 9172
Email openroadfilms@blueyonder.co.uk

Development Executive *Sophie Prideaux*
Producer *Andrew Holmes*

Company, formed by **Holmes Associates** to produce low to medium budget British feature films. OUTPUT *Chunky Monkey; Ashes & Sand.* Four projects in development. Unsolicited drama/film scripts will be considered but may take some time for response.

Orlando TV Productions

Up-the-Steps, Little Tew, Chipping Norton,
Oxfordshire OX7 4JB
☎01608 683218 Fax 01608 683364
Email orlando.tv@btinternet.com

Website www.orlandodigital.co.uk

Contact *Mike Tomlinson*

Producer of TV documentaries and digital multimedia content, with science subjects as a specialisation. OUTPUT includes programmes for *Horizon* and *QED* (BBC). Approaches by established writers/journalists to discuss proposals for collaboration are welcome.

Orpheus Productions

6 Amyand Park Gardens, Twickenham,
Middlesex TW1 3HS
☎020 8892 3172 Fax 020 8892 4821
Email richard-taylor@blueyonder.co.uk

Contact *Richard Taylor*

Television documentaries and corporate work. OUTPUT has included programmes for BBC Current Affairs, Music and Arts, and the African-Caribbean Unit as well as documentaries for the Shell Film Unit and Video Arts. Unsolicited scripts are welcomed with caution. 'We have a preference for visually stirring documentaries with quality writing of the more personal and idiosyncratic kind, not straight reportage.'

Outcast Production

1 Lewin Road, London SW14 8DR
☎020 8878 9486
Email xisle@bluecarrots.com

Contact *Andreas Wisniewski*

Low-budget feature films. No unsolicited mss; send synopsis or treatment only. 'We are actively searching for and encouraging new writing.'

Ovation

One Prince of Wales Passage, 117 Hampstead
Road, London NW1 3EF
☎020 7387 2342 Fax 020 7380 0404

Contact *John Plews*

Corporate video and conference scripts. Unsolicited mss not welcome. 'We talk to new writers from time to time.' Ovation also runs the fringe theatre, 'Upstairs at the Gatehouse' in Highgate, north London, and welcomes new plays.

Oxford Scientific Films Ltd

Lower Road, Long Hanborough, Oxfordshire
OX8 8LL
☎01993 881881 Fax 01993 882808
Email enquiries@osf.uk.com
Website www.osf.uk.com

Chief Executive *Claire Birks*

Directors *Sean Morris, Suzanne Aitzetmuller*

Established media company with specialist knowledge and expertise in award-winning natural history films and science-based programmes. Film, video and TV documentaries. Scripts welcome. Operates an extensive stills and film footage library specialising in wildlife and special effects (see entry under **Picture Libraries**).

Barry Palin Associates Ltd
Unit 10 Princeton Court, 55 Felsham Road, London SW15 1AZ
☎020 8394 5660 Fax 020 8785 0440
Email mail@barrypalinassociates.com

Contact *Barry Palin*

Film, video and TV production for drama, documentary, commercials and corporate material. OUTPUT *Harmfulness of Tobacco* Anton Chekhov short story – BAFTA Best Short Film Awardwinner (Ch4); Corporate: Philip Morris, York International, Republic Bank of New York.

Panther Pictures Ltd
3rd Floor, 16 Golden Square, London W1F 9JQ
☎07976 256 610 Fax 020 7734 8858
Website www.pantherpictures.co.uk

Contact *Robert Sutton*

Feature films, including *Inside/Out*, a US/UK/Canada/France co-production.

Paper Moon Productions
Wychwood House, Burchetts Green Lane, Littlewick Green, Nr. Maidenhead, Berkshire SL6 3QW
☎01628 829819 Fax 01628 825949
Email david@paper-moon.co.uk

Contact *David Haggas*

Television and video: medical and health education documentaries. OUTPUT includes *Shamans and Science*, a medical documentary examining the balance between drugs discovered in nature and those synthesised in laboratories. Unsolicited scripts welcome. Interested in new writing 'from people who really understand television programme-making'.

Parallax Pictures Ltd
7 Denmark Street, London WC2H 8LS
☎020 7836 1478 Fax 020 7497 8062
Website www.parallaxpictures.co.uk

Contact *Sally Hibbin*

Feature films/television drama. OUTPUT *RiffRaff*; *Bad Behaviour*; *Raining Stones*; *Ladybird,* *Ladybird*; *I.D.*; *Land and Freedom*; *The Englishman Who Went up a Hill But Came Down a Mountain*; *Bliss*; *Jump the Gun*; *Carla's Song*; *The Governess*; *My Name Is Joe*; *Stand and Deliver*; *Dockers*; *Hold Back the Night*; *Bread and Roses*; *Princesa*; *The Navigators*; *Sweet Sixteen*; *Innocence*.

Passion Pictures
25–27 Riding House Street, London W1W 7DU
☎020 7323 9933 Fax 020 7323 9030
Email info@passion-pictures.com

Managing Director *Andrew Ruhemann*

Documentary and drama includes: *One Day in September* (Academy Award-winner for Best Feature Documentary, 2000); also commercials and music videos: Carphone Warehouse, Mini, Aero, Gorillaz, Coldplay and Robbie Williams. Unsolicited mss welcome.

Pathé Pictures
14–17 Kent House, Market Place, London W1N 8AR
☎020 7323 5151 Fax 020 7631 3568

Head of Development *Matthew Gannon*
Development Executives *Lucy Ryan,* *Celine Haddad*
Development Assistant *Erol Arguden*

Produces 4–6 theatrical feature films each year. 'We are pleased to consider all material that has representation from an agent or production company.'

PBF Motion Pictures
The Little Pickenhanger, Tuckey Grove, Ripley, Surrey GU23 6JG
☎01483 225179 Fax 01483 224118
Email peter@pbf.co.uk

Contact *Peter B. Fairbrass*

Film, video and TV: drama, documentary, commercials and corporate. Also televised chess series and chess videos. No scripts; send one-page synopsis only in the first instance. 'Good scripts which relate to current projects will be followed up, otherwise not, as PBF do not have the time to reply to proposals which do not interest them. Only good writing stands a chance.'

Pearson Television
See **FremantleMedia Ltd**

Pelicula Films
59 Holland Street, Glasgow G2 4NJ
☎0141 287 9522 Fax 0141 287 9504

Contact *Mike Alexander*

Television producer. Maker of drama docu-mentaries and music programmes for the BBC and Ch4. OUTPUT *As an Eilean (From the Island); The Trans-Atlantic Sessions 1 & 2; Nanci Griffith, Other Voices 2; Follow the Moonstone.*

Penumbra Productions Ltd

80 Brondesbury Road, London NW6 6RX
☎020 7328 4550 Fax 020 7328 3844
Email nazpenumbra@compuserve.com

Contact *H.O. Nazareth*

Film, video, TV and radio: drama and social issues documentaries. OUTPUT includes *Fugitive Pieces* (Radio 3 play); *Stories My Country Told Me* (BBC2, 'Arena'); *Repomen* (Ch4, 'Cutting Edge'). Send synopses only, preferably by e-mail. Keen to assist in the development of new writing but only interested in social issue-based material.

Photoplay Productions Ltd

21 Princess Road, London NW1 8JR
☎020 7722 2500 Fax 020 7722 6662
Email photoplay@compuserve.com

Contact *Patrick Stanbury*

Documentaries for film, television and video plus restoration of silent films and their theatrical pre-sentation. OUTPUT includes *Cinema Europe: The Other Hollywood; Universal Horror; D.W. Griffith: Father of Film; Lon Chaney, Man of 1000 Faces* and the 'Channel 4 Silents' series of silent film restoration, including *The Wedding March* and *The Iron Mask.* Recently completed *The Tramp and the Dictator.* No unsolicited mss; 'we tend to create and write all our own programmes.'

Picardy Media Group

1 Park Circus, Glasgow G3 6AX
☎0141 333 1200 Fax 0141 332 6002
Email jr@picardy.co.uk
Website www.picardy.co.uk

Senior Producer *John Rocchiccioli*

Television and video: arts documentaries, training and promotional videos, education projects, multi-media productions, and TV and cinema commercials. Unsolicited mss wel-come; 'keen to encourage new writing.'

Picture Palace Films Ltd

13 Egbert Street, London NW1 8LJ
☎020 7586 8763 Fax 020 7586 9048
Email info@picturepalace.com
Website www.picturepalace.com

Contacts *Malcolm Craddock, Katherine Hedderly*

FOUNDED 1971. Leading independent producer of film and TV drama. OUTPUT *Rebel Heart*

(BBC1); *Extremely Dangerous* and *A Life for A Life* (both for ITV); *Sharpe's Rifles* (14 films for Carlton TV); *Little Napoleons* (comedy drama, Ch4); *The Orchid House* (drama serial, Ch4); *Tandoori Nights; 4 Minutes; When Love Dies* (all for Ch4); *Ping Pong* (feature film); *Acid House* (Picture Palace North). Material will only be considered if submitted through an agent.

Phil Pilley Productions

Ferryside, Felix Lane, Shepperton, Middlesex TW17 8NG
☎01932 702916 Fax 01932 702916
Email pilley@tinyworld.co.uk

Programmes for TV and video, mainly sports. Now specialising in sporting history books, particularly golf.

Planet 24 Productions Ltd

195 Marsh Wall, London E14 9SG
☎020 7345 2424 Fax 020 7345 9400
Email info@planet24.co.uk
Website www.planet24.com

Managing Director *Mary Durkan*

Television producer of light and factual enter-tainment, comedy, music, features and computer animation. Wholly owned subsidiary of Carlton Communications plc. OUTPUT *The Big Breakfast; The Word; The Messiah* (live recording); *Hotel Babylon; Gaytime TV; Delicious; Extra Time, Nothing But the Truth; Watercolour Challenge; Andi Meets ...; Richard Whiteley Unbriefed; The Richard Blackwood Show; A Family of My Own.*

Plantagenet Films Limited

Ard-Daraich Studio B, Ardgour, Nr Fort William, Inverness-shire PH33 7AB
☎01855 841384 Fax 01855 841384
Email plantagenetfilms@aol.com

Contact *Norrie Maclaren*

Film and television: documentary and drama programming such as *Dig* (gardening series for Ch4); various 'Dispatches' for Ch4 and 'Omnibus' for BBC. Keen to encourage and promote new writing; unsolicited mss welcome.

Platinum Film & TV Production Ltd

1b Murray Street, London NW1 9RE
☎020 7916 9091 Fax 020 7916 5238
Email inquiries@platinumtv.co.uk

Contact *Terry Kelleher*

Television documentaries, including drama-documentary. OUTPUT *South Africa's Black Economy* (Ch4); *Murder at the Farm* (Thames

TV); *The Biggest Robbery in the World* (major investigative true-crime drama-documentary for Carlton TV); *Dead Line* (original drama by Chilean-exiled writer, Ariel Dorfman, for Ch4). Scripts and format treatments welcome.

Portobello Pictures
64A Princedale Road, London W11 4NL
☎020 7379 5566 Fax 020 7379 5599

Contact *Eric Abraham*

Film drama, including Jan Sverak's *Dark Blue World* and *Kolya*; Jez Butterworth's *Birthday Girl* and *Mojo*; Tim Roth's *The War Zone*, plus BBC1's *Dalziel & Pascoe* (series 1–3).

Gavin Prime Television
Christmas House, 213 Chester Road, Castle Bromwich, Solihull, West Midlands B36 0ET
☎0121 749 7147/4144

Contact *Gavin Prime*

Film and television: comedy, entertainment and animation. No unsolicited mss.

Renaissance Films
34–35 Berwick Street, London W1F 8RP
☎020 7287 5190 Fax 020 7287 5191
Website www.renaissance-films.com

Co-Managing Directors *Stephen Evans, Angus Finney*
Director of Development *Caroline Wood*

Feature films: *The Luzhin Defense; The Wings of the Dove; The Madness of King George* (as Close Call Films); *Twelfth Night; Much Ado About Nothing; Peter's Friends; Henry V.* No unsolicited mss.

Renaissance Vision
256 Fakenham Road, Taverham, Norwich, Norfolk NR8 6QW
☎01603 260280 Fax 01603 864857
Email bfg@renvision.demon.co.uk

Contact *B. Gardner*

Video: full range of corporate work (training, sales, promotional, etc.). Producers of educational and special-interest video publications. Willing to consider good ideas and proposals.

Richmond Films & Television Ltd
PO Box 33154, London NW3 4AZ
☎020 7722 6464 Fax 020 7722 6232
Email mail@richmondfilms.com

Contact *Development Executive*

Film and TV: drama and comedy. OUTPUT *Press Gang; The Lodge; The Office; Wavelength;*

Privates. 'No unsolicited scripts. We will accept *two pages only* consisting of a brief treatment of your project (either screenplay or TV series) which includes its genre and its demographics. Please tell us also where the project has been submitted previously and what response you have had. *Your two pages will not be returned.*'

Rocking Horse
See **Isis Productions**

Rose Bay Film Productions
13 Austin Friars, London EC2N 2JX
☎020 7670 1609 Fax 020 8357 0845
Email info@rosebay.co.uk

Contacts *Matthew Steiner, Simon Usiskin*

Formats and TV production: entertainment and comedy. Unsolicited scripts (with s.a.e.) welcome.

Brenda Rowe Productions
42 Wellington Park, Clifton, Bristol BS8 2UW
☎0117 973 0390 Fax 0117 973 8254
Email br007b3169@blueyonder.co.uk

Contact *Brenda Rowe*

Produces observational, investigative, current affairs TV documentaries, and training and promotional videos for business organisations. Open to new work; unsolicited mss welcome.

RS Productions
47 Laet Street, Newcastle upon Tyne NE29 6NN
☎0191 259 1184/07710 064632 (Mobile)
Fax 0191 259 1184
Email enquiries@rsproductions.co.uk
Website www.rsproductions.co.uk

Contact *Mark Lavender*

Feature films, television and new media: drama series/serials and singles. Targeting TV docs and series. Working with established and new talent. Submissions – one- or two-page outline, synopsis or treatment.

Sands Films
119 Rotherhithe Street, London SE16 4NF
☎020 7231 2209 Fax 020 7231 2119
Website www.sandsfilms.co.uk

Contacts *Christine Edzard, Olivier Stockman*

Film and TV drama. OUTPUT *Little Dorrit; The Fool; As You Like It; A Dangerous Man; The Long Day Closes; A Passage to India; The Nutcracker; Seven Years in Tibet; The Children's Midsummer Night's Dream.* No unsolicited scripts.

Scala Productions Ltd

15 Frith Street, London W1D 4RE
☎020 7734 7060 Fax 020 7437 3248
Email scalaprods@aol.com

Contacts *Nik Powell*

Production company set up by ex-Palace
Productions Nik Powell and Stephen Woolley,
who have an impressive list of credits including
*Company of Wolves; Absolute Beginners; Mona Lisa;
Scandal; Crying Game; Backbeat; Neon Bible; 24:7;
Little Voice; Divorcing Jack; Welcome to Woop
Woop; The Lost Son; Fanny and Elvis; The Last
September; Wild About Harry; Last Orders; A
Christmas Carol – The Movie; Black and White.* In
development: *Leopold Bloom; Boswell for the
Defence; The Night We Called It a Day; I'll Sleep
When I'm Dead; A Passionate Woman; A Single
Shot; Haroun and the Sea of Stories; Level; St Agnes'
Stand; Johnny Bollywood; One Love; English
Passengers; He Kills Coppers.*

Scope Productions Ltd

Keppie House, 147 Blythswood Street,
Glasgow G2 4EN
☎0141 332 7720 Fax 0141 332 1049
Website www.scopeproductions.co.uk

Corporate *Bill Gordon*

Corporate film and video; broadcast documentaries and sport; TV commercials. Unsolicited,
realistic scripts/ideas welcome.

Screen First Ltd

The Studios, Funnells Farm, Down Street,
Nutley, East Sussex TN22 3LG
☎01825 712034 Fax 01825 713511
Email info@screenfirst.co.uk

Contacts *M. Thomas, P. Madden*

Television dramas, documentaries, arts and animation programmes. Developing major drama
series, feature films, animated specials and
series. No unsolicited scripts.

Screen Ventures Ltd

49 Goodge Street, London W1T 1TE
☎020 7580 7448
Email sales@screenventures.com

Contacts *Christopher Mould, Naima Mould*

Film and TV sales and production: documentary,
music videos and drama. OUTPUT *Life and Limb*
(documentary, Discovery Health Channel);
Pavement Aristocrats (SABC); *Woodstock Diary;
Vanessa Redgrave* and *Genet* (both LWT 'South
Bank Show'); *Mojo Working; Burma: Dying for
Democracy* (Ch4); *Dani Dares* (Ch4 series on
strong women); *Pagad* (Ch4 news report).

Screenhouse Productions Ltd

378 Meanwood Road, Leeds, West Yorkshire
LS7 2JF
☎0113 239 2292 Fax 0113 239 2293
Email info@screenhouse.co.uk
Website www.screenhouse.co.uk/screenhouse

Contacts *Paul Bader, Barbara Govan*

Factual programmes, mainly popular science and
history. Also new media. OUTPUT includes
Science Shack, BBC2 series presented by Adam
Hart-Davis; six series of *Local Heroes*, factual programmes about the greats of science; two series
of *Hart-Davis on History*, a magazine series about
local history and how to become involved in historical research (both for BBC2); two history
series for BBC Knowledge, *History Quest* and
History Fix. Contact with one-page outline of
idea in the first instance.

Screenprojex.com – a division of Screen Production Associates Ltd

☎020 7287 1170 Fax 020 7287 1123
Email enquiries@screenprojex.com
Website screenprojex.com

Contacts *Doug Abbott, John Jaquiss,
Julia Vickers*

Feature films: *The Fourth Man; The Case; Black
Badge* (all in association with The Writers'
Studio); *The Truth Game; Club Le Monde;
Midnight Warriors.* No unsolicited mss. Send
preliminary letter outlining project and c.v.

September Films Ltd

Glen House, 22 Glenthorne Road, London
W6 0NG
☎020 8563 9393 Fax 020 8741 7214
Email september@septemberfilms.com
Website www.septemberfilms.com

Head of Production *Elaine Day*
Head of Drama and Film Development
Nadine Mellor

Factual entertainment and documentary specialists expanding further into television drama and
film. Feature film OUTPUT includes *Breathtaking;
House of America; Solomon & Gaenor.*

Serendipity Picture Company

Media Centre, Emma-Chris Way,
Abbeywood Park, Bristol BS34 7JU
☎0117 906 6541 Fax 0117 906 6542
Email tony@serendipitypictures.com

Contacts *Tony Yeadon, Nick Dance*

Television and video; corporate and documentary programming. Encourages new writing
and will consider scripts.

Seventh House Films

1 Hall Farm Place, Bawburgh, Norwich,
Norfolk NR9 3LW
☎01603 749068 Fax 01603 749069
Email caflo.dunn@virgin.net

Contacts *Clive Dunn, Angela Rule*

Documentary for film, video and TV on subjects
ranging from arts to history and science to social
affairs. OUTPUT *The Last Fling* (life for a paralysed
jump-jockey); *Dark Miracle* (an investigation into
a near nuclear disaster in East Anglia); *A Pleasant
Terror* (life and ghosts of M.R. James); *Piano
Pieces* (musical excursion exploring different
aspects of the piano); *Rockin' the Boat* (memories
of pirate radio); *White Knuckles* (on the road with
a travelling funfair); *King Romance* (life of Henry
Rider Haggard); *A Drift of Angels* (three women
and the price of art); *Bare Heaven* (the life and fiction of L.P. Hartley); *A Swell of the Soil* (life of
Alfred Munnings); *Light Out of the Sky* (the art
and life of Edward Seago). 'We welcome programme proposals with a view to collaborative
co-production. Always interested in original and
refreshing expressions for visual media.'

Sianco Cyf

7 Ffordd Segontiwm, Caernarfon, Gwynedd
LL55 2LL
☎01286 673436/07831 726111 (Mobile)
Fax 01286 677616
Email sianco@treannedd.demon.co.uk

Contact *Siân Teifi*

Children's, youth and education programmes
and children's drama.

SilentSound Films Ltd

Cambridge Court, Cambridge Road, Frinton
on Sea, Essex CO13 9HN
☎01255 676381 Fax 01255 676381
Email thj@silentsoundfilms.co.uk
Website www.silentsoundfilms.co.uk *or*
   www.londonfoodfilmfiesta.co.uk

Contact *Timothy Foster*

Active in European film co-production with
mainstream connections in the USA. Special
interest in developing new projects for live
orchestral accompaniment. Also film musicals
and documentaries on the arts. Synopses considered via e-mail or post.

Siriol Productions

3 Mount Stuart Square, Butetown, Cardiff
CF1 6RW
☎029 2048 8400 Fax 029 2048 5962
Email enquiries@siriol.co.uk

Website www.siriolproductions.com

Contact *Andrew Offiler*

Animated series, mainly for children. OUTPUT
includes *Meeow; Hilltop Hospital; The Hurricanes;
Tales of the Toothfairies; Billy the Cat; The Blobs*, as
well as the feature films, *Under Milkwood* and *The
Princess and the Goblin*. Write with ideas and sample script in the first instance.

Skyline Productions

10 Scotland Street, Edinburgh EH3 6PS
☎0131 557 4580 Fax 0131 556 4377
Email leslie@skyline.uk.com

Producer/Writer *Leslie Hills*

Film and television drama and documentary.
Encourages new writers but telephone first
before sending material.

SMG & Ginger TV Productions Ltd

116 New Oxford Street, London WC1A 1HH
☎020 7663 2300
Website www.ginger.com

Also: SMG TV Productions (Glasgow),
200 Renfield Street, Glasgow G2 3PR
☎0141 300 3000

Managing Director *Jagdip Jagpal*
Head of Drama *Erina Rayner, Eric Coulter*
   (Glasgow)
Executive Producer for Drama *Judy
   Counihan*
Head of Development and Children's
   Elizabeth Partyka
Head of Factual Programming *John Farren,
   Helen Alexander* (Glasgow)

SMG (Scottish Media Group) TV Productions
Ltd, which incorporates Ginger Television,
makes programmes for the national television
networks, including ITV, Ch4 and Sky.
Specialises in drama, factual entertainment and
children's programming. OUTPUT includes
*Taggart; Rebus; Take Me; TFI Friday;
Remembering Lockerbie; The Priory; How2*.

Specific Films

25 Rathbone Street, London W1T 1NQ
☎020 7580 7476 Fax 020 7494 2676
Email specificfilms@compuserve.com

Contacts *Michael Hamlyn*

FOUNDED 1991. OUTPUT includes *Mr Reliable*
(feature film co-produced by PolyGram and
the AFFC); *The Adventures of Priscilla, Queen of
the Desert*, co-produced with Latent Image
(Australia) and financed by PolyGram and
AFFC; *U2 Rattle and Hum*, full-length feature
– part concert film/part cinema verité docu-

mentary; *Paws* (executive producer); *The Last Seduction 2* (Polygram); and numerous pop promos for major international artists.

Spellbound Productions Ltd

90 Cowdenbeath Path, Islington, London N1 0LG
☎020 7713 8066 Fax 020 7713 8067
Email phspellbound@hotmail.com

Contact *Paul Harris*

Specialises in feature films for cinema and drama for television. Keen to support and encourage new writing. Material will only be considered if in correct screenplay format and accompanied by s.a.e.

Spice Factory (UK) Ltd

81 The Promenade, Brighton, East Sussex BN10 8LS
☎01273 585275 Fax 01273 585304
Email info@spicefactory.co.uk

Contacts *Lucy Shuttleworth, Emily Kyriakides*

FOUNDED 1995. Film producers. OUTPUT *Pilgrim* (starring Ray Liotta); *Sabotage* (David Suchet, Stephen Fry); *Anazupta* (Lena Headey, Jason Fleming); *Mr In-Between* (Andrew Howard); *Plots With a View* (Christopher Walken, Brenda Blethyn, Alfred Molina, Lee Evans). 'Treatment and/or synopsis for feature-length films. Please enclose s.a.e.'

'Spoken' Image Ltd

8 Hewitt Street, Manchester M15 4GB
☎0161 236 7522 Fax 0161 236 0020
Email multimedia@spoken-image.com

Contacts *Geoff Allman, Steve Foster*

Film, video and TV production for documentary and corporate material. Specialises in high-quality brochures and reports, CD-ROMs, exhibitions, conferences, film and video production for broadcast, industry and commerce.

Standish Films

320 Woodhouse Lane, Wigan, Lancashire WN6 7TD
☎077193 75575
Email mail@sirco.co.uk
Website www.sirco.co.uk

Contact *Rosemary Allen*

Film, video and TV: documentary, drama, commercials and corporate, including dramatised training videos. Currently looking for feature film scripts with Anglo/American/European themes. 'Interested in supporting and encouraging new talent and experienced writers looking

for new and imaginative ways to express their ideas.' No unsolicited materal; send synopses and enquiries via e-mail. Check website for current needs.

Stirling Film & TV Productions Limited

137 University Street, Belfast BT7 1HP
☎028 9033 3848 Fax 028 9043 8644
Email anne@stirlingtelevision.co.uk

Contact *Anne Stirling*

Producer of broadcast and corporate programming – documentary, sport, entertainment and magazine programmes.

Storm Film Productions Ltd

32–34 Great Marlborough Street, London W1F 7JB
☎020 7439 1616 Fax 020 7439 4477
Email sophie.storm@btclick.com

Contact *Nic Auerbach*

Producer of commercials for clients such as British Airways and Shell. Unsolicited mss welcome.

Straight Forward Film & Television Productions Ltd

Ground Floor, Crescent House, 14 High Street, Holywood, Co. Down BT18 9AZ
☎028 9042 6298 Fax 028 9042 3384
Email enquiries@sforward.prestel.co.uk

Contacts *John Nicholson, Ian Kennedy*

Northern Ireland-based production company specialising in documentary, feature and lifestyle series for both regional and network transmission. OUTPUT includes *We Shall Overcome* (winner of Best Documentary at 1999 Celtic Television Festival for BBC); *Conquering the Normans* (Ch4 Learning – history of Normans in Ireland); *Gift of the Gab* (Ch4 Learning – contemporary Irish writing); *Fire School* (BBC NI – training of a team of fire-fighters); *Fish Out of Water* (BBC NI – job swaps north and south of the Irish border); *Just Jones* (BBC Radio Ulster daily show); *Sportsweek* (BBC Radio Ulster); *School Challenge* (3rd series, BBC NI); *World Indoor Bowls* (BBC NI); *Awash With Colour* (series, BBC Daytime).

Strawberry Productions Ltd

36 Priory Avenue, London W4 1TY
☎020 8994 4494 Fax 020 8742 7675

Contact *John Black*

Film, video and TV: drama and documentary; corporate and video publishing.

Sunset + Vine Productions Ltd
30 Sackville Street, London W1S 3DY
☎020 7478 7300   Fax 020 7478 7403

Sports, children's and music programmes for television. No unsolicited mss. 'We hire free-lancers only upon receipt of a commission.'

Sweetheart Films
15 Quennel Mansions, Weir Road, London SW12 0NQ
☎020 8673 3855

Producer *Karel Bata*

Low-to-medium-budget feature films. No unsolicited mss; 'an introductory letter with, perhaps, a treatment and short extract would receive consideration. We are constantly on the look-out for talent. Tip: study your craft!'

Table Top Productions
1 The Orchard, Chiswick, London W4 1JZ
☎020 8742 0507   Fax 020 8742 0507
Email alvin@tabletopproductions.com

Contact *Alvin Rakoff*

TV and film. OUTPUT *Paradise Postponed* (TV mini-series); *A Voyage Round My Father; The First Olympics 1896; Dirty Tricks; A Dance to the Music of Time.* No unsolicited mss. Also Dancetime Ltd.

Talisman Films Limited
5 Addison Place, London W11 4RJ
☎020 7603 7474   Fax 020 7602 7422
Email email@talismanfilms.com

Contact *Richard Jackson*

Drama for film and TV: developing the full range of drama – TV series, serials and single films, as well as theatric features. 'We will only consider material submitted via literary agents.' Interested in supporting and encouraging new writing.

TalkBack Productions
20–21 Newman Street, London W1T 1PG
☎020 7861 8000   Fax 020 7861 8001
Email reception@talkback.co.uk

Chief Executive *Peter Fincham*
Managing Director *Sally Debonnaire*

TalkBack Productions is a **FremantleMedia** company. Specialises in comedy, comedy drama and drama; also feature lifestyle programmes. OUTPUT *Smith and Jones; Murder Most Horrid; The Day Today; Knowing Me Knowing You with Alan Patridge; I'm Alan Patridge; They Think It's All Over; Never Mind the Buzzcocks; Brass Eye; House Doctor; She's Gotta Have It; Grand Designs; Sword of Honour; In a Land of Plenty; Shooting the Past; 11 o'clock Show; Smack the Pony; Big Train; Los Dos Bros; Your Money or Your Life; Property Ladder; Would Like to Meet.*

Tandem TV & Film Ltd
10 Bargrove Avenue, Hemel Hempstead, Hertfordshire HP1 1QP
☎01442 261576   Fax 01442 219250
Email info@tandemtv.com
Website www.tandemtv.com

Contact *Barbara Page*

Produces training videos, especially health and safety; construction and civil engineering documentaries; drama-doc life stories for satellite television; Christian church and charity documentary, training and promotional programmes. Welcomes unsolicited mss.

Telemagination Ltd
Royalty House, 72–74 Dean Street, London W1V 6AE
☎020 7434 1551   Fax 020 7434 3344
Email mail@tmation.co.uk
Website www.telemagination.co.uk

Contact *Marion Edwards*

Producer of television animation. OUTPUT includes *The Animals of Farthing Wood; Noah's Island; The Last Polar Bears.* No unsolicited material.

Televideo Productions
The Riverside, Furnival Road, Sheffield, South Yorkshire S4 7YA
☎0114 249 1500   Fax 0114 249 1505
Email gking@televideo.co.uk
Website www.televideo.co.uk

Contact *Graham King*

Video and television: TV news and sports coverage, documentary and corporate work; sell-through videos (distributed on own label). OUTPUT includes *The Premier Collection* (football club videos); varied sports coverage for cable, satellite and terrestrial broadcasters plus a wide range of corporate work from drama-based material to documentary.

Teliesyn
Chapter Arts Centre, Market Road, Canton, Cardiff CF5 1QE
☎029 2030 0876   Fax 029 2030 0877
Email tv@teliesyn.demon.co.uk
Website www.teliesyn.co.uk

Contact *Chris Davies*

Film and video: produces drama, documentary,

music and social action in English and Welsh. Celtic Film Festival, BAFTA Cymru, Grierson and Indie award winner. OUTPUT *Llafur Cariad* (epic drama, S4C); *How Red Was My Valley* (documentary series on the Labour Party, BBC2W); *Suckerfish* (35mm short); *Subway Cops and the Mole Kings* (Ch4); *Navida Nuestra* (Christmas mass from Argentina, S4C). Will consider unsolicited scripts only if accompanied by synopsis and c.v. Encourages new writing wherever possible in close association with a producer.

Tern Television Productions Ltd
73 Crown Street, Aberdeen AB11 6EX
☎01224 211123 Fax 01224 211199
Email office@terntv.com
Website www.terntv.com
Also at: The Pentagon Centre, 36 Washington Street, Glasgow G3 8AZ ☎0141 248 2180
Contacts *David Strachan, Gwyneth Hardy* (Aberdeen), *Harry Bell* (Glasgow)

Broadcast, television and corporate video productions. Specialises in factual entertainment. Currently developing drama. Unsolicited mss welcome.

Testimony Films
12 Great George Street, Bristol BS1 5RS
☎0117 925 8589 Fax 0117 925 7608
Email stevehumphries@testimonyfilms.force9. co.uk
Contact *Steve Humphries*

TV documentary producer. Specialises in social history exploring Britain's secret past in the twentieth century. OUTPUT includes *Hooked: History of Addictions* (Ch4 series); *A Secret World of Sex* (BBC series).

Theatre of Comedy Company
See **Theatre Producers**

Tiger Aspect Productions Ltd
5 Soho Square, London W1D 3QA
☎020 7434 0672 Fax 020 7287 1448
Email general@tigeraspect.co.uk
Website www.tigeraspect.co.uk
Contact *Charles Brand*

TV producer of comedy, drama, documentary and entertainment. OUTPUT *Births, Marriages & Deaths; Kid in the Corner; Country House; Gimme Gimme Gimme; Harry Enfield & Chums; Howard Goodalls' Big Bangs; Playing the Field I, II & III; Streetmate I & II; Let Them Eat Cake; The Vicar of Dibley.* Only considers material submitted via an agent or from writers with a known track record.

Tonfedd Eryri
Hen Ysgol Aberpwll, Y Felinheli, Bangor, Gwynedd LL56 4JS
☎01248 671167 Fax 01248 671172
Email swyddfa@ff-eryri.demon.co.uk
Contacts *Hefin Elis, Norman Williams*

Light entertainment, comedy, music and drama.

Touch Productions Ltd
The Malt House Studios, Donhead St Mary, Dorset SP7 9DN
☎01747 828030 Fax 01747 828004
Email touch.productions@virgin.net
Contacts *Erica Wolfe-Murray, Malcolm Brinkworth*

Over the past 15 years has produced 'investigative documentary films, history based films with a strong contemporary relevance, powerful observational series and innovative films that stretch the form.' Television documentaries such as *Life of a £10 Note; Falklands 20th Anniversary; OJ – The Untold Story; Simon Weston V; Siege Doctors* (all for BBC); *The Good Life; The Surgery; Coast of Dreams; A French Affair; Watching the Detectives; Brown Babies* (all for Ch4); *Fame School* and *Fame School – the Graduates* (both for Meridian). Also has a drama section based on real-life stories and unsolicited mss are welcome.

Transatlantic Films Production and Distribution Company
Studio One, 3 Brackenbury Road, London W6 0BE
☎020 8735 0505 Fax 020 8735 0605
Email mail@transatlanticfilms.com
Website www.transatlanticfilms.com
Executive Producer *Revel Guest*

Producer of TV documentaries. OUTPUT *Belzoni* (Ch4 Schools); *Science of Sleep and Dreams, Science of Love* and *Extreme Body Parts* (all for Discovery Health); *Legends of the Living Dead* (Discovery Travel/S4C International); *2025* (Discovery Digital); *How Animals Tell the Time* (Discovery); *Trailblazers* (Travel Channel). No unsolicited scripts. Interested in new writers to write 'the book of the series', e.g. for *Greek Fire* and *The Horse in Sport*, but not usually drama script writers.

TV Choice Ltd
22 Charing Cross Road, London WC2H 0HR
☎020 7379 0873 Fax 020 7379 0263
Email tvchoiceuk@aol.com
Website www.tvchoice.uk.com

Contact *Norman Thomas*

Produces a range of educational videos for schools and colleges on subjects such as history, geography, business studies and economics. No unsolicited mss; send proposals only.

Twentieth Century Fox Film Co

Twentieth Century House, 31–32 Soho Square, London W1D 3AP
☎020 7437 7766 Fax 020 7734 3187
Website www.fox.co.uk

London office of the American giant.

Twofour Productions Limited

Quay West Studios, Old Newnham, Plymouth, Devon PL7 5BH
☎01752 333900 Fax 01752 344224
Email enq@twofour.co.uk
Website www.twofour.co.uk

Managing Director *Charles Wace*
Director of Broadcasting *Jill Lourie*

Specialises in factual and leisure programming for network and regional television; corporate presentations for national/international business and charities; special interest videos for retail/mail order; and, through its subsidiary twofourtv, webcasting and Internet-based TV.

Tyburn Film Productions Limited

Pinewood Studios, Iver Heath, Buckinghamshire SL0 0NH
☎01753 651700 Fax 01753 656050

Feature films. Subsidiary of **Arlington Productions Limited**. No unsolicited submissions.

UBA Ltd

21 Alderville Road, London SW6 2EE
☎01984 623619 Fax 01984 623733
Email shawjshaw@aol.com *or* petershaw@btinternet.com

Contacts *Peter Shaw, Joanna Shaw*

Feature films and TV for an international market. OUTPUT *Windprints; The Lonely Passion of Judith Hearne* (co-production with HandMade Films Ltd); *Taffin; Castaway; Turtle Diary; Sweeney Todd; Keep the Aspidistra Flying*. In development: *Kinder Garden; Rebel Magic; No Man's Land*. Prepared to commission new writing whether adapted from another medium or based on a short outline/treatment. Concerned with the quality of the script (*Turtle Diary* was written by Harold Pinter) and breadth of appeal. 'Exploitation material' not welcome.

UK Film and TV Production Company Plc

3 Colville Place, London W1T 2BH
☎020 7255 1650

Contact *Henrietta Fudakowski*

Film and television. Currently looking for feature film or TV drama scripts, with a preference for stories with humour. Return postage and list of credits essential. Please phone before submitting material.

Vanson Productions

PO Box 16926, London SW18 3ZP
☎020 8874 4241 Fax 020 8874 3600
Email vansonproductions@btinternet.com

Contact *Yvette Vanson*

Twenty years as documentary producer, then films and drama. OUTPUT *The Murder of Stephen Lawrence* by Paul Greengrass (a film with Granada for ITV; BAFTA 2000 Best Single Drama); *Doomwatch* by John Howlett and Ian McDonald (science drama with **Working Title Films** for Ch5). Films in development: *Guts & Glitter* by Jo Leigh; *Algeria* by Greg Dinner. Latest venture: co-partner in Zephaniah Films with Benjamin Zephaniah – *Face*, a six-part children's drama and *Refugee Boy*, children's feature, both based on Zephaniah's novels. Please ring before sending anything on spec.

Vera Productions

66–68 Margaret Street, London W1W 8SR
☎020 7436 6116 Fax 020 7436 6117

Contact *Rachel Sutherland*

Produces television comedy such as *Alistair McGowan's Big Impression*; *Rory Bremner* and *Mark Thomas*.

Video Enterprises

12 Barbers Wood Road, High Wycombe, Buckinghamshire HP12 4EP
☎01494 534144/0831 875216 (Mobile)
Fax 01494 534144
Email maurice@vident.u-net.com
Website www.vident.u-net.com

Contact *Maurice R. Fleisher*

Video and TV, mainly corporate: business and industrial training, promotional material and conferences. No unsolicited material 'but always ready to try out good new writers'.

Brian Waddell Productions Ltd

Strand Studios, 5/7 Shore Road, Holywood, Co. Down BT18 9HX
☎028 9042 7646 Fax 028 9042 7922

Email strand@bwpltv.co.uk

Contacts *Brian Waddell*

Producer of a wide range of television programmes in leisure activities, the arts, music, children's, comedy, travel/adventure and documentaries. Currently developing several film and drama projects.

Wall to Wall

8–9 Spring Place, London NW5 3ER
☎020 7485 7424 Fax 020 7267 5292
Website www.walltowall.co.uk

Chief Executive *Alex Graham*

Factual and drama programming. OUTPUT includes *A Rather English Marriage; Glasgow Kiss; Sex, Chips & Rock 'n' Roll; The 1940s House; Body Story* and *Neanderthal.* Drama ideas welcomed through established agents.

Jane Walmsley Productions

See **JAM Pictures**

The Walnut Partnership

Crown House, Armley Road, Leeds,
West Yorkshire LS12 2EJ
☎08707 427070 Fax 08707 427080
Email mail@walnutpartnership.co.uk
Website www.walnutpartnership.co.uk

Contact *Geoff Penn*

A multi-service production company specialising in business communication using video, live events and new media solutions. Clients include HSBC, Yorkshire Electricity, Clydesdale and Yorkshire Bank.

Walsh Bros. Limited

4 The Heights, London SE7 8JH
☎020 8858 5870/8854 5557
Fax 020 8858 6870
Email walshbros@lycosmail.com

Producer/Director *John Walsh*
Producer/Head of Finance *David Walsh, ACA*
Producer/Head of Development *Maura Walsh*

Award-winning producer of drama documentaries and feature films. OUTPUT *Monarch* (feature film on the events on the eve of the death of King Henry VIII); *Trex* (factual series shooting in China, Mexico, Vancouver and Alaska); *Nu Model Armi* (documentary); *TUEX2* (shot in Romania, India, Iceland and Louisiana); *Boyz & Girlz,* (documentary series); *Cowboyz & Cowgirlz* (US sequel to the first hit series); *Ray Harryhausen* (profile of the work of

Hollywood special effects legend); *The Comedy Store* (behind-the-scenes view of the birthplace of alternative comedy); *The Sceptic & The Psychic; The Sleeper* and *A State of Mind* (film dramas).

Warner Sisters Film & TV Ltd

The Cottage, Pall Mall Deposit, 124 Barlby Road, London W10 6BL
☎020 8960 3550 Fax 020 8960 3880
Email sisters@warnercine.com

Chief Executives *Lavinia Warner, Jane Wellesley, Dorothy Viljoen*

FOUNDED 1984. Drama and comedy. TV and feature films. OUTPUT includes *Selling Hitler; Rides; Life's a Gas; She-Play; A Village Affair; Dangerous Lady; Dressing for Breakfast; The Spy that Caught a Cold; The Bite; Jilting Joe; The Jump; Lady Audley's Secret; Do or Die.* Developing a wide range of projects including *The Letters* (feature film).

Paul Weiland Film Company

14 Newburgh Street, London W1F 7RT
☎020 7287 6900 Fax 020 7434 0146
Email action@paulweiland.com

Contact *Mary Francis*

Television commercials and pop promos.

Western Eye

Easton Business Centre, Felix Road, Easton, Bristol BS5 0HE
☎0117 941 5854 Fax 0117 941 5851
Email westerneyetv@cs.com

Contact *Jayne Cotton*

Corporate video production for Re-Solv, NACAB, Water Aid and other national charities. Looking for experienced writers in the above field.

Michael White Productions Ltd

See **MW Entertainments Ltd**

Windrush Productions Ltd

7 Woodlands Road, Moseley, Birmingham B13 4EH
☎0121 449 6439/07977 059378 (Mobile)
Fax 0121 449 6439
Email beboyyaa@hotmail.com

Contacts *Pogus Caesar, Shawn Caesar*

Television documentaries, including a multicultural series for Carlton TV (*Xpress and Respect*); *The A-Force* (BBC); *I'm Black in Britain* (Central TV); *Drumbeat* (Carlton). Also produces *Windrush E. Smith Show* (comedy) and

Pogus Caesar's *Off the Hook* for BBC Radio Pebble Mill. Produces pop promos/corporate videos for a range of clients. Encourages new writing, especially from the regions. 'We try to seek scripts from writers interested in developing new Black fiction/comedy.'

Working Title Films Ltd

Oxford House, 76 Oxford Street, London W1D 1BS
☎020 7307 3000 Fax 020 7307 3001/2/3
Co-Chairmen (Films) *Tim Bevan, Eric Fellner*
Head of Development (Films) *Debra Hayward*
Development Executive (Films) *Chris Clark*
Television *Simon Wright*

Feature films, TV drama; also family/children's entertainment and TV comedy. OUTPUT Films: *Bridget Jones's Diary; Captain Corelli's Mandolin; Ali G in da House; Notting Hill; Elizabeth; Plunkett & Macleane; The Borrowers; The Matchmaker; Fargo; Dead Man Walking; French Kiss; Four Weddings and a Funeral; The Hudsucker Proxy; The Tall Guy; Wish You Were Here; My Beautiful Laundrette*. Television: *More Tales of the City; The Borrowers I & II; Armisted Maupin's Tales of the City; News Hounds; Randall & Hopkirk Deceased; Doomwatch*. No unsolicited mss at present, but keen to encourage new writing nevertheless via New Writers Scheme - contact *Dan Shepherd*.

Worldview Pictures

Units 1&2, Leeds Place, off Tollington Park, London N4 3RQ
☎020 7916 4696 Fax 020 7916 4696
Email anyone@worldviewpictures.co.uk
Contacts *Stephen Trombley*

Documentaries and series for television, plus theatrical. OUTPUT *A Death in the Family; Project X; War and Civilization; Nuremberg; Raising Hell: The Life of A.J. Bannister; The Execution Protocol; Drancy: A Concentration Camp in Paris; The Lynchburg Story; 99% Woman*.

Worthwhile Productions

16 Biddulph Road, London W6 1JB
☎020 7266 9166 Fax 020 7266 9166
Contact *Jeremy Wootliff*

Feature films, video; documentary, corporate and commercials. Unsolicited mss welcome.

Wortman Productions UK

48 Chiswick Staithe, London W4 3TP
☎020 8994 8886/07976 805976 (Mobile)
Email nevillewortman@beeb.net
Producer *Neville Wortman*

Co-producers with Polestar Pictures Ltd. Feature film and TV production for drama, documentary, commercials and corporate. OUTPUT *House in the Country* John Julius Norwich (ITV series); *Tribute to Ellington* (jazz special); *Lost Ships* (maritime historical drama series; Discovery Channel); *Criminal Chronicles* (Russian crime series; BBC TV/Court TV co-production). In preparation: *Samuel's Last Summer* (feature film). Open to new writing, preferably through agents; single page outline, some pages of dialogue; s.a.e. for reply.

W.O.W. Productions

12 Rutland Park Gardens, London NW2 4RG
☎020 8451 7922
Email wow@dircon.co.uk
Contacts *Carl Schonfeld, Dom Rotheroe*

Film and television drama and documentary programming. OUTPUT includes *A Sarajevo Diary* (documentary) and *My Brother Tom* (feature).

Yoda Productions Ltd

Brooklands Cottage, Guildford Road, Westcott, Dorking, Surrey RH4 3LB
☎01306 886916 Fax 01306 889352
Email gail@yodaproductions.co.uk
Contact *Gail Lowe*

Medical, scientific, technical marketing and promotional, training videos and multimedia. No unsolicited mss.

Zenith Entertainment Ltd

43–45 Dorset Street, London W1U 7NA
☎020 7224 2440 Fax 020 7224 3194
Email general@zenith-entertainment.co.uk
Head of Drama Development *Judith Hackett*

Feature films and TV drama. OUTPUT Films: Todd Haynes' *Velvet Goldmine; Wisdom of Crocodiles*; Nicole Holofcener's *Walking and Talking*. Television: *Hamish Macbeth; Rhodes; Bodyguards; The Uninvited; Bomber; 2000 Acres of Sky*. No unsolicited scripts.

Curtain Up on How to Become a Playwright

James Roose-Evans

If getting a novel published today is difficult enough (not to mention the difficulty of getting it reviewed once published), then for anyone contemplating writing for the stage there ought to be danger warnings! Of the thousands of plays written, only a few see the light of a production. And just as most novelists have to earn their living by some other means, so do most playwrights. While it is true that for those under the age of twenty-six there are many more opportunities today to learn their craft and even to see their work staged, for anyone over that age it is much more difficult. Even a script sent with a stamped addressed envelope may never be acknowledged, let alone returned, but more often will pile up on a producer's desk unread and eventually be dumped in the wastepaper basket. So an author has to be able to afford to send out a large number of scripts, each with an s.a.e., in the hope that he may receive at least one response. Even if a management expresses interest, few any more will take an option on the play, thereby remunerating the author a little for his investment, but will call the author to numerous meetings, even a rehearsed reading, and then drop the whole thing. Where commercial managements are concerned (as opposed to subsidised theatre), their prime concern is to secure a star who will sell the play; for mounting a play today, as well as the need to market it, is an increasingly costly venture. In 1953, West End managers commissioned and financed twenty-six new plays, a number that is inconceivable today, especially when stars can no longer be tempted to do a long run.

But for anyone willing to enter the fray it is important to look at what has been happening in the theatre over the last thirty years and, in particular, over the past decade.

From the mid-1950s to the late 1970s the Royal Court Theatre in London was unquestionably the main home of the best new writing talent. It was also the home of many of our best directors, who were eager to encourage new writing. Meanwhile, at the Royal Shakespeare Company, Harold Pinter was the company's number two dramatist, while at the National Theatre there were Tom Stoppard and Peter Nichols. At the same time a flourishing fringe theatre was producing new writing responsive to the student movement and political questioning of the late 1960s. Then, during the 1980s, all these theatres, including the fringe, lost their identities as far as new writing was concerned.

With certain exceptions, such as David Hare at the National and Caryl Churchill at the Royal Court, writers were no longer identified with the policies of an individual theatre or director. In fact, there were no artistic policies because theatres could no longer afford them.

It is not surprising therefore that at the beginning of the 1990s newspaper articles were being written about the theatre's crisis in new writing. Then, in 1990, Dominic Dromgoole took over the Bush Theatre, a small pub theatre in London, and inaugurated an eclectic policy of new writing in which there were to be no rules, no ideologies, and where writers were free to follow their own imaginations. First came Jonathan Harvey's *Beautiful Thing*, which told the story of two working-class boys discovering their gay sexuality, followed by Philip Ridley's *The Pitchfork Disney*, in which the characters ate cockroaches, broke fingers and vomited. Shortly after, at the Glasgow Mayfest, Irvine Walsh's *Trainspotting* explored the culture of poverty, boredom and violence. But it was Sarah Kane's *Blasted* at the Royal Court, with its explicit scenes of sexual abuse and cannibalism, that finally brought the new writing to the fore.

Vilified by the critics, with strident calls to bring back censorship, it resulted in the Royal Court, under its radical new director, Stephen Daldry, rediscovering its roots as a theatre of controversy. There followed plays by Joe Penhall, Anthony Neilsen, Judy Upton and Nick Grosso, and then came Mark Ravenhill's *Shopping and Fucking*, which finally consolidated the new wave, fulfilling Ken Tynan's observation in 1965: 'Unless we can use the theatre as a platform on which to demonstrate the serious problems of today, particularly violence, we feel that we are not serving a useful purpose in society.' The critic James Christopher wrote of Ravenhill's 'unnerving knack of opening our eyes to the horrors of our daily lives', but what particularly shocked many was that his young characters were not heroin addicts on a Glasgow housing estate but the children of middle-class Britons. By 1998 *Shopping and Fucking*, Patrick Marber's study of sexual relations, *Closer*, and Ben Elton's *Popcorn* were running next to each other on Shaftesbury Avenue. The new writing had become commercial.

By 1996 Michael Billington in the *Guardian* was writing: 'I cannot recall a time when there were so many exciting dramatists in the twenty-something age group. What is more they are speaking to audiences of their own generation.'

At the Bush, at Hampstead, the Tricycle, the Royal Court, the Finborough Arms, the Old Red Lion, there was suddenly a burst of new writing, as well as up and down the country in regional theatres. Most importantly, as Billington observed, these theatres were also attracting younger audiences who were discovering plays that explored a world they could recognise as their own.

All these theatres gave their writers complete freedom. More and more the rules taught in playwriting courses were being broken. As John Mortimer observed: 'The new writing reflects the strident, anarchic, aimless world of England today, not in anger, or even bitterness, but with humour and a kind of love.' Rape, fellatio, anal intercourse, defecation, torture, violence, gross language and sick jokes, all were permissible. The writing was aggressive and emotionally dark as audiences were reminded that not everything in the garden was lovely. Pandora's box had been opened and every skeleton came tumbling out of domestic cupboards, but behind the violence was a response by young people to the difficulties of living in a fragmented, post-Christian, post-feminist and postmodern society. Stephen Daldry was absolutely right when, in 1993, he said, 'Why is our audience so fucking middle aged? We have to listen to the kids.'

And so going to the theatre in the 1990s meant the risk of the spectator being unmasked, caught off guard, enraged, frightened. Never perhaps has the theatre so fully reflected Hamlet's definition of it: 'to hold, as 'twere, the mirror up to nature, to show virtue her own feature, scorn her own image, and the very age and body of the time his form and pressure.'

But by 2000 there were signs that the theatre of outrage was coming to an end, signalled by the enormous success of Conor McPherson's *The Weir*. Where the next wave of new writing will go is anyone's guess. All a writer, setting out today to write for theatre, can do is to follow her or his instincts, writing from the heart, from the guts. In the meantime, however, much can be learned about the craft of writing, the variety of techniques available and how to make the best of what opportunities exist to encourage new writing.

In the theatre, unlike a novel, the writer has to decide where in the story to start. To begin at the beginning and carry on remorselessly to the end can become ponderous. It is best to start as late as one can without leaving an audience terminally perplexed. Plays today no longer have to have a chronological development but can flash back and forth in time, using the simplest of staging. The heavy hampering world of naturalistic sets is, by and large, a thing of the past. Today, with the use of sound, music and light, a play can move almost cinematically. Compared to plays of the 1970s and 1980s, the new drama has faster dialogue, language is more highly coloured and the expressions of emotions are more extreme. There is a greater vitality and immediacy about most writing for theatre today.

What playwrights have to remember is that they are there to tell a story in front of a live audience. It is the task of the author and the actor to find a way of engaging that audience. As Peter Brook observed in *There Are No Secrets* (Methuen, 1993), an audience becomes quickly bored. The story, and its storytellers, have to lure, beguile, seduce, startle, surprise, disturb and delight the listener and spectator.

Playwrights also have to have a very clear idea of the *through-line* of the whole play, as well as within each scene. When an actor enters the stage he has to know where he has come from and where he is going, why he is here, when (time of year or day), and so forth. The text may be as ordinary and even as banal as the words 'I love you', and yet the actor, knowing the given circumstances of the character and the scene, will discover that these words can take on a variety of possible interpretations. Different authors, of course, present different problems, which is why the craft of acting is so complex. Rightly to be able to play a great variety of roles an actor has to be a chameleon, but he is only as good as the text he is given!

Each night the text must be recreated by the actors as though being spoken for the first time. This immediate communal test is unique to theatre. The novelist never has to face it. A playwright, however, has to be able to grab the audience each night. And so the relationship of the author with his actors and their director is crucial. If a play is savaged by the critics the author can retire and lick his wounds but the actor still has to go out there each night before a live audience. It is possible that the single most useful preparation for writing plays, says Alan Ayckbourn, is to be an actor. Noël Coward, Harold Pinter, Ayckbourn himself, John Osborne, Anthony Neilsen, Patrick Marber, Kevin Elyot, Hugh Whitemore have all been actors.

The relationship of the playwright to the director is very important, and fortunate is the writer who is able to work closely with a director on a new script. As the innovative Russian director, Meyerhold, once remarked, 'In every director there potentially sits a dramatist.'

Kevin Elyot, the award-winning author of the play *My Night with Reg*, has described working with Richard Wilson on one of his earliest plays, *Coming Clean*, which was produced at the Bush Theatre and which it had been suggested Richard might direct. 'We worked on the script over several months. Richard would say, "Well, maybe I will direct it but, if I do, I would want this or that altered," and undoubtedly he improved the text with his suggestions. Then he decided not to direct it and it was very disappointing at the time. But he was great to work with on the text. I will always remember one thing he said: "You should never have a character say what he means, such as 'I love you', or 'I hate you', but rather 'I'll go and put the kettle on', or 'Will you have another drink?' " In real life it is often what is not said that is important. It is the tone of voice used with such ordinary statements which tells us what is really going on between people.' Elyot says that whenever he was in doubt while he was working on *My Night with Reg*, he recalled Richard's advice and so he'd never have his characters say what they meant but 'Will you have another drink?' 'There's a lot of that in the play!' he added.

The task of a director is to understand the author's intention and, like a sculptor faced with block of stone, to unearth the form within. A director seeks the heart of a play, the reason for its having been written, which is why it is important for the writer to be present at rehearsals. The search should always be for what the American critic Stark Young once described as 'the original design', rather than for what a 'clever' director thinks he can impose on the text.

On the surface the director studies the narrative, for theatre is a form of storytelling; but then he begins to go deeper, exploring the subtext. On one level there is the storyline, the plot, which carries the action forward, and on another level there is an inner storyline for each character as well as for the play itself. Of necessity any play will also require the director to do a good deal of preliminary research. This information has then to be infiltrated among the actors. A play about a hospital, or a major auction house, will require that the actors be familiar with the history, the practices, the jargon and the attitudes of such a milieu. It may even be necessary for the cast to visit a hospital or an auction house. The playwright does not necessarily provide all the information, although where he does have experience of such a milieu the playwright will then be the best person to talk to the cast.

Not surprisingly dialogue is the key to theatre. Unless the author is attempting to create a particular period when language was more formal, as in Tom Stoppard's *Arcadia*, dialogue should not be overly literary, nor too wordy. A novel can afford to be leisurely, even tangential, for the reader can easily refer back and forth, or if he chooses, put the book down and go off and do something else. Almost all plays benefit from editing. If too much is explained nothing is left for the actor to discover.

What counts first and foremost in theatre (and even more so on the screen, as in the movie *In the Bedroom*), is the subtext: the unspoken thoughts and feelings of a character which are expressed primarily through the actor's use of nuance of tone, silences, gestures and movements. Eva La Gallienne has described how Eleanora Duse could hold a pause for two minutes, during which time she would keep the audience entranced by her reactions and interior thought processes.

And so it is important for the playwright to remember that acting is as much about reacting as it is about acting, about being as much as about doing. Henry Irving once, in a lecture, remarked that an actor does not just come on as Othello and say baldly: 'Oh! Oh! Oh! Desdemona!' It is how he fills those sounds with emotion that matters. An actor can, by the mere use of a particular tone, or emphasis, open up whole new dimensions of meaning even in a very familiar text.

For those under twenty-five there are a number of schemes set up to give young people who have ideas and imagination a sense of the craft of theatre. Some of these are listed below. Practical work with them includes finding out what actors can bring to a piece; how the rehearsal process works; and what can be achieved by working with the audience's imagination. Quite a number of theatres now run workshop programmes as well as offering rehearsed readings and other initiatives designed to give writers a sense of their work in performance.

In July 2000 the Birmingham Repertory Theatre embarked on a marathon staging of sixteen new plays by new writers aged between twelve and twenty-five, under the direction of Carl Miller who, previously, had been in charge of a similar programme at the Royal Court in London. Writing in the *Independent*, he observed, 'Nothing helps playwrights of any age understand their craft more than by hanging around theatres.' After nine months of working, the writers pile into the theatre with easy familiarity, whereas before they started most of them had the same idea about theatre which kept their friends away. As Chris Rivers, one of the young writers, commented, 'I thought it would be a bit uptight. I thought theatre people would be all polo necks, vodkas and roll-ups.' Even for those who knew about the Birmingham Rep, its image was that of a place for old classics, not the kind of new talent that the theatre's literary manager, Ben Payne, and Carl Miller, have fostered there over the past two years. As Carl

Miller writes, 'Sitting in the theatre among a packed and excited audience that is more like a movie crowd, this audience – young and old, Asian, black and white – actually reflects the range of people on the street outside. And that's because the range of young writers presented also reflects that reality. This isn't just about new writers; it's about new audiences too.'

The Birmingham Rep, under Ben Payne, has a literary panel that meets once a week to discuss the most promising plays and playwrights. If a decision is made to take a play further there can then follow a meeting between the writer and a member of the literary panel, where the writer is offered feedback and advice, and a script-development workshop where actors and a director will work together with the writer on the script. This can lead to a rehearsed reading of the play to a public audience. The National Theatre Studio operates in a similar way, and even established authors such as Patrick Marber, Pam Gems and others have benefited from this approach.

The Royal Court also has a Young Writers' Programme (see entry under **Festivals**), which is open to anyone between the ages of thirteen and twenty-five. It also offers a biannual Young Writers' Festival, and during the autumn of

---

Schemes

Writernet Offers a service on all aspects of the live and recorded performing industry for both writers and producers (see entry under **Professional Associations and Societies**).

The Royal Court Young Writers Programme (See entry under **Festivals**.)

Traverse Theatre, Edinburgh Aims to nurture, develop and produce contemporary Scottish and international playwrights. All scripts go straight to the Literary Department (see entry under **Theatre Producers**).

Birmingham Repertory Theatre (See entry under **Theatre Producers**.)

Hampstead Theatre The Hampstead Theatre website is especially helpful to writers as it provides advice on how to submit a play as well as answering various other questions. (www.hampstead-theatre.co.uk/writers)

Books
State of Play: Playwrights on Playwriting edited by David Edgar (Faber & Faber)
The Full Room: An A-Z of Contemporary Playwrights by Dominic Dromgoole (Methuen)
In-Yer-Face Theatre: British Drama Today by Aleks Sierz (Faber & Faber)
Experimental Theatre, from Stanislavsky to Peter Brook by James Roose-Evans (Routledge)

2000 there was a weekly online workshop. Members of the scheme are also entitled to tickets for Royal Court shows at £1 each. This is an imaginative scheme because it is not only by studying scripts that a writer learns, but by seeing texts in performance and analysing what works in theatre and what does not. Whereas a novelist can work in a physical vacuum, on a mountain top, or in a remote Yorkshire valley, a playwright needs to relate to the camaraderie of theatre, learning the intricacies of lighting, staging, acting and directing, as well as audience responses. It is said of that outstanding producer, Binkie Beaumont, the head of what was in the 1940s and '50s the largest West End management, H.M. Tennent's, that he would never come to a rehearsal of a new play but only to the previews. He would then stand at the back of the stalls and watch, not the play, but the audience. Wherever the audience became restless or lost interest he would say to the director: 'That scene needs looking at, it isn't working!'

'Theatre,' says Peter Brook, 'only exists at the precise moment when the two worlds of the actors and the audience meet: a society in miniature, a microcosm brought together every evening within a space. Theatre's role is to give this microcosm a burning and fleeting taste of another world, in which our present world is integrated and transformed.' And, because theatre, unlike the cinema or television, is so immediate in its impact, a living relationship between actors and audience, happening now, it is also a revolutionary art.

James Roose-Evans is the founder of the Hampstead Theatre and was its artistic director for ten years. Among his many West End productions are Hugh Whitemore's The Best of Friends *and his own adaptation of Helene Hanff's* 84 Charing Cross Road, *which he also directed on Broadway, winning awards on both sides of the Atlantic for Best Play and Best Director. He also adapted Laurie Lee's* Cider With Rosie *for the stage and wrote, especially for Maureen Lipman,* Re:Joyce!, *an entertainment about Joyce Grenfell. He is the author of* London Theatre: From the Globe to the National *(Phaidon),* Directing a Play *(Studio Vista),* Experimental Theatre *(Routledge) and* One Foot on the Stage: the biography of Richard Wilson *(Weidenfeld & Nicolson).*

Theatre Producers

Actors Touring Company (ATC)

Alford House, Aveline Street, London
SE11 5DQ
☎020 7735 8311
Fax 020 7735 1031 attn. ATC
Email judith@atc-online.com
Website www.atc-online.com

Artistic Director *Gordon Anderson*

Collaborates with writers on adaptation and/or translation work and unsolicited mss will be considered in this category as well as new writing. 'We endeavour to read mss but do not have the resources to do so quickly.' As a small-scale company, all plays must have a cast of six or less.

Almeida Theatre Company

Almeida at King's Cross, Omega Place, off Caledonian Road, London N1 9DR
☎020 7226 7432 Fax 020 7704 9581
Website www.almeida.co.uk

Artistic Director *Michael Attenborough*

FOUNDED 1980. Now in its thirteenth year as a full-time producing theatre, presenting a year-round theatre and music programme in which international writers, composers, performers, directors and designers are invited to work with British artists on challenging new and classical works. Previous productions: *Galileo; Moonlight; The School for Wives; Hamlet; Who's Afraid of Virginia Woolf; Ivanov; Naked; The Judas Kiss; The Iceman Cometh; The Jew of Malta; Celebration; The Room; Richard II; Coriolanus; Lulu; The Shape of Things; King Lear*. No unsolicited mss: 'our producing programme is very limited and linked to individual directors and actors'.

Alternative Theatre Company Ltd

Bush Theatre, Shepherds Bush Green, London W12 8QD
☎020 7602 3703 Fax 020 7602 7614
Email info@bushtheatre.co.uk

Literary Manager *Nicola Wilson*

FOUNDED 1972. Trading as The Bush Theatre. Produces nine new plays a year (principally British) including up to three visiting companies also producing new work: 'we are a writer's theatre'. Previous productions: *Kiss of the Spiderwoman* Manuel Puig; *Raping the Gold* Lucy

Gannon; *The Wexford Trilogy* Billy Roche; *Love and Understanding* Joe Penhall; *This Limetree Bower* Conor McPherson; *Discopigs* Enda Walsh; *The Pitchfork Disney* Philip Ridley; *Caravan* Helen Blakeman; *Beautiful Thing* Jonathan Harvey; *Killer Joe* Tracy Letts; *Shang-a-Lang* Catherine Johnson; *Howie the Rookie* Mark O'Rowe. Scripts are read by a team of associates, then discussed with the management, a process which takes about four months. The theatre offers a small number of commissions, recommissions to ensure further drafts on promising plays, and a guarantee against royalties so writers are not financially penalised even though the plays are produced in a small house. Writers should send scripts (full-length plays only) with small s.a.e. for acknowledgement and large s.a.e. for return of script.

Yvonne Arnaud Theatre

Millbrook, Guildford, Surrey GU1 3UX
☎01483 440077 Fax 01483 564071
Website www.yvonne-arnaud.co.uk

Contact *James Barber*

Credits include: *The Caretaker* Harold Pinter; *Alarms and Excursions* Michael Frayn; *Tom and Clem* Stephen Churchett; *Life Support* Simon Gray; *Equally Divided* Ronald Harwood; *Comic Potential* Alan Ayckbourn; *The Prisoner of Second Avenue* Neil Simon; *A Passionate Woman* Kay Mellor; *Indian Ink* Tom Stoppard; *Home* David Storey; *Cellmates* Simon Gray; *Letter of Resignation* Hugh Whitemore; *Quartet* Ronald Harwood.

Birmingham Repertory Theatre

Centenary Square, Broad Street, Birmingham B1 2EP
☎0121 245 2000 Fax 0121 245 2100
Website www.birmingham-rep.co.uk

Associate Director (Literary) *Ben Payne*
Literary Officer *Caroline Jester*

The Birmingham Repertory Theatre aims to provide a platform for the best work from new writers from both within and beyond the West Midlands region. The Rep is committed to a policy of integrated casting and to the production of new work which reflects the diversity of contemporary experience. The commissioning of new plays takes place across the full range of the theatre's activities: in the Main House, The Door (which is a dedicated new writing space) and on tour to community venues in the region. 'Writers are advised that the Rep is very unlikely to produce an unsolicited script. We usually assess unsolicited submissions on the basis of whether it indicates a writer with whom the theatre may be interested in working. The theatre runs a programme of writers' attachments every year in addition to its commissioning policy and maintains close links with *Stagecoach* (the regional writers' training agency) and the **MA in Playwriting Studies** at the University of Birmingham.' For more information contact the Literary Officer.

Black Theatre Co-op
See **NITRO**

Bootleg Theatre Company
23 Burgess Green, Bishopdown, Salisbury, Wiltshire SP1 3El
☎01722 421476
Email colin@thebootlegtheatrecompany. fsnet.co.uk

Contact *Colin Burden*

FOUNDED 1984. Tries to encompass as wide an audience as possible and has a tendency towards plays with socially relevant themes. A good bet for new writing since unsolicited mss are very welcome. 'Our policy is to produce new and/or rarely seen plays and anything received is given the most serious consideration.' Actively seeks to obtain grants to commission new writers for the company. Productions include: *Clubland* by Giles, Harris, Suthers and Mordell; *Hanging Hanratty* by Michael Burnham; *The Truth About Blokes* by Trevor Suthers; *Cool Blokes: Decent Suits* by Russell Mardell.

Borderline Theatre
Darlington New Church, North Harbour Street, Ayr KA8 8AA
☎01292 281010 Fax 01292 263825
Email enquiries@borderlinetheatre.co.uk
Website www.borderlinetheatre.co.uk

Producer *Eddie Jackson*

FOUNDED 1974. Borderline is one of Scotland's leading touring companies. Committed to new writing, it tours an innovative programme of new plays and radical adaptations/translations of classic texts in an accessible and entertaining style. Tours to main-house theatres and small venues throughout Scotland. Productions include the world premières of *The Angels' Share* by Chris Dolan; *The Prince and the Pilot* Anita Sullivan. Previous writers have included Dario Fo, Liz Lochhead and John Byrne. Borderline is also committed to commissioning and touring new plays for young people. Send synopsis with cast size in the first instance.

Bristol Old Vic Theatre Company (Theatre Royal, New Vic Studio & Basement)
Theatre Royal, King Street, Bristol BS1 4ED
☎0117 949 3993 Fax 0117 949 3996
Email admin@bristol-old-vic.co.uk
Website www.bristol-old-vic.co.uk

Bristol Old Vic is committed to the commissioning and production of new writing in the Theatre Royal (650 seats). Plays must have enough popular appeal to attract an audience of significant size. In the New Vic Studio (150 seats) up to four plays a year are produced. The theatre will read and report on unsolicited scripts, and asks for a fee of £15 per script to cover the payments to readers. 'We also seek to attract emerging talent to the Basement, a profit-share venue (50 seats) committed to producing one-act plays. Plays for the Basement will be read free of charge although no report can be provided.' In all cases, if return of script is required, please supply s.a.e.

Bush Theatre
See **Alternative Theatre Company Ltd**

Carnival (Films & Theatre) Ltd
See entry under **Film, TV and Video Production Companies**

Guy Chapman Productions Ltd
1–2 Henrietta Street, London WC2E 8PS
☎020 7379 7474 Fax 020 7379 8484
Email guy@g-c-a.co.uk

Contacts *Guy Chapman*

Performs to young audiences with innovative, experimental theatre. Productions include: *Shopping and Fucking*; *Love Upon the Throne*; *Crave*; *Disco Pigs*; *Resident Alien*; *Corpus Christi*; *New Boy*.

Chester Gateway Theatre Trust Ltd
Hamilton Place, Chester, Cheshire CH1 2BH
☎01244 344238 Fax 01244 317277
Website www.gateway-theatre.org

Chief Executive *Jasmine Hendry*

FOUNDED 1968. 440-seater main house and

120-seater Manweb Studio. Committed to producing two in-house productions a year and aims to present a varied programme of theatre, dance, music, opera and comedy. The Education and Access Department works in schools and the community, and a writers' group meets fortnightly. Each year the group presents rehearsed readings using professional actors and directors.

Citizens Theatre

Gorbals, Glasgow G5 9DS
☎0141 429 5561 Fax 0141 429 7374
Email info@citz.co.uk
Website www.citz.co.uk
Artistic Director *Giles Havergal*

No formal new play policy. The theatre has a play reader but opportunities to do new work are limited.

Clwyd Theatr Cymru

Mold, Flintshire CH7 1YA
☎01352 756331 Fax 01352 701558
Email drama@celtic.co.uk
Website www.clwyd-theatr-cymru.co.uk
Literary Manager *William James*
 (wjames@clwyd-theatr-cymru.co.uk)

Clwyd Theatr Cymru produces a season of plays each year performed by a core ensemble, along with tours throughout Wales (in English and Welsh). Plays are a mix of classics, revivals, contemporary drama. Recent new writing includes: *The Rabbit* Meredydd Barker; *Journey of Mary Kelly* Siân Evans; *Rape of the Fair Country*, *Hosts of Rebecca* and *Song of the Earth* all adapt. Manon Eames; *The Changelings* Gregg Cullen; *Celf* by Yasmina Reza; *Damwain a Hap* by Dario Fo, both translated by Manon Eames; *Flora's War/Rhyfel Flora*, *Word for Word/Gair am Air* and *The Secret/Y Gyfrinach* by Tim Baker. Plays by Welsh writers or with Welsh themes will be considered.

Michael Codron Plays Ltd

Aldwych Theatre Offices, Aldwych, London WC2B 4DF
☎020 7240 8291 Fax 020 7240 8467
General Manager *Paul O'Leary*

Michael Codron Plays Ltd manages the Aldwych Theatre in London's West End. The plays it produces don't necessarily go into the Aldwych but always tend to be big-time West End fare. Previous productions: *Bedroom Farce; Blue Orange; Copenhagen; The Invention of Love; Hapgood; Uncle Vanya; Rise and Fall of Little Voice; Arcadia; Dead Funny.* No particular rule of thumb on subject matter or treatment. The acid test is whether 'something appeals to Michael'. Straight plays rather than musicals.

Colchester Mercury Theatre Limited

Balkerne Gate, Colchester, Essex CO1 1PT
☎01206 577006 Fax 01206 769607
Email mercury.theatre@virgin.net
Artistic Producer *Gregory Floy*
Associate Director *Adrian Stokes*

Producing theatre with a wide-ranging audience. Unsolicited scripts welcome. The theatre has a free playwright's group for adults with a serious commitment to writing plays.

The Coliseum, Oldham

Fairbottom Street, Oldham, Lancashire OL1 3SW
☎0161 624 1731 Fax 0161 624 5318
Chief Executive *Kenneth Alan Taylor*

The policy of the Coliseum is to present high quality work that is unashamedly 'popular'. Has a special interest in new work that has a Northern flavour, however this does not rule out other plays. Unsolicited scripts are all read but will only be returned if a s.a.e. is included.

Contact Theatre Company

Oxford Road, Manchester M15 6JA
☎0161 274 3434 Fax 0161 274 0640
Email info@contact-theatre.org.uk
Artistic Director *John E. McGrath*

'In partnership with the BBC, we are investing in innovative approaches to the discovery of new writers – and new kinds of writing – for stage, screen, radio and new media.' In general, Contact works primarily with the 13–30 age group and is particularly interested in materials that relate to the lives and culture of young people. 'We welcome work from writers of all ages. Hearing from a variety of voices, from different cultures and backgrounds, is also important to us. We encourage concise pitches from writers – no more than 10 pages – including a summary and some sample pages.'

Crucible Theatre

55 Norfolk Street, Sheffield S1 1DA
☎0114 249 5999 Fax 0114 249 6003
Associate Director *Michael Grandage*
Literary Associates *Matthew Byam Shaw, Anna Mackmin*

'Most of the new work we present will be the result of commissions or a prolonged exchange of ideas and script development with writers in whom we have expressed an interest. However, we are interested in all new work and offer a free script reading service for unsolicited scripts. NB We do not offer readers' reports. Please ring or send s.a.e. for full details of script reading service.'

Cwmni Theatr Gwynedd
Deiniol Road, Bangor, Gwynedd LL57 2TL
☎01248 351707 Fax 01248 351915
Email theatr@theatregwynedd.co.uk
Contact *Artistic Director*

FOUNDED 1984. A mainstream company, performing in major theatres on the Welsh circuit. Welsh-language work only at present. Classic Welsh plays, translations of European repertoire and new work, including adaptations from novels. New Welsh work always welcome; works in English considered if appropriate for translation (i.e. dealing with issues relevant to Wales). 'We are keen to discuss projects with established writers and offer commissions where possible.'

Derby Playhouse
Eagle Centre, Derby DE1 2NF
☎01332 363271 Fax 01332 547200
Website www.derbyplayhouse.co.uk
Artistic Director *Mark Clements*

Derby Playhouse is interested in new work and has produced several world premières over the last year. 'We have a discrete commissioning budget but already have several projects under way. Due to the amount of scripts we receive, we now ask writers to send a letter accompanied by a synopsis of the play, a résumé of writing experience and any ten pages of the script they wish to submit. We will then determine whether we think it is suitable for the Playhouse, in which case we will ask for a full script.' Writers are welcome to send details of rehearsed readings and productions as an alternative means of introducing the theatre to their work.

Druid Theatre Company
Chapel Lane, Galway, Republic of Ireland
☎00 353 91 568660 Fax 00 353 91 563109
Email info@druidtheatre.com
Website www.druidtheatre.com
Contact *Literary Manager*

FOUNDED 1975. Based in Galway and playing nationally and internationally, the company operates a major programme for the development of new writing. While focusing on Irish

work, the company also accepts unsolicited material from outside Ireland.

The Dukes Playhouse Ltd
Moor Lane, Lancaster LA1 1QE
☎01524 598505 Fax 01524 598519
Chief Executive *Amanda Belcham*
Artistic Director *Ian Hastings*

FOUNDED 1971. The only producing house in Lancashire. Wide target market for cinema and theatre. Plays in a 320-seater end-on auditorium and in a 198-seater in-the-round studio. In the summer months open-air promenade performances are held in Williamson Park. Also, community based Youth Arts Centre.

Dundee Repertory Theatre
Tay Square, Dundee DD1 1PB
☎01382 227684 Fax 01382 228609
Email hglen@dundeereptheatre.co.uk
Website www.dundeereptheatre.co.uk
Artistic Director *Hamish Glen*

FOUNDED 1939. Plays to a varied audience. Translations and adaptations of classics, and new local plays. Most new work is commissioned. Interested in contemporary plays in translation and in new Scottish writing. No scripts except by prior arrangement.

Eastern Angles Theatre Company
Sir John Mills Theatre, Gatacre Road, Ipswich, Suffolk IP1 2LQ
☎01473 218202 Fax 01473 384999
Email admin@easternangles.co.uk
Website www.easternangles.co.uk
Artistic Director *Ivan Cutting*
General Manager *Jill Streatfeild*

FOUNDED 1982. Plays to a rural audience for the most part. New work only: some commissioned, some devised by the company, some researched documentaries. Unsolicited mss welcome from regional writers. 'We are always keen to develop and produce new writing, especially that which is germane to a rural area.'

Edinburgh Royal Lyceum Theatre
See **Royal Lyceum Theatre Company**

English Touring Theatre
25 Short Street, London SE1 9LJ
☎020 7450 1990 Fax 020 7450 1991
Email admin@englishtouringtheatre.co.uk
Website www.englishtouringtheatre.co.uk
Artistic Director *Stephen Unwin*

FOUNDED 1993. National touring company visiting middle-scale receiving houses and arts centres throughout England. Mostly mainstream. Largely classical programme, but with increasing interest to tour one modern English play per year. Strong commitment to education work. No unsolicited mss.

Robert Fox Ltd

6 Beauchamp Place, London SW3 1NG
☎020 7584 6855 Fax 020 7225 1638
Email rf@robertfoxltd.com

Contact *Robert Fox*

Producer and co-producer of work suitable for West End production. Previous productions: *Another Country; Chess; Lettice and Lovage; Burn This; When She Danced; The Ride Down Mount Morgan; The Importance of Being Earnest; The Seagull; Goosepimples; Vita & Virginia; The Weekend; Three Tall Women; Skylight; Who's Afraid of Virginia Woolf; Masterclass; A Delicate Balance; Amy's View; Closer; The Lady in the Van; The Caretaker.* Scripts, while usually by established playwrights, are always read.

Gate Theatre Company Ltd

11 Pembridge Road, London W11 3HQ
☎020 7229 5387 Fax 020 7221 6055

Literary Manager *Kate Wild*

FOUNDED 1979. Plays to a mixed, London-wide audience, depending on production. Aims to produce British premières of plays which originate from abroad and translations of neglected classics. Most work is with translators. Recent productions: *Ion* by Euripides, transl. by Stephen Sharkey; *Les Justes* by Albert Camus, transl. by Gillian Hannah. Positively encourages writers from abroad to send in scripts or translations. Most unsolicited scripts are read but it is extremely unlikely that new British, Irish or North American plays will have any future at the theatre due to emphasis on plays translated from foreign languages. The Gate does not welcome primary anglophone material and will not read these plays. Always enclose s.a.e. if play needs returning.

Graeae Theatre Company

Interchange Studios, Hampstead Town Hall Centre, 213 Haverstock Hill, London NW3 4QP
☎020 7681 4755 Fax 020 7681 4756
Email info@graeae.org
Website www.graeae.org
Minicom 020 7267 3167

Artistic Director *Jenny Sealey*

Executive Producer *Roger Nelson*

Europe's premier theatre company of disabled people, the company tours nationally and internationally with innovative theatre productions highlighting both historical and contemporary disabled experience. Graeae also runs Forum Theatre and educational programmes available to schools, youth clubs and day centres nationally, provides vocational training in theatre arts (including playwriting). Unsolicited scripts – from disabled writers – welcome. New work examining disability issues is commissioned.

Hampstead Theatre

Swiss Cottage Centre, Avenue Road, London NW3 3EX
☎020 7722 9224 Fax 020 7722 3860
Website www.hampstead-theatre.co.uk

Literary Manager *Jeanie O'Hare*

A brand new Hampstead Theatre is due to open in the winter of 2002. The building will be an intimate space with a flexible stage and an auditorium capable of expanding to seat 325 (double the current capacity). The artistic policy will continue to be the production of British and international new plays and the development of important young writers. 'We are looking for writers who recognise the power of theatre and who have a story to tell. All plays are read and discussed. We give feedback to all writers with potential.' Writers produced at Hampstead include: Michael Frayn, Roy Williams, Shelagh Stephenson, Simon Block, Philip Ridley, Frank McGuinness, Rona Munro, Brad Fraser and Abi Morgan.

Harrogate Theatre Company

Oxford Street, Harrogate, North Yorkshire HG1 1QF
☎01423 502710 Fax 01423 563205
Email staff.name@harrogatetheatre.demon.co.uk

Artistic Director *Rob Swain*

Produces four to five productions a year on the main stage, one of which may be a new play but is most likely to be commissioned. Annual mainstage Youth Theatre production may also be commissioned. Over the next two years it is planned to workshop and read new plays by local writers and possibly stage them in the sudio. Unsolicited scripts from outside Yorkshire are unlikely to receive a production or workshop. Please write with a brief synopsis initially.

Heritage Theatre Ltd

See entry under **Film, TV and Video Production Companies**

The Hiss & Boo Company Ltd

1 Nyes Hill, Wineham Lane, Bolney, West Sussex RH17 5SD Fax 01444 882057
Email hissboo@msn.com
Website www.hissboo.co.uk
Contact *Ian Liston*

Particularly interested in new thrillers, comedy thrillers, comedy and melodrama – must be commercial full-length plays. Also interested in plays/plays with music for children. No one-acts. Previous productions: *The Shakespeare Revue; Come Rain Come Shine; Sleighrider; Beauty and the Beast; An Ideal Husband; Mr Men's Magical Island; Mr Men and the Space Pirates; Nunsense; Corpse!; Groucho: A Life in Revue; See How They Run; Christmas Cat and the Pudding Pirates; Pinocchio* and traditional pantos written by Roy Hudd for the company. 'We are keen on revue-type shows and compilation shows but *not* tribute-type performances.' No unsolicited scripts; no telephone calls. Send synopsis and introductory letter in the first instance.

Hull Truck Theatre Company

Spring Street, Hull HU2 8RW
☎01482 224800 Fax 01482 581182
Executive Director *Joanne Gower*

John Godber, of *Teechers, Bouncers, Up 'n' Under* fame, the artistic director of this high-profile Northern company since 1984, has very much dominated the scene in the past with his own successful plays. The emphasis is still on new writing but Godber's work continues to be toured extensively. Most new plays are commissioned. Previous productions: *Dead Fish* Gordon Steel; *Off Out* and *Fish and Leather* both by Gill Adams; *Happy Families* John Godber. The company receives a large number of unsolicited scripts but cannot guarantee a quick response. Bear in mind the artistic policy of Hull Truck, which is 'accessibility and popularity'. In general they are not interested in musicals, or in plays with casts of more than eight.

Stephen Joseph Theatre

Westborough, Scarborough, North Yorkshire YO11 1JW
☎01723 370540 Fax 01723 360506
Artistic Director *Alan Ayckbourn*
Literary Manager *Laura Harvey*

A two-auditoria complex housing a 165-seat end stage theatre/cinema (the McCarthy) and a 400-seat theatre-in-the-round (the Round). Positive policy on new work. For obvious reasons, Alan Ayckbourn's work features quite strongly but a new writing programme ensures plays from other sources are actively encouraged. Also runs a lunchtime season of one-act plays each summer. Writers are advised however that the SJT is very unlikely to produce an unsolicited script – synopses are preferred. Recent commissions and past productions include: *A Listening Heaven* and *Clockwatching* Torben Betts; *Larkin with Women* Ben Brown; *Amaretti Angels* Sarah Phelps; *Something Blue* Gill Adams; *The Star Throwers* Paul Lucas; *Man for Hire* Meredith Oakes; *Safari Party* Tim Firth; *Gameplan, Flatspin, Roleplay* and *House and Garden* Alan Ayckbourn. 'Writers are welcome to send details of rehearsed readings and productions as an alternative means of introducing the theatre to their work.' Submit to *Laura Harvey* enclosing an s.a.e. for return of mss.

Bill Kenwright Ltd

BKL House, 106 Harrow Road, London W2 1RR
☎020 7446 6200 Fax 020 7446 6222
Contact *Bill Kenwright*

Presents both revivals and new shows for West End and touring theatres. Although new work tends to be by established playwrights, this does not preclude or prejudice new plays from new writers. Scripts should be addressed to Bill Kenwright with a covering letter and s.a.e. 'We have enormous amounts of scripts sent to us although we very rarely produce unsolicited work. Scripts are read systematically. Please do not phone; the return of your script or contact with you will take place in time.'

Komedia

Gardner Street, North Lane, Brighton, East Sussex BN1 1UN
☎01273 647101 Fax 01273 647102
Email info@komedia.co.uk
Website www.komedia.co.uk
Contact *David Lavender*

FOUNDED in 1994, Komedia promotes, produces and presents new work. Mss of new plays welcome.

Leeds Playhouse

See **West Yorkshire Playhouse**

Leicester Haymarket Theatre

Belgrave Gate, Leicester LE1 3YQ
☎0116 253 0021 Fax 0116 251 3310
Website www.leicesterhaymarkettheatre.org

Artistic Directors *Paul Kerryson,*
Kully Thiarai

Leicester Haymarket Theatre aims for a balanced programme of original and established works. It is a multi-cultural, racially integrated company with educational projects attached to all productions and areas of work. Forthcoming productions include two new plays, *Unsuitable Girls* by Dolly Dhingra and *Bali – The Sacrifice* by Girish Karnad. There is also a full studio programme and thriving youth theatre.

Library Theatre Company

St Peter's Square, Manchester M2 5PD
☎0161 234 1913 Fax 0161 228 6481
Email ltc@libraries.manchester.gov.uk
Website www.libtheatreco.org.uk
Artistic Director *Christopher Honer*

Produces new and contemporary work, as well as occasional classics. No unsolicited mss. Send outline of the nature of the script first. Encourages new writing through the commissioning of new plays and through a programme of rehearsed readings to help writers' development.

Live Theatre Company

7/8 Trinity Chare, Newcastle upon Tyne
NE1 3DF
☎0191 261 2694 Fax 0191 232 2224
Email info@live.org.uk
Website www.live.org.uk
Artistic Director *Max Roberts*
Executive Director *Jim Beirne*

FOUNDED 1973. Produces shows at its refurbished 200-seat venue, and also tours regionally and nationally. Company policy is to produce work that is rooted in the culture of the region, particularly for those who do not normally get involved in the arts. The company is particularly interested in promoting new writing. As well as full-scale productions the company organises workshops, rehearsed readings and other new writing activities. The company also enjoys a close relationship with **New Writing North**. Productions include: *Buffalo Girls* by Karin Young; *Two* Jim Cartwright; *Cabaret*, and an ambitious cycle of plays – *Twelve Tales of Tyneside* – which involved 12 writers; *Falling Together* Tom Hadaway; *Cooking With Elvis* Lee Hall; *Bones* Peter Straughan; *Laughter When We're Dead* Sean O'Brien and *ne1* and *Tales From the Backyard* Alan Plater.

London Bubble Theatre Company

3–5 Elephant Lane, London SE16 4JD
☎020 7237 4434 Fax 020 7231 2366
Email peth@londonbubble.org.uk
Website www.londonbubble.org.uk
Artistic Director *Jonathan Petherbridge*

Produces workshops, plays and events for a mixed audience of theatregoers and non-theatregoers, wide-ranging in terms of age, culture and class. Previous productions: *Gilgamesh; Sleeping Beauty; Growing People.* Unsolicited mss are received but 'our reading service is extremely limited and there can be a considerable wait before we can give a response'. Commissions approximately one new project a year, often inspired by a promenade site, specific community of interest or workshop group.

Lyric Theatre Hammersmith

King Street, London W6 0QL
☎020 8741 0824 Fax 020 8741 5965
Email enquiries@lyric.co.uk
Website www.lyric.co.uk
Artistic Director *Neil Bartlett*
Executive Director *Simon Mellor*

The main theatre stages an eclectic programme of new and revived classics with a particular interest in music theatre. Interested in developing projects with writers, translators and adaptors. The Lyric does not accept unsolicited scripts. Its 110-seat studio focuses on work for children, young people and families.

MAC – The Centre for Birmingham

Cannon Hill Park, Birmingham B12 9QH
☎0121 440 4221 Fax 0121 446 4372
Email enquiries@mac-birmingham.org.uk
Website www.birminghamarts.org.uk/
   organisations/mac.asp
Director *Dorothy Wilson*

Home of the Geese Theatre Company, Sampad South Asian Arts, Stan's Café Theatre Company and a host of other arts/performance-related organisations based in Birmingham. Details on Geese, the touring theatre company, available from the Centre.

Cameron Mackintosh

1 Bedford Square, London WC1B 3RA
☎020 7637 8866

Musical producer. Productions include *Oliver!; Little Shop of Horrors; Side by Side by Sondheim; Cats; Les Misérables; Phantom of the Opera; Miss*

Saigon. Will not consider unsolicited material; no new projects for the foreseeable future.

Manchester Library Theatre
See **Library Theatre Company**

Midland Arts Centre
See **MAC - The Centre for Birmingham**

New Vic Theatre
Etruria Road, Newcastle under Lyme, Staffordshire ST5 0JG
☎01782 717954 Fax 01782 712885

Artistic Director *Gwenda Hughes*

The New Vic is a purpose-built theatre-in-the-round. Plays to a fairly broad-based audience which tends to vary from one production to another. A high proportion are not regular theatre-goers and new writing has been one of the main ways of contacting new audiences. Synopses preferred to unsolicited scripts.

Newpalm Productions
26 Cavendish Avenue, London N3 3QN
☎020 8349 0802 Fax 020 8346 8257

Contact *Lionel Chilcott*

Rarely produces new plays (*As Is* by William M. Hoffman, which came from Broadway to the Half Moon Theatre, was an exception to this). National tours of productions such as *Peter Pan (The Musical); Noises Off, Seven Brides for Seven Brothers* and *Rebecca*, at regional repertory theatres, are more typical examples of Newpalm's work. Unsolicited mss, both plays and musicals, are, however, welcome; scripts are preferable to synopses.

NITRO
6 Brewery Road, London N7 9NH
☎020 7609 1331 Fax 020 7609 1221
Email btc@dircon.co.uk
Website www.nitro.co.uk

Artistic Director *Felix Cross*

FOUNDED 1978. Formerly Black Theatre Co-op. Plays to a mixed audience, approximately 65% female. Usually tours nationally twice a year. 'A music theatre company, we are committed in the first instance to new writing by Black British writers and work which relates to the Black culture and experience throughout the Diaspora.' Unsolicited mss welcome.

Northcott Theatre
Stocker Road, Exeter, Devon EX4 4QB
☎01392 223999 Fax 01392 223996
Website www.northcott-theatre.co.uk

Artistic Director *Ben Crocker*

FOUNDED 1967. The Northcott is the South-west's principal subsidised producing theatre, situated on the University of Exeter campus. Describes its audience as 'geographically diverse, with a core audience of AB1s (40–60 age range)'. Continually looking to broaden the base of its audience profile, targeting younger and/or non-mainstream theatregoers. Aims to develop, promote and produce quality new writing which reflects the life of the region and addresses the audience it serves. Generally works on a commission basis but occasionally options existing new work. Unsolicited mss welcome – current turnaround on script-reading service is approximately three months and no mss can be returned unless a correct value s.a.e. is included with the original submission.

Northern Stage
Newcastle Playhouse, Barras Bridge, Newcastle upon Tyne NE1 7RH
☎0191 232 3366 Fax 0191 261 8093
Email directors@northernstage.com
Website www.northernstage.com

Artistic Director *Alan Lyddiard*
Executive Director *Caroline Routh*

A contemporary performance company whose trademarks are a strongly visual and physical style, international influences, appeal to young people and strongly linked programmes of community work. As likely to produce devised work as conventional new writing. Before submitting unsolicited scripts, please contact *Brenda Gray*, PA to the Directors.

Norwich Puppet Theatre
St James, Whitefriars, Norwich, Norfolk NR3 1TN
☎01603 615564 Fax 01603 617578
Email norpuppet@hotmail.com
Website www.geocities.com/norwichpuppets

Artistic Director *Luis Boy*
General Manager *Ian Woods*

Plays to a young audience (aged 3–12) but developing shows for adult audiences interested in puppetry. All year round programme plus tours to schools and arts venues. Unsolicited mss welcome if relevant.

Nottingham Playhouse
Nottingham Theatre Trust, Wellington Circus, Nottingham NG1 5AF
☎0115 947 4361 Fax 0115 947 5759

Artistic Director *Giles Croft*

Aims to make innovation popular, and present the best of world theatre, working closely with the communities of Nottingham and Nottinghamshire. Unsolicited mss will be read. It normally takes about six months, however, and 'we have never yet produced an unsolicited script. All our plays have to achieve a minimum of 60 per cent audiences in a 732-seat theatre. We have no studio.'

Nottingham Playhouse Roundabout Theatre in Education

Wellington Circus, Nottingham NG1 5AF
☎0115 947 4361 Fax 0115 953 9055
Email andrewb@nottinghamplayhouse.co.uk
Website www.roundabout.org.uk

Contact *Andrew Breakwell*

FOUNDED 1973. Theatre-in-Education company of the **Nottingham Playhouse**. Plays to a young audience aged 5–18 years of age. 'Most of our current work uses existing scripts but we try and commission at least one new play every year. We are committed to the encouragement of new writing as and when resources permit. With other major producers in the East Midlands we will share the resources of the literary manager who will be based at the Playhouse in 2002/3. See website for philosophy and play details. Please make contact before submitting scripts.'

N.T.C. Touring Theatre Company

The Playhouse, Bondgate Without, Alnwick, Northumberland NE66 1PQ
☎01665 602586 Fax 01665 605837
Email admin@ntc-touringtheatre.co.uk
Website www.ntc-touringtheatre.co.uk

Contact *Gillian Hambleton*
Administrator *Anna Flood*

FOUNDED 1978. Formerly Northumberland Theatre Company. A Northern Arts revenue funded organisation. Predominantly rural, small-scale touring company, playing to village halls and community centres throughout the Northern region, the Scottish Borders and countrywide. Productions range from established classics to new work and popular comedies, but must be appropriate to their audience. Unsolicited scripts welcome but are unlikely to be produced. All scripts are read and returned with constructive criticism within six months. Writers whose style is of interest may then be commissioned. The company encourages new writing and commissions when possible. Financial constraints restrict casting to a *maximum* of five.

Nuffield Theatre

University Road, Southampton, Hampshire SO17 1TR
☎023 8031 5500 Fax 023 8031 5511

Artistic Director *Patrick Sandford*
Script Executive *John Burgess*

Well known as a good bet for new playwrights, the Nuffield gets an awful lot of scripts. They do a couple of new main stage plays every season. Previous productions: *Exchange* by Yuri Trifonov (transl. Michael Frayn) which transferred to the Vaudeville Theatre; *The Floating Light Bulb* Woody Allen (British première); new plays by Claire Luckham: *Dogspot; The Dramatic Attitudes of Miss Fanny Kemble;* and by Claire Tomalin: *The Winter Wife.* Open-minded about subject and style, producing musicals as well as straight plays. Also opportunities for some small-scale fringe work. Scripts preferred to synopses in the case of writers new to theatre. All will, eventually, be read 'but please be patient. We do not have a large team of paid readers. We read everything ourselves.'

Octagon Theatre Trust Ltd

Howell Croft South, Bolton, Lancashire BL1 1SB
☎01204 529407 Fax 01204 380110

Executive Director *John Blackmore*

FOUNDED 1967. The Octagon Theatre has pursued a dynamic policy of commissioning new plays in recent years. These have been by both established writers such as Paul Abbott, Tom Elliott, Henry Livings and Les Smith as well as new and emerging writers through partnerships with organisations such as **North West Playwrights** and the national new writing company **Paines Plough**. Whilst there is no prescriptive 'house style' at the Octagon, the theatre is nevertheless keen to encourage the development of writers from the North West region, telling stories that will resonate with the local audience. The Associate Director, *Sue Reddish,* coordinates the new writing initiative at the Octagon and any unsolicited scripts are processed through North West Playwrights.

Orange Tree Theatre

1 Clarence Street, Richmond, Surrey TW9 2SA
☎020 8940 0141 Fax 020 8332 0369
Email admin@orange-tree.demon.co.uk
Website www.orangetreetheatre.co.uk

Artistic Director *Sam Walters*

One of those theatre venues just out of London

which are good for new writing, both full-scale productions and rehearsed readings. Productions from September 2001: *Flyin' West* Pearl Cleage; *Whispers Along the Patio* David Cregan; *The Caucasian Chalk Circle* Bertolt Brecht; *Have You Anything To Declare?* Maurice Hennequin and Pierre Veber; *The Three Sisters* Anton Chekhov. Unsolicited mss are read, but patience (and s.a.e.) required.

Out of Joint

7 Thane Works, Thane Villas, London N7 7PH
☎020 7609 0207 Fax 020 7609 0203
Email ojo@outofjoint.co.uk
Website www.outofjoint.co.uk
Director *Max Stafford-Clark*
Producer *Graham Cowley*
Literary Manager *Jenny Worton*

FOUNDED 1993. Award-winning theatre company with new writing central to its policy. Produces new plays which reflect society and its concerns, placing an emphasis on education activity to attract young audiences. Welcomes unsolicited mss. Productions include: *Blue Heart* Caryl Churchill; *Our Lady of Sligo, The Steward of Christendom* and *Hinterland* Sebastian Barry; *Shopping and Fucking* and *Some Explicit Polaroids* Mark Ravenhill; *Rita, Sue and Bob Too* Andrea Dunbar; *A State Affair* Robin Soans; *Sliding with Suzanne* Judy Upton.

Oxford Stage Company

131 High Street, Oxford OX1 4DH
☎01865 723238 Fax 01865 790625
Website www.oxfordstage.co.uk
Artistic Director *Dominic Dromgoole*

A middle-scale touring company producing established and new plays. At least one new play or new adaptation a year. Due to forthcoming projects not considering unsolicited scripts at present.

Paines Plough

4th Floor, 43 Aldwych, London WC2B 4DN
☎020 7240 4533 Fax 020 7240 4534
Email office@painesplough.com
Website www.painesplough.com
Artistic Director *Vicky Featherstone*
Associate Director *John Tiffany*
Literary Associate *Lucy Morrison*

Tours new plays nationally. Works with writers to develop their skills and voices through workshops, rehearsed readings and playwriting projects. Provides a supportive environment for commissioned writers to push themselves and challenge their craft. Will consider unso-

licited material from UK writers (please send s.a.e. for return of script).

Palace Theatre, Watford

Clarendon Road, Watford, Hertfordshire WD17 1JZ
☎01923 235455 Fax 01923 819664
Website www.watfordtheatre.co.uk
Artistic Director *Lawrence Till*

An important part of artistic and cultural policy is the commissioning of new plays and translations. Recent new plays: *Elton John's Glasses* David Farr (1997 Writers' Guild Best Regional Play award); *The Talented Mr Ripley* Phyllis Nagy; *The Dark* Jonathan Holloway; *The Late Middle Classes* Simon Gray (1999 Barclays/TMA Best New Play Award); *Morning Glory* Sarah Daniels; *The True-Life Fiction of Mata Hari* Diane Samuels; *Full House* and *The Hairless Diva* (after Ionesco) John Mortimer; *Big Night Out at the Little Palace Theatre* Sandi Toksvig and Dillie Keane.

Perth Repertory Theatre Ltd

185 High Street, Perth PH1 5UW
☎01738 472700 Fax 01738 624576
Email theatre@perth.org.uk
Website www.perth.org.uk/perth/theatre.htm
Artistic Director *Michael Winter*
General Manager *Paul Hackett*

FOUNDED 1935. Combination of one- to four-weekly repertoire of plays and musicals, incoming tours and studio productions. Unsolicited mss are read when time permits, but the timetable for return of scripts is lengthy. New plays staged by the company are usually commissioned under the SAC scheme.

Plymouth Theatre Royal

See **Theatre Royal**

Polka Theatre for Children

240 The Broadway, Wimbledon, London SW19 1SB
☎020 8545 8320 Fax 020 8545 8365
Email info@polkatheatre.com
Website www.polkatheatre.com
Artistic Director *Vicky Ireland*
Administrator *Stephen Midlane*

FOUNDED in 1967 and moved into its Wimbledon base in 1979. Leading children's theatre committed to commissioning and producing new plays. Programmes are planned two years ahead and at least three new plays are commissioned each year. 'Because of our specialist needs and fixed budgets, all our scripts are commissioned from established writers with whom we work very closely. Writers are selected via recommendation and previous work. We do not perform unsolicited scripts. Potential new writers' work is read and discussed on a regular basis; thus we constantly add to our pool of interesting and interested writers. This department is now headed by a new position, Director of New Writing.'

Praxis Theatre Company Ltd
24 Wykeham Road, London NW4 2SU
☎020 8203 1916 Fax 020 8203 1916
Email praxisco@globalnet.co.uk
Website www.users.globalnet.co.uk/~praxisco
Artistic Director *Sharon Kennet*

FOUNDED 1993. Performs to a mixed European audience, 'crossing the divide between text-based theatre and visual theatre'. No unsolicited mss. Previous productions and films: *Seed*; *My Brother Whom I Love*; *The Sacred Penman*; *She's Well Out of Order*; *Dot*.

Queen's Theatre, Hornchurch
Billet Lane, Hornchurch, Essex RM11 1QT
☎01708 456118 Fax 01708 452348
Email info@queens-theatre.co.uk
Website www.queens-theatre.co.uk

Artistic Director *Bob Carlton*

The Queen's Theatre is a 500-seat producing theatre in the London Borough of Havering and within the M25. ESTABLISHED in 1953, the theatre has been located in its present building since 1975 and produces up to nine in-house productions per year, including pantomime. The Queen's has re-established a permanent core company of actor/musicians under the artistic leadership of Bob Carlton. Aims to produce distinctive and accessible performances in an identifiable house style focused upon actor/musician shows but, in addition, embraces straight plays, classics and comedies. 'New play/musical submissions are welcome but should be submitted in treatment and not script form.' Each year there is a large-scale community play commissioned from a local writer culminating in a summer event beside the theatre. A new writers' group has been established, led currently by David Eldridge. Enquiries about joining should be directed to the education manager.

The Really Useful Group Ltd
22 Tower Street, London WC2H 9TW
☎020 7240 0880 Fax 020 7240 1204
Website www.reallyuseful.com
Commercial/West End theatre producer whose output has included *Jesus Christ Superstar*; *Sunset Boulevard*; *Joseph and the Amazing Technicolor Dreamcoat*; *Cats*; *Phantom of the Opera*; *Starlight Express*; *Daisy Pulls It Off*; *Lend Me a Tenor*; *Arturo Ui*; *The Beautiful Game*; *Whistle Down the Wind*; *Aspects of Love*; *Bombay Dreams*.

Red Ladder Theatre Company
3 St Peter's Buildings, York Street, Leeds, West Yorkshire LS9 8AJ
☎0113 245 5311 Fax 0113 245 5351
Email wendy@redladder.co.uk
Website www.redladder.co.uk
Artistic Director/Literary Manager
  Wendy Harris
Administrator *Janis Smyth*

FOUNDED 1968. Commissioning company touring 2–3 shows a year with a strong commitment to new work and new writers. Aimed at an audience of young people aged between 14–25 years who have little or no access to theatre. Performances held in youth clubs and similar venues where young people choose to meet. Recent productions: *Hold Ya* Chris O'Connell; *LowDown Highnotes* Andrea Earl. The company is particularly keen to enter into a dialogue with writers with regard to creating new work for young people. Red Ladder is running an attachment scheme, *Outwrite In*, in partnership with BBC northern exposure for writers from or based in Bradford. E-mail the artistic director for more information at the address above.

Red Shift Theatre Company
TRG2 Trowbray House, 108 Weston Street, London SE1 3QB
☎020 7378 9787 Fax 020 7378 9789
Email mail@redshifttheatreco.co.uk
Website www.redshifttheatreco.co.uk
Contact *Jonathan Holloway, Artistic Director*
General Manager *Jess Lammin*

FOUNDED 1982. Small-scale touring company which plays to a theatre-literate audience. Unlikely to produce an unsolicited script as most work is commissioned. Welcomes contact with writers – 'we try to see their work' – and receipt of c.v.s and treatments. Occasionally runs workshops bringing new scripts, writers and actors together. These can develop links with a reservoir of writers who may feed the company. Interested in new plays with subject matter which is accessible to a broad audience and concerns issues of importance; also new translations and adaptations. 2001–2002 productions: *Nicholas Nickleby* and *The Love Child*.

Ridiculusmus

c/o me&him&her, BAC, Lavender Hill,
London SW11 5TN
Email ridiculusmus@meandhim.net
Website www.ridiculusmus.com
Artistic Directors *Jon Hough, David Woods*

FOUNDED 1992. Touring company which plays to a wide range of audiences. Productions have included adaptations of *Three Men In a Boat; The Third Policeman; At Swim Two Birds* and original work: *The Exhibitionists; Yes, Yes, Yes* and *Say Nothing*. Unsolicited scripts not welcome.

Royal Court Theatre

Sloane Square, London SW1W 8AS
☎020 7565 5050
Fax 020 7565 5002 (Literary office)
Website www.royalcourttheatre.com
Literary Manager *Graham Whybrow*

The Royal Court is a leading international theatre producing up to 17 new plays each year in its 400-seat proscenium theatre and 80-seat studio. In 1956 its first director George Devine set out to find 'hard-hitting, uncompromising writers whose plays are stimulating, provocative and exciting'. This artistic policy helped transform post-war British theatre, with new plays by writers such as John Osborne, Arnold Wesker, John Arden, Samuel Beckett, Edward Bond and David Storey, through to Caryl Churchill, Jim Cartwright, Kevin Elyot and Timberlake Wertenbaker. Since 1994 it has produced a new generation of writers such as Joe Penhall, Rebecca Prichard, Sarah Kane, Jez Butterworth, Martin McDonagh, Mark Ravenhill, Ayub Khan-Din, Conor McPherson, Roy Williams and many other first-time writers. The Royal Court has programmes for young writers and international writers, and it is always searching for new plays and new playwrights.

Royal Exchange Theatre Company

St Ann's Square, Manchester M2 7DH
☎0161 833 9333 Fax 0161 832 0881
Website www.royalexchange.co.uk
Literary Manager *Sarah Frankcom*

FOUNDED 1976. The Royal Exchange has developed a new writing policy which it finds is attracting a younger audience to the theatre. The company has produced new plays by Shelagh Stephenson, Brad Fraser, Simon Burke, Jim Cartwright, Peter Barnes and Alex Finlayson. Also English and foreign classics, modern classics, adaptations and new musicals. The Royal Exchange receives 500–2000 scripts a year. These are read by Sarah Frankcom and a team of experienced readers. Only a tiny percentage is suitable, but a number of plays are commissioned each year.

Royal Lyceum Theatre Company

Grindlay Street, Edinburgh EH3 9AX
☎0131 248 4800 Fax 0131 228 3955
Artistic Director *Kenny Ireland*
Administration Manager *Ruth Butterworth*
Administration Director *Sadie McKinlay*

FOUNDED 1965. Repertory theatre which plays to a mixed urban Scottish audience. Produces classic, contemporary and new plays. Would like to stage more new plays, especially Scottish. No full-time literary staff to provide reports on submitted scripts.

Royal National Theatre

South Bank, London SE1 9PX
☎020 7452 3333 Fax 020 7452 3350
Website www.nationaltheatre.org.uk
Literary Manager *Jack Bradley*

The majority of the National's new plays come about as a result of direct commission or from existing contacts with playwrights. There is no quota for new work, though so far more than a third of plays presented have been the work of living playwrights. Writers new to the theatre would need to be of exceptional talent to be successful with a script here, though the Royal National Theatre Studio helps a limited number of playwrights, through readings, workshops and discussions. In some cases a new play is presented for a shorter-than-usual run in the Cottesloe Theatre. Scripts considered (send s.a.e).

Royal Shakespeare Company

Dramaturgy, Royal Shakespeare Theatre,
Waterside, Stratford upon Avon,
Warwickshire CV37 6BB
☎01789 412200
Website www.rsc.org.uk
Dramaturg *Paul Sirett*

The RSC is a classical theatre company based in Stratford upon Avon. It has recently transformed intself to create the opportunity for different esemble companies to work on distinct projects that will open both in Stratford upon Avon and at various venues around London. The company also has an annual residency in Newcastle upon Tyne and tours both nationally and internationally. As well as Shakespeare, English classics and foreign classics in translation, new plays counterpoint the RSC's repertory, especially those which celebrate language. 'The dramaturgy department is proactive rather than reactive and seeks out the plays and playwrights it wishes to commission. It will read all translations of classic foreign works submitted, or of contemporary works where the original writer and/or translator is known. It is unable to read unsolicited work from less established writers. It can only return scripts if an s.a.e. is enclosed with submission.'

7:84 Theatre Company Scotland

333 Woodlands Road, Glasgow G3 6NG
☎0141 334 6686 Fax 0141 334 3369
Email admin@784theatre.fsnet.co.uk
Artistic Director *Gordon Laird*

FOUNDED 1973. One of Scotland's foremost touring theatre companies committed to producing work that addresses current social, cultural and political issues. Recent productions include commissions by Scottish playwrights such as Peter Arnott (*A Little Rain*); Stephen Greenhorn (*Dissent*); David Greig (*Caledonia Dreaming*) and the Scottish premières of Tony Kushner's *Angels in America* and Athol Fugard's *Valley Song*. 'The company is committed to a new writing policy that encourages and develops writers at every level of experience, to get new voices and strong messages on to the stage.' New writing development has always been central to 7:84's core activity and has included Summer Schools and the 7:84 Writers Group. The company continues to be committed to this work and its development. 'Happy to read unsolicited scripts.'

Shared Experience

The Soho Laundry, 9 Dufours Place, London W1F 7SJ
☎020 7434 9248 Fax 020 7287 8763
Email admin@setheatre.co.uk
Joint Artistic Directors *Nancy Meckler, Polly Teale*

FOUNDED 1975. Varied audience depending on venue, since this is a touring company. Recent productions have included: *Anna Karenina* (adapt. Helen Edmundson); *Mill on the Floss* (adapt. Helen Edmundson); *The Danube* Maria Irene Fornes; *Desire Under the Elms* Eugene O'Neill; *War and Peace* (adapt. Helen Edmundson); *The Tempest* William Shakespeare; *Jane Eyre* (adapt. Polly Teale); *I Am Yours* Judith Thompson; *The House of*

Bernarda Alba (transl. Rona Munro); *Mother Courage* (transl. Lee Hall); *A Doll's House* (transl. Michael Meyer); *The Magic Toyshop* (adapt. Bryony Lavery); *The Clearing* Helen Edmundson. No unsolicited mss. Primarily not a new writing company but 'we are interested in innovative new scripts'.

Sherman Theatre Company

Senghennydd Road, Cardiff CF24 4YE
☎029 2064 6901 Fax 029 2064 6902
Artistic Director *Phil Clark*

FOUNDED 1973. Theatre for Young People, with main house and studio. Encourages new writing; has produced 86 new plays in the last ten years. Previous productions include a David Wood adaptation of Roald Dahl's *James and the Giant Peach*, plays by Frank Vickery (*Pullin the Wool*); Helen Griffin (*Flesh and Blood*); Patrick Jones (*Everything Must Go*); Terry Deary (*Horrible Histories Crackers Christmas*); Mike Kenny (*Puff the Magic Dragon*); Brendan Murray (*Something Beginning With ...*); Roald Dahl (*The Enormous Crocodile*); Roger Williams (*Pop*); Arnold Wesker (*Break, My Heart*). The company has presented four seasons of six new plays live on stage and broadcast on BBC Radio Wales, and four series of one-act lunchtime plays on stage and then filmed for HTV Wales. Priority will be given to Wales-based writers.

Show of Strength

74 Chessel Street, Bedminster, Bristol BS3 3DN
☎0117 902 0235 Fax 0117 902 0196
Email sheila@showofstrength.freeserve.co.uk
Artistic Director *Sheila Hannon*

FOUNDED 1986. Plays to an informal, younger than average audience. Aims to stage at least one new play each season with a preference for work from Bristol and the South West. Will read unsolicited scripts but a lack of funding means they are unable to provide written reports. OUTPUT *Blue Murder, So Long Life,* and *Nicholodeon* Peter Nichols; *Lags* Ron Hutchinson; *A Busy Day* Fanny Burney. Also, rehearsed readings of new work.

Snap People's Theatre Trust

29 Raynham Road, Bishop's Stortford, Hertfordshire CM23 5PE
☎01279 461607 Fax 01279 506694
Website www.snaptheatre.co.uk
Contacts *Andy Graham, Mike Wood*

FOUNDED 1979. Plays to young people (5–11; 12–19), and to the thirty-something-plus age group. Classic adaptations and new writing. Writers should make contact in advance of sending material. New writing is encouraged and should involve, be written for or by young people. 'Projects should reflect the writer's own beliefs, be thought-provoking, challenging and accessible. The writer should be able to work with designers, directors and musicians in the early stages to develop the text and work alongside other disciplines.'

Soho Theatre Company
21 Dean Street, London W1D 3NE
☎020 7287 5060 Fax 020 7287 5061
Email writers@sohotheatre.com
Website www.sohotheatre.com
Artistic Director *Abigail Morris*
Literary Manager *Ruth Little*

Dedicated to new writing, the company has an extensive research and development programme consisting of a free script-reading service, workshops and readings. Also runs many courses for new writers. The company produces around four plays a year. Previous productions include: *Office* Shan Khan, winner of the 2000 Verity Bargate Award; *Angels and Saints* Jessica Townsend, joint winner of the 1998 Peggy Ramsay Award; *Jump Mr Malinoff Jump* Toby Whithouse, winner of the 1998 Verity Bargate Award; *Gabriel* Moira Buffini, winner of the 1996 LWT Award; *Be My Baby* Amanda Whittington; *Kindertransporte* Diane Samuels. Runs the **Verity Bargate Award**, a biennial competition (see entry under **Prizes**).

Sphinx Theatre Company
25 Short Street, London SE1 8LJ
☎020 7401 9993 Fax 020 7401 9995
Email sphinxtheatre@demon.co.uk
Website www.sphinxtheatre.co.uk
Artistic Director *Sue Parrish*
General Manager *Amanda Rigali*

FOUNDED 1973. Tours new plays by women nationally to small and mid-scale venues. Synopses and ideas are welcome.

The Steam Industry
Finborough Theatre, 118 Finborough Road, London SW10 9ED
☎020 7244 7439 Fax 020 7835 1853
Website www.steamindustry.co.uk *or* www.finboroughtheatre.co.uk
Artistic Director *Phil Willmott*
Director, Finborough Theatre *Neil McPherson*

Since June 1994, the Finborough Theatre has been a base for The Steam Industry who produce in and out of the building. Their output is diverse and prolific and includes a high percentage of new writing alongside radical adaptations of classics and musicals. The space is also available for a number of hires per year and the hire fee is sometimes negotiable to encourage innovative work. Unsolicited scripts are no longer welcome. The company has developed new work by writers such as Chris Lee, Anthony Neilson, Naomi Wallace, Conor McPherson, Tony Marchant, Diane Samuels and Mark Ravenhill.

Swan Theatre
The Moors, Worcester WR1 3EF
☎01905 726969 Fax 01905 723738
Email swan_theatre@lineone.net
Website www.worcesterswantheatre.co.uk
Artistic Director *Jenny Stephens*

Repertory company producing a wide range of plays to a mixed audience coming largely from the City of Worcester and the county of Worcester. A writing group meets at the theatre. Unsolicited scripts are discouraged.

Swansea Little Theatre Ltd
Dylan Thomas Theatre, Maritime Quarter, Gloucester Place, Swansea SA1 1TY
☎01792 473238
Secretary *Gwynn Roberts*

A wide variety of plays, from pantomime to the classics. New writing encouraged. New plays considered by the Artistic Committee.

Talawa Theatre Company Ltd
3rd Floor, 23–25 Great Sutton Street, London EC1V 0DN
☎020 7251 6644 Fax 020 7251 5969
Email hq@talawa.com
Website www.talawa.com
Administrator *Suzannah Bedford*

FOUNDED 1985. 'Aims to provide high quality productions that reflect the significant creative role that Black theatre plays within the national and international arena and also to enlarge theatre audiences from the Black community.' Previous productions include all-Black performances of *The Importance of Being Earnest* and *Antony and Cleopatra*; plus Jamaican pantomime *Arawak Gold; The Gods Are Not to Blame; The Road* Wole Soyinka; *Beef, No Chicken* Derek Walcott; *Flying West* Pearl Cleage; *Othello* William Shakespeare. Seeks to provide a platform for new work from up and coming Black British writers. Send synopsis in the first instance. Runs a black script development project. Talawa is funded by the **London Arts Board** (for three years).

Theatre Absolute

57–61 Corporation Street, Coventry CV1 1GQ
☎024 7625 7380 Fax 024 7655 0680
Email julia@theatreabsolute.demon.co.uk
Website www.theatreabsolute.demon.co.uk
Artistic Director/Writer *Chris O'Connell*
Producer *Julia Negus*
FOUNDED 1992. An independent theatre company which commissions, produces and tours new plays which are based on a strong narrative text and aimed at audiences aged 15 and upwards. Productions include: *Car*, winner of an Edinburgh Fringe First Award 1999 and a *Time Out* Live Award – Best New Play on the London Fringe 1999; and most recently, *Raw*, winner of a Fringe First Award 2001. Alongside the Belgrade Theatre, the company also runs The Writing House, a script development scheme.

Theatre of Comedy Company

210 Shaftesbury Avenue, London WC2H 8DP
☎020 7379 3345 Fax 020 7836 8181
Email info@toc.dltentertainment.co.uk
Chief Executive *Richard Porter*
Creative Director *Keith Murray*
FOUNDED 1983 to produce new work as well as classics and revivals. Interested in strong comedy in the widest sense – Chekhov comes under the definition as does farce. Also has a light entertainment division, developing new scripts for television, namely situation comedy and series.

Theatre Royal, Plymouth

Royal Parade, Plymouth, Devon PL1 2TR
☎01752 230347 Fax 01752 225892
Email d.prescott@theatreroyal.com
Website www.theatreroyal.com
Artistic Director *Simon Stokes*
Artistic Associate *David Prescott*
Stages small, middle and large-scale drama and music theatre. Commissions and produces new plays. Unsolicited scripts with s.a.e. are read and responded to. Send only one script at a time.

Theatre Royal Stratford East

Gerry Raffles Square, London E15 1BN
☎020 8534 7374 Fax 020 8534 8381
Email jperies@stratfordeast.com
Website www.stratfordeast.com
New Writing Manager *James Peries*

Lively East London theatre, catering for a very mixed audience, both local and London-wide. Produces plays, musicals, youth theatre and local community plays/events, all of which is new work. Special interest in Asian and Black British work, and contemporary London/UK stories. New initiatives include developing contemporary British musicals. Unsolicited scripts which are fully completed and have never been produced are welcome. Feedback is given only on scripts that closely meet the artistic remit.

Theatre Royal Windsor

Windsor, Berkshire SL4 1PS
☎01753 863444 Fax 01753 831673
Email info@theatreroyalwindsor.co.uk
Website www.theatreroyalwindsor.co.uk
Executive Producer *Bill Kenwright*
Executive Director *Mark Piper*

Plays to a middle-class, West End-type audience. Produces thirteen plays a year and 'would be disappointed to do fewer than two new plays in a year; always hope to do half a dozen'. Modern classics, thrillers, comedy and farce. Only interested in scripts along these lines.

Theatre Workshop Edinburgh

34 Hamilton Place, Edinburgh EH3 5AX
☎0131 225 7942 Fax 0131 220 0112
Artistic Director *Robert Rae*

First ever professional producing theatre to fully include disabled actors in all its productions. Plays to a young, broad-based audience with many pieces targeted towards particular groups or communities. OUTPUT has included *D.A.R.E.* Particularly interested in issues-based work for young people and minority groups. Frequently engages writers for collaborative work and devised projects. Commissions a significant amount of new writing for a wide range of contexts, from large-scale community plays to small-scale professional productions. Favours writers based in Scotland, producing material relevant to a contemporary Scottish audience.

Tiebreak Theatre

Heartsease High School, Marryat Road, Norwich, Norfolk NR7 9DF
☎01603 435209 Fax 01603 435184
Email info@tiebreak-theatre.com
Website www.tiebreak-theatre.com
Artistic Director *David Farmer*

FOUNDED 1981. Specialises in high-quality theatre for children and young people, touring schools, youth centres, small-scale theatres, museums and festivals. Productions: *Time and*

Tide; The Snow Egg; One Dark Night; Suitcase Full of Stories; Flint People; Intake/Outake; Fast Eddy; Breaking the Rules; George Speaks; Frog and Toad; Singing in the Rainforest; The Invisible Boy; My Friend Willy; The Ugly Duckling. New writing encouraged. Interested in low-budget, small-cast material only. School and educational material of special interest. 'Scripts welcome but please ring first to discuss any potential submission.'

The Torch Theatre
St Peter's Road, Milford Haven,
Pembrokeshire SA73 2BU
☎01646 694192 Fax 01646 698919
Email info@torchtheatre.co.uk
Website www.torchtheatre.org.uk
Artistic Director *Peter Doran*

FOUNDED 1977. Stages a mixed programme of in-house and middle-scale touring work. Unsolicited scrips will be read and guidance offered but production unlikely due to restricted funding. Please include s.a.e. for return of script and notes; mark clearly, 'FAO Peter Doran'. Torch Theatre Company productions include: *Dancing at Lughnasa; Neville's Island; The Woman in Black; Abigail's Party; Taking Steps; Blue Remembered Hills; A Prayer for Wings; Little Shop of Horrors; The Caretaker,* plus annual Christmas musicals.

Traverse Theatre
Cambridge Street, Edinburgh EH1 2ED
☎0131 228 3223 Fax 0131 229 8443
Email roxana@traverse.co.uk
Website www.traverse.co.uk
Artistic Director *Philip Howard*
Literary Director *Roxana Silbert*
International Literary Associate *Katherine Mendelsohn*
Literary Development Officer *Hannah Rye*

The Traverse is Scotland's new writing theatre, with a particular commitment to producing new Scottish plays. However, it also has a strong international programme of work in translation and visiting companies. Previous productions: *Gagarin Way* Gregory Burke; *Wiping My Mother's Arse* Iain Heggie; *The Speculator* David Greig; *The Juju Girl* Aileen Ritchie; *Perfect Days* Liz Lochhead. Please address unsolicited scripts to *Roxana Silbert*, Literary Director.

Trestle Theatre Company
Birch Centre, Hill End Lane, St Albans,
Hertfordshire AL4 0RA
☎01727 850950 Fax 01727 855558
Artistic Director *Toby Wilsher*

FOUNDED 1981. Physical, mask touring theatre company. Usually devised work but does work with writers to create new writing for physical/visual theatre. No unsolicited scripts.

Tricycle Theatre
269 Kilburn High Road, London NW6 7JR
☎020 7372 6611 Fax 020 7328 0795
Website www.tricycle.co.uk
Artistic Director *Nicolas Kent*

FOUNDED 1980. Plays to a very mixed audience, in terms of both culture and class. Previous productions: *Stones in his Pockets* Marie Jones; *The Stephen Lawrence Enquiry – The Colour of Justice* adapt. from the enquiry transcripts by Richard Norton-Taylor; *Nuremberg* adapt. from transcripts of the trials by Richard Norton-Taylor; *Joe Turner's Come and Gone, The Piano Lesson* and *Two Trains Runnin'* all by August Wilson; *Kat and the Kings* David Kramer. New writing welcome from women and ethnic minorities (particularly Black, Asian and Irish). Looks for a strong narrative drive with popular appeal, not 'studio' plays. Can only return scripts if postage coupons or s.a.e. are enclosed with original submission.

Tron Theatre Company
63 Trongate, Glasgow G1 5HB
☎0141 552 3748 Fax 0141 552 6657
Email neil@tron.co.uk
Website www.tron.co.uk
Administrative Director *Neil Murray*

FOUNDED 1981. Plays to a broad cross-section of Glasgow and beyond, including international tours. Recent productions: *Our Bad Magnet* Douglas Maxwell; *Further Than the Furthest Thing* Zinnie Harris (co-production with the **Royal National Theatre**). Interested in ambitious plays by UK and international writers. No unsolicited mss.

Unicorn Theatre for Children
St Mark's Studios, Chillingworth Road,
London N7 8QJ
☎020 7700 0702 Fax 020 7700 3870
Email <name>@unicorntheatre.com
Website www.unicorntheatre.com
Artistic Director *Tony Graham*

FOUNDED 1947 as a touring company, and was resident at the Arts Theatre from 1967 until April 1999. Produces seasons at The Pleasance theatre in north London, a summer show at Regent Park's Open Air Theatre, and tours both nationally and internationally. Plays to children, aged 4–12, their teachers and families. New work in 2001: *Pinocchio* Michael Rosen; *Red, Red Shoes* Charles Way; *1001 Nights* Shahrukh Husein. 2002: *Peter Rabbit* adapt. Adrian Mitchell; *Great Expectations* adapt. John Clifford; *Merlin the Magnificent* adapt. Stuart Paterson. Plans to build Unicorn Children's Centre with two auditoria in central London, to open in 2004.

Upstairs at the Gatehouse
See **Ovation Productions** under **Film, TV and Video Production Companies**

Charles Vance Productions
Hampden House, 2 Weymouth Street, London W1N 3FD
☎020 7636 4343 Fax 020 7636 2323
Email cvtheatre@aol.com
Contact *Charles Vance*

In the market for medium-scale touring productions and summer-season plays. Hardly any new work and no commissions but writing of promise stands a good chance of being passed on to someone who might be interested in it. Occasional try-outs for new work in the Sidmouth repertory theatre. Send s.a.e. for return of mss.

Warehouse Theatre
62 Dingwall Road, Croydon CR0 2NF
☎020 8681 1257 Fax 020 8688 6699
Email warehous@dircon.co.uk
Website www.warehousetheatre.co.uk
Artistic Director *Ted Craig*

South London's new writing theatre (adjacent to East Croydon railway station) seats 100–120 and produces up to six new plays a year. Also co-produces with, and hosts, selected touring companies who share the theatre's commitment to new work. Continually building upon a tradition of discovering and nurturing new writers, with activities including a monthly writers' workshop and the annual **International Playwriting Festival**. Also hosts youth theatre workshops and Saturday morning children's theatre. Previous productions: *Iona Rain* by Peter Moffat and *Fat Janet is Dead* by Simon Smith (both past winners of the International Playwriting Festival); *The Shagaround* Maggie Neville; *Coming Up* James Martin Charlton and M.G. 'Monk' Lewis; *The Castle Spectre* edited by Phil Willmott; *Dick*

Barton Special Agent; Dick Barton and the Curse of the Pharaoh's Tomb and *Dick Barton: The Tango of Terror* Phil Willmott. Unsolicited scripts welcome but it is more advisable to submit plays through the theatre's International Playwriting Festival.

Watford Palace Theatre
See **Palace Theatre**

West Yorkshire Playhouse
Playhouse Square, Leeds, West Yorkshire LS2 7UP
☎0113 213 7800 Fax 0113 213 7250
Email alex.chisholm@wyp.org.uk
Website www.wyp.co.uk
Literary Manager *Alex Chisholm*

Committed to working with new writing originating from or set in the Yorkshire and Humberside region. New writing from outside the region is programmed usually where writer or company is already known to the theatre. The Playhouse runs workshops, courses and writers' events including Thursday Night Live, an open platform held at the theatre for local writers and performers. For more information contact the Literary Manager on extension 357 or e-mail to address above. Samples of scripts should be submitted with s.a.e. for return.

Whirligig Theatre
14 Belvedere Drive, Wimbledon, London SW19 7BY
☎020 8947 1732 Fax 020 8879 7648
Email whirligig-theatre@virgin.net
Contact *David Wood*

One play a year in major theatre venues, usually a musical for primary school audiences and weekend family groups. Interested in scripts which exploit the theatrical nature of children's tastes. Previous productions: *The See-Saw Tree; The Selfish Shellfish; The Gingerbread Man; The Old Man of Lochnagar; The Ideal Gnome Expedition; Save the Human; Dreams of Anne Frank; Babe, the Sheep-Pig.*

Michael White Productions Ltd
See **MW Entertainments Ltd** under **Film, TV and Video Production Companies**

White Bear Theatre Club
138 Kennington Park Road, London SE11 4DJ
Administration: 3 Dante Road, Kennington, London SE11 4RB
☎020 7793 9193 Fax 020 7793 9193

Contact *Michael Kingsbury*
Administrator *Julia Parr*

FOUNDED 1988. OUTPUT primarily new work for an audience aged 20–35. Unsolicited scripts welcome, particularly new work with a keen eye on contemporary issues, though not agitprop. *Absolution* by Robert Sherwood was nominated by the Writers' Guild for 'Best Fringe Play' and *Spin* by the same author was the *Time Out* Critics' Choice in 2000. The theatre received the *Time Out* award for Best Fringe Venue in 2001 and a Peter Brook award for best up-and-coming venue. The Writers' Guild, sponsored by the Mackintosh Foundation, is leading writer workshops and readings throughout the year.

Windsor Theatre Royal
See **Theatre Royal Windsor**

The Young Vic
66 The Cut, London SE1 8LZ
☎020 7633 0133 Fax 020 7928 1585

Email info@youngvic.org
Website www.youngvic.org

Artistic Director *David Lan*
Executive Director *Kevin Fitzmaurice*

FOUNDED 1970. The Young Vic is a theatre for everyone but, above all, for younger artists and audiences. Produces revivals of classics – old and new – as well as new plays and annual events that embrace both young people and adults. The main house is one of London's most exciting spaces and seats up to 450. A smaller, flexible space, the Young Vic Studio, seats 80 and is used for research, experiment and performance. Each main house production is accompanied by an extensive programme of Teaching Participation and Research aimed at local schools and colleges. Under the Funded Ticket Scheme 10% of the audience see productions for nothing or very little. Recent productions include *Six Characters Looking For an Author, A Raisin in the Sun* and *Afore Night Come*.

Freelance Rates –
Subsidised Repertory Theatres
(excluding Scotland)

The following minimum rates were negotiated by the **Writers' Guild** and Theatrical Management Association and are set out under the TMA/Writers Agreement.

Theatres are graded by a 'middle range salary level' (MRSL), worked out by dividing the 'total basic salaries' paid by the total number of 'actor weeks' in the year.

	MRSL 1	MRSL 2	MRSL 3
Commissioned Play			
Commission payment	£3,465	£2,810	£2,186
Delivery payment	£1,562	£1,249	£1,249
Acceptance payment	£1,562	£1,249	£1,249
Non-Commissioned Play			
Delivery payment	£4,998	£4,058	£3,434
Acceptance payment	£1,562	£1,249	£1,249
Rehearsal Attendance	£46.09	£40.03	£37.27

Options

UK (excluding West End)	£1,948
West End/USA	£3,249
Rest of the World (English speaking productions)	£2,598

Festivals

Aberdeen Arts Carnival

Aberdeen Arts Centre, 33 King Street,
Aberdeen AB24 5AA
☎01224 635208
Website www.aberdeenartscentre.org.uk
Venue Manager *Arthur Deans*

Performances – mainly by local amateurs and
arts workshops in drama, music, art, dance and
creative writing – take place each summer during the school holidays.

Abergavenny Arts Festival

c/o T.I.C., Swan Meadows, Cross Street,
Abergavenny NP7 5HH
☎01873 857588 Fax 01873 850217
Email abergavenny.tic@monmouthshire.
  gov.uk

FOUNDED 1993. Annual two-week festival held
July/August in various venues in Abergavenny.
Programme includes music, drama, outdoor
concerts, creative writing workshops, poetry in
the street, storytelling, readings, children's
events, art exhibitions, gardens open, etc.
Programmes available at the end of May.

Aberystwyth Rich Text Literature Festival

Aberystwyth Arts Centre, Penglais,
Aberystwyth SY23 3DE
☎01970 622889/622883
Email lla@aber.ac.uk

FOUNDED 2000. Annual weekend festival held
in October (3rd to 6th in 2002). Previous guest
writers have included Robin Young, John
Stoddart and Menna Elfyn.

Aldeburgh Poetry Festival

Reading Room Yard, The Street, Brockdish,
Diss, Norfolk IP21 4JZ
☎01379 668345 Fax 01379 668844
Email aldeburghpoetry.trust@virgin.net
Website www.aldeburghpoetryfestival.org
Festival Director *Naomi Jaffa*

Now in its fourteenth year, an annual international festival of contemporary poetry held
on the first weekend of November in
Aldeburgh, attracting large audiences. Regular
features include a four-week residency leading
up to the festival, poetry readings, children's
event, workshops, public masterclass, lecture,
performance spot and the festival prize for the
year's best first collection (see entry under
Prizes). Also full fringe programme.

Arundel Festival

The Arundel Festival Society, 3 Castle Mews,
Tarrant Street, Arundel, West Sussex
BN18 9DG
☎01903 883690 Fax 01903 884243
Email arundelfestival@btopenworld.com
Website www.argonet.co.uk/arundel.festival
Festival Manager *Debbie Levenson*

Annual summer festival (23rd to 31st August in
2002). Events include small-scale theatre,
open-air theatre in Arundel Castle, concerts
with internationally known artists, jazz, visual
arts and active fringe.

Aspects Literature Festival

North Down Borough Council, Tower
House, 34 Quay Street, Bangor BT20 5ED
☎028 9127 8032 Fax 028 9146 7744
Festival Director *Kenneth Irvine*
Administrator *Paula Clamp*

FOUNDED 1992. 'Ireland's Premier Literary
Festival' is held at the end of September and
celebrates the richness and diversity of living
Irish writers with occasional special features on
past generations. It draws upon all disciplines
– fiction (of all types), poetry, theatre, non-
fiction, cinema, song-writing, etc. It also
includes a day of writing for young readers and
sends writers to visit local schools during the
festival. Highlights of recent festivals include
appearances by Bernard MacLaverty, Marion
Keyes, Alice Taylor, Frank Delaney, Seamus
Heaney, Brian Keenan and Fergal Keane.

Bath Fringe Festival

The Bell, 103 Walcot Street, Bath BA1 5BW
☎01225 480079 Fax 01225 480079
Email admin@bathfringe.co.uk
Website www.bathfringe.co.uk
Contact *Wendy Matthews*

FOUNDED 1981 to complement the international

music festival, the Fringe presents theatre, poetry, jazz, blues, comedy, cabaret, street performance and more in venues, parks and streets of Bath during late May and early June.

Bath Literature Festival
5 Broad Street, Bath BA1 5LJ
☎01225 462231 Fax 01225 445551
Festival Director *Nicola Bennett*
FOUNDED 1995. Annual festival (1–9 March in 2003). Wide range of debates, performances, storytelling, author discussions and workshops. Previous guests: Melvyn Bragg, A.S. Byatt, Louis de Bernières, Terry Jones, John McGahern, Iain Sinclair and Jeanette Winterson.

Belfast Festival at Queen's
Festival House, 25 College Gardens, Belfast BT9 6BS
☎028 9066 7687 Fax 028 9066 3733
Email festival@qub.ac.uk
Website www.belfastfestival.com
Director *Stella Hall*
FOUNDED 1964. Annual three-week festival held in the autumn. Organised by Queen's University in association with the **Arts Council of Northern Ireland**, the festival covers a wide variety of events, including literature. Programme available in September.

Between the Lines –
Belfast Literary Festival
Crescent Arts Centre, 2–4 University Road, Belfast BT7 1NH
☎028 9024 2338 Fax 028 9024 6748
Email info@crescentarts.org
Website www.crescentarts.org
Artistic Director *Jo Baker*
FOUNDED 1998. Annual 7–10-day international event held in March. Features readings, workshops, open platforms, quizzes and performance. All genres covered: playwriting, prose, poetry, screenwriting, etc. and special events for children. Previous guests include David Lodge, Lemn Sissay, Sheila O'Flanagan, Matthew Sweeney, Medbh McGuckian, Conor O'Callaghan, Merlin Holland, Ciaran Carson. Telephone to join free mailing list.

Beyond the Border International Storytelling Festival
St Donats Arts Centre, St Donats Castle, Vale of Glamorgan CF61 1WF
☎01446 799100 Fax 01446 799101
Email info@beyondtheborder.com
Website www.beyondtheborder.com
Festival Directors *David Ambrose, Ben Haggarty*
FOUNDED 1993. Annual event held over the first full weekend in July when storytellers from around the world gather in the grounds of a medieval cliff-top castle. Features formal and informal story sessions, ballad singing, storywalks, folk and world music, dance and a full programme of events for children.

Birmingham Book Festival
c/o Book Communications, Unit 116, The Custard Factory, Gibb Street, Birmingham B9 4AA
☎0121 246 2777/2770 Fax 0121 246 2771
Email info@bookcommunications.co.uk
Contacts *Helen Thomas, Jonathan Davidson*
FOUNDED 1999. Annual two-week-long festival held the last two weeks of October at various venues around Birmingham. Includes performances, lectures, discussion events, workshops.

Book Now!
The Arts Office, 1st Floor, Regal House, London Road, Twickenham TW1 3QB
☎020 8831 6138 Fax 020 8894 7568
Website www.richmond.gov.uk
FOUNDED 1992. Annual festival which runs throughout the month of November, administered by the Arts Section of Richmond Council. Principal focus is on poetry and serious fiction, but events also cover biography, writing for theatre, children's writing. Programme includes readings, discussions, workshops, debates, exhibitions, schools events. Writers to appear at past festivals include Beryl Bainbridge, Sally Beauman, Andrew Motion, A.S. Byatt, Penelope Lively, Benjamin Zephaniah, Roger McGough, Rose Tremain, John Mortimer, P.D. James and P.J. O'Rourke.

Bradford Book Festival
Central Library, Princes Way, Bradford, West Yorkshire BD1 1NN
☎01274 754096
Email tom.palmer@bradford.gov.uk
Contact *Tom Palmer*
FOUNDED 1999. Month-long festival coordinated by Bradford Libraries' Reader to Reader Project, held during May/June.

Brighton Festival
Festival Office, 12a Pavilion Buildings, Castle Square, Brighton, East Sussex BN1 1EE
☎01273 700747 Fax 01273 707505

Email info@brighton-festival.org.uk
Website www.brighton-festival.org.uk
Contact *General Manager*
FOUNDED 1966. For 24 days every May,
Brighton hosts England's largest mixed arts
festival. Music, dance, theatre, film, opera,
literature, comedy and exhibitions. Literary
enquiries will be passed to the literature officer.
Deadline October for following May.

Bristol Poetry Festival
The Poetry Can, Unit 11, 20–23 Hepburn
Road, Bristol BS2 8UD
☎0117 942 6976 Fax 0117 944 1478
Email festival@poetrycan.demon.co.uk
Website www.poetrycan.demon.co.uk
Festival Director *Hester Cockcroft*
FOUNDED 1996. Annual festival taking place
across the city every October. A celebration of
the best in contemporary poetry, from readings
and performances to cabaret and multimedia.
Local, national and international poetry is
showcased and explored in all its manifesta-
tions, with events for everyone including performances and workshops, competitions and
commissions, public poetry interventions,
community work and cross art form and digital
projects. Telephone for further details.

Broadstairs Dickens Festival
10 Lanthorne Road, Broadstairs, Kent
CT10 3NH
☎01843 861827
Website www.broadstairs.gov.uk/
   DickensFestivel.html
Organiser *Sylvia Hawkes*
FOUNDED 1937 to commemorate the 100th
anniversary of Charles Dickens' first visit to
Broadstairs in 1837, which he continued to visit
until 1859. The Festival lasts for eight days in
June and events include an opening gala concert,
a parade, a performance of a Dickens play
(*Sketches by Boz* in 2002), duels, melodramas,
Dickens readings, a Victorian cricket match,
Victorian bathing parties, talks, music hall, three-
day Victorian country fair. Costumed
Dickensian ladies in crinolines with top-hatted
escorts promenade during the week.

Canterbury Festival
Christ Church Gate, The Precincts,
Canterbury, Kent CT1 2EE
☎01227 452853 Fax 01227 781830
Email info@canterburyfestival.co.uk
Festival Director *Mark Deller*

FOUNDED 1984. Annual two-week festival
held in October (11th to 25th in 2003). A
mixed programme of events including concerts
in the cathedral by international artistes, opera,
dance, drama, jazz and folk, visual arts open-
house trail, community events and street
theatre, talks and walks.

The Cheltenham Festival of Literature
Town Hall, Imperial Square, Cheltenham,
Gloucestershire GL50 1QA
☎01242 263494 Fax 01242 256457
Email sarahsm@cheltenham.gov.uk
Website www.cheltenhamfestivals.co.uk
Festival Director *Sarah Smyth*
FOUNDED 1949. Annual festival held in
October. The first purely literary festival of its
kind, this festival has over the past decade
developed from an essentially local event into
the largest and most popular in Europe. A wide
range of events including talks and lectures,
poetry readings, novelists in conversation,
exhibitions, discussions and a large bookshop.

Chester Literature Festival
8 Abbey Square, Chester CH1 2HU
☎01244 319985 Fax 01244 341200
Chairman *John Scrivener*
FOUNDED 1989. Annual festival always held in
early October (5th to 20th in 2002). Events
include international and nationally known writers, as well as events by local literary groups.
There is a Literary Lunch, events for children,
workshops, competitions, etc. Free mailing list.

Children's Books Ireland – Annual Festival
See **Children's Books Ireland** under
Professional Associations and Societies

Dartington Literary Festival
See **Ways With Words**

Dorchester Festival
Dorchester Arts Centre, School Lane, The
Grove, Dorchester, Dorset DT1 1XR
☎01305 266926 Fax 01305 266926
Contact *Artistic Director*
FOUNDED 1996. A biennial four-day festival
over early May Bank Holiday weekend (next
to be held in 2004) which includes performing,
media and visual arts, with associated educational and community projects in the three
weeks around the Festival. Includes a wide

range of events, in many venues, for all age groups, including some literature and poetry.

The Daphne du Maurier Festival of Arts & Literature

Restormel Borough Council, Penwinnick Road, St Austell, Cornwall PL25 5DR
☎01726 223439

Annual festival, held in Fowey over ten days in May. Guests at the 2002 Festival included Iain Banks, Sally Beauman, Michael Holroyd, Helen Fielding, Bob Geldof and Tony Benn.

Dublin Writers' Festival

Dublin City Council Arts Office, 20 Parnell Square, Dublin 1, Republic of Ireland
☎00 353 1 872 2816 Fax 00 353 1 872 2933
Email info@dublinwritersfestival.com
Website www.dublinwritersfestival.com

Programme Director *Pat Boran*

Annual festival held in mid-June, including Bloomsday. Features readings, public interviews and discussions, along with a poetry slam and beginners' workshops. Major Irish and international poets and writers.

Dumfries and Galloway Arts Festival

Gracefield Arts Centre, 28 Edinburgh Road, Dumfries DG1 1JQ
☎01387 260447 Fax 01387 260447
Email dgartsfestival@ukgateway.net

Festival Organiser *Mrs Jill Hardy*

FOUNDED 1980. Annual week-long festival held at the end of May with a variety of events including classical and folk music, theatre, dance, literary events, exhibitions and children's events.

Durham Literature Festival

Durham City Arts, Byland Lodge, Hawthorn Terrace, Durham City DH1 4TD
☎0191 301 8245 Fax 0191 301 8821
Website www.durhamcityarts.demon.co.uk

Festival Coordinator *Alison Lister*

FOUNDED 1989. Annual 2–3-week festival held in June at various locations in the city. Performances plus workshops, cabaret, exhibitions and other events.

Edinburgh International Book Festival

Scottish Book Centre, 137 Dundee Street, Edinburgh EH11 1BG
☎0131 228 5444 Fax 0131 228 4333

Email admin@edbookfest.co.uk
Website www.edbookfest.co.uk

Director *Catherine Lockerbie*

FOUNDED 1983. Europe's largest and liveliest public book event, now taking place on an annual basis, is a 17-day event held during the Edinburgh International Festival. Presents an extensive programme for both adults and children including discussions, readings, lectures, demonstrations and workshops.

Exeter Festival

Festival Office, Civic Centre, Exeter, Devon EX1 1JN
☎01392 265200 Fax 01392 265366
Email lesley.waters@exeter.gov.uk
Website www.exeter.gov.uk/festival

Festival Organiser *Lesley Waters*

FOUNDED 1980. Annual two-week summer festival with a variety of events including concerts, theatre, dance and exhibitions.

Fife Festival of Authors

Fife Council Libraries – Central Area, Libraries HQ, East Fergus Place, Kirkcaldy, Fife KY1 1XT
☎01592 412930
Email david.spalding@fife.gov.uk

Contact *David Spalding*

FOUNDED 1996. Annual festival running in March/April for adults and children. Aims to bring the best of modern writing to the public as well as stimulate and foster creative writing within the local communities. Author readings, poetry events, writing workshops, literary competitions and dramatic presentations feature in the programme.

Frome Festival

10 The Retreat, Frome, Somerset BA11 5JU
☎01373 453889 Fax 01373 464912
Email fromefestival@ukonline.co.uk
Website www.fromefestival.co.uk

Festival Director *Martin Bax*

An annual festival held from the first Friday in July for ten days celebrating all aspects of visual and performing arts and entertainment. Features classical, jazz, folk and world music, film, drama and dance plus exhibitions of arts and crafts and a strong literary element. Previous guests: Fay Weldon and Brian Patten.

Graham Greene Festival

See **Graham Greene Birthplace Trust** under **Literary Societies**

Greenwich + Docklands Festivals

6 College Approach, London SE10 9HY
☎020 8305 1818 Fax 020 8305 1188
Email info@festival.org
Website www.festival.org

Director *Bradley Hemmings*

Greenwich + Docklands Festivals (GDF) is an arts development and festival production organisation working across east London in the boroughs of Greenwich, Tower Hamlets, Newham and Lewisham. GDF covers the International Festival, London's largest multi-arts festival in July which, in 2001, attracted 130,000 people; First Night, a celebration of New Year's Eve through the arts; and various training and education projects, including work with young people and a disability arts initiative, which takes place during the year.

The Guardian Hay Festival

Festival Office, Hay-on-Wye HR3 5BX
☎01497 821217 Fax 01497 821066
Website www.hayfestival.co.uk

Festival Director *Peter Florence*

FOUNDED 1988. Annual May festival sponsored by *The Guardian*. Guests have included Paul McCartney, Bill Clinton, Salman Rushdie, Toni Morrison, Stephen Fry, Joseph Heller, Carlos Fuentes, Maya Angelou, Amos Oz, Arthur Miller.

Guildford Book Festival

c/o Arts Office, University of Surrey, Guildford, Surrey GU2 5XH
☎01483 689167 Fax 01483 300803
Email book-festival-director@surrey.ac.uk
Website www.guildford.org.uk

Book Festival Director *Glenis Pycraft*

FOUNDED 1990. Held annually, during October/November. Two-week festival which includes workshops, poetry performances, children's events, competitions, literary lunches and teas. Its appeal lies in its diversity and its aim is to involve, instruct and entertain all who care about literature and to encourage in children a love of reading. In 2001, guest authors included Terry Waite, Douglas Hurd, Penny Vincenzi, Jenny Colgan, Kathy Lette, Ann Granger, Timothy West, John Drummond, Ranulph Fiennes, Fay Weldon, Anne Fine, Sandi Toksvig, Nigel Planer, George Melly, Tracy Chevalier, Jonathan Miller, Simon Callow, Louis de Bernières, Terry Pratchett and Sally Beauman.

Hallam Literature Festival and Book Fair

School of Cultural Studies, Sheffield Hallam University, 32 Colegiate Crescent Campus, Sheffield S10 2BP
☎0114 225 2228 Fax 0114 225 4403

Festival Coordinator *E.A. Markham*

FOUNDED 1997. The third festival was held in association with *Mslexia* magazine at Easter in 2002. Events featured 'Poet to Poet', and 'Writing the Life' discussions, and guests included Michele Roberts, Sean O'Brien, Penny Faith and Gareth Creer.

Haringey Literature Festival

Haringey Arts Council, The Chocolate Factory, Clarendon Road, London N22 6XJ
☎020 8365 7500 Fax 020 8365 8686
Email dana@haringeyartscouncil.org

Festival Organiser *Dana Captainino*

FOUNDED 1995. Annual festival. The programme is a mixture of poetry and literature in the form of readings, discussions, workshops and masterclasses. Writers at past festivals include: Diran Adebayo, Peter Lovesey, Michael Donaghy, Anna Pavord, Louis de Bernières, Nick Hornby, Blake Morrison, Bernice Rubens, James Kelman, Jean Binta Breeze, Beryl Bainbridge and Deborah Moggach.

Harrogate International Festival

1 Victoria Avenue, Harrogate, North Yorkshire HG1 1EQ
☎01423 562303 Fax 01423 521264
Email info@harrogate-festival.org.uk
Website www.harrogate-festival.org.uk

Festival Director *William Culver-Dodds*
Festival Manager *Fiona Goh*

FOUNDED 1966. Annual two-week festival at the end of July and beginning of August. Events include international symphony orchestras, chamber concerts, ballet, celebrity recitals, contemporary dance, opera, drama, jazz, comedy plus an international street theatre festival.

Hastings International Poetry Festival

'The Snoring Cat', 16 Marianne Park, Dudley Road, Hastings, East Sussex TN35 5PU

Contact *Josephine Austin*

FOUNDED 1968. Annual weekend poetry festival held in November in the Sussex Hall, White Rock Theatre, Hastings. Runs the Hastings National Poetry Competition; entry forms available from the address above.

The Hay Festival
See **The Guardian Hay Festival**

Hebden Bridge Arts Festival
c/o Tourist Information Centre, West End,
Hebden Bridge, West Yorkshire HX7 9EX
☎01422 842684
Email hbartsfestival@hotmail.com
Website www.hebdenbridge.co.uk/festival
Contact *Enid Stephenson*

FOUNDED 1994. Annual arts festival with
increasingly strong adult and children's literature events. Previous guest writers include
Roger McGough, Benjamin Zephaniah, Carol
Ann Duffy, Juliet Barker, Jacqueline Wilson,
Anthony Browne, Ian McMillan, Adele Geras.

Hull Literature Festival
See **The Humber Mouth**

Humber Mouth –
Hull Literature Festival
City Arts Unit, Central Library, Albion Street,
Kingston upon Hull HU1 3TF
☎01482 616875/6 Fax 01482 616827
Email humber.mouth@hullcc.gov.uk
Website www.humbermouth.org.uk
Contact *City Arts Unit*

FOUNDED 1992. Annual festival running in
November. Features an array of readings, performances and workshops by writers and artists
from around the world and from the city.

Ilkley Literature Festival
The Manor House, Ilkley, West Yorkshire
LS29 9DT
☎01943 601210 Fax 01943 817079
Email admin@ilkleyliteraturefestival.org.uk
Website www.ilkleyliteraturefestival.org.uk
Director *Dominic Gregory*

FOUNDED 1973. Major literature festival in the
north with events running throughout the
year. Large-scale annual festival each October.
Recent guests: A.S. Byatt, Germaine Greer,
V.S. Naipaul, Tony Parsons and Will Self.
Telephone or e-mail to join free mailing list.

The International Festival of Mountaineering Literature
University of Leeds, Bretton Hall Campus,
Wakefield, West Yorkshire WF4 4LG
☎01924 830261 Fax 01924 832018
Email tgifford@leeds.ac.uk
Website www.terrygifford.co.uk
Director *Terry Gifford*

FOUNDED 1987. Annual one-day festival held
at the end of November celebrating recent
books, commissioning new writing, overviews
of national literatures, debates of issues, book
signings, discussion with Chair of Judges of the
adjudication of the annual **Boardman Tasker
Award** for the best mountaineering book of
the year. Announces the winner of the festival
writing competition run in conjunction with
High magazine. Write to join free mailing list.

International Playwriting Festival
Warehouse Theatre, Dingwall Road,
Croydon CR0 2NF
☎020 8681 1257 Fax 020 8688 6699
Email warehous@dircon.co.uk
Website www.warehousetheatre.co.uk
Festival Administrator *Rose Marie Vernon*

FOUNDED 1985. Annual competition for full-length unperformed plays, judged by a panel of
theatre professionals. Finalists given rehearsed
readings during the festival week in November.
Entries welcome from all parts of the world.
Scripts plus two s.a.e.s (one script-sized) should
reach the theatre by the end of June, accompanied by an entry form (available from the
theatre). Previous winners produced at the
theatre include: Kevin Hood *Beached*; Ellen Fox
*Conversations with George Sandburgh After a Solo
Flight Across the Atlantic*; Guy Jenkin *Fighting for
the Dunghill*; James Martin Charlton *Fat Souls*;
Peter Moffat *Iona Rain*; Dino Mahoney *YoYo*;
Simon Smith *Fat Janet is Dead*; Dominic McHale
The Resurrectionists; Philip Edwards *51 Peg*;
Roumen Shomov *The Dove*; Maggie Nevill *The
Shagaround*; Andrew Shakeshaft *Just Sitting*.
Shares plays with its partner festival in Italy, the
Premio Candoni Arta Terme.

Isle of Man Literature Festival
Isle of Man Arts Council, 10 Villa Marina
Arcade, Douglas, Isle of Man IM1 2HN
☎01624 611316 Fax 01624 615423
Email maddrell@artscounciliom.
freeserve.co.uk
Contact *Arts Development Manager*

FOUNDED 1997. Annual festival of literature,
poetry and music. The 2002 Festival takes
place from 10th to 13th October when the
guests will include Gervaise Phinn, Nick
Toczek and Christopher Cook.

Kent Literature Festival
The Metropole Galleries, The Leas,
Folkestone, Kent CT20 2LS
☎01303 255070

Festival Director *Nick Ewbank*
FOUNDED 1980. Annual week-long festival of readings, performances, talks, screenings, book launches, debates, signings and special events. The 2002 Festival will be held from 23rd to 29th September.

King's Lynn, The Fiction Festival
19 Tuesday Market Place, King's Lynn, Norfolk PE30 1JW
☎01553 691661 (office hours) or 761919
Fax 01553 691779
Contact *Anthony Ellis*
FOUNDED 1989. Annual weekend festival held in March. Over the weekend there are readings and discussions, attended by guest writers of which there are usually eight. Guests at the 2002 festival included Beryl Bainbridge, Nina Bawden, D.J. Taylor, Emma Richler, Michel Faber, Andrew O'Hagan, Georgina Hammick, Jane Rogers, Andrew Cowan and Ali Smith.

King's Lynn, The Poetry Festival
19 Tuesday Market Place, King's Lynn, Norfolk PE30 1JW
☎01553 691661 (office hours) or 761919
Fax 01553 691779
Contact *Anthony Ellis*
FOUNDED 1985. Annual weekend festival held at the end of September (27th to 29th in 2002), with guest poets (usually eight). Previous guests have included Carol Ann Duffy, Paul Durcan, Gavin Ewart, Peter Porter, Stephen Spender. Events include readings and discussion panels and the presentation of the King's Lynn Award; current Laureate is C.K. Stead.

Lancaster LitFest
Sun Street Studios, 23–29 Sun Street, Lancaster LA11 1EW
☎01524 62166 Fax 01524 841216
Email andy.darby@litfest.org
Website www.litfest.org
FOUNDED 1978. Regional Literature Development Agency, organising workshops, readings, residencies, publications. Year-round programme of literature-based events and annual festival in October featuring a wide range of writers from the UK and overseas. Organises annual poetry competition with winners receiving cash prizes and anthology publication.

Ledbury Poetry Festival
Town Council Offices, Church Lane, Ledbury, Herefordshire HR8 1DH
☎01531 634156

Email info@poetry-festival.com
Website www.poetry-festival.com
Contact *Charles Bennett*
FOUNDED 1997. Annual ten-day festival held in July. Includes readings, discussions, workshops, exhibitions, music and walks. There are also writers in residence at local schools and residential homes, a national poetry competition and the Town Party. Past guests have included Andrew Motion, Benjamin Zephaniah, Simon Armitage, Roger McGough, John Hegley and Germaine Greer. Full programme available in May.

Leicester Literature Festival
See **Words Out**

Lichfield International Arts Festival
7 The Close, Lichfield, Staffordshire WS13 7LD
☎01543 306270 Fax 01543 306274
Email lichfieldfest@lichfield-arts.org.uk
Website www.lichfieldfestival.org
Festival Director *Meurig Bowen*
FOUNDED 1982. Annual July festival with events taking place in the 13th century Cathedral, Guildhall and Hawksyard Priory as well as various country churches and outdoor venues. Mainly music but also includes literary events such as schools poetry competitions, talks and lectures. Lichfield is the birthplace of Samuel Johnson and Johnson-related events feature strongly in the festival programme.

City of London Festival
230 Bishopsgate, London EC2M 4HW
☎020 7377 0540 Fax 020 7377 1972
Email admin@colf.org
Website www.colf.org
Director *Kathryn McDowell*
FOUNDED 1962. Annual three-week festival held in June and July. Features over fifty classical and popular music events alongside poetry and prose readings, street theatre and open-air extravaganzas, in some of the most outstanding performance spaces in the world.

London New Play Festival
40/7 Altenburg Gardens, London SW11 1JW
☎07050 641959 Fax 07050 642929
Website www.lnpf.co.uk
Literary Manager *Julia Parr*
Education Director *Christopher Preston*
FOUNDED 1989. Annual festival of new plays

held in venues around London each September, centring on a short play platform season held in the West End in association with Really Useful Theatres. LNPF specialises in developing and producing new plays, normally working with early career playwrights. As well as the annual festival, LNPF stages education and production programmes throughout the year. Full information can be found on the website. Script submissions should be sent to *Julia Parr* at the address above.

Lowdham Book Festival

Mansfield Library, Westgate, Mansfield, Nottinghamshire NG18 1NH
☎01623 647229 Fax 01623 629276
Email ross.bradshaw@nottsscc.gov.uk

Contact *Ross Bradshaw*

FOUNDED 1999. Annual week-long festival combining a village fête atmosphere with that of a major literature festival. Guests have included Carol Anne Duffy, Pete McCarthy, Ian McMillan, Alan Sillitoe, Jackie Kay, Sarah Harrison and Carole Blake. Talks on everything from St Kilda to the Jewish roots of rock 'n' roll. Free mailing list includes *County Lit* magazine.

Ludlow Festival

Castle Square, Ludlow, Shropshire SY8 1AY
☎01584 875070 (Admin)/872150 (Box Office) Fax 01584 877673
Email info@ludlowfestival.co.uk
Website www.ludlowfestival.co.uk

Contact *Festival Administrator*

FOUNDED 1959. Annual two-week festival held in the last week of June and first week of July with an open-air Shakespeare production held at Ludlow Castle and a varied programme of events including recitals, opera, dance, popular and classical concerts, literary and historical lectures.

Manchester Festival of Writing

Manchester Central Library, St Peter's Square, Manchester M2 5PD
☎0161 234 1981
Email janem@libraries.manchester.gov.uk

Contact *Jane Mathieson*

FOUNDED 1990. An annual event organised by Manchester Libraries and Commonword community publishers. It consists of a short programme of practical writing workshops on specific themes/genres run by well-known writers. Attendance at all workshops is free to Manchester residents.

Manchester Poetry Festival

114 Fog Lane, Didsbury, Manchester M20 6SP
☎0161 438 0550 Fax 0161 438 0660
Email mpf@dial.pipex.com

Contact *Richard Michael*

Held in the autumn (2nd to 10th November in 2002), the Festival aims to bring the world's best poets to Manchester and promote Manchester poets to the rest of the world. Includes workshops and events for children.

Mere Literary Festival

Lawrence's, Old Hollow, Mere, Wiltshire BA12 6EG
☎01747 860475/861211 (Tourist Information)

Contact *Adrienne Howell*

FOUNDED 1997. Annual festival held in the second week of October in aid of registered charity, The Mere & District Linkscheme. Events include readings, quiz, workshop, writer's lunch and talks. Finale is adjudication of the festival's writing competition (see entry under **Prizes**) and presentation of awards.

Mole Valley Literature Festival

See **Wordswork**

National Association of Writers' Groups (NAWG) Open Festival of Writing

The Arts Centre, Washington, Tyne & Wear NE38 2AB
☎0191 416 9751
Email briannawgfestival@yahoo.co.uk
Website www.nawg.co.uk

Festival Administrator *Brian Lister*

FOUNDED 1997. Annual festival held at St Aidan's College, University of Durham in September or October. Three days of creative writing tuition covering poetry, short and long fiction, playwriting, journalism, TV sitcom and many other subjects all led by professional writer-tutors. 36 workshops, 32 surgeries plus seminars and fringe events. Saturday gala dinner and awards ceremony. Full- or part-residential weekend, or single workshops only. Open to all, no qualifications or NAWG membership required.

National Eisteddfod of Wales

40 Parc Ty Glas, Llanishen, Cardiff CF14 5WU
☎029 2076 3777 Fax 029 2076 3737
Website www.eisteddfod.org.uk

The National Eisteddfod, held in August, is the

largest arts festival in Wales, attracting over 170,000 visitors during the week-long celebration of more than 800 years of tradition. Competitions, bardic ceremonies and concerts.

National Student Drama Festival
See **University of Hull** under **Writers' Courses, Circles and Workshops**

Norfolk and Norwich Festival
42–58 St George's Street, Norwich, Norfolk NR3 1AB
☎01603 614921 Fax 01603 632303
Email info@n-joy.org.uk
Website www.n-joy.org.uk
Festival Director *Peter Bolton*
FOUNDED 1772, this performing arts festival is the second oldest in the UK. Held annually in May, the festival includes talks by writers along with poetry and storytelling events.

Northern Children's Book Festival
Durham Clayport Library, Millennium Place, Durham DH1 1WA
☎0191 386 4003
Secretary *Carol Attewell* (at address above)
FOUNDED 1984. Annual two-week festival during November. Events in schools and libraries for children in the North East region. One Saturday during the festival sees the staging of a large book event hosted by one of the local authorities involved.

Off the Page Literature Festival
County Library Support Services, Glaisdale Parkway, Nottingham NG8 4GP
☎0115 985 4242 Fax 0115 928 6400
Email pam.middleton@nottscc.gov.uk
Contact *Pam Middleton*
Author visits aimed at making authors accessible to readers. In 2002 the series takes place at Nottingham Central Library in November. Programme available from late summer/early autumn.

Off the Shelf Literature Festival
Central Library, Surrey Street, Sheffield S1 1XZ
☎0114 273 4716/4400 Fax 0114 273 5009
Email off-the-shelf@pop3.poptel.org.uk
Website www.offtheshelf.org.uk
Festival Organisers *Maria de Souza, Susan Walker*
FOUNDED 1992. Annual two-week festival

held during the last fortnight in October. Lively and diverse mix of readings, workshops, children's events, storytelling and competitions. Previous guests have included Bill Bryson, Doris Lessing, Benjamin Zephaniah, Terry Pratchett, Michael Palin, Carol Ann Duffy and Louis de Bernières.

Oxford Literary Festival
301 Woodstock Road, Oxford OX2 7NY
☎01865 514149 Fax 01865 514804
Email oxford.literary.festival@ntlworld.com
Directors *Sally Dunsmore, Angela Prysor-Jones*
FOUNDED 1997. Annual four-day festival held two weekends prior to Easter. Authors speaking about their books, covering a wide variety of writing: fiction, poetry, biography, travel, food, gardening, children's art. Previous guests have included William Boyd, Andrew Motion, Candia McWilliam, Beryl Bainbridge, Sophie Grigson, Jamie McKendrick, Bernard O'Donoghue, Philip Pullman and Korky Paul.

The Round Festival
c/o Word And Action (Dorset), 75 High Street, Wimborne, Dorset BH21 1HS
☎01202 883197 Fax 01202 881061
Email info@roundfestival.org.uk
Website www.roundfestival.org.uk
Contact *Anne Jennings*
FOUNDED 1990. International festival of theatre-in-the-round held in July offering a variety of workshops and performances celebrating and exploring the form. Programme includes performances and playreading (including new plays) in the round.

Royal Court Young Writers Programme
The Site, Royal Court Theatre, Sloane Square, London SW1W 8AS
☎020 7565 5050 Fax 020 7565 5001
Email ywp@royalcourttheatre.com
Website www.royalcourttheatre.com
Associate Director *Ola Animashawun*
Open to young people up to the age of 25. The YWP focuses on the process of playwriting by running a series of writers groups throughout the year at its base in Sloane Square. Additionally the YWP welcomes unsolicited scripts from all young writers from across the country. 'We are always looking for scripts for development and possible production (not film scripts).'

Royal Festival Hall
Literature & Talks
Performing Arts Department, Royal Festival Hall, London SE1 8XX
☎020 7921 0906 Fax 020 7928 2049
Email shoare@rfh.org.uk
Website www.sbc.org.uk

Head of Literature & Talks *Ruth Borthwick*

The Royal Festival Hall presents a year-round literature programme covering all aspects of writing. Regular series range from A Life Indeed! to Fiction International and there are two biennial festivals: Poetry International and Imagine: Writers and Writing for Children. Literature events are now programmed in the Voice Box, Purcell Room and Queen Elizabeth Hall. To join the free mailing list, ☎020 7921 0971 or e-mail: Literature&Talks @rfh.org.uk

Rye Festival
PO Box 33, Rye, East Sussex TN31 7YB
☎01797 224982

Artistic Director *David Willison*

FOUNDED 1972. Annual two-week September event, plus short winter series. Variety of events with strong emphasis on literature (nominated by the *Independent on Sunday* as one of ten best British festivals), classical and modern music, visual arts, workshops and masterclasses. Write or phone to join free mailing list.

Salisbury Festival
Festival Office, 75 New Street, Salisbury, Wiltshire SP1 2PH
☎01722 332241 Fax 01722 410552
Email info@salisburyfestival.co.uk
Website www.salisburyfestival.co.uk

Director *Trevor Davies*

FOUNDED 1972. Annual festival held at the end of May/beginning of June, including classical music, theatre, jazz and exhibitions.

The Scottish Book Town Festival
Book Town Office, 26 South Main Street, Wigtown DG8 9EH
☎01988 402036 Fax 01988 402506
Email booktown-wigit@btinternet.com
Website www.wigtown-booktown.co.uk

Contact *Jennifer Bradley*

FOUNDED 1999. A rural literary festival which takes place annually at the end of September over three days in Wigtown town centre,

many of the town's 16 bookshops and the nearby Bladnoch Distillery. Authors' readings including children's authors, debates, poetry, music and film.

Southwold Festival
See **Ways with Words**

Stoke Newington Festival
Old Town Hall, Stoke Newington Church Street, London N16 0JR
☎020 8356 6410 Fax 020 8356 6435
Email fiona@stokenewingtonfestival.co.uk
Website www.stokenewingtonfestival.co.uk

Programme Producer *Fiona Fieber*

FOUNDED 1993. The 2002 Festival, held over ten days in June, featured WordontheStreet, a one-day programme of literature, text, spoken word and artistic interventions to do with the Word, held in Stoke Newington Church Street. Other literature events featured Writers Surgery, Poetry Workout and Turkish Storytelling for Children.

Stratford-upon-Avon
Poetry Festival
The Shakespeare Centre, Henley Street, Stratford-upon-Avon, Warwickshire CV37 6QW
☎01789 204016/292176 (Box office)
Fax 01789 296083
Email director@shakespeare.org.uk

Festival Director *Roger Pringle*

FOUNDED 1953. Annual festival held on Sunday evenings during July and August. Readings by poets and professional actors.

Swansea Festivals
Dylan Thomas Centre, Somerset Place, Swansea SA1 1RR
☎01792 463980 Fax 01792 463993
Email dylan.thomas@cableol.co.uk
Website www.dylanthomas.org

Contact *David Woolley*

Wordplay (2nd to 7th October): seventh annual festival of literature and arts for young people. The Dylan Thomas Celebration (27th October to 9th November) is two weeks of performances, talks, lectures, films, music, poetry, exhibitions and celebrity guests.

Swindon Festival of Literature
Lower Shaw Farm, Shaw, Swindon, Wiltshire SN5 9PJ
☎01793 771080 Fax 01793 771080

Email swindonlitfest@lsfarm.globalnet.co.uk
Website www.swindonlink.com
Festival Director *Matt Holland*
FOUNDED 1994. Annual festival held in May, starting with 'Dawn Chorus' at sunrise on May Day. Includes a wide range of authors, speakers, discussions, performances and workshops, plus the Clive Brain Memorial Lecture and the Swindon Performance Poetry Slam competition.

The Dylan Thomas Celebration
See **Swansea Festivals**

Warwick & Leamington Festival
Warwick Arts Society, Northgate, Warwick CV34 4JL
☎01926 410747   Fax 01926 407606
Email admin@warwickarts.org.uk
Website www.welcome.to/warwickarts.org.uk
Festival Director *Richard Phillips*
FOUNDED 1980. Annual festival lasting 12 days in the first half of July (2nd to 13th in 2003). Basically a chamber and early music festival, with some open-air, large-scale concerts in Warwick Castle, the Festival also promotes plays by Shakespeare in historical settings. Large-scale education programme. Interested in increasing its literary content, both in performances and workshops.

Warwick Literary Weekend
Warwick Events Group, Northgate, Warwick CV34 4JL
☎01926 497000   Fax 01926 407606
Email admin@warwickarts.org.uk
Website www.WarwickLive.com

A new venture to be launched over the weekend of 4th/6th October 2002. Plans to be annual at that time and feature both living writers and those who have had connections with Warwick – Tolkien, Larkin and Landor in particular. Based on The Dream Factory, Bridge House Theatre, St Mary's Church, the Lord Leycester Hospital and other historic buildings. Also workshops and education programme.

Ways with Words
Droridge Farm, Dartington, Totnes, Devon TQ9 6JQ
☎01803 867373   Fax 01803 863688
Email admin@wayswithwords.co.uk
Website www.wayswithwords.co.uk
Festival Director *Kay Dunbar*
Ways with Words runs a major literature festival at Dartington Hall in south Devon for ten days in July each year (11th to 21st in 2003). Features over 200 writers giving lectures, readings, interviews, discussions, performances, masterclasses and workshops.

Also, Words by the Water, a Cumbrian literature festival held in Keswick. The 2003 festival runs from 18th to 23rd March. There is a regular festival in held in Southwold, Suffolk (provisional dates for 2003 are 13th to 18th November). Organises writing, reading and painting courses in Italy.

Wellington Literary Festival
Civic Offices, Larkin Way, Tan Bank, Wellington, Telford, Shropshire TF1 1LX
☎01952 222935   Fax 01952 222936
Email WellTownCl@aol.com
Website www.wellington-shropshire.gov.uk
Contact *Derrick Drew*
FOUNDED 1997. Annual festival held throughout October. Events include story telling, writers' forum, 'Pints and Poetry', children's poetry competition, story competition, theatre review and guest speakers.

Wells Festival of Literature
Tower House, St Andrew Street, Wells, Somerset BA5 2UN
☎01749 673385   Fax 01749 673385
Website www.somersite.co.uk/wellsfest.htm
Contact *Pamela Egan*
FOUNDED 1992. Annual weekend-plus festival held at the end of October. Main venue is the historic, moated Bishop's Palace. A wide range of speakers caters for different tastes in reading; previous guests: Douglas Hurd, Eric Newby, Elizabeth Jennings, P.D. James, Anthony Howard, Terry Pratchett, Joan Aiken. Short story and poetry competitions and writing workshops are run in conjunction with the Festival.

Wessex Poetry Festival
38 Hod View, Stourpaine, Blandford Forum, Dorset DT11 8TN
☎01258 456803
Email esp@euphony.net
Website www.wanderingdog.co.uk
Festival Director *David Caddy*
FOUNDED 1995. Annual international poetry

festival held at the end of October, organised by David Caddy and friends. Previous guests have included Irina Ratushinskaya, Michele Roberts, Iain Sinclair, Jon Silkin, Ketaki Kushari Dyson, Jim Burns, Jay Ramsay, Edwin Morgan, Pansy Maurer-Alvarez, Julian Bell.

WordontheStreet
See **Stoke Newington Festival**

Wordplay
See **Swansea Festivals**

Words by the Water
See **Ways with Words**

'Words Live' Literature Festival
London Borough of Harrow, Arts and Leisure Service, Civic Centre, PO Box 22, Milton House, Station Road, Harrow, Middlesex HA1 2UW
☎020 8424 1076 Fax 020 8424 1817
Website www.Harrow.gov.uk
Festival Organiser *Arts Development Officer*
FOUNDED 1999. Annual two-week community based literature festival held in March, combining readings from established authors with workshops and innovative literature development activities for all ages. Previous guests have included: Courttia Newland, Bernadine Everisto, Alexie Sayle, Ian McEwan, Leslie Glaister, Deborah Moggach, E.A. Markham, Dotun Adebayo and Claire Rayner. The festival is part of a year-long development programme.

Words Out –
Leicester Literature Festival
Leicester City Council, Arts and Leisure, Block A, New Walk Centre, Welford Place, Leicester LE1 6ZG
☎0116 252 7347
Email libraries@leicester.gov.uk
Literature Development Officer *Sarah Butler*
Biannual festival held in October. A mixture of author events, workshops, profiles of community arts and spotlights on local writing held in a range of community/library/arts venues around the city.

Words Work
See **Northamptonshire Libraries & Information Service** under **Library Services**

Wordswork – Mole Valley Literature Festival
Mole Valley Leisure Services, Pippbrook, Dorking, Surrey RH4 1SJ
☎01273 478943 Fax 01273 478943
Email jo@koenig48.freeserve.co.uk
Literature Development Worker *Jo König*
A festival which celebrates literary talent both past and present throughout the Mole Valley. Includes a programme of readings, workshops, exhibitions, storytelling, performance poetry, children's and young people's events. Dedicated to encouraging, promoting and developing literature in its broadest sense. Initiates sustainable literary projects for all the community.

European Publishers

Austria

Springer-Verlag KG
PO Box 89, A–1200 Vienna
☎00 43 1 3302415 Fax 00 43 1 3302426
Website www.springer.at
FOUNDED 1924. *Publishes* anthropology, architecture, art, business, chemistry, computer science, communications, electronics, economics, education, environmental studies, engineering, law, maths, dentistry, medicine, nursing, philosophy, physics, psychology, technology and general science.

Verlag Carl Ueberreuter GmbH
Postfach 306, A–1091 Vienna
☎00 43 1 404440 Fax 00 43 1 404445
Website www.ueberreuter.de
FOUNDED 1548. *Publishes* fiction and general non-fiction: art, government, history, economics, political science, general science, health and nutrition, science fiction, fantasy, music and dance.

Paul Zsolnay Verlag GmbH
Postfach 142, A–1041 Vienna
☎00 43 1 50576610 Fax 00 43 1 505766110
Website www.zsolnay.at
FOUNDED 1923. *Publishes* biography, fiction, general non-fiction, history, poetry.

Belgium

Brepols Publishers NV
Begijnhof 67, 2300 Turnhout
☎00 32 14 448020 Fax 00 32 14 428919
FOUNDED 1796. *Publishes* academic monographs and collections in the humanities.

Facet NV
Willem Linnigstr 13, 2060 Antwerp
☎00 32 3 2274028 Fax 00 32 3 2273792
FOUNDED 1986. *Publishes* children's books.

Uitgeverij Lannoo NV
Kasteelstr 97, B-8700 Tielt
☎00 32 51 424211 Fax 00 32 51 401152
Website www.lannoo.com

FOUNDED 1909. *Publishes* general non-fiction, art, architecture and interior design, cookery, biography, economics, gardening, health, history, management, nutrition, photography, self-help, poetry, government, political science, religion, travel.

Standaard Uitgeverij
Belgiëlei 147a, 2018 Antwerp
☎00 32 3 2395900 Fax 00 32 3 2308550
Website www.standard.com
FOUNDED 1919. *Publishes* education, fiction, humour.

Denmark

Forlaget Apostrof ApS
Postboks 2580, DK–2100 Copenhagen O
☎00 45 39 208420 Fax 00 45 39 208453
Website www.apostrof.dk
FOUNDED 1980. *Publishes* psychology and psychiatry.

Aschehoug Dansk Forlag A/S
PO Box 2179, DK–1017 Copenhagen K
☎00 45 33 305522 Fax 00 45 33 305822
Website www.aschehoug.dk
FOUNDED 1977. Part of the Egmont Group. *Publishes* fiction, biography, cookery, health, how-to, maritime and nutrition.

Borgens Forlag A/S
Valbygardsvej 33, DK–2500 Valby
☎00 45 36 153615 Fax 00 45 36 153616
Website www.borgens.dk
FOUNDED 1948. *Publishes* fiction, literature, literary criticism, general non-fiction, art, crafts, education, environmental studies, essays, games, hobbies, health, nutrition, humour, music, dance, philosophy, poetry, psychology, psychiatry, religion.

Egmont Lademann A/S
Gerdasgade 37, DK–2500 Valby
☎00 45 36 156600 Fax 00 45 36 441162
Website www.egmont.com
FOUNDED 1954. *Publishes* general illustrated non-fiction, fiction and children's books.

Egmont Wangel AS
Gerdasgade 37, DK–2500 Valby
☎00 45 36 156600 Fax 00 45 36 441162
Website www.egmont.com
FOUNDED 1946. *Publishes* commercial fiction.

Forum Publishers
Snaregade 4, DK–1205 Copenhagen K
☎00 45 33 147714 Fax 00 45 33 147791

FOUNDED 1940. *Publishes* fiction and mysteries.

GEC Gads Forlags Aktieselskab
Vimmelskaftet 32, DK–1161 Copenhagen K
☎00 45 33 150558 Fax 00 45 33 110800

FOUNDED 1855. *Publishes* general non-fiction, biological sciences, cookery, crafts, games, economics, education, English as a second language, environmental studies, gardening, history, mathematics, natural history, physics, plants, travel.

Gyldendalske Boghandel- Nordisk Forlag A/S
Klareboderne 3, DK–1001 Copenhagen K
☎00 45 33 755555 Fax 00 45 33 755556
Website www.gyldendal.dk
FOUNDED 1770. *Publishes* fiction, art, biography, dance, dentistry, education, history, how-to, medicine, music, poetry, nursing, philosophy, psychology, psychiatry, general and social sciences, sociology.

Hekla Forlag
Valbygaardsvej 33, DK–2500 Valby
☎00 45 36 153615 Fax 00 45 36 153616
FOUNDED 1979. *Publishes* general fiction and non-fiction.

Høst & Søns Publishers Ltd
PO Box 2212, DK–1018 Copenhagen K
☎00 45 33 382888 Fax 00 45 33 382898
FOUNDED 1836. *Publishes* fiction, crafts, environmental studies, games, hobbies, regional interests, travel.

Lindhardt og Ringhof
Frederiksborggade 1, DK–1360 Copenhagen K
☎00 45 33 695000 Fax 00 45 33 695001
FOUNDED 1971. *Publishes* fiction and general non-fiction.

Munksgaard International Publishers Ltd
PO Box 2148, DK–1016 Copenhagen K
☎00 45 77 127030 Fax 00 45 77 129387

Website www.munksgaard.dk
FOUNDED 1917. *Publishes* dentistry, medicine, nursing, psychology, psychiatry, general science.

Nyt Nordisk Forlag Arnold Busck A/S
Købmagergade 49, DK–1150 Copenhagen K
☎00 45 33 733575 Fax 00 45 33 733576
Website www.nytnordiskforlag.dk

FOUNDED 1896. *Publishes* fiction, art, biography, dance, dentistry, history, how-to, music, philosophy, religion, medicine, nursing, psychology, psychiatry, general and social sciences, sociology.

Samlerens Forlag A/S
Snaregade 4/1, DK–1205 Copenhagen K
☎00 45 33 131023 Fax 00 45 33 144314

FOUNDED 1942. *Publishes* essays, fiction, government, history, literature, literary criticism, political science.

Det Schønbergske Forlag
Landemaerket 5, DK–1119 Copenhagen K
☎00 45 33 733585 Fax 00 45 33 733586

FOUNDED 1857. *Publishes* art, biography, fiction, history, humour, philosophy, poetry, psychology, psychiatry, travel

Spektrum Forlagsaktieselskab
Snaregade 4, DK–1205 Copenhagen K
☎00 45 33 147714 Fax 00 45 33 147791
FOUNDED 1990. *Publishes* general non-fiction.

Tiderne Skifter Forlag A/S
Pilestraede 51/5, DK–1001 Copenhagen K
☎00 45 33 325772 Fax 00 45 33 144205

FOUNDED 1979. *Publishes* fiction, literature and literary criticism, essays, ethnicity, photography, behavioural sciences.

Finland

Gummerus Publishers
PO Box 749, SF–00101 Helsinki
☎00 358 9 584301 Fax 00 358 9 58430200

FOUNDED 1872. *Publishes* fiction, general non-fiction and textbooks.

Karisto Oy
PO Box 102, SF–13101 Hämeenlinna
☎00 358 3 6161551 Fax 00 358 3 6161565

FOUNDED 1900. *Publishes* fiction and general non-fiction.

Kirjayhtymä Oy
Urho Kekkosen Katu 4–6E, SF–00100 Helsinki
☎00 358 9 6937641 Fax 00 358 9 69376366
Website www.kirjayhtyma.fi
FOUNDED 1958. *Publishes* fiction and general
non-fiction.

Otava Publishing Co. Ltd
PO Box 134, SF–00121 Helsinki
☎00 358 9 19961 Fax 00 358 9 643136
Website www.otava.fi
FOUNDED 1890. *Publishes* fiction, general non-
fiction, how-to.

Werner Söderström Osakeyhtiö (WSOY)
PO Box 222, SF–00121 Helsinki
☎00 358 9 61681 Fax 00 358 9 6168467
FOUNDED 1878. *Publishes* fiction, general non-
fiction, education.

Tammi Publishers
PO Box 410, SF–00101 Helsinki
☎00 358 9 6937621 Fax 00 358 9 69376266
Website www.tammi.net
FOUNDED 1943. *Publishes* fiction, general non-
fiction.

France

Editions Arthaud SA
26 rue Racine, F–75006 Paris Cedex 06
☎00 33 1 4051 3008 Fax 00 33 1 4325 0118
FOUNDED 1890. Imprint of **Flammarion SA**.
Publishes art, history, literature, literary criticism, essays, sport, travel.

Editions Belfond
12 avenue d'Italie, F–75627 Paris
☎00 33 1 4416 0500 Fax 00 33 1 4416 0505
FOUNDED 1963. *Publishes* fiction, literature, literary criticism, essays, mysteries, romance,
poetry, general non-fiction, art, biography,
dance, health, history, how-to, music, nutrition.

Editions Bordas
21 rue Saint-Suplice, F–75006 Paris Cedex 06
☎00 33 1 4325 0451 Fax 00 33 1 4325 4784
FOUNDED 1946. *Publishes* education and general non-fiction.

Editions Calmann-Lévy SA
3 rue Auber, F–75009 Paris
☎00 33 1 4742 3833 Fax 00 33 1 4742 7781
FOUNDED 1836. Part of **Hachette-Livre**.

Publishes fiction, science fiction, fantasy, biography, history, humour, economics, philosophy, psychology, psychiatry, social sciences,
sociology, sport.

Editions Denoël Sàrl
9 rue du Cherche-Midi, F–75006 Paris
☎00 33 1 4439 7373 Fax 00 33 1 4439 7390
FOUNDED 1932. *Publishes* art, economics, fiction, science fiction, fantasy, government, history, philosophy, political science, psychology,
psychiatry.

Librairie Arthème Fayard
75 rue des Saints-Pères, F–75278 Paris
Cedex 06
☎00 33 1 4549 8200 Fax 00 33 1 4222 4017
FOUNDED 1854. *Publishes* biography, fiction,
history, dance, music, philosophy, religion,
social sciences, sociology, general science,
technology.

Flammarion SA
26 rue Racine, F–75006 Paris Cedex 06
☎00 33 1 4051 3008 Fax 00 33 1 4325 0118
FOUNDED 1875. *Publishes* general fiction and
non-fiction, art, architecture, gardening,
plants, interior design, literature, literary criticism, essays, medicine, nursing, dentistry, wine
and spirits.

Editions Gallimard
5 rue Sébastien-Bottin, F–75341 Paris
Cedex 07
☎00 33 1 4954 4200 Fax 00 33 1 4954 1616
FOUNDED 1911. *Publishes* fiction, poetry, art,
biography, dance, history, music, philosophy.

Editions Grasset & Fasquelle
61 rue des Saints-Pères, F–75006 Paris
☎00 33 1 4439 2200 Fax 00 33 1 4222 6418
Website www.grasse.fr
FOUNDED 1907. *Publishes* fiction and general
non-fiction, essays, literature, literary criticism,
philosophy.

Hachette-Livre
43 quai de Grenelle, F–75905 Paris Cedex 15
☎00 33 1 4392 3000 Fax 00 33 1 4392 3030
FOUNDED 1826. *Publishes* fiction and general
non-fiction, architecture and interior design,
art, economics, education, general engineering,
government, history, language and linguistics,
political science, philosophy, general science,
self-help, social sciences, sociology, sport,
travel.

Editions Robert Laffont, Julliard, Nil, Seghers, Fixot
24 ave Marceau, F–75381 Paris Cedex 08
☎00 33 1 5367 1400 Fax 00 33 1 5367 1414
Website www.laffont.fr
FOUNDED 1941. *Publishes* fiction and non-fiction; literature, literary criticism, essays, poetry, biography, philosophy, self-help, general science, psychology.

Librairie Larousse
21 rue de Montparnasse, F–75298 Paris Cedex 06
☎00 33 1 4439 4400
Fax 00 33 1 4439 4343
FOUNDED 1852. *Publishes* general and social sciences, sociology, language arts, linguistics, technology.

Editions Jean-Claude Lattès
17 rue Jacob, F–75006 Paris
☎00 33 1 4441 7400 Fax 00 33 1 4325 3047
FOUNDED 1968. Part of **Hachette-Livre**. *Publishes* fiction and general non-fiction.

Les Editions Magnard Sàrl
20 rue Berbier-du-Mets, F–75647 Paris Cedex 13
☎00 33 1 4408 8585 Fax 00 33 1 4408 4979
FOUNDED 1933. *Publishes* education.

Michelin et Cie (Services de Tourisme)
46 ave de Breteuil, F–75324 Paris Cedex 07
☎00 33 1 4566 1234 Fax 00 33 1 4566 1163
FOUNDED 1900. *Publishes* travel.

Les Editions de Minuit SA
7 rue Bernard-Palissy, F–75006 Paris
☎00 33 1 4439 3920 Fax 00 33 1 4544 8236
FOUNDED 1942. *Publishes* fiction, essays, literature, literary criticism, philosophy, social science, sociology.

Fernand Nathan
9 rue Méchain, F–75676 Paris Cedex 14
☎00 33 1 4587 5000 Fax 00 33 1 4331 2169
FOUNDED 1881. *Publishes* education, history, philosophy, psychology, psychiatry, general and social sciences, sociology.

Presses de la Cité
12 ave d'Italie, F–75627 Paris Cedex 13
☎00 33 1 4416 0500 Fax 00 33 1 4416 0505
FOUNDED 1947. Imprint of **Editions Belfond**.

Publishes fiction and general non-fiction, science fiction, fantasy, biography, mysteries.

Presses Universitaires de France (PUF)
12 rue Jean-de-Beauvais, F–75005 Paris 06
☎00 33 1 4441 3939 Fax 00 33 1 4354 7887
Website www.puf.com
FOUNDED 1921. *Publishes* art, biography, dance, dentistry, government, general engineering, geography, geology, history, law, medicine, music, nursing, philosophy, psychology, psychiatry, religion, political science, social science, sociology.

Editions du Seuil
27 rue Jacob, F–75261 Paris Cedex 06
☎00 33 1 4046 5050 Fax 00 33 1 4329 0829
FOUNDED 1935. *Publishes* fiction, literature, literary criticism, essays, poetry, art, biography, dance, government, history, how-to, music, photography, philosophy, psychology, psychiatry, religion, general and social sciences, sociology.

Les Editions de la Table Ronde
7 rue Corneille, F–75006 Paris
☎00 33 1 4046 7070 Fax 00 33 1 4046 7101
FOUNDED 1944. *Publishes* fiction and general non-fiction, biography, history, psychology, psychiatry, religion.

Librairie Vuibert
20 rue Babier-du-Mets, F–75647 Paris Cedex 13
☎00 33 1 4408 4900 Fax 00 33 1 4408 4929
FOUNDED 1877. *Publishes* biological and earth sciences, chemistry, chemical engineering, economics, law, mathematics, physics.

Germany
Verlag C.H. Beck (OHG)
Postfach 400340, 80703 Munich
☎00 49 89 381890 Fax 00 49 89 38189398
Website www.beck.de
FOUNDED 1763. *Publishes* general non-fiction, anthropology, archaeology, art, dance, economics, essays, history, language, law, linguistics, literature, literary criticism, music, philosophy, social sciences, sociology, theology.

C. Bertelsmann Verlag GmbH
Postfach 800360, 81603 Munich 80
☎00 49 89 431890 Fax 00 49 89 43189440
Website www.bertelsmann.com

FOUNDED 1835. *Publishes* fiction and general non-fiction, art, biography, government and political science.

Carlsen Verlag GmbH
Postfach 500380, 22703 Hamburg
☎00 49 40 3910090 Fax 00 49 40 39100962
Website www.carlsen.de
FOUNDED 1953. *Publishes* humour and children's books.

Deutscher Taschenbuch Verlag GmbH & Co. KG (dtv)
Postfach 400422, 80704 Munich
☎00 49 89 38167-0 Fax 00 49 89 346428
Email info@dtv.de
Website www.dtv.de
FOUNDED 1961. *Publishes* fiction and general non-fiction; art, astronomy, biography, child care and development, cookery, computer science, dance, education, government, history, how-to, music, poetry, psychiatry, psychology, philosophy, political science, religion, medicine, dentistry, nursing, social sciences, literature, literary criticism, essays, humour, travel.

Econ-Verlag GmbH
Paul-Heyse-Strasse 28, 80336 Munich
☎00 49 89 5148-0 Fax 00 49 89 5148-2229
Website www.econ-verlag.de
FOUNDED 1950. *Publishes* general non-fiction and fiction, economics, general science.

S Fischer Verlag GmbH
Postfach 700355, 60553 Frankfurt am Main
☎00 49 69 60620 Fax 00 49 69 60623532
Website www.s-fischer.de
FOUNDED 1886. Part of the **Holtzbrinck Group**. *Publishes* fiction, general non-fiction, essays, literature, literary criticism.

Carl Hanser Verlag
Postfach 860420, 81631 Munich
☎00 49 89 998300 Fax 00 49 89 9834809
Email info@hanser.de
Website www.hanser.de
Managing Director, Non-Fiction
Wolfgang Beisler
Managing Director, Fiction *Michael Krüger*
FOUNDED in 1928 in Munich. *Publishes* international and German contemporary literature; classics, anthropology, non-fiction on social sciences and the arts; children's and juveniles; specialist books on engineering, natural science, plastics, computers and computer science, economics and management, dentistry. *Subsidiaries* **Paul**

Zsolnay Verlag, Vienna; Sanssouci Verlag, Zurich; Verlag Nagel & Kimche, Zurich; Fachbuchverlag Leipzig, Leipzig; Hanser Gardner Publications, Cincinatti.

Wilhelm Heyne Verlag
Postfach 200143, 80001 Munich
☎00 49 89 286350 Fax 00 49 89 2800943
Website www.heyne.de
FOUNDED 1934. *Publishes* fiction, mystery, romance, humour, science fiction, fantasy, astrology, biography, cookery, film, history, how-to, occult, psychology, psychiatry, video.

Hoffmann und Campe Verlag
Postfach 130444, 20139 Hamburg
☎00 49 40 441880 Fax 00 49 40 44188-290
Website www.hoffmann-und-campe.de
FOUNDED 1781. *Publishes* fiction and general non-fiction; art, biography, dance, history, music, poetry, philosophy, psychology, psychiatry, general science, social sciences, sociology.

Verlagsgruppe Georg von Holtzbrinck GmbH
Gänsheidestrasse 26, 70184 Stuttgart
☎00 49 711 21500 Fax 00 49 711 2150100
Email info@holtzbrinck.com
Website www.holtzbrinck.com
FOUNDED 1948. One of the world's largest publishing groups with 12 book publishing houses and 40 imprints. Also publishes the newspapers, *Handelsblatt* and *Die Zeit*.

Hüthig GmbH & Co. KG
Postfach 102869, 69018 Heidelberg
☎00 49 6221 489-0 Fax 00 49 6221 489-279
Email info@huethig.de
Website www.huethig.de
FOUNDED 1925. Germany's fourth largest professional publisher.

Ernst Klett Verlag GmbH
Postfach 106016, 70049 Stuttgart
☎00 49 711 6671333
Fax 00 49 711 6672-2000
Website www.klett-verlag.de
FOUNDED 1897. *Publishes* education, geography, geology.

Langenscheidt Verlagsgruppe
Postfach 401120, 80711 Munich 40
☎00 49 89 35096-0 Fax 00 49 89 36096-222
Website www.langenscheidt.de
FOUNDED 1856. *Publishes* dictionaries, reference, maps, travel guides, how-to, language.

Gustav Lübbe Verlag GmbH
Postfach 200180, 51469 Bergisch Gladbach
☎00 49 2202 1210 Fax 00 49 2202 121928
Website www.lubbe.de
FOUNDED 1963. *Publishes* fiction and general
non-fiction, archaeology, biography, history,
how-to.

Propylän Verlag, Zweigniederlassung Berlin der Ullstein Buchverlage
Postfach 8030, 10888 Berlin
☎00 49 30 2593570 Fax 00 49 30 25913533
FOUNDED 1903. *Publishes* fiction and general
non-fiction, romance, mysteries, architecture
and interior design, art, biography, dance, film,
video, education, essays, ethnology, geography, geology, government, health, history,
how-to, humour, literature, literary criticism,
maritime, military science, music, nutrition,
poetry, political science, general science, social
sciences, sociology, travel.

Rowohlt Taschenbuch Verlag GmbH
Postfach 1349, 21462 Reinbeck
☎00 49 40 72720 Fax 00 49 40 7272319
Website www.rowohlt.de
FOUNDED 1953. *Publishes* fiction and general
non-fiction; archaeology, art, computer science,
crafts, education, essays, games and hobbies, government, history, literature, literary criticism,
philosophy, psychology, psychiatry, religion,
general science, social sciences, sociology.

Springer-Verlag GmbH & Co KG
Postfach 311340, 10643 Berlin
☎00 49 30 827870 Fax 00 49 30 8214092-93
Website www.springer.de
FOUNDED 1842. *Publishes* agriculture, architecture and interior design, astronomy, behavioural
sciences, business, biological sciences, chemical
engineering, chemistry, civil engineering, computer science, dentistry, economics, finance,
geography, geology, health, nutrition, library
and information sciences, management, marketing, mechanical engineering, electronics, electrical engineering, general engineering, earth sciences, environmental studies, law, mathematics,
medicine, nursing, psychology, psychiatry,
physics, general science, technology.

Suhrkamp Verlag
Postfach 101945, 60019 Frankfurt am Main
☎00 49 69 756010 Fax 00 49 69 75601314
Website www.suhrkamp.de

FOUNDED 1950. *Publishes* fiction, poetry, biography, philosophy, psychology, psychiatry,
general science.

Taschen GmbH
Hohenzollernring 53, 50672 Cologne
☎00 49 221 201800 Fax 00 49 221 254919
Email info@taschen.com
Website www.taschen.com
FOUNDED 1980. *Publishes* photography, art,
architecture and interior design.

K. Thienemanns Verlag
Blumenstr 36, 70182 Stuttgart
☎00 49 711 210550 Fax 00 49 711 2105539
Website www.thienemanns.de
FOUNDED 1849. *Publishes* fiction and general
non-fiction.

WEKA Firmengruppe GmbH & Co KG
Postfach 1209, 86425 Kissing
☎00 49 8233 230 Fax 00 49 8233 23195
FOUNDED 1973. Germany's largest professional
publisher.

Italy

Adelphi Edizioni SpA
Via S. Giovanni sul Muro 14, 20121 Milan
☎00 39 2 72000975 Fax 00 39 2 89010337
FOUNDED 1962. *Publishes* fiction, art, biography, dance, music, philosophy, psychology,
psychiatry, religion, general science.

Bompiana–RCS Libri
Via Mecenate 91, 20138 Milan
☎00 39 2 50951 Fax 00 39 2 5065361
Website www.rcslibri.it
FOUNDED 1929. *Publishes* fiction and general
non-fiction, art, drama, theatre and general science.

Bulzoni Editore SRL (Le Edizioni Universitarie d'Italia)
Via Dei Liburni 14, 00185 Rome
☎00 39 6 4455207 Fax 00 39 6 4450355
FOUNDED 1969. *Publishes* fiction, literature,
literary criticism, essays, art, drama, general
engineering, film, law, language, linguistics,
philosophy, general science, social sciences,
sociology, theatre, video.

Nuova Casa Editrice Licinio Cappelli GEM srl
Via Farini 14, 40124 Bologna
☎00 39 51 239060 Fax 00 39 51 239286
Website www.cappellieditore.com
FOUNDED 1851. *Publishes* fiction, art, biography, drama, film, government, history, music, dance, poetry, medicine, nursing, dentistry, philosophy, political science, psychology, psychiatry, religion, general science, social sciences, sociology, theatre, video.

Garzanti Editore
Via Newton 18A, 20148 Milan
☎00 39 2 487941 Fax 00 39 2 48794292
FOUNDED 1861. *Publishes* fiction, literature, literary criticism, essays, art, biography, history, poetry, government, political science.

Giunti Publishing Group
Via Bolognese 165, 50139 Florence
☎00 39 55 66791 Fax 00 39 55 6679298
FOUNDED 1840. *Publishes* fiction, literature, literary criticism, essays, art, chemistry, chemical engineering, education, history, how-to, language arts, linguistics, mathematics, psychology, psychiatry, general science. Italian publishers of National Geographical Society books.

Ernesto Gremese Editore SRL
Via Agnelli 88, 00151 Rome
☎00 39 6 65740507 Fax 00 39 6 65740509
Website www.gremese.com
FOUNDED 1954. *Publishes* fiction, art, astrology, cookery, crafts, dance, drama, fashion, games, hobbies, essays, literature, literary criticism, music, occult, sport, travel, theatre, television, radio.

Longanesi & C
Corso Italia 13, 20122 Milan
☎00 39 2 8692640 Fax 00 39 2 72000306
Website www.longanesi.it
FOUNDED 1946. *Publishes* fiction, art, biography, dance, history, how-to, medicine, nursing, dentistry, music, philosophy, psychology, psychiatry, religion, general and social sciences, sociology.

Arnoldo Mondadori Editore SpA
Via Mondadori, 20090 Segrate (Milan)
☎00 39 2 75421 Fax 00 39 2 75422302
Website www.mondadori.com
FOUNDED 1907. *Publishes* fiction, mystery, romance, art, biography, dance, dentistry, history, how-to, medicine, music, poetry, philosophy, psychology, psychiatry, religion, nursing, general science, education.

Società Editrice Il Mulino
Str Maggiore 37, 40125 Bologna
☎00 39 51 256011 Fax 00 39 51 256034
Website www.mulino.it
FOUNDED 1954. *Publishes* economics, government, history, law, language, linguistics, philosophy, political science, psychology, psychiatry, social sciences, sociology.

Gruppo Ugo Mursia Editore SpA
Via Tadino 29, 20124 Milan
☎00 39 2 2057201 Fax 00 39 2 205720217
FOUNDED 1922. *Publishes* fiction, poetry, art, biography, education, history, maritime, philosophy, religion, sport, general and social sciences, sociology.

RCS Libri SpA
Via Mecenate 91, 20138 Milan
☎00 39 2 50951 Fax 00 39 2 5065361
Website www.rcslibri.it
FOUNDED 1945. *Publishes* art, crafts, dance, business, games, hobbies, history, music, medicine, nursing, dentistry, outdoor recreation, general science.

Societa Editrice Internazionale – SEI
Corso Regina Margherita 176, 10152 Turin
☎00 39 11 52271 Fax 00 39 11 5211320
FOUNDED 1908. *Publishes* literature, literary criticism, essays, education, geography, geology, history, mathematics, philosophy, physics, religion, psychology, psychiatry.

Sonzogno
Via Mecenate 91, 20138 Milan
☎00 39 2 50951 Fax 00 39 2 5065361
Website www.rcslibri.it
FOUNDED 1818. *Publishes* fiction, mysteries, and general non-fiction.

Sperling e Kupfer Editori SpA
Via Durazzo 4, 20134 Milan
☎00 39 2 217211 Fax 00 39 2 21721277
FOUNDED 1899. *Publishes* fiction and general non-fiction, biography, economics, health, how-to, management, nutrition, general science, sport, travel.

Sugarco Edizioni SRL
Via Fermi 9, 21040 Carnago (Varese)
☎00 39 331 985511 Fax 00 39 331 985385
FOUNDED 1956. *Publishes* fiction, biography, history, how-to, philosophy.

Todariana Editrice
Via Gardone 29, 20139 Milan
☎00 39 2 56812953 Fax 00 39 2 55213405
FOUNDED 1967. *Publishes* fiction, poetry, science fiction, fantasy, literature, literary criticism, essays, language arts, linguistics, psychology, psychiatry, social sciences, sociology, travel.

The Netherlands

A.W. Bruna Uitgevers BV
Postbus 40203, 3504 AA Utrecht
☎00 31 30 247 0411 Fax 00 31 30 241 0018
FOUNDED 1868. *Publishes* fiction and general non-fiction; thrillers, suspense, mysteries, computer science, history, philosophy, psychology, psychiatry, general and social science, sociology.

BZZTÔH Publishers
Laan van Meerdervoort 10,
2517 AJ Gravenhage
☎00 31 70 363 2934 Fax 00 31 70 363 1932
Website www.bzztoh.nl
FOUNDED 1970. *Publishes* fiction, mysteries, literature, literary criticism, essays, general nonfiction, animals, astrology, biography, cookery, dance, humour, music, philosophy, self-help, health and nutrition, occult, pets, religion (Buddhist, Hindhu, Jewish), romance, sport, travel.

Elsevier Science BV
Sara Burgehartst. 25, 1055 KV Amsterdam
☎00 31 20 586 2911 Fax 00 31 20 485 2457
Website www.elsevier.nl
FOUNDED 1946. Parent company – Reed Elsevier. *Publishes* sciences (all fields), medicine, nursing, dentistry, economics, engineering (computer, chemical and general), mathematics, physics, technology.

Kluwer Academic Publishers
Postbus 17, 3300 AA Dordrecht
☎00 31 78 657 6000 Fax 00 31 78 657 6254
Website www.wkap.nl
FOUNDED 1889. *Publishes* education, medical, technical encyclopedias, trade books and journals, law, life sciences, humanities, social sciences, environmental sciences, engineering.

Uitgeversmaatschappij J. H. Kok BV
PO Box 5019, 8260 GA Kampen
☎00 31 38 339 2555 Fax 00 31 38 332 7331
FOUNDED 1894. *Publishes* fiction, poetry, history, religion, general and social sciences, sociology.

M & P Publishing House
Postbus 170, 3990 DD Houten
☎00 31 30 637 7736 Fax 00 31 30 637 7764
FOUNDED 1974. *Publishes* general non-fiction.

J.M. Meulenhoff & Co BV
Postbus 100, 1000 AC Amsterdam
☎00 31 20 553 3500 Fax 00 31 20 625 8511
FOUNDED 1895. *Publishes* international co-productions, fiction and general non-fiction. Specialises in Dutch and translated literature.

Pearson Education
Concertgebouwplein 25, 1071 LM Amsterdam
☎00 31 20 575 5800 Fax 00 31 20 675 2141
Website www.pearsoneducation.nl
FOUNDED 1942. *Publishes* education, business, computer science, economics, management, technology.

Uitgeverij Het Spectrum BV
Postbus 2073, 3500 GB Utrecht
☎00 31 30 265 0650 Fax 00 31 30 262 0850
FOUNDED 1935. *Publishes* science fiction, fantasy, literature, literary criticism, essays, mysteries, criminology, general non-fiction, computer science, history, astrology, occult, management, environmental studies, travel.

Unieboek BV
Postbus 97, 3990 DB Houten
☎00 31 30 637 7660 Fax 00 31 30 637 7600
FOUNDED 1891. *Publishes* fiction, general nonfiction, architecture and interior design, government, political science, literature, literary criticism, essays, archaeology, cookery, history.

Uniepers BV
Postbus 69, 1390 AB Abcoude
☎00 31 29 428 5111 Fax 00 31 29 428 3013
FOUNDED 1961. *Publishes* (mostly in co-editions) antiques, anthropology, archaeology, architecture and interior design, art, culture, dance, history, music, natural history.

Norway

H. Aschehoug & Co (W. Nygaard) A/S
Postboks 363, 0102 Sentrum, Oslo
☎00 47 22 400400 Fax 00 47 22 206395
FOUNDED 1872. *Publishes* fiction and general non-fiction, general and social science, sociology.

J.W. Cappelens Forlag A/S
Postboks 350, 0101 Sentrum, Oslo
☎00 47 22 365000 Fax 00 47 22 365040
FOUNDED 1829. *Publishes* fiction, general non-fiction, religion.

N.W. Damm og Søn A/S
Postboks 1755, Vika, 0122 Oslo
☎00 47 22 471000 Fax 00 47 22 360874
FOUNDED 1845. Owned by the Egmont Group. *Publishes* general non-fiction, education, reference and translated fiction.

Ex Libris Forlag A/S
Postboks 2130, Grünerløkka, 0505 Oslo
☎00 47 22 809500 Fax 00 47 22 385160
FOUNDED 1982. *Publishes* cookery, health, nutrition, humour, human relations, publishing and book trade reference.

Gyldendal Norsk Forlag A/S
Postboks 6860, 0130 St Olaf, Oslo
☎00 47 22 034100 Fax 00 47 22 034105
Website www.gyldendal.no
FOUNDED 1925. *Publishes* fiction, science fiction, fantasy, art, dance, biography, government, political science, history, how-to, music, social sciences, sociology, poetry, philosophy, psychology, psychiatry, religion.

NKS-Forlaget
Postboks 5853, 0308 Oslo
☎00 47 22 596000 Fax 00 47 22 596300
Website www.nksforlaget.no
FOUNDED 1971. *Publishes* childcare and development, English as a second language, health, nutrition, mathematics, natural history, general and social sciences, sociology.

Tiden Norsk Forlag
PO Box 8813, Youngstorget, 0028 Oslo
☎00 47 22 007100 Fax 00 46 22 426458
FOUNDED 1933. *Publishes* fiction, general non-fiction; essays, literature, literary criticism, science fiction, fantasy, management.

Portugal

Bertrand Editora Lda
Rua Anchieta 29–1, 1200 Lisbon
☎00 351 1 3468286 Fax 00 351 1 3479728
FOUNDED 1727. *Publishes* art, essays, literature, literary criticism, social sciences, sociology.

Editorial Caminho SARL
Al Santo Antonio dos Capuchos 6B, 1100 Lisbon
☎00 351 1 3152683 Fax 00 351 1 534346
FOUNDED 1977. *Publishes* fiction, government, political science.

Livraria Civilizacão (Américo Fraga Lamares & Ca Lda)
Rua Alberto Aires de Gouveia 27, 4000 Porto
☎00 351 2 20002286
FOUNDED 1921. *Publishes* fiction, art, economics, history, social science, political science, government, sociology.

Publicações Dom Quixote Lda
Rua Luciano Cordiero 116–2, 1098 Lisbon
☎00 351 21 538079 Fax 00 351 21 574595
FOUNDED 1965. *Publishes* fiction, poetry, education, history, philosophy, general and social sciences, sociology.

Publicações Europa-América Lda
Estrada Nacional 249 (Lisboa-Sintra), Km 14, 2725–397 Mem Martins
☎00 351 21 926 7700
Fax 00 351 21 926 7771
FOUNDED 1945. *Publishes* fiction, poetry, art, biography, dance, education, general engineering, history, how-to, music, philosophy, medicine, nursing, dentistry, psychology, psychiatry, general and social sciences, sociology, technology.

Gradiva–Publicações Lda
Rua Almeida e Sousa 21–r/c Esq, 1300 041 Lisbon
☎00 351 1 3974067 Fax 00 351 1 3953471
Website www.gravida.pt
FOUNDED 1981. *Publishes* fiction, literature, literary criticism, essays, science fiction, fantasy, romance, anthropology, Asian studies, astronomy, archaeology, behavioural and biological science, communications, computer science, crafts, education, games, hobbies, economics, general engineering, geography, geology, government, political studies, journalism, natural history, history, humour, environmental studies,

human relations, management, philosophy, general science, physics, psychology, psychiatry, social sciences, sociology.

Livros Horizonte Lda
Rua Chagas 17 - 1 Dto, 1200 Lisbon
☎00 351 1 3466917 Fax 00 351 1 3326921
FOUNDED 1953. *Publishes* art, education, history, psychology, psychiatry, social sciences, sociology.

Editorial Verbo SA
Rua Carlos Testa 1–2, 1000 Lisbon
☎00 351 1 3562131 Fax 00 351 1 3865396
FOUNDED 1959. *Publishes* education, history, general science.

Spain
Alianza Editorial SA
Juan Ignacio Luca de Tena 15, 28027 Madrid
☎00 349 1 393 8888 Fax 00 349 1 320 7480
Website alianzaeditorial.es
FOUNDED 1965. *Publishes* fiction, poetry, art, history, mathematics, dance, music, philosophy, government, political and social sciences, sociology, general science.

Ediciones Anaya SA
Juan Ignacio Luca de Tena 15, 28027 Madrid
☎00 349 1 393 8800 Fax 00 349 1 742 6631
FOUNDED 1959. *Publishes* education.

Editorial Don Quijote
Compãs del Porvenir 6, 41013 Seville
☎00 349 5 423 5080
FOUNDED 1981. *Publishes* fiction, literature, literary criticism, poetry, essays, drama, theatre, history.

EDHASA (Editora y Distribuidora Hispano – Americana SA)
Av Diagonal 519–521, 08029 Barcelona
☎00 349 3 494 9720 Fax 00 349 3 419 4584
Website www.edhasa.es
FOUNDED 1946. *Publishes* fiction, literature, literary criticism, essays, history.

Editorial Espasa-Calpe SA
Apdo de correos 547, Carreterade Irún Km 12, 200, 28049 Madrid
☎00 349 1 358 9689 Fax 00 349 1 358 8679
FOUNDED 1925. *Publishes* fiction, science fiction, fantasy, English as a second language,

general non-fiction, art, child care and development, cookery, biography, essays, history, literature, literary criticism, self-help, social sciences, sociology.

Grijalbo Mondadori SA
Arago 385, 08013 Barcelona
☎00 349 3 476 7110 Fax 00 349 3 476 7119
Website www.grijalbo.com
FOUNDED 1962. *Publishes* fiction, general non-fiction, architecture, interior design, gardening, humour, literature, literary criticism, essays, poetry, human relations.

Grupo CEAC SA
Arago 472, 08013 Barcelona
☎00 349 3 247 2424 Fax 00 349 3 231 5115
Website www.ceacedit.com
Publishes education, technology, science fiction, fantasy.

Ediciónes Hiperión SL
Calle Salustiano Olózaga 14, 28001 Madrid
☎00 349 1 557 6015 Fax 00 349 1 435 8690
Website www.hiperion.com
FOUNDED 1976. *Publishes* literature, literary criticism, essays, poetry, religion (Islamic and Jewish).

Editorial Luis Vives (Edelvives)
C/Xaudaró 25, 28034 Madrid
☎00 349 1 334 4890 Fax 00 349 1 334 4892
FOUNDED 1890. *Publishes* education.

Editorial Molino
Calabria 166 baixos, 08015 Barcelona
☎00 349 3 226 0625 Fax 00 349 3 226 6998
Website www.editorialmolino.com
FOUNDED 1933. *Publishes* education, sport, fiction.

Pearson Educacion SA
Nunez de Balboa 120, 28006 Madrid
☎00 349 1 590 3432 Fax 00 349 1 590 3448
FOUNDED 1942. *Publishes* art, education, history, language arts, linguistics, medicine, nursing, dentistry, general science, psychology, psychiatry, philosophy.

Editorial Planeta SA
Córsega 273–277, 08008 Barcelona
☎00 349 3 228 5800 Fax 00 349 3 217 7140
Website www.planeta.com
FOUNDED 1952. *Publishes* fiction and general non-fiction.

Plaza y Janés Editores SA
Travessera de Gracia 47–49,
08008 Barcelona
☎00 349 3 366 0421   Fax 00 349 3 366 0444
FOUNDED 1959. *Publishes* fiction and general
non-fiction, biography, history.

Editorial Seix Barral SA
Corsega 270, Apdo 5023, 08008 Barcelona
☎00 349 3 496 7003   Fax 00 349 3 496 7004
Website www.seix-barral.es
FOUNDED 1945. Part of Grupo Planeta.
Foreign language publisher of literature.

Tusquets Editores
Cesare Cantù 8, 08017 Barcelona
☎00 349 3 253 0400   Fax 00 349 3 417 6703
FOUNDED 1969. *Publishes* fiction, biography,
essays, literature, literary criticism, general science.

Ediciones Versal SA
Calabria 108, 08015 Barcelona
☎00 349 3 325 7404   Fax 00 349 3 423 6898
FOUNDED 1984. *Publishes* general non-fiction,
biography, literature, literary criticism, essays.

Sweden

Albert Bonniers Förlag
Box 3159, S-103 63 Stockholm
☎00 46 8 6968000   Fax 00 46 8 6968361
FOUNDED 1837. *Publishes* fiction and general
non-fiction.

Bokförlaget Bra Böcker AB
Södra Vägen, S-26380 Höganäs
☎00 46 42 339000   Fax 00 46 42 330504
FOUNDED 1965. *Publishes* fiction, geography,
geology, history.

Brombergs Bokförlag AB
Box 12886, S-112 98 Stockholm
☎00 46 8 56262080   Fax 00 46 8 56262085
Website www.brombergs.se
FOUNDED 1973. *Publishes* fiction and general
non-fiction.

Bokförlaget Forum AB
PO Box 70321, S-107 23 Stockholm
☎00 46 8 6968440   Fax 00 46 8 6968367
FOUNDED 1944. *Publishes* fiction and general
non-fiction.

Natur och Kultur Bokförlaget
PO Box 27323, S-102 54 Stockholm
☎00 46 8 4538600   Fax 00 46 8 4538790
Website www.nok.se
FOUNDED 1922. *Publishes* fiction and general
non-fiction; biography, history, psychology,
psychiatry and general science.

Norstedts Förlag
Box 2052, S-103 12 Stockholm
☎00 46 8 7698700   Fax 00 46 8 7698864
Website www.norstedt.se
FOUNDED 1823. *Publishes* fiction and general
non-fiction.

Rabén och Sjögren Bokförlag
PO Box 2052, S-103 12 Stockholm
☎00 46 8 7698800   Fax 00 46 8 7698813
Website www.raben.se
FOUNDED 1942. *Publishes* general non-fiction.

Richters Egmont
Ostra Förstadsgatan 46, 205 75 Malmö
☎00 46 40 380600   Fax 00 46 40 933708
FOUNDED 1942. *Publishes* fiction.

B. Wählströms Bokförlag AB
Box 30022, S-104 25 Stockholm
☎00 46 8 6198600   Fax 00 46 8 6189761
Website www.wahlstroms.se
FOUNDED 1911. *Publishes* fiction and general
non-fiction.

Switzerland

Arche Verlag AG, Raabe und Vitali
Postfach 112, CH-8030 Zurich
☎00 41 1 2522410   Fax 00 41 1 2611115
FOUNDED 1944. *Publishes* literature and literary
criticism, essays, biography, fiction, poetry,
music, dance, travel.

Diogenes Verlag AG
Sprecherstr 8, CH-8032 Zurich
☎00 41 1 2528111   Fax 00 41 1 2528407
FOUNDED 1952. *Publishes* fiction, essays, literature, literary criticism, mysteries, art, drama,
theatre, philosophy.

Langenscheidt AG Zürich-Zug
Postfach 326, CH-8021 Zurich
☎00 41 1 2115000   Fax 00 41 1 2122149

Part of the **Langenscheidt Group**, Germany. *Publishes* language arts and linguistics.

Larousse (Suisse) SA

c/o Acces-Direct, 3 Route du Grand-Mont, CH-1052 Le Mont-sur-Lausanne
☎00 41 21 335336
Publishes dictionaries, reference and textbooks. Part of **Librairie Larousse**, France.

Neptun-Verlag

Postfach 307, CH-8280 Kreuzlingen
☎00 41 72 727262 Fax 00 41 72 642023
FOUNDED 1946. *Publishes* history and travel.

Orell Füssli Verlag

Nuschelerstrasse 22, CH-8022 Zurich
☎00 41 1 2113630 Fax 00 41 1 4667412
Website www.orell-fuessli-verlag.ch
FOUNDED 1519. *Publishes* art, biography, economics, education, geography, geology, history, how-to.

Editions Payot Lausanne

CP 529, CH-1001 Lausanne
☎00 41 21 3290264 Fax 00 41 21 3290266
FOUNDED 1875. *Publishes* general non-fiction, anthropology, archaeology, architecture and interior design, dance, education, history, law, medicine, nursing, dentistry, music, philosophy, literature, literary criticism, essays, general science, social sciences and sociology.

Sauerländer AG

Laurenzenvorstadt 89, CH-5001 Aarau
☎00 41 64 8268626 Fax 00 41 64 8245780
Website www.sauerlaender.ch
FOUNDED 1807. *Publishes* education and general non-fiction.

Scherz Verlag AG

Theaterplatz 4–6, CH-3000 Berne 7
☎00 41 31 3277117 Fax 00 41 31 3277171
Website www.scherzverlag.ch
FOUNDED 1939. *Publishes* fiction and general non-fiction; biography, history, psychology, psychiatry, philosophy, parapsychology.

European TV Companies

Austria

ORF (Österreichisher Rundfunk)
Würzburggasse 30, A–1136 Vienna
☎00 43 1 87 8780 Fax 00 43 1 87 8782550
Website www.orf.at

Belgium

Radio–Télévision Belge de la Communauté Française (RTBF)
Boulevard Auguste Reyers 52,
B–1044 Brussels
☎00 32 2 737 2111 Fax 00 32 2 737 2556
Website www.rtbf.be

Vlaamse Radio en Televisieomroep (VRT)
Omroepcentrum, Reyerslaan 52,
B–1043 Brussels
☎00 32 2 741 3111 Fax 00 32 2 739 9351
Email info@vrt.be
Website www.vrt.be

Vlaamse Televisie Maatschappij (VTM) (cable)
Medialaan 1, B–1800 Vilvoorde
☎00 32 2 255 3211 Fax 00 32 2 252 5141
Email info@vtm.be
Website www.vtm.be

Denmark

Danmarks Radio–TV
TV-Byen, DK–2860 Søborg
☎00 45 35 20 3040 Fax 00 45 35 20 2644
Email dr@dr.dk
Website www.dr.dk

TV Danmark
Langebrogade 6A, DK–1411 Copenhagen K
☎00 45 70 10 1010 Fax 00 45 32 69 9699
Email info@tvdanmark.dk
Website www.tvdanmark.dk

TV–2 Danmark
Rugaardsvej 25, DK–5100 Odense C
☎00 45 65 91 9191 Fax 00 45 65 91 3322
Website www.tv2.dk

Finland

MTV3 Finland
Ilmalantori 2, FIN–00240 Helsinki
☎00 358 9 15001 Fax 00 358 9 1500707
Website www.mtv3.fi

Yleisradio Oy (YLE)
PO Box 90, FIN–00024 Yleisradio
☎00 358 9 14801 Fax 00 358 9 14803215
Email fbc@yle.fi
Website www.yle.fi

France

Arte France (cable & satellite)
8 rue Marceau, 92785 Issy les Moulineaux
Cedex 9
☎00 33 1 55 00 77 77
Fax 00 33 1 55 00 77 00
Website www.arte-tv.com

Canal + (pay TV)
85–89 quai André Citroën, 75906 Paris
Cedex 15
☎00 33 1 44 25 10 00
Website www.cplus.fr

France Télévision (France 2/ France 3)
7 Esplanade Henri de France, 75907 Paris
Cedex 15
☎00 33 1 56 22 42 42(France 2)/
  30 30 (France 3)
Website www.france2.fr and www.france3.fr

France 5
10–12 rue Horace-Vernet, 92785 Issy-les-Moulineaux Cedex 9
☎00 33 1 56 22 91 91
Fax 00 33 1 56 22 95 95
Website www.france5.fr

M6 (Métropole Télévision)
89 ave Charles de Gaulle, 92575 Neuilly-sur-Seine Cedex
☎00 33 1 41 92 66 66
Fax 00 33 1 41 92 66 10
Website www.m6.fr

RFO (Radio Télévision Française d'Outre-mer)
5 ave du Recteur Poincaré, 75016 Paris
☎00 33 1 42 15 71 00
Email rfo@rfo.fr
Website www.rfo.fr

TF1 (Télévision Française 1)
1 quai du Pont du Jour, 92656 Boulogne
☎00 33 1 41 41 12 34
Fax 00 33 1 41 41 28 40
Website www.tf1.fr

Germany
ARD – Das Erste
ARD Büro, Bertramstr 8,
60320 Frankfurt am Main
☎00 49 69 59 0607 Fax 00 49 69 15 52075
Website www.ard.de

Arte Germany (cable & satellite)
Schützenstrasse 1, 76530 Baden-Baden
☎00 49 7221 9369-0
Website www.arte.de

ZDF (Zweites Deutsches Fernsehen)
Postfach 40 40, 55100 Mainz
☎00 49 61 31/701 Fax 00 49 61 31 702157
Email info@zdf.de
Website www.zdf.de

Republic of Ireland
Radio Telefís Éireann (RTE – RTE 1)
Donnybrook, Dublin 4
☎00 353 1 208 3111 Fax 00 353 1 208 3080
Website www.rte.ie

Teilefís na Gaelige
Baile na hAbhann, Co. na Gaillimhe
☎00 353 91 505050 Fax 00 353 91 505021
Website www.tg4.ie

Italy
RAI (RadioTelevisione Italiana)
Viale Mazzini 14, 00195 Rome
☎00 39 06 3878-1 Fax 00 39 06 372 5680
Website www.rai.it

Tele piu' (pay TV)
Via Piranesi 44/46, 20137 Milan
☎00 39 02 700 271 Fax 00 39 02 700 27201
Email infopiu@telepiu.it
Website www.telepiu.it

The Netherlands
AVRO (Algemene Omroep Vereniging)
Postbus 2, 1200 JA Hilversum
☎00 31 35 671 79 11
Fax 00 31 35 671 74 39
Website www.omroep.nl/avro

IKON
Postbus 10009, 1201 DA Hilversum
☎00 31 35 672 72 72
Fax 00 31 35 621 51 00
Email ikon@ikon.nl
Website www.omroep.nl/ikon

NCRV (Nederlandse Christelijke Radio Vereniging)
Postbus 25000, 1202 HB Hilversum
☎00 31 35 671 99 11
Fax 00 31 35 671 92 85
Website www.ncrv.nl

NOS (Nederlandse Omroep Stichting)
Postbus 26600, 1202 JT Hilversum
☎00 31 35 677 92 22
Fax 00 31 35 624 20 23
Website www.omroep.nl/nos/noshome/
  index.html

NPS (Nederlandse Programma Stichting)
Postbus 29000, 1202 MA Hilversum
☎00 31 35 677 9333 Fax 00 31 35 677 4959
Email publiek@nps.nl
Website www.omroep.nl/nps

TROS (Televisie en Radio Omroep Stichting)
Postbus 28450, 1202 LL Hilversum
☎00 31 35 671 57 15
Fax 00 31 35 671 52 36
Website www.omroep.nl/tros

VARA
Postbus 175, 1200 AD Hilversum
☎00 31 35 671 19 11 Fax 00 31 35 671 13 33

Email vara@vara.nl
Website www.omroep.nl/vara

VPRO

Postbus 11, 1200 JC Hilversum
☎00 31 35 671 29 11
Fax 00 31 35 671 22 54
Email info@vpro.nl
Website www.vpro.nl

Norway

NRK (Norsk Rikskringkasting), N–0340 Oslo

☎00 47 23 04 7000 Fax 00 47 23 04 7575
Email info@nrk.no
Website www.nrk.no

TVNorge

Biskop Gunnerus gt. 6, N–0155 Oslo
☎00 47 21 02 2000
Website www.tvnorge.no

TV2

Postboks 7222, N–5020 Bergen
☎00 47 55 90 8070 Fax 00 47 55 90 8090
Website www.tv2.no

Portugal

Radiotelevisão Portuguesa (RTP)

Avenida 5 de Outubro 197, 1050–054 Lisbon
☎00 351 21 794 7000
Email rtp@rtp.pt
Website www.rtp.pt

TVI (Televisão Independente)

Rua Mário Castelhano 40, Queluz de Baixo,
2749–502 Barcarena
☎00 351 21 434 7500
Fax 00 351 21 434 7654
Website www.tvi.pt

Spain

RTVE (RadioTelevision Española)

Edificio Prado del Rey, E–28223 Madrid
☎00 349 1 581 7238 Fax 00 349 1 581 7239
Website www.rtve.es

TVE (Televisión Española, SA)

C/ Alcalde Saénz de Baranda 92, 28036
Madrid
☎00 349 1 346 4000 Fax 00 349 1 346 8533
Website www.tve.es

Sweden

Sveriges Television AB–SVT, S–105 10 Stockholm

☎00 46 8 784 0000 Fax 00 46 8 784 1500
Email information@svt.se
Website www.svt.se

TV4

Tegeluddsvägen 3, S–115 79 Stockholm
☎00 46 8 459 4000 Fax 00 46 8 459 4444
Website www.tv4.se

Switzerland

RTR (Radio e Televisiun Rumantscha) (Romansch language TV)

Via dal Teater 1, CH–7002 Cuira
☎00 41 81 255 7575 Fax 00 41 81 255 7500

RTSI (Radiotelevisione svizzera di lingua Italiana) (Italian language TV)

Casella postale, CH–6903 Lugano
☎00 41 91 803 51 11 Fax 00 41 91 803 5355
Email info@rtsi
Website www.rtsi.ch

SF DRS (Schweizer Fernsehen) (German language TV)

Fernsehenstrasse 1–4, CH–8052 Zurich
☎00 41 1 305 66 11 Fax 00 41 1 305 50 94
Email sfdrs@sfdrs
Website www.sfdrs.ch

SRG SSR idée suisse (Swiss Broadcasting Corp.)

Giacomettistr 3, CH–3000 Berne15
☎00 41 31 350 91 11 Fax 00 41 31 350 97 09
Website www.srg-ssr.ch

TSR (Télévision Suisse Romande)

Quai Ernest Ansermet 20, CH–1211 Geneva 8
☎00 41 22 708 99 11 Fax 00 41 22 708 98 00
Website www.tsr.ch

US Publishers

Anyone corresponding with the big American publishers should know that following the terrorist attacks of 11 September they are very wary of any package or letter that looks in any way suspicious. Of course, this begs the question what is or what is not suspicious which is as difficult to answer as what makes or does not make a good novel. The best policy is to make an initial enquiry by e-mail.

International Reply Coupons (IRCs)
For return postage, send IRCs, available from post offices. Letters, 60 pence; mss according to weight.

ABC–CLIO
PO Box 1911, Santa Barbara CA 93116–1911
☎001 805 968 1911 Fax 001 805 685 9685
Email sales@abc-clio.com
Website www.abc-clio.com
CEO *Ronald J. Boehm*

FOUNDED 1953. *Publishes* academic and reference, focusing on history and social studies; books and multimedia. No unsolicited mss; synopses and ideas welcome.
Royalties paid annually. *UK subsidiary* **ABC-Clio Ltd**, Oxford.

Abingdon Press
PO Box 801, Nashville TN 37202–0801
☎001 615 749 6290 Fax 001 615 749 6056
Website www.abingdon.org
Snr. VP/Editorial Director *Harriett Jane Olson*

Publishes non-fiction: religious (lay and professional), children's religious and academic texts. Over 100 titles a year. Approach in writing only with synopsis and samples; ms submission guidelines available on the website. IRCs essential.

Harry N. Abrams, Inc.
100 Fifth Avenue, New York NY 10011
☎001 212 206 7715 Fax 001 212 645 8437
Website www.abramsbooks.com
Editor-in-Chief *Eric Himmel*

FOUNDED 1950. *Publishes* illustrated books: art, architecture, nature, entertainment and children's. No fiction. About 200 titles a year. Submit completed mss (no dot matrix), together with sample illustrations.

Academy Chicago Publishers
363 W. Erie Street, Chicago IL 60610
☎001 312 751 7300 Fax 001 312 751 7306
Email academy363@aol.com
Website www.academychicago.com
President/Senior Editor *Anita Miller*

FOUNDED 1975. *Publishes* mainstream fiction; non-fiction: history, books for women. No romance, children's, young adult, religious, sexist or avant-garde. Send first three consecutive chapters with synopsis only, accompanied by IRCs.
Royalties paid twice-yearly. *Distributed* in the UK and Europe by Gazelle, Lancaster.

Ace/Putnam
See **Penguin Putnam Inc.**

Adams Media Corporation
55 Littlefield Street, Avon MA 02322
☎001 508 427 7100 Fax 001 508 427 6790
Website www.adamsmedia.com
Publishing Director *Gary M. Krebs*

FOUNDED 1980. *Publishes* general non-fiction: self-help, business, personal finance, relationships, parenting, psychology/self-improvement, reference, cooking and fitness. Send query letter with IRCs.

Addison Wesley
75 Arlington Street, Suite 300, Boston, MA 02116
☎001 617 848 6000
Website www.awl.com

Part of Pearson Education. *Publishes* academic textbooks, multimedia and learning programs in computer science, economics, finance, mathematics and statistics. See the website for submission guidelines.

University of Alabama Press
Box 870380, Tuscaloosa AL 35487–0380
☎001 205 348 5180   Fax 001 205 348 9201
Director *Nicole Mitchell*
FOUNDED 1945. *Publishes* American history, Latin American history, American religious history; African-American and Native American studies, Judaic studies, theatre. Submissions are not invited in poetry, fiction or drama. About 50 titles a year.

Aladdin Books
See **Simon & Schuster Children's Publishing**

University of Alaska Press
PO Box 756240, University of Alaska, Fairbanks AK 99775–6240
☎001 907 474 5831   Fax 001 907 474 5502
Email fypress@uaf.edu
Website www.uaf.edu/uapress
Director *Claus. M. Naske*
Senior Editor *Carla Helfferich*
Acquisitions *Pam Odom*

Traces its origins back to 1927 but was relatively dormant until the early 1980s. *Publishes* scholarly works about Alaska and the North Pacific rim, with a special emphasis on circumpolar regions. 5–10 titles a year. No fiction or poetry.
DIVISIONS
Ramuson Library Historical Translation Series; **Oral Biography Series**; **Monograph Series**; **Classic Reprint Series**; **Lanternlight Library** Informal non-fiction covering Northern interest. Unsolicited mss, synopses and ideas welcome.

Allen Lane The Penguin Press
See **Penguin Putnam Inc.**

Alyson Publications
6922 Hollywood Boulevard, Suite 1000, Los Angeles CA 90028
☎001 323 860 6065   Fax 001 323 467 0152
Email mail@alyson.com
Website www.alyson.com
Publisher *Greg Constante*
Editor-in-Chief *Scott Brassort*
FOUNDED 1980. *Publishes* fiction and non-fiction books of general interest to the gay and lesbian community. 52 titles in 2001. No unsolicited mss. Synopses and ideas for books welcome; initial contact by mail or e-mail.
Royalties paid twice-yearly.

AMACOM Books
1601 Broadway, New York NY 10019–7406
☎001 212 586 8100   Fax 001 212 903 8083
Website www.amacombooks.org
President & Publisher *Harold V. Kennedy*
FOUNDED 1972. Owned by American Management Association. *Publishes* business books only, including general management, business communications, sales and marketing, finance, computers and information systems, human resource management and training, career/personal growth skills, research development, project management and manufacturing, quality/customer service titles. About 70 titles a year. Proposals welcome.
Royalties paid twice-yearly.

Anchor
See **Random House, Inc.**

Anvil
See **Krieger Publishing Co.**

Shaye Areheart Books
See **The Crown Publishing Group**

University of Arizona Press
355 S. Euclid Avenue, Ste. 103, Tucson AZ 85719–6654
☎001 520 621 1441   Fax 001 520 621 8899
Website www.uapress.arizona.edu
Director *Christine Szuter*
FOUNDED 1959. *Publishes* academic non-fiction, particularly with a regional/cultural link, plus Native-American and Hispanic literature. About 50 titles a year.

University of Arkansas Press
McIlroy House, 201 Ozark Avenue, Fayetteville AR 72701
☎001 501 575 3246   Fax 001 501 575 6044
Website www.uapress.com
Director *Lawrence J. Malley*
FOUNDED 1980. *Publishes* scholarly monographs, poetry and general trade including biography, etc. Particularly interested at present in scholarly works in history, politics and literary criticism. About 30 titles a year.
Royalties paid annually.

ASM Press
1752 N. Street NW, Washington DC 20036
Fax 001 202 942 9342
Email books@asmusa.org
Website www.asmpress.org
Managing Director *Jeff Hoffmeier*
FOUNDED 1899. The book publishing division of the American Society for Microbiology. *Publishes* monographs, texts, reference books and manuals in microbiological sciences. 20 titles in 2001. Unsolicited mss, synopses and ideas welcome; approach by mail or e-mail in the first instance. No fiction.
Royalties paid annually.

Aspect
See **Warner Books Inc.**

Atheneum Books for Young Readers
See **Simon & Schuster Children's Publishing**

Atlantic Monthly Press
See **Grove/Atlantic Inc.**

Atria Books
See **Simon & Schuster Adult Publishing Group**

AUP (Associated University Presses)
AUP New Jersey titles are handled in the UK by **Golden Cockerel Press** (see entry under **UK Publishers**).

Avery Publishing Group, Inc.
375 Hudson Street, New York NY 10014
☎001 212 366 2000 Fax 001 212 366 2643
Website www.penguinputnam.com
Publisher *John Duff*
Executive Editor *Laura Shepherd*
FOUNDED 1976. Imprint of **Penguin Putnam Inc.** *Publishes* alternative and complimentary health care, nutrition, disease prevention, diet, supplements, functional foods, mind/body therapies, holistic healing. About 50 titles a year. No unsolicited mss; synopses and ideas welcome if accompanied by s.a.e./IRCs.
Royalties paid twice-yearly.

Avon Books
10 East 53rd Street, New York NY 10022
☎001 212 207 7000 Fax 001 212 702 2525
Website www.harpercollins.com
Editor-in-Chief *Larry Ashmead*
FOUNDED 1941. An imprint of **HarperCollins**

Publishers, Inc.** *Publishes* hardcover; trade and mass-market paperback reprints and originals including fiction, non-fiction, adult, juvenile and young adult. 500 titles a year. Submit query letter and sample chapter.

Baker Book House
PO Box 6287, Grand Rapids MI 49516–6287
☎001 616 676 9185 Fax 001 616 676 9573
Website www.bakerbooks.com
President *Dwight Baker*
Director of Publications *Don Stephenson*
FOUNDED 1939. Began life as a used-book store and began publishing in earnest in the 1950s, primarily serving the evangelical Christian market. About 165 titles a year. Additional information for authors on website.

DIVISIONS/IMPRINTS
Baker Books *Publishes* religious non-fiction and fiction, Bible reference, professional (pastors and church leaders) books, children's books. About 80 titles a year. No unsolicited proposals.
  Baker Academic *Jim Kinney* *Publishes* college/seminary textbooks, religious reference books, biblical studies monographs. About 30 titles a year. No unsolicited proposals.
Fleming
  H. Revell *Lonnie Hull Du Pont* FOUNDED 1870. A family-owned business until 1978, Revell was one of the first Christian publishers to take the step into secular publishing. Joined Baker Book House in 1992. *Publishes* adult fiction and non-fiction for evangelical Christians. About 45 titles a year. No unsolicited proposals.
  Brazos Press *Rodney Clapp* *Publishes* academic and trade books in theology, biblical studies, ethics, cultural criticism and spirituality (trade editions only). About 15 titles a year. No unsolicited mss.
  Chosen Books *Jane Campbell* FOUNDED 1971; joined Baker Book House in 1992. *Publishes* charismatic adult non-fiction for evangelical Christians. About 10 titles a year. No unsolicited proposals.

Ballantine Books
1540 Broadway, 11th Floor, New York
NY 10036 Fax 001 212 782 8439
Website www.randomhouse.com
President/Publisher *Gina Centrello*
FOUNDED 1952. A division of **Random House, Inc.** since 1973. *Publishes* fiction and non-fiction, science fiction.

DIVISIONS/IMPRINTS
Ballantine Books; **Del Rey**; **Fawcett Books**

Mystery; **Ivy** Romance; **Library of Contemporary Thought**; **Lucas Books**; **One World**; **Wellspring**. No unsolicited mss.

Banner Books
See **University Press of Mississippi**

Bantam Dell Publishing Group
1540 Broadway, New York NY 10036
☎001 212 782 9000 Fax 001 212 302 7985
President/Publisher *Irwyn Applebaum*
FOUNDED 1945. The largest mass market paperback publisher in the USA. A division of **Random House, Inc.** *Publishes* general commercial fiction and non-fiction, young readers and children's.

DIVISIONS/IMPRINTS **Bantam Classics**; **Delacorte Press**; **Dell**; **Delta Books**; **Dial Press**; **DTP**; **Island Books**.

Barron's Educational Series, Inc.
250 Wireless Boulevard, Hauppauge
NY 11788–3917
☎001 516 434 3311 Fax 001 516 434 3723
Email info@barronseduc.com
Website www.barronseduc.com
President *Manuel H. Barron*
Acquisitions Editor *Wayne Barr*
FOUNDED 1942. *Publishes* adult non-fiction, children's fiction and non-fiction, test preparation materials and language materials, cookbooks, pets, hobbies, sport, photography, health, business, law, computers, travel, business, art and painting. No adult fiction. 400 titles a year. Unsolicited mss, synopses and ideas for books welcome.
Royalties paid twice-yearly.

Basic Books
See **Perseus Books Group**

Beacon Press
25 Beacon Street, Boston MA 02108
☎001 617 742 2110 Fax 001 617 723 3097
Website www.beacon.org
Director *Helene Atwan*
FOUNDED 1854. *Publishes* general non-fiction. About 85 titles a year. Does not accept unsolicited mss. For further information, refer to website page.

Beech Tree Books
See **HarperCollins Publishers, Inc.**

Belknap Press
See **Harvard University Press**

Berkley Books
See **Penguin Putnam Inc.**

H.&R. Block
See **Simon & Schuster Adult Publishing Group**

BlueHen Books
See **Penguin Putnam Inc.**

Boulevard
See **Penguin Putnam Inc.**

Boyds Mills Press
815 Church Street, Honesdale PA 18431
☎001 570 253 1164 Fax 001 570 253 0179
Website www.boydsmillspress.com
Publisher *Kent Brown Jr*
Manuscript Coordinator *Kathryn Yerkes*
A subsidiary of Highlights for Children, Inc. FOUNDED 1990 as a publisher of children's trade books. *Publishes* children's fiction, non-fiction and poetry. About 50 titles a year. Unsolicited mss, synopses and ideas for books welcome. No romance or fantasy novels.
Royalties paid twice-yearly.

Bradford Books
See **The MIT Press**

Brassey's, Inc.
22841 Quicksilver Drive, Dulles VA 20166
☎001 703 661 1569 Fax 001 703 661 1547
Email djacobs@bookintl.com
Publisher *Don McKeon*
Senior Assistant Editor *Donald Jacobs*
FOUNDED 1983. *Publishes* non-fiction titles on topics of history (especially military history), world and US affairs, US foreign policy, defence, intelligence, biography, transport (especially automobiles) and sports. About 80 titles a year. No unsolicited mss; synopses and ideas welcome.
Royalties paid annually.

Brazos Press
See **Baker Book House**

Broadway Books
See **Doubleday Broadway Publishing Group**

University of California Press
2000 Center Street, Suite 303, Berkeley
CA 94704
☎001 510 642 4247 Fax 001 510 643 7127
Director *James H. Clark*

FOUNDED 1893. *Publishes* scholarly and scientific non-fiction; some fiction and poetry in translation. Preliminary letter with outline preferred.

Carolrhoda Books, Inc.
241 First Avenue North, Minneapolis MN 55401
☎001 612 332 3344 Fax 001 612 332 7615
Submissions Editor *Rebecca Poole*
FOUNDED 1969. *Publishes* children's: nature, biography, history, beginners' readers, world cultures, photo essays, historical fiction and picture books. Please send s.a.e. for author guidelines, making sure guideline requests are clearly marked on the envelope or they will be returned. 'We are *only* accepting submissions twice a year – from March 1–31 and October 1–31. Submissions postmarked with other dates will be returned unopened. Also, only submissions with s.a.e./IRCs will receive a response.'

Charlesbridge Publishing
85 Main Street, Watertown MA 02472
☎001 617 926 0329 Fax 001 617 926 5720
Email books@charlesbridge.com
Website www.charlesbridge.com
Chairman *Brent Farmer*
Managing Editor, School Division
Elena Dworkin Wright
Senior Editor, Trade Division *Dominic Barth*
FOUNDED 1980 as an educational publisher focused on a strategic approach to reading, writing, maths and science. *Publishes* children's educational programmes, non-fiction picture books and fiction for 3- to 12-year-olds. School division publishes mathematical fiction, *Maths Adventures*, in picture-book format and astronomy-related picture books. Complete mss or proposals welcome with self-addressed envelope and IRCs. Unsolicited mss are accepted but must be exclusive submissions. Responses are sent within three months.

University of Chicago Press
1427 East 60th Street, Chicago IL 60637–2954
☎001 773 702 7700 Fax 001 773 702 9756
Email general@press.uchicago.edu
Website www.press.uchicago.edu
FOUNDED 1891. *Publishes* academic non-fiction only.

Children's Press
See **Grolier Publishing**

Chosen Books
See **Baker Book House**

Chronicle Books LLC
85 Second Street, Sixth Floor, San Francisco CA 94105
☎001 415 537 4200 Fax 001 415 537 4440
Website www.chroniclebooks.com
President/Publisher *Jack Jensen*
FOUNDED 1966. *Publishes* illustrated and non-illustrated adult trade and children's books as well as stationery and gift items. About 200 titles a year. Query or submit outline/synopsis and sample chapters and artwork. Guidelines for ms submissions on the website.
Royalties paid twice-yearly.

Clarkson Potter
See **The Crown Publishing Group**

Contemporary Books
1 Prudential Plaza, Suite 900, Chicago IL 60601
☎001 312 233 7500 Fax 001 312 233 7570
FOUNDED 1947. *Publishes* general adult non-fiction. About 400 titles a year. Submissions require s.a.e./IRCs for response.

Copper Beech Books
See **The Millbrook Press, Inc.**

Counterpoint Press
See **Perseus Books Group**

Crocodile Books, USA
See **Interlink Publishing Group, Inc.**

The Crown Publishing Group
299 Park Avenue, New York NY 10171
☎001 212 751 2600 Fax 001 212 751 6192
Website www.randomhouse.com
FOUNDED 1933. Division of **Random House, Inc.** *Publishes* popular trade fiction and non-fiction.
IMPRINTS
Clarkson Potter Editorial Director *Lauren Shakely* Illustrated books – cookery, gardening, style, decorating and design; **Crown Business** Editorial Director *Steve Ross* Business books; **Crown Publishers** Editorial Director *Steve Ross* General fiction and non-fiction; **Harmony Books** Editorial Director *Shaye Areheart* New Age, spirituality, religion, some fiction; **Shaye Areheart Books** Editorial Director *Shaye Areheart* Fiction; **House of Collectibles**

Director *Dottie Harris* Antiques and collectibles; **Three Rivers Press** Executive Editor *Becky Cabaza* Non-fiction paperbacks.

Cumberland House Publishing
431 Harding Industrial Drive, Nashville TN 37211
☎001 615 832 1171 Fax 001 615 832 0633
Email info@cumberlandhouse.com
Website www.cumberlandhouse.com

FOUNDED 1996. *Publishes* fiction, non-fiction, cookery and sports. 60 titles in 2001. Unsolicited mss, synopses and ideas welcome; approach by mail. No children's books or poetry.
Royalties paid annually.

Benjamin Cummings
1301 Sansome Street, San Francisco CA 94111
☎001 415 402 2500
Website www.awl.com

Part of Pearson Education. *Publishes* academic textbooks, multimedia and learning programs in chemistry, health and life science. See the website for submission guidelines.

Currency
See **Doubleday Broadway Publishing Group**

Da Capo Press
See **Perseus Books Group**

DAW Books, Inc.
375 Hudson Street, 3rd Floor, New York NY 10014–3658
☎001 212 366 2096/Submissions: 366 2095
Fax 001 212 366 2090
Email daw@penguinputnam.com
Website www.dawbooks.com
Publishers *Elizabeth R. Wollheim, Sheila E. Gilbert*
Submissions Editor *Peter Stampfel*

FOUNDED 1971 by Donald and Elsie Wollheim as the first mass-market publisher devoted to science fiction and fantasy. *Publishes* science fiction/fantasy, and some horror. No short stories, anthology ideas or non-fiction. Unsolicited mss, synopses and ideas for books welcome. About 36 titles a year.
Royalties paid twice-yearly.

Dearborn Financial Publishing, Inc.
155 N. Wacker Drive, Chicago IL 60606–1719
☎001 312 836 4400 Fax 001 312 836 1021
Website www.dearborn.com
President *Eric Cantor*

FOUNDED 1967. A niche publisher serving the financial services industries. *Publishes* real estate, insurance, financial planning, securities, commodities, investments, banking, professional education, motivation and reference titles, investment reference and how-to books for the consumer (personal finance, real estate) and small business owner. About 200 titles a year. Unsolicited mss, synopses and ideas welcome.
Royalties paid twice-yearly.

Del Rey
See **Ballantine Books**

Delacorte Press
See **Bantam Dell Publishing Group**

Dell
See **Bantam Dell Publishing Group**

Delta Books
See **Bantam Dell Publishing Group**

Dial Books for Young Readers
345 Hudson Street, New York NY 10014–3657
☎001 212 366 2800
Queries *Submissions Coordinator*

FOUNDED 1961. A division of Penguin Putnam Books for Young Readers. *Publishes* children's books, including picture books, beginning readers, fiction and non-fiction for middle grade and young adults. 50 titles a year.
IMPRINTS Hardcover only: **Dial Books for Young Readers**; **Dial Easy-to-Read**. No unsolicited mss accepted; query letters with return postage only.
Royalties paid twice-yearly.

Dial Press
See **Bantam Dell Publishing Group**

Dolphin Books
See **Doubleday Broadway Publishing Group**

Doubleday Broadway Publishing Group
1540 Broadway, New York NY 10036
☎001 212 782 9000 Fax 001 212 302 7985
Website www.randomhouse.com
President & Publisher *Stephen Rubin*

The Doubleday Broadway Publishing Group, a division of **Random House, Inc.** was formed by a merger of Doubleday and Broadway Books in 1999. *Publishes* fiction and non-fiction.

DIVISION/IMPRINTS
Broadway Books; Currency; Doubleday; Doubleday Religious Publishing; Image Books; Dolphin Books; Nan A. Talese. No unsolicited material.

Lisa Drew Books
See **Simon & Schuster Adult Publishing Group**

DTP
See **Bantam Dell Publishing Group**

Thomas Dunne Books
See **St Martin's Press LLC**

Sanford J. Durst Publications
11 Clinton Avenue, Rockville Centre,
New York NY 11570
☎001 516 766 4444 Fax 001 516 766 4520
Owner *Sanford J. Durst*
FOUNDED 1975. *Publishes* non-fiction: numismatic and related, philatelic, legal and art. Also children's books. About 12 titles a year.
Royalties paid twice-yearly.

Dushkin
See **The McGraw-Hill Companies, Inc.**

Dutton/Dutton's Children's Books
See **Penguin Putnam Inc.**

The Ecco Press
See **HarperCollins Publishers, Inc.**

William B. Eerdmans Publishing Co.
255 Jefferson Avenue SE, Grand Rapids
MI 49503
☎001 616 459 4591 Fax 001 616 459 6540
Email sales@eerdmans.com
Website www.eerdmans.com
President *William B. Eerdmans Jr*
Vice President/Editor-in-Chief *Jon Pott*
FOUNDED 1911 as a theological and reference publisher. Gradually began publishing in other genres with authors like C.S. Lewis, Dorothy Sayers and Malcolm Muggeridge on its lists. *Publishes* religious: theology, biblical studies, ethical and social concern, social criticism and children's, religious history, religion and literature. 120 titles in 2000.
DIVISIONS
Children's *Judy Zylstra*; **Other** *Jon Pott*. Unsolicited mss, synopses and ideas welcome.
Royalties paid twice-yearly.

M. Evans & Co., Inc.
216 East 49th Street, New York NY 10017
☎001 212 688 2810 Fax 001 212 486 4544
Email editorial@mevans.com
Website www.mevans.com
President *George C. de Kay*
FOUNDED 1954 as a packager. Began publishing in 1962. Best known for its popular psychology and health books, with titles like *Dr Atkins' New Diet Revolution*, *This is How Love Works*, *Bragging Rights* and *Robert Crayhon's Nutrition Made Simple*. *Publishes* general non-fiction and fiction. About 30 titles a year. No unsolicited mss; query first. Synopses and ideas welcome.
Royalties paid twice-yearly.

Everyman's Library
See **Random House, Inc.**

Faber & Faber, Inc.
19 Union Square West, New York NY 10003
☎001 212 741 6900 Fax 001 212 633 9385
Editor *Denise Oswald*
FOUNDED 1976. An affiliate of **Farrar, Straus & Giroux, Inc.** *Publishes* primarily non-fiction books for adults with a focus on film, theatre, music, popular culture and literary and cultural criticism. Unsolicited mss accepted; please query first and include IRCs with letter.
Royalties paid twice-yearly.

Facts On File, Inc.
132 West 31st Street, New York NY 10001
☎001 212 967 8800 Fax 001 212 967 9196
President *Mark McDonnell*
Publisher *Laurie E. Likoff*
Started life in the early 1940s with News Digest subscription series to libraries. Began publishing on specific subjects with the Facts On File imprint and developed its current reference and trade book programme in the 1970s. *Publishes* general trade, young adult trade and academic reference for the school and library markets. *Specialises* in single subject encyclopedias, atlases and biographical dictionaries. About 150 titles a year. No fiction, cookery or popular non-fiction.
DIVISIONS
General Reference *Laurie Likoff*; **Academic Reference** *Owen Lancer*; **Adult Trade** *James Chambers*; **Young Adult & US History** *Nicole Bowen*; **Electronic Publishing** *James Housley*; **Literary Studies** *Anne Savarese*. Unsolicited synopses and ideas welcome; no mss. Send query letter in the first instance.
Royalties paid twice-yearly.

Farrar, Straus & Giroux, Inc.

19 Union Square West, New York NY 10003
☎001 212 741 6900
FOUNDED 1946. *Publishes* general fiction, non-fiction, juveniles. No unsolicited material.

Fawcett Books

See **Ballantine Books**

Frederick Fell Publishers, Inc.

2131 Hollywood Boulevard, Ste 305,
Hollywood FL 33020
☎001 954 925 5242 Fax 001 954 925 5244
Email info@fellpub.com
Website www.fellpub.com
Chairman *Donald L. Lessne*
Managing Director *Barbara Newman*
FOUNDED 1943. *Publishes* trade non-fiction. 40
titles in 2001. Unsolicited mss, synopses and
ideas welcome; send query letter with two chapters and table of contents in the first instance. No
fiction.
Royalties twice-yearly.

Fireside

See **Simon & Schuster Adult Publishing Group**

Fodor's Travel Publications

See **Random House, Inc.**

The Free Press

See **Simon & Schuster Adult Publishing Group**

Samuel French, Inc.

45 West 25th Street, New York
NY 10010–2751
☎001 212 206 8990 Fax 001 212 206 1429
Email samuelfrench@earthlink.net
Website www.samuelfrench.com
Senior Editor *Lawrence Harbison*
FOUNDED 1830. *Publishes* plays in paperback:
Broadway and off-Broadway hits, light comedies, mysteries, one-act plays and plays for
young audiences. Unsolicited mss welcome.
No synopses.
Royalties paid annually (books); twice-yearly
(amateur productions); monthly (professional
productions). *Overseas associates* in London,
Toronto, Sydney and Johannesburg.

Gale Group

27500 Drake Road, Farmington Hills
MI 48331
☎001 248 699 4253 Fax 001 248 699 8070
Website www.galegroup.com
CEO *Allen Paschal*
FOUNDED 1954. A subsidiary of The Thomson
Corporation, the Gale Group is a world leader in
e-information publishing. *Publishes* electronic
reference material for libraries, schools and businesses. IMPRINTS **Graham & Whiteside Ltd**;
Thorndike Press; **Greenhaven Press**; **Lucent
Books**.

The Globe Pequot Press

PO Box 480, Guildford CT 06437–0480
☎001 203 458 4500 Fax 001 203 458 4601
Website www.globe-pequot.com
President *Linda Kennedy*
Associate Publisher *Michael K. Urban*
Publishes regional and international travel,
how-to, regional and outdoor recreation. Also
publishes the *Insiders'* guides. About 250 titles a
year. Unsolicited mss, synopses and ideas welcome, particularly for travel and outdoor recreation books.
Royalties paid 'occasionally'.

Great Source Education Group

See **Houghton Mifflin Co.**

Greenhaven Press

See **Gale Group**

Greenwillow Books

See **HarperCollins Publishers, Inc.**

Griffin

See **St Martin's Press LLC**

Grolier Publishing

90 Sherman Turnpike, Danbury CT 06816
☎001 203 797 3500
Website www.publishing.grolier.com
President *Joseph Tessitore*
FOUNDED 1895. Acquired by Scholastic, Inc. in
2000. *Publishes* juvenile non-fiction, encyclopedias, speciality reference sets, children's fiction
and picture books. Aout 600 titles a year.
DIVISIONS/IMPRINTS **Children's Press**;
Grolier Educational; **Grolier Classroom
Publishing**; **Franklin Watts**.

Grosset & Dunlap/Grosset Putnam

See **Penguin Putnam Inc.**

Grove/Atlantic Inc.

841 Broadway, New York NY 10003–4793
☎001 212 614 7850 Fax 001 212 614 7886
President/Publisher *Morgan Entrekin*

Managing Editor *Michael Hornburg*

FOUNDED 1952. *Publishes* general fiction and non-fiction. IMPRINTS **Atlantic Monthly Press; Grove Press.**

Gulliver Books
See **Harcourt Trade Division**

Harcourt School Publishers
6277 Sea Harbor Drive, Orlando FL 32887
☎001 407 345 2000 Fax 001 407 352 3445
Website www.harcourt.com
President/CEO *Anthony Lucki*

A division of Harcourt Inc., FOUNDED 1919. *Publishes* education materials – books, CD-ROMs, Internet and audio.

Harcourt Trade Division
525 'B' Street, Suite 1900, San Diego
CA 92101–4495
☎001 619 231 6616 Fax 001 619 699 6777
Website www.harcourt.com
Managing Editor *David Hough*

A division of Harcourt Inc. *Publishes* fiction, poetry and non-fiction covering a wide range of subjects: biography, environment and ecology, history, travel, science and current affairs for children and young adults. About 175 titles a year.

IMPRINTS **Gulliver Books; Harcourt Children's Books; Harcourt Paperbacks; Odyssey Classics** Novels; **Red Wagon Books** For ages 6 months to 3 years; **Voyager Paperbacks** Picture books; **Silver Whistle.** No unsolicited mss.

Harlequin Historicals
See **Silhouette Books**

Harmony Books
See **The Crown Publishing Group**

HarperCollins Publishers, Inc.
10 East 53rd Street, New York NY 10022
☎001 212 207 7000 Fax 001 212 207 6968
Website www.harpercollins.com
President/Chief Executive Officer *Jane Friedman*

FOUNDED 1817. Owned by News Corporation. *Publishes* general and literary fiction, general non-fiction, business, children's, reference and religious books. About 1700 titles a year. No unsolicited material.

DIVISIONS/IMPRINTS
Adult Trade; HarperCollins/HarperCollins Children's Books; HarperResource (reference); **HarperAudio; Avon Books** (see entry); **Beech Tree Books; Greenwillow Books; Hearst Books; Lothrop, Lee & Shepard; Mulberry Books; Quill; Regan Books; The Ecco Press; William Morrow.**

SUBSIDIARY **Zondervan Publishing House** (see entry).

Harvard University Press
79 Garden Street, Cambridge
MA 02138–1499
☎001 617 495 2600 Fax 001 617 495 5898
Website www.hup.harvard.edu
Director *William P. Sisler*

FOUNDED 1913. *Publishes* scholarly non-fiction only: medical and scientific. IMPRINT **Belknap Press.**

University of Hawai'i Press
2840 Kolowalu Street, Honolulu HI 96822
☎001 808 956 8694 Fax 001 808 988 6052
Email pcrosby@hawaii.edu
Website www.uhpress.hawaii.edu
Chairman *William Hamilton*
Executive Editor *Patricia Crosby*

FOUNDED 1947. *Publishes* scholarly books pertaining to East Asia, Southeast Asia, Hawaii and the Pacific. 81 titles in 2001.

IMPRINT **Lattitude 20.** Unsolicited mss; synopses and ideas welcome; approach by mail. No poetry, children's books or any topics other than Asia and the Pacific.

Royalties paid twice-yearly.

Hearst Books
See **HarperCollins Publishers, Inc.**

Hidden Spring
See **Paulist Press**

Hill Street Press
191 E. Broad Street, Suite 209, Athens
GA 30601–2848
☎001 706 613 7200 Fax 001 706 613 7204
Email info@hillstreetpress.com
Senior Editor *Patrick Allen*

FOUNDED 1998. *Publishes* books on the American South – fiction and non-fiction: literary history/criticism, memoirs, history, current issues, cookery. No poetry, erotica, romance, children's or young adults. 20 titles in 2000. Unsolicited material welcome; approach in writing in the first instance.

Royalties paid twice-yearly.

Hippocrene Books, Inc.
171 Madison Avenue, New York NY 10016
☎001 212 685 4371 Fax 001 212 779 9338
Email hippocrene.books@verizon.net
Website www.hippocrenebooks.com
President/Editorial Director *George Blagowidow*
Foreign Language Editor *Caroline Gates*
Cookbook Editor *Anne McBride*
FOUNDED 1971. *Publishes* general non-fiction and reference books. Particularly strong on foreign language dictionaries, language studies and international cookbooks. No fiction. Send brief summary, table of contents and one chapter for appraisal. S.a.e. essential for response. For manuscript return include sufficient postage cover (IRCs).

Holiday House, Inc.
425 Madison Avenue, New York NY 10017
☎001 212 688 0085 Fax 001 212 421 6134
Vice President/Editor-in-Chief
Regina Griffin
Publishes children's general fiction and non-fiction (pre-school to secondary). About 50 titles a year. Send query letters only. IRCs for reply must be included.

Henry Holt & Company Inc.
115 West 18th Street, New York NY 10011
☎001 212 886 9200 Fax 001 212 633 0748
Website www.henryholt.com
President/Publisher *John Sterling*
Editor-in-Chief *Jennifer Barton*
Executive Editor, Books for Young Readers *Nina Ignatowicz*
Associate Publisher, Books for Young Readers *Laura Godwin*
FOUNDED in 1866, Henry Holt is one of the oldest publishers in the United States. Part of Holtzbrinck Publishing Holdings. *Publishes* fiction, by both American and international authors, biographies, and books on history and politics, ecology and psychology. 230 titles a year.
DIVISIONS/IMPRINTS **Adult Trade**; **Books for Young Readers**; **John Macrae Books** *John Macrae*; **Metropolitan Books** *Sara Bershtel*; **Owl Books**; **Times Books** *David Sobel*.

Houghton Mifflin Co.
222 Berkeley Street, Boston MA 02116–3764
☎001 617 351 5000 Fax 001 617 351 1125
Website www.hmco.com
Contact *Submissions Editor*

FOUNDED 1832. Acquired by Vivendi in June 2001. *Publishes* literary fiction and general non-fiction, including autobiography, biography and history. Also school and college textbooks; children's fiction and non-fiction. Average 100 titles a year. Unsolicited adult mss no longer accepted. Send synopses, outline and sample chapters for children's non-fiction; complete mss for children's fiction. IRCs required with all submissions/queries.
DIVISIONS/SUBSIDIARY COMPANIES
Houghton Mifflin College Division; **Houghton Mifflin School Division**; **Houghton Mifflin Trade & Reference Division**; **Great Source Education Group**; **McDougal Littell Inc.**; **The Riverside Publishing Co.**; **Sunburst Technology** (multimedia and video).

House of Collectibles
See **The Crown Publishing Group**

HPBooks
See **Penguin Putnam Inc.**

University of Illinois Press
1325 South Oak Street, Champaign
IL 61820–6903
☎001 217 333 0950 Fax 001 217 244 8082
Email uipress@uillinois.edu
Website www.press.uillinois.edu
Editorial Director *Willis Regier*
Publishes non-fiction, scholarly and general, with special interest in Americana, women's studies, African–American studies, film, religion, American music and regional books. About 140–150 titles a year.

Image Books
See **Doubleday Broadway Publishing Group**

Indiana University Press
601 North Morton Street, Bloomington
IN 47404–3797
☎001 812 855 8817 Fax 001 812 855 8507
Email iupress@indiana.edu
Website www.indiana.edu/~iupress
Director *Peter-John Leone*
Publishes scholarly non-fiction in the following subject areas: African studies, anthropology, Asian studies, Afro-American studies, environment and ecology, film, folklore, history, Jewish studies, literary criticism, medical ethics, Middle East studies, military, music, paleontology, philanthropy, philosophy, politics, reli-

gion, semiotics, Russian and East European studies, Victorian studies, women's studies. Query in writing in first instance.

Interlink Publishing Group, Inc.
46 Crosby Street, Northampton MA 01060
☎001 413 582 7054 Fax 001 413 582 7057
Email info@interlinkbooks.com
Website www.interlinkbooks.com
Publisher *Michel Moushabeck*
FOUNDED 1987. *Publishes* fiction, travel, children's, politics, cookbooks. *Specialises* in Middle East titles and ethnicity. 60 titles in 2001. IMPRINTS **Crocodile Books, USA** Editorial Head *Ruth Lane Moushabeck*; **Olive Branch Press** Editorial Head *Phyllis Bennis*. See submission guidelines on the website before making an approach.
Royalties paid annually.

University of Iowa Press
Kuhl House, 119 West Park Road, Iowa City IA 52242
☎001 319 335 2000 Fax 001 319 335 2055
Website www.uiowa.edu/~uipress
Director *Holly Carver*
FOUNDED 1969 as a small scholarly press publishing about five books a year. Now publishing about 35 a year in a variety of scholarly fields, plus local interest, short stories, creative non-fiction and poetry anthologies. No unsolicited mss; query first. Unsolicited ideas and synopses welcome.
Royalties paid annually.

Iowa State University Press
2121 State Avenue, Ames IA 50010
☎001 515 292 0140 Fax 001 515 292 3348
Email vanhouten@iowastatepress.com
Website www.iowastatepress.com
Publishing Director *Gretchen Van Houten*
FOUNDED 1934 as an offshoot of the university's journalism department. Now a Blackwell Science company. *Publishes* reference books and textbooks on agriculture, aviation, food science, human dentistry, dietetics, journalism, and veterinary medicine. No fiction, trade books or poetry.
Royalties paid annually.

Irwin
See **The McGraw-Hill Companies, Inc.**

Island Books
See **Bantam Dell Publishing Group**

Ivy
See **Ballantine Books**

Jove
See **Penguin Putnam Inc.**

University Press of Kansas
2501 West 15th Street, Lawrence KS 66049–3905
☎001 785 864 4154 Fax 001 785 864 4586
Email unewpress@ku.edu
Website www.kansaspress.ku.edu
Director *Fred M. Woodward*
FOUNDED 1946. Became the publishing arm for all six state universities in Kansas in 1976. *Publishes* scholarly books in American history studies, legal studies, presidential studies, American studies, political philosophy, political science, military history and environmental. About 50 titles a year. Proposals welcome.
Royalties paid annually.

Jean Karl Books
See **Simon & Schuster Children's Publishing**

Kent State University Press
Kent OH 44242–0001
☎001 330 672 7913 Fax 001 330 672 3104
Director (Interim) *Will Underwood*
Editor-in-Chief *Joanna Hildebrand Craig*
FOUNDED 1965. *Publishes* scholarly works in history and biography, literary studies and general non-fiction with an emphasis on American studies. 25–30 titles a year. Queries welcome; no mss.
Royalties paid annually.

Kluwer Academic Publishers
101 Philip Drive, Assinippi Park, Norwell MA 02061
☎001 781 871 6600 Fax 001 781 871 6528
Email kluwer@wkap.com
Website www.wkap.nl
President *Jay Lippencott*
Managing Editor *Claire Stanton*
FOUNDED 1972. *Publishes* scholarly scientific, technical, medical, business and professional books and journals. Over 300 titles a year. Queries only.
IMPRINTS **Kluwer Academic Publishers/ Plenum Publishers**.

Alfred A. Knopf
See **Random House, Inc.**

Krieger Publishing Co.
PO Box 9542, Melbourne FL 32902–9542
☎001 321 724 9542 Fax 001 321 951 3671
Email info@krieger-pub.com
Website www.krieger-publishing.com
Chairman *Robert E. Krieger*
President *Donald E. Krieger*
Vice-President *Maxine D. Krieger*
FOUNDED 1970. *Publishes* science, education, ecology, humanities, history, mathematics, chemistry, space science, technology and engineering. IMPRINTS/SERIES **Anvil**; **Exploring Community History**; **Open Forum**; **Orbit**; **Professional Practices**; **Public History**. Unsolicited mss welcome. Not interested in synopses/ideas or trade type titles.
Royalties paid yearly.

Lanternlight Library
See **University of Alaska Press**

Lattitude 20
See **University of Hawai'i Press**

Lehigh University Press
See **Golden Cockerel Press** under **UK Publishers**

Lerner Publications Co. (A division of Lerner Publishing Group)
241 First Avenue North, Minneapolis MN 55401
☎001 612 332 3344 Fax 001 612 332 7615
Website www.lernerbooks.com
Submissions Editor *Jennifer Zimian*
Publishes primarily non-fiction for readers of all grade levels. List includes titles on nature, geography, natural and physical science, current events, ancient and modern history, world art, special interest, sports, world cultures and numerous biography series. Some young adult and middle grade fiction. No alphabet, puzzle, song or text books, religious subject matter or plays. Submissions are accepted in the months of March and October *only*. Work received in any other month will be returned unopened. S.a.e./IRCs required for authors who wish to have their material returned. Please allow two to six months for a response. No phone calls.

Library of Contemporary Thought
See **Ballantine Books**

Little Simon
See **Simon & Schuster Children's Publishing**

Little, Brown and Company
Adult Trade Division: 1271 Avenue of the Americas, New York NY 10020
☎001 212 522 8700 Fax 001 212 522 2067
Website www.twbookmark.com
CHILDREN'S BOOKS DIVISION: 3 Center Plaza, Boston, MA 02108–2084. ☎001 617 227 0730 Fax 001 617 263 2864
Imprint of the AOL Time Warner Book Group. FOUNDED 1837. *Publishes* fiction, non-fiction and children's. DIVISIONS **Adult Trade** VP/Publisher *Michael Pietsch*; **Children's Books** VP/Editor-in-Chief *Maria Modugno*. No unsolicited mss.

Living Language
See **Random House, Inc.**

Llewellyn Publications
PO Box 64383, St Paul MN 55164–0383
☎001 612 291 1970 Fax 001 612 291 1908
Email nancym@llewellyn.com
Website www.llewellyn.com
President/Publisher *Carl L. Weschcke*
Acquisitions Manager *Nancy J. Mostad*
Division of Llewellyn Worldwide Ltd. FOUNDED 1901. *Publishes* self-help and how-to: astrology, alternative health, tantra, Fortean studies, tarot, yoga, Santeria, dream studies, metaphysics, magic, witchcraft, herbalism, shamanism, organic gardening, women's spirituality, graphology, palmistry, parapsychology. Also fiction with an authentic magical or metaphysical theme. About 100 titles a year. Unsolicited mss welcome; proposals preferred. IRCs essential in all cases.

Lothrop, Lee & Shepard
See **HarperCollins Publishers, Inc.**

Louisiana State University Press
Baton Rouge LA 70803
☎001 225 578 6295 Fax 001 225 578 6461
Email lsupress@lsu.edu
Website www.lsu.edu/lsupress
Director *L.E. Phillabaum*
Publishes non-fiction: Southern history, American history, Southern literary criticism, American literary criticism, biography, political science, music (jazz) and Latin American studies. About 80 titles a year. Send IRCs for mss guidelines.

Love Inspired
See **Silhouette Books**

Lucas Books
See **Ballantine Books**

Lucent Books
See **Gale Group**

The Lyons Press Inc.
123 West 18th Street, Sixth Floor, New York
NY 10011
☎001 212 620 9580 Fax 001 212 929 1836
Website www.lyonspress.com
Senior Vice-President *Tony Lyons*
Managing Editor *Richard Rothschild*

FOUNDED 1978. *Publishes* general fiction and
non-fiction; outdoor, natural history, sports,
gardening, cookery and art. About 180 titles a
year. No unsolicited mss; synopses and ideas
welcome.
Royalties paid twice-yearly.

McDougal Littell Inc.
See **Houghton Mifflin Co.**

Margaret K. McElderry Books
See **Simon & Schuster Children's
Publishing**

McFarland & Company, Inc.,
Publishers
PO Box 611, Jefferson NC 28640
☎001 336 246 4460 Fax 001 336 246 5018
Email info@mcfarlandpub.com
Website www.mcfarlandpub.com
President/Editor-in-Chief *Robert Franklin*
Vice President *Rhonda Herman*
Senior Editor *Steve Wilson*
Editor *Virginia Tobiassen*

FOUNDED 1979. A library reference and upper-
end speciality market press publishing scholarly
books in many fields: international studies, performing arts, popular culture, sports, automotive history, women's studies, music and
fine arts, chess, history and librarianship.
Specialises in general reference. Especially
strong in cinema studies. No fiction, poetry,
children's, New Age or inspirational/devo-
tional works. About 220 titles a year. No unsolicited mss; send query letter first. Synopses and
ideas welcome; submissions by mail preferred.
Royalties paid annually.

The McGraw-Hill Companies, Inc.
1221 Avenue of the Americas, New York
NY 10020
☎001 212 512 2000
Website www.mcgraw-hill.com

President/CEO *Harold McGraw, III*

FOUNDED 1888. Parent of **McGraw-Hill
Education** which has offices in the UK (see
under **UK Publishers**. *Publishes* a wide range
of educational, professional, business, science,
engineering and computing books. HIGHER
EDUCATION AND PROFESSIONAL DIVISIONS
**McGraw-Hill Professional; McGraw-Hill
Trade; McGraw-Hill/Osborne Media;
McGraw-Hill Higher Education; McGraw-
Hill/Irwin; McGraw-Hill/Dushkin;
McGraw-Hill/Primis Custom Publishing;
McGraw-Hill/Contemporary**.

John Macrae Books
See **Henry Holt & Company Inc.**

Magic Attic Press
See **The Millbrook Press, Inc.**

University of Massachusetts Press
PO Box 429, Amherst MA 01004–0429
☎001 413 545 2217 Fax 001 413 545 1226
Website www.umass.edu/umpress
Director *Bruce Wilcox*
Senior Editor *Clark Dougan*

FOUNDED 1964. *Publishes* scholarly, general
interest, African-American, ethnic, women's
and gender studies, cultural criticism, architecture and environmental design, literary criticism, poetry, philosophy, biography, history.
Unsolicited mss considered but query letter
preferred in the first instance. Synopses and
ideas welcome. 40 titles a year.
Royalties paid annually.

Mentor
See **Penguin Putnam Inc.**

Meridian
See **Penguin Putnam Inc.**

Metropolitan Books
See **Henry Holt & Company Inc.**

The University of Michigan Press
PO Box 1104, Ann Arbor MI 48106–1104
☎001 734 764 4388 Fax 001 734 615 1540
Email um.press@umich.edu
Website www.press.umich.ef

FOUNDED 1930. *Publishes* non-fiction, textbooks, literary criticism, theatre, economics,
political science, history, classics, anthropology,
law studies, gender studies, English as a second
language.
Royalties paid twice-yearly.

The Millbrook Press, Inc.
2 Old New Milford Road, PO Box 335,
Brookfield CT 06804
☎001 203 740 2220 Fax 001 203 775 5643
Website www.millbrookpress.com
School/Library Publisher *Jean Reynolds*
Publisher (Roaring Brook Press) *Simon Boughton*
Managing Editor *Colleen Seibert*
FOUNDED 1989. *Publishes* mainly non-fiction, children's and young adult, for trade, school and public library. About 180 titles a year. IMPRINTS **Copper Beech Books**; **Twenty-First Century Books**; **Magic Attic Press**; **Roaring Brook Press** Fiction.
Royalties paid twice-yearly.

Minotaur
See **St Martin's Press LLC**

University Press of Mississippi
3825 Ridgewood Road, Jackson
MS 39211–6492
☎001 601 432 6205 Fax 001 601 432 6217
Email press@ihl.state.ms.us
Website www.upress.state.ms.us
Director *Seetha Srinivasan*
Editor-in-Chief *Craig Gill*
FOUNDED 1970. Non-profit book publisher partially supported by the eight State universities. *Publishes* scholarly and trade titles in literature, history, American culture, Southern culture, African-American, women's studies, popular culture, folklife, ethnic, performance, art and photography, and other liberal arts. About 60 titles a year.
IMPRINTS
Muscadine Books *Craig Gill* Regional trade titles. **Banner Books** Paperback reprints of significant fiction and non-fiction. Send letter of enquiry, prospectus, table of contents and sample chapter prior to submission of full mss.
Royalties paid annually. *Represented* worldwide. UK representatives: **Roundhouse Publishing Group**.

University of Missouri Press
2910 LeMone Boulevard, Columbia
MO 65201
☎001 573 882 7641 Fax 001 573 884 4498
Website www.system.missouri.edu/upress
Director *Beverly Jarrett*
FOUNDED 1958. *Publishes* academic: history, literary criticism, intellectual history and related

humanities disciplines and short stories – usually four volumes a year. Best approach is by letter. Send one short story for consideration, and synopses for academic work. About 60 titles a year.

The MIT Press
5 Cambridge Ctr., Cambridge MA 02142
☎001 617 253 5646 Fax 001 617 258 6779
Website www.mitpress.mit.edu
Editor-in-Chief *Laurence Cohen*
FOUNDED 1961. *Publishes* scholarly and professional, technologically sophisticated books, including computer science and artificial intelligence, economics, finance, architecture, cognitive science, neuroscience, environmental studies, linguistics and philosophy. IMPRINT **Bradford Books**.

The Modern Library
See **Random House, Inc.**

Monograph Series
See **University of Alaska Press**

William Morrow
See **HarperCollins Publishers, Inc.**

MTV Books
See **Pocket Books**

Mulberry Books
See **HarperCollins Publishers, Inc.**

Muscadine Books
See **University Press of Mississippi**

Mysterious Press
See **Warner Books Inc.**

NAL
See **Penguin Putnam, Inc.**

University of Nevada Press
MS 166, Reno NV 89557–0076
☎001 775 784 6573 Fax 001 775 784 6200
Director *Ronald Latimer*
Editor-in-Chief *Joanne O'Hare*
FOUNDED 1960. *Publishes* scholarly and popular books; serious fiction, Native American studies, natural history, Western Americana, Basque studies and regional studies. About 40 titles a year including reprints. Unsolicited material welcome if it fits in with areas published, or offers a 'new and exciting' direction.
Royalties paid twice-yearly.

University Press of New England
23 South Main Street, Hanover
NH 03755–2055
☎001 603 643 7100 Fax 001 603 643 7117
Website www.upne.com
Director & Editor-in-Chief *Richard Abel*
Executive Editor *Phyllis Deutsch*

FOUNDED 1970. A scholarly book publisher
sponsored by five institutions of higher education
in the region: Brandeis, Dartmouth, Middlebury,
Tufts and the University of New Hampshire.
Publishes general and scholarly non-fiction and
Hardscrabble Books fiction of New England.
About 80 titles a year. Unsolicited material wel-
come.

Royalties paid annually. *Overseas associates:*
Canada – University of British Columbia; UK,
Europe, Middle East – University Presses
Marketing; Australia, New Zealand, Asia & the
Pacific – East-West Export Books.

University of New Mexico Press
1720 Lomas Boulevard NE, Albuquerque
NM 87131–1591
☎001 505 277 2346 Fax 001 505 277 9270
Website www.unmpress.com
Director *Elizabeth C. Hadas*
Editor *Larry Durwood Ball*

FOUNDED 1929. *Publishes* scholarly and
regional books. No fiction, how-to, children's,
humour, self-help, technical or textbooks.

University of North Texas Press
PO Box 311336, Denton TX 76203–1336
☎001 940 565 2142 Fax 001 940 565 4590
Email rchrisman@unt.edu
Website www.unt.edu/untpress
Director *Ronald Chrisman*

FOUNDED 1987. *Publishes* folklore, regional
interest, contemporary, social issues, Texas
history, military history, women's issues, multi-
cultural. Publishes the Vassar Miller Poetry Prize
winner each year. About 20 titles a year. No
unsolicited mss; synopses and ideas welcome.

Royalties paid annually.

W.W. Norton & Company, Inc.
500 Fifth Avenue, New York NY
10110–0017
☎001 212 354 5500 Fax 001 212 869 0856
Website www.wwnorton.com
Vice-President/Managing Editor
Nancy K. Palmquist

FOUNDED 1923. *Publishes* fiction and non-

fiction, college textbooks and professional
books. About 300 titles a year.

Odyssey Classics
See **Harcourt Trade Division**

University of Oklahoma Press
1005 Asp Avenue, Norman OK 73019–6051
☎001 405 325 2000 Fax 001 405 325 4000
Website www.ou.edu/oupress
Director *John N. Drayton*

FOUNDED 1928. *Publishes* general scholarly
non-fiction only: American Indian studies, history of American West, classical studies, literary
theory and criticism, anthropology, archaeology, natural history, political science and
women's studies. About 100 titles a year.

Olive Branch Press
See **Interlink Publishing Group, Inc.**

One World
See **Ballantine Books**

Onyx
See **Penguin Putnam Inc.**

Open Forum
See **Krieger Publishing Co.**

Orbit
See **Krieger Publishing Co.**

Osborne Media
See **The McGraw-Hill Companies, Inc.**

Owl Books
See **Henry Holt & Company Inc.**

Palgrave
See **St Martin's Press LLC**

Pantheon Books
See **Random House, Inc.**

Paper Star
See **Penguin Putnam Inc**

Paragon House
2700 University Avenue, Suite 200, St Paul
MN 55114–1016
☎001 651 644 3087 Fax 001 651 644 0997
Email paragon@paragonhouse.com
Website www.paragonhouse.com
Executive Director *Dr Gordon L. Anderson*

FOUNDED 1982. *Publishes* non-fiction: reference and academic. Subjects include history, religion, philosophy, spirituality, Jewish interest, political science, international relations, psychology.

Royalties paid twice-yearly.

Paulist Press
997 Macarthur Boulevard, Mahwah NJ 07430
☎001 201 825 7300 Fax 001 201 825 8345
Email sales@paulistpress.com
Website www.paulistpress.com
Owner *Missionary Society of St Paul the Apostle, New York*
CSP/Publisher *Fr. Lawrence Boadt*
Managing Editor *Paul McMahon*

FOUNDED in 1866 by the Paulist Fathers as the Catholic Publication Society. One of the largest Catholic Publishing houses in the world, the Paulist Press *publishes* religious, spiritual, theology and children's religious books. 90 titles a year. IMPRINTS **Paulist Press** *Paul McMahon* Spirituality, ministry resources, ethics and social issues, ecumenical and inter-religious; *Chris Bellitto* Theology and philosophy; *Susan O'Keefe* Children's religious. **HiddenSpring** *Jan-Erik Guerth* General religious trade books. Unsolicited mss, synopses and ideas welcome; approach through direct mail with IRCs for return postage of material and/or letter. No New Age, Evangelical Christian books.

Pelican Publishing Company
Box 3110, Gretna LA 70054–3110
☎001 504 368 1175
Website www.pelicanpub.com
Editor-in-Chief *Nina Kooij*

Publishes general non-fiction: popular history, cookbooks, travel, art, business, children's, editorial cartoon, architecture, golf, Scottish interest, collectibles guides and motivational. About 100 titles a year. Initial enquiries required for all submissions.

Pelion Press
See **The Rosen Publishing Group, Inc.**

Penguin Putnam Inc.
375 Hudson Street, New York NY 10014
☎001 212 366 2000 Fax 001 212 366 2666
Email online@penguinputnam.com
Website www.penguinputnam.com
President/CEO *David Shanks*

Penguin Putnam is a division of the Penguin Group, which is owned by Pearson plc. The Group is the second-largest trade book publisher in the world. *Publishes* fiction and non-fiction in hardback and paperback; adult and children's. About 2500 titles a year. No unsolicited mss.

PENGUIN GROUP IMPRINTS
Hardback: **Dutton**; **Viking**; **Viking Studio**; **Allen Lane The Penguin Press**; **DAW Books, Inc.** (see entry); Paperback: **Penguin**; **Plume**; **Signet/Signet Classics**; **Onyx**; **Roc**; **Topaz**; **Mentor**; **Meridian**. CHILDREN'S DIVISION **Dial Books for Young Readers** (see entry); **Dutton's Children's Books**; **Viking Children's Books**; **Puffin**; **Grosset & Dunlap**; **NAL**; **Frederick Warne**.

PUTNAM BERKLEY IMPRINTS
Hardback: **G.P. Putnam's Sons** (see entry); **Riverhead Books**; **BlueHen Books**; **Jeremy P. Tarcher**; **Avery** (see entry); **Grosset/Putnam**; **Ace/Putnam**; **Boulevard**; **Putnam**; **Price Stern Sloan**; Paperbacks: **Berkley Books**; **Jove**; **Perigee**; **Prime Crime**; **HPBooks**; Children's Division: **Philomel**; **Paper Star**; **Planet Dexter**.
Royalties paid twice-yearly.

University of Pennsylvania Press
4200 Pine Street, Philadelphia
PA 19104–4011
☎001 215 898 6261 Fax 001 215 898 0404
Website www.upenn.edu/pennpress
Director *Eric Halpern*

FOUNDED 1890. *Publishes* serious non-fiction: scholarly, reference, professional, textbooks and semi-popular trade. No original fiction or poetry. About 75 titles a year. No unsolicited mss but synopses and ideas for books welcome.
Royalties paid annually.

Perigee
See **Penguin Putnam Inc.**

Perseus Books Group
10 East 53rd Street, New York NY 10022
☎001 212 207 7600 Fax 001 212 207 7635
Website www.perseusbooksgroup.com
President/CEO *Jack McKeown*

FOUNDED 1997. Subsidiary of Perseus Capital LLC. *Publishes* general, academic and professional. 350 titles in 2001. IMPRINTS **Basic Books** *John Donatich*; **Perseus Publishing** *David Goehring*; **Counterpoint Press** *Jack Schumacher*; **Perseus Press** *Don Fehr*; **Da Capo Press** *John Radziewicz*; **Westview Press** *Holly Hodder*; **Public Affairs** *Peter Osnos*. No unsolicited mss.

Philomel
See **Penguin Putnam Inc.**

Picador USA
See **St Martin's Press LLC**

Planet Dexter
See **Penguin Putnam Inc.**

Players Press
PO Box 1132, Studio City CA 91614-0132
☎001 818 789 4980
CEO *William-Alan Landes*
FOUNDED 1965 as a publisher of plays; now publishes across the entire range of performing arts: plays, musicals, theatre, film, cinema, television, costume, puppetry, plus technical theatre and cinema material. No unsolicited mss; synopses/ideas welcome. Send query letter.
Royalties paid twice-yearly. *Overseas subsidiaries* in Canada, Australia, Germany and the UK.

Plenum Publishers
See **Kluwer Academic Publishers**

Plume
See **Penguin Putnam Inc.**

Pocket Books
1230 Avenue of the Americas, New York NY 10020
☎001 212 698 1260 Fax 001 212 698 1253
Executive VP/Publisher *Louise Burke*
FOUNDED 1939. A division of Simon & Schuster Adult Publishing Group. *Publishes* trade paperbacks and hardcovers; mass-market, reprints and originals. IMPRINTS **Pocket Books/Pocket Star Books**; **Sonnet Books**; **MTV Books**.

PowerKids Press
See **The Rosen Publishing Group, Inc.**

Price Stern Sloan
See **Penguin Putnam Inc.**

Prime Crime
See **Penguin Putnam Inc.**

Princeton Review
See **Random House, Inc.**

Professional Practices
See **Krieger Publishing Co.**

Public Affairs (US)
See **Perseus Books Group**

Public History
See **Krieger Publishing Co.**

Puffin
See **Penguin Putnam Inc**

G.P. Putnam's Sons (Children's)
345 Hudson Street, New York NY 10014
☎001 212 366 2000
Website www.penguinputnam.com
President/Publisher *Nancy Paulsen*
Executive Editor *Kathy Dawson*
A children's book imprint of Penguin Putnam Books for Young Readers, a member of **Penguin Putnam Inc.** *Publishes* picture books, middle-grade fiction and young adult fiction.

Quill
See **HarperCollins Publishers, Inc.**

Rand McNally
PO Box 7600, Chicago IL 60680
☎001 847 329 8100 Fax 001 847 673 0539
Website www.randmcnally.com
President/CEO *Richard Davis*
FOUNDED 1856. *Publishes* world atlases and maps, road atlases of North America and Europe, city and state maps of the United States and Canada, educational wall maps, atlases and globes, plus children's products. Includes electronic multimedia products.

Random House, Inc.
1540 Broadway, New York NY 10036
☎001 212 782 9000 Fax 001 212 726 0600
Website www.randomhouse.com
Chairman/Chief Executive Officer
Peter Olson
FOUNDED 1925. The world's largest English-language general trade book publisher. A division of the Bertelsmann Book Group AG, one of the foremost media companies in the world. The reach of Random House, Inc. is global with subsidiaries and affiliated companies in Canada, the UK, Australia, New Zealand and South Africa. Through Random House International, the books published by the imprints of Random House, Inc. are sold in virtually every country in the world. Submissions via agents preferred.
DIVISIONS/IMPRINTS
Random House Adult Books; **Ballantine Books** (see entry); **Bantam Dell Publishing Group** (see entry); **Crown Publishing Group** (sce entry); **Doubleday Broadway Publishing Group** (see entry). **Alfred A. Knopf** (including

Everyman's Library, Knopf, Pantheon Books, Schocken Books, Vintage and **Anchor**) FOUNDED 1915. Fiction and non-fiction. **Random House Audio Publishing Group**; **Random House Children's Books** (including **Random House Books for Young Readers, Alfred A. Knopf Books for Young Readers, Crown Books for Young Readers, Delacorte Press** and **Doubleday Books for Young Readers**); **Random House Large Print**; **Random House Value Publishing**; **Random House New Media**; **Fodor's Travel Publications**; **Living Language**; **Princeton Review**; **Random House Reference**; **Villard**; **The Modern Library**. *Royalties* paid twice-yearly.

Rawson Associates
See **Simon & Schuster Adult Publishing Group**

Reader's Digest Association Inc
Reader's Digest Road, Pleasantville, NY 10570–7000
☎001 914 238 1000 Fax 001 914 238 4559
Website www.rd.com
Chairman/CEO *Thomas Ryder*
Publishes home maintenance reference, cookery, DIY, health, gardening, children's books; videos and magazines.

Red Wagon Books
See **Harcourt Trade Division**

Regan Books
See **HarperCollins Publishers, Inc.**

Fleming H. Revell
See **Baker Book House**

Riverhead Books
See **Penguin Putnam Inc.**

The Riverside Publishing Co.
See **Houghton Mifflin Co.**

Roaring Brook Press
See **The Millbrook Press, Inc.**

Roc
See **Penguin Putnam Inc.**

The Rosen Publishing Group, Inc.
29 East 21st Street, New York NY 10010
☎001 212 777 3017 Fax 001 212 777 0277
Website www.rosenpublishing.com
President *Roger Rosen*

Associate Editor, PowerKids Press
    Gina Strazzabosco-Hayn
Editorial Director *Erin Hovanec*
FOUNDED 1950. *Publishes* non-fiction books (supplementary to the curriculum, reference and self-help) for a young adult audience. Reading levels are years 7–12, 4–6 (books for teens with literacy problems), and 5–9. Areas of interest include careers, self-esteem, sexuality, personal safety, science, sport, African studies, Holocaust studies and a wide variety of other multicultural titles. About 180 titles a year.
IMPRINTS
Pelion Press Music titles; **PowerKids Press** Non-fiction books for Reception up to Year 4 that are supplementary to the curriculum. Subjects include conflict resolution, character building, health, safety, drug abuse prevention, history, self-help, religion and multicultural titles. 144 titles a year. For all imprints, write with outline and sample chapters.

Rutgers University Press
100 Joyce Kilmer Avenue, Piscataway NJ 08854–8099
☎001 732 445 7762 Fax 001 732 445 7039
Website rutgerspress.rutgers.edu
Director *Marlie Wasserman*
Associate Director/Editor-in-Chief
    Leslie Mitchner
FOUNDED 1936. *Publishes* scholarly books, regional, social sciences and humanities. Unsolicited mss, synopses and ideas for books welcome. No original fiction or poetry. About 80 titles a year.
Royalties paid annually.

St Martin's Press LLC
175 Fifth Avenue, New York NY 10010
☎001 212 674 5151 Fax 001 212 420 9314
Email inquiries@stmartins.com
Website www.stmartins.com
CEO (Holtzbrinck) *John Sargent*
President/Publisher (Trade Division)
    Sally Richardson
FOUNDED 1952. A subsidiary of **Macmillan Publishers** (UK), St Martin's Press made its name and fortune by importing raw talent from the UK to the States and has continued to buy heavily in the UK. *Publishes* general fiction, especially mysteries and crime; and adult non-fiction: history, self-help, political science, travel, biography, scholarly, popular reference, college textbooks. All submissions via legitimate literary agents only.

IMPRINTS
Picador USA; **Griffin** (Trade paperbacks); **St Martin's Paperbacks** (Mass market); **Thomas Dunne Books**; **Minotaur**; **Palgrave**; **Truman Talley Books**.

Scarecrow Press Inc.
4720 Boston Way, Lanham MD 20706
☎001 301 459 3366 Fax 001 301 429 5747
Website www.scarecrowpress.com

Editorial Director/Associate Publisher
Shirley Lambert

FOUNDED 1950 as a short-run publisher of library reference books. Acquired by **University Press of America, Inc.** in 1995 which is now part of Rowman and Littlefield Publishing Group. *Publishes* reference, scholarly and monographs (all levels) for libraries. Reference books in all areas except sciences, specialising in the performing arts, music, cinema and library science. About 165 titles a year. Unsolicited mss welcome but material will not be returned unless requested and accompanied by return postage. Unsolicited synopses and ideas for books welcome.
Royalties paid annually.

Schocken Books
See **Random House, Inc.**

Anne Schwartz Books
See **Simon & Schuster Children's Publishing**

Scott Foresman
1900 E Lake Avenue, Glenview IL 60025
☎001 847 729 3000 Fax 001 847 729 8910
Website www.scottforesman.com

President *Paul McFall*

FOUNDED 1896. *Publishes* elementary education materials. No unsolicited material.

Scribner
See **Simon & Schuster Adult Publishing Group**

Seven Stories Press
140 Watts Street, New York NY 10013
☎001 212 226 8760 Fax 001 212 226 1411
Email info@sevenstories.com
Website www.sevenstories.com

CEO *Daniel Simon*

FOUNDED 1995. Named by *Publishers Weekly* in 2001 as the fastest growing independent publisher in America. *Publishes* fiction, literature, literary translations, memoirs, political non-fiction,

health, history, current affairs. 40 titles in 2001. DIVISION **Siete Cuentos Editorial** *Juana Ponce de Leon*. No unsolicited mss; synopses and ideas from agents welcome or send query letter. No children's or business books.
Royalties paid twice-yearly. *Overseas subsidiaries:* Turnaround Publishing Services, UK; Tower Books, Australia; Hushion House, Canada.

Signet/Signet Classics
See **Penguin Putnam Inc.**

Silhouette Books
300 East 42nd Street, New York NY 10017
☎001 212 682 6080 Fax 001 212 682 4539

Editorial Director *Tara Gavin*

FOUNDED 1979 as an imprint of Simon & Schuster and was acquired by a wholly owned subsidiary of Toronto-based Harlequin Enterprises Ltd in 1984. *Publishes* category, contemporary romance fiction and historical romance fiction only. Over 360 titles a year across a number of lines.
IMPRINTS
Silhouette Romance *Mary Theresa Hussey*; **Silhouette Desire** *Joan Marlow Golan*; **Silhouette Special Edition** *Karen Taylor Richman*; **Silhouette Intimate Moments** *Leslie Wainger*; **Harlequin Historicals** *Tracy Farrell*; **Steeple Hill** *Tracy Farrell*. Imprint, launched in 1997, **Love Inspired** publishes a line of inspirational contemporary romances with stories designed to 'lift readers' spirits and gladden their hearts'. No unsolicited mss. Submit query letter in the first instance or write for detailed submission guidelines/tip sheets. See also **Harlequin Mills & Boon Ltd** under **UK Publishers**.
Royalties paid twice-yearly. *Overseas associates* worldwide.

Silver Whistle
See **Harcourt Trade Division**

Simon & Schuster Adult Publishing Group (Division of Simon & Schuster, Inc)
1230 Avenue of the Americas, New York NY 10020
☎001 212 698 7000 Fax 001 212 698 7007
Website www.simonsays.com

President/Publisher *Carolyn K. Reidy*

Publishes fiction and non-fiction.
DIVISIONS
The Free Press VP & Senior Editor *Fred W.*

Hills; **Fireside/Touchstone** VP & Editor-in-Chief *Trish Todd*; **Scribner** VP & Editor-in-Chief *Nan Graham*; **Simon and Schuster** Senior VP & Editor-in-Chief *Michael V. Korda*; **Trade Paperbacks** VP & Editor-in-Chief *Trish Todd*; **Pocket Books** (see entry).
IMPRINTS
Atria Books; **H.&R. Block**; **Lisa Drew Books**; **Fireside**; **The Free Press**; **Rawson Associates**; **Scribner**; **Scribner Classics**; **Scribner Paperback Fiction**; **S&S Libros en Espanol**; **Simon & Schuster**; **Touchstone**. No unsolicited mss.
Royalties paid twice-yearly.

Simon & Schuster Children's Publishing

1230 Avenue of the Americas, New York NY 10020
☎001 212 698 2112
President/Publisher *Kristina Peterson*
VP/Publisher, Hardcover & Paperback Imprints *Brenda Bowen*

A division of the Simon & Schuster Consumer Group. *Publishes* pre-school to young adult, picture books, hardcover and paperback fiction, non-fiction, trade, library and mass-market titles. About 480 titles a year.

IMPRINTS
Aladdin Books *Ellen Krieger* Picture books, paperback fiction and non-fiction reprints and originals, and limited series for ages pre-school to young adult; **Atheneum Books for Young Readers** *Ginee Seo* Picture books, hardcover fiction and non-fiction books across all genres for ages three to young adult. Two lines within this imprint are **Jean Karl Books** quality fantasy-fiction and **Anne Schwartz Books** distinct picture books and high-quality fiction; **Little Simon** *Robin Corey* Mass-market novelty books (pop-ups, board books, colouring & activity) and merchandise (book and audiocassette) for ages birth through eight; **Margaret K. McElderry Books** *Margaret K. McElderry, Emma Dryden* Picture books, hardcover fiction and non-fiction trade books for children ages three to young adult; **Simon & Schuster Books for Young Readers** *Steve Geck* Picture books, hardcover fiction and non-fiction for children ages three to young adult. **Simon Spotlight** *Jennifer Koch* New imprint devoted exclusively to children's media tie-ins and licensed properties.
   For submissions to all imprints: send envelope (US size 10) for guidelines, attention: *Manuscript Submissions Guidelines*.

Simon Spotlight
See **Simon & Schuster Children's Publishing**

Sonnet Books
See **Pocket Books**

Southern Illinois University Press
PO Box 3697, Carbondale IL 62902–3697
☎001 618 453 2281 Fax 001 618 453 1221
Email jstetter@siu.edu
Website www.siu.edu/siupress
Director *John F. Stetter*
FOUNDED 1956. *Publishes* scholarly and general interest non-fiction books and educational materials. 50 titles a year.
   Royalties paid annually.

Stackpole Books
5067 Ritter Road, Mechanicsburg PA 17055
☎001 717 796 0411 Fax 001 717 796 0412
Website www.stackpolebooks.com
President *David Ritter*
Vice President/Editorial Director *Judith Schnell*
FOUNDED 1933. *Publishes* outdoor sports, fishing, nature, photography, military reference, history. About 80 titles a year.
   Royalties paid twice-yearly.

Stanford University Press
521 Lomita Mall, Stanford CA 94305-2235
☎001 650 723 9434 Fax 001 650 725 3457
Website www.sup.org
ManagingDirector *Geoffrey R.H. Burn*
FOUNDED 1925. *Publishes* non-fiction: scholarly works in all areas of the humanities, social sciences, history and literature, also professional lists in business, economics and law. About 120 titles a year. No unsolicited mss; query in writing first.

Steeple Hill
See **Silhouette Books**

Sterling Publishing Co. Inc.
387 Park Avenue South, 5th Floor, New York NY 10016–8810
☎001 212 532 7160 Fax 001 212 213 2495
Website www.sterlingpub.com
President *Lincoln A. Boehm*
Executive Vice-President *Charles Nurnberg*
Editorial Director *John Woodside*
FOUNDED 1949. *Publishes* non-fiction: refer-

ence and information books, science, business, nature, arts and crafts, home improvement, history, photography, children's humour, complementary health, wine and food, sports, music, psychology, occult, woodworking, pets, hobbies, gardening, puzzles.

Sunburst Technology
See **Houghton Mifflin Co.**

Susquehanna University Press
See **Golden Cockerel Press** under **UK Publishers**

Syracuse University Press
621 Skytop Road, Suite 110, Syracuse NY 13244–5290
☎001 315 443 5534 Fax 001 315 443 5545
Acting Director *John Fruehwirth*

FOUNDED 1943. *Publishes* scholarly books in the following areas: contemporary Middle East studies, Middle East literature in translation, international affairs, Irish studies, Iroquois studies, women and religion, Jewish studies, medieval studies, religion and politics, television, geography. About 70 titles a year. Also co-publishes with a number of organisations such as the American University of Beirut. No unsolicited mss. Send query letter with IRCs.
Royalties paid annually.

Nan A. Talese
See **Doubleday Broadway Publishing Group**

Jeremy P. Tarcher
See **Penguin Putnam Inc**

Temple University Press
1601 N. Broad Street, 083–42, Philadelphia PA 19122–6099
☎001 215 204 8787 Fax 001 215 204 4719
Website www.temple.edu/tempress
Editor-in-Chief *Janet M. Francendese*

FOUNDED 1969. *Publishes* scholarly books. About 60 titles a year. Authors generally academics. Letter of inquiry with brief outline. Include fax/e-mail address.

University of Tennessee Press
110 Conference Center Bldg., Knoxville TN 37996
☎001 865 974 3321 Fax 001 865 974 3724
Website www.utpress.org
Managing Editor *Stan Ivester*

FOUNDED in 1940. *Publishes* scholarly and regional non-fiction. *Royalties* paid annually.

University of Texas Press
PO Box 7819, Austin TX 78713-7819
☎001 512 471 7233/Editorial: 471 4278
Fax 001 512 232 7178
Website www.utexas.edu/utpress/
Director *Joanna Hitchcock*
Assistant Director/Executive Editor-in-Chief *Theresa J. May*

Publishes scholarly and regional non-fiction: anthropology, architecture, classics, environmental studies, humanities, social sciences, geography, language studies, literary modernism; Latin American/Latino/Mexican American/Middle Eastern/Native American studies, natural history and ornithology, regional books (Texas and the southwest). Unsolicited material welcome in above subject areas only. About 90 titles a year and 12 journals.
Royalties paid annually.

Thorndike Press
See **Gale Group**

Three Rivers Press
See **The Crown Publishing Group**

Times Books
See **Henry Holt & Company Inc.**

Topaz
See **Penguin Putnam Inc.**

Touchstone
See **Simon & Schuster Adult Publishing Group**

Transaction Publishers Ltd
c/o Rutgers University, 35 Berrue Circle, Piscataway NJ 08854–8042
☎001 732 445 2280 Fax 001 732 445 3138
Email ihorowitz@transactionpub.com
Website www.transactionpub.com
Chairman *I.L. Horowitz*
Managing Director *Mary E. Curtis*

FOUNDED 1962. Independent publisher of academic social scientific books, periodicals and serials. 125 titles in 2001.

Truman Talley Books
See **St Martin's Press LLC**

Twenty-First Century Books
See **The Millbrook Press, Inc.**

Tyndale House Publishers, Inc.

PO Box 80, Wheaton IL 60189
☎001 630 668 8310 Fax 001 630 668 3245
Website www.tyndale.com
President *Mark D. Taylor*
FOUNDED 1962. Non-denominational religious publisher of around 300 titles a year for the evangelical Christian market. Books cover a wide range of categories from non-fiction to gift books, theology, doctrine, Bibles, children's and youth. Also produces video material, calendars and audio books for the same market. No poetry. No unsolicited mss. Synopses and ideas considered. Send query letter summarising contents of book and length. Include a brief biography, detailed outline and 3 sample chapters. IRCs essential for response or return of material. No audio cassettes, disks or video tapes in lieu of mss. Response time around 12–16 weeks. No phone calls or e-mail submissions. Send s.a.e. for submission guidelines.
Royalties paid annually.

University Press of America, Inc.

4720 Boston Way, Lanham MD 20706
☎001 301 459 3366 Fax 001 301 459 2118
Website www.univpress.com
President/Publisher *James E. Lyons*
Director *Judith L. Rothman*
FOUNDED 1974. *Publishes* scholarly monographs, college and graduate level textbooks. No children's, elementary or high school. About 450 titles a year. Submit outline or request proposal questionnaire.
Royalties paid annually.

Viking/Viking Children's Books

See **Penguin Putnam Inc**

Villard

See **Random House, Inc.**

Vintage Books

See **Random House, Inc.**

University of Virginia Press

PO Box 400318, Charlottesville
VA 22904–4318
☎001 434 924 3468 Fax 001 434 982 2655
Email upressva@virginia.edu
Website www.upress.virginia.edu
Director *Penelope Kaiserlian*
FOUNDED 1963. *Publishes* academic books in humanities and social science with concentrations in American history, African-American

studies, architecture, Victorian literature, Caribbean literature and ecocriticism. 52 titles in 2001. No unsolicited mss; will consider synopses and ideas for books if in their specific areas of concentration. Approach by mail for full proposal; e-mail for short inquiry. No fiction, children's, poetry or academic books outside interests specified above.
Royalties paid annually.

Voyager Paperbacks

See **Harcourt Trade Division**

J. Weston Walch, Publisher

PO Box 658, Portland ME 04102
☎001 207 772 2846 Fax 001 207 772 3105
Website www.walch.com
President *John Thoreson*
Editor-in-Chief *Susan Blair*
FOUNDED 1927. *Publishes* supplementary educational materials for middle and secondary schools across a wide range of subjects, including English/language arts, literacy, special needs, mathematics, social studies, science and school-to-career. Always interested in ideas from secondary school teachers who develop materials in the classroom. Proposal letters, synopses and ideas welcome.
Royalties

Walk Worthy Press

See **Warner Books Inc.**

Walker & Co.

435 Hudson Street, New York NY 10014
☎001 212 727 8300 Fax 001 212 727 0984
Contact *Submissions Editor*
FOUNDED 1959. *Publishes* mystery, children's and non-fiction. Please contact the following editors in advance before sending any material to be sure of their interest, then follow up as instructed: **Mystery** *Michael Seidman* 65–70,000 words. Send first three chapters and two-page synopsis. **Trade Non-fiction** *George Gibson* Permission and documentation must be available with mss. Submit prospectus first, with sample chapters and marketing analysis. **Books for Young Readers** *Emily Easton* Fiction and non-fiction for all ages. Query before sending non-fiction proposals. Especially interested in young science and picture books, historical and contemporary fiction for middle grades and young adults. BFYR will consider unsolicited submissions.

Frederick Warne

See **Penguin Putnam Inc**

Warner Books Inc.

1271 Avenue of the Americas, New York
NY 10020
☎001 212 522 7200 Fax 001 212 522 7991
Website www.twbookmark.com

Senior Vice-President/Publisher *Jamie Raab*

Associate Publisher *Les Pockell*

FOUNDED 1961. A subsidiary of Time Warner
Book Group. *Publishes* fiction and non-fiction,
audio books. About 250 titles a year.
IMPRINTS **Aspect** *Jaime Levine*; **Mysterious
Press** *Sara Ann Freed*; **Time Warner Audio
Books**; **Warner Vision**; **Walk Worthy
Press**; **Warner Faith**. No unsolicited mss.

Washington State University Press

PO Box 645910, Pullman WA 99164-5910
☎001 509 335 3518 Fax 001 509 335 8568
Email wsupress@wsu.edu
Website www.wsu.edu/wsupress

Editor *Glen Lindeman*

FOUNDED 1928. *Publishes* hardcover originals,
trade paperbacks and reprints. *Publishes* mainly
on the history, prehistory, culture, politics and
natural history of the Northwest United States
(Washington, Idaho, Oregon, Montana, Alaska)
and British Columbia, but works that focus on
national topics or other regions may also be considered if they have a Northwest connection.
Subjects include history, biography, cooking/
food history, nature/environment, politics.
8–10 titles a year. Queries welcome.
  Royalties paid annually.

Franklin Watts

See **Grolier Publishing**

Wellspring

See **Ballantine Books**

Westview Press

See **Perseus Books Group**

John Wiley & Sons, Inc.

605 Third Avenue, New York NY 10158
☎001 212 850 6000 Fax 001 212 850 6088
Email info@wiley.com
Website www.wiley.com

Chief Executive Officer *William J. Pesce*

FOUNDED 1807. Acquired a major stake in
Oxford-based business publisher Capstone
Publishing Ltd in 2000. *Publishes* professional
and trade print and electronic products in the
following fields: culinary arts and hospitality,
architecture/design, business, accounting, psychology, non-profit institution management,
computers, engineering and general interest.
Educational products: the sciences, mathematics,
engineering, accounting, business, teacher education, modern languages, religion. Scientific,
technical and medical publishers of journals,
encyclopedias, available in print and electronic
media. About 1500 titles a year. Unsolicited mss
not accepted.

The University of Wisconsin Press

1930 Monroe Street, 3rd Floor, Madison
WI 53711–2059
☎001 608 263 1110 Fax 001 608 263 1120
Email uwiscpress@uwpress.wisc.edu
Website www.wisc.edu/wisconsinpress

Director *Robert A. Mandel*

FOUNDED 1936. *Publishes* scholarly, general
interest non-fiction and regional books about
Wisconsin and the mid-west. About 50 titles a
year. No unsolicited mss; proposals (sent by
mail) welcome. 'No unrevised dissertations, no
Festschrifts, no genre, no how-to.'

Zondervan Publishing House

5300 Patterson Avenue SE, Grand Rapids
MI 49530
☎001 616 698 6900 Fax 001 616 698 3421

President/Chief Executive
  Bruce E. Ryskamp

FOUNDED 1931. Subsidiary of **HarperCollins
Publishers, Inc.** *Publishes* Protestant religion,
Bibles, books, audio & video, computer soft-
ware, calendars and speciality items.

US Literary Agents

Adler & Robin Books, Inc.

3000 Connecticut Avenue, NW, Suite 317,
Washington DC 20008
☎001 202 986 9275 Fax 001 202 986 9485
Email dmorris@morrisbelt.com
Website www.adlerbooks.com
President Bill Adler Jr
Senior Agents Laura Belt, Djana Pearson
   Morris
Editor Jeanne Tyrrell Welsh

FOUNDED 1988. Handles computer books and
non-fiction. Unsolicited synopses and queries
welcome with s.a.e./IRCs. Electronic submissions accepted. No reading fee. Commission
Home 15%; UK 20%.

Altair Literary Agency★

141 Fifth Avenue, Suite 8N, New York
NY 10010
☎001 212 505 3320 Fax 001 212 505 3319
Email APedolsky or
NSmith@AltairLiteraryAgency.com
Website www.AltairLiteraryAgency.com
Contacts Andrea Pedolsky, Nicholas T. Smith

FOUNDED 1996. Handles historical, pre-20th
century, literary and women's related fiction;
children's books; and non-fiction covering
how-to, popular science, contemporary issues,
museum-exhibit-related books, illustrated/
photography, history of science. No true crime
or memoirs. Send query letter and proposal for
non-fiction; query letter and synopsis for fiction. Return postage essential. No reading fee.
Commission Home 15%; Foreign 20%.

Miriam Altshuler Literary Agency★

53 Old Post Road North, Red Hook
NY 12571
☎001 845 758 9408 Fax 001 845 758 3118
Email malalit@ulster.net
Contact Sara McGhee

FOUNDED 1994. Handles literary and commercial fiction; general non-fiction, psychology,
biography. No romance, science fiction, mysteries, thrillers or self-help. Send query letter
and synopsis in the first instance with return
postage. No reading fee. Commission Home
15%; Foreign/Translation 20%.

AMG/Renaissance

9465 Wilshire Boulevard, Beverly Hills
CA 90212
☎001 310 860 8000 Fax 001 310 860 8100
President Joel Gotler
Literary Associates Alan Nevins, Irv Schwartz,
   Judi Farkas, Michael Prevett, Noah Lukeman

FOUNDED 1934. Fiction and non-fiction; film
and TV rights. No unsolicited mss. Send query
letter with IRCs in the first instance. No reading fee. Commission Home 10–15%.

Marcia Amsterdam Agency

41 West 82nd Street, New York
NY 10024–5613
☎001 212 873 4945
Contact Marcia Amsterdam

FOUNDED 1969. Specialises in mainstream fiction,
horror, suspense, young adult, TV and film
scripts. No poetry, books for the 8–10 age group
or how-to. No unsolicited mss. First approach
by letter only and enclose IRCs. No reading fee
for outlines and synopses. Commission Home
15%; Foreign 20%.

Bart Andrews & Associates Inc

7510 Sunset Boulevard, Suite 100, Los
Angeles CA 90046–3418
☎001 310 271 9916
Contact Bart Andrews

FOUNDED 1982. General non-fiction: show
business, biography and autobiography, film
books, trivia, TV and nostalgia. No scripts. No
fiction, poetry, children's or science. No books
of less than major commercial potential.
Specialises in working with celebrities on autobiographies. No unsolicited mss. 'Send a brilliant
letter (with IRCs for response) extolling your
manuscript's virtues. Sell me!' No reading fee.
Commission Home & Translation 15%. Overseas
associate **Abner Stein**, UK.

Malaga Baldi Literary Agency

204 84th Street, Suite 3C, New York
NY 10024
☎001 212 579 5075 Fax 001 212 579 5078
Email MBALDI@aol.com
Contact Malaga Baldi

FOUNDED 1986. *Handles* quality fiction and non-fiction. No scripts. No westerns, men's adventure, science fiction/fantasy, romance, how-to, young adult or children's. Writers of fiction should send query letter describing the novel plus IRCs. Allow ten weeks *minimum* for response. For non-fiction, approach in writing with a proposal, table of contents and two sample chapters. No reading fee. *Commission* 15%. *Overseas associates* **Abner Stein**, UK; Japan Uni; Eliane Benisti, France; **Marsh Agency**.

The Balkin Agency, Inc.★
PO Box 222, Amherst MA 01004
☎001 413 548 9835 Fax 001 413 548 9836
Email balkin@crocker.com
Contact *Richard Balkin*
FOUNDED 1973. *Handles* adult non-fiction only. No reading fee for outlines and synopses. *Commission* Home 15%; Foreign 20%.

Loretta Barrett Books, Inc.★
101 Fifth Avenue, New York NY 10003
☎001 212 242 3420 Fax 001 212 807 9579
Contacts *Loretta Barrett, Nick Mullendore*
FOUNDED 1990. *Handles* all non-fiction and fiction genres except children's, poetry, science fiction/fantasy. *Specialises* in women's fiction, history, spirituality. No scripts. Send query letter with biography and return postage only in the first instance. *Commission* Home 15%; Foreign 20%.

Meredith Bernstein Literary Agency, Inc.★
2112 Broadway, Suite 503A, New York NY 10023
☎001 212 799 1007 Fax 001 212 799 1145
Contacts *Meredith Bernstein, Elizabeth Cavanaugh*
FOUNDED 1981. *Handles* commercial and literary fiction, mysteries and non-fiction (women's issues, business, memoirs, health, current affairs, crafts). *Commission* Home & Dramatic 15%; Translation 20%. *Overseas associates* **Abner Stein**, UK; Lennart Sane, Holland, Scandinavia and Spanish language; Thomas Schluck, Germany; Bardon Chinese Media Agency; William Miller, Japan; Frederique Porretta, France; Agenzia Letteraria, Italy.

Bleecker Street Associates, Inc.★
532 LaGuardia Place #617, New York NY 10012
☎001 212 677 4492 Fax 001 212 388 0001
FOUNDED 1984. *Handles* fiction – women's,

mystery, suspense, literary; non-fiction – history, women's interests, parenting, health, relationships, psychology, sports, sociology, current events, biography, spirituality, New Age, business. No poetry, children's, westerns, science fiction, professional, academic. Send query letter in the first instance. Will only respond if envelope and return postage enclosed. No phone calls, faxes or e-mails. No reading fee. *Commission* Home 15%; Foreign 25%.

Reid Boates Literary Agency
PO Box 328, Pittstown NJ 08867-0328
☎001 908 730 8523 Fax 001 908 730 8931
Contact *Reid Boates*
FOUNDED 1985. *Handles* general fiction and non-fiction. New clients by personal introduction only. *Commission* Home & Dramatic 15%; Translation 20%. *Overseas associates* worldwide.

Book Deals, Inc.★
417 North Sangamon Street, Chicago IL 60622
☎001 312 491 0300 Fax 001 312 491 8091
Email BookDeals@aol.com
Website www.BookDealsInc.com
President *Caroline Carney*
FOUNDED 1997. *Handles* health, finance, business, self-help, parenting, narrative non-fiction and literary fiction. No scripts, genre fiction, cookbooks, illustrated children's, coffee table books, travel guides, military history, paranormal experience. No unsolicited material; query letter welcome. No reading fee. *Commission* Home 15%; Foreign/Translation 20%.

Georges Borchardt, Inc.★
136 East 57th Street, New York NY 10022
☎001 212 753 5785 Fax 001 212 838 6518
FOUNDED 1967. Works mostly with established/published authors. *Specialises* in fiction, biography, and general non-fiction of unusual interest. Unsolicited mss not read. *Commission* Home, UK & Dramatic 15%; Translation 20%. *UK associate* **Sheil Land Associates Ltd** (Richard Scott Simon), London.

Brandt & Hochman Literary Agents, Inc.★
1501 Broadway, New York NY 10036
☎001 212 840 5760
Contacts *Carl D. Brandt, Gail Hochman, Marianne Merola, Charles Schlessiger*
FOUNDED 1914. *Handles* non-fiction and fiction. No poetry. No unsolicited mss. Approach

by letter describing background and ambitions; include return postage. No reading fee. *Commission* Home & Dramatic 15%; Foreign 20%. *UK associate* **A.M. Heath & Co. Ltd.**

Pema Browne Ltd, Illustration and Literary Agents

HCR Box 104B, Neversink NY 12765
☎001 845 985 2936/2062
Fax 001 845 985 7635
Email ppbltd@catskill.net
Website www.geocities.com/pemabrowneltd
Contacts *Pema Browne, Perry Browne*

FOUNDED 1966. ('Pema rhymes with Emma.') *Handles* mass-market mainstream and hard-cover fiction: romance, business, children's picture books and young adult; non-fiction: how-to and reference. No unsolicited mss; send query letter with IRCs. No fax or e-mail queries. Also handles illustrators' work. *Commission* Home 15%; Translation 20%; Dramatic 10%; Overseas authors 20%.

Sheree Bykofsky Associates, Inc.★

16 West 36th Street, 13th Floor, New York NY 10018
☎001 212 244 4144
Contact *Sheree Bykofsky*

FOUNDED 1985. *Handles* adult fiction and non-fiction. No scripts. No children's, young adult, horror, science fiction, romance, westerns, occult or supernatural. No unsolicited mss. Send query letter first with brief synopsis or outline and writing sample (1–3 pp) for fiction. IRCs essential for reply or return of material. No phone calls. No reading fee. *Commission* Home 15%; UK (including sub-agent's fee) 25%.

Carlisle & Company LLC★

24 East 64th Street, New York NY 10021
☎001 212 813 1881 Fax 001 212 813 9567
Email ep@carlisleco.com
Website www.carlisleco.com
Contacts *Michael V. Carlisle, Christy Fletcher, Emma Parry, Michelle Tessler*

FOUNDED 1998. *Handles* history, science, travel, narrative non-fiction, literary and category fiction. No scripts, children's, juvenile, romance, science fiction/fantasy, mysteries. No unsolicited mss. Query letter for fiction by mail or through website; proposal with query for non-fiction. No reading fee. *Commission* Home 15%; Foreign/Translation 20%.

Associates Co-agents in every major territory.

Maria Carvainis Agency, Inc.★

1350 Avenue of the Americas, Suite 2905, New York NY 10019
☎001 212 245 6365 Fax 001 212 245 7196
Email mca@mariacarvainisagency.com
President *Maria Carvainis*
Executive *Frances Kuffel*

FOUNDED 1977. *Handles* fiction: literary and mainstream, contemporary women's, mystery, suspense, historical, young adult novels; non-fiction: business, finance, women's issues, politics, film, memoirs, reportage, biography, medicine, psychology and popular science. No film scripts unless from writers with established credits. No science fiction. No faxed or e-mailed queries. No unsolicited mss; they will be returned unread. Queries only, with IRCs for response. No reading fee. *Commission* Domestic & Dramatic 15%; Translation 20%.

Martha Casselman, Literary Agent

PO Box 342, Calistoga CA 94515
☎001 707 942 4341
Contact *Martha Casselman*

FOUNDED 1979. *Handles* all types of non-fiction. No fiction at present. Main interest: food/cookery. No scripts, children's, text-books, poetry, coming-of-age fiction or science fiction. Especially interested in cookery with an appeal to the American market for possible co-publication in UK. Send queries and brief summary, with return postage. No mss. If you do not wish return of material, please state so. Also include, where applicable, any material on previous publications, reviews, brief biography. No proposals via fax. No reading fee. *Commission* Home 15%.

Castiglia Literary Agency★

1155 Camino del mar, #510, Del Mar CA 92014
☎001 858 755 8761 Fax 001 858 755 7063
Email jaclagency@aol.com
Contacts *Julie Castiglia, Winifred Golden*

FOUNDED 1993. *Handles* fiction: literary, mainstream, ethnic; non-fiction: narrative, biography, science, health, parenting, memoirs, psychology, women's and contemporary issues. *Specialises* in science, biography and literary fiction. No scripts, horror or true crime. No unsolicited material; send query letter only in the first instance. No reading fee. *Commission* Home 15%; Foreign/Translation 25%.

The Catalog Literary Agency
PO Box 2964, Vancouver WA 98668
☎001 360 694 8531
Contact *Douglas Storey*

FOUNDED 1986. *Handles* popular, professional and textbook material in all subjects, especially business, health, money, science, technology, computers, electronics and women's interests; also how-to, self-help, mainstream fiction and children's non-fiction. No genre fiction. No scripts, articles, screenplays, plays, poetry or short stories. No unsolicited mss. Query with an outline and sample chapters, and include IRCs. No reading fee. *Commission* 15%.

Linda Chester & Associates★
Rockefeller Center, 630 Fifth Avenue, New York NY 10111
☎001 212 218 3350   Fax 001 212 218 3343
Website www.lindachester.com
Contact *Joanna Pulcini, Associate*

FOUNDED 1978. *Handles* literary and commercial fiction and non-fiction in all subjects. No scripts, children's or textbooks. No unsolicited mss or queries. No reading fee for solicited material. *Commission* Home & Dramatic 15%; Translation 25%.

Clausen, Mays & Tahan Literary Agency
249 West 34th Street, Suite 605, New York NY 10001
☎001 212 239 4343   Fax 001 212 239 5248
Email cmtassist@aol.com
Contacts *Stedman Mays, Mary M. Tahan*

Handles non-fiction work such as memoirs, biography, true crime, true stories, how-to, psychology, spirituality, relationships, style, health/nutrition, fashion/beauty, women's issues, humour and cookbooks. Some fiction. Send query letter only. Include IRCs. *UK associate* **David Grossman Literary Agency Ltd**.

Hy Cohen Literary Agency Ltd
66 Brookfield, Montclair NJ 07043
☎001 973 783 9494   Fax 001 973 783 9867
Email cogency@comcast.net
President *Hy Cohen*

FOUNDED 1975. Fiction and non-fiction. No scripts. Unsolicited mss welcome, but synopsis with sample 100 pages preferred. IRCs essential. No reading fee. *Commission* Home & Dramatic 10%; Foreign 20%. *Overseas associate* **Abner Stein**, UK.

Frances Collin Literary Agent★
PO Box 33, Wayne PA 19087–0033
☎001 610 254 0555   Fax 001 610 254 5029
Contact *Frances Collin*

FOUNDED 1948. Successor to Marie Rodell. *Handles* general fiction and non-fiction. No scripts. No unsolicited mss. Send query letter only, with IRCs for reply, for the attention of *Marsha Kear*. No reading fee. Rarely accepts non-professional writers or writers not represented in the UK. *Overseas associates* worldwide.

Don Congdon Associates, Inc.★
156 Fifth Avenue, Suite 625, New York NY 10010–7002
☎001 212 645 1229   Fax 001 212 727 2688
Contacts *Don Congdon, Michael Congdon, Susan Ramer*

FOUNDED 1983. *Handles* fiction and non-fiction. No academic, technical, romantic fiction, or scripts. No unsolicited mss. Query letter with return postage in the first instance. No reading fee. *Commission* Home 10%; UK & Translation 19%. *Overseas associates* worldwide.

Cornerstone Literary Agency★
4500 Wilshire Boulevard, Los Angeles CA 90010
☎001 323 930 6039   Fax 001 323 930 0407
Email info@cornerstoneliterary.com
Website www.cornerstoneliterary.com
Contact *Helen Breitwieser*

FOUNDED 1998. *Handles* commercial fiction and non-fiction. *Specialises* in thrillers and commercial women's fiction. No scripts, children's, self-help, science fiction or fantasy. No unsolicited mss; send three sample chapters and a synopsis via fax or mail (enclosing return postage with latter). No reading fee. *Commission* Home 10%; Foreign/Translation 20%.

Richard Curtis Associates, Inc.
171 East 74th Street, Second Floor, New York NY 10021
☎001 212 772 7363   Fax 001 212 772 7393
Email info@curtisagency.com
Website www.curtisagency.com
Contact *Richard Curtis*

FOUNDED 1969. *Handles* genre and mainstream fiction, plus commercial non-fiction. No children's books or scripts.

Curtis Brown Ltd★
10 Astor Place, New York NY 10003
☎001 212 473 5400

Book Rights *Laura Blake Peterson, Ellen Geiger,*
Peter L. Ginsberg, Emilie Jacobson, Ginger
Knowlton, Marilyn E. Marlow, Maureen
Walters, Mitchell Walters
Film, TV, Audio Rights *Timothy Knowlton,*
Edwin Wintle
Translation *Dave Barbor*

FOUNDED 1914. Handles general fiction and
non-fiction. Also some scripts for film, TV and
theatre. No unsolicited mss; queries only, with
IRCs for reply. No reading fee. *Overseas associates*
Representatives in all major foreign countries.

Joan Daves Agency
21 West 26th Street, New York
NY 10010-1003
☎001 212 685 2663 Fax 001 212 685 1781

Director *Jennifer Lyons*

FOUNDED 1952. See also **Writers House
LLC**. Literary fiction and non-fiction. No
romance or textbooks. No scripts. Send query
letter in the first instance. 'A detailed synopsis
seems valuable only for non-fiction work.
Material submitted should specify the author's
background, publishing credits and similar pertinent information.' No reading fee.
Commission Home 15%; Dramatic/Film 15%;
Foreign 20%.

Sandra Dijkstra Literary Agency★
PMB 515, 1155 Camino Del Mar, Del Mar
CA 92104–3115
☎001 858 755 3115 Fax 001 858 794 2822

Contact *Babette Sparr*

FOUNDED 1981. *Handles* quality and commercial non-fiction and fiction, including some
genre fiction. No scripts. No westerns, contemporary romance or poetry. Willing to look
at children's projects. *Specialises* in quality fiction, mystery/thrillers, narrative non-fiction,
psychology, self-help, science, health, business,
memoirs, biography. 'Dedicated to promoting
new and original voices and ideas.' For fiction:
send brief synopsis (one page) and first 50
pages; for non-fiction: send proposal with
overview, chapter outline, author biog, two
sample chapters and profile of competition. All
submissions should be accompanied by IRCs.
No reading fee. *Commission* Home 15%;
Translation 20%. *Overseas associates* **Abner
Stein**, UK; Ursula Bender, Agence Hoffman,
Germany; Licht & Burr, Scandinavia; Luigi
Bernabo, Italy; Sandra Bruna, Spain; Caroline

Van Gelderen, Netherlands; M. Kling (La
Nouvelle Agence), France; William Miller,
The English Agency, Japan.

Dunham Literary★
156 Fifth Avenue, Suite 625, New York
NY 10010
☎001 212 929 0994 Fax 001 212 929 0904
Website www.dunhamlit.com

Contacts *Jennie Dunham, Donna H. Liberman*

FOUNDED 2000. *Handles* literary fiction and
non-fiction, New Age spirituality, mysteries
and children's (from picture books through
young adult). No scripts, romance, westerns,
horror, science-fiction/fantasy or poetry. No
unsolicited material. Send query letter (with
return postage) giving information on the
author and ms. No e-mail or faxed queries; see
the website for further contact information.
No reading fee. *Commission* Home 15%;
Foreign/Translation 20%. *Overseas associate* UK
& Europe – **A.M. Heath & Co. Ltd**.

Jane Dystel Literary Management★
One Union Square West, Suite 904, New
York NY 10003
☎001 212 627 9100 Fax 001 212 627 9313
Website www.dystel.com

Contacts *Jane Dystel, Miriam Goderich,*
Jo Fagan, Stacey Glick, Michael Bourret

FOUNDED 1991. *Handles* non-fiction and fiction. *Specialises* in politics, history, biography,
cookbooks, current affairs, celebrities, commercial and literary fiction. No reading fee.

Educational Design Services, Inc.
PO Box 253, Wantagh NY 11793
☎001 718 539 4107/516 221 0995
Email linder.eds@juno.com *or*
eselzer@nyc.rr.com

President *Bertram Linder*
Vice President *Edwin Selzer*

FOUNDED 1979. *Specialises* in educational ma-
terial and textbooks for sale to school markets.
IRCs must accompany submissions. *Commission*
Home 15%; Foreign 25%.

Elek International Rights Agents
(a subsidiary of **The Content
Company, Inc.**)
5111 JFK Boulevard East, West New York
NJ 07093
☎001 201 558 0323 Fax 001 201 558 0307
Email info@theliteraryagency.com
Website www.theliteraryagency.com

Contact *Lauren Mactas*

FOUNDED 1979. *Handles* adult non-fiction and children's picture books. No scripts, fiction, psychology, New Age, poetry, short stories or autobiography. No unsolicited mss; send letter of enquiry with IRCs for reply; include résumé, credentials, brief synopsis. No reading fee. *Commission* Home 15%; Dramatic & Foreign 20%.

Ethan Ellenberg Literary Agency*
548 Broadway, #5E, New York NY 10012
☎001 212 431 4554 Fax 001 212 941 4652
Email agent@ethanellenberg.com
Website www.ethanellenberg.com

Contacts *Ethan Ellenberg, Michael Psaltis*

FOUNDED 1984. *Handles* fiction: commercial, genre, literary and children's; non-fiction: history, biography, business, science, health, cooking, current affairs. No scripts, poetry or short stories. *Specialises* in commercial fiction, thrillers, suspense and romance. All communication should be by mail with return postage. For fiction send synopsis and three chapters; for non-fiction send proposal and sample chapters, if available. No reading fee. *Commission* Home 15%; Translation 20%.

Ann Elmo Agency, Inc.*
60 East 42nd Street, New York NY 10165
☎001 212 661 2880/1 Fax 001 212 661 2883

Contacts *Lettie Lee, Mari Cronin, Andree Abecassis*

FOUNDED in the 1940s. *Handles* literary and romantic fiction, mysteries and mainstream; also non-fiction in all subjects, including biography and self-help. Some children's (8–12-year-olds). Query letter with outline of project in the first instance. No reading fee. *Commission* Home 15–20%. *Overseas associate* **John Johnson Ltd**, UK.

The Fogelman Literary Agency*
7515 Greenville Avenue, Suite 712, Dallas TX 75231
☎001 214 361 9956 Fax 001 214 361 9553
Email FogLit@aol.com
Website www.fogelman.com

Also at: 919 Third Avenue, Suite 2700, New York, NY 10022

Contacts *Evan Fogelman, Linda Kruger, Kim Leak*

FOUNDED 1989. *Handles* non-fiction and fiction: romance (including historical and contemporary) and some mystery/suspense. No scripts, poetry,

westerns, science fiction/fantasy or children's books. No unsolicited material. Published authors are welcome to call but unpublished authors should send query by e-mail or letter with return postage. No reading fee. *Commission* Home 15%; Foreign/Translation 10%. *Overseas associates* Thomas Schluck Agency; Shin Won Literary Agency; Bastei Lubbe Taschenbucher; Big Apple Tuttle-Mori Agency.

ForthWrite Literary Agency & Speakers Bureau
23852 W. Pacific Coast Highway, Suite 701, Malibu CA 90265
☎001 310 456 5698 Fax 001 310 456 6589
Email agent@KellerMedia.com
Website www.KellerMedia.com

Contact *Wendy L. Keller*

FOUNDED 1988. *Specialises* in non-fiction: biography, business (marketing, finance, management and sales), alternative health, cookery, gardening, nature, popular psychology, history, self-help, home and health, crafts, computer, how-to, animal care by experts known in the field. Handles electronic, foreign (translation and distribution) and resale rights for previously published books. Send query letter with IRCs. No reading fee. *Commission* Foreign 20%.

Jeanne Fredericks Literary Agency, Inc.*
221 Benedict Hill Road, New Canaan CT 06840
☎001 203 972 3011 Fax 001 203 972 3011
Email jfredrks@optonline.net

Contact *Jeanne Fredericks*

FOUNDED 1997. *Handles* quality adult non-fiction, usually of a practical and popular nature by authorities in their fields. *Specialises* in health, gardening, business, self-help, reference, careers. No fiction, juvenile, poetry, essays, politics, academic or textbooks. No unsolicited material; send query by e-mail (no attachments) or letter with return postage in the first instance. No reading fee. *Commission* Home 15%; Foreign 25% (with co-agent) or 20% (direct).

Robert A. Freedman Dramatic Agency, Inc.*
Suite 2310, 1501 Broadway, New York NY 10036
☎001 212 840 5760

President *Robert A. Freedman*

Vice President *Selma Luttinger*

FOUNDED 1928 as Brandt & Brandt Dramatic Department, Inc. Took its present name in 1984. Works mostly with established authors. *Specialises* in plays, film and TV scripts. Unsolicited mss not read. *Commission* Dramatic 10%.

Max Gartenberg, Literary Agent

521 Fifth Avenue, Suite 1700, New York NY 10175
☎001 212 292 4354 Fax 001 973 535 5033
Email gartenbook@att.net

Contact *Max Gartenberg*

FOUNDED 1954. Works mostly with established/published authors. *Specialises* in non-fiction and trade fiction. Query first. *Commission* Home & Dramatic 10%; 15% on initial sale, 10% thereafter; Foreign 15/20%.

Gelfman Schneider Literary Agents, Inc.★

250 West 57th Street, Suite 2515, New York NY 10107
☎001 212 245 1993 Fax 001 212 245 8678

Contacts *Deborah Schneider, Jane Gelfman*

FOUNDED 1919 (London), 1980 (New York). Formerly John Farquharson Ltd. Works mostly with established/published authors. *Specialises* in general trade fiction and non-fiction. No poetry, short stories or screenplays. No reading fee for outlines. Submissions must be accompanied by IRCs. *Commission* Home 15%; Dramatic 15%; Foreign 20%. *Overseas associate* **Curtis Brown Group Ltd**, UK.

The Sebastian Gibson Agency

PO Box 13350, Palm Desert CA 92255–3350
☎001 760 322 2446 Fax 001 760 322 3857

Contact *Sebastian Gibson*

FOUNDED 1994. *Handles* all categories of fiction; psychological thrillers, historical novels, mysteries/suspense, action/adventure, crime/police, medical dramas. Also non-fiction written by celebrities, cookbooks or photography, children's and juvenile books. No poetry, textbooks, essays, short stories, child development, how-to, gardening, erotic, autobiography, drug recovery, religious books or scripts. 'We are constantly seeking something fresh and new with novel plot lines or a story told in a way that has never been told before. Grab our imagination and you may grab the imagination of a publisher as well.' Send query letter, synopsis and first three chapters with sufficient IRCs for return. No phone calls, faxes or e-mails. *Commission* Home 20%; Overseas & Translation 20%; Film & Ancilliary Rights 15%.

Graybill & English, LLC★

1875 Connecticut Avenue, NW, Suite 712, Washington DC 20009
☎001 202 861 0106 Fax 001 202 457 0662
Website www.graybillandenglish.com

FOUNDED 1997. *Handles* fiction: literary, commercial women's, romance, mystery; plus serious and commercial non-fiction. No scripts, poetry or children's books. No unsolicited mss; send query letter with biog and writing sample (enclose return postage). See website for contact information. No reading fee. *Commission* Home 15%; Foreign 20%.

Sanford J. Greenburger Associates, Inc.★

15th Floor, 55 Fifth Avenue, New York NY 10003
☎001 212 206 5600 Fax 001 212 463 8718
Website www.greenburger.com

Contacts *Heide Lange, Faith Hamlin, Beth Vesel, Theresa Park, Elyse Cheney, Daniel Mandel*

Handles fiction and non-fiction. No unsolicited mss. First approach with query letter, sample chapter and synopsis. No reading fee.

The Charlotte Gusay Literary Agency

10532 Blythe Avenue, Los Angeles CA 90064
☎001 310 559 0831 Fax 001 310 559 2639
Email gusay1@aol.com
Website www.mediastudio.com/gusay

Contact *Charlotte Gusay*

FOUNDED 1988. *Handles* fiction, both literary and commercial, plus non-fiction: children's and adult humour, parenting, gardening, women's and men's issues, feminism, psychology, memoirs, biography, travel. No science fiction, horror, short pieces or collections of stories. No unsolicited mss; send query letter first, then if your material is requested, send succinct outline and first three sample chapters for fiction, or proposal for non-fiction. No response without IRCs. No reading fee. *Commission* Home 15%; Dramatic 10%; Translation & Foreign 25%.

Joy Harris Literary Agency, Inc.★

156 Fifth Avenue, Suite 617, New York NY 10010
☎001 212 924 6269 Fax 001 212 924 6609

Email gen.office@jhlitagent.com

Contacts *Joy Harris, Stephanie Abou, Leslie Daniels, Alexia Paul*

Handles adult non-fiction and fiction. No unsolicited mss. Query letter in the first instance. No reading fee. *Commission* Home & Dramatic 15%; Foreign 20%. *Overseas associates* Michael Meller, Germany; **Abner Stein**, UK; Roberto Santachiara, Italy; various Japanese agencies; **Andrew Nurnberg Associates**, rest of the territories.

John Hawkins & Associates, Inc.★

71 West 23rd Street, Suite 1600, New York NY 10010
☎001 212 807 7040 Fax 001 212 807 9555
Email jha@jhaliterary.com
Website www.jhaliterary.com

Contacts *John Hawkins, William Reiss*

FOUNDED 1893. *Handles* film and TV rights. No unsolicited mss; send queries with 1–3-page outline and one-page c.v. IRCs necessary for response. No reading fee. *Commission* Apply for rates.

The Jeff Herman Agency, LLC

332 Bleecker Street, Suite 631, New York NY 10014
☎001 212 941 0540 Fax 001 212 941 0614
Email jeff@jeffherman.com
Website www.jeffherman.com

Contact *Jeffrey H. Herman*

Handles all areas of non-fiction, textbooks and reference. No scripts. No unsolicited mss. Query letter with IRCs in the first instance. No reading fee. Jeff Herman publishes a useful reference guide to the book trade called *The Writer's Guide to Book Editors, Publishers & Literary Agents* (Prima). *Commission* Home 15%; Translation 10%.

Frederick Hill Bonnie Nadell Inc.

1842 Union Street, San Francisco CA 94123
☎001 415 921 2910 Fax 001 415 921 2802

Contacts *Fred Hill, Bonnie Nadell, Irene Moore*

FOUNDED 1979. General fiction and non-fiction. No scripts. Send query letter detailing past publishing history if any. IRCs required. *Commission* Home & Dramatic 15%; Foreign 20%. *Overseas associate* **Mary Clemmey Literary Agency**, UK.

IMG Literary

See entry under **UK Literary Agents**

Janklow & Nesbit Associates

445 Park Avenue, New York NY 10022
☎001 212 421 1700 Fax 001 212 980 3671

Partners *Morton L. Janklow, Lynn Nesbit*
Senior Vice-President *Anne Sibbald*
Agents *Tina Bennett, Luke Janklow, Richard Morris, Eric Simonoff*

FOUNDED 1989. *Handles* fiction and non-fiction; commercial and literary. No unsolicited mss. See also **Janklow & Nesbit (UK) Ltd** under **UK Literary Agents**.

JCA Literary Agency, Inc★

27 West 20th Street, Suite 1103, New York NY 10011
☎001 212 807 0888 Fax 001 212 807 0461

Contacts *Jeff Gerecke, Tony Outhwaite, Peter Steinberg*

FOUNDED 1978. *Handles* general fiction and non-fiction. No scripts, poetry, science fiction/fantasy or children's books. No unsolicited mss; send query letter with return postage. No reading fee. *Commission* Home 15%; Foreign 20%. *Overseas associate* **Vanessa Holt**, UK.

Kidde, Hoyt & Picard★

333 East 51st Street, New York NY 10022
☎001 212 755 9461/9465
Fax 001 212 223 2501

Chief Associate *Katharine Kidde*

FOUNDED 1981. *Specialises* in mainstream and literary fiction, mysteries, romantic fiction (historical and contemporary), and quality non-fiction in humanities and social sciences (biography, history, current affairs, the arts). No unsolicited mss. Query first, include return postage. No reading fee. *Commission* 15%.

Kirchoff/Wohlberg, Inc.★

866 United Nations Plaza, Suite 525, New York NY 10017
☎001 212 644 2020 Fax 001 212 223 4387

Authors' Representative *Elizabeth Pulitzer-Voges*

FOUNDED 1930. *Handles* books for children and young adults, specialising in children's picture books. No adult material. No scripts for TV, radio, film or theatre. Send letter of enquiry with synopsis or outline and writing sample plus IRCs for reply or return. No reading fee.

Harvey Klinger, Inc.★

301 West 53rd Street, New York NY 10019
☎001 212 581 7068 Fax 001 212 315 3823
Email Klingerinc@aol.com

Contact *Harvey Klinger*

FOUNDED 1977. *Handles* mainstream fiction and non-fiction. Specialises in commercial and literary fiction, psychology, health and science. No scripts, poetry, computer or children's books. Welcomes unsolicited material; send by e-mail or post (no faxes). No reading fee. *Commission* Home 15%; Foreign 25%. *Overseas associates* in all principal countries.

The Knight Agency, Inc★
PO Box 550648, Atlanta GA 30355
Fax 001 404 237 3439
Email knightagency@msn.com
Website www.knightagency.net
Contacts *Deidre Knight, Pamela Harty, Lisa Payne*

FOUNDED 1996. *Handles* romance and women's fiction; general non-fiction including business, finance, African American, religion, health. No scripts, horror, science fiction, action/adventure, mystery, short story or poetry collections. No unsolicited material. Prefers a well-written one-page query sent via e-mail (no attachments) or post. If sent by the latter, include return postage. No reading fee. *Commission* Home 15%; Foreign 20–25 %.

Paul Kohner, Inc.
9300 Wilshire Boulevard, Suite 555, Beverly Hills CA 90212
☎001 310 550 1060 Fax 001 310 276 1083
Contacts *Pearl Wexler, Stephen Moore, Deborah Obad*

FOUNDED 1938. *Handles* a broad range of books for subsidiary rights sales to film and TV. Few direct placements with publishers as film and TV scripts are the major part of the business. *Specialises* in true crime, biography and history. Non-fiction preferred to fiction for the TV market but anything 'we feel has strong potential' will be considered. No short stories, poetry, science fiction or gothic. Unsolicited material will be returned unread, if accompanied by s.a.e. Approach via a third-party reference or send query letter with professional résumé. No reading fee. *Commission* Home & Dramatic 10%; Publishing 15%.

Linda Konner Literary Agency★
10 West 15 Street, Suite 1918, New York NY 10011
☎001 212 691 3419
Email ldkonner@cs.com
Contact *Linda Konner*

FOUNDED 1996. *Handles* non-fiction only, specialising in health, self-help, diet/fitness, pop psychology, relationships, parenting, personal finance. Also some pop culture/celebrities. Books must be written by or with established experts in their field. No scripts, fiction, poetry or children's books. No unsolicited material; send one-page query with return postage. No reading fee. *Commission* Home 15%; Foreign 25%.

Barbara S. Kouts, Literary Agent★
PO Box 560, Bellport NY 11713
☎001 516 286 1278 Fax 001 516 286 1538
Contact *Barbara S. Kouts*

FOUNDED 1980. *Handles* fiction, non-fiction and children's. No romance, science fiction or scripts. No unsolicited mss. Query letter in the first instance. No reading fee. *Commission* Home 15%; Foreign 20%.

Peter Lampack Agency, Inc.
551 Fifth Avenue, Suite 1613, New York NY 10176
☎001 212 687 9106 Fax 001 212 687 9109
Email renboPLA@aol.com
Contact *Loren Soeiro*

FOUNDED in 1977. *Handles* commercial fiction: male action and adventure, contemporary relationships, historical, mysteries and suspense, literary fiction; also non-fiction from recognised experts in a given field, plus biographies, autobiographies. Also handles theatrical, motion picture, and TV rights from book properties. No original scripts or screenplays, series or episodic material. Best approach by letter in first instance. No reply without s.a.e. 'We will respond within three weeks and invite the submission of manuscripts which we would like to examine.' No reading fee. No unsolicited mss. *Commission* Home & Dramatic 15%; Translation & UK 20%.

The Lazear Agency, Inc./ Talkback, A Speaker's Bureau
800 Washington Avenue N., Suite 660, Minneapolis MN 55401
☎001 612 332 8640 Fax 001 612 332 4648
Contacts *Christi Cardenas, Jonathon Lazear, Wendy Lazear, Anne Blackstone, Julie Mayo*

FOUNDED 1984. *Handles* fiction: mysteries, suspense, young adult, commercial and literary; also commercial and serious non-fiction of all types; and children's books. No poetry or stage plays. Approach by letter, with description of mss, short autobiography and IRCs. No reading fee. Also book packaging division and select entertainment management. Talkback is the agency's speaker's bureau. *Commission* Home & Dramatic 15%; Translation 20%.

Ellen Levine, Literary Agency, Inc.★
Suite 1801, 15 East 26th Street, New York NY 10010-1505
☎001 212 899 0620 Fax 001 212 725 4501
Contacts *Diana Finch, Elizabeth Kaplan, Louise Quayle, Ellen Levine*
FOUNDED 1980. *Handles* all types of books. No scripts. No unsolicited mss, nor any other material unless requested. No telephone calls. First approach by letter; send US postage or IRCs for reply, otherwise material not returned. No reading fee. *Commission* Home 15%; Foreign 20%. *UK Associate* **A.M. Heath & Co. Ltd**.

Wendy Lipkind Agency★
165 East 66th Street, New York NY 10021
☎001 212 628 9653 Fax 001 212 628 2693
Contact *Wendy Lipkind*
FOUNDED 1977. *Handles* parenting, fitness, diet, memoirs, social history and women's issues. *Specialises* in medical, psychology, history and psychological thrillers. No scripts, science fiction/fantasy, mystery series. No unsolicited material; send query letter with return postage. No reading fee. *Commission* Home 15%; Foreign 20%. *Overseas associates* worldwide.

Literary & Creative Artists Inc.★
3543 Albemarle Street NW, Washington DC 20008–4213
☎001 202 362 4688 Fax 001 202 362 8875
Website www.lcadc.com
Contacts *Muriel G. Nellis, Jane F. Roberts, Stephen Rowe*
FOUNDED 1981. *Specialises* in a broad range of general non-fiction. No poetry, pornography, academic or educational textbooks. No unsolicited mss; query letter in the first instance. Include IRCs for response. No reading fee. *Commission* Home 15%; Dramatic 20%; Translation 20–25%.

Sterling Lord Literistic, Inc.
65 Bleecker Street, New York NY 10012
☎001 212 780 6050 Fax 001 212 780 6095
Contacts *Peter Matson, Sterling Lord*

FOUNDED 1979. *Handles* all genres, fiction and non-fiction, plus scripts for TV and film. No unsolicited mss. Prefers letter outlining all non-fiction. No reading fee. *Commission* Home 15%; UK & Translation 20%.

Barbara Lowenstein Associates★
121 West 27th Street, Suite 601, New York NY 10001
☎001 212 206 1630 Fax 001 212 727 0280
Agents *Barbara Lowenstein, Nancy Yost, Eileen Cope, Dorian Karchmar*
FOUNDED 1976. *Handles* fiction: literary and commercial, women's, mainstream, romance, mystery, thrillers. Non-fiction: narrative, health, business, women's issues, adventure travel, science, spirituality, psychology, social issues, ethnic and cultural issues, history, biography and the arts. No textbooks, westerns, science fiction, cookery or children's books. No reading fee. Fiction – send query letter, synopsis and first chapter; nonfiction – send query with proposal, if available, or overview. Include return postage. *Commission* Home 15%; Foreign/Translation 20%. *Overseas associates* in all major countries.

McIntosh & Otis, Inc.★
353 Lexington Avenue, New York NY 10016
☎001 212 687 7400 Fax 001 212 687 6894
Email info@mcintoshandotis.com
President *Eugene H. Winick*
Adult Books *Sam Pinkus, Elizabeth Winick*
Children's *Dorothy Markinko, Tracey Adams*
Motion Picture/Television *Evva Pryor*
FOUNDED 1928. Adult and juvenile literary fiction and non-fiction. No textbooks or scripts. No unsolicited mss. Query letter indicating nature of the work plus details of background. IRCs for response. No reading fee. *Commission* Home & Dramatic 15%; Foreign 20%. *Overseas Associates* **Abner Stein** and **Curtis Brown**, UK; Bardon-Chinese Media, China; Luigi Bernabo, Italy; Bookman, Scandinavia; Julio F-Yanez, Latin America, Portugal, Spain; Japan Uni and Tuttle Mori, Japan; Nuricham Kesim, Turkey; La Nouvelle Agence, France; Lex Copyright Office, Hungary; Mohrbooks, Germany; Prava I Prevodi Agency, E. Europe; Van Geldren, Netherlands.

Carol Mann Agency★
55 Fifth Avenue, New York NY 10003
☎001 212 206 5635 Fax 001 212 674 4809
Contacts *Carol Mann, Jim Fitzgerald, Gareth Esersky*

FOUNDED 1977. *Handles* literary fiction and narrative non-fiction, including psychology, biography, memoirs, history, pop culture, spirituality. No scripts or genre fiction. No unsolicited material; send query letter with return postage. No reading fee. *Commission* Home 15%; Foreign 20%.

Manus & Associates Literary Agency, Inc.★

375 Forest Avenue, Palo Alto CA 94301
Email ManusLit@ManusLit.com
Website www.ManusLit.com
Also at: 445 Park Avenue, New York, NY 10022
Contacts *Janet Manus, Jillian Manus, Jandy Nelson, Stephanie Lee*

Handles commercial and literary fiction; non-fiction, including true crime, pop culture and popular science. No scripts, science fiction/fantasy, westerns, romance, horror, poetry or children's books. No unsolicited mss. Fiction: send query letter and first 30 pages; non-fiction: query letter and proposal. Include return postage. No reading fee. *Commission* Home 15%; Foreign 25%.

The Evan Marshall Agency★

Six Tristam Place, Pine Brook NJ 07058–9445
☎001 973 882 1122 Fax 001 973 882 3099
Email evanmarshall@TheNovelist.com
Website www.TheNovelist.com
Contact *Evan Marshall*

FOUNDED 1987. *Handles* general adult fiction. No unsolicited mss; send query letter first. *Commission* Home 15%; UK & Translation 20%.

Helen Merrill Ltd★

295 Lafayette Street, Suite 915, New York NY 10012–2700
☎001 212 226 5015 Fax 001 212 226 5079
Email info@hmlartists.com
Contacts *Patrick Herold, Morgan Jenness, Beth Blickers*

FOUNDED 1974. *Handles* film and television scripts only. No unsolicited material. New clients through professional reference only.

Mews Books Ltd

c/o Sidney B. Kramer, 20 Bluewater Hill, Westport CT 06880
☎001 203 227 1836 Fax 001 203 227 1144
Contacts *Sidney B. Kramer, Fran Pollak*
Email mewsbooks@aol.com (initial contact only; submission by regular mail)

FOUNDED 1970. *Handles* adult fiction and non-fiction, children's, pre-school and young adult. No scripts, short stories or novellas (unless by established authors). *Specialises* in cookery, medical, health and nutrition, scientific non-fiction, children's and young adult. Unsolicited material welcome. Presentation must be professional and should include summary of plot/characters, one or two sample chapters, personal credentials and brief on target market, all suitable for forwarding to a publisher. No reading fee. If material is accepted, agency asks $350 circulation fee (4–5 publishers), which will be applied against commissions (waived for published authors). Charges for photocopying, postage expenses, telephone calls and other direct costs. Principal agent is an attorney and former publisher (a founder of Bantam Books). Offers consultation service through which writers can get advice on a contract or on publishing problems. *Commission* Home 15%; Film & Translation 20%. *Overseas associate* **Abner Stein**, UK.

Maureen Moran Agency

PO Box 20191, Parkwest Station, New York NY 10025
☎001 212 222 3838 Fax 001 212 531 3464
Email maureenm@erols.com
Contact *Maureen Moran*

Formerly Donald MacCampbell, Inc. *Handles* novels only. No scripts, non-fiction, science fiction, westerns or suspense. *Specialises* in romance. No unsolicited mss; approach by letter. No reading fee. *Commission* US Book Sales 10%; First Novels US 15%.

Howard Morhaim Literary Agency★

841 Broadway, Suite 604, New York NY 10003
☎001 212 529 4433 Fax 001 212 995 1112
Contact *Howard Morhaim*

FOUNDED 1979. *Handles* general adult fiction and non-fiction. No scripts. No children's or young adult material, poetry or religious. No unsolicited mss. Send query letter with synopsis and sample chapters for fiction; query letter with outline or proposal for non-fiction. Include return postage. No reading fee. *Commission* Home 15%; UK & Translation 20%. *Overseas associates* worldwide.

Henry Morrison, Inc.

PO Box 235, Bedford Hills NY 10507
☎001 914 666 3500 Fax 001 914 241 7846
Contact *Henry Morrison*

FOUNDED 1965. *Handles* general fiction, crime

and science fiction, and non-fiction. No scripts unless by established writers. Unsolicited material welcome but send query letter with outline (1–5 pp) in the first instance. No reading fee. *Commission* Home 15%; UK & Translation 25%.

Multimedia Product Development, Inc.★
410 S. Michigan Avenue, Suite 724, Chicago IL 60605
☎001 312 922 3063 Fax 001 312 922 1905
President *Jane Jordan Browne*
Vice-President *Scott Mendel*
Assistants *Nik Vargas, Janie McAdams*
FOUNDED 1971. *Handles* commercial and literary fiction, and practical non-fiction with wide appeal. No scripts, science fiction or poetry. In the first instance, send query letter with return postage. No unsolicited material; no e-mail queries. No reading fee. *Commission* Home 15%; Foreign/Translation 20%. *Overseas associates* in Europe, Latin America, Japan and Asia.

The Jean V. Naggar Literary Agency★
216 East 75th Street, New York City NY 10021
Contacts *Jean Naggar, Alice Tasman*
FOUNDED 1978. *Handles* strong mainstream fiction, literary fiction, memoir, biography, sophisticated self-help, popular science and psychology. No scripts. No unsolicited material; send query letter *only* with return postage initially. No reading fee. *Commission* Home 15%; Foreign 20%.

Ruth Nathan Agency
141 East 33rd Street, New York NY 10016–4606
☎001 212 889 2696 Fax 001 212 481 1185
FOUNDED 1984. *Specialises* in illustrated books, fine art & decorative arts, historical fiction with emphasis on Middle Ages, true crime, showbiz. Query first. No unsolicited mss. No reading fee. *Commission* 15%.

B.K. Nelson Literary Agency
84 Woodland Road, Pleasantville NY 10570
☎001 914 741 1322 Fax 001 914 741 1324
Website www.bknelson.com
Also at: 1565 Paseo Vida, Palm Springs, CA 92264 ☎001 760 880 7800
President *Bonita K. Nelson*
Vice President *Leonard 'Chip' Ashbach*

Editorial Director *John W. Benson*
FOUNDED 1979. *Specialises* in novels, business, self-help, how-to, political, autobiography, celebrity biography. Major motion picture and TV documentary success. No unsolicited mss. Letter of inquiry. Reading fee charged. *Commission* 20%. Lecture Bureau for Authors founded 1994; Foreign Rights Catalogue established 1995; BK Nelson Infomercial Marketing Co. 1996, primarily for authors and endorsements, and BKNelson, Inc. for motion picture production in 1998. Signatory to Writers Guild of America, West (WGAW).

New England Publishing Associates, Inc.★
Box 5, Chester CT 06412
☎001 860 345 7323 Fax 001 860 345 3660
Email nepa@nepa.com
Website www.nepa.com
Contacts *Elizabeth Frost-Knappman, Edward W. Knappman, Kris Schiavi, Ron Formica, Victoria S. Harlow* (photo/research editor)
FOUNDED 1983. *Handles* non-fiction and (clients only) fiction. *Specialises* in current affairs, history, science, women's studies, reference, psychology, politics, biography, true crime and literature. No textbooks or anthologies. No scripts. Unsolicited mss considered but query letter or phone call preferred first. No reading fee. *Commission* Home 15%. *Overseas associates* throughout Europe and Japan; Scott-Ferris, UK. Dramatic rights: Artists Management Group, Los Angeles.

Richard Parks Agency★
138 East 16th Street, Suite 5B, New York NY 10003
☎001 212 254 9067
Contact *Richard Parks*
FOUNDED 1989. *Handles* general trade fiction and non-fiction: literary novels, mysteries and thrillers, commercial fiction, science fiction, biography, pop culture, psychology, self-help, parenting, medical, cooking, gardening, history, etc. No scripts. No technical or academic. No unsolicited mss. Fiction read by referral only. No reading fee. *Commission* Home 15%; UK & Translation 20%. *Overseas associates* **The Marsh Agency**; **Barbara Levy Literary Agency**.

James Peter Associates, Inc.★
PO Box 358, New Canaan CT 06840
☎001 203 972 1070 Fax 001 203 972 1759
Email gene_brissie@msn.com
President *Eugene Brissie*

FOUNDED 1971. Non-fiction only. 'Many of our authors are historians, psychologists, physicians – all are writing trade books for general readers.' No scripts. No fiction or children's books. *Specialises* in history, popular culture, business, health, biography and politics. No unsolicited mss. Send query letter first with brief project outline, samples and biographical information. No reading fee. *Commission* 15%.

Alison J. Picard Literary Agent

PO Box 2000, Cotuit MA 02635
☎001 508 477 7192 Fax 001 508 477 7192
(notify before faxing)
Email ajpicard@aol.com

Contact *Alison Picard*

FOUNDED 1985. *Handles* mainstream and literary fiction, contemporary and historical romance, children's and young adult, mysteries and thrillers; plus non-fiction. No short stories or poetry. Rarely any science fiction and fantasy. Particularly interested in expanding non-fiction titles. Approach with written query. No reading fee. *Commission* 15%. *Overseas associate* **A.M. Heath & Co. Ltd**, UK.

Pinder Lane & Garon-Brooke Associates Ltd★

159 West 53rd Street, Suite 14–E, New York NY 10019
☎001 212 489 0880 Fax 001 212 489 7104

Owner Agents *Dick Duane, Robert Thixton*
Consulting Agent *Nancy Coffey*

FOUNDED 1951. Fiction and non-fiction. No category romance, westerns or mysteries. No unsolicited mss. First approach by query letter. No reading fee. *Commission* Home 15%; Dramatic 10–15%; Foreign 30%. *Overseas associates* **Abner Stein**, UK; Translation: Rights Unlimited.

PMA Literary & Film Management, Inc.

PO Box 1817, Old Chelsea Sta., New York NY 10011
☎001 212 929 1222 Fax 001 212 206 0238
Email pmalitfilm@aol.com
Website www.pmalitfilm.com

President *Peter Miller*
Associate *Nathan Rice*

FOUNDED 1976. Commercial fiction and non-fiction. *Specialises* in books with motion picture and television potential, and in true crime. No poetry, pornography, non-commercial or academic. No unsolicited mss. Approach by letter

with one-page synopsis. *Commission* Home 15%; Dramatic 10–15%; Foreign 20–25%.

Susan Ann Protter Literary Agent★

110 West 40th Street, Suite 1408, New York NY 10018
☎001 212 840 0480

Contact *Susan Ann Protter*

FOUNDED 1971. *Handles* general fiction, mysteries, thrillers, science fiction and fantasy; non-fiction: history, general reference, biography, science, health and parenting. No romance, poetry, westerns, religious, children's or sport manuals. No scripts. First approach with letter, including IRCs. No reading fee. *Commission* Home & Dramatic 15%. *Overseas associates* **Abner Stein**, UK; agents in all major markets.

Quicksilver Books, Literary Agents

50 Wilson Street, Hartsdale NY 10530
☎001 914 946 8748

President *Bob Silverstein*

FOUNDED 1973. *Handles* literary fiction and mainstream commercial fiction: blockbuster, suspense, thriller, contemporary, mystery and historical; and general non-fiction, including self-help, psychology, holistic healing, ecology, environmental, biography, fact crime, New Age, health, nutrition, cookery, enlightened wisdom and spirituality. No scripts, science fiction and fantasy, pornographic, children's or romance. UK material being submitted must have universal appeal for the US market. Unsolicited material welcome but must be accompanied by IRCs for response, together with biographical details, covering letter, etc. No reading fee. *Commission* Home & Dramatic 15%; Translation 20%.

Reece Halsey North★

98 Main Street, #704, Tiburon CA 94920
☎001 415 789 9191 Fax 001 415 789 9177
Email bookgirl@worldnet.att.net
Website www.kimberleycameron.com

Also: Reece Halsey Agency, 8733 Sunset Blvd. #101, Los Angeles, CA 90069
☎001 310 652 2409 Fax 001 310 652 7595

Contact (Tiburon) *Kimberley Cameron*
Contact (Los Angeles) *Dorris Halsey*

FOUNDED 1957. *Handles* literary and mainstream fiction. No scripts, poetry or children's books.No unsolicited material; send query letter with first 10 pages together with return postage. No e-mail submissions. No reading fee. *Commission* Home 15%; Foreign 20%.

Helen Rees Literary Agency★

123 N. Washington Street, 2nd Floor, Boston
MA 02114
☎001 617 723 5232 ext 222
Fax 001 617 723 5211
Email wwhelen@aol.com *or*
joanmaz@aol.com *or* brifkind@mediaone.com
or acoll10702@aol.com

Contact *Joan Mazmanian*
Associates *Barbara Rifkind, Ann Collette*

FOUNDED 1982. *Specialises* in books on health
and business; also handles biography, autobiography and history; quality fiction. No scholarly
or technical books. No scripts, science fiction,
children's, poetry, photography, short stories,
cooking. No unsolicited mss. Send query letter
with IRCs. No reading fee. *Commission* Home
15%; Foreign 20%.

Rights Unlimited, Inc.★

101 West 55th Street, Suite 2D, New York
NY 10019
☎001 212 246 0900 Fax 001 212 246 2114
Email bkurman@rightsunlimited.com

Contact *Bernard Kurman*

FOUNDED 1985. *Handles* adult fiction, non-fiction. No scripts, poetry, short stories, educational or literary works. Query letter with synopsis preferred in the first instance. No reading
fee. *Commission* Home 15%; Translation 20%.

The Angela Rinaldi Literary Agency★

PO Box 7877, Beverly Hills CA 90212–7877
☎001 310 842 7665 Fax 001 310 837 8143
Email ARinaldiLitAgcy@aol.com

Contact *Angela Rinaldi*

FOUNDED 1995. *Handles* commercial and literary fiction; narrative non-fiction, practical and
pro-active self-help. No scripts, cookery, science fiction, westerns, romance, poetry, children's/young adult. Send brief e-mail or query
letter with return postage in the first instance.
No reading fee. *Commission* Home 15%;
Foreign 20%.

B.J. Robbins Literary Agency★

5130 Bellaire Avenue, North Hollywood
CA 91607
☎001 818 760 6602 Fax 001 818 760 6616
Email robbinsliterary@aol.com

Contacts *B.J. Robbins, Robert McAndrews*

FOUNDED 1992. *Handles* literary fiction, narrative
and general non-fiction. No scripts, genre
fiction, romance, horror, science fiction or

children's books. Send covering letter with first
three chapters or e-mail query in the first
instance. No reading fee. *Commission* Home
15%; Foreign/Translation 10%. *Overseas associates*
Abner Stein and **The Marsh Agency**, UK.

Linda Roghaar Literary Agency, Inc.★

133 High Point Drive, Amherst MA 01002
☎001 413 256 1921 Fax 001 413 256 2636
Email LRoghaar@aol.com
Website www.LindaRoghaar.com

Contact *Linda L. Roghaar*

FOUNDED 1997. *Handles* fiction and non-fiction, specialising in religious titles. No science fiction or horror. Scripts through sub-agents. Send query by e-mail or letter with
return postage (for fiction, include the first five
pages). No reading fee. *Commission* Home
15%; Foreign/Translation rate varies.

The Rosenberg Group★

2800 Harlanwood Drive, Fort Worth
TX 76109
Website www.rosenberggroup.com

Contact *Barbara Collins Rosenberg*

FOUNDED 1998. *Handles* fiction, specialising in
romance (single title and category) and women's;
non-fiction, specialising in college textbooks. No
scripts, science fiction, true crime, inspirational
fiction, children's and young adult. No unsolicited material; send query letter by post only.
No reading fee. *Commission* Home 15%; Foreign
25%. NB Moving offices in the summer of 2002.
Check website for details.

Rosenstone/Wender★

38 East 29th Street, 10th Floor, New York
NY 10016
☎001 212 725 9445 Fax 001 212 725 9447

Contacts *Phyllis Wender, Susan Perlman Cohen,
Sonia E. Pabley*

FOUNDED 1981. *Handles* fiction, non-fiction,
children's, and scripts for film, TV and theatre.
No material for radio. No unsolicited mss. Send
letter outlining the project, credits, etc. No reading fee. *Commission* Home 15%; Dramatic 10%;
Foreign 20%. *Overseas associates* La Nouvelle
Agence, France; Andrew Nurnberg, Netherlands; The English Agency, Japan; Mohrbooks,
Germany; Ole Licht, Scandinavia.

Gail Ross Literary Agency★

1666 Connecticut Avenue, NW, Suite 500,
Washington DC 20009
☎001 202 328 3282 Fax 001 202 328 9162

Email jennifer@gailross.com
Website www.gailross.com

Contacts *Jennifer Manguera, Gail Ross*

FOUNDED 1998. *Handles* non-fiction, self-help, health, financial. No scripts, poetry, science fiction or children's books. No unsolicited mss; send query letter with sample material. No reading fee.

Jane Rotrosen Agency LLC★
318 East 51st Street, New York NY 10022
☎001 212 593 4330 Fax 001 212 935 6985

Contacts *Meg Ruley, Andrea Cirillo, Annelise Robey*

Handles commercial fiction: romance, horror, mysteries, thrillers and popular non-fiction. No scripts, educational, professional or belles lettres. Query by referral only. No reading fee. *Commission* Home 15%; UK & Translation 20%. *Overseas associates* worldwide and film agents on the West Coast.

The Sagalyn Literary Agency★
4825 Bethesda Avenue #302, Bethesda MA 20814
Email query@sagalyn.com
Website www.sagalyn.com
Contact *Ethan Kline*

FOUNDED 1980. *Handles* mostly upmarket nonfiction with some fiction. No screenplays, romance, science fiction/fantasy, children's literature. No unsolicited material. See website for submissions procedure. No reading fee.

Victoria Sanders & Associates LLC★
241 Avenue of the Americas, Suite 11H, New York NY 10014
☎001 212 633 8811 Fax 001 212 633 0525
Email queriesvsa@hotmail.com
Website www.victoriasanders.com

Contacts *Victoria Sanders, Diane Dickensheid*

FOUNDED 1993. *Handles* general trade fiction and non-fiction, plus ancillary film and television rights. *Commission* Home & Dramatic 15%; Translation 20%.

Sandum & Associates
144 East 84th Street, New York NY 10028
☎001 212 737 2011
Contact *Howard E. Sandum*

FOUNDED 1987. *Handles* all categories of general adult non-fiction, plus occasional fiction. No scripts. No children's, poetry or short stories. No unsolicited mss. Third-party referral preferred but direct approach by letter, with

synopsis, brief biography and IRCs, is accepted. No reading fee. *Commission* Home & Dramatic 15%; Translation & Foreign 20%. *Overseas associate* Scott Ferris Associates.

Jack Scagnetti
Talent & Literary Agency
5118 Vineland Avenue, Suite 102, North Hollywood CA 91601
☎001 818 762 3871
Contact *Jack Scagnetti*

FOUNDED 1974. Works mostly with established/published authors. *Handles* non-fiction, fiction, film and TV scripts. No reading fees. *Commission* Home & Dramatic 10% (scripts), 15% (books); Foreign 15%.

Schiavone Literary Agency, Inc.
236 Trails End, West Palm Beach FL 33413–2135
☎001 561 966 9294 Fax 001 561 966 9294
Email profschia@aol.com
Website www.freeyellow.com/members8/
schiavone/index.html

Branch office (June/July/Aug. only):
3671 Hudson Manor Terrace, Suite 11H, Bronx, NY 10463
☎/Fax 001 718 543 5093

President *James Schiavone*

FOUNDED 1996. *Handles* fiction and non-fiction (all genres). *Specialises* in biography, autobiography, celebrity memoirs. No poetry. No unsolicited mss; send query with brief biog-sketch, synopsis, outline and sample chapters (enclose IRCs). No reading fee. *Commission* Home 15%; Foreign & Translation 20%. *Overseas associates* in Europe.

Susan Schulman,
A Literary Agency★
454 West 44th Street, New York NY 10036
☎001 212 713 1633/4/5
Fax 001 212 581 8830
Email schulman@aol.com
Website www.susanschulmanagency.com

Submissions Editor (Books) *Christine Maren*
Submissions Editor (Plays) *Brian Leifert*

FOUNDED 1979. *Specialises* in non-fiction of all types but particularly in health and psychology-based self-help for men, women and families. Other interests include business, the social sciences, biography, language and international law. Fiction interests include contemporary fiction, including women's, mysteries, historical and thrillers 'with a cutting edge'. Always looking for 'something original and fresh'. No unsolicited mss. Query first, including outline and three sample chapters with IRCs. No reading fee. Represents properties for film and television, and works with agents in appropriate territories for translation rights. *Commission* Home & Dramatic 15%; Translation 20%. *Overseas associates* Plays: **Rosica Colin Ltd** and **The Agency Ltd**, UK; Children's books: Marilyn Malin, UK, Commercial fiction: Laura Morris, UK.

Scovil Chichak Galen, Inc.*
381 Park Avenue South, New York NY 10016
☎001 212 679 8686 Fax 001 212 679 6710
Email mailroom@scglit.com

Contacts *Russell Galen, Anna M. Ghosh, Jack Scovil*

FOUNDED 1993. *Handles* all categories of books. No scripts. No unsolicited material; send query by e-mail or letter. No reading fee. *Commission* Home 15%; Foreign 20%.

Shapiro-Lichtman – Talent Agency
8827 Beverly Boulevard, Los Angeles CA 90048
☎001 310 859 8877 Fax 001 310 859 7153

FOUNDED 1969. Works mostly with established/published authors. *Handles* film and TV scripts. Unsolicited mss will not be read. *Commission* Home & Dramatic 10%; Foreign 20%.

The Shepard Agency
M&T Bank Building, Suite 3, 1525 Rte. 22, Brewster NY 10509
☎001 914 279 2900/3236
Fax 001 914 279 3239
Email shepardagcy@mindspring.com
Website home.mindspring.com/~shepardagcy

Contacts *Jean Shepard, Lance Shepard*

FOUNDED 1987. *Handles* non-fiction: business, food, self-help and travel; some fiction: adult, children's and young adult and the occasional script. No pornography. *Specialises* in business. Send query letter, table of contents, sample chapters and IRCs for response. No reading fee. *Commission* Home & Dramatic 15%; Translation 20%.

Lee Shore Agency Ltd
The Sterling Building, 440 Friday Road, Pittsburgh PA 15209
☎001 412 821 0440 Fax 001 412 821 6099
Email LeeShore1@aol.com

Website www.leeshoreagency.com

Contacts *Jennifer Piemme, Danielle Chiotti*

FOUNDED 1988. *Handles* non-fiction, including textbooks, and mass-market fiction: horror, romance, mystery, westerns, science fiction. Also some young adult and, more recently, screenplays. *Specialises* in New Age, self-help, how-to and quality fiction. No children's. No unsolicited mss. Send IRCs for guidelines before submitting work. Reading fee charged. *Commission* Home 15%; Dramatic 20%.

Bobbe Siegel Literary Agency
41 West 83rd Street, New York NY 10024
☎001 212 877 4985 Fax 001 212 877 4985

Contacts *Bobbe Siegel, Pete Siegel*

FOUNDED 1975. Works mostly with established/published authors. *Specialises* in literary fiction, detective, suspense, historical, fantasy, biography, how-to, women's interest, fitness, health, beauty, sports, pop psychology. No scripts. No cookbooks, crafts, children's, short stories or humour. First approach with letter including IRCs for response. Will not accept queries via fax. No reading fee. Critiques given if the writer is taken on for representation. *Commission* Home 15%; Dramatic & Foreign 20%. (Foreign/Dramatic split 50/50 with sub-agent.) Also handles foreign rights for many US agents. *Overseas associates* in various countries, including **John Pawsey** in the UK.

Rosalie Siegel, International Literary Agency, Inc.*
1 Abey Drive, Pennington NJ 08534
☎001 609 737 1007 Fax 001 609 737 3708
Email rsiegel@ix.netcom.com

Contact *Rosalie Siegel*

FOUNDED 1978. A one-woman, highly selective agency that takes on only a limited number of new projects. *Handles* fiction, non-fiction, especially narrative non-fiction, memoir, biography, history, current affairs, social history, psychology, botany, art history, zoology, neuroscience, social science and anthropology. *Specialises* in French history and literature; Europe in general; American history, social history. No science fiction, photography, illustrated art books or children's. No unsolicited material; send query letter citing background, previously published books and brief description of current book. Include return postage. No reading fee. *Commission* Home 15%; Foreign 20%. *Overseas associate* **Louise Greenberg**, UK; plus associates worldwide.

Michael Snell Literary Agency

PO Box 1206, Truro MA 02666–1206
☎001 508 349 3718
President *Michael Snell*
Vice President *Patricia Smith*

FOUNDED 1980. Adult non-fiction, especially science, business and women's issues. *Specialises* in business and computer books (professional and reference to popular trade how-to); general how-to and self-help on all topics, from diet and exercise to parenting, relationships, health, sex, psychology and personal finance, plus literary and suspense fiction. No unsolicited mss. Send outline and sample chapter with return postage for reply. No reading fee for outlines. Brochure available on how to write a book proposal. Author of *From Book Idea to Bestseller*, published by Prima. Rewriting, developmental editing, collaborating and ghostwriting services available on a fee basis. Send IRCs. *Commission* Home 15%.

The Spieler Agency

154 West 57th Street, Room 135, New York NY 10019
☎001 212 757 4439 Fax 001 212 333 2019
Email SpielerLit@aol.com
The Spieler Agency/West, 4096 Piedmont Avenue, Oakland, CA 94611
☎001 510 985 1422 Fax 001 510 985 1323
Contacts *Joseph Spieler, John Thornton, Lisa M. Ross, Dierdre Mullane, Ada Muellner* (NY); *Victoria Shoemaker* (Oakland)

FOUNDED 1980. *Handles* literary fiction and non-fiction. No how-to or genre romance. *Specialises* in history, science, ecology, social and political issues and business. No scripts. Approach in writing with IRCs. No reading fee. *Commission* Home 15%; Translation 20%. *Overseas associates* **Abner Stein**; **The Marsh Agency**, UK.

Philip G. Spitzer Literary Agency★

50 Talmage Farm Lane, East Hampton NY 11937
☎001 631 329 3650 Fax 001 631 329 3651
Email spitzer516@aol.com
Contact *Philip Spitzer*

FOUNDED 1969. Works mostly with established/published authors. *Specialises* in general non-fiction and fiction – thrillers. No reading fee for outlines. *Commission* Home & Dramatic 15%; Foreign 20%.

Lyle Steele & Co. Ltd
Literary Agents

511 East 73rd Street, Suite 6, New York NY 10021
☎001 212 288 2981
President *Lyle Steele*

FOUNDED 1985. *Handles* general non-fiction and category fiction. Also North American rights to titles published by major English publishers. No scripts unless derived from books already being handled. No romance. No unsolicited mss: query with IRCs in first instance. No reading fee. *Commission* 10%. *Overseas associates* worldwide.

Steele–Perkins Literary Agency★

26 Island Lane, Canandaigua NY 14424
☎001 716 396 9290 Fax 001 716 396 3579
Email pattiesp@aol.com
Contact *Pattie Steele-Perkins*

Handles mainstream women's fiction, romance. *Specialises* in sailing titles. No scripts. Send query letter, synopsis, three chapters and return postage. No reading fee. *Commission* Home 15%.

Gloria Stern Agency (Hollywood)

12535 Chandler Boulevard, Suite 3, North Hollywood CA 91607
☎001 818 508 6296 Fax 001 818 508 6296
Email wryter21@excite.com
Contact *Gloria Stern*

FOUNDED 1984. *Handles* film scripts, genre (romance, detective, thriller and sci-fi) and mainstream fiction; electronic media. Accepts interactive material, games and electronic data. 'No books containing gratuitous violence.' Approach with letter, biography and synopsis. Reading fee charged by the hour. *Commission* Home 15%; Offshore 20%.

Stimola Literary Studio★

210 Crescent Avenue, Leonia NJ 07605
☎001 201 944 9886 Fax 001 201 944 9886
Email LtryStudio@aol.com
Contact *Rosemary B. Stimola*

FOUNDED 1997. *Handles* children's books – pre-school through young adult – fiction and non fiction. Specialises in picture books, middle/young adult novels. No adult fiction. No unsolicited material; send query e-mail. No reading fee. *Commission* Home 15%; Foreign 20%.

Gunther Stuhlmann Author's Representative

PO Box 276, Becket MA 01223
☎001 413 623 5170

Contacts *Gunther Stuhlmann, Barbara Ward*

FOUNDED 1954. *Handles* literary fiction, biography and serious non-fiction. No film/TV scripts unless from established clients. No short stories, detective, romance, adventure, poetry, technical or computers. Query first with IRCs, including sample chapters and synopsis of project. *'We take on few new clients.'* No reading fee. *Commission* Home 10%; Foreign 15%; Translation 20%.

Roslyn Targ*

105 West 13th Street, 15 E, New York NY 10011
☎001 212 206 9390 Fax 001 212 989 6233
Email roslyntarg@aol.com

Contact *Roslyn Targ*

FOUNDED 1970. *Handles* non-fiction, particularly biography, self-help, and literary fiction. No scripts or cookbooks. No unsolicited material; send query e-mail or letter describing the work. No reading fee. *Commission* Home 15%; Foreign 20%.

Scott Treimel NY*

434 Lafayette Street, New York NY 10003
☎001 212 505 8353 Fax 001 212 505 0664
Email st.ny@verizon.net

FOUNDED 1995. *Handles* children's books only – from concept/board books to teen fiction. No scripts. No unsolicited material. 'Not accepting anyone unless recommended by professional authors or editors.' No reading fee. *Commission* Home 15%; Foreign 20%.

2M Communications Ltd

121 West 27th Street, Suite 601, New York NY 10001
☎001 212 741 1509 Fax 001 212 691 4460

Contact *Madeleine Morel*

FOUNDED 1982. *Handles* non-fiction only: everything from pop psychology and health to cookery books, biographies and pop culture. No scripts. No fiction, children's, computers or science. No unsolicited mss; send letter with sample pages and IRCs. No reading fee. *Commission* Home & Dramatic 15%; Translation 20%. *Overseas associates* Thomas Schluck Agency, Germany; Asano Agency, Japan; EAIS, France;

Living Literary Agency, Italy; Nueva Agencia Literaria Internacional, Spain.

Van der Leun & Associates

32 Gramercy Park South #11L, New York City NY 10003
☎001 212 982 6165
Website www.publishersmarketplace.com/members/pvanderleun

Contact *Patricia Van der Leun*

FOUNDED 1984. *Handles* fiction and non-fiction. No scripts. No science fiction, fantasy or romance. *Specialises* in art and architecture, science, cookbooks, wine, reference, lifestyle, religious, biography and fiction. No unsolicited mss; query first, with letter and short biography. No reading fee. *Commission* 15%. *Overseas associates* **Abner Stein**, UK; Michelle Lapautre, France; English Agency, Japan; Carmen Balcells, Spain; Lucia Riff, South America; Susanna Zevi, Italy.

The Vines Agency, Inc.*

648 Broadway, Suite 901, New York NY 10012
☎001 212 777 5522 Fax 001 212 777 5978
Email JV@vinesagency.com
Website www.vinesagency.com

Contacts *James C. Vines, Kate Payne*

FOUNDED 1995. *Handles* fiction – literary, women's, thrillers, love stories; narrative non-fiction, historical, biography, advice, how-to. No children's picture books or poetry. *Specialises* in women's fiction and thrillers. Unsolicited mss, synopses and sample chapters welcome. Send query with one-page letter and return postage. No reading fee. *Commission* Home 15%; Foreign/Translation 25%. *Overseas associate* Baror International (foreign rights).

Wales Literary Agency, Inc.*

PO Box 9428, Seattle WA 98109–0428
☎001 206 284 7114
Email waleslit@aol.com

Contacts *Elizabeth Wales, Meg Lemke, Adrienne Reed*

FOUNDED 1988. *Handles* quality fiction and non-fiction. No genre fiction, westerns, romance, science fiction or horror. Special interest in 'Pacific Rim', West Coast and Pacific Northwest stories. No unsolicited mss; send query letter with publication list and writing sample. No e-mail queries longer than one page and no attachments. No reading fee. *Commission* Home 15%; Dramatic & Translation 20%.

John A. Ware Literary Agency
392 Central Park West, New York NY 10025
☎001 212 866 4733 Fax 001 212 866 4734
Contact *John Ware*

FOUNDED 1978. *Specialises* in non-fiction: biography, history, current affairs, investigative journalism, science, nature, inside looks at phenomena, medicine and psychology (academic credentials required). Also handles literary fiction, mysteries/thrillers, sport, oral history, Americana and folklore. Unsolicited mss not read. Send query letter first with IRCs to cover return postage. No reading fee. *Commission* Home & Dramatic 15%; Foreign 20%.

Waterside Productions, Inc.
2191 San Elijo Avenue, Cardiff by the Sea CA 92007
☎001 760 632 9190 Fax 001 760 632 9295
Website www.waterside.com
Contact *William Gladstone*

FOUNDED 1982. *Handles* general non-fiction: computers and technology, science, business, sports. All types of multimedia. No unsolicited mss; send query letter. No reading fee. *Commission* Home 15%; Dramatic 20%; Translation 25%. *Overseas associates* Asano Agency, Japan; Ruth Liepman, Germany; Vera Le Marie, EAIS, France; Bardon Chinese Media Agency, China; DRT, Korea.

Watkins Loomis Agency, Inc.
133 East 35th Street, Suite 1, New York NY 10016
☎001 212 532 0080 Fax 001 212 889 0506
Contact *Katherine Fausset*

FOUNDED 1904. *Handles* fiction and non-fiction. No scripts for film, radio, TV or theatre. No science fiction, fantasy or horror. No reading fee. No unsolicited mss. Approach in writing with enquiry or proposal and s.a.e. *Commission* Home 15%; UK & Translation 20%. *Overseas associates* **Abner Stein**; **The Marsh Agency**, UK.

Wecksler-Incomco
170 West End Avenue, New York NY 10023
☎001 212 787 2239 Fax 001 212 496 7035
Contacts *Sally Wecksler, Joann Amparan-Close*

FOUNDED 1971. *Handles* literary fiction and non-fiction: business, reference, biography, performing arts and heavily illustrated books; also some children's books. Send queries only. No unsolicited mss. No submissions by fax or e-mail; hard copy only. No reading fee. Foreign rights. *Commission* Home 15%; Translation & UK 20%.

Cherry Weiner Literary Agency
28 Kipling Way, Manalapan NJ 07726
☎001 732 446 2096 Fax 001 732 792 0506
Email Cherry8486@aol.com
Contact *Cherry Weiner*

FOUNDED 1977. *Handles* all types of fiction: science fiction and fantasy, mainstream, romance, mystery, westerns. No submissions except through referral. No reading fee. *Commission* 15%. *Overseas associates* **Abner Stein**, UK; Thomas Schluck, Germany; International Editors Inc., Spain; Prava Prevodi Agency (Eastern Europe), Serbia; Elaine Benisti Agency, France; Borderline Literary Agency, Italy; Nucihan Kesim Literary Agency, Turkey; English Agency (Japan) Ltd; Alex Korzhenevski Agency, Russia; Renaissance Media – movie agent. Also deals with various e-book publishers.

Wieser & Wieser, Inc.
25 East 21st Street, New York NY 10010
☎001 212 260 0860
Contacts *Olga B. Wieser, Jake Elwell*

FOUNDED 1976. Works mostly with established/published authors. *Specialises* in literary and mainstream fiction, serious and popular historical fiction, and general non-fiction: business, finance, aviation, sports, travel and popular medicine. No poetry, children's, science fiction or religious. No unsolicited mss. First approach by letter with IRCs. No reading fee for outlines. *Commission* Home & Dramatic 15%; Foreign 20%.

Ann Wright Representatives
165 West 46th Street, Suite 1105, New York NY 10036–2501
☎001 212 764 6770 Fax 001 212 764 5125
Contact *Dan Wright*

FOUNDED 1961. *Specialises* in material with strong film potential. *Handles* screenplays and novels, drama and fiction. No academic, scientific or scholarly. Approach by letter; no reply without IRCs. Include outline and credits only. 'Has reputation for encouraging new writers.' No reading fee. Signatory to the Writers Guild of America Agreement. *Commission* Literary 10–20%; Screenplays 10% of gross.

Writers House, LLC.★

21 West 26th Street, New York NY 10010
☎001 212 685 2400 Fax 001 212 685 1781

Contacts *Albert Zuckerman, Amy Berkower, Merrilee Heifetz, Susan Cohen, Susan Ginsburg, Robin Rue, Simon Lipskar, Steven Malk, Jennifer Lyons* (see **Joan Daves Agency**), *Jodi Reamer*

FOUNDED 1974. See also **Joan Daves Agency**. *Handles* all types of fiction, including children's and young adult, plus narrative nonfiction: history, biography, popular science, pop and rock culture as well as how-to, business and finance, and New Age. *Specialises* in popular fiction, women's novels, thrillers and children's. No scripts. No professional or scholarly. For consideration of unsolicited mss, send letter of enquiry, 'explaining why your book is wonderful, briefly what it's about and outlining your writing background'. No reading fee. *Commission* Home & Dramatic 15%; Foreign 20%. Albert Zuckerman is author of *Writing the Blockbuster Novel*, published by Little, Brown & Co. and Warner Paperbacks.

The Zack Company, Inc.★

243 West 70th Street, Suite 8D, New York NY 10023–4366
☎001 212 712 2400 Fax 001 212 712 9110
Website www.zackcompany.com

Contact *Andrew Zack*

FOUNDED 1996. *Handles* serious narrative nonfiction by qualified experts: history, particularly military, politics, current affairs, science and technology, biography, autobiography, memoirs, personal finance, parenting, health and medicine, business, relationships. Commercial fiction – thrillers, mysteries, crime, science fiction/fantasy. No women's fiction, westerns, gay or lesbian, scripts. See website for full listing of areas of representation and submission guidelines. No unsolicited material. For nonfiction, send query letter, resume and 1–2 pages describing project; fiction – query letter should include publishing history (title, publisher and year), if any, and a 2–3 paragraph summary of the work. No reading fee. *Commission* Home 15% (published authors)/20% (new, unpublished); Foreign/Translation 25%.

US Media Contacts in the UK

ABC News Intercontinental Inc.
3 Queen Caroline Street, Mail Code 2303,
London W6 9PE
☎020 8222 5000 Fax 020 8222 5020
**Bureau Chief & Director of News
Coverage, Europe, Middle East &
Africa** *Rex Granum*

Alaska Journal of Commerce
16 Cavaye Place, London SW10 9PT
☎0702 092 4480 Fax 0702 092 4482
Bureau Chief *Robert Gould*

The Associated Press
12 Norwich Street, London EC4A 1BP
☎020 7353 1515 Fax 020 7353 8118
**Chief of Bureau/Managing Director,
AP Ltd** *Myron L. Belkind*

The Baltimore Sun
11 Kensington Court Place, London W8 5BJ
☎020 7460 2200 Fax 020 7460 2211
Bureau Chief *Bill Glauber*

Bloomberg Business News
City Gate House, 39–45 Finsbury Square,
London EC2A 1PQ
☎020 7330 7500 Fax 020 7392 6666
London Bureau Chief *Ed Roussel*

Boston Globe
34 West Heath Road, London NW3 7UR
☎020 7431 5797 Fax 020 7431 5807
Bureau Chief *Charles Sennott*

Business Week
1 Albemarle Street, London W1S 4DT
☎020 7491 8985 Fax 020 7409 7152
Bureau Chief *Stanley Reed*

Cable News Network Inc. (CNN)
Turner House, 16 Great Marlborough Street,
London W1P 1DF
☎020 7693 1000 Fax 020 7693 1552
Bureau Chief *Thomas Mintier*

CBC Television and Radio
43/51 Great Titchfield Street, London
W1P 8DD

☎020 7412 9200 Fax 020 7412 9226
London Bureau Manager *Ann Macmillan*

CBS News
68 Knightsbridge, London SW1X 7LL
☎020 7581 4801 Fax 020 7581 4431
Vice President/Bureau Chief *John Paxson*

Chicago Tribune Press Service
169 Piccadilly, London W1J 9EH
☎020 7499 8769 Fax 020 7499 8781
Chief European Correspondent *Tom
Huntley*

CNBC
10 Fleet Place, Limeburner Lane, London
EC4M 7QS
☎020 7653 9451 Fax 020 7653 9393
News Editor *Robert McKenzie*

Dallas Morning News
☎020 8742 0495 Fax 020 8747 3131
European Bureau Chief *Gregory Katz*

Dow Jones Newswires
10 Fleet Place, Limeburner Lane, London
EC4M 7QN
☎020 7842 9900
Editor (Europe, Middle East, Africa)
Gabriella Stern

**Fairchild Publications of
New York**
20 Shorts Gardens, London WC2H 9AU
☎020 7240 0420 Fax 020 7240 0290
Bureau Chief *Samantha Conti*

Forbes Magazine
10 Rotherwick Road, London
NW11 7DA
☎020 8455 0463 Fax 020 8455 0512
European Bureau Chief *Richard C. Morais*

Fox News Channel
6 Centaurs Business Park, Grant Way,
Isleworth, Middlesex TW7 5QD
☎020 7805 7143 Fax 020 7805 1111
Producer/Bureau Chief *Paul Tyson*

The Globe and Mail
43–51 Great Titchfield Street, London
W1W 7DA
☎020 7323 0449 Fax 020 7323 0428
European Correspondent *Alan Freeman*

International Herald Tribune
40 Marsh Wall, London E14 9TP
☎020 7510 5718 Fax 020 7987 3470
London Correspondent *Eric Pfanner*
(See entry under **National Newspapers**)

Los Angeles Times
150 Brompton Road, London SW3 1HX
☎020 7823 7315 Fax 020 7823 7308
Bureau Chief *Marjorie Miller*

Market News International
167 Fleet Street, 8th Floor, London
EC4A 2EA
☎020 7353 4462 Fax 020 7353 9122
Bureau Chief *Gavin Friend*

National Public Radio
Room G-10 East Wing, Bush House, Strand,
London WC2B 4PH
☎020 7557 1089 Fax 020 7379 6486
Bureau Chief *Julie McCarthy*

NBC News Worldwide Inc.
4th Floor, 3 Shortlands, Hammersmith,
London W6 8HX
☎020 8600 6600 Fax 020 8600 6601
Bureau Chief *Chris Hampson*

The New York Times
66 Buckingham Gate, London
SW1E 6AU
☎020 7799 5050 Fax 020 7799 2962
Chief Correspondent *William Hoge*

Newsweek
18 Park Street, London W1K 2HQ
☎020 7629 8361 Fax 020 7408 1403
Bureau Chief *Stryker McGuire*

People Magazine
Brettenham House, Lancaster Place, London
WC2E 7TL
☎020 7322 1134 Fax 020 7322 1125
Bureau Chief *Bryan Alexander*

Philadelphia Inquirer
2 Cranley Mews, London SW7 3BX
☎020 7460 6800 Fax 020 7460 6800
Bureau Chief *Andrea Gerlin*

Reader's Digest Association Ltd
11 Westferry Circus, Canary Wharf, London
E14 4HE
☎020 7715 8046 Fax 020 7715 8716
(See under **UK Publishers** and **Magazines**)

Time Magazine
Brettenham House, Lancaster Place, London
WC2E 7TL
☎020 7499 4080 Fax 020 7322 1230
Bureau Chief *Jef McAllister*
(See entry under **Magazines**)

USA Today
69 New Oxford Street, London WC1A 1DG
☎020 7559 5859 Fax 020 7559 5895
European Correspondents *Elliott Blair Smith*

Voice of America
International Press Centre, 76 Shoe Lane,
London EC4A 3JB
☎020 7410 0960 Fax 020 7410 0966
Bureau Chief/Senior Editor *Gary Edquist*

Wall Street Journal
10 Fleet Place, Limeburner Lane, London
EC4M 7RB
☎020 7842 9200 Fax 020 7842 9201
London Bureau Chief *James R. Hagerty*

Washington Post
18 Park Street, London W1Y 4HH
☎020 7629 8958 Fax 020 7629 8950
Bureau Chief *T.R. Reid*

US Writers' Courses

In general, courses are open to students from overseas though, of course, in some cases the financial aid information varies for international students.

California

Chapman University
Master of Fine Arts Degree, Office of Admissions, Orange CA 92866
☎001 714 997 6770
Email shoover@chapman.edu
Contact *Saundra Hoover, Admissions*

Three-year Master of Fine Arts (MFA) course in *Creativing Writing* which includes courses in fiction writing, poetry and screenwriting as well as courses in world and comparative literature. Programme connected with the John Fowles Center for Creative Writing.

Saint Mary's College of California
MFA Program in Creative Writing, PO Box 4686, Moraga CA 94575–4686
☎001 925 631 4762 Fax 001 925 631 4471
Email writers@stmarys-ca.edu
Programme Coordinator *Thomas Cooney*

Two-year MFA course in *Fiction, Playwriting* or *Poetry*. Students have the opportunity to gain knowledge of the world of publishing through internships in the College's in-house press, Momotombo Press and literary journal, *26.*

Strawberry Mansion Films
13586 Mahogany Place, Tustin CA 92780
☎001 714 997 6586
Email axelrod@chapman.edu
Contact *Mark Axelrod*

One-day, three-day and five-day seminar/workshops in *Screenwriting*. A practising screenwriter, Mark Axelrod has conducted such programmes at the Escuela Internacional de Cine y TV in San Antonio de los Baños, Cuba (founded by García Márquez); the Goethe Institute, Santiago, Chile (with Antonio Skármeta – *Il Postino*); the National Film School of Denmark, as well as the University of East Anglia in Norwich, University of Washington and Columbia College.

Florida

University of West Florida
Department of English and Foreign Languages, College of Arts and Sciences, 11000 University Parkway, Pensacola FL 32514
☎001 850 474 2923 Fax 001 850 474 2935
Email English@uwf.edu
Website uwf.edu/english

BA in *English (Writing Specialization)*: students who choose to develop their creative writing skills or editing can take courses in poetry, fiction, creative non-fiction, magazine writing and editing, and feature writing. *MA in English (Creative Writing Specialization)*: workshop courses in the specialisation include fiction, creative non-fiction, poetry, editing, teaching creating writing and special topics in creative writing.

Georgia

Georgia State University
Department of English, University Plaza, Atlanta, GA 30303
Email tmchaney@gsu.edu
Website www.gsu.edu/~wwweng/
Contact *Director of Creative Writing*

BA, MA, MFA and PhD programmes in *Creative Writing* – fiction or poetry.

Illinois

Southern Illinois University
Department of English, Carbondale IL 62901–4503
☎001 618 453 6849 Fax 001 618 453 3253
Email crwr@siu.edu
Contact *Professor Beth Lordan*

Three-year MFA in *Creative Writing*. The programme accepts a maximum of eight students each year, so workshops are small and faculty members work closely with students.

Indiana

Taylor University

Department of English, 1025 West Rudisill Boulevard, Fort Wayne IN 46807
☎001 219 744 8647
Email DNHensley@TaylorU.edu
Contact *Dr Dennis E. Hensley*

One-day seminars on *Freelance Writing* and *Fiction Writing* held on Saturdays each spring and autumn. Taught by Dr Hensley, Director of the Professional Writing major at the University.

Louisiana

Louisiana State University

English Department, 213 Allen Hall, Baton Rouge LA 70803
Website www.english.lsu.edu
Contacts *James Wilcox, Judy Kahn*

Master of Fine Arts (MFA) course with a focus in *Poetry, Fiction, Playwriting, Screenwriting* or *Creative Non-fiction*. Includes opportunity to meet and/or work with visiting writers. Teaching and editorial assistantships are available.

Maryland

Goucher College

Welch Center for Graduate and Continuing Studies, 1021 Dulaney Valley Road, Baltimore MD 21204–2794
☎001 800 697 4646 Fax 001 410 337 6085
Email center@goucher.edu
Course Director *Patsy Sims* (☎001 800 697 4646)

The two-year MFA Program in *Creative Nonfiction* is a limited-residency course that allows students to complete most of the requirements off campus while developing their skill as non-fiction writers under the close supervision of a faculty mentor. Provides instruction in the following areas: the personal essay, memoir, literary journalism, travel/nature/science writing, biography/profiles, and narrative non-fiction.

New York

New York University

19 University Place, 2nd Floor, New York NY 10003
Email creative.writing@nyu.edu
Website www.nyu.edu/gsas/program/cwp
Contact *Russell Carmony*
Director *Melissa Hammerle*

Offers MFA in *Creative Writing* and MA in *English* with focus in *Creative Writing* in poetry and fiction. Includes writing workshops and craft courses, literary outreach programmes, a public reading series, student readings, special literary seminars and student teaching opportunities. Publishes two literary journals: *Washington Square* and *Calabash*. Contact the department via e-mail.

Texas

University of Texas at Austin

Department of Radio-Television-Film, Austin TX 78712
☎001 512 475 7399 (Admissions)
Website www.utexas.edu/ftp/coc/rtf

Four-year BSc course in *Radio-Television-Film* during which writing for film and television may be studied in the third and fourth years. At graduate level, a MA in *Screenwriting* is offered.

Commonwealth Publishers

Australia

ACER Press
19 Prospect Hill Road, Camberwell
Victoria 3124
☎00 61 3 9277 5555
Fax 00 61 3 9277 5678
FOUNDED 1930. *Publishes* Education, human
relations, psychology, psychiatry.

Allen & Unwin Pty Ltd
PO Box 8500, St Leonards, Sydney
NSW 1590
☎00 61 2 8425 0100 Fax 00 61 2 9906 2218
Website www.allenandunwin.com
FOUNDED 1976. *Publishes* fiction, literature, literary criticism, essays; general non-fiction, art,
Asian studies, business, cookery, earth sciences,
economics, education, gay and lesbian, government, political science, health and nutrition,
history, industrial relations, general science.

Edward Arnold (Australia) Pty Ltd
PO Box 885, Kew Victoria 3101
☎00 61 3 859 9011 Fax 00 61 3 859 9141
FOUNDED 1966. Part of Hodder & Stoughton
(Australia) Pty Ltd. *Publishes* general non-
fiction: accountancy, Asian studies, career
development, computer science, cookery,
geography, geology, government, political science, health and nutrition, law, mathematics,
psychology and psychiatry, technology.

Blackwell Science Pty Ltd
PO Box 378, South Carlton Victoria 3053
☎00 61 3 9347 0300 Fax 00 61 3 9347 5552
FOUNDED 1971. Part of Blackwell Science Ltd,
UK. *Publishes* general science, medicine, nursing, dentistry, engineering, computer science,
mathematics, physical sciences, physics, psychology, psychiatry.

Currency Press Pty Ltd
PO Box 2287, Strawberry Hills NSW 2012
☎00 61 2 9319 5877 Fax 00 61 2 9319 3649
Website www.currency.com.au
FOUNDED 1971. Performing arts publisher –
drama, theatre, music, dance, film and video.

Dangaroo Press
PO Box 93, New Lambton NSW 2305
☎00 61 2 4925 1761 Fax 00 61 4 951 7430
FOUNDED 1978. *Publishes* general non-fiction,
art, literature, literary criticism, essays, poetry,
social sciences, women's studies.

E.J. Dwyer (Australia) Pty Ltd
Locked Bag 71, Alexandria NSW 2015
☎00 61 2 9550 2355 Fax 00 61 2 9519 3218
FOUNDED 1904. *Publishes* self-help, marketing,
social sciences, sociology, religion, theology.

Harcourt Australia Pty Ltd
Locked Bag 16, Marrickville NSW 2044
☎00 61 2 9517 8999 Fax 00 61 2 9517 2204
FOUNDED 1972. *Publishes* business, education,
general science, medicine, nursing, dentistry,
psychology, psychiatry, veterinary science,
social sciences, mathematics.

HarperCollins Publishers (Australia) Pty Ltd
PO Box 321, Pymble NSW 2073
☎00 61 2 9952 5445 Fax 00 61 2 9952 5544
FOUNDED 1872. Part of the HarperCollins
Publishers Group. *Publishes* fiction and general
non-fiction, biography, children's, gardening,
humour, government, political science,
regional interests, literature, literary criticism,
essays, women's studies.

Hodder Headline Australia
Level 22, 201 Kent Street, Sydney NSW 2000
☎00 61 2 8248 0800 Fax 00 61 2 8248 0810
Website www.hha.com.au
FOUNDED 1958. Owned by **Hodder
Headline**, UK. *Publishes* general non-fiction
and fiction (adult and children's), education.

Hyland House Publishing Pty Ltd
PO Box 122, Flemington Victoria 3031
☎00 61 3 9376 4461
FOUNDED 1976. *Publishes* general non-fiction,
Asian studies, biography, cookery, animals,
pets, history, essays, fiction, gardening, literature, literary criticism.

LexisNexis Butterworths Australia Ltd
Tower 2, 475–495 Victoria Avenue, Chatswood NSW 2067
☎00 61 2 9422 2222 Fax 00 61 2 9422 2444
Website www.lexisnexis.com.au
FOUNDED 1910. A division of Reed Elsevier Australia Pty Ltd. *Publishes* accountancy, business and law.

Thomas C. Lothian Pty Ltd
11 Munro Street, Port Melbourne Victoria 3207
☎00 61 3 9645 1544 Fax 00 61 3 9646 4882
FOUNDED 1888. *Publishes* general non-fiction: business, health and nutrition, New Age, astrology, occult, self-help.

Macmillan Education Australia Pty Ltd
Locked Bag 1400, South Yarra Victoria 3141
☎00 61 3 9825 1025 Fax 00 61 3 9825 1010
Website www.macmillan.com.au
FOUNDED 1896. Part of **Macmillan Publishers**, UK. *Publishes* accountancy, economics, education, geography, geology, government, political science, history, management, mathematics, physics, general science, social sciences, sociology.

McGraw-Hill Book Company Australia Pty Ltd
4 Barcoo Street, Roseville NSW 2069
☎00 61 2 9415 9899 Fax 00 61 2 9417 8872
Website www.mcgraw-hill.com.au
FOUNDED 1964. Owned by **McGraw-Hill Companies Inc.**, USA. *Publishes* accountancy, education, health and nutrition, advertising, aeronautics, aviation, anthropology, architecture and interior design, art, chemistry, child care and development, computer science, criminology, economics, electronics, electrical engineering, general engineering, English as a second language, environmental studies, film and video, geography, geology, journalism, industrial relations, language arts, linguistics, management, maritime, mathematics, mechanical engineering, medicine, nursing, dentistry, philosophy, photography, physics, psychology, psychiatry, sport, social sciences and sociology.

Melbourne University Press
PO Box 278, Carlton South Victoria 3053
☎00 61 3 9342 0300 Fax 00 61 3 9342 0399
FOUNDED 1922. *Publishes* general non-fiction, biography, essays, history, literature, literary criticism, natural history, psychology, psychiatry, travel.

Openbook Publishers
GPO Box 1368J, Adelaide SA 5001
☎00 61 8 8223 4568 Fax 00 61 8 8223 4552
Website www.openbooks.com.au
FOUNDED 1913. *Publishes* religious and educational books.

Oxford University Press Australia and New Zealand
PO Box 2784Y, Melbourne 3001 Victoria 3001
☎00 61 3 9934 9123 Fax 00 61 3 9934 9100
Website www.oup.com.au
FOUNDED 1908. Owned by **Oxford University Press**, UK. *Publishes* for the college, school and trade markets.

Pan Macmillan Australia
Level 18, St Martin's Tower, 31 Market Street, Sydney NSW 2000
☎00 61 2 9261 5611 Fax 00 61 2 9261 5047
Email panpublishing@www.macmillan.com.au
Website www.macmillan.com.au
FOUNDED 1983. Part of **Macmillan Publishers**, UK. *Publishes* fiction, science fiction/fantasy, essays, literature, literary criticism; general non-fiction, biography, government, political science, health and nutrition, self-help, sport, travel.

Pearson Education Australia
LMB 507, Frenchs Forest NSW 1640
☎00 61 3 9454 2200 Fax 00 61 3 9453 0089
Website www.awl.com.au
Australia's largest educational publisher.

Penguin Books Australia Ltd
PO Box 157, Ringwood Victoria 3134
☎00 61 3 9871 2400 Fax 00 61 3 9870 9618
FOUNDED 1946. *Publishes* general non-fiction and fiction; biography, cookery, humour, literature, literary criticism, essays, science fiction, fantasy, self-help, travel.

University of Queensland Press
PO Box 6042, St Lucia Queensland 4067
☎00 61 7 3365 2127 Fax 00 61 7 3365 7579
Website www.uqp.uq.edu.au
FOUNDED 1948. *Publishes* Aboriginal studies, reference, social and political issues; general non-fiction and fiction, literature, literary criticism, essays, poetry, biography, history, sport, travel.

Random House Australia Pty Ltd
20 Alfred Street, Milsons Point NSW 2061
☎00 61 2 8923 9893 Fax 00 61 2 9954 4562
Email random@randomhouse.com.au
Website www.randomhouse.com.au
Subsidiary of **Bertelsmann AG**. *Publishes* fiction and non-fiction.

Reader's Digest (Australia) Pty Ltd
PO Box 4353, Sydney NSW 2001
☎00 61 2 9690 6935 Fax 00 61 2 9690 6390
FOUNDED 1946. Associate company of **Reader's Digest Association, Inc.** (USA). Educational publisher.

Reed Educational & Professional Publishing Australia
PO Box 460, Port Melbourne Victoria 3207
☎00 61 3 9245 7188 Fax 00 61 3 9245 7265
Website www.reededucation.com.au
FOUNDED 1982. *Publishes* art, chemistry, chemical engineering, environmental studies, geography, geology, health and nutrition, history, mathematics, physics.

Scholastic Australia Pty Limited
PO Box 579, Gosford NSW 2250
☎00 61 2 4328 3555 Fax 00 61 2 4329 1106
FOUNDED 1968. Educational publisher.

Science Press
Fitzroy & Chapel Streets, Marrickville NSW 2204
☎00 61 2 9516 1122 Fax 00 61 2 9550 1915
FOUNDED 1945. Educational publisher.

Simon & Schuster Australia Pty Ltd
PO Box 507, East Roseville NSW 2069
☎00 61 2 9417 3255 Fax 00 61 2 9417 3188
FOUNDED 1987. Part of **Simon & Schuster Inc.**, USA. *Publishes* general non-fiction.

University of Western Australia Press
35 Stirling Highway, Crawley WA 6009
☎00 61 8 9380 3182 Fax 00 61 8 9380 1027
FOUNDED 1954. *Publishes* general non-fiction, essays, literature, literary criticism, history, social sciences, sociology, natural history, autobiography.

John Wiley & Sons Ltd
PO Box 1226, Milton Queensland 4064
☎00 61 7 3859 9755 Fax 00 61 7 3859 9715
Email brisbane@johnwiley.com.au
Website www.johnwiley.com.au
FOUNDED 1954. Owned by **John Wiley & Sons Inc.**, USA. *Publishes* general non-fiction and education books.

Canada

Arnold Publishing Ltd
11016 127th Street, Edmonton
Alberta T5M 0T2
☎001 780 454 7477 Fax 001 780 454 7463
Email info@arnold.ca
Website www.arnold.ca
FOUNDED 1967. Educational textbooks and CD-ROMS.

Butterworths Canada Ltd
75 Clegg Road, Markham Ontario L6G 1A1
☎001 905 479 2665 Fax 001 905 479 2826
Website www.butterworths.ca
FOUNDED 1912. Division of **Reed Elsevier plc**. *Publishes* law books, CD-ROMs, journals, newsletters, law reports and newspapers.

Canadian Scholars' Press, Inc
180 Bloor Street W, Suite 1202, Toronto
Ontario M5S 2V6
☎001 416 929 2774 Fax 001 416 929 1926
Email info@cspi.org
Website www.cspi.org
FOUNDED 1987. *Publishes* academic books in English and French.

Fenn Publishing Co Ltd
34 Nixon Road, Bolton Ontario L7E 1W2
☎001 905 951 6600 Fax 001 905 951 6601
Website www.hbfenn.com
FOUNDED 1977. *Publishes* fiction and non-fiction, children's.

Fitzhenry & Whiteside Limited
195 Allstate Parkway, Markham
Ontario L3R 4T8
☎001 905 477 9700 Fax 001 905 477 9179
Email godwit@fitzhenry.ca
Website www.fitzhenry.ca
FOUNDED 1966. *Publishes* reference and children's books; educational material.

Golden Books Publishing (Canada) Inc
73 Water Street N., No 501, Cambridge
Ontario N1R 5X2
☎001 519 623 3590 Fax 001 519 623 3598

Website www.goldenbooks.com
FOUNDED 1942. *Publishes* (in English and French) juvenile and adult books, Bibles.

Harcourt Canada Ltd
55 Horner Avenue, Toronto
Ontario M8Z 4X6
☎001 416 255 4491 Fax 001 416 255 4046
Website www.harcourtcanada.com
FOUNDED 1922. *Publishes* educational material.

HarperCollins Publishers Limited
55 Avenue Road, Suite 2900, Hazelton Lanes,
Toronto Ontario M5R 3L2
☎001 416 975 9334 Fax 001 416 975 9884
Website www.harpercanada.com
FOUNDED 1989. *Publishes* fiction and non-fiction, children's and religious.

Irwin Publishing
325 Humber College Blvd., Toronto
Ontario M9W 7C3
☎001 416 798 0424 Fax 001 416 798 1384
Email irwin@irwin-pub.com
Website www.irwin-pub.com
FOUNDED 1945. *Publishes* (in English and French) education.

McClelland & Stewart Ltd
481 University Avenue, Suite 900, Toronto
Ontario M5G 2E9
☎001 416 598 1114 Fax 001 416 598 7764
Website www.mcclelland.com
FOUNDED 1906. *Publishes* fiction and non-fiction, poetry.

McGraw-Hill Ryerson Ltd
300 Water Street, Whitby Ontario L1N 9B6
☎001 905 430 5000 Fax 001 905 430 5020
Website www.mcgrawhill.ca
FOUNDED 1944. Subsidiary of the **McGraw-Hill Companies**. *Publishes* education and professional.

Nelson Thomson Learning
1120 Birchmount Road, Scarborough Ontario
M1K 5G4
☎001 416 752 9100 Fax 001 416 752 9646
Website www.nelson.com
FOUNDED 1914. Division of Thomson Canada Ltd. *Publishes* educational, professional and reference.

New Star Books Ltd
107–3477 Commercial Street, Vancouver
BC V5N 4E8

☎001 604 738 9429 Fax 001 604 738 9332
Email info@newstarbooks.com
Website www.newstarbooks.com
FOUNDED 1974. *Publishes* social issues and current affairs, fiction, literature, history, international politics, labour, feminist, gay and lesbian studies.

Oxford University Press, Canada
70 Wynford Drive, Don Mills
Onatario M3C 1J9
☎001 416 441 2941 Fax 001 416 444 0427
Website www.oup.com/ca
FOUNDED 1904. Owned by **Oxford University Press**, UK. *Publishes* for college, school and trade markets.

Pearson Canada
26 Prince Andrew Place, Torontor
Ontario M3C 2T8
☎001 416 447 5101 Fax 001 416 443 0948
Website www.pearsoned.com
FOUNDED 1966. Fourth-largest educational publisher in Canada. Publishes in English and French.

Penguin Books Canada Ltd
10 Alcorn Avenue, Suite 300, Toronto
Ontario M4V 3B2
☎001 416 925 2249 Fax 001 416 925 0068
Website www.penguin.ca
FOUNDED 1974. Division of the Pearson Group. *Publishes* fiction and non-fiction books and audio cassettes.

Random House of Canada Ltd
2775 Matheson Blvd. East, Mississauga
Ontario L4W 4P7
☎001 905 624 0672 Fax 001 905 624 6217
Website www.randomhouse.com
FOUNDED 1944. *Publishes* fiction and non-fiction and children's.

Scholastic Canada Ltd
175 Hillmount Road, Markham
Ontario L6C 1Z7
☎001 905 887 7323 Fax 001 905 887 1131
Website www.scholastic.ca
FOUNDED 1957. *Publishes* (in English and French) children's books and educational material.

Tundra Books
481 University Avenue, Suite 900, Toronto
Ontario M5G 2E9
☎001 416 598 4786 Fax 001 416 598 0247

FOUNDED 1967. Division of **McClelland & Stewart Ltd**. *Publishes* (in English and French) children's illustrated books.

John Wiley & Sons Canada Ltd
22 Worcester Road, Etobicoke Ontario
M9W 1L1
☎001 416 236 4433 Fax 001 416 236 4447
Website www.wiley.com
FOUNDED 1968. Subsidiary of **John Wiley & Sons Inc.**, USA. *Publishes* professional, reference and textbooks.

India
Affiliated East West Press Pvt Ltd
104 Nirmal Tower, 26 Barakhamba Road,
New Delhi 110 001
☎00 91 11 331 5398 Fax 00 91 11 326 0538
FOUNDED 1962. *Publishes* aeronautics, aviation, agriculture, anthropology, biological sciences, chemistry, engineering (chemical, civil, electrical, mechanical), computer science, economics, electronics, mathematics, management, microcomputers, physical sciences, physics, general science, veterinary science, women's studies.

Arnold Heinman Publishers (India) Pvt Ltd
AB-9, 1st Floor, Safdarjang Enclave,
New Delhi 110 029
☎00 91 11 688 3422 Fax 00 91 11 687 7571
FOUNDED 1969. Associate company of **Edward Arnold (Publishers) Ltd**, UK. *Publishes* fiction, poetry, essays, literature, literary criticism, art, general engineering, government, political science, philosophy, religion, medicine, nursing, dentistry, social sciences and sociology.

S. Chand & Co Ltd
PO Box 5733, New Delhi 110 055
☎00 91 11 777 208011
Fax 00 91 11 777 7446
FOUNDED 1917. *Publishes* art, business, economics, government, political science, medicine, nursing, dentistry, philosophy, social sciences, sociology, general science, technology.

Current Books
Round West, Trichur 680 001
☎00 91 487 335642 Fax 00 91 487 335660
FOUNDED 1952. *Publishes* fiction and general non-fiction.

General Book Depot
PO Box 1220, Delhi 110 006
☎00 91 11 326 3695
Fax 00 91 11 294 0861
FOUNDED 1936. *Publishes* general nonfiction; business, career development, how-to, English as a second language, language arts, linguistics, self-help, travel.

HarperCollins Publishers India Pty Ltd
7/61 Ansari Road, Daryaganj,
New Delhi 110 002
☎00 91 11 327 8586 Fax 00 91 11 327 7294
FOUNDED 1991. *Publishes* fiction, poetry, biography and education.

Hind Pocket Books Private Ltd
18–19 Dilshad Garden G T Road,
Delhi 110 095
☎00 91 11 202 046 Fax 00 91 11 228 2332
FOUNDED 1958. *Publishes* fiction and general non-fiction; biography, how-to and self-help.

Jaico Publishing House
121–125 Mahatma Gandhi Road,
Mumbai 400 023
☎00 91 22 267 6702 Fax 00 91 22 204 1673
FOUNDED 1945. *Publishes* biography, language arts, linguistics, health and nutrition, cookery, law, criminology, astrology, occult, philosophy, religion, general engineering, economics, humour, history, government, political science, psychology, psychiatry.

Macmillan India Ltd
315/316 Raheja Chambers, 12 Museum
Road, Bangalore 560 052
☎00 91 80 558 6563 Fax 00 91 80 558 8713
Email macmillan@aindia.com
Website www.macmillan-india.com
FOUNDED 1903. Part of **Macmillan Publishers**, UK. *Publishes* scientific and mathematical books and journals.

Munshiram Manoharlal Publishers Pvt Ltd
PO Box 5715, New Delhi 110 055
☎00 91 11 777 3650 Fax 00 91 11 751 2745
FOUNDED 1952. *Publishes* art, architecture and interior design, anthropology, archaeology, astrology, occult, religion (Buddhist, Hindu, Islamic), philosophy, history, language arts and linguistics, music, dance, drama, theatre, Asian studies.

National Book Trust India

H–29, Green Park Extension,
New Delhi 110 016
☎00 91 11 664 9962 Fax 00 91 11 685 1795

FOUNDED 1957. *Publishes* human relations and foreign countries.

National Publishing House

23 Daryaganj, New Delhi 110 002
☎00 91 11 327 4161

FOUNDED 1950. *Publishes* human relations, ethnicity, social sciences, sociology.

Orient Paperbacks

1590 Madarsa Road, Kashmere Gate,
Delhi 110 006
☎00 91 11 296 2267 Fax 00 91 11 296 2935

FOUNDED 1948. *Publishes* fiction and general non-fiction; business, career development, cookery, crafts, games, hobbies, drama, theatre, health and nutrition, how-to, poetry, astrology, occult, self-help, sport.

Oxford University Press India

YMCA Library Building, 1st Floor, Jai Singh Road, PO Box 43, New Delhi 110 001
☎00 91 11 374 2990 Fax 00 91 11 374 2312
Email admin@oupin.com

FOUNDED 1912. Owned by **Oxford University Press**, UK. Academic publishers.

Rajpal & Sons

Madarasa Road, Kashmere Gate,
Delhi 110 006
☎00 91 11 296 3904 Fax 00 91 11 296 7791

FOUNDED 1891. *Publishes* fiction, literature, literary criticism, essays, dictionaries, human relations, general science.

Tata McGraw-Hill Publishing Co Ltd

4/12 Asaf Ali Road, 3rd Floor,
New Delhi 110 002
☎00 91 11 278 251

FOUNDED 1970. *Publishes* general engineering and science, business, social sciences, sociology and management.

Vidyarthi Mithram Press

Baker Road, Kottayam 686 001
☎00 91 481 563 281 Fax 00 91 481 562 616

FOUNDED 1928. *Publishes* child care and development, cookery, drama and theatre, economics, biography, biological sciences, chemistry and chemical engineering, computer science.

A.H. Wheeler & Co Ltd

411 Surya Kiran Building, 19 K G Marg, New Delhi 110 001
☎00 91 11 331 2629 Fax 00 91 11 335 7798

FOUNDED 1879. *Publishes* computer science, behavioural sciences, accountancy, advertising, business, career development, civil engineering, communications.

New Zealand

Auckland University Press

University of Auckland, 1–11 Short Street,
Auckland
☎00 64 9 373 7528 Fax 00 64 9 373 7465
Website www.auckland.ac.nz/aup

FOUNDED 1966. *Publishes* art, archaeology, biography, government, political science, history, social sciences, sociology, women's studies, essays, poetry, literature, literary criticism.

Butterworths of New Zealand Ltd

PO Box 472, Wellington 1
☎00 64 4 385 1479 Fax 00 64 4 385 1598
Website www.butterworths.co.nz

FOUNDED 1914. *Publishes* law.

Canterbury University Press

University of Canterbury, Private Bag 4800,
Christchurch
☎00 64 3 364 2914 Fax 00 64 3 364 2044
Email mail@cup.canterbury.ac.nz

FOUNDED 1960. *Publishes* general non-fiction; biography, biological sciences, history, natural history.

The Caxton Press

PO Box 25088, Christchurch
☎00 64 3 366 8516 Fax 00 64 3 365 7840

FOUNDED 1935. *Publishes* general non-fiction; biography, gardening and plants.

HarperCollins Publishers (New Zealand) Ltd

31 View Road, Auckland
☎00 64 9 443 9400 Fax 00 64 9 443 9403
Website www.harpercollins.co.nz

FOUNDED 1888. *Publishes* fiction, art, history, humour, natural history, biography, gardening, sport, travel, self-help.

Hodder Moa Beckett Publishers Ltd

PO Box 3858, Auckland
☎00 64 9 444 3640 Fax 00 64 9 444 3646

FOUNDED 1971. Owned by **Hodder Headline**, UK. *Publishes* fiction and general non-fiction, biography.

Huia Publishers
PO Box 17335, Karori, Wellington
☎00 64 4 473 9262 Fax 00 64 4 473 9265
Website www.huia.co.nz
FOUNDED 1991. *Publishes* Maori cultural history and language, children's books in Maori and English, history of colonisation in New Zealand.

University of Otago Press
PO Box 56, Dunedin
☎00 64 3 479 8807 Fax 00 64 3 479 8385
Email university.press@otago.ac.nz
Website www.otago.ac.nz
FOUNDED 1958. *Publishes* fiction, essays, literature, literary criticism, history, education, biography, anthropology, natural history, environmental studies, government and political science.

Oxford University Press New Zealand
See **Oxford University Press Australia and New Zealand** under Australia.

Pearson Education New Zealand
Private Bag 102908, North Shore Mail Centre, Glenfield, Auckland 10
☎00 64 9 444 4968 Fax 00 64 9 444 4957
FOUNDED 1968. Educational publishers.

Penguin Books (NZ) Ltd
182–190 Wairau Road (Glenfield), Private Bag, Takapuna, Auckland 9
☎00 64 9 444 4965
FOUNDED 1976. Owned by **Penguin UK**.

Reed Publishing (NZ) Ltd
Private Bag 34901, Birkenhead, Auckland 10
☎00 64 9 480 4950 Fax 00 64 9 419 4999
Website www.reed.co.nz
FOUNDED 1988. *Publishes* fiction and general non-fiction, biography, cookery, history, natural history, regional interests, travel.

Southern Press Ltd
R D 1, Porirua 6221
☎00 64 4 239 9068 Fax 00 64 4 239 9835
FOUNDED 1971. *Publishes* aviation, aeronautics, maritime, transport, technology, mechanical and civil engineering, archaeology.

Tandem Press
2 Rugby Road, Birkenhead, Auckland 10
☎00 64 9 480 1452 Fax 00 64 9 480 1455
FOUNDED 1990. *Publishes* fiction and general non-fiction; cookery, business, alternative, ethnicity, health and nutrition, photography, psychology, psychiatry, self-help, women's studies.

Victoria University Press
PO Box 600, Wellington
☎00 64 4 496 6580 Fax 00 64 4 471 1701
Website www.vup.vuw.ac.nz
FOUNDED 1979. *Publishes* government, political science, essays, poetry, literature, literary criticism, drama, theatre, history, social sciences and sociology, anthropology, language and linguistics, law, architecture and interior design.

Viking Sevenseas NZ Ltd
PO Box 152, Paraparaumu 6150, Wellington
☎00 64 4 902 9990
FOUNDED 1957. *Publishes* general non-fiction; astrology, occult, health and nutrition, medicine, nursing and dentistry, ethnicity.

Bridget Williams Books Ltd
PO Box 5482, Wellington
☎00 64 4 473 8317 Fax 00 64 4 473 8417
FOUNDED 1990. *Publishes* general non-fiction, biography, education, government, political science, history, women's studies.

South Africa

Butterworths South Africa
PO Box 4, Mayville, Durban 4058
☎00 27 31 268 3111
Fax 00 27 31 268 3100
Website www.butterworths.za
Owned by Butterworths UK. *Publishes* general science, medicine, nursing and dentistry, economics, education, law.

Flesch Financial Publications (Pty) Ltd
PO Box 3473, Cape Town 8000
☎00 27 21 461 7472
Fax 00 27 21 461 3758
FOUNDED 1966. *Publishes* aviation, aeronautics, maritime, animals, pets, business.

Heinemann Educational Publishers Southern Africa

PO Box 781940, Sandton 21461, Johannesburg
☎00 27 11 322 8600 Fax 00 27 11 322 8717
Website www.heinemann.co.za

FOUNDED 1986. Parent company: **Reed Educational & Professional Publishing**, UK. *Publishes* economics, education, English as a second language, mathematics, mechanical engineering.

Maskew Miller Longman

PO Box 396, Cape Town 8000
☎00 27 21 531 7750 Fax 00 27 21 531 4877

FOUNDED 1893. *Publishes* education, language arts and linguistics, essays, literature, literary criticism.

University of Natal Press

PB X01, Scottsville, Pietermaritzburg 3209
☎00 27 331 260 5226
Fax 00 27 331 260 5599
Email books@press.unp.ac.za

FOUNDED 1947. *Publishes* essays, literature and literary criticism, natural history, history, women's studies.

Oxford University Press Southern Africa

PO Box 12119, N1 City, Goodwood 7460
☎00 27 21 595 4400 Fax 00 27 21 595 4430
Email oxford@oup.co.za

FOUNDED 1915. Parent company: **Oxford University Press**, UK. *Publishes* academic, educational and general books.

Ravan Press (Pty) Ltd

PO Box 145, Randburg, Johannesburg 2125
☎00 27 11 789 7636 Fax 00 27 11 789 7653

FOUNDED 1972. Part of Hodder & Stoughton Educational South Africa. *Publishes* fiction and general non-fiction; anthropology, biography, business, economics, education, environmental studies, ethnicity, government, political science, history, labour and industrial relations, management, music, dance, social studies and sociology, women's studies.

Shuter & Shooter (Pty) Ltd

PO Box 618, Ferndale 2160
☎00 27 11 792 8363 Fax 00 27 11 792 7024

FOUNDED 1925. *Publishes* general non-fiction; biography, history, ethnicity, general science, technology, social sciences and sociology.

Struik Publishers (Pty) Ltd

PO Box 1144, Cape Town 8000
☎00 27 21 517128 Fax 00 27 21 4624379

FOUNDED 1962. *Publishes* child care and development, cookery, gardening, environmental studies, natural history.

Witwatersrand University Press

PO Wits, Johannesburg 2050
☎00 27 11 484 5907 Fax 00 27 11 484 5971
Website www.wirs.ac.za/wup.html

FOUNDED 1922. *Publishes* essays, literature and literary criticism, drama, theatre, history, business, anthropology, archaeology, natural history, religion (Jewish), medicine, nursing and dentistry.

Professional Associations and Societies

Academi (Yr Academi Gymreig)
3rd Floor, Mount Stuart House, Mount Stuart Square, Cardiff CF10 5FQ
☎029 2047 2266 Fax 029 2049 2930
Email post@academi.org
Website www.academi.org

North West Wales office: Tŷ Newydd, Llanystumdwy, Cricieth, Gwynedd LL52 0LW
☎01766 522817 Fax 01766 523095
Email academi.gog@dial.pipex.com

West Wales office: Dylan Thomas Centre, Somerset Place, Swansea SA1 1RR
☎01792 463980 Fax 01792 463993
Email academi.dylan.thomas@business.ntl.com

North East Wales office: Yr Hen Garchar, 46 Clwyd Street, Ruthin, Denbighshire LL15 1HP
☎01824 708218 Fax 01824 708202
Email academi@denbighshire.gov.uk

Chief Executive *Peter Finch*

Academi is the trading name of Yr Academi Gymreig, the national society of Welsh writers. The Society exists to promote the literature of Wales. Yr Academi Gymreig was FOUNDED in 1959 as an association of Welsh language writers. An English language section was established in 1968. Membership, for those who have made a significant contribution to the literature of Wales, is by invitation. Membership currently stands at 500. The Academi runs courses, competitions (including the **Cardiff International Poetry Competition**), conferences, tours by authors, festivals and represents the interests of Welsh writers and Welsh writing both inside Wales and beyond. Its publications include *Taliesin*, a quarterly literary journal in the Welsh language, *The Oxford Companion to the Literature of Wales*, *The Welsh Academy English-Welsh Dictionary* and a variety of translated works.

In 1998 the Academi won the franchise from the Arts Council of Wales to run the Welsh National Literature Promotion Agency. The new, much enlarged organisation now administers a variety of schemes including Writers on Tour, Writers Residencies and a number of literature development projects. It promotes an annual literary festival alternating between North and South Wales, runs its own programme of literary activity and publishes *A470*, a bi-monthly literature information magazine. The Academi is also in receipt of a lottery grant to publish the first Welsh National Encyclopedia. This is expected to be ready towards the end of 2003.

Those with an interest in literature in Wales can become an associate of the Academi (which carries a range of benefits). Rates are £15 p.a. (waged); £7.50 (unwaged).

ALCS
See **Authors' Licensing & Collecting Society**

Alliance of Literary Societies
22 Belmont Crescent, Havant, Hampshire PO9 3PU
☎023 9247 5855 Fax 08700 560330
Email rosemary@sndc.demon.co.uk
Website www.sndc.demon.co.uk/als.htm

Honorary Secretary *Mrs Rosemary Culley*

FOUNDED 1974. Aims to help and support its 90+ member societies and, when necessary, to act as a pressure group. Produces a handbook which holds useful information that is deemed important for the successful running of a literary society. It also contains details of the member societies and events to publicise them to the ALS members and the wider public. In addition, the Alliance produces two newsletters and *The Open Book*, an annual publication.

Arts & Business (A&B)
Nutmeg House, 60 Gainsford Street, Butlers Wharf, London SE1 2NY
☎020 7378 8143 Fax 020 7407 7527
Email head.office@AandB.org.uk
Website www.AandB.org.uk

The purpose of Arts & Business (formerly the Association for Business Sponsorship of the Arts) is to help strengthen communities by developing creative and effective partnership between Business and the Arts. It provides a wide range of services to over 350 business members as well as to 700 arts organisations and museums through the Development Forum. The Arts & Business Skills Bank, Board

Bank and mentoring schemes enable individual business people to share their skills with arts managers. On behalf of the Department for Culture, Media and Sport, it manages the Arts & Business New Partners Programme, an incentive programme for new and established sponsors of the arts. Arts & Business is working with forward-looking businesses to determine the future of business/arts partnerships. With the support of its President, HRH The Prince of Wales, it is exploring and developing new ways for business, the arts and society to interact. Arts & Business has 15 offices offering a range of services throughout the UK.

Arvon Foundation

See entry under **Writers' Courses, Circles and Workshops**

ASLS

See **Association for Scottish Literary Studies**

Association for Business Sponsorship of the Arts (ABSA)

See **Arts & Business**

Association for Scottish Literary Studies

c/o Department of Scottish History, 9 University Gardens, University of Glasgow, Glasgow G12 8QH
☎0141 330 5309 Fax 0141 330 5309
Email d.jones@scothist.arts.gla.ac.uk
Website www.asls.org.uk

Contact *Duncan Jones*
Subscription £34 (Individual);
 £63 (Institutional)

FOUNDED 1970. ASLS is an educational charity promoting the languages and literature of Scotland. *Publishes* works of Scottish literature; essays, monographs and journals; and *Scotnotes*, a series of comprehensive study guides to major Scottish writers. Also produces *New Writing Scotland*, an annual anthology of contemporary poetry and prose in English, Gaelic and Scots (see entry under **Magazines**).

Association of American Correspondents in London

c/o Time Magazine, Brettenham House, Lancaster Place, London WC2E 7TL
☎020 7499 4080 Fax 020 7322 1230

Contact *Elizabeth Lea*
Subscription £90 (Organisations)

FOUNDED 1919 to serve the professional interests of its member organisations, promote social cooperation among them, and maintain the ethical standards of the profession. (An extra £30 is charged for each department of an organisation which requires separate listing in the Association's handbook and a charge of £10 for each full-time editorial staff listed, up to a maximum of £120 regardless of the number listed.)

Association of American Publishers, Inc

71 Fifth Avenue, 2nd Floor, New York, NY 10003–3004 USA
☎001 212 255 0200 Fax 001 212 255 7007
Website www.publishers.org

Also at: 50 f Street, NW, Washington, DC 20001–1564
☎001 202 347 3375 Fax 001 202 347 3690

Contact *Judith Platt*

FOUNDED 1970. For information, visit the Association's website.

Association of Authors' Agents

c/o Curtis Brown Group Ltd, 4th Floor, Haymarket House, 28/29 Haymarket, London SW1Y 4SP
☎020 7396 6600 Fax 020 7396 0110/1
Email jlloyd@curtisbrown.co.uk
Website www.agentsassoc.co.uk

President *Jonathan Lloyd*
Membership £50 p.a.

FOUNDED 1974. Membership voluntary. The AAA maintains a code of practice, provides a forum for discussion and represents its members in issues affecting the profession. For a full list of members visit the AAA website.

Association of Authors' Representatives

PO Box 237201, Ansonia Station, New York, NY 10023 USA
☎001 212 252 3695
Email aarinc@mindspring.com
Website www.aar-online.org

Administrative Secretary *Leslie Carroll*

FOUNDED in 1991 through the merger of the Society of Authors' Representatives and the Independent Literary Agents Association. Membership of this US organisation is restricted to agents of at least two years' operation. Provides information, education and support for its members and works to protect their best interests.

Association of British Editors

See **Society of Editors**

Association of British Science Writers (ABSW)

23 Savile Row, London W1X 2NB
☎020 7439 1205 Fax 020 7973 3051
Email absw@absw.org.uk
Website www.absw.org.uk
Chairman *Pallab Ghosh*
Administrator *Barbara Drillsma*
Membership £35 p.a.; £30 (Associate);
    £5 (Student)

ABSW has played a central role in improving the standards of science journalism in the UK over the last 40 years. The Association seeks to improve standards by means of networking, lectures and organised visits to institutional laboratories and industrial research centres. Puts members in touch with major projects in the field and with experts worldwide. A member of the European Union of Science Journalists' Associations, ABSW is able to offer heavily subsidised places on visits to research centres in most other European countries, and hosts reciprocal visits to Britain by European journalists. Membership open to those who are considered to be *bona fide* science writers/editors, or their film/TV/radio equivalents, who earn a substantial part of their income by promoting public interest in and understanding of science. Runs the administration and judging of the **Glaxo Science Writers' Awards**, for outstanding science journalism in newspapers, journals and broadcasting and, with The Wellcome Trust, awards bursaries for science undergraduates taking a science communication course.

Association of Canadian Publishers

110 Eglinton Avenue West, Suite 401,
Toronto, Ontario M4R 1A3 Canada
☎001 416 487 6116 Fax 001 416 487 8815
Email info@canbook.org
Website www.publishers.ca
Executive Director *Monique M. Smith*

FOUNDED 1971. ACP represents over 140 Canadian-owned book publishers countrywide from the literary, general trade, scholarly and education sectors. Aims to encourage the writing, publishing, distribution and promotion of Canadian books and to support the development of a 'strong, independent and vibrant Canadian-owned publishing industry'. The organisation's website has information on getting published and links to many of their member publishers' websites.

Association of Christian Writers

All Saints Vicarage, 43 All Saints Close,
Edmonton, London N9 9AT
☎020 8884 4348 Fax 020 8884 4348
Email admin@christianwriters.org.uk
Website www.christianwriters.org.uk
Administrator *Mrs Jenny Kyriacou*
Subscription Single: £17 (£15 Direct Debit);
    Joint Husband/Wife: £20 (£18 DD);
    Overseas: £23 (£21 DD on UK a/c)

FOUNDED in 1971 'to inspire and equip men and women to use their talents and skills with integrity to devise, write and market excellent material which comes from a Christian worldview. In this way we seek to be an influence for good and for God in this generation.' *Publishes* a quarterly magazine. Runs three training events each year, biennial conference, competitions, postal workshops, area groups, prayer support and manuscript criticism. Charity No. 1069839.

Association of Freelance Editors, Proofreaders & Indexers (Ireland)

Skeagh, Skibbereen, Co. Cork, Republic of Ireland
☎00 353 28 38259 Fax 00 353 28 38004
Email gloria@redbarn-publishing.ie
Contact *Gloria Greenwood*
Subscription €25 p.a.

The organisation was established in Ireland to protect the interests of its members and to provide information to publishers on freelancers working in the relevant fields. Membership is restricted to freelancers with experience and/or references (but does not test or evaluate the skills of members). New category of membership – Associate Member – available for trainees in proofreading/editing who are taking the Book House Training Centre correspondence courses in Proofreading and Copy-editing.

Association of Freelance Journalists

2 Glen Cottage, Brick Hill Lane, Ketley,
Telford, Shropshire TF2 6SB
Email afj_UK@Yahoo.com
Website www.afj.home-page.org
Official Patron *Dr Carl Chinn, PhD, MBE*
Founding President *Martin Scholes*
Subscription £30 p.a.

Offers membership to all who work in the field of journalism but especially local correspondents, stringers, freelance journalists, news photographers, those at the beginning of their careers or long established. Also welcomes those who make a modest income writing for the specialist press or who self-publish; who have written for a hobby but now wish to make a career of their writing. Members receive a regular newsletter, a laminated press card, a free postal/e-mail advice service, the opportunity to network with other members (through the newsletter and a special Internet service) and editors who contact the AFJ. There are discounts on products and services, including the AFJ writing course.

Association of Freelance Writers

Sevendale House, 7 Dale Street, Manchester M1 1JB
☎0161 228 2362, ext 210 Fax 0161 228 3533
Email fmn@writersbureau.com

Contact *Angela Cox*
Subscription £29 p.a.

FOUNDED in 1995 to help and advise new and established freelance writers. Members receive a copy of *Freelance Market News* each month which gives news, views and the latest advice and guidelines about publications at home and abroad. Other benefits include one free appraisal of prose or poetry each year, reduced entry to **The Writers Bureau** writing competition, reduced fees for writing seminars and discounts on books for writers.

Association of Golf Writers

106 Byng Drive, Potters Bar, Hertfordshire EN6 1UJ
☎01707 654112 Fax 01707 654112
Email pasport@markgarrod.fsbusiness.co.uk

Honorary Secretary *Mark Garrod*

FOUNDED 1938. Aims to cooperate with golfing bodies to ensure best possible working conditions.

Association of Illustrators

81 Leonard Street, London EC2A 4QS
☎020 7613 4328 Fax 020 7613 4417
Email info@a-o-illustrators.demon.co.uk
Website www.aoisupplement.co.uk

Contact *Harriet Booth*

FOUNDED 1973 to promote illustration, protect illustrators' rights, and encourage professional standards. The AOI is a non-profit-making trade association dedicated to its members, to protecting their interests and promoting their work. Talks, seminars, a newsletter, regional groups, legal and portfolio advice as well as a number of related publications: *Rights, The Illustrator's Guide to Professional Practice, Survive, The Illustrator's Guide to a Professional Career* and *Images*, the only jury-selected annual of British illustration.

Association of Independent Libraries

Leeds Library, 18 Commercial Street, Leeds, West Yorkshire LS1 6AL
☎0113 245 3071

Chairman *Geoffrey Forster*
Secretary *Krystyna Smithers*

Established to 'further the advancement, conservation and restoration of a little-known but important living portion of our cultural heritage'. Members include the **London Library, Devon & Exeter Institution, Linen Hall Library** and **Plymouth Proprietary Library**.

Association of Learned and Professional Society Publishers

South House, The Street, Clapham, Worthing, West Sussex BN13 3UU
☎01903 871686 Fax 01903 871457
Email sec-gen@alpsp.org
Website www.alpsp.org

Secretary-General *Sally Morris*
Business Manager *Jill Tolson*
Editor, Learned Publishing *Michele Benjamin*

FOUNDED in 1972 to serve, represent and strengthen the community of not-for-profit publishers and those who work with them to disseminate academic and professional information. 'ALPSP believes that this is a time of unprecedented change in the publishing environment and intends to play an active part in shaping the future of academic and professional communication, demonstrating the essential role that its member publishers have to play.'

Association of Scottish Motoring Writers

c/o Scottish and Universal Newspapers, 5/15 Bank Street, Airdrie ML6 6AF
☎01236 748048 Fax 01236 748098

Secretary *John Murdoch*
Subscription £45 (Full); £25 (Associate)

FOUNDED 1961. Aims to co-ordinate the activities of, and provide shared facilities for, motoring writers resident in Scotland. Membership is by invitation only.

Australian Copyright Council

PO Box 1986, Strawberry Hills, NSW 2016, Australia
☎00 61 29318 1788 Fax 00 61 29698 3536
Email info@copyright.org.au
Website www.copyright.org.au

Contact *Customer Service*

FOUNDED 1968. The Council's activities and services include a range of publications, organising and speaking about copyright at seminars, research, consultancies and free legal advice. Aims include assistance for copyright owners to exercise their rights effectively, raising awareness about the importance of copyright and seeing changes to the law of copyright.

Australian Society of Authors

PO Box 1566, Strawberry Hills, NSW 2012, Australia
☎00 61 2 9318 0877 Fax 00 61 2 9318 0530
Email asa@asauthors.org
Website www.asauthors.org
Executive Director *José Borghino*

FOUNDED 1963. The ASA aims to promote and protect the professional interests of Australian authors. Provides contract advice and assists authors on industry standards and practices. *Publishes Australian Author magazine.*

Author-Publisher Network

12 Mercers, Hawkhurst, Kent TN18 4LH
☎01580 753346
Website www.author.co.uk
Administrator *John Dawes*
Newsletter Editor *David Bosworth*
Subscription £15 p.a.

FOUNDED 1993. The association aims to provide an active forum for writers publishing their own work. An information network of ideas and opportunities for self-publishers. Explores the business and technology of writing and publishing. Regular newsletter (*Write to Publish!*), supplements, seminars and workshops, etc.

Authors North

c/o The Society of Authors, 84 Drayton Gardens, London SW10 9SB
☎020 7373 6642
Secretary *Emma Boniwell*

A group within the **Society of Authors** which organises meetings for members living in the north of England.

Authors' Club

40 Dover Street, London W1S 4NP
☎020 7499 8581 Fax 020 7409 0913
Secretary *Mrs Ann de La Grange*

FOUNDED in 1891 by Sir Walter Besant, the Authors' Club welcomes as members writers, agents, publishers, critics, journalists, academics and anyone involved with literature and the written word. Administers the **Authors' Club** **Best First Novel Award** and **Sir Banister Fletcher Award**, and organises regular talks and dinners with well-known guest speakers. Membership fee: apply to secretary.

Authors' Licensing & Collecting Society Limited (ALCS)

Marlborough Court, 14–18 Holborn, London EC1N 2LE
☎020 7395 0600 Fax 020 7395 0660
Email alcs@alcs.co.uk
Website www.alcs.co.uk
Chief Executive *Dafydd Wyn Phillips*
Subscription £7.50 incl. VAT (UK; free to members of **Society of Authors**, **Writers' Guild**, **NUJ**, **BAJ** and **CIOJ**); £7.50 (EU residents); £10 (Overseas)

FOUNDED 1977. The UK collecting society for all writers and their successors, ALCS is a non-profit organisation whose principle purpose is to ensure that hard-to-collect revenues due to writers are efficiently collected and speedily distributed. Established to give assistance to writers in their battle to make a better living through the protection and exploitation of collective rights, ALCS has distributed over £75m. to writers since its creation. On joining, members give ALCS a mandate to administer on their behalf those rights which the law determines must be received or which are best handled collectively. Chief among these are: photocopying, cable retransmission (including the fees for BBC Prime and BBC World Service programming), rental and lending rights (but not British Public Lending Right), off-air recording, electronic rights, the performing right and public reception of broadcasts. The society is a prime resource and a leading authority on copyright matters and writers' collective interests. It maintains a watching brief on all matters affecting copyright both in Britain and abroad, making representations to UK government authorities and the EU. Consult the ALCS website or contact the office for application forms and further information.

BACB

See **British Association of Communicators in Business**

BAFTA (British Academy of Film and Television Arts)

195 Piccadilly, London W1J 9LN
☎020 7734 0022 Fax 020 7437 0473
Website www.bafta.org

FOUNDED 1947. Membership limited to 'those who have made a significant contribution to the industry' over a minimum period of three years. Best known for its annual awards ceremonies, now held separately for film, television, craft, children's programmes and interactive entertainment, the Academy runs a full programme of screenings, seminars, masterclasses, debates, lectures, etc. It also actively supports training and educational projects.

Also, BAFTA Scotland, BAFTA Wales, BAFTA North, BAFTA LA, BAFTA East Coast (USA) run separate programmes and, in the case of Scotland, Wales and the North, hold their own awards.

BAPLA (British Association of Picture Libraries and Agencies)

18 Vine Hill, London EC1R 5DZ
☎020 7713 1780 Fax 020 7713 1211
Email enquiries@bapla.org.uk
Website www.bapla.org.uk

Represents the interests of the British picture library industry. Works on UK and world-wide levels on such issues as copyright and technology. Offers researchers free telephone referrals from its database and through its website. With access to 350 million images through its membership, BAPLA is a good place to start. *Publishes Directory*, the definitive guide to UK picture libraries and the quarterly magazine, *Light Box*.

BFC

See **British Film Commission**

The Bibliographical Society

c/o The Wellcome Library, 183 Euston Road, London NW1 2BE
☎020 7611 7244 Fax 020 7611 8703
Email jm93@dial.pipex.com
President *M.M. Foot*
Honorary Secretary *D. Pearson*
Subscription £33 p.a.

Aims to promote and encourage the study and research of historical, analytical, descriptive and textual bibliography, and the history of printing, publishing, bookselling, bookbinding and collecting; to hold meetings at which papers are read and discussed; to print and publish works concerned with bibliography; to form a bibliographical library. Awards grants and bursaries for bibliographical research. *Publishes* a quarterly magazine called *The Library*.

Book Packagers Association

8 St John's Road, Saxmundham, Suffolk IP17 1BE
☎01728 604204 Fax 01728 604029

Treasurer *Charles Perkins*
Subscription £150 p.a.; £75 (Associate); £100 (Overseas)

Aims to provide members with a forum for the exchange of information, to improve the image of packaging and to represent the interests of members. Activities include meetings, seminars and the provision of standard contracts.

Booksellers Association of the UK & Ireland Ltd

Minster House, 272 Vauxhall Bridge Road, London SW1V 1BA
☎020 7834 5477 Fax 020 7834 8812
Email mail@booksellers.org.uk
Website www.booksellers.org.uk
Chief Executive *Tim Godfray*

FOUNDED 1895. The BA helps 3200 independent, chain and multiple members to sell more books, reduce costs and improve efficiency. It represents members' interests to the UK Government, European Commission, publishers, authors and others in the trade as well as offering marketing assistance, running training courses, conferences, seminars and exhibitions. Together with **The Publishers Association**, coordinates World Book Day. *Publishes* directories, catalogues, surveys and various other publications connected with the book trade and administers the **Whitbread Book Awards** and the **Samuel Johnson Prize for Non-fiction**.

Booktrust

Book House, 45 East Hill, London SW18 2QZ
☎020 8516 2977 Fax 020 8516 2978
Email info@booktrust.org.uk
Website www.booktrust.org.uk *and*
www.booktrusted.com
Director *Chris Meade*
Subscription £25 p.a.

FOUNDED 1925. Booktrust, the independent educational charity promoting books and reading, runs the Book Information Line giving accurate facts about topical books and the book world (☎0906 516 1193, weekdays 10 am to 2 pm; calls charged at £1.50 per minute). Runs Booktrusted.com, their website for all those who care what young people read which includes details of Bedtime Reading Week, Children's Book Week and Booktrusted publications. Administers many literary prizes such as the Orange and Booker, creative reading projects like Breathtaker and Bookscapes, and runs Bookstart, the acclaimed national scheme which aims to supply a free introductory bag of baby books to all babies at their eight-month health check.

British Academy of Composers and Songwriters

2nd Floor, British Music House,
25–27 Berners Street, London W1T 3LR
☎020 7636 2929 Fax 020 7636 2212
Email info@britishacademy.com
Website www.britishacademy.com

Head of Membership *Fergal Kilroy*

The Academy represents the interests of music writers of all genres, providing advice on professional and artistic matters. *Publishes* quarterly magazine, *The Works*. Administers the annual Ivor Novello Awards.

British Academy of Film and Television Arts

See **BAFTA**

British Association of Communicators in Business (BACB)

42 Borough High Street, London SE1 1XW
☎020 7378 7139 Fax 020 7387 7140
Email enquiries@bacb.org
Website www.bacb.org

Secretary General *Kathie Jones*

FOUNDED 1949. The Association aims to be the 'market leader for those involved in corporate media management and practice by providing professional, authoritative, dynamic, supportive and innovative services'.

British Association of Journalists

88 Fleet Street, London EC4Y 1PJ
☎020 7353 3003 Fax 020 7353 2310

General Secretary *Steve Turner*

Subscription National newspaper, broadcasting and news agency staff: £12.50 a month. Other seniors, including magazine journalists, PRs and freelances who earn the majority of their income from journalism: £7.50 a month. Journalists under 24: £5 a month.

FOUNDED 1992. Aims to protect and promote the industrial and professional interests of journalists.

British Association of Picture Libraries and Agencies

See **BAPLA**

British Centre for Literary Translation

University of East Anglia, Norwich, Norfolk NR4 7TJ
☎01603 592134/592785 Fax 01603 592737
Email c.fuller@uea.ac.uk
Website www.literarytranslation.com

Contact *Catherine Fuller*

FOUNDED 1989. Aims to promote literary translation and the status of the literary translator by working in the UK and overseas with translator associations and centres (e.g. European network of Translation Centres), cultural policy-makers, teachers and researchers of literary translation, Regional Arts Boards, publishers and the media, libraries and schools. PhD programme in literary translation. Coordinates activities, mostly in collaboration with other organisations, include a summer school, conferences (e.g. British Council seminars on literary translation) and seminars, workshops and readings. With European and other funding, BCLT runs a translator-in-residence programme for translators to spend one calendar month in Norwich. *Publishes* proceedings and reports of its activities where possible, a journal *In Other Words* jointly with the **Translators Association**. Free mailing list; website in conjunction with the **British Council**.

British Copyright Council

Copyright House, 29–33 Berners Street, London W1T 3AB
☎01986 788122 Fax 01986 788847
Email copyright@bcc2.demon.co.uk

Contact *Janet Ibbotson*

Works for the national and international acceptance of copyright and acts as a lobby/watchdog organisation on behalf of creators, publishers and performers on copyright and associated matters. Publications include *Guide to the Law of Copyright and Rights in Performances in the UK*; *Photocopying from Books and Journals*. An umbrella organisation which does not deal with individual enquiries.

The British Council

10 Spring Gardens, London SW1A 2BN
☎020 7930 8466/7389 4268 (Press Office)
Fax 020 7839 6347
Website www.britishcouncil.org

Head of Literature *Margaret Meyer*

The British Council promotes Britain abroad. It provides access to British ideas, expertise and experience in education, the English language, literature and the arts, science and technology and governance. Works in 109 countries running a mix of offices, libraries, resource centres and English teaching operations.

British Equestrian Writers' Association

Priory House, Station Road, Swavesey,
Cambridge CB4 5QJ
☎01954 232084 Fax 01954 231362
Email gnewsumn@aol.com

Contact *Gillian Newsum*
Subscription £15

FOUNDED 1973. Aims to further the interests of equestrian sport and improve, wherever possible, the working conditions of the equestrian press. Membership is by invitation of the committee. Candidates for membership must be nominated and seconded by full members and receive a majority vote of the committee.

British Film Commission (BFC)

10 Little Portland Street, London W1W 7JG
☎020 7861 7860 Fax 020 7861 7864
Email info@bfc.co.uk
Website www.bfc.co.uk

FOUNDED in 1991, the British Film Council is now a division of the Film Council. Its remit is to promote the UK as an international production centre by encouraging the use of British artists and technicians, technical services, facilities and locations, and to provide wide-ranging support to those filming and contemplating filming in the UK.

British Film Institute

21 Stephen Street, London W1T 1LN
☎020 7255 1444 Fax 020 7436 0439
Website www.bfi.org.uk

Chair *Joan Bakewell, CBE*
Director *Jon Teckman*
24-hour *bfi* events line: 0870 240 4050

'The *bfi* offers opportunities to experience, enjoy and discover more about the world of film and television.' Its three main departments are: *bfi* Education, comprising the *bfi* National Library, *bfi* Publishing, *Sight and Sound* magazine and *bfi* Education Projects, which encourages life-long learning about the moving image; *bfi* Exhibition, which runs the National Film Theatre on London's South Bank and the annual London Film Festival, and supports local cinemas and film festivals UK-wide; and *bfi* Collections, which preserves the UK's moving image heritage and promotes access to it through a variety of means, including film, video and DVD releases and touring exhibitions. The *bfi* also runs the *bfi* London IMAX Cinema at Waterloo, featuring the UK's largest screen.

British Guild of Beer Writers

15 Sollershott West, Letchworth,
Hertfordshire SG6 3PU
☎01462 685844 Fax 01462 685783
Email bsb@tccnet.co.uk
Website www.beerguild.com

Secretary *Barry Bremner*
Subscription £30 p.a.

FOUNDED 1988. Aims to improve standards in beer writing and at the same time extend public knowledge of beers and brewing. *Publishes* a directory of members with details of their publications and their particular areas of interest; this is then circulated to newspapers, magazines, trade press and broadcasting organisations. Also *publishes* a monthly newsletter, the *BGBW Newsletter*. As part of the plan to improve writing standards and to achieve a higher profile for beer, the Guild offers annual awards, The Gold and Silver Tankard Awards, to writers and broadcasters judged to have made the most valuable contribution towards this end in their work. Meetings are held regularly.

British Guild of Travel Writers

91 Amesbury Avenue, Streatham Hill,
London SW2 3AF
☎020 8674 7406
Website www.bgtw.org

Chairman *Mary Johns*
Honorary Secretary *Melissa Shales*
Subscription £100 p.a.

The professional association of travel writers, broadcasters, photographers and editors which aims to serve its members' professional interests by acting as a forum for debate, discussion and 'networking'. The Guild *publishes* an annual Year Book giving full details of all its members, holds monthly meetings and has a monthly newsletter. Members are required to spend the majority of their working time on travel.

British Science Fiction Association

1 Long Row Close, Everdon, Daventry,
Northants NN11 3BE
☎01327 361661
Email bsfa@enterprise.net

Membership Secretary *Paul Billinger*
Subscription £21 p.a. (reduction for unwaged)

FOUNDED originally in 1958 by a group of authors, readers, publishers and booksellers interested in science fiction. With a worldwide membership, the Association aims to promote the reading, writing and publishing of science fiction and to encourage SF fans to maintain contact with each other. Also offers postal writers workshop, a magazine chain and an information service. *Publishes Matrix* bi-monthly newsletter with comment and opinions, news of conventions, etc. Contributions from members welcomed; *Vector* bi-monthly critical journal – reviews of books and magazines; *Focus* biannual magazine with articles, original fiction and letters column. For further information, contact the Membership Secretary at the address above or via e-mail.

British Society of Comedy Writers

61 Parry Road, Ashmore Park,
Wolverhampton, West Midlands WV11 2PS
☎01902 722729 Fax 01902 722729
Email comedy@bscw.co.uk
Website www.bscw.co.uk

Contact *Ken Rock*

FOUNDED 1999. The Society aims to develop good practice and professionalism among comedy writers while bringing together the best creative professionals, and working to standards of excellence agreed with the light entertainment industry. Offers a network of industry contacts and a range of products, services and training initiatives including specialised workshops, an annual international conference, script assessment service and opportunities to visit international festivals.

British Society of Magazine Editors (BSME)

137 Hale Lane, Edgware, Middlesex
HA8 9QP
☎020 8906 4664 Fax 020 8959 2137
Email bsme@cix.co.uk

Contact *Gill Branston*

Holds regular industry forums and events as well as an annual awards dinner.

Broadcasting Press Guild

Tiverton, The Ridge, Woking, Surrey
GU22 7EQ
☎01483 764895 Fax 01483 765882
Email torin.douglas@bbc.co.uk

Membership Secretary *Richard Last*
Subscription £15 p.a.

FOUNDED 1974 to promote the professional interests of journalists specialising in writing or broadcasting about the media. Organises monthly lunches addressed by leading industry figures, and annual TV and radio awards. Membership by invitation.

BSME

See **British Society of Magazine Editors**

Bureau of Freelance Photographers

Focus House, 497 Green Lanes, London
N13 4BP
☎020 8882 3315 Fax 020 8886 5174
Email info@thebfp.com

Membership Secretary *Joanna Georgiou*
Subscription £45 p.a. (UK); £60 p.a. (Overseas)

FOUNDED 1965. Assists members in selling their pictures through monthly *Market Newsletter*, and offers advisory, legal assistance and other services.

Campaign for Press and Broadcasting Freedom

Second Floor, 23 Orford Road,
Walthamstow, London E17 9NL
☎020 8521 5932 Fax 020 8521 5932
Email freepress@cpbf.org.co.uk
Website www.cpbf.org.co.uk

Subscription £15 p.a. (concessions available); £25 p.a. (Institutions/Organisations)

Broadly based pressure group working for more accountable and accessible media in Britain. Advises on right of reply and takes up the issue of the portrayal of minorities. Members receive *Free Press* (bi-monthly), discounts on publications and news of campaign progress.

Canadian Authors Association

National Office: Box 419, 320 South Shores Road, Campbellford, ON K0L 1L0 Canada
☎001 705 653 0323 Fax 001 705 653 0593
Email canauth@redden.on.ca
Website www.CanAuthors.org

Administrator *Alec McEachern*

FOUNDED 1921. The CAA 'has expanded from a group of published authors concerned with protection of their own property to one that now includes those not yet published who want protection of what they might eventually produce and who need help producing it.' The Association has branches across the country providing support to local members in the form of advice, local contests, publications and writers' circles. *Publishes National Newsline* (quarterly) and *The Canadian Writer's Guide*.

Canadian Publishers' Council

250 Merton Street, Suite 203, Toronto,
Ontario M4S 1B1 Canada
☎001 416 322 7011 Fax 001 416 322 6999
Email pubadmin@pubcouncil.ca

Website www.pubcouncil.ca

Executive Director, External Relations
Jacqueline Hushion

FOUNDED 1910. Trade association of English-language publishers which represents the domestic and international interests of member companies.

The Caravan Writers' Guild
2 Harbury Field Cottage, Harbury, Leamington Spa, Warwickshire CV33 8JN
☎01926 613186 Fax 01926 613186
Email caratesters@hotmail.com

Membership Officer *Adrian French*
Subscription £5 Joining fee plus £20 p.a.; Associates: £12.50

Guild for writers active in the specialist fields of caravan and camping journalism.

Careers Writers' Association
16 Caewal Road, Llandaff, Cardiff CF5 2BT
☎029 2056 3444 Fax 029 2065 8190
Email anne.goodman5@ntlworld.com

Membership Secretary *Anne Goodman*

FOUNDED 1979. An association of professional careers writers whose work meets its high standards of accuracy and impartiality. It provides a network for members to exchange information and experience and holds meetings on topics of interest to its members. Forges links with organisations that share related interests and maintains regular contact with national education and training bodies, government agencies and publishers. 'The association can provide a list of its members to organisations that require high standards of careers writing.'

Chartered Institute of Journalists
2 Dock Offices, Surrey Quays Road, London SE16 2XU
☎020 7252 1187 Fax 020 7232 2302
Email memberservices@ioj.co.uk
Website www.ioj.co.uk

General Secretary *Christopher Underwood*
Subscription £180 p.a.; £15 (monthly)

FOUNDED 1884. The Institute is concerned with professional journalistic standards and with safeguarding the freedom of the media. It is open to writers, broadcasters and journalists (including self-employed) in all media. Affiliate membership (£115) is available to part-time or occasional practitioners and to overseas journalists who can join the Institute's International Division. Members also belong to the IOJ (TU), an independent trade union which pro-tects, advises and represents them in their employment or freelance work; negotiates on their behalf and provides legal assistance and support. The IOJ (TU) is a certificated independent trade union which represents members' interests in the workplace, and is also a constituent member of the National Council in the Training of Journalists, the Independent Unions Training Council and the **British Copyright Council**.

Children's Book Circle
c/o HarperCollins Publishers Ltd, 77–85 Fulham Palace Road, London W6 8JB
☎020 8307 4680 Fax 020 8307 4199

Membership Secretary *Jo Williamson*

The Children's Book Circle provides a discussion forum for anybody involved with children's books. Monthly meetings are addressed by a panel of invited speakers and topics focus on current and controversial issues. Administers the **Eleanor Farjeon Award**.

Children's Books Ireland
17 Lower Camden Street, Dublin 2 Republic of Ireland
☎00 353 1 872 5854 Fax 00 353 1 872 5854
Email childrensbooksire@eircom.net

Contact *Claire Ranson*
Subscription €25 p.a. (Individual); €35 (Institutions); €15 (Students); €45/US$40 (Overseas)

Aims to promote quality children's books and reading. Holds annual spring seminar, summer school and autumn conference for adults. Quarterly magazine, *Children's Books in Ireland*. Annual children's book festival in October; Bisto/CBI Book of the Year Award. *Publishes Book Choice for Primary Schools; Book Choice for Post Primary Schools; The Big Guide 2: Irish Children's Books.*

CILIP: The Chartered Institute of Library and Information Professionals
7 Ridgmount Street, London WC1E 7AE
☎020 7255 0500 Fax 020 7255 0501
Email info@cilip.org.uk
Website www.cilip.org.uk

Chief Executive *Bob McKee*

The leading membership body for library and information professionals, formed in 2002 following the unification of the Library Association and the Institute of Information Scientists. **Facet Publishing** (successor to LA Publishing) produces 25–30 new titles each year and has over 200 in print from the LA's back catalogue. Further information from Marketing & External Relations, CILIP.

Circle of Wine Writers

166 Meadvale Road, London W5 1LS
☎020 8930 0181
Email andrea.warren@btinternet.com
Administrator *Andrea Warren*
Membership £45 p.a.

FOUNDED 1962. Open to all *bona fide* authors, broadcasters, journalists and photographers currently being published, as well as lecturers and tutors, all of whom are professionally engaged in communicating about wines and spirits. Aims to improve the standard of writing, broadcasting and lecturing about wines, spirits and beers; to contribute to the growing knowledge and interest in wine; to promote wines and spirits of quality and to comment adversely on faulty products or dubious practices; to establish and maintain good relations with the news media and the wine trade; to provide members with a strong voice with which to promote their views; to provide a programme of workshops, meetings, talks and tastings.

Cleveland Arts

Third Floor, Melrose House, Melrose Street, Middlesbrough TS1 2HZ
☎01642 264651   Fax 01642 264955
Contact *Programme Manager (Literature)*

Not one of the Regional Arts Boards, Cleveland Arts is an independent arts development agency working in the areas of Middlesbrough, Stockton on Tees, Hartlepool and Redcar & Cleveland. It works in partnership with local authorities, public agencies, the business sector, schools, colleges, individuals and organisations to coordinate, promote and develop the arts – crafts, film, video, photography, music, drama, dance, literature, public arts, disability, Black arts, community arts. The Word Foundation is the literature development unit which promotes writing classes, reading promotions, poetry readings and residencies, issues a free newsletter and assists local publishers and writers.

Clé, The Irish Book Publishers' Association

43/44 Temple Bar, Dublin 2, Republic of Ireland
☎00 353 1 670 7393   Fax 00 353 1 670 7642
Email info@publishingireland.com
Website www.publishingireland.com

President *Fergal Tobin*
Executive Director *Orla Martin*

FOUNDED 1970 to promote Irish publishing, protect members' interests and train the industry.

Comedy Writers' Association UK

11 Wandsworth Road, Norris Green, Liverpool L11 1DR
☎0151 287 2982
Email pauloulton@genius11.fsnet.co.uk
Website www.cwauk.co.uk
Honorary President *Ken Dodd*
Chairman *Bob Orr*
Membership Secretary *Paul Oulton* (at address above)

FOUNDED 1981 to assist and promote the work of comedy writers, the Association has grown to become the largest group of independent comedy writers in the UK. Holds annual and one-day seminars. Members receive a monthly newsletter and regular market opportunities.

Comhairle nan Leabhraichean/ The Gaelic Books Council

22 Mansfield Street, Glasgow G11 5QP
☎0141 337 6211   Fax 0141 341 0515
Email fios@gaelicbooks.net
Website www.gaelicbooks.net
Chairman *Donalda MacKinnon*
Director *Ian MacDonald*

FOUNDED 1968 and now a charitable company with its own bookshop. Encourages and promotes Gaelic publishing by giving grants to publishers and writers; providing editorial and word-processing services; retailing Gaelic books; producing a catalogue of all Gaelic books in print and answering enquiries about them; mounting occasional literary evenings and training courses.

Commercial Radio Companies Association

77 Shaftesbury Avenue, London W1D 5DU
☎020 7306 2603   Fax 020 7470 0062
Email info@crca.co.uk
Chairman *Lord Eatwell*
Chief Executive *Paul Brown*
Research and Communications Manager
   Alison Winter
Public Affairs Manager *Lisa Kerr*

The CRCA is the trade body for the independent radio stations. It represents members' interests to Government, the **Radio Authority**, trade unions, copyright organisations and other bodies.

Copyright Advice and Anti-Piracy Hotline

Clivemont House, 54 Clivemont Road, Maidenhead, Berkshire SL6 7BZ
☎0845 603 4567
Email contact@copyright-info.org
Website www.copyright-info.org

Copyright Line Administrator *Keith Lowde*

FOUNDED 1999 to offer advice and information to anyone who wants to use film, music and software copyrights. The Hotline also helps the public and law enforcement agencies to identify and report piracy, and the intellectual property industries to monitor infringements and coordinate their responses. (See also the **Federation Against Copyright Theft (FACT) Limited**.)

The Copyright Licensing Agency Ltd

90 Tottenham Court Road, London W1T 4LP
☎020 7631 5555   Fax 020 7631 5500
Email cla@cla.co.uk
Website www.cla.co.uk

Chief Executive *Peter Shepherd*

FOUNDED 1982 by the **Authors' Licensing and Collecting Society (ALCS)** and the **Publishers Licensing Society Ltd (PLS)**, the CLA administers collectively photocopying and other copying rights that it is uneconomic for writers and publishers to administer for themselves. The Agency issues collective and transactional licences, and the fees it collects, after the deduction of its operating costs, are distributed at regular intervals to authors and publishers via their respective societies (i.e. ALCS or PLS). Since 1986, CLA has distributed approximately £83 million.

Council for British Archaeology

Bowes Morrell House, 111 Walmgate, York YO1 9WA
☎01904 671417   Fax 01904 671384
Email info@britarch.ac.uk
Website www.britarch.ac.uk

Information Officer *Mike Heyworth*

FOUNDED 1944 to represent and promote archaeology at all levels. Its aims are to improve the public's awareness in and understanding of Britain's past; to carry out research; to survey, guide and promote the teaching of archaeology at all levels of education; to publish a wide range of academic, educational, general and bibliographical works (see **CBA Publishing** under **UK Publishers**).

Council of Academic and Professional Publishers

See **The Publishers Association**

Crime Writers' Association (CWA)

(New secretary not yet appointed. Check website for contact details.)
Website www.thecwa.co.uk

Secretary *To be appointed*
Membership £45

Full membership is limited to professional crime writers, but publishers, literary agents, booksellers, etc. who specialise in crime, are eligible for Associate membership. The Association has regional chapters throughout the country, including Scotland. Meetings are held regularly in central London, with informative talks frequently given by police, scenes of crime officers, lawyers, etc., and a weekend conference is held annually in different parts of the country. Produces a monthly newsletter for members called *Red Herrings* and presents various annual awards (see **Prizes**).

The Critics' Circle

c/o Catherine Cooper, 69 Marylebone Lane, London W1U 2PH
☎020 7224 1410
Website www.criticscircle.org.uk

President *Jane Edwards*
Honorary General Secretary *Charles Hedges*
Subscription £18 p.a.

Membership by invitation only. Aims to uphold and promote the art of criticism (and the commercial rates of pay thereof) and preserve the interests of its members: professionals involved in criticism of film, drama, music and dance.

Cyngor Llyfrau Cymru

See **Welsh Books Council**

Department for Culture, Media and Sport

2–4 Cockspur Street, London SW1Y 5DH
☎020 7211 6000   Fax 020 7211 6270
Email toby.sargent@culture.gsi.gov.uk

Head of News *Paddy Feeny*

The Department for Culture, Media and Sport has responsibilities for Government policies relating to the arts, museums and galleries, public libraries, sport, gambling, broadcasting, Press standards, the built heritage, the film and music industries, tourism and the National Lottery. It funds the **Arts Council**, national museums and galleries, the **British Library**, the Public Lending Right and the Royal Commission on Historical Manuscripts. It is responsible within Government for the public library service in England, and for library and information matters generally, where they are not the responsibility of other departments.

Directory & Database Publishers Association

PO Box 23034, London W6 0RJ
☎020 8846 9707
Website www.directory-publisher.co.uk
Contact *Rosemary Pettit*
Subscription £120 – £1200 p.a.

FOUNDED 1970 to promote the interests of *bona fide* directory and database publishers and protect the public from disreputable and fraudulent practices. The objectives of the Association are to maintain a code of professional practice to safeguard public interest; to raise the standard and status of directory publishing throughout the UK; to promote business directories as a medium for advertising; to protect the legal and statutory interests of directory publishers; to foster bonds of common interest among responsible directory publishers and to provide for the exchange of technical, commercial and management information between members. Meetings, seminars, conference, newsletter, awards, exhibitions, business support helpline.

Drama Association of Wales

The Old Library Building, Singleton Road, Splott, Cardiff CF24 2ET
☎029 2045 2200 Fax 029 2045 2277
Email aled.daw@virgin.net
Contact *Teresa Hennessy*

Runs a large playscript lending library; holds an annual playwriting competition (see entry under **Prizes**); offers a script-reading service (£15 per script) which usually takes three months from receipt of play to issue of reports. From plays submitted to the reading service, selected scripts are considered for publication of a short run (70–200 copies). Writers receive a percentage of the cover price on sales and a percentage of the performance fee.

Edinburgh Bibliographical Society

Edinburgh University Library, George Square, Edinburgh EH8 9LJ
☎0131 650 6823 Fax 0131 650 6863
Email p.freshwater@ed.ac.uk *or*
   warrenmcdougall@aol.com
Website www.edbibsoc.lib.ed.ac.uk
Honorary Treasurer *Peter B. Freshwater*

Honorary Secretary *Warren McDougall*
Subscription £10; £15 (Institution); £7 (Students)

FOUNDED 1890. Organises lectures on bibliographical topics and visits to libraries. *Publishes* an occasional journal called *Transactions*, which is free to members, and other occasional publications.

Educational Publishers Council

See **The Publishers Association**

Electronic Publishers' Forum

See **The Publishers Association**

The English Association

University of Leicester, University Road, Leicester LE1 7RH
☎0116 252 3982 Fax 0116 252 2301
Email engassoc@le.ac.uk
Website www.le.ac.uk/engassoc/
Chief Executive *Helen Lucas*

FOUNDED 1906 to promote understanding and appreciation of the English language and its literatures. Activities include sponsoring a number of publications and organising lectures and conferences for teachers, plus annual sixth-form conferences. Publications include *Year's Work in Critical and Cultural Theory, English, Use of English, English 4–11, Essays and Studies* and *Year's Work in English Studies*.

Federation Against Copyright Theft (FACT) Limited

Unit 7, Victory Business Centre, Worton Road, Isleworth, Middlesex TW7 6DB
☎020 8568 6646 Fax 020 8560 6364
Email davidlowe@fact-uk.co.uk
Director General *David Lowe*

FOUNDED in 1983, FACT is an investigative organisation funded by its members to combat counterfeiting piracy and misuse of their products. It assists all law enforcement authorities and will undertake private criminal prosecutions wherever possible. Membership is made up of major companies in the British and American film, video and television industries.

Federation of Entertainment Unions

1 Highfield, Twyford, Nr Winchester, Hampshire SO21 1QR
☎01962 713134 Fax 01962 713134
Email harris@interalpha.co.uk
Secretary *Steve Harris*

Plenary meetings six times annually and meetings of the Film and Electronic Media Committee six times annually on alternate months. Additionally, there are Training & European Committees. Represents the following unions: British Actors' Equity Association; Broadcasting Entertainment Cinematograph and Theatre Union; Musicians' Union; AEEU; **National Union of Journalists**; **The Writers' Guild of Great Britain**.

The Federation of Worker Writers and Community Publishers (FWWCP)

Burslem School of Art, Queen Street, Stoke on Trent ST6 3EJ
☎01782 822327 Fax 01782 822327
Email thefwwcp@tiscali.co.uk
Website www.thefwwcp.org.uk

Administrator/Coordinator *Tim Diggles*

The FWWCP is a federation of writing groups committed to writing and publishing based on working-class experience and creativity. The FWWCP is the membership's collective national voice and has for some time been given funding by the **Arts Council**. Founded in 1976, it comprises around 60 member groups, each one with its own identity, reflecting its community and membership.

These groups represent over 5000 people who regularly (often weekly) meet to offer constructive criticism, produce books and tapes, perform and share skills, offering creative and critical support. There are writers' workshops of long standing; adult literacy organisations; groups working mainly in oral and local history; groups and local networks of writers who come together to publish, train or perform; groups with a specific remit to further the aims of a section of the community such as the homeless or disabled.

Although diverse in nature, member organisations share the aim of making writing and publishing accessible to people and encourage them to take an active, cooperative and democratic role in writing, performing and publishing. The main activities include training days and weekends to learn and share skills, a quarterly magazine, a quarterly broadsheet of members' writing, a major annual festival of writing and networking between member organisations.

The FWWCP has published a number of anthologies and is willing to work with other organisations on publishing projects. Membership is open only to groups but individuals will be put in touch with groups which can help them and become friends of the Federation. Contact the address above for an information leaflet.

Fellowship of Authors and Artists

PO Box 158, Hertford SG13 8FA
☎0870 747 2514 Fax 0870 747 2557
Email fellowship@compassion-in-business.co.uk
Website www.author-fellowship.co.uk

Contact *Graham Irwin*

FOUNDED in 2000 to promote and encourage the use of writing and all art forms as a means of therapy and self healing; to provide a valuable resource and meeting point for all interested parties including, but not limited to, writers, artists, counsellors and healers; to publish as web pages or e-books any suitable works that may help to support or promote the aims of the fellowship.

Film Council

10 Little Portland Street, London W1W 7JG
☎020 7861 7861 Fax 020 7861 7862
Email info@filmcouncil.org.uk
Website www.filmcouncil.org.uk

A recently formed strategic agency responsible for developing the film industry in the UK. By helping those already in the business of film-making through its funding and training initiatives and also those wishing to become part of the film-making process and film culture in the UK, the Council aims to create a sustainable film industry for the future.

Foreign Press Association in London

11 Carlton House Terrace, London SW1Y 5AJ
☎020 7930 0445 Fax 020 7925 0469
Email secretariat@foreign-press.org.uk
Website www.foreign-press.org.uk

General Manager *Bob Jenner*
Membership (incl. VAT) £128 p.a. (Full); £119 (Associate Journalists); £178 (Associate Non-Journalists)

FOUNDED 1888. Non-profit-making service association for foreign correspondents based in London, providing a variety of press-related services.

The Gaelic Books Council

See **Comhairle nan Leabhraichean**

The Garden Writers' Guild

c/o Institute of Horticulture, 14/15 Belgrave Square, London SW1X 8PS
☎020 7245 6943
Email gwg@horticulture.org.uk
Website www.gardenwriters.co.uk

Contact *Angela Clarke*
Subscription £45; (£40 to Institute of Horticulture members); £55 (Associate members)

FOUNDED 1990. Aims to raise the quality of gardening communication, to help members operate efficiently and profitably, to improve liaison between garden communicators and the horticultural industry. Administers an annual awards scheme. Operates a mailing service and organises press briefing days.

General Practitioner Writers' Association
See **Medical Writers' Association**

Guild of Agricultural Journalists
Charnwood, 47 Court Meadow, Rotherfield, East Sussex TN6 3LQ
☎01892 853187 Fax 01892 853551
Email don.gomery@farmline.com
Website www.gaj.org.uk
Honorary General Secretary *Don Gomery*
Subscription £40 p.a.

FOUNDED 1944 to promote a high professional standard among journalists who specialise in agriculture, horticulture and allied subjects. Represents members' interests with representative bodies in the industry; provides a forum through meetings and social activities for members to meet eminent people in the industry; maintains contact with associations of agricultural journalists overseas; promotes schemes for the education of members and for the provision of suitable entrants into agricultural journalism.

Guild of Editors
See **Society of Editors**

The Guild of Food Writers
48 Crabtree Lane, London SW6 6LW
☎020 7610 1180 Fax 020 7610 0299
Email gfw@gfw.co.uk
Website www.gfw.co.uk
Administrator *Christina Thomas*
Subscription £70

FOUNDED 1985. The Guild's objects include: 'to bring together professional food writers including journalists, broadcasters and authors, to print and issue an annual list of members, to extend the range of members' knowledge and experience by arranging discussions, tastings and visits, and to encourage the development of new writers by every means including competitions and awards. The Guild aims to contribute to the growth of public interest in, and knowledge of, the subject of food and to campaign for improvements in the quality of food.'

Guild of Motoring Writers
30 The Cravens, Smallfield, Surrey RH6 9QS
☎01342 843294 Fax 01342 844093
Email sharon@scott-fairweather.freeserve.co.uk
Website www.newspress.co.uk/guild
General Secretary *Sharon Scott-Fairweather*

FOUNDED 1944. Represents members' interests and provides a forum for members to exchange information.

Horror Writers Association
UK Contact: 24 Pearl Road, Walthamstow, London E17 4QZ
Email hwa@horror.org
Website www.horror.org

US Contact: HWA Membership, PO Box 50577, Palo Alto, CA 94303, USA
☎001 650 322 4610
Contact (UK) *Jo Fletcher*

FOUNDED 1987. World-wide organisation of writers and publishers dedicated to promoting the interests of writers of horror and dark fantasy. *Publishes* a bi-monthly newsletter, issues e-mail bulletins, gives access to lists of horror agents, reviewers and bookstores; and keys to the 'Members Only' area of the HWA website. Presents the annual **Bram Stoker Awards** (see entry under **Prizes**).

HTML Writers Guild
Email membership-questions@hwg.org
Website www.hwg.org

FOUNDED in 1994 by a small group of HTML writers, the Guild is an international organisation for Internet designers with over 123,000 members world-wide and is open to anyone with an interest in the craft of web design. Provides extensive resources through the Guild website and mailing lists. Online classes to support members' efforts from the professional designer to the hobbyist designing a homepage. Various levels of membership available.

HWA
See **Horror Writers Association**

Independent Publishers Guild
PO Box 93, Royston, Hertfordshire SG8 5GH Fax 01763 246293
Email sheila@ipg.uk.com

Website www.ipg.com
Secretary *Sheila Bounford*
Subscription £99.88 p.a.
FOUNDED 1962. Membership open to independent publishers, packagers and suppliers, i.e. professionals in allied fields. Regular meetings, annual conference, seminars, mailings and e-mail bulletin.

Independent Television Association
See **ITV Network Ltd**

Independent Television Commission (ITC)
33 Foley Street, London W1W 7TL
☎020 7255 3000 Fax 020 7306 7800
Website www.itc.org.uk
Chief Executive *Patricia Hodgson*
The ITC issues licences and regulates commercial television in the UK; maintains standards of the programmes which appear plus advertising and technical quality. Complaints against the service are investigated by the Commission which frequently publishes its findings and it is empowered to impose penalties on licensees that do not comply with their licence conditions.

Independent Theatre Council
12 The Leathermarket, Weston Street, London SE1 3ER
☎020 7403 1727 Fax 020 7403 1745
Email c.jones@itc-arts.org
Website www.itc-arts.org
Contact *Charlotte Jones*
The management association and representative body for small/middle-scale theatres (up to around 450 seats) and touring theatre companies. Negotiates contracts and has established standard agreements with Equity on behalf of all professionals working in the theatre. Negotiations with the WGGB for a contractual agreement covering rights and fee structure for playwrights were concluded in 1991. Terms and conditions were renegotiated and updated in September 1998. Copies of the minimum terms agreement can be obtained from the **Writers' Guild**. *Publishes* a booklet, *A Practical Guide for Writers and Companies* (£3.50 plus p&p), giving guidance to writers on how to submit scripts to theatres and guidance to theatres on how to deal with them.

Institute of Copywriting
Honeycombe House, Bagley, Wedmore BS28 4TD
☎01934 713563 Fax 01934 713492
Email copy@inst.org

Website www.inst.org/copy
Secretary *Lynn Hall*
FOUNDED 1991 to promote copywriters and copywriting (writing publicity material). Maintains a code of practice. Membership is open to students as well as experienced practitioners. Runs training courses (see entry under **Writers' Courses**). Has a list of approved copywriters. Answers queries relating to copywriting. Contact the Institute for a free booklet.

Institute of Linguists
Saxon House, 48 Southwark Street, London SE1 1UN
☎020 7940 3100 Fax 020 7940 3101
Email info@iol.org.uk
Website www.iol.org.uk
Chief Executive Officer *Henry Pavlovich*
Marketing Manager *Stephen Eden*
FOUNDED 1910. Professional association for translators, interpreters and trainers; examining body for languages at degree level and above for vocational purposes; the National Register of Public Service Interpreters is managed by NRPSI Limited, an IoL subsidiary. Subscription rates on application. The Institute's limited company, Language Services Ltd, provides customised assessments of language-oriented requirements, skills, etc.

Institute of Translation and Interpreting (ITI)
Exchange House, 494 Midsummer Boulevard, Milton Keynes, Buckinghamshire MK9 2EA
☎01908 255905 Fax 01908 255700
Email info@iti.org.uk
Website www.iti.org.uk
FOUNDED 1986. The ITI is a professional association of translators and interpreters aiming to promote the highest standards in translating and interpreting. It has strong corporate membership and runs professional development courses and conferences, sometimes in conjunction with its language, regional and subject network. Membership is open to those with a genuine and proven involvement in translation and interpreting (including students). ITI's *Directory of Members*, its bi-monthly *Bulletin* and other publications are available from the Secretariat, which also offers a free referral service whereby enquirers can be given the names of suitable members for any interpreting/translating assignment. ITI is a full and active member of FIT (International Federation of Translators).

Irish Book Publishers' Association

See **Clé**

Irish Copyright
Licensing Agency Ltd

Irish Writers' Centre, 19 Parnell Square,
Dublin 1, Republic of Ireland
☎00 353 1 872 9202 Fax 00 353 1 872 2035
Email icla@esatlink.com

Executive Director *Samantha Holman*

FOUNDED 1992 by writers and publishers in
Ireland to provide a scheme through which
rights holders can give permission, and users of
copyright material can obtain permission, to
copy.

Irish Playwrights and
Screenwriters Guild

Irish Writers' Centre, 19 Parnell Square,
Dublin 1 Republic of Ireland
☎00 353 1 872 1302 Fax 00 353 1 872 6282
Email moffats@indigo.ie
Website www.writerscentre.ie/IPSG.html

Contact *Sean Moffatt*
Subscription Details available on request

FOUNDED in 1969 to safeguard the rights of
scriptwriters for radio, stage and screen.

Irish Translators' & Interpreters'
Association

Irish Writers' Centre, 19 Parnell Square,
Dublin 1 Republic of Ireland
☎00 353 1 285 9137 Fax 00 353 1 872 6282
Email translation@eircom.net
Website www.translatorsassociation.ie

Honorary Secretary *Miriam Lee*
Subscription €35 p.a. (ordinary); €15 (students,
unwaged, pensioners, members of affiliated
organisations); €80 (corporate);
€55 (professional: membership by application
to Professional Membership Committee only)

FOUNDED 1986. The Association is for all translators: technical, commercial, literary and cultural, both written and spoken. It is also for those
with an interest in translation such as teachers
and students. Provides legal advice to members,
issues a register of translators and *publishes* a
quarterly newsletter, *Translation Ireland*.

Irish Writers' Union

Irish Writers' Centre, 19 Parnell Square,
Dublin 1 Republic of Ireland
☎00 353 1 872 1302 Fax 00 353 1 872 6282

Secretary *Helen Brennan*
Chair *Tony Hickey*

Subscription €45 p.a.

FOUNDED 1986 to promote the interests and
protect the rights of writers in Ireland.

ISBN Agency

Woolmead House, Bear Lane, Farnham,
Surrey GU9 7LG
☎01252 742590 Fax 01252 742526
Email isbn@whitaker.co.uk
Website www.whitaker.co.uk/isbn.htm

ISBNs are product numbers used by all sections
of the book trade for ordering and listing purposes. While ISBNs have no links to copyright
and carry no form of legal protection for the
book, they will enable your books to be listed
on bibliographic databases and may therefore
help sales. The UK Standard Book Numbering
Agency is the national ISBN agency, responsible for assigning ISBN prefixes to publishers
based in the UK or Republic of Ireland. Its services include advising publishers on the correct
implementation of the ISBN system and maintaining a database of publishers and their prefixes, as well as providing technical advice and
assistance to publishers and the booktrade on all
aspects of ISBN usage. Applications for ISBNs
for new publishers, help with calculating
ISBNs and additional prefixes are all available
from the Agency.

Isle of Man Authors

24 Laurys Avenue, Ramsey, Isle of Man
IM8 2HE
☎01624 815634

Secretary *Mrs Beryl Sandwell*
Subscription £5 p.a.

An association of writers living on the Isle of
Man, which has links with the **Society of
Authors**.

ITC

See **Independent Television Commission**

ITI

See **Institute of Translation and
Interpreting**

ITV Network Ltd.

200 Gray's Inn Road, London WC1X 8HF
☎020 7843 8000 Fax 020 7843 8158
Website www.itv.com

Director of Programmes *David Liddiment*

The ITV Network Ltd., wholly owned by the
ITV companies, independently commissions and
schedules the television programmes which are

shown across the ITV network. As a successor to the Independent Television Association, it also provides a range of services to the ITV companies where a common approach is required.

IVCA (International Visual Communication Association)

19 Pepper Street, Glengall Bridge, London E14 9RP
☎020 7512 0571 Fax 020 7512 0591
Email info@ivca.org
Website www.ivca.org
Chief Executive *Wayne Drew*

The IVCA is a professional association representing the interests of the users and suppliers of visual communications. In particular it pursues the interests of producers, commissioners and manufacturers involved in the non-broadcast and independent facilities industries and also business event companies. It represents all sizes of company and freelance individuals, offering information and advice services, publications, a professional network, special interest groups, a magazine and a variety of events including the UK's Film and Video Communications Festival.

Learning on Screen (The Society for Screen Based Learning)

9 Bridge Street, Tadcaster, North Yorkshire LS24 9AW
☎01937 530520 Fax 01937 530520
Email josie.key@learningonscreen.u-net.com
Website www.learningonscreen.org.uk
Administrator *Josie Key*

Learning on Screen brings together individuals and organisations with a common interest in helping people to learn via any kind of screen be it television or computer. The Society is a meeting place, a skills forum and resource for all those who want to exploit screen-based media in their roles as managers, trainers, lecturers, teachers, producers and communicators in the field of education, training, government and commerce. Annual conference and production awards. New members welcome.

The Library Association

See **CILIP: The Chartered Institute of Library and Information Professionals**

The Media Society

56 Roseneath Road, London SW11 6AQ
Contact *Peter Dannheisser*
Subscription £35 p.a.; £10 Entry fee
FOUNDED 1973. A registered charity which

aims to provide a forum for the exchange of knowledge and opinion between those in public and political life, the professions, industry and education. Meetings (about 10 a year) usually take the form of luncheons and dinners in London with invited speakers. The society also acts as a 'think tank' and submits evidence and observations to royal commissions, select committees and review bodies.

Medical Journalists' Association

(Access the website for contact details)
Website www.medicaljournalists.org.uk
Chairman *John Illman*
Honorary Secretary *Philippa Pigache*
Subscription £30 p.a.

FOUNDED 1967. Aims to improve the quality and practice of medical and health journalism and to improve relationships and understanding between medical and health journalists and the health and medical professions. Regular meetings with senior figures in medicine and medico politics; educational workshops on important subject areas or issues of the day; debates; awards for medical journalists from commercial sponsors, plus the MJA's own awards financed by members. *Publishes* a detailed directory of members and freelances and a newsletter five times a year.

Medical Writers' Association

The Barn, Tonacliffe Road, Whitworth OL12 8SJ
Contact *Dr David Brooks*
Subscription £30 p.a.; £40 (Joint)

FOUNDED in 1986 and expanding rapidly in membership and influence. Exists to promote and improve professional and lay writing activities within and for general practice. Open to doctors and other health professionals especially those working in the field of general practice; also to professional journalists writing on anything pertaining to general practice. Keen to develop input from interested parties who work mainly outside the profession. Regular workshops held around Britain. *Publishes* a twice-yearly journal (*The GP Writer*), anthologies and books from members, and a register of members and their writing interests.

Medical Writers' Group

The Society of Authors, 84 Drayton Gardens, London SW10 9SB
☎020 7373 6642 Fax 020 7373 5768
Email info@societyofauthors.org
Contact *Dorothy Sym*

FOUNDED 1980. A specialist group within the

Society of Authors offering advice and help to authors of medical books.

Mystery Writers of America, Inc.
17 East 47th Street, 6th Floor, New York, NY 10017 USA
☎001 212 888 8171   Fax 001 212 888 8107
Email mwa_org@earthlink.net
Website www.mysterywriters.org
Admin Director *Mary Beth Becker*
Subscription $80 (US); $60 (Corresponding members)

FOUNDED 1945. Aims to promote and protect the interests of writers of the mystery genre in all media; to educate and inform its membership on matters relating to their profession; to uphold a standard of excellence and raise the profile of this literary form to the world at large. Holds an annual banquet at which the 'Edgars' are awarded (named after Edgar Allan Poe).

National Association for Literature Development
PO Box 140, Ilkley, West Yorkshire LS29 6RH
☎01943 872546
Email steve@nald.org
Website www.nald.org
Coordinator *Steve Dearden*

NALD exists to enable literature professionals to talk to each other, develop their professional skills and make the case for increased investment in their work. Offers individual, organisational or corporate membership.

National Association of Writers Groups
The Arts Centre, Biddick Lane, Washington, Tyne & Wear NE38 2AB
☎01262 609228
Email mikediane@tesco.net
Website www.nawg.co.uk
Secretary *Diane Wilson*
Subscription £20 p.a. + £5 registration (Group); £10 p.a. (Individual)

FOUNDED 1995 with the object of furthering the interests of writers' groups throughout the UK. A registered charity, No: 1059047, NAWG is strictly non-sectarian and non-political. *Publishes* a bi-monthly newsletter, distributed to member groups; gives free entry to competitions for group anthologies, poetry, short stories, articles, novels and sketches; holds an annual open festival of writing with 36 workshops, seminars,

individual surgeries led by professional, high-profile writers. Membership is open to all writers' groups and individual writers – there are no restrictions or qualifications required for joining; 140 groups are affiliated to-date.

National Association of Writers in Education
PO Box 1, Sheriff Hutton, York YO60 7YU
☎01653 618429
Email paul@nawe.co.uk
Website www.nawe.co.uk
Contact *Paul Munden*
Subscription £20 p.a. (Individual); £10 (Student); £60 (Institution); £30 (Overseas)

FOUNDED 1991. Aims to promote the contribution of living writers to education and to encourage both the practice and the critical appreciation of creative writing. Has over 500 members. Organises national conferences and training courses. A directory of over 1200 writers who work in schools, colleges and the community is available online. *Publishes* a magazine, *Writing in Education*, issued free to members three times per year.

National Campaign for the Arts
Pegasus House, 37–43 Sackville Street, London W1S 3EH
☎020 7333 0375   Fax 020 7333 0660
Email nca@artscampaign.org.uk
Website www.artscampaign.org.uk
Director *Victoria Todd*
Deputy Director *Anna Leatherdale*

FOUNDED 1984 to represent the cultural sector in Britain and to make sure that the problems facing the arts are properly put to Government, at local and national level. The NCA is an independent body relying on finance from its members. Involved in all issues which affect the arts: public finance, education, broadcasting and media affairs, the fight against censorship, the rights of artists, the place of the arts on the public agenda and structures for supporting culture. Membership open to all arts organisations and to individuals. Literature subscriptions available.

National Literacy Trust
Swire House, 59 Buckingham Gate, London SW1E 6AJ
☎020 7828 2435   Fax 020 7931 9986
Email contact@literacytrust.org.uk
Website www.literacytrust.org.uk *and* www.rif.org.uk
Director *Neil McClelland*

FOUNDED 1993. A registered charity (No: 1015539) which aims to make 'an independent, strategic contribution to the creation of a society in which all can enjoy the appropriate skills, confidence and pleasures of literacy to support their educational, economic, social and cultural goals.' Maintains an extensive website with literacy issues, research news and information on literacy practice nationwide; promotes and facilitates literacy partnerships; organises an annual conference, courses and training events; *publishes* quarterly magazine, *Literacy Today* (the Educational Publishing Company, subscription £18). Organised and implemented the National Year of Reading 1998–99 and is coordinating the National Reading Campaign. It also incorporates Reading Is Fundamental, UK, which provides books free to children.

National Union of Journalists
Headland House, 308 Gray's Inn Road, London WC1X 8DP
☎020 7278 7916 Fax 020 7837 8143
Email acorn.house@nuj.org.uk
Website www.gn.apc.org/media/

General Secretary *Jeremy Dear*
Subscription £171 p.a. (Freelance) or 1% of annual income if lower; or 0.5% if income less than £12,000 p.a.

Represents journalists in all sectors of publishing, print and broadcast. Responsible for wages and conditions agreements which apply across the industry. Provides advice and representation for its members, as well as administering unemployment and other benefits. *Publishes* various guides and magazines: *On-Line Freelance Directory, Fees Guide, The Journalist* and *The Freelance*.

New Playwrights Trust
See **Writernet**

New Producers Alliance (NPA)
9 Bourlet Close, London W1W 7BP
☎020 7580 2480 Fax 020 7580 2484
Email queries@npa.org.uk
Website www.newproducer.co.uk

FOUNDED 1993; current membership of over 1000. Aims to encourage the production of commercial feature films for an international audience and to educate and inform film producers, writers and directors. The NPA is an independent networking organisation providing members with access to contacts, free legal advice and general help regarding film production. *Publishes* a monthly newsletter and organises meetings, workshops and seminars. The NPA also actively lobbies for better access to funds for first- and second-time film makers. The NPA does not produce films so please do not send scripts or treatments.

The New SF Alliance (NSFA)
c/o BBR, PO Box 625, Sheffield, South Yorkshire S1 3GY
Website www.bbr-online.com/writers
Contact *Chris Reed*

FOUNDED 1989. Committed to supporting the work of new writers and artists by promoting independent and small press publications worldwide. 'Helps with finding the right market for your material by providing a mail-order service which allows you to sample magazines, and various publications including *The Fix* magazine which features the latest market news and tips.'

New Writing North
7/8 Trinity Chare, Quayside, Newcastle upon Tyne NE1 3DF
☎0191 232 9991 Fax 0191 230 1883
Email subtext.nwn@virgin.net
Website www.newwritingnorth.com

Director *Claire Malcolm*
Administrator *John McGagh*

New Writing North is the literature development agency for the **Northern Arts** region and offers many useful services to writers, organising events, readings and courses. NWN produces writing guides and has a website with literary news, events and opportunities. Administers the **Northern Rock Foundation Writer Award** (see entry under **Bursaries, Fellowships and Grants**), the New Playwriting Panel (aiding new drama) and the Northern Writers' Awards, which include tailored development packages (mentoring and financial help). NWN has strong links with the post of Northern Literary Fellow. NWN also programmes the **Durham Literature Festival**.

The Newspaper Society
Bloomsbury House, 74–77 Great Russell Street, London WC1B 3DA
☎020 7636 7014 Fax 020 7631 5119
Email ns@newspapersoc.org.uk
Website www.newspapersoc.org.uk

Director *David Newell*

FOUNDED in 1836, the Newspaper Society is the voice of Britain's regional and local newspapers. It represents and promotes the interests of around 1300 regional daily and weekly, paid for and free, titles. The range of activities and services provided by the Society can be split into two broad areas: marketing and lobbying. Holds a series of conferences and seminars each year and runs the annual Local Newspaper Week.

NPA
See **New Producers Alliance**

NSFA
See **The New SF Alliance**

Outdoor Writers' Guild
PO Box 520, Bamber Bridge, Preston, Lancashire PR5 8LF
☎01772 696732 Fax 01772 696732
Secretary *Terry Marsh*
Subscription £60 p.a.

FOUNDED 1980 to promote, encourage and assist the development and maintenance of professional standards among those involved in all aspects of outdoor journalism. Membership is not limited to writers but includes other outstanding professional media practitioners in the outdoor world such as broadcasters, photographers, filmmakers, editors, publishers and illustrators. *Publishes* a quarterly journal, *Bootprint*, and an annual *Directory* (£30; free to members). Presents five Awards for Excellence plus other awards in recognition of achievement.

PACT (Producers Alliance for Cinema and Television)
45 Mortimer Street, London W1W 8HJ
☎020 7331 6000 Fax 020 7331 6700
Email enquiries@pact.co.uk
Website www.pact.co.uk
Chief Executive *John McVay*
Information Manager *David Alan Mills*

FOUNDED 1991. PACT is the trade association of the UK independent television and feature film production sector and is a key contact point for foreign producers seeking British co-production, co-finance partners and distributors. Works for producers in the industry at every level and operates a members' regional network throughout the UK with a divisional office in Scotland. Membership services include: a dedicated industrial relations unit; discounted legal advice; a varied calendar of events; business advice; representation at international film and television markets; a comprehensive research programme; various publications: a monthly magazine, an annual members' directory; affiliation with European

and international producers' organisations; extensive information and production advice. Lobbies actively with broadcasters, financiers and governments to ensure that the producer's voice is heard and understood in Britain and Europe on all matters affecting the film and television industry.

PEN
152–156 Kentish Town Road, London NW1 9QB
☎020 7267 9444 Fax 020 7267 9304
Email enquiries@pen.org.uk
Website www.pen.org.uk
Director *Diana Reich*
Membership cheque/standing order: £45/£40 (London/Overseas); £40/£35 (Country)

English PEN is part of International PEN, a worldwide association of writers and other literary professionals which promotes literature, fights for freedom of expression and speaks out for writers who are imprisoned or harassed for having criticised their governments, or for publishing other unpopular views. FOUNDED in London in 1921, International PEN now consists of over 130 centres in almost 100 countries. PEN originally stood for poets, essayists and novelists, but membership is now open to all literary professionals. It is also possible to become a 'Friend of English PEN'. A programme of talks and discussions, and other activities such as social gatherings, is supplemented by mailings, website and annual congress at one of the centre countries.

Performing Right Society
29–33 Berners Street, London W1T 3AB
☎020 7580 5544 Fax 020 7306 4455
Email info@prs.co.uk
Website www.prs.co.uk

Collects and distributes royalties arising from the performance and broadcast of copyright music on behalf of its composer, lyricist and music publisher members and members of affiliated societies worldwide.

Periodical Publishers Association (PPA)
Queens House, 28 Kingsway, London WC2B 6JR
☎020 7404 4166 Fax 020 7404 4167
Email info1@ppa.co.uk
Website www.ppa.co.uk

FOUNDED 1913 to promote and protect the interests of magazine publishers in the UK.

The Personal Managers' Association Ltd

1 Summer Road, East Molesey, Surrey
KT8 9LX
☎020 8398 9796 Fax 020 8398 9796
Email info@thepma.com

Co-chairs *Marc Berlin, Tim Corrie, Nicholas Young*
Secretary *Angela Adler*
Subscription £250 p.a.

An association of artists' and dramatists' agents (membership not open to individuals). Monthly meetings for exchange of information and discussion. Maintains a code of conduct and acts as a lobby when necessary. Applicants screened. A high proportion of play agents are members of the PMA.

The Picture Research Association

Head Office: 2 Culver Drive, Oxted, Surrey
RH8 9HP
☎01883 730123 Fax 01883 730144
Email pra@lippmann.co.uk
Website www.picture-research.org.uk

Chair *Charlotte Lippmann*
Subscription Members: £45 (Introductory); £55 (Full); £50 (Associate).
Magazine only: £25

FOUNDED 1977 as the Society of Picture Researchers & Editors. The Picture Research Association is a professional body for picture researchers, managers, picture editors and all those involved in the research, management and supply of visual material to all forms of the media. The Association's main aims are to promote the interests and specific skills of its members internationally; to promote and maintain professional standards; to bring together those involved in the research and publication of visual material; to provide a forum for the exchange of information and to provide guidance to its members. Free advisory service for members, regular meetings, quarterly magazine, monthly newsletter and Freelance Register.

Player–Playwrights

9 Hillfield Park, London N10 3QT
☎020 8883 0371
Email P-P@dial.pipex.com

President *Olwen Wymark*
Contact *Peter Thompson* (at the address above)
Subscription £10 (Joining fee); £6 p.a.
thereafter, plus £1.50 per attendance

FOUNDED 1948. A society giving opportunity for writers new to stage, radio and television, as well as others finding difficulty in achieving results, to work with writers established in those media. At weekly meetings (7.45 pm–10.00 pm, Mondays, upstairs at the Horse and Groom, 128 Great Portland Street, London W1), members' scripts are read or performed by actor members and afterwards assessed and dissected in general discussion. Newcomers and new acting members are always welcome.

PLS
See **Publishers Licensing Society Ltd**

PMA
See **The Personal Managers' Association Ltd**

Poetry Book Society
See **Organisations of Interest to Poets**

Poetry Ireland
See **Organisations of Interest to Poets**

The Poetry Society
See **Organisations of Interest to Poets**

Press Complaints Commission

1 Salisbury Square, London EC4Y 8JB
☎020 7353 1248 Fax 020 7353 8355
Email pcc@pcc.org.uk
Website www.pcc.org.uk

Director *Guy Black*
Information Officer *Tonia Milton*

FOUNDED in 1991 to deal with complaints from members of the public about the editorial content of newspapers and magazines. Administers the editors' Code of Practice covering such areas as accuracy, privacy, harrassment and intrusion into grief. Publications available: *Code of Practice* and *How to Complain*.

Private Libraries Association

16 Brampton Grove, Kenton, Harrow,
Middlesex HA3 8LG
☎020 8907 6802 Fax 020 8907 6802
Email Frank@plantage.demon.co.uk

Honorary Secretary *Frank Broomhead*
Membership £25 p.a.

FOUNDED 1956. An international society of book collectors. The Association's objectives are to promote and encourage the awareness of the benefits of book ownership, and the study of books, their production and ownership; to publish works concerned with this, particularly those which are not commercially profitable, to hold meetings at which papers on cognate subjects can be read and discussed. Lectures and exhibitions are open to non-members.

Producers Alliance for Cinema and Television
See **PACT**

The Publishers Association
29B Montague Street, London WC1B 5BH
☎020 7691 9191 Fax 020 7691 9199
Email mail@publishers.org.uk
Website www.publishers.org.uk
Chief Executive *Ronnie Williams, OBE*

The national UK trade association for books, learned journals, and electronic publications, with around 200 member companies in the industry. Very much a trade body representing the industry to Government and the European Commission, and providing services to publishers. *Publishes* the *Directory of Publishing* in association with **Continuum**. Also home of the Educational Publishers Council (school books), PA's International Division (BDCI), the Council of Academic and Professional Publishers, and the Electronic Publishers' Forum.

Publishers' Association of South Africa
PO Box 22640, Fish Hoek 7974 South Africa
☎00 27 21 7827677 Fax 00 27 21 7827679
Email pasa@publishsa.co.za
Website www.publishsa.co.za

FOUNDED in 1992 to represent publishing in South Africa, a small but key industry sector. With a membership of approximately 120 companies, the Association includes commercial organisations, university presses, one-person privately-owned publishers as well as importers and distributors.

Publishers Licensing Society Ltd
5 Dryden Street, Covent Garden, London WC2E 9NB
☎020 7829 8486 Fax 020 7829 8488
Email pls@pls.org.uk
Website www.pls.org.uk
Chief Executive *Jens Bammel*
Manager *Caroline Elmslie*

FOUNDED in 1981, the PLS obtains mandates from publishers which grant PLS the authority to license photocopying of pages from published works. Some licences for digitisation of printed works are available. PLS aims to maximise revenue from licences for mandating publishers and to expand the range and repertoire of mandated publishers available to licence holders. It supports the **Copyright Licensing Agency (CLA)** in its efforts to increase the number of legitimate users through the issuing of licences and vigorously pursues any infringements of copyright works belonging to rights' holders.

Publishers Publicity Circle
65 Airedale Avenue, London W4 2NN
☎020 8994 1881
Email ppc-@lineone.net
Website www.publisherspublicitycircle.co.uk
Contact *Heather White*

Enables book publicists from both publishing houses and freelance PR agencies to meet and share information regularly. Meetings, held monthly in central London, provide a forum for press journalists, television and radio researchers and producers to meet publicists collectively. A directory of the PPC membership is published each year and distributed to over 2500 media contacts.

Radio Authority
Holbrook House, 14 Great Queen Street, London WC2B 5DG
☎020 7430 2724 Fax 020 7405 7062
Email info@radioauthority.org.uk
Website www.radioauthority.org.uk

The Radio Authority plans frequencies, awards licences, regulates programming and advertising, and plays an active role in the discussion and formulation of policies which affect the Independent Radio industry and its listeners. The Authority also licenses digital radio services. The national commercial digital radio service was launched on 15 November 1999. The number of Independent Radio stations, now over 250, continues to increase with new licences being advertised on a regular basis.

Romance Writers of America
3707 FM 1960 W, Suite 555, Houston, TX 77068, USA
☎001 281 440 6885 Fax 001 281 440 7510
Email info@rwanational.org
Website www.rwanational.org
Communications Assistant *Nicole Kennedy*
Subscriptions $75 p.a. plus $25 joining fee

FOUNDED 1980. RWA, a non-profit association with more than 8400 members worldwide, provides a service to authors at all stages of their careers as well as to the romance publishing industry and its readers. Anyone pursuing a career in romantic fiction may join RWA. Holds an annual conference, and provides contests for both published and unpublished writers through the RITA Awards and Golden Hearts Awards.

The Romantic Novelists' Association

Highcroft, Church Place, Rodborough, Stroud, Gloucestershire GL5 3NF
Email ffordes@aol.com
Website www.rna-uk.org
Contact *Katie Fforde*
Subscription Full & Associate: £28 p.a.; £33 (Overseas, non-EU); New Writers: £78; £83 (Overseas, non-EU)

Membership is open to published writers of romantic fiction (modern or historical), or those who have had two or more full-length serials published. Associate membership is open to publishers, editors, literary agents, booksellers, librarians and others having a close connection with novel writing and publishing. Membership in the New Writers' Scheme is available to writers who have not yet had a full-length novel published. New Writers must submit a manuscript each year. The mss receive a report from experienced published members and the reading fee is included in the subscription of £78. Meetings are held in London and the regions with guest speakers. The *RNA News* is published quarterly and issued free to members. The Association makes two annual awards: **The Major Award** for the Romantic Novel of the Year, and **The New Writers Award** for the best published novel by a new writer.

Royal Festival Hall Literature & Talks

See entry under **Festivals**

Royal Society of Literature

Somerset House, Strand, London WC2R 1LA
☎020 7845 4676 Fax 020 7845 4679
Email info@rslit.org
Website www.rslit.org
President *Lord Jenkins of Hillhead*
Chairman *Ronald Harwood*
Subscription £30 p.a.

FOUNDED 1820. Membership by application to the Secretary. Fellowships are conferred by the Society on the proposal of two Fellows. Membership benefits include lectures, discussion meetings, poetry readings and two annual joint meetings with the Royal Society.

Lecturers have included John Carey, Michael Holroyd, P.D. James, Jan Morris and Philip Pullman. Presents the **W.H. Heinemann Award**, the **Winifred Holtby Prize** and the **V.S. Pritchett Memorial Prize**.

Royal Television Society

Holborn Hall, 100 Gray's Inn Road, London WC1X 8AL
☎020 7430 1000 Fax 020 7430 0924
Email info@rts.org.uk
Website www.rts.org.uk
Subscription £70 p.a.

FOUNDED 1927. Covers all disciplines involved in the television industry. Provides a forum for debate and conferences on technical, social and cultural aspects of the medium. Presents various awards including journalism, programmes, technology, design and commercials. *Publishes Television Magazine* nine times a year for members and subscribers.

Science Fiction Foundation

Membership Secretary: D28, Department of Arts and Media, Buckinghamshire Chilterns University College, High Wycombe, Buckinghamshire HP11 2JZ
Email ambutler@enterprise.net
Website www.sf-foundation.org
Membership Secretary *Andrew M. Butler*

The SFF is an international academic body for the furtherance of science fiction studies. *Publishes* a thrice-yearly magazine, *Foundation* (see entry under **Magazines**), which features academic articles and reviews of new fiction. It also has a reference library (see entry under **Library Services**), housed at Liverpool University.

Scottish Book Trust

The Scottish Book Centre, 137 Dundee Street, Edinburgh EH11 1BG
☎0131 229 3663 Fax 0131 228 4293
Email scottish.book.trust@dial.pipex.com
Website www.scottishbooktrust.com
Contact *Lindsey Fraser*

FOUNDED 1956. Scottish Book Trust works with schools, libraries, writers, artists, publishers, bookshops and individuals to promote the pleasures of reading to people of all ages. It provides a book information service which draws on the children's reference library (a copy of every children's book published in the previous twelve months) and a range of press cuttings on Scottish literary themes. Scottish Book Trust administers the Blue Peter Book Awards and *publishes* age-ranged book lists, reading resources and guides to Scottish books and writers, both adult and children's. It administers the *Writers in Scotland* scheme, coordinates National Poetry Day and World Book Day in Scotland and produces a range of posters and literary guides.

Scottish Daily Newspaper Society

48 Palmerston Place, Edinburgh EH12 5DE
☎0131 220 4353 Fax 0131 220 4344
Email info@sdns.org.uk
Director *Mr J.B. Raeburn*

FOUNDED 1915. Trade association representing publishers of Scottish daily and Sunday newspapers.

Scottish Library Association

Scottish Centre for Information & Library Services, 1 John Street, Hamilton, Strathclyde ML3 7EU
☎01698 458888 Fax 01698 458899
Email sla@slainte.org.uk
Website www.slainte.org.uk
Director *Robert Craig*

FOUNDED 1908 to bring together everyone engaged in or interested in library work in Scotland. The Association has over 2300 members, covering all aspects of library and information work. Its main aims are the promotion of library services and the qualifications and status of librarians.

Scottish Newspaper Publishers Association

48 Palmerston Place, Edinburgh EH12 5DE
☎0131 220 4353 Fax 0131 220 4344
Email info@snpa.org.uk
Website www.snpa.org.uk
Director *Mr J.B. Raeburn*

FOUNDED around 1905. The representative body for the publishers of paid-for weekly and associated free newspapers in Scotland. Represents the interests of the industry to Government, public and other bodies and provides a range of services including marketing of *The Scottish Weekly Press*, industrial relations, and education and training. It is an active supporter of the Press Complaints Commission.

Scottish Print Employers Federation

48 Palmerston Place, Edinburgh EH12 5DE
☎0131 220 4353 Fax 0131 220 4344
Email info@spef.org.uk
Website www.spef.org.uk
Director *Mr J.B. Raeburn*

FOUNDED 1910. Employers' organisation and trade association for the Scottish printing industry. Represents the interests of the industry to Government, public and other bodies and provides a range of services including industrial relations, education, training and commercial activities. Negotiates a national wages and conditions agreement with the Graphical, Paper and Media Union. The Federation is a member of Intergraf, the international confederation for employers' associations in the printing industry. In this capacity its views are channelled on the increasing number of matters affecting print businesses emanating from the European Union.

Scottish Publishers Association

Scottish Book Centre, 137 Dundee Street, Edinburgh EH11 1BG
☎0131 228 6866 Fax 0131 228 3220
Email a.rae@scottishbooks.org
Website www.scottishbooks.org
Director *Lorraine Fannin*
Administrator *Carol Lothian*
Marketing Manager *Alison Rae*
Promotions & Training Manager
  Allan Shanks

The Association represents over 80 Scottish publishers, from multinationals to small presses, in a number of capacities, but primarily in the cooperative promotion and marketing of their books. The SPA also acts as an information and advice centre for both the trade and general public. *Publishes* seasonal catalogues, membership lists, the annual *Directory of Publishing in Scotland* and regular newsletters. Represents members at international book fairs; runs an extensive training programme in publishing skills; carries out market research; and encourages export initiatives. Also provides administrative back-up for the Scottish Book Marketing Group, a cooperative venture with Scottish booksellers.

Scottish Young Playwrights

Scottish Youth Theatre, 3rd Floor, Forsyth House, 111 Union Street, Glasgow G1 3TA
☎0141 221 5127 Fax 0141 221 9123
Email info@scottishyouththeatre.org.
Website www.scottishyouththeatre.org
Artistic Director *Mary McCluskey*

Scottish Youth Theatre is involved in and operates various projects supporting young writers in Scotland. Further details from the address above.

Society for Children's Book Writers & Illustrators

Flat 3, 124 Norwood Road, London SE24 9AY
Email scbwi_bi@hotmail.com

British Isles Regional Advisor *Natascha Biebow*

FOUNDED in 1968 by a group of Los Angeles-based writers, the Society acts as a network for the exchange of knowledge between writers, illustrators, editors, publishers, agents and others involved with literature for young people. With a membership of over 10,000 worldwide, it is the largest organisation of its kind in the world. Holds an annual national conference plus a number of regional ones, *publishes* a bi-monthly newsletter and awards grants for works in progress. The Golden Kite Award, which is presented annually, is for best fiction and non-fiction books. For membership enquiries, contact *Natascha Biebow* at the address above.

Society for Editors and Proofreaders (SfEP)

1 Riverbank House, 1 Putney Bridge Approach, London SW6 3JD
☎020 7736 3278 Fax 020 7736 3318
Email admin@sfep.org.uk
Website www.sfep.org.uk

Chair *Naomi Laredo*
Vice-chair *Adrian Sumner*
Secretary *Katie Lewis*

Subscription £65 p.a. (Individuals) plus £25 joining fee; Corporate membership available

FOUNDED 1988 in response to the growing number of freelance editors and their increasing importance to the publishing industry. Aims to promote high editorial standards by disseminating information through advice and training, and to achieve recognition of the professional status of its members. The Society also supports moves towards recognised standards of training and accreditation for editors and proofreaders. It launched its own Accreditation in Proofreading test in 2002.

Society for Technical Communications (STC)

901 N. Stuart Street, Suite 904, Arlington, Virginia 22203–1822 USA
☎001 703 522 4114 Fax 001 703 522 2075
Email stc@stc.org *and (UK Chapter)*
stc_uk_chapter@yahoo.co.uk
Website www.stc.org *and*
   www.stc-europe.org/uk

UK Chapter Contact *Liz Hale* (07970 649579)

Subscription US$158 p.a. (Individual)

Dedicated to advancing the arts and sciences of technical communication, the STC has 25,000 members world-wide, including technical writers, editors, graphic designers, videographers, multimedia artists, Web and intranet page information designers, translators and others whose work involves making technical information available to those who need it. *Publishes* a quarterly scholarly journal, *Technical Communications* and the magazine, *Intercom*, ten times a year (both available to members only). The UK Chapter, which has about 120 members, hosts meetings and seminars, runs an annual technical publications competition, and publishes its own newsletter six times a year.

The Society of Authors

84 Drayton Gardens, London SW10 9SB
☎020 7373 6642 Fax 020 7373 5768
Email info@societyofauthors.org
Website www.societyofauthors.org

General Secretary *Mark Le Fanu*
Subscription £70/£75 p.a.

FOUNDED 1884. The Society of Authors is an independent trade union with some 7000 members. It advises on negotiations with publishers, broadcasting organisations, theatre managers and film companies; assists with complaints and takes action for breach of contract, copyright infringement, etc. Together with the **Writers' Guild**, the Society has played a major role in advancing the Minimum Terms Agreement for authors. Among the Society's publications are *The Author* (a quarterly journal) and the *Quick Guides* series to various aspects of writing (all free of charge to members). Other services include vetting of contracts, emergency funds for writers, and various special discounts. There are groups within the Society for scriptwriters, children's writers and illustrators, educational writers, academic writers, medical writers and translators. Authors under 35 or over 65, not earning a significant income from their writing, may apply for lower subscription rates. Contact the Society for a free booklet and a copy of *The Author*.

The Society of Authors in Scotland

Bonnyton House, Arbirlot, Angus DD11 2PY
☎01241 874131 Fax 01241 874131
Email info@eileenramsay.co.uk
Website www.writersorg.co.uk

Secretary *Eileen Ramsay*

The Scottish branch of the **Society of Authors,**

which organises business meetings, social and bookshop events throughout Scotland.

Society of Civil and Public Service Writers

17 The Green, Corby Glen, Grantham, Lincolnshire NG33 4NP
Email jhykin@talk21.com
Membership Secretary *Mrs Joan Hykin*
Subscription £15 p.a.

FOUNDED 1935. Welcomes serving and retired members of the Civil Service, armed forces, Post Office and BT, nursing profession and other public servants who are aspiring or published writers. Offers competitions for short story, article and poetry; postal folios for short story and article; AGM, occasional meetings and luncheon held in London; quarterly magazine, *Civil Service Author*, to which members may submit material; Poetry Workshop (extra £3) offers annual weekend outside London, anthology, newsletter, postal folio, competitions. S.a.e. to Secretary for details.

Society of Editors

University Centre, Granta Place, Mill Lane, Cambridge CB2 1RU
☎01223 304080 Fax 01223 304090
Email info@societyofeditors.org
Website www.societyofeditors.org
Executive Director *Bob Satchwell*

Formed by a merger of the Association of British Editors and the Guild of Editors, the Society of Editors has nearly 500 members in national, regional and local newspapers, magazines, broadcasting, new media, journalism education and media law. Campaigns for media freedom and self-regulation. For further information contact *Bob Satchwell* at the address above or on pager number 07625 155366.

Society of Indexers

Globe Centre, Penistone Road, Sheffield, South Yorkshire S6 3AE
☎0114 281 3060 Fax 0114 281 3061
Email admin@socind.demon.co.uk
Website www.socind.demon.co.uk
Secretary *Ann Kingdom*
Administrator *Wendy Burrow*
Subscription £50 p.a.; Institutions: from £100

FOUNDED 1957. Publishes *The Indexer* (biannual, April and October) and a quarterly newsletter. Issues an annual list of members and *Indexers Available (IA)*, which lists members and their subject expertise. In addition, the Society

runs an open-learning course entitled *Training in Indexing* and recommends rates of pay (currently £15–20 per hour).

Society of Picture Researchers & Editors

See **The Picture Research Association**

Society of Women Writers & Journalists

4 Larch Way, Haywards Heath, West Sussex RH16 3TY
☎01444 412087 Fax 01444 416866
Email swwriters@aol.com
Honorary Secretary *Jennie Davidson*
Subscription £35 (Town); £30 (Country); £25 (Overseas). £15 Joining fee

FOUNDED 1894. The first of its kind to be run as an association of women engaged in journalism. Aims to encourage literary achievement, uphold professional standards, and establish social contacts with other writers. Lectures given at monthly lunchtime meetings. Offers advice to members and has regular seminars, etc. *Publishes* a society journal, *The Woman Writer*.

Society of Young Publishers

Endeavour House, 189 Shaftesbury Avenue, London WC2H 8JT
Email info@thesyp.org.uk
Website www.thesyp.org.uk
Subscription £25 p.a.; £15 (Student/Unwaged); £30 (Associate)

Provides facilities whereby members can increase their knowledge and widen their experience of all aspects of publishing, and holds regular social events. Open to those in related occupations, with associate membership available for over-35s. *Publishes* a monthly newsletter called *Inprint* and holds meetings on the last Wednesday of each month. Please enclose an s.a.e. when writing to the Society.

The South and Mid-Wales Association of Writers (SAMWAW)

c/o I.M.C. Consulting Group, Denham House, Lambourne Crescent, Cardiff CF14 5ZW
☎029 2076 1170 Fax 029 2076 1304
Email info@imcconsultinggroup.co.uk
Subscription £10 (Single); £15 (Joint)

FOUNDED 1971 to foster the art and craft of writing in all its forms. Provides a common meeting ground for writers, critics, editors, adjudicators from all over the UK and abroad. Organises residential weekend conferences and day seminars throughout the year. Holds competitions, two for members only and two which are open to the public, in addition to **The Mathew Prichard Award for Short Story Writing** (see entry under **Prizes**).

Spoken Word Publishing Association (SWPA)

c/o Macmillan Audio, 120 New Wharf Road, London N1 9RR
☎020 7014 6000 Fax 020 7014 6001
Email audio@penguin.co.uk
Website www.swpa.co.uk
Chairman *Ali Muirden*
Secretary *Zoe Howes*

FOUNDED 1994. SWPA is the UK trade association for the spoken word industry with membership open to all those involved in the publishing of spoken word audio. *Publishes SWPA Resources Directory* available from the address above.

Sports Writers' Association of Great Britain

c/o Sport England External Affairs, 16 Upper Woburn Place, London WC1H 0QP
☎020 7273 1789 Fax 020 7383 0273
Subscription £23.50 p.a. incl. VAT (London); £11.75 (Regional)

FOUNDED 1948 to promote and maintain a high professional standard among journalists who specialise in sport in all its branches and to serve members' interests. *Publishes* a quarterly bulletin for members and promotes jointly with Sport England the annual British Sports Personalities of the Year Awards, the British Sports Journalism Awards and the Sports Photographer of the Year award.

SWPA
See **Spoken Word Publishing Association**

Theatre Writers' Union
See **The Writers' Guild of Great Britain**

The Translators Association

84 Drayton Gardens, London SW10 9SB
☎020 7373 6642 Fax 020 7373 5768
Email info@societyofauthors.org
Secretary *Dorothy Sym*

FOUNDED 1958 as a subsidiary group within the **Society of Authors** to deal exclusively with the special problems of literary translators into the English language. Benefits to members include free legal and general advice and assistance on all business matters relating to translators' work,

including the vetting of contracts and advice on rates of remuneration. Membership is normally confined to translators who have had their work published in volume or serial form or produced in this country for stage, television or radio. The Association administers several prizes for translators of published work (see **Prizes**) and maintains a database to enable members' details to be supplied to publishers who are seeking a translator for a particular work.

Voice of the Listener and Viewer (VLV)

101 Kings Drive, Gravesend, Kent DA12 5BQ
☎01474 352835 Fax 01474 351112
Email vlv@btinternet.com

VLV represents the citizen and consumer interest in broadcasting. It is an independent, non-profit-making society working to ensure independence, quality and diversity in broadcasting. VLV is the only consumer body speaking for listeners and viewers on the full range of broadcasting issues. VLV is funded by its members and is free from sectarian, commercial and political affiliations. Holds public lectures, seminars and conferences, and has frequent contact with MPs, civil servants, the BBC and independent broadcasters, regulators, academics and other consumer groups. Produces a quarterly news bulletin and regular briefings on broadcasting issues. Holds its own archive and those of the former Broadcasting Research Unit (1980–90) and BACTV (British Action for Children's Television). Maintains a panel of speakers, the VLV Forum for Children's Broadcasting, and the VLV Forum for Educational Broadcasting, and acts as secretariat for the European Alliance of Listeners' and Viewers' Associations (EURALVA). VLV has responded to all major public enquiries on broadcasting since 1984 and to all consultation documents issued by the ITC and Radio Authority since 1990. The VLV does not handle complaints.

W.A.T.C.H.
See **Writers, Artists and their Copyright Holders**

Welsh Academy
See **Academi**

Welsh Books Council (Cyngor Llyfrau Cymru)

Castell Brychan, Aberystwyth, Ceredigion SY23 2JB
☎01970 624151 Fax 01970 625385

Email castellbrychan@cllc.org.uk
Website www.cllc.org.uk *and*
www.gwales.com

Director *Gwerfyl Pierce Jones*
Head of Editorial Department *Dewi Morris Jones*

FOUNDED 1961 to stimulate interest in Welsh literature and to support authors. The Council distributes the government grant for Welsh language publications and promotes and fosters all aspects of both Welsh and Welsh-interest book production. Its Editorial, Design, Marketing and Children's Books departments and wholesale distribution centre offer central services to publishers in Wales. Writers in Welsh and English are welcome to approach the Editorial Department for advice on how to get their manuscripts published.

Welsh National Literature Promotion Agency

See **Academi**

West Country Writers' Association

High Wootton, Wootton Lane, Limpstone, Exmouth, Devon EX8 5AY
☎01395 222749
Email jjoss@josser.freeserve.co.uk
Website www.westcountrywriters.co.uk

President *Christopher Fry*
Honorary Secretary *Judy Joss*

FOUNDED 1951 in the interest of published authors with an interest in the West Country. Meets to discuss news and views and to listen to talks. Conference and newsletters.

Women in Publishing

Email wipub@hotmail.com
Website www.cyberiacafe.net/wip

Contact *Information Officer* (at e-mail address above)
Membership £25 p.a. (Waged);
£15 (Unwaged/Student); £30 (if paid for by company)

Aims to promote the status of women working in publishing and related trades by helping them to develop their careers. Through WiP there are opportunities for members to learn more about their area of work, share information and expertise, give and receive support and partake in practical training for career and personal development. Monthly meetings provide a forum for discussion on various topics of interest within the industry while other meetings are oriented towards giving careers advice and networking. Meetings are held on the second Wednesday of each month. See website for further information. *Publishes* monthly newsletter, *WiPlash* and *Women in Publishing Directory.*

Women Writers Network (WWN)

23 Prospect Road, London NW2 2JU
☎020 7794 5861

Membership Secretary *Cathy Smith*
Subscription £40 p.a. (Full); £30 p.a. (Overseas); £25 p.a. ('Newsletter only' UK membership)

FOUNDED 1985. Provides a forum for the exchange of information, support, career and networking opportunities for working women writers. Meetings, seminars, excursions, newsletter and directory. Full membership includes free admission to monthly meetings, a directory of members and a monthly newsletter. Details from the Membership Secretary at the address above.

Writernet

Cabin V, Clarendon Buildings, 25 Horsell Road, Highbury, London N5 1XL
☎020 7609 7474 Fax 020 7609 7557
Email writernet@btinternet.com
Website www.writernet.org.uk

Executive Director *Jonathan Meth*
Subscription (information on rates available by post or on website)

Writernet (formerly the New Playwrights Trust) is the national research and development organisation for writing for all forms of live and recorded performance. *Publishes* a range of information pertinent to writers on all aspects of development and production in the form of pamphlets, and a six-weekly journal which also includes articles and interviews on aesthetic and practical issues. Writernet also runs a script-reading service and a link service between writers and producers, organises seminars and conducts research projects. The latter includes research into the use of bilingual techniques in playwriting (*Two Tongues*), documentation of training programmes for writers (*Going Black Under the Skin*) and an investigation of the relationship between live art and writing (*Writing Live*).

The Writers' Guild of Great Britain

430 Edgware Road,, London W2 1EH
☎020 7723 8074 Fax 020 7706 2413
(moving to new premises, summer 2002; check website for details)

Email admin@writersguild.org.uk
Website www.writersguild.org.uk
General Secretary *Bernie Corbett*
Assistant General Secretaries *Anne Hogben,*
Christine Paris
Annual subscription 1% of that part of the
author's income earned in the areas in
which the Guild operates, with a basic
subscription of £125 and a maximum of
£1250

FOUNDED 1959. The Writers' Guild is the writers' trade union, affiliated to the TUC. It represents writers in film, radio, television, theatre and
publishing. The Guild has negotiated agreements
on which writers' contracts are based with the
BBC, Independent Television companies, and
PACT (the Producers' Alliance for Cinema and
Television). Those agreements are regularly
renegotiated, both in terms of finance and conditions. In 1997, the Guild membership joined
with that of the Theatre Writers' Union to create
a new, more powerful union.

In 1979, together with the Theatre Writers'
Union, the Guild negotiated the first ever
industrial agreement for theatre writers, the
TNC Agreement, which covers the **Royal
National Theatre**, the **Royal Shakespeare
Company**, and the **Royal Court**. Further
agreements have been negotiated with the
Theatrical Management Association which
covers regional theatre and the **Independent
Theatre Council**, the organisation which
covers small theatres and the Fringe.

The Guild initiated a campaign over ten years
ago which achieved the first ever publishing
agreement for writers with the publisher W.H.
Allen. Jointly with the **Society of Authors**,
that campaign has continued and most years see
new agreements with more publishers. Perhaps
the most important breakthrough came with
Penguin on 20 July 1990. The Guild now also
has agreements covering **HarperCollins**,
Random House Group, **Transworld** and
others.

The Guild regularly provides individual help
and advice to members on contracts, conditions of work, and matters which affect a member's life as a professional writer. Members are
given the opportunity of meeting at craft meetings, which are held on a regular basis throughout the year. Writers can apply for Full
Membership if they have one piece of written
work for which payment has been received

under a contract with terms not less than those
negotiated by the Guild. Writers who do not
qualify for Full Membership can apply for
Candidate Membership. This is open to all
those who wish to be involved in writing but
have not yet had work published. The subscription fee for this is £55.

Writers, Artists and their Copyright Holders (W.A.T.C.H.)

The Library, The University of Reading,
PO Box 223, Whiteknights, Reading,
Berkshire RG6 6AE
☎0118 931 8783 Fax 0118 931 6636
Website www.watch-file.com
Contact *Dr David Sutton*

FOUNDED 1994. Provides an online database of
information about the copyright holders of literary authors and artists. The database is available free of charge on the Internet and the
Web. W.A.T.C.H. is the successor project to
the Location Register of English Literary
Manuscripts and Letters, and continues to deal
with location register enquiries.

Yachting Journalists' Association

3 Friars Lane, Maldon, Essex CM9 6AG
☎01621 855943/0776 896 2936 (mobile)
Fax 01621 852212
Email Yjauk@cs.com
Honorary Secretary *Peter Cook*
Subscription £30 p.a.

To further the interest of yachting, sail and
power, and to provide support and assistance to
journalists in the field; current membership is just
over 260 with 31 from overseas. A handbook,
listing details of members and subscribing PR
organisations, press facility recommendations,
forthcoming events and other useful information, is published annually at a cost to non-
members and non-advertisers of £10. Information for inclusion should be submitted by
the end of August. The YJA organises the
Yachtsman of the Year and Young Sailor of
the Year Awards, that form part of the British
Nautical Awards, presented annually at the
beginning of January on the first Friday of the
London International Boat Show.

Yr Academi Gymreig

See **Academi**

What is Mine is Yours – At a Price

Kate Pool gives an update on the law of copyright

Copyright is the legal right of authors, dramatists, artists and composers to prevent others from exploiting their work without their permission. All original material qualifies for protection, regardless of its artistic merit, immediately it is recorded in writing or in another form. There are no formalities in any country which is a member of the Berne Copyright Union – which includes virtually all the principal countries of the world. Contrary to some popular misunderstandings, and while it may sometimes be harder to police infringements, copyright applies as much to work appearing on the Internet as it does to work appearing anywhere else.

Generally, the owner of the copyright in a work is the author who created it. The main exceptions are when you do work in the course of your employment, in which case your employer will own the copyright; or when you assign your copyright to someone else. A translator owns copyright in the translation, in addition to any copyright which exists in the original work. Likewise a screen-writer owns copyright in a screenplay, in addition to any copyright in the work from which the script was adapted.

Length of copyright

Throughout the European Economic Area, and also the USA, copyright lasts until 70 years from the end of the year of the author's death. In most other countries of the world (including Canada and Australia) copyright lasts until 50 years from the end of the year of the author's death. However, there are many exceptions to this general rule. In particular:

Literary, dramatic and musical works unpublished during the author's lifetime (including letters and private papers)
If the author died before 1 August 1989, copyright lasts until 50 years from the end of the year of first posthumous publication or until 31 December 2039, whichever is the sooner. If life plus 70 years is longer than that period, then the life plus 70 rule will prevail, but not otherwise. Where the author died after 1 August 1989, the period is 70 years from death; and artistic works, whenever the artist died and whether published or not, are protected for life plus 70, with the exception of old photographs, portraits and engravings.

The works of non-European authors
These are protected in Europe only for as long as they are protected in their country of origin.

The copyright status of old works in the USA

This is a complex affair. The Society of Authors' *Quick Guide to Copyright* has a section covering American copyright law as it relates to British authors.

The works of European authors who died between 1 January 1925 and 31 December 1944, which went out of copyright 50 years after their death

On 1 January 1996 these works went back into copyright for what remains of 70 years from their death. The new period of protection is known as 'revived copyright'. You may use revived copyright material without permission from the rights holder but you have to give notice of your intentions and may have to pay a reasonable royalty.

The copyright in the typographical arrangement of a published work is owned by the publisher

This means the work cannot, for example, be photocopied without the publisher's consent. The protection lasts for 25 years from the end of the year of first publication.

There is no copyright in ideas or information. In general, anyone may use published ideas and facts provided they do not copy the precise wording in which they are expressed. But be careful. It is an infringement of copyright to rely on someone else's 'skill and labour' in creating a work. For instance, the second writer is expected to check all facts at their original source.

Protecting material when submitting it to publishers

Copyright is yours, and applies as soon as something is recorded. When sending out a typescript, you should include a copyright line: © [your name] 2002 (although copyright is not forfeited if you forget to do so). Always send your proposal to a specific person by name (not just The Commissioning Editor), with a covering letter making clear that all rights in it are yours, you are showing it to them in confidence, and you would be pleased to discuss terms if they are interested in publishing it. Always send a copy, not the original.

You can establish proof of when your work was created by putting a copy in a sealed, dated envelope, and depositing it with a bank or solicitor – or even by posting it to yourself and storing it in a safe place.

Submitting an article to a journal

Find out what terms the journal will want before, not after, committing yourself. Ideally you should be granting 'first serial rights' only – which means the publisher has the right to be the first to publish the article (in paper and electronic form), but having done so all further rights in it belong to you. But be aware that many journals seek a wider grant of rights. Indeed academic and learned journals frequently seek an outright assignment of copyright from their contributors (something that the writers' unions deplore).

A book publishing contract
You should be keeping your copyright and giving the publisher the 'exclusive licence' to publish the work.

Assigning copyright
If you do have to assign copyright, make sure that there is a termination clause under which you can get your rights back if things go wrong (e.g. you are not paid). Also make sure that no major changes will be made to the text without your agreement; that you will be credited as the author and that your moral right of paternity is asserted (see Moral rights below); and that if the work is exploited in some further way, you will be paid for and credited on the adaptation. It should also be clear that the assignment is not valid until you have received full payment of any monies due to you.

Small complete items like short stories, poems and illustrations
In most cases it will be appropriate to grant only a non-exclusive licence to reproduce the material in a particular anthology or journal, leaving you free to use the work elsewhere.

Moral rights

The main moral rights conferred by the Copyright, Designs and Patents Act 1988 are the right of paternity (the right of an author to be identified whenever a work is published, performed or broadcast: in other words, book writers, scriptwriters, illustrators, and translators must be properly credited); and the right of integrity (the right of an author to object to 'derogatory' treatment of a work. Treatment is 'derogatory' if it amounts to 'distortion or mutilation . . . or is otherwise prejudicial to the honour or reputation of the author . . . ')

While the right of integrity is automatic, the right of paternity must be 'asserted' in writing. The easiest way is to include a suitable clause in your publishing contract – the assertion should also appear in the book, generally under the copyright line.

The rights of paternity and integrity do not apply when the work is published in a newspaper, magazine or similar periodical. Nor do the rights benefit authors contributing to an encyclopaedia, dictionary, yearbook or other collective work of reference.

When do you need permission to make use of someone else's copyright work?

The simple answer is 'On most occasions', but there are exceptions worth noting.

First, there are special provisions covering educational use – the Society of

Authors can give further information on this.

Second, if the quotation can be regarded as 'fair dealing . . . for purposes of criticism or review', whether of the work quoted or of another work, you need not ask permission, but must ensure that either in the text itself or in an acknowledgements page you give the title and the author of the work quoted. It is not possible to give specific guidance on what constitutes 'fair dealing'; it is a matter of impression and common sense according to the circumstances. However, it may be relevant to take into account:

- the length and importance of the quotation;
- the amount quoted in relation to your commentary;
- the extent to which your work competes with or rivals the work quoted;
- the extent to which works quoted are saving you work.

Some years ago the Society of Authors and the Publishers Association stated that they would usually regard as 'fair dealing' the use of a single extract of up to 400 words or a series of extracts (of which none exceeds 300 words) to a total of 800 words from a prose work, or of extracts to a total of 40 lines from a poem, provided that this did not exceed a quarter of the poem. The words must be quoted in the context of 'criticism or review'. While this statement does not have the force of law, it has carried weight with a judge experienced in copyright in a leading infringement case. It does not mean, however, that a quotation 'for purposes of criticism or review' in excess of these limits cannot rank as 'fair dealing' in some circumstances.

For quotations other than those in the above categories you should ask permission to use any 'substantial' extract from a copyright work. The difficulty, once again, is that the meaning of 'substantial' is not defined but is a matter of fact and degree. A short extract may be a vital part of a work. It has often been said that the test is much more about the quality than the quantity of what has been used. A few sentences taken from a long novel or biography are unlikely to a 'substantial part' of the original work, but a few lines of poetry may be. The only safe course, if in doubt, is to ask permission.

Permission should be obtained for the use of any quotation of copyright material, however short, to be included in an anthology. And if you want to quote from song lyrics that are in copyright, beware that permission fees can be much higher than those charged by book publishers.

When reproducing extracts from letters or private papers, remember that they may still be in copyright long after the author's death. The letter itself belongs to the recipient, but the copyright in it belongs to the writer of the letter and, after death, to the writer's estate.

Who grants permission?

With published material, it is best to write first to the publishers of the original edition of the book. Address your letter to the Permissions Department. It is very much in your interest to clear permissions as early as possible. If the publisher cannot help, or if the work is unpublished, the Society of Authors' *Quick Guide to Permissions* (also on its website at www.societyofauthors.org) gives suggestions as to how to track down rights holders.

What will the fee be?

When assessing fees, copyright owners should bear in mind that they may well on occasion be on the other side of the fence, and wishing to quote from other authors' works.

The lower figures in the scales given below may be considered as recommended 'basic minimum fees', with the top figures representing the suggested rates appropriate to major works. Factors such as the importance of the author quoted, the proportion of the original work that the user intends to quote, its value to the author or publisher requesting permission, and the expected size of the print run will most likely be taken into consideration and may affect the fee.

Rates given are for world rights; where more limited rights are required it is usual for fees to be adjusted proportionately. The rate for UK and Commonwealth, or the USA alone, for example, is usually 50 per cent of the world rate, and for a single major country, 25 per cent of the world rate. The Society of Authors can advise on appropriate rates for other territories.

These fees will generally cover just one edition. An additional fee may be required if material is used in a reset or offset edition or in a new format or new binding (e.g. a paperback edition), or if the publisher sub-licenses rights to another publisher.

Prose: £120 to £146 per 1,000 words Where an extract is complete in itself (e.g. a chapter or short story) an additional fee is sometimes charged at half the rate applicable for 1,000 words. It is usual to halve the fees for quotations to be used in critical or scholarly works with low print runs.

Poetry: £90 to £120 for the first ten lines; thereafter £2.10 to £2.30 per line for the next 20 lines and £1.30 to £1.50 per line thereafter The rate per line/poem may be reduced by a third if the poem appears in a literary or scholarly journal, or an anthology which contains more than 40 poems in copyright, or in a book with a print run of less than 1,500 copies. For subsequent editions or for separate publication elsewhere (e.g. in the US, Australasia, Europe, Canada) it is accepted practice to charge further but reduced fees of not less than half of the original fee when new poets are involved. Established poets may well command full fees.

Further information on copyright

The Quick Guide to Copyright and Moral Rights, available from the Society of Authors (free to members, £2 post free in the UK to non-members); *The Quick Guide to Copyright in Artistic Works, including Photographs*, available from the Society (free to members, £2 post free in the UK to non-members).

For details about copyright in the US refer to the Library of Congress

Copyright Office at www.loc.gov/copyright/ or call the Public Information Office on 001 202 707 3000.

Some useful websites when tracing rights holders

ALCS: www.alcs.co.uk/
Association of Authors' Agents: www.agentsassoc.co.uk
British Library: http//blpc.bl.uk/
Location Register of Literary Mss: www.rdg.ac.uk/SerDepts/vl/Lib/
    Projects/locreg.html
National Library of Scotland: www.nls.uk/
US Library of Congress Copyright Office: www.loc.gov/copyright/
WATCH (Writers Artists and Their Copyright Holders):   www.watch-file.com

Kate Pool is the Deputy General Secretary of the Society of Authors.

Literary Societies

Most literary societies exist on a shoestring budget; it is a good idea to enclose an A5 s.a.e. with all correspondence needing a reply.

Margery Allingham Society
2B Higham Green, Winchelsea, East Sussex TN36 4HB
☎01797 222363 Fax 01797 222363
Website www.geocities.com/margeryallingham
Contact *Mrs Pamela Bruxner*
Subscription £14 p.a.

FOUNDED 1988 to promote interest in and study of the works of Margery Allingham. The Society *publishes* two issues of the newsletter, *The Bottle Street Gazette*, per year. Contributions welcome. Two social events a year. Open membership.

Jane Austen Society
22 Belmont Grove, Bedhampton, Havant, Hampshire PO9 3PU
☎023 9247 5855
Email rosemary@sndc.demon.co.uk
Website www.sndc.demon.co.uk/jas.htm
Membership Secretary *Mrs Rosemary Culley*
Subscription UK: £5 (Student);
£10 (Annual); £15 (Joint); £30 (Corporate);
£150 (Life); Overseas: £12 (Annual);
£18 (Joint); £33 (Corporate); £180 (Life)

FOUNDED 1940 to promote interest in and enjoyment of Jane Austen's novels and letters. The society has branches in Bath & Bristol, Midlands, London, Oxford, Kent and Hampshire. There are independent Societies in North America and Australia.

The Baskerville Hounds
6 Bramham Moor, Hill Head, Fareham, Hampshire PO14 3RU
☎01329 667325
Chairman *Philip Weller*
Subscription £6 p.a.

FOUNDED 1989. An international Sherlock Holmes society specialising solely in studies of *The Hound of the Baskervilles* and its Dartmoor associations. *Publishes* an annual journal and specialist monographs. It also organises many social functions, usually on Dartmoor. Open membership.

The BB Society
8 Park Road, Solihull, West Midlands B91 3SU
☎01564 741847
Email bryan@barbryn.co.uk
Chairman *Bill Humphreys*
Secretary *Bryan Holden* (at address above)
Subscription £10 (Individual); £17.50
(Family); £50 (Corporate); £5 (Unwaged)

FOUNDED in 2000 to bring together the fans of the country writer BB (Denys Watkins-Pitchford). The Society holds regular meetings, events and *publishes* newsletters and an annual journal.

The Beckford Society
15 Healey Street, London NW1 8SR
☎020 7267 7750 Fax 01985 213239
Email Sidney.Blackmore@btinternet.com
Secretary *Sidney Blackmore*
Subscription £10 (min.) p.a.

FOUNDED 1995 to promote an interest in the life and works of William Beckford (1760–1844) and his circle. Encourages Beckford studies and scholarship through exhibitions, lectures and publications, including an annual journal, *The Beckford Journal*, and occasional newsletters.

Thomas Lovell Beddoes Society
11 Laund Nook, Belper, Derbyshire DE56 1GY
☎01773 828066 Fax 01773 828066
Email john@beddoes.demon.co.uk
Website
www.nortexinfo.net/McDaniel/tlb.htm
Chairman *John Lovell Beddoes*
Secretary *Annette Eley*

Formed to research the life, times and work of poet Thomas Lovell Beddoes (1803–1849), encourage relevant publications, further the reading and appreciation of his works by a wider public and liaise with other groups and organisations. *Publishes* an annual newsletter.

Arnold Bennett Society
106 Scotia Road, Burslem, Stoke on Trent ST6 4ET
☎01782 816311

Website www.arnoldbennett.co.uk

Secretary *Mrs Jean Potter*
Subscription £7 (Single); £9 (Family) plus
£2 for membership outside the EEC

Aims to promote interest in the life and works of
'Five Towns' author Arnold Bennett and other
North Staffordshire writers. Annual dinner.
Regular functions in and around Burslem plus
annual seminar in London. Three newsletters a
year. Open membership.

E.F. Benson Society
The Old Coach House, High Street, Rye,
East Sussex TN31 7JF
☎01797 223114

Secretary *Allan Downend*
Subscription £7.50 (UK/Europe);
£12.50 (Overseas)

FOUNDED 1985 to promote the life and work
of E.F. Benson and the Benson family.
Organises social and literary events, exhibitions, talks and Benson interest walks in Rye.
Publishes a quarterly newsletter and annual
journal, *The Dodo*, postcards and reprints of
E.F. Benson articles and short stories in a series
called 'Bensoniana'. Holds an archive which
includes the Seckersen Collection (transcrip-
tions of the Benson collection at the Bodleian
Library in Oxford).

E.F. Benson/The Tilling Society
5 Friars Bank, Guestling, Hastings, East Sussex
TN35 4EJ Fax 01424 813237
Contact *Cynthia Reavell*
Subscription Full starting membership
(members receive all back newsletters)
£30 (UK); £34 (Overseas); or Annual
Membership (members receive only current
year's newsletters) £8 (UK); £10 (Overseas).

FOUNDED 1982 for the exchange of news,
information and speculation about E.F. Benson,
his works and, in particular, his *Mapp & Lucia*
novels. Readings, talks and substantial biannual
newsletter. Annual get-together in Rye/
'Tilling'. Acts as a clearing house for every sort
of news and activity concerning E.F. Benson.

The Betjeman Society
35 Eaton Court, Boxgrove Avenue,
Guildford, Surrey GU1 1XH
☎01483 560882

Honorary Secretary *John Heald*
Subscription £10 (Individual); £12
(Family); £3 (Student); £3 additional for
Overseas members

Aims to promote the study and appreciation of
the work and life of Sir John Betjeman. Annual
programme includes poetry readings, lectures,
discussions, visits to places associated with
Betjeman, and various social events. Meetings
are held in London and other centres. Regular
newsletter and annual journal, *The Betjemanian*.

The Bewick Society
c/o The Hancock Museum, Newcastle upon
Tyne NE2 4PT
☎01207 562196
Email juneholmes@lineone.net
Membership Secretary *June Holmes*
Subscription £7 p.a. (Individual);
£10 (Family)

FOUNDED 1988 to promote an interest in the
life and work of Thomas Bewick, wood-
engraver and naturalist (1753–1828). Organises
related events and meetings, and is associated
with the Bewick birthplace museum.

Birmingham Central Literary Association
23 Arden Grove, Ladywood, Birmingham
B16 8HG
☎0121 454 9352
Email bakerbrum@netscapeonline.co.uk
Contact *The Secretary*

Holds fortnightly meetings in central Birmingham to discuss the lives and work of authors
and poets. Holds an annual dinner to celebrate
Shakespeare's birthday.

The George Borrow Society
60 Upper Marsh Road, Warminster, Wiltshire
BA12 9PN
Email borrow@mskillman.freeserve.co.uk
Website www.clough5.fsnet.co.uk/gb.html
Chairman/Bulletin Editor *Dr Ann M. Ridler*
Membership Secretary *Michael Skillman*
Honorary Treasurer *David Pattinson*
Bulletin Editor: St Mary's Cottage, 61 Thame
Road, Warborough, Wallingford, Oxford
OX10 7EA ☎01865 858379 Fax 01865
858575
Subscription £12.50 p.a.

FOUNDED 1991 to promote knowledge of the
life and works of George Borrow (1803–81),
traveller, linguist and writer. The Society holds
biennial conferences (with published proceedings) and informal intermediate gatherings, all at
places associated with Borrow. *Publishes* the
George Borrow Bulletin twice yearly, containing

scholarly articles, reviews of publications relating to Borrow, reports of past events and news of forthcoming events. Member of the **Alliance of Literary Societies** and corporate associate member of the Centre of East Anglian Studies (CEAS) at the University of East Anglia, Norwich (Borrow's home city for many years).

Elinor Brent-Dyer

See **Friends of the Chalet School** and **The New Chalet Club**

British Fantasy Society

201 Reddish Road, South Reddish, Stockport, Cheshire SK5 7HR
☎0161 476 5368 (after 6pm)
Email faliol@yahoo.com
Website www.britishfantasysociety.org.uk

President *Ramsey Campbell*
Chairman *Gary Couzens*
Secretary *Robert Parkinson*
Subscription from £25 p.a. (apply to Secretary.)

FOUNDED 1971 for devotees of fantasy, horror and related fields in literature, art and the cinema. *Publishes* a regular newsletter with information and reviews of new books and films, plus related fiction and non-fiction magazines. Annual conference at which the **British Fantasy Awards** are presented. These awards are voted on by the membership and are not an open competition.

The Brontë Society

Brontë Parsonage Museum, Haworth, Keighley, West Yorkshire BD22 8DR
☎01535 642323   Fax 01535 647131
Email bronte@bronte.prestel.co.uk
Website www.bronte.org.uk

Contact *Membership Secretary*
Subscription £17.50 p.a. (UK/Europe); £7.50 (Student); £5 (Junior – up to age 14); £30 (Overseas); Joint subscriptions available

FOUNDED 1893. Aims and activities include the preservation of manuscripts and other objects related to or connected with the Brontë family, and the maintenance and development of the museum and library at Haworth. The society holds regular meetings, lectures and exhibitions; and *publishes* information relating to the family and a biannual *Gazette*. Freelance contributions for either publication should be sent to the Publications Secretary at the address above. Members can receive the journal, *Brontë Studies*, at a reduced subscription of £12 p.a.

The Rupert Brooke Society

The Orchard, 45/47 Mill Way, Grantchester, Cambridge CB3 9ND
☎01223 845788   Fax 01223 842331
Email rbs@callan.co.uk
Website www.rupert-brooke-society.com

Contact *Robin Callan*
Subscription £7.50 (UK); £10.50 (Overseas)

FOUNDED in 1999 to foster an interest in the work of Rupert Brooke, help preserve places associated with him and to increase knowledge and appreciation of the village of Grantchester. Members receive a newsletter with information about events, new books and activities.

The Browning Society

163 Wembley Hill Road, Wembley Park, Middlesex HA9 8EL
☎020 8904 8401

Honorary Secretary *Ralph Ensz*
Subscription £15 p.a.

FOUNDED 1969 to promote an interest in the lives and poetry of Robert and Elizabeth Barrett Browning. Meetings are arranged in the London area, one of which occurs in December at Westminster Abbey to commemorate Robert Browning's death.

The John Buchan Society

Greenmantle, Main Street, Kings Newton, Melbourne, Derbyshire DE73 1BX
☎01332 865315
Email moonfleet@greenmantle63.freeserve.co.uk

Secretary *Kenneth Hillier*
Subscription £10 (Full/Overseas); £4 (Associate); £6 (Junior); £20 (Corporate); £90 (Life)

To perpetuate the memory of John Buchan and to promote a wider understanding of his life and works. Holds regular meetings and social gatherings, *publishes* a journal, and liaises with the John Buchan Centre at Broughton in the Scottish borders.

The Robert Burns World Federation Ltd

Dean Castle Country Park Dower House, Kilmarnock, Strathclyde KA3 1XB
☎01563 572469   Fax 01563 572469
Email robertburnsfederation@kilmarnock26.freeserve.co.uk

Chief Executive *Shirley Bell*
Subscription £20 p.a.(Individual); £25 (Family); £40 (Club subscription)

FOUNDED 1885 to encourage interest in the life and work of Robert Burns and keep alive the old Scottish Tongue. The Society's interests go beyond Burns himself in its commitment to the development of Scottish literature, music and arts in general. *Publishes* the quarterly *Burns Chronicle/Burnsian.*

The Byron Society

Byron House, 6 Gertrude Street, London SW10 0JN
☎020 7352 5112

Honorary Director, Byron Society
  Mrs Elma Dangerfield CBE
Subscription £20 p.a.

FOUNDED 1876; revived in 1971. Aims to promote knowledge and discussion of Lord Byron's life and works, and those of his contemporaries, through lectures, readings, concerts, performances and international conferences. *Publishes* annually in April *The Byron Journal*, a scholarly journal – £5.50 plus £2 postage.

Randolph Caldecott Society

Clatterwick House, Little Leigh, Northwich, Cheshire CW8 4RJ
☎01606 891303 (day)/781731 (evening)

Honorary Secretary *Kenneth N. Oultram*
Subscription £7–£10 p.a.

FOUNDED 1983 to promote the life and work of artist/book illustrator Randolph Caldecott. Meetings held in the spring and autumn in Caldecott's birthplace, Chester. Guest speakers, outings, newsletter, exchanges with the society's American counterpart. (Caldecott died and was buried in St Augustine, Florida.) A medal in his memory is awarded annually in the US for children's book illustration.

The Carlyle Society, Edinburgh

Dept of English Literature, The University of Edinburgh, David Hume Tower, George Square, Edinburgh EH8 9JX
Fax 0131 650 6898
Email ian.campbell@ed.ac.uk

President *Ian Campbell*
Subscription £2 p.a.; £10 (Life); $20 (US)

FOUNDED 1929 to examine the lives of Thomas Carlyle and his wife Jane, their writings, contemporaries, and influences. Meetings are held about six times a year and occasional papers are published annually. Enquiries should be addressed to the President of the Society at the address above or to the Secretary at 16a Blackford Road, Edinburgh EH9 2DS.

Lewis Carroll Society

69 Cromwell Road, Hertford, Hertfordshire SG13 7DP
☎01992 584530
Email alanwhite@tesco.net
Website aznet.co.uk/lcs

Secretary *Alan White*
Subscription Individual: £13 (UK); £15 (Europe); £17 (Outside Europe); £10 (Retired rate); £2 (Additional family members); Institutions: £26 (UK); £28 (Europe); £30 (Outside Europe)

FOUNDED 1969 to bring together people with an interest in Charles Dodgson and promote research into his life and works. *Publishes* bi-annual journal *The Carrollian*, featuring scholarly articles and reviews; a newsletter (*Bandersnatch*) which reports on Carrollian events and the Society's activities; and *The Lewis Carroll Review*, a book reviewing journal. Regular meetings held in London with lectures, talks, outings, etc.

Lewis Carroll Society (Daresbury)

Clatterwick House, Little Leigh, Northwich, Cheshire CW8 4RJ
☎01606 891303 (day)/781731 (evening)

Honorary Secretary *Kenneth N. Oultram*
Subscription £5 p.a.

FOUNDED 1970. To promote the life and work of Charles Dodgson, author of the world-famous *Alice's Adventures*. Holds meetings in the spring and autumn in Carroll's birthplace, Daresbury, Cheshire. Guest speakers and theatre visits. Appoints annually a 10-year-old 'Alice' who is available for public invitations.

The New Chalet Club

94 Bangor Street, Y Felinheli, Gwynedd LL56 4PJ
Website users.powernet.co.uk/tanquen

Membership Secretary *Sera Roberts*
Subscription £18 p.a. (UK under 18); £10 (UK Adults & Europe); £12 (RoW)

FOUNDED 1995 for all those with an interest in the books of Elinor Brent-Dyer. *Publishes* a quarterly journal and occasional supplements, including *The A-Z of Chalet Characters*, and regularly holds local and national meetings.

Friends of the Chalet School

4 Rock Terrace, Coleford, Bath, Somerset BA3 5NF
☎01373 812705 Fax 01373 813517
Email focs@rockterrace.co.uk
Website www.rockterrace.demon.co.uk/FOCS

Contacts *Ann Mackie-Hunter, Clarissa Cridland*
Subscription £7.50 p.a.; £6 (Under–18);
   Outside UK: details on application

FOUNDED 1989 to promote the works of
Elinor Brent-Dyer. The society has members
worldwide; *publishes* four magazines a year and
runs a lending library.

The Chesterton Society UK
11 Lawrence Leys, Bloxham, Near Banbury,
Oxfordshire OX15 4NU
☎01295 720869/07747 786428 (mobile)
Honorary Secretary *Robert Hughes, KHS*
Subscription £12.50 p.a.

FOUNDED 1964 to promote the ideas and writings of G.K. Chesterton.

The Children's Books History Society
25 Field Way, Hoddesdon, Hertfordshire
EN11 0QN
☎01992 464885   Fax 01992 464885
Email cbhs@abcgarrett.demon.co.uk
Membership Secretary *Mrs Pat Garrett*
Subscription £10 p.a. (UK/Europe); write
for Overseas subscription details

ESTABLISHED 1969. Aims to promote an appreciation of children's books and to study their
history, bibliography and literary content. The
Society holds approximately six meetings per
year in London and a summer meeting to a collection, or to a location with a children's book
connection. Three substantial newsletters issued
annually, also an occasional paper. The Society
constitutes the British branch of the Friends of
the Osborne and Lillian H. Smith Collections in
Toronto, Canada, and also liaises with **CILIP**
(formerly The Library Association). In 1990, the
Society established its biennial Harvey Darton
Award for a book, published in English, which
extends our knowledge of some aspect of British
children's literature of the past. 2002 winner:
Nigel Tattersfield *John Bewick, engraver on wood.*

The John Clare Society
The Stables, 1a West Street, Helpston,
Peterborough PE6 7DU
☎01733 252678   Fax 01733 252678
Email moyse.helpston@talk21.com
Website vzone.virgin.net/linda.curry/
   jclaresociety.htm *or*
   human.ntu.ac.uk/clare/clare.html
Honorary Secretary *Peter Moyse*
Subscription £9.50 (Individual);
£12.50 (Joint); £7.50 (Fully Retired);

£9.50 (Joint Retired); £10 (Group/Library);
£3 (Student, Full-time); £12.50 sterling
draft/$25 (Overseas)

FOUNDED 1981 to promote a wider appreciation of the life and works of the poet John
Clare (1793–1864). Organises an annual festival
in Helpston in July; arranges exhibitions, poetry
readings and conferences; and *publishes* an
annual society journal and quarterly newsletter.

William Cobbett Society
10 Grenehurst Way, Petersfield, Hampshire
☎01730 262060
Chairman *Molly Townsend*
Subscription £8 p.a.

Also: Boynell House, Outlands Lane,
Curdridge, Southampton SO30 2HR
☎01489 782453
Contact *David Chun*

FOUNDED in 1976 to bring together those with
an interest in the life and works of William
Cobbett (1763–1835) and to extend the interest
to a wider public. Society activities include an
annual Memorial Lecture; publication of an
annual journal (*Cobbett's New Register*) containing
articles on various aspects of his life and times; an
annual expedition retracing routes taken by
Cobbett on his Rural Rides in the 1820s; visits
to his birthplace and his tomb in Farnham,
Surrey. In association with the Society, the
Museum of Farnham holds bound volumes of
Cobbett's *Political Register*, a large collection of
Cobbett's works, books about Cobbett, and has
various Cobbett artefacts on display.

The Friends of Coleridge
87 Richmond Road, Montpelier, Bristol
BS6 5EP
☎0117 942 6366
Email gcddavidson@compuserve.com
Membership Secretary *Shirley Watters*
   (11 Castle Street, Nether Stowey, Somerset
   TA5 1LN)
Editor (Coleridge Bulletin) *Graham Davidson*
Subscription £10 (UK); £15/£20 (Overseas)

FOUNDED in 1987 to advance knowledge about
the life, work and times of Samuel Taylor
Coleridge and his circle, and to support his
Nether Stowey Cottage, with the National
Trust, as a centre of Coleridge interest. Holds
study weekends and a biennial international academic conference. *Publishes The Coleridge Bulletin*
biannually. Short articles on Coleridge-related
topics may be sent to the editor at the (Bristol)
address above.

Wilkie Collins Society
4 Ernest Gardens, London W4 3QU
Email paul@wilkiecollins.org
Website www.wilkiecollins.org
Chairman *Andrew Gasson*
Membership Secretary *Paul Lewis* (at address above)
Subscription £10 (UK/Europe); £16 (RoW – remittance must be made in UK sterling)

FOUNDED 1980 to provide information on and promote interest in the life and works of Wilkie Collins, one of the first English novelists to deal with the detection of crime. *The Woman in White* appeared in 1860 and *The Moonstone* in 1868. *Publishes* newsletters, reprints of Collins' work and an annual academic journal.

The Arthur Conan Doyle Society
PO Box 1360, Ashcroft, British Columbia Canada V0K 1A0
☎001 250 453 2045 Fax 001 250 453 2075
Email ashtree@ash-tree.bc.ca
Website www.ash-tree.bc.ca/acdsocy.html
Joint Organisers *Christopher Roden, Barbara Roden*
Membership Contact R. *Dixon-Smith*, 59 Stonefield, Bar Hill, Cambridge CB3 8TE
Subscription £16 (UK); £16 (Overseas); Family rates available

FOUNDED 1989 to promote the study and discussion of the life and works of Sir Arthur Conan Doyle. Occasional meetings, functions and visits. *Publishes* a biannual journal together with reprints of Conan Doyle's writings.

Joseph Conrad Society (UK)
c/o P.O.S.K., 238–246 King Street, Hammersmith, London W6 0RF
Fax 020 8240 4365
Email AllanSimmons@compuserve.com
Website www.bathspa.ac.uk/conrad
Secretary *Hugh Epstein*
Treasurer/Editor (The Conradian) *Allan Simmons*
Subscription £15 p.a. (Individual); £20 p.a. (Institutions)

FOUNDED in 1973 to promote the study of the works and life of Joseph Conrad (1857–1924). A scholarly society, supported by the Polish Library at the Polish Cultural Association where a substantial library of Conrad texts and criticism is held in the Study Centre. *Publishes* a journal of Conrad studies – *The Conradian* – biannually and holds an annual International Conference in the first week of July.

The Rhys Davies Trust
10 Heol Don, Whitchurch, Cardiff CF14 2AU
☎029 2062 3359 Fax 029 2052 9202
Contact *Professor Meic Stephens*

FOUNDED 1990 to perpetuate the literary reputation of the Welsh prose writer, Rhys Davies (1901–78), and to foster Welsh writing in English. Organises competitions in association with other bodies such as the **Welsh Academy**, puts up plaques on buildings associated with Welsh writers, offers grant-aid for book production, etc.

The Walter de la Mare Society
Flat 15, Trinity Court, Vicarage Road, Twickenham, Middlesex TW2 5TY
Website www.bluetree.co.uk/wdlmsociety
Honorary President *John Bayley, CBE*
Honorary Secretary & Treasurer *Julie de la Mare*
Subscription £15 p.a.

FOUNDED in 1997 to honour the memory of Walter de la Mare; to promote the study and deepen the appreciation of his works; to widen the readership of his works; to facilitate research by making available the widest range of contacts and information about de la Mare; and to encourage and facilitate new Walter de la Mare publications. Produces a regular newsletter and organises events. Membership information from the address above.

The Dickens Fellowship
48 Doughty Street, London WC1N 2LX
☎020 7405 2127 Fax 020 7831 5175
Email arwilliams33@compuserve.com
Website www.dickens.fellowship.btinternet.co.uk
Joint Honorary General Secretaries *Mrs Thelma Grove, Dr Tony Williams*
Subscription £5 (First year); £8.50 (Renewal)

FOUNDED 1902. The Society's particular aims and objectives are: to bring together lovers of Charles Dickens; to spread the message of Dickens, his love of humanity ('the keynote of all his work'); to remedy social injustice for the poor and oppressed; to assist in the preservation of material and buildings associated with Dickens. Annual conference. *Publishes* journal called *The Dickensian* (available at special rate to members) and organises a full programme of lectures, discussions, visits and conducted walks throughout the year. Branches worldwide.

Early English Text Society
Christ Church, Oxford OX1 1DP
Fax 01865 286581

Executive Secretary *R.F.S. Hamer*
(at address above)
Editorial Secretary *Dr H.L. Spencer*
(at Exeter College, Oxford OX1 3DP)
Membership Secretary *Mrs J.M. Watkinson*
(at 12 North End, Durham DH1 4NJ)
Subscription £15 p.a. (UK); $30 (US);
$35 (Canada)

FOUNDED 1864. Concerned with the publication of early English texts. Members receive annual publications (one or two a year) or may select titles from the backlist in lieu.

The George Eliot Fellowship
71 Stepping Stones Road, Coventry,
Warwickshire CV5 8JT
☎024 7659 2231

Contact *Mrs Kathleen Adams*
Subscription £10 p.a.; £100 (Life);
Concessions for pensioners

FOUNDED 1930. Exists to honour George Eliot and promote interest in her life and works. Readings, memorial lecture, birthday luncheon and functions. Issues a quarterly newsletter and an annual journal. Awards an annual prize for a George Eliot essay.

The John Meade Falkner Society
Greenmantle, Main Street, Kings Newton,
Melbourne, Derbyshire DE73 1BX
☎01332 865315
Email moonfleet@greenmantle63.
freeserve.co.uk

Secretary *Kenneth Hillier*
Subscription £5

FOUNDED in 1999 to promote the appreciation and study of John Meade Falkner's life, times and works. Produces three newsletters a year and an annual journal.

Folly (Fans of Light Literature for the Young)
21 Warwick Road, Pokesdown,
Bournemouth, Dorset BH7 6JW
☎01202 432562
Email folly@sims.abel.co.uk

Contact *Mrs Sue Sims*
Subscription £7.50 p.a. (UK); £9 (Europe);
£11 (Worldwide)

FOUNDED 1990 to promote interest in a wide variety of children's authors – with a bias towards writers of girls' books and school stories. *Publishes* three magazines a year.

C.S. Forester Society
11 Park Town, Oxford OX2 6SN
☎01865 515292 Fax 01865 515292
Email csforester@hotmail.com
Website www.csforester.com

Contact *Colin Blogg*
Subscription £5 or $10 p.a.

FOUNDED in 1999 to provide an informal forum to promote knowledge and enjoyment of the works and life of C.S. Forester; to write a definitive bibliography and, ultimately, a biography. *Publishes* a newsletter 3–4 times a year containing contributions from members and holds meetings for film shows, readings and lectures.

The Franco-Midland Hardware Company
6 Bramham Moor, Hill Head, Fareham,
Hampshire PO14 3RU
☎01329 667325
Email franco.midland@btinternet.com
Website www.btinternet.com/~sherlock.fmhc

Chairman *Philip Weller*
Subscription £12 p.a. (UK); £13 (Europe);
£15 (RoW)

FOUNDED 1989. 'The world's leading Sherlock Holmes correspondence study group and the most active Holmesian society in Britain.' *Publishes* annual journal, a biannual news magazine and an individual case study as a subscription package. Also publishes at least two specialist monographs a year. It provides certificated self-study courses and organises monthly functions at Holmes-associated locations. Open membership.

The Friends of Shandy Hall (The Laurence Sterne Trust)
Shandy Hall, Coxwold, York YO61 4AD
☎01347 868465 Fax 01347 868465
Website www.shandy-hall.org.uk

Honorary Secretary *Mrs J. Monkman*
Subscription £7 (Annual); £70 (Life)

Promotes interest in the works of Laurence Sterne and aims to preserve the house in which they were created (open to the public). *Publishes* annual journal, *The Shandean*. An Annual Memorial Lecture is delivered at Shandy Hall each summer.

The Gaskell Society

Far Yew Tree House, Over Tabley,
Knutsford, Cheshire WA16 0HN
☎01565 634668
Email JoanLeach@aol.com
Website gaskellsociety.users.btopenworld.com
   and lang.nagoya-u.ac.jp/~matsuoka/
      EG-Society.html
Honorary Secretary *Joan Leach*
Subscription £12 p.a.; £16 (Corporate &
   Overseas)

FOUNDED 1985 to promote and encourage the
study and appreciation of the life and works of
Elizabeth Cleghorn Gaskell. Meetings held in
Knutsford, Manchester, Bath and London; residential study weekends and visits; annual journal
and biannual newsletter. On alternate years holds
either a residential weekend conference or overseas visit.

The Ghost Story Society

PO Box 1360, Ashcroft, British Columbia
Canada V0K 1A0
☎001 250 453 2045 Fax 001 250 453 2075
Email ashtree@ash-tree.bc.ca
Website www.ash-tree.bc.ca/GSShtml
Joint Organisers *Barbara Roden,*
   Christopher Roden
Subscription UK: £16 (Surface mail)/
   £18 (Airmail); $27.50 (US); $34 (Canadian)

FOUNDED 1988. Devoted mainly to supernatural
fiction in the literary tradition of M.R. James,
Walter de la Mare, Algernon Blackwood, E.F.
Benson, A.N.L. Munby, R.H. Malden, etc.
Publishes a thrice-yearly journal, *All Hallows*,
which includes new fiction in the genre and
non-fiction of relevance to the genre.

Graham Greene Birthplace Trust

Rhenigidale, Ivy House Lane, Berkhamsted,
Hertfordshire HP4 2PP
☎01442 865158
Email secretary@grahamgreenebt.org
Website www.grahamgreenebt.org
Secretary *Ken Sherwood*
Subscription £7.50 (UK, £18 for 3 years);
   £10 (Europe, £25); £14 (RoW, £37)

FOUNDED on 2 October 1997, the 93rd anniversary of Graham Greene's birth, to promote the
appreciation and study of his works. *Publishes* a
quarterly newsletter and occasional papers.
Organises the annual four-day Graham Greene
Festival during the weekend nearest to the
writer's birthday (2nd October) and adminis-
trates the Graham Greene Memorial Awards.

Rider Haggard Society

27 Deneholm, Whitley Bay, Tyne & Wear
NE25 9AU
☎0191 252 4516 Fax 0191 252 4516
Email RB27Allen@aol.com
Website www.riderhaggardsociety.org.uk
Contact *Roger Allen*
Subscription £9 p.a. (UK); £10 (Overseas)

FOUNDED 1985 to promote appreciation of the
life and works of Sir Henry Rider Haggard,
English novelist, 1856–1925. News/books
exchange and meetings every two years.

James Hanley Network

Old School House, George Green Road,
George Green, Wexham, Buckinghamshire
SL3 6BJ
☎01753 578632
Email gostick@altavista.net
Website www.jameshanley.mcmail.com/
   index.htm
Network Coordinator *Chris Gostick*

An informal international association FOUNDED
in 1997 for all those interested in exploring and
publicising the works and contribution to literature of the novelist and dramatist James
Hanley (1901–1985). *Publishes* an annual newsletter. Occasional conferences are planned for the
future. All enquiries welcome.

The Thomas Hardy Society

PO Box 1438, Dorchester, Dorset DT1 1YH
☎01305 251501 Fax 01305 251501
Honorary Secretary *Mrs Olive Blackburn*
Subscription £18 (Individual); £25
   (Corporate); £22.50 (Individual Overseas);
   £30 (Corporate Overseas)

FOUNDED 1967 to promote the reading and
study of the works and life of Thomas Hardy.
Thrice-yearly journal, events and a biennial
conference.

The Henty Society

Old Foxes, Kelshall, Royston, Hertfordshire
SG8 9SE
☎01763 287208
Honorary Secretary *Mrs Ann J. King*
Subscription £13 p.a. (UK); £16 (Overseas)

FOUNDED 1977 to study the life and work of
George Alfred Henty, and to publish research,
bibliographical data and lesser-known works,
namely short stories. Organises conferences and
social gatherings in the UK and North America,
and *publishes* bulletins to members. Published in

1996: *G.A. Henty (1832–1902) a Bibliographical Study* by Peter Newbolt.

James Hilton Society
49 Beckingthorpe Drive, Bottesford,
Nottingham NG13 0DN
Honorary Secretary *J.R. Hammond*
Subscription £10 (UK/EU); £7 Concessions

FOUNDED 2000 to promote interest in the life and work of novelist and scriptwriter James Hilton (1900–1954). *Publishes The James Hilton Newsletter* (quarterly) and organises meetings and conferences.

Sherlock Holmes Society
(Northern Musgraves)
Hallas Lodge, Greenside Lane, Cullingworth,
Bradford, West Yorkshire BD13 5AP
☎01535 273468
Email hallaslodge@btinternet.com
Contacts *John Hall, Anne Jordan*
Subscription £17 p.a. (UK)

FOUNDED 1987 to promote enjoyment and study of Sir Arthur Conan Doyle's Sherlock Holmes through publications and meetings. One of the largest Sherlock Holmes societies in Great Britain. Honorary members include Bert Coules, Richard Lancelyn Green, Edward Hardwicke, Clive Merrison and Douglas Wilmer. Past honorary members: Dame Jean Conan Doyle, Peter Cushing, Jeremy Brett and Michael Williams. Open membership. Lectures, presentations and consultation on matters relating to Holmes and Conan Doyle available.

Sherlock Holmes
See **The Franco-Midland Hardware Company**

Hopkins Society
35 Manor Park, Gloddaeth Avenue,
Llandudno LL30 2SE
☎01492 878334
Email carolinemay@hopkinsoc.freeserve.co.uk
Website www.hopkinsoc.freeserve.co.uk
Contact *Ambrose Boothby*
Subscription £7 p.a. (UK); £10 (Overseas)

FOUNDED 1990 to celebrate the life and work of Gerard Manley Hopkins; to inform members of any publications, courses or events about the poet. Holds an annual lecture on Hopkins in the spring; produces two newsletters a year; sponsors and organises educational projects based on Hopkins' life and works.

Housman Society
80 New Road, Bromsgrove, Worcestershire
B60 2LA
☎01527 874136 Fax 01527 837274
Email jimpage@btinternet.com
Website www.housman-society.co.uk
Contact *Jim Page*
Subscription £10 (UK); £12.50 (Overseas)

FOUNDED 1973 to promote knowledge and appreciation of the lives and work of A.E. Housman and other members of his family, and to promote the cause of literature and poetry. Sponsors a lecture at the **Hay Festival** each year under the title of 'The Name and Nature of Poetry'. *Publishes* an annual journal and biannual newsletter.

W.W. Jacobs Appreciation Society
3 Roman Road, Southwick, West Sussex
BN42 4TP
☎01273 871017 Fax 01273 871017
Contact *A.R. James*

FOUNDED 1988 to encourage and promote the enjoyment of the works of W.W. Jacobs, and stimulate research into his life and works. No subscription charge. Material available for purchase includes *W.W. Jacobs*, a biography published in 1999, price £12, post paid, and *WWJ Book Hunter's Field Guide*, a narrative biography published in 2001, price £6, post paid.

Richard Jefferies Society
Eidsvoll, Bedwells Heath, Boars Hill, Oxford
OX1 5JE
☎01865 735678
Website www.bath.ac.uk/~lissmc/rjeffs.htm
Honorary Secretary *Lady Phyllis Treitel*
Membership Secretary *Mrs Margaret Evans*
Subscription £7 p.a. (Individual); £8 (Joint);
    Life membership for those over 50

FOUNDED 1950 to promote understanding of the work of Richard Jefferies, nature/country writer, novelist and mystic (1848–87). Produces newsletters, reports and an annual journal; organises talks, discussions and readings. Library and archives. Assists in maintaining the museum in Jefferies' birthplace at Coate near Swindon. Membership applications should be sent to *Margaret Evans*, 23 Hardwell Close, Grove, Nr Wantage, Oxon OX12 0BN.

Jerome K. Jerome Society
c/o Fraser Wood, Mayo and Pinson,
15/16 Lichfield Street, Walsall, West Midlands
WS1 1TS
☎01922 629000 Fax 01922 721065

Email tonygray@jkj.demon.co.uk
Website www.jeromekjerome.com
Honorary Secretary *Tony Gray*
Subscription £7 p.a. (Ordinary);
£25 (Corporate); £6 (Joint); £2.50 (Under 21/Over 65)

FOUNDED 1984 to stimulate interest in Jerome K. Jerome's life and works (1859–1927). One of the Society's principal activities is the support of a small museum in the author's birthplace, Walsall. Meetings, lectures, events and a twice-yearly newsletter, *Idle Thoughts*. Annual dinner in Walsall near Jerome's birth date (2nd May).

The Captain W.E. Johns Appreciation Society
Nottingham meeting: Wendover, Windy Harbour Lane, Bromley Cross, Bolton, Lancashire BL7 9AP
☎01204 306051
Email Biggles.uk@LineOne.net
Website website.lineone.net/~biggles.uk

Contacts *Mrs A. Thompson* (Nottingham), *Joy Tilley* (Hertford, Tel 01785 240299)
Hertford meeting: 8 Holmes Close, Castlefields, Stafford ST16 1AR

Society for the appreciation of W.E. Johns, creator of Biggles. Meets twice a year in Nottingham and Hertford. See contacts above.

Johnson Society
Johnson Birthplace Museum, Breadmarket Street, Lichfield, Staffordshire WS13 6LG
☎01543 264972
Hon. General Secretary *Mrs Norma Hooper*
Subscription £7.50 p.a.; £10 (Joint)

FOUNDED 1910 to encourage the study of the life, works and times of Samuel Johnson (1709–1784) and his contemporaries. The Society is committed to the preservation of the Johnson Birthplace Museum and Johnson memorials.

Johnson Society of London
255 Baring Road, Grove Park, London SE12 0BQ
☎020 8851 0173
Email JSL@nbbl.demon.co.uk
Website www.nbbl.demon.co.uk/index.html

President *Mary, Viscountess Eccles, PhD, DLitt*
Honorary Secretary *Mrs Z.E. O'Donnell*
Subscription £12.50 p.a.; £15 (Joint)

FOUNDED 1928 to promote the knowledge and appreciation of Dr Samuel Johnson and his works. *Publishes* an annual journal, *New Rambler* and occasional newsletter. Regular meetings from October to April in the meeting room of Wesley's Chapel, City Road, London on the second Saturday of each month, and a commemoration ceremony around the anniversary of Johnson's death (December) held in Westminster Abbey.

The Just William Society
7 Church Lane, Costock, Loughborough LE12 6UZG
Secretary/Treasurer *Paula Cross*
Subscription £7 p.a. (UK); £10 (Overseas); £5 (Juvenile/Student); £15 (Family)

FOUNDED 1994 to further knowledge of Richmal Crompton's *William* and *Jimmy* books. An annual 'William' meeting is held in April. The Honorary President of the Society is Richmal Crompton's niece, Richmal Ashbee. (NB Change of address for the Secretary/Treasurer from 1 September 2002: Easter Badbea, Dundonnell, Wester Ross IV23 2QX.)

The Keats–Shelley Memorial Association (Inc)
(Registered office): 1 Satchwell Walk, Royal Priors, Leamington Spa, Warwickshire CV32 4QE
☎01926 427400 Fax 01926 335133
Contact *Honorary Secretary*
Subscription £10 p.a.

FOUNDED 1903 to promote appreciation of the works of Keats and Shelley, and their circle. One of the Society's main tasks is the preservation of 26 Piazza di Spagna in Rome as a memorial to the British Romantic poets in Italy, particularly Keats and Shelley. *Publishes* an annual review of Romantic Studies called the *Keats-Shelley Review*, arranges events and lectures for Friends and promotes bursaries and competitive writing on Romantic Studies (see **Keats-Shelley Prize** under **Prizes**). The *Review* is edited by *Angus Graham-Campbell*, c/o Eton College, Windsor, Berkshire SL4 6EA.

The Kenny/Naughton Society
Aghamore, Ballyhaunis, Co Mayo, Republic of Ireland
Email paulwdrogers@hotmail.com
Chairman *Paul W.D. Rogers*
Patron *Mrs Erna Naughton*

FOUNDED in 1993 to commemorate two writers who had links with Aghamore: P.D. Kenny (1862–1944), who wrote under the pseudonym

'Pat' and Bill Naughton (1910–1992), best known as the author of *Alfie*. Holds an annual school over the October bank holiday weekend which includes lectures, drama, debate and competition (the **Bill Naughton Short Story Competition** – see entry under **Prizes**).

Kent & Sussex Poetry Society

39 Rockington Way, Crowborough,
East Sussex TN6 2NJ
☎01892 662781
Email joyce345@yahoo.co.uk
Publicity Secretary *John Arnold*
Subscription £10 p.a. (Full); £6 (Concessionary – country members living farther afield, senior citizens, under-16s, unemployed)

FOUNDED 1946 to promote the enjoyment of poetry. Monthly meetings are held in Tunbridge Wells, including readings by major poets, a monthly workshop and an annual writing retreat week. *Publishes* an annual folio of members' work based on Members' Competition, adjudicated and commented upon by a major poet. Runs an annual Open Poetry Competition (see entry under **Prizes**) and Saturday workshops twice a year with leading poets.

The Kilvert Society

The Old Forge, Kinnersley, Hereford
HR3 6QB
☎01544 327426
Secretary *Mr M. Sharp*
Subscription £6 p.a.; £9 (Two persons at same address)

FOUNDED 1948 to foster an interest in the Diary, the diarist and the countryside he loved. *Publishes* three journals each year; during the summer holds three weekends of walks, commemoration services and talks.

The Kipling Society

6 Clifton Road, London W9 1SS
☎020 7286 0194 Fax 020 7286 0194
Email jane@keskar.fsworld.co.uk
Website www.kipling.org.uk
Honorary Secretary *Jane Keskar*
Subscription £20 p.a.

FOUNDED 1927. The Society's main activities are: maintaining a specialised library in London; answering enquiries from the public (schools, publishers, writers and the media); arranging a regular programme of lectures, especially in London and in Sussex, and an annual luncheon with guest speaker; maintaining a small museum and reference at The Grange, in Rottingdean near Brighton; issuing a quarterly journal. (For the Kipling mailbox discussion list, e-mail to: Rudyard-Kipling@jiscmail.ac.uk) This is a literary society for all who enjoy the prose and verse of Rudyard Kipling (1865–1936) and are interested in his life and times. Please contact the Secretary by letter, telephone, fax or e-mail for further information.

The Kitley Trust

Toadstone Cottage, Edge View, Litton,
Derbyshire SK17 8QU
☎01298 871564
Email stottie2@waitrose.com
Contact *Rosie Ford*

FOUNDED 1990 by a teacher in Sheffield to promote the art of creative writing, in memory of her mother, Jessie Kitley. Activities include: biannual poetry competitions; a 'Get Poetry' day (distribution of children's poems in shopping malls); annual sponsorship of a writer for a school; campaigns; organising conferences for writers and teachers of writing. Funds are provided by donations and profits (if any) from competitions.

Charles Lamb Society

BM Elia, London WC1N 3XX
Subscription £12 p.a. (Single); £18 (Joint & Corporate); US$28 (Overseas Personal); US$42 (Overseas Corporate)

FOUNDED 1935 to promote the study of the life, works and times of English essayist Charles Lamb (1775–1834). Holds regular bi-monthly meetings and lectures in London and organises society events over the summer. Annual luncheon in February. *Publishes* a quarterly bulletin, *The Charles Lamb Bulletin*. Contributions of Elian interest are welcomed by the editor *Rick Tomlinson* at 669 South Monroe Street, Decatur, Illinois 62522–3225, USA (E-mail: romanticism@ameritech.net). Membership applications should be sent to the box number address above. The Society's library is housed in the **Guildhall Library**, Aldermanbury, London EC2P 2EJ. Requests to consult printed sources must be made 48 hours in advance by letter to the Principal Reference Librarian, in person at the Printed Books Enquiry Desk or by telephone (☎020 7332 1868/1870). Member of the **Alliance of Literary Societies**. Registered Charity No: 803222.

Lancashire Authors' Association

Heatherslade, 5 Quakerfields, Westhoughton,
Bolton, Lancashire BL5 2BJ
☎01942 791390
Email eholt@cwctv.net

General Secretary *Eric Holt*
Subscription £9 p.a.; £12 (Joint); £1 (Junior)
FOUNDED 1909 for writers and lovers of Lancashire literature and history. Aims to foster and stimulate interest in Lancashire history and literature as well as in the preservation of the Lancashire dialect. Meets four times a year on Saturday at various locations. *Publishes* a quarterly journal called *The Record*, which is issued free to members, and holds eight annual competitions (open to members only) for both verse and prose. Comprehensive library with access for research to members.

The Landor Society of Warwick
11 Watersfield Gardens, Sydenham, Leamington Spa, Warwickshire CV31 1NT
☎01926 337874
Email portlandbooks@quicknet.com
Honorary Secretary *Mrs Jean Field*
Subscription £5 p.a.

FOUNDED 2000 to promote interest in the life and works of the Warwick-born writer Walter Savage Landor (1775–1864). Holds a Landor Birthday Dinner on 30th January each year, and reading and discussion meetings most months. *Publishes* newsletter twice a year.

The Philip Larkin Society
c/o Department of English, The University of Hull, Hull HU6 7RX
☎01482 465637 Fax 01482 465641
Email j.booth@hull.ac.uk
Website www.philiplarkin.com
Contact *Dr James Booth*
Subscription £18 (Full rate); £12 (Unwaged/ Senior Citizen); £8 (Student)

FOUNDED in 1995 to promote awareness of the life and work of Philip Larkin (1922–1985) and his literary contemporaries; to bring together all those who admire Larkin's work as a poet, writer and librarian; to bring about publications on all things Larkinesque. Organises a programme of events ranging from lectures to rambles exploring the countryside of Larkin's schooldays and *publishes* a biannual newsletter, *About Larkin*.

The D.H. Lawrence Society
24 Briarwood Avenue, Nottingham NG3 6JQ
☎0115 950 3008
Secretary *Ron Faulks*
Subscription £11; £10 (Concession); £13 (European); £16 (RoW)
FOUNDED 1974 to increase knowledge and the

appreciation of the life and works of D.H. Lawrence. Monthly meetings, addressed by guest speakers, are held in the library at Eastwood (birthplace of DHL). Organises visits to places of interest in the surrounding countryside, supports the activities of the D.H. Lawrence Centre at Nottingham University, and has close links with DHL Societies worldwide. *Publishes* two newsletters and one journal each year, free to members.

The T.E. Lawrence Society
PO Box 728, Oxford OX2 6YP
Website www.telawrencesociety.org
Contact *Gigi Horsfield*
Subscription £18 (UK); £23 (Overseas)

FOUNDED 1985 as a non-profit making, educational, registered charity to advance awareness of the life and work of Thomas Edward Lawrence and to promote research into his life and work. *Publishes* four newsletters and two journals per year. A biennial symposium is held, usually in Oxford, to bring members together to share both academic and social interests. The Society encourages the formation of regional groups of which, currently, there are seven: three in England (Northwest, London, Dorset), one in Europe (Netherlands), two in the USA (Eastern and Western States) and one in Japan.

The Leamington Literary Society
52 Newbold Terrace East, Leamington Spa, Warwickshire CV32 4EZ
☎01926 425733
Honorary Secretary *Mrs Margaret Watkins*
Subscription £10 p.a.

FOUNDED 1912 to promote the study and appreciation of literature and the arts. Holds regular meetings every second Tuesday of the month (except August) at the Royal Pump Rooms, Leamington Spa. The Society has published various books of local interest.

Lewes Monday Literary Club
c/o 12 Little East Street, Lewes, East Sussex BN7 2NU
☎01273 472658
Email derekmason@onetel.net.uk
Contact *Mrs Christine Mason*
Subscription £15 p.a.; £5 (Guest, per meeting)

FOUNDED in 1948 for the promotion and enjoyment of literature. Seven meetings are held during the winter on the last Monday of each month (from October to April) at the

White Hart Hotel in Lewes. The Club attracts speakers of the highest quality and a balance between all forms of literature is aimed for. Guests are welcome to attend meetings.

The George MacDonald Society

The Library, Kings College, Strand, London WC2R 2LS
☎01342 823859
Email macdonaldsociety@britishlibrary.net
Website www.gmsociety.org.uk *linked with* www.george-macdonald.com
Contact *John Docherty*
Subscription £10 p.a. (Individual);
    £13 (Joint); £7 (Unwaged); £11 (Overseas)
FOUNDED 1981 to increase awareness of 'the uniqueness and importance of MacDonald's writings'. Notable among Victorian writers for his radical mixture of genres: MacDonald's fantasy works influenced H.G. Wells, C.S. Lewis and J.R.R. Tolkien, and his 'realistic' novels offered a fascinating glimpse into Victorian Scottish life. The Society organises conferences and workshops in Britain and abroad, often in association with other societies with related interests. *Publishes* an annual journal, *North Wind*, with contributions from most of the leading MacDonald scholars worldwide and a newsletter, *Orts*, three times a year.

The Friends of Arthur Machen

Clemendy Cottage, 14 New Market Street, Usk, Gwent NP5 1AT
☎01291 672869
Email gvbrangham@hotmail.com
Website www.machensoc.demon.co.uk/welcome.htm
Contact *Godfrey Brangham*
Subscription £15 p.a. (UK); £18 (US)
FOUNDED 1998. (Formerly the Arthur Machen Society.) Promotes a wider readership of Arthur Machen and a greater understanding of his life and work. Members receive hardback journals (*Faunus*) and newsletters (*Machenalia*). 'While stocks last', new members also receive *Precious Balms* and a new biography of Machen.

The Marlowe Society

7 Rushworth House, Rushworth Close, Cheltenham, Gloucestershire GL51 0JR
☎01242 579472 Fax 01242 579472
Email marsoct@ntlworld.com
Website www.marlowe-society.org
Membership Secretary *Frieda Barker*
Treasurer *Peter Barker*

Subscription £12 p.a. (Individual);
    £7 p.a. (Pensioners/Student/Unwaged);
    £15 p.a. (Overseas); £200 (Group);
    £100 (Individual Life Membership)
FOUNDED 1955. Holds meetings, lectures and discussions, stimulates research into Marlowe's life and works, encourages production of his plays and *publishes* a biannual newsletter. Currently promoting a memorial to the playwright and poet in Poets' Corner in Westminster Abbey.

The John Masefield Society

The Frith, Ledbury, Herefordshire HR8 1LW
☎01531 631647 Fax 01531 631647
Email petercarter@btinternet.com
Website www.my.genie.co.uk/masefield
Chairman *Peter Carter*
Subscription £5 p.a. (Individual);
    £8 (Family, Institutions, Libraries);
    £10 (Overseas); £2.50 (Junior, Student)
FOUNDED in 1992 to stimulate the appreciation of and interest in the life and works of John Masefield (Poet Laureate 1930–1967). The Society is based in Ledbury, the Herefordshire market town of his birth and holds various public events in addition to publishing a journal and occasional papers.

William Morris Society

Kelmscott House, 26 Upper Mall, Hammersmith, London W6 9TA
☎020 8741 3735 Fax 020 8748 5207
Email william.morris@care4free.net
Website www.morrissociety.org
Contact *Helen Elletson*
Subscription £15 p.a.
FOUNDED 1953 to promote interest in the life, work and ideas of William Morris (1834–1896), English poet and craftsman.

The Neil Munro Society

8 Briar Road, Kirkintilloch, Glasgow G66 3SA
☎0141 776 4280
Email brian@bdosborne.fsnet.co.uk
Website www.neilmunro.co.uk
Secretary *Brian D. Osborne*
Subscription £10 (Annual); £11 (Family);
    £5 (Unwaged); £15 (Institutional)
FOUNDED in 1996 to encourage interest in the works of Neil Munro (1863–1930), the Scottish novelist, short story writer, poet and journalist. An annual programme of meetings is held in Glasgow and Munro's home-town of Inveraray. *Publishes ParaGraphs*, a twice-yearly magazine,

sponsors reprints of Munro's work and is developing a Munro archive.

Bill Naughton

See **The Kenny/Naughton Society**

Violet Needham Society

c/o 19 Ashburnham Place, London
SE10 8TZ
☎020 8692 4562
Honorary Secretary *R.H.A. Cheffins*
Subscription £7.50 p.a. (UK & Europe);
£11 (RoW)

FOUNDED 1985 to celebrate the work of children's author Violet Needham and stimulate critical awareness of her work. *Publishes* thrice-yearly *Souvenir*, the Society journal with an accompanying newsletter; organises meetings and excursions to places associated with the author and her books. The journal includes articles about other children's writers of the 1940s and '50s and on ruritanian fiction. Contributions welcome.

The Edith Nesbit Society

21 Churchfields, West Malling, Kent
ME19 6RJ
Website www.imagix.dial.pipex.com
Chairman *Nicholas Reed*
Secretary *Margaret McCarthy*
Subscription £6 p.a.; £8 (Joint); £75 (Life)

FOUNDED in 1996 to celebrate the life and work of Edith Nesbit (1858–1924), best known as the author of *The Railway Children*. The Society's activities include a regular newsletter, booklets, talks and visits to relevant places.

The Wilfred Owen Association

192 York Road, Shrewsbury, Shropshire
SY1 3QH
☎01743 460089
Website www.wilfred.owen.mcmail.com
Chairman *Michael Grayer*
Subscription Adults £4 (£6 Overseas);
£2 (Senior Citizens/Students/Unemployed);
£10 (Groups/Institutions)

FOUNDED 1989 to commemorate the life and works of Wilfred Owen by promoting readings, visits, talks and performances relating to Owen and his work, and supporting appropriate academic and creative projects. Membership is international with 600 members. *Publishes* a newsletter twice a year. Speakers are available for schools or clubs, etc.

The Elsie Jeanette Oxenham Appreciation Society

32 Tadfield Road, Romsey, Hampshire
SO51 5AJ
☎01794 517149 Fax 01794 517149
Email abbey@bufobooks.demon.co.uk
Website www.bufobooks.demon.co.uk/
abbeylnk.htm
Contact *Ms Ruth Allen* (Editor, *The Abbey Chronicle*)
Subscription £6 p.a.; enquire for Overseas rates

FOUNDED 1989 to promote the works of Elsie J. Oxenham. Publishes a newsletter for members, *The Abbey Chronicle*, three times a year.

Thomas Paine Society

43 Eugene Gardens, Nottingham NG2 3LF
☎0115 986 0010
President *The Rt. Hon. Michael Foot*
Honorary Secretary *R.W. Morrell, MBE* (at address above)
Treasurer *Stuart Wright*
Subscription (Minimum) £12 p.a. (UK);
$35 (Overseas); £5 (Unwaged/Pensioners/
Students)

FOUNDED 1963 to promote the life and work of Thomas Paine, and continues to expound his ideals. Meetings, newsletters, lectures and research assistance. Membership badge. The Society has members worldwide and keeps in touch with American and French Thomas Paine associations. *Publishes* magazine, *The Journal of Radical History*, twice yearly (Editor: *R.W. Morrell*) and a newsletter. Holds occasional exhibitions and lectures, including the annual Thomas Paine Memorial Lecture.

Mervyn Peake Society

Rupera, Trinity Road, Mistley, Manningtree,
Essex CO11 2HL
Secretary *Yvonne McLean*

FOUNDED 1975 to promote a wider understanding of Mervyn Peake's achievements as novelist, poet, painter and illustrator. Membership is open to all, irrespective of native language or country of residence. *Publishes The Mervyn Peake Review* annually and the *MPS Newsletter* quarterly.

The John Polidori Literary Society

PO Box 6078, Nottingham NG16 4HX
Founder & President *Franklin Bishop*
Subscription £50 p.a.

FOUNDED 1990 to promote and encourage

appreciation of the life and works of John William Polidori MD (1795–1821) – novelist, poet, tragedian, philosopher, diarist, essayist, reviewer, traveller and one of the youngest students to obtain a medical degree (at the age of 19). He was one-time intimate of the leading figures in the Romantic movement and travelling companion and private physician to Lord Byron. He was a pivotal figure in the infamous Villa Diodati ghost story sessions in which he assisted Mary Shelley in the creation of her *Frankenstein* tale. Polidori introduced into literature the enduring icon of the vampire portrayed as an aristocratic, handsome seducer with his seminal work *The Vampyre – A Tale*, published in 1819. Polidori was honoured in 1998 by the erection of a City of Westminster Plaque at his birthplace – 38 Great Pulteney Street, Westminster, London – officially unveiled by the Italian ambassador. The Society issues unique publications of the rare works of Polidori. International membership in Italy, USA, Canada and Spain.

The Beatrix Potter Society

9 Broadfields, Harpenden, Hertfordshire AL5 2HJ
☎01582 769755 Fax 01582 769755
Email bps@akester.freeserve.org.uk
Website www.beatrixpottersociety.org.uk
Subscription UK: £15 p.a. (Individual); £20 (Institution); Overseas: £20 (Individual); £25 (Institution)

FOUNDED 1980 to promote the study and appreciation of the life and works of Beatrix Potter (1866–1943). Potter was not only the author of *The Tale of Peter Rabbit* and other classics of children's literature; she was also a landscape and natural history artist, diarist, farmer and conservationist, and was responsible for the preservation of large areas of the Lake District through her gifts to the National Trust. The Society upholds and protects the integrity of the inimitable and unique work of Potter, her aims and bequests; holds regular talks and meetings in London with visits to places connected with Beatrix Potter. Biennial International Study Conferences are held in the UK and occasionally in the USA. The Society has an active publishing programme.

The Anthony Powell Society

76 Ennismore Avenue, Greenford, Middlesex UB6 0JW
☎020 8864 4095 Fax 020 8864 6109
Email secretary@anthonypowell.org.uk
Website www.anthonypowell.org.uk

Patron *John Powell*
President *Hugh Massingberd*
Honorary Secretary *Dr Keith C. Marshall*
Subscription £20 p.a. (Individual); £30 (Joint/Gold); £12 (Students); £100 (Organisation)

FOUNDED in June 2000 by a group of scholars and enthusiasts following Powell's death earlier that year at the age of 94. The Society's initial project was the First Biennial Anthony Powell Conference, held at Eton College (Powell's old school); the second conference is planned for April 2003 at Balliol College, Oxford (Powell's *alma mater*). Also organises events for members, ranging from 'pub meets' to talks and visits to places of Powell interest. *Publishes* a quarterly newsletter. The Society is a member of the **Alliance of Literary Societies**.

The Powys Society

82 Linden Road, Gloucester GL1 5HD
☎01452 304539
Email pjf@retepssof.freeserve.co.uk
Website www.powys-society.org
Honorary Secretary *Peter J. Foss*
Subscription £13.50 (UK); £16 (Overseas); £6 (Students)

The Society (with a membership of 350) aims to promote public education and recognition of the writings, thought and contribution to the arts of the Powys family; particularly of John Cowper, Theodore and Llewelyn, but also of the other members of the family and their close associates. The Society holds two major collections of Powys published works, letters, manuscripts and memorabilia. *Publishes* the *Powys Society Newsletter* in April, June and November and *The Powys Journal* in August. Organises an annual conference as well as lectures and meetings in Powys places.

The J.B. Priestley Society

Eldwick Crag Farm, High Eldwick, Bingley, West Yorkshire BD16 3BB
☎01274 563078
Email reavill@globalnet.co.uk
Website www.jbpriestley-society.com
President *Roy Hattersley*
Chairman *The Revd. John Waddington-Feather*
Honorary Secretary *R.E.Y. Slater*
Membership Secretary *Tony Reavill*
Subscription £10 (Individual); £5 (Concession); £15 (Group/Family)

FOUNDED 1997 to widen the knowledge and understanding of Priestley's works; promote the study of his life and his social, cultural and political influences; provide members of the Society with lectures, seminars, films, journals and stimulate education projects; promote public performances of his works and the distribution of material associated with him. For further information, contact the Membership Secretary at the address above.

The Queen's English Society

Membership Secretary: Fernwood, Nightingales, West Chiltington, Pulborough, West Sussex RH20 2QT
☎01798 813001
Website www.queens-english-society.co.uk
Hon. Membership Secretary *David Ellis*
Subscription £10 p.a. (Ordinary); £12 (Family/Corporate); £100 (Life member); reduced rates available for students and long-term unemployed

FOUNDED in 1972 to promote and uphold the use of good English and to encourage the enjoyment of the language. Holds regular meetings to which speakers are invited, an annual luncheon and *publishes* a quarterly journal, *Quest*, for which original articles are welcome.

The Arthur Ransome Society Ltd

Abbot Hall Art Gallery & Museum, Kendal, Cumbria LA6 5AL
☎01539 722464 Fax 01539 722494
Email tarsinfo@arthur-ransome.org
Website www.arthur-ransome.org/ar
Trustee Chairman *Robin Anderson*
Company Secretary *Bill Janes*
Subscription UK: £5 (Junior); £10 (Student); £15 (Adult); £20 (Family); £40 (Corporate); Overseas: £5 (Junior); £10 (Student); £20 (Adult); £25 (Family) Payable in local currency in US, Canada & Australia

FOUNDED in 1990 to celebrate the life and to promote the works and ideas of Arthur Ransome, author of *Swallows and Amazons* titles for children, biographer of Oscar Wilde, works on the Russian Revolution and extensive articles on fishing. TARS seeks to encourage children and adults to engage in adventurous pursuits, to educate the public about Ransome and his works, and to sponsor research into his literary works and life.

The Followers of Rupert

31 Whiteley, Windsor, Berkshire SL4 5PJ
☎01753 865562
Email followersofrupert@hotmail.com
Website www.rupertbear.info
Membership Secretary *Mrs Shirley Reeves*

Subscription UK: £12; £14 (Joint); Europe, airmail: £13 (Individual); £15 (Joint); RoW, airmail: £17 (Individual); £19 (Joint)

FOUNDED in 1983. The Society caters for the growing interest in the Rupert Bear stories, past, present and future. *Publishes* the *Nutwood Newsletter* quarterly which gives up-to-date news of Rupert and information on Society activities. A national get-together of members – the Followers Annual – is held during the autumn.

The Ruskin Society

49 Hallam Street, London W1W 6JP
☎020 7580 1894
Honorary Secretary *Dr Cynthia. J. Gamble*
Honorary Treasurer *The Hon. Mrs Catherine Edwards*
Subscription £10 p.a. (payable January 1st)

FOUNDED in 1997 to encourage a wider understanding of John Ruskin and his contemporaries. Organises lectures and events which seek not only to explain to the public at large the nature of Ruskin's theories but also to place these in a modern context.

The Ruskin Society of London

351 Woodstock Road, Oxford OX2 7NX
☎01865 310987/515962 Fax 01865 240448
Honorary Secretary *Miss O.E. Forbes-Madden*
Subscription £10 p.a.

FOUNDED 1986 to promote interest in John Ruskin (1819–1900) and his contemporaries. All aspects of Ruskinia are introduced. Functions are held in London. *Publishes* the annual *Ruskin Gazette*, a journal concerned with Ruskin's influence. Affiliated to other literary societies.

The Malcolm Saville Society

10 Bilford Road, Worcester WR3 8QA
Email mystery@witchend.demon.co.uk
General Secretary *Mark O'Hanlon*
Subscription £7.50 p.a. (UK); £12 (Overseas)

FOUNDED in 1994 to remember and promote interest in the work of the popular children's author. Regular social activities, booksearch, library, contact directory and three magazines per year.

The Dorothy L. Sayers Society

Rose Cottage, Malthouse Lane, Hurstpierpoint, West Sussex BN6 9JY
☎01273 833444 Fax 01273 835988
Website www.sayers.org.uk
Contact *Christopher Dean*

Subscription £14 p.a. (UK);
£16.50 (Europe); $28 (US)

FOUNDED 1976 to promote the study of the life, works and thoughts of Dorothy Sayers; to encourage the performance of her plays and publication of her books and books about her; to preserve original material and provide assistance to researchers. Acts as a forum and information centre, providing material for study purposes which would otherwise be unavailable. Annual seminars and other meetings. Co-founder of the Dorothy L. Sayers Centre in Witham. *Publishes* bi-monthly bulletin, annual proceedings and other papers.

The Bernard Shaw Information & Research Service
27 Cavendish Avenue, South Ruislip HA4 6QJ
Email diane@georgebernardshaw.com
Website www.georgebernardshaw.com
President *Diane S. Uttley*

ESTABLISHED in 1997 by writer and Shaw specialist Diane S. Uttley who was custodian of and lived in the writer's home, Shaw's Corner, from 1989 to 1997. The service is used by enthusiasts and academics; literary, theatrical and biographical.

The Shaw Society
51 Farmfield Road, Downham, Bromley, Kent BR1 4NF
☎020 8697 3619   Fax 020 8697 3619
Email anthnyellis@aol.com
Honorary Secretary *Ms Barbara Smoker*
Subscription £15 p.a. (Individual); £22 (Joint)

FOUNDED 1941 to promote interest in the life and works of G. Bernard Shaw. Meetings are held on the last Friday of every month (except July, August and December) at Conway Hall, Red Lion Square, London WC1 (6.30 pm for 7.00 pm) at which speakers are invited to talk on some aspect of Shaw's life or works. Monthly playreadings are held on the first Friday of each month (except August). A 'Birthday Tribute' is held at Shaw's Corner, Ayot St Lawrence in Hertfordshire, on the weekend nearest to Shaw's birthday (26th July). *Publishes* a quarterly newsletter and a magazine, *The Shavian*, which appears approximately every nine months. (No payment for contributors.)

The Robert Southey Society
1 Lewis Terrace, Abergarwed, Neath SA11 4DL
☎01639 711480
Contact *Robert King*

Subscription £10 p.a.

FOUNDED 1990 to promote the work of Robert Southey. *Publishes* an annual newsletter and arranges talks on his life and work. Open membership.

The Laurence Sterne Trust
See **The Friends of Shandy Hall**

Robert Louis Stevenson Club
37 Lauder Road, Edinburgh EH9 1UE
☎0131 667 6256   Fax 0131 662 0353
Email MBeanConferences@aol.com
Contact *Margaret Bean, MA*
Subscription £15 p.a. (Individual); £20 p.a. (Overseas); £100 (Ten-year); £180 (Life)

FOUNDED in 1920 to foster interest in Robert Louis Stevenson's life and works. The Club organises an annual lunch and other events. *Publishes RLS Club News* twice a year.

The Bram Stoker Society
Regent House, Trinity College, Dublin 2
Republic of Ireland   Fax 00 353 1 671 9003
(attn: David Lass)
Email dlass@tcd.ie
Website www.vampyremag.com
Honorary Secretary *David Lass*
Honorary Treasurer *Dr Albert Power*
(43 Castle Court, Killiney Hill Road, Killiney, Co. Dublin, Republic of Ireland)
Subscription £10 p.a. (UK/Europe); $20 (US/RoW)

FOUNDED 1980. Aims to promote the study and appreciation of Bram Stoker's works, including his place in the Gothic horror tradition, and his influence on later writers in the areas of cinema, music and theatre. *Publishes* a quarterly newsletter, an annual journal of scholarly articles and organises a regular programme of activities with its affiliated body, The Bram Stoker Club of Trinity College Dublin. These include screenings, annual memorial lectures and the annual summer school held in July. Subscription payments by cheque or postal order (made out to The Bram Stoker Society) should be sent to the Hon. Treasurer at his address above.

The R.S. Surtees Society
Manor Farm House, Nunney, Near Frome, Somerset BA11 4NJ
☎01373 836937   Fax 01373 836574
Website www.clique.co.uk/r.s.surteessociety
Contact *Orders and Membership Secretary*

Subscription £10

FOUNDED 1979 to republish the works of R.S. Surtees and others.

The Tennyson Society

Central Library, Free School Lane, Lincoln LN2 1EZ
☎01522 552862 Fax 01522 552858
Email kathleenjefferson@lincolnshire.gov.uk
Honorary Secretary *Miss K. Jefferson*
Subscription £8 p.a. (Individual); £10 (Family); £15 (Corporate); £125 (Life)

FOUNDED 1960. An international society with membership worldwide. Exists to promote the study and understanding of the life and work of Alfred, Lord Tennyson. The Society is concerned with the work of the Tennyson Research Centre, 'probably the most significant collection of mss, family papers and books in the world'. *Publishes* annually the *Tennyson Research Bulletin*, which contains articles and critical reviews; and organises lectures, visits and seminars. Annual memorial service at Somersby in Lincolnshire.

The Angela Thirkell Society

54 Belmont Park, London SE13 5BN
☎020 8244 9339
Email penny.aldred@tesco.net
Website www.sndc.demon.co.uk/als.htm *and* www.angelathirkell.org (N. American branch)
Honorary Secretary *Mrs. P. Aldred*
Subscription £7 p.a.

FOUNDED in 1980 to honour the memory of Angela Thirkell as a writer and to make her works available to new generations. *Publishes* an annual journal, holds an AGM in early October and a spring meeting which usually takes the form of a visit to a location associated with Thirkell. Has a flourishing North American branch which has frequent contact with the UK parent society.

The Dylan Thomas Society of Great Britain

5 Church Park, Mumbles, Swansea SA3 4DE
☎01792 520080
Contact *Mrs Eryl Jenkins*
Subscription £5 (Individual); £8 (2 adults from same household)

FOUNDED 1977 to foster an understanding of the work of Dylan Thomas and to extend members' awareness of other 20th century writers, especially Welsh writers in English. Meetings take place monthly, mainly in Swansea.

The Edward Thomas Fellowship

Butlers Cottage, Halswell House, Goathurst, Bridgwater, Somerset TA5 2DH
☎01278 662856
Secretary *Richard Emeny*
Subscription £7 p.a. (Single); £10 p.a. (Joint)

FOUNDED 1980 to perpetuate and promote the memory of Edward Thomas and to encourage an appreciation of his life and work. The Fellowship holds a commemorative birthday walk on the Sunday nearest the poet's birthday, 3 March; issues newsletters and holds various events.

The Tolkien Society

65 Wentworth Crescent, Ash Vale, Surrey GU12 5LF Fax 0870 0525569
Email membership@tolkiensociety.org
Website www.tolkiensociety.org
Membership Secretary *Trevor Reynolds*
Subscription £20 p.a. (UK); £22 (Overseas)

An international organisation which aims to encourage and further interest in the life and works of the late Professor J.R.R. Tolkien, CBE, author of *The Hobbit* and *Lord of the Rings*. Current membership stands at 900. *Publishes Mallorn* annually and *Amon Hen* bi-monthly.

The Trollope Society

9A North Street, Clapham, London SW4 0HN
☎020 7720 6789 Fax 020 7978 1815
Email trollsoc@barset.fsnet.co.uk
Contacts *John Letts, Phyllis Eden*

FOUNDED 1987 to study and promote Anthony Trollope's works. *Publishes* the complete works of Trollope's novels and travel books.

Edgar Wallace Society

84 Ridgefield Road, Oxford OX4 3DA
Website www.edgarwallace.org
Organiser *Miss Penny Wyrd*
Subscription £15 p.a.; £10 (Senior Citizen/Student); Overseas: £20; £15 (Senior Citizen/Student)

FOUNDED in 1969 by Wallace's daughter, Penelope, to bring together all who have an interest in Edgar Wallace. Members receive a brief biography of Edgar by Penelope Wallace, with a complete list of all published book titles. A newsletter, *Crimson Circle*, is published three times a year.

The Walmsley Society

April Cottage, No 1 Brand Road, Hampden Park, Eastbourne, East Sussex BN22 9PX
☎01323 506447

Email walmsley@haughshw.demon.co.uk
Honorary Secretary *Fred Lane*
Subscription £9 p.a.; £11 (Family);
£8 (Students/Senior Citizens);
£15 (Overseas, £25 for 2 years)

FOUNDED 1985 to promote interest in the art and writings of Ulric and Leo Walmsley. Two annual meetings – one held in Robin Hood's Bay on the East Yorkshire coast, spiritual home of the author Leo Walmsley. The Society also seeks to foster appreciation of the work of his father Ulric Walmsley. *Publishes* a journal twice-yearly and newsletters, and is involved in other publications which benefit the aims of the Society.

Sylvia Townsend Warner Society
2 Vicarage Lane, Dorchester, Dorset DT1 1LH
☎01305 266028
Email tartarus@pavilion.co.uk
Website www.freepages.pavilion.net/users/
tartarus/warner1.htm
Contact *Eileen Johnson*
Subscription £10 p.a.; $20 (Overseas)

FOUNDED in 2000 to promote a wider readership and better understanding of the writings of Sylvia Townsend Warner.

Mary Webb Society
8 The Knowe, Willaston, Neston, Cheshire
CH64 1TA
☎0151 327 5843
Email suehigginbotham@yahoo.co.uk
Website www.marywebb.2ya.com
Secretary *Sue Higginbotham*
Subscription £8 p.a. (Individual);
£11 p.a. (Joint/Overseas)

FOUNDED 1972. Attracts members from the UK and overseas who are devotees of the literature of Mary Webb and of the beautiful Shropshire countryside of her novels. *Publishes* annual journal in September, organises summer schools in various locations related to the authoress's life and works. Archives; lectures; tours arranged for individuals and groups.

H.G. Wells Society
49 Beckingthorpe Drive, Bottesford,
Nottingham NG13 0DN
Website hgwellsusa.50megs.com
Honorary Secretary *J.R. Hammond*
Subscription £16 (UK/EU); £19 (Overseas);
£20 (Corporate); £10 (Concessions)

FOUNDED 1960 to promote an interest in and appreciation of the life, work and thought of Herbert George Wells. *Publishes The Wellsian* (annual) and *The H.G. Wells Newsletter* (three issues yearly). Organises meetings and conferences.

The Oscar Wilde Society
100 Peacock Street, Gravesend, Kent
DA12 1EQ
☎01474 535978
Email vanessa@salome.co.uk
Honorary Secretary *Vanessa Harris*

FOUNDED 1990 to promote knowledge, appreciation and study of the life, personality and works of the writer and wit Oscar Wilde. Activities include meetings, lectures, readings and exhibitions, and visits to locations associated with Wilde. Members receive a journal, *The Wildean*, twice-yearly and a newsletter, *Intentions* (six per year).

The Charles Williams Society
35 Broomfield, Stacey Bushes, Milton Keynes,
Buckinghamshire MK12 6HP
Email charles_wms_soc@yahoo.co.uk
Website www.geocities.com/charles_wm_soc
Contact *Honorary Secretary*

FOUNDED 1975 to promote interest in, and provide a means for the exchange of views and information on the life and work of Charles Walter Stansby Williams (1886–1945).

The Henry Williamson Society
16 Doran Drive, Redhill, Surrey RH1 6AX
☎01737 763228
Email mm@misterman.freeserve.co.uk
Website www.henrywilliamson.org
Membership Secretary *Mrs Margaret Murphy*
Subscription £12 p.a.; £15 (Family);
£5 (Students)

FOUNDED 1980 to encourage, by all appropriate means, a wider readership and deeper understanding of the literary heritage left by the 20th-century English writer Henry Williamson (1895–1977). *Publishes* annual journal.

The P.G. Wodehouse Society (UK)
16 Herbert Street, Plaistow, London E13 8BE
Website www.eclipse.co.uk/wodehouse
Membership Secretary *Helen Murphy*
Subscription £15 p.a.

Relaunched in May 1997 to advance the genius of P.G. Wodehouse. Publications include the *Wooster Source* quarterly journal and the *By The Way* newsletter. Regular national and international group meetings. Members in most countries throughout the world. Society patrons include Rt. Hon. Tony Blair MP and Stephen Fry. Wodehouse's grandson, Sir Edward Cazalet, is on the committee.

The Parson Woodforde Society
22 Gaynor Close, Wymondham, Norfolk NR18 0EA
☎01953 604124
Email mabrayne@supanet.com
Website www.cix.co.uk~kcm/pwsoc.htm
Membership Secretary *Mrs Ann Elliott*
Subscription £12.50 (UK); £25 (Overseas)
FOUNDED 1968. Aims to extend and develop knowledge of James Woodforde's life and the society in which he lived and to provide the opportunity for fellow enthusiasts to meet together in places associated with the diarist. *Publishes* a quarterly journal and newsletter. The Society is producing a complete edition of the diary of James Woodforde. To date, twelve volumes of diary material have been published covering the period 1759–1790.

The Virginia Woolf Society of Great Britain
Fairhaven, Charnleys Lane, Banks, Southport PR9 8HJ
Email snclarke@talk21.com
Website orlando.jp.org/vwsgb/index.html
Contact *Stuart N. Clarke*
Subscription £12 p.a.; £15 (Overseas)
FOUNDED 1998 to promote interest in the life and work of Virginia Woolf, author, essayist and diarist. The Society's activities include trips away, walks, reading groups and talks. *Publishes* a literary journal, *Virginia Woolf Bulletin*, three times a year.

WW2 HMSO PPBKS Society
3 Roman Road, Southwick, West Sussex BN42 4TP
☎01273 871017 Fax 01273 871017
Contact *A.R. James*
FOUNDED 1994 to encourage collectors and to promote research into HMSO's World War II series of paperbacks. Most of them were written by well-known authors, though in many cases anonymously. No subscription charge. Available for purchase: Collectors' Guide (£5); Bibliography (£3); Handbook, *Informing the People* (£10).

The Yeats Society Sligo
Yeats Memorial Building, Douglas Hyde Bridge, Sligo, Republic of Ireland
☎00 353 71 42693 Fax 00 353 71 42780
Email info@yeats-sligo.com
Website www.yeats-sligo.com
President *E.J. Wylie-Warren*
Subscription E25 (Single); E38 (Couple); E127 (Corporate)
FOUNDED in 1958 to promote the heritage of W.B. Yeats and the Yeats family. Attractions include continuous updated Yeats exhibitions for public viewing, annual Yeats International Summer School in August and Yeats Winter School in January. The Yeats Summer Festival is held each August and lectures are held in the winter and spring, sponsored by the Institute of Technology, Sligo. *Publishes* a newsletter and organises year-round events/programmes in arts, culture, education for writers' groups, poetry/drama groups, etc.

Yorkshire Dialect Society
51 Stepney Avenue, Scarborough, North Yorkshire YO12 5BW
Secretary *Michael Park*
Subscription £7 p.a.
FOUNDED 1897 to promote interest in and preserve a record of the Yorkshire dialect. *Publishes* dialect verse and prose writing. Two journals to members annually. Details of publications available from YDS, Rosebank Cottage, Main Street, Great Heck, West Yorkshire DN14 0BQ.

Francis Brett Young Society
92 Gower Road, Halesowen, West Midlands B62 9BT
☎0121 422 8969
Website www.fbysociety.co.uk
Honorary Secretary *Mrs Jean Hadley*
Subscription £7 p.a. (Individuals); £10 (Couples sharing a journal); £5 (Students); £7 (Organisations/Overseas); £70 (Life); £100 (Joint, Life)
FOUNDED 1979. Aims to provide a forum for those interested in the life and works of English novelist Francis Brett Young and to collate research on him. Promotes lectures, exhibitions and readings; *publishes* a regular newsletter.

Arts Councils and Regional Arts Boards

The Arts Council of England
14 Great Peter Street, London SW1P 3NQ
☎020 7333 0100/Minicom: 020 7973 6564
Fax 020 7973 6590
Email enquiries@artscouncil.org.uk
Website www.artscouncil.org.uk
Chairman *Gerry Robinson*
Chief Executive *Peter Hewitt*

The Arts Council of England is the national policy body for the arts in England. It develops, sustains and champions the arts. It distributes public money from government and from the National Lottery to artists and arts organisations both directly and through the 10 Regional Arts Boards. The Arts Council works independently and at arm's length from government. Information about Arts Council funding programmes are available on the website, by e-mail or by contacting the enquiry line on 020 7973 6517. Information about funding available from the Regional Arts Boards can be found on the website (www.arts.org.uk) or by contacting your Regional Arts Board.

The Irish Arts Council/
An Chomhairle Ealaíon
70 Merrion Square, Dublin 2
☎00 353 1 6180200 Fax 00 353 1 6761302
Email info@artscouncil.ie
Website www.artscouncil.ie

Literature Officer *Sinead MacAodha*

The Irish Arts Council has programmes under six headings to assist in the area of literature and book promotion: a) Writers; b) Literary Organisations; c) Publishers; d) Literary Magazines; e) Participation Programmes; f) Literary Events and Festivals. It also awards a number of annual bursaries (see **Arts Council Literature Bursaries, Ireland** in the section **Bursaries, Fellowships and Grants**).

The Arts Council of
Northern Ireland
MacNeice House, 77 Malone Road, Belfast BT9 6AQ
☎028 9038 5200 Fax 028 9066 1715
Website www.artscouncil-ni.org

Literature Arts Officer *John Brown*

Funds book production by established publishers, programmes of readings, literary festivals, writers-in-residence schemes and literary magazines and periodicals. Occasional schools programmes and anthologies of children's writing are produced. Annual awards and bursaries for writers are available. Holds information also on various groups associated with local arts, workshops and courses.

Scottish Arts Council
12 Manor Place, Edinburgh EH3 7DD
☎0131 226 6051 Fax 0131 225 9833
Email administrator@scottisharts.org.uk
Website www.sac.org.uk

Chairman *James Boyle*
Acting Director *Graham Berry*
Literature Director *Jenny Brown*
Literature Officers *Gavin Wallace,*
  Jenny Attala
Literature Secretary *Catherine Allan*

Principal channel for government funding of the arts in Scotland. The Scottish Arts Council (SAC) is funded by the Scottish Executive. It aims to develop and improve the knowledge, understanding and practice of the arts, and to increase their accessibility throughout Scotland. It offers around 1300 grants a year to artists and arts organisations concerned with the visual arts, crafts, dance and mime, drama, literature, music, festivals and traditional, ethnic and community arts. It is also a distributor of National Lottery funds to the arts in Scotland. SAC's support for Scottish-based writers with a track record of publication includes bursaries, writing and translation fellowships and book awards (see entries under **Bursaries, Fellowships and Grants** and **Prizes**). Information offered includes lists of literary awards, literary magazines, agents and publishers.

The Arts Council of Wales
Museum Place, Cardiff CF10 3NX
☎029 2037 6500 Fax 029 2022 1447
Website www.ccc-acw.org.uk
Senior Literature Officer *Tony Bianchi*

Senior Officer: Drama *Sandra Wynne*

Funds literary magazines and book production; *Writers on Tour* and bursary schemes; **Welsh Academy, Welsh Books Council, Hay-on-Wye Literature Festival** and **Tŷ Newydd Writers' Centre** at Criccieth; also children's literature, annual awards and translation projects. The Council aims to develop theatrical experience among Wales-based writers through a variety of schemes – in particular, by funding writers on year-long attachments.

English Regional Arts Boards

English Regional Arts Boards are support and development agencies for the arts in the regions. Policies are developed in response to regional demand, and to assist new initiatives in areas of perceived need; they may vary from region to region. The RABs are now responsible for the distribution of Arts Council Lottery funding for capital and revenue projects under £100,000.

SUPPORT FOR WRITERS

All the Regional Arts Boards offer support for professional creative writers through a range of grants, awards, advice, information and contacts. Interested writers should contact the Board in whose region they live.

At the time of writing the current system of RABs is under review and anyone experiencing problems getting in touch with their RAB is advised to contact the Arts Council of England.

East England Arts

Eden House, 48–49 Bateman Street, Cambridge CB2 1LR
☎01223 454400 Fax 0870 2421271
Email info@eearts.co.uk
Website www.arts.org.uk

Literature Officer *Lucy Sheerman*
Drama Officer *Alan Orme*
Cinema & Broadcast Media Officer
  Martin Ayres

Covers Bedfordshire, Cambridgeshire, Essex, Hertfordshire, Norfolk and Suffolk and the non-metropolitan authorities of Luton, Peterborough, Southend-on-Sea and Thurrock. Policy emphasises quality and access. Support is given to publishers and literature promoters based in the EEB region, also to projects which develop audiences for literature performances and publishing, including electronic media. Also provides advice on applying for National Lottery funds.

East Midlands Arts

Mountfields House, Epinal Way, Loughborough, Leicestershire LE11 0QE
☎01509 218292 Fax 01509 262214
Email info@em-arts.co.uk

Literature Officer *To be appointed*
Drama Officer *Michaela Waldram*

Covers Derbyshire, Leicestershire, Lincolnshire, Northamptonshire, Nottinghamshire, and the unitary authorities of Derby, Leicester, Nottingham and Rutland. A comprehensive information service for regional writers includes an extensive *Writers' Information Pack*, with details of local groups, workshops, residential writing courses, publishers and publishing information, regional magazines, advice on approaching the media, on unions, courses and grants. Also available is a directory of writers, primarily to aid people wishing to organise workshops, readings or writer's residencies. Literature grants are given for work on a specific project – local history and biography are ineligible for support. Writing for the theatre can come under the aegis of both Literature and Drama. A list of writers' groups is available, plus contact details for the East Midlands Literature Development Officer network.

London Arts

2 Pear Tree Court, London EC1R 0DS
☎020 7608 6100 Fax 020 7670 4100
Email sarah.sanders@lonab.co.uk
Website www.arts.org.uk/londonarts

Literature Administrator *Sarah Sanders*

London Arts is the Regional Arts Board for the Capital, covering the 32 boroughs and the City of London. Grants are available to support a variety of literature projects, focusing on three main areas: live literature, including storytelling; support for small presses and literary magazines in the publishing of new or under-represented creative writing; bursaries for writers who have published one book and are working on their second work of fiction or poetry. There are two deadlines each year for applications. Please contact the Literature Unit for more information and an application form.

North West Arts Board

Manchester House, 22 Bridge Street, Manchester M3 3AB
☎0161 834 6644 Fax 0161 834 6969
Email info@nwarts.co.uk

Arts Officer – Literature *Bronwen Williams*
  (Email bwilliams@nwarts.co.uk)

Arts Officer – Drama *Ian Tabbron* (Email itabbron@nwarts.co.uk)

NWAB covers Cheshire, Cumbria, Lancashire, the metropolitan districts of Bolton, Bury, Knowsley, Liverpool, Manchester, Oldham, Rochdale, St Helens, Salford, Sefton, Stockport, Tameside, Trafford, Wigan and Wirral, and the non-metropolitan districts of Blackburn with Darwen, Blackpool, Halton and Warrington. Offers financial assistance to a great variety of organisations and individuals through a number of schemes, including Writers' Bursaries, Residencies and Placements and the Live Writing scheme. NWAB publishes a directory of local writers' groups, a directory of writers and a range of information covering topics such as performance and publishing. For further details please contact the Literature or Drama Department.

Northern Arts Board

Central Square, Forth Street, Newcastle upon Tyne NE1 3PJ
☎0191 255 8500 Fax 0191 230 1020
Email info@northernarts.org.uk
Website www.arts.org.uk
Head of Film, Media and Literature
Mark Robinson
Literature Officer *Kate Griffin*

Covers County Durham, Northumberland, Teesside and Tyne and Wear, and was the first regional arts association in the country to be set up by local authorities. It supports both organisations and writers and aims to stimulate public interest in artistic events. The Northern Writers Awards scheme is operated through **New Writing North** (see entry under **Professional Associations and Societies**). Northern Arts makes drama awards to producers. Also funds writers' residencies, and has a fund for publications. Contact list of regional groups available.

South West Arts

Bradninch Place, Gandy Street, Exeter, Devon EX4 3LS
☎01392 218188 Fax 01392 229229
Email info@swa.co.uk
Website www.swa.co.uk
Director of Visual Arts and Media
David Drake
Visual Arts and Media Administrators
Sara Williams, Kate Offord, Lis Spencer

Covers Cornwall, Devon, Dorset (excluding Bournemouth, Christchurch and Poole), Gloucestershire, Somerset and the unitary authorities of Bristol, Bath and North East Somerset, South Gloucestershire, North Somerset, Torbay and Plymouth. The central theme running through the Board's aims are 'promoting quality and developing audiences for new work'. Specific policies aim to support the development and promotion of new writing and performance work in all areas of contemporary literature and published arts. There is direct investment in small presses and magazine publishers, literary festivals, writer residencies and training, and marketing bursaries for individual writers. There is also a commitment to supporting the development of new writing in the performing arts, and critical writing within the visual arts and media department.

Southern and South East Arts (Tunbridge Wells office)

Union House, Eridge Road, Tunbridge Wells, Kent TN4 8HF
☎01892 507200 Fax 01892 549383
Email info@seab.co.
Website www.arts.org.uk
Literature Officer *Suzy Joinson*
Drama Officer *Judith Hibberd*

Covers Kent, Surrey, East Sussex, West Sussex, Brighton and Hove and Medway (excluding the London boroughs). Grant schemes accessible to all art forms in the areas of new work, presentation of work and venue development. Awards for individuals include training bursaries and writers' awards schemes. The literature programme aims to raise the profile of contemporary literature in the region and encourage creative writing and reading development projects. Priorities include live literature, writers and readers in residence and training bursaries for writers resident in the region. A regular feature on literature appears in the *Arts News* newsletter.

Southern and South East Arts (Winchester office)

13 St Clement Street, Winchester, Hampshire SO23 9DQ
☎01962 855099 Fax 0870 242 1257
Email info@southernarts.co.uk
Website www.arts.org.uk/sa
Literature Officer *Keiren Phelan*
Theatre Officer *Nic Young*

Covers Berkshire, Buckinghamshire, Hampshire, the Isle of Wight, Oxfordshire, Wiltshire and South East Dorset. The Literature Department funds festivals, magazines, publications and residencies. Development funds are available for programming and events, support for individual artists and new commissions.

West Midlands Arts

82 Granville Street, Birmingham B1 2LH
☎0121 631 3121 Fax 0121 643 7239
Website www.arts.org.uk/directory/regions/west-mid

Literature Officer *Adrian Johnson*

Covers Shropshire, Staffordshire, Warwickshire, Worcestershire; also the metropolitan districts of Birmingham, Coventry, Dudley, Sandwell, Solihull, Walsall and Wolverhampton, and the non-metropolitan districts of Herefordshire, Stoke-on-Trent, Telford and Wrekin. There are special criteria across the art forms, so contact the Information Office for details of general support funds for the arts, especially *Creative Ambition Awards* for writers (six application dates throughout the year) and other arts lottery schemes, as well as for the *Reading (Correspondence Mss Advice) Service.* There are contact lists of writers, storytellers, writing groups, etc. WMA supports the regional publication, *Raw Edge Magazine*: contact PO Box 4867, Birmingham B3 3HD, the Virtual Literature Centre for the West Midlands (and beyond) called 'Lit-net' (www.lit-net.org) and the major storytelling and poetry festivals in Shropshire and Ledbury respectively.

Yorkshire Arts

21 Bond Street, Dewsbury, West Yorkshire WF13 1AY
☎01924 455555 Fax 01924 466522
Email <firstname.surname>@yarts.co.uk
Website www.arts.org.uk

Literature Officer *Jane Stubbs*
Theatre Development Officer *Maric Hollander*
Literature & Audience Development Administrator *Kelly McMichael*

'Libraries, publishing houses, local authorities and the education service all make major contributions to the support of literature. Recognising the resources these agencies command, Yorkshire Arts actively seeks ways of acting in partnership with them, while at the same time retaining its particular responsibility for the living writer and the promotion of activities currently outside the scope of these agencies.' Funding goes to a range of independent publishers, festivals and literature development agencies. Yorkshire Arts also offers a range of development funds to support the individual and the promotion and distribution of literature. Holds lists of writers' groups throughout the region and *publishes Write Angles*, a bimonthly newsletter. Contact *Kelly McMichael* for further information.

Writers' Courses, Circles and Workshops

Writers' Courses

UK – ENGLAND

Berkshire

University of Reading
Department of Continuing Education,
London Road, Reading, Berkshire RG1 5AQ
☎0118 931 8347
Email Cont-Ed@reading.ac.uk
Website www.reading.ac.uk/ContEd

An expanding programme of creative writing courses, including *Life into Fiction; Poetry Workshop; Getting Started; Writing Fiction; Becoming Independent; Publishing Poetry; Adventures in Writing* and *Scriptwriting*. There is also a public lecture by a writer and a reading by students of their work, and various Saturday workshops. Tutors include the science fiction writer Brian Stableford, novelist Leslie Wilson and poets Jane Draycott, Elizabeth James and Susan Utting. Fees vary depending on the length of course. Concessions available.

Buckinghamshire

Missenden Abbey Continuing Education
Chilterns Consortium, The Misbourne Centre, Great Missenden, Buckinghamshire HP16 0BN
☎01494 862904 Fax 01494 890087
Email conedchil@buckscc.gov.uk
Website www.aredu.org.uk/missendenabbey

Residential and non-residential weekend workshops and summer school. Programmes have included *Writing Stories for Children; Writing for Self-Discovery; Travel to Success; Writers' Toolkit; Writing Poetry*. Missenden Abbey is a member of the Adult Residential Colleges Association.

National Film & Television School
Beaconsfield Studios, Station Road,
Beaconsfield, Buckinghamshire HP9 1LG
☎01494 731425 Fax 01494 674042
Email admin@nftsfilm-tv.ac.uk
Website www.nftsfilm-tv.ac.uk

Intensive, one-year, full-time screenwriting course for people with established writing skills but little or no experience of writing for the screen. One-year, part-time course for people with some screenwriting experience who are ready to focus on feature script development. Completion of both courses, plus short dissertation, is required for the award of an MA. Courses develop an understanding of the practical stages involved in the making of film and television drama. Range of work covers comedy, TV series and serials, short-film, adaptation and narrative. The ability to collaborate successfully is developed through exercises and projects shared with students in other specialisations. 'We encourage the formation of working partnerships which will continue after graduation.'

Cambridgeshire

National Extension College
Michael Young Centre, Purbeck Road,
Cambridge CB2 2HN
☎01223 400200 Fax 01223 400399
Email info@nec.ac.uk
Website www.nec.ac.uk

Runs a number of home-study courses on writing. Courses include: *Essential Editing; Creative Writing; Writing for Money; Copywriting; Essential Desktop Publishing; Essential Design.* Contact the NEC for copy of the *Guide to Courses* which includes details of fees.

PMA Training
PMA House, Free Church Passage, St Ives,
Cambridgeshire PE27 5AY
☎01480 300653 Fax 01480 496022
Email training@pma-group.com
Website www.pma-group.com

One-/two-/three-day editorial, PR, design and publishing courses held in central London. High-powered, intensive courses run by Fleet Street journalists and magazine editors. Courses include: *News-Writing; Writing and Surviving as a Freelance; Feature Writing; Investigative Reporting; Basic Writing Skills.* Fees range from £170 to £750 plus VAT. Special rates for freelances.

University of Cambridge Institute of Continuing Education

Madingley Hall, Madingley, Cambridge
CB3 8AQ
☎01954 280399 Fax 01954 280200
Website www.cont-ed.cam.ac.uk

A wide range of weekend, five-day and week long creative writing courses for adults are offered by the University at the Institute of Continuing Education's residential headquarters at Madingley Hall. Evening courses are also available in Cambridgeshire and surrounding area. Details of all courses can be found on the website or phone for a brochure.

Cheshire

Burton Manor College

Burton Village, Neston, Cheshire CH64 5SJ
☎0151 336 5172 Fax 0151 336 6586
Email enquiry@burtonmanor.com
Website www.burtonmanor.org

Wide variety of short courses, residential and non-residential on writing and literature, including *Writing About Travel; Plays and Players; The Internet for Writing; Writing for Drama*; Easter Writing and a Literature Summer School. Full details in brochure.

The College of Technical Authorship – Distance Learning Course

The College of Technical Authorship,
PO Box 7, Cheadle, Cheshire SK8 3BY
☎0161 437 4235 Fax 0161 437 4235
Email crossley@coltecha.u-net.com
Website www.coltecha.com

Contact *John Crossley*, DipDistEd, DipM, MCIM, FISTC, LCGI

Distance learning courses for City & Guilds Tech 5360, Part 1, Technical Communication Techniques, and Part 2, Technical Authorship. Individual tuition by letter or e-mail; includes some practical work done at home. A member of the British Association for Open Learning.

Cornwall

Falmouth College of Art

Woodlane, Falmouth, Cornwall TR11 4RH
☎01326 211077
Website www.falmouth.ac.uk *and* (magazine) www.hackwriters.com

Contact *Admissions Secretary*

Postgraduate professional writing programme.

An intensive vocational writing programme developing skills in children's fiction, magazine journalism/features, screenwriting. Students have the opportunity to work on an extended writing project and form links with other PgDips such as broadcast TV and radio. The course won Guardian Media Award 1999 and was nominated again in 2000.

The Indian King Arts Centre

Fore Street, Camelford, Cornwall PL32 9PG
☎01840 212111
Email info@indianking.co.uk
Website www.indianking.co.uk

Director *Helen Jagger Wood*

FOUNDED in 1994 to offer people from all walks of life the opportunity to explore and develop their creative writing skills with the support of published writers. The annual programme of residential writing courses starts with the annual Poetry Festival in memory of Jon Silkin, held on the last weekend before Easter, and continues into the autumn. Visiting writers offer two-day courses (Saturday/Sunday) or four-and-a-half-day courses (Monday evening to Friday evening inclusive) in poetry, short and long fiction and drama. The Centre offers writing classes, readings and book launches throughout the year on a weekly, fortnightly and monthly basis as well as having a poetry library.

Cumbria

Higham Hall College

Bassenthwaite Lake, Cockermouth, Cumbria
CA13 9SH
☎01768 776276 Fax 01768 776013
Email admin@higham-hall.org.uk
Website www.higham-hall.org.uk

Winter and summer residential courses. Programme has included *Creative Writing*. Brochure available.

Derbyshire

Real Writers

PO Box 170, Chesterfield, Derbyshire S40 1FE
☎01246 238492 Fax 01246 238492
Email info@real-writers.com
Website www.real-writers.com

Correspondence service with personal tuition from working writers. In addition to the support and appraisal service, runs an annual short story competition. Send s.a.e. for details.

University of Derby

Student Information Centre, Kedleston Road, Derby DE22 1GB
☎01332 622236 Fax 01332 622754
Email J.Bains@derby.ac.uk (prospectus requests only)
Website www.derby.ac.uk

Contact *Graham Parker*

With upwards of 300 students, *Creative Writing* runs 21 modules as part of the undergraduate degree programme. These include: *Storytelling, Poetry, Playwriting, Writing for TV and Radio, Screenwriting, The Short Story, Journalism, Writing for Children.* The courses are all led by practising writers.

Writers' Summer School, Swanwick

The Hayes, Swanwick, Derbyshire
Website www.wss.org.uk

Secretary *Jean Sutton*

A week-long summer school of informal talks and discussion groups, forums, panels, quizzes, competitions, and 'a lot of fun'. Open to everyone, from absolute beginners to published authors. Held mid-August from Saturday to Friday morning. Cost (2002) from £225, all inclusive. Contact the Secretary, at 10 Stag Road, Lake, Sandown, Isle of Wight PO36 8PE (☎01983 406759) or e-mail.

Devon

Arvon Foundation (Devon)

See entry under Greater London

Dartington College of Arts

Totnes, Devon TQ9 6EJ
☎01803 862224 Fax 01803 861666
Email registry@dartington.ac.uk
Website www.dartington.ac.uk

BA(Hons) course in *Performance Writing*: exploratory approach to writing as it relates to performance. The course is part of a performance arts programme which encourages interdisciplinary work with arts management, music, theatre, visual performance. The programme includes a range of elective modules in digital media and emerging art forms which are available to all students. Contact Subject Director, Performance Writing: *Rick Allsopp*.

Exeter Phoenix

Bradninch Place, Gandy Street, Exeter, Devon EX4 3LS
☎01392 667080 Fax 01392 667599

Website www.exeterphoenix.org.uk

Exeter Phoenix has regular literature events, focusing on readings by living poets and other writers and is often linked to aspects of a wider performance programme. Tutors in a wide range of writing skills run classes and workshops, listed in the brochure of Phoenix activities.

University of Exeter

Exeter, Devon EX4 4QW
☎01392 264580
Website www.ex.ac.uk/drama

Contact *The Secretary* (Drama Department, Thornlea, New North Road, Exeter EX4 4LA)

BA(Hons) in *Drama* with a third-year option in *Playwriting*. MPhil and PhD in *Performance Practice* (including *Playwriting*).

Dorset

Bournemouth University

Bournemouth Media School, Poole House, Talbot Campus, Fern Barrow, Poole, Dorset BH12 5BB
☎01202 595553 Fax 01202 595530

Contact *Katrina King, Programme Administrator*

Three-year, full-time BA(Hons) course in *Scriptwriting for Film and Television.*

Essex

National Council for the Training of Journalists

Latton Bush Centre, Southern Way, Harlow, Essex CM18 7BL
☎01279 430009 Fax 01279 438008
Email info@nctj.com
Website www.nctj.com

For details of journalism courses, both full-time and via distance learning, please write to the NCTJ enclosing a large s.a.e. or visit the website.

Gloucestershire

Chrysalis – The Poet In You with Jay Ramsay, BA Hons (Oxon)

5 Oxford Terrace, Uplands, Stroud, Gloucestershire GL5 1TW
☎01453 759436/020 7794 8880
Email ramsay@chrysalis37.fsnet.co.uk

Offers postal courses, workshops (including 'The Sacred Space of the Word'), one-to-one sessions, and individual therapy related to the participant's creative process. The course consists of Part 1, 'for those who feel drawn to reading more poetry as well as wanting to start to write their own', and Part 2, 'a more in-depth course designed for those who are already writing and who want to go more deeply into its process and technique'. Editing and information about publication also provided. Brochure and workshop dates available from the address above.

Wye Valley Arts Centre

The Coach House, Mork, St Briavel's, Lydney, Gloucestershire GL15 6QH
☎01594 530214/01291 689463
Fax 01594 530321
Email wyeart@cwcom.net
Website www.wyeart.cwc.net

Residential courses (Monday to Friday) – held at The Coach House, a country house near Tintern Abbey in the Wye Valley – include *Creative Writing*, *Writing for Radio* and *Fiction Workshop*. 'All styles and abilities. Companions and other guests not taking the courses are welcome to stay.'

Hampshire

Annual Writers' Conference Winchester

'Chinook', Southdown Road, Winchester, Hampshire SO21 2BY
☎01962 712307
Email WriterConf@aol.com
Website www.gmp.co.uk/writers/conference
and www.awc-workshops.ndo.co.uk

Conference Director *Barbara Large, MBE, FRSA*

This festival of writing, now in its 22nd year, attracts international authors, playwrights, poets, agents and editors who give workshops, mini courses, editor appointments, lectures and seminars to help writers harness their creativity and develop technical skills. Fifteen writing competitions are attached to the conference. All first-place winners are published in *The Best of* series annually. The 2002 Conference was held over the last weekend of June at King Alfred's University College, Winchester, with workshops in July. The Bookfair offers delegates a wide choice of exhibits including Internet author services, publishers, booksellers, printers and trade associations. See also **Pitstop Refuelling Writers' Weekend Workshops**.

Highbury College, Portsmouth

Dovercourt Road, Cosham, Portsmouth, Hampshire PO6 2SA
☎023 9238 3131 Fax 023 9237 8382
Website www.highbury.ac.uk

Contact *Secretary* (☎ 023 9231 3287)

The 20-week fast-track courses include: *Pre-entry Magazine Journalism*, run under the auspices of the Periodicals Training Council; *Pre-entry Newspaper Journalism*, run under the auspices of the National Council for Training of Journalists; and Postgraduate Diploma in *Broadcasting Journalism*, run under the auspices of the Broadcast Journalism Training Council.

King Alfred's College

Winchester, Hampshire SO22 4NR
☎01962 841515 Fax 01962 842280
Website www.kingalfreds.ac.uk

Three-year degree course in *Drama, Theatre and Television Studies*, including *Writing for Devised Community Theatre* and *Writing for Television Documentary*. Contact the Admissions Office (☎ 01962 827262).

MA course in *Theatre for Development* – one year, full-time course with major project overseas or in the UK. MA course in *Writing for Children* available on either a one- or two-year basis. Enquiries: Admissions Officer (☎01962 827235).

University of Southampton New College

The Avenue, Southampton SO17 1BG
☎023 8059 7261 Fax 023 8059 7271
Email vah@soton.ac.uk

Creative writing courses and writers' workshops. Courses are held in local/regional centres.

Hertfordshire

Liberato Breakaway Writing Courses

9 Bishop's Avenue, Bishop's Stortford, Hertfordshire CM23 3EJ
☎01279 833690
Email Liberato@tesco.net
Website www.liberato.co.uk

Contact *Maureen Blundell*

Specialises in beginner fiction writers with day, weekend and week-long courses. Day courses on short stories, novels and poetry held in Harlow and Sawbridgeworth on the Herts/Essex border. Weekend courses on all aspects of fiction writing held at Polstead in Suffolk or Hertford. Five-day fiction and poetry course at Leiston,

Suffolk in September. Greek weeks on small island near Aegina, May/June. Emphasis on individual writing with written manuscript critiques and one-to-one sessions. Also offers postal manuscript critiques on all fiction/autobiography.

West Herts College

Creative Industries, Hempstead Road, Watford, Hertfordshire WD1 3EZ
☎01923 812654
Email gaym@westherts.ac.uk

Contact *Admissions*

The college offers a postgraduate diploma in *Publishing* with an option in *Multimedia Publishing*.

Kent

North West Kent College

Miskin Road, Dartford, Kent DA1 2LU
☎01322 629436 Fax 01322 629468
Website www.nwkent.ac.uk

Contact *Neil Nixon, Head of School, Media & Communications*

Two-year, full-time course that explores writing from a number of angles, teaching essential skills, market and academic aspects of the subject. Successful students progress to work or the University of Greenwich, the latter option allowing them to gain a BA(Hons) in Humanities from a further year of study. Staff include scriptwriters, novelists and a book publishers. Students produce their own creative work, compiling a portfolio in the final year under guidance from staff.

University of Kent at Canterbury

Unit for Regional Learning, Keynes College, Canterbury, Kent CT2 7NP
☎01227 823507 Fax 01227 458745
Email part-time@ukc.ac.uk
Website www.ukc.ac.uk/url

Certificate courses in *Practical Writing* and *Imaginative Writing*. Also combined studies – *English and Creative Writing*.

Lancashire

Alston Hall College

Alston Lane, Longridge, Preston, Lancashire PR3 3BP
☎01772 784661 Fax 01772 785835
Email alston.hall@ed.lancscc.gov.uk
Website www.alstonhall.u-net.com

Holds regular day-long creative writing workshops, also weekend residential courses. Brochure available.

Edge Hill College of Higher Education

St Helen's Road, Ormskirk, Lancashire L39 4QP
☎01695 575171
Email shepparr@edgehill.ac.uk

Contact *Dr R. Sheppard*

Offers a two-year, part-time MA in *Writing Studies*. Combines advanced-level writers' workshops with closely related courses in the poetics of writing and contemporary writing in English. There is also provision for MPhil and PhD-level research in writing and poetics. A full range of creative writing courses is available at undergraduate level, in poetry and fiction writing which may be taken as part of a modular BA.

Lancaster University

Department of Creative Writing, Lonsdale College, Bailrigg, Lancaster LA1 4YN
☎01524 594169 Fax 01524 843934
Email l.kellett@lancaster.ac.uk

Contact *Lyn Kellett*

Offers practical graduate and undergraduate courses in writing fiction, poetry and scripts. All based on group workshops – students' work-in-progress is circulated and discussed. Distance learning MA now available. Graduates include Andrew Miller, Justin Hill, Monique Roffey, Alison MacLeod, Jacob Polley.

The Written Word

43 Green Lane, Beaumont, Lancaster LA1 2ES
☎01524 35215 Fax 01524 35215
Email steve@ashton01.freeserve.co.uk

Contact *Steve Ashton*

Postal course in all categories of short and full-length non-fiction work, with an emphasis on writing magazine feature articles and getting them published. Personal tuition from a working professional with 15 years' experience. £275 fee includes comprehensive course book plus detailed guidance and feedback on eight realistic assignments. Also, script evaluation service (£45 for articles, £120 for three chapters plus the synopsis of a book). Send for information leaflet.

Leicestershire

Leicester Adult Education College, Writing School

2 Wellington Street, Leicester LE1 6HL
☎0116 233 4343 Fax 0116 233 4344
Email valerie.moore@leicester-adult-ed.ac.uk
Website www.leicester-adult-ed.ac.uk

Contact *Valerie Moore*

Offers a wide range of creative writing and journalism courses throughout the year. The programme offers a mix of critical workshops, one-day courses and short craft modules. Specialises in supporting new and more experienced writers through to publication and has strong links with local media. Occasional masterclasses and talks. Visiting writers have included Melvyn Bragg, Simon Brett, John Harvey, Roy Hattersley, Susan Hill, Rose Impey, Graham Joyce, Deric Longden, Simon Armitage and Andrew Motion.

Greater London

Arvon Foundation

Administration: 2nd Floor, 42A Buckingham Palace Road, London SW1W 0RE
☎020 7931 7611 Fax 020 7963 0961
Website www.arvonfoundation.org

President *Terry Hands*

Totleigh Barton, Sheepwash, Beaworthy, Devon EX21 5NS
☎01409 231338 Fax 01409 231144
Email t-barton@arvonfoundation.org

Lumb Bank, Heptonstall, Hebden Bridge, West Yorkshire HX7 6DF
☎01422 843714 Fax 01422 843714
Email l-bank@arvonfoundation.org

Moniack Mhor, Teavarran, Kiltarlity, Beauly, Inverness-shire IV4 7HT
☎01463 741675
Email m-mhor@arvonfoundation.org

Chairman *Prue Skene, CBE*
National Director *Helen Chaloner*

FOUNDED 1968. Offers people of any age (over 16) and any background the opportunity to live and work with professional writers. Four-and-a-half-day residential courses are held throughout the year at Arvon's three centres, covering poetry, fiction, drama, writing for children, songwriting and the performing arts. Bursaries towards the cost of course fees are available for those on low incomes, the unemployed, students and pensioners. Runs a biennial poetry competition (see entry under **Prizes**).

Blaze the Trail

2nd Floor, 241 High Street, London E17 7BH
☎020 8520 4569
Email training@coralmedia.co.uk
Website www.blaze-the-trail.com

ScriptCity at Blaze the Trail provides creative and professional training in screenwriting and story editing skills for writers, readers and script editors. *New Perspectives*: a 12-month intensive script development programme in association with professional editors and incorporating workshops and masterclasses; *Do the Write Thing*: for writers new to the screen; *Reading Room*: professional development for script readers; *Final Edition*: foundation and advanced training for script editors and producers; also one-on-one creative surgeries with professionals. Please call course coordinator for full details.

The Central School of Speech and Drama

Embassy Theatre, Eton Avenue, London NW3 3HY
☎020 7722 8183 Fax 020 7722 4132

Contact *Nick Wood, Writing and Dramaturgy Tutor*

MA in *Advanced Theatre Practice*. One-year, full-time course aimed at providing a grounding in principal areas of professional theatre practice – *Writing, Dramaturgy, Directing, Performance, Design* and *Puppetry*, with an emphasis on collaboration between the various strands. 'The Writing and Dramaturgy strands are particularly suitable for those wishing to work in a lively and stimulating atmosphere creating, with other practitioners, new work for the theatre.' Prospectus available.

The City Literary Institute

Humanities Dept, Stukeley Street, London WC2B 5LJ
☎020 7430 0542 Fax 020 7405 3347
Email humanities@citylit.ac.uk

The Writing School offers a wide range of courses from *Ways Into Creative Writing* and *Writing for Children* to *Playwriting* and *Writing Short Stories*. The creative writing classes may be one-day Saturday classes, weekly sessions over one or more terms, or one-week intensive workshops. The Department offers information and advice during term time.

City University

Department of Continuing Education, Northampton Square, London EC1V 0HB
☎020 7040 5060
Email conted@city.ac.uk
Website www.city.ac.uk/conted/cfa.htm

Creative writing classes include: *Writer's Workshop; Wordshop* (poetry); *Writing Comedy; Playwright's Workshop; Writing Freelance Articles for Newspapers; Writing about Travel; Creative Writing; Fiction: Short and Long; Feature Journalism; Writing for Children.*

The Complete Creative Writing Course at the Groucho Club

☎020 7249 3711 Fax 020 7683 8141
Email maggie.h@blueyonder.co.uk
Website www.creative-writing.pwp.
  blueyonder.co.uk

Contact *Maggie Hamand*

Courses of ten two-hour sessions held at the Groucho Club in London's Soho, starting in January, April and September, Monday or Saturday afternoons, 2.30 pm – 4.30 pm. Beginners and advanced courses offered. Each week looks at a different aspect of fiction writing and includes stimulating exercises, discussion and weekly homework. The tutors are novelists Maggie Hamand and Henrietta Soames. £195 for whole course.

The Drill Hall

16 Chenies Street, London WC1B 7EX
☎020 7307 5061 Fax 020 7307 5062
Email admin@drillhall.co.uk

Holds a number of writing classes and workshops. Regular tutors include Carol Burns and Peter Carty.

London College of Printing

Elephant & Castle, London SE1 6SB
☎020 7514 6562
Website www.lcptraining.co.uk

Intensive courses in journalism. Short courses run by DALI (Developments at the London Institute) at the Elephant & Castle address above: *Guide to Magazine Writing/News Writing/ Feature Writing/Freelance Journalism/Proof Reading/ Subbing on the Screen; Sub-editing.* Also offers two-day specialist journalism courses in food writing, travel writing, writing for the music press, sports journalism and fashion writing, health and medicine writing, electronic journalism, business journalism, plus scriptwriting and documentary making. One-day specialist courses: interviewing techniques for print/ broadcast journalism; law for journalists. For individuals and companies 'tailor-made training' services can be provided. Prospectus and information leaflets available; ☎020 7514 6770 or access the website where course bookings can be made securely online.

London School of Journalism

22 Upbrook Mews, London W2 3HG
☎020 7706 3790 Fax 020 7706 3780
Email info@lsjournalism.com
Website www.home-study.com

Contact *Student Administration Office*

Correspondence courses with an individual and personal approach. Students remain with the same tutor throughout their course. Options include: *Short Story Writing; Writing for Children; Poetry; Freelance Journalism; Internet Journalism; Media Law; Improve Your English; Cartooning; Thriller Writing; English for Business; Journalism and Newswriting.* Fees vary but range from £215 for *Enjoying English Literature* to £395 for *Journalism and Newswriting.* NUJ-recognised Postgraduate Journalism Diploma (three and six-month attendance).

Middlesex University

School of Humanities, White Hart Lane, London N17 8HR
☎020 8411 5000 Fax 020 8411 6652
Email tmadmissions@mdx.ac.uk
Website www.mdx.ac.uk

The UK's longest established writing degree offers a Single or Joint Honours programme in *Writing & Media* (full- or part-time). This modular programme in creative and media writing gives an opportunity to explore journalism, poetry, prose fiction and dramatic writing for a wide range of genres and audiences. Option for work experience in the media and publishing. Contact Admissions or *Maggie Butt*, Programme Leader. (Email m.butt@mdx.ac.uk)

MA in *Writing* (full-time, part-time; day and evening classes) includes a specialist strand in Asian and Black British writing, approaches to the short story and novel; lectures and workshops from established writers. Options in Poetry and Scriptwriting are awaiting validation. Contact *Sue Gee.* ☎020 8411 5941. (Email s.gee@mdx.ac.uk)

Soho Theatre Company

See entry under **Theatre Producers**

University of Surrey Roehampton

School of Arts, Roehampton Lane, London SW15 5PU
☎020 8392 3230 Fax 020 8392 3289
Website www.roehampton.ac.uk

Three-year BA(Hons) programmes in *Drama and Theatre Studies* and *Film and Television Studies* include courses on writing for stage and screen.

University of Westminster

School of Communication and Creative Industries, Harrow Campus, Watford Road, Harrow, Middlesex HA1 3TP
☎020 7911 5903 Fax 020 7911 5955
Email harrow-admissions@wmin.ac.uk

Website www.wmin.ac.uk

Courses include part-time MAs available in *Journalism Studies; Film and Television Studies.*

Greater Manchester

Manchester Metropolitan University – The Writing School

Department of English, Geoffrey Manton Building, Rosamond Street West, off Oxford Road, Manchester M15 6LL
☎0161 247 1732/1 Fax 0161 247 6345
Course Convenor *Michael Schmidt*

Closely associated with **Carcanet Press Ltd** and *PN Review*, The Writing School offers four 'routes' for students to follow: *Poetry, The Novel, Life Writing* and *Writing for Children.* A key feature of the programme is regular readings, lectures, workshops and masterclasses by writers, publishers, producers, booksellers, librarians and agents. Tutors include Simon Armitage, Carol Ann Duffy, Sophie Hannah, Jacqueline Roy and Jeffrey Wainwright.

University of Manchester

Department of English & American Studies, Arts Building, Oxford Road, Manchester M13 9PL
☎0161 275 3144 Fax 0161 275 3256
Email english@man.ac.uk
Website www.art.man.ac.uk/english/
pgdegree/ma.htm#novel

Offers a one-year MA in *Novel Writing.*

Password Training Ltd

23 New Mount Street, Manchester M4 4DE
☎0161 953 4071 Fax 0161 953 4001

Password Training provides training for publishers, writers' groups and individual writers in Internet publishing, planning, production, design, marketing, costing and distribution.

University of Salford

Postgraduate Admissions, Dept. of Arts, Media & Social Sciences, Adelphi Building, Peru Street, Salford, Greater Manchester M3 6EQ
☎0161 295 6027
Email r.humphrey@salford.ac.uk
Website www.smmp.salford.ac.uk

MA in *Television and Radio Scriptwriting.* Two-year, part-time course taught by professional writers and producers. Also offers a number of masterclasses with leading figures in the radio and television industry.

The Writers Bureau

Sevendale House, 7 Dale Street, Manchester M1 1JB
☎0161 228 2362 Fax 0161 236 9440
Email advisory@writersbureau.com
Website www.writersbureau.com

Comprehensive home-study writing course with personal tuition service from professional writers (fee: £249). Fiction, non-fiction, articles, short stories, novels, TV, radio and drama all covered in detail. Trial period, guarantee and no time limits. ODLQC accredited. Quote Ref. EH03. Free enquiry line: 0800 856 2008

The Writers Bureau College of Journalism

Address etc. as The Writers Bureau above

Home-study course covering all aspects of journalism. Real-life assignments assessed by qualified tutors with the emphasis on getting into print and enjoying the financial rewards. Comprises 28 modules and three handbooks with special introductory offers. Ref: EHJ03. Free enquiry line: 0800 298 7008.

The Writers College

Address etc. as The Writers Bureau above

The Art of Writing Poetry Course from The Writers Bureau sister college. A home-study course with a more 'recreational' emphasis. The 60,000-word course has 17 modules and lets you complete six written assignments for tutorial evaluation. Fees: £99. Quote Ref. EHP03. Free enquiry line: 0800 856 2008.

The Writer's Muse

5 Churchdale Road, Higher Blackley, Manchester M9 8NE
☎0161 720 9307
Secretary *Wendy Creighton*

Offers postal workshops and courses designed to meet aspiring writers' individual needs with one-to-one tuition by writer/teacher, Rosetta Moore, BSc Hons, MBPsS, TDip. Twelve monthly assignments; £50 p.a. (No poetry.) Also offers evaluation service; send A4 s.a.e. for full details.

Merseyside

University of Liverpool

Centre for Continuing Education, 19 Abercromby Square, Liverpool L69 7ZG
☎0151 794 6900/6952 (24 hours)
Fax 0151 794 2544

Website www.liv.ac.uk/conted

Head of Creative Arts *Keith Birch*

Courses include: *Introduction to Creative Writing; The Short Story and the Novel; Introduction to Writing Poetry; Introduction to Scripting for Radio and Television; Introduction to Writing Journalism; Science Fiction and Fantasy; Travel Writing; Songwriting; Theatre Playwrights Workshop; Scriptwriting: Situation Comedy; Scriptwriting: Film and Television.* Most courses are run in the evening over 10 or 20 weeks but there are some linked Saturday and weekday courses on offer. Students have the option of accreditation towards a university award in Creative Writing. Some of the above courses are also part of the university's part-time Flexible Degree pathway (Comb. Hons., Arts). No pre-entry qualifications required. Fees vary with concessions for the unwaged and those in receipt of benefit.

Norfolk

University of East Anglia

School of English & American Studies, Norwich, Norfolk NR4 7TJ
☎01603 593262   Fax 01603 593799
Email l.faith@uea.ac.uk
Website www.uea.ac.uk/eas

Contact *Lorraine Faith, Postgraduate Admissions*

UEA has a history of concern with contemporary literary culture. Among its MA programmes is one in *Creative Writing*, Stream 1: Prose Fiction; Stream 2: Poetry; Stream 3: Scriptwriting.

Nottinghamshire

The Nottingham Trent University

Humanities Faculty Office (Post Graduate Studies), Clifton Lane, Nottingham NG11 8NS
☎0115 848 6677   Fax 0115 848 6339
Email hum.postgrad@ntu.ac.uk
Website human.ntu.ac.uk/pg/courses/writing.html

MA in *Writing*. Hands-on and workshop-based, the course concentrates primarily on the practice and production of writing. A choice of options from *Fiction, Poetry, Creative Non-Fiction, New Media* and *Scriptwriting*. Assignments and a dissertation of your writing to complete for award of degree. No formal exams. Staff are all established writers. Current visiting professors: Peter Porter, Michele

Roberts and Miranda Seymour. Also a full programme of visiting speakers. Study either full-time (three evenings per week) or part-time (two evenings per week over two years). Further details and application forms from the Faculty Office (details above).

Oxfordshire

University of Oxford Department for Continuing Education

Rewley House, 1 Wellington Square, Oxford OX1 2JA
☎01865 270368   Fax 01865 270309
Website www.conted.ox.ac.uk

Creative writing schools, usually held during the autumn and spring terms. Courses for 2001/2 were: *The Novel, The Art of Lying* and *Writing for Children.* Each course is a series of three-day schools with student numbers limited to 20. Early booking is advised.

Somerset

Bath Spa University College

Newton Park, Bath BA2 9BN
☎01225 875875   Fax 01225 875444
Email enquiries@bathspa.ac.uk
Website www.bathspa.ac.uk

Admissions Officer *Clare Brandram Jones*

Postgraduate Diploma/MA in *Creative Writing.* A course for creative writers wanting to develop their work. Teaching is by published writers in the novel, poetry, short stories and scriptwriting. In recent years, several students from this course have received contracts from publishers for novels, awards for poetry and short stories and have had work produced on BBC Radio.

Dillington House

Ilminster, Somerset TA19 9DT
☎01460 52427/Minicom: 01460 258640
Fax 01460 52433
Email dillington@somerset.gov.uk
Website www.dillington.co.uk

Contact *Ruth Mankelow, Bookings Assistant*

Offers a range of day schools, residential weekends and a summer school in a variety of writing subjects and literary appreciation. Courses in 2001/2 included *Write On!* (creative writing); *Writing From Experience; Writing Your Life Story; Writing the Commercial Short Story;*

William Blake and the Poetry of Protest. Full details of programme available in free brochure and on the website.

Institute of Copywriting
Honeycombe House, Bagley, Wedmore, Somerset BS28 4TD
☎01934 713563 Fax 01934 713492
Email copy@inst.org
Website www.institute.org/copy

Comprehensive home-study course covering all aspects of copywriting, including advice on becoming a self-employed copywriter. Each student has a personal tutor who is an experienced copywriter and who provides detailed feedback on the student's assignments.

University of Bristol
Department of English, 3/5 Woodland Road, Bristol BS8 1TB
☎0117 954 6969 Fax 0117 928 8860
Email rowena.fowler@bris.ac.uk
Website www.bris.ac.uk/Depts/English/ce_creat.html

Courses: *Women and Writing*, for women who write or would like to begin to write (poetry, fiction, non-fiction, journals) and various other writing courses for the general public. *Certificate in Creative Writing* and *Certificate in Creative Writing for Therapeutic Purposes*. Detailed brochure available.

Staffordshire
Keele University
The Centre for Continuing and Professional Education, Keele University, (Freepost ST1666), Newcastle under Lyme, Staffordshire ST5 5BG
☎01782 583436

Evening and weekend courses on literature and creative writing. The 2002 programme included fiction writing and writing for children. Also runs study days where major novelists or poets read and discuss their work.

Surrey
Royal Holloway
University of London, Egham Hill, Egham, Surrey TW20 0EX
☎01784 443922 Fax 01784 431018
Email drama@rhul.ac.uk
Contacts *Dan Rebellato, David Wiles*
Three-year BA course in *Theatre Studies* during which playwriting can be studied as an option in the second or third year. MA *Theatre (Playwriting)*, a one- or two-year (full- or part-time) postgraduate degree.

University of Surrey
School of Educational Studies, University of Surrey, Guildford, Surrey GU1 5XH
☎01483 876172 Fax 01483 876171
Email r.curtis@surrey.ac.uk

The Open Studies programme includes several *Creative Writing* courses. For autumn 2002 these will be held at the Guildford Institute (in the centre of Guildford), Caterham and Reigate. The courses carry credits and can build to a university award. For details, contact *Rachel Curtis*, Enrolment Secretary or *Lynda Strudwick, BEd, MSc*, Programme Director and Subject Leader in Creative Writing.

Sussex
University College Chichester
Bishop Otter Campus, College Lane, Chichester, West Sussex PO19 4PE
☎01243 816000 Fax 01243 816080
Email s.norgate@ucc.ac.uk

Contact *Stephanie Norgate*, Route Leader, MA in Creative Writing (01243 816296)

Postgraduate Certificate/Diploma/MA in *Creative Writing*, both full- and part-time.

The Earnley Concourse
Earnley, Chichester, West Sussex PO20 7JL
☎01243 670392 Fax 01243 670832
Email info@earnley.co.uk
Website www.earnley.co.uk

Offers a range of residential and non-residential courses throughout the year. Previous programme has included *Writing for Publication; You Can Sell What You Write*. Brochure available.

University of Sussex
Centre for Continuing Education, Education Development Building, Falmer, Brighton, East Sussex BN1 9RG
☎01273 678537 Fax 01273 678848
Email y.d.barnes@sussex.ac.uk
Website www.sussex.ac.uk
Contact (for all courses) *Yvonne Barnes*

Postgraduate Diploma in *Dramatic Writing*: the student is treated as a commissioned writer working in theatre, TV, radio or film with professional directors and actors. Includes workshops, masterclasses and a residential weekend.

Sixteen-months, part-time. Convenor: *Richard Crane*. Certificate in *Creative Writing*: short fiction, novel and poetry for imaginative writers. Two-year, part-time. Convenors: *Richard Crane, Mark Slater*.

Tyne & Wear

University of Newcastle upon Tyne

Centre for Lifelong Learning, King George VI Building, Newcastle upon Tyne NE1 7RU
☎0191 222 5680 Fax 0191 222 7090
Website www.cll.ncl.ac.uk

Courses held in 2002 included: *Creative Writing: Fictionalising the Family* and *Writing From the Inside Out*, a workshop for women. Contact the Secretary, Adult Education Programme.

Warwickshire

University of Warwick

Open Studies, Continuing Education Department, Coventry, Warwickshire CV4 7AL
☎024 7652 3831
Email k.rainsley@warwick.ac.uk *or* l.downs@warwick.ac.uk

Creative writing courses held at the university or in regional centres. Subjects include: *Starting to Write; Prose and Poetry Writing; Writing for Radio; Screenwriting for Beginners*. A one-year certificate in *Creative Writing* is available.

West Midlands

Sandwell College

Smethwick Campus, Crocketts Lane, Smethwick B66 3BU
☎0121 556 6000
Contact *Tony Martin*

Creative writing courses held afternoons/evenings, from September to July. General courses covering short stories, poetry, autobiography, etc. Also women's writing courses.

University of Birmingham

School of Education, Selly Oak, Birmingham B29 6LL
☎0121 414 3413 Fax 0121 414 8067
Email S.G.Roseten@bham.ac.uk

Certificate of Higher Education in *Creative Writing* – two years, part-time in Birmingham and Worcester. Day or evening plus occasional classes, depending on venue, including theory and practice of writing in a wide range of literary genres. Course brochures are available from the address above. Please specify which course you are interested in. Progression routes to Diploma and Degree. Students who can demonstrate qualifications/writing skills equivalent to Certificate Level may apply to join the Diploma of Creative Writing. Additional courses are available at the Selly Oak Campus and in Worcestershire.

The University also offers an MPhil in *Playwriting Studies* established by playwright David Edgar in 1989. Contact *April Di Angelis*, Course Director at the Department of Drama and Theatre Arts (☎0121 414 5790).

Wiltshire

Marlborough College Summer School

Marlborough, Wiltshire SN8 1PA
☎01672 892388/9 Fax 01672 892476
Email summer.school@marlboroughcollege.wilts.sch.uk
Website www.marlboroughcollege.org

Summer School with literature and creative writing included in its programme. Caters for residential and day students. Brochure available giving full details and prices.

Yorkhire

Arvon Foundation (Yorkshire)

See entry under Greater London

Hull College

Queen's Gardens, Hull, East Yorkshire HU1 3DG
☎01482 329943 Fax 598733219079
Email jbillaney@hull-college.ac.uk
Contact *Julia Billaney*

Offers part-time day/evening writing courses in *Novel Writing* and *Short Story Writing*, at Hull College, Park Street Centre. Courses begin each academic term. Writers are encouraged to contribute stories for a collection.

University of Hull

Scarborough Campus, Filey Road, Scarborough, North Yorkshire YO11 3AZ
☎01723 362392 Fax 01723 370815
Website www.hull.ac.uk
Director of Studies *David Hughes*

BA Single Honours in *Theatre Studies* incorporates *Writing for Performance* and *Writing for Theatre*. Works closely with the Stephen Joseph Theatre and its artistic director Alan Ayckbourn. The theatre sustains a policy for staging new writers. (See entry under **Theatre Producers**.) The campus hosts the annual National Student Drama Festival which includes the International Student Playscript Competition (details from The National Information Centre for Student Drama; e-mail: nsdf@hull.ac.uk).

University of Leeds
Springfield Mount, Leeds, West Yorkshire LS2 9JT
Email r.k.o'rourke@leeds.ac.uk
Contact *Rebecca O'Rourke*
Also at: Adult Education Centre, 37 Harrow Road, Middlesbrough, Cleveland, TS5 5NT
☎01642 814987

Creative writing courses held throughout Cleveland, North and West Yorkshire in the autumn, spring and summer terms. These are held weekly and as non-residential summer schools. Courses carry undergraduate credit, are part-time and offered in a range of subjects, at beginners, intermediate and advanced levels. Professional development courses for writers and writing development workers which carry post-graduate credit are also offered.

University of Leeds, Bretton Hall Campus
School of Performance and Cultural Industries, Bretton Hall Campus, West Bretton, Wakefield, West Yorkshire WF4 4LG
☎01924 830261 Fax 01924 832006
Email rwatson@leeds.ac.uk
Contact *Rob Watson*

Offers one-year full-time/two-year part-time MA course in *Creative Writing* designed for competent though not necessarily published writers.

Leeds Metropolitan University
H505, City Site, Calverley Street, Leeds, West Yorkshire LS1 3HE
☎0113 283 2600 ext 3860
Email s.morton@lmu.ac.uk
Website www.lmu.ac.uk
Administrator *Samantha Morton*

Offers a Postgraduate Certificate/Diploma/MA in *Screenwriting (Fiction)*.

Open College of the Arts
Unit 1B, Redbrook Business Park, Wilthorpe Road, Barnsley, South Yorkshire S75 1JN
☎01226 730495 Fax 01226 730838
Email open.arts@ukonline.co.uk
Website www.oca-uk.com

The OCA correspondence course, *Starting to Write*, offers help and stimulus from experienced writers/tutors. Emphasis is on personal development rather than commercial genre. Subsequent levels available include specialist poetry, fiction and autobiographical writing courses. OCA writing courses are accredited to the University of Glamorgan. Prospectus and guide to courses available on request.

Sheffield Hallam University
School of Cultural Studies, Sheffield Hallam University, Collegiate Crescent, Sheffield S10 2BP
☎0114 225 2607 Fax 0114 225 2603
Email cspgenquiry@shu.ac.uk
Website www.shu.ac.uk/schools/cs/english/
  english.htm

Offers MA in *Creative Writing* (one-year, full-time; also part-time).

University of Sheffield
Institute for Lifelong Learning,
196–198 West Street, Sheffield S1 4ET
☎0114 222 7000 Fax 0114 222 7001
Website www.shef.ac.uk/till

Certificate in *Creative Writing* (Degree Level 1) and a wide range of courses, from foundation level to specialist writing areas, open to all members of the public. Courses in poetry, prose, journalism, scriptwriting, comedy, travel writing, writing using ICT/Web, writing for children. Brochures and information available from the address above.

Yorkshire Art Circus
School Lane, Glasshoughton, Castleford WF10 4QH
☎01977 550401
Email lorna@artcircus.org.uk
Website www.artcircus.org.uk
Course Administrator *Lorna Hey*

Organises courses designed to meet the needs of people living in the region who are looking to find out more about the arts. Writing courses cover a wide range of topics, from fiction and poetry workshops, to scriptwriting, selfpublishing and multimedia art on the Internet. Course brochure available on request.

IRELAND

Dingle Writing Courses Ltd

Ballyneanig, Ballyferriter, Tralee, Co. Kerry, Republic of Ireland
☎00 353 66 9154990 Fax 00 353 66 9154992
Email info@dinglewriting.com
Website www.dinglewriting.com

Directors *Abigail Joffe, Nicholas McLachlan*

A summer and autumn programme of weekend and five-day residential courses for beginners and experienced writers alike. Tutored by professional writers the courses take place in 'an inspirational setting overlooking Inch strand'. The programme includes poetry, fiction, starting to write and writing for theatre as well as special themed courses.

Past tutors have included Jennifer Johnston, Paul Durcan, Anne Enright, Paula Meeham, Jim Perrin, Mary O'Malley, Graham Mort and Michael Donaghy. Writing courses for schools are also available. Brochures and further information from programme director *Camilla Dinkel* at the address above.

University of Dublin (Trinity College)

Graduate Studies Office, Arts Building, Trinity College, Dublin 2, Republic of Ireland
☎00 353 1 608 1166 Fax 00 353 1 671 2821
Email gradinfo@tcd.ie
Website www.tcd.ie/owc

Contact *Admissions*

Offers an MPhil *Creative Writing* course. A one-year, full-time course intended for students who are seriously committed to writing, are practising, or prospective authors.

Queen's University of Belfast

Institute of Lifelong Learning, Belfast BT7 1NN
☎028 9027 3323 Fax 028 9023 6909
Email ill@qub.ac.uk
Website www.qub.ac.uk/ill

Courses have included *Creative Writing*; *Writing for Profit and Pleasure*; *Scriptwriting* and *Creative Writing for Beginners*.

University of Ulster

Conference & Professional Development Unit, Room 17C21, University of Ulster, Belfast BT37 0QB
☎028 9036 5131 Fax 028 9036 6060

Creative writing course/workshop, usually held in the autumn and spring terms. Concessions available.

SCOTLAND

University of Aberdeen

KEY Learning Opportunities, Regent Building, Regent Walk, Aberdeen AB24 3FX
☎01224 273528 Fax 01224 272478
Email evening-classes@abdn.ac.uk

Creative writing evening class held weekly, taught by published author. Participants may join at any time.

Arvon Foundation (Inverness-shire)

See entry under Greater London

University of Dundee

Continuing Education, Nethergate, Dundee DD1 4HN
☎01382 344128 Fax 01382 221057
Email k.mackle@dundee.ac.uk
Website www.dundee.ac.uk/education

Various creative writing courses held at the University and elsewhere in Dundee, Perthshire and Angus. Detailed course brochure available.

Edinburgh University

Office of Lifelong Learning, 11 Buccleuch Place, Edinburgh EH8 9LW
☎0131 650 4400 Fax 0131 667 6097
Email cce@ed.ac.uk
Website www.cce.ed.ac.uk *or*
www.lifelong.ed.ac.uk

Several writing-orientated courses and summer schools. Course brochure available.

University of Glasgow

Department of Adult and Continuing Education, 1 Park Drive, Glasgow G3 6LP
☎0141 330 4394/1829 (Enquiries/Brochure)
Fax 0141 330 1821
Email enquiry@ace.gla.ac.uk
Website www.gla.ac.uk/Acad/AdultEd

Runs writers' workshops and courses at all levels; all friendly and informal. Daytime and evening meetings. Tutors are all experienced published writers in various fields.

University of St Andrews

School of English, The University, St Andrews, Fife KY16 9AL
☎01334 462666 Fax 01334 462655
Email english@st-andrews.ac.uk
Website www.st-andrews.ac.uk

Offers postgraduate study in *Creative Writing*. Candidates choose two topics from: *Fiction: The Novel; Craft and Technique in Poetry* and all take the *Short Story* module. In September students submit a dissertation of original writing – prose fiction of 15,000 words or a collection of around 30 short poems. Taught by John Burnside, Robert Crawford, Douglas Dunn and Kathleen Jamie.

7:84 Summer School
See **7:84 Theatre Company Scotland** under **Theatre Producers**

WALES

Tŷ Newydd Writers' Centre
Llanystumdwy, Criccieth, Gwynedd LL52 0LW
☎01766 522811 Fax 01766 523095
Email tynewydd@dial.pipex.com

Residential writers' centre set up by the Taliesin Trust with the support of the **Arts Council of Wales** to encourage and promote writing in both English and Welsh. Most courses run from Monday evening to Saturday morning. Each course has two tutors and takes a maximum of 16 participants. The centre offers a wide range of specific courses for writers at all levels of experience. Early booking essential. Fee: £320 (single)/£345 (twin-bedded) inclusive. People on low incomes may be eligible for a grant or bursary. Course leaflet available. (See also **Organisations of Interest to Poets**.)

University of Glamorgan
Treforest, Pontypridd CF37 1DL
☎01443 482551
Website www.glam.ac.uk

Director, The National Centre for Writing *Professor Tony Curtis, FRSL*

MPhil in *Writing* – a two-year part-time Masters degree for writers of fiction and poets. ESTABLISHED 1993. Contact: *Professor Tony Curtis* at the School of Humanities and Social Sciences.

MA in *Scriptwriting (Theatre, TV or Radio)* – a two-year part-time Masters degree for scriptwriters. Contact: *Dr Richard J. Hand.*

Also, BA *Creative and Professional Writing* – a three-year course for undergraduates. Contact: *Dr Matthew Francis.*

University of Wales, Aberystwyth
Department of English, Hugh Owen Building, Aberystwyth, Ceredigion SY23 3DY
☎01970 622534 Fax 01970 622530
Website www.aber.ac.uk/~engwww/

BA *English and Creative Writing*, a three-year

course taught in part by practising writers, including novelist Patricia Duncker and poet Tiffany Atkinson. Also offers an MA in *Writing* with modules in narratology and poetry, writing and publication.

University of Wales, Bangor
Department of English, College Road, Bangor LL57 2DG
☎01248 382102 Fax 01248 382102
Email els029@bangor.ac.uk

PhD *Creative and Critical Writing*; MA *Creative Studies (Creative Writing)*; BA *English Literature with Creative Writing*; BA *English Language with Creative Writing*; BA *French wtih Creative Writing*; BA *German with Creative Writing*. Also MA *Creative Studies (Film Practice)*; MA *Creative Studies (Drama Practice)*; MA *Creative Studies (Media Practice)*. The Centre for the Creative and Performing Arts launched the UK national database on creative writing education in universities and colleges and was the location of the first national and international conferences on creative writers on campus. It is the location of the research programme, Creative Writing in Universities.

Writers' Holiday at Caerlon
School Bungalow, Church Road, Pontnewydd, Cwmbran NP44 1AT
☎01633 489438
Email writersholiday@lineone.net
Website www.writersholiday.net

Contact *Anne Hobbs*

Annual six-day conference for writers of all standards held in the summer at the University of Wales' Caerlon Campus. Courses, lectures, concert and excursion all included in the fee (£324 in 2002). Private, single and en-suite, full board accommodation. Courses in 2002 included *Writing for Publication*, *Writing Poetry*, *Writing Romantic Fiction* and *Writing for the Radio*.

EUROPE – FRANCE
Creative in Calvados
1 Ormelie Terrace, Joppa, Edinburgh EH15 2EX
☎0131 669 4025
Email steveharvey@creativeincalvados.co.uk
Website www.creativeincalvados.co.uk

Contact *Steve Harvey*

Residential writing courses and retreats, readers' breaks and creative workshops based in an old watermill and outbuildings in a forest valley in

Normandy. Courses are tutored by well-known writers and generally run Tuesday to Friday and Friday to Monday in spring and autumn. Tuition is friendly and information, and group numbers are limited to seven per course.

Full Moon Productions
See entry under **Film, TV and Video Production Companies**

GREECE

Great Escapes
Casa Lucia, Sgombou, Corfu 49083 Greece
☎00 30 661 091419 Fax 00 30 661 091732
Email wendyhol@otenet.gr

A variety of writing and related courses held on the island of Corfu from April to October. For details of courses and fees, contact *Wendy Holborow* by post or e-mail.

Circles and Workshops

Directory of Writers' Circles
39 Lincoln Way, Harlington, Bedfordshire
LU5 6NG
☎01525 873197
Email diana@writers-circles.com
Website www.writers-circles.com

Directory of writers' circles in the UK and Republic of Ireland, listing contact details and information about meetings. Contact the editor, *Diana Hayden*, for details.

Writers' Circles Handbook
Oldacre, Horderns Park Road, Chapel-en-le-Frith, High Peak SK23 9SY
☎01298 812305
Email jillie@cix.co.uk *or*
oldacre@btinternet.com
Website www.cix.co.uk/~oldacre/

New handbook for writers' circles, with invaluable information, articles and a comprehensive list of all known circles and groups meeting in the UK. Some overseas entries too. Free regular updates available after initial purchase (£5, post free). Contact *Jill Dick* at the address above for further details.

Ayr Writers' Club
Meeting place: Wallace Tower, High Street, Ayr
Website www.ayrwritersclub.co.uk
Contact *May Stevenson* (☎01292 2637900)

FOUNDED in 1970, this well-established writers' club is strong on encouraging its members towards achieving success in various genres and many of them have been published. Meetings are held every Wednesday from September to April at 7.30 pm. These take the form of club nights and workshops at which published authors are invited to speak once a month.

Carmarthern Writers' Circle
Lower Carfan, Tavernspite, Whitland, Pembrokeshire SA34 0NP
☎01994 240441
Contact *Jenny White*

FOUNDED 1989. The Circle meets on the second Monday of every month upstairs at the Queen's Hotel in Carmarthen. Both beginners and experienced writers are welcome. In addition to monthly meetings, activities include workshops and 'poets and pints' evenings. More information available from address above.

Children's Novel Writers' Folio
See **Short Story Writers' Folio**

Chiltern Writers' Group
151 Chartridge Lane, Chesham, Buckinghamshire HP5 2SE
☎01494 772308
Email chilwriters@netscept.net
Website www.chilternwriters.netfirms.com

Guest speakers, workshops, manuscript critiques; monthly meetings at Wendover Public Library. Regular newsletter and competitions. Annual subscription: £15; concessions: £10. Non-members meeting: £3.

Concordant Poets Folios
17 Stone Close, Braintree, Essex CM7 1LJ
☎01376 342095
Email whogg@onetel.net.uk

An independent postal workshop for poets which at present consists of two folios of eight members each. The purpose of the folios is to submit work for appreciation and criticism by folio members. Send s.a.e. for details.

The Cotswold Writers' Circle

Bliss's Cottage, Lower Chedworth,
Cheltenham, Gloucestershire GL54 4AN
☎01285 720668
Email elaine@pandlunt.co.uk

Patron *Elizabeth Webster*
Membership Secretary *Mrs E. Lunt*
Honorary Treasurer *Charles Hooker*

The Circle meets fortnightly during the day
(10.30 am to 12.30 pm) in Cirencester. Circle
activities include organising an International
Open Writing Competition – closing date 31
January; details from the address above (enclose
s.a.e.). Publishes an anthology to include winning entries of the Competition. Arranges
writing workshops conducted by well-known
authors. Contact the Membership Secretary at
the address above for further details.

Cumbrian Literary Group

'Calgarth', The Brow, Flimby, Maryport,
Cumbria CA15 8TD
☎01900 813444

President *George Bott*
Secretary *Joyce E. Fisher*

FOUNDED in 1946 to provide a meeting place
for readers and writers in Cumbria. The Group
meets once a month (April to November), usually in Windermere. Invites speakers to meetings and holds annual competitions for poetry
and prose. *Publishes* a magazine, *Bookshelf.*
Subscription: £8 p.a. For further details contact the Secretary at the address above.

'Sean Dorman' Manuscript Society

Cherry Trees, Crosemere Road, Cockshutt,
Ellesmere, Shropshire SY12 0JP
☎01939 270293

Director *Mary Driver*

FOUNDED 1957. The Society provides mutual
help among writers and aspiring writers in
England, Wales and Scotland. By means of cir-
culating manuscript parcels, members receive
constructive criticism of their own work and
read and comment on the work of others. Each
'Circulator' has up to nine participants and
members' contributions may be in any medium:
short stories, chapters of a novel, poetry, magazine articles, etc. Members may join two such
circulators if they wish. Each circulator has a
technical section and a letters section in which
friendly communication between members is
encouraged, and all are of a general nature apart
from one, specialising in mss for the Christian

market. Full details and application forms available on receipt of s.a.e. Subscription: £6.50 p.a.

East Anglian Writers

52 Riverside Road, Norwich, Norfolk
NR1 1SR
☎01603 629088   Fax 01603 629088
Email Anthony.vivis@tesco.net

Contact *Anthony Vivis (Chair)*

A group of over 80 professional writers living
in Norfolk, Cambridgeshire and Suffolk.
Affiliated to the **Society of Authors**. Informal
pub meetings, occasional speakers' evenings
and contact point for professional writers new
to the area.

Eastbourne's Anderida Writers

20 Vian Avenue, Eastbourne, East Sussex
BN23 6EY
☎01323 737677

Secretary *Stella Freshney*

Creative writing group of Sussex authors, both
published and aspiring as well as beginners.
Main meetings are held at 8 pm on the first
Tuesday of each month (except January) for
talks, workshops, competitions and other activities at Chaseley Trust, Bolsover Road,
Eastbourne; holds two evening meetings catering for articles/short stories/poetry and novel
writing plus one afternoon open meeting.
Produces annual anthology of members' work.
For information on joining the group, contact
the Membership Secretary at the address above.
Subscription: £15 p.a.

Equinoxe Screenwriting Workshops

Association Equinoxe, 4 Square du Roule,
75008 Paris France
☎00 33 1 5353 4488   Fax 00 33 1 5353 4489
Email equinoxef@wanadoo.fr

Contact *Claire Dubert*

FOUNDED 1993, with Jeanne Moreau as president, to promote screenwriting and to establish a
link between European and American film production. In association with Canal+, Sony
Pictures Entertainment, Fondation Daniel
Langlais and Media Programme of the European
Union, Château Beychevelle, Equinoxe supports
young writers of all nationalities by creating a
screenwriting community capable of appealing
to an international audience. Open to selected
professional screenwriters able to speak either
English or French fluently. To-date, Equinoxe
has helped 160 European and American authors
to perfect and promote scripts. 54 of these have

been brought to the screen and several are in production.

Euroscript

Suffolk House, 1–8 Whitfield Place, London W1P 5SF

☎020 7387 5880 Fax 020 7387 5880

Email euroscript@netmatters.co.uk

Website www.euroscript.co.uk

Euroscript is a script development organisation aimed at professional writers and producers seeking creative and editorial input on their projects. Develops screenplays through an intensive modular programme, including residential script workshops; provides script reports and runs two film story competitions per year: deadlines 30 April and 31 October. Open to writers of any nationality. Write or access the website for further information.

Gay Authors Workshop

BM Box 5700, London WC1N 3XX

☎020 8520 5223

Contact *Kathryn Byrd*

Established 1978 to encourage and support lesbian/gay writers. Regular meetings and a newsletter. GAW gave rise to Paradise Press (see entry under **Small Presses**).

Historical Novel Folio

17 Purbeck Heights, Mount Road, Parkstone, Poole, Dorset BH14 0QP

☎01202 741897

Contact *Doris Myall-Harris*

An independent postal workshop – single folio dealing with any period before World War II. Send s.a.e. for details.

Kops and Ryan Advanced Playwriting Workshops

41B Canfield Gardens, London NW6 3JL

☎020 7624 2940/7263 8740

Tutors *Bernard Kops, Tom Ryan*

Three ten-week terms per year beginning in September. Students may join course any term. Workshops on Tuesday, 7 pm–10 pm or Thursday, 7 pm–10 pm, or Saturday, 2 pm–5 pm. Small groups. Focuses on structure, character, language, meaning and style through written and improvised exercises; readings of scenes from students' current work; and readings of full-length plays. Two actors attend each session. Also, instruction in film technique and private tutorials. Call for details.

London Writer Circle

27 Braycourt Avenue, Walton-on-Thames, Surrey KT12 2AZ

☎01932 702874

Email wendy.stickler@org.uk

Contact *Wendy Hughes (Editor & Membership Secretary)*

FOUNDED 1924. Aims to help and encourage writers of all grades. Monthly evening meetings with well-known speakers on aspects of literature and journalism, and workshops for short story writing, poetry and feature writing. Occasional social events and quarterly magazine. Subscription: £20 (London); £10 (Country); £6 (Overseas).

North West Playwrights (NWP)

18 St Margaret's Chambers, 5 Newton Street, Manchester M1 1HL

☎0161 237 1978 Fax 0161 237 1978

Email newplaysnw@hotmail.com

Website www.newplaysnw.com

FOUNDED 1982. Award-winning organisation whose aim is to develop and promote new theatre writing. Operates a script-reading service, classes and script development scheme and *The Lowdown* newsletter. Services available to writers in the region only. Also disburses grants to support commissions, residencies, etc.

Pier Playwrights

PO Box 141, Brighton, East Sussex BN2 1LZ

☎01273 625132

Email admin@pierplaywrights.co.uk

Website www.pierplaywrights.co.uk

Contact *Chris Taylor*

Run by playwrights for playwrights in the south east region, Pier Playwrights meets regularly to support writers in all drama forms. Workshops by visiting professionals and skill-sharing workshops in particular media such as screenwriting or writing for radio. The monthly newsletter keeps members informed of writing opportunities and in touch with the industry. Subscription: £15 (Individual); £5 (Unwaged); £30 (Company).

Pitstop Refuelling Writers' Weekend Workshops

'Chinook', Southdown Road, Winchester, Hampshire SO21 2BY

☎01962 712307

Email WriterCon@aol.com

Website www.gmp.co.uk/writers/conference *and* www.awc-workshops.ndo.co.uk

Director *Barbara Large, MBE, FRSA*

Following on from the **Annual Writers'**
Conference in Winchester, these workshops
are an opportunity for writers to work in small
groups to improve fiction and non-fiction projects under the guidance of professional writers.

QueenSpark Books

See entry under **Small Presses**

Screenwriters' Workshop

Suffolk House, 1–8 Whitfield Place, London
W1T 5JU
☎020 7387 5511
Email screenoffice@tiscali.co.uk
Website www.lsw.org.uk

ESTABLISHED 1983. Formerly London Screenwriters Workshop, the SW is open to writers
from all over Britain and Europe. The Workshop is an educational charity whose aim is to
help writers into the film and TV industries.
Many high-profile members. Offers a rolling
programme of tuition, networking and events
including guest speakers and showcasing opportunities. Membership: £40 p.a. Runs *Feedback*
– a script-reading service with reduced rates for
SW members – contact *R. Wheeler* (e-mail
ritaw@tiscali.co.uk).

Scribo

1/31 Hamilton Road, Boscombe,
Bournemouth, Dorset BH1 4EQ
☎01202 302533
Contact *K. & P. Sylvester*

Scribo (established for more than 20 years) is a
postal workshop for novelists. Mss criticism
foilos cover fantasy/sci-fi, crime/thrillers,
mainstream, women's fiction, literary. Forums
offer information, discussion on all topics relating to writing and literature. No annual subscription. £5 joining fee only. Full details from
the address above; enclose s.a.e., please.

Short Story Writers' Folio/
Children's Novel Writers' Folio

5 Park Road, Brading, Sandown, Isle of
Wight PO36 0HU
☎01983 407697
Email dawn.wortley-nott@lineone.net
Contact *Mrs Dawn Wortley-Nott*

Postal workshops – members receive constructive criticism of their work and read and offer
advice on fellow members' contributions. Send
an s.a.e. for further details.

Society of Sussex Authors

Bookends, Lewes Road, Horsted Keynes,
Haywards Heath, West Sussex RH17 7DP
☎01825 790755   Fax 01825 790755
Email michael@bookends.claranet.com
Contact *Michael Legat*

FOUNDED 1968 to promote the interests of its
members and of literature, particularly within
the Sussex area. Regular meetings and
exchange of information; plus social events.
Membership restricted to writers who live in
Sussex and who have had at least one book
commercially published, or other writings used
professionally. Meetings are held six times a
year in Lewes. Annual subscription: £10.

South Eastern Writers' Association

35 Leighton Avenue, Leigh-on-Sea, Essex
SE9 1QB
☎01702 470983
President *Marion Hough*
Secretary *Zoe Massey*

FOUNDED 1989 to bring together experienced
and novice writers, in an informal atmosphere.
Non-profit-making, the Association holds an
annual residential weekend each spring at
Bulphan, Essex. Free workshops and discussion
groups included in the overall cost. Previous
guest speakers: Simon Brett, Bernard
Cornwell, Maureen Lipman, Deric Longden,
Terry Pratchett, Jack Rosenthal. Contact the
Secretary at the address above.

South Manchester
Writer's Workshop

c/o Didsbury Methodist Church Hall,
Sandhurst Road, Didsbury, Manchester M20
☎0161 431 4717
Email Philcave@aol.com
Website www.manchester-
writers.freeserve.co.uk
Contact *Philip Caveney*

The Workshop, which has been running for
around 20 years, provides a lively and informative forum where writers at all levels of their
craft can meet to read and discuss their work.
Meetings held every Tuesday, 7.30 pm–9.30
pm. The first session is free and thereafter a
small charge (currently £1.50) is made. Write
or access the website for more details.

Southwest Scriptwriters

☎0117 909 5522   Fax 0117 907 3816
Website www.southwest-scriptwriters.co.uk
Secretary *John Colborn*

FOUNDED 1994 to offer encouragement and advice to those writing for stage, screen, radio and TV in the region. The group, which attracts professional writers, enthusiasts and students, meets regularly at the Theatre Royal, Bristol to read aloud and provide critical feedback on members' work, discuss writing technique and exchange market information. Mike Bullen, writer of ITV's *Cold Feet*, acts as Honorary President. Subscription: £5 p.a.

Speakeasy – Milton Keynes Writers' Group

46 Wealdstone Place, Springfield, Milton Keynes MK6 3JG
☎01908 663860
Email speakeasywriters@aol.com
Contact *Martin Brocklebank*

Invites lovers of the written and spoken word to their monthly meetings on the first Tuesday of each month at 8.00 pm. Full and varied programme including Local Writers Nights where work can be read and performed, Guest Nights where writers, poets and journalists are invited to speak. Mini-workshops and information nights are also in the programme. Invites entries to their Open Creative Writing Competitions. Phone, e-mail or send s.a.e. for details to address above.

Sussex Playwrights' Club

2 Brunswick Mews, Hove, East Sussex BN3 1HD
☎01273 730106
Website www.newventure.org.uk
Secretary *Dennis Evans*

FOUNDED 1935. Aims to encourage the writing of plays for stage, radio and TV by giving monthly dramatic readings of members' work by experienced actors, mainly from local drama groups. Gives constructive, critical suggestions as to how work might be improved, and suggests possible marketing. Membership is not confined to writers but to all who are interested in theatre in all its forms, and all members are invited to take part in discussions. Guests are always welcome at a nominal £1. Meetings held at New Venture Theatre, Bedford Place, Brighton, East Sussex. Subscription: £7 p.a. Contact the Secretary for details or visit the 'features' page on the website.

Tally Ho! Writers' Group

124 Friern Park, London, N12 9PN
Contact *Rosalyn Rappaport* (☎020 8446 3690) or *John Burns* (at the address above)

Formerly known as the Finchley Writers' Group. Encourages people who are writing with a view to being published. Members include aspiring and established authors. The Group meets every Tuesday at 7.30 pm upstairs at the Tally Ho! pub in north Finchley in London.

Ver Poets

Haycroft, 61–63 Chiswell Green Lane, St Albans, Hertfordshire AL2 3AL
☎01727 867005
Chairman *Ray Badman*
Editor/Organiser *May Badman*

FOUNDED 1966 to promote poetry and to help poets. With postal and local members, holds meetings in St Albans; runs a poetry bookstall for members' books and publications from other groups; publishes members' work in anthologies and organises poetry competitions, including the annual **Ver Poets Open** competition. Gives help and advice whenever they are sought and makes information available to members about other poetry groups, events and opportunities for publication. Membership: £12.50 p.a.; £15 or US$30 (Overseas).

Workers' Educational Association

National Office: Temple House, 17 Victoria Park Square, London E2 9PB
☎020 8983 1515   Fax 020 8983 4840
Email national@wea.org.uk
Website www.wea.org.uk

FOUNDED in 1903, the WEA is a voluntary body with members drawn from all walks of life. It runs writing courses and workshops throughout the country and all courses are open to everyone. Branches in most towns and many villages, with 13 district offices in England and one in Scotland. Contact your district WEA office for courses in your region. All correspondence should be addressed to the District Secretary.

Cheshire, Merseyside & West Lancashire:
7/8 Bluecoat Chambers, School Lane, Liverpool L1 3BX (☎0151 709 8023)

Eastern: Botolph House, 17 Botolph Lane, Cambridge CB2 3RE (☎01223 350978)

East Midlands: 39 Mapperley Road, Mapperley Park, Nottingham NG3 5AQ (☎0115 962 8400)

London: 4 Luke Street, London EC2A 4NT (☎ 020 7613 7550)

Northern: 51 Grainger Street, Newcastle upon Tyne NE1 5JE (☎0191 232 3957)

North Western: 4th Floor, Crawford House, University Precinct Centre, Oxford Road, Manchester M13 9GH (☎0161 273 7652)

South Eastern: 57 Riverside 2, Sir Thomas Longley Road, Rochester, Kent ME2 4DP (☎01634 730101)

South Western: Sandon Court, The Millfields, 1 Craigie Drive, Plymouth, Devon PL1 3JB (☎01752 664989)

Thames & Solent: 6 Brewer Street, Oxford OX1 1QN (☎01865 246270)

Western: 40 Morse Road, Redfield, Bristol BS5 9LB (☎0117 935 1764)

West Mercia: 78–80 Sherlock Street, Birmingham B5 6LT (☎0121 666 6101)

Yorkshire North: 6 Woodhouse Square, Leeds, W. Yorkshire LS3 1AD (☎0113 245 3304)

Yorkshire South: Chantry Buildings, 6–20 Corporation Street, Rotherham S60 1NG (☎01709 837001)

Scottish Association: Riddle's Court, 322 Lawnmarket, Edinburgh EH1 2PG (☎0131 226 3456)

Writers in Oxford

6 Princes Street, Oxford OX4 1DD
☎01865 791202
Email brian@levison.fslife.co.uk

Membership Secretary *Brian Levison*

FOUNDED 1992. Open to published authors, playwrights, poets and journalists. Linked to the **Society of Authors** but organised locally. Arranges a programme of meetings, seminars and social functions. Publishes newsletter, *The Oxford Writer*. Subscription: £20 p.a.

The Writers' Workshop

Cowfields Farm, Rotherfield Greys, Henley-on-Thames, Oxfordshire RG9 4PX
☎01491 628819   Fax 01491 628581

The Writers' Workshop runs regular daytime sessions on aspects of creative writing together with talks from guest speakers. Published writers and beginners are equally welcome.

Yorkshire Playwrights

3 Trinity Road, Scarborough, North Yorkshire YO11 2TD
☎01723 367449   Fax 01723 367449
Email ScarTam@aol.com
Website www.yorkshireplaywrights.com

Administrator *Ian Watson*

FOUNDED 1989 out of an initiative by Jude Kelly and William Weston of the **West Yorkshire Playhouse**. A group of professional writers of plays for stage, TV and radio whose aims are to encourage the writing and performance of new plays in Yorkshire. Open to any writers living in Yorkshire who are members, preferably, of the **Writers' Guild**, or the **Society of Authors**. Contact the Administrator for an information sheet.

The Words Complained of . . .

David Hooper gives advice on how to avoid an expensive court appearance

The main area of risk in libel is in non-fiction. The best working test is whether the tendency of the words used is to diminish the reputation of the claimant. If you were in the claimant's position, could you validly object to what was written about you? It is sensible to ask yourself who might complain about what you have written and how you would respond to that complaint, bearing in mind that the burden of proving by legally admissible evidence will be upon you. There is unfortunately no substitute for careful research and checking. Some errors pass into mythology. A British police officer called Morton collected damages on no less than three occasions, from W.H. Allen, Secker & Warburg and Weidenfeld & Nicolson, for the repetition of the canard that he was responsible for the shooting in cold blood of Abram Stern, head of the Stern gang in Palestine.

The issue is what readers would reasonably conclude that the words meant. The fact that the author did not intend to libel the claimant is not a defence. The readers are in any event unlikely to know what the author's intention was and would form their own view on the interpretation of the words on the page. The fact that a libel was the result of an honest mistake rather than deliberate would be relevant to the amount of damages awarded. Unhappily, experience shows that libel is, particularly in the area of publishing, the product of mistake rather than the product of a failed exposé. Publishers are in any event increasingly reluctant to run the risk of publishing investigative books. Cases involving the exposure of the wrongdoing of footballers, policemen or doctors normally involve newspapers or television companies. Writers need therefore to check the accuracy of what they write. They would have done well, for example, not to confuse the Chancellor of Glasgow University, Sir Alec Cairncross, with his brother, a suspected member of the Cambridge spy ring. Nor is it wise to suggest that a Nigerian-born singer said that 'it was time to support apartheid' when in reality she had said nothing more sinister than 'it was time to support a party'.

The writer should focus on all people who might bring a claim. Often controversial books successfully avoid an action from the principal target only to invite a claim from some minor character over a relatively trivial indiscretion. Claims can come from unlikely sources. *The Sunday Telegraph* can scarcely have expected to be sued by the son of Gaddafi but when he turned up at court he obtained an apology although no damages. Recently, a Russian businessman, Grigori Loutchansky, successfully sued *The Times* over a report linking him with money laundering even though the paper may have felt such a claim was unlikely as he was banned from this country because his presence was deemed undesirable by the Home Secretary and he had served a lengthy prison sentence for dishonesty in the USSR. Unfortunately, the libel laws in this country have attracted a number of libel tourists wishing to impress on the world their spotless reputation. Writers should bear in mind that the libel laws in the United States are unfavourable to plaintiffs, with the result that people such as Dr Armand Hammer sued the English edition of a hostile biography in this country whereas he had decided not to bring a claim in the USA.

If a claim for libel is notified, advice should be sought from a specialist lawyer, preferably one recommended by the publisher. An outraged response can raise the level of damages. If a claim is made, immediate consideration must be given as to whether any amendment or footnote is required in respect of any electronic version of the article which can be accessed by third parties. Section 2 of the Defamation Act 1996 has significantly amended the defence of offer of amends, which enables a swift and less expensive resolution of a claim where a mistake has been made. It involves an admission of liability, and if the parties cannot agree, an assessment of damages by the judge, but it can stop the greed of the claimant in its tracks. Writers need to discover whether they are covered by the publisher's insurance and, if so, what excess attaches to any claim. Increasingly libel insurance only cuts in after the claim has cost five figures – scant consolation for the author who is likely to have warranted in the publishing contract that the book is free from libel. Very often publishers will not enforce that indemnity in the absence of serious blameworthy conduct on the part of the writer, but again that is little consolation as publishers will not commit themselves in advance to their probable reaction to a libel claim. It is important therefore to consider whether the book should be read for libel and, if so, whether it is necessary to have it all read or simply part of it.

Many publishing contracts are silent on the question of who pays for the libel reading. Writers who try to modify the standard form indemnity given to publishers normally face a thankless task, but it is worth considering whether there is scope for agreeing that the writer's liability should be modified in respect of potential defamations of which the publisher is aware where the writer has complied with all the requirements of the lawyer reading the book for libel. Practical steps which can be taken include considering whether a particular passage should be sent to the person written about. If it can be shown that the person consented to what was written, that is a defence to a claim for libel. The problem, however, is that normally such persons will not give consent.

Libel actions cannot be brought on behalf of those who are dead. The death of a plaintiff in the course of a libel action, as happened with Robert Maxwell's claim against Faber, brings the claim to an immediate halt, but each side is left bearing their own legal costs. Writers are well advised to consult a helpful volume called *Who was Who*.

Another defence is justification, which involves the author proving that what was written was true. If what was written was fair comment on a matter of public interest based on facts which were substantially true the writer will have a defence. By virtue of the Human Rights Act 1998 the English courts will increasingly take note of the decisions made under Article 10 of the European Convention of Human Rights, which upholds the freedom of speech and which has a greater tendency to rule that criticisms made of a claimant were matters of comment rather than allegations of fact which have to be justified.

One of the most promising developments has been the expansion of the defence of qualified privilege in the libel action brought by the former Irish Prime Minister Albert Reynolds against the *Sunday Times*. If the writer can prove that on a matter of public interest there was a duty to inform the public, who had a corresponding interest in receiving that information, there will be a defence which does not require proving that the particular allegation was true. The court will, however, look very carefully at the research carried out, the language used and the attempt to put both sides of the matter.

Qualified privilege was the issue in the Loutchansky case, where the newspaper argued that it required the protection of qualified privilege to write about his alleged activities, which were by their nature very difficult to prove. The judge concluded, however, that the paper had made insufficient attempts to contact Loutchansky and should not have published until it had done so. The most helpful development for writers is the recognition by the courts of the importance of freedom of speech. The press has to discharge vital functions as a bloodhound as well as a watchdog and any lingering doubts should be resolved in favour of publication. The courts have recognized that freedom of speech is essential to informed political debate and that restrictions imposed upon that freedom must be proportionate and no more than is necessary to promote the legitimate object of the restriction. The courts also recognize that news is a perishable commodity and that the decision to publish must be assessed in the light of the facts then known. To date, however, despite all the ringing endorsements of the freedom of the press, the courts have often been unwilling to uphold defences of qualified privilege. Too often they have found that there was some step which ought to have been taken before going into print. Journalists with publication deadlines may have a better prospect of establishing qualified privilege than authors, who may be expected to undertake more research to get to the truth of the matter. The existence of the defence and the unpredictability of the view which the judge may take of the research carried out is likely to deter many claimants, particularly those in public life. The Court of Appeal has recently held that a balanced account of the allegations made by a Saudi dissident was protected by qualified privilege. Previously, a writer repeating the allegations was likely to have had to prove that they were true.

Writers of fiction face fewer libel problems. However, their use of autobiographical material can lead to some of their characters being identifiable. The inadvertent use of the name of a real peer has led to a novel being pulped. Directories should, where possible, be consulted to ensure there are no similarly named people in a comparable occupation. Care should be taken to see on whom characters are based and whether any of the surrounding events actually happened; often there is much to be said for a carefully worded disclaimer of reference to living individuals. Compton Mackenzie used to pick names from old telephone directories. Unfortunately, when this expedient was used by the novelist Paul Watkins, in his book *Stand up before your God*, a randomly chosen name of a villainous character was by ill-fortune the name of one of his contemporaries at Eton College. Damages had to be paid since checks in the school directories could have avoided this error.

Writers of fiction will benefit from the defence of accidental defamation under Section 2 of the Defamation Act, which will limit damages and costs but, even so, failure to make these checks can be expensive. Derek Jameson's experiences in accidentally changing the name of a sergeant who had been convicted of treason to spare that man's family's feelings to a randomly chosen name which turned out to be that of a journalist showed that the road to libel can be paved with good intentions.

The growth of faction and the introduction of living people into works of fiction do increase the risk of libel claims by blurring the distinction between fact and imagination. A *roman-à-clef* can present significant libel problems and it was perhaps not surprising that recently a publisher could not be found for a novel featuring unattractive characteristics of a person described as the wife of a Labour Prime Minister who as 'a young chap with a phoney smile' was felt not to be sufficiently unrecognizable.

Changes introduced by the Defamation Act 1996 and procedural changes regarding the conduct of libel actions to make them less tortuous and expensive and to require each side to disclose the strengths and weaknesses of their cases at an earlier stage certainly are an improvement. Libel nevertheless remains a very costly pitfall, even if the damages awarded are much less. Damages are now capped at £150,000 for the most serious libels, but on top of that there are the legal costs. Most cases settle for a fraction of that. There are fast-track procedures where libel damages will be capped at £10,000. This is little consolation to writers as these changes together with the willingness of lawyers to bring libel claims on a conditional fee basis – that is to say the lawyer does not get paid unless he wins the case, but he can recover from the defendant a success fee on top of his not inconsiderable normal legal fees – serve only to encourage the bringing of smaller, but nevertheless expensive, claims. Things are improving but at present the only certainty about libel is its expense.

Article 8 of the European Convention of Human Rights protects the right to respect for private and family life. To date, claims have related either to intrusive tabloid exposés or to celebrities exploiting publicity rights, for example Michael Douglas seeking to prevent *Hello!* magazine publishing photographs of his wedding when he had sold the rights to *OK!*. Naomi Campbell recovered £3,500 in respect of photographs of her leaving a drugs rehabilitation clinic and Amanda Holden and her husband received £40,000 from the *Daily Star*, which had published intrusive pictures of them on holiday. Although the Court of Appeal has restricted the scope of privacy claims in the case brought by the footballer Gary Flitcroft, claims based in privacy or breach of confidence claims can be brought where the writer knew or ought to have known that the other person could reasonably expect his privacy to be protected. Certain kinds of information about a person, for example relating to health, private relationships or finances, might well be viewed by the court as private, as could certain kinds of activity which a reasonable person applying contemporary standards of morals and behaviour would understand to be meant to be unobserved. A useful practical test of what is private is whether the disclosure of that information or conduct would be highly offensive to a reasonable person or ordinary sensibilities. Writers who are publishing details of people's private lives or their personal finances need to be able to justify the publication of such material and they may need to limit the amount of detail they do in fact publish.

David Hooper is media partner of Pinsent Curtis Biddle and author of Reputations under Fire, *published by Little Brown (2001).*

Miscellany

Arjay Research

20 Rookery View, Little Thurrock, Grays, Essex RM17 6AS
☎01375 372199 Fax 01375 372199
Email RogWJ@aol.com
Contact *Roger W. Jordan*

All aspects of international merchant shipping and naval research undertaken by former shipping archivist and editor. Extensive maritime library and comprehensive databases on *inter alia* ships wrecked/lost and passenger and cruise ships. Terms by arrangement.

Authors' Research Services

32 Oak Village, London NW5 4QN
☎020 7284 4316 Fax 020 7284 4316
Email rmwindserv@aol.com
Contact *Richard Wright*

Research and document supply service, particularly to authors, academics and others without easy access to London libraries and sources of information. Also indexing of books and journals. Rates negotiable.

Combrógos

10 Heol Don, Whitchurch, Cardiff CF14 2AU
☎029 2062 3359 Fax 029 2052 9202
Email meic@heoldon.fsnet.co.uk
Contact *Professor Meic Stephens*

FOUNDED 1990. Arts and media research, editorial services, specialising in books about Wales or by Welsh authors. 'Encyclopaedic knowledge of Welsh history, language, literature and culture.'

CopyPlus of Monmouth

Hadnock Road, Monmouth NP25 3NQ
☎01600 772600 Fax 01600 712896
Email books@copyplus.demon.co.uk
Contact *Anne King*

Advice and technical assistance for those wishing to self-publish plus full design, printing and binding services. Yearbooks, commemorative books, personal, family, local histories, etc. Print runs as low as 25 copies.

Jacqueline Edwards

104 Earlsdon Avenue South, Coventry, Warwickshire CV5 6DQ
Contact *Jacqueline Edwards, MA, LLB(Hons)*

Historical research – family, local and 19th and 20th century legal history. Covers Warwickshire, Gloucestershire, Wiltshire, Worcestershire, Cambridgeshire and the Public Record Office, Kew, London.

Facts&nfo Research Service for Writers

12 Kenbury Street, London SE5 9BS
☎020 7326 4215/07966 386304 (mobile)
Fax 020 7326 4215
Email factsinfo@beeb.net
Contact *Thecla Schreuders*

Facts&nfo specialises in global research for fiction and non-fiction writers. Offers biographical and character research; social backgrounds and domestic life; popular culture; medical, scientific and technical research; and history, from classical Greece to the late 20th century. Also archive and journal searches, art and film references; and source experts of all kinds. Over 12 years' experience in research for factual television.

International Booksearch Service

8 Old James Street, London SE15 3TS
☎020 7639 8900
Email scfordham@talk21.com
Website www.scfordham.com
Contact *S.C. Fordham*

FOUNDED 1992. International book search service for out-of-print books. A free service with no obligation to buy the book when found. Experienced in finding books for authors, researchers, TV and film companies, newspapers, magazines, etc.

Caroline Landeau

8 Elystan Place, London SW3 3LF
☎07050 600420 Fax 07050 605641
Email winmacweb@hotmail.com
Contact *Caroline Landeau*

Experienced research and production – films, multimedia, books, magazines, exhibitions, animation, general interest, art, music, crime, travel, food, film, theatre.

Murder Files

81 Churchfields Drive, Bovey Tracey, Devon TQ13 9QU
☎01626 833487 Fax 01626 835797
Email enquiry@murderfiles.com
Website www.murderfiles.com
Contact *Paul Williams*

FOUNDED 1994. Crime writer and researcher specialising in UK murders. Holds information on thousands of well-known and less well-known murders dating from 1400 to the present day. Copies of press cuttings available from 1920 onwards. Details of executions, particularly at the Tyburn and Newgate. Information on British hangmen. CD-Rom *The Ultimate Price – The Unlawful Killing of British Police Officers*, Part 1 (1700–1899) & Part 2 (1900–2000), available £15 each or £26 for both including p&p. Specialist in British police murders since 1700. Service available to general enquirers, writers, researchers, TV, radio, video, etc.

Ormrod Research Services

Weeping Birch, Burwash, East Sussex TN19 7HG
☎01435 882541 Fax 01435 882541
Contact *Richard Ormrod*

ESTABLISHED 1982. Comprehensive research service: literary, historical, academic, biographical, commercial. Verbal quotations available. Also editing, indexing and ghost-writing.

Roger Palmer Limited, Media Contracts

Antonia House, 262 Holloway Road, London N7 6NE
☎020 7609 4828 Fax 020 7609 4878
Email contracts@rogerpalmerltd.co.uk
Contact *Peter Palmer*

ESTABLISHED 1993. Drafts, advises on and negotiates all media contracts (on a regular or *ad hoc* basis) for publishers, literary and merchandising agents, authors, packagers, charities and others. Manages and operates clients' complete contracts functions, undertakes contractual audits, devises contracts and permissions systems, advises on copyright and related issues and provides training and seminars on an individual or group basis. Extensive private client list, with special rates for members of the **Society of Authors** and the **Writers' Guild**.

Patent Research

Dachsteinstr. 12a, D–81825 Munich, Germany
☎00 49 89 430 7833
Contact *Gerhard Everwyn*

All world, historical patents for researchers, authors, archives, museums and publishers. Rates on application.

Teral Research Services

45 Forest View Road, Moordown, Bournemouth, Dorset BH9 3BH
☎01202 516834 Fax 01202 516834
Contact *Terry C. Treadwell*

All aspects of research undertaken but specialises in all military, aviation, naval and defence subjects, both past and present. Extensive book and photographic library, including a leading collection of World War One aviation photographs. Terms by arrangement.

The United Kingdom Copyright Bureau

110 Trafalgar Road, Portslade, East Sussex BN41 1GS
☎01273 277333 Fax 01273 705451
Email info@copyrightbureau.co.uk
Website www.copyrightbureau.co.uk
Contact *Ralph de Straet von Kollman*

The UKCB provides a secure copyright service at reasonable cost, enabling multiple copyrights to be registered nominally when required. Prices are advertised on the website including the UKCB's solicitors, etc. Copyrights preferred on floppy disk or CD-Rom; mss discouraged but are accepted.

Melanie Wilson

72 High Street, Syston LE7 1GQ
☎0116 260 4442 Fax 0116 260 1396
Email MelanieWilson@bigfoot.com
Contact *Melanie Wilson*

Comprehensive research service for books, magazines, newspapers, documentaries, films, radio, education, TV drama. Includes free worldwide booksearch service and groundwork for factual basis for all media presentations, particularly in historical research, costume and textiles, crafts, food and cooking, weapons and uniforms, traditional storytelling, past technology, living history displays and exhibitions.

Press Cuttings Agencies

BMC Clipserver
89½ Worship Street, London EC2A 2BF
☎020 7377 1742 Fax 020 7377 6103
Email info@bmcnews.com
Website www.clipserver.com

Television, radio, national and European press monitoring agency. Cuttings from national and all major European press available seven days a week, with early morning delivery. Also monitoring of all news and current affairs programmes – national, international and satellite. Retrospective research service and free telephone notification. Sponsorship evaluation from all media sources.

Durrants Press Cuttings Ltd
Discovery House, 28–42 Banner Street, London EC1Y 8QE
☎020 7674 0200 Fax 020 7674 0222
Email contact@durrants.co.uk
Website www.durrants.co.uk

Wide coverage of all print media sectors plus Internet, newswire and broadcast monitoring; foreign press in association with agencies abroad. High speed, early morning press cuttings from the national press e-mailed to your desktop. Overnight delivery via courier to most areas or first-class mail. Well presented, laser printed, A4 cuttings. Rates on application.

International Press-Cutting Bureau
224–236 Walworth Road, London SE17 1JE
☎020 7708 2113 Fax 020 7701 4489
Email ipcb2000@aol.com

Contact *Robert Podro*

Covers national, provincial, trade, technical and magazine press. Cuttings are normally sent twice weekly by first-class post and there are no additional service charges or reading fees. Subscriptions are valid for six months; 100 cuttings: £300; 250: £500 (plus VAT).

Romeike Media Intelligence
Hale House, 290–296 Green Lanes, London N13 5TP
☎0800 289543 Fax 020 8882 6716
Email info@romeike.com
Website www.romeike.com

Contact *Mary Michael*

Monitors national and international dailies and Sundays, provincial papers, consumer magazines, trade and technical journals, teletext services as well as national radio and TV networks. Back research, advertising checking and Internet monitoring, plus analysis and editorial summary service available.

We Find It (Press Clippings)
103 South Parade, Belfast BT7 2GN
☎028 9064 6008 Fax 028 9064 6008

Contact *Avril Forsythe*

Specialises in Northern Ireland press and magazines, both national and provincial. Rates on application.

Bursaries, Fellowships and Grants

Amazon.co.uk Writers' Bursaries
Amazon.co.uk., Patriot Court, 1–9 The
Grove, Slough, Berkshire SL1 1QP
☎020 8636 9200 Fax 020 8636 9400
Website www.amazon.co.uk
Contact *Lisa Ramshaw*
FOUNDED 2000. Annual scheme 'to mark
Amazon.co.uk.'s commitment to literature'.
Entrants must have published one previous
novel or volume of short stories in the past two
years. Recommendations by publishers only.
2002 winners: Danny King, Sarah May.
   Award £3500 each plus three-month sabbatical post.

Aosdána
An Chomhairle Ealaíon (The Irish Arts
Council), 70 Merrion Square, Dublin 2,
Republic of Ireland
☎00 353 1 6180200 Fax 00 353 1 6761302
Email aosdana@artscouncil.ie
Website www.artscouncil.ie/aosdana
Aosdána is an affiliation of creative artists
engaged in literature, music and the visual arts,
and consists of not more than 200 artists who
have gained a reputation for achievement and
distinction. Membership is by competitive
sponsored selection and is open to Irish citizens
or residents only. Members are eligible to
receive an annuity for a five-year term to assist
them in pursuing their art full-time.

**Arts Council
Literature Bursaries, Ireland**
An Chomhairle Ealaíon (The Irish Arts
Council), 70 Merrion Square, Dublin 2,
Republic of Ireland
☎00 353 1 6180200 Fax 00 353 1 6761302
Email info@artscouncil.ie
Website www.artscouncil.ie
Literature Officer *Sinéad Mac Aodha*
Bursaries in literature awarded to creative writers
of fiction, poetry and drama in Irish and
English to enable development or completion
of, specific projects. A limited number of bursaries
may also be given to non-fiction projects

of a contemporary nature. Open to Irish citizens
or residents only.
   Awards up to €12,000.

**Arts Council Theatre
Writing Bursaries**
Arts Council of England, 14 Great Peter
Street, London SW1P 3NQ
☎020 7973 6431 Fax 020 7973 6983
Email jemima.lee@artscouncil.org.uk
Website www.artscouncil.org.uk
Contact *Theatre Writing Section*
Intended to provide experienced playwrights
with an opportunity to research and develop a
play for the theatre independently of financial
pressures and free from the need to write for a
particular market. Bursaries are also available
for theatre translation projects. Writers must be
resident in England.
   Award £5500.

**Arts Council Theatre
Writing Commission Award**
Arts Council of England, 14 Great Peter
Street, London SW1P 3NQ
☎020 7973 6431 Fax 020 7973 6983
Email jemima.lee@artscouncil.org.uk
Website www.artscouncil.org.uk
Contact *Theatre Writing Section*
Theatre companies and groups based in England
can apply for a grant of up to half the cost of paying
a writer a commission or fee to write a new
play, to secure the rights to an unperformed play
or to rewrite an unperformed play. The theatre
company or organisation is expected to find at
least half the cost of the fee from their own
resources. Commissions are also available for
theatre translation projects. Further details available
from the theatre writing section.

The Authors' Contingency Fund
The Society of Authors, 84 Drayton Gardens,
London SW10 9SB
☎020 7373 6642 Fax 020 7373 5768
Email info@societyofauthors.org
This fund makes modest grants to published
authors who find themselves in sudden financial

difficulties. Contact the **Society of Authors** for an information sheet and application form.

The Authors' Foundation

The Society of Authors, 84 Drayton Gardens, London SW10 9SB
☎020 7373 6642 Fax 020 7373 5768
Email info@societyofauthors.org

Grants to writers whose publisher's advance is insufficient to cover the costs of research involved. Application by letter to The Authors' Foundation giving details, in confidence, of the advance and royalties, together with the reasons for needing additional funding. Grants are sometimes given even if there is no commitment by a publisher, so long as the applicant has had a book published and the new work will almost certainly be published. About £80,000 is distributed each year. Contact the **Society of Authors** for full entry details. Final entry dates: 30 April and 31 October.

The K. Blundell Trust

The Society of Authors, 84 Drayton Gardens, London SW10 9SB
☎020 7373 6642 Fax 020 7373 5768
Email info@societyofauthors.org

Grants to writers whose publisher's advance is insufficient to cover the costs of research. Author must be under 40, has to submit a copy of his/her previous book and the work must 'contribute to the greater understanding of existing social and economic organisation'. Application by letter. Contact the **Society of Authors** for full entry details. Final entry dates: 30 April and 31 October.

Alfred Bradley Bursary Award

c/o BBC Radio Drama, Room 1119, New Broadcasting House, Oxford Road, Manchester M60 1SJ
☎0161 244 4260 Fax 0161 244 4248

Contact *Coordinator*

ESTABLISHED 1992. Biennial award in commemoration of the life and work of the distinguished radio producer Alfred Bradley. Aims to encourage and develop new radio writing talent in the BBC North region. There is a change of focus for each award, e.g. previous years have targeted comedy drama, verse drama, etc. Entrants must live or work in the North region. The award is given to help writers to pursue a career in writing for radio. The next award was launched in spring 2002, with a deadline for scripts in autumn 2002. Previous winners: Lee Hall, Mandy Precious, Peter Straughan, Pam Leeson.

Award Up to £6000 over two years and a BBC Radio Drama commission, the opportunity to develop further ideas with Radio Drama.

British Academy Small Personal Research Grants

10 Carlton House Terrace, London SW1Y 5AH
☎020 7969 5200 Fax 020 7969 5300
Website www.britac.ac.uk

Contact *Assistant Secretary, Research Grants*

Quarterly award to further original creative research at postdoctoral level in the humanities and social sciences. Entrants must no longer be registered for postgraduate study and must be resident in the UK. Final entry dates: end of September, November, February and April.
Award £5000 (maximum).

Lar Cassidy Award

An Chomhairle Ealaíon (The Irish Arts Council), 70 Merrion Square, Dublin 2, Republic of Ireland
☎00 353 1 6180200 Fax 00 353 1 6761302
Email info@artscouncil.ie
Website www.artscouncil.ie

The award commemorates the life and work of the late Lar Cassidy, pioneering arts administrator and former Arts Council Literature and Community Arts Officer. The aim of the award in 2002 is to support an individual writer working on a new or experimental fiction project. (In alternate years, the award will be offered to an arts practitioner working in the field of combined arts.) Information sheet/application form available.
Award €15,000.

Cholmondeley Awards

The Society of Authors, 84 Drayton Gardens, London SW10 9SB
☎020 7373 6642 Fax 020 7373 5768

FOUNDED 1965 by the late Dowager Marchioness of Cholmondeley. Annual honorary awards to recognise the achievement and distinction of individual poets. 2001 winners: Ian Duhig, Paul Durcan, Kathleen Jamie, Grace Nichols.
Award £8000 (total).

The Economist/ Richard Casement Internship

The Economist, 25 St James's Street, London SW1A 1HG
☎020 7830 7000
Website www.economist.com

Contact *Science Editor (re. Casement Internship)*

For an aspiring journalist under 25 to spend three months in the summer writing for *The Economist* about science and technology. Applicants should write a letter of introduction along with an article of approximately 600 words suitable for inclusion in the Science and Technology Section. Competition details normally announced in the magazine late January or early February and 4–5 weeks allowed for application.

European Jewish Publication Society

PO Box 19948, London N3 3ZJ
☎020 8346 1668 Fax 020 8346 1776
Email cs@ejps.org.uk
Website www.ejps.org.uk

Contact *Dr Colin Shindler*

ESTABLISHED in 1995 to help fund the publication of books of European Jewish interest which would otherwise remain unpublished. Helps with the marketing, distribution and promotion of such books. Publishers who may be interested in publishing works of Jewish interest should approach the Society with a proposal and manuscript in the first instance. Books which have been supported include: *The Vanished Shtetl* Stanislav Brunstein; *Tidings from Zion* Jennifer Glynn; *Botchki* David Zagier; *Just One More Dance* Ernest Levy. Also supports the publication of poetry, and translations from and into other European languages.
Grant £3000 (maximum).

Fulbright Awards

The Fulbright Commission, Fulbright House, 62 Doughty Street, London WC1N 2JZ
☎020 7404 6880 Fax 020 7404 6834
Website www.fulbright.co.uk

Contact *British Programme Manager*

The Fulbright Commission has a number of scholarships at postgraduate level and above, open to any field (science and the arts) of study/research to be undertaken in the USA. Length of award is typically an academic year. Application deadline for postgraduate awards is usually late October/early November of preceding year of study; and mid-March/early April for distinguished scholar awards. Further details and application forms are available on the website. Alternatively, send A4 envelope with sufficient postage for 100g with a covering letter explaining which level of award is of interest.

Fulton Fellowship

David Fulton (Publishers) Ltd, The Chiswick Centre, 414 Chiswick High Road, London W4 5TF
☎020 8996 3333 Fax 020 8742 8390
Email david.fulton@fultonbooks.co.uk
Website www.fultonbooks.co.uk

Chairman and Publisher *David Fulton*
Managing Director *David Hill*

The Fulton Fellowship in Special Education was ESTABLISHED in 1995 and is administered by the Centre for Special Education, University College, Worcester. The Fellowship, worth £2000, has been extended to offer schools as well as individual teachers the chance to share work their staff have done or are doing collaboratively through written publication to a wider audience. 2000 Fellow: Mordaunt School, Southampton.

Tony Godwin Memorial Trust

c/o 67a Prince of Wales Mansions, Prince of Wales Drive, London SW11 4BJ
☎020 7627 4244
Email info@tgmt.org.uk
Website www.tgmt.org.uk

Chairman *Iain Brown*

Biennial award established to commemorate the life of Tony Godwin, a prominent publisher in the 1960s/70s. Open to all young people (under 35 years old) who are UK nationals and working, or intending to work, in publishing. The award provides the recipient with the means to spend at least one month as the guest of an American publishing house in order to learn about international publishing. The recipient is expected to submit a report upon return to the UK. Next award: 2004; final entry date: 31 December 2003. Previous winners: George Lucas (Hodder), Clive Priddle (Fourth Estate), Richard Scrivener (Penguin), Lisa Shakespeare (Weidenfeld & Nicolson), Fiona Stewart (HarperCollins).
Award Bursary of approx. US$5000.

Eric Gregory Trust Fund

The Society of Authors, 84 Drayton Gardens, London SW10 9SB
☎020 7373 6642 Fax 020 7373 5768
Email info@societyofauthors.org

Annual awards of varying amounts are made for the encouragement of poets under the age of 30 on the basis of a submitted collection. Open only to British-born subjects resident in the UK. Final entry date: 31 October. Contact the **Society of**

Authors for full entry details. 2001 winners: Tishani Doshi, Leontia Flynn, Kathryn Gray, Patrick Mackie, Sally Read, Thomas Warner. *Award* £24,000 (total).

The Guardian Research Fellowship

Nuffield College, Oxford OX1 1NF
☎01865 288540 Fax 01865 278676
Contact *The Academic Administrator*

One-year fellowship endowed by the Scott Trust, owner of *The Guardian*, to give someone working in the media the chance to put their experience into a new perspective, publish the outcome and give a *Guardian* lecture. Applications welcomed from journalists and management members, in newspapers, periodicals or broadcasting. Research or study proposals should be directly related to experience of working in the media. Accommodation and meals in college will be provided and a stipend. Advertised biennially in November.

Hawthornden Castle Fellowship

Hawthornden Castle, The International Retreat for Writers, Lasswade, Midlothian EH18 1EG
☎0131 440 2180 Fax 0131 440 1989
Contact *The Administrator*

ESTABLISHED 1982 to provide a peaceful setting where published writers can work without disturbance. The Retreat houses five writers at a time, who are known as Hawthornden Fellows. Writers from any part of the world may apply for the fellowships. No monetary assistance is given, nor any contribution to travelling expenses, but once arrived at Hawthornden, the writer is the guest of the Retreat. Applications on forms provided must be made by the end of September for the following calendar year. Previous winners include: Les Murray, Alasdair Gray, Helen Vendler, Olive Senior, Hilary Spurling.

Francis Head Bequest

The Society of Authors, 84 Drayton Gardens, London SW10 9SB
☎020 7373 6642 Fax 020 7373 5768
Email info@societyofauthors.org

Provides grants to published British authors over the age of 35 who need financial help during a period of illness, disablement or temporary financial crisis. Contact the **Society of Authors** for an information sheet and application form.

Ralph Lewis Award

University of Sussex Library, Brighton, East Sussex BN1 9QL
☎01273 678158 Fax 01273 678441
Email p.a.ringshaw@sussex.ac.uk

ESTABLISHED 1985. Occasional award set up by Ralph Lewis, a Brighton author and art collector who left money to fund awards for promising manuscripts which would not otherwise be published. The award is given in the form of a grant to a UK-based publisher in respect of an agreed three-year programme of publication of literary works by new authors or by established authors using new styles or forms. No direct applications from writers. Previous winners: **Peterloo Poets** (1989–91); **Serpent's Tail** (1992–94); **Stride Publications** (1997–99).

Macaulay Fellowship

An Chomhairle Ealaíon (The Irish Arts Council), 70 Merrion Square, Dublin 2, Republic of Ireland
☎00 353 1 6180200 Fax 00 353 1 6761302
Email info@artscouncil.ie
Website www.artscouncil.ie
Literature Officer *Sinéad Mac Aodha*

To further the liberal education of a young creative artist. Candidates for this triennial award must be under 30 on 30 June, or 35 in exceptional circumstances, and must be Irish citizens or residents. The Fellowship is offered on rotation between Music, Visual Arts and Literature (Literature in 2002). *Award* €5000.

The John Masefield Memorial Trust

The Society of Authors, 84 Drayton Gardens, London SW10 9SB
☎020 7373 6642 Fax 020 7373 5768
Email info@societyofauthors.org

This trust makes occasional grants to professional poets (or their immediate dependants) who are faced with sudden financial problems. Contact the **Society of Authors** for an information sheet and application form.

Somerset Maugham Trust Fund

The Society of Authors, 84 Drayton Gardens, London SW10 9SB
☎020 7373 6642 Fax 020 7373 5768
Email info@societyofauthors.org

Annual awards designed to encourage writers under the age of 35 to travel. Given on the basis of a published work of fiction, non-fiction or poetry. Open only to British-born subjects resident in the UK. Final entry date: 20 December. 2001 winners: Edward Platt *Leadville*; Ben Rice *Pobby and Dingan*.

Awards £12,000 (total).

The Airey Neave Trust

PO Box 36800, 40 Bernard Street, London WC1N 1WJ
☎020 7833 4440 Fax 020 7833 4949

Contact *Hannah Scott*

INITIATED 1989. Annual research fellowships for up to three years – towards a book or paper – for serious research connected with national and international law, and human freedom. Must be attached to a particular university in Britain. Interested applicants should come forward with ideas, preferably before March in any year.

New Playwriting Panel

See **New Writing North** under **Professional Associations and Societies**

Newspaper Press Fund

Dickens House, 35 Wathen Road, Dorking, Surrey RH4 1JY
☎01306 887511 Fax 01306 888212

Director/Secretary *David Ilott*

Aims to relieve distress among journalists and their dependants. Continuous and/or occasional financial grants; also retirement homes for eligible beneficiaries. Further information and subscription details available from the Secretary or via the Reuters Foundation website on: www.foundation.reuters.com/

Northern Arts Literary Fellowship

Northern Arts, Central Square, Forth Street, Newcastle upon Tyne NE1 3PJ
☎0191 255 8500 Fax 0191 230 1020

Contact *Film, Media & Literature Department*

A competitive fellowship in association with the Universities of Durham and Newcastle upon Tyne. Contact Northern Arts for details.

Northern Rock Foundation Writer Award

New Writing North, 7–8 Trinity Chare, Quayside, Newcastle upon Tyne NE1 3DF
☎0191 232 9991 Fax 0191 230 1883
Email subtext.nwn@virgin.net
Website www.newwritingnorth.com

Contacts *John McGagh, Claire Malcolm*

Annual award ESTABLISHED in 2002 with the aim of liberating established writers who live in the region from work other than writing.

Applicants must have at least two books published by a recognised publisher and *must* live in Northumberland, Tyne and Wear, County Durham or Teesside. Closing date: 28 January. The first winner of the award in 2002 was poet, Anne Stevenson.

Award £20,000 per year (for three years).

Northern Writers' Awards

See **New Writing North** under **Professional Associations and Societies**

PAWS (Public Awareness of Science) Drama Script Fund

The PAWS Office,
OMNI Communications, Chancel House, Neasden Lane, London NW10 2TU
☎020 8214 1543 Fax 020 8214 1544
Email pawsomni@globalnet.co.uk

Contacts *Barrie Whatley, Andrew Millington*

ESTABLISHED 1994. Annual award aimed at encouraging television scriptwriters to include science and engineering scenarios in their work. Grants (currently £2000) are given to selected writers to develop their script ideas into full treatments; prizes are awarded for the best of these treatments. The PAWS Fund holds meetings enabling writers to meet scientists and engineers and also offers a contacts service to put writers in 'one-to-one' contact with specialists who can help them develop their ideas. See also the **EuroPAWS Midas Prize** under **Prizes**.

Pearson Playwrights' Scheme

80 Strand, London WC2R 0RL
Website www.pearson.com

Administrator *Jack Andrews, MBE*

Awards four bursaries to playwrights annually, each worth £5000. Applicants must be sponsored by a theatre which then submits the play for consideration by a panel. Each award allows the playwright a twelve-month attachment. Applications invited via theatres in October each year. For up-to-date information, contact *Jack Andrews* (☎020 8943 8176).

Charles Pick Fellowship

School of English and American Studies, University of East Anglia, Norwich, Norfolk NR4 7TJ
☎01603 492810 Fax 01603 507728
Email v.striker@uea.ac.uk
Website www.uea.ac.uk/eas/Fellowships/ fellowschol.html

Contact *Val Striker*

An annual award, FOUNDED in 2001 by the Charles Pick Consultancy in memory of the publisher and literary agent who died in 2000, to support a new unpublished writer of fictional or non-fictional prose. Award of the fellowship, which is residential from August to January, is judged on the quality of writing and reference from a literary agent, editor or accredited creative writing teacher.

Award £10,000 plus free campus accommodation.

Peggy Ramsay Foundation

Hanover House, 14 Hanover Square, London W1S 1HP

☎020 7667 5000 Fax 020 7667 5100

Email laurence.harbottle@harbottle.com

Website www.peggyramsayfoundation.org

Contact *G. Laurence Harbottle*

FOUNDED 1992 in accordance with the will of the late Peggy Ramsay, the well-known agent. Grants are made to writers for the stage who have some experience and who need time and resources to make writing possible. Grants are also made for writing projects by organisations connected with the theatre. The Foundation does not support production costs or any project that does not have a direct benefit to playwriting. Writers must have some record of successful writing for the stage.

Grants total £150,000 to £200,000 per year.

The Margaret Rhondda Award

The Society of Authors, 84 Drayton Gardens, London SW10 9SB

☎020 7373 6642 Fax 020 7373 5768

Email info@societyofauthors.org

Competitive award given to a woman writer as a grant-in-aid towards the expenses of a research project in journalism. Contact the **Society of Authors** for an information sheet. Triennial (next award: 2005). Final entry date: 20 December 2004. 1999 winner: Sue Branford.

Award approx. £1000.

The Royal Literary Fund

3 Johnson's Court, off Fleet Street, London EC4A 3EA

☎020 7353 7150 Fax 020 7353 1350

Email egunnrlf@globalnet.co.uk

Secretary *Eileen Gunn*

Grants and pensions are awarded to published authors in financial need, or to their dependants. Examples of author's works are needed for assessment by Committee. Write for further details and application form.

Scottish Arts Council Book Awards

Scottish Arts Council, 12 Manor Place, Edinburgh EH3 7DD

☎0131 226 6051 Fax 0131 225 9833

Email gavin.wallace@scottisharts.org.uk

Website www.sac.org.uk

Contact *Gavin Wallace, Literature Officer*

A minimum of three awards is made annually in the spring. The current value of award is £1000 to each author but due to be increased from 2002. Preference is given to literary fiction but literary non-fiction is also considered. Authors should be Scottish or resident in Scotland, but books of Scottish interest by other authors are eligible for consideration. Applications from publishers only.

Scottish Arts Council Creative Scotland Awards

Scottish Arts Council, 12 Manor Place, Edinburgh EH3 7DD

☎0131 240 6051/ Help Desk: 0845 603 6000 Fax 0131 225 9833

Email helpdesk@scottisharts.org.uk

Website www.sac.org.uk

The details of this scheme are currently under review but substantial awards or commissions will be available to established artists based in Scotland working in any medium, including writing.

Scottish Arts Council New Writers' Bursaries

Scottish Arts Council, 12 Manor Place, Edinburgh EH3 7DD

☎0131 226 6051 Fax 0131 225 9833

Email jenny.brown@scottisharts.org.uk

Website www.sac.org.uk

Contact *Jenny Brown, Head of Literature*

Ten bursaries of £2000 awarded annually to enable previously unpublished writers of literary work more time to devote to their writing. Applicants should be based in Scotland.

Scottish Arts Council Writers' Bursaries

Scottish Arts Council, 12 Manor Place, Edinburgh EH3 7DD

☎0131 226 6051 Fax 0131 225 9833

Email jenny.brown@scottisharts.org.uk

Website www.sac.org.uk

Contact *Jenny Brown, Head of Literature*

Bursaries to enable published writers of literary work and recognised playwrights to devote more time to their writing. Around 20 bursaries of up to £15,000 awarded annually; deadline for aplications in June and December. Application open to writers based in Scotland.

Laurence Stern Fellowship

Department of Journalism, City University, Northampton Square, London EC1V 0HB
☎020 7040 8224   Fax 020 7040 8594
Email B.Jones@city.ac.uk
Website www.city.ac.uk/journalism

Contact *Bob Jones*

FOUNDED 1980. Awarded to a young journalist experienced enough to work on national stories. It gives them the chance to work on the national desk of the *Washington Post*. Benjamin Bradlee, the *Post*'s Vice-President-at-Large, selects from a shortlist drawn up in March/April. 2002 winner: Helen Rumbelow of *The Times*. Full details available on the website.

Tom-Gallon Trust

The Society of Authors, 84 Drayton Gardens, London SW10 9SB
☎020 7373 6642   Fax 020 7373 5768
Email info@societyofauthors.org

A biennial award made on the basis of a sub-mitted story to fiction writers of limited means who have had at least one short story accepted for publication. Contact the **Society of Authors** for an entry form. Final entry date 20 September 2002.
Award £1000.

The Betty Trask Awards

The Society of Authors, 84 Drayton Gardens, London SW10 9SB
☎020 7373 6642   Fax 020 7373 5768
Email info@societyofauthors.org

These annual awards are for authors who are under 35 and Commonwealth citizens, awarded on the strength of a first novel (published or unpublished) of a traditional or romantic nature. The awards must be used for a period or periods of foreign travel. Final entry date: 31 January. Contact the **Society of Authors** for an entry form. 2001 winners: Zadie Smith *White Teeth*; Justin Hill *The Drink and Dream Teahouse*; Maggie O'Farrell *After You'd Gone*; Vivien Kelly *Take One Young Man*; Mohsin Hamid *Moth Smoke*; Patrick Neate *Musungu Jim and the Great Chief Tuloko*.
Award £25,000 (total).

The Travelling Scholarships

The Society of Authors, 84 Drayton Gardens, London SW10 9SB

☎020 7373 6642   Fax 020 7373 5768
Annual honorary grants to established British writers. 2001 winners: Alan Judd, Christina Koning, Tessa Ransford, Maurice Riordan.
Award £6000 (total).

UEA Writing Fellowship

School of English and American Studies, University of East Anglia, University Plain, Norwich, Norfolk NR4 7TJ
☎01603 592734   Fax 01603 593522
Website www.uea.ac.uk/eas/Fellowships/ fellowschol.html

Director of Personnel & Registry Services *J.R.L. Beck*

ESTABLISHED 1971. Awarded to a writer of established reputation in prose fiction and poetry for a period of six months, January to end June. The duties of the Fellowship are discussed at an interview. It is assumed that one activity will be the pursuit of the Fellow's own writing. In addition the Fellow will be expected to (a) offer an undergraduate creative writing workshop in the School of English and American Studies during the Spring semester; (b) make contact with groups around the county in association with **East England Arts**. Office space and some limited secretarial assistance will be provided, and some additional funds will be available to help the Fellow with the activities described above. Applications for the fellowship should be lodged with the Director of Personnel & Registry Services in the autumn; candidates should submit two examples of recent work. Previous winner: Bernadine Evaristo.
Award £7500 plus free flat on campus.

David T.K. Wong Fellowship

School of English and American Studies, University of East Anglia, University Plain, Norwich, Norfolk NR4 7TJ
☎01603 592810   Fax 01603 507728
Email v.striker@uea.ac.uk
Website www.uea.ac.uk/eas/Fellowships/ fellowschol.html

Contact *Val Striker*

FOUNDED 1998. An annual endowment to enable a writer of promise to spend a year at the University writing a work of fiction on some aspect of life in the Far East. Judged on the basis of submitted written work, the award is open to all nationalities. Final entry date: 31 October. 2001 winner: Liisa Laing.
Award £25,000.

Prizes

ABSW/Glaxo
Science Writers' Awards
Association of British Science Writers,
23 Savile Row, London W1X 2NB
☎020 7439 1205 Fax 020 7973 3051
ABSW Administrator *Barbara Drillsma*

A series of annual awards for outstanding science
journalism in newspapers, journals and broadcasting.

J.R. Ackerley Prize
English Centre of International PEN, 152–156
Kentish Town Road, London NW1 9QB
☎020 7267 9444 Fax 020 7267 9304
Email enquiries@pen.org.uk
Website www.pen.org.uk

Commemorating the novelist/autobiographer
J.R. Ackerley, this prize is awarded for a literary
autobiography, written in English and published
in the year preceding the award. Entry restricted
to nominations from the Ackerley Trustees only
('please do not submit books'). Previous winner:
Mark Frankland *Child of My Time*.
   Prize £1000, plus silver pen.

Acorn-Rukeyser Chapbook Contest
Mekler & Deahl, Publishers, 237 Prospect
Street South, Hamilton, Ontario, Canada
L8M 2Z6
☎001 905 312 1779 Fax 001 905 312 2285
Email james@meklerdeahl.com
Website www.meklerdeahl.com
Contacts *James Deahl, Gilda Mekler*

ESTABLISHED in 1996, this annual award is
named after the poets Milton Acorn and Muriel
Rukeyser in order to honour their achievements
as populist poets. Poets may enter as many as
30 poems for a fee of £5. Final entry date: 30
September. Contact the above address for a copy
of the rules or access the website.
   Prizes 1st and 2nd, US$100 and publication
of the manuscript.

Aldeburgh Poetry Festival Prize
Reading Room Yard, The Street, Brockdish,
Diss, Norfolk IP21 4JZ
☎01379 668345 Fax 01379 668844
Contact *Naomi Jaffa*

ESTABLISHED 1989 by the Aldeburgh Poetry
Trust. Sponsored by the Aldeburgh Bookshop
for the best first collection published in Britain
or the Republic of Ireland in the preceding
twelve months. Open to any first collection of
poetry of at least 40 pages. Final entry date:
1 October. Previous winners include: Donald
Atkinson, Susan Wicks, Gwyneth Lewis, Glyn
Wright, Robin Robertson, Tamar Yoseloff,
Colette Bryce.
   Prize £500, plus an invitation to read at the
following year's festival.

Alexander Prize
Royal Historical Society, University College
London, Gower Street, London WC1E 6BT
☎020 7387 7532 Fax 020 7387 7532
Contact *Executive Secretary*

Awarded for a historical essay of not more than
8000 words. Competitors may choose their own
subject for the essay. Closing date: 1 November.
   Prize £250 or a silver medal.

ALPSP Awards/ALPSP
Charlesworth Awards
South House, The Street, Clapham,
Worthing, West Sussex BN13 3UU
☎01903 871686 Fax 01903 871457
Email sec-gen@alpsp.org
Website www.alpsp.org
Contact *Sally Morris*

Presented in recognition of significant achievement in the field of learned and professional publishing by the **Association of Learned and
Professional Society Publishers** and the
Charlesworth Group. The awards were originally for excellence in design and typography in
journals but since 2001 they also recognise innovation, contribution to not-for-profit publishing,
library-publiser relations and for service to the
ALPSP. The awards are international and open
to publishers, organisations and individuals.
Details available on the Association's website.

An Duais don bhFilíocht i nGaeilge
An Chomhairle Ealaíon (The Irish Arts
Council), 70 Merrion Square, Dublin 2,
Republic of Ireland

☎00 353 1 6180200 Fax 00 353 1 6761302
Email info@artscouncil.ie
Website www.artscouncil.ie
Literature Officer *Sinéad Mac Aodha*
Triennial award for the best book of Irish
poetry. Works must have been published in the
Irish language in the preceding three years.
Next award in 2004.
Prize €4000.

Hans Christian Andersen Awards
IBBY, Nonnenweg 12, Postfach,
CH-4003 Basel, Switzerland
☎00 41 61 272 2917 Fax 00 41 61 272 2757
Email ibby@eye.ch
Website www.ibby.org
Executive Director *Leena Maissen*
The highest international prizes for children's lit-
erature: The Hans Christian Andersen Award for
Writing ESTABLISHED 1956; The Hans Christian
Andersen Award for Illustration ESTABLISHED
1966. Candidates are nominated by National
Sections of IBBY (The International Board on
Books for Young People). Biennial prizes are
awarded, in even-numbered years, to an author
and an illustrator whose body of work has made
a lasting contribution to children's literature.
2002 winners: Award for Writing: Aidan
Chambers (UK); Award for Illustration: Quentin
Blake (UK).
Award Gold medals.

Angus Book Award
Angus Council Cultural Services, County
Buildings, Forfar DD8 3WF
☎01307 461460 Fax 01307 462590
Contact *Norman Atkinson, Director of Cultural
Services*
ESTABLISHED 1995. Designed to try to help
teenagers develop an interest in and enthusiasm
for reading. Eligible books are read and voted on
by third-year schoolchildren in all eight Angus
secondary schools. 2001 winner: Malcolm Rose
Plague.
Prize £250 cheque, plus trophy in the form
of a replica Pictish stone.

Annual Theatre Book Prize
See **The Society for Theatre Research
Annual Theatre Book Prize**

Arts Council Children's Award
Arts Council of England, 14 Great Peter
Street, London SW1P 3NQ
☎020 7973 6431 Fax 020 7973 6983
Email jemima.lee@artscouncil.org.uk

Website www.artscouncil.org.uk
Contact *Theatre Writing Section*
A new annual award for playwrights who write
for children. The plays, which must have been
produced professionally between 1 July 2002 and
30 June 2003, should be suitable for children up
to the age of 12 and be at least 45 minutes long.
The playwright must be resident in England.
Closing date for entries: 4 July 2003. Contact the
Theatre Writing Section for full details and
application form.
Award £6000.

Arvon Foundation International Poetry Competition
2nd Floor, 42a Buckingham Palace Road,
London SW1W 0RE
☎020 7931 7611 Fax 020 7963 0961
Email london@arvonfoundation.org
Website www.arvonfoundation.org
Contact *National Administration*
ESTABLISHED 1980. Biennial competition (next
in 2004) for poems written in English and not
previously broadcast or published. There are
no restrictions on the number of lines, themes,
age of entrants or nationality. No limit to the
number of entries. Entry fee: £5 per poem.
Previous winners: Paul Farley *Laws of Gravity*;
Don Paterson *A Private Bottling*.
Prize (1st) £5000 and £5000 worth of other
prizes sponsored by Duncan Lawrie Limited.

Authors' Club First Novel Award
Authors' Club, 40 Dover Street, London
W1S 4NP
☎020 7499 8581 Fax 020 7409 0913
Contact *Mrs Ann de La Grange*
ESTABLISHED 1954. This award is made for the
most promising work published in Britain by a
British author, and is presented at a dinner held
at the Authors' Club in April. Entries for the
award are accepted from publishers by the end
of November of the year in question and must
be full-length – short stories are not eligible.
2002 winner: Carl Tighe *Burning Worm*.
Award £1000 (sponsored by the Marsh
Christian Trust).

Aventis Prizes for Science Books
Copus, c/o The Royal Society, 6–9 Carlton
House Terrace, London SW1Y 5AG
☎020 7451 2579 Fax 020 7451 2693
Email bookprize@copus.org
Website www.aventissciencebookprizes.com
Contact *Natasha Martineau*

Annual prizes ESTABLISHED in 1988 to celebrate the best in popular science writing. Awarded to books that make science more accessible to readers of all ages and backgrounds. Organised by Copus (The Science Communication Partnership) and sponsored by Aventis Pharma Ltd. All entries must be written in English and their first publication in the UK must have been between 1 January and 31 December; submission by publishers only. Educational textbooks published for professional or specialist audiences are not eligible. 2001 winners: Robert Kunzig *Mapping the Deep – The Extraordinary Story of Ocean Science* (General Prize); Michael Allaby *DK Guide to Weather* (Junior Prize).

Prizes (total) £30,000.

The BA/Book Data Author of the Year Award

Booksellers Association Ltd, 272 Vauxhall Bridge Road, London SW1V 1BA
☎020 7834 5477 Fax 020 7834 8812
Email denise.bayat@booksellers.org.uk
Website www.booksellers.org.uk

Contact *Denise Bayat*

Founded as part of the BA Annual Conference to involve authors more closely in the event. Authors must be British or Irish. Not an award open to entry but voted on by the BA's membership. 2001 winner: Philip Pullman.

Award £1000, plus trophy.

BAAL Book Prize

BAAL Publications Secretary, Centre for Language and Communication, Cardiff University, Colum Drive, PO Box 94, Cardiff CF10 3XB
☎029 2087 4243 Fax 029 2087 4242
Email sarangi@cardiff.ac.uk
Website www.baal.org.uk

Contact *Dr Srikant Sarangi*

Annual award made by the British Association for Applied Linguistics to an outstanding book in the field of applied linguistics. Final entry at the end of Oct/Nov. Nominations from publishers only. Previous winners: Susan Berk-Seligson *The Bilingual Courtroom*; Joshua A. Fishman *Reversing Language Shift*; Deborah Cameron *Verbal Hygiene*; Marco Jacquemet *Credibility in Court*; Ana Celia Zentella *Growing Up Bilingual*; Daniel Nettle and Suzanne Romaine *Vanishing Voices: the extinction of the world's languages*.

Barclays Bank Prize

See **Lakeland Book of the Year Awards**

Verity Bargate Award

The Soho Theatre Company, 21 Dean Street, London W1D 3NE
☎020 7287 5060 Fax 020 7287 5061
Email writers@sohotheatre.com

Contact *Jo Ingham, Literary Officer*

The award was set up to commemorate the late Verity Bargate, co-founder and director of the **Soho Theatre Company**. This national award is presented biennially for a new and unperformed play (next in 2004). To go on the mailing list, please e-mail or send s.a.e. to *Jo Ingham*. Previous winners include: Shan Khan, Fraser Grace, Lyndon Morgans, Adrian Pagan, Diane Samuels, Judy Upton and Toby Whithouse.

The Herb Barrett Award

Mekler & Deahl, Publishers, 237 Prospect Street South, Hamilton, Ontario Canada L8M 2Z6
☎001 905 312 1779 Fax 001 905 312 8285
Email james@meklerdeahl.com
Website www.meklerdeahl.com

Contact *James Deahl*

ESTABLISHED in 1996, this annual award is named in honour of Herb Barrett, founder of the Hamilton Chapter of the Canadian Poetry Association. Poets may enter up to 10 haiku for a fee of £5. Final entry date: 30 November. Contact the address above for a copy of the rules or access the website.

Prize (US) $200, $150 and $100; anthology publication for the winners and all other worthy entries.

BBC Wildlife Magazine Awards for Nature Writing

PO Box 229, Bristol BS99 7JN
☎0117 973 8402 Fax 0117 946 7075
Email nina.epton@bbc.co.uk

Contact *Nina Epton*

Annual competition for professional and amateur writers. Entries (no longer than 1000 words) should be based on personal observations of, or thoughts about, nature – general or specific. The entry form appears in the magazine; closing date varies. Contact the magazine for entry information.

Prizes Winner: cash prize, plus publication in the magazine; runners-up: cash prizes, plus publication; two young writers' awards.

BBC Wildlife Magazine Poet of the Year Awards

PO Box 229, Bristol BS99 7JN

☎0117 973 8402   Fax 0117 946 7075
Email nina.epton@bbc.co.uk
Contact *Nina Epton*

Annual award for a poem, the subject of which must be the natural world and/or our relationship with it. Entrants may submit one poem only of no more than 50 lines with the entry form which appears in the magazine. Closing date for entries varies from year to year. Contact the magazine for entry information.

Prizes Poet of the Year: £500, publication in the magazine, plus reading of the poem on Radio 4's *Poetry Please*; runners-up: cash prizes, plus publication in the magazine; four young poets awards.

BBC Wildlife Magazine Travel Writing Award

PO Box 229, Bristol BS99 7JN
☎0117 973 8402   Fax 0117 946 7075
Email nina.epton@bbc.co.uk
Contact *Nina Epton*

Awarded to a travel essay that is a true account involving an intimate encounter with wildlife, either local or exotic. The essay should convey a strong impression of the environment and incorporate the idea of travel and discovery. Maximum 800 words. Contact the magaine for entry information.

Prize Publication in the magazine, plus 'holiday of a lifetime'.

The BBCFour Samuel Johnson Prize for Non-fiction

The Booksellers Association, Minster House, 272 Vauxhall Bridge Road, London SW1V 1BA
☎020 7834 5477   Fax 020 7834 8812
Contact *Sharon Down*

ESTABLISHED 1998. Annual prize sponsored by BBCFour. Eligible categories include the arts, autobiography, biography, business, commerce, current affairs, history, natural history, popular science, religion, sport and travel. Entries submitted by publishers only. 2001 winner: Michael Burleigh *The Third Reich*.

Prize £30,000; £2500 to each shortlisted author.

Bedford Open Poetry Competition

PO Box 6079, Leighton Buzzard, Bedfordshire LU7 2NB
Email gavin.stewart@interpreters-house
Contact *Gavin Stewart*

Annual award, FOUNDED 1997. Open to anyone of 16 years of age and over, competitors may submit an unlimited number of poems for a fee of £3 per poem. Entry information leaflet available. The aim of the competition is to find good poems for publication in *The Interpreter's House* magazine. Previous winners: Julian Van Hauson and Mary Michaels.

Prizes £300 (1st); £100 (Runners-up); £50 (Bedfordshire Prize).

David Berry Prize

Royal Historical Society, University College London, Gower Street, London WC1E 6BT
☎020 7387 7532   Fax 020 7387 7532
Contact *Executive Secretary*

Annual award for an essay of not more than 10,000 words on Scottish history. Closing date: 31 October.

Prize £250.

Besterman/McColvin Medal

See **CILIP: The Chartered Institute of Library and Information Professionals Besterman/McColvin Medal**

The Biographers' Club Prize

17 Sutherland Street, London SW1V 4JU
☎020 7828 1274   Fax 020 7828 7608
Email lownie@globalnet.co.uk
Website www.booktrust.org.uk
Contact *Andrew Lownie*

ESTABLISHED 1999 by literary agent, biographer and founder of the Biographers' Club, Andrew Lownie, to finance and encourage first-time writers researching a biography. Sponsored by the *Daily Mail*. Deadline for submissions: 2 September 2002. Open to previously un-commissioned writers producing a proposal of 15–20 pages, broken down by chapter with a note of author's credentials, the market for the book, sources used and competing/comparable books. 2001 winner: Adrian Fort.

Prize £1000.

Birdwatch Bird Book of the Year

c/o Birdwatch Magazine, 3D/F Leroy House, 436 Essex Road, Islington, London N1 3QP
☎020 7704 9495
Contact *Dominic Mitchell*

ESTABLISHED in 1992 to acknowledge excellence in ornithological publishing – an increasingly large market with a high turnover. Annual award. Entries, from publishers, must offer an original and comprehensive treatment of their particular ornithological subject matter and must have a broad appeal to British-based readers. 2001 winner: *Sylvia Warblers, Identification, taxonomy and phylogeny of the genus Sylvia* Hadoram Shirihai, Gabriel Gargallo, Andreas J. Helbig.

Biscuit Poetry and Fiction Prizes

Biscuit Publishing, PO Box 123, Washington, Newcastle upon Tyne NE37 2YW
☎0191 431 1263 Fax 0191 431 1263
Email biscuitpub@yahoo.co.uk

Contacts *Brian Lister, Jacqui Lister*

FOUNDED 2000. Annual award that aims to support new writers of short fiction and poetry. The 'Top Twenty' winners from each category are published in an anthology. In addition, the winning poet and fiction author will each have separate publications. Closing date: 31 May. Previous winners: Ruth Henderson *The Art of Living*; Chris Preddle *Bonobos*.
  Prizes Publication and advance royalties.

Bisto/CBI Book of the Year Award
See **Children's Books Ireland** under **Professional Associations and Societies**

James Tait Black Memorial Prizes
University of Edinburgh, David Hume Tower, George Square, Edinburgh EH8 9JX
☎0131 650 3619 Fax 0131 650 6898
Website www.ed.ac.uk/englit/jtbint.htm

Contact *Department of English Literature*

ESTABLISHED 1918 in memory of a partner of the publishing firm of **A.&C. Black Ltd**. Two prizes, one for biography and one for fiction. Closing date for submissions: 30 September. Each prize is awarded for a book published in Britain in the previous twelve months. Prize winners are announced in February each year. 2001 winners: Sid Smith *Something Like a House* (fiction); Robert Skidelsky *John Maynard Keynes, Vol. 3: Fighting for Britain 1937–1946*.
  Prizes £3000 each.

Blue Peter Book Awards
See **Scottish Book Trust** under **Professional Associations and Societies**

Boardman Tasker Award
Pound House, Llangennith, Swansea, West Glamorgan SA3 1JQ
☎01792 386215 Fax 01792 386215
Email margaretbody@lineone.net
Website www.boardmantasker.com

Contact *Maggie Body, Honorary Secretary*

ESTABLISHED 1983, this award is given for a work of fiction, non-fiction or poetry, whose central theme is concerned with the mountain environment and which can be said to have made an outstanding contribution to mountain literature. Authors of any nationality are eligible, but the book must have been published or distributed in the UK for the first time between 1 November 2001 and 31 October 2002. Entries from publishers only. 2001 winner: Roger Hubank *Hazard's Way*.
  Prize £2000 (at Trustees' discretion).

Bollinger Everyman Wodehouse Prize
Everyman Publishers, Gloucester Mansions, 140A Shaftesbury Avenue, London WC2H 8HD
☎020 7539 7608 Fax 020 7379 4060
Email dcampbell@everyman.uk.com
Website www.everyman.uk.com

Contact *Becke Parker*

ESTABLISHED in 2000 by David Campbell, publisher of Everyman's Library, Bollinger and the Hay Festival to celebrate comic writing in memory of P.G. Wodehouse. Books are nominated by readers of the *Sunday Times* and visitors to www.bol.com. 2001 winner: Jonathan Coe *The Rotters' Club*.

The Booker Prize for Fiction
See **The Man Booker Prize for Fiction**

The Books for Children Award
BCA, Greater London House, Hampstead Road, London NW1 7TZ
☎020 7760 6500 Fax 020 7760 6829

Contact *Books for Children Editor*

ESTABLISHED 1979. Formerly known as the BFC Mother Goose Award. Annual award open to writers and illustrators of a first children's work published in the UK. 2002 winner: Peter Horacek *What Is Black and White?* and *Strawberries Are Red*.
  Prize £1000.

Border Television Prize
See **Lakeland Book of the Year Awards**

The BP Natural World Book Prize
Booktrust, Book House, 45 East Hill, London SW18 2QZ
☎020 8516 2972 Fax 020 8516 2978
Email tarryn@booktrust.org.uk
Website www.booktrust.org.uk

Contact *Tarryn McKay*

ESTABLISHED in 1996 as an amalgamation of the

Natural World Book Prize (the magazine of the Wildlife Trusts) and the BP Conservation Book Prize. Award for a book on creative conservation of the environment. Entries from UK publishers only. 2000 winner: Brian Clarke *The Stream*.
Prizes (1st) £5000; Runner-up: £1000.

The Branford Boase Award
18 Grosvenor Road, Portswood,
Southampton, Hampshire SO17 1RT
☎023 8055 5057
Email lo@loisb.fsnet.co.uk
Website www.henriettabranford.co.uk
Administrator *Lois Beeson*

ESTABLISHED in 2000 in memory of children's novelist, Henrietta Branford and editor and publisher, Wendy Boase. To be awarded annually to encourage and celebrate the most promising novel by a new writer of children's books, while at the same time highlighting the importance of the editor in nurturing new talent. 2001 winners: Marcus Sedgwick *Floodland* (book); Fiona Kennedy, **Orion Children's Books** (editor).
Award £1000.

The Bridport Prize
Bridport Arts Centre, South Street, Bridport, Dorset DT6 3NR
☎01308 459444 Fax 01308 459166
Website www.bridportprize.org.uk
Contact *Competition Secretary*

Annual competition for poetry and short story writing. Unpublished work only, written in English. Winning stories are read by a literary agent (**A.M. Heath**), the winning poems are put forward to *Poetry Review* and the **Forward Prize**, and an anthology of winning entries is published. Final entry date: 30 June. Send s.a.e. for entry forms.
Prizes £3000, £1000 & £500 in each category, plus various supplementary prizes.

Katharine Briggs Folklore Award
The Folklore Society, c/o The Warburg Institute, Woburn Square, London WC1H 0AB
☎020 7862 8564/8562
Email folklore-society@talk21.com
Website www.folklore-society.com
Contact *The Convenor*

ESTABLISHED 1982. An annual award in November for the book, published in Britain and Ireland between 1 June in the previous calendar year and 30 May, which has made the most distinguished non-fiction contribution to folklore studies. Intended to encourage serious research in the field which Katharine Briggs did so much to establish. The term folklore studies is interpreted broadly to include all aspects of traditional and popular culture, narrative, belief, custom and folk arts.
Prize £50, plus engraved goblet.

The British Academy Book Prize
10 Carlton House Terrace, London
SW1Y 5AH
☎020 7969 5263 Fax 020 7969 5414
Email jbreckon@britac.ac.uk
Website www.britishacademy.ac.uk
Contact *Dr Jonathan Breckon*

Annual award FOUNDED in 2001 to celebrate outstanding scholarly books in the humanities and social sciences that are accessible to the general reader. Nominations from publishers only; final entry date: 20 February 2003. 2001 joint winners: Ian Kershaw *Hitler: 1936–1945, Nemesis*; Rees Davies *The First English Empire*.

British Book Awards
Publishing News, 39 Store Street, London
WC1E 7DB
☎020 7692 2900 Fax 020 7419 2111
Email mailbox@publishingnews.co.uk
Website www.publishingnews.co.uk

ESTABLISHED 1988. Viewed by the book trade as the one to win, 'The Nibbies' are presented annually in February. The awards are made in various categories. Each winner receives the prestigious Nibbie and the awards are presented to those who have made the most impact in the book trade during the previous year. Recent winners have included: Philip Pullman, Pete McCarthy, Pamela Stephenson, Alan Bennett, Eoin Colfer, Mark Barty-King, Martyn Goff, Blackwell's, and the publishers **HarperCollins**. For further information contact: Merric Davidson, 12 Priors Heath, Goudhurst, Cranbrook, Kent TN17 2RE (☎/Fax 01580 212041; e-mail nibbies@mdla.co.uk).

British Comparative Literature Association/British Centre for Literary Translation Competition
School of Language, Linguistics and Translation Studies, University of East Anglia, Norwich, Norfolk NR4 7TJ
Fax 01603 250599
Email transcomp@uea.ac.uk
Website www.bcla.org
Competition Organiser *Dr Jean Boase-Beier*

ESTABLISHED 1983. Annual competition open to unpublished literary translations from all languages. Maximum submission: 25 pages.

Prizes £350 (1st); £200 (2nd); £100 (3rd); plus publication for all winning entries in the Association's annual journal *Comparative Criticism* (**Cambridge University Press**). Other entries may receive commendations.

British Fantasy Awards

201 Reddish Road, South Reddish, Stockport, Cheshire SK5 7HR
☎0161 476 5368 (after 6.00 pm)
Email faliol@yahoo.com
Website www.britishfantasysociety.com

Secretary *Robert Parkinson*

Awarded by the **British Fantasy Society** by members at its annual conference for Best Novel and Best Short Story categories, among others. Not an open competition. Previous winners include: Ramsey Campbell, Dan Simmons, Michael Marshall Smith, Thomas Ligotti.

British Press Awards

Press Gazette, Quantum House, 19 Scarbrook Road, Croydon, Surrey CR9 1LX
☎020 8565 4200 Fax 020 8565 4395
Email pged@qpp.co.uk

'The Oscars of British journalism.' Open to all British morning and Sunday newspapers sold nationally and news agencies. March event. Run by *Press Gazette*.

British Science Fiction Association Award

8 Century House, Armoury Road, London SE8 4LH
☎020 8469 3354
Email awards@amaranth.aviators.net
Website www.bsfa.co.uk

Award Administrator *Tanya Brown*

ESTABLISHED 1966. Categories for novel, short story, artwork and non-fiction. The awards are announced and presented at the British Annual SF Convention every Easter. 2001 winners: Alastair Reynolds *Chasm City* (novel); Eric Brown *The Children of Winter* (short fiction); Stephen Baxter *Omegatropic* (non-fiction); Colin Odell for the cover of *Omegatropic* (artwork).

British Sports Journalism Awards

See **Sports Writers' Association of Great Britain** under **Professional Associations and Societies**

The Caine Prize for African Writing

2 Drayson Mews, London W8 4LY
☎020 7376 0440 Fax 020 7938 3728
Email caineprize@jftaylor.com
Website www.caineprize.com

Administrator *Nick Elam*
Secretary *Jan Hart*

Annual award FOUNDED in 1999 in memory of Sir Michael Caine, former chairman of Booker plc, to recognise the worth of African writing in English. Awarded for a short story by an African writer, published in English anywhere in the world. 'An African writer' is someone who was born in Africa, or who is a national of an African country, or whose parents are African, and whose work has reflected African sensibilities. Final entry date: 31 January; submissions by publishers only. 2001 winner: Helon Habila.
Prize $15,000.

The Calouste Gulbenkian Prize
See **The Translators Association Awards**

James Cameron Award

City University, Department of Journalism, Northampton Square, London EC1V 0HB
☎020 7477 8221 Fax 020 7477 8594

Contact *The Administrator*

Annual award for journalism to a reporter of any nationality, working for the British media, whose work is judged to have contributed most during the year to the continuance of the Cameron tradition. Administered by the City University Department of Journalism. 2001 winner: Suzanne Goldenberg, *Guardian*.

Canadian Poetry Association Annual Poetry Contest

Box 22571, St George Postal Outlet, 264 Bloor Street West, Toronto, Ontario, Canada M5S 1V8
Website www.mirror.org/cpa

Annual contest open to members and non-members of the CPA worldwide. Submission fee: $5 per poem. See the website for entry details. All winning poems are published on the CPA website.

Six cash *Prizes* and publication in *Poetmata*.

Canadian Poetry Association Shaunt Basmajian Award

Box 22571, St George Postal Outlet, 264 Bloor Street West, Toronto, Ontario M5S 1V8, Canada
Website www.mirror.org/cpa

Annual poetry contest open to members and non-members of the CPA worldwide. Entry fee: C$15; cheque or money order payable to the Canadian Poetry Association. Submit a manuscript of poems up to 24 pages in length, published or unpublished, and in any style or tradition. See the website for full details. The author of the winning manuscript receives 50 copies of the resulting chapbook as well as C$100 cash.

The Canongate Prize
Canongate Books, 14 High Street, Edinburgh EH1 1TE
☎0131 557 5111 Fax 0131 557 5211
Email info@canongate.co.uk
Website www.canongate-prize.com

ESTABLISHED in 1999 by **Canongate Books** and Waterstone's to stimulate innovative new prose writing. The competition was under review at the time of going to press.

Cardiff International Poetry Competition
PO Box 438, Cardiff CF10 5YA
☎029 2047 2266 Fax 029 2049 2930
Email post@academi.org
Website www.academi.org
Contact *Peter Finch*

ESTABLISHED 1986. An annual competition for unpublished poems in English of up to 50 lines. Closing date in October.
Prize £5000 (total) .

Carey Award
Society of Indexers, Globe Centre, Penistone Road, Sheffield, South Yorkshire S6 3AE
☎0114 281 3060 Fax 0114 281 3061
Email admin@socind.demon.co.uk
Website www.socind.demon.co.uk
Secretary *Ann Kingdom*

A private award made by the Society to a member who has given outstanding services to indexing. The recipient is selected by Council with no recommendations considered from elsewhere.

Carnegie Medal
See **CILIP: The Chartered Institute of Library and Information Professionals Carnegie Medal**

Sid Chaplin Short Story Competition
Shildon Town Council, Civic Centre Square, Shildon, Co Durham DL4 1AH
☎01388 772563 Fax 01388 775227
Contact *Mrs J.M. Stafford*

ESTABLISHED 1986. Annual themed short story competition (2001 subject was 'Good & Evil'). Maximum 3000 words; £2 entrance fee (juniors free). All stories must be unpublished and not broadcast and/or performed. Application forms available from September 2002.
Prizes £300 (1st); £150 (2nd); £75 (3rd); £50 (Junior).

Children's Book Award
The Federation of Children's Book Groups, The Old Malt House, Aldbourne, Wiltshire SN8 2DW
☎01672 540629 Fax 01672 541280
Email marianneadey@cs.com
Coordinator *Marianne Adey*

ESTABLISHED 1980. Awarded annually for best book of fiction suitable for children. Unique in that it is judged by the children themselves. 2001 winner: *Eat Your Peas* by Kes Gray, illus. Nick Sharratt.
Award Portfolio of letters, drawings and comments from the children who took part in the judging.

Children's Book Circle Eleanor Farjeon Award
See **Eleanor Farjeon Award**

The Children's Laureate
18 Grosvenor Road, Portswood, Southampton, Hampshire SO17 1RT
☎023 8055 5057
Email lo@loisb.fsnet.co.uk
Website www.waterstones.co.uk
Administrator *Lois Beeson*

ESTABLISHED 1998. Sponsored by Waterstone's, the Laureate is awarded biennially to an eminent British writer or illustrator of children's books both in celebration of a lifetime's achievement and to highlight the role of children's book creators in making the readers of the future. 2001 winner: Anne Fine.
Award Medal and £10,000.

CILIP: The Chartered Institute of Library and Information Professionals Besterman/ McColvin Medal
7 Ridgmount Street, London WC1E 7AE
☎020 7255 0650 Fax 020 7255 0501

Annual award for an outstanding reference work first published in the UK during the preceding year. Consists of two categories: printed and electronic. Works eligible for consideration include: encyclopedias, general and special dictionaries; annuals, yearbooks and directories; handbooks and compendia of data; atlases. Nominations are invited from members of **CILIP**, publishers and others.

Award Medal and cash prize for each category.

CILIP: The Chartered Institute of Library and Information Professionals Carnegie Medal

7 Ridgmount Street, London WC1E 7AE
☎020 7255 0650 Fax 020 7255 0501

ESTABLISHED 1936. Presented for an outstanding book for children written in English and first published in the UK during the preceding year. Fiction, non-fiction and poetry are all eligible. 2000 winner: Beverley Naidoo *The Other Side of Truth*.

Award Medal.

CILIP: The Chartered Institute of Library and Information Professionals Kate Greenaway Medal

7 Ridgmount Street, London WC1E 7AE
☎020 7255 0650 Fax 020 7255 0501

ESTABLISHED 1955. Presented annually for the most distinguished work in the illustration of children's books first published in the UK during the preceding year. 2000 winner: Lauren Child *I Will Not Ever, Never Eat a Tomato*.

Award Medal. The Colin Mears Award (£5000 cash) is given annually to the winner of the Kate Greenaway Medal.

CILIP: The Chartered Institute of Library and Information Professionals Walford Award

7 Ridgmount Street, London WC1E 7AE
☎020 7255 0650 Fax 020 7255 0501

Awarded to an individual who has made a sustained and continual contribution to British bibliography over a period of years. The nominee need not be resident in the UK. The award is named after Dr A.J. Walford, a bibliograper of international repute. Previous winners include: Prof. J.D. Pearson, Prof. R.C. Alston and Prof. John McIlwaine.

Award Cash prize and certificate.

CILIP: The Chartered Institute of Library and Information Professionals Wheatley Medal

7 Ridgmount Street, London WC1E 7AE
☎020 7255 0650 Fax 020 7255 0501

ESTABLISHED 1962. Annual award for an outstanding index first published in the UK during the preceding three years. Whole work must have originated in the UK and recommendations for the award are invited from members of **CILIP**, the **Society of Indexers**, publishers and others. Previous winners include: Paul Nash *The World of Environment 1972–1992*; Richard Raper *The Works of Charles Darwin*; David Crystal and Hilary Crystal *Words on Words*.

Award Medal and cash prize.

Arthur C. Clarke Award for Science Fiction

60 Bournemouth Road, Folkestone, Kent CT19 5AZ
☎01303 252939 Fax 01303 252939
Email clarke@appomattox.demon.co.uk

Administrator *Paul Kincaid*

ESTABLISHED 1986. The Arthur C. Clarke Award is given annually to the best science fiction novel with first UK publication in the previous calendar year. Both hardcover and paperback books qualify. Made possible by a generous donation from Arthur C. Clarke, this award is selected by a rotating panel of judges nominated by the **British Science Fiction Association**, the **Science Fiction Foundation** and the Science Museum. 2002 winner: Gwyneth Jones *Bold as Love*.

Award £2002 (award increases by £1 per year), plus trophy.

The Cló Iar-Chonnachta Literary Award

Cló Iar-Chonnachta Teo, Indreabhán, Conamara, Co. Galway, Republic of Ireland
☎00 353 91 593307 Fax 00 353 91 593362
Website www.cic.ie

Editor *Róisín Ní Mhianànn*

An annual prize for a newly written and unpublished work in the Irish language. 2003 award will be for the best collection of short stories or long play. 2001 winner: Pádraig Ó Siadhail for his collection of short stories, *Na Seacht gCineál Meisce*.

Prize €6350.

David Cohen
British Literature Prize

Arts Council of Great Britain, 14 Great Peter Street, London SW1P 3NQ
☎020 7333 0100 Fax 020 7973 6520
Website www.artscouncil.org.uk

Literature Director *Gary McKeone*
Literature Assistant *Pippa Shoubridge*

ESTABLISHED 1993 by the Arts Council and awarded biennially, the British Literature Prize is one of the most distinguished literary prizes in Britain. It recognises writers who use the English language and who are British citizens, encompassing dramatists as well as novelists, poets and essayists. Anyone may suggest candidates for the award. The prize is for a lifetime's achievement rather than a single play or book and is donated by the David Cohen Family Charitable Trust. Set up in 1980 by David Cohen, general practitioner and son of a property developer, the Trust has helped composers, choreographers, dancers, poets, playwrights and actors. The Council is providing a further £10,000 to enable the winner to commission new work, with the dual aim of encouraging young writers and readers. 2001 winner: Doris Lessing. Previous winners: William Trevor, Dame Muriel Spark, Harold Pinter, V.S. Naipaul.
Award £30,000, plus £10,000 towards new work.

The Commonwealth Writers Prize

Booktrust, Book House, 45 East Hill, London SW18 2QZ
☎020 8516 2972 Fax 020 8516 2978
Email tarryn@booktrust.org.uk
Website www.booktrust.org.uk *or* www.commonwealthwriters.com

Contact *Tarryn McKay*

ESTABLISHED 1987. An annual award to reward and encourage the upsurge of new Commonwealth fiction. Any work of prose or fiction is eligible, i.e. a novel or collection of short stories. No drama or poetry. The work must be first written in English by a citizen of the Commonwealth and be first published in the year before its entry for the prize. Entries must be submitted by the publisher to the region of the writer's Commonwealth citizenship. The four regions are: Africa, Eurasia, S.E. Asia and South Pacific, Caribbean and Canada. 2002 winners: Richard Flanagan *Gould's Book of Fish* (Best Book); Manu Herbstein *Alma* (Best First Book).
Prizes £10,000 for Best Book; £3000 for Best First Book; 8 prizes of £1000 for each best and first best book in four regions.

The Thomas Cook
Travel Book Award

Thomas Cook Publishing, PO Box 227, Peterborough PE3 8XX
☎01733 402009 Fax 01733 416688
Email joan.lee@thomascook.com

Contact *Joan Lee, Publishing*

ESTABLISHED in 1980 by The Thomas Cook Group. Annual award given to the author of the book, published (in the English language) in the previous year, which most inspires the reader to want to travel. Submissions by publishers only. 2001 winner: Stanley Stewart *In the Empire of Genghis Khan.*
Award £10,000.

The Duff Cooper Prize

54 St Maur Road, London SW6 4DP
☎020 7736 3729 Fax 020 7731 7638

Contact *Artemis Cooper*

An annual award for a literary work of biography, history, politics or poetry, published by a recognised publisher (member of the **Publishers Association**) during the previous 12 months. The book must be submitted by the publisher, not the author. Financed by the interest from a trust fund commemorating Duff Cooper, first Viscount Norwich (1890–1954). 2001 winner: Margaret MacMillan *Peacemakers.*
Prize £3000.

Rose Mary Crawshay Prize

The British Academy, 10 Carlton House Terrace, London SW1Y 5AH
☎020 7969 5200 Fax 020 7969 5300
Website www.britac.ac.uk

Contact *British Academy Secretary*

ESTABLISHED 1888 by Rose Mary Crawshay, this prize is given for a historical or critical work by a woman of any nationality on English literature, with particular preference for a work on Keats, Byron or Shelley. The work must have been published in the preceding three years.
Prizes Normally two of approximately £500 each.

Crime Writers' Association
(Cartier Diamond Dagger)

PO Box 338, Ashford, Kent TN23 5WQ
Website www.thecwa.co.uk
Contact *The Secretary*

An annual award for a lifetime's oustanding contribution to the genre. 2002 winner: Sara Paretsky.

Crime Writers' Association (The CWA Ellis Peters Historical Dagger)

PO Box 338, Ashford, Kent TN23 5WQ
Website www.thecwa.co.uk
Contact *The Secretary*

ESTABLISHED 1999. Annual award for the best historical crime novel. Nominations from publishers only. 2001 winner: Andrew Taylor *The Office of the Dead*.

Award Dagger, plus cheque.

Crime Writers' Association (The Ian Fleming Steel Dagger)

PO Box 388, Ashford, Kent TN23 5WQ
Website www.thecwa.co.uk
Contact *The Secretary*

FOUNDED 2002. Annual award for the best thriller, adventure or spy novel. Sponsored by Ian Fleming (Glidrose) Publications Ltd to celebrate the best of contemporary thriller writing.

Award Dagger, plus cheque.

Crime Writers' Association (The Macallan Gold Dagger for Non-Fiction)

PO Box 388, Ashford, Kent TN23 5WQ
Website www.thecwa.co.uk
Contact *The Secretary*

Annual award for the best non-fiction crime book published during the year. Nominations from publishers only. 2001 winner: Philip Etienne and Martin Maynard with Tony Thompson *The Infiltrators*.

Award Dagger, plus cheque (sum varies).

Crime Writers' Association (The Macallan Gold and Silver Daggers for Fiction)

PO Box 388, Ashford, Kent TN23 5WQ
Website www.thecwa.co.uk
Contact *The Secretary*

Two annual awards for the best crime fiction published during the year. Nominations for Gold Dagger from publishers only. 2001 winners: Henning Mankell *Sidetracked* transl. Steven T. Murray (Gold); Giles Blunt *Forty Words for Sorrow* (Silver).

Award Dagger, plus cheque (sum varies).

Crime Writers' Association (The Macallan Short Story Dagger)

PO Box 388, Ashford, Kent TN23 5WQ
Website www.thecwa.co.uk

Contact *The Secretary*

ESTABLISHED 1993. An award for a published crime story. Publishers should submit three copies of the story by 30 September. 2001 winner: Marion Arnott *Prussian Snowdrops*.

Prize Dagger, plus cheque.

Crime Writers' Association (The Creasey Dagger for Best First Crime Novel)

PO Box 388, Ashford, Kent TN23 5WQ
Website www.thecwa.co.uk
Contact *The Secretary*

ESTABLISHED 1973 following the death of crime writer John Creasey, founder of the **Crime Writers' Association**. This award, sponsored by **Chivers Press**, is given annually for the best crime novel by an author who has not previously published a full-length work of fiction. Nominations from publishers only. 2001 winner: Susanna Jones *The Earthquake Bird*.

Award Dagger, plus cheque.

Curtis Brown University of Manchester Prize

Curtis Brown Group Ltd, Haymarket House, 28/29 Haymarket, London SW1Y 4SP
☎020 7396 6600 Fax 020 7396 0110
Email cb@curtisbrown.co.uk

Contact *Giles Gordon*
(Giles@Curtisbrown.co.uk)

ESTABLISHED 1998. Annual prize for the best novel, in the opinion of Curtis Brown, written by a student on the MA in Novel Writing programme run by the University of Manchester. Open to all those not currently represented by a literary agent or under contract to a publisher.

Prize £1000. (Curtis Brown reserves the right to offer to act as literary agent to the winner.)

Harvey Darton Award

See **The Children's Books History Society** under **Literary Societies**

Hunter Davies Prize

See **Lakeland Book of the Year Awards**

Isaac & Tamara Deutscher Memorial Prize

SML, University of Southampton, Highfield, Southampton, Hampshire SO17 1BJ
Email ed2@soton.ac.uk
Contact *Professor Elizabeth Dore*

An annual award in recognition of, and as an encouragement to, outstanding research in or

about the Marxist tradition. Made to the author of an essay or full-scale work published or in manuscript. Final entry date: 1 May.
Award £250.

George Devine Award
17A South Villas, London NW1 9BS
☎020 7267 9793 (evenings only)

Contact *Christine Smith*

Annual award for a promising new playwright writing for the stage in memory of George Devine, artistic director of the **Royal Court Theatre**, who died in 1965. The play, which can be of any length, does not need to have been produced. Send two copies of the script, plus outline of work, to Christine Smith. Closing date: March. Information leaflet available from January on receipt of s.a.e.
Prize £10,000.

Denis Devlin Memorial Award for Poetry
An Chomhairle Ealaíon (The Irish Arts Council), 70 Merrion Square, Dublin 2, Republic of Ireland
☎00 353 1 6180200 Fax 00 353 1 6761302
Email info@artscouncil.ie
Website www.artscouncil.ie

Literature Officer *Sinéad Mac Aodha*

Triennial award for the best book of poetry in English by an Irish poet, published in the preceding three years. Next award 2004.
Award €2500.

Dingle Prize
British Society for the History of Science, 31 High Street, Stanford in the Vale, Farringdon, Oxfordshire SN7 8LH
☎01367 718963 Fax 01367 718963
Email bshs@hidex.demon.co.uk
Website www.bshs.org.uk

Biennial award made by the BSHS to the best book in the history of science (broadly construed) which is accessible to a wide audience of non-specialists. Next award: 2003. Previous winners: Deborah Cadbury *The Dinosaur Hunters*; Steven Shapin *The Scientific Revolution*.
Prize £300.

Drama Association of Wales Playwriting Competition
The Old Library, Singleton Road, Splott, Cardiff CF24 2ET
☎029 2045 2200 Fax 029 2045 2277
Email aled.daw@virgin.net

Contact *Teresa Hennessy*

Annual competition held to promote the writing of one-act plays in English and Welsh of between 20 and 45 minutes' playing time. The competition format is reviewed annually, looking at different themes, genres and markets. Application forms from the address above.

S.T. Dupont Golden PEN Award for Lifetime Distinguished Service to Literature
English Centre of International PEN, 152–156 Kentish Town Road, London NW1 9QB
☎020 7267 9444 Fax 020 7267 9304
Email enquiries@pen.org.uk
Website www.pen.org.uk

Awarded to a senior writer, with a distinguished body of work over many years, who has made a significant and constructive impact on fellow writers, the reading public and the literary world. Nominations by members of English PEN only.

Eccles Prize
Columbia Business School, Uris Hall, 3022 Broadway, New York NY 10027, USA
☎001 212 854 2747 Fax 001 212 854 3050
Email mag177@columbia.edu

Contact *Maria Graham*

ESTABLISHED 1986 by Spencer F. Eccles in commemoration of his uncle, George S. Eccles, a 1922 graduate of the Business School. Annual award for excellence in economic writing. One of the US's most prestigious book prizes. Books must have a business theme and be written for a general audience. Previous winners: Ron Chernow *The Warburgs*; Jagdish Bhagwati *A Stream of Windows: Unsettling Reflections on Trade, Immigration and Democracy*.

The T.S. Eliot Prize
The Poetry Book Society, Book House, 45 East Hill, London SW18 2QZ
☎020 8870 8403/8874 6361
Fax 020 8877 1615
Email info@poetrybooks.co.uk
Website www.poetrybooks.co.uk

Contact *Clare Brown, Director*

ESTABLISHED 1993. Annual award named after T.S. Eliot, one of the founders of the **Poetry Book Society**. Open to books of new poetry published in the UK and Republic of Ireland during the year and over 32 pages in length. At least 75 per cent of the collection must be previously unpublished in book form. Final entry date is in August. 2001 winner: Anne Carson *The Beauty of the Husband*. Previous winners: Michael Longley *The Weather in Japan*; Hugo Williams *Billy's Rain*; Ted Hughes *Birthday Letters*; Don Paterson *God's Gift to Women*; Les Murray *Subhuman Redneck Poems*. *Award £10,000.*

The Encore Award

The Society of Authors, 84 Drayton Gardens, London SW10 9SB
☎020 7373 6642 Fax 020 7373 5768
Email info@societyofauthors.org
ESTABLISHED 1990. Awarded for the best second published novel or novels of the year. Final entry date: 30 November. Details from the **Society of Authors**. 2002 winner: Ali Smith *Hotel World*.
Prize £10,000.

Envoi Poetry Competition

Envoi, 44 Rudyard Road, Biddulph Moor, Stoke on Trent, Staffordshire ST8 7JN
☎01782 517892
Contact *Roger Elkin*

Run by *Envoi* poetry magazine. Competitions are featured regularly, with prizes of £300, plus three annual subscriptions to *Envoi*. Winning poems along with full adjudication report are published. Send s.a.e. to Competition Secretary, 17 Millcroft, Bishops Stortford, Hertfordshire CM23 2BP.

EuroPAWS (European Public Awareness of Science) Midas Prize

The EuroPAWS Office, OMNI Communications, Chancel House, Neasden Lane, London NW10 2TU
☎020 8214 1543 Fax 020 8214 1544
Email pawsomni@globalnet.co.uk
Contacts *Barrie Whatley, Andrew Millington*
ESTABLISHED 1998. Annual prize awarded to the writer and producer of the best television drama, first transmitted in the year up to the end of October, that bears in a significant way on science or engineering. The drama may be a single play or an episode of a series, serial or soap. It need not necessarily be centred on a science or engineering theme, although clearly it can be. The context and quality of the drama and the audience size all weigh alongside the science in making the Award. To enter a programme or suggest that a programme should be entered, contact the EuroPAWS office above.

Euroscript Film Story Competitions

See **Euroscript** under **Writers' Courses, Circles and Workshops**

Geoffrey Faber Memorial Prize

Faber & Faber Ltd, 3 Queen Square, London WC1N 3AU
☎020 7465 0045 Fax 020 7465 0034
ESTABLISHED 1963 as a memorial to the founder and first chairman of **Faber & Faber**, this prize is awarded in alternate years for the volume of verse and the volume of prose fiction published in the UK in the preceding two years, which is judged to be of greatest literary merit. Authors must be under 40 at the time of publication and citizens of the UK, Commonwealth, Republic of Ireland or South Africa. 2001 winner: Trezza Azzopardi *The Hiding Place*.
Prize £1000.

Eleanor Farjeon Award

Children's Book Circle, c/o Random House Children's Books, 61–63 Uxbridge Road, London W5 5SA
☎020 8231 6768 Fax 020 8231 6737
Contact *Kate Giles*

This award, named in memory of the much-loved children's writer, is for distinguished services to children's books either in this country or overseas, and may be given to a librarian, teacher, publisher, bookseller, author, artist, reviewer, television producer, etc. Nominations from members of the **Children's Book Circle**. Sponsored by **Scholastic**. 2001 winner: Amelia Edwards, co-founder of **Walker Books**.
Award £750.

The Fish Short Story Prize

Fish Publishing, Durrus, Bantry, Co. Cork Republic of Ireland
☎00 353 27 61246
Email info@fishpublishing.com
Website www.fishpublishing.com
Contact *Clem Cairns*

FOUNDED 1994. Annual international award which aims to discover, encourage and publish exciting new literary talent. Honorary Patrons: Roddy Doyle, Dermot Healy and Frank McCourt. The best 15–20 stories are published in an anthology. Previously unpublished stories up to 5000 words are eligible. Entry fee: £10 (€14) for first, £7 (€9) for subsequent entries; concession rate: £7 (€9). Closing date: 30 November. Previous winners: Gina Oschner *From the Bering Strait*; Kathy Hughes *Five O'Clock*

Shadow; Maureen O'Neill *Asylum 1928*.

First Prize: £1000/€1500; Second Prize: one-week residence at Anam Cara Writers' and Artists' Retreat in West Cork.

Sir Banister Fletcher Award

Authors' Club, 40 Dover Street, London
W1S 4NP
☎020 7499 8581   Fax 020 7409 0913
Contact *Mrs Ann de La Grange*

This award was created by Sir Bannister Fletcher, President of the **Authors' Club** for many years, and is presented annually. The prize alternates between books on architecture and the fine arts. In 2002 the prize was awarded for the best book on the fine arts published during the previous two years. Submissions to Mrs Ann de La Grange at the Authors' Club. Previous winners: David Alan Brown *Leonardo da Vinci*; Richard Weston *Alvar Aalto*; Dr Megan Aldrich *Gothic Revival*; Professor Thomas Markus *Building and Power*; John Onians *Bearers of Meaning: Classical Orders in Antiquity*; Sir Michael Levey *Gianbattista Tiepolo: his life and art*; John Allan *Berthold Lubetkin – Architecture and The Tradition of Progress*.

The John Florio Prize

See **The Translators Association Awards**

The Forward Prizes for Poetry

Colman Getty PR, 17 & 18 Margaret Street, London W1W 8RP
☎020 7631 2666   Fax 020 7631 2699
Email pr@colmangettypr.co.uk
Contact *Truda Spruyt*

ESTABLISHED 1992. Three awards: the Forward Prize for Best Collection, the Waterstone's Prize for Best First Collection and the Tolman Cunard Prize for Best Single Poem which is not already part of an anthology or collection. All entries must be published in the UK or Eire and submitted by poetry publishers (collections) or newspaper and magazine editors (single poems). Individual entries of poets' own work are not accepted. 2001 winners: Sean O'Brian (best collection), John Stammers (best first collection), Ian Duhig (best single poem).

Prizes £10,000 for best collection; £5000 for best first collection; £1000 for best single poem.

The Frogmore Poetry Prize

42 Morehall Avenue, Folkestone, Kent
CT19 4EF
Website www.frogmorepress.co.uk
Contact *Jeremy Page*

ESTABLISHED 1987. Awarded annually and sponsored by the Frogmore Foundation. The winning poem, runners-up and short-listed entries are all published in the magazine. Previous winners: David Satherley, Caroline Price, Bill Headdon, John Latham, Diane Brown, Tobias Hill, Mario Petrucci, Gina Wilson, Ross Cogan, Joan Benner, Ann Alexander, Gerald Watts.

Prize The winner receives 200 guineas and a life subscription to the biannual literary magazine, *The Frogmore Papers*.

R.H. Gapper Book Prize

Society for French Studies, Taylor Institution, St Giles, Oxford OX1 3NA
Email editor@sfs.ac.uk
Website www.sfs.ac.uk
Contact *The Editor*

FOUNDED in 2000 to promote excellence in scholarship in French Studies. Awarded for critical and scholarly distinction and likely impact on wider critical debate. The winner is chosen from all books received for review by *French Studies* quarterly journal in the previous calendar year. The author must be based in an institution of higher education in the UK or Ireland. 2001 winner: David Baguley *Napoleon III and His Regime: An Extravaganza*.

Prize £2000, presented at the Society for French Studies annual conference.

Martha Gellhorn Trust Prize

Rutherfords, Herbert Road, Salcombe, Devon
TQ8 8HN

Annual prize for journalism in honour of one of the twentieth century's greatest reporters. Open for journalism published in English, giving 'the view from the ground – a human story that penetrates the established version of events and illuminates an urgent issue buried by prevailing fashions of what makes news'. The subject matter can involve the UK or abroad. 2001 winner: Jeremy Harding.

Prize £5000.

The Gladstone History Book Prize

Royal Historical Society, University College London, Gower Street, London WC1E 6BT
☎020 7387 7532   Fax 020 7387 7532
Contact *Executive Secretary*

ESTABLISHED 1998. Annual award for the best new work on any historical subject which is not primarily related to British history, published in the UK in the preceding calendar year. The

book must be the author's first (solely written) history book and be an original and scholarly work of historical research. Closing date: 31 December. 2000 winner: Matthew Innes *State and Society in the Middle Ages: The Middle Rhine Valley 400–1000*.
Prize £1000.

Glaxo Science Writers' Awards
See **ABSW/Glaxo Science Writers' Awards**

Glenfiddich Food & Drink Awards
4 Bedford Square, London WC1B 3RA
☎020 7255 1100   Fax 020 7631 0602

Known as the 'Cooker Bookers' or the 'Oscars' of the gastronomic world, the awards aim to recognise excellence in writing, publishing and broadcasting on the subjects of food and drink. There are 12 category winners from work published or broadcast in the UK and the Republic of Ireland. 2002 winners: Food Book: *The River Cottage Cookbook* Hugh Fearnley-Whittingstall; Drink Book: *Drink! … Never Mind the Peanuts* Susy Atkins and Dave Broom; Food Writer: Clarissa Hyman for work in *Country Living*; Magazine Cookery Writer: Sybil Kapoor for work in *Waitrose Food Illustrated*; Newspaper Cookery Writer: Rowley Leigh for work in *The Sunday Telegraph Magazine*; Restaurant Critic: Caroline Stacey for work in *The Independent*; Drink Writer: Dave Broom for work in *Wine* and *Harpers On Trade*; Wine Writer: John Stimpfig for articles in *The Weekend FT How to spend it*; Regional Writer: Joanna Blythman for work in the *Sunday Herald*; Television Programme: not awarded in 2002; Radio Programme: *Woman's Hour* 'Forgotten Fruit and Vegetables', presented by Anna McNamee with Sybil Kapoor and Fred Foster, for BBC Radio 4; Visual Work: John Reardon for work in *The Observer Food Monthly*; Independent Spirit Award: Patricia Llewellyn, in recognition of her progressive contribution to food and drink broadcasting; 2002 Glenfiddich Trophy Winner: Hugh Fearnley-Whittingstall.
Award Overall winner (chosen from the category winners) £3000, plus the Glenfiddich Trophy (which is held for one year); category winners £1000 each, plus a case of Glenfiddich Single Malt Scotch Whisky.

Golden Kite Award
See **Society for Children's Book Writers & Illustrators** under **Professional Associations and Societies**

The Phillip Good Memorial Prize
QWF Magazine, PO Box 1768, Rugby CV21 4ZA
Email jo.good@ntlworld.com
Website www.qwfmagazine.co.uk
Contact *Competition Secretary*

ESTABLISHED in 1997, the competition is run by *QWF Magazine* . The prize commemorates the memory of Phillip Good (late husband of *QWF* editor, Jo Good) and is for short stories of less than 5000 words in any style or genre (except children's). Open entry. Entrants may request in-depth critique of their stories for an extra fee. For entry forms send s.a.e. to the address above. Closing date: 21 August.
Prizes (total) at least £525, plus free subscription to *QWF Magazine*; also book prizes and publication for winning authors.

Edgar Graham Book Prize
c/o Development Studies, School of Oriental and African Studies, Thornhaugh Street, Russell Square, London WC1H 0XG
☎020 7898 4485   Fax 020 7898 4519

Contact *Professor Henry Bernstein*

ESTABLISHED 1984. Biennial award in memory of Edgar Graham. Aims to encourage research work in Third World agricultural and industrial development. At the time of going to press the award was under review.

Kate Greenaway Medal
See **CILIP: The Chartered Institute of Library and Information Professionals Kate Greenaway Medal**

The Griffin Poetry Prize
6610 Edwards Boulevard, Mississauga, Ontario Canada L5T 2V6
☎001 905 565 5993   Fax 001 905 564 3645
Email info@griffinpoetryprize.com
Website www.griffinpoetryprize.com
Contact *Ruth Smith, Manager*

Annual award ESTABLISHED in 2000 by Toronto-based entrepreneur, Scott Griffin, for books of poetry written in or translated into English. Trustees include Margaret Atwood and Michael Ondaatje. Submissions from publishers only.
Prizes A total of C$80,000, divided into two categories: International and Canadian.

The Guardian Children's Fiction Award
The Guardian, 119 Farringdon Road, London EC1R 3ER
☎020 7239 9694   Fax 020 7713 4366

Children's Book Editor *Julia Eccleshare*
ESTABLISHED 1967. Annual award for an out-standing work of fiction for children aged seven and over by a British or Commonwealth author, first published in the UK in the preceding year, excluding picture books. Final entry date: 1 June. No application form necessary. 2001 winner: Kevin Crossley-Holland *The Seeing Stone.*
Award £1500.

The Guardian First Book Award

The Guardian, 119 Farringdon Road, London EC1R 3ER
☎020 7239 9694 Fax 020 7713 4366
Contact *Literary Editor*
ESTABLISHED 1999. Annual award for first time authors published in English in the UK. All genres of writing eligible, apart from academic, guidebooks, children's, educational, manuals, reprints and TV, radio and film tie-ins. 2001 winner: Jimmy Corrigan *The Smartest Kid on Earth.*
Award £10,000, plus *Guardian/Observer* advertising package.

Guild of Food Writers Awards

48 Crabtree Lane, London SW6 6LW
☎020 7610 1180 Fax 020 7610 0299
Email awards@gfw.co.uk
Website www.gfw.co.uk
Contact *Christina Thomas*
ESTABLISHED 1985. Annual awards in recognition of outstanding achievement in all areas in which food writers work and have influence. Entry is not restricted to members of the Guild. Entry form available from the address above. 2001 winners: Michael Smith Award: Hugh Fearnley-Whittingstall *The River Cottage Cookbook*; Cookery Book of the Year: Gordon Ramsay and Roz Denny *Just Desserts*; Food Book of the Year: Anthony Bourdain *A Cook's Tour*; Jeremy Round Award for Best First Book of the Year: Fuschia Dunlop *Sichuan Cookery*; Derek Cooper Award for Investigative or Campaigning Food: Andy Jones *Eating Oil: Food Supply in a Changing Climate*; Cookery Journalist of the Year: Jill Dupleix for work in *The Times*; Food Journalist of the Year: Fiona Beckett for work in *The Times, Decanter* and *Sainsbury's The Magazine.*

Gwobr Llyfr y Flwyddyn
See **Arts Council of Wales Book of the Year Awards**

James W. Hackett Award
See **The British Haiku Society** under **Organisations of Interest to Poets**

Hastings National Poetry Competition
See **Hastings International Poetry Festival** under **Festivals**

W.H. Heinemann Award

Royal Society of Literature, Somerset House, Strand, London WC2R 1LA
☎020 7845 4676 Fax 020 7845 4679
Email info@rslit.org
Website www.rslit.org
ESTABLISHED 1945. Works of any kind of literature may be submitted by publishers under this award, which aims to encourage genuine contributions to literature. Books must be written in the English language and have been published in the previous year; translations are not eligible for consideration nor are single poems, nor collections of pieces by more than one author, nor may individuals put forward their own work. Preference tends to be given to publications which are unlikely to command large sales: poetry, biography, criticism, philosophy, history. Publishers must contact the Secretary for details of how to submit works. Final entry date: 15 December. Up to three awards may be given. Previous winner: Catherine Merridale *Night of Stone: Death and Memory in Russia.*
Prize £5000.

Hellenic Foundation Prize
See **The Translators Association Awards**

Felicia Hemans Prize for Lyrical Poetry

University of Liverpool, PO Box 147, Liverpool, Merseyside L69 3BX
☎0151 794 2458 Fax 0151 794 2454
Email wilderc@liv.ac.uk
Contact *The Registrar*
ESTABLISHED 1899. Annual award for published or unpublished verse. Open to past or present members and students of the University of Liverpool. One poem per entrant only. Closing date 1 May.
Prize £30.

The Hessell-Tiltman Prize for History

English Centre of International PEN, 152–156 Kentish Town Road, London NW1 9QB
☎020 7267 9444 Fax 020 7267 9304

Email enquiries@pen.org.uk
Website www.pen.org.uk

FOUNDED 2002. Awarded for a history book, written in English (including translations) and aimed at a wide audience. Submissions by publishers only.
Prize Silver pen.

Heywood Hill Literary Prize
10 Curzon Street, London W1J 5HH
☎020 7629 0647

Contact *John Saumarez Smith*

ESTABLISHED 1995 by the Duke of Devonshire to reward a lifetime's contribution to the enjoyment of books. Three judges chosen annually. No applications are necessary for this award. 2001 winner: Michael Holroyd.
Prize £15,000.

Hidden Brook Press International Poetry Anthology Contests
412–701 King Street West, Toronto, Ontario Canada M5V 2W7
☎001 416 504 3966   Fax 001 801 751 1837
Email writers@hiddenbrookpress.com
Website www.HiddenBrookPress.com

International poetry competitions: No Love Lost Poetry Anthology Contest; The Open Window Poetry Anthology Contest and Seeds International Poetry Chapbook Anthology Contest. Electronic and hard copy submissions are required. Closing dates and full entry details can be found on the website. Cash prizes and anthology publication.

William Hill
Sports Book of the Year
Greenside House, Station Road, Wood Green, London N22 7TP
☎020 8918 3731   Fax 020 8918 3728

Contact *Graham Sharpe*

ESTABLISHED 1989. Annual award introduced by Graham Sharpe of bookmakers William Hill. Sponsored by William Hill and thus dubbed the 'bookie' prize, it is the first, and only, Sports Book of the Year award. Final entry date: September. 2001 winner: Laura Hillenbrand *Seabiscuit*.
Prize (reviewed annually) £15,000 package including £12,000 cash, hand-bound copy, £1000 free bet. Runners-up prizes.

Calvin & Rose G. Hoffman Prize
King's School, Canterbury, Kent CT1 2ES
☎01227 595501

Contact *The Headmaster*

Annual award for distinguished publication on Christopher Marlowe, established by the late Calvin Hoffman, author of *The Man Who was Shakespeare* (1955) as a memorial to himself and his wife. For unpublished works of at least 5000 words written in English for their scholarly contribution to the study of Christopher Marlowe and his relationship to William Shakespeare. Final entry date: 1 September. 2001 joint winners: Prof. Michael Hattaway and Michael Rubb.

Winifred Holtby Prize
Royal Society of Literature, Somerset House, Strand, London WC2R 1LA
☎020 7845 4676   Fax 020 7845 4679
Email info@rslit.org
Website www.rslit.org

ESTABLISHED 1966 by Vera Brittain who gave a sum of money to the RSL to provide an annual prize in honour of Winifred Holtby who died at the age of 37. Administered by the **Royal Society of Literature**. The prize is for the best regional novel of the year written in the English language. The writer must be of British or Irish nationality, or a citizen of the Commonwealth. Translations, unless made by the author himself of his own work, are not eligible for consideration. If in any year it is considered that no regional novel is of sufficient merit the prize money may be awarded to an author, qualified as aforesaid, of a literary work of non-fiction or poetry, concerning a regional subject. Publishers are invited to submit works published during the current year and must contact the Secretary for details. Final entry date: 15 December. Previous winners: Donna Morrissey *Kit's Law*; Eden Robinson *Traplines*; Andrew O'Hagan *Our Fathers*.
Prize £1000.

L. Ron Hubbard's
Writers of the Future Contest
PO Box 218, East Grinstead, West Sussex RH19 4GH
Contest Administrator *Andrea Grant-Webb*

ESTABLISHED 1984 by L. Ron Hubbard to encourage new and amateur writers of science fiction, fantasy and horror. Quarterly awards with an annual grand prize. Entrants must submit a short story of up to 10,000 words, or a novelette less than 17,000 words, which must not have been published previously. The contest is open only to those who have not been published professionally. Previous winners:

Roge Gregory, Malcolm Twigg, Janet Martin, Alan Smale, Janet Barron. Send s.a.e. for entry form.

Prizes £640 (1st), £480 (2nd) and £320 (3rd) each quarter; Annual Grand Prize: £2500. All winners are awarded a trip to the annual L. Ron Hubbard Achievement Awards which include a series of professional writers' workshops, and are published in the *L. Ron Hubbard Presents Writers of the Future* anthology.

The Richard Imison Memorial Award

The Society of Authors, 84 Drayton Gardens, London SW10 9SB
☎020 7373 6642 Fax 020 7373 5768
Email info@societyofauthors.org
Contact *The Secretary, The Broadcasting Committee*

Annual award established 'to perpetuate the memory of Richard Imison, to acknowledge the encouragement he gave to writers working in the medium of radio, and in memory of the support and friendship he invariably offered writers in general, and radio writers in particular'. Administered by the **Society of Authors** and generally sponsored by the Peggy Ramsay Foundation, the purpose is 'to encourage new talent and high standards in writing for radio by selecting the radio drama by a writer new to radio which, in the opinion of the judges, is the best of those submitted.' An adaptation for radio of a piece originally written for the stage, television or film is not eligible. Any radio drama first transmitted in the UK between 1 January and 31 December by a writer or writers new to radio, is eligible, provided the work is an original piece for radio and it is the first dramatic work by the writer(s) that has been broadcast. Submission may be made by any party to the production in the form of two copies of an audio cassette (not-returnable) accompanied by a nomination form. 2001 winner: Murray Gold *Electricity*.
Prize £1500.

The Independent Foreign Fiction Prize

c/o Literature Department, Arts Council of England, 14 Great Peter Street, London SW1P 3NQ
☎020 7973 6519 Fax 020 7973 6590

Awarded for translated fiction by living authors first published in Britain in the year preceding the award. 2002 winner: *Austerlitz* by W.G. Sebald; translated by Anthea Bell.

Prize £10,000 shared equally between author and translator.

Individual Screenwriter Awards

SGRÎN – Media Agency for Wales, The Bank, 10 Mount Stuart Square, Cardiff CF10 5EE
☎029 2033 3300 Fax 029 2033 3320
Email anneli.jones@acw-ccc.org.uk
Contact *Anneli Jones*

FOUNDED 2001. A pilot scheme, offering funding towards the development of a feature-length screenplay. Open to any individual, excluding those in full-time education. Entry requirements: completion of application form and submission of 12-page treatment and c.v.
Individual awards of up to £5000.

The International IMPAC Dublin Literary Award

Dublin City Public Libraries, Administrative Headquarters, Cumberland House, Fenian Street, Dublin 2, Republic of Ireland
☎00 353 1 6644800 Fax 00 353 1 6761628
Email dubaward@iol.ie
Website www.impacdublinaward.ie

ESTABLISHED 1995. Sponsored by Dublin City Council and a US-based productivity improvement firm, IMPAC, this prize is awarded for a work of fiction written and published in the English language or written in a language other than English and published in English translation. Initial nominations are made by municipal public libraries in major and capital cities worldwide, each library putting forward up to three books to the international panel of judges in Dublin. 2002 winner: Michel Houellebecq *Atomised*.
Prize €100,000 (if the winning book is in English translation, the prize is shared €75,000 to the author and €25,000 to the translator).

International Reading Association Literacy Award

International Reading Association, 800 Barksdale Road, PO Box 8139, Newark, Delaware 19714-8139 USA
☎001 302 731 1600 Fax 001 302 731 1057
Executive Director *Alan E. Farstrup*

The International Reading Association is a non-profit education organisation devoted to improving reading instruction and promoting literacy worldwide. In addition to the US $15,000 award presented each year on International Literacy Day (September 8), the organisation gives more than 25 awards in recognition of achievement in reading research, writing for children, media coverage of literacy and literacy instruction.

International Student Playscript Competition
See **University of Hull** under **Writers' Courses, Circles and Workshops**

Irish Times International Fiction Prize
The Irish Times Ltd, 10–16 D'Olier Street, Dublin 2, Republic of Ireland
☎00 353 1 679 2022 Fax 00 353 1 670 9383

Biennial prize awarded for any work of fiction (novel, novella or collection of short stories) in the English language. Books are nominated by literary editors and critics, and are then called in from publishers. Next award to be announced in autumn 2003. Previous winner: Michael Ondaatje *Anil's Ghost.*

Irish Times Irish Literature Prizes
The Irish Times Ltd, 10–16 D'Olier Street, Dublin 2, Republic of Ireland
☎00 353 1 679 2022 Fax 00 353 1 670 9383
Administrator, Book Prizes *Gerard Cavanagh*

ESTABLISHED 1989. Biennial prizes awarded in four different categories: fiction (a novel, novella or collection of short stories), non-fiction prose (history, biography, autobiography, criticism, politics, sociological interest, travel, current affairs and belles-lettres), poetry (collection or a long poem or a sequence of poems, or a revised/updated edition of a previously published selection/collection) and for a work in the Irish language (fiction, poetry or non-fiction). The author must have been born in Ireland or be an Irish citizen, but may live in any part of the world. Books are nominated by literary editors and critics, and are then called in from publishers. Next awards to be announced in autumn 2003. Previous winners: William Trevor *The Hill Bachelors* (fiction); Angela Bourke *The Burning of Bridget Cleary* (non-fiction); Michael Longley *The Weather in Japan*; Cathal O'Searcaigh *Ag Tnúth Leis an tSolas* (Irish language).

JazzClaw Alternative Poetry Competition
Searle Publishing, 36 Wolfe Road, Norwich, Norfolk NR1 4HT
Email jazzclaw@lycos.co.uk
Website www.searlepublishing.co.uk

Ten finalists are selected by a team of JazzClaw published poets. Entry fee: £2 per poem or £10 for unlimited entries. Information leaflet available.

Prizes £50, plus publication by JazzClaw (1st); £20, plus trophy (2nd); £10 (3rd).

Jewish Quarterly Literary Prizes
PO Box 35042, London NW1 7XH
☎020 7284 1117 Fax 020 7284 1117
Contact *Gerald Don*

Formerly the H.H. Wingate Prize. Annual awards (one for fiction and one for non-fiction) for works which best stimulate an interest in and awareness of themes of Jewish interest. Books must have been published in the UK in the year of the award and be written in English by an author resident in Britain, the Commonwealth, Israel, Republic of Ireland or South Africa. 2002 winners: W.G. Sebald *Austerlitz* (fiction); Oliver Sacks *Uncle Tungsten* (non-fiction).

Prizes Fiction: £4000; Non-fiction: £3000.

Mary Vaughan Jones Award
Cyngor Llyfrau Cymru (Welsh Books Council), Castell Brychan, Aberystwyth, Dyfed SY23 2JB
☎01970 624151 Fax 01970 625385
Email castellbrychan@cllc.org.uk
Website www.wbc.org.uk
Contact *The Administrator*

Triennial award for distinguished services in the field of children's literature in Wales over a considerable period of time. 2000 winner: J. Selwyn Lloyd.

Award Silver trophy.

Keats–Shelley Prize
Keats–Shelley Memorial Association, 117 Cheyne Walk, London SW10 0ES
☎020 7352 2180 Fax 020 7352 6705
Website www.demon.co.uk.heritage/Keats.House.Rome
Contact *Harriet Cullen*

ESTABLISHED 1998. Annual award to promote the study and appreciation of Keats and Shelley, especially in the universities, and of creative writing inspired by the younger Romantic poets. Two categories: essay and poem; open to all ages and nationalities. Previous winners: Sarah Wootton, Rukmini Maria Callimachi, James Burton, Cate Parish, Antony Nichols, Helena Nelson, Robert Saxton, Toby Venables.

Prize £3000 distributed between the winners of the two categories.

The Keeley-Sherrard Translation Award

Poetry Greece, Mitropolitou Athanasiou 10, 3rd Parados, Triklino, Corfu 49100 Greece
☎00 30 661 047990 Fax 00 30 661 047990
Email poetrygreece@hotmail.com
Website users.otenet.gr/~wendyhol/
   poetry_greece/
Contact *Wendy Holborow*

Annual award in memory of the late Philip Sherrard who worked closely with Edmund Keeley translating many Greek poets into English. The award is for Greek poetry translated into English. Potential translators should contact Poetry Greece for further information.

The Petra Kenney Poetry Competition

PO Box 32, Filey, Yorkshire YO14 9YG
Email morgan@petrapoetrycompetition.co.uk
Website www.petrapoetrycompetition.co.uk
Contact *Secretary*

ESTABLISHED 1995. Annual poetry award. Original, unpublished poems up to 80 lines on any theme. Closing date: 1 December. Entry fee: £3 per poem. Send s.a.e. for rules and entry form. 2000 winners: Brian Bartlett, Linda Rogers, Ben Murray, Lucy Brennan, Valerie Darville, Doreen Hinchcliffe.
   Prizes £1000 (1st); £500 (2nd); £250 (3rd) and three highly commended prizes of £125 each; plus publication in *Writers' Forum* and inscribed Royal Brierley Crystal Vase to each winner.

Kent & Sussex Poetry Society Open Competition

13 Ruscombe Close, Southborough, Tunbridge Wells, Kent TN4 0SG
☎01892 543862
Chairman *Clive R. Eastwood*

Annual competition. Entry fee: £3 per poem, maximum 40 lines.
   Prizes £1000 (total).

Kent Short Story Competition

13 Wave Crest, Whitstable, Kent CT5 1EH
☎01227 762504
Contact *Narissa Knights*

Competition for a short story of up to 2500 words. Send s.a.e. for entry form and full details.

Kraszna-Krausz Book Awards

122 Fawnbrake Avenue, London SE24 0BZ
☎020 7738 6701 Fax 020 7738 6701
Email awards@k-k.org.uk
Website www.k-k.org.uk
Administrator *Andrea Livingstone*

ESTABLISHED 1985. Annual award to encourage and recognise oustanding achievements in the publishing and writing of books on the art, practice, history and technology of photography and the moving image (film, television, video and related screen media). Books in any language, published worldwide, are eligible. Entries must be submitted by publishers only. Prizes for books on still photography alternate annually with those for books on the moving image (2002: photography). 2001 winners: Pearl Bowser and Louise Spence *Writing Himself Into History: Oscar Micheaux, His Silent Films and His Audiences*; Richard Rickitt *Special Effects: The History and Technique*.
   Prizes £5000 in each of the main categories; £1000 special commendations.

Lakeland Book of the Year Awards

Cumbria Tourist Board, Ashleigh, Holly Road, Windermere, Cumbria LA23 2AQ
☎01539 444444 Fax 01539 444041
Email mail@cumbria-tourist-board.co.uk
Contact *Annette Vidler*

Six annual awards set up by Cumbrian author Hunter Davies and the Cumbria Tourist Board. The **Hunter Davies Prize** was established in 1984 and is awarded for the book which best helps visitors or residents enjoy a greater love or understanding of any aspect of life in Cumbria and the Lake District. The **Barclays Bank Prize**, established in 1993, is for the best researched book on any aspect of Cumbrian life, its people or culture. The **Border Television Prize**, also established in 1993, is for the book which best illustrates the beauty and character of Cumbria. A further two prizes were established in 1999: the **Ron Sands Prize**, for the best book on a cultural theme; and the **Titus Wilson and Son Prize**, for the best book on people. The **Bill Rollinson Award** was given in 2001 for the best book on the Cumbrian landscape and tradition. Final entry date mid-March. 2001 winners: Hunter Davies Prize and Border Television Prize: John and Eilean Malden *Rex Malden's Whitehaven*; Barclays Bank Prize: David A. Cross *A Striking Likeness: The Life of George Romney*; Bill Rollinson Award: Helen Caldwell, John Caldwell, Jennifer Forsyth and Beryl Offley *Life on the Fell*; Ron Sands Prize: John Batchelor *John Ruskin: No Wealth but Life*;

Titus Wilson & Son Prize: David W.V. Weston *Carlisle Cathedral History*.
Prize £100 and certificate.

Lancashire County Library Children's Book of the Year Award

Lancashire County Library Headquarters, County Hall, PO Box 61, Preston, Lancashire PR1 8RJ
☎01772 264040 Fax 01772 264043
Manager, Young People's Service *Jean Wolstenholme*

ESTABLISHED 1986. Annual award, presented in June for a work of original fiction suitable for 12–14-year-olds. The winner is chosen by 13–14-year-old secondary school pupils in Lancashire. Books must have been published between 1 September and 31 August in the year of the award and authors must be UK residents. Final entry date: 1 September each year. 2001 winner: Mallorie Blackman *Naughts and Crosses*.
Prize £500, plus engraved glass decanter.

Lannan Literary Award

Lannan Foundation, 313 Read Street, Santa Fe, New Mexico 87501 USA
☎001 505 986 8160
Website www.lannan.org

ESTABLISHED 1989. Annual awards given to writers of exceptional poetry, fiction and non-fiction who have made a significant contribution to English-language literature, as well as emerging writers of distinctive literary merit who have demonstrated potential for outstanding future work. On occasion, the Foundation recognises a writer for lifetime achievement. Candidates for the awards are recommended to the Foundation by a network of writers, literary scholars, publishers and editors. Applications for the awards are not accepted.

Legend Writing Award

Hastings Writers' Group, 39 Emmanuel Road, Hastings, East Sussex TN34 3LB
Contact *Legend Coordinator*

ESTABLISHED 2001. Annual award to encourage new fiction writers resident in the UK. Entries (2000 words maximum) may be either short stories or extracts from novels. Closing date: 31 August. Entry fee: £4. Please send s.a.e. for rules and entry form (essential). The competition is organised by Hastings Writers' Group and sponsored by its patron, author David Gemmell, who also selects the prize-winning entries.
Prizes £500 (1st); £250 (2nd); £100 (3rd); plus two runners-up prizes of £25.

The Library Association Awards

See **CILIP: The Chartered Institute of Library and Information Professionals** individual awards

Literary Review Grand Poetry Competition

See *Literary Review* under **Magazines**

The London Writers Competition

Room 224a, The Town Hall, Wandsworth High Street, London SW18 2PU
☎020 8871 8711 Fax 020 8871 8712
Email arts@wandsworth.gov.uk
Website www.wandsworth.gov.uk
Contact *Wandsworth Arts Office*

Arranged by Wandsworth Borough Council in association with Waterstone's. An annual competition, open to all writers of 16 or over who live, work or study in the Greater London area. Work must not have been published previously. There are three sections: poetry, short story and play.
Prizes £1000 for each section, with a first prize of £600. Poetry and story winners are published and the winning play is showcased in a London venue.

Longman–History Today Book of the Year Award

c/o History Today, 20 Old Compton Street, London W1D 4TW
☎020 7534 8000
Contacts *Peter Furtado, Marion Soldan*

ESTABLISHED 1993. Annual award set up as joint initiative between the magazine *History Today* and the publisher Longman (**Pearson Education**) to mark the past links between the two organisations, to encourage new writers, and to promote a wider public understanding of, and enthusiasm for, the study and publication of history. Submissions are made by publishers only. 2002 joint winners: Jonathan Rose *The Intellectual Life of the British Working Classes* and Peter Biller *The Measure of Multitude: Population in Medieval Thought*.
Prize £1000 (see *History Today* from July 2002).

Sir William Lyons Award

The Guild of Motoring Writers, 30 The Cravens, Smallfield, Surrey RH6 9QS
☎01342 843294 Fax 01342 844093
Email sharon@scott-fairweather.freeserve.co.uk
Contact *Sharon Scott-Fairweather*

An annual competitive award to encourage young people in automotive journalism and to foster interests in motoring and the motor industry. Entrance by two essays and interview with Awards Committee. Applicants must be British, aged 17–23 and resident in UK. Final entry date: 31 August. Presentation date in December.
Award £1000 plus trophy.

The Macallan/Scotland on Sunday Short Story Competition

Scotland on Sunday, 108 Holyrood Road, Edinburgh EH8 8AS
☎0131 620 8620 Fax 0131 523 0330
Contact *Competition Administrator*
ESTABLISHED 1990. Annual competition to recognise the best in new Scottish writing. Stories are accepted from those who were born or are living in Scotland, or from Scots living abroad. Up to three stories per applicant permitted. Maximum 3000 words per story. Final entry date: end of August. Previous winners: David Strachan, Alan Spence, Ali Smith, Chris Dolan, Michel Faber, Anne Donovan.
Prizes £6000 (1st); £2000 (2nd); four runners-up receive £500 each. Winning story is published in *Scotland on Sunday*.

McColvin Medal

See **CILIP: The Chartered Institute of Library and Information Professionals Besterman/McColvin Medal**

W.J.M. Mackenzie Book Prize

Political Studies Association, Department of Politics, University of Newcastle, Newcastle upon Tyne NE1 7RU
☎0191 222 8021 Fax 0191 222 3499
PSA Executive Director *Jack Arthurs*
ESTABLISHED 1987. Annual award to best work of political science published in the UK during the previous year. Submissions from publishers only. Final entry date: end of October. 2000 winner: Professor Brian Barry *Culture and Equality*.

McKitterick Prize

Society of Authors, 84 Drayton Gardens, London SW10 9SB
☎020 7373 6642 Fax 020 7373 5768
Email info@societyofauthors.org
Contact *Awards Secretary*
Annual award for a full-length novel in the English language, first published in the UK or unpublished. Open to writers over 40 who have not had any novel published other than the one submitted (excluding works for children). Closing date: 20 December. 2001 winner: Giles Waterfield *The Long Afternoon*.
Prize £4000.

Enid McLeod Prize

Franco-British Society, Room 623, Linen Hall, 162–168 Regent Street, London W1R 5TB
☎020 7734 0815 Fax 020 7734 0815
Executive Secretary *Lady Strabolgi*
ESTABLISHED 1982. Annual award to the author of the work of literature published in the UK which, in the opinion of the judges, has contributed most to Franco-British understanding. Any full-length work written in English by a citizen of the UK, Commonwealth, Republic of Ireland, Pakistan, Bangladesh and South Africa. No English translation of a book written originally in any other language will be considered. Nominations from publishers for books published between 1 January and 31 December of the year of the prize. 2000 winner: Graham Robb *Rimbaud*.
Prize Cheque.

Macmillan Prize for a Children's Picture Book

Macmillan Children's Books, 20 New Wharf Road, London N1 9RR
☎020 7014 6219 Fax 020 7014 6142
Contact *Marketing Dept., Macmillan Children's Books*
Set up in order to stimulate new work from young illustrators in art schools, and to help them start their professional lives. Fiction or non-fiction. **Macmillan** have the option to publish any of the prize winners.
Prizes £1000 (1st); £500 (2nd); £250 (3rd).

Macmillan Silver PEN Award

The English Centre of International PEN, 152–156 Kentish Town Road, London NW1 9QB
☎020 7267 9444 Fax 020 7267 9304
Email enquiries@pen.org.uk
Website www.pen.org.uk
Sponsored by **Macmillan Publishers**. An annual award for a volume of short stories written in English by a British author and published in the UK in the year preceding the prize. Nominations by the PEN Executive Committee only. Please do not submit books. Previous winner: Cressida Connolly *The Happiest Days*.
Prize £500, plus silver pen.

The Mail on Sunday Novel Competition

Postal box address changes each year (see below)

Annual award ESTABLISHED 1983. Judges look for a story/character that springs to life in the 'tantalising opening 50–150 words of a novel'. Details of the competition, including the postal box address, are published in *The Mail on Sunday* in July/August. 2001 winner: Jonathan Amberston.

Awards (1st) £400 book tokens and a writing course at the **Arvon Foundation**; (2nd) £300 tokens; (3rd) £200 tokens; three further prizes of £150 tokens each.

The Mail on Sunday/ John Llewellyn Rhys Prize

Booktrust, Book House, 45 East Hill, London SW18 2QZ
☎020 8516 2972 Fax 020 8516 2978
Email tarryn@booktrust.org.uk
Website www.booktrust.org.uk

Contact *Tarryn McKay*

ESTABLISHED 1942. An annual young writer's award for a memorable work of any kind. Entrants must be under the age of 35 at the time of publication; books must have been published in the UK in the year of the award. The author must be a citizen of Britain or the Commonwealth, writing in English. 2000 winner: Edward Platt *Leadville*.

Prize £5000 (1st); £500 for shortlisted entries.

The Man Booker Prize for Fiction

Booktrust, Book House, 45 East Hill, London SW18 2QZ
☎020 8516 2972 Fax 020 8516 2978
Email tarryn@booktrust.org.uk
Website www.booktrust.org.uk

Contact *Tarryn McKay*

The leading British literary prize, set up in 1968 by Booker McConnell Ltd, with the intention of rewarding merit, raising the stature of the author in the eyes of the public and increasing the sale of the books. The announcement of the winner has been televised live since 1981 and all books on the shortlist experience a substantial increase in sales. With a new sponsor (the finance house, Man Group plc) the prospect of opening the prize to US fiction is under discussion.

Eligible novels must be written in English by a citizen of Britain, the Commonwealth, the Republic of Ireland or South Africa, and must be published in the UK for the first time between 1 October and 30 September of the year of the prize. Self-published books are no longer accepted. Entries are accepted from UK publishers who may each submit two novels, as well as any author with a new novel who has previously won or been shortlisted for the prize, within the appropriate scheduled publication dates. The judges may also ask for certain other eligible novels to be submitted to them. Annual award. 2001 winner: Peter Carey *True History of the Kelly Gang*. Previous winners include: Margaret Atwood, *The Blind Assassin*; J.M. Coetzee *Disgrace*; Ian McEwan *Amsterdam*; Arundhati Roy *God of Small Things*.

Prize £50,000 winner; £1000, shortlist.

Marsh Award for Children's Literature in Translation

National Centre for Research in Children's Literature, University of Surrey Roehampton, Digby Stuart College, Roehampton Lane, London SW15 5PH
☎020 8392 3008 Fax 020 8392 3819
Email g.lathey@roehampton.ac.uk

Contact *Dr Gillian Lathey*

ESTABLISHED 1995 and sponsored by the Marsh Christian Trust, the award aims to encourage translation of foreign children's books into English. It is a biennial award (next award: 2003), open to British translators of books for 4–16-year-olds, published in the UK by a British publisher. Any category will be considered with the exception of encyclopedias and reference books. No electronic books. 2001 winner: Betsy Rosenberg for her translation of *Duel* by David Grossman.

Prize £750.

Marsh Biography Award

The English-Speaking Union, Dartmouth House, 37 Charles Street, London W1J 5ED
☎020 7529 1565 Fax 020 7495 6108
Email tim_rolph@esu.org
Website www.esu.org

Contact *Ann Ferrier-Ilic*

A biennial award for the most significant biography published over a two-year period by a British publisher. Next award October 2003. 2001 winner: Anthony Sampson *Mandela: The Authorised Biography*. Previous winners: Richard Holmes *Coleridge: Darker Reflections*; Jim Ring *Erskine Childers*; Selina Hastings *Evelyn Waugh*; Patrick Marnham *The Man Who Wasn't Maigret*.

Award A year's membership of the ESU and £4000, plus a silver trophy presented at a dinner.

Colin Mears Award
See **CILIP: The Chartered Institute of Library and Information Professionals Kate Greenaway Medal**

Medical Book Awards
The Society of Authors, 84 Drayton Gardens, London SW10 9SB
☎020 7373 6642 Fax 020 7373 5768
Email info@society of authors.org
Contact *Secretary, Medical Writers Group*

Annual awards sponsored by the Royal Society of Medicine. Nine categories for medical texts published in the twelve months preceding the deadline. Contact the **Society of Authors** for entry details. Closing date: 30 April.
Prizes £6500 (total).

The Mercedes–Benz Award for the Montagu of Beaulieu Trophy
Guild of Motoring Writers, 30 The Cravens, Smallfield, Surrey RH6 9QS
☎01342 843294 Fax 01342 844093
Email sharon@scott-fairweather.freeserve.co.uk
Contact *Sharon Scott-Fairweather*

First presented by Lord Montagu on the occasion of the opening of the National Motor Museum at Beaulieu in 1972. Awarded annually to a member of the **Guild of Motoring Writers** who, in the opinion of the nominated jury, has made the greatest contribution to recording in the English language the history of motoring or motor cycling in a published book or article, film, television or radio script, or research manuscript available to the public. Cash prize sponsored by Mercedes-Benz UK.
Prize £1000, plus trophy.

Mere Literary Festival Open Competition
'Lawrences', Old Hollow, Mere, Wiltshire BA12 6EG
☎01747 860475
Contact *Mrs Adrienne Howell (Events Organiser)*

Annual open competition which alternates between short stories and poetry. The winners are announced at the Mere Literary Festival during the second week of October. The 2003 competition is for poetry with a closing date for entries in July. For further details, including entry fees and form, contact the address above from 1 March with s.a.e.
Cash prizes.

Meyer-Whitworth Award
Arts Council of England, 14 Great Peter Street, London SW1P 3NQ
☎020 7973 6431 Fax 020 7973 6983
Email jemima.lee@artscouncil.org.uk
Website www.artscouncil.org.uk
Contact *Theatre Writing Section*

In 1908 the movement for a National Theatre joined forces with that to create a memorial to William Shakespeare. The result was the Shakespeare Memorial National Theatre Committee, the embodiment of the campaign for a National Theatre. This award was established to commemorate all those who worked with the SMNT. The Award, endowed by residual funds of the SMNT and now transferred to the Royal National Theatre Foundation, is intended to help further the careers of UK playwrights who are not yet established, and to draw contemporary theatre writers to the public's attention. The award is given to the writer whose play most nearly satisfies the following criteria: a play which embodies Geoffrey Whitworth's dictum that 'drama is important in so far as it reveals the truth about the relationships of human beings with each other and the world at large'; a play which shows promise of a developing new talent; a play in which the writing is of individual quality. Nominations are from professional theatre companies. Plays must have been written in the English language and produced professionally in the UK in the 12 months between 1 August 2002 and 31 July 2003. *Candidates will have had no more than two of their plays professionally produced. No writer who has won the award previously may reapply and no play that has been submitted previously for the award is eligible.* Closing date: 31 August 2003.
Award £8000.

Milton Acorn Prize for Poetry
Poetry Forever, PO Box 68018, Hamilton, Ontario Canada L8M 3M7
☎001 905 312 1779 Fax 001 905 312 8285

ESTABLISHED 1998. Open to poets worldwide who write in English. All types of poetry welcome; maximum 30 lines. Entry fee: £1 per poem (cheques payable to Poetry Forever). All profits from the contest will be used to fund publication of full-size collections by Milton Acorn, 'the People's Poet' (1923–86). Also runs the Orion Prize for Poetry to fund publication of work by Ottawa poet Marty Flomen (1942–97) and the Tidepool Prize for Poetry for work by Hamilton poet Herb Barrett (1912–95).
Cash prizes.

MIND Book of the Year

Granta House, 15–19 Broadway, London
E15 4BQ
☎020 8519 2122 Fax 020 8522 1725
Email publications@mind.org.uk
Website www.mind.org.uk

ESTABLISHED 1981. Annual award, in memory
of Sir Allen Lane, for the author of a book
published in the current year (fiction or non-
fiction), which furthers public understanding of
mental health problems. 2001 winner: Kate
Rankin *Growing Up Severely Autistic: They Call
Me Gabriel.*

The Mitchell Prize for Art History/ The Eric Mitchell Prize

c/o The Burlington Magazine, 14–16 Duke's
Road, London WC1H 9SZ
☎020 7388 8157 Fax 020 7388 1230
Executive Director *Caroline Elam*

ESTABLISHED 1977 by art collector, philan-
thropist and businessman, Jan Mitchell, to draw
attention to exceptional achievements in the history of art. Consists of two prizes: The Mitchell
Prize, given for an outstanding and original contribution to the study and understanding of visual
arts, and The Eric Mitchell Prize, given for the
outstanding exhibition catalogue of the year.
The prizes are awarded to authors of books in
English that have been published in the previous
12 months. Books are submitted by publishers
before the end of February. Previous winners:
The Mitchell Prize: *Nicolas Poussin* Elizabeth
Cropper and Charles Dempsey; The Eric
Mitchell Prize: *The Triumph of Vulcan* Suzanne
Brown Butters.
Prizes $10,000 each.

Scott Moncrieff Prize

See **The Translators Association Awards**

The Oscar Moore Screenwriting Prize

The Oscar Moore Foundation, c/o Screen
International, 33–39 Bowling Green Lane,
London EC1R 0DA
☎020 7505 8080 Fax 020 7505 8087
Email michelle.connery@media.emap.com
Website www.screendaily.com
Coordinator *Michelle Connery*

ESTABLISHED 1997. Annual prize in honour of
Oscar Moore, former *Guardian* columnist and
editor-in-chief of *Screen International*, who died in
1996. The genre for the competition changes
each year (comedy for 2002) , as does the closing

date. Contact the Foundation to obtain an entry
form. 2001 winner: Marcus Lloyd *Cuckoo.*
Award £10,000 cash, plus week-long script
development course courtesy of Arista, and
performance of the winning script by the Script
Factory.

Mother Goose Award

See **The Books for Children Award**

Shiva Naipaul Memorial Prize

The Spectator, 56 Doughty Street, London
WC1N 2LL
☎020 7405 1706 Fax 020 7242 0603
Email emma@spectator.co.uk
Contact *Emma Bagnall*

ESTABLISHED 1985. Annual prize given to an
English language writer of any nationality
under the age of 35 for an essay of not more
than 4000 words describing a culture alien to
the writer. Final entry date is 30 April. 2000
winner: Mary Wakefield.
Prize £3000.

NASEN Special Educational Needs Book Awards

The Educational Publishers Council, The
Publishers Association, 29B Montague Street,
London WC1B 5BH
☎020 7691 9191 Fax 020 7691 9199
Email mail@publishers.org.uk
Website www.publishers.org.uk

ESTABLISHED 1992. Organised by the National
Association for Special Education Needs
(NASEN) and the Educational Publishers
Council. Two awards: The Children's Book
Award, for the book that most successfully provides a positive image of children with special
needs; The Academic Book Award celebrates
the work of authors and editors who have
made an outstanding contribution to the
theory and practice of special education. Books
must have been published in the UK within
the year preceding the award. A new award,
Books for Teaching and Learning, will be
established in 2003. 2001 winners: Jack Gantos
Joey Pigza Swallowed the Key (Children's); Paul
Cooper, Mary Jane Drummond, Susan Hart,
Jane Lovey, Colleen McLaughlin *Positive
Alternatives to Exclusion* (Academic).
Prize £500.

National Poetry Competition

The Poetry Society, 22 Betterton Street,
London WC2H 9BX
☎020 7420 9880 Fax 020 7240 4818

Email info@poetrysoc.com
Website www.poetrysoc.com

Contact *Competition Organiser (WH)*

One of Britain's major open poetry competitions. Closing date: 31 October. Poems on any theme, up to 40 lines. For rules and entry form send s.a.e. to the competition organiser or enter the competition via the website.

Prizes £5000 (1st); £1000 (2nd); £500 (3rd); plus 10 commendations of £50.

Bill Naughton Short Story Competition

Box No. 2003, Aghamore, Ballyhaunis, Co. Mayo, Republic of Ireland

Organised by the **Kenny/Naughton Society** (see entry under **Literary Societies**). Stories may be on any topic and no more than 2500 words in length. All work must be unpublished; typed scripts only with no name or address appearing on the work. Entry fee: £3 per story; three stories may be submitted for the price of two. Closing date: 1 September each year. No entry form required.

Prizes £150 (1st); £100 (2nd); £50 (3rd). Best stories published in a collection entitled *Splinters*.

Nestlé Smarties Book Prize

Booktrust, Book House, 45 East Hill, London SW18 2QZ
☎020 8516 2972 Fax 020 8516 2978
Email tarryn@booktrust.org.uk
Website www.booktrusted.com

Contact *Tarryn McKay*

ESTABLISHED 1985 to encourage high standards and stimulate interest in books for children, this prize is given for a children's book (fiction), written in English by a citizen of the UK or an author resident in the UK, and published in the UK in the year ending 31 October. There are three age-group categories: 5 and under, 6–8 and 9–11. 2001 Gold Award winners: Catherine and Laurence Anholt *Chimp and Zee* (5 and under); Emily Smith *The Shrimp* (6–8); Eva Ibbotson *Journey to the River Sea* (9–11); Raymond Briggs *Ug* (Kids' Club Network Special Award).

Prizes in each category: £2500 (gold); £1000 (silver); £500 (bronze).

The New Writer Prose & Poetry Prizes

The New Writer, PO Box 60, Cranbrook, Kent TN17 2ZR
☎01580 212626 Fax 01580 212041

Email admin@thenewwriter.com
Website www.thenewwriter.com

Contact *Merric Davidson*

ESTABLISHED 1997. Annual award founded by *The New Writer* poetry editor and poet, Abi Hughes-Edwards. Open to all poets writing in the English language for an original, previously unpublished poem or collection of six to ten poems. Also open to writers of short stories and novellas/serials, features, articles, essays and interviews. Final entry date: 30 November. Previous winners: Mark Granier, Ros Barber, Celia de Fréine, John Hilton.

Prizes (total) £3000, plus publication in collection.

'The Nibbies'

See **British Book Awards**

No Love Lost Poetry Anthology Contest

See **Hidden Brook Press International Poetry Anthology Contest**

Nobel Prize

The Nobel Foundation, PO Box 5232, 102 45 Stockholm, Sweden
☎00 46 8 663 0920 Fax 00 46 8 660 3847
Website www.nobel.se

Contact *Information Section*

Awarded yearly for outstanding achievement in physics, chemistry, physiology or medicine, literature and peace. FOUNDED by Alfred Nobel, a chemist who proved his creative ability by inventing dynamite. In general, individuals cannot nominate someone for a Nobel Prize. The rules vary from prize to prize but the following are eligible to do so for Literature: members of the Swedish Academy and of other academies, institutions and societies similar to it in constitution and purpose; professors of literature and of linguistics at universities or colleges; Nobel Laureates in Literature; presidents of authors' organisations which are representative of the literary production in their respective countries. British winners of the literature prize, first granted in 1901, include Rudyard Kipling, John Galsworthy and Winston Churchill. Recent winners: Nadine Gordimer (South Africa); Derek Walcott (St Lucia); Toni Morrison (USA); Kenzaburo Oe (Japan); Seamus Heaney (Ireland); Wislawa Szymborska (Poland); Dario Fo (Italy); José Saramago (Portugal); Günter Grass (Germany); Gao Xingjian (France). Nobel Laureate in Literature 2001: V.S. Naipaul (Great Britain).

The Noma Award for Publishing Africa

PO Box 128, Witney, Oxfordshire OX8 5XU
☎01993 775235 Fax 01993 709265
Email maryljay@aol.com

Contact *Mary Jay, Secretary, Managing Committee*

ESTABLISHED 1979. Annual award, founded by the late Shoichi Noma, President of Kodansha Ltd, Tokyo. The award is for an outstanding book, published in Africa by an African writer, in three categories: scholarly and academic; literature and creative writing; children's books. Entries, by publishers only, by 28 February for a title published in the previous year. Maximum number of three entries. Previous winners: Kitia Touré *Destins Parallèles*; A. Adu Boahen *Mfantsipim and the Making of Ghana: A Centenary History 1876–1976*; Peter Adwok Nyaba *The Politics of Liberation in South Sudan; An Insider's View*; Djibril Samb *L'intérpretation des rêves dans la région Sénégambienne. Suivi de la clef des songes de la Sénégambie, de l'Egypte pharaonique et de la tradition islamique*; Kimari Njogu and Rocha Chimerah *Ufundishaji wa Fasihi. Nadharia na Mbinu*; Abosede Emanuel *Odun Ifa/Ifa Festival*.
Prize US$10,000 and presentation plaque.

C.B. Oldman Prize

Aberdeen University Library, Queen Mother Library, Meston Walk, Aberdeen AB24 3UE
☎01224 272592 Fax 01224 487048
Email r.turbet@abdn.ac.uk

Contact *Richard Turbet*

ESTABLISHED 1989 by the International Association of Music Libraries, UK Branch. Annual award for best book of music bibliography, librarianship or reference published the year before last (i.e. books published in 1999 considered for the 2001 prize). Previous winners: Michael Talbot, Donald Clarke, John Parkinson, John Wagstaff, Stanley Sadie, William Waterhouse, Richard Turbet, John Gillaspie, David Fallows, Arthur Searle.
Prize £150.

Open Window Poetry Anthology Contest

See **Hidden Brook Press International Poetry Anthology Contests**

Orange Prize for Fiction

Booktrust, 45 East Hill, London SW18 2QZ
☎020 8516 2972 Fax 020 8516 2978
Email tarryn@booktrust.org.uk
Website www.orangeprize.com

Contact *Tarryn McKay*

ESTABLISHED 1996. Annual award founded by a group of senior women in publishing to 'create the opportunity for more women to be rewarded for their work and to be better known by the reading public'. Awarded for a full-length novel written in English by a woman of any nationality, and published in the UK between 1 April and 31 March of the following year. 2001 winner: Kate Grenville *The Idea of Perfection*.
Prize £30,000 and a work of art (a limited edition bronze figurine known as 'The Bessie' in acknowledgement of anonymous prize endowment).

Orion Prize for Poetry

See **Milton Acorn Prize for Poetry**

The Orwell Prize

Simage Communications Ltd, Fulton House, Fulton Road, Wembley Park, Middlesex HA9 0TF
☎020 8584 0444 Fax 020 8584 0443
Email orwell@simage-comms.co.uk
Website www.simage-comms.co.uk

Contact *Maxine Vlieland*

Jointly ESTABLISHED in 1993 by the George Orwell Memorial Fund and the *Political Quarterly* to encourage and reward writing in the spirit of Orwell's 'What I have most wanted to do ... is to make political writing into an art'. Two categories: book or pamphlet; newspaper and/or articles, features, columns, or sustained reportage on a theme. Submissions by editors, publishers or authors. 2001 winners: Miranda Carter *Anthony Blunt: His Lives*; (book); Yasmin Alibhai-Brown (journalism).
Prizes £1000 for each category.

Outposts Poetry Competition

Outposts, 22 Whitewell Road, Frome, Somerset BA11 4EL
☎01373 466653

Contact *Roland John*

Annual competition for an unpublished poem of not more than 60 lines run by **Hippopotamus Press**.
Prizes £500 (1st), £200 (2nd), £100 (3rd).

The Wilfred Owen Award for Poetry

192 York Road, Shrewsbury, Shropshire SY1 3QH
☎01743 460089
Website www.wilfred.owen.mcmail.com

Contact *Michael Grayer*

Biennial award ESTABLISHED in 1988 by the **Wilfred Owen Association**. Given to a poet whose poetry reflects the spirit of Owen's work in its thinking, expression and inspiration. Applications are not sought; the decision is made by the Association's committee. Previous winner: Seamus Heaney.

Award A silver and gunmetal work of art, suitably decorated and engraved.

OWG Awards for Excellence

Outdoor Writers' Guild, PO Box 520, Bamber Bridge, Preston, Lancashire PR5 8LF
☎01772 696732 Fax 01772 696732

Contact *Terry Marsh*

ESTABLISHED 1980. Annual awards by the **Outdoor Writers' Guild** to raise the standard of outdoor writing, journalism and broadcasting. Winning categories include guidebook, outdoor book, feature (one-off), feature (regular), photography. Open to OWG members only. Final entry date: March.

Catherine Pakenham Award

The Sunday Telegraph, 1 Canada Square, Canary Wharf, London E14 5DT
☎020 7538 6257 Fax 020 7513 2512
Email charlotte.ibarra@telegraph.co.uk

Contact *Charlotte Ibarra*

ESTABLISHED in 1970, the award is designed to ecourage women journalists as they embark on their careers. Open to women aged 18–25 who have had at least one piece of work published, however small. 2001 winner: Alice Wignall.

Award £1000 and a writing commission with one of the Telegraph publications; three runner-up prizes of £200 each.

The Parker Romantic Novel of the Year

2 Broad Oak Lane, Wigginton, York YO32 2SB
☎01904 765035

Award Organiser *Joan Emery*

ESTABLISHED 1960. Formerly known as the Romantic Novelists' Association Major Award. Sponsorship for the 2001 award is by Parker Pen. Annual award for the best romantic novel of the year, open to non-members as well as members of the **Romantic Novelists' Association**. Novels must be published in the UK between specified dates. Authors must be based in the UK unless members of the RNA.

2002 winner: Philippa Gregory *The Other Boleyn Girl.* Send s.a.e. to the Organiser for entry form.
Award £10,000.

PEN Awards

See **J.R. Ackerley Prize**; **Golden PEN Award for Lifetime Distinguished Services to Literature**; **The Hessell-Tiltman Prize for History**; **Macmillan Silver PEN Award**

Peterloo Poets Open Poetry Competition

The Old Chapel, Sand Lane, Calstock, Cornwall PL18 9QX
☎01822 833473

Contact *Harry Chambers*

ESTABLISHED 1986. Annual competition for unpublished English language poems of not more than 40 lines. Final entry date: 1 March. Send s.a.e. for rules and entry form. Previous winners: John Watts, Jem Poster, David Craig, Rodney Pybus, Debjani Chatterjee, Donald Atkinson, Romesh Gunesekera, Anna Crowe, Carol Ann Duffy, Mimi Khalvati, John Lyons, M.R. Peacocke, Alison Pryde, Carol Shergold, Maureen Wilkinson, Chris Woods.

Prizes £2000 (1st); £1000 (2nd); £500 (3rd); £100 (4th); plus 10 prizes of £50; 15–19 age group: 5 prizes of £100.

Pets on Parade Short Story Competition

Bridlington and District RSPCA, 42 Quay Road, Bridlington, East Yorkshire YO16 2AP
Website www.rspca-bridlington.org.uk

Competition Organiser *Viv Stamford*

Annual short story competition. The winning stories are published in book form which is sold to raise funds to help animals. Closing date: 31 October. For further details send s.a.e. to the address above.
Prize £100 (1st).

Poetry Business Competition

The Studio, Byram Arcade, Westgate, Huddersfield, West Yorkshire HD1 1ND
☎01484 434840 Fax 01484 426566
Email edit@poetrybusiness.co.uk
Website www.poetrybusiness.co.uk

Contact *The Competition Administrator*

ESTABLISHED 1986. Annual award which aims to discover and publish new writers. Entrants should submit a manuscript of poems. Winners will have their work published by the **Poetry**

Business under the Smith/Doorstop imprint. Final entry date: end of October. Previous winners include: Pauline Stainer, Michael Laskey, Mimi Khalvati, David Morley, Julia Casterton, Liz Cashdan, Moniza Alvi, Selima Hill. Send s.a.e. for full details.

Prizes Publication of full collection; runners-up have pamphlets; 20 complimentary copies. Also cash prize (£1000) to be shared equally between all winners.

Poetry Life Poetry Competition
1 Blue Ball Corner, Water Lane, Winchester, Hampshire SO23 0ER
Email adrian.abishop@virgin.net
Website freespace.virgin.net/poetry.life/
Contact *Adrian Bishop*

ESTABLISHED 1993. Open competition for original poems in any style which have not been published in a book. Maximum length of 80 lines. Entry fee of £3 per poem. Send s.a.e. for details.

Prizes £500 (1st); £100 (2nd); £50 each (3rd & 4th).

The Poetry Society's National Poetry Competition
See **National Poetry Competition**

Peter Pook Humorous Novel Competition
See **Emissary Publishing** under **UK Publishers**

The Portico Prize
The Portico Library, 57 Mosley Street, Manchester M2 3HY
☎0161 236 6785 Fax 0161 236 6803
Email librarian@theportico.org.uk
Website www.theportico.org.uk
Contact *Miss Emma Marigliano*

ESTABLISHED 1985. Administered by the Portico Library in Manchester. Biennial award for a work of fiction or non-fiction published between the two closing dates. Set wholly or mainly in the North-West of England, including Cumbria and the High Peak District of Derbyshire. Next award: June 2002. Previous winners include: John Stalker *Stalker*; Alan Hankinson *Coleridge Walks the Fells*; Jenny Uglow *Elizabeth Gaskell: A Habit of Stories*.
Prize £3000.

The Dennis Potter Screenwriting Award
BBC Broadcasting House, Whiteladies Road, Bristol BS8 2LR
☎0117 974 7586
Email BBC2Awards@bbc.co.uk
Editor *Jeremy Howe*

Annual award ESTABLISHED in 1995 in memory of the late television playwright to 'nurture and encourage the work of new writers of talent and personal vision'. Submissions should be made through a BBC TV drama producer or an independent production company (no start date confirmed; contact the editor for further information).

The Premio Valle Inclán
See **The Translators Association Awards**

The Mathew Prichard Award for Short Story Writing
Competition Secretary, 2 Rhododendron Close, The Greenways, Cyn Coed, Cardiff CF23 7HS
Competition Organiser *Philip Beynon*
Competition Secretary *Marjorie Williams*

ESTABLISHED 1996 to provide sponsorship and promote Wales and its writers. Entry fee: £5; NB scripts are not returned. Competition open to all writers in English; the final entry date is 28 February each year.
Prizes A total of £2000.

V.S. Pritchett Memorial Prize
Royal Society of Literature, Somerset House, Strand, London WC2R 1LA
☎020 7845 4676 Fax 020 7845 4679
Email info@rslit.org
Website www.rslit.org

ESTABLISHED 1999. Awarded for a previously unpublished short story of between 2000 and 5000 words. For entry forms, please contact the Secretary.

Pulitzer Prizes
The Pulitzer Prize Board, 709 Journalism, Columbia University, New York NY 10027, USA
☎001 212 854 3841/2 Fax 001 212 854 3342
Email pulitzer@www.pulitzer.org
Website www.pulitzer.org

Awards for journalism in US newspapers, and for published literature, drama and music by American nationals. Deadlines: 1 February (journalism); 1 March (music); 1 March (drama); 1 July for books published between 1 Jan–30 June, and 1 Nov for books published between 1 July–31 Dec (literature). Previous winners include: Michael Chabon *The Amazing Adventures of Kavalier & Clay*; Joseph J. Ellis *Founding Brothers: The Revolutionary Generation*; David Levering Lewis *W.E.B. Du Bois: The Fight for Equality and the American Century, 1919–1963*; Stephen Dunn *Different Hours*; Herbert P. Bix *Hirohito and the Making of Modern Japan*.

The *Real* Writers/The Book Pl@ce Short Story Awards

PO Box 170, Chesterfield, Derbyshire
S40 1FE
☎01246 238492 Fax 01246 238492
Email info@real-writers.com
Website www.real-writers.com

Formerly the *Real* Writers Short Story Competition, ESTABLISHED 1994. Sponsored by www.thebookplace.com Closing date: 3 September. Entry fee: £5. Optional critiques. S.a.e. to the address above for entry forms, etc.

Prizes (1st) £2500, plus 10 regional awards.

Trevor Reese Memorial Prize

Institute of Commonwealth Studies, University of London, 28 Russell Square, London WC1B 5DS
☎020 7862 8844 Fax 020 7862 8820
Contact *Events & Publicity Officer*

ESTABLISHED 1979 with the proceeds of contributions to a memorial fund to Dr Trevor Reese, Reader in Commonwealth Studies at the Institute and a distinguished scholar of imperial history (d.1976). Biennial award (next award 2004) for a scholarly work, usually by a single author, in the field of Imperial and Commonwealth History published in the preceding two academic years. All correspondence relating to the prize should be marked 'Trevor Reese Memorial Prize'.

Prize £1000.

Regional Press Awards

Press Gazette, Quantum House, 19 Scarbrook Road, Croydon, Surrey CR9 1LX
☎020 8565 4463 Fax 020 8565 4462
Email pged@qpp.co.uk

A comprehensive range of journalist and newspaper awards for the regional press. There are five newspapers of the year, by circulation and frequency, and a full list of journalism categories. Open to all regional journalists, whether freelance or staff. July event. Run by the *Press Gazette*.

Renault UK Journalist of the Year Award

Guild of Motoring Writers, 30 The Cravens, Smallfield, Surrey RH6 9QS
☎01342 843294 Fax 01342 844093
Email sharon@scott-fairweather.freeserve.co.uk
Contact *Sharon Scott-Fairweather*

Originally the Pierre Dreyfus Award and ESTABLISHED 1977. Awarded annually by Renault UK Ltd in honour of Pierre Dreyfus, president director general of Renault 1955–75, to the member of the **Guild of Motoring Writers** who is judged to have made the most outstanding journalistic effort during the year.

Prize (1st) £1500, plus trophy.

John Llewellyn Rhys Prize
See **The Mail on Sunday/John Llewellyn Rhys Prize**

Bill Rollinson Award
See **Lakeland Book of the Year Awards**

Romantic Novelists' Association Major Award
See **The Parker Romantic Novel of the Year**

Rooney Prize for Irish Literature

Rooney Prize, Strathin, Templecarrig, Delgany, Co. Wicklow, Republic of Ireland
☎00 353 1 287 4769
Fax 00 353 1 287 2595
Email rooney-prize@ireland.com
Contacts *Jim Sherwin, Thelma Cloake*

ESTABLISHED 1976. Annual award to encourage young Irish writing to develop and continue. Authors must be Irish, under 40 and published. A non-competitive award with no application procedure.

Prize €7500.

Royal Economic Society Prize

c/o University of York, York YO10 5DD
☎01904 433575 Fax 01904 433575
Contact *Professor Mike Wickens*

Annual award for the best article published in *The Economic Journal*. Open to members of the Royal Economic Society only. Previous winners: Professors Kip Viscusi, Mark Armstrong, Jim Heckman and Jeffrey Smith.

Prize £3000.

Royal Society of Literature Awards
See **Winifred Holtby Memorial Prize** and **W.H. Heinemann Prize**

Runciman Award
The Anglo-Hellenic League, c/o The Hellenic Centre, 16–18 Paddington Street, London W1U 5AS
☎020 7486 9410 Fax 020 7486 4254
Contact *The Administrator*

ESTABLISHED 1985. Annual award, sponsored by the National Bank of Greece. Founded by the Anglo-Hellenic League to promote Anglo-Greek understanding and friendship, for a work wholly or mainly about some aspect of Greece or the Hellenic scene, which has been published in its first English edition in the UK during the previous year and listed in Whitaker's Books in Print. Named after the late Sir Steven Runciman, former chairman of the Anglo-Hellenic League. The Award may be given for a work of fiction, drama or non-fiction; concerned academically or non-academically with the history of any period; biography or autobiography, the arts, archaeology; a guide book or a translation from the Greek of any period. Final entry date in February; award presented in May/June. 2001 winner: Dr Cyprian Broodbank *An Island Archaeology of the Early Cyclades* .
Award £5000.

Sagittarius Prize
Society of Authors, 84 Drayton Gardens, London SW10 9SB
☎020 7373 6642 Fax 020 7373 5768
Email info@societyofauthors.org

ESTABLISHED 1990. For first published novel by an author over the age of 60. Final entry date: 20 December. Full details available from the **Society of Authors**. 2001 winner: Michael Richardson *The Pig Bin*.
Prize £2000.

Sainsbury's Baby Book Award
Booktrust, Book House, 45 East Hill, London SW18 2QZ
☎020 8516 2972 Fax 020 8516 2978
Email tarryn@booktrust.org.uk
Website www.booktrust.org.uk
Contact *Tarryn McKay*

ESTABLISHED 1999. Annual award, set up by **Booktrust** with sponsorship from Sainsbury's, for the best book for a baby under one year old, published in the UK. 2001 winner: Sandra Lousada *Baby Faces*.

Prize £2000 and trophy to the winner; certificate and trophy to the winning publisher.

The David St John Thomas Charitable Trust Competitions and Awards
PO Box 6055, Nairn IV12 4YB
☎01667 453351
Competition & Awards Manager *Lorna Edwardson*

A large programme of writing competitions and awards including annual ghost story and love story competitions (each 1600–1800-words with £1000 first prize), and open poetry competition (poems up to 32 lines, total prize money £1200). Publication of winning entries is guaranteed, usually in *Writers' News/Writing Magazine* and/or annual anthology. The awards are led by the annual Self-Publishing Award, ESTABLISHED in 1993, which is open to anyone who has self-published a book during the preceding calendar year. There are four categories each with a £250 prize; the overall winner is declared self-publisher of the year with a total award of £1000. For full details, send large s.a.e. to the address above.

The Saltire Literary Awards
Saltire Society, 9 Fountain Close, 22 High Street, Edinburgh EH1 1TF
☎0131 556 1836 Fax 0131 557 1675
Administrator *Kathleen Munro*

ESTABLISHED 1982. Annual awards, one for Book of the Year, the other for Best First Book by an author publishing for the first time. Open to any author of Scottish descent or living in Scotland, or to anyone who has written a book which deals with either the work and life of a Scot or with a Scottish problem, event or situation. Nominations are invited from editors of leading newspapers, magazines and periodicals. Previous winners: Saltire Scottish Book of the Year: Liz Lochhead *Medea*; The Post Office/Saltire Best First Book: Meaghan Delahunt *In the Bluehouse*.
Prizes £5000 (Scottish Book); £1500 (First Book).

Sandburg-Livesay Anthology Contest
Mekler & Deahl, Publishers, 237 Prospect Street South, Hamilton, Ontario, Canada L8M 2Z6
☎001 905 312 1779 Fax 001 905 312 8285
Email james@meklerdeahl.com

Website www.meklerdeahl.com

Contacts *James Deahl, Gilda Mekler*

FOUNDED 1996. Annual award named after the poets Carl Sandburg and Dorothy Livesay to honour their achievement as populist poets. Up to ten poems may be entered for a fee of £6. A copy of the rules is available from the address above or from the website. Final entry date: 31 October.

Prizes US$250 (1st); US$150 (2nd); US$100 (3rd); anthology publication for the winners and all other worthy entries.

Ron Sands Prize
See **Lakeland Book of the Year Awards**

The Biennial Sasakawa Prize
British Haiku Society, Lenacre Ford, Woolhope, Hereford HR1 4RF
☎01432 860328
Email davidawalker@btinternet.com
Website www.britishhaikusociety.org

Contact *David Walker*

ESTABLISHED 1999. Biennial prize (next in 2003) for original contributions in the field of haikai (haiku and related genres). Open to entrants domiciled in either the UK or Japan. Closing date: 31 December 2003. Entry details available from the British Haiku Society at the address above or on the website.

Prize £2500, partly in the form of a return air ticket to Japan (or to the UK for a Japanese winner).

Schlegel–Tieck Prize
See **The Translators Association Awards**

Scottish Arts Council Children's Book Awards
Scottish Arts Council, 12 Manor Place, Edinburgh EH3 7DD
☎0131 226 6051 Fax 0131 225 9833
Email jenny.brown@scottisharts.org.uk
Website www.sac.org.uk

Head of Literature *Jenny Brown*

A number of awards are given annually (spring) to authors of published books in recognition of high standards in children's fiction or non-fiction from new or established writers. Authors should be Scottish or resident in Scotland, or books must be of Scottish interest. Applications from publishers only. 2001 winners: Julie Lacome *Ruthie's Big Old Coat*; Tom Pow and Robert Ingpen *Who is the World For?*; Diana Hendry *Harvey Angell Beats Time*; J.K. Rowling *Harry*

Potter and the Goblet of Fire; Lindsay MacRae *How to Avoid Kissing Your Parents in Public*; Alison Prince *Second Chance.*

Awards under review but minimum of £1000 each.

Scottish Book of the Year
See **The Saltire Literary Awards**

Scottish Historical Book of the Year
The Saltire Society, 9 Fountain Close, 22 High Street, Edinburgh EH1 1TF
☎0131 556 1836 Fax 0131 557 1675
Email saltire@saltire.org.uk
Website www.saltire-society.demon.co.uk

Administrator *Kathleen Munro*

ESTABLISHED 1965. Annual award in memory of the late Dr Agnes Mure Mackenzie for a published work of distinguished Scottish historical research of scholarly importance (including intellectual history and the history of science). Editions of texts are not eligible. Nominations are invited and should be sent to the Administrator. Previous winner: Marcus Merriman *The Rough Wooings: Mary Queen of Scots 1542–1551.*

Prize Bound and inscribed copy of the winning publication.

SEEDS International Poetry Chapbook Anthology Contest
See **Hidden Brook Press International Poetry Anthology Contests**

SES Book Prizes
Institute of Education, University of London, 20 Bedford Way, London WC1H 0AL
☎020 7612 6003 Fax 020 7612 6330

Contact *Professor G. Grace (Chair of Book Prize Committee)*

Annual awards given by the Society for Educational Studies for the best books on Education published during the preceding year. Nomination by members of the Standing Conference and publishers or by individual authors based in the UK.

Prizes £1000, £800 and £400.

Bernard Shaw Translation Prize
See **The Translators Association Awards**

André Simon Memorial Fund Book Awards
5 Sion Hill Place, Bath BA1 5SJ
☎01225 336305 Fax 01225 421862
Email tessa@tantraweb.co.uk

Contact *Tessa Hayward*

ESTABLISHED 1978. Awards given annually for the best book on drink, best on food and special commendation in either. 2001 winners: Stephen Skelton *The Wines of Britain and Ireland*; Hugh Fearnley-Whittingstall *River Cottage Cookbook*; Bennet Alan Weinberg and Bonnie K. Bealer *The World of Caffeine* (special commendation); Tom Jaine (special award).

Awards £2000 (best books); £1000 (special commendation); £200 to shortlisted books.

WHSmith Book Awards

WHSmith PLC, Nations House, 103 Wigmore Street, London W1U 1WH
☎020 7514 9623 Fax 020 7514 9635
Email elizabeth.walker@group-whsmith.co.uk
Website www.whsmith.co.uk/bookawards2002

Contact *Elizabeth Walker, Awards Manager*

The only UK book awards that can truly lay claim to be the 'people's choice' for the book industry in this country. With 65,000 votes cast in the first year, there are eight categories open to public voting which include: Fiction; Business; Autobiography/Biography; Travel; Home & Leisure; New Talent; Children's and General Knowledge. A panel of judges for each category, consisting of a member of the public, an author and a celebrity, shortlists the books for each category with voting commencing in January for a period of one month. Votes are gathered in-store, by freepost and online. The ninth category incorporates the long-standing WHSmith Literary Award and is decided by a panel of nine judges, which includes three public judges.

WHSmith's Thumping Good Read Award

WHSmith PLC, Greenbridge Road, Swindon, Wiltshire SN3 3LD
☎01793 616161 Fax 01793 562590

Contact *Award Administrator*

ESTABLISHED 1992 to promote writers of popular fiction. Books must have been published in the twelve months preceding the award. Submissions, made by publishers, are judged by a panel of customers to be the most un-put-down-able from a shortlist of ten. 2001 winner: Jeffery Deaver *The Empty Chair*.

Award £5000.

The Society for Theatre Research Annual Theatre Book Prize

c/o The Theatre Museum, 1e Tavistock Street, London WC2E 7PA

Email e.cottis@btinternet.com
Website www.str.org.uk

ESTABLISHED 1997. Annual award for books, in English, of original research into any aspect of the history and technique of the British Theatre. Not restricted to authors of British nationality nor books solely from British publishers. Books must be first published in English (no translations) during the calendar year. Play texts and those treating drama as literature are not eligible. Publishers submit books directly to the independent judges and should contact the Book Prize Administrator for further details. 2001 winner: Jim Davis and Victor Emeljanow *Reflecting the Audience: London Theatregoing, 1840–1880*.

Award £400.

Sony Radio Academy Awards

Alan Zafer & Associates, 47–48 Chagford Street, London NW1 6EB
☎020 7723 0106 Fax 020 7724 6163
Email secretariat@radioawards.org
Website www.radioawards.org

Contact *The Secretariat*

ESTABLISHED 1982 in association with the **Society of Authors** and Sony UK. Presented in association with the Radio Academy. Annual awards to recognise excellence in radio broadcasting. Entries must have been broadcast in the UK between 1 January and 31 December in the year preceding the award. The categories for the awards are reviewed each year.

Southport Writers' Circle Poetry Competition

32 Dover Road, Southport, Merseyside PR8 4TB

Contact *Mrs Hilary Tinsley*

For previously unpublished work. Entry fee: £2 per poem. Any subject, any form; maximum 40 lines. Closing date: end April. Poems must be entered under a pseudonym, accompanied by a sealed envelope marked with the pseudonym and title of poem, containing s.a.e. Entries must be typed on A4 paper and be accompanied by the appropriate fee payable to Southport Writers' Circle. No application form is required. Envelopes should be marked 'Poetry Competition'. Postal enquiries only. No calls.

Prizes £250 (1st); £50 (2nd); £25 (3rd); additional £25 Humour Prize.

The Spoken Word Awards

The Spoken Word Publishing Association, Macmillan Audio Books, 20 New Wharf Road, London N1 9RR

☎020 7014 6041
Email z.howes@macmillan.co.uk
Contact *Zoe Howes*

Hosted by the **Spoken Word Publishing Association**, the Awards are for excellence in the spoken word industry and recognise the valuable work of all those involved with the production of audio books. There are 22 categories of award, consisting of 14 Consumer Awards (including Drama, Biography, Poetry, Children's and Comedy), four Trade Awards (including Best Retailer and Best Media Coverage) and four Performance Awards (Male and Female Performer of the Year, Publisher of the Year and Spoken Word Audio of the Year).

Prizes Glass trophy for the 'Gold' awards; certificates for Silver and Bronze.

Bram Stoker Awards for Superior Achievement

Horror Writers Association, PO Box 50577, Palo Alto, CA 94303 USA
☎001 650 322 4610
Email hwa@horror.org
Website www.horror.org
Contact *Nancy Etchemendy*

FOUNDED 1988 and named in honour of Bram Stoker, author of *Dracula*. Presented annually by the **Horror Writers Association** (HWA) for works of horror first published in the English language. Works are eligible during their first year of publication. HWA members recommend works for consideration in twelve categories: novel, first novel, short fiction, long fiction, fiction collection, anthology, non-fiction, illustrated narrative, screenplay, work for young readers, poetry, and other media. In addition, Lifetime Achievement Stokers are occasionally presented to individuals whose entire body of work has substantially influenced horror.

Strokestown International Poetry Prize

Strokestown Poetry Festival, Strokestown, Co. Roscommon, Republic of Ireland
☎00 353 78 33759
Email twiggezvous@eircom.net
Website www.strokestownpoetryprize.com
Contacts *M. Harpur, Pat Compton*

Annual competition ESTABLISHED in 1999 by Strokestown Community Development Association to reward excellence in poetry. A centrepiece of the Strokestown International Poetry Festival held the first weekend in May. Final entry date: mid-February. Maximum length: 70 lines. All short-listed poets are expected to attend the festival and read their poem.

Prizes €4000; €1250; €600; and nine runner-up prizes of €130 each. Also prizes totalling €2500 for a poem in Irish (max. 50 lines); and a total of €1000 for a political satire in verse.

Sunday Times Award for Small Publishers

Independent Publishers Guild, PO Box 93, Royston, Hertfordshire SG8 5GH
Fax 01763 246293
Email sheila@ipg.uk.com
Contact *Sheila Bounford*

ESTABLISHED 1988, the first winner was **Fourth Estate**. Open to any publisher producing between five and forty titles a year, which must primarily be original titles, not reprints. Entrants are invited to submit their catalogues for the last twelve months, together with two representative titles. Award presented at the London Book Fair. 2001 winner: **Hambledon and London**. Previous winners include: **Carcanet Press**; **Profile Books**; **Nick Hern Books**; **Tarquin Publications**; Ellipsis; **Bradt Publications**.

Sunday Times Writer of the Year Award

The Sunday Times, 1 Pennington Street, London E1 9XW
☎020 7782 5770 Fax 020 7782 5798

ESTABLISHED 1987. Annual award to fiction and non-fiction writers. The panel consists of *Sunday Times* journalists and critics. Previous winners: Anthony Burgess, Seamus Heaney, Stephen Hawking, Ruth Rendell, Muriel Spark, William Trevor, Martin Amis, Margaret Atwood, Ted Hughes, Harold Pinter, Tom Wolfe, Robert Hughes. No applications; prize at the discretion of the Literary Editor.

Sunday Times Young Writer of the Year Award

The Society of Authors, 84 Drayton Gardens, London SW10 9SB
☎020 7373 6642 Fax 020 7373 5768
Email info@societyofauthors.org
Contact *Awards Secretary*

ESTABLISHED 1991. Annual award given on the strength of the promise shown by a full-length published work of fiction, non-fiction, poetry or drama. Entrants must be British citizens, resident in Britain and under the age of 35. The panel consists of *Sunday Times* journalists and critics. Closing date: 20 December. The work must be by one author, in the English language, and published in Britain. Applications by publishers via the **Society of Authors**. 2001 winner: Zadie Smith *White Teeth*.

Tabla Poetry Competition

Department of English, University of Bristol, 3–5 Woodland Road, Bristol BS8 1TB
Fax 0117 928 8860
Email stephen.james@bristol.ac.uk
Website www.bris.ac.uk/tabla
Contact *Stephen James*

ESTABLISHED 1991. Annual award for poems of any length which have not been published or broadcast. Minimum age of entrants must be 16. Final entry date: 1 March. No poems by e-mail, please. Winning and other selected entries are published, alongside leading names, in the annual *Tabla Book of New Verse*. Previous winners: Philip Gross, Henry Shukman.
   Prizes £500 (1st); £200 (2nd); 3 runners-up, £100 each.

Reginald Taylor and Lord Fletcher Essay Prize

Journal of the British Archaeological Association, Institute of Archaelogy, 36 Beaumont Street, Oxford OX1 2PG
Contact *Dr Martin Henig*

A biennial prize, in memory of the late E. Reginald Taylor and of Lord Fletcher, for the best unpublished essay, not exceeding 7500 words, on a subject of archaeological, art history or antiquarian interest within the period from the Roman era to AD 1830. The essay should show *original* research on its chosen subject, and the author will be invited to read the essay before the Association. The essay may be published in the journal of the Association if approved by the Editorial Committee. Closing date for entries is 1 June 2004. All enquiries by post please. No phone calls. Send s.a.e. for details.
   Prize £300 and a medal.

Tidepool Prize for Poetry

See **Milton Acorn Prize for Poetry**

The Times Educational Supplement Book Awards

Times Educational Supplement, Admiral House, 66–68 East Smithfield, London E1W 1BX
☎020 7782 3000
Website www.tes.co.uk

ESTABLISHED 1973. The Awards are under review at present.

The Tir Na N-Og Award

Cyngor Llyfrau Cymru (Welsh Books Council), Castell Brychan, Aberystwyth, Dyfed SY23 2JB
☎01970 624151 Fax 01970 625385
Email castellbrychan@cllc.org.uk
Website www.wbc.org.uk

An annual award given to the best original book published for children in the year prior to the announcement. There are three categories: Best Welsh Fiction; Best Welsh Non-fiction; Best English Book with an authentic Welsh background.
   Awards £1000 (each category).

TLS/Blackwells Poetry Competition

Times Literary Supplement, Admiral House, 66–68 East Smithfield, London E1W 1BX
☎020 7782 3000
Website www.the-tls.co.uk
Contact *Mick Imlah (Poetry Editor, TLS)*

ESTABLISHED 1997. Annual open competition. Final entry date in January. 2001-02 winner: Jane Griffiths.
   Prizes £2000; three runners-up £500 each.

Tolman Cunard Prize

See **The Forward Prizes for Poetry**

Marten Toonder Award

An Chomhairle Ealaíon (The Irish Arts Council), 70 Merrion Square, Dublin 2, Republic of Ireland
☎00 353 1 6180200 Fax 00 353 1 6761302
Email info@artscouncil.ie
Website www.artscouncil.ie
Contact *Music Officer*

The award, made possible by Dutch artist Marten Toonder, honours established artists in music, literature and the visual arts. In 2002 the award was made for visual art; in 2003 it will be for music. Applicants should enclose a detailed c.v. as well as an excerpt or copy of their work. The standard application form for individuals should be used and is available on request.
   Award €10,000.

The Translators Association Awards

The Translators Association, 84 Drayton Gardens, London SW10 9SB
☎020 7373 6642 Fax 020 7373 5768
Email info@societyofauthors.org

Contact *Awards Secretary*

Various awards for published translations into English from Dutch and Flemish (The Vondel Translation Prize), French (Scott Moncrieff Prize), German (Schlegel-Tieck Prize), Greek (Hellenic Foundation Prize), Italian (The John Florio Prize), Portuguese (The Calouste Gulbenkian Prize), Spanish (The Premio Valle Inclán), Swedish (Bernard Shaw Translation Prize) and Japanese (Sasakawa Prize). Contact the **Translators Association** for full details.

The Betty Trask Prize

See entry under **Bursaries, Fellowships and Grants**

Travelex Travel Writers' Awards

Ingrams, 120–122 Seymour Place, London W1H 1EL
☎020 7339 7777 Fax 020 7339 7878

ESTABLISHED in 1993 to reward excellence in UK travel journalism. Details for 2003 still to be determined at the time of going to press.

The Trewithen Poetry Prize

Chy-an-Dour, Trewithen Moor, Stithians, Truro, Cornwall TR3 7DU

Contact *Competition Secretary*

ESTABLISHED 1995 in order to promote poetry with a rural theme. The competition supports one environmental and one animal welfare charity each year. Entry forms available from the address above (enclose s.a.e.). Closing date: 31 October. Entry fee of £3 for first poem, £2 for subsequent entries. Previous winners include: Elizabeth Rapp, David Smart, Ann Drysdale, Roger Elkin, Lesley Quayle.

Prizes (total) £800 plus publication in *The Trewithen Chapbook*.

The Trollope Society Short Story Prize

9A North Street, London SW4 0HN
☎020 7720 6789 Fax 020 7978 1815
Email trollsoc@barset.fsnet.co.uk

Contacts *Pamela Neville-Sington, John Williams*

ESTABLISHED in 2001 to encourage interest in Trollope's novels among young people with the emphasis on reading – and writing – for fun. The competition, which is held annually, focuses on a different Trollope book each year; contact the Society for details. Open to secondary-school (pre-university) students of all countries from the ages of 15 to 19. Final entry date: 15 January. The winning story will be published in the Society's quarterly journal, *Trollopiana*.

Prize £1000; the winner's school receives a set of books from the Society's edition of Trollope's works.

UNESCO Prize for Children's and Young People's Literature in the Service of Tolerance

Division of Arts and Cultural Enterprise, UNESCO, 1 rue Miollis, 75732–Paris Cedex 15, France
☎00 33 1 45 68 43 40
Fax 00 33 1 45 68 55 95
Email m.bulos@unesco.org
Website www.unesco.org/culture/ toleranceliterature

Contact *Ms Maha Bulos*

The UNESCO Prize is awarded every two years in recognition of works for the young that 'best embody the concepts and ideals of tolerance and peace, and promote mutual understanding based on respect for other people and cultures'. The works may be novels, collections of short stories or illustrated picture books, and fall within two categories: for children up to the age of 12 and for young people aged 13 to 18. Submissions by publishers only. The International Jury will select the 2003 winners in December 2002.

Prizes US$8000 in each category.

The V.B. Poetry Prize

20 Clifton House, Club Row, London E2 7HB
Email LOOKLEARN@aol.com
Website www.looklearn.com

Contact *Nicholas Morgan*

Annual open competition for original single unpublished poem, any style, maximum length 40 lines. Entry fee: £3 for first two poems, £1.50 for each additional poem. Closing date: 30 June 2003. Send s.a.e. for full details and entry form.

Prizes £400 (1st), £150 (2nd), £50 (3rd). Winning poems will be published on the Look and Learn Productions' website.

Ver Poets Open Competition

Haycroft, 61–63 Chiswell Green Lane, St Albans, Hertfordshire AL2 3AL
☎01727 867005

Contact *May Badman*

Various competitions are organised by **Ver Poets**, the main one being the annual Open for unpublished poems of no more than 30 lines written in English. Entry fee: £3 per poem. Entries must be made under a pseudo-nym, with name and address on form or separate sheet. Two copies of poems typed on A4 white paper. *Vision On*, the anthology of winning and selected poems, and the adjudicators' report are normally available from mid-June. Final entry date: 30 April. Back numbers of the anthology are available for £3, post-free; one copy each free to those included.

Prizes £500 (1st); £300 (2nd); two runner-up prizes of £100.

Vogue Talent Contest

Vogue, Vogue House, Hanover Square, London W1S 1JU
☎020 7499 9080 Fax 020 7408 0559

Contact *Frances Bentley*

ESTABLISHED 1951. Annual award for young writers and journalists (under 25 on 1 January in the year of the contest). Final entry date is in April. Entrants must write three pieces of journalism on given subjects.

Prizes £1000, plus a month's paid work experience with *Vogue*; £500 (2nd).

The Vondel Translation Prize

See **The Translators Association Awards**

Wadsworth Prize
for Business History

Business Archives Council, 3rd and 4th Floors, 101 Whitechapel High Street, London E1 7RE
☎020 7247 0024 Fax 020 7422 0026

Contact *Mrs Lenore Symons*

ESTABLISHED 1978. Annual award for the best book published on British business history. 2000 winner: David Kynaston *The City of London; Vol. 3: Illusions of Gold 1914–1945.*

Prize £500.

Arts Council of Wales
Book of the Year Awards

Arts Council of Wales, Museum Place, Cardiff CF10 3NX
☎029 2037 6500 Fax 029 2022 1447
Email information@ccc-acw.org.uk

Contact *Tony Bianchi*

Annual non-competitive prizes awarded for works of exceptional literary merit written by Welsh authors (by birth or residence), published in Welsh or English during the previous calendar year. There is one major prize in English, the Book of the Year Award, and one major prize in Welsh, Gwobr Llyfr y Flwyddyn. Shortlists of three titles in each language are announced in

April; winners announced in May. 2001 winners: Stephen Knight *Mr Schnitzel*; Owen Martell *Cadw Dy Ffydd Brawd.*

Prizes £3000 (each); £1000 to each of four runners-up.

Walford Award
See **CILIP: The Chartered Institute of Library and Information Professionals Walford Award**

Waterstone's Prize
See **The Forward Prizes for Poetry**

The David Watt Prize

Rio Tinto plc, 6 St James's Square, London SW1Y 4LD
☎020 7753 2277 Fax 020 7930 3249
Email davidwattprize@riotinto.com

Contact *The Administrator*

INITIATED in 1987 to commemorate the life and work of David Watt. Annual award, open to writers currently engaged in writing for English language newspapers and journals, on international and national affairs. The winners are judged as having made 'outstanding contributions towards the greater understanding of national, international or global issues'. Entries must have been published during the year preceding the award. Final entry date 31 March. The 2001 winner was Robert Fisk for 'Dead Reckoning', published in *The Independent.*

Prize £7500.

The Harri Webb Prize

10 Heol Don, Whitchurch, Cardiff CF14 2AU
☎029 2062 3359 Fax 029 2052 9202
Email meic@heoldon.fsnet.co.uk

Contact *Professor Meic Stephens*

ESTABLISHED 1995. Annual award to commemorate the Welsh poet, Harri Webb (1920–94), for a single poem in any of the categories in which he wrote: ballad, satire, song, polemic or a first collection of poems. The poems are chosen by three adjudicators; no submissions. Previous winner: Grahame Davies.

Prizes £100/£200.

The Weidenfeld Translation Prize

New College, Oxford OX1 3BW
☎01865 279525 Fax 01865 279590
Email karen.leeder@new.ox.ac.uk

Contact *The Fellows' Secretary*

ESTABLISHED in 1996 by publisher Lord Weidenfeld to encourage good translation into English. Annual award to the translator(s) of a

work of fiction, poetry or drama written in any living European language. Submissions from publishers only. For further information, contact Dr David Constantine at the Queen's College address above. 2001 winner: Edwin Morgan for his translation of *Phaedra* by Jean Racine.
Prize £1000.

The Wellcome Trust Prize
Consultation and Education Dept., The Wellcome Trust, 210 Euston Road, London NW1 2BE
☎020 7611 7221 Fax 020 7611 8269
Email r.birse@wellcome.ac.uk
Website www.wellcome.ac.uk
Contact *Ruth Birse*
ESTABLISHED 1997. Biennial award for a non-fiction book that 'will educate, captivate and inspire the non-specialist lay reader', to be written by a professional life scientist who is unpublished and resident in the UK or Ireland. Contact the Wellcome Trust for rules and guidelines or visit the website. The winning book will be published by **Weidenfeld & Nicolson**. Previous winners: Dr Guy Brown, Professor Chris McManus, Dr Michael Morgan.
Prize £25,000 (in four instalments, depending on progress of the book).

Wellington Town Council Award
Civic Offices, Larkin Way, Tan Bank, Wellington, Telford, Shropshire TF1 1LX
☎01952 222935 Fax 01952 222936
Email WellTownCl@aol.com
Website www.wellington-shropshire.gov.uk
Contact *Derrick Drew*
ESTABLISHED 1995. Annual short story competition to promote the ancient town of Wellington, now part of the annual **Wellington Literary Festival**. Open to all for a minimum fee of £2.50; prizes are sponsored so all entry fee monies go to charity. 2001 winners: D. Ballantine, Belfast (Open category); A. Frazer, Telford (Best Shropshire Entry); R. Howard (Best Story for Children).
Prizes Trophies and money.

Wheatley Medal
See **CILIP: The Chartered Institute of Library and Information Professionals Wheatley Medal**

Whitbread Book Awards
The Booksellers Association, Minster House, 272 Vauxhall Bridge Road, London SW1V 1BA
☎020 7834 5477 Fax 020 7834 8812
Email denise.bayat@booksellers.co.uk
Website www.whitbread-bookawards.co.uk
Contact *Denise Bayat*
ESTABLISHED 1971. The awards celebrate and promote the best contemporary British writing. They are judged in two stages and offer a total of £50,000 prize money. The awards are open to Novel, First Novel, Biography, and Poetry, each judged by a panel of three judges. The winner of each award receives £5000. Three adult judges and two young judges select a shortlist of four books from which the Whitbread Children's Book of the Year is chosen, the winner receiving £5000. The Whitbread Book of the Year (£25,000) is chosen from the category winners. Writers must have lived in Britain and Ireland for three or more years. Submissions received from publishers only. Closing date: early July. Sponsored by Whitbread PLC. 2001 winners: Philip Pullman *The Amber Spyglass* (children's and overall winner); Patrick Neate *Twelve Bar Blues* (novel); Sid Smith *Something Like a House* (first novel); Diana Souhami *Selkirk's Island* (biography); Selima Hill *Bunny* (poetry).

Whitfield Prize
Royal Historical Society, University College London, Gower Street, London WC1E 6BT
☎020 7387 7532 Fax 020 7387 7532
Contact *Executive Secretary*
ESTABLISHED 1977. An annual award for the best new work within a field of British history, published in the UK in the preceding calendar year. The book must be the author's first (solely written) history book and be an original and scholarly work of historical research. Final entry date: 31 December. 2000 winner: Adam Fox *Oral and Literate Culture in England, 1500–1700*.
Prize £1000.

John Whiting Award
Arts Council of England, 14 Great Peter Street, London SW1P 3NQ
☎020 7973 6431 Fax 020 7973 6983
Email jemima.lee@artscouncil.org.uk
Website www.artscouncil.org.uk
Contact *Theatre Writing Section*
FOUNDED 1965. Annual award to commemorate the life and work of the playwright John Whiting (*The Devils, A Penny for a Song*). Any writer who has received during 2002 and 2003: (a) an award through the **Arts Council's Theatre Writing Schemes**; (b) a commission

from a theatre company in receipt of an annual or revenue subsidy from either the Arts Council or a Regional Arts Board; or (c) a première production by a theatre company in receipt of annual subsidy is eligible to apply. The play must have been written during 2002 and/or 2003. Awarded to the writer whose play most nearly satisfies the following criteria: a play in which the writing is of special quality; a play of relevance and importance to contemporary life; a play of potential value to the British theatre. No writer who has won the award previously may reapply and no play that has been submitted for the award previously is eligible. Closing date for entries: 9 January 2004.
Prize £6000.

Alfred and Mary Wilkins Memorial Poetry Competition and Lecture

Birmingham & Midland Institute, 9 Margaret Street, Birmingham B3 3BS
☎0121 236 3591 Fax 0121 212 4577
Administrator *Mr P.A. Fisher*

Alternating competition and lecture. The next competition, to be held in 2004, is for an unpublished poem, not exceeding 40 lines, written in English by an author over the age of 15. The poem should not have been entered for any other poetry competition. Details from the address above.
Prizes (total) £1000.

Titus Wilson and Son Prize
See **Lakeland Book of the Year Awards**

H.H. Wingate Prize
See **Jewish Quarterly Literary Prizes**

Wolf Web

PO Box 136, Norwich, Norfolk NR3 3NJ
☎01603 440940 Fax 01603 440940
Email poems@sayanawolf.org
Website www.sayanawolf.org

Contact *Tricia Frances*

Sayana Wolf Trust publishes *Wolf Web* twice a year and runs one poetry competiton annually. Closing date: 12 December. Unpublished poems only on the theme of 'wolf'. All profits go to the work of The Sayana Wolf Trust which funds personal development, educational and community projects for British and North American children and adults. For more details, write to the address above (no replies without s.a.e.).
Prizes One-year's membership to Wolf Web and publication in *Wolf Web*.

Wolfson History Prizes

Wolfson Foundation, 8 Queen Anne Street, London W1G 9LD
☎020 7323 5730 Fax 020 7323 3241
Contact *Executive Secretary*

The Wolfson History Prize, ESTABLISHED in 1972, is awarded annually to promote and encourage standards of excellence in the writing of history for the general reading public. 2000 winners: Ian Kershaw *Hitler, 1936–1945: Nemesis*; Mark Mazower *The Balkans*; Roy Porter *Enlightenment: Britain and the Creation of the Modern World*.
Prizes vary each year.

The David T.K. Wong Short Story Prize

International PEN, 9/10 Charterhouse Buildings, Goswell Road, London EC1M 7AT
☎020 7253 4308 Fax 020 7253 5711
Email intpen@dircon.co.uk
Website www.oneworld.org/internatpen
Contact *Gilly Vincent*

ESTABLISHED 2000. An international, biannual prize to promote literary excellence in the form of the short story written in English. Unpublished stories (6000 words maximum) are welcome from writers worldwide, as long as their entries are submitted via their local PEN Centre and incorporate one or more of International PEN's ideals as set out in its Charter. Writers in those few countries without a PEN Centre can be directed to the nearest appropriate centre by International PEN. See website for full prize details and PEN Centres. 2001 winner: Rachel Seiffert *The Crossing*.
Prize £7500 (1st).

World Wide Writers Award

PO Box 3229, Bournemouth, Dorset BH1 1ZS
☎01202 589828 Fax 01202 587758
Email writintl@globalnet.co.uk
Website www.worldwidewriters.com
Contacts *John Jenkins, Mary Hogarth*

ESTABLISHED 1997. Quarterly and annual competitions for original, unpublished short stories of between 2500 and 5000 words. Entries are published in *World Wide Writers* magazine. Entry fee: £10 (£6 for subscribers to *World Wide Writers*). Entry fee includes back issue of the magazine. Closing dates: end of January, March, June and September. Previous winners: Sally Zigmond, Shirley Nunes, Judi Moore,

Gerald Phillipson, Brian Dixon, L. Morgana Braveraven. Annual *prize* £3000 and medal.

The Writers Bureau Poetry and Short Story Competition

The Writers Bureau, Sevendale House, 7 Dale Street, Manchester M1 1JB
☎0161 228 2362 Fax 0161 228 3533
Email compent@writersbureau.com
Website www.writersbureau.com

Competition Secretary *Angela Cox*

ESTABLISHED 1994. Annual award. Poems should be no longer than 40 lines and short stories no more than 2000 words. £4 entry fee. Closing date: 31 July 2003.

Prizes in each category: £1000 (1st); £400 (2nd); £200 (3rd); £100 (4th); £50 x 6.

Yorkshire Post Book of the Year Award

The Rectory, Ripley, Near Harrogate, North Yorkshire HG3 3AY
☎01423 772217 Fax 01423 772217

Contact *Margaret Brown*

An annual award for the book (either fiction or non-fiction) which, in the opinion of the judges, is the best work published in the preceding year. Closing date: 31 December. Previous winner:

John Ehrman *The Younger Pitt, Vol. III: The Consuming Struggle.*
Prize £1200.

Young Science Writer Award

The Daily Telegraph, 1 Canada Square, Canary Wharf, London E14 5DT
☎020 7538 6960/Hotline: 020 7704 5315
Email enquiries@science-writer.co.uk
Website www.science-writer.co.uk

Contact *Amelia Watson-Steele*

ESTABLISHED 1987, this award is designed to bridge the gap between science and writing, challenging the writer to come up with a piece of no more than 700 words that is friendly, informative and, above all, understandable. Sponsored by BASF, the award is open to two age groups: 16–19 and 20–28.

Award Winners and runners-up receive cash prizes and have the opportunity to have their pieces published on the science pages of *The Daily Telegraph*. The winner in each category also gets an all expenses paid trip to the USA for the meeting of the American Association for the Advancement of Science and an invitation to meet Britain's most distinguished scientists at the British Association's Festival of Science. Visit the website, telephone the hotline number or e-mail for further information.

Holding Readers to Account

Has Public Lending Right had its day?
Barry Turner considers the evidence

There are rumours flying about that the government is out of love with Public Lending Right, the £7 million fund that compensates authors for loans of their books from public libraries. Set against state spending in other areas, the sum distributed is petty cash, but the question remains: Does the scheme do its job and is it right for our time? The critics argue that the book scene has changed out of all recognition since PLR was introduced over twenty years ago. Then, public libraries were the standard-bearers of popular literacy. Now, of those that remain open, many are sad social relics more interested in pushing videos and discs than in lending books. As book buying has increased along with higher living standards, so loans from libraries have fallen, down from 500 million at the turn of the century to around 430 million today.

Jim Parker, PLR registrar, bemoans the decline as 'sad and remorseless' but expects loan figures to bottom out before long. Possibly, but this may well be wishful thinking. The whole nature of book borrowing and book buying is going through a revolution. Anecdotal evidence suggests that more people borrow from each other. When I buy a cheap paperback I invariably hand it on, a habit well known to the journal trade, where total readership of a magazine always far outpaces the sales figure.

Then again, many of the serious books, those that used to be stocked by the public libraries because otherwise they were virtually unobtainable except at a high price, have moved over to university, college and specialist libraries, none of which is covered by PLR. Why not? The quick answer is that there is simply not enough money to go round. The latest payout at 2.67 pence per loan means that just 130 authors qualify for the maximum of £6,000. Most of those who have books registered for PLR get under £100. It won't be long before audio books and the reference works, which are referred to in libraries but are seldom taken home, qualify for PLR. Then, average payments will be lower still unless the government argues a substantial increase in funding, which seems unlikely. The arts minister has only to look at the names at the top of the PLR list – Dick Francis, Jack Higgins, Ruth Rendell, Patricia Cornwell among them – to know that Chancellor Brown is not likely to see such well-heeled luminaries as qualifying for a public subsidy.

So is there any point in continuing with PLR? As the Society of Authors argues, there are writers who are so strapped that even £100 is a welcome addition to income. It would help them if the maximum payout was reduced from £6,000 to, say, £1,000, allowing for an extra £750,000 or so for distribution to those who need the money. A change to the copyright rule would also be welcome. Currently, PLR continues for the life of the author plus seventy years, much to the joy of such as the heirs of Agatha Christie and Catherine Cookson. Would it not be fairer to reduce this to, perhaps, ten years?

The publishing sector where PLR does deserve to be taken seriously is children's books. Youngsters who read can get through a huge number of books, which is why library loans in this category are up by 7 per cent over ten years. Moreover, it is not the megasellers like J.K. Rowling that do best out of PLR, presumably because the Harry Potter books are for reading and rereading and so thought to be worth buying. Since the government is keen on children acquiring the reading habit, there must be a case for a discriminatory grant to give further encouragement to children's writers.

While the argument over the future of PLR hots up, there is encouraging news for authors from the Authors' Licensing & Collecting Society (ALCS), which distributes fees to writers whose work has been copied, broadcast or recorded. A long drawn-out fight with the universities over the page rate for copying has ended with an agreed blanket fee of £4 per full-time student to allow for the copying of up to 5 per cent of any work. Authors of academic books, not to mention poets, playwrights and novelists, should soon get a welcome addition to income. And this is where the future lies. Copying and, longer term, online transmission will take over from the traditional library loan system as the meaty bone of contention between authors and readers. There needs to be a radical rethink of PLR if it is not to be left behind.

PLR application forms and details can be obtained from the Registrar of Public Lending Right at Richard House, Sorbonne Close, Stockton-on-Tees TS17 6DA. ☎ *01642 604699; fax 01642 615641; e-mail: authorservices@plr.uk.com; website www.plr.uk.com.*

The Authors' Licensing & Collecting Society Ltd (ALCS), is at Marlborough Court, 14–18 Holborn, London EC1N 2LE. ☎ *020 7395 0600; fax 020 7395 0660; e-mail: alcs@alcs.co.uk; website www.alcs.co.uk.*

Library Services

Aberdeen Central Library

Rosemount Viaduct, Aberdeen AB25 1GW
☎01224 652500 Fax 01224 641985
Email centlib@arts-rec.aberdeen.net.uk

Open 9.00 am to 7.00 pm Monday to
Thursday; 9.00 am to 5.00 pm Friday
(Reference & Local Studies: 9.00 am to
8.00 pm); 9.00 am to 5.00 pm Saturday.
Branch library opening times vary

Open access
General reference and loans. Books, pamphlets, periodicals and newspapers; videos, CDs; arts equipment lending service; Internet and Learning Centre for public access; photographs of the Aberdeen area; census records, maps; online database, patents and standards. The library offers special services to housebound readers. Non-resident administrative fee.

Armitt Library

Ambleside, Cumbria LA22 9BL
☎015394 31212 Fax 015394 31313
Website www.armitt.com

Open 10.00 am to 12.30 pm and 1.30 pm to
4.00 pm Monday to Friday

Free access (To view original material please
give prior notice)
A small but unique reference library of rare books, manuscripts, pictures, antiquarian prints and museum items, mainly about the Lake District. It includes early guidebooks and topographical works, books and papers relating to Ruskin, H. Martineau, Charlotte Mason and others; fine art including work by W. Green, J.B. Pyne, John Harden, K. Schwitters, and Victorian photographs by Herbert Bell; also a major collection of Beatrix Potter's scientific watercolour drawings and microscope studies. Museum and Exhibition open seven days per week from 10.00 am to 5.00 pm. Entry charge.

The Athenaeum, Liverpool

Church Alley, Liverpool L1 3DD
☎0151 709 7770 Fax 0151 709 0418
Email library@athena.force9.net
Website www.athena.force9.co.uk

Open 9.00 am to 4.00 pm Monday to Friday

Access To club members; researchers by application only
General collection, with books dating from the 15th century, now concentrated mainly on local history with a long run of Liverpool directories and guides. *Special collections* Liverpool playbills; William Roscoe; Blanco White; Robert Gladstone; 18th-century plays; 19th-century economic pamphlets; the Norris books; Bibles; Yorkshire and other genealogy. Some original drawings, portraits, topographical material and local maps.

Bank of England Information Centre

Threadneedle Street, London EC2R 8AH
☎020 7601 4715 Fax 020 7601 4356
Email informationcentre@bankofengland.co.uk
Website www.bankofengland.co.uk

Open 9.30 am to 5.30 pm Monday to Friday

Access For research workers by prior arrangement only, when material is not readily available elsewhere
50,000 volumes of books and periodicals. 2000 periodicals taken. UK and overseas coverage of banking, finance and economics. *Special collections* Central bank reports; UK 17th–19th-century economic tracts; Government reports in the field of banking.

Barbican Library

Barbican Centre, London EC2Y 8DS
☎020 7638 0569 Fax 020 7638 2249
Email barbicanlib@corpoflondon.gov.uk
Website www.cityoflondon.gov.uk

Open 9.30 am to 5.30 pm Monday,
Wednesday, Thursday, Friday; 9.30 am to
7.30 pm Tuesday; 9.30 am to 12.30 pm
Saturday

Open access
Situated on Level 2 of the Barbican Centre, this is the Corporation of London's largest lending library. Study facilities are available plus free Internet access. In addition to a large general lending department, the library seeks to reflect the Centre's emphasis on the arts and includes strong collections (including DVDs, videos and CD-ROMs), on painting, sculpture, theatre, cinema and ballet, as well as a

large music library with books, scores and CDs (sound recording loans available at a small charge). Also houses the City's main children's library and has special collections on finance, natural resources, conservation, socialism and the history of London. Service available for housebound readers. A literature events programme is organised by the Library which supplements and provides cross-arts planning opportunities with the Barbican Centre artistic programme.

Barnsley Public Library
Central Library, Shambles Street, Barnsley, South Yorkshire S70 2JF
☎01226 773930 Fax 01226 773955
Email Librarian@Barnsley.ac.uk
Website www.barnsley.gov.uk/service/libraries/index.asp
Open Lending & Reference: 9.30 am to 7.00 pm Monday and Wednesday; 9.30 am to 5.30 pm Tuesday and Friday; 9.30 am to 4.00 pm Saturday. Please telephone to check hours of other departments.

Open access
General library, lending and reference. Archive collection of family history and local firms; local studies: coal mining, local authors, Yorkshire and Barnsley; large junior library. (Specialist departments are closed on certain weekday evenings and Saturday afternoons.)

BBC Written Archives Centre
Peppard Road, Caversham Park, Reading, Berkshire RG4 8TZ
☎0118 948 6281 Fax 0118 946 1145
Email wac.enquiries@bbc.co.uk
Website www.bbc.co.uk/thenandnow
Contact *Jacqueline Kavanagh*
Open 9.30 am to 5.30 pm Monday to Friday
Access For reference, by appointment only on Wednesday to Friday.
Holds the written records of the BBC, including internal papers from 1922 to 1979 and published material to date. 20th century biography, social history, popular culture and broadcasting. Charges for certain services.

Bedford Central Library
Harpur Street, Bedford MK40 1PG
☎01234 350931/270102 (Reference Library)
Fax 01234 342163
Website www.bcclgis.gov.uk/gateway
Open 9.30 am to 7.00 pm Monday and

Wednesday; 9.30 am to 5.30 pm Tuesday, Thursday, Friday; 9.30 am to 5.00 pm Saturday
Open access
Lending library with a wide range of stock, including books, music (CDs and cassettes), audio books and videos; reference and information library, children's library, local history library, Internet facilities and gallery.

Belfast Public Libraries: Central Library
Royal Avenue, Belfast BT1 1EA
☎028 9050 9150 Fax 028 9033 2819
Email info@libraries.belfast-elb.gov.uk
Website www.belb.org.uk
Open 9.30 am to 8.00 pm Monday and Thursday; 9.30 am to 5.30 pm Tuesday, Wednesday, Friday; 9.30 am to 1.00 pm Saturday
Open access To lending libraries; reference libraries by application only
Over two million volumes for lending and reference. *Special collections* United Nations depository; complete British Patent Collection; Northern Ireland Newspaper Library; British and Irish government publications. The Central Library provides the following Reference Departments: General Reference; Belfast, Ulster and Irish Studies; Music. A Learning Gateway includes public Internet facilities and a Learndirect Centre. The Lending Library is one of over 20 branches along with a range of outreach services to hospitals, care homes and housebound readers.

BFI National Library
21 Stephen Street, London W1T 1LN
☎020 7255 1444 Fax 020 7436 2338
Email library@bfi.org.uk
Website www.bfi.org.uk
Open 10.30 am to 5.30 pm Monday and Friday; 10.30 am to 8.00 pm Tuesday and Thursday; 1.00 pm to 8.00 pm Wednesday; Telephone Enquiry Service operates from 10.00 am to 5.00 pm
Access For reference only; annual, 5-day and limited day membership available
The world's largest collection of information on film and television including periodicals, cuttings, scripts, related documentation, personal papers. Information available through SIFT (Summary of Information on Film and Television).

Birmingham and Midland Institute

9 Margaret Street, Birmingham B3 3BS
☎0121 236 3591 Fax 0121 212 4577
Website www.bmi.org.uk

Administrator & General Secretary
Philip Fisher

Access Members only
ESTABLISHED 1854. Later merged with the
Birmingham Library which was founded in
1779. The Library specialises in the humanities,
with approximately 100,000 volumes in stock.
Founder member of the **Association of
Independent Libraries**. Meeting-place of
many affiliated societies devoted to poetry and
literature.

Birmingham Library Services

Central Library, Chamberlain Square,
Birmingham B3 3HQ
☎0121 303 4511
Email central.library@birmingham.gov.uk
Website www.birmingham.gov.uk/libraries

Open 9.00 am to 8.00 pm Monday to Friday;
9.00 am to 5.00 pm Saturday

Over a million volumes. *Research collections*
include the Shakespeare Library; War Poetry
Collection; Parker Collection of Children's
Books and Games; Johnson Collection; Milton
Collection; Cervantes Collections; Early and
Fine Printing Collection (including the William
Ridler Collection of Fine Printing); Joseph
Priestley Collection; Loudon Collection;
Railway Collection; Wingate Bett Transport
Ticket Collection; Labour, Trade Union and
Co-operative Collections. Photographic
Archives: Sir John Benjamin Stone; Francis
Bedford; Francis Frith; Warwickshire
Photographic Survey; Boulton and Watt
Archive; Charles Parker Archive; Birmingham
Repertory Theatre Archive and Sir Barry
Jackson Library; Local Studies (Birmingham);
Patents Collection; Song Sheets Collection;
Oberammergau Festival Collection.

Book Data Ltd

Globe House, 1 Chertsey Road,
Twickenham, Middlesex TW1 1LR
☎020 8843 8620 Fax 020 8843 8744
Email sales@bookdata.co.uk
Website www.bookdata.co.uk *and*
www.ehaus.co.uk

Contact *Sales Department*

The leading supplier of content-rich book information and other published media to the book
industry. Book Data takes information from

publishers and creates a unique title record which
includes bibliographic details, text summaries,
tables of contents, extensive subject-related
information, market-rights details, jacket images,
etc. This information is then available through a
variety of services: record supply, CD-ROM
and online (BookFind-Online). *Record Supply*
supplies the data in a format specified by the customer for easy integration into existing database
systems. *BookFind-Online* is a fully searchable,
web-based bibliographic service with daily
updates containing over 1.9 million titles on the
UK service and over 4 million titles on the international service. Produces a variety of CD-
ROMs. Offers web hosting and design services
for publishers through its *e-haus* department.

Bournemouth Library

22 The Triangle, Bournemouth, Dorset
BH2 5RQ
☎01202 454848 Fax 01202 454840

Open 10.00 am to 7.00 pm Monday; 9.30 am
to 7.00 pm Tuesday, Thursday, Friday; 9.30
am to 5.00 pm Wednesday; 9.00 am to 1.00
pm Saturday

Open access
Main library for Bournemouth with lending,
reference and music departments, plus the
Heritage Zone – local and family history.

Bradford Central Library

Princes Way, Bradford, West Yorkshire
BD1 1NN
☎01274 753600 Fax 01274 395108
Email public.libraries@bradford.gov.uk

Open 9.00 am to 7.30 pm Monday to Friday;
9.00 am to 5.00 pm Saturday

Open access
Wide range of books and media loan services.
Comprehensive reference and information services, including major local history collections
and specialised business information service.
Bradford Libraries run *Reader2Reader*, a ground-
breaking, reader–centred literature development
project (www.Reader2Reader.com)

Brighton Central Library

Vantage Point, New England Street, Brighton,
East Sussex BN1 2GW
☎01273 290800 Fax 01273 296951

Local Studies Library: Church Street,
Brighton BN1 2UE

Open 10.00 am to 7.00 pm Monday to Friday
(closed Wednesday); 10.00 am to 4.00 pm
Saturday

Access Limited stock on open access; material for reference use and lending

FOUNDED 1869, the library has a large stock covering most subjects. Specialisations include art and antiques, history of Brighton and Sussex, family history, local illustrations, TSO, business and large bequests of antiquarian books and ecclesiastical history.

Bristol Central Library

College Green, Bristol BS1 5TL
☎0117 903 7200 Fax 0117 922 1081
Website www.bristol-city.gov.uk *or*
www.digitalbristol.org

Open 9.30 am to 7.30 pm Monday, Tuesday
and Thursday; 9.30 am to 5.00 pm
Wednesday, Friday and Saturday; 1.00 pm
to 4.00 pm Sunday

Open access

Lending, reference, art, music, business and local studies are particularly strong. Facilities available: PCs (large screen with Jaws and Zoomtext), Internet, printing; videophone on site.

British Architectural Library

Royal Institute of British Architects, 66
Portland Place, London W1B 1AD
☎020 7580 5533 Fax 020 7631 1802
Email bal@inst.riba.org
Website www.architecture.com

Members' Information Line: 020 7307 3600
(membership number required);
Public Information Line (50p per min.):
0906 302 0400

Open 10.00 pm to 8.00 pm Tuesday; 10.00
am to 5.00 pm Wednesday to Friday; 10.00
am to 1.30 pm Saturday; Closed Sunday,
Monday and any Saturday preceding a Bank
Holiday; full details on the website

Access Free to RIBA members; non-members must buy a day ticket (£10/£6 concessions, but on Tuesdays between 5.00 pm–8.00 pm and Saturdays £6/£3); subscriber membership available (write for details); loans available to RIBA and library members only

Collection of books, drawings, manuscripts, photographs and periodicals. All aspects of architecture, current and historical. Material both technical and aesthetic, covering related fields including: interior design, landscape architecture, topography, the construction industry and applied arts. Brochure available; queries by telephone, letter, e-mail or in person. Charge for research (min. charge £30).

The British Library

Admission to St Pancras Reading Rooms

The British Library does not provide access to all those who request admission to use its research facilities but operates an admissions policy which grants access to those who need to use the collection because they cannot find the material they require in other libraries.

Admission is by interview and applicants are required to demonstrate that they need access to the reading rooms because: (a) material they need to consult is not available elsewhere; (b) their work or studies require the facilities of a large research library; (c) they need access to the Library's public records.

For further information, contact the Reader Admissions Office, The British Library, 96 Euston Road, London NW1 2DB Email reader-admissions@bl.uk ☎020 7412 7677 Fax 020 7412 7794

British Library
Business Information Service (BIS)

96 Euston Road, London NW1 2DB
Email business-information@bl.uk
Website www.bl.uk/bis

Free enquiry service ☎020 7412 7977
Fax 020 7412 7453

Free enquiry service: ☎020 7412 7977
Fax 020 7412 945

Priced enquiry service: ☎020 7412 7457
Fax 020 7412 7453

Open 10.00 am to 8.00 pm Monday; 9.30 am
to 8.00 pm Tuesday to Thursday; 9.30 am
to 5.00 pm Friday and Saturday; closed for
public holidays

Access Pass required for access

BIS holds the most comprehensive collection of business information literature in the UK. This includes market research reports and journals, directories, company annual reports, trade and business journals, house journals, trade literature and CD-ROM services.

British Library
Early Printed Collections

96 Euston Road, London NW1 2DB
☎020 7412 7676 Fax 020 7412 7577
Email rare-books@bl.uk
Website www.bl.uk

Open 10.00 am to 8.00 pm Monday; 9.30 am
to 8.00 pm Tuesday to Thursday; 9.30 am
to 5.00 pm Friday and Saturday; closed for
public holidays

Access By British Library reader's pass

General enquiries about reader services and advance reservations: ☎020 7412 7676 Fax 020 7412 7609 E-mail reader-services@bl.uk

Early Printed Collections, which is an integral part of British Library Scholarship and Collections, selects, acquires, researches and provides access to material printed in the British Isles to 1914 and in Western European languages before 1851. The collections are available in the Rare Books and Music Reading Room at St Pancras which also functions as the focus for the British Library's extensive collection of humanities microforms.

Further information about Early Printed Collections can be found at the British Library website.

British Library Humanities Reading Room

96 Euston Road, London NW1 2DB
☎020 7412 7676 Fax 020 7412 7609
Email reader-services-enquiries@bl.uk
Website www.bl.uk

Open 10.00 am to 8.00 pm Monday; 9.30 am to 8.00 pm Tuesday, Wednesday, Thursday; 9.30 am to 5.00 pm Friday and Saturday; closed for public holidays

Access By British Library reader's pass

This reading room is the focus for the Library's modern collections service in the humanities. It is on two levels, Humanities 1 and Humanities 2 and provides access to the Library's comprehensive collections of books and periodicals in all subjects in the humanities and social sciences and in all languages apart from Oriental. These collections are not available for browsing at the shelf. Material is held in closed access storage and needs to be identified and ordered from store using an online catalogue. A selective open access collection on most humanities subjects can be found in Humanities 1 whilst in Humanities 2 there are open access reference works relating to periodicals and theses, to recorded sound and to librarianship and information science.

To access British Library catalogues, go to the website at blpc.bl.uk

British Library Manuscript Collections

96 Euston Road, London NW1 2DB
☎020 7412 7513 Fax 020 7412 7745
Email mss@bl.uk
Website www.bl.uk

Open 10.00 am to 5.00 pm Monday; 9.30 am to 5.00 pm Tuesday to Saturday; closed for public holidays

Access Reading facilities only, by British Library reader's pass; a written letter of recommendation and advance notice is required for certain categories of material

Two useful publications, *Index of Manuscripts in the British Library*, Cambridge 1984–6, 10 vols, and *The British Library: Guide to the Catalogues and Indexes of the Department of Manuscripts* by M.A.E. Nickson, help to guide the researcher through this vast collection of manuscripts dating from Ancient Greece to the present day. Approximately 300,000 mss, charters, papyri and seals are housed here.

For information on British Library collections and services and to access British Library catalogues, including the Manuscripts online catalogue, visit the website.

British Library Map Collections

96 Euston Road, London NW1 2DB
☎020 7412 7702 Fax 020 7412 7780
Email maps@bl.uk
Website www.bl.uk/collections/maps

Open 10.00 am to 5.00 pm Monday; 9.30 am to 5.00 pm Tuesday to Saturday; closed for public holidays

Access By British Library reader's pass

A collection of about five million maps, charts and globes with particular reference to the history of British cartography. Maps for all parts of the world in a wide range of scales and dates, including the most comprehensive collection of Ordnance Survey maps and plans. *Special collections* King George III Topographical Collection and Maritime Collection, and the Crace Collection of maps and plans of London.

For information on British Library collections and services, visit the website.

To access main British Library catalogues, go to the website at blpc.bl.uk (NB Map Library catalogue on CD-ROM; not yet available online.)

British Library Music Collections

96 Euston Road, London NW1 2DB
☎020 7412 7772 Fax 020 7412 7751
Email music-collections@bl.uk
Website www.bl.uk

Open 10.00 am to 8.00 pm Monday; 9.30 am to 8.00 pm Tuesday to Thursday; 9.30 am to 5.00 pm Friday and Saturday; closed for public holidays

Access By British Library reader's pass
Special collections The Royal Music Library

(containing almost all Handel's surviving auto-graph scores) and the Paul Hirsch Music Library. Also a large collection (about one and a quarter million items) of printed music and about 100,000 items of manuscript music, both British and foreign.

Ther British Library website contains details of collections and services, and provides access to the catalogues.

British Library
National Sound Archive
96 Euston Road, London NW1 2DB
☎020 7412 7440   Fax 020 7412 7441
Email nsa@bl.uk
Website cadensa.bl.uk

Open 10.00 am to 8.00 pm Monday; 9.30 am to 8.00 pm Tuesday to Thursday; 9.30 am to 5.00 pm Friday and Saturday; closed for public holidays

Listening service (by appointment)

Northern Listening Service
British Library Document Supply Centre, Boston Spa, West Yorkshire: 9.15 am to 4.30 pm Monday to Friday

Open access
An archive of over 1,000,000 discs and more than 200,000 hours of tape recordings, including all types of music, oral history, drama, wildlife, selected BBC broadcasts and BBC Sound Archive material. Produces a thrice-yearly newsletter, *Playback*.

For information on British Library National Sound Archive collections and services, visit the website.

British Library Newspaper Library
Colindale Avenue, London NW9 5HE
☎020 7412 7353   Fax 020 7412 7379
Email newspaper@bl.uk
Website www.bl.uk/collections/
    newspapers.html

Open 10.00 am to 4.45 pm Monday to Saturday (last newspaper issue 4.15 pm); closed for public holidays

Access By British Library reader's pass or Newspaper Library pass (available from and valid only for Colindale)

Major collections of English provincial, Scottish, Welsh, Irish, Commonwealth and selected overseas foreign newspapers from c.1700 are housed here. Some earlier holdings are also available. London newspapers from 1801 and many weekly and fortnightly periodicals are also in stock. (London newspapers pre-dating 1801

are housed at the new library building in St Pancras – 96 Euston Road, NW1 2DB – though many are available at Colindale Avenue on microfilm.) Readers are advised to check avail-ability of material in advance.

For information on British Library Newspaper Library collections and services, visit the website.

British Library Oriental and India Office Collections
96 Euston Road, London NW1 2DB
☎020 7412 7873   Fax 020 7412 7641
Email oioc-enquiries@bl.uk
Website www.bl.uk

Open 10.00 am to 5.00 pm Monday; 9.30 am to 5.00 pm Tuesday to Saturday; closed for public holidays

Access By British Library reader's pass (identi-fication required)

A comprehensive collection of printed vol-umes and manuscripts in the languages of North Africa, the Near and Middle East and all of Asia, plus records of the East India Company and British government in India until 1947. Also prints, drawings and paintings by British artists of India.

For information on British Library collec-tions and services, visit the website.

To access British Library catalogues, go to the website at blpc.bl.uk

British Library Science, Technology and Innovation Information Services
96 Euston Road, London NW1 2DB
☎020 7412 7494/7496 (General Enquiries)
Fax 020 7412 7495
Email scitech@bl.uk
Website www.bl.uk

British/EPO patent equiries: 020 7412 7919

Business enquiries: 020 7412 7454/7977 (Business quick enquiry line available 9.00 am to 5.00 pm Monday to Friday)

Open 10.00 am to 8.00 pm Monday; 9.30 am to 8.00 pm Tuesday to Thursday; 9.30 am to 5.00 pm Friday and Saturday; closed for public holidays

Engineering, business information on com-panies, markets and products, physical science and technologies. British, European and Patent Co-operation Treaty patents and trade marks.

For information on British Library collec-tions and services, visit the website.

To access British Library catalogues go to the website at blpc.bl.uk

British Library Social Policy Information Service

96 Euston Road, London NW1 2DB
☎020 7412 7536 Fax 020 7412 7761
Website www.bl.uk/services/stb/spis.html

Open 10.00 am to 8.00 pm Monday; 9.30 am to 8.00 pm Tuesday to Thursday; 9.30 am to 5.00 pm Friday and Saturday; closed for public holidays

Access By British Library reader's pass

Provides an information service on social policy, public administration, and current and international affairs, and access to current and historical official publications from all countries and intergovernmental bodies, including House of Commons sessional papers, UK legislation, UK electoral registers, up-to-date reference books on official publications and on the social sciences, a major collection of statistics and a browsing collection of recent social science books and periodicals. Also offers a priced research service providing literature surveys, current awareness and topic briefings for clients on demand.

To access British Library catalogues, go to the website at blpc.bl.uk

British Museum Department of Ethnography – Anthropology Library

6 Burlington Gardens, London W1S 3EX
☎020 7323 8031 Fax 020 7323 8013

Open 10.00 am to 4.45 pm Monday to Friday

Access By appointment; ticket-holders only. Tickets are given to scholars and postgraduate students, with special privileges accorded to Fellows of the Royal Anthropological Institute. Reference tickets are issued to *bona fide* researchers provided that the material is not available elsewhere. Undergraduates are admitted only if engaged in a research project

In 1976 the important library of the Royal Anthropological Institute (RAI) was donated to the Department of Ethnography Library and the RAI continues to support the library with donations of books and periodicals.

The collection consists of books (120,000), periodicals (1400 current titles), congress reports, newsletters, maps, microforms, manuscripts. It covers every aspect of anthropology: cultural anthropology (notably material culture and the arts), archaeology, biological anthropology and linguistics, together with such related fields as history, sociology, description and travel. Geographically the collection's scope

is worldwide. Particular strengths are in British Commonwealth, Eastern Europe and the Americas. Mesoamerica is well represented as the library holds the Sir John Eric Thompson (1898–1970) collection. The Henry Christie Collection is also held by the library.

British Psychological Society Library

c/o Psychology Library, University of London Library, Senate House, Malet Street, London WC1E 7HU
☎020 7862 8451/8461 Fax 020 7862 8480
Email enquiries@ull.ac.uk
Website www.ull.ac.uk

Open Term-time: 9.00 am to 9.00 pm Monday to Thursday; 9.00 am to 6.30 pm Friday; 9.30 am to 5.30 pm Saturday (Holidays: 9.00 am to 6.00 pm Monday to Friday; 9.30 am to 5.30 pm Saturday)

Access Members only; Non-members £7 day ticket

Reference library, containing the British Psychological Society collection of periodicals – over 140 current titles housed alongside the University of London's collection of books and journals. Largely for academic research. General queries referred to **Swiss Cottage Library** in London which has a good psychology collection.

Bromley Central Library

London Borough of Bromley - Leisure & Community Services, High Street, Bromley, Kent BR1 1EX
☎020 8460 9955 Fax 020 8313 9975
Email reference.library@bromley.gov.uk
Website www.bromley.gov.uk

Open 9.30 am to 6.00 pm Monday, Wednesday, Friday; 9.30 am to 8.00 pm Tuesday and Thursday; 9.30 am to 5.00 pm Saturday

Open access

A large selection of fiction and non-fiction books for loan, both adult and children's. Also DVDs, videos, CDs, cassettes, language courses, open learning packs, CD-ROM and Playstation games for hire. Other facilities include a business information service (email bis@bromley.gov. uk), CD-ROM, computer hire, Internet, local studies library, 'Upfront' teenage section, large reference library with photocopying, fax, microfiche and film facilities and specialist 'Healthpoint', 'Signpost' – online community information and 'Careerpoint' sections. *Specialist collections* include: H.G. Wells, Walter de la Mare, Crystal Palace, The Harlow Bequest, and the history and geography of Asia, America, Australasia and the Polar regions.

Bromley House Library
Angel Row, Nottingham NG1 6HL
☎0115 947 3134

Librarian *Julia Wilson*

Open 9.30 am to 5.00 pm Monday to Friday; also first Saturday of each month from 10.00 am to 12.30 pm

Access For members only

FOUNDED 1816 as the Nottingham Subscription Library. Collection of 30,000 books including local history, topography, biography, travel and fiction.

CAA Library and Information Centre
Aviation House, Gatwick Airport, West Sussex RH6 0YR
☎01293 573725 Fax 01293 573181
Website www.caa.co.uk

Open 9.30 am to 4.30 pm Monday to Friday; 10.00 am to 4.30 pm first Wednesday of the month

Open access
Books, periodicals and reports on air transport, air traffic control, electronics, radar and computing.

Cambridge Central Library (Reference Library & Information Service)
7 Lion Yard, Cambridge CB2 3QD
☎01223 712000 Fax 01223 712036
Email cambridge.central.library@ cambridgeshire.gov.uk
Website www.cambridgeshire.gov.uk/library/ ver1/cam.htm

Open 9.00 am to 7.00 pm Monday to Friday; 9.00 am to 5.30 pm Saturday

Open access
Large stock of books, periodicals, newspapers, maps, plus comprehensive collection of directories and annuals covering UK, Europe and the world. Microfilm and fiche reading and printing services. Online access to news and business databases. News databases on CD-ROM; Internet access. Monochrome and colour photocopiers.

Camomile Street Library
12–20 Camomile Street, London EC3A 7EX
☎020 7247 8895

Open 9.30 am to 5.30 pm Monday to Friday

Open access
Corporation of London lending library. Wide range of fiction and non-fiction books and language courses on cassette, foreign fiction, paperbacks, maps and guides for travel at home and abroad, children's books, a selection of large print, and collections of DVDs, videos and music CDs. Free Internet access.

Cardiff Central Library
Frederick Street, St David's Link, Cardiff CF10 2DU
☎029 2038 2116 Fax 029 2087 1599
Email robboddy@hotmail.com
Website www.libraries.cardiff.gov.uk

Open 9.00 am to 6.00 pm Monday, Tuesday, Wednesday, Friday; 9.00 am to 7.00 pm Thursday; 9.00 am to 5.30 pm Saturday

General lending library with the following departments: leisure, music, children's, local studies, information, science and humanities.

Carmarthen Public Library
St Peter's Street, Carmarthen SA31 1LN
☎01267 224830 Fax 01267 221839
Email dpthomas@carmarthenshire.gov.uk

Open 9.30 am to 7.00 pm Monday, Tuesday, Wednesday, Friday; 9.30 am to 5.00 pm Thursday and Saturday

Open access
Comprehensive range of fiction, non-fiction, children's books and reference works in English and in Welsh. Large local history library. Free Internet access and CD-ROM facilities. Large Print books, books on tape, CDs, CD-ROMs, cassettes and videos available for loan.

Catholic Central Library
Lancing Street, London NW1 1ND
☎020 7383 4333 Fax 020 7388 6675
Email librarian@catholic-library.org.uk
Website www.catholic-library.org.uk

Open 10.30 am to 5.00 pm Monday, Tuesday, Thursday, Friday; 10.30 am to 7.00 pm Wednesday

Open access For reference (non-members must sign in; loans restricted to members)

Contains books, many not readily available elsewhere, on theology, religions worldwide, scripture and the history of churches of all denominations.

The Centre for the Study of Cartoons and Caricature
See entry under **Picture Libraries**

City Business Library

1 Brewers' Hall Garden, London EC2V 5BX
☎020 7332 1812 Fax 020 7332 1847
Email cbl@corpoflondon.gov.uk
Website www.cityoflondon.gov.uk
Open 9.30 am to 5.00 pm Monday to Friday

Open access
Local authority public reference library run
by the Corporation of London. Books, pamphlets, periodicals and newspapers of current
business interest, mostly financial. Aims to satisfy
the day-to-day information needs of the City's
business community, and in so doing has
become one of the leading public resource centres in Britain in its field. Strong collection of
directories for both the UK and overseas, plus
companies information, market research
sources, management, law, banking, insurance,
statistics and investment. No academic journals
or textbooks.

Commonwealth Institute

Commonwealth Resource Centre,
Kensington High Street, London W8 6NQ
☎020 7603 4535 Fax 020 7603 2807
Email crc@commonwealth.org.uk
Website www.commonwealth.org.uk
Open 10.00 am to 4.00 pm Monday to
Saturday

Open access to the public
The Commonwealth Literature collection
includes fiction, poems, drama and critical
writings. *Special collection* Books and periodicals
on the 54 Commonwealth countries. Also a
collection of directories and reference books
on the Commonwealth and information on
arts, geography, history and literature, cultural
organisations and bibliography.

Commonwealth Secretariat Library

Marlborough House, Pall Mall, London
SW1Y 5HX
☎020 7747 6164/5/6/7 Fax 020 7747 6168
Email library@commonwealth.int
Website www.thecommonwealth.org
Librarian *David Blake*
Open 9.15 am to 5.00 pm Monday to Friday

Access For reference only, by appointment
Extensive reference source concerned with
economy, development, trade, production and
industry of Commonwealth countries; also
human resources including women, youth,
health, management and education. Includes
the archives of the Secretariat.

Corporation of London Libraries

See **Barbican Library; Camomile Street
Library; City Business Library; Guildhall**

Coventry Central Library

Smithford Way, Coventry, Warwickshire
CV1 1FY
☎024 7683 2314/2395 (Minicom)
Fax 024 7683 2440
Email central.library@coventry.gov.co.uk
Website www.coventry.gov.uk/accent.htm
Open 9.00 am to 8.00 pm Monday, Tuesday,
Thursday; 9.30 am to 8.00 pm Wednesday;
9.00 am to 5.00 pm Friday; 9.00 am to 4.30
pm Saturday

Open access
Located in the middle of the city's main shopping centre. Approximately 120,000 items
(books, cassettes, CDs and DVDs) for loan; plus
reference collection of business information and
local history. *Special collections* Cycling and motor
industries; George Eliot; Angela Brazil; Tom
Mann Collection (trade union and labour
studies); local newspapers on microfilm from
1740 onwards. Over 300 periodicals taken.
'Peoplelink' community information database
available.

Department for Environment, Food and Rural Affairs

Nobel House, 17 Smith Square, London
SW1P 3JR
☎020 7238 3000 Fax 020 7238 6591
DEFRA Helpline 08459 335577 (local call
rate): a general contact point providing
information on DEFRA work, either directly
or by referring callers to appropriate contacts.
Available 9.00 am to 5.00 pm Monday to
Friday (excluding Bank Holidays)
Open 9.30 am to 5.00 pm Monday to Friday
Access For reference (but at least 24 hours
notice must be given for intended visits)
Large stock of volumes on temperate agriculture.

Derby Central Library

Wardwick, Derby DE1 1HS
☎01332 255398 Fax 01332 369570
Website www.derby.gov.uk/libraries
Open 9.30 am to 7.00 pm Monday, Tuesday,
Thursday, Friday; 9.30 am to 1.00 pm
Wednesday and Saturday

LOCAL STUDIES LIBRARY
25B Irongate, Derby DE1 3GL
☎01332 255393 Fax 01332 255381

Open 9.30 am to 7.00 pm Monday and
Tuesday; 9.30 am to 5.00 pm Wednesday,
Thursday, Friday; 9.30 am to 1.00 pm
Saturday

Open access
General library for lending, information and
Children's Services. The Central Library also
houses specialist private libraries: Derbyshire
Archaeological Society; Derby Philatelic Society.
The Local Studies Library houses the largest
multimedia collection of resources in existence
relating to Derby and Derbyshire. The collection
includes mss deeds, family papers, business
records including the Derby Canal Company,
Derby Board of Guardians and the Derby China
Factory. Both libraries offer Internet access for a
small charge.

Devon & Exeter Institution Library

7 Cathedral Close, Exeter, Devon EX1 1EZ
☎01392 251017
Email M.Midgley@exeter.ac.uk
Website www.devonandexeterinstitution.org.uk

Open 9.00 am to 5.00 pm Monday to Friday

Access Members only (Temporary membership available)
FOUNDED 1813. Under the administration
of Exeter University Library. Contains over
36,000 volumes, including long runs of 19th-
century journals, theology, history, topography, early science, biography and literature. A
large and growing collection of books, journals, newspapers, prints and maps relating to
the South West.

Doncaster Libraries and Information Services

Central Library, Waterdale, Doncaster, South
Yorkshire DN1 3JE
☎01302 734305 Fax 01302 369749
Email Reference.Library@doncaster.gov.uk

Open 9.30 am to 6.00 pm Monday; 9.00 am
to 6.00 pm Tuesday to Friday; 9.00 am to
4.00 pm Saturday

Open access
Books, cassettes, CDs, videos, picture loans.
Reading aids unit for people with visual handi-
cap; activities for children during school holidays, including visits by authors, etc. Occasional funding available to support literature
activities. Also reference library.

Dorchester Library (part of Dorset County Library)

Colliton Park, Dorchester, Dorset DT1 1XJ
☎01305 224440 (lending)/224448 (reference)
Fax 01305 266120
Email Dorchesterreflibrary@dorset-cc.gov.uk

Open 10.00 am to 7.00 pm Monday; 9.30 am
to 7.00 pm Tuesday, Wednesday, Friday;
9.30 am to 5.00 pm Thursday; 9.00 am to
4.00 pm Saturday

Open access
General lending and reference library,
including Local Studies Collection, special collections on Thomas Hardy, the Powys Family
and William Barnes. Periodicals, children's
library, CD-ROMs, free Internet access. Video
lending service.

Dundee Central Library

The Wellgate, Dundee DD1 1DB
☎01382 434318 Fax 01382 434642
Email central.library@dundeecity.gov.uk
Website www.dundeecity.gov.uk

Open Lending & Local Studies Departments:
9.30 am to 6.00 pm Monday, Tuesday,
Friday; 10.00 am to 6.00 pm Wednesday;
9.30 am to 8.00 pm Thursday; 9.30 am to
5.00 pm Saturday. General Reference
Department: 9.30 am to 9.00 pm Monday,
Tuesday, Thursday, Friday; 10.00 am to
9.00 pm Wednesday; 9.30 am to 5.00 pm
Saturday.

Access Reference services available to all;
lending services to those who live, work, study
or were educated within Dundee City
Adult lending, reference and children's ser-
vices. Art, music, audio, video and DVD lend-
ing services. Internet access. Schools service
(Agency). Housebound and mobile services.
Special collections: The Wighton Collection of
National Music; The Wilson Photographic
Collection; The Lamb Collection.

Durning-Lawrence Library
See **University of London Library**

English Nature

Northminster House, Peterborough,
Cambridgeshire PE1 1UA
☎01733 455000 Fax 01733 568834
Email enquiries@english-nature.org.uk
Website www.english-nature.org.uk

Open 8.30 am to 5.00 pm Monday to
Thursday; 8.30 am to 4.30 pm Friday

Access To *bona fide* students only. Telephone

library for appointment on 01733 455094

Information on nature conservation, nature reserves, SSSIs, planning, legislation, etc. English Nature is the government-funded body whose purpose is to promote the conservation of England's wildlife and natural features.

Equal Opportunities Commission

Arndale House, Arndale Centre, Manchester M4 3EQ
☎0845 601 5901 Fax 0161 838 1733
Email info@eoc.org.uk
Website www.eoc.org.uk

The Library at the EOC is not open to the public. The Customer Contact Point is available to deal with/pass on calls or mail publications.

Essex County Council Libraries

County Library Headquarters, Goldlay Gardens, Chelmsford, Essex CM2 0EW
☎01245 284981 Fax 01245 492780
Email essexlib@essexcc.gov.uk
Website www.essexcc.gov.uk

Essex County Council Libraries has 74 static libraries throughout Essex as well as 13 mobile libraries and three special-needs mobiles. Services to the public include books, newspapers, periodicals, CDs, cassettes, videos, pictures, CD-ROMs and Internet access as well as postal cassettes for the blind and subtitled videos. Specialist subjects and collections are listed below at the relevant library.

Chelmsford Library

PO Box 882, Market Road, Chelmsford, Essex CM1 1LH
☎01245 492758 Fax 01245 492536

Open 9.00 am to 7.00 pm Monday, Tuesday, Thursday, Friday; 10.00 am to 7.00 pm Wednesday; 9.00 am to 5.00 pm Saturday; 1.00 pm to 4.00 pm Sunday

Science and technology, business information and social sciences.

Colchester Library

Trinity Square, Colchester, Essex CO1 1JB
☎01206 245900 Fax 01206 245901

Open 9.00 am to 7.30 pm Monday, Tuesday, Friday; 10.00 am to 7.30 pm Wednesday; 9.00 am to 5.00 pm Thursday and Saturday; 1.00 pm to 4.00 pm Sunday

Local studies, music scores and education. Harsnett collection (early theological works 16th/17th-century); Castle collection (18th-century subscription library); Cunnington collec-

tion; Margaret Lazell collection; Taylor collection.

Harlow Library

The High, Harlow, Essex CM20 1HA
☎01279 413772 Fax 01279 424612

Open 9.00 am to 7.00 pm Monday, Tuesday, Thursday, Friday; 10.00 am to 7.00 pm Wednesday; 9.00 am to 5.00 pm Saturday; 1.00 pm to 4.00 pm Sunday

Fiction, language and literature. Sir John Newson Memorial collection; Maurice Hughes Memorial collection.

Loughton Library

Traps Hill, Loughton, Essex IG10 1HD
☎020 8502 0181 Fax 020 8508 5041

Open 9.30 am to 7.00 pm Monday and Friday; 10.00 am to 7.00 pm Tuesday and Wednesday; 9.30 am to 1.30 pm Thursday; 9.00 am to 5.00 pm Saturday; 1.00 pm to 4.00 pm Sunday
National Jazz Foundation Archive.

Saffron Walden Library

2 King Street, Saffron Walden, Essex CB10 1ES
☎01799 523178 Fax 01799 513642

Open 9.00 am to 7.00 pm Monday, Tuesday, Thursday, Friday; 9.00 am to 5.00 pm Saturday; 1.00 pm to 4.00 pm Sunday (closed Wednesday)

Victorian studies collection.

Witham Library

18 Newland Street, Witham, Essex CM8 2AQ
☎01376 519625 Fax 01376 501913

Open 9.00 am to 7.00 pm Monday, Tuesday, Thursday, Friday; 9.00 am to 5.00 pm Saturday (closed Wednesday)

Drama. Dorothy L. Sayers and Maskell collections.

The Fawcett Library
See **The Women's Library**

Foreign and Commonwealth Office Library

King Charles Street, London SW1A 2AH
☎020 7270 3925 Fax 020 7270 3270
Website www.fco.gov.uk

Access By appointment only

An extensive stock of books, pamphlets and other reference material on all aspects of historical, socio-economic and political subjects relating to countries covered by the Foreign and Commonwealth Office. Particularly strong on colonial history, early works on travel, and photograph collections, mainly of Commonwealth countries and former colonies, c. 1850s–1960s.

Forestry Commission Library
Forest Research Station, Alice Holt Lodge, Wrecclesham, Farnham, Surrey GU10 4LH
☎01420 22255 Fax 01420 23653
Email library@forestry.gsi.gov.uk
Website www.forestry.gov.uk/forest_research
Open 9.00 am to 5.00 pm Monday to Thursday; 9.00 am to 4.30 pm Friday
Access By appointment for personal visits
Approximately 20,000 books on forestry and arboriculture, plus 500 current journals. CD-ROMS include TREECD (1939 onwards). Offers a Research Advisory Service for advice and enquiries on forestry (☎01402 23000) with a charge for consultations and diagnosis of tree problems exceeding ten minutes.

French Institute Library
Institut français, 17 Queensberry Place, London SW7 2DT
☎020 7073 1350 Fax 020 7073 1363
Email library@ambafrance.org.uk
Website www.institut.ambafrance.org.uk
Open 12 noon to 7.00 pm Tuesday to Friday; 12 noon to 6.00 pm Saturday; Children's Library: 12 noon to 6.00 pm Tuesday to Saturday
Open access For reference and consultation (loans restricted to members)
A collection of over 40,000 volumes mainly centred on French cultural interests with special emphasis on language, literature and history. Books in French and English. Collection of videos, periodicals, CDs (French music), CD-ROMs; children's library (8000 books); also a special collection about 'France Libre'. Inter-library loans; quick information service; Internet access. Group visits on request.

John Frost Newspapers
22b Rosemary Avenue, Enfield, Middlesex EN2 0SS
☎020 8366 1392/0946 Fax 020 8366 1379
Email andrew@johnfrostnewspapers.com
Website www.johnfrostnewspapers.co.uk
Contacts *Andrew Frost, John Frost*
A collection of 80,000 original newspapers (1630 to the present day) and 200,000 press cuttings available, on loan, for research and rostrum/stills work (TV documentaries, book and magazine publishers and audiovisual presentations). His-

toric events, politics, sports, royalty, crime, wars, personalities, etc., plus many in-depth files.

Gloucestershire County Council Library Services
Quayside House, Shire Hall, Gloucester GL1 2HY
☎01452 425020 Fax 01452 425042
Email gclams@gloscc.gov.uk
Website www.gloscc.gov.uk
Head of Library Services *Colin Campbell, MBA, ALA*
Open access
The service includes 39 local libraries and six mobile libraries. The website (GlosNet) includes library opening hours, mobile library route schedules; the library catalogue; and a book renewal/reservations facility.

Goethe-Institut Library
50 Princes Gate, Exhibition Road, London SW7 2PH
☎020 7596 4040 Fax 020 7594 0230
Email Library@London.goethe.org
Website www.goethe.de/london
Librarian *Gerlinde Buck*
Open 12.00 am to 8.00 pm Monday to Thursday; 11.00 am to 5.00 pm Saturday
Library specialising in German literature and books/audiovisual material on German culture and history: 25,000 books (4800 of them in English), 140 periodicals, 14 newspapers, 2800 audiovisual media (including 1000 videos), selected press clippings on German affairs from the German and UK press, information service, photocopier, video facility. Also German language teaching material for teachers and students of German.

Goldsmiths' Library
See **University of London Library**

Greater London Record Office
See **London Metropolitan Archives**

Guildford Institute of the University of Surrey Library
Ward Street, Guildford, Surrey GU1 4LH
☎01483 562142
Email c.miles@surrey.ac.uk
Librarian *Clare Miles*
Open 10.00 am to 3.00 pm Tuesday to Friday
Open access To members only but open to enquirers for research purposes
FOUNDED 1834. Some 12,000 volumes of which 7500 were printed before the First World

War. The remaining stock consists of recently published works of fiction, biography and travel. Newspapers and periodicals also available. *Special collections* include an almost complete run of the *Illustrated London News* from 1843–1906, a collection of Victorian scrapbooks, and about 400 photos and other pictures relating to the Institute's history and the town of Guildford. Publishes Library newsletter twice-yearly.

Guildhall Library

Aldermanbury, London EC2P 2EJ
☎See below Fax 020 7600 3384
Website www.corpoflondon.gov.uk

Access For reference (but much of the material is kept in storage areas and is supplied to readers on request; proof of identity is required for consultation of certain categories of stock)

Part of the Corporation of London libraries. Seeks to provide a basic general reference service but its major strength, acknowledged worldwide, is in its historical collections. The library is divided into three sections, each with its own catalogues and enquiry desks. These are: Printed Books; Manuscripts; the Print & Maps Room.

PRINTED BOOKS
☎020 7332 1868/1870

Open 9.30 am to 5 pm Monday to Saturday
NB closes on Saturdays preceding Bank
Holidays; check for details

Strong on all aspects of London history, with wide holdings of English history, topography and genealogy, including local directories, poll books and parish register transcripts. Also good collections of English statutes, law reports, parliamentary debates and journals, and House of Commons papers. Home of several important collections deposited by London institutions: the Marine collection of the Corporation of Lloyd's, the Stock Exchange's historical files of reports and prospectuses, the Clockmakers' Company library and museum (currently under refurbishment; call for further information), the Gardeners' Company, Fletchers' Company, the Institute of Masters of Wine, International Wine and Food Society and Gresham College.

MANUSCRIPTS
☎020 7332 1863
Email manuscripts.guildhall@corpoflondon.gov.uk
Website ihr.sas.ac.uk/gh/

Open 9.30 am to 4.45 pm Monday to Saturday (no requests for records after 4.30

pm) NB closes on Saturdays preceding Bank Holidays; check for details

The official repository for historical records relating to the City of London (except those of the Corporation of London itself, which are housed at the Corporation Records Office). Records date from the 11th century to the present day. They include archives of most of the City's parishes, wards and livery companies, and of many individuals, families, estates, schools, societies and other institutions, notably the Diocese of London and St Paul's Cathedral, as well as the largest collection of business archives in any public repository in the UK. Although mainly of City interest, holdings include material for the London area as a whole and beyond.

PRINT & MAPS ROOM
☎020 7332 1839
Email print&maps@corpoflondon.gov.uk
Website collage.nhil.com

Open 9.30 am to 5.00 pm Monday to Friday

An unrivalled collection of prints and drawings relating to London and the adjacent counties. The emphasis is on topography, but there are strong collections of portraits and satirical prints. The map collection includes maps of the capital from the mid-16th century to the present day and various classes of Ordnance Survey maps. Other material includes photographs, theatre bills and programmes, trade cards, book plates and playing cards as well as a sizeable collection of Old Master prints. Over 30,000 items have been digitally imaged on Collage, including topographical prints, some maps, a small number of photographs and all the Guildhall art collection. Free, *limited* enquiry service available. Also a fee-based service for in-depth research – ☎020 7332 1854 Fax 020 7600 3384 E-mail search.guildhall@corpoflondon.gov.uk Website www.cityoflondon.gov.uk/search_guildhall

Guille–Alles Library

Market Street, St Peter Port, Guernsey, Channel Islands GY1 1HB
☎01481 720392 Fax 01481 712425
Email ga@library.gg
Website www.library.gg

Open 9.00 am to 5.00 pm Monday, Thursday, Friday, Saturday; 10.00 am to 5.00 pm Tuesday; 9.00 am to 8.00 pm Wednesday

Open access For residents; payment of returnable deposit by visitors. Music CD collection: £10 for two-year subscription
Lending, reference and information services. Public Internet service.

Herefordshire Libraries and Information Service

Shirehall, Hereford HR1 2HY
☎01432 359830 Fax 01432 260744
Website www.libraries.herefordshire.gov.uk

Open Opening hours vary in the libraries across the county

Access Information and reference services open to anyone; loans to members only (membership criteria: resident, being educated, working, or an elector in the county or neighbouring authorities; temporary membership to visitors. Proof of identity and address required)

Information service, reference and lending libraries. Non-fiction and fiction for all age groups, including normal and large print, spoken word cassettes, sound recordings (CD and cassette), videos, maps, local history, CD-ROMs for reference at Hereford and Leominster Libraries. Internet access at all libraries. *Special collections* Cidermaking; Beekeeping; Alfred Watkins; John Masefield; Pilley.

University of Hertfordshire Library

College Lane, Hatfield, Hertfordshire
AL10 9AB
☎01707 284678 Fax 01707 284666
Website www.herts.ac.uk/lis

Open See website for term-time and vacation opening hours

Access For reference use of printed collections. Appropriate ID required for Visitor's pass.

There are currently four sites: Art & Design, Engineering & Information Sciences, Health & Human Sciences, Interdisciplinary Studies, Natural Sciences at the main Hatfield campus; the Business School at Hertford, Humanities & Education at the Watford campus near Radlett and law at the Faculty of Law at St Albans.

Highgate Literary and Scientific Institution Library

11 South Grove, London N6 6BS
☎020 8340 3343 Fax 020 8340 5632
Email admin@hlsi.demon.co.uk

Open 10.00 am to 5.00 pm Tuesday to Friday; 10.00 am to 4.00 pm Saturday (closed Sunday and Monday)

Annual membership £42 (individual); £68 (household)

25,000 volumes of general fiction and non-fiction, with a children's section and extensive local archives. *Special collections* on local history,

London, and local poets Samuel Taylor Coleridge and John Betjeman.

Highland Libraries, The Highland Council, Cultural and Leisure Services

Library Support Unit, 31a Harbour Road, Inverness IV1 1UA
☎01463 235713 Fax 01463 236986
Email libraries@highland.gov.uk
Website www.highland.gov.uk

Open Library opening hours vary to suit local needs. Contact administration and support services for details (8.00 am to 6.00 pm Monday to Friday)

Open access
Comprehensive range of lending and reference stock: books, pamphlets, periodicals, newspapers, compact discs, audio and video cassettes, maps, census records, genealogical records, photographs, educational materials, etc. Highland Libraries provides the public library service throughout the Highlands with a network of 41 static and 12 mobile libraries.

Holborn Library

32–38 Theobalds Road, London WC1X 8PA
☎020 7974 6345/6

Open 10.00 am to 7.00 pm Monday and Thursday; 10.00 am to 6.00 pm Tuesday and Friday; 10.00 am to 5.00 pm Saturday (closed all day Wednesday)

Open access
London Borough of Camden public library. Includes a law collection and the London Borough of Camden Local Studies and Archive Centre.

Sherlock Holmes Collection (Westminster)

Marylebone Library, Marylebone Road, London NW1 5PS
☎020 7641 1206 Fax 020 7641 1019
Email c.cooke@dial.pipex.com
Website www.westminster.gov.uk/el/libarch/services/special/sherlock.html

Open 9.30 am to 8.00 pm Monday, Tuesday, Thursday, Friday; 10.00 am to 8.00 pm Wednesday; Closed Saturday and Sunday (unless by prior arrangement)

Access By appointment only
Located in Westminster's Marylebone Library. An extensive collection of material from all over the world, covering Sherlock Holmes

and Sir Arthur Conan Doyle. Books, pamphlets, journals, newspaper cuttings and photos, much of which is otherwise unavailable in this country. Some background material.

Imperial College Central Library
See **Science Museum Library**

Imperial War Museum
Department of Printed Books, Lambeth Road, London SE1 6HZ
☎020 7416 5342 Fax 020 7416 5246
Email books@iwm.org.uk
Website www.iwm.org.uk

Open 10.00 am to 5.00 pm Monday to Saturday (restricted service Saturday; closed on Bank Holiday Saturdays and one week during the year for annual stock check)

Access For reference (but at least 24 hours' notice must be given for intended visits)
A large collection of material on 20th-century life with detailed coverage of the two world wars and other conflicts. Books, pamphlets and periodicals, including many produced for short periods in unlikely wartime settings; also maps, biographies and privately printed memoirs, and foreign language material. Additional research material available in the following departments: Art, Documents, Exhibits and Firearms, Film, Sound Records, Photographs. Active publishing programme based on reprints of rare books held in library. Catalogue available.

Instituto Cervantes
102 Eaton Square, London SW1W 9AN
☎020 7201 0757 Fax 020 7235 0329
Email biblon@cervantes.es
Website www.cervantes.es

Open 12 noon to 6.30 pm Monday to Thursday; 9.30 am to 1.30 pm Saturday (closed Friday)

Open access For reference and lending
Spanish literature, history, art, philosophy. The library houses a collection of books, periodicals, videos, slides, tapes, CDs, cassettes, films and CD-ROMs specialising entirely in Spain and Latin America.

Italian Institute Library
39 Belgrave Square, London SW1X 8NX
☎020 7396 4425 Fax 020 7235 4618
Website www.italcultur.org.uk

Open 10.00 am to 1.00 pm and 2.00 pm to 5.00 pm Monday to Friday

Open access For reference

A collection of over 21,000 volumes relating to all aspects of Italian culture. Texts are mostly in Italian, with some in English.

Jersey Library
Halkett Place, St Helier, Jersey JE2 4WH
☎01534 59991 (lending)/59992 (reference)
Fax 01534 69444
Email piano@itl.net
Website www.jsylib.gov.je

Open 9.30 am to 5.30 pm Monday, Wednesday, Thursday, Friday; 9.30 am to 7.30 pm Tuesday; 9.30 am to 4.00 pm Saturday

Open access
Books, periodicals, newspapers, CDs, cassettes, CD-ROMs, videos, microfilm, specialised local studies collection, public Internet access. Branch Library at Les Quennevais School, St Brelade. Mobile library and homes services.

Kent County Central Library
Kent County Council Arts & Libraries, Springfield, Maidstone, Kent ME14 2LH
☎01622 696511 Fax 01622 696494

Open 9.30 am to 5.30 pm Monday, Wednesday, Friday; 9.30 am to 6.00 pm Tuesday; 9.30 am to 7.00 pm Thursday; 10.00 am to 5.00 pm Saturday

Open access
50,000 volumes available on the floor of the library plus 250,000 volumes of non-fiction, mostly academic, available on request to staff. English literature, poetry, classical literature, drama (including play sets), music (including music sets). Strong, too, in sociology, art history, business information and government publications. Loans to all who live or work in Kent; those who do not may consult stock for reference or arrange loans via their own local library service.

Leeds Central Library
Calverley Street, Leeds, West Yorkshire LS1 3AB
☎0113 247 8274 Fax 0113 247 8426
Website www.leeds.gov.uk/libraries

Open 9.00 am to 8.00 pm Monday and Wednesday; 9.00 am to 5.30 pm Tuesday and Friday; 9.30 am to 5.30 pm Thursday; 10.00 am to 5.00 pm Saturday

Open access to lending libraries; reference material on request

Lending Library covering all subjects.

Music Library contains scores, books, video and audio. ☎0113 247 8273

Business & Research Library Company information, market research, statistics, directories, journals and computer-based information. Extensive files of newspapers and periodicals plus all government publications since 1960. *Special collections* include military history, Judaic, early gardening books and mountaineering. ☎0113 247 8426/8282 E-mail information.for.business @leeds.gov.uk *and* research.and.studies@leeds.gov.uk

Art Library Major collection of material on fine and applied arts. ☎0113 247 8247

Local Studies Library Extensive collection on Leeds and Yorkshire, including maps, books, pamphlets, local newspapers, illustrations and playbills. Census returns for the whole of Yorkshire also available. International Genealogical Index and parish registers. Free public Internet access. ☎0113 247 8290 E-mail local.studies@leeds.gov.uk

Leeds City Libraries has an extensive network of 65 branch and mobile libraries.

Leeds Library

18 Commercial Street, Leeds, West Yorkshire LS1 6AL
☎0113 245 3071 Fax 0113 243 8218

Open 9.00 am to 5.00 pm Monday to Friday

Access To members; research use upon application to the librarian

FOUNDED 1768. Contains over 120,000 books and periodicals from the 15th century to the present day. *Special collections* include Reformation pamphlets, Civil War tracts, Victorian and Edwardian children's books and fiction, European language material, spiritualism and psychical research, plus local material.

Lincoln Central Library

Free School Lane, Lincoln LN2 1EZ
☎01522 510800 Fax 01522 535882
Email lincoln.library@lincolnshire.gov.uk
Website www.lincolnshire.gov.uk

Open 9.30 am to 7.00 pm Monday to Friday; 9.30 am to 4.00 pm Saturday

Open access to the library; appointment required for the Tennyson Research Centre

Lending and reference library. Special collections include Lincolnshire local history (printed and published material, photographs, maps, directories and census data) and the Tennyson Research Centre (contact *Susan Gates*).

Linen Hall Library

17 Donegall Square North, Belfast BT1 5GB
☎028 9032 1707 Fax 028 9043 8586
Email info@linenhall.com
Website www.linenhall.com

Librarian *John Gray*

Open 9.30 am to 5.30 pm Monday to Friday; 9.30 am to 4.00 pm Saturday

Open access For reference (loans restricted to members)

FOUNDED 1788. Contains about 200,000 books. Major Irish and local studies collections, including the Northern Ireland Political Collection relating to the current troubles (c. 250,000 items).

Literary & Philosophical Society of Newcastle upon Tyne

23 Westgate Road, Newcastle upon Tyne NE1 1SE
☎0191 232 0192 Fax 0191 261 4494
Email library@litandphil.org.uk
Website www.litandphil.org.uk

Librarian *Kay Easson*

Open 9.30 am to 7.00 pm Monday, Wednesday, Thursday, Friday; 9.30 am to 8.00 pm Tuesday; 9.30 am to 1.00 pm Saturday

Access Members; research facilities for *bona fide* scholars on application to the Librarian

200-year-old library of 140,000 volumes, periodicals (including 130 current titles), classical music on vinyl recordings and CD, plus a collection of scores. A programme of lectures and recitals provided. Recent publications include: *The Reverend William Turner: Dissent and Reform in Georgian Newcastle upon Tyne* Stephen Harbottle; *History of the Literary and Philosophical Society of Newcastle upon Tyne, Vol. 2 (1896–1989)* Charles Parish; *Bicentenary Lectures 1993* ed. John Philipson.

Liverpool City Libraries

William Brown Street, Liverpool L3 8EW
☎0151 233 5829 Fax 0151 233 5886
Email refbt.central.library@liverpool.gov.uk
Website www.liverpool.gov.uk

Open 9.00 am to 8.00 pm Monday to Thursday; 9.00 am to 7.00 pm Friday; 9.00 am to 5.00 pm Saturday; 12 noon to 4.00 pm Sunday

Open access

Humanities Reference Library A total stock in excess of 120,000 volumes and 24,000 maps, plus book plates, prints and autographed letters. *Special collections* Walter Crane and Edward Lear illustrations, Kelmscott Press, Audubon.

Business and Technology Reference Library Extensive stock dealing with all aspects of science, commerce and technology, including British and European standards and patents and trade directories.

Audio Visual Library Extensive stock relating to all aspects of music. Includes 128,000 volumes and music scores, over 3000 CDs, 2,000 videos and 600 DVDs.

Record Office and Local History Department Printed and audiovisual material relating to Liverpool, Merseyside, Lancashire and Cheshire, together with archive material mainly on Liverpool. Some restrictions on access, with 30-year rule applying to archives.

University of London Library

Senate House, Malet Street, London
WC1E 7HU
☎020 7862 8461/62 (Information Centre)
Fax 020 7862 8480
Email enquiries@ull.ac.uk
Website www.ull.ac.uk

Open Term-time: 9.00 am to 9.00 pm Monday to Thursday; 9.00 am to 6.30 pm Friday; 9.30 am to 5.30 pm Saturday. Vacation: 9.00 am to 6.00 pm Monday to Friday; 9.30 am to 5.30 pm Saturday.

Membership Desk: ☎020 7862 8439/40
Email userservices@ull.ac.uk

The University of London Library is a major academic research library predominantly based across the Humanities and Social Sciences. Housed within its 16 floors in Senate House are some two million titles including 5,500 current periodicals and a wide range of electronic resources. It contains a number of outstanding research collections which, as well as supporting the scholarly activities of the University, attract researchers from throughout the United Kingdom and internationally. These include: English (e.g. the Durning-Lawrence Library and Sterling Collection of first editions); Economic and Society History (the Goldsmiths' Library, containing 70,000 items ranging from 15th to early 19th century); Modern Languages (primarily Romance and Germanic); Palaeography (acclaimed as being the best open access collection in its field in Europe); History (complementary to the Institute of Historical Research); Music, Philosophy (acts as the Library of the Royal Institute of Philosophy); Psychology (includes the BPS library); Major area studies collections (Latin-American – including

Caribbean; United States and Commonwealth Studies, British Government Publications and maps). Check the website for full details of current access arrangements.

The London Institute – London College of Printing: Library and Learning Resources

Elephant and Castle, London SE1 6SB
☎020 7514 6527 (Elephant)/6882 (Back Hill)
Fax 020 7514 6597
Website www.linst.ac.uk/library

Access By arrangement

Library and Learning Resources operates from the two sites of the college at: Elephant & Castle and Back Hill (Clerkenwell, EC1). Books, periodicals, slides, CD-ROMs, videos and computer software on all aspects of the art of the book, printing, management, film/photography, graphic arts, plus retailing. *Special collections* history and development of published and unpublished scripts and the art of the western book.

The London Library

14 St James's Square, London SW1Y 4LG
☎020 7930 7705 Fax 020 7766 4766
Email membership@londonlibrary.co.uk
Website www.londonlibrary.co.uk

Librarian *Miss Inez Lynn*
Open 9.30 am to 5.30 pm Monday, Friday, Saturday; 9.30 am to 7.30 pm Tuesday, Wednesday, Thursday

Access For members only (£150 p.a., 2002)

With over a million books and 8400 members, The London Library 'is the most distinguished private library in the world; probably the largest, certainly the best loved'. Founded in 1841, it is a registered charity and wholly independent of public funding. Its permanent collection embraces most European languages as well as English. Its subject range is predominantly within the humanities, with emphasis on literature, history, fine and applied art, architecture, bibliography, philosophy, religion, and topography and travel. Some 6000–7000 titles are added yearly. Most of the stock is on open shelves to which members have free access. Members may take out up to 10 volumes; 15 if they live more than 20 miles from the Library. The comfortable Reading Room has an annexe for users of personal computers. There are photocopiers, CD-ROM workstations, free access to the Internet, and the Library also offers a postal loans service.

Prospective members are required to submit a refereed application form in advance of admission, but there is at present no waiting list for membership. The London Library Trust may make grants to those who are unable to afford the full annual fee; details on application.

London Metropolitan Archives

40 Northampton Road, London EC1R 0HB
☎020 7332 3820 Fax 020 7833 9136
Email ask.lma@corpoflondon.gov.uk
Website www.cityoflondon.gov.uk
Minicom 020 7278 8703

Open 9.30 am to 4.45 pm Monday, Wednesday, Friday; 9.30 pm to 7.30 pm Tuesday and Thursday; call the Archives for details of Saturday opening hours

Access For reference only
Formerly, the Greater London Record Office Library. Covers all aspects of the life and development of London, specialising in the history and organisation of local government in general, and London in particular. Books on London history and topography, covering many subjects. Also London directories dating back to 1677, plus other source material including Acts of Parliament, Hansard reports, statistical returns, atlases, yearbooks and periodicals.

Lord Louis Library

Orchard Street, Newport, Isle of Wight
PO30 1LL
☎01983 527655/823800 (Reference Library)
Fax 01983 825972
Email reflib@llouis.demon.co.uk

Open 9.00 am to 5.30 pm Monday to Wednesday and Friday; 9.00 am to 8.00 pm Thursday; 9.00 am to 5.00 pm Saturday; 10.00 am to 4.00 pm Sunday

Open access
General adult and junior fiction and non-fiction collections; local history collection and periodicals. Also the county's main reference library.

Manchester Central Library

St Peters Square, Manchester M2 5PD
☎0161 234 1900 Fax 0161 234 1963
Email mclib@libraries.manchester.gov.uk
Website www.manchester.gov.uk/libraries

Open 10.00 am to 8.00 pm Monday to Thursday; 10.00 am to 5.00 pm Friday and Saturday; Commercial and European Units: 10.00 am to 6.00 pm Monday to Thursday; 10.00 am to 5.00 pm Friday and Saturday

Open access
One of the country's leading reference libraries with extensive collections covering all subjects. Departments include: Commercial, European, Technical, Social Sciences, Arts, Music, Local Studies, Chinese, General Readers, Language & Literature. Large lending stock and VIP (visually impaired) service available.

Marylebone Library (Westminster)

See **Sherlock Holmes Collection**

The Mitchell Library

North Street, Glasgow G3 7DN
☎0141 287 2999 Fax 0141 287 2915
Website www.mitchelllibrary.org

Open 9.00 am to 8.00 pm Monday to Thursday; 9.00 am to 5.00 pm Friday and Saturday

Open access
One of Europe's largest public reference libraries with stock of over 1,200,000 volumes. It subscribes to 48 newspapers and more than 2000 periodicals. There are collections in microform, records, tapes and videos, as well as CD-ROMs, electronic databases, illustrations, photographs, postcards, etc.
The library contains a number of special collections, e.g. the Robert Burns Collection (5000 vols), the Scottish Poetry Collection (12,000 items) and the Scottish Drama Collection (1650 items).

Morrab Library

Morrab House, Morrab Gardens, Penzance, Cornwall TR18 4DA
☎01736 364474

Librarian *Annabelle Read*
Open 10.00 am to 4.00 pm Tuesday to Friday; 10.00 am to 1.00 pm Saturday

Access Non-members may use the library for a small daily fee, but may not borrow books
Formerly known as the Penzance Library. An independent subscription lending library of over 40,000 volumes covering virtually all subjects except modern science and technology, with large collections on history, literature and religion. There is a comprehensive Cornish collection of books, newspapers and manuscripts including the Borlase letters; a West Cornwall photographic archive; many runs of 18th- and 19th-century periodicals; a collection of over 2000 books published before 1800.

National Library of Scotland

George IV Bridge, Edinburgh EH1 1EW
☎0131 226 4531 Fax 0131 622 4803
Email enquiries@nls.uk
Website www.nls.uk

Open Main Reading Room: 9.30 am to 8.30 pm Monday, Tuesday, Thursday, Friday; 10.00 am to 8.30 pm Wednesday; 9.30 am to 1.00 pm Saturday. Map Library: 9.30 am to 5.00 pm Monday, Tuesday, Thursday, Friday; 10.00 am to 5.00 pm Wednesday; 9.30 am to 1.00 pm Saturday.

Access To all reading rooms, for research not easily done elsewhere, by reader's ticket

Collection of over seven million volumes. The library receives all British and Irish publications. Large stock of newspapers and periodicals. Many special collections, including early Scottish books, theology, polar studies, baking, phrenology and liturgies. Also large collections of maps, music and manuscripts including personal archives of notable Scottish persons.

National Library of Wales

Aberystwyth, Ceredigion SY23 3BU
☎01970 632800 Fax 01970 615709
Website www.llgc.org.uk

Open 9.30 am to 6.00 pm Monday to Friday; 9.30 am to 5.00 pm Saturday (closed Bank Holidays and first week of October)

Access To reading rooms by reader's ticket, available on application. Open acess to regular exhibition programme and to permanent exhibition 'The Treasures of the Nation'

Collection of over four million books and including large collections of periodicals, maps, manuscripts and audiovisual material. Particular emphasis on humanities in printed foreign material, and on Wales and other Celtic areas in all collections.

National Meteorological Library and Archive

London Road, Bracknell, Berkshire RG12 2SZ
☎01344 854841 Fax 01344 854840
Email metlib@metoffice.com
Website www.metoffice.com

Open Library & Archive: 8.30 am to 4.30 pm Monday to Friday; Archive closed between 1.00 pm and 2.00 pm

Access By Visitor's Pass available from the reception desk; advance notice of a planned visit is appreciated

The major repository of most of the important literature on the subjects of meteorology, climatology and related sciences from the 16th century to the present day. The Library houses a collection of books, journals, articles and scientific papers, plus published climatological data from many parts of the world. The Technical Archive (The Scott Building,

Sterling Centre, Eastern Road, Bracknell, Berks RG12 2PW, ☎01344 855960; Fax 01344 855961) holds the document collection of meteorological data and charts from England, Wales and British overseas bases, including ships' weather logs. Records from Scotland are stored in Edinburgh and those from Northern Ireland in Belfast.

The Natural History Museum Library

Cromwell Road, London SW7 5BD
☎020 7942 5460 Fax 020 7942 5559
Email library@nhm.ac.uk
Website www.nhm.ac.uk/library/index.html

Open 10.00 am to 4.30 pm Monday to Friday

Access To *bona fide* researchers, by reader's ticket on presentation of identification (telephone first to make an appointment)

The library is in five sections: general; botany; zoology; entomology; earth sciences. The sub-department of ornithology is housed at the Zoological Museum, Akeman Street, Tring, Herts HP23 6AP (☎01442 834181). Resources available include books, journals, maps, manuscripts, drawings and photographs covering all aspects of natural history, including palaeontology and mineralogy, from the 14th century to the present day. Also archives and historical collection on the museum itself.

Newcastle upon Tyne City Library

Princess Square, Newcastle upon Tyne NE99 1DX
☎0191 277 4100 Fax 0191 277 4168
Email city.information@newcastle.gov.uk *or* city.reference.library@newcastle.gov.uk *or* business.information.gateway@newcastle. gov.uk
or local.studies@newcastle.gov.uk

Open 9.30 am to 8.00 pm Monday and Thursday; 9.30 am to 5.00 pm Tuesday, Wednesday, Friday; 9.00 am to 5.00 pm Saturday

Open access

Extensive local studies collection, including newspapers, illustrations and genealogy. Also business, science, humanities and arts, open learning resource centre, marketing advice centre. Patents advice centre.

Norfolk Library & Information Service

Norfolk and Norwich Millennium Library, The Forum, Millennium Plain, Norwich, Norfolk NR2 1AW

Website www.norfolk.gov.uk/council/
departments/lis/libhome.htm

Open Lending Library, Reference and
Information Service and Norfolk Studies:
9.00 am to 8.00 pm Monday to Friday; 9.00
am to 5.00 pm Saturday. EXPRESS: 9.00
am to 10.30 pm Monday to Friday; 9.00 am
to 8.30 pm Saturday; 10.30 am to 4.30 pm
Sunday.

Open access
Reference lending library (stock merged
together) with wide range, including books,
recorded music, music scores, plays and videos.
Houses the 2nd Air Division Memorial Library
and has a strong Norfolk Heritage Library.
Extensive range of reference stock including
business information. Online database and CD-
ROM services. Public fax and colour photocopying, free access to the Internet. EXPRESS
(fiction, sound & vision library within a library)
– selection of popular fiction, videos, CDs and
DVDs available, with extended opening hours.

Northamptonshire Libraries & Information Service
Library HQ, PO Box 216, John Dryden
House, 8–10 The Lakes, Northampton
NN4 7DD
☎01604 237959 Fax 01604 237937
Email nrowland@northamptonshire.gov.uk

Since 1991, the Libraries and Information
Service has offered its 'Words Work' diary of literature events. The programme now attracts
exciting literary names as well as new and
locally-based writers. There are three diaries each
year for an adult audience. Poets have an opportunity to read at a variety of venues. Literature
workshops, activities and other events are supported. Regular book displays and dedicated
notice boards in libraries support the programme
across the county.

Northumberland Central Library
The Willows, Morpeth, Northumberland
NE61 1TA
☎01670 534518/534514 Fax 01670 534513

Open 10.00 am to 8.00 pm Monday,
Tuesday, Wednesday, Friday; 9.30 am to
12.30 pm Saturday (closed Thursday)

Open access
Books, periodicals, newspapers, cassettes,
CDs, videos, microcomputers, CD-ROMs,
Internet access, prints, microforms, vocal scores,
playsets, community resource equipment. *Special
collections* **Northern Poetry Library**: 15,000
volumes of modern poetry (see entry under

Organisations of Interest to Poets); Cinema:
comprehensive collection of about 5000 volumes covering all aspects of the cinema; Family
History.

Nottingham Central Library
Angel Row, Nottingham NG1 6HP
☎0115 915 2828 Fax 0115 915 2850
Email arts.library@nottinghamcity.gov.co.uk
Website www.nottinghamcity.gov.uk

Open 9.30 am to 7.00 pm Monday to Friday;
9.00 am to 1.00 pm Saturday

Open access
General public lending library: business
information, online information, the arts, local
studies, religion, community languages, literature. Videos, periodicals, spoken word,
recorded music, CD-ROM service – textual
information on CD-ROM on public access
machines. People's Network Internet, providing free public access. *Special collection* on D.H.
Lawrence. Extensive back-up reserve stocks.
Drama and music sets for loan to groups. Art
gallery – contemporary exhibitions; coffee
shop.

Nottingham Subscription Library Ltd
See **Bromley House Library**

Office for National Statistics, National Statistics Information and Library Service
1 Drummond Gate, London SW1V 2QQ
☎0845 601 3034/Minicom: 01633 812399
Fax 01633 652747
Email info@statistics.gov.uk
Website www.statistics.gov.uk

Open 9.00 am to 5.00 pm; no appointment
required

Also: National Statistics Information and
Library Service, Government Buildings,
Cardiff Road, Newport NP9 1XG

Open as above

Wide range of government statistical publications and access to government Internet-based
data. Census statistical data from 1801; population and health data from 1837; government
social survey reports from 1941; recent international statistical data (UN, Eurostat, etc.);
monograph and periodical collections of statistical methodology. The library in south Wales
holds a wide range of government economic
and statistical publications.

Orkney Library

Laing Street, Kirkwall, Orkney KW15 1NW
☎01856 873166 Fax 01856 875260
Email orkney.library@orkney.gov.uk

Open 9.00 am to 7.00 pm Monday,
Wednesday, Thursday; 9.00 am to 5.00 pm
Tuesday, Friday, Saturday. Archives: 9.00
am to 1.00 pm and 2.00 pm to 4.45 pm
Tuesday to Friday

Open access
Local studies collection. Archive includes
sound and photographic departments.

Oxford Central Library

Westgate, Oxford OX1 1DJ
☎01865 815549 Fax 01865 721694
Email centlib.occdla@dial.pipex.com
Website www.oxfordshire.gov.uk

Open Call 01865 815509 for details
General lending and reference library including the Centre for Oxfordshire Studies. Also
periodicals, audio visual materials, music library,
children's library and Business Information
Point.

PA News Centre

Central Park, New Lane, Leeds,
West Yorkshire LS11 5DZ
☎0870 830 6824 Fax 0870 830 6801
Email palibrary@pa.press.net
Website www.pa.press.net

Open 8.00 am to 8.00 pm Monday to Friday;
10.00 am to 6.00 pm Saturday and Sunday

Open access
PA News, the 24-hour national news and
information group, offers public access to its
press cuttings archive. Covering a wide range of
subjects, the library includes over 14 million cuttings dating back to 1928. Personal callers welcome or research undertaken by in-house staff.

Penzance Library

See **Morrab Library**

City of Plymouth Library and Information Services

Central Library, Drake Circus, Plymouth,
Devon PL4 8AL
Website www.pgfl.plymouth.gov.uk/libraries
and www.webopac.plymouth.uk

Open access

CENTRAL LIBRARY LENDING DEPARTMENTS:
Lending ☎01752 305912
Children's Department ☎01752 305916
Music & Drama Department ☎01752

305914 Email music@plymouth.gov.uk

Open 9.30 am to 7.00 pm Monday and
Friday; 9.30 am to 5.30 pm Tuesday,
Wednesday, Thursday; 9.30 am to 4.00 pm
Saturday

The Lending departments offer books on all
subjects; language courses on cassette and foreign language books; the Holcenberg Jewish
Collection; books on music and musicians,
drama and theatre; music parts and sets of
music parts; play sets; DVDs, videos; song
index; cassettes and CDs.

CENTRAL LIBRARY REFERENCE DEPARTMENTS:
Reference ☎01752 305907/8
Email ref@plymouth.gov.uk
Business Information ☎01752 305906
Email keyinfo@plymouth.gov.uk
**Local Studies & Naval History
Department** ☎01752 305909
Email localstudies@plymouth.gov.uk

Open 9.00 am to 7.00 pm Monday to Friday;
9.00 am to 4.00 pm Saturday

The Reference departments include an extensive collection of Ordnance Survey maps and
town guides; community and census information; marketing and statistical information;
Patents; books on every aspect of Plymouth;
naval history; Mormon Index on microfilm;
Baring Gould manuscript of 'Folk Songs of the
West'.

Plymouth Proprietary Library

Alton Terrace, 111 North Hill, Plymouth,
Devon PL4 8JY
☎01752 660515

Librarian *John R. Smith*
Open Monday to Saturday from 9.30 am
(closing time varies)

Access To members; visitors by appointment
only
FOUNDED 1810. The library contains
approximately 17,000 volumes of mainly 20th-
century work. Member of the **Association of
Independent Libraries**.

The Poetry Library

See entry under **Organisations of Interest
to Poets**

Polish Library

238–246 King Street, London W6 0RF
☎020 8741 0474 Fax 020 8741 7724
Email bibliotekapolska@posk.library.fsnet.co.uk

Librarian *Jadwiga Szmidt*
Open 10.00 am to 8.00 pm Monday and

Wednesday; 10.00 am to 5.00 pm Friday; 10.00 am to 1.00 pm Saturday (library closed Tuesday and Thursday)

Access For reference to all interested in Polish affairs; limited loans to members and *bona fide* scholars only through inter-library loans

Books, pamphlets, periodicals, maps, music, photographs on all aspects of Polish history and culture. *Special collections* Emigré publications; Joseph Conrad and related works; Polish underground publications; bookplates.

Poole Central Library

Dolphin Centre, Poole, Dorset BH15 1QE
☎01202 262424 Fax 01202 262442
Email poolelendlib@hotmail.com

Open 8.00 am to 7.00 pm Monday; 8.30 am to 6.30 pm Tuesday, Wednesday, Thursday; 8.00 am to 6.30 pm Friday; 9.00 am to 5.00 pm Saturday

Open access
General lending and reference library, including Healthpoint health information centre, business information, children's library, periodicals and newspapers, cafe, IT suite and meeting room.

Press Association Library
See **PA News Centre**

Harry Price Library of Magical Literature
University of London Library, Senate House, Malet Street, London WC1E 7HU

Housed at the **University of London Library**. See entry for details of opening times and access.

The collection of Harry Price (1881–1948), the publicist of psychical research, which contains 18,000 books, journals, pamphlets and broadsides. Its holdings are strong from the early modern period onwards and are of particular significance for the history of psychical research and spiritualism in the late 19th and early 20th centuries. Subjects covered include psychic phenomena (especially in England), frauds, conjuring, hypnotism, magic and witchcraft.

Public Record Office
Ruskin Avenue, Kew, Richmond, Surrey TW9 4DU
☎020 8876 3444 Fax 020 8878 8905
Email enquiry@pro.gov.uk
Website www.pro.gov.uk

Also at: The Family Record Centre, 1 Myddleton Street, London EC1R 1UW

Open 9.00 am to 5.00 pm Monday, Wednesday, Friday; 10.00 am to 7.00 pm Tuesday; 9.00 am to 7.00 pm Thursday; 9.30 am to 5.00 pm Saturday

Access For reference, by reader's ticket, available free of charge on production of proof of identity (UK citizens: banker's card or driving licence; non-UK: passport or national identity card. Telephone for further information)

Over 168 kilometres of shelving house the national repository of records of central Government in the UK and law courts of England and Wales, which extend in time from the 11th–20th century. Medieval records and the records of the State Paper Office from the early 16th–late 18th century, plus the records of the Privy Council Office and the Lord Chamberlain's and Lord Steward's departments. Modern government department records, together with those of the Copyright Office dating mostly from the late 18th century. Under the Public Records Act, records are normally only open to inspection when they are 30 years old.

Reading Central Library
Abbey Square, Reading, Berkshire RG1 3BQ
☎0118 901 5955 Fax 0118 901 5954
Email info@readinglibraries.org.uk
Website www.readinglibraries.org.uk

Open 9.30 am to 5.30 pm Monday and Friday; 9.30 am to 7.00 pm Tuesday and Thursday; 9.30 am to 5.00 pm Wednesday and Saturday

Open access
Lending library; reference library; local studies library, bringing together every aspect of the local environment and human activity in Berkshire; business library; music and drama library. Special collections: Mary Russell Mitford; local illustrations.

Public meeting room available.

Religious Society of Friends Library
Friends House, 173 Euston Road, London NW1 2BJ
☎020 7663 1135 Fax 020 7663 1001
Email library@quaker.org.uk
Website www.quaker.org.uk

Open 1.00 pm to 5.00 pm Monday, Tuesday, Thursday, Friday; 10.00 am to 5.00 pm Wednesday

Open access A letter of introduction from a college/employer/publisher/Friends meeting is required for researchers who are not members of the Society

Quaker history, thought and activities from the 17th century onwards. Supporting collections on peace, anti-slavery and other subjects in which Quakers have maintained long-standing interest. Also archives and manuscripts relating to the Society of Friends.

Richmond Central Reference Library

Old Town Hall, Whittaker Avenue, Richmond, Surrey TW9 1TP
☎020 8940 5529 Fax 020 8940 6899
Email reference.services@richmond.gov.uk
Website www.richmond.gov.uk

Open 10.00 am to 6.00 pm Monday, Thursday, Friday (Tuesday until 1.00 pm; Wednesday until 8.00 pm and Saturday until 5.00 pm)

Open access
General reference library serving the needs of local residents and organisations. Internet access and online databases for public use.

Royal Anthropological Institute Library
See **British Museum Department of Ethnography – Anthropology Library**

Royal Geographical Society Library (with the Institute of British Geographers)
1 Kensington Gore, London SW7 2AR
☎020 7591 3040 Fax 020 7591 3001
Website www.rgs.org

The Library and Map Room are closed for major refurbishment until December 2003. The Archives remain open to Fellows and non-Fellows by appointment only on Thursdays and Fridays. All enquiries should be made in writing to the Archives Assistant (archives@rgs.org). For information on the Picture Library see entry under **Picture Libraries**.

Royal Institute of Philosophy
See **University of London Library**

Royal Society Library
6 Carlton House Terrace, London SW1Y 5AG
☎020 7451 2606 Fax 020 7930 2170
Email library@royalsoc.ac.uk
Website www.royalsoc.ac.uk

Open 10.00 am to 5.00 pm Monday to Friday

Access For research only, to *bona fide*

researchers; contact the Library in advance of first visit

History of science, scientists' biographies, science policy reports, and publications of international scientific unions and national academies from all over the world.

RSA (Royal Society for the Encouragement of Arts, Manufactures & Commerce)
8 John Adam Street, London WC2N 6EZ
☎020 7930 5115 Fax 020 7839 5805
Website www.rsa.org.uk

Open Library: 8.30 am to 8.00 pm every weekday. Archive material by appointment

Access to Fellows of RSA; by application and appointment to non-Fellows (Contact *Julie Cranage* Library Services Coordinator, ☎020 7451 6874 or e-mail julie.cranage@rsa.org.uk)

Archives of the Society since 1754. A collection of approximately 10,000 volumes; international exhibition material.

Royal Society of Medicine Library
1 Wimpole Street, London W1G 0AE
☎020 7290 2940 Fax 020 7290 2939
Email library@rsm.ac.uk
Website www.rsm.ac.uk

Director of Information Services *Ian Snowley*
Head of Customer Services *Sheron Burton*
Open 9.00 am to 8.30 pm Monday to Friday; 10.00 am to 5.00 pm Saturday

Access For reference only, on introduction by Fellow of the Society (temporary membership is available to non-members; £10 per day; £25 per week; £75 per month)

Books and periodicals on general medicine, biochemistry and biomedical science. Extensive historical material and portrait collection.

St Bride Printing Library
Bride Lane, London EC4Y 8EE
☎020 7353 4660 Fax 020 7583 7073
Email stbride@corpoflondon.gov.uk
Website www.stbride.org

Open 9.30 am to 5.30 pm Monday to Friday

Open access
Corporation of London public reference library. Appointments advisable for consultation of special collections. Every aspect of printing and related matters: publishing and bookselling, newspapers and magazines, graphic design, calligraphy and type, papermaking and bookbinding. One of the world's largest specialist

collections in its field, with over 50,000 volumes, over 3000 periodicals (200 current titles), and extensive collection of drawings, manuscripts, prospectuses, patents and materials for printing and typefounding. Noted for its comprehensive holdings of historical and early technical literature.

Science Fiction Foundation Research Library

Liverpool University Library, PO Box 123, Liverpool L69 3DA
☎0151 794 3142 Fax 0151 794 2681
Email asawyer@liverpool.ac.uk
Website www.liv.ac.uk/~asawyer/sffchome.html

Contact *Andy Sawyer*

Access For research, by appointment only (telephone first)

This is the largest collection outside the US of science fiction and related material – including autobiographies and critical works. *Special collection* Runs of 'pulp' magazines dating back to the 1920s. Foreign-language material (including a large Russian collection), and the papers of the Flat Earth Society. The collection also features a growing range of archive and manuscript material, including the Eric Frank Russell archive. The University of Liverpool also holds the Olaf Stapledon and John Wyndham archives.

Science Museum Library

Imperial College Road, London SW7 5NH
☎020 7942 4242 Fax 020 7942 4243
Email smlinfo@nmsi.ac.uk
Website www.nmsi.ac.uk/library

Open 9.30 am to 9.00 pm Monday to Friday (closes 5.30 pm outside academic terms); 9.30 am to 5.30 pm Saturday

Open access Reference only; no loans

National reference library for the history and public understanding of science and technology, with a large collection of source material. Operates jointly with Imperial College Central Library.

Scottish Poetry Library

See entry under **Organisations of Interest to Poets**

Sheffield Libraries, Archives and Information

Central Library, Surrey Street, Sheffield S1 1XZ
☎0114 273 4712 Fax 0114 273 5009

Central Lending Library
☎0114 273 4727 (enquiries)/4729 (renewals)

Open 10.00 am to 8.00 pm Monday; 9.30 am to 5.30 pm Tuesday and Friday; 9.30 am to 8.00 pm Wednesday; 9.30 am to 5.30 pm Saturday (closed Thursday)

Books, talking books, large print, language courses, European fiction, books in cultural languages, play sets. Writers' Resource Centre, Wednesday evenings, 5.00 pm to 7.00 pm. Proof of signature and a separate proof of address required to join.

Sheffield Archives
52 Shoreham Street, Sheffield S1 4SP
☎0114 203 9395 Fax 0114 203 9398
Email sheffield.archives@dial.pipex.com

Open 10.00 am to 5.30 pm Monday; 9.30 am to 5.30 pm Tuesday to Thursday; 9.30 am to 1.00 pm and 2.00 pm to 5.00 pm Saturday (documents should be ordered by 5.00 pm Thursday for Saturday); closed Friday

Access By reader's pass

Holds documents relating to Sheffield and South Yorkshire, dating from the 12th century to the present day, including records of the City Council, churches, businesses, landed estates, families and individuals, institutions and societies.

Arts and Social Sciences Reference Service
☎0114 273 4747/8

Open 10.00 am to 8.00 pm Monday; 9.30 am to 5.30 pm Tuesday and Friday; 9.30 am to 8.00 pm Wednesday; 9.30 am to 5.30 pm Saturday (closed Thursday)

Access For reference only

A comprehensive collection of books, periodicals and newspapers covering all aspects of arts (excluding music) and social sciences.

Music and Video Service
☎0114 273 4733

Open as for Arts and Social Sciences above

Access For reference (loans to ticket holders only)

An extensive range of books, CDs, cassettes, scores, etc. related to music. Also a video cassette and DVD loan service.

Local Studies Service
☎0114 273 4753

Open as for Arts & Social Sciences above (except Wednesday 9.30 am to 5.30 pm)

Access For reference

Extensive material covering all aspects of Sheffield and its population, including maps, photos and videos.

Business, Science and Technology Reference Services

☎0114 273 4736/7 or 273 4742

Open as for Arts & Social Sciences above

Access For reference only

Extensive coverage of science and technology as well as commerce and commercial law. British patents and British and European standards with emphasis on metals. Hosts the World Metal Index. The business section holds a large stock of business and trade directories, plus overseas telephone directories and reference works with business emphasis.

Sheffield Information Service

☎0114 273 4761/4712 Fax 0114 275 7111

Email nd54@dial.pipex.com

Website dis.shef.ac.uk/help_yourself

Open 10.00 am to 5.30 pm Monday; 9.30 am to 5.30 pm Tuesday, Wednesday, Friday; 9.30 am to 4.30 pm Saturday (closed Thursday)

Full local information service covering all aspects of the Sheffield community and a generalist advice service on a sessional basis.

Children's and Young People's Library Service

☎0114 273 4734

Open 10.30 am to 5.00 pm Monday and Friday; 1.00 pm to 5.00 pm Tuesday and Wednesday; 9.30 am to 4.30 pm Saturday (closed Thursday)

Books, spoken word sets, videos; under-five play area; teenage reference section; readings and promotions; storytime sessions.

Sports Library

☎0114 273 5929

Email sports.library@dial.pipex.com

Open 10.00 am to 1.00 pm and 2.00 pm to 6.00 pm Monday and Wednesday; 10.00 pm to 1.00 pm and 2.00 pm to 4.30 pm Tuesday and Friday (closed Thursday and Saturday)

Information on all aspects of sport and physical recreation including sports medicine, physiology, nutrition, coaching, recreation management, sports history. Special collection on mountaineering.

Shetland Library

Lower Hillhead, Lerwick, Shetland ZE1 0EL

☎01595 693868 Fax 01595 694430

Email info@shetland-library.gov.uk

Website www.shetland-library.gov.uk

Open 10.00 am to 7.00 pm Monday, Wednesday, Thursday; 10.00 am to 5.00 pm Tuesday, Friday, Saturday

General lending and reference library; extensive local interest collection including complete set of *The Shetland Times, The Shetland News* and other local newspapers on microfilm and many old and rare books; audio collection including talking books/newspapers. Junior room for children. Disabled access and Housebound Readers Service (delivery to reader's home). Mobile library services to rural areas. Open Learning Service. Same day photocopying service. Publishing programme of books in dialect, history, literature.

Shoe Lane Library

Hill House, Little New Street, London EC4A 3JR

☎020 7583 7178 Fax 020 7353 0884

Email shoelane@corpoflondon.gov.uk

Website www.corpoflondon.gov.uk

Open 9.30 am to 5.30 pm Monday, Wednesday, Thursday, Friday; 9.30 am to 6.30 pm Tuesday

Open access

Corporation of London general lending library, with a comprehensive stock of 50,000 volumes, most of which are on display.

Shrewsbury Library

Castlegates, Shrewsbury, Shropshire SY1 2AS

☎01743 255300 Fax 01743 255309

Email shrewsbury.library@shropshire-cc. gov.uk

Website www.shropshire-cc.gov.uk/library.nsf

Open 9.30 am to 5.00 pm Monday and Wednesday; 9.30 am to 1.00 pm Thursday; 9.30 am to 7.30 pm Tuesday and Friday; 9.30 am to 4.00 pm Saturday

Open access

The largest public lending library in Shropshire. Books, cassettes, CDs, talking books, DVDs, videos, language courses. Open Learning, homework and study centre with public use computers for word processing, CD-ROMs and Internet access. Strong music, literature and art book collection. Reference and local studies provision in adjacent buildings.

Spanish Institute Library
See **Instituto Cervantes**

Sterling Collection
See **University of London Library**

Suffolk County Council Libraries & Heritage
St Andrew House, County Hall, St Helens Street, Ipswich, Suffolk IP4 1LJ
☎01473 584564 Fax 01473 584549
Email infolink@libher.suffolkcc.gov.uk (general enquiries)
Website www.suffolkcc.gov.uk/libraries

Open Details on application to St Andrew House above. Major libraries open six days a week

Access A single user registration card gives access to the lending service of 42 libraries across the county
Full range of lending and reference services. Free public access to the Internet and multimedia CD-ROMs in all libraries. Catalogue with self-service facilities for registered borrowers available on the website. *Special collections* include Suffolk Archives and Local History Collection; Benjamin Britten Collection; Edward Fitzgerald Collection; Seckford Collection and Racing Collection (Newmarket). The Suffolk Infolink service gives details of local groups and societies and is available in libraries throughout the county and on the website.

Sunderland City Library and Arts Centre
28–30 Fawcett Street, Sunderland, Tyne & Wear SR1 1RE
☎0191 514 1235 Fax 0191 514 8444
Email enquiry.desk@edcom.sunderland.gov.uk

Open 9.30 am to 7.30 pm Monday and Wednesday; 9.30 am to 5.00 pm Tuesday, Thursday, Friday; 9.30 am to 4.00 pm Saturday

The city's main library for lending and reference services. Local studies and children's sections, plus Sound and Vision department (CDs, cassettes, videos, CD-ROMs, talking books). The City of Sunderland also maintains community libraries of varying size, offering a range of services, plus mobile libraries. Free Internet access is available in all libraries across the city. A Books on Wheels service is available to housebound readers; the Schools Library Service serves teachers and schools. Two writ-

ers' groups meet at the City Library and Arts Centre: Janus Writers, every Wednesday, 1.30 pm to 3.30 pm. Tuesday Writers, every Tuesday, 7.30 pm to 9.30 pm.

Swansea Central Reference Library
Alexandra Road, Swansea SA1 5DX
☎01792 516753/516757 Fax 01792 615759
Email central.library@swansea.gov.uk
Website www.swansea.gov.uk/culture/ libraries/libraryIntro.htm

Open 9.00 am to 7.00 pm Monday, Tuesday, Wednesday, Friday; 9.00 am to 5.00 pm Thursday and Saturday. The library has a lending service but hours tend to be shorter – check in advance (☎01792 516750/1)

Access For reference only (Local Studies closed access: items must be requested on forms provided)
General reference material; also British standards, statutes, company information, maps, European Community information. Local studies: comprehensive collections on Wales; Swansea & Gower; Dylan Thomas. Local maps, periodicals, illustrations, local newspapers from 1804. B&w and colour photocopying facilities, access to the Internet and microfilm/microfiche copying facility.

Swiss Cottage Central Library
88 Avenue Road, London NW3 3HA
☎020 7974 6522

Open 10.00 am to 7.00 pm Monday and Thursday; 10.00 am to 6.00 pm Tuesday, Wednesday, Friday; 10.00 am to 5.00 pm Saturday

Open access
Over 300,000 volumes in the lending and reference libraries. Home of the London Borough of Camden's Information and Reference Services. Refurbishment during 2002 means no access to some categories of stock.

Theatre Museum Library & Archive
1e Tavistock Street, London WC2E 7PR
☎020 7943 4700 Fax 020 7943 4777
Website theatremuseum.org

Open 10.30 am to 4.30 pm Tuesday to Friday

Access By appointment only
The Theatre Museum was founded as a separate department of the Victoria & Albert Museum in 1974 and moved to its own building in Covent Garden in 1987. The museum (open Tuesday to Sunday 10.00 am to 6.00 pm) houses

permanent displays, temporary exhibitions, a studio theatre, and organises a programme of special events, performances, lectures, guided visits and workshops. The library houses the UK's largest performing arts research collections, including books, photographs, designs, engravings, programmes, press cuttings, etc. All the performing arts are covered but strengths are in the areas of theatre, dance, musical theatre and stage design. The Theatre Museum has acquired much of the British Theatre Association's library and is providing reference access to its collections of play texts and critical works.

Thurrock Council Leisure, Libraries & Cultural Services Department

Grays Library, Orsett Road, Grays, Essex RM17 5DX
☎01375 383611 Fax 01375 370806
Email acairns@thurrock.gov.uk (Virtual Enquiry Desk)

Open 9.00 am to 7.00 pm Monday, Tuesday, Thursday; 9.00 am to 5.00 pm Wednesday, Friday, Saturday; branch library opening times vary

Open access
General library lending and reference through ten libraries and a mobile library. Services include books, magazines, newspapers, audiocassettes, CDs, videos and language courses. Large collection of Thurrock materials. Internet and word processing.

Truro Library

Union Place, Pydar Street, Truro, Cornwall TR1 1EP
☎01872 279205 (lending)/272702 (reference)

Open 9.30 am to 5.00 pm Monday to Thursday; 9.30 am to 7.00 pm Friday; 9.00 am to 4.00 pm Saturday

Books, cassettes, CDs, videos and DVDs for loan through branch or mobile networks. Reference collection. *Special collections* on local studies.

United Nations Information Centre

Millbank Tower (21st Floor), 21–24 Millbank, London SW1P 4QH
☎020 7630 1981 Fax 020 7976 6478
Email info@uniclondon.org
Website www.unitednations.org.uk

Open Library: 9.00 am to 1.00 pm and 2.00 pm to 6.00 pm Monday to Thursday

Access By appointment only
A full stock of official publications and documentation from the United Nations.

Western Isles Libraries

Public Library, 19 Cromwell Street, Stornoway, Isle of Lewis HS1 2DA
☎01851 708631 Fax 01851 708676

Open 10.00 am to 5.00 pm Monday to Thursday; 10.00 am to 7.00 pm Friday; 10.00 am to 5.00 pm Saturday

Open access
General public library stock, plus local history and Gaelic collections including maps, printed music, cassettes and CDs; census records and Council minutes; music collection (cassettes). Branch libraries on the isles of Barra, Benbecula, Harris and Lewis.

City of Westminster Archives Centre

10 St Ann's Street, London SW1P 2DE
☎020 7641 5180/Minicom: 020 7641 4879
Fax 020 7641 5179
Email archives@westminster.gov.uk
Website www.westminster.gov.uk

Open 9.30 am to 5.00 pm Monday, Friday, Saturday; 9.30 am to 7.00 pm Tuesday, Wednesday, Thursday

Access For reference
Comprehensive coverage of the history of Westminster and selective coverage of general London history. 22,000 books, together with a large stock of maps, prints, photographs, local newspapers, theatre programmes and archives.

Westminster Music Library

Victoria Library, 160 Buckingham Palace Road, London SW1W 9UD
☎020 7641 4292 Fax 020 7641 4281
Email westmuslib@dial.pipex.com
Website www.westminster.gov.uk/libraries/ special/music

Open 11.00 am to 7.00 pm Monday to Friday; 10 am to 5.00 pm Saturday

Open access
Located at Victoria Library, this is the largest public music library in the South of England, with extensive coverage of all aspects of music, including books, periodicals and printed scores. No recorded material, notated only. Lending library includes a small collection of CDs and videos.

Westminster Reference Library

35 St Martin's Street, London WC2H 7HP
☎020 7641 4636 Fax 020 7641 4606
Email westreflib@dial.pipex.com
Website www.westminster.gov.uk/libraries/
libraries/westref

General Reference & Performing Arts:
☎020 7641 4636

Art & Design: ☎020 7641 4638

Business and Official Publications:
☎020 7641 4634

Open 10.00 am to 8.00 pm Monday to
Friday; 10.00 am to 5.00 pm Saturday

Access For reference only
General reference library with emphasis on:
Art & Design – fine and decorative arts, architecture, graphics and design; Performing Arts –
theatre, cinema, radio, television and dance;
Official Publications – major collection of
HMSO publications from 1947, plus parliamentary papers dating back to 1906; Business – UK
directories, trade directories, company and
market data; Official EU Depository Library –
carries official EU material; Periodicals – long
files of many titles. One working day's notice is
required for some government documents, some
monographs and most older periodicals.

The Wiener Library

4 Devonshire Street, London W1W 5BH
☎020 7636 7247 Fax 020 7436 6428
Email info@wienerlibrary.co.uk
Website wienerlibrary.co.uk

Director *Ben Barkow*
Education and Outreach Coordinator
Katherin Klinger
Open 10.00 am to 5.30 pm Monday to Friday

Access By letter of introduction (readers needing to use the Library for any length of time
should become members)
Private library – one of the leading research
centres on European history since the First
World War, with special reference to the era of
totalitarianism and to Jewish affairs. Founded
by Dr Alfred Wiener in Amsterdam in 1933, it
holds material that is not available elsewhere.
Books, periodicals, press archives, documents,
pamphlets, leaflets and brochures. Much of the
material can be consulted on microfilm.

Vaughan Williams Memorial Library

English Folk Dance and Song Society, Cecil
Sharp House, 2 Regent's Park Road, London
NW1 7AY

☎020 7485 2206 ext. 18/19
Fax 020 7284 0523
Email library@efdss.org
Website www.efdss.org

Open 9.30 am to 5.30 pm Tuesday to Friday;
10.00 am to 4.00 pm 1st & 3rd Saturday
(sometimes closed between 1.00 pm and
2.00 pm)

Access For reference to the general public, on
payment of a daily fee; members may borrow
books and use the library free of charge
A multimedia collection: books, periodicals,
manuscripts, tapes, records, CDs, films, videos.
Mostly British traditional culture and how this
has developed around the world. Some foreign
language material, and some books in English
about foreign cultures. Also, the history of the
English Folk Dance and Song Society.

Dr Williams's Library

14 Gordon Square, London WC1H 0AR
☎020 7387 3727

Open 10.00 am to 5.00 pm Monday,
Wednesday, Friday; 10.00 am to 6.30 pm
Tuesday and Thursday

Open access to reading room (loans restricted
to subscribers). Visitors required to supply
identification

Annual subscription £10; ministers of religion and certain students £5
Primarily a library of theology, religion and
ecclesiastical history. Also philosophy, history
(English and Byzantine). Particularly important
for the study of English Nonconformity.
Trustees of Dr William's Library manage the
Congregational Library on behalf of the
Memorial Hall Trustees.

Wolverhampton Central Library

Snow Hill, Wolverhampton WV1 3AX
☎01902 552025 (lending)/552026 (reference)
Fax 01902 552024
Email wolverhampton.libraries@dial.pipex.com
Website www.wolverhampton.gov.uk

Open 9.00 am to 7.00 pm Monday to
Thursday; 9.00 am to 5.00 pm Friday and
Saturday

Archives & Local Studies Collection
42–50 Snow Hill, Wolverhampton WV2 4AB
☎01902 552480

Open 10.00 am to 5.00 pm Monday,
Tuesday, Friday, 1st and 3rd Saturday of
each month; 10.00 am to 7.00 pm
Wednesday; closed Thursday

General lending and reference libraries, plus

children's library and audiovisual library holding cassettes, CDs, videos and music scores. Internet access.

The Women's Library

Old Castle Street, London E1 7NT
☎020 7320 2222 Fax 020 7320 2333
Email moreinfo@thewomenslibrary.ac.uk
Website www.thewomenslibrary.ac.uk
Open Reading Room: 9.30 am to 5.00 pm
Tuesday to Friday (8.00 pm Thursday);
10.00 am to 4.00 pm Saturday

Open access

The Women's Library, national research library for women's history, is the UK's oldest and most comprehensive research library on all aspects of women in society, with both historical and contemporary coverage. The Library includes materials on feminism, work, education, health, the family, law, arts, sciences, technology, language, sexuality, fashion and the home. The main emphasis is on Britain but many other countries are represented, especially the Commonwealth and the Third World. Established in 1926 as the library of the London Society of Women's Service (formerly Suffrage), a non-militant organisation led by Millicent Fawcett. In 1953 the Society was renamed after her and the library became the Fawcett Library.

Collections include: women's suffrage, work, education; women and the church, the law, sport, art, music; abortion, prostitution. Mostly British materials but some American, Commonwealth and European works. Books, journals, pamphlets, archives, photographs, posters, postcards, audiovisual materials, artefacts, scrapbooks, albums and press cuttings dating mainly from the 19th century although some materials date from the 17th century.

The Library's new building, which opened in February 2002, includes a reading room, exhibition space, café, education areas and a conference room, and is the cultural and research centre for anyone interested in women's lives and achievements.

Worcestershire Libraries and Information Service

Cultural Services, Worcestershire County Council, County Hall, Spetchley Road, Worcester WR5 2NP
☎01905 766231 Fax 01905 766244
Website www.worcestershire.gov.uk/libraries
Open Opening hours vary in the 22 libraries,

the History Centre and mobile libraries covering the county; all full-time libraries open at least one evening a week until 7.00 pm or 8.00 pm, and on Saturday until 1 pm; 8 largest libraries open until 4.00 pm on Saturday; part-time libraries vary

Access Information and reference services open to anyone; loans to members only (membership criteria: resident, being educated, working, or an elector in the county or neighbouring authorities; temporary membership to visitors. Proof of identity and address required. No charge for membership or for borrowing books.)

Information service, and reference and lending libraries. Non-fiction and fiction for all age groups, including normal and large print, spoken word cassettes, sound recordings (CD, cassette), videos, maps, local history, CD-ROMs for reference at main libraries, free public Internet access in all libraries. Joint Libraries Service/County Record Office History Centre with resources for local and family history. *Special collections* Carpets and Textiles; Needles & Needlemaking; Stuart Period; A.E. Housman.

York Central Library

Museum Street, York YO1 7DS
☎01904 655631 Fax 01904 611025

Lending Library
Open 9.30 am to 8.00 pm Monday, Tuesday, Friday; 9.30 am to 5.30 pm Wednesday and Thursday; 9.30 am to 4.00 pm Saturday

General lending library including videos, CDs, music cassettes, audio books, children's storytapes language courses and printed music. Photocopying and fax facilities.

Reference Library
Open 9.00 am to 8.00 pm Monday, Tuesday, Wednesday, Friday; 9.00 am to 5.30 pm Thursday; 9.00 am to 4.00 pm Saturday

General reference library; organisations database; local studies library for York and surrounding area; business information service; microfilm/fiche readers for national and local newspapers; census returns and family history resource; general reference collection. Maintains strong links with other local history resource centres, namely the Borthwick Institute, York City Archive and York Minster Library. CD-ROM and Internet facilities. Room 18: IT resource centre available to the public. In addition, 14 branch libraries and one mobile, serving the City of York Council area.

Young Booktrust Children's Reference Library

Book House, 45 East Hill, London
SW18 2QZ
☎020 8516 2985 Fax 020 8516 2978
Email ed@booktrust.org.uk
Website www.booktrust.org.uk *and*
www.booktrusted.com
Contact *Mr E. Zaghini*
Open 9.00 am to 5.00 pm Monday to Friday
(by appointment only)
Access For reference only

A comprehensive collection of children's literature, related books and periodicals. Aims to hold most of all children's titles published within the last two years. An information service covers all aspects of children's literature, including profiles of authors and illustrators. Reading room facilities.

Zoological Society Library

Regent's Park, London NW1 4RY
☎020 7449 6293 Fax 020 7586 5743
Email library@zsl.org
Website www.zsl.org
Open 9.30 am to 5.30 pm Monday to Friday

Access To members and staff; non-members by application and on payment of fee

160,000 volumes on zoology including 5000 journals (1300 current) and a wide range of books on animals and particular habitats. Slide collection available and many historic zoological prints.

Picture Libraries

A–Z Botanical Collection Ltd

192 Goswell Road, London EC1V 7DT
☎020 7253 0991 Fax 020 7253 0992
Email azbotanical@yahoo.com
Website www.a–z.picture-library.com

Contact *James Wakefield*

300,000 transparencies, specialising in plants and related subjects.

Acme

See **Popperfoto**

Action Plus

54–58 Tanner Street, London SE1 3PH
☎020 7403 1558 Fax 020 7403 1526
Email info@actionplus.co.uk
Website www.actionplus.co.uk

FOUNDED 1986. Specialist sports and action library with a vast comprehensive collection of small-format colour and b&w images covering all aspects of over 130 professional and amateur sports from around the world. As well as personalities, events, venues, etc, also covers themes such as success, celebration, dejection, teamwork, effort and exhaustion. 35mm colour stock and online digital archive.

Lesley & Roy Adkins Picture Library

Ten Acre Wood, Whitestone, Exeter, Devon EX4 2HW
☎01392 811357 Fax 01392 811435
Email mail@adkinsarchaeology.com
Website www.adkinsarchaeology.com

Colour coverage of archaeology, heritage and related subjects in the UK, Europe, Egypt and Turkey. Subjects include towns, villages, housing, landscape and countryside, churches, temples, castles, monasteries, art and architecture, gravestones and tombs, inscriptions and antiquarian views. No service charge if pictures are used.

The Advertising Archive Limited

45 Lyndale Avenue, London NW2 2QB
☎020 7435 6540 Fax 020 7794 6584
Email suzanne@advertisingarchives.co.uk
Website www.advertisingarchives.co.uk

Contacts *Suzanne Viner, Larry Viner*

With over one million images, the largest collection of British and American press ads, TV commercial stills and magazine cover illustrations in Europe. Material spans the period from 1850 to the present day. Expert in-house research; rapid service, competitive rates. On-line database and digital delivery available. Visitors by appointment.

AKG London Ltd, The Arts and History Picture Library

5 Melbray Mews, 158 Hurlingham Road, London SW6 3NS
☎020 7610 6103 Fax 020 7610 6125
Email enquiries@akg-london.co.uk
Website www.akg-london.co.uk

Contact *Julia Engelhardt*

Collection of 250,000 images with direct access to ten million (100,000 available via ISDN as high resolution scans) kept in the Berlin AKG Library. *Specialises* in art, archaeology, history, topography, music, personalities and film.

Bryan & Cherry Alexander Photography

Higher Cottage, Manston, Sturminster Newton, Dorset DT10 1EZ
☎01258 473006 Fax 01258 473333
Email alexander@arcticphoto.co.uk
Website www.arcticphoto.co.uk

Contact *Cherry Alexander*

Arctic and Antarctic specialists; indigenous peoples, wildlife and science in polar regions; Norway, Iceland, Siberia and Alaska.

Allsport (UK)

3 Greenlea Park, Prince George's Road, London SW19 2JD
☎020 8685 1010 Fax 020 8648 5240
Email allsportlondon@gettyimages.com *and* www.mhomes@allsport.co.uk
Website www.allsport.com

Part of **Getty Images** (UK) Ltd, Allsport is a large specialist library with six million colour transparencies, covering 140 different sports and top sports personalities. Represented in 27 countries worldwide. Digital wiring facilities through Macintosh picture desk. Online digital archive access available via ISDN and Internet.

Alpine Garden Society

AGS Centre, Avon Bank, Pershore, Worcester WR10 3JP
☎01386 554790 Fax 01386 554801
Email ags@alpinegardensociety.org
Website www.alpinegardensociety.org

Contact *Peter Sheasby*

Over 16,000 colour transparencies (35mm) covering plants in the wild from many parts of the world; particularly strong in plants from mountain and sub-alpine regions, and from Mediterranean climates – South Africa, Australia, California and the Mediterranean. Extensive coverage of show alpines in pots and in gardens and of European orchids. Full slide list available.

Alvey & Towers

Enterprise House, Ashby Road, Coalville, Leicestershire LE67 3LA
☎01530 450011 Fax 01530 450011
Email alveytower@aol.com
Website www.alveyandtowers.com

Contact *Emma Rowen*

Houses one of the country's most comprehensive collections of transport images depicting not only actual transport systems but their surrounding industries as well. Also specialist modern railway image collection.

Andalucia Slide Library

Apto 499, Estepona, Malaga 29 680 Spain
☎00 34 952 793647 Fax 00 34 952 880138
Email library@andalucia.com
Website www.andalucia.com/slidelibrary

Library Manager *Michelle Chaplow*

Specialist library covering all aspects of Spain and Spanish life and culture. Cities, white villages, landscapes, festivals, art, gastronomy, leisure, tourism. Also images of Portugal, Madiera and Malta. Commissions undertaken.

Andes Press Agency

26 Padbury Court, London E2 7EH
☎020 7613 5417 Fax 020 7739 3159
Email apa@andespressagency.com

Contacts *Val Baker, Carlos Reyes*

80,000 colour transparencies and 300,000 b&w, specialising in social documentary, world religions, Latin America and Britain.

Heather Angel/Natural Visions

Highways, 6 Vicarage Hill, Farnham, Surrey GU9 8HJ
☎01252 716700 Fax 01252 727464
Email hangel@naturalvisions.co.uk
Website www.naturalvisions.co.uk

Contact *Valerie West*

Constantly expanding worldwide natural history, wildlife and landscapes: polar regions, tropical rainforest flora and fauna, all species of plants and animals in natural habitats from Africa, Asia (notably China and Malaysia), Australasia, South America and USA, urban wildlife, pollution, biodiversity, global warming. Also worldwide gardens and cultivated flowers. Transparencies only loaned to publishers after contract exchanged with author.

Ansel Adams

See **Corbis Images**

Aquarius Library

PO Box 5, Hastings, East Sussex TN34 1HR
☎01424 721196 Fax 01424 717704
Email aquarius.lib@clara.net
Website www.aquariuscollection.com

Contact *David Corkill*

Over one million images specialising in cinema past and present, television, pop music, ballet, opera, theatre, etc. The library includes various American showbiz collections. Film stills date back to the beginning of the century. Interested in film stills, the older the better. Current material is supplied by own suppliers.

Aquila Wildlife Images

PO Box 1, Studley, Warwickshire B80 7JG
☎01527 852357 Fax 01527 857507
Email interbirdnet@birder.co.uk
Website www.birder.co.uk

Natural history library specialising in birds, British and European wildlife, North America, Africa and Australia, environmental subjects, farming, habitats and related subjects, domestic animals and pets.

Architectural Association Photo Library

36 Bedford Square, London WC1B 3ES
☎020 7887 4078 Fax 020 7414 0782
Email valerie@aaschool.ac.uk
Website www.aaschool.ac.uk

Contacts *Valerie Bennett, Sarah Franklin, Sarah Farmer*

100,000 35mm transparencies on architecture,

historical and contemporary. Archive of large-format b&w negatives from the 1920s and 1930s.

Art Directors & Trip Photo Library

57 Burdon Lane, Cheam, Surrey SM2 7BY
☎020 8642 3593/8661 7104
Fax 020 8395 7230
Email images@artdirectors.co.uk
Website www.artdirectors.co.uk

Contacts *Helene Rogers, Bob Turner*

Extensive coverage, with over 750,000 images, of all countries, lifestyles, peoples, etc. with detailed coverage of all religions. Backgrounds a speciality. Catalogues available free to professionals.

art71

PO Box One, Newtown, Powys SY16 2WP
☎07005 963956 Fax 07005 963957
Email photo@art71.com
Website www.art71.com/photo

Contact *Mike Slater*

Specialist collection of photo-art images, abstract colour and form; close-up nature photography. Available as transparencies and also supplied as prints, including framed prints of any size.

Artbank Illustration Library

8 Woodcroft Avenue, London NW7 2AG
☎020 8906 2288 Fax 020 8906 2289
Email info@artbank.com
Website www.artbank.com

Illustration and art library holding thousands of 'protected rights' images by many renowned contemporary illustrators. Large-format transparencies and digital files. Catalogue available on faxed request. Represents a diverse group of UK and American illustrators for commissioned work. Portfolios and stock images available for viewing online.

Aspect Picture Library Ltd

40 Rostrevor Road, London SW6 5AD
☎020 7736 1998/7731 7362
Fax 020 7731 7362
Email Aspect.Ldn@btinternet.com
Website www.aspect-picture-library.co.uk

Colour and b&w worldwide coverage of countries, events, industry and travel, with large files on art, namely paintings, space, China and the Middle East.

Atlantic Syndication Partners
See **Solo Syndication Ltd**

Australia Pictures

28 Sheen Common Drive, Richmond TW10 5BN
☎020 7602 1989 Fax 020 7602 1989

Contact *John Miles*

Collection of 4000 transparencies covering all aspects of Australia: Aboriginal people, paintings, Ayers Rock, Kakadu, Tasmania, underwater, reefs, Arnhem Land, Sydney. Also Africa, Middle East and Asia.

Aviation Images – Mark Wagner

42B Queens Road, London SW19 8LR
☎020 8944 5225 Fax 020 8944 5335
Email mark.wagner@aviation-images.com
Website www.aviation-images.com

Contacts *Mark Wagner, Mark Steele*

500,000+ aviation images, civil and military, technical and generic. Mark Wagner is the photographer for *Flight International* magazine. Member of **BAPLA** and RAeS.

Aviation Photographs International

15 Downs View Road, Swindon, Wiltshire SN3 1NS
☎01793 497179 Fax 01793 434030

250,000 photographs comprise a comprehensive coverage of army, naval and airforce hardware ranging from early pistols to the latest ships. Extensive coverage of military and civil aviation includes modern together with many air-to-air views of vintage/warbird types. Collections available on disk. Commissions undertaken for additional photography and research. CD-ROM available of part of the library collection.

Aviation Picture Library

116 The Avenue, St Stephens, West Ealing, London W13 8JX
☎020 8566 7712 Fax 020 8566 7714
Email avpix@aol.com

Contact *Austin John Brown*

Specialists in the aviation field but also a general library which includes travel, architecture, transport, landscapes and skyscapes. *Special collections* Aircraft and all aspects of the aviation industry, including the archival collection of John Stroud; aerial obliques of Europe, USA, Caribbean and West Africa; architectural and town planning. Photographers for *Flyer* magazine in the UK. Commissions undertaken on the ground and in the air.

Axel Poignant Archive

115 Bedford Court Mansions, Bedford
Avenue, London WC1B 3AG
☎020 7636 2555 Fax 020 7636 2555
Email Rpoignant@aol.com

Contact *Roslyn Poignant*

Anthropological and ethnographic subjects,
especially Australia and the South Pacific. Also
Scandinavia (early history and mythology),
Sicily and England.

Barnaby's Picture Library

See **Mary Evans Picture Library**

Barnardos Photographic and Film Archive

Tanners Lane, Barkingside, Ilford, Essex
IG6 1QG
☎020 8550 8822 Fax 020 8550 0429
Email marissa.dowling@barnardos.org.uk
Website www.barnardos.org.uk

Contact *Marissa Dowling*

Specialises in social history (1874 to present day),
child care, education, war years, emigration/
migration. Half a million prints, slides, negatives.
Images are mainly b&w, colour since late
1940s/early '50s. Archive of 200 films dating
back to 1905. Visitors by appointment Monday
to Friday, 9.30 am to 4.30 pm.

Colin Baxter Photography Limited

Woodlands Industrial Estate, Grantown-on-
Spey PH26 3NA
☎01479 873999 Fax 01479 873888
Email colin.baxter@zetnet.co.uk
Website www.colinbaxter.co.uk

Contacts *Colin B. Kirkwood* (Marketing),
Mike Rensner (Editorial)

Over 50,000 images specialising in Scotland.
Also the Lake District, Yorkshire, France, Iceland and a special collection on Charles Rennie
Mackintosh's work. *Publishes* guidebooks plus
books, calendars, postcards and greetings cards
on landscape, cityscape and natural history containing images which are primarily, but not
exclusively, Colin Baxter's. Also publishers of
the *Worldlife Library* of natural history books.

BBC Natural History Unit Picture Library

See **Nature Picture Library**

The Photographic Library Beamish, The North of England Open Air Museum

The North of England Open Air Museum,
Beamish, County Durham DH9 0RG
☎0191 370 4000 Fax 0191 370 4001
Email museum@beamish.org.uk
Website www.beamish.org.uk

Keeper of Resource Collections *Jim Lawson*

Comprehensive collection; images relate to the
North East of England and cover agricultural,
industrial, topography, advertising and shop
scenes, people at work and play. Also on laser
disk for rapid searching. Visitors by appointment weekdays.

Francis Bedford

See **Birmingham Library Services** under
Library Services

Ivan J. Belcher Colour Picture Library

57 Gibson Close, Abingdon, Oxfordshire
OX14 1XS
☎01235 521524 Fax 01235 521524

Extensive colour picture library specialising in
top-quality medium-format transparencies depicting the British scene. Particular emphasis on
tourist, holiday and heritage locations, including
famous cities, towns, picturesque harbours,
rivers, canals, castles, cottages, rural scenes and
traditions photographed throughout the seasons.
Mainly of recent origin and constantly updated.

Andrew Besley PhotoLibrary

'Trenerth Barton', Fraddam, Near Hayle,
Cornwall TR27 5EP
☎01736 850086 Fax 01736 850086
Email bes.pix@btinternet.com
Website www.andrewbesley-
photolibrary.co.uk

Contact *Andrew Besley*

Specialist library of 20,000 images of West
Country faces, places and moods.

Bettmann Archive

See **Corbis Images**

BFI Stills, Posters and Designs

British Film Institute, 21 Stephen Street,
London W1T 1LN
☎020 7957 4797 Fax 020 7323 9260
Email stills.films@bfi.org.uk
Website ww.bfi.org.uk/collections/stills/
index.html

A unique collection of photographs from cinema and TV containing over seven million stills and transparencies from over 80,000 titles. Capturing on and off screen moments, the material features not only portraits of the world's most famous stars – and those behind the camera who made them famous – but shots of studios, cinemas and special events. The collection provides a comprehensive visual history of film and TV from their inception to the present day. Also holds original posters, set and costume designs. Research requests can be made by e-mail, telephone, fax or letter. Visits by appointment only (Tuesday to Thursday, 11 am to 4 pm).

Blackwoods Picture Library
See **Geoslides Photography**

Anthony Blake Photo Library
20 Blades Court, Deodar Road, Putney, London SW15 5AL
☎020 8877 1123 Fax 020 8877 9787
Email info@abpl.co.uk
Website ww.abpl.co.uk

'Europe's premier source' of food and wine related images. From the farm and the vineyard to the plate and the bottle. Cooking and kitchens, top chefs and restaurants, country trades and markets, worldwide travel with an extensive Italian section. Many recipes available to accompany transparencies. Free brochure available.

Peter Boardman Collection
See **Chris Bonnington Picture Library**

Boats & Boating Features (Keith Pritchard)
9 High Street, Southwell, Portland, Dorset DT5 2EH
☎01305 861006 Fax 0870 132 4192
Email boats@btinternet.com
Website www.boats.btinternet.co.uk
Contact *Keith Pritchard*

International marine photojournalist – photographs, features and news on up-market speedboats, classic sail, eco-tourism, '999' craft, ethnic fishing. Images of more than 300 kinds of craft.

Chris Bonington Picture Library
Badger Hill, Nether Row, Hesket Newmarket, Wigton, Cumbria CA7 8LA
☎016974 78286 Fax 016974 78238
Email frances@bonington.com
Website www.bonington.com

Contact *Frances Daltrey*

Based on the personal collection of climber and author Chris Bonington and his extensive travels and mountaineering achievements; also work by Doug Scott and other climbers, including the Peter Boardman and Joe Tasker Collections. Full coverage of the world's mountains, from British hills to Everest, depicting expedition planning and management stages, the approach march showing inhabitants of the area, flora and fauna, local architecture and climbing action shots on some of the world's highest mountains.

Boulton and Watt Archive
See **Birmingham Library Services** under **Library Services**

The Bridgeman Art Library
17–19 Garway Road, London W2 4PH
☎020 7727 4065 Fax 020 7792 8509
Email info@bridgeman.co.uk
Website www.bridgeman.co.uk
Head of Marketing *Vivien Wheeler*

Fine art photo archive acting as an agent to more than 1000 museums, galleries and picture owners around the world. Large-format colour transparencies of private collections, artists, paintings, sculptures, prints, manuscripts, antiquities and the decorative arts. The Library is currently expanding at the rate of 500 new images each week and has offices in Paris and New York. Collections represented by the library include the British Library, the National Galleries of Scotland, the National Library of Australia, and the National Gallery of South Africa. Fully searchable catalogue online and printed catalogue available.

British Library Reproductions
British Library, 96 Euston Road, London NW1 2DB
☎020 7412 7614 Fax 020 7412 7771
Email bl-repro@bl.uk
Website www.bl.uk

Twelve million books and approximately five million other items available for photography, microfilming or photocopying by Library staff. Specialist subjects include illuminated manuscripts, stamps, music, maps, botanical and zoological illustration, portraits of historical figures, history of India and South East Asia. All copies should be ordered as far in advance as possible.

For photographs for commercial reproduction a picture library service is available which enables orders to be processed more quickly. The Picture Library also has a small but unique collection of colour and b&w images mainly covering royalty, religion, medieval life and world maps plus a selection of natural history for hire. Customers are welcome to visit the collection.

Brooklands Museum Picture Library

Brooklands Museum, Brooklands Road, Weybridge, Surrey KT13 0QN
☎01932 857381 Fax 01932 855465
Email brooklands@dial.pipex.com
Website www.motor-software.co.uk/
brooklands

Contacts *John Pulford* (Curator of Collections), *Julian Temple* (Curator of Aviation)

About 40,000 b&w and colour prints and slides. Subjects include: Brooklands Motor Racing 1907–1939; British aviation and aerospace 1908–present day – particularly BAC, Hawker, Sopwith and Vickers aircraft built at Brooklands.

Hamish Brown MBE Scottish Photographic

26 Kirkcaldy Road, Burntisland, Fife KY3 9HQ
☎01592 873546

Contact *Hamish M. Brown, MBE*

Coverage of most topics and areas of Scotland (sites, historic, buildings, landscape, mountains), also travel and mountains abroad, Ireland and Morocco. Commissions undertaken.

Capital Pictures

49–51 Central Street, London EC1V 8AB
☎020 7253 1122 Fax 020 7253 1414
Email sales@capitalpictures.com
Website www.capitalpictures.com

Contact *Phil Loftus*

500,000 images. *Specialises* in photographs of famous people from the worlds of showbusiness, rock and pop, television, politics, royalty and film stills.

The Centre for the Study of Cartoons and Caricature

The Templeman Library, University of Kent at Canterbury, Canterbury, Kent CT2 7NU
☎01227 823127 Fax 01227 823127
Email N.P.Hiley@ukc.ac.uk *or*
J.M.Newton@ukc.ac.uk
Website library.ukc.ac.uk/cartoons/

Contacts *Dr Nicholas Hiley, Jane Newton*

A national research archive of over 85,000

twentieth century cartoons and caricatures, supported by a library of books, papers, journals, catalogues and assorted ephemera. A computer database of 70,000 cartoons provides quick and easy catalogued access. A source for exhibitions and displays as well as a picture library service. *Specialises* in historical, political and social cartoons from British newspapers.

Cephas Picture Library

Hurst House, 157 Walton Road, East Molesey, Surrey KT8 0DX
☎020 8979 8647 Fax 020 8224 8095
Email pictures@cephas.co.uk
Website www.cephas.co.uk

The wine industry and vineyards of the world is the subject on which Cephas has made its reputation. 100,000 images, mainly original $6 \times 7''$ make this the most comprehensive and up-to-date archive in Britain. Almost all wine-producing countries and all aspects of the industry are covered in depth. Spirits, beer and cider also included. A major food and drink collection now also exists, through preparation and cooking, to eating and drinking.

Giles Chapman Library

2 Peacock Yard, Iliffe Street, London SE17 3LH
☎020 7708 5818 Fax 020 7701 8672

Contact *Giles Chapman*

Around 100,000 colour and b&w images of cars and motoring, from 1945 to the present day. No research fees.

Christel Clear Marine Photography

Roselea, Church Lane, Awbridge, Near Romsey, Hampshire SO51 0HN
☎01794 341081 Fax 01794 340890
Email christel.clear@btinternet.com
Website www.christelclear.com

Contacts *Nigel Dowden, Christel Dowden*

Over 70,000 images on 35mm and 645 transparencies: yachting and boating from Grand Prix sailing to small dinghies, cruising locations and harbours. Recent additions include angling, fly fishing and travel. Visitors by appointment.

Christian Aid Photo Section

PO Box 100, London SE1 7RT
☎020 7523 2235 Fax 020 7620 0719

Pictures are mainly from Africa, Asia and Latin America, relating to small-scale, community-based programmes. Mostly development themes: health, agriculture, education, urban and rural life.

Christie's Images Ltd
1 Langley Lane, London SW8 1TJ
☎020 7582 1282 Fax 020 7582 5632
Email imageslondon@christies.com
Website www.christiesimages.com

Contact *Emma Strouts*

The UK's largest fine art photo library. 150,000 images of fine and decorative art. An extensive list of subjects is covered through paintings, drawings and prints of all periods as well as silver, ceramics, jewellery, sculpture, textiles and many other decorative and collectable items. Staff will search files and database to locate specific requests or supply a selection for consideration. Visits by appointment. Search fee.

Chrysalis Images
64 Brewery Road, London N7 9NT
☎020 7697 3000 Fax 020 7697 3001
Email Tforshaw@chrysalisbooks.co.uk

Contact *Terry Forshaw*

One million photographs and illustrations, colour and b&w, on military, history, transport, cookery, crafts, natural history, space and travel.

The Cinema Museum
The Master's House, Old Lambeth Workhouse, off Renfrew Road, London SE11 4TH
☎020 7840 2200 Fax 020 7840 2299
Email martin@cinemamuseum.org.uk

Colour and b&w coverage (including stills) of the motion picture industry throughout its history, including the Ronald Grant Archive. Smaller collections on theatre, variety, television and popular music.

John Cleare/Mountain Camera
Hill Cottage, Fonthill Gifford, Salisbury, Wiltshire SP3 6QW
☎01747 820320 Fax 01747 820320
Email cleare@btinternet.com
Website www.mountaincamera.com

Colour and b&w coverage of mountains and wild places, climbing, ski-touring, trekking, expeditions, wilderness travel, landscapes, people and geographical features from all continents. *Specialises* in the Himalaya, Andes, Antarctic, Alps and the British countryside, and a range of topics from reindeer in Lapland to camels in Australia, from whitewater rafting in Utah to ski-mountaineering in China. Commissions and consultancy work undertaken. Researchers welcome by appointment. Member of **BAPLA** and the **OWG**.

Michael Cole Camerawork
The Coach House, 27 The Avenue, Beckenham, Kent BR3 2DP
☎020 8658 6120 Fax 020 8658 6120
Website www.tennisphotos.com

Contacts *Michael Cole, Derrick Bentley*

Probably the largest and most comprehensive collection of tennis pictures in the world. Over 50 years' coverage of the Wimbledon Championships. M.C.C. incorporates the tennis archives of Le Roye Productions, established in 1945.

Collections
13 Woodberry Crescent, London N10 1PJ
☎020 8883 0083 Fax 020 8883 9215
Email collections@btinternet.com

Contact *Brian Shuel*

Extensive coverage of the British and Ireland from the Shetlands to the Channel Islands, and Connemara to East Anglia, including people, traditional customs, workers, religions and pastimes, as well as places both well known and obscure, and an extensive collection of 'things'. Includes the landscapes of Fay Godwin. Visitors are welcome but please make an appointment.

Concannon Golf History Library
See **Phil Sheldon Golf Picture Library**

Corbis Images
111 Salusbury Road, London NW1 6RG
☎020 7644 7644 Fax 020 7644 7645
Email info@uk.corbis.com
Website www.corbis.com

Contact *Anna Calvert*

A unique and comprehensive resource containing more than 65 million images, with over 2.1 million of them available online. The images come from professional photographers, museums, cultural institutions and public and private collections worldwide, including images from the Bettmann Archive, Ansel Adams, Lynn Goldsmith, the Turnley Collection and Hulton Deutsch. Subjects include history, travel, celebrities, events, science, world art and cultures. Free catalogues are available or register for a free password to search, save and order online.

Sylvia Cordaiy Photo Library
45 Rotherstone, Devizes, Wiltshire SN10 2DD
☎01380 728327 Fax 01380 728328
Email sylviacordaiy@compuserve.com
Website www.sylvia-cordaiy.com

Over 160 countries on file from the obscure to main stock images – Africa, North, Central and South America, Asia, Atlantic, Indian and Pacific Ocean islands, Australasia, Europe, polar regions. Covers travel, architecture, ancient civilisations, people worldwide, environment, wildlife, natural history, Antarctica, domestic pets, livestock, marine biology, veterinary treatment, equestrian, ornithology, flowers. UK files cover cities, towns villages, coastal and rural scenes, London collection. Transport, railways, shipping and aircraft (military and civilian). Aerial photography. Backgrounds and abstracts. Also the Paul Kaye B/W archive.

Country Collections
Unit 9, Ditton Priors Trading Estate, Bridgnorth, Shropshire WV16 6SS
☎01746 712533/861330
Contact *Robert Foster*

Small select collection of colour transparencies specialising in sundials, Celtic culture, villages, churches and ancient monuments. Assignments undertaken.

Country Images Picture Library
27 Camwood, Bamber Bridge, Preston, Lancashire PR5 8LA
☎01772 321243 Fax 0870 137 8888
Email mail@countryimages.uk.net
Website www.countryimages.uk.net
Contact *Terry Marsh*

35mm and 645 colour coverage of landscapes and countryside features generally throughout the UK (Cumbria, North Yorkshire, Lancashire, southern Scotland, Isle of Skye, Scottish islands, Wales, Cornwall), France (French Alps, French Pyrenees, Provence) and Australia. Commissions undertaken.

Country Life Picture Library
King's Reach Tower, Stamford Street, London SE1 9LS
☎020 7261 6337 Fax 020 7261 6216
Email camilla_costello@ipcmedia.com
Website www.countrylifelibrary.co.uk
Contact *Camilla Costello*

Over 150,000 b&w negatives dating back to 1897, and 80,000 colour transparencies. Country houses, stately homes, churches and town houses in Britain and abroad, interiors of architectural interest (ceilings, fireplaces, furniture, paintings, sculpture), and exteriors showing many landscaped gardens, sporting and social events, crafts, people and animals. Visitors by appointment. Open Tuesday to Friday.

Philip Craven
Worldwide Photo-Library
Surrey Studios, 21 Nork Way, Nork, Banstead, Surrey SM7 1PB
☎0870 220 2121
Website www.philipcraven.com
Contact *Philip Craven*

Extensive coverage of British scenes, cities, villages, English countryside, gardens, historic buildings and wildlife. Worldwide travel and wildlife subjects on medium- and large-format transparencies.

CTC Picture Library
CTC Ltd, Longfield, Midhurst Road, Fernhurst, Haslemere, Surrey GU27 3HA
☎01428 661441 Fax 01428 641071
Email ctcreate@globalnet.co.uk
Website www.crightonthomascreative.com
Contact *Vic Thomas*

One of the biggest specialist libraries in the UK with 250,000 slides covering world and UK agriculture, horticulture, and environmental subjects. Also a small section on travel.

Cumbria Picture Library
See **Eric Whitehead Photography**

Sue Cunningham Photographic
56 Chatham Road, Kingston upon Thames, Surrey KT1 3AA
☎020 8541 3024 Fax 020 8541 5388
Email pictures@scphotographic.com
Website www.scphotographic.com

Extensive coverage of many geographical areas: South America (especially Brazil), Eastern Europe from the Baltic to the Balkans, various African countries, Western Europe including the UK. Colour and b&w. Member of **BAPLA**.

Dalton–Watson Collection
See **The Ludvigsen Library Limited**

James Davis Travel Photography
65 Brighton Road, Shoreham, West Sussex BN43 6RE
☎01273 452252 Fax 01273 440116
Email library@eyeubiquitous.com

Travel collection: people, places, emotive scenes and tourism. Constantly updated by James Davis and a team of photographers, both at home and abroad. Same-day service available.

The Defence Picture Library

Sherwell House, 54 Staddiscombe Road,
Plymouth, Devon PL9 9NB
☎01752 401800 Fax 01752 402800
Email picdesk@defencepictures.com
Website www.defencepictures.com

Contacts *David Reynolds, Jessica Kelly,
James Rowlands, Andrew Chittock*

Leading source of military photography covering
all areas of the UK Armed Forces, supported by a
research agency of facts and figures. More than
500,000 images with a significant number on
CD-ROM. Campaigns in Aden, the Falklands,
Ulster, the Gulf and Kosovo. Specialist collections include the Chinese Armed Forces, US
Special Forces, as well as military units of Italy,
Spain and France. Visitors welcome by appointment.

Douglas Dickins Photo Library

2 Wessex Gardens, Golders Green, London
NW11 9RT
☎020 8455 6221

Sole Proprietor *Douglas Dickins, FRPS*

Worldwide colour and b&w coverage, specialising in Asia, particularly India, Indonesia and
Japan. *In Grandpa's Footsteps*, highly illustrated
book of world travel published by Book Guild
in 2000.

CM Dixon

The Orchard, Marley Lane, Kingston,
Canterbury, Kent CT4 6JH
☎01227 830075 Fax 01227 831135

Colour coverage of ancient civilisations, archaeology and art, ethnology, mythology, world religion, museum objects, geography, geology,
meteorology, landscapes, people and places from
many countries including most of Europe, former USSR, Ethiopia, Iceland, Jordan, Morocco,
Sri Lanka, Tunisia, Turkey, Egypt, Uzbekistan.

Dominic Photography

4B Moore Park Road, London SW6 2JT
☎020 7381 0007 Fax 020 7381 0008

Contacts *Zoë Dominic, Catherine Ashmore*

Colour and b&w coverage of the entertainment world from 1957 onwards: dance, opera,
theatre, ballet, musicals and personalities.

E&E Picture Library – Ecclesiastical and Eccentricities

Beggars Roost, Woolpack Hill, Brabourne
Lees, Ashford, Kent TN25 6RR
☎01303 812608 Fax 01303 812608

Email isobel@picture-library.freeserve.co.uk
Website www.picture-library.freeserve.co.uk

Contact *Isobel Sinden*

Specialises in world religions, buildings, artifacts,
clothes, festivals, clergy, arts, culture, history, pil-
grimages, ancient stones, Bible lands, death and
burial worldwide, ancient to modern. Curiosities
such as follies, mazes, towers, pyramids. Also
wind and water.

Patrick Eagar Photography

1 Queensberry Place, Richmond, Surrey
TW9 1NW
☎020 8940 9269 Fax 020 8332 1229
Email patrick@patrickeagar.com
Website www.patrickeagar.com

The cricket library consists of Patrick Eagar's
work over the last 30 years with coverage of over
250 Test matches worldwide, unique coverage
of all seven World Cups, countless one-day
internationals and player action portraits of over
2000 cricketers. The wine library consists of
vineyards, grapes and festivals from Argentina to
New Zealand. France and Australia are specialist
areas. Photographs can be supplied by ISDN, on
CD, prints and transparencies.

Ecoscene

The Oasts, Headley Lane, Passfield, Liphook,
Hampshire GU30 7RX
☎01428 751056 Fax 01428 751057
Email sally@ecoscene.com
Website www.ecoscene.com

Contact *Sally Morgan*

Expanding colour library of over 80,000 transparencies specialising in all aspects of the environment: pollution, conservation, recycling,
restoration, wildlife (especially underwater),
habitats, education, landscapes, industry and
agriculture. All parts of the globe are covered
with specialist collections covering Antarctica,
Australia, North America. Sally Morgan, who
runs the library, is a professional ecologist and
expert source of information on all environmental topics. Photographic and writing commissions undertaken. Images delivered by post,
on CD-ROM, by e-mail and ISDN.

Edifice

14 Doughty Street, London WC1N 2PL
☎020 7242 0740 Fax 020 7267 3632
Email info@edificephoto.com
Website www.edificephoto.com

Contacts *Philippa Lewis, Gillian Darley*

Colour coverage of architecture, buildings of

all possible descriptions, gardens, urban and rural landscape. *Specialises* in details of ornament, period style and material. British Isles, USA, Africa, Europe and Japan all covered. Detailed list available, visits by appointment.

Edinburgh Photographic Library
14 Garscube Terrace, Edinburgh EH12 6BQ
☎0131 337 7615 Fax 0131 337 0303
Email epl@mercat.co.uk
Website www.mercat.co.uk

Contact *James Young*

15,000 transparencies of Scotland: cities, towns and villages, castles, bridges, scenery, mountains, lochs, activities, wildlife, traditional industries. Visitors by appointment only.

Education Photos
April Cottage, Warners Lane, Albury Heath, Guildford, Surrey GU5 9DE
☎01483 203846 Fax 01483 203846
Email johnwalmsley@educationphotos.co.uk
Website www.educationphotos.co.uk

Formerly the John Walmsley Photo Library. Specialist library of learning/training/working subjects. Comprehensive coverage of learning environments such as playgroups, schools, colleges and universities. Images reflect a multiracial Britain. Commissions undertaken. Subject list and CD available on request.

English Heritage Photo Library
23 Savile Row, London W1S 2ET
☎020 7973 3338/9 Fax 020 7973 3027
Email celia.sterne@english-heritage.org.uk
Website www.english-heritage.org.uk

Contact *Celia Sterne*

Images of English castles, abbeys, houses, gardens, Roman remains, ancient monuments, battlefields, industrial and post-war buildings, interiors, paintings, artifacts, architectural details, conservation, archaeology, scenic views, landscapes.

Mary Evans Picture Library
59 Tranquil Vale, Blackheath, London SE3 0BS
☎020 8318 0034 Fax 020 8852 7211
Email lib@mepl.co.uk
Website www.mepl.co.uk

Collection of historical illustrations documenting social, political, cultural, technical, geographical and biographical themes from ancient times to the recent past (up to mid-20th century). Photographs, prints and ephemera backed by large book and magazine collection. Many special collections including Sigmund Freud, the

Women's Library (women's rights), the paranormal, the Meledin Collection (20th-century Russian history) and individual photographers such as Roger Mayne and Grace Robertson. Recently acquired the Weimar Archive and Barnaby's Picture Library. Brochure sent on request. Compilers of the *Picture Researcher's Handbook* by Pira International.

Exile Images
1 Mill Row, West Hill Road, Brighton, East Sussex BN1 3SU
☎01273 208741 Fax 01273 382782
Email pics@exileimages.co.uk
Website www.exileimages.co.uk

Contact *Howard Davies*

Over 15,000 b&w and colour 35mm slides of refugees, asylum seekers, conflict, third world development and daily life, UK protests, travel. CD-ROM available via the website to picture editors and researchers.

Express Newspapers Syndication
Ludgate House, 245 Blackfriars Road, London SE1 9UX
☎020 7922 7884 Fax 020 7922 7871
Email syndication@express.co.uk

Manager *Adam Williams*

Two million images updated daily, with strong collections on personalities, royalty, showbiz, sport, fashion, nostalgia and events. Also includes the *OK! Magazine* collection. Electronic transmission available. Daily news and feature service.

Eye Ubiquitous
65 Brighton Road, Shoreham, East Sussex BN43 6RE
☎01273 440113 Fax 01273 440116
Email library@eyeubiquitous.com

Contact *Stephen Rafferty*

General stock specialising in social documentary worldwide, including the work of Tim Page, and now incorporating the **James Davis Travel** library (see entry).

EyeWire
See **Getty Images**

Famous Pictures & Features Agency
13 Harwood Road, London SW6 4QP
☎020 7731 9333 Fax 020 7731 9330
Email info@famous.uk.com
Website www.famous.uk.com

Pictures and features agency with a growing library of interviews and colour transparencies dating back to 1985. Portrait, party and concert shots of rock and pop stars plus international entertainers, film and TV celebrities. The library is supplied by a team of photographers and journalists from the UK and around the world, keeping it up-to-date on a daily basis. 'We are always looking out for new writers who specialise in celebrity material.'

ffotograff
10 Kyveilog Street, Pontcanna, Cardiff CF11 9JA
☎029 2023 6879 Fax 029 2022 9326
Email ffotograff@easynet.co.uk

Contact *Patricia Aithie*

Library and agency specialising in travel, exploration, the arts, architecture, traditional culture, archaeology and landscape. Based in Wales but specialising in the Middle and Far East; Africa, Central and South America; Yemen and Wales are strong aspects of the library. Churches and cathedrals of Britain and Crusader castles.

Financial Times Pictures
One Southwark Bridge, London SE1 9HL
☎020 7873 3671 Fax 020 7873 4606
Email richard.pigden@ft.com

Photographs from around the world ranging from personalities in business, politics and the arts, people at work and other human interests and activities. 'FT Graphics are outstanding in their ability to make complex issues comprehensible.' Delivery via ISDN or e-mail.

Fine Art Photographic Library Ltd
2A Milner Street, London SW3 2PU
☎020 7589 3127 Fax 020 7584 1944
Email info@fineartphotolibrary.com
Website www.finartphotolibrary.com

Contact *Linda Hammerbeck*

Over 30,000 large-format transparencies, with a specialist collection of 19th and 20th century paintings. CD-ROM available.

Firepix International
68 Arkles Lane, Anfield, Liverpool, Merseyside L4 2SP
☎0151 260 0111/0777 5930419 (mobile)
Fax 0151 260 0111
Email info@firepix.com
Website www.firepix.com

Contact *Tony Myers*

The UK's only fire photo library. 23,000 images of fire-related subjects, firefighters, fire

equipment manufacturers. Website contains 15 categories from industrial fire, domestic, digital images and abstract flame. Member of **BAPLA**.

Fogden Wildlife Photographs
Flat 1, 78 High Street, Perth PH1 5TH
☎01738 580811 Fax 01738 580811
Email susan.fogden@virgin.net
Website www.fogdenphotos.com

Contact *Susan Fogden*

Natural history collection, with special reference to rain forests and deserts. Emphasis on quality rather than quantity; growing collection of around 15,000 images.

Food Features
Farnham Forge, 5 Upper Church Lane, Farnham, Surrey GU9 7PW
☎01252 735240 Fax 01252 735242
Email frontdesk@foodpix.co.uk
Website www.foodpix.co.uk

Contacts *Steve Moss, Alex Barker*

Specialised high-quality food and drink photography, features and tested recipes. Clients' specific requirements can be incorporated into regular shooting schedules.

FoodPix
See **Getty Images**

Christine Foord Colour Picture Library
155B City Way, Rochester, Kent ME1 2BE
☎01634 847348 Fax 01634 847348

Specialist library with over 1000 species of British and European wild flowers, plus garden flowers, trees, indoor plants, pests and diseases, mosses, lichen, cacti and the majority of larger British insects.

Forest Life Picture Library
231 Corstorphine Road, Edinburgh EH12 7AT
☎0131 314 6411 Fax 0131 314 6285
Email n.campbell@forestry.gsi.gov.uk
Website www.forestry.gov.uk/pictures

Contacts *Douglas Green, Neill Campbell*

The official image bank of the Forestry Commission, the library provides a single source for all aspects of forest and woodland management. The comprehensive subject list includes tree species, scenic landscapes, employment, wildlife, flora and fauna, conservation, sport and leisure.

Werner Forman Archive Ltd

36 Camden Square, London NW1 9XA
☎020 7267 1034 Fax 020 7267 6026
Email wfa@btinternet.com
Website www.werner-forman-archive.com

Colour and b&w coverage of ancient civilisations, oriental and primitive societies around the world. A number of rare collections. Searchable website.

Format Photographers

19 Arlington Way, London EC1R 1UY
☎020 7833 0292 Fax 020 7833 0381
Email format@formatphotogs.demon.co.uk
Website www.formatphotographers.co.uk

Contact *Maggie Murray*

Over 100,000 documentary images in colour and b&w covering education, health, disability and women's issues in the UK and abroad.

Formula One Pictures

29 Merlin Close, Waltham Abbey, Essex
EN9 3NG
☎01992 787800 Fax 01992 714366
Email jt@f1pictures.com
Website www.f1pictures.com

Contacts *John Townsend, Erika Townsend*

500,000 35mm colour slides, b&w and colour negatives of all aspects of Formula One grand prix racing including driver profiles and portraits.

Robert Forsythe Picture Library

16 Lime Grove, Prudhoe, Northumberland
NE42 6PR
☎01661 834511 Fax 01661 834511
Email robert@forsythe.demon.co.uk
Website www.forsythe.demon.co.uk

Contacts *Robert Forsythe, Fiona Forsythe*

25,000 transparencies of industrial and transport heritage; plus a unique collection of 50,000 items of related publicity ephemera from 1945. Image finding service available. Robert Forsythe is a transport/industrial heritage historian and consultant. Nationwide coverage, particularly strong on Northern Britain. A bibliography of published material is available.

Fortean Picture Library

Henblas, Mwrog Street, Ruthin LL15 1LG
☎01824 707278 Fax 01824 705324
Email janet.bord@forteanpix.demon.co.uk
Website www.forteanpix.demon.co.uk

Contact *Janet Bord*

30,000 colour and 45,000 b&w images: mys-
teries and strange phenomena worldwide, including ghosts, UFOs, witchcraft and monsters; also antiquities, folklore and mythology. Subject list available.

The Fotomas Index

12 Pickhurst Rise, West Wickham, Kent
BR4 0AL
☎020 8776 2772 Fax 020 8776 2236/2772

Contact *John Freeman*

General historical collection, mostly pre-1900. Subjects include London, topography, art, satirical, social and political history. Large portrait section.

The Francis Frith Collection

Frith's Barn, Teffont, Salisbury, Wiltshire
SP3 5QP
☎01722 716376 Fax 01722 716881
Email john_buck@francisfrith.co.uk
Website www.francisfrith.co.uk

Contact *John Buck*

Publishers of *Frith's Photographic Memories* series of illustrated local books, all featuring nostalgic photographs from the archive, founded by Frith in 1860. The archive now contains over 360,000 images of 7000 British towns.

John Frost Newspapers

See entry under **Library Services**

Andrew N. Gagg's Photo Flora

Town House Two, Fordbank Court,
Henwick Road, Worcester WR2 5PF
☎01905 748515
Email a.n.gagg@ntlworld.com
Website homepage.ntlworld.com/a.n.gagg/
   photo/photoflora.html

Specialist in British and European wild plants, flowers, ferns, grasses, trees, shrubs, etc. with colour coverage of most British and many European species (rare and common) and habitats; also travel in India, Sri Lanka, Nepal, Egypt, China, Mexico, Thailand, Tibet, Vietnam and Cambodia.

Galaxy Picture Library

1 Milverton Drive, Ickenham, Uxbridge,
Middlesex UB10 8PP
☎01895 637463 Fax 01895 623277
Email robin@galaxypix.com
Website www.galaxypix.com

Contact *Robin Scagell*

Specialises in astronomy, space, telescopes, observatories, the sky, clouds and sunsets.

Composites of foregrounds, stars, moon and planets prepared to commission. Editorial service available.

Garden and Wildlife Matters Photo Library

'Marlham', Henley's Down, Battle,
East Sussex TN33 9BN
☎01424 830566 Fax 01424 830224
Email gardens@gmpix.com
Website www.gardenmatters.uk.com *and*
  www.gmpix.com

Contact *Dr John Feltwell*

Collection of 110,000 6×4″ and 35mm images. General gardening techniques and design; cottage gardens and USA designer gardens. 9000 species of garden plants and over 1000 species of trees. Flowers, wild and house plants, trees and crops. Environmental, ecological and conservation pictures, including sea, air, noise and freshwater pollution, SE Asian and Central and South American rainforests; Eastern Europe, Mediterranean. Recycling, agriculture, forestry, horticulture and oblique aerial habitat shots from Europe and USA. 24/7 service. Digital images supplied worldwide by ISDN.

Garden Picture Library

Unit 12, Ransome's Dock, 35 Parkgate Road,
London SW11 4NP
☎020 7228 4332 Fax 020 7924 3267
Email info@gardenpicture.com
Website www.gardenpicture.com

Picture Research Manager *Lorraine Shill*,

'Our inspirational images of gardens, plants and gardening offer plenty of scope for writers looking for original ideas to write about.' Special collections include al fresco food, floral graphics and the still life photography of Linda Burgess. From individual stock photos to complete features, photographers submit material from the UK, Europe, USA and Australia on 35mm and medium formats. In-house picture research can be undertaken on request or review 10,000 images on 'The Collection' page of the website. Visitors to the library are welcome by appointment and copies of promotional literature are available on request.

Ed Geldard Photo Collection

9 Sunderland Bridge Village, Durham
DH6 5HB
☎0191 378 2592

Contact *Ed Geldard*

Approximately 20,000 colour transparencies and b&w negs, all by Ed Geldard, specialising in mountain landscapes: particularly the mountain regions of the Lake District; and the Yorkshire limestone areas, from valley to summit. Commissions undertaken. Books published: *Wainwright's Tour of the Lake District; Wainwright in the Limestone Dales; The Lake District.*

Genesis Space Photo Library

Greenbanks, Robins Hill, Raleigh, Bideford,
Devon EX39 3PA
☎01237 471960 Fax 01237 472060
Email tim@spaceport.co.uk
Website www.spaceport.co.uk

Contact *Tim Furniss*

Contemporary and historical colour and b&w spaceflight collection including rockets, spacecraft, spacemen, Earth, moon and planets. Catalogue of 775 images on website.

Geo Aerial Photography

4 Christian Fields, London SW16 3JZ
☎020 8764 6292/0115 981 9418
Fax 020 8764 6292/0115 981 9418
Email geo.aerial@geo-group.co.uk
Website www.geo-group.co.uk

Contact *Kelly White*

Established 1990. Now a growing collection of aerial oblique photographs from the UK, Scandinavia, Asia and Africa – landscapes, buildings, industrial sites, etc. Commissions undertaken.

GeoScience Features

6 Orchard Drive, Wye, Kent TN25 5AU
☎01233 812707 Fax 01233 812707
Email gsf@geoscience.demon.co.uk
Website www.geoscience.demon.co.uk

Fully computerised and comprehensive library containing the world's principal source of volcanic phenomena. Extensive collections, providing scientific detail with technical quality, of rocks, minerals, fossils, microsections of botanical and animal tissues, animals, biology, birds, botany, chemistry, earth science, ecology, environment, geology, geography, habitats, landscapes, macro/microbiology, peoples, sky, weather, wildlife and zoology. Over 300,000 original colour transparencies in medium- and 35mm-format. Subject lists and CD-ROM catalogue available on application. Incorporates the RIDA photolibrary.

Geoslides Photography

4 Christian Fields, London SW16 3JZ
☎020 8764 6292/0115 981 9418
Fax 020 8764 6292/0115 981 9418

Email geoslides@geo-group.co.uk
Website www.geo-group.co.uk
Contact *John Douglas*

Established in 1968. Landscape and human interest subjects from the Arctic, Antarctica, Scandinavia, UK, Africa (south of Sahara), Middle East, Asia (south and southeast); also Australia, via Blackwoods Picture Library. Also specialist collections of images from British India (the Raj) and Boer War.

Getty Images
101 Bayham Street, London NW1 0AG
☎0800 376 7977 Fax 020 7544 3334
Email info@getty-images.com
Website www.gettyone.com
Contact *Sales Dept.*

Hosts a variety of collections including The Image Bank, EyeWire, FoodPix, Hulton Archive, Illustration Works and Tony Stone Images. With over 15 million images, Getty Images is the largest picture resource in Europe with coverage from ancient history through the early years of photography up to the present day. As well as many old newspaper archives, the extensive contemporary collections cover lifestyles, travel, science, business.

Lynn Goldsmith
See **Corbis Images**

Martin and Dorothy Grace
40 Clipstone Avenue, Mapperley, Nottingham NG3 5JZ
☎0115 920 8248 Fax 0115 962 6802
Email graces@lineone.net

Colour coverage of Britain's natural history, specialising in trees, shrubs and wild flowers. Also ferns, birds and butterflies, habitats, landscapes, ecology.

Ronald Grant Archive
See **The Cinema Museum**

Sally and Richard Greenhill
357 Liverpool Road, London N1 1NL
☎020 7607 8549 Fax 020 7607 7151
Email sr.greenhill@virgin.net
Website www.srgreenhill.co.uk
Photo Librarian *Denise Lalonde*

Social documentary photography in colour and b&w of working lives: pregnancy and birth, child development, education, work, old people, medical, urban. Also Modern China, 1971

to the present; most London statues. Some material from Borneo, USA, India, Israel, Philippines and Sri Lanka.

V.K. Guy Ltd
Silver Birches, Troutbeck, Windermere, Cumbria LA23 1PN
☎015394 33519 Fax 015394 32971
Email vic@vk.guy.co.uk
Website www.vk.guy.co.uk
Contacts *Vic Guy, Pauline Guy, Mike Guy, Paul Guy, Nicola Guy*

British landscapes and architectural heritage. 20,000 5×4″ transparencies, suitable for tourism brochures, calendars, etc. Colour catalogue available.

Angela Hampton 'Family Life Picture Library'
Holly Tree House, The Street, Walberton, Arundel, West Sussex BN18 0PH
☎01243 555952 Fax 01243 555952
Contact *Angela Hampton*

Over 50,000 transparencies on all aspects of contemporary lifestyle, including pregnancy, childbirth, babies, children, parenting, behaviour, education, medical, holidays, pets, family life, relationships, teenagers, women and men's health, over-50s and retirement. Also comprehensive stock on domestic and farm animal life. Environmental and travel pictures in 35mm. Commissions undertaken. Offers fully illustrated text packages on most subjects and welcomes ideas for collaboration from writers with proven, successful background.

Tom Hanley
41 Harefield, Esher, Surrey KT10 9TG
☎020 8972 9165 Fax 020 8972 9164
Email Tomhanley31@hotmail.com

Colour and b&w coverage of London, England, Europe, Canada, India, the Philippines, Brazil, China, Japan, Korea, Taiwan, the Seychelles, Cayman Islands, USA. Also pop artists of the 1960s, First World War trenches, removal of London Bridge to America, and much more. Current preoccupation with Greece, Turkey, Spain and Egypt, ancient and modern.

Robert Harding Picture Library
58–59 Great Marlborough Street, London W1F 7JY
☎020 7478 4000 Fax 020 7631 1070
Email info@robertharding.com
Website www.robertharding.com

A leading source of stock photography with over two million colour images covering a wide range of subjects – worldwide travel and culture, geography and landscapes, people and lifestyle, architecture, business and industry, medicine, sports, food and drink. Rights protected and royalty-free images. Can supply images as transparencies, on CD or ISDN. Visitors welcome; telephone or visit the website.

Dennis Hardley Photography, Scottish Photo Library

Rosslynn, Benderloch, Oban, Argyll PA37 1ST
☎01631 720434 Fax 01631 720434
Email dennis.hardley@btinternet.com *and* info@scotphoto.com
Website www.scottishphotographs.com *and* www.englishphotographs.com

Contacts *Dennis Hardley, Tony Hardley*

ESTABLISHED 1974. About 30,000 images ($6 \times 7''$, $6 \times 9''$ format colour transparences) of Scotland: castles, historic, scenic landscapes, islands, transport, etc. Also English views – Liverpool, Chester, Bath, Weston Super Mare, Sussex, Somerset and Cambridge.

Jim Henderson Photographer & Publisher

Crooktree, Kincardine O'Neil, Aboyne, Aberdeenshire AB34 4JD
☎01339 882149 Fax 01339 882149
Email JHende7868@aol.com
Website www.jimhendersonphotography.com

Contact *Jim Henderson, AMPA, ARPS*

Scenic and general activity coverage of the north east Scotland/Grampian region and Highlands for tourist, holiday and activity illustration. Specialist collection of over 150 Aurora Borealis displays from 1989–2002 in Grampian and co-author of *The Aurora* (pub. 1997). Large collection of recent images of Egypt: Cairo through to Abu-Simbel. Commissions undertaken.

Heritage and Natural History Photographic Library

37 Plainwood Close, Summersdale, Chichester, West Sussex PO19 4YB
☎01243 533822 Fax 01243 533822

Contact *Dr John B. Free*

Specialises in insects (particularly bees and beekeeping), tropical and temperate agriculture and crops, archaeology and history worldwide.

John Heseltine Archive

Mill Studio, Frogmarsh Mill, South Woodchester, Gloucestershire GL5 5ET
☎01453 873792 Fax 01453 873793
Email john@heseltine.co.uk
Website www.heseltine.co.uk

Contact *John Heseltine*

Over 150,000 colour transparencies of landscapes, architecture, food and travel with particular emphasis on Italy and the UK.

Christopher Hill Photographic Library

17 Clarence Street, Belfast BT2 8DY
☎028 9024 5038 Fax 028 9023 1942
Email ChrisHillPhotographic@btclick.com
Website www.scenic-ireland.com

Contact *Christopher Hill*

A comprehensive collection of landscapes of Northern Ireland, from Belfast to the Giant's Causeway, updated daily. Images of farming, food and industry. 'We will endeavour to supply images overnight.'

Hobbs Golf Collection

5 Winston Way, New Ridley, Stocksfield, Northumberland NE43 7RF
☎01661 842933 Fax 01661 842933
Email hobbs.golf@btinternet.com
Website www.hobbsgolfcollection.com

Contact *Michael Hobbs*

Specialist golf collection: players, courses, art, memorabilia and historical topics (1300–present). 40,000+ images – mainly 35mm colour transparencies and b&w prints. Commissions undertaken. Author of 30 golf books.

David Hoffman Photo Library

c/o BAPLA, 18 Vine Hill, London EC1R 5DZ
☎020 8981 5041 Fax 020 8980 2041
Email info@hoffmanphotos.com
Website www.hoffmanphotos.com

Contact *David Hoffman*

Commissioned photography and stock library with a strong emphasis on social issues built up from 35mm journalistic and documentary work dating from the late 1970s. Files on drugs and drug use, policing, disorder, riots, youth, protest, homelessness, housing, environmental demonstrations and events, waste disposal, alternative energy, industry and pollution. Wide range of images especially from UK and Europe but also USA, Canada, Venezuela, Mexico and Thailand. General files on topical issues and current affairs plus specialist files from leisure cycling to local authority services.

Holt Studios International Ltd
The Courtyard, 24 High Street, Hungerford, Berkshire RG17 0NF
☎01488 683523 Fax 01488 683511
Email library@holt-studios.co.uk
Website www.holt-studios.co.uk

Director *Nigel Cattlin*

Specialist photo library covering world agriculture, horticulture, gardens and gardening from pictorial and technical aspects. Worldwide assignments undertaken.

Bill Hopkins Collection
See **The Special Photographers Library**

Houghton's Horses/ Kit Houghton Photography
Radlet Cottage, Spaxton, Bridgwater, Somerset TA5 1DE
☎01278 671362 Fax 01278 671739
Email kit@enterprise.net
Website www.houghtonshorses.com

Contacts *Kit Houghton, Debbie Cook*

Specialist equestrian library of over 200,000 transparencies on all aspects of the horse world, with images ranging from the romantic to the practical, step-by-step instructional and competition pictures in all equestrian disciplines worldwide. Online picture delivery with ISDN facility.

Houses and Interiors
192 Goswell Road, London EC1V 7DT
☎020 7253 0991 Fax 020 7253 0992
Email housesandinteriors@yahoo.com

Manager *James Wakefield*

Stylish house interiors and exteriors, home dossiers, renovations, architectural details, interior design, gardens, houseplants and cookery. Also step-by-step photographic sequences of DIY subjects and gardening techniques. Large format and 35mm. Member of **BAPLA**.

Chris Howes/ Wild Places Photography
51 Timbers Square, Cardiff CF24 3SH
☎029 2048 6557 Fax 029 2048 6557
Email photos@wildplaces.co.uk

Contacts *Chris Howes, Judith Calford*

Expanding collection of over 50,000 colour transparencies and b&w prints covering travel, topography and natural history worldwide, plus action sports such as climbing. *Specialist areas* include caves, caving and mines (with historical coverage using engravings and early photographs), wildlife, landscapes and the environment, including pollution and conservation. Europe (including Britain), USA, Africa and Australia are all well represented within the collection. Commissions undertaken.

Hulton Archive
See **Getty Images**

Hulton Deutsch
See **Corbis Images**

Huntley Film Archive
78 Mildmay Park, Islington, London N1 4PR
☎020 7923 0990 Fax 020 7241 4929
Email films@huntleyarchives.com
Website www.huntleyarchives.com

Contact *Amanda Huntley*

Originally a private collection, the library is now a comprehensive archive of rare and vintage documentary film dating from 1895. 30,000–35,000 films on all subjects of a documentary nature, plus 50,000 feature film stills. Hollywood and the British film studios plus a television archive of rare stills and films. On-line catalogue available.

Jacqui Hurst
66 Richford Street, Hammersmith, London W6 7HP
☎020 8743 2315/07970 781336 (mobile)
Fax 020 8743 2315
Email jacquih@dircon.co.uk

Contact *Jacqui Hurst*

A specialist library of traditional and contemporary designers and crafts, regional food producers and markets. The photos form illustrated essays of how something is made and finish with a still life of the completed object. The collection is always being extended and a list is available on request. Commissions undertaken.

Hutchison Picture Library
118B Holland Park Avenue, London W11 4UA
☎020 7229 2743 Fax 020 7792 0259
Email library@hutchisonpic.demon.co.uk
Website www.hutchisonpictures.co.uk

Worldwide contemporary images from the straight-forward to the esoteric and quirky. With over half a million documentary colour photographs on file and more than 200 photographers continually adding new work, this is an ever-growing resource covering people, places, customs and faiths, agriculture, industry and transport. *Special collections* include the environment and climate, family life (including pregnancy and birth), ethnic minorities worldwide (including Disappearing World archive), conventional and alternative medicine, and music around the world. Search service available.

Illustrated London News Picture Library

20 Upper Ground, London SE1 9PF
☎020 7805 5585 Fax 020 7805 5905
Email iln.pictures@ilng.co.uk
Website www.ilng.co.uk

Engravings, photographs and illustrations from 1842 to the present day, taken from magazines published by Illustrated Newspapers: *Illustrated London News*; *Graphic*; *Sphere*; *Tatler*; *Sketch*; *Illustrated Sporting and Dramatic News*; *Illustrated War News 1914–18*; *Bystander*; *Britannia & Eve*. Social history, London, Industrial Revolution, wars, travel. CD-ROM available. Visitors by appointment.

Illustration Works
See **Getty Images**

The Image Bank
See **Getty Images**

Images of Africa Photobank

11 The Windings, Lichfield, Staffordshire WS13 7EX
☎01543 262898 Fax 01543 417154
Email info@imagesofafrica.co.uk
Website www.imagesofafrica.co.uk

Contact *Jacquie Shipton*
Owner *David Keith Jones, FRPS*

Over 135,000 images covering the following African countries: Botswana, Chad, Egypt, Ethiopia, Kenya, Lesotho, Madagasca, Malawi, Namibia, Rwanda, South Africa, Swaziland, Tanzania, Uganda, Zaire, Zambia, Zanzibar and Zimbabwe. 'Probably the best collection of photographs of Kenya in Europe.' Wide range of topics covered. Particularly strong on African wildlife with over 80 species of mammals including many sequences showing action and behaviour. Popular animals like lions and elephants are covered in encyclopædic detail. Other strengths include National Parks and reserves, natural beauty, tourism facilities, traditional and modern people. Most work is by David Keith Jones, FRPS; several other photographers are represented.

Images of India
See **Link Picture Library**

ImageState Europe

Ramillies House, 1–2 Ramillies Street, London W1F 7LN
☎020 7734 7344 Fax 020 7287 3933
Email sales@imagestate.co.uk
Website www.imagestate.co.uk

Markets royalty free and rights protected images, footage, music and sound effects. Image and footage subjects include people and lifestyles, business and industry, sport, travel, nature and animals and more. Visit the website for details.

Imperial War Museum Photograph Archive

All Saints Annexe, Austral Street, London SE1 4SL
☎020 7416 5333 Fax 020 7416 5355
Email photos@iwm.org.uk
Website www.iwm.org.uk

A national archive of over six million photographs illustrating all aspects of 20th century conflict. Emphasis on the two world wars but includes material from other conflicts involving Britain and the Commonwealth. Majority of material is b&w, although holdings of colour material increases with more recent conflicts. Visitors welcome by appointment, Monday to Friday, 10.00 am. to 5.00 pm.

Infoterra

Arthur Street, Barwell, Leicestershire LE9 8GZ
☎01455 849207 Fax 01455 841785
Email joanne.burchnall@infoterra-global.com
Website www.infoterra-global.com

Contact *Joanne Burchnall*

Leading supplier of earth observation data, including satellite imagery, aerial photography and airborne remote sensing.

International Photobank

Loscombe Barn Farmhouse, West Knighton, Dorchester, Dorset DT2 8LS
☎01305 854145 Fax 01305 853065
Email peter@internationalphotobank.co.uk
Website www.internationalphotobank.co.uk

Over 360,000 transparencies, mostly medium-format. Colour coverage of travel subjects: places, people, folklore, events. Assignments undertaken for guide books and brochure photography.

Robbie Jack Photography

45 Church Road, Hanwell, London W7 3BD
☎020 8567 9616 Fax 020 8567 9616
Email rjackphoto@aol.com

Contact *Robbie Jack*

Built up over the last 19 years, the library contains over 300,000 colour transparencies of the performing arts – theatre, dance, opera and music. Includes West End shows, the RSC and Royal National Theatre productions, English National Opera and Royal Opera. The dance section contains images of the Royal Ballet, English National Ballet, the Rambert Dance Company, plus many foreign companies. Also holds the largest selection of colour material from the Edinburgh International Festival. Researchers are welcome to visit by appointment.

Jayawardene Travel Photo Library

7A Napier Road, Wembley, Middlesex
HA0 4UA
☎020 8902 3588 Fax 020 8902 7114
Email rjayawarde@aol.com
Website members.aol.com/rjayawarde

Contact *Rohith Jayawardene*

170,000 colour transparencies of travel and travel-related subjects, covering countries worldwide. Most places have been photographed in depth, with more than 600 images per destination. Shot in 35mm and medium format and regularly updated. Commissions undertaken. Contributing photographers welcome (please telephone first) – minimum initial submission: 200 transparencies.

Trevor Jones
Thoroughbred Photography

The Hornbeams, 2 The Street, Worlington,
Suffolk IP28 8RU
☎01638 713944 Fax 01638 713945
Email trevorjones@thoroughbredphoto.com
Website www.thoroughbredphoto.com

Contacts *Trevor Jones, Gill Jones, Laura Green*

Extensive library of high-quality colour transparencies depicting all aspects of thoroughbred horse racing dating from 1987. Major group races, English classics, studs, stallions, mares and foals, early morning scenes, personalities, jockeys, trainers and prominent owners. Also international work: USA Breeders Cup, Arc de Triomphe, French Classics, Irish Derby, Dubai racing scene, Japan Cup and Hokkaido stud farms; and more unusual scenes such as racing on the sands at low tide, Ireland, and on the frozen lake at St Moritz. Visitors by appointment.

Katz Pictures/FSP

109 Clifton Street, London EC2A 4LD
☎020 7749 6000 Fax 020 7749 6001
Email katzpictures@katzpictures.com
Website www.katzpictures.com

Contact *Sarah Bennett*

Contains an extensive collection of colour and b&w material covering a multitude of subjects from around the world – business, environment, industry, lifestyles, politics plus celebrity portraits from the entertainment world. Also Hollywood portraits and film stills dating back to the twenties.

David King Collection

90 St Pauls Road, London N1 2QP
☎020 7226 0149 Fax 020 7354 8264
Email davidkingcollection@btopenworld.com

Contact *David King*

250,000 b&w original and copy photographs and colour transparencies of historical and present-day images. Russian history and the Soviet Union from 1900 to the fall of Khrushchev; the lives of Lenin, Trotsky and Stalin; the Tzars, Russo-Japanese War, 1917 Revolution, World War I, Red Army, the Great Purges, Great Patriotic War, etc. Special collections on China, Eastern Europe, the Weimar Republic, John Heartfield, American labour struggles, Spanish Civil War. Open to qualified researchers by appointment, Monday to Friday, 10.00 am to 6.00 pm. Staff will undertake research; negotiable fee for long projects. David King's latest photographic book, *The Commissar Vanishes*, documents the falsification of photographs and art in Stalin's Russia.

The Kobal Collection

2 The Quadrant, 135 Salusbury Road,
London NW6 6RJ
☎020 7624 3300 Fax 020 7624 3311
Email info@picture-desk.com
Website www.picture-desk.com

Colour and b&w coverage of Hollywood films: portraits, stills, publicity shots, posters, ephemera. Visitors by appointment.

Kos Picture Source Ltd

7 Spice Court, Ivory Square, Plantation
Wharf, London SW11 3UE
☎020 7801 0044 Fax 020 7801 0055
Email images@kospictures.com
Website www.kospictures.com

Specialists in water-related images including international yacht racing and cruising, classic boats and superyachts, and extensive range of watersports. Also worldwide travel including seascapes, beach scenes, underwater photography and the weather.

Ed Lacey Collection
See **Phil Sheldon Golf Picture Library**

Frank Lane Picture Agency Ltd
Pages Green House, Wetheringsett, Stowmarket, Suffolk IP14 5QA
☎01728 860789 Fax 01728 860222
Email pictures@flpa-images.co.uk
Website www.flpa-images.co.uk

Colour and b&w coverage of natural history, environment, pets and weather. Represents Sunset from France, Foto Natura from Holland, Minden Pictures from the US and works closely with Eric and David Hosking, plus 270 freelance photographers.

Last Resort Picture Library
Manvers Studios, 12 Ollerton Road, Tuxford, Newark, Nottinghamshire NG22 0LF
☎01777 870166 Fax 01777 871739
Email LRPL@dmimaging.co.uk
Website www.dmimaging.co.uk

Contact *Jo Makin*

Images of agriculture, architecture, education, social issues, landscape, industry, food, people at work, computing and new technology. Images cover a wide variety of areas rather than specialising, ranging from the everyday to the obscure.

LAT Photographic
Somerset House, Somerset Road, Teddington TW11 8RU
☎020 8251 3000 Fax 020 8251 3001
Email lat.photo@haynet.com
Website www.latphoto.co.uk

Motor sport collection of over nine million images dating from 1895 to the present day.

André Laubier Picture Library
4 St James Park, Bath BA1 2SS
☎01225 420688 Fax 01225 420688

An extensive library of photographs from 1935 to the present day in 35mm and medium-format. Main subjects are: archaeology and architecture, art and artists (wood carving, sculptures, contemporary glass), botany, historical buildings, sites and events, landscapes, nature, leisure sports, events, experimental artwork and photography, people and travel. Substantial stock of many other subjects including: birds, buildings and

cities, folklore, food and drink, gardens, transport. Special collection: Images d'Europe (Austria, Britain, France, Greece, S.W. Ireland, Italy, Spain, Turkey, Egypt – from Cairo to Abu Simbel), Norway and former Yugoslavia). Private collection: World War II to D-Day. List available on request. Correspondence welcome in English, French or German.

Lebrecht Music Collection
58b Carlton Hill, London NW8 0ES
☎020 7625 5341/7372 8233
Fax 020 7625 5341
Email pictures@lebrecht.co.uk
Website www.lebrecht.co.uk

Contact *Elbie Lebrecht*

50,000 prints and transparencies covering classical music, from antiquity to 21st century minimalists. Instruments, opera singers, concert halls and opera houses, composers and musicians.

The Erich Lessing Archive of Fine Art & Culture
c/o AKG London Ltd, The Arts and History Picture Library, 5 Melbray Mews, 158 Hurlingham Road, London SW6 3NS
☎020 7610 6103 Fax 020 7610 6125
Email enquiries@akg-london.co.uk
Website www.akg-london.co.uk

Archive of large-format transparencies depicting the contents of many of the world's finest art galleries as well as ancient archaeological and biblical sites. High resolution scans available via ISDN. Mac and PC-compatible CD-ROMs. Represented by **AKG London Ltd**.

Life File Ltd
76 Streathbourne Road, London SW17 8QY
☎020 8767 8832 Fax 020 8672 8879
Email simontaylor@attglobal.net

Contact *Simon Taylor*

300,000 images of people and places, lifestyles, industry, environmental issues, natural history and customs, from Afghanistan to Zimbabwe. Stocks most of the major tourist destinations throughout the world, including the UK.

Lindley Library, Royal Horticultural Society
80 Vincent Square, London SW1P 2PE
☎020 7821 3053 Fax 020 7828 3022

Contact *Jennifer Vine*

20,000 original drawings and approx. 8000 books with hand-coloured plates of botanical illustrations. Appointment is absolutely essential; all photography is done by own photographer.

Link Picture Library

33 Greyhound Road, London W6 8NH
☎020 7381 2261/2433 Fax 020 7385 6244
Email lib@linkpicturelibrary.com
Website www.linkphotographers.com

Contact *Orde Eliason*

100,000 images of South Africa, India, China, Vietnam and Israel. A more general collection of colour transparencies from 100 countries worldwide. Link Picture Library and its partner, Images of India, has an international network and can source material not in its file from Japan, Scandinavia, India and South Africa. Original photographic commissions undertaken.

London Aerial Photo Library

PO Box 25, Ashwellthorpe, Norwich, Norfolk NR16 1HL
☎01508 488320 Fax 01508 488282
Email aerialphotos@btinternet.com
Website www.londonaerial.co.uk

Contact *Sandy Stockwell*

80,000 colour negatives of aerial photographs covering most of Britain, with particular emphasis on London and surrounding counties. No search fee. Photocopies of library prints are supplied free of charge to enquirers. Welcomes enquiries in respect of either general subjects or specific sites and buildings.

The London Film Archive

78 Mildmay Park, Islington, London N1 4PR
☎020 7923 4074 Fax 020 7241 4929
Email info@londonfilmarchive.org
Website www.londonfilmarchive.org

Contact *Robert Dewar*

Archive which concentrates on all aspects of commercial, political and social life in the City and suburbs of London. The collection is primarily a film collection but also has stills, glass plate negatives, posters, advertising and documents of London interest.

London Metropolitan Archives

40 Northampton Road, London EC1R 0HB
☎020 7332 3820 Fax 020 7833 9136
Email ask.lma@corpoflondon.gov.uk
Website www.cityoflondon.gov.uk

Contact *The Senior Librarian*

Approximately 500,000 images of London, mostly topographical and architectural. Subjects include education, local authority housing, transport, the Thames, parks, churches, hospitals, war damage, pubs, theatres and cinemas. Also major redevelopments like the South Bank, the City, Covent Garden and Docklands.

London's Transport Museum Photographic Library

39 Wellington Street, London WC2E 7BB
☎020 7379 6344 Fax 020 7565 7252
Website www.ltmuseum.co.uk

Contacts *Hugh Robertson, Simon Murphy, Martin Harrison-Putnam*

Around 100,000 b&w images from the 1860s and 20,000 colour images from c.1975. *Specialist collections* Poster archive, Underground construction, corporate design and architecture, street scenes, London Transport during the war. Collection available for viewing by appointment on Monday and Tuesday. No loans system but prints and transparences can be purchased. Digital images available on CD-ROM.

Lonely Planet Images

See **Lonely Planet Publications** under **UK Publishers**

Ludvigsen Library Limited

73 Collier Street, London N1 9BE
☎020 7837 1700 Fax 020 7837 1776
Email library@ludvigsen.com
Website www.ludvigsen.com

Contact *Karl Ludvigsen*

Extensive information research facilities for writers and publishers. Approximately 400,000 images (both b&w and many colour transparencies) of automobiles and motorsport, from 1920s through 1980s. Glass plate negatives from the early 1900s; Formula One, Le Mans, motor car shows, vintage, antique and classic cars from all countries. Includes the Dalton-Watson Collection and the work of noted photographers such as John Dugdale, Edward Eves, Peter Keen, Max le Grand, Karl Ludvigsen, Rodolfo Mailander, Ove Nielsen, Stanley Rosenthall and others.

MacQuitty International Photographic Collection

7 Elm Lodge, River Gardens, Stevenage Road, London SW6 6NZ
☎020 7385 5606 Fax 020 7385 5606
Email miranda.macquitty@btinternet.com

Contact *Dr Miranda MacQuitty*

Colour and b&w collection on aspects of life in over 70 countries: dancing, music, religion, death, archaeology, buildings, transport, food, drink, nature. Visitors by appointment.

Magnum Photos Ltd
Moreland Buildings, 2nd Floor, 5 Old Street, London EC1V 9HL
☎020 7490 1771 Fax 020 7608 0020
Email magnum@magnumphotos.co.uk
Website www.magnumphotos.com
Head of Library *Hamish Crooks*

FOUNDED 1947 by Cartier Bresson, George Rodger, Robert Capa and David 'Chim' Seymour. Represents over 50 of the world's leading photo-journalists. Coverage of all major world events from the Spanish Civil War to present day. Also a large collection of personalities.

The Raymond Mander & Joe Mitchenson Theatre Collection
Jerwood Library of the Performing Arts, Trinity College of Music, King Charles Court, Old Royal Naval College, London SE10 9JF
☎020 8305 3893 Fax 020 8305 3993
Email rmangan@tcm.ac.uk
Website www.mander-and-mitchenson.co.uk
Contact *Richard Mangan*

Enormous collection covering all aspects of the theatre: plays, actors, dramatists, music hall, theatres, singers, composers, etc. Visitors welcome by appointment.

S&O Mathews Photography
The Old Rectory, Calbourne, Isle of Wight PO30 4JE
☎01983 531247 Fax 01983 531253
Email oliver@mathews-photography.com
Website www.mathews-photography.com
Library of colour transparencies of gardens, plants and landscapes.

Institution of Mechanical Engineers
1 Birdcage Walk, London SW1H 9JJ
☎020 7973 1265 Fax 020 7222 8762
Email k_moore@imeche.org.uk
Website www.imeche.org.uk
Senior Librarian & Archivist *Keith Moore*

Historical and contemporary images on mechanical engineering. Open 9.15 am to 5.30 pm, Mon. to Fri. Telephone for appointment.

Medimage
32 Brooklyn Road, Coventry CV1 4JT
☎024 7666 8562 Fax 024 7666 8562
Email chambersking@ntlworld.com
Contacts *Anthony King, Catherine King*

Medium format colour transparencies of Mediterranean countries, also some from the Czech Republic, covering a wide range of subjects: agriculture, archaeology, architecture, arts, crafts, education, festivals, flora, geography, history, industry, landscapes, markets, recreation, seascapes, sports and transport. The collection is added to on a regular basis and commissions are undertaken. No search fees. Pictures by other photographers are not accepted.

Meledin Collection
See **Mary Evans Picture Library**

The MerseySlides Collection
c/o Tropix Photo Library, 156 Meols Parade, Meols, Meols, Wirral CH47 6AN
☎0151 632 1698 Fax 0151 632 1698
Email tropixphoto@talk21.com
Website www.tropix.co.uk
Contact *Veronica Birley*

The MerseySlides Collection comes from **Tropix Photo Library** and contains powerful images of Liverpool, Merseyside, Wirral, Cheshire and much of North West England. Also North Wales, Scotland, other parts of England, Ireland and some Europe. Assignment and studio photography are regularly undertaken for a wide range of clients, both commercial and editorial. Photography is available in all formats including digital and panoramic.

Lee Miller Archives
Farley Farm House, Chiddingly, Near Lewes, East Sussex BN8 6HW
☎01825 872691 Fax 01825 872733
Email archives@leemiller.co.uk
Website www.leemiller.co.uk

The work of Lee Miller (1907–77). As a photojournalist she covered the war in Europe from early in 1944 to VE Day with further reporting from the Balkans. Collection includes photographic portraits of prominent Surrealist artists: Ernst, Eluard, Miró, Picasso, Penrose, Carrington, Tanning, and others. Surrealist and contemporary art, poets and writers, fashion, the Middle East, Egypt, the Balkans in the 1930s, London during the Blitz, war in Europe and the liberation of Dachau and Buchenwald.

Monitor Picture Library
The Forge, Roydon, Harlow, Essex CM19 5HH
☎01279 792700 Fax 01279 792600
Email info@monitorpicturelibrary.com
Website www.monitorpicturelibrary.com

Colour and b&w coverage of leading international personalities. Politics, entertainment, royals, judicial, commerce, religion, trade unions, well-known buildings. Also an archive library dating back to 1840, and a specialist file on Lotus cars. Syndication to international, national and local media.

Moroccan Scapes

Seend Park, Seend, Wiltshire SN12 6NZ
☎01380 828533 Fax 01380 828630
Email chris@morocco-travel.com
Website www.realmorocco.com

Contact *Chris Lawrence*

Specialist collection of Moroccan material: scenery, towns, people, markets and places, plus the Atlas Mountains. Over 18,000 images.

Motoring Picture Library

National Motor Museum, Beaulieu, Hampshire SO42 7ZN
☎01590 614656 Fax 01590 612655
Email motoring.pictures@beaulieu.co.uk
Website www.alamay.com/mpl *and* www.heritage-images.com

Contact *Jonathan Day*

Three-quarters of a million b&w images, plus 90,000 colour transparencies covering all forms of motoring history from the 1880s to the present day. Commissions undertaken. Own studio.

Mountain Camera

See **John Cleare**

Moving Image Communications

61 Great Titchfield Street, London W1W 7PP
☎020 7580 3300 Fax 020 7580 2242
Email mail@milibrary.com
Website www.milibrary.com

Contact *Kevin Smalley*

Over 11,350 hours of quality archive and contemporary footage, including: Channel X Communications; TVAM Archive 1983–92; Leo & Mandy Dickinson Action & Adventure Sports Archive; The Lonely Planet (TV travel series); Shark Bay Films (tropical and subaqua); British Tourist Authority – BTA (1930 to present day); TIDA Public Information Films (BTA's predecessor); Buff Films (aviation archive/NATO planes and ships); Drummer Films (travel classics, 1950–70); Universal Newsreels (1950s-60s); The Freud Archive (1930–39); Natural World; Stockshots (time-lapse, cityscapes, land and seascapes, chroma-key); Space Exploration (NASA); Wild Islands; Flying Pictures; National Trust.

Museum of Antiquities Picture Library

University and Society of Antiquaries of Newcastle upon Tyne, Newcastle upon Tyne NE1 7RU
☎0191 222 7846 Fax 0191 222 8561
Email m.o.antiquities@ncl.ac.uk
Website www.ncl.ac.uk/antiquities

Contact *Lindsay Allason-Jones*

25,000 images, mostly b&w, of special collections including: Hadrian's Wall Archive (b&ws taken over the last 100 years); Gertrude Bell Archive (during her travels in the Near East, 1900–26); and aerial photographs of archaeological sites in the North of England. Visitors welcome by appointment.

Museum of London Picture Library

150 London Wall, London EC2Y 5HN
☎020 7814 5604 Fax 020 7600 1058
Email picturelib@museumoflondon.org.uk

The Museum of London Picture Library tells the story of London from its earliest settlers to the present day. Suffragettes: photographs and memorabilia; Museum Objects: gallery and reserve collections – Prehistoric, Roman, Saxon, Medieval, Tudor, Stuart, Georgian, Victorian, London Now; Photographs: social history of the capital – working life, East End, inter-war years, the Blitz, post-war; Prints and Caricatures: political and social satire, architecture; Paintings: dating from the 17th century, portraits, landscapes, cityscapes.

National Galleries of Scotland Picture Library

The Dean Gallery, Belford Road, Edinburgh EH4 3DS
☎0131 624 6258/6260 Fax 0131 623 7135
Email picture.library@nationalgalleries.org

Contact *Deborah Hunter*

Over 30,000 b&w and several thousand images in colour of works of art from the Renaissance to present day. Specialist subjects cover fine art (painting, sculpture, drawing), portraits, Scottish, historical, still life, photography and landscape. Colour leaflet, scale of charges and application forms available on request.

National Maritime Museum Picture Library

Greenwich, London SE10 9NF
☎020 8312 6631/6704 Fax 020 8312 6533
Email picturelibrary@nmm.ac.uk
Website www.nmm.ac.uk

Contacts *David Taylor, Chris Rich*

Over three million maritime-related images and artefacts, including oil paintings from the 16th century to present day, prints and drawings, historic photographs, plans of ships built in the UK since the beginning of the 18th century, models, rare maps and charts, instruments, etc. Over 50,000 items within the collection are now photographed and with the Historic Photographs Collection form the basis of the picture library's stock.

National Meteorological Library and Archive
See entry under **Library Services**

National Monuments Record
National Monuments Record Centre, Kemble Drive, Swindon, Wiltshire SN2 2GZ
☎01793 414600 Fax 01793 414606
Email nmrinfo@english-heritage.org.uk
Website www.english-heritage.org.uk

The National Monuments Record is the first stop for photographs and information on England's heritage. Over 10 million photographs, documents and drawings are held. English architecture from the first days of photography to the present, air photographs covering every inch of England from the first days of flying to the present, and archaeological sites. The record is the public archive of English Heritage. The London office specialises in the architecture of the capital city. For more information e-mail nmrlondon@english-heritage.org.uk or phone 020 7208 8200.

National Portrait Gallery Picture Library
St Martin's Place, London WC2H 0HE
☎020 7312 2474/5/6 Fax 020 7312 2464
Email picturelibrary@npg.org.uk
Website www.npg.org.uk

Contact *Tom Morgan*

Access to over 900,000 portraits of famous British men and women dating from the middle ages to the present. Images can be searched, viewed and ordered on the website.

National Railway Museum Picture Library
Leeman Road, York YO26 4XJ
☎01904 621261 Fax 01904 611112
Email nrm@nmsi.ac.uk
Website www.nrm.org.uk

1.5 million images, mainly b&w, covering every aspect of railways from 1850s to the present day. Visitors by appointment.

The National Trust Photo Library
36 Queen Anne's Gate, London SW1H 9AS
☎020 7447 6788/9 Fax 020 7447 6767
Email photolibrary@ntrust.org.uk
Website www.nationaltrust.org.uk/photolibrary

Contact *Amanda Russell*

Collection of mixed-format transparencies covering landscape and coastline throughout England, Wales and Northern Ireland; also architecture, interiors, gardens, paintings and conservation, plus a new collection of wildlife photographs. Award-winning brochure available on request. Profits from the picture library are reinvested in continuing the work of the Trust.

Natural History Museum Picture Library
Cromwell Road, London SW7 5BD
☎020 7942 5401/5324 Fax 020 7942 5443
Email nhmpl@nhm.ac.uk
Website www.nhm.ac.uk/piclib

Contacts *Hillary Smith, Dawn Hathaway*

Pictures from the Museum's collections, including dinosaurs, man's evolution, extinct species and fossil remains. Also pictures of gems, minerals, birds and animals, plants and insect specimens, plus historical artworks depicting the natural world.

Natural History Photographic Agency
See **NHPA**

Natural Science Photos
33 Woodland Drive, Watford, Hertfordshire WD17 3BY
☎01923 245265 Fax 01923 246067

Colour coverage of natural history subjects worldwide. The work of some 150 photographers, it includes angling, animals, birds, reptiles, amphibia, fish, insects and other invertebrates, habitats, plants, fungi, geography, weather, scenics, horticulture, agriculture, farm animals and registered dog breeds. Researched by experienced scientists, Peter and Sondra Ward. Visits by appointment. Commissions undertaken.

Nature Photographers Ltd
West Wit, New Road, Little London, Tadley, Hampshire RG26 5EU
☎01256 850661 Fax 01256 851157

Email info@naturephotographersco.uk
Website www.naturephotographers.co.uk

Contact *Dr Paul Sterry*

Over 150,000 images on worldwide natural history and environmental subjects. The library is run by a trained biologist and experienced author on his subject.

Nature Picture Library
BBC Broadcasting House, Whiteladies Road, Bristol BS8 2LR
☎0117 974 6720 Fax 0117 923 8166
Email info@naturepl.com
Website www.naturepl.com

Contact *Helen Gilks*

A collection of 120,000 transparencies of wildlife from around the world, especially animal portraits and behaviour. Other subjects covered include plants, landscapes, environmental issues and photos relating to the making of the BBC natural history films. Thousands of images can be viewed online and downloaded for reproduction.

Peter Newark's Picture Library
3 Barton Buildings, Queen Square, Bath BA1 2JR
☎01225 334213 Fax 01225 480554

Over one million images covering world history from ancient times to the present day. Includes an extensive military collection of photographs, paintings and illustrations. Also a special collection on American history covering Colonial times, exploration, social, political and the Wild West and Native-Americans in particular. Subject list available. Telephone, fax or write for further information.

NHPA (Natural History Photographic Agency)
Little Tye, 57 High Street, Ardingly, West Sussex RH17 6TB
☎01444 892514 Fax 01444 892168
Email nhpa@nhpa.co.uk
Website www.nhpa.co.uk

Library Manager *Tim Harris*

Extensive coverage on all aspects of natural history – animals, plants, landscapes, environmental issues, gardens and pets. 150 photographers worldwide provide a steady input of high-quality transparencies. Specialist files include the unique high-speed photography of Stephen Dalton, extensive coverage of African and American wildlife, also rainforests, marine life and the polar regions. UK agents for the

ANT collection of Australasian material. Loans are generally made direct to publishers; individual writers must request material via their publisher.

Odhams Periodicals Library
See **Popperfoto**

Offshoot
See **Skishoot**

Only Horses Picture Agency
27 Greenway Gardens, Greenford, Middlesex UB6 9TU
☎020 8578 9047 Fax 020 8575 7244
Email onlyhorsespics@aol.com
Website www.onlyhorsespictures.com

Colour and b&w coverage of all aspects of the horse. Foaling, retirement, racing, show jumping, eventing, veterinary, polo, breeds, personalities.

Oxford Picture Library
15 Curtis Yard, North Hinksey Lane, Oxford OX2 0LX
☎01865 723404 Fax 01865 725294
Email chris.andrews@virgin.net
Website www.cap-ox.co.uk

Contacts *Annabel Webb, Chris Andrews*

Specialist collection on Oxford: the city, university and colleges, events, people, spires and shires. Also, the Cotswolds, architecture and landscape from Stratford-upon-Avon to Bath; the Thames and Chilterns, including Henley on Thames and Windsor; Channel Islands, especially Guernsey and Sark. Aerial views of all areas specified above. General collection includes wildlife, trees, plants, clouds, sun, sky, water and teddy bears. Commissions undertaken.

Oxford Scientific Films Photo Library
Lower Road, Long Hanborough, Oxfordshire OX29 8LL
☎01993 881881 Fax 01993 882808
Email photo.library@osf.uk.com
Website www.osf.uk.com

Head of Film & Photo Library *Suzanne Aitzetmuller*
Account Managers *Nick Jessop, Rebecca Warren, Ruth Blair, Charlotte Jones*

Collection of 350,000 colour transparencies of wildlife and natural science images supplied by over 300 photographers worldwide, covering all aspects of wildlife plus landscapes, weather, seasons, plants, environment, anthropology, habitats, industry, space, creative textures and backgrounds, and geology. Macro and micro photography. UK agents for Animals Animals, USA, Okapia, Germany and Dinodia, India. Research by experienced researchers for specialist and creative briefs. Visits welcome, by appointment.

PA News Photo Library

PA News Centre, 292 Vauxhall Bridge Road, London SW1V 1AE
☎020 7963 7990 Fax 020 7963 7066
Email paphotos@pa.press.net
Website www.paphotos.com

PA News, the 24-hour national news and information group, offers public access to its photographic archives. Photographs, dating from 1890 to the present day, cover everything from news and sport to entertainment and royalty, with around 50 new pictures added daily.

PAL (Performing Arts Library)

First Floor, Production House, 25 Hackney Road, London E2 7NX
☎020 7749 4850 Fax 020 7749 4858
Email performingartspics@pobox.com
Website www.PerformingArtsLibrary.co.uk

Continually updated specialist image collection covering classical music, opera, theatre, musicals, instruments, festivals, venues, circus, ballet and contemporary dance. Almost one million images from late 19th century onwards. Please phone, fax or e-mail to make a selection.

Hugh Palmer

Knapp House, Shenington, Near Banbury, Oxfordshire OX15 6NE
☎01295 670433 Fax 01295 670709
Email hupalmer@msn.com
Website www.hughpalmer.com

Extensive collection of landscapes, rural life and architecture from Britain and Europe, as featured in *The Most Beautiful Villages* series of books published by Thames & Hudson.

Panos Pictures

1 Chapel Court, Borough High Street, London SE1 1HH
☎020 7234 0010 Fax 020 7357 0094
Email pics@panos.co.uk
Website www.panos.co.uk

Documentary colour and b&w library specialising in Third World and Eastern Europe, with emphasis on environment and development issues. Leaflet available. Fifty per cent of all profits from this library go to the Panos

Institute to further its work in international sustainable development.

Papilio

The Oasts, Headley Lane, Passfield, Liphook, Hampshire GU30 7RX
☎01428 751056 Fax 01428 751057
Email library@papiliophotos.com
Website www.papiliophotos.com

Contacts *Robert Pickett, Vicki Coombs*

More than 100,000 colour transparencies of natural history, including birds, animals, insects, flowers, plants, fungi and landscapes; plus travel worldwide including people, places and cultures. Commissions undertaken. Colour catalogue and digital slide show on disk available; call for further information. Visits by appointment only.

Charles Parker Archive

See **Birmingham Library Services** under **Library Services**

Ann & Bury Peerless Picture Library

St David's, 22 King's Avenue, Minnis Bay, Birchington-on-Sea, Kent CT7 9QL
☎01843 841428 Fax 01843 848321
Website www.peerlessimages.com

Contacts *Ann or Bury Peerless*

Specialist collection on world religions: Hinduism, Buddhism, Jainism, Christianity, Islam, Sikhism. Geographical areas covered: India, Afghanistan (Bamiyan Valley of the Buddhas), Pakistan, Bangladesh, Sri Lanka, Cambodia (Angkor), Java (Borobudur), Bali, Thailand, Russia, Republic of China, Spain, Poland, Uzbekistan (Samarkand and Bukhara), Vietnam. 10,000 35mm colour transparencies.

Performing Arts Library

See **PAL**

Photo Resources

The Orchard, Marley Lane, Kingston, Canterbury, Kent CT4 6JH
☎01227 830075 Fax 01227 831135

Colour and b&w coverage of archaeology, art, ancient art, ethnology, mythology, world religion, museum objects.

Photofusion

17A Electric Lane, London SW9 8LA
☎020 7738 5774 Fax 020 7738 5509
Email library@photofusion.org
Website www.photofusion.org

Contact *Liz Somerville*

Colour and b&w coverage of contemporary social issues including babies and children, disability, education, the elderly, environment, family, health, housing, homelessness, people and work. Brochure available.

The Photolibrary Wales

2 Bro-nant, Church Road, Pentyrch, Cardiff CF15 9QG
☎029 2089 0311 Fax 029 2089 2650
Email info@photolibrarywales.com
Website www.photolibrarywales.com

Contacts *Steve Benbow, Kate Benbow*

Over 60,000 colour transparences covering all areas and subjects of Wales. Represents the work of 140 photographers, living and working in Wales.

Photos Horticultural

PO Box 105, Ipswich, Suffolk IP1 4PR
☎01473 257329 Fax 01473 233974
Email library@photos.keme.co.uk
Website www.photos-horticultural.co.uk

Wide coverage of gardens and all aspects of gardening from library established in 1968. Now incorporates the Kenneth Scowen Collection. 'Extensive travelling ensures the best material from around the world is on file.'

PictureBank Photo Library Ltd

Parman House, 30–36 Fife Road, Kingston upon Thames, Surrey KT1 1SY
☎020 8547 2344 Fax 020 8974 5652
Website www.picturebank.co.uk

Over 400,000 colour transparencies covering people (girls, couples, families, children), travel and scenic (UK and world), moods (sunsets, seascapes, deserts, etc.), industry and technology, environments and general. Commissions undertaken. Visitors welcome. Member of **BAPLA**. New material on medium/large format welcome.

Pictures Colour Library

10 James Whatman Court, Turkey Mill, Ashford Road, Maidstone, Kent ME14 5SS
☎01622 609809 Fax 01622 609806
Email Researcher@PicturesColourLibrary.co.uk
Website www.picturescolourlibrary.co.uk

Travel and travel-related images depicting lifestyles and cultures, people and places, attitudes and environments from around the world, including a comprehensive section on Great Britain.

H.G. Ponting

See **Popperfoto**

Popperfoto

The Old Mill, Overstone Farm, Overstone, Northampton NN6 0AB
☎01604 670670 Fax 01604 670635
Email popperfoto@msn.com
Website www.popperfoto.com

Home to over 14 million images, covering 150 years of photographic history. Renowned for its archival material, a world-famous sports library and stock photography. Popperfoto's credit line includes Reuters, Bob Thomas Sports Photography, UPI, Acme, INP, Planet, Paul Popper, Exclusive News Agency, Victory Archive, Odhams Periodicals Library, Illustrated, Harris Picture Agency, and H.G. Ponting which holds the Scott 1910–1912 Antarctic expedition. Colour from 1940, b&w from 1870 to the present. Major subjects covered worldwide include events, personalities, wars, royalty, sport, politics, transport, crime, history and social conditions. Material available on the same day to clients throughout the world. Mac-desk available. Researchers welcome by appointment. Free catalogue available.

PPL (Photo Agency) Ltd

Bookers Yard, The Street, Walberton, Arundel, West Sussex BN18 0PF
☎01243 555561 Fax 01243 555562
Email ppl@mistral.co.uk
Website www.pplmedia.com

Contacts *Barry Pickthall, Jo Bennett*

Two million pictures covering watersports, business and commerce, travel and tourism and a fast growing achive on Sussex. Pictures available in high resolution directly from website.

Premaphotos Wildlife

Amberstone, 1 Kirland Road, Bodmin, Cornwall PL30 5JQ
☎01208 78258 Fax 01208 72302
Email authors@premaphotos.co.uk
Website www.premaphotos.co.uk

Library Manager *Jean Preston-Mafham,*

Natural history worldwide. Subjects include flowering and non-flowering plants, fungi, slime moulds, fruits and seeds, galls, leaf mines, seashore life, mammals, birds, reptiles, amphibians, insects, spiders, habitats, scenery and cultivated cacti. Commissions undertaken. Visitors welcome. 'Make sure your name is on our mailing list to receive regular, colourful mailers.'

Professional Sport UK Ltd
18–19 Shaftesbury Quay, Hertford,
Hertfordshire SG14 1SF
☎01992 505000 Fax 01992 505020
Email pictures@prosport.co.uk
Website www.professionalsport.com

Photographic coverage of tennis, soccer, athletics, golf, cricket, rugby, winter sports and many minor sports. Major international events including the Olympic Games, World Cup soccer and all Grand Slam tennis events. Also news and feature material supplied worldwide. Online photo archive; photo transmission services available for editorial and advertising.

Public Record Office
Image Library
Ruskin Avenue, Kew, Richmond, Surrey
TW9 4DU
☎020 8392 5225 Fax 020 8392 5266
Email image-library@pro.gov.uk

Contacts *Paul Johnson, Hugh Alexander*

British and colonial history from the Domesday Book to the 1960s, shown in photography, maps, illuminations, posters, advertisements, textiles and original manuscripts. Approximately 30,000 5x4″ and 35mm colour transparencies and b&w negatives. Open: 9.00 am to 5.30 pm, Monday to Friday.

Punch Cartoon Library
Suite 5, 3 Hans Crescent, London
SW1X 0LN
☎020 7225 6710/6793 Fax 020 7225 6712
Email punch.library@harrods.com
Website www.punch.co.uk

Owner *Liberty Publishing*

Gives access to the 500,000 cartoons published in *Punch* magazine between 1841–1992. The library has a 500+ subject listing and can search on any topic. Social history, politics, fashion, fads, famous people and more by the world's most famous cartoonists, including Tenniel, du Maurier, Pont, Fougasse, E.H. Shepard and Emmett.

PWA International Ltd
City Gate House, 399–425 Eastern Avenue, Gants Hill, Ilford, Essex IG2 6LR
☎020 8518 2057 Fax 020 8518 2241
Email pwaint@dircon.co.uk

Contact *Terry Allen*

Leading comprehensive library of story illustrations comprising work by some of the UK's best-known illustrators, including book covers and magazines. Also over half a million images of beauty, cookery and craft.

Railfotos
Millbrook House Ltd., Unit 1, Oldbury
Business Centre, Pound Road, Oldbury,
West Midlands B68 8NA
☎0121 544 2970
Fax 0121 253 6836 (quote Millbrook House)

One of the largest specialist libraries dealing comprehensively with railway subjects worldwide. Colour and b&w dating from the turn of the century to present day. Up-to-date material on UK, South America and Far East. Visitors by appointment.

Redferns Music Picture Library
7 Bramley Road, London W10 6SZ
☎020 7792 9914 Fax 020 7792 0921
Email info@redferns.com
Website www.musicpictures.com

Music picture library covering every aspect of popular music from 1920's jazz to present day. Over 15,000 artists on file plus other subjects including musical instruments, recording studios, crowd scenes, festivals, etc. Brochure available.

Retna Pictures Ltd
Ground Floor, 53–56 Great Sutton Street,
London EC1V 0DG
☎020 7608 4800 Fax 020 7608 4805
Email london@retna.com
Website www.retna.com

Established 1978, Retna Pictures Ltd is a leading picture agency with two libraries: celebrity and lifestyle. The former specialises in images of international and national celebrities, early and contemporary music, films and personalities and has an exclusive syndication deal with the *LA Times*. The lifestyle library specialises in people, family life, work, leisure and food. Both libraries are constantly receiving new material from established and up and coming photographers.

Retrograph Nostalgia Archive Ltd
164 Kensington Park Road, London W11 2ER
☎020 7727 9378 Fax 020 7229 3395
Email retropix1@aol.com
Website www.Retrograph.com

Contact *Jilliana Ranicar-Breese*

'Number One for nostalgia!' A vast archive of commercial and decorative art (1860–1960). Worldwide labels and packaging for food, wine, chocolate, soap, perfume, cigars and cigarettes; fine art and commercial art journals, fashion and lifestyle magazines, posters, Victorian greetings cards, scraps, Christmas cards, Edwardian post-cards, wallpaper and gift-wrap sample books, music sheets, folios of decorative design and ornament – Art Nouveau and Deco; hotel, air-line and shipping labels; memorabilia, tourism, leisure, food and drink, transport and entertain-ment. Lasers for book dummies, packaging, mock-ups, film/TV action props. Colour brochure on request. Picture research service. Design consultancy service. Victorian-style montages conceived, designed and styled (RetroMontages).

Rex Features Ltd

18 Vine Hill, London EC1R 5DZ
☎020 7278 7294 Fax 020 7696 0974
Email library@rexfeatures.com
Website www.rexfeatures.com

Contact *Glen Marks*, Library Sales Manager

Extensive picture library established in the 1950s. Daily coverage of news, politics, per-sonalities, show business, glamour, humour, art, medicine, science, landscapes, royalty, etc.

Royal Air Force Museum

Grahame Park Way, Hendon, London
NW9 5LL
☎020 8205 2266 Fax 020 8200 1751
Email christine.gregory@rafmuseum.com

Contact *Christine Gregory*

About a quarter of a million images, mostly b&w, with around 1500 colour in all formats, on the history of aviation. Particularly strong on the activities of the Royal Air Force from the 1870s to 1970s. Researchers are requested to enquire in writing only.

The Royal Collection, Photographic Services

Windsor Castle, Windsor, Berks SL4 1NJ
☎01753 868286 Fax 01753 620046
Email photoservices@royalcollection.org.uk

Contact *Shruti Patel*

Photographic material of items in the Royal Collection, particularly oil paintings, drawings and watercolours, works of art, and interiors and exteriors of royal residences. 35,000 colour transparencies, plus 25,000 b&w negatives.

Royal Geographical Society Picture Library

1 Kensington Gore, London SW7 2AR
☎020 7591 3060 Fax 020 7591 3061
Email pictures@rgs.org

Website www.rgs.org/picturelibrary

Contact *Joanna Wright*

A strong source of geographical and historical images, both archival and modern, showing the world through the eyes of photographers and explorers dating from the 1830s to the present day. The RGS Contempory Collection pro-vides up-to-date transparencies from around the world, highlighting aspects of cultural activity, environmental phenomena, anthropology, architectural design, travel, mountaineering and exploration. Offers a professional and com-prehensive service for both commercial and academic use.

RSPB Images

That's Good, Britannia Walk, 151 City Road, London EC1V 1JH
☎020 7253 5411 Fax 020 7336 8170
Email rspb@thatsgood.biz
Website www.rspb-images.com

Contact *Zana Nel*

Colour and b&w images of birds, butterflies, moths, mammals, reptiles and their habitats. Also colour images of all RSPB reserves. Growing selection of various habitats. Over 52,000 slides available digitally or in any desired format.

RSPCA Photolibrary

RSPCA Trading Limited, Wilberforce Way, Southwater, Horsham, West Sussex RH13 7WN
☎0870 754 0150 Fax 0870 753 0048
Email pictures@rspcaphotolibrary.com
Website www.rspcaphotolibrary.com

Photolibrary Manager *Andrew Forsyth*

Over 70,000 colour transparencies and over 5000 b&w/colour prints. A comprehensive col-lection of natural history images whose subjects include mammals, birds, domestic and farm ani-mals, amphibians, insects and the environment, as well as a unique photographic record of the RSPCA's work. Also includes the Wild Images collections. Catalogue available. No search fees.

Russia and and Eastern Images

'Sonning', Cheapside Lane, Denham, Uxbridge, Middlesex UB9 5AE
☎01895 833508 Fax 01895 831957
Email easteuropix@btinternet.com

Architecture, cities, landscapes, people and travel images of Russia and the former Soviet Union. Considerable background knowledge available and Russian language spoken.

Peter Sanders Photography

24 Meades Lane, Chesham, Buckinghamshire
HP5 1ND
☎01494 773674/771372 Fax 01494 773674
Email photos@petersanders.com
Website www.petersanders.com

Contacts *Peter Sanders, Hafsa Garwatuk*

Specialises in the world of Islam in all its aspects
from culture, arts, industry, lifestyles, celebra-
tions, etc. Areas included are north, east and
west Africa, the Middle East (including Saudi
Arabia), China, Asia, Europe and USA. A continually expanding library.

Science & Society Picture Library

Science Museum, Exhibition Road, London
SW7 2DD
☎020 7942 4400 Fax 020 7942 4401
Email piclib@nmsi.ac.uk
Website www.nmsi.ac.uk/piclib/

Contact *Angela Murphy*

25,000 reference prints and 100,000 colour
transparencies, incorporating many from collections at the Science Museum, the National
Railway Museum and the National Museum of
Photography Film and Television. Collections
illustrate the history of science, industry, technology, medicine, transport and the media.
Plus three archives documenting British society
in the twentieth century.

Science Photo Library

327–329 Harrow Road, London W9 3RB
☎020 7432 1100 Fax 020 7286 8668
Email info@sciencephoto.com
Website www.sciencephoto.com

Subjects covered include the human body,
health and medicine, research, genetics, technology and industry, space exploration and
astronomy, earth science, satellite imagery,
environment, nature and wildlife and the history of science. The whole collection, more
than 100,000 images, is available online.

Kenneth Scowen Collection

See **Photos Horticultural**

Seaco Picture Library

Sea Containers House, 20 Upper Ground,
London SE1 9PF
☎020 7805 5831 Fax 020 7805 5807
Email seaco.pictures@seacontainers.com

Contact *Maureen Elliott*

Approx. 250,000 images of containerisation,
shipping, fast ferries, manufacturing, fruit farming, ports, hotels and leisure.

Mick Sharp Photography

Eithinog, Waun, Penisarwaun, Caernarfon,
Gwynedd LL55 3PW
☎01286 872425 Fax 01286 872425
Email mick.jean@virgin.net

Contacts *Mick Sharp, Jean Williamson*

Colour transparencies (6×4.5cm and 35mm)
and black & white prints (5×4" and 6×4.5cm
negatives) of subjects connected with archaeology, ancient monuments, buildings, churches,
countryside, environment, history, landscape,
past cultures and topography from Britain and
abroad. Photographs by Mick Sharp and Jean
Williamson, plus access to other specialist collections on related subjects. Commissions
undertaken.

Phil Sheldon Golf Picture Library

40 Manor Road, Barnet, Hertfordshire
EN5 2JQ
☎020 8440 1986 Fax 020 8440 9348
Email GolfSnap@aol.com

An expanding collection of over 500,000
quality images of the 'world of golf'. In-depth
worldwide tournament coverage including
every Major championship & Ryder Cup since
1976. Instruction, portraits, trophies and over
400 golf courses from around the world. Also
the Dale Concannon collection covering the
period 1870 to 1940, the classic 1960s collection by photographer Sidney Harris and the Ed
Lacey Collection.

Skishoot–Offshoot

Hall Place, Upper Woodcott, Whitchurch,
Hampshire RG28 7PY
☎01635 255527 Fax 01635 255528
Email skishootsnow@aol.com
Website www.skishoot.net

Contacts *Kate Parker, Jo Crossley*

Skishoot ski and snowboarding picture library
has 300,000 images. Offshoot travel library
specialises in France.

The Skyscan Photolibrary

Oak House, Toddington, Cheltenham,
Gloucestershire GL54 5BY
☎01242 621357 Fax 01242 621343
Email info@skyscan.co.uk
Website www.skyscan.co.uk

As well as the Skyscan Photolibrary collection of
unique balloon's-eye views of Britain, the
library now includes the work of photographers

from across the aviation spectrum; air to ground, aviation, aerial sports – 'in fact, anything aerial!' Links have been built with photographers across the world; photographs can be handled on an agency basis and held in house, or as a brokerage where the collection stays with the photographer; terms 50/50 for both. Commissioned photography arranged. Enquiries welcome.

SMG Newspapers Ltd
200 Renfield Street, Glasgow G2 3PR
☎0141 302 7364 Fax 0141 302 7383

Over six million images: b&w and colour photographs from *c*.1900 from the *Herald* (Glasgow) and *Evening Times*. Current affairs, Scotland, Glasgow, Clydeside shipbuilding and engineering, personalities, World Wars I and II, sport.

Snookerimages (Eric Whitehead Photography)
Postal Buildings, Ash Street, Bowness-on-Windermere, Cumbria LA23 3EB
☎015394 48894 Fax 015394 48294
Email eric@snookerimages.co.uk
Website www.snookerimages.co.uk

Over 20,000 images of snooker from 1982 to the present day. The agency covers local news events, PR and commercial material.

SOA Photo Library
Lovells Farm, Dark Lane, Stoke St Gregory, Taunton, Somerset TA3 6EU
☎0870 333 6062 Fax 0870 333 6082
Email info@soaphotoagency.com
Website www.soaphotoagency.com
Contact *Sabine Oppenlander*

85,000 colour slides, 15,000 b&w photos covering *Stern* productions, sports, travel and geographic, advertising, social subjects. Representatives of Voller Ernst, Interfoto, Picture Press, Look and many freelance photographers. Free catalogues available.

Solo Syndication Ltd (trading as Atlantic Syndication Partners)
17–18 Haywards Place, Clerkenwell, London EC1R 0EQ
☎020 7566 0360 Fax 020 7566 0388
Syndication Director *Trevor York*
Sales *Danny Howell, Nick York*
Online transmissions *Geoff Malyon*
  (☎020 7566 0370)
Three million images from the archives of the *Daily Mail, Mail on Sunday, Evening Standard*

and *Evening News*. Hard prints or Mac-to-mac delivery. 24-hour service.

Sotheby's Picture Library
34–35 New Bond Street, London W1A 2AA
☎020 7293 5383 Fax 020 7293 5062
Email piclib.london@sothebys.com
Contacts *Joanna Ling, David Johnson*

The library consists mainly of over 50,000 selected transparencies of pictures sold at Sotheby's. Images from the 15th to the 20th century. Oils, drawings, watercolours, prints and decorative items. 'Happy to do searches or, alternatively, visitors are welcome by appointment.'

South American Pictures
48 Station Road, Woodbridge, Suffolk IP12 4AT
☎01394 383963/380423 Fax 01394 380176
Email morrison@southamericanpictures.com
Website www.southamericanpictures.com *and specialist site:* www.nonesuchinfo.info
Contact *Marion Morrison*

Colour and b&w images of South/Central America, Cuba, Mexico, New Mexico (USA), Dominican Republic and Haiti, including archaeology and the Amazon. There is an archival section, with pictures and documents from most countries. Now with 40 contributing photographers.

The Special Photographers Library
21 Kensington Park Road, London W11 2EU
☎020 7221 3489 Fax 020 7792 9112
Email info@specialphotographers.com
Website www.specialphotographers.com
Contacts *Chris Kewbank*

Represents over 100 contemporary fine art photographers who are unusual in style, technique or subject matter. Also has exclusive access to the Bill Hopkins Collection – an archive of thousands of vintage pictures dating back to the early 20th century.

Frank Spooner Pictures (FSP)
See **Katz Pictures**

The Still Moving Picture Co.
157 Broughton Road, Edinburgh EH7 4JJ
☎0131 557 9697 Fax 0131 557 9699
Email info@stillmovingpictures.com
Website www.stillmovingpictures.com
Contact *John Hutchinson*

Over 100,000 colour images of Scotland and

sport. Scottish agents for **Allsport (UK) Ltd.** (Fully digitised service via www.stilldigital.co.uk)

Still Pictures' Whole Earth Photolibrary

199 Shooters Hill Road, Blackheath, London SE3 8UL
☎020 8858 8307 Fax 020 8858 2049
Email info@stillpictures.com
Website www.stillpictures.com

Contacts *Theresa de Salis, Mark Edwards*

FOUNDED 1970, the library is a leading source of pictures illustrating the human impact on the environment, Third World development issues, industrial ecology, nature and wildlife, endangered species and habitats. 400,000 colour medium-format transparencies, 100,000 b&w prints. Over 400 leading photographers from around the world supply the library with stock pictures. Write, phone or fax for Still Pictures' Environment and Third World catalogue and Still Pictures' Nature and Wildlife catalogue.

Stockfile

5 High Street, Sunningdale, Berkshire SL5 0LX
☎01344 872249 Fax 01344 872263
Email info@stockfile.co.uk
Website www.stockfile.co.uk

Contacts *Jill Behr, Steven Behr*

Specialist cycling collection with emphasis on mountain biking. Expanding adventure sports section covering snow, land, air and water activities.

Stockscotland Photo Library

Croft Roy, Crammond Brae, Tain, Ross-shire IV19 1JG
☎01862 892298 Fax 01862 892298
Email info@stockscotland.com
Website www.stockscotland.com

Contact *Hugh Webster*

150,000 colour transparencies of Scotland. Not just a travel library; images cover industry, agriculture, fisheries and many other subjects. Submissions from photographers welcome. Commissions undertaken. Call for CD catalogue.

Sir John Benjamin Stone

See **Birmingham Library Services** under **Library Services**

Tony Stone Images

See **Getty Images**

Jessica Strang Photo Library

504 Brody House, Strype Street, Spitalfields, London E1 7LQ
☎020 7247 8982 Fax 020 7247 8982
Email Jessica.Strang@virgin.net

Contact *Jessica Strang*

Approximately 60,000 transparencies covering architecture, interiors (contemporary), gardens, 'obsessive and not just small but tiny, or from almost no space at all', men, women, couples and animals in architecture, and vanishing London details. Recycled ideas for the home.

Syndication International

22nd Floor, 1 Canada Square, Canary Wharf, London E14 5AP
☎020 7293 3700 Fax 020 7293 2712
Email desk@mirrorpix.com
Website www.mirrorpix.com

General Manager *John Churchill*

Major photo library specialising in current affairs, personalities, royalty, sport, pop and glamour, plus extensive British and world travel pictures. Major motion picture archive up to 1965. Agents for Mirror Group Newspapers. Syndicator of photos and text for news/features.

Joe Tasker Collection

See **Chris Bonnington Picture Library**

Tate Enterprises Picture Library

20 John Islip Street, London SW1P 4LL
☎020 7887 8867 Fax 020 7887 8805
Email picture.library@tate.org.uk
Website www.tate.org.uk

Contact *Chris Webster*

Approximately 8000 images of British art from the 16th century; international 20th century painting and sculpture. Artists include William Blake, William Hogarth, J.M.W. Turner, Dante Gabriel Rossetti, Barbara Hepworth, Henry Moore, Stanley Spencer, Pablo Picasso, Mark Rothko, Salvador Dali, Lucien Freud and David Hockney. Colour transparencies of more than half the works in the main collection are available for hire. For a fee, new photography is available depending on the location and condition of the art work. B&w prints of nearly all the works in the collection can be purchased. Colour slides and prints can be made on request providing a colour transparency exists. Picture researchers must make an appointment to visit the library. All applications must be made by fax or letter.

Bob Thomas Sports Photography
See **Popperfoto**

Patrick Thurston Photography
The Gallery, 12 High Street, Chesterton,
Cambridge CB4 1NG
☎01223 368109
Colour photography of Britain: scenery, people, museums, churches, coastline. Also various countries abroad. Commissions undertaken.

Rick Tomlinson Marine Photo Library
18 Hamble Yacht Services, Port Hamble,
Hamble, Southampton, Hampshire SO31 4NN
☎023 8045 8450 Fax 023 8045 8350
Email ricktom@compuserve.com
Website www.rick-tomlinson.com
Contacts *Rick Tomlinson, Jessica Wollen*
ESTABLISHED 1985. *Specialises* in marine subjects. 100,000 35mm transparencies of yachting, racing, cruising, Whitbread Round the World Race, Volvo Ocean Race, Americas Cup, Tall Ships, RNLI Lifeboats, Antarctica, wildlife and locations.

Topham Picturepoint
PO Box 33, Edenbridge, Kent TN8 5PB
☎01732 863939 Fax 01732 860215
Email admin@topfoto.co.uk
Website www.topfoto.co.uk
Contact *Alan Smith*
Eight million contemporary and historical images, ideal for advertisers, publishers and the travel trade. Delivery online.

B.M. Totterdell Photography
Constable Cottage, Burlings Lane, Knockholt,
Kent TN14 7PE
☎01959 532001 Fax 01959 532001
Email btrial@btinternet.com
Contact *Barbara Totterdell*
Specialist volleyball library covering all aspects of the sport.

Tessa Traeger Library
7 Rossetti Studios, 72 Flood Street, London
SW3 5TF
☎020 7352 3641 Fax 020 7352 4846
Food, gardens, travel and artists.

Travel Ink Photo & Feature Library
The Old Coach House, 14 High Street,
Goring on Thames, Nr Reading, Berkshire
RG8 9AR
☎01491 873011 Fax 01491 875558
Email info@travel-ink.co.uk
Website www.travel-ink.co.uk
Contact *Abbie Enock*
Around 100,000 colour images covering about 130 countries (including the UK). Close links with other specialist libraries mean most topics can be accessed. Subjects include travel, tourism, lifestyles, business, industry, transport, children, religion, history, activities. Specialist collections on Hong Kong (including construction of the Tsing Ma bridge), Greece, North Wales, Germany, the Cotswolds, France and many others.

Peter Trenchard's Image Store Ltd
The Studio, West Hill, St Helier, Jersey,
Channel Islands JE2 3HB
☎01534 769933 Fax 01534 789191
Email peter-trenchard@2000net.com
Website www.peter-trenchard.com
Contact *Peter Trenchard, FBIPP, AMPA, PPA*
Slide library of the Channel Islands – mainly tourist and financial-related. Commissions undertaken.

Tropix Photo Library
156 Meols Parade, Meols, Wirral CH47 6AN
☎0151 632 1698 Fax 0151 632 1698
Email tropixphoto@talk21.com
Website www.tropix.co.uk
Contact *Veronica Birley*
Specialises in images of developing nations: travel and editorial pictures emphasising the attractive and progressive, not just the problems. Evocative photos concerning the economies, environment, culture and society of 100+ countries across Africa, Central and South America, Caribbean, Eastern Europe, Middle East, Indian sub-continent, South East Asia, CIS and Far East; also Antarctica. Also incorporating **MerseySlides Collection** (see entry). Assignment photography available worldwide. All photos supplied with detailed captions. Rapid response with one-hour digital delivery available. Established 21 years. **BAPLA** member.

True North Picture Source
26 New Road, Hebden Bridge, West
Yorkshire HX7 8EF
☎01422 845532 Fax 01422 845532
Email john@trunorth.demon.co.uk
Website www.trunorth.demon.co.uk
Contact *John Morrison*
30,000 transparencies on 35mm and 6×4.5cm

format on the life and landscape of the north of England, photographed by John Morrison.

Turnley Collection
See **Corbis Images**

Ulster Museum Picture Library
Botanic Gardens, Belfast BT9 5AB
☎028 9038 3000 ext 3113
Fax 028 9038 3103
Email patricia.mclean.um@nics.gov.uk
Website www.ulstermuseum.org.uk

Contact *Mrs Pat McLean*

Specialist subjects: art – fine and decorative, late 17th–20th century, particularly Irish art, archaeology, ethnography, treasures from the Armada shipwrecks, geology, botany, zoology, local history and industrial archaeology. Commissions welcome for objects not already photographed.

Universal Pictorial Press & Agency Ltd
29–31 Saffron Hill, London EC1N 8SW
☎020 7421 6000   Fax 020 7421 6006
Email postmaster@uppa.demon.co.uk

News Editor *Peter Dare*

Photo archive dates back to 1944 and contains approximately four million pictures. Colour and b&w coverage of news, royalty, politics, sport, arts, and many other subjects. Commissions undertaken for press and public relations. Fully interactive digital photo archive in addition to bulletin board accessible via ISDN or modem. Full digital scanning, retouching and transmission facilities.

UPI
See **Popperfoto**

V&A Picture Library
Victoria and Albert Museum, South Kensington, London SW7 2RL
☎020 7942 2486/2489   Fax 020 7942 2482
Email picture.library@vam.ac.uk

85,000 colour and 350,000 b&w photos from the collections of the world's largest museum of the decorative arts. Definitive image collections include European Ceramics and Glass; European Furniture; Jewellery and Metalwork; Far Eastern Objects, Textiles and Dress; Indian and South East Asian Objects, Textiles and Dress; European Textiles and Dress; the Art of Photography; Toys and Games.

Valley Green
Barn Ley, Valley Lane, Buxhall, Stowmarket, Suffolk IP14 3EB
☎01449 736090   Fax 01449 736090
Email pics@valleygreen.co.uk

Contacts *Joseph Barrere, Colette Barrere*

'Profusion of perennials – all correctly labelled.' Over 10,000 hardy plant transparencies in stock, plus watercolours and line drawings available. Commissions undertaken as well as creative copywriting.

Victory Archive
See **Popperfoto**

Vin Mag Archives Ltd
203–213 Mare Street, London E8 3QE
☎020 8533 7588   Fax 020 8533 7283
Email piclib.vintage@ndirect.co.uk
Website www.vinmag.com

Formerly the Vintage Magazine Company. A large collection of movie stills and posters, photographs, illustrations and advertisements covering music, glamour, social history, theatre posters, ephemera, postcards.

John Walmsley Photo Library
See **Education Photos**

Christopher Ware Pictures
65 Trinity Street, Barry, Glamorgan CF62 7EX
☎01446 732816/07802 865999 (mobile)
Fax 01446 413471
Email crware@ntlworld.com
Website www.soundandvision-wales.co.uk

Contact *Christopher Ware*

Large collection of images (b&w and colour) of S.E. Wales, including Barry docks and the Steam Graveyard, railways, Vale of Glamorgan landscapes, civil and military aircraft over the last 40 years. Images available on CD-ROM or via e-mail. Digital post-production. Commissions. Other photographers' work not accepted.

Warwickshire Photographic Survey
See **Birmingham Library Services** under **Library Services**

Waterways Photo Library
39 Manor Court Road, Hanwell, London W7 3EJ
☎020 8840 1659   Fax 020 8567 0605
Email watphot39@aol.com

Contact *Derek Pratt*

A specialist photo library on all aspects of

Britain's inland waterways. Top-quality 35mm and medium-format colour transparencies, plus a large collection of b&w. Rivers and canals, bridges, locks, aqueducts, tunnels and waterside buildings. Town and countryside scenes, canal art, waterway holidays, boating, fishing, windmills, watermills, watersports and wildlife.

Philip Way Photography
2 Green Moor Link, Winchmore Hill, London N21 2ND
☎020 8360 3034
Contact *Philip Way*

Over 10,000 images of St Paul's Cathedral – historical exteriors, interiors and events (1686–2002).

Weimar Archive
See **Mary Evans Picture Library**

Wellcome Photo Library
210 Euston Road, London NW1 2BE
☎020 7611 8348   Fax 020 7611 8577
Email photolib@wellcome.ac.uk
Website www.wellcome.ac.uk
Contacts *Sonya Brown, Julie Dorrington*

Approximately 180,000 images on the history of medicine and human culture worldwide, including modern clinical medicine, healthcare, family life and biomedica.

Eric Whitehead Photography
Postal Buildings, Ash Street, Bowness-on-Windermere, Cumbria LA23 3EB
☎015394 48894   Fax 015394 48284
Email info@ewphotography.com
Website www.ewphotography.com

Incorporates the Cumbria Picture Library. The agency covers local news events, PR and commercial material, also leading library of snooker images (see **Snookerimages**).

Wild Images
See **RSPCA Photolibrary**

Wilderness Photographic Library
Mill Barn, Broad Raine, Sedbergh, Cumbria LA10 5ED
☎015396 20196   Fax 015396 21293
Contact *John Noble*

Striking colour images from around the world, from polar wastes to the Himalayas and Amazon jungle. Subjects: mountains, Arctic, deserts, icebergs, wildlife, rainforests, glaciers, geysers, exploration, caves, rivers, eco-tourism, people and cultures, canyons, seascapes, marine life, weather, volcanoes, mountaineering, skiing, geology, conservation, adventure sports, national parks.

David Williams Picture Library
50 Burlington Avenue, Glasgow G12 0LH
☎0141 339 7823   Fax 0141 337 3031

Specialises in travel photography with wide coverage of Scotland, Iceland and Spain. Many other European countries also included plus smaller collections of Western USA and Canada. The main subjects in each country are: cities, towns, villages, 'tourist haunts', buildings of architectural or historical interest, landscapes and natural features. The Scotland and Iceland collections include many pictures depicting physical geography and geology. Photographic commissions and illustrated travel articles undertaken. Catalogue available.

The Neil Williams Classical Collection
22 Avon, Hockley, Tamworth, Staffordshire B77 5QA
☎01827 286086   Fax 01827 286086
Email TNWCC@aol.com
Website members.aol.com/TNWCC/TNWCC.htm
Contact *Neil Williams, BA(Hons), Dip Mus.*

Archive specialising in classical music ephemera, particularly portraits of composers, musicians, conductors and opera singers comprising of old and sometimes very rare photographs, postcards, antique prints, cigarette cards, stamps, First Day Covers, concert programmes, Victorian newspapers, etc. Also modern photos of composer references such as museums, statues, busts, paintings, monuments, memorials and graves. Other subjects covered include ballet, musical instruments, concert halls, opera houses, 'music in art', manuscripts, opera scenes, music-caricatures, bands, orchestras and other music groups.

Vaughan Williams Memorial Library
English Folk Dance and Song Society, Cecil Sharp House, 2 Regent's Park Road, London NW1 7AY
☎020 7485 2206 ext. 18/19
Fax 020 7284 0523
Email library@efdss.org
Website www.efdss.org

Mainly b&w coverage of traditional/folk music, dance and customs worldwide, focusing on Britain and other English-speaking nations. Photographs date from the late 19th century to the 1990s.

The Wilson Photographic Collection

See **Dundee Central Library** under **Library Services**

Windrush Photos, Wildlife and Countryside Picture Agency

99 Noah's Ark, Kemsing, Sevenoaks, Kent TN15 6PD
☎01732 763486 Fax 01732 763285
Website www.windrushphotos.com

Contact *David Tipling*

Specialists in birds (worldwide) and British wildlife. Photographic and features commissions are regularly undertaken for publications in the UK and overseas. The agency acts as ornithological consultants for all aspects of the media. Offers expert captioning service. **BAPLA** member.

Woodfall Wild Images

17 Bull Lane, Denbigh, Denbighshire LL16 3SN
☎01745 815903 Fax 01745 814581
Email WWImages@btinternet.com
Website www.woodfall.com

Contact *David Woodfall*

Specialist environmental, conservation, landscape and wildlife photographic library. A constantly expanding collection of images reflecting the natural world and man's effect upon it, both positively and negatively. New pictures of agriculture, sharks and whales. Please call for a brochure, stock cards or prospective photographer notes. New specialist panoramic coverage available including world city scapes.

World Pictures

85a Great Portland Street, London W1W 7LT
☎020 7437 2121/7436 0440
Fax 020 7439 1307
Email worldpictures@btinternet.com
Website www.worldpictures.co.uk

Contacts *David Brenes, Carlo Irek*

600,000 colour transparencies of travel and emotive material.

WWF UK Photolibrary

Panda House, Weyside Park, Catteshall Lane, Godalming, Surrey GU7 1XR
☎01483 412336 Fax 01483 861360

Contact *Patricia Patton*

Specialist library covering natural history, endangered species, conservation, environment, forests, habitats, habitat destruction, and pollution in the UK and abroad. 25,000 colour slides (35mm).

Yemen Pictures

28 Sheen Common Drive, Richmond TW10 5BN
☎020 7602 1989 Fax 020 7602 1989

Large collection (4000 transparencies) covering all aspects of Yemen – culture, people, architecture, dance, qat, music. Also Africa, Australia, Middle East, and Asia.

York Archaeological Trust Picture Library

Cromwell House, 13 Ogleforth, York YO1 7FG
☎01904 663000 Fax 01904 663024
Email enquiries@yorkarchaeology.co.uk
Website www.yorkarchaeology.co.uk

Specialist library of rediscovered artifacts, historic buildings and excavations, presented by the creators of the highly acclaimed Jorvik Viking Centre. The main emphasis is on the Roman, Anglo-Saxon and Viking periods.

The John Robert Young Collection

61 De Montfort Road, Lewes, East Sussex BN7 1SS
☎01273 475216 Fax 01273 475216

Contact *Jennifer Barrett*

50,000 transparencies and monochrome prints on religion, travel and military subjects. Major portfolios: religious communities; the French Foreign Legion; the Spanish Legion; the Royal Marines; the People's Liberation Army (China).

Settling Accounts

*Ian Spring takes an expert look at the latest Budget
and explains how writers can be tax wise*

'No man in the country is under the smallest obligation, moral or other, to
arrange his affairs as to enable the Inland Revenue to put the largest possible shovel in his stores.

The Inland Revenue is not slow, and quite rightly, to take every advantage which is open to it ... for the purpose of depleting the taxpayer's
pockets. And the taxpayer is, in like manner, entitled to be astute to prevent as far as he honestly can the depletion of his means by the Inland
Revenue.'

Lord Clyde, *Ayrshire Pullman v Inland Revenue Commissioners, 1929*

Income Tax

What is a professional writer for tax purposes?

Writers are professionals while they are writing regularly with the intention of
making a profit; or while they are gathering material, researching or otherwise
preparing a publication.

A professional freelance writer is taxed under Case II of Schedule D of the
Income and Corporation Taxes Act 1988. The taxable income is the amount
receivable, either directly or by an agent, on his behalf, less expenses wholly and
exclusively laid out for the purpose of the profession. If expenses exceed
income, the loss can either be set against other income of the same or preceding
years or carried forward and set against future income from writing. If tax has
been paid on that other income, a repayment can be obtained, or the sum can be
offset against other tax liabilities. Special loss relief can apply in the opening
years of the profession. Losses made in the first four years can be set against
income of up to three earlier years.

Where a writer receives very occasional payments for isolated articles, it may
not be possible to establish that these are profits arising from carrying on a continuing profession. In such circumstances these 'isolated transactions' may be
assessed under Case VI of Schedule D of the *Income and Corporation Taxes Act*
1988. Again, expenses may be deducted in arriving at the taxable income but, if
expenses exceed income, the loss can only be set against the profits from future
isolated transactions, or other income assessable under Case VI.

In the tax year 1996/97 a new tax system came into effect called Self Assessment.
Under Self Assessment the onus is on the individual to declare income and

expenses correctly. Each writer therefore has to decide whether profits arise from a professional or occasional activity. The consequences of getting it wrong can be expensive by way of interest, penalties and surcharges on additional tax subsequently found to be due. If in any doubt the writer should seek professional advice.

Income

A writer's income includes fees, advances, royalties, commissions, sale of copyrights, reimbursed expenses, etc., from any source anywhere in the world whether or not brought to the UK (non UK resident or domiciled writers should seek professional advice).

Agents

It should be borne in mind that the agent stands in the shoes of the principal. It is not always realised that when the agent receives royalties, fees, advances, etc. on behalf of the author those receipts became the property of the author on the date of their receipt by the agent. This applies for Income Tax and Value Added Tax purposes.

Expenses

A writer can normally claim the following expenses:

(a) Secretarial, typing, proofreading, research. Where payment for these is made to the author's wife or husband they should be recorded and entered in the spouse's tax return as earned income which is subject to the usual personal allowances. If payments reach relevant levels, PAYE should be operated.

(b) Telephone, faxes, Internet costs, computer software, postage, stationery, printing, equipment maintenance, insurance, dictation tapes, batteries, any equipment or office requisites used for the profession.

(c) Periodicals, books (including presentation copies and reference books) and other publications necessary for the profession, but amounts received from the sale of books should be deducted.

(d) Hotels, fares, car running expenses (including repairs, petrol, oil, garaging, parking, cleaning, insurance, road fund tax, depreciation), hire of cars or taxis in connection with:

(i) business discussions with agents, publishers, co-authors, collaborators, researchers, illustrators, etc.

(ii) travel at home and abroad to collect background material.

As an alternative to keeping details of full car running costs, a mileage rate can be claimed for business use. This rate depends on the engine size and varies from year to year. This is known as the Fixed Profit Car Scheme and is available to writers whose turnover does not exceed the VAT registration limit, currently £55,000.

(e)   Publishing and advertising expenses, including costs of proof corrections, indexing, photographs, etc.

(f)   Subscriptions to societies and associations, press cutting agencies, libraries, etc., incurred wholly for the purpose of the profession.

(g)   Rent, council tax and water rates, etc., the proportion being determined by the ratio of the number of rooms used exclusively for the profession, to the total number of rooms in the residence. But see note on *Capital Gains Tax* below.

(h)   Lighting, heating and cleaning. A carefully calculated figure of the business use of these costs can be claimed as a proportion of the total.

(i)   Agent's commission, accountancy charges and legal charges incurred wholly in the course of the profession including cost of defending libel actions, damages in so far as they are not covered by insurance, and libel insurance premiums. However, where in a libel case damages are awarded to punish the author for having acted maliciously the action becomes quasi-criminal and costs and damages may not be allowed.

(j)   TV and video rental (which may be apportioned for private use), and cinema or theatre tickets, if wholly for the purpose of the profession.

(k)   Capital allowances for business equipment. These are now divided into three categories:

    (i)   Computer equipment including printers, scanners, cabling, etc. For any such equipment purchased subsequent to 1 April 2000 there is a First Year Allowance of 100%. Prior to that the First Year Allowance was 40% of the cost of the equipment purchased after 1 July 1998 and 50% on equipment purchased after 1 July 1997. For equipment purchased prior to 1 April 2000, after the first year there is an annual Writing Down Allowance of 25% of the reducing balance.

    (ii)   On motor cars the allowance is 25% in the first year and 25% of the reducing balance in each successive year limited to £3000 each year.

    (iii)   For all other business equipment, e.g. TV, radio, hi-fi sets, tape and video recorders, Dictaphones, office furniture, photographic equipment, etc. there is a First Year Allowance of 40%. After the first year there is an annual Writing Down Allowance of 25% of the reducing balance. The allowances for all the three categories mentioned above will be reduced to exclude personal (non-professional) use where necessary.

(l)   Lease rent. The cost of lease rent of equipment is allowable; also on cars, subject to restrictions for private use, and for expensive cars.

(m)   Other expenses incurred wholly and exclusively for professional purposes. (Entertaining expenses are not allowable in any circumstances.)

NB It essential to keep detailed records. Diary entries of appointments, notes of fares and receipted bills are much more convincing to the Inland Revenue who are very reluctant to accept estimates. **The Self Assessment regime makes it**

a legal requirement for proper accounting records to be kept. These records must be sufficient to support the figures declared in the tax return.

In addition to the above, tax relief is available on:

(a)   Premiums to pension schemes such as the *Society of Authors Retirement Benefits Scheme*. Depending on age, up to 40% of net earned income can be paid into a personal pension plan.
(b)   Covenants to charities. (Deeds executed prior to 6 April 2000.)
(c)   Gift Aid payments to charities. Any amount. (Prior to 6 April 2000, single payments of £250 or more.)

Capital Gains Tax

The exemption from Capital Gains Tax which applies to an individual's main residence does not apply to any part of that residence which is used exclusively for business purposes. The effect of this is that the appropriate proportion of any increase in value of the residence since 31 March 1982 can be taxed when the residence is sold, subject to adjustment for inflation to March 1998 and subsequent length of ownership, at the individual's highest rate of tax.

Writers who own their houses should bear this in mind before claiming expenses for the use of a room for writing purposes. Arguments in favour of making such claims are that they afford some relief now, while Capital Gains Tax in its present form may not stay for ever. Also, where a new house is bought in place of an old one, the gain made on the sale of the first study may be set off against the cost of the study in the new house, thus postponing the tax payment until the final sale. For this relief to apply, each house must have a study and the author must continue his profession throughout. On death there is an exemption of the total Capital Gains of the estate.

Alternatively, writers can claim that their use is non-exclusive and restrict their claim to the cost of extra lighting, heating and cleaning to avoid any Capital Gains Tax liability.

Can a writer average out his income over a number of years for tax purposes?

The Budget in March 2001 introduced measures which will enable writers to average their profits (made wholly or mainly from creative works) over two or more consecutive years. If the profits of the lower year are less than 70% of the profits of the higher year or the profits of one year (but not both) are nil, the author will be able to claim to have the profits averaged. Where the profits of the lower year are more than 70% but less than 75% of the profits of the higher year a pro-rata adjustment is made to both years to reduce the difference between them.

The first years that can be averaged are 2000/1 and 2001/2. These new provisions will be of much greater relevance to the circumstances of many more authors than the previous ones. These (under Section 534 of the Income and Corporation Taxes Act 1988) enabled a writer, in certain circumstances, to spread over two or three fiscal years lump sum payments whenever received and royalties received during two years from the date of first publication or performance of work. These old rules now only apply to sums received before 6 April 2001.

It is also possible to average out income within the terms of publishers' contracts, but professional advice should be taken before signature. Where a husband and wife collaborate as writers, advice should be taken as to whether a formal partnership agreement should be made or whether the publishing agreement should be in joint names.

Is a lump sum paid for an outright sale of the copyright or is part of the copyright exempt from tax?
No. All the money received from the marketing of literary work, by whatever means, is taxable. Some writers, in spite of clear judicial decisions to the contrary, still seem to think that an outright sale of, for instance, the film rights in a book is not subject to tax.

Remaindering
To avoid remaindering authors can usually purchase copies of their own books from the publishers. Monies received from sales are subject to income tax but the cost of books sold should be deducted because tax is only payable on the profit made.

Is there any relief where old copyrights are sold?
Section 535 of the *Income and Corporation Taxes Act 1988* prior to 5 April 2001 gave relief where not less than ten years after the first publication of the work the author of a literary, dramatic, musical or artistic work assigned the copyright therein wholly or partially, or granted any interest in the copyright by licence, and:

(a)   the consideration for the assignment or grant consisted wholly or partially of a lump sum payment, the whole amount of which would, but for this section, be included in computing the amount of his/her profits or gains for a single year of assessment, and

(b)   the copyright or interest is not assigned or granted for a period of less than two years.

In such cases, the amount received could be spread forward in equal yearly instalments for a maximum of six years, or, where the copyright or interest was assigned or granted for a period of less than six years, for the number of whole years in that period. A 'lump sum payment' is defined to include a non-returnable advance on account of royalties.

It should be noted that a claim could not be made under this section in respect of a payment if a prior claim had been made under Section 534 of the *Income and Corporation Taxes Act 1988* (see section on spreading lump sum payments over two or three years) or vice versa. Relief under Sections 534 and 535 was withdrawn from partnerships some years ago and is withdrawn altogether for sums received after 5 April 2001. Claims for the tax year 2000/01 have to be made by January 2003.

Are royalties payable on publication of a book abroad subject to both foreign tax as well as UK tax?

Where there is a Double Taxation Agreement between the country concerned and the UK, then on the completion of certain formalities no tax is deductible at source by the foreign payer, but such income is taxable in the UK in the ordinary way. When there is no Double Taxation Agreement, credit will be given against UK tax for overseas tax paid. A complete list of countries with which the UK has conventions for the avoidance of double taxation may be obtained from FICO, Inland Revenue, St John's House, Merton Road, Bootle, Merseyside L69 9BB, or a local tax office.

Residence abroad

Writers residing abroad will, of course, be subject to the tax laws ruling in their country of residence, and as a general rule royalty income paid from the United Kingdom can be exempted from deduction of UK tax at source, providing the author is carrying on his profession abroad. A writer who is intending to go and live abroad should make early application for future royalties to be paid without deduction of tax to FICO, address as above. In certain circumstances writers resident in the Irish Republic are exempt from Irish Income Tax on their authorship earnings.

Are grants or prizes taxable?

The law is uncertain. Some Arts Council grants are now deemed to be taxable, whereas most prizes and awards are not, though it depends on the conditions in each case. When submitting the Self Assessment annual returns, such items should be excluded, but reference made to them in the 'Additional Information' box on the self-employment (or partnership) pages.

What is the item 'Class 4 N.I.C.' which appears on my Self Assessment return?

All taxpayers who are self-employed pay an additional national insurance contribution if their earned income exceeds a figure which varies each year. This contribution is described as Class 4 and is calculated when preparing the return. It is additional to the self-employed Class 2 contribution but confers no additional benefits and is a form of levy. It applies to men aged under 65 and women under 60.

Value Added Tax

Value Added Tax (VAT) is a tax currently levied at 17.5% on:

(a) the total value of taxable goods and services supplied to consumers,
(b) the importation of goods into the UK,
(c) certain services or goods from abroad if a taxable person receives them in the UK for the purpose of their business.

Who is taxable?

A writer resident in the UK whose turnover from writing and any other business, craft or art on a self-employed basis is greater than £55,000 annually, before deducting agent's commission, must register with HM Customs & Excise as a taxable person. Turnover includes fees, royalties, advances, commissions, sale of copyright, reimbursed expenses, etc. A business is required to register:

● at the end of any month if the value of taxable supplies in the past twelve months has exceeded the annual threshold; or
● if there are reasonable grounds for believing that the value of taxable supplies in the next twelve months will exceed the annual threshold.

Penalties will be claimed in the case of late registration. A writer whose turnover is below these limits is exempt from the requirements to register for VAT but may apply for voluntary registration and this will be allowed at the discretion of HM Customs & Excise.

A taxable person collects VAT on outputs (turnover) and deducts VAT paid on inputs (taxable expenses) and where VAT collected exceeds VAT paid, must remit the difference to HM Customs & Excise. In the event that input exceeds output, the difference will be refunded by HM Customs & Excise.

Outputs (Turnover)

A writer's outputs are taxable services supplied to publishers, broadcasting organisations, theatre managements, film companies, educational institutions, etc. A taxable writer must invoice, i.e. collect from, all the persons (either individuals or organisations) in the UK for whom supplies have been made, for fees, royalties or other considerations plus VAT. An unregistered writer cannot and must not invoice for VAT. A taxable writer is not obliged to collect VAT on royalties or other fees paid by publishers or others overseas. In practice, agents usually collect VAT for the registered author.

Remit to Customs

The taxable writer adds up the VAT which has been paid on taxable inputs, deducts it from the VAT received and remits the balance to Customs. Business with HM Customs is conducted through the local VAT offices of HM Customs which are listed in local telephone directories, except for VAT returns which are sent direct to the Customs & Excise VAT Central Unit, Alexander House, 21 Victoria Avenue, Southend on Sea, Essex SS99 1AA.

Inputs

Taxable at the standard rate if supplier is registered	Taxable at the zero or special rate	Not liable to VAT
Rent of certain commercial premises	Books (zero)	Rent of non-commercial premises
Advertisements in newspapers, magazines, journals and periodicals	Coach, rail and air travel (zero)	Postage
Agent's commission (unless it relates to monies from overseas)	Agent's commission (on monies from overseas)	Services supplied by unregistered persons
Accountant's and solicitor's fees for business matters	Domestic gas and electricity (5%)	Subscriptions to the Society of Authors, PEN, NUJ, etc.
Agency services (typing, copying, etc.)		Insurance
Word processors, typewriters and stationery		
Artists' materials		
Photographic equipment		
Tape recorders and tapes		
Hotel accommodation		*Outside the scope of VAT*
Taxi fares		
Motorcar expenses		PLR (Public Lending Right)
Telephone		Profit shares
Theatres and concerts		Investment income
NB This list is not exhaustive		

Accounting

A taxable writer is obliged to account to HM Customs & Excise at quarterly intervals. Returns must be completed and sent to VAT Central Unit by the dates shown on the return. Penalties can be charged if the returns are late.

It is possible to account for the VAT liability under the Cash Accounting Scheme (leaflet 731), whereby the author accounts for the output tax when the invoice is paid or royalties, etc., are received. The same applies to the input tax, but as most purchases are probably on a 'cash basis', this will not make a considerable difference to the author's input tax. This scheme is only applicable to those with a taxable turnover of less than £600,000 and, therefore, is available to the majority of authors. The advantage of this scheme is that the author does not have to account for VAT before receiving payments, thereby relieving the author of a cash flow problem.

It is also possible to pay VAT by nine estimated direct debits, with a final balance at the end of the year (see leaflet 732). This annual accounting method also means that only one VAT return is submitted.

Flat Rate Scheme

Charges announced in the Budget in April 2002 introduced the 'flat rate scheme' (FRS) for small businesses. This is initially open to businesses with business income up to £125,000 a year. Under the normal VAT accounting rules, each item of turnover and every claimed expense must be recorded and supported by evidence, e.g. invoices, receipts etc. Under the FRS, detailed records of sales and purchases do not have to be kept. A record of gross income (including zero-rated and exempt income) is maintained and a flat rate percentage is applied to the total. This percentage is then paid over to HM Customs. The percentage varies from one profession or business to another but for authors is 11%.

The aim of the scheme is to reduce the amount of time and money spent in complying with VAT regulations and this is to be welcomed. However, there are disadvantages:

- The detailed records of income and expenses are still going to be required for taxation purposes.
- Invoices on sales are issued in the normal way.
- The percentage is applied to all business income. So 11% VAT will effectively be paid on income from abroad, zero-rated under the normal basis, and PLR, otherwise exempt.
- For many authors, normal VAT accounting has imposed a good, timely discipline for dealing with accounting and taxation matters.

Registration

A writer will be given a VAT registration number which must be quoted on all VAT correspondence. It is the responsibility of those registered to inform those to whom they make supplies of their registration number. The taxable turnover limit which determines whether a person who is registered for VAT may apply for cancellation of registration is £53,000.

Voluntary registration

A writer whose turnover is below the limits may apply to register. If the writer is paying a relatively large amount of VAT on taxable inputs – agent's commission, accountant's fees, equipment, materials, or agency services, etc. – it may make a significant improvement in the net income to be able to offset the VAT on these inputs. A writer who pays relatively little VAT may find it easier, and no more expensive, to remain unregistered.

Fees and royalties

A taxable writer must notify those to whom he makes supplies of the VAT Registration Number at the first opportunity. One method of accounting for and paying VAT on fees and royalties is the use of multiple stationery for 'self-billing', one copy of the royalty statement being used by the author as the VAT invoice. A second method is for the recipient of taxable outputs to pay fees, including authors' royalties, without VAT. The taxable writer then renders a tax invoice for the VAT element and a second payment, of the VAT element, will be made. This scheme is cumbersome but will involve only taxable authors. Fees and royalties from abroad will count as payments of the exported services and will accordingly be zero-rated.

Agents and accountants

A writer is responsible to HM Customs for making VAT returns and payments. Neither an agent nor an accountant nor a solicitor can remove the responsibility, although they can be helpful in preparing and keeping VAT returns and accounts. Their professional fees or commission will, except in rare cases where the adviser or agent is himself unregistered, be taxable at the standard rate and will represent some of a writer's taxable inputs.

Income Tax – Schedule D

An unregistered writer can claim some of the VAT paid on taxable inputs as a business expense allowable against income tax. However, certain taxable inputs fall into categories which cannot be claimed under the income tax regulations. A taxable writer, who has already claimed VAT on inputs, cannot charge it as a business expense for the purposes of income tax.

Certain services from abroad

A taxable author who resides in the United Kingdom and who receives certain services from abroad must account for VAT on those services at the appropriate tax rate on the sum paid for them. Examples of the type of services concerned include: services of lawyers, accountants, consultants, provision of information and copyright permissions.

Inheritance Tax

Inheritance Tax was introduced in 1984 to replace Capital Transfer Tax, which had in turn replaced Estate Duty, the first of the death taxes of recent times. Paradoxically, Inheritance Tax has reintroduced a number of principles present under the old Estate Duty.

The general principle now is that all assets owned at death are chargeable to tax (currently 40%) except the first £250,000 of the estate and any assets passed to a surviving spouse or a charity. Gifts made more than seven years before death are exempt, but those made within this period may be taxed on a sliding scale. No tax is payable at the time of making the gift.

In addition, each individual may currently make gifts of up to £3000 in any year and these will be considered to be exempt. A further exemption covers any number of annual gifts not exceeding £250 to any one person.

If the £3000 is not fully utilised in one year, any unused balance can be carried forward to the following year (but no later). Gifts out of income, which do not reduce one's living standards, are also exempt if they are part of normal expenditure.

At death all assets are valued; they will include any property, investments, life policies, furniture and personal possessions, bank balances and, in the case of authors, the value of copyrights. All, with the sole exception of copyrights, are capable (as assets) of accurate valuation and, if necessary, can be turned into cash. The valuation of copyright is, of course, complicated and frequently gives rise to difficulty. Except where they are bequeathed to the owner's husband or wife, very real problems can be left behind by the author.

Experience has shown that a figure based on two to three years' past royalties may be proposed by the Inland Revenue in their valuation of copyright. However, this may not be reasonable and may require negotiation. If a book is running out of print or if, as in the case of educational books, it may need revision at the next reprint, these factors must be taken into account. In many cases the fact that the author is no longer alive and able to make personal appearances, or provide publicity, or write further works, will result in lower or slower sales. Obviously, this is an area in which help can be given by the publishers, and in particular one needs to know what their future intentions are, what stocks of the books remain, and what likelihood there will be of reprinting.

There is a further relief available to authors who have established that they have been carrying on a business, normally assessable under Case II of Schedule D, for at least two years prior to death. It has been possible to establish that copyrights are treated as business property and in these circumstances, Inheritance Tax 'business property relief' is available. This relief at present is 100% so that the tax saving can be quite substantial. The Inland Revenue may wish to be assured that the business is continuing and consideration should therefore be given to the appointment, in the author's will, of a literary executor who should be a qualified business person or, in certain circumstances, the formation of partnership between the author and spouse, or other relative, to ensure that it is established the business is continuing after the author's death.

If the author has sufficient income, consideration should be given to building up a fund to cover future Inheritance Tax liabilities. One of a number of ways would be to take out a whole life assurance policy which is assigned to the children, or other beneficiaries, the premiums on which are within the annual exemption of £3000. The capital sum payable on the death of the assured is exempt from inheritance tax.

Anyone wondering how best to order his affairs for tax purposes should consult an accountant with specialised knowledge in this field. Experience shows that a good accountant is well worth his fee which, incidentally, so far as it relates to professional matters, is an allowable expense.

Ian Spring of Moore Stephens, Chartered Accountants will be pleased to answer questions on tax problems. Write c/o The Writer's Handbook, *34 Ufton Road, London N1 5BX.*

Company Index

Subject Index